**Fromm**

W9-CSK-298

# Southeast Asia

## 4th Edition

### by Charles Agar & Jennifer Eveland

Here's what the critics say about Frommer's:

"Amazingly easy to use. Very portable, very complete."

—*Booklist*

"Detailed, accurate, and easy-to-read information for all price ranges."
—*Glamour Magazine*

"Hotel information is close to encyclopedic."

—*Des Moines Sunday Register*

"Frommer's Guides have a way of giving you a real feel for a place."
—*Knight Ridder Newspapers*

WILEY

Wiley Publishing, Inc.

Published by:

## Wiley Publishing, Inc.

111 River St.
Hoboken, NJ 07030-5774

ISBN 10: 0-7645-7829-4
ISBN 13: 978-0-7645-7829-8

Editor: John Vorwald
Production Editor: M. Faunette Johnston
Cartographer: Nicholas Trotter
Photo Editor: Richard Fox
Production by Wiley Indianapolis Composition Services

Front cover photo: Thailand: Kanchanaburi Province, novice monk blowing
bubble gum.
Back cover photo: Thailand: Vendors selling produce from boats.

For information on our other products and services or to obtain technical support,
please contact our Customer Care Department within the U.S. at 800/762-2974,
outside the U.S. at 317/572-3993 or fax 317/572-4002.

Wiley also publishes its books in a variety of electronic formats. Some content that
appears in print may not be available in electronic formats.

Manufactured in the United States of America

5   4   3   2

# Contents

## 4 Thailand 85

*by Charles Agar*

## 5 Laos 237

*by Charles Agar*

## 6  Vietnam
287

*by Charles Agar*

## 7  Cambodia
407

*by Charles Agar*

## 8  Singapore
446

*by Jennifer Eveland*

# List of Maps

## An Invitation to the Reader

In researching this book, we discovered many wonderful places—hotels, restaurants, shops, and more. We're sure you'll find others. Please tell us about them, so we can share the information with your fellow travelers in upcoming editions. If you were disappointed with a recommendation, we'd love to know that, too. Please write to:

*Frommer's Southeast Asia,* 4th Edition
Wiley Publishing, Inc. • 111 River St. • Hoboken, NJ 07030-5774

## An Additional Note

Please be advised that travel information is subject to change at any time—and this is especially true of prices. We therefore suggest that you write or call ahead for confirmation when making your travel plans. The authors, editors, and publisher cannot be held responsible for the experiences of readers while traveling. Your safety is important to us, however, so we encourage you to stay alert and be aware of your surroundings. Keep a close eye on cameras, purses, and wallets, all favorite targets of thieves and pickpockets.

## About the Authors

**Charles Agar** (Vietnam, Laos, Bali, Cambodia, and Myanmar)—After completing a Masters in English Literature at the University of Rochester, work as an English teacher in Japan first brought Charles to Asia. The years since have found him in the region whenever possible, practicing Buddhism, teaching and studying language. This is his first assignment with Frommer's and he'd like to thank the many people who helped him, among them: Rick Tuggey and Tim Miner for teaching him how to work, Bill Indick for being at the airport rain or shine, Eunice Agar for the tea, sympathy, and editing, Annette Monreal for sharing the roads of Laos, Mr. Abhay, Mr. Sousath, Kerry Howley, Tony Tran, and Ms. Phuoc. A special thanks to Connell McGrath for his help and encouragement, Keith Cahalan, Chaula Hopefisher, the Mandels for all the groovy dinners and above all his loving family as well as the many kind expats and fellow travelers he met while trudging along the happy road.

**Jennifer Eveland** (Thailand, Singapore, and Malaysia)—She was a child when she and her family first moved to Singapore, and after returning to the United States, she was drawn again and again to the magic of Singapore, East Asia, and Southeast Asia. She is the author of *Frommer's Singapore & Malaysia* and currently lives in Singapore.

## Other Great Guides for Your Trip:

*Frommer's Singapore & Malaysia*
*Frommer's Thailand*
*Frommer's Hong Kong*

## Frommer's Star Ratings, Icons & Abbreviations

Every hotel, restaurant, and attraction listing in this guide has been ranked for quality, value, service, amenities, and special features using a **star-rating system.** In country, state, and regional guides, we also rate towns and regions to help you narrow down your choices and budget your time accordingly. Hotels and restaurants are rated on a scale of zero (recommended) to three stars (exceptional). Attractions, shopping, nightlife, towns, and regions are rated according to the following scale: zero stars (recommended), one star (highly recommended), two stars (very highly recommended), and three stars (must-see).

In addition to the star-rating system, we also use **eight feature icons** that point you to the great deals, in-the-know advice, and unique experiences that separate travelers from tourists. Throughout the book, look for:

| | |
|---|---|
| **Finds** | Special finds—those places only insiders know about |
| **Fun Fact** | Fun facts—details that make travelers more informed and their trips more fun |
| **Kids** | Best bets for kids, and advice for the whole family |
| **Moments** | Special moments—those experiences that memories are made of |
| **Overrated** | Places or experiences not worth your time or money |
| **Tips** | Insider tips—great ways to save time and money |
| **Value** | Great values—where to get the best deals |
| **Warning** | Warning—traveler's advisories are usually in effect |

The following **abbreviations** are used for credit cards:

| | | | | | |
|---|---|---|---|---|---|
| AE | American Express | DISC | Discover | V | Visa |
| DC | Diners Club | MC | MasterCard | | |

## Frommers.com

Now that you have the guidebook to a great trip, visit our website at **www.frommers.com** for travel information on more than 3,000 destinations. With features updated regularly, we give you instant access to the most current trip-planning information available. At Frommers.com, you'll also find the best prices on airfares, accommodations, and car rentals—and you can even book travel online through our travel booking partners. At Frommers.com, you'll also find the following:

- Online updates to our most popular guidebooks
- Vacation sweepstakes and contest giveaways
- Newsletter highlighting the hottest travel trends
- Online travel message boards with featured travel discussions

# What's New in Southeast Asia

Much of what is so fascinating to travelers in Southeast Asia is the ephemeral: that friendly shopkeeper who invites you to sample something new, a hole-in-the-wall antiques store, a local specialty served at street side, seeming impromptu festivals, and the kindness of strangers. These serendipitous moments—some call it "Trail Magic"—are what make exploring this part of the world so memorable and yet so maddening for the publisher of a guidebook to chronicle. Those quaint little corners are as fickle as shooting stars and can often only be found by searching, and often disappear or change if sought after again. Our advice: Search away! Follow a passion—an interest in local cuisine, history, or architecture—and ask around. Go where the locals go. Accept invites where appropriate and take time—things unfold slowly in this part of the world. Visitors come away with their own unique experiences and impressions in even the shortest visit to this diverse region.

Below we list a few of the major changes in this updated edition. Travelers to Southeast Asia need to be hip to fluctuations in the international airline scene in today's cautious climate. While some Asian airlines have eliminated North American routes, many North American carriers have begun offering rock-bottom rates for premium flights, and there are even some new international connections. Check with ticket consolidators or carriers that sell regional multistop tickets: See Cathay Pacific (www.cathay.com), for example, or specials like the unique "Hip-Hop Pass" arranged by ASEAN (access the ASEAN website at www.asean-tourism.com).

Safety is on the mind of every traveler these days, and despite the public relations disaster of the SARS crisis, avian influenza, and some political hot spots in the region, the well-informed traveler in Southeast Asia can be sure of a trouble-free trip and manageable adventures.

## THAILAND

One of the Asian "tiger economies," Thailand is growing exponentially. Thais are wealthier, and Thai infrastructure is expanding. Recent years have seen large public works projects; the building of dams, bridges, and highways; rural development; and growth in agricultural productivity. Bangkok's new international airport is nearly complete, and the Thai capital now boasts a subway line to augment the services of the elevated BTS Skytrain.

Politically, the country has seen a conservative shift with the ascendancy of Prime Minister Thaksin Shinawatra, who is enacting aggressive fiscal and infrastructural reforms in an effort to make Thailand a leader in Asia. The PM's "War on Dark Influences" is more than your average PR campaign, but an across-the-board crackdown on corruption. Palm greasing and kickbacks are still the norm in local government and business, but laws once ignored are now being strictly enforced.

## The Tsunami of 2004

On December 26, 2004, just as we were going to press with this edition, an earthquake measuring 9 on the Richter scale, the largest in 40
years, struck Aceh near Indonesia; the resulting tsunami, a wall of
water some 12m high (40 ft.) in some areas, pounded the coastal areas
throughout the region, leaving an estimated death toll of over
250,000 people, mostly in the western part of Indonesia and Sri Lanka.
Coastal areas throughout the region were devastated. International
relief continues to pour in and the situation is rapidly improving. Loss
of life in Thailand was estimated at over 5,000; the resort areas were
hit hard. Khao Lak in the Pha Nga region and the island of Ko Phi Phi
were nearly flattened. Damage to the large resort island of Phuket
was considerable, but rebuilding and cleanup are under way, and most
hotels were fully operational just days after the disaster. Parts of
coastal Malaysia were also hit. A coalition of nations on the Indian
Ocean are at work to implement an early warning system similar to
those in countries on the Pacific in the hope that this tragedy will not
be repeated. For this edition, it is important to note that only the
southwestern peninsula of Thailand and the west coast of Malaysia
were affected. Vietnam, Cambodia, and Bali were untouched.

Recent news from Thailand focuses on the troubles in the far south along the Malay border. Sectarian tensions and small-scale terror attacks by isolated extremist groups since January 2004 have provoked a swift and deadly response from the Thai military. Thai police and military installations, schools, and Buddhist temples have been targeted by extremists, and retaliation from Thai troops has left hundreds dead; in fact, much of the international criticism cites excessive use of military force against young militants, particularly in the wake of a massacre at a temple in April 2004. The southern border area, near Pattani and Sungai Kolok, has been under periodic martial law, and travelers are discouraged from any unnecessary travel to the far south; few international tourists visit the area, however, and any violence so far has been directed at Thai establishments and places that cater to Malay tourists (mostly weekend revelers).

The situation along the border is being watched closely, and things have been calm of late. Deferring travel to the south coast islands (which are far removed from the violence) would only mean a triumph for extremists.

The big news is that Bangkok's long-awaited subway is finally open! The subway connects Hualamphang Train Station with the northern Mo Chit bus terminal via an inverted C route through the city, with access to the existing skytrain at Silom and at the Asok stop on Sukhumvit Road. One ride will cost between 15B and 35B (40¢–90¢).

Bangkok is also awaiting the completion of a new airport. Suvanabhumi International Airport is slated for opening in the fall of 2005. The current airport, Don Muang International, will be transformed into the domestic terminal. In other airline news, there have been some exciting changes on the domestic air scene, with many new, smaller carriers vying for domestic routes. **Nok Air** (*nok* means bird) is a small, no-frills subsidiary of Thai Airways (www.thaiair.com); **Air Asia** (www.airasia.com), a budget Malay carrier, runs budget hops to all major tour destinations in the kingdom; and **Valuejet** is making connections from a number of international destinations.

Along with its fine resorts in Hua Hin, Bangkok, and the Golden Triangle, Anantara has just opened 108 rooms of the **Anantara Resort and Spa Koh Samui** (© 02477-0795; www.anantara.com) on a quiet stretch of beach on Bo Phut Bay.

On Koh Chang, a lush little hideaway just short of the Cambodian border on Thailand's eastern seaboard, the folks at the Amari hotel chain have just finished construction on the **Amari Emerald Cove Resort** (© 03955-2000; www.amari.com).

In Bangkok, the luxury Siam Intercontinental, once a top hotel in the heart of the city at Siam Square, has been torn down, and in it's place the **Paragon,** a massive five- star, is under construction. **The Inter-Continental** is now open in style in a building once housing Le Meridien. The **Hilton Nai-Lert,** a park-side five-star also near the city center, is rebranding and opening as a **Raffles Hotel** (© 02253-0123). Bangkok's latest luxury catwalk is the newly opened **Metropolitan** (© 02625-3333) on the site of the old YMCA.

Elsewhere, luxury properties are springing up like mushrooms on a wet log. On Phuket, the **JW Marriott** (© 07633-8000) is a secluded, luxury oasis on the northernmost tip of the busy tourist island. On Koh Samui, don't miss the newly opened **Buriraya** (© 07742-9300), a luxury resort overlooking Lamai Beach, an area once reserved for budget travelers. In Krabi, the **Sheraton Krabi Beach Resort** (© 07562-8000) is new to

this edition and a luxury find. These same resort areas still support a host of good midrange and budget accommodations with newer small resorts opening every day.

Islands like Ko Pha Ngan (near Koh Samui), Ko Lanta (near Krabi), and Ko Chang (east of Bangkok), once virtually untouched by mass tourism are, for good or for ill, sprouting high-end properties and luring the more well heeled. **Amari Emerald Cove Resort** (© 03955-2000) is a cozy new choice on Ko Chang. **Panviman Resorts** has fine properties on Ko Chang (© 03955-1290) and Ko Pha Ngan (© 07723-8543). Ko Lanta, south of Krabi, now hosts the **Pimalai Resort and Spa** (© 07560-7999), a luxurious hideaway on a backpacker's isle.

In Chiang Mai, **Tamarind Village** (© 05341-8896) is a unique semiluxe compound at the city center. In the far north, near Chiang Rai, don't miss the reopened **Anantara Resort and Spa Golden Triangle** (© 800/225-5843 or 05378-4084) overlooking the Golden Triangle and near the large **Hall of Opium,** a new interactive museum about the history and cultivation of the poppy.

**Spa tourism** has taken off in leaps and bounds in Thailand: from luxury properties offering extensive health and beauty packages and superluxe accommodations at prices comparable to Europe or the U.S., to smaller day spas and affordable destination spas with relaxing treatments and healthy living for all that ails you. Tops are places like the **Banyan Tree** in Phuket (© 07632-4374) or the **Four Seasons Resort & Spa** in Chiang Mai (© 05329-8181). For high-end health destinations, nothing compares with **Chiva-Som** in Hua Hin (© 03253-6536), a longtime leader in spa treatments with a very proactive, "peel the onion" approach.

## LAOS

French military men in the early 19th century bemoaned the posting of disciplined officers to Laos, telling of how the languid pace and earthly delights spoiled the man and made mush out of good soldiers. Things haven't change much; in fact, after a visit to Laos it's hard to get back into the rat race.

The Lao economy still lags, and any improvements in infrastructure since the last edition of this book come with the incursion of foreign investors and international aid: the Japanese building bridges in the south; China's efforts to pave the far north; and increased trade with both China and neighboring Thailand, has sparked some growth. But in general, the predominantly rural population of Laos eke out a basic living from the land, and a visit here is stepping into a bygone era.

Security for travelers is not an issue, but some reports over the last decade give pause (see the special box at the head of the Laos chapter); however the main north-south highway, Route 13, has been free of insurgent activity for some time now. The national carrier, once called Lao Aviation, has renamed itself **Lao Airlines** (www.laoairlines. com) and has acquired a number of new planes and flies new routes, offering better service and a stronger commitment to safety (though still has yet to pass international safety standards).

Rural roads are still reserved for the hardy. One good way to get around in style is to book with **Luangsay Cruises** (✆ 071/252-553; www.mekongcruises.com), either for its northern trip from the Thai border to Luang Prabang—with an overnight at its luxurious eco-lodge—or on the luxury **Wat Phou** flagship in the far south. **Diethelm** (✆ 021/213-833; www.diethelm-travel.com) is still the country's leader for deluxe classic tours.

**Luang Prabang,** a UNESCO World Heritage city of quaint French colonial buildings and stunning original temples along the Mekong, is the country's premiere attraction. The picturesque **Villa Santi Hotel** has long set the standard for downtown boutique luxury, but a number of unique new hotels are following suit. **3 Nagas** (✆ 071/252-079; www.3nagas.com) is exemplary of the cool, new boutique renovations going on in town. Originally a royal building in the 19th century, later an ice-cream factory, rooms here are kingly and atmospheric. **Sala Prabang** is another stylish innovator; this a more budget choice—a boutique guesthouse, really—down by the riverside (✆ 071/252-460; www. salalao.com). The former **L'hotel Souvannaphoum,** a latter-day remodeling of what was once the home of a prince of the same name, is now under construction again, this time by a Singaporean firm, and is scheduled to reopen in 2005 in a new incarnation.

**L'Elephant** (✆ 071/252-482), an upscale French bistro in the heart of Luang Prabang, is still the town's top dog. **Café Reginé** (✆ 071/253-397), a small street-side restaurant in Luang Prabang, is new to this guide and serves some of the best pizza in the region and good French and Mediterranean from a little storefront. **The Hive,** just next door to L'étranger and run by the same folks, is the one and only nightspot in town. Drum-and-bass and hip-hop pump late into the evening and the dancing is fast and furious behind Phoussi hill until 12 or 1am.

Day trips from Luang Prabang to waterfalls and small villages are a hoot, but, sadly, you can no longer rent motorbikes in town, and must instead rely on local transport.

In the capital, **Vientiane,** a new riverside hotel, the behemoth **Donchane Palace,** is scheduled to open in 2005 and greet business conventions and international delegates. A unique new restaurant called **Le Na Dao** (© **020/550-484**) sets a new standard in town for authentic French—no fusion, no foolin'—a real find.

**Eco-tourism** is still what brings so many off the track to rural Laos, and the folks at **Wildside Eco Group** (54 Setthathirat Rd., Vientiane; © **021/ 223-022;** www.lao-wildside.com) lead adventurous trips out into the back of beyond, and now even further into the bush.

## VIETNAM

Vietnam is a trudging into the modern world with its head held high. Long a world leader in the export of rice, Vietnam now exports coffee, catfish, and shrimp on a level that has turned world markets upside down. Sloughing off years of isolation and recent economic collapse in the late 1990s, Vietnam is rushing pell-mell into the global economy, and international investments following bilateral trade agreements with Western countries has meant a GDP growth in 2002 to 2003 of 8%, second only to bubbling China. Vietnam is in the queue for membership in the World Trade Organization. Hosting the Southeast Asian (SEA) Games in 2003 was a great boost to Vietnam's status and relations in the region.

As recent as the fall of 2004, remains of American soldiers from the war era were unearthed and returned to the U.S., and the process of reconciliation between the two one-time enemies has been slow, marred by disagreements over missing American POWs, and Vietnam's continued aggression in the region and human rights violations at home. But trade and diplomatic ties have been redrawn, and cooperation is now the rule. An American naval ship, the USS *Vandergrift,* docked in Vung Tao in '04, the first since the war years, and the U.S. and Vietnam now even exchange military intelligence.

Further evidence of international cooperation, an extension of the *doi moi* beginning in the 1980s, is the comprehensive airline agreement between Vietnam and the U.S., which means that American carriers now fly directly to Vietnam from the U.S. West Coast. Loosening of restrictions on visas for people from neighboring nations—South Korea and Japan—is a good sign, and there are hints that visa-on-arrival will be available for Western visitors in coming years. **Vietnam Airlines,** the country's only domestic carrier, has purchased a fleet of new, safer planes and has expanded its schedule, both foreign and domestic. And the exponential growth in the number of ATMs in Vietnam means convenience for the international traveler.

Three-quarters of Vietnam's landmass is mountainous and covered by lush tropical forests, great for trekking and mountain biking. Wide rivers and beautiful coastline attracts paddlers worldwide, and the country's long stretch of beaches is great for watersports and relaxing. The major cities of Hanoi and Saigon are exciting and cosmopolitan, with countless cultural and historical attractions as well as accommodations from budget to ultradeluxe. Below are some exciting additions to this edition.

Despite development, busy Hanoi retains all of its charms: the chaos of the busy Old Quarter, tranquil Hoan Kiem at dawn, or a visit to the sites venerating Ho Chi Minh (even his actual body lying in state). Accommodations in the Vietnam capital are many. The **Sheraton Hanoi Hotel** (© **04/719-9000;** www.sheraton. com) is finally up and running after a prolonged stall caused by economic collapse in the late 1990s. The Sheraton is a short ride from the town center and a good, comfortable choice, just one of many five-star hotels in town. On the budget end, **Hong**

**Ngoc Hotels** (☎ **04/826-7566**) are an ever-expanding local chain of tidy minihotels, all with good locations in the heart of the Old Quarter (now a total of four buildings).

A visit to Hanoi is not complete without visiting **Cha Ca La Vong** (☎ **04/825-3929**), a unique local restaurant, and new to this edition are the likes of the **Green Tangerine** (☎ **04/825-1286**), an upmarket French bistro set in a charming colonial, and **Mediterraneo** (☎ **04/826-6288**), with good Italian fare.

Tours to picturesque Ha Long Bay, just 4 hours from Hanoi, are popular, and new luxury options abound. **Buffalo Tours** (www.buffalotours.com/jewel) runs overnight trips on its luxury *The Jewel of the Bay* (the best of many similar junkets), and the *Emeraude* (www.emeraude-cruises.com), a copy of an early-20th-century French steamer, trolls the bay in style.

The hotel scene in the colonial capital of **Hue,** once rather grim, gets a good goose from the new high-end rooms at the old **Hotel Saigon Morin** (☎ **054/823-526**; www.morinhotel.com.vn), the only international standard in town.

The UNESCO World Heritage town of **Hoi An** has seen a rise in tourists and fine high-end hotels and resorts to accommodate. New this edition is the **Life Resort** (☎ **510/914-555**; www.life-resorts.com) with a unique semiluxe campus near the old town proper. Development on nearby Hoi An Island, within walking distance from town, starts with mid-range **Vinh Hung Resort** (☎ **0510/910-577**; www.vinhhunghotels.com), a trend likely to continue. Also new is the **Hoi An Cargo Club and Patisserie** (☎ **0510/910-489**; www.hoianhospitality.com), a high-end restaurant and bakery that offers cooking classes.

In coastal Nha Trang, Vietnam's Ocean City, the finest resort is still the **Ana Mandara,** but the same developers, Six Senses (www.sixsenses.com), have just finished **Evason Hideaway Ana Mandara,** a superluxe resort of pool villas reachable only by boat. New **VinPearl Resort** (☎ **058/598-188**; www.vinpearlresort.com) is notable for its size (over 450 rooms) and unique location on an island just off shore (reached only by boat). In town, the new **Sunrise Beach Resort Nha Trang** (☎ **058/920-999**; www.sunrisenhatrang.com) brings high-end luxury to the main Nha Trang strip. New minihotels abound.

Phan Thiet, a beachside resort close to Ho Chi Minh, is crowded with good accommodations; add to this the **Pandanus Beach Resort** (☎ **062/849-849**; www.pandanusresort.com) in a newly developed area near the Red Dunes (quite far from town), or the latest budget venture by **Sinh Café** (www.sinhcafevn.com), one of Vietnam's convenient budget travel agents.

In busy Ho Chi Minh, you can't miss the city's latest addition: the 23-floor **Sheraton Saigon** (☎ **08/827-2828**; www.sheraton.com/saigon) is a top business standard, with close competition from longtime favorite the **Caravelle** and soon a **Hyatt** now under construction. On the budget end, and new to this edition, is the convenient **Riverside Hotel** (☎ **08/822-4038**; www.riversidehotelsg.com) and, in the backpacker area, the **Que Huong—Liberty 3** (☎ **08/836-9522**; www.libertyhotels.com.vn), both spartan but comfortable.

Dining choices are many in old Saigon, and new to this edition is luxury **Port Orient** at the Caravelle Hotel (☎ **08/823-4999**), serving good fusion. Also try **Skewers** (☎ **08/829-2216**), with fine Mediterranean and barbecue. The new Sheraton Hotel's **Top of 23** is a cool new live music venue.

On the picturesque Mekong Delta, just south of Saigon, the **Victoria Can**

Tho (☎ 071/810-111; www.victoria
hotels-asia.com) is new to this edition
and the luxury companion to nearby
**Victoria Chau Doc,** both colonial-
style hotels at river side.

## CAMBODIA
Cambodia is receiving more and more
Western visitors and greeting them in
style. Cambodia's rough, rural roads
are still best left to the adventurous,
though, and it is important to stay
abreast of the political situation, but
travel to Phnom Penh and Siem Reap
is now convenient and comfortable.
New flights connect Cambodia's
premier attraction, the magnificent
temples of Angkor Wat, with nearby
air hubs and accommodations in Siem
Reap, the access town to the temples,
which is rife with comfortable
amenities.

Popular for its fine hotels in Vietnam, **Victoria Hotels** (www.victoria
hotels-asia.com) introduces their latest—and arguably best—endeavor,
the **Victoria Angkor Hotel** (☎ 063/
760-428). The hotel dominates the
central green just across from the classic **Raffles Grand Hotel D'Angkor.**

**Angkor Village** is still one of the
most popular, atmospheric choices in
Siem Reap, so much so that they've
opened the **Angkor Village Hotel**
(☎ 063/963-5613; www.angkor
village.com), a larger version of the
older favorite.

**Aman Resorts** (www.amanresorts.
com), one of the most luxurious hoteliers in the region, now hosts the
**Amansara** (☎ 063/760-333) just
outside town, with private villas from
$700 that rent to the rock stars and
royalty.

Also new to this edition in Siem
Reap are the following: **Shinta Mani**
(☎ 063/761-998; www.sanctuary
resorts.com/shintamani), a small, boutique resort supported by its own
hospitality institute; **Bopha Angkor**

(☎ 063/964-928; www.bopha-
angkor.com), a midrange Khmer-
themed gem. For dining in Siem
Reap, check out **Khmer Kitchen
Restaurant** (☎ 012/763-468) or the
**Soup Dragon** (☎ 063/964-933),
both new to this edition, but popular
old standbys in Siem Reap that serve
authentic local cuisine.

It is important to note that visitors
to Angkor are now prohibited from
riding rented motorbikes to the temple sites, but new motorbikes with
small, shaded surreys on the back are a
good, affordable option. Officials cite
safety concerns, but it is likely more
about creating jobs for local drivers.
Makes sense, really.

For dining, check out **Rendezvous
Café** (☎ 023/986-466), a cool new
riverfront spot on the north end of
Sisowath Quay. New to this edition is
cool, laid-back **Comme á la Maison**
(☎ 023/360-801; www.commeala
maison-delicatessen.com), a bakery
and cafe south of town.

Air connections to and from
Phnom Penh and Siem Reap are frequent. Boats now connect Phnom
Penh with Chau Doc on the border of
Vietnam and convenient speedboats
still ply the Tonle Sap between Phnom
Penh and Siem Reap. Don't miss the
new luxury services provided by
**Mekong Express** (☎ 023/427-518;
www.mekongexpresstourboat.com);
$35 buys a ride from Phnom Penh to
Siem Reap in style, and the company
also runs comfortable air-conditioned
buses. Rural travel is four-wheel-drive
only, and in-country tour operators
can arrange exciting tours.

## SINGAPORE
Singapore is booming with culture. In
2003, the Lion City opened the
much-anticipated **Asian Civilisations
Museum, Empress Place** (1 Empress
Place; ☎ 65/6332-7798), a stunning
display of Asian history and heritage

in a gorgeous colonial building at the mouth of the Singapore River. The building also hosts eateries and a fabulous museum gift shop. Check the website (www.nhb.gov.sg) before you come, to see if you can catch a free lecture. Book early, as they're very popular. Nearby, the charming **Old Parliament House** (1 Old Parliament Lane; ℂ **65/6332-6900**), perhaps the oldest building in Singapore, was recently restored and reopened to welcome arts exhibits, performances, and lectures.

The bad news is the **Singapore History Museum** is closed. The good news is, when it reopens in 2006 it will be twice the size and house completely new exhibits. In the meantime, they've set up a small display along the Singapore River (Riverside Point, 30 Merchant Rd., #03-09/17; ℂ **65/6332-3659**) documenting the history of river life.

Speaking of construction, if it looks like the **Singapore Art Museum** (Bras Basah Rd.; ℂ **65/6332-3222**) is closed, it's not. It's just unfortunately surrounded by barricades to protect people from wandering into neighboring construction of a new MRT station just beneath. In fact, **Bras Basah Park,** which sits between the history and art museums, will open soon as the new campus of the Singapore Management University, a move that might turn the downtown area into a college town in the next couple years. Until then, it is one enormous construction site and traffic jam.

Meanwhile, over in **Kampong Glam,** the **Istana,** the former palace of Singapore's ruling Sultan Hussein, got a complete facelift and now offers up the best glimpse into local Malay culture that Singapore has ever had. The new **Malay Heritage Centre** (85 Sultan's Gate; ℂ **65/6391-0450**), in addition to exhibits, also has demonstrations and tours.

Two exciting developments in **Pasir Ris,** in the northeast part of the island, are **Escape Theme Park** (Downtown East 1, Pasir Ris Close; ℂ **65/6581-9112**) and **Wild Wild Wet** (Downtown East 1, Pasir Ris Close; ℂ **65/6581-9135**), great options for traveling families looking to stave off heat and boredom.

## MALAYSIA

**AirAsia** is exciting news for travelers to Malaysia (www.airasia.com). The budget, no-frills airline has survived its first 3 years with flying colors and offers some of the cheapest airfares around the country. What you save in airfare you can use to upgrade to a more deluxe resort. In similar news, **Berjaya Air** (ℂ **603/7846-8228;** www.berjaya-air.com). recently opened flights from Kuala Lumpur to Redang island off the east coast of peninsular Malaysia, making this fantastic dive resort very accessible.

Not so exciting, in recent years Malaysia has suffered a rise in **purse snatching,** what they call "snatch-thieving," which is an unfortunate mar on this otherwise safe country. Keep your bag close.

**KUALA LUMPUR**   The **Bird Park** (Jalan Perdana, Lake Gardens; ℂ **03/2273-5423**) has reopened and it is really something—the world's largest walk-in aviary is home to some 3,000 birds. They did a fantastic job. There's a new hot nightspot called **Asian Heritage Row** along Jalan Doraisamy with about a half dozen trendy restaurants and bars, and more to come.

My favorite new attraction in KL has to be the **Berjaya Times Square** shopping mall, not for its 900 shops, food, and entertainment venues, but for the world's largest indoor roller-coaster (1 Jalan Imbi; ℂ **03/2117-3118**). Even if you don't ride it, you'll feel a rush when it rumbles above your head at breakneck speeds. Very cool.

**MALACCA**    This city has been busy restoring all of its museums (and there are quite a few). The newer exhibits are a welcome improvement and much recommended for those who find adventure in learning about history and heritage.

**PENANG**    In my last visit to Penang I discovered that the **Cheong Fatt Tze Mansion** (13 Leith St.; ✆ 04/262-0006) opens its doors to overnight guests. This opulent Chinese baroque mansion, which belonged to one of Penang's richest fat cats, has renovated rooms with en suite bathrooms that carry over the eye-popping style of the rest of the mansion. If you choose not to stay, staff members still conduct daily tours to show off the unbelievable renovation job.

**TERENGGANU**    On the east coast, the state of Terengganu ushered in new political leadership that is committed to reversing the previous conservative government's antitourism policies. A **new highway** connecting the capital to Kuantan in the east coast is expected to extend to Terengganu by the end of 2005, opening up this fascinating state's rich heritage to visitors.

**SABAH**    Across the sea in Sabah, scuba divers headed for **Sipadan,** one of the top 10 dive sites in the world, should note that the Malaysian government is turning the island into a protected park. After December 2004, no dive operators will be allowed to run resorts on the island. Divers can still appreciate the site, however, but only via day trips.

## BALI

In the aftermath of the huge drop in tourism following the Bali bombings in 2001, the island is getting back to full speed, but things aren't the same. The shakeup has changed the Balinese tourist market, and price ranges across the board have dropped. Some services have fallen away; there are no more high-speed ferry connections to Lombok, for example; but services that remain are tops, and great discounts are available across the board.

**Aman Resorts** (www.amanresorts. com) has ultraluxurious resorts in the major destinations in Bali: Ubud, Candi Dasa and Nusa Dua—a great place to go rock star if you can afford it.

New to this edition is the **Royal Seminyak** (✆ 361/730730) a four-star at beach side on the north end of **Kuta.** The hotel is at the end of **Dhyana Pura Street,** Kuta's newest and hippest area with some of Bali's finest fine dining and cool clubs that go all night. Check out *The Yak,* a free local glossy featuring the best of the best. Nearby **Puri Cendana** (✆ 361/730869) is a great budget choice.

In **Ubud,** Bali's cultural locus at the island center, there are lots of good, high-end choices. Ubud's **Amandari** and **Four Seasons** are without rival, but **Alila** (✆ 361/975963; www.alila hotels.com) is a more affordable luxury hotel outside of town among lush rice terraces. **Maya Ubud** (✆ 361/977888; www.mayaubud.com) is a fine four-star on the city outskirts, cozy, stylish, and removed with great spa service overlooking a verdant river valley. **Ubud Sari Health Resort** (✆ 361/974393; www.ubudsari.com) is new to this edition and a great choice for spa service and bungalows, fine style, and service at budget prices.

Dining in Ubud gets a real shot of class and innovation with new **Mozaic** (✆ 361/975768; www.mozaic-bali. com), a refined, atmospheric restaurant serving good Balinese-influenced French cuisine—nothing like it. **Lamak** (✆ 361/974663; www.lamak bali.com) is a newer, stylish bistro serving Western favorites from a chic two-tiered site in the center of Ubud.

Dining in the busy tourist center of **Kuta** is fast and furious. **Ku De Ta** (✆ 361/736969; www.kudeta.net), in Seminyak (the north end of Kuta), is arguably the best, but certainly typical of new fine dining options in the area. If you eat all of your meals in Bali at ritzy restaurants, you've missed out; don't miss the chance to eat suckling pig—called *babi guling*—or crispy duck and good local seafood and rice dishes at the island's many local restaurants, called *warung*.

Travelers to neighboring **Lombok** have slowed to a trickle, what with the suspension of ferry services and secular tensions in the region, but a visit to the **Oberoi Lombok** (© 370/638444; www.oberoihotels.com) is replete with kingly comforts—there is also a luxurious property in Seminyak.

**Bali Adventure Tours** (© 361/721480; www.baliadventuretours. com) and **Sobek** (© 361/287059) still run great adventures around the island, and newcomer **Matangi Tours** (© 361/739820; www.traditional balitours.com) brings a whole new compliment of home stay and immersion programs to the table.

# 1

# The Best of Southeast Asia

To the Western visitor, Southeast Asia is an assault on the senses, an immersion into a way of life utterly unlike that to which we're accustomed. From bustling cities like Bangkok, Singapore, and Kuala Lumpur to tiny fishing villages and thatched rural hamlet, from the jungles of Malaysian Borneo to the deluxe resorts of Bali, from the temples of Luang Prabang in Laos to the bacchanal of Patpong in Thailand, Southeast Asia offers a glimpse of the extraordinary, an explosion of colors, sounds, smells, textures, and life that will send you home with a wider vision of the human experience. In this chapter, we share our picks of the region's unrivaled highlights.

## 1 The Most Unforgettable Travel Experiences

- **Making Merit (Thailand).** In Thailand, Buddhist monks do not earn income; they survive on gifts of food and necessary items given by devoted Buddhists in the lay community. But the tonsured monk in his gold-colored robes who walks from house to house each morning is not begging for food; instead, he is offering an opportunity for the giver to receive merit. In contributing to the monk's survival, the giver of food and gifts is supporting the *sangha,* the monkhood, and therefore gets closer to Buddhist ideals. If you are interested in making merit this way, talk to your hotel's concierge. You might be able to join kitchen staff as they head to a nearby monastery in the early morning or wait on the right byway to greet and feed a column of monks. See chapter 4.

- **Sailing the South China Sea (Vietnam).** With the sky above us a deep, red afterglow, we rounded a buoy marking the shipping lane off coastal Nha Trang and, with the wind now at our backs, settled the Hobie Cat into a perfect fan-tail, the mainsail and jib billowing on opposite sides as the rudders gave a low moan and the boat gained speed. Riding low swells, we sped toward a coast where twinkling lights might have belonged to a child's train set, and the sky continued its show, now in orange. Heavenly. Opportunities for watersports and sailing are many as you travel along Vietnam's coast. Most resorts have boats for rent, and Nha Trang is a good bet, as is the area off Mui Ne Beach near Phan Thiet, which is becoming a very popular wind- and kite-surfing spot. See chapter 6.

- **Staying in a Hill-Tribe Village near the China Border (Laos).** They're still asking visitors, "Why do you come here, anyway?" in villages along the NamHa River in northern Laos. Thanks to the folks who run the NamHa Project, these vast tracts of pristine jungle won't be overrun by tourists anytime soon, and the many ethnic minority groups who've lived

# Southeast Asia

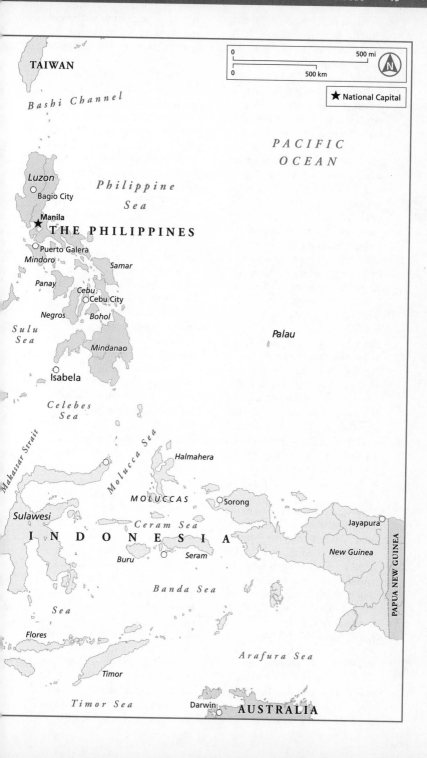

here in isolation won't be turned into human zoo exhibits. It is heartening to know that the money you spend on a trek goes to support a model of sustainable eco-tour development in a fragile region. And it is good, hearty jungle trekking or river kayak that takes you through lush jungle terrain where you're likely to see monkeys and exotic birds. Arrive in villages where kayaks are still an oddity, and spend fun evenings around the fire communicating by charades or stick figures in a notebook. It's not about the villages being "pristine"; it's about the fact that your visit is part of a cultural exchange, not about disparate currency exchange rates. You can have a positive effect on people with your heart *and* your tourist dollars. See chapter 5.

- **Participating in a Baci Ceremony (Laos).** The Baci is a touching Lao ceremony used to say welcome or farewell and to honor achievements. Participants sit in a circle and receive group blessings, after which there is traditional dancing and *lao lao,* rice wine. It's a chance for the ultrafriendly Lao people to express their hospitality to you, their honored guest. See chapter 5.

- **Sipping a Singapore Sling in the Long Bar (Raffles Hotel, Singapore).** Ah, the Long Bar, home of the Singapore Sling. I like to come in the afternoons before the tourist rush. Sheltered by long timber shutters that close out the tropical sun, the air cooled by lazy punkahs (small fans that wave gently back and forth above), you can sit back in old rattan chairs and have your saronged waitress serve you sticky alcoholic creations while you toss back a few dainty crab cakes. Life can be so decadent. Okay, so the punkahs

are electric and, come to think of it, the place is air-conditioned (not to mention that it costs a small fortune), but it's fun to imagine the days when Somerset Maugham, Rudyard Kipling, or Charlie Chaplin would be sitting at the bar sipping Slings and spinning exotic tales of their world travels. Drink up, my friend; it's a lovely high. See chapter 8.

- **Walking the Streets of Georgetown (Penang, Malaysia).** Evidence of former British colonization and early Chinese, Indian, and Arab immigration is apparent in many major cities in Malaysia, but Penang has a special charm. In some ways, the city still operates the way it did half a century ago. The shop houses are filled with small businesses—bicycle-repair shops, hardware stores, Chinese medicine halls, and coffee shops. From upstairs windows, you can still see laundry hanging on bamboo poles. Life hums in these streets, and for anyone who has witnessed the homogenization of Singapore or the modernization of Kuala Lumpur, Penang is a charming reminder of what life might have been like in these old outposts. See chapter 9.

- **Observing Open-Air Public Cremations (Bali).** Hindus believe that cremation is the only way a soul can be freed of its earthly body and travel to its next incarnation (or to enlightenment), so cremations are joyous occasions, full of floats and fanfare that can resemble a Mardi Gras parade. Complicated towers hold the body, carried aloft by cheering men. At the burning ground, the body is placed in a receptacle resembling a winged lion, a bull, or some other fabulous creature, and is set on fire. It's beautiful and awesome, a marvelous show of pageantry and faith, and yet a natural part of everyday life. Western visitors are welcomed. See chapter 10.

- **The Magic Hour at Angkor Wat (Cambodia).** You'll want to plan your day around it, and temple aficionados all have their favorite spots; but whether from a hillside overlooking a glowing temple facade or from the heights of the main temple itself with the horizon framed by the famed ancient towers, be sure to see an Angkor sunset. Sunrise is equally worth the early morning ride. At the more popular viewing spots, like Bakeng Hill, you'll ooh and aah in concert with lots of other travelers. Nobody likes crowds, but there is a certain cool oneness here, and the odd didgeridoo player or cross-legged character in meditation is all a nice throwback to the old hippy-trail days in the region. See chapter 7.

## 2 The Best Towns & Villages

- **Chiang Saen (Thailand).** Crumbling 11th-century temples take you back to the birthplace of the Lanna Kingdom, one of Thailand's wealthiest and most influential. The nearby **Golden Triangle,** a notorious trade point for the international opium industry, has a new museum and riverside views of Laos, Thailand, and Burma. See chapter 4.

- **Hoi An (Vietnam).** The small size of Hoi An belies its importance to Vietnam; it was once a major trading port, with canals leading right up to merchants' quarters for easy delivery of goods. The canals are now peaceful streets, but little else has changed. Almost every building in central Hoi An is a historic Vietnamese-, Japanese-, and Chinese-influenced residence or meeting hall. See chapter 6.

- **Luang Prabang (Laos).** This town, sanctioned a World Heritage site by UNESCO for its glorious Buddhist temples, is also a charming retreat. Shady lanes are lined with French-style country homes that have been restored and converted to house cafes, galleries, shops, and some quaint guesthouses. The sunset over the lazy Mekong is the perfect end to a day spent in Luang Prabang. See chapter 5.

- **Ubud (Bali).** This is the cultural heart of Bali, bursting with art and greenery and some of the best food on the island. Even though it's dependent on tourism and is far from a typical Bali village, you still get a sense of a real town, with real life going on around you. Ubud is the richest region in Bali for art production and, because of its central location, the town is the perfect base for exploring the rest of the island. See chapter 10.

- **Phnom Penh (Cambodia).** Few countries' capitals could be called quaint or fall under the category of a "town," and that's the very charm of this riverside burg. They say you either love it or hate it, that it's a place for expats and not tourists, but in a short stroll through the town center, you'll come across a unique mix. First you'll encounter a row of tourist cafes, streets buzzing with motorbikes and choked with dust, but turn the corner and find a quiet alley, a row of colonials, a lone kid kicking a soccer ball, and a grim-looking grandmother breaking into a smile as you walk by. There's something special here. See chapter 7.

## 3 The Best Beaches

- **Chaweng Beach (Koh Samui, Thailand).** Chaweng is real fun in the sun. The beach itself is gorgeous, with bungalows nestled in the trees just beyond the sand. Behind the beach lies a small town full of life, from wonderful Thai and seafood eateries to shopping and wild nightlife options. See chapter 4.

- **Phan Thiet (Vietnam).** Just a few hours from Saigon, Phan Thiet is the latest getaway in Vietnam. Oceanside development is in full swing here, and there are some great boutique resorts along the stunning white sands of Mui Ne Beach. There's a golf course designed by Nick Faldo, and the town of Phan Thiet itself is an interesting little fishing port worth a wander. The seafood is good, and there are some great day trips to enormous remote dunes and smaller fishing villages. See chapter 6.

- **Tanjung Rhu (Langkawi, Malaysia).** This huge secluded cove has one of the longest stretches of private beach I've ever seen. Wide with soft sand, the beach has cooling shady spots provided by palm trees overhead and beautiful deep blue waters for good swimming. Best of all, there's only one resort here (and the beach is kept picture perfect), so you won't have to elbow for space or suffer jet skis. See chapter 9.

- **Juara Bay (Tioman Island, Malaysia).** This beach is what they meant when they coined the word *isolated*. Be prepared to live like Robinson Crusoe—in tiny huts with cold-water showers and many with no electricity. But, oh, the beach! A wide crescent of palm-lined sand hugs the clearest blue water, with very few other people in sight. See chapter 9.

- **Lombok (Indonesia).** The pure white-sand beaches of Lombok, with clear aqua-blue water lapping against them, are sometimes so private that you can have one all to yourself. And Lombok is just a short hop from neighboring Bali. See chapter 10.

## 4 The Best Outdoor Adventures

- **Phang-nga Bay (Thailand).** From the island of Phuket, sea canoe operators guide visitors through the caves hidden deep inside the craggy island-rocks of Phang-nga Bay. Outside, the islands thrust up to the sky, their jagged edges laced with scattered trees. Lie flat in your canoe to slip through the small cave openings, inside which you'll find magnificent chambers believed to have once hidden pirate operations. See chapter 4.

- **Sea Kayaking in Halong Bay (Vietnam).** The more than 3,000 arresting limestone karst formations rising out of Halong Bay's peaceful blue-green waters provide a natural obstacle course for paddling. Moving among them, you'll pass in and among intriguing grottos and caverns. Nights are spent camping out in natural parks or on the deck of a mother ship. See chapter 6.

- **Hill-Tribe Village Treks in Sapa (North Vietnam).** Dressed in elaborate costume of leggings, tunic, and headdress, Hmong and Yao people (among other groups) gather to sell their weavings, fine dyed clothing, or crude but intricate metalwork in the central market. In fact, the town of Sapa is famed for an ephemeral "Love Market," where people from surrounding villages converge to find that special someone. A trip to Sapa means that the hill tribes come to you, but don't limit your trip to the town; be sure to get off into the countryside and trek in the shadow of Fansipan, the highest mountain in the region. Among lush terraced rice fields, you can visit many villages in even the shortest trek and experience different hill-tribe traditions and cultures. See chapter 6.

- **Caving and Kayaking in Vang Vieng (Laos).** Countless caves and caverns are hidden in the magnificent mountains surrounding Vang Vieng, a small village along the Nam Song River. Some of them are well known and some are barely on the map. Kayak tours on the Nam Song include some fun caves that you'll swim into and can test your mettle on natural mud slides. Spend your days exploring and evenings talking about it over drinks in this laid-back little backpacker town. See chapter 5.
- **Jungle Trekking in Taman Negara (Malaysia).** With suitable options for all budgets, levels of comfort, and desired adventure, Malaysia's largest national park opens the wonders of primary rain forest and the creatures who dwell in it to everyone. From the canopy, walk high atop the forest to night watches for nocturnal life. This adventure is as stunning as it is informative. See chapter 9.
- **Hiking Gunung Agung (Bali).** Bali's highest mountain/volcano, Gunung Agung (3,014m/9,886 ft. high), is sacred to the Balinese, whose traditions call it "the center of the world." Climbing the steaming peak is a serious trek that calls for a guide and proper supplies. Most hotels can arrange for it, but you will have to start out in the middle of the night or very early in the morning to make the top by sunrise. Nearby **Gunung Batur** is a less strenuous and no less rewarding half-day climb. See chapter 10.
- **Born to Be Wild (Cambodia).** If you ride motorbikes, get your motor runnin' and head out on the dirt-track back roads. Rural Cambodia is just opening up for exploration, and the pioneers here are leading the way to the back of beyond on dirt bikes (find a bike with the best suspension). It's certainly a choice for the hearty and a great adventure. See chapter 7.

## 5  The Most Intriguing Temples, Shrines, Palaces & Archaeological Sites

- **The Grand Palace & Wat Phra Kaeo (Bangkok, Thailand).** These two places are number one on every travel itinerary to Bangkok, and rightly so. The palace is indeed grand, with mixtures of traditional Thai and European Victorian architecture. Wat Phra Kaeo, the royal temple that houses Thailand's revered and mysterious Emerald Buddha, is a small city in itself, with a dozen or more picturesque outer buildings and monuments that devour rolls of film. See chapter 4.
- **Ayutthaya (Thailand).** Before Bangkok, there was Ayutthaya. This was the thriving capital of Siam that the first Europeans saw when they visited amazing Thailand. Ruling a rich and powerful kingdom of over a million

inhabitants, the monarchy supported the arts, especially literature. As the city grew, international trade was encouraged. All that remains are brick remnants of a grand palace and many temples that were sacked during the Burmese invasion. It's best to hire a guide who can walk you through and point out the significance of each site. See chapter 4.

- **The Cao Dai Holy See (Tay Ninh) (North of Ho Chi Minh, Vietnam).** This is the spiritual home base of the Cao Dai religion, a faith characterized by philosophical inclusion and influence gathered from all beliefs, including the world's great scientists and humanitarians. Its headquarters is like a fantasyland of colored mosaic and elaborate painting. Followers are dressed in white turbans during the picturesque daily procession. It's quite unique. See chapter 6.

- **Tomb of Khai Dinh (Hue, Vietnam).** Khai Dinh was an egotistical, eccentric emperor who was bad for the people of Vietnam but great for the tomb he left behind. A gaudy mix of Gothic, baroque, and classical Chinese architecture, the exterior is remarkable. The stunning interior is completely covered with intricate glass and ceramic mosaic work. See chapter 6.

- **Wat Xieng Thong (Luang Prabang, Laos).** The glittering Xieng Thong, built in 1560, sits grandly on a peninsula jutting out into the Mekong River. The facades of two of its buildings are covered by glittering glass mosaics; another building contains an ornate chariot with the heads of seven dragons and the remains of a king. About a dozen English-speaking monks roam the premises; all are

excellent conversationalists. See chapter 5.

- **Plain of Jars (Xieng Khouang, Laos).** How did hundreds of huge stone urns, some measuring 2.7m tall (9 ft.), come to be placed on a few meadows in northern Laos? No one really knows, and that's what's fun here. The most prevalent explanation is that the urns were made by prehistoric folk in the area about 2,000 years ago to be used as sarcophagi, but there's lots of room for conjecture. See chapter 5.

- **Thian Hock Keng (Singapore).** One of Singapore's oldest Chinese temples, it is a fascinating testimony to Chinese Buddhism combined with traditional Confucian beliefs and natural Taoist principles. Equally fascinating is the modern world that carries on just outside the old temple's doors. See chapter 8.

- **Jame Mosque (Kuala Lumpur, Malaysia).** Built at the central point of the city, this is one of the oldest mosques in Kuala Lumpur. It is the heart of Malay Islam, as evidenced by the Muslim shops, eateries, and daily activities carried on in the streets surrounding it. See chapter 9.

- **Jalan Tokong (Malacca, Malaysia).** This street, in the historical heart of the city, has a Malay mosque, a Chinese temple, and a Hindu temple living peacefully side by side—the perfect example of how the many foreign religions that came to Southeast Asia shaped its communities and learned to coexist in harmony. See chapter 9.

- **Basakih Temple (Central Bali, Indonesia).** Built in homage of Gunung Agung, the island's feisty, smoke-belching creator, the Basakih Temple does justice to the awe and grandeur of the Balinese creation myths surrounding the volcano. The spires of individual family shrines and temples are something like Chinese pagodas, and the place is always abuzz with local worshippers. You're likely to get pulled into a ceremony. See chapter 10.

- **Angkor Wat (Cambodia).** One of the world's man-made wonders, Angkor Wat is the Disneyland of temples in Asia. This ancient city

was known to the Western world only in myth until it was rediscovered and hacked free of jungle overgrowth in the late 1800s. The magnificent temples are arrayed over a 97-sq.-km (37-sq.-mile) compound that dates from the rise and fall of the mighty Angkor Civilization (A.D. 802–1295). A visit here is unforgettable. See chapter 7.

## 6 The Best Museums

- **National Museum (Bangkok, Thailand).** From prehistory to recent events, this museum—the former palace of the brother of King Rama I—answers many questions about Thai history and culture through the ages. Inside buildings that are themselves works of fine Thai design, you'll find Buddha images, ancient arts, royal paraphernalia, and fine arts. Rama's sister also lived here, and her house is decorated in the same style as it was in the late 1700s. See chapter 4.

- **Vietnam National Museum of Fine Arts (Hanoi, Vietnam).** Proper art museums are few and far between in the region, and this large colonial house is a nice collection of newer works and historical pieces. You'll find nothing too controversial or groundbreaking, but some good examples of lacquer and silk painting, woodblock, and folk and expressive work in oil. If you see anything you like, you're sure to find good copies in any of the city's many galleries. See chapter 6.

- **The Cham Museum (Danang, Vietnam).** This open-air colonial structure houses the largest collection of Cham sculpture in the world. Not only are relics of this ancient Hindu-inspired culture

rare, but the religious artwork itself—more than 300 pieces of sandstone—is voluptuous, captivating, and intense. See chapter 6.

- **Images of Singapore (Sentosa Island, Singapore).** No one has done a better job than this museum in chronicling for the public the horrors of the Pacific theater and Japanese occupation in Southeast Asia. Video and audio displays take you on a chronological journey through Singapore's World War II experience. The grand finale is the Surrender Chambers, life-size wax dioramas of the fateful events. There's also dioramas depicting historical figures throughout Singapore's early development, as well as depictions of traditional cultural festivals. See chapter 8.

- **National Museum (Phnom Penh, Cambodia).** Don't miss this repository for the statues and relief sculpture that have been recovered from the Angkor temples and other ancient sites throughout Cambodia. Organized in a convenient chronology, it's a short course in Khmer art history. Later pieces are particularly quite expressive. See chapter 7.

- **Tuol Sleng, Museum of Genocide (Phnom Penh, Cambodia).** Be warned that a visit here is quite intense—too much for some. The museum is simply the shell of Cambodia's largest prison from 1975 to 1979, when the entire country was turned into a concentration camp. Originally a high school, Tuol Sleng was the site of horrible atrocities and, though there are some exhibits of photos, the experience of the museum is in wandering the small cells and learning the tragic tale from experienced local guides. See chapter 7.

## 7 The Best Festivals & Celebrations

- **Chinese New Year (Singapore).** If you're in Southeast Asia around the end of January or the beginning of February, hop up to Hong Kong or down to Singapore for the festivities. It's a 3-day party, with parades (complete with dragons and stilt walkers) and fireworks. See chapter 8.

- **Songkran (Thailand).** Every year from April 13 to 15, Thais welcome the New Year (according to their calendar). Because Songkran falls in the middle of the hottest season in an already hot country, how do you think people celebrate? Every Thai heads out into the streets with water guns and buckets of ice water (sometimes laced with talcum powder, just to add to the mess), and spends the next 3 days soaking each other— and *you.* Foreigners are especially favorite targets. Don't get mad— arm thyself: Water bazookas are on sale everywhere. Have a ball! See chapter 4.

- **That Luang Festival (Vientiane, Laos).** Thousands of Buddhist followers from all over the country, and even a few neighboring countries, converge on the spectacular That Luang temple in Vientiane. There are alms-giving ceremonies and flower processions, and then the whole affair dissolves into a carnival that stretches over several days. See chapter 5.

- **Bun Song Hua/Dragon Boat Races (Laos).** Celebrating the end of Buddhist Lent, Dragon Boat races are held in every riverside town in Laos (and that's most towns, really). The races are exciting, the betting is frenzied, and there's always a small carnival with handmade rides and the standard rigged skill games. See chapter 5.

- **Thaipusam (Singapore and Malaysia).** Around the end of January and the beginning of February, Hindus celebrate Thaipusam. Men give thanks for prayers answered by carrying *kavadis,* huge steel racks attached to their bodies with skewers piercing the skin. Cheeks are pierced, and fruits are hung from the skin using sharp hooks. A parade of devotees carry these things in a deep trance—and the next day they wake up virtually unharmed. See chapters 8 and 9.

## 8 The Biggest Cultural No-Nos

- **Photographing a member of a Hill Tribe Without Permission.** There's nothing a visitor wants more than to take away indelible images of the colorful, rustic lifestyles of the Vietnamese ethnic minorities. However, many rural people are superstitious about photographs or might resent the intrusion of privacy. Ask first. See "Etiquette Tips," in chapter 2.

- **Losing Your Temper in Laos or Thailand.** The Lao and Thai people follow Buddhist traditions in their daily life, approaching even unfortunate events with calm cheerfulness. They would be shocked and dismayed at anger or ill temper, and raising your voice won't achieve any purpose whatsoever. No matter how frustrated you become, keep it under wraps, or the people around you will see to it that you never get where you need to go. See "Etiquette Tips," in chapter 2.

• **Looking (or Being) Poor in Singapore.** You probably won't run into too many cultural faux pas in cosmopolitan Singapore, but poverty is the pits in this city. Bring your smartest clothes if you want to impress people here. See chapter 8.

• **Using Offensive Body Language in Bali, Malaysia, Thailand, or Laos.** Muslims, Hindus, and Buddhists all reserve the left hand for "unclean" toilet duties, never for pointing at anyone or anything, handing objects to others, eating, or touching other people. Similarly, in Buddhist and Hindu

cultures, the head is revered as the most sacred part of the body, while the feet are the lowest. Never touch another person's head or shoulders, not even a child's. Never point or gesture with your feet or use your feet to perform any tasks other than walking. See "Etiquette Tips," in chapter 2.

• **Hanging Clothes out to Dry in Bali.** Or otherwise out in public (off hotel balconies and chairs and the like).

• **Showing Too Much Skin (Regional).** Except perhaps in Hong Kong, Singapore and Bangkok or other heavily touristed areas, modest Southeast Asians accept beachwear at the beach, revealing vacation clothing at resorts, and sexy attire at discos. Everywhere else, dress with respect for the locals and their traditions. See "Etiquette Tips," in chapter 2.

• **Wearing Shorts or Short Skirts to a Temple or Mosque (Regional).** It'll get you tossed out. See "Etiquette Tips," in chapter 2.

## 9 The Best Resorts & Luxury Hotels

• **The Oriental (Bangkok, Thailand).** The original address in Thailand, The Oriental has seen modernization detract from its charms of yesterday, but there's still ambience all around. See p. 109.

• **Rayavadee (Krabi, Thailand).** This seductive bungalow resort in exquisite Thai style will thrill even the most discerning guests. See p. 206.

• **The Regent (Cha-Am, Thailand).** Luxurious Thai-style suites, excellent restaurants, a multitude of activities, and the most amazing swimming pool you've ever seen await you. Don't forget to meet the resident water buffalo

family—they work the resort's private rice paddies. See p. 156.

• **Sofitel Metropole (Hanoi, Vietnam).** The history of the Metropole, one of Vietnam's premier grand dames, tells the history of the last tumultuous century in Vietnam. If the walls could only talk. Though everything is luxurious and comfortable and you're in a prime downtown location, you'll certainly feel like you've walked into old Indochina. See p. 309.

• **Ana Mandara (Nha Trang, Vietnam).** The details are perfect in this small-scale resort, from the incense burning in the open longhouse-style lobby to the small signs identifying tropical fish in the lobby's pond. Each stylish room has the air of a secluded hut with its own verandah, many overlooking the palm-lined coast. Both the food and the staff's smiles are perfect. Also check out the new **Evason Hideaway** nearby. See p. 361.

- **Sofitel Dalat Palace (Dalat, Vietnam).** It's real old-world colonial opulence in the king's former castle in Vietnam's Central Highlands. Private spaces are decorated in a cool colonial baroque, and lobby and service are, in short, kingly. See p. 370.

- **Settha Palace (Vientiane, Laos).** Once the address of note for visitors to the French colony, the Settha Palace only recently returned from obscurity and is now one of the finest hotels in the region. It's a nice marriage of colonial elegance and modern comfort. See p. 256.

- **La Résidence Phou Vao (Luang Prabang, Laos).** Lording it over the town in boutique luxury, the gardens and large suite rooms of the Phou Vao (formerly the **Pansea**) are comfort and atmosphere done to a T. This is typical of other **Orient Express** properties in the region. See p. 271.

- **Raffles Hotel (Singapore).** For old-world opulence, Raffles is second to none. This is a pure fantasy of the days when tigers still lurked around the perimeters. See p. 468.

- **Four Seasons Hotel (Singapore).** Elegance and warmth combine to make this place a good bet. Consider a regular room here before you book a suite elsewhere. See p. 474.

- **The Regent (Kuala Lumpur, Malaysia).** For my money, the Regent offers the smartest decor, best service, and best selection of facilities in the whole city. See p. 554.

- **Four Seasons (Jimbaran, Bali).** With its individual bungalows and plunge pools overlooking the blue sea and its famous Four Seasons pampering, this is one of the great hotels in the world. See p. 621.

- **Amandari (Ubud, Bali).** Its individual bungalows overlook a deep green gorge, and the Amandari offers another sybaritic Bali experience. If you can afford it (or the Four Seasons Jimbaran), do. Even if you can't, do. See p. 626.

- **Raffles Grand Hotel D'Angkor (Siem Reap, Cambodia).** A classic Indochine colonial, the Grand is indeed grand. With fine services to connect you to nearby Angkor Wat, a great central pool and spa/massage facility, and beautiful rooms, it doesn't get any better. See p. 436.

## 10 The Best Hotel Bargains

- **The Atlanta (Bangkok, Thailand).** Located in a prime spot off of central Sukhumvit, the Atlanta is the oldest hotel in Bangkok (without structural renovation) and quite quirky and atmospheric. See p. 119.

- **Tamarind Village (Chiang Mai, Thailand).** If you're going to travel on a budget, do it with style—and style is what Tamarind

Village has wrapped up in its quiet courtyard in the middle of Old Town. Rooms are new and rather spartan in concrete and rattan, but everything is tiptop. See p. 219.

- **Spring Hotel/Mua Xuan (Saigon, Vietnam).** Not especially luxurious, rooms in this privately owned downtown property (one of few nongovernment places in Saigon) start at $34. It's light on amenities but very comfortable, convenient, and friendly. See p. 394.

- **Day Inn (Vientianne, Laos).** So it's just a few notches above your average guesthouse, but there's a comfortable, laid-back feel here and many long-stay visitors can't be wrong. You'll find rooms for $25. See p. 257.

- **RELC International Hotel (Singapore).** For a safe and simple place to call home in Singapore, RELC can't be beat. You might wonder how they keep costs so low when their location is so good. See p. 479.

- **Traders Hotel (Singapore).** "Value for money" is the name of the game, with all sorts of promotional packages, self-service launderettes, vending machines, and a checkout lounge—just a few of the offerings that make this the most convenient hotel in the city. See p. 479.

- **Swiss-Inn (Kuala Lumpur, Malaysia).** Tucked behind the market tents in Chinatown, this bargain find has the look of a higher-quality hotel, but in mini-size. If you plan on spending your time out exploring the city, why pay more for empty space? See p. 557.

- **Heeren House (Malacca, Malaysia).** Bargain or no bargain, this boutique hotel in the heart of the old city is *the* place to stay in Malacca if you want to really get a feel for the local atmosphere. See p. 566.

- **Telang Usan Hotel (Kuching, Malaysia).** An informal place, Telang Usan is homey and quaint, and within walking distance of many major attractions in Kuching. See p. 588.

- **The Home Stays/Losmen of Bali.** These small-time accommodations will give you a large, comfortable (though no-frills) room or bungalow with a big, often fancy breakfast for about $5 a night for two. See chapter 10.

- **Goldiana (Phnom Penh, Cambodia).** It's no frills but friendly and cheap here in a quiet neighborhood south of the town center. It's popular with long-staying visitors and NGO workers. See p. 426.

## 11 The Best Local Dining Experiences

- **Street Food (Bangkok, Thailand).** On every street, down every alley, you'll find someone setting up a cart with an umbrella. Noodles, salads, and satay are favorites, and some hawkers set up tables and stools on the sidewalk for you to take a load off. This is Thai cafe life! See chapter 4.

- *Pho* **(Vietnam).** Don't leave the country without sampling one, if not many, bowls of this delicate noodle soup, made with vermicelli-thin rice noodles, chicken *(ga)* or beef *(bo)*, and several fresh accompaniments, according to the chef's whim or local flavor: basil, mint, chile peppers, and bean sprouts. See chapter 6.

- **Ngon Restaurant (Ho Chi Minh, Vietnam).** It's a restaurant, but really like the classroom for Vietnam Cuisine 101. It's loud and busy, but diners have their choice of food from the many authentic street stalls that line the central courtyard. Locals eat here; though they have an English menu, go with a Vietnamese friend or ask for a recommendation from the friendly (but always busy) staff. See p. 398.

- **Kua Lao (Vientiane, Laos).** Kua Lao is traditional Lao cuisine in a similar setting, including music. Situated in a restored colonial, with a series of dining rooms, it is the premier Lao restaurant in the country. The extensive menu goes on for pages. There is an entire page of vegetarian entrees and another entire page of something you don't see often: traditional Lao desserts. See p. 260.

- **Hawker Centers (Singapore).** Think of them as shopping malls for food—great food! For local cuisine, who needs a menu with pictures when you can walk around and select anything you want as it's prepared before your eyes? See chapter 8.

- **Gurney Drive (Penang, Malaysia).** Penang is king for offering a variety of Asian cuisine, from Chinese to Malay, Indian, and everything else in between. Visiting this large hawker center by the sea is like taking Intro to Penang 101. See p. 577.

- **Balinese *Warungs* (Bali).** Just a local cafe, the Balinese equivalent of the greasy-spoon diner in America, *warungs* can be found on every street corner. Our favorite is **Satri's** in Ubud. With 24-hours advance notice, Satri's will cook you a smoked duck or banana chicken feast, a whole bird, plus three plates of salad or fabulous vegetables, rice, and fruit for dessert, for about $7 for two. See p. 632.

## 12 The Best Markets

- **Chatuchak Weekend Market (Bangkok, Thailand).** One word describes it: huge. You can easily get lost and certainly spend hours wandering this labyrinth. Don't buy anything until you spend at least a half-day wandering down the endless aisles eyeballing the multitude of merchandise available. See chapter 4.

- **Night Bazaar (Chiang Mai, Thailand).** Most of those gorgeous handicrafts you find all over Thailand are made in the north, and at Chiang Mai's sprawling Night Bazaar, you'll find the widest selection, best quality, and best prices. See chapter 4.

- **Central Market (Hoi An, Vietnam).** On the banks of the busy Perfume River lies this entire city block of narrow, roofed aisles. Produce of every description is for sale inside—handicrafts, household items, and services such as facials and massages. On the outskirts, an entire warehouse is devoted to silk and silk tailoring. See chapter 6.

- **Morning Market (Vientiane, Laos).** Laos's famous market is three huge buildings with traditional tiered roofs. Silver handicrafts, fabrics, jewelry, electronics, books, and much, much more occupy each building's several floors. The aisles are wide and made for wandering and poking through the wares, and the proprietors are friendly, gentle bargainers. See chapter 5.

- **Arab Street (Singapore).** Sure, Singapore is a shopper's paradise, but it needs more places like Arab Street, where small shops lining the street sell everything from textiles to handicrafts. Bargaining is welcome. See chapter 8.

- **Central Market (Kuala Lumpur, Malaysia).** This is one-stop shopping for all the rich arts and handicrafts Malaysia produces—and it's air-conditioned, too. See chapter 9.

- **Central Market (Phnom Penh, Cambodia).** This is where it all happens in Phnom Penh. The main building is a massive Art

Deco rotunda with wings extending in all directions. It's an anthill of activity on any given day, and you can get some interesting bargains and unique finds. See chapter 7.

## 13 The Best Shopping Bargains

- **Antiques (Thailand).** Before you head out on vacation, visit some Asian galleries in your home country and take a look at the prices of the items you like. Once you're here, you'll be amazed at how little these things really cost. Most places will be glad to pack and ship purchases for you, and you'll still come out ahead. See chapter 4.

- **Tailored Silk Suits (Thailand and Hanoi, Hoi An, and Saigon, Vietnam).** For a fraction of what you'd pay at home, you can have a lined silk (or wool) suit tailored in a day or less, including a fitting or two. Bring pictures of your favorite designer outfits for a clever copy, and an empty suitcase or two for the trip home. See chapters 4 and 6.

- **Silver or Lacquer Handicrafts (Vietnam).** The workmanship is tops and the prices low throughout Vietnam, particularly for lacquer ware. Bargain hard and make sure that the silver is genuine. See chapter 6.

- **Hand-Woven Textiles (Laos).** The Laos hand weave textured fabrics piece by piece on primitive wooden looms. Such painstaking work costs more than a few dollars, but, ranging from sophisticated silk to gaily colored ethnic prints, the designs are pure art and uniquely Laotian. See chapter 5.

- **Silver Filigree Jewelry (Malaysia).** This fine silver is worked into detailed filigree jewelry designs to make brooches, necklaces, bracelets, and other fine jewelry. See chapter 9.

- **Pewter (Malaysia).** Malaysia is the home of Selangor Pewter, one of the largest pewter manufacturers in the world. Its many showrooms have all sorts of items to choose from. See chapter 9.

- **Fabric and Woodcarvings (Bali).** Even with the "rich man's tax" for tourists in Bali, just about anything you buy on the island is a bargain compared with the same stuff back home. Commissioned fabric and woodcarvings are a particularly good deal. See chapter 10.

## 14 The Hottest Nightlife Spots

- **Patpong (Bangkok, Thailand).** Yes, *that* Patpong. If go-go bars and sex shows aren't your style, you'll still find plenty to do. After you're finished shopping in the huge night market, you'll find plenty of restaurants, pubs, and discos that cater to folks who prefer more traditional nightlife. See chapter 4.

- **Saigon (Vietnam).** From the tawdry to the socialite scene, you'll find it in Saigon. With rooftop garden bars like Saigon-Saigon and cool spots like Q-Bar, Saigon has a rollicking scene. Most evenings begin with an elegant (but very reasonable) French or Vietnamese dinner; then it's bar-hopping time in the city's compact downtown, mingling with trendy locals and fun-loving expats. See chapter 6.

- **Disco Lives! (Laos).** Go to a disco . . . any disco. It's like a bad junior high dance and just as innocent. In the basement of Vientiane's Lao Plaza Hotel is a reasonable big-city facsimile, but ask around in any small town for what's on. The music is Asian pop, but it's refreshing to watch young gentlemen ask the ladies to the floor with a bit of pomp and circumstance, and then it's cheek-to-cheek or stilted boogie until the big cheer when the music stops. It hearkens to an America of the 1950s. See chapter 5.

• **Singapore.** Nightlife is becoming increasingly sophisticated in Singapore, where locals have more money for recreation and fun. Take the time to choose the place that suits your personality. Jazz club? Techno disco? Cocktail lounge? Wine bar? Good old pub? It has it all. See chapter 8.

• **Bangsar (near Kuala Lumpur, Malaysia).** Folks in Kuala Lumpur know to go to Bangsar for nighttime excitement. A couple blocks of concentrated restaurants, cafes, discos, pubs, and wine bars will tickle any fancy. There's good people-watching, too. See chapter 9.

# 2

# Introducing Southeast Asia

While the rest of the world's continents fit into nice, tidy compartments, the nations that make up Southeast Asia—Cambodia, Indonesia, Laos, Malaysia, Singapore, Thailand, and Vietnam—many times have more differences than similarities. Diverse geographical features, history, religious and cultural heritage, economy, and politics across the region mean that the shortest journey offers cross-cultural comparison and new perspective.

Safety is a primary concern for travelers these days, and while it is important to stay updated on internal issues in any given country and steer clear of any hot spots, the adventurous tourist paths through this vibrant region are ripe for exploration and replete with mystery, beauty, and ancient culture and wisdom.

## 1 The Region Today

The region's many differences mean an array of choices for vacationers. With so many options, how can you decide which is the perfect beach or the most intriguing cultural or adventure locale? In this chapter, we provide an overall view of the region and explain some of the special features and unique attractions of each destination to help you decide. And in the chapters that follow, we'll help you plan your trip from soup to nuts.

Geographically, Southeast Asia is diverse and stunning. The lush tropical rainforests of peninsular Malaysia and Borneo are some of the oldest in the world. Beautiful islands and beaches are many, including large resort areas like Thailand's Phuket or Bali (Indonesia), plus countless other gorgeous islands, atolls, and beaches that are relatively unexploited. Divers and snorkelers flock from around the world for stunning coral reefs bursting with colorful life in Thailand, Malaysia, and Indonesia. Find adventures in the wild while jungle trekking, sea and river kayaking, or visiting ethnic villages and sacred peaks.

Southeast Asia is also a cultural melting pot, a crossroads of influences from China, south Asia, and Tibet. Consider the Sri Lankans, who transplanted Theravada Buddhism, with its serene and orthodox ways, from Myanmar to Thailand and Laos. Or the Indian traders, who brought ancient Hinduism to Cambodia, influencing the architecture of the magical city of Angkor; or consider the Hindus who settled on Bali, mixing their dogma with local animism to create a completely unique sect. Meanwhile, seafaring Arab merchants imported Islam to coastal areas of Malaysia and Indonesia, adding another interesting facet to the region. In Vietnam, the only Southeast Asian nation to fall directly under the control of past Chinese empires, China's cultural influences are still strong. And, on top of that, Europeans from the late 1400s onward imported Western culture to cities such as Hong Kong, Singapore, Penang, and Malacca; the European colonial imprint is still visible in the architecture and cuisine of most countries in the region. Crossing an international border in Southeast Asia is stepping into another world.

Economic and political developments have changed the face of tourism in the region. While cosmopolitan stops like Singapore, Kuala Lumpur, and Bangkok guarantee the best luxury hotels, finest dining, and most refined cultural attractions, up-and-coming cities such as Hanoi, Ho Chi Minh City, or Chiang Mai promise cultural curiosities around every street corner as they struggle to justify traditional customs with modern development. Thailand's 3 decades of tourism development have created very familiar facilities for travelers, for example, but those looking for a more down-and-dirty experience can head off to nearby Cambodia or Laos, countries still off the beaten path of most tour agendas. For every luxurious Bali, there's a laid-back Tioman Island (Malaysia). For every busy Bangkok, there's a charming Luang Prabang (Laos).

It is important, of course, to talk about those Southeast Asian nations that have political or safety concerns, and the sections that follow discuss political turmoil in more detail. Steer clear of any sectarian or political tension, and know that the relative stability of many countries in Southeast Asia is rather short-lived and flash political upheavals are not uncommon. Contact your country's overseas affairs bureau or check the U.S. Department of State's website posting current travel warnings (http://travel. state.gov).

## THAILAND

Thailand sees more international travelers each year than any of its neighbors, enticing everyone from luxury vacationers to young shoestring backpackers, Japanese junkets, and European group tours. You'll meet young professionals on hiatus, naive tourists prowling for that "One Night in Bangkok," and soul-searchers hanging around for the Buddhist Dharma and Asian hospitality. Many trips to Southeast Asia either start here or end up here, and it is a good orientation.

Travelers usually arrive in **Bangkok,** staying for a few days to take in the city's bizarre mix of royal palaces and skyscrapers, pious monks amid rush-hour commuters, and sidewalk noodle vendors serving bankers in suits. That's not to mention the city's nightlife, with that seedy element that makes Bangkok infamous. Heading south, find the legendary beaches and resorts of **Phuket** island, while **Koh Samui,** in the Gulf of Thailand, is a comparable alternative to Phuket. Another attraction to Thailand, the northern hills around **Chiang Mai,** presents a world of adventure trekking and tribal culture along well-worn—but well-worth-it—travel trails. Throughout the country are opportunities for **outdoor adventure** and **extreme sports,** organized by very professional firms that you can count on for safety and reliability.

And at the end of the day, there's that unbeatable taste of the **Thai cuisine**—tangy soups, hearty coconut curries, and the freshest seafood.

## VIETNAM

If the thought of Vietnam stirs flashbacks of televised war coverage or scenes from dark movies, guess again. One of the fastest-growing destinations in the region also happens to be one of the most beautiful, most friendly, and most convenient places to travel.

Vietnam's major destinations fall in a line, and most travelers choose to travel from north to south, starting in Hanoi and ending in Ho Chi Minh City, or vice versa. Convenient tourist buses connect the main coastal stops, and there are increasing options for individual travelers and more unique stops along the way.

Ho Chi Minh City, or Saigon, is the gateway to the beautiful **Mekong Delta** region. Heading north, pass through **Dalat,** a hill station in the cool mountains, and then on to **Nha Trang,** an emerging seaside getaway. Farther north, **Hoi An** is one of the region's most charming villages and a picturesque labyrinth of cobblestone streets, historic buildings, and lots of shopping. Still farther north, the former capital city at **Hue** is filled with many architectural gems of Chinese and European influence. The cultural amalgam is best defined in **Hanoi,** where Vietnamese, French, and Chinese cultures collide. From here, head east to see the gorgeous **Halong Bay,** with hundreds of craggy rock formations plunging straight up from the sea, or travel north to **Sapa** and visit Vietnam's hill-tribe people in the mountains that divide northern Vietnam from China.

## LAOS

Travelers who complain that Thailand has become too touristy can look to Laos. Here is a country where foreigners are still greeted as gracious guests rather than cash cows. Rarely will you find tacky souvenir stalls or tourist kitsch—just quiet towns with laid-back markets, townsfolk carrying on their trades, and farmers tending to their chores. Life is set to the pace of Buddhism, tranquillity and compassion the hallmarks, and Lao people are very kind and welcoming.

Some people fear that Laos will follow Thailand's accelerated development model, that the ethnic villages in the north will be turned into safari parks and the country's beautiful temples turned into theme attractions. But the infrastructure of this developing nation won't yet support that, and Lao people are in no rush to cash in on the nation's tranquility.

For a capital city, Vientiane is startlingly parochial. With every other building dedicated to an international development agency, it's an eye-opening reminder that Laos is one of the top 10 poorest countries in the world. Next stop is **Luang Prabang,** UNESCO World Heritage site, a paradise of gorgeous Buddhist temples— dozens of them amid shady streets that lead to the Mekong River. If you have time, **Xieng Khouang,** in the east of Vientiane, is the home of Southeast Asia's Stonehenge, the **Plain of Jars,** huge mysterious stone monoliths that have somehow survived bombs and guerilla insurgents. **Eco-tourism** is growing rapidly, and some new and interesting avenues into the Lao jungle and rivers connect remote ethnic villages (especially in the north).

## SINGAPORE

All of Southeast Asia's cultures seem to converge on Singapore, making it perhaps one of the best places to begin your exploration of the region. Excellent **museums** explore Asian civilizations, Southeast Asian art, and even World War II history. The city's hundreds of restaurants provide a wealth of choices in terms of **cuisine,** for a glimpse of regional specialties in one stop. And some of the best regional **fine arts, crafts, and antiques** end up in Singapore showrooms.

I'll be honest with you: Singapore gets trashed regularly by complaints that it is too Western, too modern, too sanitary—too Disneyland. Walk the streets of **Chinatown, Little India,** and the Malay Muslim area at **Kampong Glam,** and you can see where the buildings have been renovated and many former inhabitants have retired from traditional crafts. But some of these places have a few secrets left that are very rewarding if you are observant. For the past 200 years, Singapore has invented itself from many contributing cultures. If you consider the country today, it is still keeping up that tradition.

## Myanmar (Burma): To Go or Not to Go?

In preparing this guide, we were confronted with problematic political realities in Myanmar—realities that made us question the advisability of sending readers there. The brutality and unfairness of the military government of Myanmar has been met with sanctions and embargo from the international community. Political leaders, like the resilient Aung San Suu Kyi, are punished and any dissent is met with house arrest and jail. Since the early 1990s, the junta has encouraged tourism, and a visit to Myanmar is in fact a unique glimpse into rich Buddhist tradition, ancient culture, and stunning natural beauty, but while some encourage tourism and believe that Western visitors give voice to the troubles of Burma, other voices shout for a moratorium on tourism to this troubled land, saying that our tourist dollars subsidize and support tyranny.

Because of the precarious political climate in Myanmar, we've decided to exclude the country from this edition. Those not so easily dissuaded, however, can find more information on the subject at the **Burma Project at the Open Society Institute** (www.soros.org/burma) or at www.burmadebate.org. If you do decide to go to Myanmar, we suggest going with a reputable international tour operator. Good regional providers include **Diethelm Travel** (1 Inya Rd., Kamayut Township; ⓒ **951/527-110** or 527-117; fax 951/527-135; www.diethelm-travel.com) and **Exotissimo** (#0303 Sakura Tower, 339 Bogyoke Aung San St., Kyauktada Township, Yangon, Myanmar; ⓒ **951/255-427** or 255-388; fax 951/255-428; myanmar@exotissimo.com).

## MALAYSIA

Possibly one of the most overlooked countries in Southeast Asia, Malaysia is one of my favorites for one very special reason: It's not Thailand! After so much time spent traveling around Thailand listening to every hawker yell "Hello! Special for you!" and every backpacker bragging about $5 roach-infested guesthouses, I look forward to Malaysia just to escape the tourism industry. Beaches on the islands of **Langkawi** and **Sabah** are just as beautiful as Thailand's, and resorts here are equally as fine. The quaint British colonial influences at **Penang, Malacca,** and **Kuching** (Sarawak) add to the beauty, as does the mysterious Arab-Islamic influences all over the country. That's not to mention an endless number of outdoor adventures, from mountain climbing to

jungle trekking to scuba diving—in fact, the rainforest here is far superior.

Why is Malaysia so underestimated? To be honest, after experiencing the relative "freedom" and tolerance of Thai culture, many travelers find Malaysian culture too strict and prohibitive. Personally, I think it's a fair trade—in Thailand, when I talk to Thai people, I'm often treated like a tourist with a fat wallet. In Malaysia, when I meet local people, I end up having interesting conversations and cherished personal experiences. And I don't have to suffer through blatant prostitution and drug abuse—the sad, sleazy side of the Thai tourism industry.

*One word of caution regarding travel in Malaysia:* On April 23, 2000, a group of tourists was kidnapped from the diving resort at

Sipadan Island, off the east coast of Sabah (Malaysian Borneo). Abu Sayyaf, the Filipino Muslim separatists who were responsible for the incident, still remain at large in the southern islands of the Philippines close to Borneo. Exercise caution when traveling to this area.

## BALI (INDONESIA)

Memories of the 2002 bombing in the town of Kuta are written large on our collective image of Bali, and no doubt the whole world is familiar with Indonesia's history of civil unrest: ethnic and religious conflict, the struggle for independence in East Timor and now Aceh, and anti-Western bombings and riots in Jakarta. Successful elections in 2004 bode well for the future, and there is hope for an improved economy.

Until the bombings, Bali was the one safe haven, an enclave of upscale resorts separate from troubles on the larger islands of Indonesia. Now, in the wake of the bombings, Bali struggles to regain its international allure. The beaches remain the stuff of legend, supporting dreamy resorts that cater to anyone from the family to escapist honeymooners and well-heeled paradise seekers. Sports enthusiasts flock to Bali for surfing, snorkeling, scuba diving, and swimming as well as wind- and kite surfing. People who can pull themselves away from the seaside will venture into villages lively with friendly local smiles and markets packed with eye-boggling local handicrafts and treasures to bargain for, or take off into the jungle or up among high volcanic peaks for rigorous trekking. The town of **Ubud** is set among delightful Hindu temples and gorgeous mountain scenery—famed for its terraced rice fields—and supports a unique community of local and expat artists. Bali still has much to offer, and the friendly Balinese islanders are eager to see a return of the Western visitors who've brought so much to this magical isle.

## CAMBODIA

It wasn't long ago that Cambodia was off the map, a land plagued by general lawlessness and banditry as the result of years of strife. In recent years, visitors have braved the remnants of the country's chaos and, by hook or crook, made their way to **Siem Reap** and Southeast Asia's premiere cultural attraction, **Angkor Wat,** the magnificent temple ruins of the mighty Angkor civilization of A.D. 800 to 1200. The good news is that, though it will take years to catch up economically with its growing neighbors, Cambodia is on the mend. It will take a few generations to heal after the tragic events of the mid-1970s, when the entire country was turned into a concentration camp under Pol Pot, but Cambodia is looking to the future. Bolstered by international humanitarian aid organizations, the country is enjoying a protracted period of peace not seen in many years. **Phnom Penh,** the capital, and **Siem Reap,** the access village for the Angkor temples, are safe, and the countryside is open to more adventurous travelers ready to brave the rough roads and basic amenities and accommodations. Many still limit their trip in Cambodia to the temples of Angkor. Convenient direct flights from the larger cities throughout the region simplify the process.

It's important to remember that the country is still littered with UXO, unexploded ordnance, including dormant bombs and landmines. In the countryside, it's important to stay on well-worn trails and, farther afield, to go with a knowledgeable guide. After a peaceful election in 2003, the situation in Phnom Penh is stable, but visitors should stay informed before going because the country has a history of flash political upheaval.

## 2 A Southeast Asian Cultural Primer

The diverse ethnic groups in the region, from socialite city dwellers to remote enclaves of subsistence farmers, each have unique history, cultural practices, and religion. The region is a veritable cornucopia of cultures that have intertwined and adopted various elements, beliefs, and practices from each other.

## THE CULTURAL MAKEUP OF SOUTHEAST ASIA
### THAILAND

Over centuries, migrating cultures have blended to create what is known as "Thai" today. Early waves of southern Chinese migrants combine with Mon peoples from Burma, Khmers from Cambodia, Malays, and Lao people—it is said that Thailand's King Rama I could trace ancestry to all these—plus European, Indian, Han Chinese, and Arab families. Of the 75% of the population that calls itself Thai, a great number of people in northeastern Isaan are of Lao ancestry. In the past century, Thailand has also become home to many migrating hill tribes in the north—tribes who've come from Vietnam, Laos, Myanmar, and southern China, many as refugees. As you travel south toward the Malaysian border, you find Thai people who share cultural and religious affinity with their southern Malay neighbors. Also in the past 50 years, Thailand has seen a boom in Chinese immigrants.

The Thais are a warm and peaceable people, with a culture that springs from Indian and Sri Lankan origins. Early Thais adopted many Brahman practices, evident in royal ceremony and social hierarchy—Thailand is a very class-oriented culture. Even their cherished national story, the *Ramakien,* the subject of almost all Thai classical dances and temple murals, finds its origin in the Indian Hindu epic the *Ramayana.* Thai Buddhism follows the Theravada sect, imported from Sri Lanka along with the classic bell-shape stupa seen in many temple grounds.

Perhaps the two main influences in Thai life today are spirituality and the royal family. In every household throughout the country, you'll find a spirit house to appease the property's former inhabitants, a portrait of the king in a prominent spot and perhaps pictures of a few previous kings, a dais for Buddha images and religious objects, and portraits of each son as he enters the monkhood, as almost all sons do.

### VIETNAM, LAOS & CAMBODIA

Together, the countries of Vietnam, Cambodia, and Laos make up one of the most ethnically diverse regions of Southeast Asia. Outside the cities, little English is spoken in any of these countries except by tour guides and others who have frequent contact with Western visitors. Much of the architecture and art in Cambodia and Laos is influenced by Buddhism and includes some of the world's most renowned temples, along with exquisitely sculpted Buddha images. The temple complexes of Angkor Wat in Cambodia are among the architectural wonders of the ancient world, while the finest temples in Laos are found in the ancient capital of Luang Prabang.

*One important note:* The ethnic minorities, or hill tribes, of northern Vietnam, Laos, and Thailand all share a common heritage with each other, originating from either Himalayan tribes or southern Chinese clans. You'll find startling similarities in the customs and languages of all these people.

### Vietnam

In Vietnam, the ethnic Vietnamese are a fusion of Viet, Tai (a southern Chinese group), Indonesian, and Chinese who first settled here between 200 B.C. and A.D. 200. Although Vietnam has no official religion, several religions have significantly impacted Vietnamese culture, including **Buddhism, Confucianism, Taoism,** and **Animism.** Animism, which is the oldest religious practice in Vietnam and many other Southeast Asian countries, is centered on belief in a spirit world. Ancient cultural traditions lean toward borrowings from the mandarins of old Chinese dynasties that claimed sovereignty over Vietnam. In the 1900s, the French added a new flavor to the mix. Modern Vietnam is defined by its pell-mell rush to capitalism.

## Laos

In Laos, approximately half the population is ethnic Lao descended from centuries of migration, mostly from southern China. A landlocked country with little natural resources, Laos has had little luck entering the global trade scene and remains dependent on the international donor community. If you think the Thais are laid-back, you'll have to check the Laos for a pulse. In fact, Lao culture is most often compared with the Thais because the two share common roots of language and culture, although the Thais will never admit it because they often look down upon their northern neighbors. Large communities of ethnic minorities live in agrarian and subsistence communities, particularly in the north, and carry on rich traditional crafts and practices.

## Cambodia

The population of Cambodia is made up primarily of ethnic Khmers who have lived here since around the 2nd century A.D. and whose religion and culture have been influenced by interaction with Indians, Javanese, Thais, Vietnamese, and Chinese. The achievements of the ancient Angkor empire were a long time ago, and modern Khmer culture still struggles in the aftermath of many years of war and terror. Relative political stability is new here and Cambodia has far to go to catch up economically and with the infrastructure of the other countries in the region. Basic medical necessities are still lacking and landmines still cover the countryside and kill an estimated four people each day. Time and effort by civil authorities and NGOs (nongovernment organizations) will only tell. Khmer life is marked by devout Buddhist ritual, much like its neighbors, which fosters a pervasive gentleness among Khmer.

## SINGAPORE

Seventy-eight percent of Singaporeans trace their heritage to migrating waves from China's southern provinces, particularly from the Hokkien, Teowchew, Hakka, Cantonese, and Hainanese dialect groups. Back then, the Chinese community was driven by rags-to-riches stories—the poor worker hawking vegetables who opened a grocery store and then started a chain of stores and now drives a Mercedes Benz. This story still motivates them today.

But it's not just Chinese who have dominated the scene. The island started off with a handful of Malay inhabitants; then came the British colonials with Indian administrators, followed by Muslim Indian moneylenders, Chinese merchants, Chinese coolie laborers, and Indian convict labor, plus European settlers and immigrants from all over Southeast Asia. Over 2 centuries of modern history, each group made its contribution to "Singaporean culture."

Today, as your average Singaporean struggles to balance traditional values with modern demands of globalization, his country is raked over the coals for being sterile and overly Westernized. Older folks are becoming frustrated by younger generations who discard traditions in their pursuit of "The 5 C's"—career, condo, car, credit

## Buddha & Buddhism in Southeast Asia

Born Siddhartha Gautama Buddha in the year 563 B.C., the historical Buddha was an Indian prince. A passing sage predicted the child's future as a great holy man and, to spare him the tortuous life of the saint, Siddhartha was kept sheltered behind palace walls. As a child, he knew nothing of sickness and death. He married, had children, and lived a carefree life, though one plagued by a certain soul sickness and discontent. His journey began when he first spied a sick man and a corpse. Renouncing his princely cloaks, he concluded that life is suffering. Resolving to search for relief from earthly pain, he went into the forest and lived there for many years as a solitary ascetic, ultimately following his moderate "middle way" and achieving enlightenment and nirvana (escape from the cycle of reincarnation) while in meditation under the Bodhi tree.

Buddha's peripatetic teaching is the basis of all Buddhism. Upon his death, two schools arose and spread throughout Asia. The oldest and probably closest to the original practice is **Theravada** (Doctrine of the Elders), sometimes referred to as **Hinayana** (the Small Vehicle), which prevails in Sri Lanka, Laos, Thailand, and Cambodia and posits the enlightenment of individuals in this life, one at a time. The other school is **Mahayana** (the Large Vehicle), practiced in eastern Asia and Vietnam, which speaks of group enlightenment (we all go up at once).

Buddhism has one aim only: to abolish suffering. To do so, according to Buddhism, one must transcend the ego, the "self," and attachment to the fleeting pleasures in an ever-changing material world, in order to see things clearly—with wisdom—and find peace.

There is no god in Buddhism; the Buddha is but an example. Buddhist practices, particularly Theravada, center on meditation and require that individuals, according to Buddha himself, look within and come to

card, and cash. Temples and ethnic neighborhoods are finding more revenue from tourists than from the communities they once served. Although many lament the loss of the good old days, most are willing to sacrifice a little tradition to be Southeast Asia's most stable and wealthy country.

## MALAYSIA

Malaysia's population consists primarily of ethnic **Malays,** labeled **Bumiputeras,** a political classification that also encompasses tribal people who live in peninsular Malaysia and Borneo. Almost all Malays are Muslim, and conservative values are the norm. The ruling government party supports an Islam that is open and tolerant to other cultures, but a growing minority favors strict Islamic law and government, further marginalizing the country's large Chinese and Indian population. These foreign cultures migrated to Malaysia during the British colonial period as trading merchants, laborers, and administrators. Today Malaysia recognizes ethnic **Chinese** and **Indian** citizens as equals under national law. However, government development and education policies always seem to favor Bumiputeras.

Among the favorite Malaysian recreational pastimes are **kite flying,** using ornately decorated paper kites, understand the Four Noble Truths: the existence of suffering; its arising; the path to eliminating suffering; and, its ultimate passing by practice of the Eightfold Path, a road map to right living and good conduct.

Buddhist philosophy pervades every aspect of life, morality, and thought in the countries of Thailand, Laos, and Cambodia. The monastic community, called the *sangha,* is supported by local people and serves as the cultural touchstone and often an important avenue for education. Monks live in the "supramundane," free from the usual human concerns of finding food, clothing, and shelter. Instead, they focus on the rigorous practice of meditation, study, and austerities prescribed by the Theravada tradition. Mahayana traditions from China hold important sway over life in parts of the Malay Peninsula, Thailand, and Vietnam.

Lay practitioners adopt the law of **karma,** in which every action has effects and the energy of past action, good or evil, which continues forever and is "reborn." Merit is gained by entering the monkhood (and most males do so for a few days or months), helping in the construction of a monastery or a stupa, contributing to education, giving alms, or performing any act of kindness, no matter how small. When monks go with their alms bowls from house to house, they are not begging, but offering laymen an opportunity to make merit by supporting them. Buddha images are honored and revered in the Eastern tradition and are said to radiate the essence of Buddha, ideals that we should revere and struggle to achieve; but the images themselves are not holy or spiritually charged, per se. Buddhism doesn't seek converts, and, if following some simple rules of conduct, tourists are welcome guests at most Buddhist fetes and festivals.

and top spinning. Some still practice **silat,** a Malaysian form of martial arts.

## BALI (INDONESIA)

No country in Southeast Asia has a more ethnically diverse population than Indonesia, with more than 350 ethnic groups with their own languages and cultures scattered among the 6,000 inhabited islands of this vast archipelago of more than 14,000 islands.

Of all the islands, Bali stands out for its especially rich cultural life, which is inextricably linked with its Hindu beliefs. Life in Bali is marked by a unique flow of ritual; whether painting, carving, dancing, or playing music, it seems that all Balinese are involved in the arts or practice devout daily rituals of beauty. Flower offerings to the gods are a common sight, and the Balinese are forever paying homage to Hindu deities at more than 20,000 temples and during the 60 annual festivals on the island.

The majority of the island's population is native Balinese; there are quite a few people from other parts of Indonesia, and they are there for work opportunities. English is widely spoken in the tourist parts of Bali, which means that just about everywhere you go someone will speak enough English to help you out.

## ETIQUETTE TIPS

"Different countries, different customs," as Sean Connery said to Michael Caine in *The Man Who Would Be King*. And although each country covered in this book proves that rule by having their own twists on etiquette, some general pointers will allow you to go though your days of traveling without inadvertently offending your hosts. (For etiquette tips on individual countries, see the country chapters.)

## GREETINGS, GESTURES & SOCIAL INTERACTION

In these modern times, the **common Western handshake** has become extremely prevalent throughout Southeast Asia, but it is by no means universal. There are a plethora of traditional greetings, so when greeting someone—especially an older man and even more especially a woman of any age—it's safest to wait for a gesture or observe those around you and then follow suit. In Muslim culture, for instance, it is not acceptable for men and women not related by blood or marriage to touch.

In interpersonal relations in strongly Buddhist areas (Laos, Vietnam, and Thailand), it helps to **take a gentle approach to human relationships.** A person showing anger or ill temper would be regarded with surprise and disapproval. A gentle approach will take you farther.

Here's an important, delicate matter: In countries with significant Muslim and Hindu cultures (Malaysia, Singapore, Indonesia, and Bali), **use only your right hand in social interaction.** Traditionally, the left hand is used only for personal hygiene. Not only should you eat with your right hand and give and receive all gifts with your right hand, but you also should make sure that you make all gestures, especially **pointing** (and even more especially, pointing in temples and mosques), with your right hand. In all the countries discussed in this book, it's also considered more polite to point with your knuckle (with your hand facing palm down) than with your finger.

In all the countries covered in this guide, ladies seated on the floor should never sit with their legs crossed in front of them—instead, always tuck your legs to the side. Men may sit with legs crossed. Both men and women should also be careful **not to show the bottoms of their feet,** which are considered the lowliest, most unclean part of the body. If you cross your legs while on the floor or in a chair, don't point your soles toward other people. Also be careful not to use your foot to point or gesture. **Shoes should be removed** when entering a temple or private home. And don't ever step over someone's body or legs.

On a similar note, in Buddhist and Hindu cultures, the head is considered the most sacred part of the body; therefore, **do not casually touch another person's head**—and this includes patting children on the head.

## DRESSING FOR CULTURAL SUCCESS

The basic rule is, **dress modestly.** Except perhaps on the grounds of resorts and in heavily tourist areas such as Bali's Kuta and Thailand's beaches, foreigners displaying navels, chests, or shoulders, or wearing short shorts or short skirts will attract stares. Although shorts and bathing suits are accepted on the beach, you should avoid parading around in them elsewhere, no matter how hot it is.

## TEMPLE & MOSQUE ETIQUETTE

Many of Southeast Asia's greatest and most remarkable sights are its places of worship, usually Buddhist *wats,* Hindu temples, and Islamic mosques (masjids). When visiting these places, more so than at any other time, it's

> ## (Tips  Everything Has a Price: Haggling
>
> Prices are never marked in the small shops and at street vendors in Southeast Asia. You must bargain. The most important thing to remember when bargaining is to keep a friendly, good-natured banter between you and the seller. Before you start out, it's good to have some idea of how much your purchase is worth, to give you a base point for negotiation. A simple "How much?" is the place to start, to which the vendor will reply with the top price. Check at a few vendors before negotiating, and never accept the first price! Try a smile and ask, "Is that your best price?" Vendors will laughingly ask for your counteroffer. Knock the price down about 50%—they'll look shocked, but it's a starting point for bidding. Just remember to smile and be friendly, and be willing to walk away (or fake it). *Caveat:* If it's a larger, more expensive item, don't get into major bargaining unless you're serious about buying. If the shopkeeper agrees on what you say you're willing to pay, it's considered rude not to make the purchase. See individual country chapters for more on shopping.

important to observe certain rules of decorum.

When visiting the **mosques,** be sure to dress appropriately. Neither men nor women will be admitted wearing shorts. Ladies should not wear short skirts or sleeveless, backless, or low-cut tops. Both men and women are required to leave their shoes outside. Also, never enter the mosque's main prayer hall; this area is reserved for Muslims only. No cameras or video cameras are allowed, and remember to turn off cellphones and pagers. Friday is the Sabbath day, and you should not plan to go to the mosques between 11am and 2pm on this day.

Visitors are welcome to walk around and explore most **temples** and *wats.* As in the mosques, remember to dress appropriately—some temples might refuse to admit you if you're showing too much skin—and to leave your shoes outside. Photography is permitted in most temples, although some, such as Wat Phra Kaeo in Thailand, prohibit it. Never climb on a Buddha image, and if you sit down, never point your feet in the direction of the Buddha. Do not cross in front of a person who is in prayer. Also, women should never touch a monk, try to shake his hand, or even give something to one directly (the monk will provide a cloth for you to lay the item upon, and he will collect it). Monks are not permitted to touch women or even to speak directly to them anywhere but inside a temple or *wat.*

# 3

# Planning Your Trip to Southeast Asia

The country chapters in this guide provide specific information on traveling to and getting around in all of Southeast Asia's individual countries, but in this chapter we give you some regionwide tips and information that will help you plan your trip.

## 1 Visitor Information

### Southeast Asia: Red-Alert Checklist

- Are you carrying a current, government-issued ID, such as a driver's license or passport?
- Are there any **special requirements** for your destination? Vaccinations? Special visas, passports, or IDs? Detailed road maps? Bug repellents? Appropriate attire?
- If you purchased traveler's checks, have you recorded the check numbers and stored the documentation separately from the checks?
- Did you stop the newspaper and mail delivery, and leave a set of keys with someone reliable?
- Did you pack your camera and an extra set of batteries, and purchase enough film? If you packed film in your checked baggage, do you have protective pouches to shield film from airport X-rays? If going digital, do you have a strategy for saving files? Enough memory?
- Do you have a safe place to carry money, like a money belt?
- Did you bring your ID cards that could entitle you to discounts, such as AAA and AARP cards, and student IDs?
- Did you bring emergency drug prescriptions and extra glasses or contact lenses?
- Did you find out your daily ATM withdrawal limit?
- Do you have your credit card PINs? Is there a daily withdrawal limit on credit card cash advances?
- To check in at a kiosk with an e-ticket, do you have the credit card you bought your ticket with or a frequent-flier card?
- Did you leave a copy of your itinerary with someone at home?
- Do you have measurements for people you plan to buy clothes for?
- Did you check if any travel advisories have been issued by the U.S. State Department (http://travel.state.gov/) regarding your destination?
- Do you have the address and phone number of your country's embassy with you?

## 2 Entry Requirements & Customs

### ENTRY REQUIREMENTS

Many countries covered in this guide require **only a valid passport** for citizens of the U.S., U.K., Canada, Australia, and New Zealand; Vietnam, Laos, and Cambodia, however, require citizens of these countries to have entry **visas.** Though most international airports offer visas upon arrival and there are more overland points where you can apply with passport photos and money when you arrive, if you plan to enter Vietnam, Laos, or Cambodia from rural overland points, you often need to obtain a visa beforehand (often you even need to specify what entry point). See individual country chapters for more specific information.

**BALI (INDONESIA)**   Visitors from the U.S., Australia, most of Europe, New Zealand, and Canada are given a visa upon arrival for a fee of US$30. The only official gateways to Bali are Ngurah Rai Airport or the seaports of Padang Bai and Benoa. If you want to stay longer than 30 days, you must get a tourist or business visa before coming to Indonesia. Tourist visas cannot be extended, while business visas can be extended for 6 months at Indonesian immigration offices.

**CAMBODIA**   All    visitors    are required to carry a passport and visa. A 1-month visa can be obtained upon entry at the Phnom Penh or Siem Reap    international    airports    for US$20. Bring two passport photos for your application. Visa on arrival is now available at the land crossing from Poi Pet (Thailand) and the boat-crossing point from Chau Doc in Vietnam for just US$22.

**LAOS**   Visitors need a valid passport and visa to visit Laos. There are a number of entry sites where visas are granted upon arrival: by air to Vientiane or Luang Prabang, or when crossing from Thailand over the Friendship Bridge between Vientiane and Nong Khai, or between Chiang Khong and Houay Xai in the far north, and Mukdahan and Savannakhet or Chong Mek and Vung Tao (near Pakse) in the far south. When coming from Vietnam, be sure to have a prearranged visa. US$30 gets you a 15-day visa. At an embassy outside of Laos, the going rate for a 30-day visa is US$35, and you'll have to wait up to 5 days for processing, less in Bangkok. For a fee, travel agents in Thailand and other countries in the region can help you jump over the bureaucratic hurdles and get a visa in 1 day. Check the Lao embassy site at **http://laoembassy.com**.

**MALAYSIA**   To enter Malaysia, you must have a valid passport. Citizens of the United States do not need visas for tourism and business visits. Citizens of Canada, Australia, New Zealand, and the United Kingdom do not require a visa for tourism or business visits not exceeding 1 month.

**SINGAPORE**   To enter Singapore, you'll need a valid passport. Visas are not necessary for citizens of the United States, Canada, the United Kingdom,    Australia,    and    New Zealand. Upon entry, visitors from these countries will be issued a 30-day pass for a social visit only, except for Americans, who get a 90-day pass.

**THAILAND**   All visitors to Thailand must carry a valid passport with proof of onward passage (either a return or through ticket). Visas are not required for stays of up to 30 days for citizens of the U.S., Australia, Canada, New Zealand, or the U.K., but 3-month tourist visas can be arranged before arrival.

**VIETNAM**   Residents of the U.S., Canada, Australia, New Zealand, and the United Kingdom need both a

## Tips  Passport Savvy

Allow plenty of time before your trip to apply for a passport; processing normally takes 3 weeks but can take longer during busy periods (especially spring). And keep in mind that if you need a passport in a hurry, you'll pay a higher processing fee. When traveling, safeguard your passport in an inconspicuous, inaccessible place like a money belt and keep a copy of the critical pages with your passport number in a separate place. If you lose your passport, visit the nearest consulate or embassy of your native country as soon as possible for a replacement.

passport and a valid visa to enter Vietnam. A tourist visa usually lasts for 30 days and costs US$60. You need to specify your date of entry and exit. Though there's no official policy, tourist visas can commonly be extended with little hassle. Multiple-entry business visas are available that are valid for up to 3 months; however, you must have a sponsoring agency in Vietnam, and it can take much longer to process. For short business trips, it's less complicated simply to enter as a tourist.

For information on how to get a passport, go to "Passports," in the "Fast Facts" section of this chapter—the websites listed provide downloadable passport applications as well as the current fees for processing passport applications. For an up-to-date country-by-country listing of passport requirements around the world, go to the "Foreign Entry Requirement" Web page of the U.S. State Department at **http://travel.state.gov/foreign entryreqs.html**.

## CUSTOMS
### WHAT YOU CAN BRING INTO SOUTHEAST ASIA

Allowable amounts of tobacco, alcohol, and currency are comparable in all countries: usually 2 cartons of cigarettes, up to 2 bottles of liquor, and between US$3,000 and US$10,000. Check individual chapters for exact amounts. Plant material and animals fall under restrictions across the board.

### WHAT YOU CAN TAKE HOME FROM SOUTHEAST ASIA

Restrictions on what you can take out of the various nations of SE Asia are loose, at best. Expect a red flag if you have any kind of plant materials or animals, but the most notable restriction has to do with antiques. To prevent the kind of wholesale looting of the region's treasures in the recent colonial past, you might be stopped if you are carrying any Buddhist statuary or authentic antiques or religious artifacts. This does not apply to tourist trinkets, however aged and interesting. In fact, despite any salesman's claim of authenticity, you'll be hard-pressed to find authentic antiques.

Returning **U.S. citizens** who have been away for at least 48 hours are allowed to bring back, once every 30 days, $800 worth of merchandise duty-free. You'll be charged a flat rate of duty on the next $1,000 worth of purchases. Any dollar amount beyond that is dutiable at whatever rates apply. On mailed gifts, the duty-free limit is $200. Be sure to have your receipts or purchases handy to expedite the declaration process. *Note:* If you owe duty, you are required to pay on your arrival in the United States, either by cash, personal check, government or traveler's check, or money order, and in some locations, a Visa or MasterCard.

To avoid having to pay duty on foreign-made personal items you owned before you left on your trip, bring along a bill of sale, insurance policy, jeweler's appraisal, or receipts of purchase. Or you can register items that can be readily identified by a permanently affixed serial number or marking—think laptop computers, cameras, and CD players—with Customs before you leave. Take the items to the nearest Customs office or register them with Customs at the airport from which you're departing. You'll receive, at no cost, a Certificate of Registration, which allows duty-free entry for the life of the item.

With some exceptions, you cannot bring fresh fruits and vegetables into the United States. For specifics on what you can bring back, download the invaluable free pamphlet *Know Before You Go* online at **www.cbp.gov**. (Click on "Travel," and then click on "Know Before You Go! Online Brochure.") Or contact the **U.S. Customs & Border Protection (CBP)**, 1300 Pennsylvania Ave., NW, Washington, DC 20229 (© **877/287-8667**) and request the pamphlet.

For a clear summary of **Canadian** rules, write for the booklet *I Declare,* issued by the **Canada Customs and Revenue Agency** (© **800/461-9999** in Canada, or 204/983-3500; www.ccra-adrc.gc.ca). Canada allows its citizens a C$750 exemption, and you're allowed to bring back duty-free 1 carton of cigarettes, 1 can of tobacco, 40 imperial ounces of liquor, and 50 cigars. In addition, you're allowed to mail gifts to Canada valued at less than C$60 a day, provided they're unsolicited and don't contain alcohol or tobacco (write on the package "Unsolicited gift, under $60 value"). All valuables should be declared on the Y-38 form before departure from Canada, including serial numbers of valuables you already own, such as expensive foreign cameras. ***Note:*** The C$750 exemption can only be used once a year and only after an absence of 7 days.

U.K. citizens returning from **a non-EU country** have a Customs allowance of: 200 cigarettes; 50 cigars; 250 grams of smoking tobacco; 2 liters of still table wine; 1 liter of spirits or strong liqueurs (over 22% volume); 2 liters of fortified wine, sparkling wine or other liqueurs; 60cc (ml) perfume; 250cc (ml) of toilet water; and £145 worth of all other goods, including gifts and souvenirs. People under 17 cannot have the tobacco or alcohol allowance. For more information, contact HM Customs & Excise at © **0845/010-9000** (from outside the U.K., 020/8929-0152), or consult the website at www.hmce.gov.uk.

The duty-free allowance in **Australia** is A$400 or, for those under 18, A$200. Citizens can bring in 250 cigarettes or 250 grams of loose tobacco, and 1,125 milliliters of alcohol. If you're returning with valuables you already own, such as foreign-made cameras, you should file form B263. A helpful brochure available from Australian consulates or Customs offices is *Know Before You Go.* For more information, call the **Australian Customs Service** at © **1300/363-263,** or log on to www.customs.gov.au.

The duty-free allowance for **New Zealand** is NZ$700. Citizens over 17 can bring in 200 cigarettes, 50 cigars, or 250 grams of tobacco (or a mixture of all three if their combined weight doesn't exceed 250g); plus 4.5 liters of wine and beer, or 1.125 liters of liquor. New Zealand currency does not carry import or export restrictions. Fill out a certificate of export, listing the valuables you are taking out of the country; that way, you can bring them back without paying duty. Most questions are answered in a free pamphlet available at New Zealand consulates and Customs offices: *New Zealand Customs Guide for Travellers, Notice no. 4.* For more information, contact **New Zealand Customs,** The Customhouse, 17–21 Whitmore St., Box 2218, Wellington (© **04/473-6099** or 0800/428-786; www.customs.govt.nz).

## 3 Money

The east Asian financial crisis is now a distant memory, and the countries of Southeast Asia are generally gaining economic clout in the world; but the rate of exchange, not to mention the price of most goods and services, means that travel in the region is very budget friendly. In places like Laos or Cambodia, you'll find that you can live quite well on very little, and the region's resort destinations and luxury accommodations in general come at a fraction of what you might pay in your home country. ATM service is good in the larger cities but can be scant, at best, in some of the region's backwaters, with no service whatsoever in places like Laos and Cambodia. Traveler's checks, an anachronism elsewhere in the world, are still not a bad idea, especially in the developing countries of the region. Note that the U.S. dollar is the de facto currency for many Southeast Asian countries, particularly in Laos, Vietnam, and Cambodia. Hotels, in particular, prefer doing business in U.S. dollars to dealing in local currency, a practice that helps them stay afloat amid fluctuating currency values. In some parts, everybody down to the smallest shop vendor quotes prices in U.S. dollars, and particularly the big-ticket items are best handled with greenbacks instead of large stacks of local currency.

While dealing in U.S. dollars can make things less complicated, always keep in mind local currency values so that you know if you're being charged the correct amount. In this book, we've listed **hotel, restaurant, and attraction rates** in whatever form the establishments quoted them—in U.S. dollars where those were quoted, and in local currencies (with U.S. dollar equivalents) where those were used.

Note that, with the exception of the Singapore dollar, Malaysian ringgit, and Hong Kong dollar (which have remained stable), all other Southeast Asian national currencies are still in a state of flux. Before you budget your trip based on rates we give in this book, be sure to check the currency's current status. CNN's website has a convenient **currency converter** at **www.xe.com/ucc**.

## CURRENCY

You will have to rely on local currency when traveling in many rural areas where neither traveler's checks nor credit cards are accepted. The U.S. dollar is the most readily accepted foreign currency throughout Southeast Asia, and it's a good idea to carry some greenbacks as backup.

It's not a bad idea to try and exchange at least some money—just enough to cover airport incidentals and transportation to your hotel—before you leave home (though don't expect the exchange rate to be ideal), so you can avoid lines at airport ATMs; most international arrival points in the region, however, have 24-hour exchange counters. You can exchange money at your local American Express or Thomas Cook office, or your bank. If you're far away from a bank with currency-exchange services, American Express offers traveler's checks and foreign currency, though with a $15 order fee and additional shipping costs, at www.american express.com or © **800/807-6233.**

Below we've listed the currencies of all countries in this guide.

**CAMBODIA**    The monetary unit is the **riel,** which is available in 50, 100, 200, 500, 1,000, 5,000, 10,000, 20,000, and 50,000 riel notes. Cambodia's volatile exchange rate typically fluctuates but is currently at **3,900 riel to US$1.** It's a good idea to bring a supply of U.S. dollars, because the dollar is considered Cambodia's second currency and is accepted—even preferred—by many hotels, guest-houses, and restaurants. If paying in dollars, you'll get the small change in riel.

**INDONESIA (BALI)** The **rupiah (Rp)** is the main currency, with bills of Rp100, Rp500, Rp1,000, Rp5,000, Rp10,000, Rp20,000, and Rp50,000, and coins in denominations of Rp25, Rp50, Rp100, and Rp500. Indonesia's currency was hit hard in 1998 and 1999, leading to exchange rates that fluctuated wildly. From a precrisis rate of approximately Rp2,300 to US$1, the rupiah plunged to Rp14,700 to US$1 in July 1998, but it has stabilized in recent years to **Rp9,094 to US$1.**

**LAOS** The primary unit of currency is the **kip** (pronounced "keep"), which comes in denominations of 5, 10, 20, 100, 500, 1,000, 2,000, 5,000, 10,000, and 20,000. The exchange rate is approximately **10,835 kip** to **US$1.** As in Cambodia, many tourist establishments prefer payment in U.S. dollars. In many areas of Laos, both U.S. dollars and Thai baht are preferred over the local currency.

**MALAYSIA** The **ringgit,** which is also referred to as the Malaysian dollar, is the unit of currency, and prices are marked RM. One ringgit equals 100 sen, and notes come in RM1, RM2, RM5, RM10, RM20, RM50, RM100, RM500, and RM1,000. Coins come in denominations of 1, 2, 5, 10, and 50 sen, and 1 ringgit coins. Since the economic crisis, the value of the ringgit has been set at **RM3.80 to US$1.**

**SINGAPORE** The **Singapore dollar** (commonly referred to as the Sing dollar) is the unit of currency, with notes issued in denominations of S$2, S$5, S$10, S$20, S$50, S$100, S$500, and S$1,000; coins come in denominations of 1, 5, 10, 20, and 50 cents and the gold-colored S$1. The exchange rate is approximately **S$1.70 to US$1.**

**THAILAND** The Thai **baht,** (noted as B), which is made up of 100 satang, comes in colored notes of 10 baht (brown), 20B (green), 100B (red), and 500B (purple). Coins come in denominations of 1B, 5B, and 10B, as well as 25 and 50 satang. The exchange rate is approximately **40B to US$1.**

**VIETNAM** The main unit of Vietnamese currency is the **dong,** (noted as VND), which comes in denominations of 200, 500, 1,000, 2,000, 5,000, 10,000, 20,000, and 50,000 notes. There are no coins. Most tourist venues accept dollars, and even in small towns you will at least be able to exchange greenbacks, if not use dollars directly. The exchange rate is approximately **15,000VND to US$1.**

## ATMs

The easiest and best way to get cash away from home is from an ATM. The **Cirrus** (✆ **800/424-7787;** www.mastercard.com) and **PLUS** (✆ **800/843-7587;** www.visa.com) networks span the globe; look at the back of your bank card to see which network you're on, then call or check online for ATM locations at your destination. Be sure you know your personal identification number (PIN) before you leave home and be sure to find out your daily withdrawal limit before you depart. Also keep in mind that many banks impose a fee every time a card is used at a different bank's ATM, and that fee can be higher for international transactions (up to $5 or more) than for domestic ones (where they're rarely more than $1.50). On top of this, the bank from which you withdraw cash may charge its own fee. To compare banks' ATM fees within the U.S., use www.bankrate.com. For international withdrawal fees, ask your bank.

You can also get cash advances on your credit card at an ATM. Keep in mind that credit card companies try to protect themselves from theft by limiting the funds someone can withdraw outside their home country, so call your credit card company before you leave home. And keep in mind that you'll pay interest from the moment of your withdrawal, even if you pay your monthly bills on time.

## TRAVELER'S CHECKS

In most parts of the world, good ATM service in major centers makes traveler's checks an anachronism from the days before the ATM made cash accessible at any time. But be forewarned that the developing countries in Southeast Asia (Laos and Cambodia) have no ATM service. In fact, in most rural areas in the region service is scant at best. Traveler's checks are a sound alternative to traveling with dangerously large amounts of cash, and they can be replaced if lost or stolen and though you'll likely pay a small commission (1% or so), you will be saving on costly ATM withdrawal fees, which are often exorbitant.

You can get traveler's checks at almost any bank. **American Express** offers denominations of $20, $50, $100, $500, and (for cardholders only) $1,000. You'll pay a service charge ranging from 1% to 4%. You can also get American Express traveler's checks over the phone by calling ✆ **800/221-7282;** Amex gold and platinum cardholders who use this number are exempt from the 1% fee.

**Visa** offers traveler's checks at Citibank locations nationwide, as well as at several other banks. The service charge ranges between 1.5% and 2%; checks come in denominations of $20, $50, $100, $500, and $1,000. Call ✆ **800/732-1322** for information.

AAA members can obtain Visa checks without a fee at most AAA offices or by calling ✆ **866/339-3378. MasterCard** also offers traveler's checks. Call ✆ **800/223-9920** for a location near you.

**Foreign currency traveler's checks** are useful if you're traveling to one country, or to the euro zone; they're accepted at locations such as bed-and-breakfasts where dollar checks may not be, and they minimize the amount of math you have to do at your destination. **American Express, Thomas Cook, Visa,** and **MasterCard** offer foreign currency traveler's checks. You'll pay the rate of exchange at the time of your purchase (so it's a good idea to monitor the rate before you take the plunge), and most companies charge a transaction fee per order (and a shipping fee if you order online).

If you choose to carry traveler's checks, be sure to keep a record of their serial numbers separate from your checks in the event that they are stolen or lost. You'll get a refund faster if you know the numbers.

## CREDIT CARDS

Credit cards are a safe way to carry money: They also provide a convenient record of all your expenses, and they generally offer relatively good exchange rates. You can also withdraw cash advances from your credit cards at banks or ATMs, provided you know your PIN. If you've forgotten yours, or didn't even know you had one, call the number on the back of your credit card and ask the bank to send it to you. It usually takes 5 to 7 business

---

### ⸤Tips⸥ Small Change

When you change money, ask for some small bills or loose change. Petty cash will come in handy for tipping and public transportation. Consider keeping the change separate from your larger bills, so that it's readily accessible and you'll be less of a target for theft.

---

**Tips  Dear Visa: I'm Off to Bangkok!**

Some credit card companies recommend that you notify them of any impending trip abroad so that they don't become suspicious when the card is used numerous times in a foreign destination and block your charges. Even if you don't call your credit card company in advance, you can always call the card's toll-free emergency number (see "Fast Facts," p. 80) if a charge is refused—a good reason to carry the phone number with you. But perhaps the most important lesson here is to carry more than one card with you on your trip; a card might not work for any number of reasons, so having a backup is the smart way to go.

---

days, though some banks will provide the number over the phone if you tell them your mother's maiden name or some other personal information. Keep in mind that when you use your credit card abroad, most banks assess a 2% fee above the 1% fee charged by Visa or MasterCard or American Express for currency conversion on credit charges. But credit cards still may be the smart way to go when you factor in things like exorbitant ATM fees and higher traveler's check exchange rates (and service fees).

For tips and telephone numbers to call if your wallet is stolen or lost, go to "Lost & Found" in the "Fast Facts" section of this chapter.

## 4  When to Go

With a few exceptions, wherever and whenever you travel in Southeast Asia you are likely to encounter hot and humid weather. All of Southeast Asia lies within the Tropics, and the countries closest to the Equator—Singapore, Malaysia, Indonesia, and southern Thailand—have the hottest annual temperatures. Vietnam, Laos, Cambodia, and the rest of Thailand located 10 to 20 degrees above the equator also have high humidity but slightly "cooler" temperatures. The mountainous northern regions of Thailand, Laos, and Vietnam get pretty chilly during the winter months between November and March, so bring a pullover.

Monsoon winds make weather patterns confusing to keep track of. The basic rule of thumb is this: Between the months of October and February, winds from the northeast create heavy rainfall and rough seas along the eastern coasts of Vietnam, Cambodia, Thailand (including Koh Samui), Malaysia, and Singapore; however, western coasts along Thailand (including Phuket) and Malaysia are peaceful and calm. In May, the winds shift, bringing rains and swelling seas from the northwest down upon the western coast of Thailand and Malaysia until October. Nearly every place feels a dry and hot spell in March and April—Bangkok swelters! The cooler months of October through March are also the most pleasant times to visit Hong Kong, while the most rain usually falls between July and September during typhoon season.

Singapore and Malaysia are hot and humid year-round, with annual average maximum and minimum daily temperatures of 90°F and 72°F (32°C and 22°C) and year-round humidity above 90%. Most major cities are located at or near sea level, where average daytime temperatures are in the range of 80°F to 90°F (27°C–32°C) range year-round. The best way to escape the heat and humidity is to

---

**Tips  Quick ID**

Tie a colorful ribbon or piece of yarn around your luggage handle, or slap a distinctive sticker on the side of your bag. This makes it less likely that someone will mistakenly appropriate it. And if your luggage gets lost, it will be easier to find.

---

head for the hills and mountains in the higher-altitude regions of Thailand, Malaysia, Vietnam, and Laos.

## HOLIDAYS, CELEBRATIONS & FESTIVALS

Some of the holidays celebrated in Southeast Asia might affect your vacation plans, either positively or negatively. Wherever you are, you won't want to miss Chinese New Year or the many lunar festivals and myriad events like dragon boat races and small Buddhist fetes, but some holidays simply mean that businesses and attractions are closed. See the individual country chapters for listings of the major holidays celebrated in each country.

## 5 Travel Insurance

Check your existing insurance policies and credit card coverage before you buy travel insurance. You may already be covered for lost luggage, canceled tickets, or medical expenses.

The cost of travel insurance varies widely, depending on the cost and length of your trip, your age, health, and the type of trip you're taking, but expect to pay between 5% to 8% of the vacation itself.

**TRIP-CANCELLATION INSURANCE**  Trip-cancellation insurance helps you get your money back if you have to back out of a trip, if you have to go home early, or if your travel supplier goes bankrupt. Allowed reasons for cancellation can range from sickness to natural disasters to the State Department declaring your destination unsafe for travel. (Insurers usually won't cover vague fears, though, as many travelers discovered who tried to cancel their trips in Oct 2001 because they were wary of flying.) In this unstable world, trip-cancellation insurance is a good buy if you're getting tickets well in advance—who knows what the state of the world, or of your airline, will be

in 9 months? Insurance policy details vary, so read the fine print—and make sure that your airline or cruise line is on the list of carriers covered in case of bankruptcy. A good resource is **"Travel Guard Alerts,"** a list of companies considered high-risk by Travel Guard International (see website below). Protect yourself further by paying for the insurance with a credit card—by law, consumers can get their money back on goods and services not received if they report the loss within 60 days after the charge is listed on their credit card statement.

***Note:*** Many tour operators, particularly those offering trips to remote or high-risk areas, include insurance in the cost of the trip or can arrange insurance policies through a partnering provider, a convenient and often cost-effective way for the traveler to obtain insurance. Make sure the tour company is a reputable one, however: Some experts suggest you avoid buying insurance from the tour or cruise company you're traveling with, saying it's better to buy from a "third party" insurer than to put all your money in one place.

For more information, contact one of the following recommended insurers: **Access America** ($\mathcal{C}$ 866/807-3982; www.accessamerica.com); **Travel Guard International** ($\mathcal{C}$ 800/826-4919; www.travelguard.com); **Travel Insured International** ($\mathcal{C}$ 800/243-3174; www.travelinsured.com); and **Travelex Insurance Services** ($\mathcal{C}$ 888/457-4602; www.travelex-insurance.com).

**MEDICAL INSURANCE** Most health insurance policies cover you if you get sick away from home—but check, particularly if you're insured by an HMO. For travel overseas, most health plans (including Medicare and Medicaid) do not provide coverage, and the ones that do often require you to pay for services upfront and reimburse you only after you return home. Even if your plan does cover overseas treatment, most out-of-country hospitals make you pay your bills upfront, and send you a refund only after you've returned home and filed the necessary paperwork with your insurance company. As a safety net, you may want to buy travel medical insurance, particularly if you're traveling to a remote or high-risk area where emergency evacuation is a possible scenario. If you require additional medical insurance, try **MEDEX Assistance** ($\mathcal{C}$ 410/453-6300; www.medexassist.com) or **Travel Assistance International** ($\mathcal{C}$ 800/821-2828; www.travelassistance.com; for general information on services, call the company's Worldwide Assistance Services, Inc., at $\mathcal{C}$ 800/777-8710).

**LOST-LUGGAGE INSURANCE** On domestic flights, checked baggage is covered up to $2,500 per ticketed passenger. On international flights (including U.S. portions of international trips), baggage coverage is limited to approximately $9.07 per pound, up to approximately $635 per checked bag. If you plan to check items more valuable than the standard liability, see if your valuables are covered by your homeowner's policy, get baggage insurance as part of your comprehensive travel-insurance package, or buy Travel Guard's "BagTrak" product. Don't buy insurance at the airport, as it's usually overpriced. Be sure to take any valuables or irreplaceable items with you in your carry-on luggage, as many valuables (including books, money, and electronics) aren't covered by airline policies.

If your luggage is lost, immediately file a lost-luggage claim at the airport, detailing the luggage contents. For most airlines, you must report delayed, damaged, or lost baggage within 4 hours of arrival. The airlines are required to deliver luggage, once found, directly to your house or destination free of charge.

## 6 Health & Safety

### STAYING HEALTHY

Health concerns should comprise much of your preparation for a trip to Southeast Asia, and staying healthy on the road takes vigilance. Tropical heat and mosquitoes are the biggest dangers, and travelers should exercise caution over dietary change and cleanliness. Just a few pretrip precautions and general prudence, though, is all that is required for a safe and healthy trip.

### GENERAL AVAILABILITY OF HEALTH CARE

The best hospitals and health-care facilities are located in the large cities and major tourist centers of countries that have the greatest number of Western tourists—Singapore, Hong Kong, Malaysia (Kuala Lumpur), and Thailand (Bangkok). In rural areas of these countries and throughout the lesser-developed countries of Vietnam,

Cambodia, and Laos, there are limited health-care facilities: Hospitals are few and far between and generally are of poor quality. Even in heavily touristed Bali, you're better off evacuating to one of the more developed countries if faced with a serious medical situation. Over-the-counter medications are available anywhere, but it's a good idea to bring some antidiarrheal medication and rehydration salts, among others.

## COMMON AILMENTS

Among Southeast Asia's tropical diseases carried by mosquitoes are **malaria, dengue fever,** and **Japanese encephalitis.** Reports about malaria prophylactics vary. While most local health agencies tell you not to waste your time with antimalarial drugs, the CDC still advises people to take tablets, most of which cause uncomfortable side effects. In truth, your only sure way to avoid mosquito-borne diseases is to avoid being bitten. Repellents that contain **DEET** are the most effective, but more gentle alternatives (see baby-care products in any pharmacy) provide terrific DEET-free mosquito protection without the chemicals. Also be aware that malaria mosquitoes bite between the hours 5 and 7 in the morning and the evening, so it's important to exercise caution at those hours (wearing long sleeves and long trousers, and burning mosquito coils is a good idea). Dengue-fever mosquitoes bite during the day.

Hepatitis A can be contracted from water or food, and cholera epidemics sometimes occur in remote areas. Bilharzia, schistosomiasis, and giardia are parasitic diseases that can be contracted from swimming in or drinking from stagnant or untreated water in lakes or streams.

Anyone contemplating sexual activity should be aware that HIV is rampant in many Southeast Asian countries, along with other STDs such as gonorrhea, syphilis, herpes, and hepatitis B.

Contact the **International Association for Medical Assistance to Travelers (IAMAT)** (② 716/754-4883 or, in Canada, 416/652-0137; www.iamat. org) for tips on travel and health concerns in the countries you're visiting, and lists of local, English-speaking doctors. The United States **Centers for Disease Control and Prevention** (② 800/311-3435; www.cdc.gov) provides up-to-date information on health hazards by region or country and offers tips on food safety.

**DIETARY RED FLAGS**   Unless you intend to confine your travels to the big cities and dine only at restaurants that serve Western-style food, you will likely be sampling some new cuisine. This could lead initially to upset stomachs or diarrhea, which usually lasts just a few days as your body adapts to the change in your diet.

Except for Singapore, where tap water is safe to drink, **always drink bottled water (never use tap water for drinking or even brushing teeth).** It's also recommended to peel all fruits and vegetables and avoid raw shellfish and seafood. Also beware of ice unless it is made from purified water. (Any suspicious water can be purified by boiling for 10 min. or treating with purifying tablets.)

If you're a vegetarian, you will find that Southeast Asia is a great place to travel; vegetarian dishes abound throughout the region. In terms of hygiene, restaurants are generally better options than street stalls, but don't forgo good local cuisine just because it's served from a cart. Be sure to carry diarrhea medication as well as any prescription medications you might need. It's acceptable to wipe down utensils in restaurants, and in some places locals even ask for a glass of hot water for just that purpose (some travelers even carry their own plastic chopsticks or cutlery). Carrying antiseptic hand-washing liquid is also not a bad idea for when you're out in the sticks.

So, how can you tell if something will upset your stomach before you eat it? Trust your instincts. Avoid buffet-style places, especially on the street, and be sure all food is cooked thoroughly and made to order. I've been plenty sick my share of times and have found that each time I get into trouble, I've usually felt dread from the start. If your gut tells you not to eat that gelatinous chicken foot, don't eat it. If your hosts insist but you are still afraid, explain about your "foreign stomach" with a regretful smile and accept a cup of tea instead. Be careful of raw ingredients, common in most Asian cuisines, but realize that questions like, "Are these vegetables washed in clean water?" are inappropriate anywhere. Use your best judgment or simply decline.

**BUGS, BITES & OTHER WILDLIFE CONCERNS** There are all kinds of creepy critters to be aware of in any tropical climate. Mosquito nets in rural accommodations are often required and, if so, are always provided by hoteliers. Check your shoes in the morning (or wear sandals) just in case some little ugly thing is taking a nap in your Nikes. Keep an eye out for snakes and poisonous spiders when in jungle terrain or when doing any trekking. Having a guide doesn't preclude exercising caution. **Rabies** is rampant, especially in rural areas of the less-developed nations, and extreme care should be taken when walking, particularly at night. In places like Thailand, dogs are simply fed and left to roam free, and you are likely to run into some ornery mutts. A walking stick or umbrella is a suitable deterrent when out in the countryside. It's also important to know that all dogs have been hit with hurled stones sometime in their life, and, a nod to Pavlov here, the very act of reaching to the ground for a handful of stones is often enough to send an angry dog on the run, for fear of being pelted. If you are bitten, wash the wound immediately and, even if you suffer just the slightest puncture or scrape, seek medical attention and a series of rabies shots (now quite a simple affair of injections in the arm in a few installments over several weeks).

**RESPIRATORY ILLNESSES** SARS hit the region hard in the winter and spring of 2003. Singapore reported some cases and essentially closed to tourism, and though most other countries in the region reported no cases of the disease, places like Thailand suffered the fallout of the regionwide scare. As of this printing in the winter of 2004 to 2005 there have been no new cases in the region. Tuberculosis is a concern in more remote areas where testing is still uncommon.

The **avian influenza,** also called the *bird flu,* is another public relations nightmare in Southeast Asia. A number of cases have been reported in Thailand and Vietnam, and millions of chickens suspected of carrying the illness have been slaughtered. The victims of the bird flu have been few in number (statistically insignificant, really) and are mostly isolated to people working in the poultry industry. The countries affected have been unusually forthright about reporting new cases, and the disease is yet limited in scope. It is important to note that you cannot contract bird flu from consuming cooked chicken.

Air quality is not good in the larger cities like Bangkok or Ho Chi Minh City; with no emissions standards, buses, trucks and cars belch some toxic stuff, so visitors with respiratory concerns or sensitivity should take caution.

## SUN/ELEMENTS/EXTREME WEATHER EXPOSURE

Sun and heatstroke are a major concern anywhere in Southeast Asia. Limit your exposure to the sun, especially during the first few days of your trip and, thereafter, from 11am to 2pm. Use a sunscreen with a high protection factor, and apply it liberally. Asians are still big fans of parasols, so don't be shy about using an umbrella to shade yourself (all the Buddhist monks do). Remember that children need more protection than adults.

Always be sure to drink plenty of bottled water, which is the best defense against heat exhaustion and the more serious, life-threatening heatstroke. Also remember that coffee, tea, soft drinks, and alcoholic beverages should not be substituted for water because they are diuretics that dehydrate the body. In extremely hot and humid weather, try to stay out of the midday heat, and confine most of your daytime traveling to early morning and late afternoon. If you ever feel weak, fatigued, dizzy, or disoriented, get out of the sun immediately and go to a shady, cool place. To prevent sunburn, always wear a hat and apply sunscreen to all exposed areas of skin.

Be aware of major weather patterns; many island destinations are prone to typhoon or severe storm.

## WHAT TO DO IF YOU GET SICK AWAY FROM HOME

Any foreign consulate can provide a list of area doctors who speak English. If you get sick, consider asking your hotel concierge to recommend a local doctor—even his or her own. You can also try the emergency room at a local hospital. Many hospitals also have walk-in clinics for emergency cases that are not life-threatening; you may not get immediate attention, but you won't pay the high price of an emergency room visit. We list hospitals and emergency numbers under "Fast Facts," in each chapter.

You will need to pay in advance for any medical treatment. In the larger cities of Southeast Asia, health care at hospitals and private clinics is of an international caliber and quite affordable. Many insurance plans reimburse any claims upon return to your home country.

If you suffer from a chronic illness, consult your doctor before your departure. For conditions like epilepsy, diabetes, or heart problems, wear a **MedicAlert identification tag** (©888/633-4298; www.medicalert.org), which will immediately alert doctors to your condition and give them access to your records through MedicAlert's 24-hour hot line.

### Avoiding "Economy-Class Syndrome"

**Deep vein thrombosis,** or as it's know in the world of flying, "economy-class syndrome," is a blood clot that develops in a deep vein. It's a potentially deadly condition that can be caused by sitting in cramped conditions—such as an airplane cabin—for too long. During a flight (especially a long-haul flight), get up, walk around, and stretch your legs every 60 to 90 minutes to keep your blood flowing. Other preventative measures include frequent flexing of the legs while sitting, drinking lots of water, and avoiding alcohol and sleeping pills. If you have a history of deep vein thrombosis, heart disease, or other conditions that puts you at high risk, some experts recommend wearing compression stockings or taking anticoagulants when you fly; always ask your physician about the best course for you. Symptoms of deep vein thrombosis include leg pain or swelling, or even shortness of breath.

Pack **prescription medications** in your carry-on luggage, and carry prescription medications in their original containers, with pharmacy labels—otherwise they won't make it through airport security. Also, bring along copies of your prescriptions in case you lose your pills or run out. Don't forget an extra pair of contact lenses or prescription glasses. Carry the generic name of prescription medicines, in case a local pharmacist is unfamiliar with the brand name.

Prescription medication is readily available, often over the counter.

For domestic trips, most reliable health-care plans provide coverage if you get sick away from home. For travel abroad, you may have to pay all medical costs upfront and be reimbursed later. See "Medical Insurance," under "Travel Insurance," above.

## STAYING SAFE

The good news is that anonymous, violent crime is not an issue in most countries in the region, but petty theft, pickpocketing, and purse snatching are common. It is a good idea to carry a hidden travel wallet with your passport and documents, and keep an eye on valuables in public.

Road conditions vary throughout the region, but most large cities, from Bangkok to Ho Chi Minh, are busy and chaotic. Even for intrepid travelers who push their limits out in the wilds, crossing big-city streets, even at prescribed crossings, can be the greatest risk on your trip; move slowly and exercise caution (Mom's advice to look both ways couldn't be more important). Rural roads in places like Laos and Cambodia are often no more

than dirt tracks. And even where the roads are good, Western visitors are often shocked at the seeming lack of rules and the fact that, on most roads, might is right: The biggest, fastest, and most aggressive vehicle takes precedence and belligerent horn blowing is the rule. It is best to rent a car with a hired driver instead of trying to drive yourself. On some bus rides you might want to just keep your eyes on the scenery and not the road ahead if you want to enjoy it.

In places like the beach towns of Thailand, you're sure to meet one or two road-rashed victims of minor motorbike accidents. Exercise extreme caution on rented bikes, especially if you're inexperienced.

Dicey political situations arise and pass with frequency and it's important to check travel warnings and double-check with the U.S. State Department (http://state.gov) or the most up-to-date sources on the region. Places like Laos, Cambodia, and Indonesia are known to flare with separatist movements and terrorism. Stay abreast of any and all news before flying.

Nancy Reagan's advice about drugs couldn't be more apt for a trip to Southeast Asia: "Just say no." Grown, produced, and shipped through the region, drugs like heroin, opium, and marijuana are readily available. There are island spots and mountain retreats where it might seem like the thing to do, but in all cases here, national laws are strict. Many visitors find themselves in an intensive language school of another variety (i.e., jail) in short order if they can't bribe their way out of it. It's certainly not worth it anywhere.

## 7 Specialized Travel Resources

### TRAVELERS WITH DISABILITIES

Most disabilities shouldn't stop anyone from traveling. There are more options

and resources out there than ever before. Larger hotels in the major cities of the region have adequate facilities for visitors with disabilities, but in rural destinations, specialized amenities are scant at best.

Many travel agencies offer customized tours and itineraries for travelers with disabilities. **Flying Wheels Travel** (© **507/451-5005;** www.flyingwheelstravel.com) offers escorted tours and cruises that emphasize sports and private tours in minivans with lifts. **Access-Able Travel Source** (© **303/232-2979;** www.access-able.com) offers extensive access information and advice for traveling around the world with disabilities. **Accessible Journeys** (© **800/846-4537** or 610/521-0339; www.disabilitytravel.com) caters specifically to slow walkers and wheelchair travelers and their families and friends.

**Avis Rent a Car** has an "Avis Access" program that offers such services as a dedicated 24-hour toll-free number (© **888/879-4273**) for customers with special travel needs; special car features such as swivel seats, spinner knobs, and hand controls; and accessible bus service.

Organizations that offer assistance to disabled travelers include **MossRehab** (www.mossresourcenet.org), which provides a library of accessible-travel resources online; **SATH (Society for Accessible Travel & Hospitality)** (© **212/447-7284;** www.sath.org; annual membership fees: $45 adults, $30 seniors and students), which offers a wealth of travel resources for all types of disabilities and informed recommendations on destinations, access guides, travel agents, tour operators, vehicle rentals, and companion services; and the **American Foundation for the Blind (AFB)** (© **800/232-5463;** www.afb.org), a referral resource for the blind or visually impaired that includes information on traveling with Seeing Eye dogs.

For more information specifically targeted to travelers with disabilities, the community website **iCan** (www.icanonline.net/channels/travel/index.cfm) has destination guides and several regular columns on accessible travel. Also check out the quarterly magazine *Emerging Horizons* ($15 per yr., $20 outside the U.S.; www.emerginghorizons.com); and *Open World* magazine, published by SATH (see above; subscription: $13 per yr., $21 outside the U.S.).

## GAY & LESBIAN TRAVELERS

Acceptance of alternative lifestyles in Southeast Asia, like anywhere, runs the gamut. One thing to remember is that many of the societies and cultures of the region are, by tradition, very modest, and public displays of affection of any kind are not acceptable. Gay nightlife choices are many and varied in larger cities like Bangkok, Singapore, and Hong Kong, but in rural areas, provincial attitudes vary and intolerance is not uncommon.

**The International Gay and Lesbian Travel Association (IGLTA)** (© **800/448-8550** or 954/776-2626; www.iglta.org) is the trade association for the gay and lesbian travel industry, and offers an online directory of gay- and lesbian-friendly travel businesses; go to its website and click on "Members."

Many agencies offer tours and travel itineraries specifically for gay and lesbian travelers. **Above and Beyond Tours** (© **800/397-2681;** www.abovebeyondtours.com) is the exclusive gay and lesbian tour operator for United Airlines. **Now, Voyager** (© **800/255-6951;** www.nowvoyager.com) is a well-known San Francisco–based gay-owned and -operated travel service. **Olivia Cruises & Resorts** (© **800/631-6277;** www.olivia.com) charters entire resorts and ships for exclusive lesbian vacations and offers smaller group experiences for both gay and lesbian travelers.

The following travel guides are available at most travel bookstores and gay and lesbian bookstores, or you can order them from **Giovanni's Room** bookstore, 1145 Pine St., Philadelphia, PA 19107 (© **215/923-2960;** www. giovannisroom.com): *Out and About* (©**800/929-2268;**www.outandabout. com), which offers guidebooks and a newsletter ($20 per yr.; 10 issues) packed with solid information on the global gay and lesbian scene; *Spartacus International Gay Guide* (Bruno Gmünder Verlag; www.spartacusworld. com/gayguide) and *Odysseus: The International Gay Travel Planner* (Odysseus Enterprises Ltd.), both good, annual English-language guide-books focused on gay men; the *Damron* guides (www.damron.com), with separate, annual books for gay men and lesbians; and *Gay Travel A to Z: The World of Gay & Lesbian Travel Options at Your Fingertips* by Mari-anne Ferrari (Ferrari International; Box 35575, Phoenix, AZ 85069), a very good gay and lesbian guidebook series.

## SENIOR TRAVEL

Seniors traveling in the region can bask in the glow of filial piety and the region's notorious Confucian respect for elders, but they are less likely to enjoy the major discounts found in the West. Mention the fact that you're a senior citizen when you make your travel reservations, though. In some cases, people over the age of 60 qualify for reduced admission to theaters, museums, and other attractions, as well as discounted fares on public transportation.

Members of **AARP** (formerly known as the American Association of Retired Persons), 601 E St. NW, Washington, DC 20049 (© **888/ 687-2277;** www.aarp.org), get dis-counts on hotels, airfares, and car rentals. AARP offers members a wide range of benefits, including *AARP: The Magazine* and a monthly newslet-ter. Anyone over 50 can join.

Many reliable agencies and organiza-tions target the 50-plus market. **Elder-hostel** (© **877/426-8056;** www.

elderhostel.org) arranges study pro-grams for those aged 55 and over (and a spouse or companion of any age) in the U.S. and in more than 80 countries around the world. Most courses last 5 to 7 days in the U.S. (2–4 weeks abroad), and many include airfare, accommodations in university dormi-tories or modest inns, meals, and tuition. **ElderTreks** (© **800/741-7956;** www.eldertreks.com) offers small-group tours to off-the-beaten-path or adventure-travel locations, restricted to travelers 50 and older. **INTRAV** (© **800/456-8100;** www. intrav.com) is a high-end tour operator that caters to the mature, discerning traveler, not specifically seniors, with trips around the world that include guided safaris, polar expeditions, pri-vate-jet adventures, and small-boat cruises down jungle rivers.

Recommended publications offering travel resources and discounts for sen-iors include: the quarterly magazine *Travel 50 & Beyond* (www.travel 50andbeyond.com); *Travel Unlim-ited: Uncommon Adventures for the Mature Traveler* (Avalon); *101 Tips for Mature Travelers,* available from Grand Circle Travel (© **800/221-2610** or 617/350-7500; www.gct. com); and *Unbelievably Good Deals and Great Adventures That You Absolutely Can't Get Unless You're Over 50* (McGraw-Hill), by Joann Rattner Heilman.

## FAMILY TRAVEL

If you have enough trouble getting your kids out of the house in the morning, dragging them thousands of miles away might seem like an insur-mountable challenge. But family travel can be immensely rewarding, giving you new ways of seeing the world through smaller pairs of eyes. The rough roads of Southeast Asia can be a bit much for the little shaver, and concerns about communicable disease in rural areas should certainly be weighed. However, more accessible destinations and larger cities offer a glimpse into ancient civilization and varied culture that delights the kid in all of us. Most hotels can arrange extra beds at little additional cost, and connecting room capability is common. To locate those accommodations, restaurants, and attractions that are particularly kid friendly, refer to the "Kids" icon throughout this guide.

Familyhostel (© 800/733-9753; www.learn.unh.edu/familyhostel) takes the whole family, including kids ages 8 to 15, on moderately priced domestic and international learning vacations. Lectures, field trips, and sightseeing are guided by a team of academics.

Recommended family travel Internet sites include **Family Travel Forum** (www.familytravelforum.com), a comprehensive site that offers customized trip planning; **Family Travel Network** (www.familytravelnetwork.com), an award-winning site that offers travel features, deals, and tips; **Traveling Internationally with Your Kids** (www.travelwithyourkids.com), a comprehensive site offering sound advice for long-distance and international travel with children; and **Family Travel Files** (www.thefamilytravelfiles.com), which offers an online magazine and a directory of off-the-beaten-path tours and tour operators for families.

## WOMEN TRAVELERS

Women traveling together or alone will find touring this region particularly pleasant and easy. The Buddhist and Islamic codes of conduct and ethics followed by many mean that you will be treated with respect and courtesy.

Wearing revealing clothing or sunbathing topless might appear to be tolerated, but that's only because your hosts wish to avoid confrontation. Deep inside, it is very embarrassing.

Although you will almost never find local women dining or touring alone, as a visitor, your behavior will be accepted. You will rarely, if ever, be approached or hassled by strangers. At the same time, you can feel free to start a conversation with a stranger without fear of misinterpretation. *Note:* If you are traveling with a man, public displays of affection are not welcome, and it's you, the female, who will be scorned. Also, you will have to take even more care than your male counterpart to dress modestly, meaning no cleavage- or midriff-baring tops, miniskirts, or short shorts. Otherwise, you risk offending people on the grounds of either religious or local moral standards.

All this said, it's still not advisable to take risks that you wouldn't normally take at home. Don't hitchhike, accept rides, or walk around late at night, particularly in dimly lit areas or in unfamiliar places. Be acutely aware of purse or jewelry snatchers in large cities. When meeting strangers in nightclubs, for example, buy your own drinks, and keep an eye on them.

Check out the award-winning website **Journeywoman** (www.journeywoman.com), a "real-life" women's travel information network where you can sign up for a free e-mail newsletter and get advice on everything from etiquette and dress to safety; or the travel guide *Safety and Security for Women Who Travel* by Sheila Swan and Peter Laufer (Travelers' Tales, Inc.), offering common-sense tips on safe travel.

## MULTICULTURAL TRAVELERS

The Internet offers a number of helpful travel sites for the black traveler. **Black Travel Online** (www.blacktravelonline.com) posts news on upcoming events and includes links to articles and travel-booking sites.

Agencies and organizations that provide resources for black travelers include: **Rodgers Travel** (© 800/825-1775; www.rodgerstravel.com), a Philadelphia-based travel agency with an extensive menu of tours in destinations worldwide, including heritage and private group tours; the **African American Association of Innkeepers International** (© 877/422-5777; www.africanamericaninns.com), which provides information on member B&Bs in the U.S., Canada, and the Caribbean; and **Henderson Travel & Tours** (© 800/327-2309 or 301/650-5700; www.hendersontravel.com).

For more information, check out the following collections and guides: *Go Girl: The Black Woman's Guide to Travel & Adventure* (Eighth Mountain Press), a compilation of travel essays by writers including Jill Nelson and Audre Lorde, with some practical information and trip-planning advice; *The African-American Travel Guide* by Wayne Robinson (Hunter Publishing; www.hunter publishing.com), with details on 19 North American cities; *Steppin' Out* by Carla Labat (Avalon), with details on 20 cities; *Travel and Enjoy Magazine* (© 866/266-6211; www.travel andenjoy.com; subscription: $38 per yr.), which focuses on discounts and destination reviews; and the more narrative *Pathfinders Magazine* (© 877/977-PATH; www.pathfinders travel.com; subscription: $15 per yr.), which includes articles on everything from Rio de Janeiro to Ghana as well as information on upcoming ski, diving, golf, and tennis trips.

## STUDENT TRAVELERS

Southeast Asia has become a very hot destination for budget-minded (I didn't say *poor*) students. Places like southern Thailand are attracting a young, spring-break crowd. Commonly, young backpackers hit the shores in SE Asia and travel for extended periods of time. From bases like Bangkok's Khao San road, budget travelers have roamed the rugged highways and byways, paving the way for high-end tourism. More rural areas are relegated to only

this hearty horde and rural roads still beckon with the promise of friendships (often through shared strife) and broadening experiences.

Any discounts to be found in Southeast Asia come from hard bargaining or tolerance for the most basic accommodations, but it's not a bad idea to have an **International Student Identity Card (ISIC),** which offers substantial savings on plane tickets and some entrance fees. It also provides you with basic health and life insurance and a 24-hour help line. The card is available for $22 from **STA Travel** (© 800/781-4040 in North America; www.statravel.com), the biggest student travel agency in the world. If you're no longer a student but are still under 26, you can get a **International Youth Travel Card (IYTC)** for the same price from the same people, which entitles you to some discounts (but not on museum admissions). (*Note:* In 2002, STA Travel bought competitors **Council Travel** and **USIT Campus** after they went bankrupt. It's still operating some offices under the Council name, but they are owned by STA.) **Travel CUTS** (© 800/667-2887 or 416/614-2887; www.travelcuts.com) offers similar services for both Canadians and U.S. residents. Irish students may prefer to turn to **USIT** (© 01/602-1600; www.usitnow.ie), an Ireland-based specialist in student, youth, and independent travel.

## SINGLE TRAVELERS

By and large, travelers in Southeast Asia are seekers of some kind, so many prefer to travel alone. For independent travelers, solo journeys are opportunities to make friends and meet locals. There is also a certain camaraderie that develops on long bus rides or in the uncertainty and wonder we share with fellow travelers, and a trip that might start out solo often ends in friendships that last a lifetime.

For advice about hopping off the track and finding your own path, check out the website **Vagabonding** by Ralf Potts (www.vagabonding.net), with information both practical and spiritual about the ways of the wanderer. Another inspiration is *The Art of Pilgrimage: The Seekers Guide to Making Travel Sacred* (Conari Press), by Phil Cousineau. For more practical information, check out Eleanor Berman's latest edition of *Traveling Solo: Advice and Ideas for More Than 250 Great Vacations* (Globe Pequot), a guide with advice on traveling alone, whether on your own or on a group tour.

If going by tour, it is important to know that single travelers are often hit with a "single supplement" to the base price of tours. To avoid it, you can agree to room with other single travelers on the trip, or you can find a compatible roommate before you go from one of the many roommate locator agencies.

Travel Buddies Singles Travel Club (✆ 800/998-9099; www.travelbuddiesworldwide.com), based in Canada, runs small, intimate, single-friendly group trips and will match you with a roommate free of charge. **TravelChums** (✆ 212/787-2621; www.travelchums.com) is an Internet-only travel-companion matching service with elements of an online personals-type site, hosted by the respected New York–based Shaw Guides travel service.

Many reputable tour companies offer singles-only trips. **Singles Travel International** (✆ 877/765-6874; www.singlestravelintl.com) offers singles-only trips to places all over the world, like London, Fiji, and the Greek Islands. **Backroads** (✆ 800/462-2848; www.backroads.com) offers more than 160 active-travel trips to 30 destinations worldwide, including Bali, Morocco, and Costa Rica.

## 8 Planning Your Trip Online

### SURFING FOR AIRFARES

The "big three" online travel agencies, **Expedia.com, Travelocity,** and **Orbitz** sell most of the air tickets bought on the Internet. (Canadian travelers should try expedia.ca and Travelocity.ca; U.K. residents can go for expedia.co.uk and opodo.co.uk.). Each has different business deals with the airlines and may offer different fares on the same flights, so it's wise to shop around. Expedia and Travelocity will also send you **e-mail notification** when a cheap fare becomes available to your favorite destination. Of the smaller travel agency websites, **SideStep** (www.sidestep.com) has gotten the best reviews from Frommer's authors. It's a browser add-on that purports to "search 140 sites at once," but in reality only beats competitors' fares as often as other sites do.

Also remember to check **airline websites,** especially those for low-fare carriers such as Southwest, JetBlue, AirTran, WestJet, or Ryanair, whose fares are often misreported or simply missing from travel agency websites. Even with major airlines, you can often shave a few bucks from a fare by booking directly through the airline and avoiding a travel agency's transaction fee. But you'll get these discounts only by **booking online:** Most airlines now offer online-only fares that even their phone agents know nothing about.

Great **last-minute deals** are available through free weekly e-mail services provided directly by the airlines. Most of these are announced on Tuesday or Wednesday and must be purchased online. Most are only valid for travel that weekend, but some (such as

Southwest's) can be booked weeks or months in advance. Sign up for weekly e-mail alerts at airline websites or check megasites that compile comprehensive lists of last-minute specials, such as **Smarter Living** (www.smarter living.com). For last-minute trips, **site59.com** and **lastminutetravel.com** in the U.S. and **lastminute.com** in Europe often have better air-and-hotel package deals than the major-label sites. A website listing numerous bargain sites and airlines around the world is **www.itravelnet.com**.

If you're willing to give up some control over your flight details, use what is called an "**opaque" fare service** like **Priceline** (www.priceline.com; www. priceline.co.uk for Europeans) or its smaller competitor **Hotwire** (www. hotwire.com). Both offer rock-bottom prices in exchange for travel on a "mystery airline" at a mysterious time of day, often with a mysterious change of planes en route. The mystery airlines are all major, well-known carriers—and the possibility of being sent from Philadelphia to Chicago via Tampa is remote; the airlines' routing computers have gotten a lot better than they used to be. But your chances of getting a 6am or 11pm flight are pretty high. Hotwire tells you flight prices before you buy; Priceline usually has better deals than Hotwire, but you have to play their "name our price" game. If you're new at this, the helpful folks at **BiddingForTravel.com** (www.bidding fortravel.com) do a good job of demystifying Priceline's prices and strategies. Priceline and Hotwire are great for flights within North America and between the U.S. and Europe. But for flights to other parts of the world, consolidators will almost always beat their fares. *Note:* In 2004 Priceline added nonopaque service to its roster. You now have the option to pick exact flights, times, and airlines from a list of offers—or opt to bid on opaque fares as before.

For much more about airfares and savvy air-travel tips and advice, pick up a copy of ***Frommer's Fly Safe, Fly Smart*** (Wiley Publishing, Inc.).

## SURFING FOR HOTELS

Shopping online for hotels is generally done one of two ways: by booking through the hotel's own website or through an independent booking agency (or a fare-service agency like Priceline; see below). These Internet hotel agencies have multiplied in mind-boggling numbers of late, competing for the business of millions of consumers surfing for accommodations around the world. This competitiveness can be a boon to consumers who have the patience and time to shop and compare the online sites for good deals—but shop they must, for prices can vary considerably from site to site. And keep in mind that hotels at the top of a site's listing may be there for no other reason than that they paid money to get the placement.

Shopping online for hotels is not too practical in the region. You'll find any number of sites, but few list the smaller boutique properties and picturesque bungalow hideaways you'll find on your own, and even the most popular websites often list inflated prices. For all hotels in the major metropolitan areas, though, online booking is cheap and convenient.

Of the "big three" sites, **Expedia.com** offers a long list of special deals and "virtual tours" or photos of available rooms so you can see what you're paying for (a feature that helps counter the claims that the best rooms are often held back from bargain booking websites). **Travelocity** posts unvarnished customer reviews and ranks its properties according to the AAA rating system. Also reliable are **Hotels.com** and **Quikbook.com**. An excellent free program, **TravelAxe** (www.travelaxe. net), can help you search multiple hotel sites at once, even ones you may never have heard of—and conveniently lists the total price of the room, including the taxes and service charges. Another booking site, **Travelweb** (www.travelweb.com), is partly owned by the hotels it represents (including the Hilton, Hyatt, and Starwood chains) and is therefore plugged directly into the hotels' reservations systems—unlike independent online agencies, which have to fax or e-mail reservation requests to the hotel, a good portion of which get misplaced in the shuffle. More than once, travelers have arrived at the hotel, only to be told that they have no reservation. To be fair, many of the major sites are undergoing improvements in service and ease of use, and Expedia.com will soon be able to plug directly into the reservations systems of many hotel chains—none of which can be bad news for consumers. In the meantime, it's a good idea to **get a confirmation number** and **make a printout** of any online booking transaction.

In the opaque website category, **Priceline** and **Hotwire** are even better for hotels than for airfares; with both, you're allowed to pick the neighborhood and quality level of your hotel before offering up your money. Priceline's hotel product even covers Europe and Asia, though it's much better at getting five-star lodging for three-star prices than at finding anything at the bottom of the scale. On the down side, many hotels stick Priceline guests in their least desirable rooms. Be sure to go to the Bidding-ForTravel.com website (see above) before bidding on a hotel room on Priceline; it features a fairly up-to-date list of hotels that Priceline uses in major cities. For both Priceline and Hotwire, you pay upfront, and the fee is nonrefundable. ***Note:*** Some hotels do not provide loyalty program credits or points or other frequent-stay amenities when you book a room through opaque online services.

## SURFING FOR RENTAL CARS

For booking rental cars online, the best deals are usually found at rental-car company websites, although all the major online travel agencies also offer rental-car reservations services. Priceline and Hotwire work well for rental

---

### Frommers.com: The Complete Travel Resource

For an excellent travel-planning resource, we highly recommend **Frommers.com** (www.frommers.com), voted Best Travel Site by *PC Magazine*. We're a little biased, of course, but we guarantee that you'll find the travel tips, reviews, monthly vacation giveaways, bookstore, and online-booking capabilities thoroughly indispensable. Among the special features are our popular **Destinations** section, where you'll get expert travel tips, hotel and dining recommendations, and advice on the sights to see for more than 3,500 destinations around the globe; the **Frommers.com Newsletter**, with the latest deals, travel trends, and money-saving secrets; our **Community** area featuring **Message Boards,** where Frommer's readers post queries and share advice (sometimes even our authors show up to answer questions); and our **Photo Center,** where you can post and share vacation tips. When your research is done, the **Online Reservations System** (www.frommers.com/book_a_trip) takes you to Frommer's preferred online partners for booking your vacation at affordable prices.

cars, too; the only "mystery" is which major rental company you get, and for most travelers the difference between Hertz, Avis, and Budget is negligible.

## 9 The 21st-Century Traveler

### INTERNET ACCESS AWAY FROM HOME

Internet cafes in Southeast Asia are many and affordable, preferable to expensive hotel business centers (you'll also meet lots of fellow travelers at Internet cafes). Of course, using your own laptop—or even a PDA (personal digital assistant) or electronic organizer with a modem—gives you the most flexibility, but connections in hotels are expensive and wireless hotspots are, as yet, few.

### WITHOUT YOUR OWN COMPUTER

In most parts of Southeast Asia you'll find a cybercafe on every street corner, anything from informed, efficient services—even help managing digital photo files and burning CDs—to basic storefront spots or a place that's just terminals under a thatch roof by the beach. Be warned that rural destinations in places like Laos have little or no service. Backpacker ghettos are always a good bet for finding cheap and reliable service. Avoid **hotel business centers** unless you're willing to pay exorbitant rates. To search availability in any area, check websites like **www.cyber captive.com** or **www.cybercafe.com**.

Most major airports now have **Internet kiosks** scattered throughout their gates. These kiosks, which you'll also see in shopping malls, hotel lobbies, and tourist information offices around the world, give you basic Web access for a per-minute fee that's usually higher than cybercafe prices. The kiosks' clunkiness and high price mean they should be avoided whenever possible.

To retrieve your e-mail, ask your **Internet Service Provider (ISP)** if it has a Web-based interface tied to your existing e-mail account. If your ISP doesn't have such an interface, you can use the free **mail2web** service (www.mail2web.com) to view and reply to your home e-mail. For more flexibility, you may want to open a free, Web-based e-mail account with **Yahoo! Mail** (http://mail.yahoo.com). (Microsoft's Hotmail is another popular option, but Hotmail has severe spam problems.) Your home ISP may be able to forward your e-mail to the Web-based account automatically.

If you need to access files on your office computer, look into a service called **GoToMyPC** (www.gotomypc. com). The service provides a Web-based interface for you to access and manipulate a distant PC from anywhere—even a cybercafe—provided your "target" PC is on and has an always-on connection to the Internet (such as with Road Runner cable). The service offers top-quality security, but if you're worried about hackers, use your own laptop rather than a cybercafe computer to access the GoToMyPC system.

### WITH YOUR OWN COMPUTER

Wi-fi (wireless fidelity) is the buzzword in computer access, and more and more hotels, cafes, and retailers are signing on as wireless "hot spots" from where you can get high-speed connection without cable wires, networking hardware, or a phone line (see below). You can get wi-fi connection one of several ways. Many laptops sold in the last year have built-in wi-fi capability (an 802.11b wireless Ethernet connection). Prepaid cards are increasingly available at upscale coffee shops (Starbucks, for example) and with your own wireless-capable computer, connection is a snap. Some places provide **free wireless networks.**

To locate these free hot spots, go to **www.personaltelco.net/index.cgi/ wirelesscommunities**.

If wi-fi is not available, most business-class hotels offer dataports for laptop modems, some using an Ethernet network cable. You can bring your own cables, but most hotels offer cables. In addition, major Internet Service Providers (ISP) have **local access numbers** around the world, allowing you to go online by simply placing a local call. Check your ISP's website or call its toll-free number and ask how you can use your current account away from home, and how much it will cost.

If you're traveling outside the reach of your ISP, the **iPass** network has dial-up numbers in most of the world's countries. You'll have to sign up with an iPass provider, who will then tell you how to set up your computer for your destination(s). For a list of iPass providers, go to www.ipass.com and click on "Individual Purchase." One solid provider is **i2roam** (www. i2roam.com; ℂ **866/811-6209** or 920/235-0475).

Wherever you go, bring a **connection kit** of the right power and phone adapters, a spare phone cord, and a spare Ethernet network cable—or find out whether your hotel supplies them to guests.

Most Southeast Asian countries runon **220-volt electrical currents.** Plugs are two-pronged, with either round or flat prongs. If you're coming from the U.S. and you must bring electrical appliances, bring your own converter and adapter (a surge protector is a good idea for a laptop). Check the "Fast Facts" section of individual country chapters. Some hotels have 110-volt service.

## USING A CELLPHONE

The three letters that define much of the world's **wireless capabilities** are GSM (Global System for Mobiles), a big, seamless network that makes for easy cross-border cellphone use throughout Europe and dozens of other countries worldwide. In the U.S., T-Mobile, AT&T Wireless, and Cingular use this quasiuniversal system; in Canada, Microcell and some Rogers customers are GSM, and all Europeans and most Australians use GSM.

If your cellphone is on a GSM system, and you have a world-capable multiband phone such as many Sony Ericsson, Motorola, or Samsung models, you can make and receive calls across civilized areas on much of the globe, from Andorra to Uganda. Just call your wireless operator and ask for "international roaming" to be activated on your account. Unfortunately, per-minute charges can be high—usually $1 to $1.50 in Western Europe and up to $5 in places like Russia and Indonesia.

That's why it's important to buy an "unlocked" world phone from the get-go. Many cellphone operators sell "locked" phones that restrict you from using any other removable computer memory phone chip (called a **SIM card**) card other than the ones they supply. Having an unlocked phone allows you to install a cheap, prepaid SIM card (found at a local retailer) in your destination country. (Show your phone to the salesperson; not all phones work on all networks.) You'll get a local phone number—and much, much lower calling rates. Getting an already locked phone unlocked can be a complicated process, but it can be done; just call your cellular operator and say you'll be going abroad for several months and want to use the phone with a local provider.

For many, **renting** a phone is a good idea. (Even world-phone owners will have to rent new phones if they're traveling to non-GSM regions, such as Japan or Korea.) While you can rent a phone from any number of overseas

## Digital Photography on the Road

Many travelers are going digital these days when it comes to taking vacation photographs. Not only are digital cameras left relatively unscathed by airport X-rays, but with digital equipment you don't need to lug armloads of film with you as you travel. In fact, nowadays you don't even need to carry your laptop to download the day's images to make room for more. With a **media storage card,** sold by all major camera dealers, you can store hundreds of images in your camera. These "memory" cards come in different configurations—from memory sticks to flash cards to secure digital cards—and different storage capacities (the more megabytes of memory, the more images a card can hold) and range in price from $30 to over $200. (**Note:** Each camera model works with a specific type of card, so you'll need to determine which storage card is compatible with your camera.) When you get home, you can print the images out on your own color printer or take the storage card to a camera store, drugstore, or chain retailer. Or have the images developed online with a service like **Snapfish** (www.snapfish.com) for something like 25¢ a shot. **Note:** The many storefront Internet cafes in the region are also important resources; for a fee as low as $1, you can burn CDs of your photos, downloading directly from your camera or by plugging-in your media storage card into an adapter. Then delete and shoot more.

sites, including kiosks at airports and at car-rental agencies, we suggest renting the phone before you leave home. That way you can give loved ones and business associates your new number, make sure the phone works, and take the phone wherever you go—especially helpful for overseas trips through several countries, where local phone-rental agencies often bill in local currency and may not let you take the phone to another country.

Phone rental isn't cheap. You'll usually pay $40 to $50 per week, plus airtime fees of at least a dollar a minute. If you're traveling to Europe, though, local rental companies often offer free incoming calls within their home country, which can save you big bucks. The bottom line: Shop around.

For trips of more than a few weeks spent in one country, **buying a phone** becomes economically attractive, as many nations have cheap, no-questions-asked prepaid phone systems. Once you arrive at your destination, stop by a local cellphone shop and get the cheapest package; you'll probably pay less than $100 for a phone and a starter calling card. Local calls may be as low as 10¢ per minute, and in many countries incoming calls are free.

True wilderness adventurers, or those heading to less-developed countries, should consider renting a **satellite phone ("satphone"),** which are different from cellphones in that they connect to satellites rather than ground-based towers. A satphone is more costly than a cellphone but works where there's no cellular signal and no towers. You can rent satellite phones from **RoadPost** (www.roadpost.com; ✆ **888/290-1606** or 905/272-5665). InTouch USA (www.intouchusa.com) offers a wider range of satphones but at higher rates. Per-minute call charges can be even cheaper than roaming charges with a regular cellphone, but the phone itself is more expensive (up to $150 a week), and depending on the service you choose, people calling you may incur high long-distance charges. As of this writing, satphones were amazingly expensive to buy, so don't even think about it.

## Online Traveler's Toolbox

Veteran travelers usually carry some essential items to make their trips easier. Following is a selection of handy online tools to bookmark and use.

- **Airplane Seating and Food.** Find out which seats to reserve and which to avoid (and more) on all major domestic airlines at www.seatguru.com. And check out the type of meal (with photos) you'll likely be served on airlines around the world at www.airline meals.com.
- **Foreign Languages for Travelers** (www.travlang.com). Learn basic terms in more than 70 languages and click on any underlined phrase to hear what it sounds like.
- **Intellicast** (www.intellicast.com) and **Weather.com** (www.weather.com). Gives weather forecasts for all 50 states and for cities around the world.
- **Time and Date** (www.timeanddate.com). See what time (and day) it is anywhere in the world.
- **Travel Warnings** (http://travel.state.gov, www.fco.gov.uk/travel, www.voyage.gc.ca, and www.dfat.gov.au/consular/advice). These sites report on places where health concerns or unrest might threaten American, British, Canadian, and Australian travelers. Generally, U.S. warnings are the most paranoid; Australian warnings are the most relaxed.
- **Universal Currency Converter** (www.xe.com/ucc). See what your dollar or pound is worth in more than 100 other countries.
- **Visa ATM Locator** (www.visa.com), for locations of PLUS ATMs worldwide, or **MasterCard ATM Locator** (www.mastercard.com), for locations of Cirrus ATMs worldwide.
- **The CIA Factbook** (www.cia.gov). Gives annotated statistics and information about countries worldwide.
- **Mekong Express** (www.visit-mekong.com). A cross-referenced site for all of the countries in Indochina.
- **The Elephant Guide** (www.elephantguide.com). A useful resource for current information in each country in the region, listing articles from international press and stories from individual travelers.

## 10 Getting There

### BY PLANE

If you're flying to Southeast Asia, you will more than likely arrive via one of the region's three main hubs: Bangkok, Singapore, or Hong Kong, from where you can pick up flights to any other destination in Southeast Asia. Your home country's national carriers will almost certainly connect with all three of these airports. Check also with Southeast Asian–based airlines for fare deals: Cathay Pacific, Thai Airways International, Malaysian Airlines, and Singapore Airlines. Check United for its new direct flights between the U.S. West Coast and Vietnam.

## TO BANGKOK

The following international airlines provide service to Bangkok's Don Muang International Airport.

### FROM THE UNITED STATES

Service is provided by the national carrier, Thai Airways International, as well as United Airlines, Northwest Airlines, Cathay Pacific Airways, All Nippon Airways, Asiana Airlines, Japan Air Lines, China Airlines, Eva Airways, Korean Air, Malaysia Airlines, and Singapore Airlines.

### FROM THE UNITED KINGDOM

Airlines with flights from the U.K. to Bangkok include Thai Airways International, British Airways, and Singapore Airlines.

### FROM CANADA

Canadian Airlines International flies to Bangkok from Vancouver via Hong Kong 4 days a week.

### FROM AUSTRALIA

Service is provided by Qantas Airways, Thai Airways International, Singapore Airlines, and British Airways.

## TO SINGAPORE

The following carriers fly to Singapore's Changi International Airport.

### FROM THE UNITED STATES

Singapore Airlines has the most weekly flights from the U.S. to Changi airport. United Airlines and Northwest Airlines are the only U.S. airlines offering flights to Singapore.

### FROM CANADA

Singapore Airlines provides service from Canada, along with Canadian Airlines International.

### FROM THE UNITED KINGDOM

You can fly to Singapore via Singapore Airlines, British Airways, and Qantas Airways.

### FROM AUSTRALIA

Singapore Airlines, Qantas Airways, Ansett Australian Airlines, British Airways, and KLM Royal Dutch Airlines all provide service to Singapore.

### FROM NEW ZEALAND

Singapore Airlines and Air New Zealand offer New Zealand–Singapore flights.

## TO HONG KONG

The following carriers fly to Hong Kong's Chek Lap Kok Airport.

### FROM THE UNITED STATES

United Airlines, Northwest Airlines, Cathay Pacific Airways, China Airlines, Singapore Airlines, Thai Airways International, and Hong Kong's Dragonair all fly to Hong Kong.

### FROM CANADA

Cathay Pacific Airways, Canadian Airlines International, Air Canada, Singapore Airlines, and China Airlines provide service.

### FROM THE UNITED KINGDOM

Cathay Pacific Airways, British Airways, Virgin Atlantic Airways, Singapore Airlines, China Airlines, and Dragonair fly into Hong Kong.

### FROM AUSTRALIA

Service is provided by Cathay Pacific Airways, Qantas Airways, Ansett Australian Airlines, Singapore Airlines, and Dragonair.

### FROM NEW ZEALAND

Airlines with flights include Air New Zealand and Cathay Pacific Airways.

## GETTING THROUGH THE AIRPORT

With the federalization of airport security, security procedures at U.S. airports are more stable and consistent than ever. Generally, you'll be fine if you arrive at the airport **1 hour** before a domestic flight and **2 hours** before an international flight; if you show up late, tell an airline employee and he or she will probably whisk you to the front of the line.

Bring a **current, government-issued photo ID** such as a driver's license or passport. Keep your ID at the ready to show at check-in, the security checkpoint, and sometimes even the gate. (Children under 18 do not need government-issued photo IDs for domestic flights, but they do for international flights to most countries.)

In 2003, the TSA phased out **gate check-in** at all U.S. airports. And **e-tickets** have made paper tickets nearly obsolete. Passengers with e-tickets can beat the ticket-counter lines by using airport **electronic kiosks** or even **online check-in** from your home computer. Online check-in involves logging on to your airlines' website, accessing your reservation, and printing out your boarding pass—and the airline may even offer you bonus miles to do so! If you're using a kiosk at the airport, bring the credit card you used to book the ticket or your frequent-flier card. Print out your boarding pass from the kiosk and simply proceed to the security checkpoint with your pass and a photo ID. If you're checking bags or looking to snag an exit-row seat, you will be able to do so using most airline kiosks. Even the smaller airlines are employing the kiosk system, but always call your airline to make sure these alternatives are available. **Curbside check-in** is also a good way to avoid lines, although a few airlines still ban curbside check-in; call before you go.

Security checkpoint lines are getting shorter than they were during 2001 and 2002, but some doozies remain. If you have trouble standing for long periods of time, tell an airline employee; the airline will provide a wheelchair. Speed up security by **not wearing metal objects** such as big belt buckles. If you've got metallic body parts, a note from your doctor can prevent a long chat with the security screeners. Keep in mind that only **ticketed passengers** are allowed past security, except for folks escorting disabled passengers or children.

Federalization has stabilized **what you can carry on** and **what you can't.** The general rule is that sharp things are out, nail clippers are okay, and food and beverages must be passed through the X-ray machine—but that security screeners can't make you drink from your coffee cup. Bring food in your carry-on rather than checking it, as explosive-detection machines used on checked luggage have been known to mistake food (especially chocolate, for some reason) for bombs. Travelers in the U.S. are allowed one carry-on bag, plus a "personal item" such as a purse, briefcase, or laptop bag. Carry-on hoarders can stuff all sorts of things into a laptop bag; as long as it has a laptop in it, it's still considered a personal item. The Transportation Security Administration (TSA) has issued a list of restricted items; check its website (www.tsa.gov/public/index.jsp) for details.

---

*Tips* **Don't Stow It—Ship It**

If ease of travel is your main concern and money is no object, you can ship your luggage and sports equipment with one of the growing number of luggage-service companies that pick up, track, and deliver your luggage (often through couriers such as Federal Express) with minimum hassle for you. Traveling luggage-free may be ultraconvenient, but it's not cheap: One-way overnight shipping can cost from $100 to $200, depending on what you're sending. Still, for some people, especially the elderly or the infirm, it's a sensible solution to lugging heavy baggage. Specialists in door-to-door luggage delivery are **Virtual Bellhop** (www.virtual bellhop.com), **SkyCap International** (www.skycapinternational.com), **Luggage Express** (www.usxpluggageexpress.com), and **Sports Express** (www. sportsexpress.com).

Airport screeners may decide that your checked luggage needs to be searched by hand. You can now purchase luggage locks that allow screeners to open and relock a checked bag if hand searching is necessary. Look for Travel Sentry–certified locks at luggage or travel shops and Brookstone stores (you can buy them online at www.brookstone.com). These locks, approved by the TSA, can be opened by luggage inspectors with a special code or key. For more information on the locks, visit www.travelsentry.org. If you use something other than TSA-approved locks, your lock will be cut off your suitcase if a TSA agent needs to hand search your luggage.

## FLYING FOR LESS: TIPS FOR GETTING THE BEST AIRFARE

Passengers sharing the same airplane cabin rarely pay the same fare. Travelers who need to purchase tickets at the last minute, change their itinerary at a moment's notice, or fly one-way often get stuck paying the premium rate. Here are some ways to keep your airfare costs down.

- Passengers who can book their ticket **long in advance,** who can **stay over Saturday night,** or who **fly midweek** or **at less-trafficked hours** may pay a fraction of the full fare. If your schedule is flexible, say so, and ask if you can secure a cheaper fare by changing your flight plans.
- You can also save on airfares by keeping an eye out in local newspapers for **promotional specials** or **fare wars,** when airlines lower prices on their most popular routes. You rarely see fare wars offered for peak travel times, but if you can travel in the off-months, you may snag a bargain.
- Search **the Internet** for cheap fares (see "Planning Your Trip Online," earlier in this chapter).

- Try to book a ticket **in its country of origin.** For instance, if you're planning a one-way flight from Johannesburg to Bombay, a South Africa–based travel agent will probably have the lowest fares. For multileg trips, book in the country of the first leg; for example, book New York–London–Amsterdam–Rome–New York in the U.S.
- **Consolidators,** also known as bucket shops, are great sources for international tickets, although they usually can't beat the Internet on fares within North America. Start by looking in Sunday newspaper travel sections; U.S. travelers should focus on the *New York Times, Los Angeles Times,* and *Miami Herald.* For less-developed destinations, small travel agents who cater to immigrant communities in large cities often have the best deals. *Beware:* Bucket shop tickets are usually nonrefundable or rigged with stiff cancellation penalties, often as high as 50% to 75% of the ticket price, and some put you on charter airlines, which may leave at inconvenient times and experience delays. One reliable agency specializing in Southeast Asia–bound flights is **Join-Us Travel** (© 800/324-5359; www.joinustravel.com).

Several reliable consolidators are worldwide and available on the Net. **STA Travel** is now the world's leader in student travel, thanks to its purchase of Council Travel. It also offers good fares for travelers of all ages. **ELTExpress (Flights.com)** (© 800/TRAV-800; www.eltexpress.com) started in Europe and has excellent fares worldwide, but particularly to that continent. It also has "local" websites in 12 countries. **Fly-Cheap** (© 800/FLY-CHEAP; www.1800flycheap.com) is owned by package-holiday megalith

MyTravel and so has especially good access to fares for sunny destinations. **Air Tickets Direct** (© **800/778-3447**; www.air ticketsdirect.com) is based in Montreal and leverages the currently weak Canadian dollar for low fares; it'll also book trips to places that U.S. travel agents won't touch, such as Cuba.

- Join **frequent-flier clubs.** Accrue enough miles, and you'll be rewarded with free flights and elite status. It's free, and you'll get the best choice of seats, faster response to phone inquiries, and prompter service if your luggage is stolen, your flight is canceled or delayed, or if you want to change your seat. You don't need to fly to build frequent-flier miles—**frequent-flier credit cards** can provide thousands of miles for doing your everyday shopping.

- For many more tips about air travel, including a rundown of the major frequent-flier credit cards, pick up a copy of *Frommer's Fly Safe, Fly Smart* (Wiley Publishing, Inc.).

## LONG-HAUL FLIGHTS: HOW TO STAY COMFORTABLE

Long flights can be trying; stuffy air and cramped seats can make you feel as if you're being sent parcel post in a small box. But with a little advance planning, you can make an otherwise unpleasant experience almost bearable.

- Your choice of airline and airplane will definitely affect your legroom. Find more details at www.seatguru. com, which has extensive details about almost every seat on six major U.S. airlines. For international airlines, research firm Skytrax has posted a list of average seat pitches at www.airlinequality.com.

- Emergency exit seats and bulkhead seats typically have the most legroom. Emergency exit seats are usually held back to be assigned the day of a flight (to ensure that the seat is filled by someone able-bodied); it's worth getting to the ticket counter early to snag one of these spots for a long flight. Many passengers find that bulkhead seating (the row facing the wall at the front of the cabin) offers more legroom, but keep in mind that bulkheads are where airlines often put baby bassinets, so you may be sitting next to an infant.

- To have two seats for yourself in a three-seat row, try for an aisle seat in a center section toward the back of coach. If you're traveling with a companion, book an aisle and a window seat. Middle seats are usually booked last, so chances are good you'll end up with three seats to yourselves. And in the event that a third passenger is assigned the middle seat, he or she will probably be more than happy to trade for a window or an aisle.

## Travel in the Age of Bankruptcy

Airlines go bankrupt, so protect yourself by **buying your tickets with a credit card,** as the Fair Credit Billing Act guarantees that you can get your money back from the credit card company if a travel supplier goes under (and if you request the refund within 60 days of the bankruptcy.) **Travel insurance** can also help, but make sure it covers against "carrier default" for your specific travel provider. And be aware that if a U.S. airline goes bust midtrip, a 2001 federal law requires other carriers to take you to your destination (albeit on a space-available basis) for a fee of no more than $25, provided you rebook within 60 days of the cancellation.

## (Tips) Coping with Jet Lag

Jetlag is a pitfall of traveling across time zones. If you're flying north-south and you feel sluggish when you touch down, your symptoms will be caused by dehydration and the general stress of air travel. When you travel east to west or vice versa, however, your body becomes thoroughly confused about what time it is, and everything from your digestion to your brain gets knocked for a loop. Traveling east, say, from Chicago to Paris, is more difficult on your internal clock than traveling west, say from Atlanta to Hawaii, as most peoples' bodies find it more acceptable to stay up late than to fall asleep early.

Here are some tips for combating jet lag:

- Reset your watch to your destination time before you board the plane.
- Drink lots of water before, during, and after your flight. Avoid alcohol.
- Exercise and sleep well for a few days before your trip.
- If you have trouble sleeping on planes, fly eastward on morning flights.
- Daylight is the key to resetting your body clock. At the website for Outside In (www.bodyclock.com), you can get a customized plan of when to seek and avoid light.
- If you need help getting to sleep earlier than you usually would, some doctors recommend taking either the hormone **melatonin** or the sleeping pill **Ambien**—but not together. Some recommend that you take 2 to 5 milligrams of melatonin about 2 hours before your planned bedtime—but again, always check with your doctor on the best course of action for you.

---

- Ask about entertainment options. Many airlines offer seatback video systems where you get to choose your movies or play video games— but only on some of their planes. (Boeing 777s are your best bet.)
- To sleep, avoid the last row of any section or a row in front of an emergency exit, as these seats are the least likely to recline. Avoid seats near highly trafficked toilet areas. Avoid seats in the back of many jets—these can be more narrow than those in the rest of coach class. You also may want to reserve a window seat so that you can rest your head and avoid being bumped in the aisle.
- Get up, walk around, and stretch every 60 to 90 minutes to keep your blood flowing. This helps avoid **deep vein thrombosis,** or "economy-class syndrome," a potentially deadly condition that can be caused by sitting in cramped conditions for too long. Other preventative measures include drinking lots of water and avoiding alcohol (see next bullet). See "Avoiding 'Economy-Class Syndrome'" box under "Health & Safety," p. 50.
- Drink water before, during, and after your flight to combat the lack of humidity in airplane cabins—which can be drier than the Sahara. Bring a bottle of water on board. Avoid alcohol, which will dehydrate you.
- If you're flying with kids, don't forget to carry on toys, books, pacifiers, and chewing gum to help them relieve ear pressure buildup during ascent and descent. Let each child pack his or her own backpack with favorite toys.

## Flying with Film & Video

Never pack film—developed or undeveloped—in checked bags, as the new, more powerful scanners in U.S. airports can fog film. The film you carry with you can be damaged by scanners as well. X-ray damage is cumulative; the faster the film, and the more times you put it through a scanner, the more likely the damage. Film under 800 ASA is usually safe for up to five scans. If you're taking your film through additional scans, U.S. regulations permit you to demand hand inspections. In international airports, you're at the mercy of airport officials. On international flights, store your film in transparent baggies, so you can remove it easily before you go through scanners. Keep in mind that airports are not the only places where your camera may be scanned: Highly trafficked attractions are X-raying visitors' bags with increasing frequency.

Most photo-supply stores sell protective pouches designed to block damaging X-rays. The pouches fit both film and loaded cameras. They should protect your film in checked baggage, but they also may raise alarms and result in a hand inspection.

You'll have nothing to worry about if you are traveling with **digital cameras.** Unlike film, which is sensitive to light, the digital camera and storage cards are not affected by airport X-rays, according to Nikon. Still, if you plan to travel extensively, you may want to play it safe and hand carry your digital equipment or ask that it be inspected by hand. See "Digital Photography on the Road," p. 61.

Carry-on scanners will not damage **videotape** in video cameras, but the magnetic fields emitted by the walk-through security gateways and handheld inspection wands will. Always place your loaded camcorder on the screening conveyor belt or have it hand inspected. Be sure your batteries are charged, as you might be required to turn the device on to ensure that it's what it appears to be.

## 11 Packages for the Independent Traveler

Before you start your search for the lowest airfare, you may want to consider booking your flight as part of a travel package. Package tours are not the same thing as escorted tours. Package tours are simply a way to buy the airfare, accommodations, and other elements of your trip (such as car rentals, airport transfers, and sometimes even activities) at the same time and often at discounted prices—kind of like one-stop shopping. Packages are sold in bulk to tour operators—who resell them to the public at a cost that usually undercuts standard rates.

One good source of package deals is the airlines themselves. Most major airlines offer air/land packages, including **American Airlines Vacations** (© 800/321-2121; www.aavacations.com), **Delta Vacations** (© 800/221-6666; www.deltavacations.com), **Continental Airlines Vacations** (© 800/301-3800; www.covacations.com), and **United Vacations** (© 888/854-3899; www.unitedvacations.com). Several big **online travel agencies**—Expedia.com, Travelocity, Orbitz, Site59, and Lastminute.com—also do a brisk business in packages. If you're unsure about the pedigree of a smaller packager, check with the Better Business Bureau in the city where the company is based, or go online at www.bbb.org. If a packager won't tell you where it's based, don't fly with it.

Travel packages are also listed in the travel section of your local Sunday newspaper. Or check ads in the national travel magazines such as *Arthur Frommer's Budget Travel Magazine, Travel & Leisure, National Geographic Traveler,* and *Condé Nast Traveler.*

Package tours can vary by leaps and bounds. Some offer a better class of hotels than others. Some offer the same hotels for lower prices. Some offer flights on scheduled airlines, while others book charters. Some limit your choice of accommodations and travel days. You are often required to make a large payment upfront. On the plus side, packages can save you money, offering group prices but allowing for independent travel. Some even let you add on a few guided excursions or escorted day trips (also at prices lower than if you booked them yourself) without booking an entirely escorted tour.

Before you invest in a package tour, get some answers. Ask about the **accommodations choices** and prices for each. Then look up the hotels' reviews in a Frommer's guide and check their rates online for your specific dates of travel. You'll also want to find out what **type of room** you get. If you need a certain type of room, ask for it; don't take whatever is thrown your way. Request a nonsmoking room, a quiet room, a room with a view, or whatever you fancy.

Finally, look for **hidden expenses.** Ask whether airport departure fees and taxes, for example, are included in the total cost.

## 12 Escorted General-Interest Tours

Escorted tours are structured group tours, with a group leader. The price usually includes everything from airfare to hotels, meals, tours, admission costs, and local transportation.

Whether you want to ride an elephant through the jungle, trek among indigenous people, shake hands with an orangutan, swim beneath a waterfall, snorkel in a clear-blue lagoon, lounge on a white-sand beach, or wander through exotic markets, there's a Southeast Asia tour packager for you, offering a wide range of travel options using the finest and most reliable travel services available in the region.

Among the most experienced and knowledgeable tour operators specializing in Southeast Asia are **Absolute Asia** and **Asia Transpacific Journeys.** In-country tour providers **Diethelm** and **Exotissimo** can do anything from arranging deluxe tours to just helping out with any small details or bookings. Most companies allow clients to design their own trip or deviate from exact schedules (often at a small cost). See individual country chapters for other in-country tour operators. Companies like **Intrepid,** among others, offer unique itineraries for solo travelers.

Here are the top outfitters.

**Abercrombie & Kent**   Well-known luxury tour operator Abercrombie & Kent offers Southeast Asia programs with numerous comprehensive itineraries. Tours include Thailand (including spa tours), Cambodia, Hong Kong, and other destinations, as well as connections with China. These tours also include stays at the finest hotels in Southeast Asia, such as the Oriental in Bangkok and the Mandarin Oriental in Hong Kong. 1520 Kensington Rd., Suite 212, Oakbrook, IL 60523-2141. ℂ 800/323-7308. Fax 630/954-3324. www.aandktours.com.

**Absolute Asia**   Founded in 1989, Absolute Asia offers an array of innovative itineraries, specializing in individual or small-group tours customized to your interests, with experienced local guides and excellent accommodations. Talk to these folks about tours that feature art, cuisine, religion, antiques, photography, wildlife study, archaeology, and soft adventure—they can plan a specialized trip to see just about anything you can dream up for any length of time. They can also book you on excellent coach programs in Indochina. 180 Varick St., 16th Floor, New York, NY 10014. ☎ 800/736-8187. Fax 212/627-4090. www.absolute asia.com.

**Asia Transpacific Journeys** Coordinating tours to every corner of South and Southeast Asia and the Pacific, Asia Transpacific Journeys deals with small groups and custom programs that include luxury hotel accommodations. The flagship package, the 23-day "Passage to Indochina" tour, takes you through Laos, Vietnam, and Cambodia's major attractions with a well-planned itinerary, and it is but one of many fun tours that promote cultural understanding. It's a model of sustainable tourism and a highly recommended choice. 2995 Center Green Court, Boulder, CO 80301. ☎ 800/642-2742 or 303/443-6789. Fax 303/443-7078. www.asiatranspacific.com.

**Backroads** For those who want to explore Southeast Asia by bicycle, cycling and hiking specialist Backroads has a 12-day Vietnam tour and an 8-day Thailand Golden Triangle tour, among others. Check out the website; it's always coming up with innovative itineraries in the region. 801 Cedar St., Berkeley, CA 94710-1800. ☎ 800/462-2848 or 510/527-1555. Fax 510/527-1444. www.backroads.com.

**Diethelm** The folks at this Swiss-based tour company, with offices throughout the region (and a popular choice for European tour groups), are friendly and helpful; they operate as de facto tourist information centers in

places like Laos. Diethelm has full tour programs and, like Exotissimo (below), can help with any details for travelers in-country, can arrange car rental or vans for small groups, and offer discount options to all locations. Kian Gwan Building II, 140/1 Wireless Rd., Bangkok 10330, Thailand. ☎ 662/255-9150. Fax 662/256-0248. www.diethelm-travel.com.

**Exotissimo** A French outfit and outbound (in-country) agency with offices in every major city in the region, Exotissimo has excellent guides on-site. Agents not only can arrange all-inclusive tours, but they also are helpful with all travel details, from ticketing to visas. See the office locations in each chapter. **In France:** 40 bis, Rue du fg Poissonniére, 75010 Paris, France ☎ 149/490-360. Fax 149/490-369. **In Saigon:** Saigon Trade Center, 37 Ton Duc Thang, District 1 Ho Chi Minh City, Vietnam.☎08/825-1723. Fax 08/829-5800. www.exotissimo.com.

**Imaginative Traveler** This U.K.–based firm gets rave reviews every time for organizing all sorts of cycling, trekking, and motorcycling adventures throughout Southeast Asia, particularly Indochina. 1 Betts Ave., Martlesham Heath, Suffolk IP5 3RH. ☎ 0208/742-8612. Fax 0280/742-3045. www.imaginative-traveler.com.

**Intrepid** This popular Australian operator is probably the best choice to get off the beaten track on a tour of Asia. Intrepid caters tours for the culturally discerning, those with humanitarian goals, those in search of comfort, adventurers, people on a budget, or those looking for a looser structure and lots of options. Its motto is its name, and with some of the best guides in Asia, these folks will take you to the back of beyond safely, in style, and with lots of laughs. Box 2781, Fitzroy, DC VIC 3065, 12 Spring St., Fitzroy, Victoria, Australia. ☎ 613/9473-2626. Fax 613/9419-4426. In the U.S.: 877/488-1616. www.intrepidtravel.com.

## THE PROS & CONS OF ESCORTED TRIPS

Many people derive a certain ease and security from escorted trips. Escorted tours—whether by bus, motorcoach, train, or boat—let travelers sit back and enjoy their trip without having to spend lots of time behind the wheel or worrying about details. You know your costs upfront, and there are few surprises. Escorted tours can take you to the maximum number of sights in the minimum amount of time with the least amount of hassle—you don't have to sweat over the plotting and planning of a vacation schedule. Escorted tours are particularly convenient for people with limited mobility. They can also be a great way to make new friends.

On the downside, an escorted tour often requires a big deposit upfront, and lodging and dining choices are predetermined. You'll get little opportunity for serendipitous interactions with locals. The tours can be jam-packed with activities, leaving little room for individual sightseeing, whim, or adventure—plus they also often focus only on the heavily touristed sites, so you miss out on the lesser-known gems.

Before you invest in an escorted tour, ask about the **cancellation policy:** Is a deposit required? Can the tour company cancel the trip if it doesn't get enough people? Do you get a refund if it cancels? If *you* cancel? How late can you cancel if you are unable to go? When do you pay in full? *Note:* If you choose an escorted tour, think strongly about purchasing trip-cancellation insurance, especially if the tour operator asks you to pay upfront. See the section on "Travel Insurance," p. 46.

You'll also want to get a complete **schedule** of the trip to find out how much sightseeing is planned each day and whether enough time has been allotted for relaxing or wandering solo.

The **size** of the group is also important to know upfront. Generally, the smaller the group, the more flexible the itinerary, and the less time you'll spend waiting for people to get on and off the bus. Find out the **demographics** of the group as well. What is the age range? What is the gender breakdown? Is this mostly a trip for couples or singles?

Discuss what is included in the **price.** You may have to pay for transportation to and from the airport. A box lunch may be included in an excursion, but drinks might cost extra. Tips may not be included. Find out if you will be charged if you decide to opt out of certain activities or meals.

Before you invest in a package tour, get some answers. Ask about the **accommodations choices** and prices for each. Then look up the hotels' reviews in a Frommer's guide and check their rates online for your specific dates of travel. You'll also want to find out what **type of room** you get. If you need a certain type of room, ask for it; don't take whatever is thrown your way. Request a nonsmoking room, a quiet room, a room with a view, or whatever you fancy.

Finally, if you plan to travel alone, you'll need to know if a **single supplement** will be charged and if the company can match you up with a roommate.

## 13 Special-Interest Trips

For cultural tours and museum tours, contact any of the smaller local travel agents listed in each section. For the amateur ethnographer, contact any of the eco-tour outfitters below or those listed in specific sections (particularly in the north of Thailand, Laos, Vietnam, or western Cambodia).

## OUTDOOR ADVENTURES & ECO-TOURS

If you live life like a Mountain Dew commercial or just like to get out into the sticks, you can find any number of small outfitters to suit you in many parts of Southeast Asia. Consider first what kind of terrain you'd like to explore—and the choices are anything from jungle to dry plains, coastal estuaries to inland rivers. The best areas to get out and get your boots wet are in the furthest reaches of Thailand, Laos, and Vietnam.

In the north of Thailand, contact **Active Thailand** for cycling, off-road, and other eco-adventures (look under trips from Chiang Mai). In the far south of Thailand, **Paddle-Asia** has some of the best nature kayaking trips where you're guaranteed to see some exciting wildlife. In rural Isan, check with the folks at **East-West Adventures** for their tours in that part of the country and across the border in Laos.

In Laos, **Wildside** runs great rafting and kayaking adventures anywhere in country and has some unique village and cultural tours as well.

In the north of Vietnam, the folks at **Handspan** as well as **Buffalo Tours** put together exciting kayaking adventures in Hao Long Bay and in the far north have good hiking trips to Sapa and by jeep up to Dien Bien Phu. In central Vietnam, the old French colonial hill station of Dalat plays host to a great outfitter, **Phat Tire Ventures,** where you can rock climb, mountain bike, or trek with the most professional guides and experienced technicians.

The folks at **Exotissimo** have offices throughout the region and are the best for arranging all kinds of rural adventures.

In Bali, **Sobek Tours** or **Bali Adventure Tours** arrange fun day and overnight itineraries to volcanoes, the jungle, and rural villages.

## DIVING

There are more dive outfits in Southeast Asia than we could possibly list, so below are only a few. Be sure to choose a PADI-accredited dive company and ask lots of questions before any trip: What is the ratio of diver to instructor? Does the company have its own boat?

For details, check specific chapters: in Thailand, look under **Phuket** or **Ko Tao;** in Vietnam, try **Nha Trang;** in Cambodia, **Sihanoukville;** in Malaysia, **Langkawi.**

## COOKING SCHOOLS

The varied cuisine of the countries of SE Asia is a veritable banquet for the gourmet or the fearless eater, and there's no better way than to learn and participate in culture than to take a cooking class. Opportunities abound.

My favorite cooking school is the upscale **Blue Elephant Restaurant and Cooking School.** Set in an old mansion in the heart of Bangkok, the restaurant is a popular luxury chain from Europe that has returned to its roots and set up shop in the Thai capital. It's not to be missed. Also, try the luxury cooking school at the **Oriental.** In the north of Thailand, try the **Chiang Mai Cookery School.** In the far south there are lots of small resorts with cooking schools attached.

In northern Laos, enjoy a fun and informative day at **Toum-Toum Cheng Restaurant and Cooking School,** where you'll not only get the dish on Lao specialties and some unique derivations, you can learn a good bit about local culture, history, and language.

In Hoi An in central Vietnam, Ms. Vy at the **Cargo Club and Patisserie** runs great programs of varying length.

## 14  Getting Around Southeast Asia

Regional flights in Southeast Asia are affordable and convenient—a great way to get around if your time is short. That said, half the fun of traveling is getting there—many walk away from land travel in this part of the world saying, "I'll never do it again, but what a trip!" When the massive Soviet 4x4 nearly lays on its side in the deep ruts of a washed-out road in Laos, or that rattle-trap motorbike you rented in hill-tribe country in the north of Vietnam catches a flat and leaves you stranded, you might curse yourself or the very road you're on, but you'll have lots of stories to tell when you get back.

### BY PLANE

International carriers cover myriad routes into the region, including Silk Air (the regional arm of Singapore Airlines), Malaysia Airlines, Thai Airways International, Cathay Pacific Airways, Vietnam Airlines, or Garuda Indonesia. Domestic carriers include Pelangi Air, Air Asia, and Berjaya Air in Malaysia; Lao Airlines in Laos; or Bangkok Airways and P.B. Air, in Thailand and Cambodia.

Bear in mind that international airports are not restricted to capital cities. In addition to Bangkok, Thailand has international access via Chiang Mai and Chiang Rai (to China and Laos), U-Tapao and Phuket (to Cambodia), and Phuket and Koh Samui (to Singapore and Kuala Lumpur). You can fly into Malaysia to Penang, Langkawi, and Tioman Island, and to Borneo destinations direct from Singapore. Laos has international access at both Luang Prabang and Pakse, in addition to the capital, Vientiane. Vietnam has international flights to Ho Chi Minh City and Hanoi. And in Cambodia, you can fly directly to Siem Reap, the access city to Angkor Wat, from Bangkok, U-Tapao (near Pattaya), Phuket, Vientiane, and Singapore.

Check out the UNESCO World Heritage routes, a new schedule of flights offered by Bangkok Airways (www.bangkokair.com). Originating in Bangkok, this tour connects Sukhothai (Thailand) with Luang Prabang (Laos), Hue (Vietnam), and Angkor Wat in Cambodia.

Ask any travel agent, and be sure to research all flight options for the most direct routes and best fares. Each chapter gives specific details for booking.

### BY TRAIN

With a few exceptions, trains that operate throughout Southeast Asia are poorly maintained, overcrowded, and slow. The most popular rail route—and the only one with interconnecting service among countries in all of Southeast Asia—runs from Singapore to Bangkok (and vice versa) through the heart of the Malaysian peninsula, with stops along the way at the cities of Johor Bahru, Malacca, Kuala Lumpur, and Butterworth (for Penang). It takes 6 hours from Singapore to Kuala Lumpur, and another 35 hours from Kuala Lumpur to Bangkok. You can board the train at the Singapore Rail Station in Tanjong Pagar, at the Kuala Lumpur Central Railway Station on Jalan Hishamuddin, and in Bangkok at the Hua Lamphong Railway Station on Rama IV Road.

Upscale travelers with unlimited budgets can book passage on one of the world's foremost luxury trains, the Eastern & Oriental Express, which covers the distance between Singapore and Bangkok in 42 hours. Find more details in the Thailand chapter.

Reliable rail service also runs north to south along coastal Vietnam with interesting new luxury cars that connect Hanoi, the capital, with the northern hill country and make a further connection to the vast rail networks of China.

## BY BUS

Buses are good on the budget, and often the best way into the back of beyond. Bus trips are myriad in the region, from VIP tours with air-conditioning and video monitors to rattle-trap, overcrowded, break-down mobiles. Thai and Malay buses are quite reliable and a good option, connecting the far north of Thailand with the far southern tip of Malaysia and on to Singapore. In Laos and Cambodia, local buses, with the exception of a few interior routes, are rough. Check specific "Getting There" sections in individual chapters before embarking on long hauls. Also, check each country's individual visa requirements because you often need to prearrange visas for land crossings.

## BY BOAT

There are lots of unique boat adventures in the region. More and more travelers are heading down the Mekong, starting from the town of Chiang Khong in northern Thailand and ending in Luang Prabang in Laos. Luxury riverboats run the same trip, as well as trips in the far south of Laos between Pakse and Si Phan Don (look for Luangsay Cruises under the relevant sections). Boat trips in Vietnam's Ha Long Bay just east of Hanoi are very popular and outfitters like Handspan and Buffalo Tours run great trips. Don't miss the new boat connections along the Mekong tributaries between Vietnam's Mekong Delta and Phnom Penh, Cambodia's capital. Boats also connect Cambodia's capital, Phnom Penh, with Siem Reap, the town that supports Angkor Wat, along the Mekong as it flows through Tonle Sap Lake.

## BY CAR

Car rental is affordable in Southeast Asia. In the developing countries—Vietnam, Laos, Cambodia—it is a good idea (and not much more) to hire a car with driver. Insurance is often unavailable. Road rules vary, and in some places seem nonexistent—though there is always a method to the madness—so it's not a bad idea to spring for a driver where affordable. Be sure to research details before heading out, and invest in good maps.

## 15  Tips on Accommodations

Affordable luxury is the name of the game in the countries of Southeast Asia. For what you might pay for a cracker-box room in big cities in the U.S. and Europe, you can go in style in Indochina and the countries on the Malay Peninsula. Pay over $100 and you are royalty. Budget travelers and young backpackers flock to the region, and a big part of the charm is spending $2 to $5 per night; it makes the budget go on and on. If your trip is short, live it up! Go for a luxury room, take advantage of affordable health and beauty or spa treatments (at a fraction of what you pay elsewhere). Midrange boutique hotels and rustic eco-friendly rural resorts are also a new trend as developers discover that *refurbished* is cool and that location—whether overlooking the Mekong, or set in a tropical rainforest—is everything.

You'll find many of the major chains represented in the region. **Sheraton** has hotels throughout Thailand and in the major stops in Vietnam. **Inter-Continental** has high-end business properties in Bangkok, Phnom Penh, and Singapore. **Hilton** has fine properties in Hanoi (Vietnam), Bangkok and Phuket (Thailand), throughout Malaysia and Singapore, and on Bali. The French hoteliers at **Accor** host a number of **Sofitel** and **Novotel** hotels in the region; many of the big-city properties are aimed at the business market, but in Vietnam

Sofitel takes the cake with some of the most unique refurbished hotels going, and in Cambodia it has a top resort. **Four Seasons** has top properties in Bangkok and outside of Chiang Mai. **JW Marriot** has a hotel in Bangkok and a luxury resort on Phuket. **Le Meridien** has top resorts and golf in Thailand and Bali (Indonesia).

There are also a few good local chains. The **Amari** group is a Swiss-managed hotel chain with semiluxurious properties in all of the major stops in Thailand; service is conscientious and there is a good consistency among their many hotels (and good rates). In Vietnam, and now Cambodia, the **Victoria** hotels are a charming blend of atmosphere and connection to place without sacrificing all of the comforts of home—quite unique. **Pansea** hotels, now individually branded under the management of the luxury **Orient Express** group, host some of the most unique and luxurious sanctuaries that take you away from it all, but remind you of local culture—find them in Laos, Thailand, and Cambodia. **Aman Resorts** are in a class all their own with their sprawling pool villa properties in Indonesia, and now in Cambodia, all at rock-star prices.

Villa rental is a popular choice in island destinations. **Balinese villas** are a particular steal, best over a longer period of time and with hired staff. In places like Thailand's Phuket you'll find timeshares and long-term rates for private, serviced, beachside places that are quite enticing (beware the hard sell, though).

Each of the countries in Southeast Asia sets their own star standards for hotels, usually one through five. Note that a five-star might only be rated so because of the quantity, not quality, of services offered.

# SAVING ON YOUR HOTEL ROOM

The **rack rate** is the maximum rate that a hotel charges for a room. Hardly anybody pays this price, however, except in high season or on holidays. To lower the cost of your room:

- **Ask about special rates or other discounts.** Always ask whether a room less expensive than the first one quoted is available, or whether any special rates apply to you. You may qualify for corporate, student, military, senior, or other discounts. Mention membership in AAA, AARP, frequent-flier programs, or trade unions which might entitle you to special deals as well. Find out the hotel policy on children—do kids stay free in the room or is there a special rate?

- **Dial direct.** When booking a room in a chain hotel, you'll often get a better deal by calling the individual hotel's reservation desk rather than the chain's main number.

- **Book online.** Many hotels offer Internet-only discounts, or supply rooms to Priceline, Hotwire, or Expedia.com at rates much lower than the ones you can get through the hotel itself. There are lots of regional websites offering very low rates, but many are unreliable fly-by-night operations. Shop around. And if you have special needs—a quiet room, a room with a view—call the hotel directly and make your needs known after you've booked online.

- **Remember the law of supply and demand.** Resort hotels are most crowded and therefore most expensive on weekends, so discounts are usually available for midweek stays. Business hotels in downtown locations are busiest during the week, so you can expect big discounts over the weekend. Many hotels have high-season and low-season prices, and booking the day after high season ends can mean big discounts.

- **Look into group or long-stay discounts.** If you come as part of a large group, you should be able to negotiate a bargain rate, since the hotel can then guarantee occupancy in a number of rooms. Likewise, if you're planning a long stay (at least 5 days), you might qualify for a discount. As a general rule, expect 1 night free after a 7-night stay.

- **Avoid excess charges and hidden costs.** When you book a room, ask whether the hotel charges for parking. Use your own cellphone, pay phones, or prepaid phone cards instead of dialing direct from hotel phones, which usually have exorbitant rates. And don't be tempted by the room's minibar offerings: Most hotels charge through the nose for water, soda, and snacks. Finally, ask about local taxes and service charges, which can increase the cost of a room by 15% or more. If a hotel insists upon tacking on a surprise "energy surcharge" that wasn't mentioned at check-in or a "resort fee" for amenities you didn't use, you can often make a case for getting it removed.

- **Book an efficiency.** A room with a kitchenette allows you to shop for groceries and cook your own meals. This is a big money saver, especially for families on long stays.

## LANDING THE BEST ROOM

Somebody has to get the best room in the house. It might as well be you. You can start by joining the hotel's frequent-guest program, which may make you eligible for upgrades. A hotel-branded credit card usually gives it owner "silver" or "gold" status in frequent-guest programs for free. Always ask about a corner room. They're often larger and quieter, with more windows and light, and they often cost the same as standard rooms. When you make your reservation, ask if the hotel is renovating; if it is, request a room away from the construction. Ask about nonsmoking rooms, rooms with views, rooms with twin, queen- or king-size beds. If you're a light sleeper, request a quiet room away from vending machines, elevators, restaurants, bars, and discos. Ask for a room that has been most recently renovated or redecorated.

If you aren't happy with your room when you arrive, ask for another one. Most lodgings will be willing to accommodate you.

In resort areas ask the following questions before you book a room:

- What's the view like? Cost-conscious travelers may be willing to pay less for a back room facing the parking lot, especially if they don't plan to spend much time in their room.

- Does the room have air-conditioning or ceiling fans? Do the windows open? If they do, and the nighttime entertainment takes place alfresco, you may want to find out when show time is over.

- What's included in the price? Your room may be moderately priced, but if you're charged for beach chairs, towels, sports equipment, and other amenities, you could end up spending more than you bargained for.

- How far is the room from the beach and other amenities? If it's far, is there transportation to and from the beach, and is it free?

## 16  Tips on Dining

Southeast Asia is a real playground for adventurous foodies; from high-class hotel restaurants and power-lunch points, to street-side stalls with local specialties, you'll find it all. The cuisine of each country is unique and crossing borders often means a new course in manners, cuisine, and culture. In this guide we list the safest of options by and large, making sure to designate any dining that could be deemed "adventurous," but the adventurous in fact have lots of opportunities to try new foods, from oddities like freshly killed snake to fried crickets and grubs. It's not all that funky though, and much of the best local cuisine is not found in restaurants but in markets and in street-side stalls, something that puts some people off. Our advice: Get adventurous! When eating in open-air joints, just be careful that things are cooked fresh and aren't just sitting out, and be careful of raw ingredients like vegetables or some fish pastes. If you find yourself playing charades to get your food, laughing, smiling, and squatting on a tiny plastic stool, talking to locals and eating a meal that costs pennies to the approving nods of your new friends, then you're in the right place. Wherever possible, ask locals what's good and you're in store for a cool, cultural adventure.

Try *pho* and the many regional specials throughout Vietnam; enjoy cover-the-table spreads in Thailand and Malaysia, where spices are fiery and a meal is always an event; and don't miss crispy duck or *babi guling*—suckling pig—in Bali. The choices are endless. The usual varieties of international fare can be found throughout the region—in fact, every big city has its Chinese, Italian, sushi, and French. In parts of Indochine, Laos and Vietnam particularly, chefs carry on long traditions from colonial times and the French cuisine is in fact as good as you'll get anywhere. Chinese communities abound and, of course, so does good Chinese in its myriad forms—from dim sum to Peking duck.

All but the fanciest restaurants are open early until late. Tipping is not expected but always appreciated, and just rounding up the bill to the next dollar amount is often more than enough.

For drinkers, there are few restrictive laws or cultural taboos—in fact, drinking is a big part of most cultures in SE Asia. Local rice wines and whiskeys abound and foreign guests are always invited. Sometimes the stuff is pretty potent—toxic even—so be warned. European visitors left their mark on the region with brewing and distilling technologies, and each country produces its own local beers to go along with the many imports. Fresh fruit is falling off the trees in the tropical climes of Southeast Asia and good fresh fruit juices are available everywhere. Coffee is grown throughout the region, and though local roasting processes are a bit different, local brews are delicious. Tap water is not potable in most regions, but bottled water is available everywhere; and perhaps the best advice for travel in the region is to stay hydrated. If you are thirsty, then it's too late. Drink lots.

## 17  Suggested Itineraries

Routes through the region are as varied as the rag-tag bunch that travels them. With the many convenient air connections, you can really just choose your destinations and connect them as you like really, but here are a few suggestions.

## INDOCHINA TOUR

Clockwise or counterclockwise routes starting in Bangkok and including northern Thailand, Laos, Vietnam, and Cambodia are popular and avoid boring backtracking. Connecting northern Thailand with Laos by boat is popular, and flying from Vientiane, the Lao capital, to Hanoi or Ho Chi Minh is a better choice than the rough overland route (which also leaves you in the middle of the north-south route where a flight will get you to a terminus). After a sweep down the coast of Vietnam, connect with Cambodia overland (or by boat from the Mekong Delta) and on to Angkor Wat by bus/boat/plane. There is frequent air service between Angkor Wat and Bangkok.

**Length** This can take anything from a few weeks to 6 months, depending on your inclinations.

**Highlights** These include the historic temple towns of Thailand, hill-tribe treks throughout the region, sleepy Luang Prabang, busy Hanoi and Ho Chi Minh, all of the stops along coastal Vietnam (historical and recreational), and, of course, Angkor Wat. After a trip like this, you'll have earned your time on the beaches of Thailand, Malaysia, or Bali.

## DOWN THE MALAY PENINSULA

Starting in Bangkok and heading south, you can connect the major resort destinations of southern Thailand with a tour down the length of Malaysia to Singapore and end in Bali.

**Length** This can take anywhere from a fly-by-night week to a few months.

**Highlights** These include pristine beaches (maybe even *The Beach*) in Thailand; great food, affordable cosmopolitan comforts, and unique cultural stops in Malaysia; "shop-till-you-drop" in Singapore; and the tranquil beaches of Bali.

## START FROM A HUB

From Bangkok, Singapore, or other major urban centers, travelers can make short forays into the countryside or to the resort of their choice from a comfortable, familiar base in a big city with all the comforts of home. Many visitors aim for the cultural and historical sites recommended by UNESCO—cities like Luang Prabang (Laos); Hoi An, Hue and Ha Long Bay (Vietnam), or Sukhothai and Ayuthaya (Thailand); and the temples of Angkor Wat (Cambodia), all reached via larger cities. Or start in a comfy hub and connect with local outfits for short adventure trips before coming back to hot showers and room service.

## 18 Recommended Books & Films

### BALI (INDONESIA)

*Bali Sekala and Nishkala: Essays on Religion, Ritual and Art*, Fred B. Eiseman, Jr., is the seminal text on the labyrinth of beliefs and practices on the island.

### CAMBODIA

Henry Kamm's *Cambodia: Report from a Stricken Land* is a good start to finding some context to the country's late troubles. *Brother Number One: A Political Biography*, by David P. Chandler, is good insight into the insanity of the Khmer Rouge.

There are many personal accounts by survivors of the years of violence and chaos in Cambodia. *Stay Alive, My Son*, by Pin Yathay, and *First They Killed My Father*, by Loung Ung, are both heart-wrenching stories of life under genocide in the mid-1970s. With the reopening of Cambodia's borders to international aid came another era of chaos, this just a general lawlessness and unrestrained vice; *Off the Rails in Phnom Penh: Into the Dark Heart of Guns, Girls, and Ganja,* by Amit Gilboa, is a portrait of that time.

On film, the best depiction of Cambodia is *The Killing Fields,* a 1984 film about the rise of the Khmer Rouge and the last days of freedom in Pnom Penh. *Tomb Raider* is a fanciful romp that was filmed at Angkor in 2000.

## LAOS

*Stalking the Elephant Kings,* by C. Kremmer, is a personal account of travel in Laos and one man's obsession to find the truth about the last dynasty—it is a good primer to Lao history and culture. *Another Quiet American,* by Brett Dakin, is a witty, personal account of recent travels in the county, and paints the state of the nation through the eyes of a young American among raucous expats in Vientiane. *The Ravens: Pilots of the Secret War of Laos* and *Air America: The Story of the CIA's Secret Airline,* both by C. Robbins, tell the heretofore untold tale of the undeclared war in Laos.

## SINGAPORE

If you're having trouble finding books about Singapore in bookstores where you live, I suggest you wait until you arrive, then browse local shelves, where you'll find tons of books about the country, its history, culture, arts, food, and local fiction. For interesting and informative reads that you can find (or order) through your neighborhood bookstore, here's a good place to start:

*From Third World to First: The Singapore Story: 1965–2000* by Lee Kuan Yew details the history and policies behind Singapore's remarkable economic success written by the man who was at the helm.

*The Singapore Story: Memoirs of Lee Kuan Yew,* by Lee Kuan Yew, offers an intimate account of Minister Mentor Lee's personal journey, and will unravel some of the mysteries behind one of the world's most talked-about leaders.

*Crossroads: A Popular History of Malaysia & Singapore,* by Jim Baker, is a readable history of Singapore and Malaysia from a long-time resident and expert.

*The Singapore Grip,* by J. G. Farrell, is a highly enjoyable work of historical fiction written by a Booker Prize winner that takes you back to Singapore on the brink of World War II to examine the last days of the British Empire.

Few knew that Louis L'Amour was a Merchant Marine in Southeast Asia. In *West from Singapore,* the famous author creates his brand of fascinating American West storytelling, only this tale takes place in the waters around pre-WWII Singapore.

## THAILAND

*Anna and the King,* the original late 19th-century work of Anna Leowens, governess for the children of the progressive King Rama IV, tells of the kingdom's opening to the West. Don't miss the film of the same name starring Jodie Foster (though due to gross historical inaccuracies the film was banned from public release in Thailand).

*The Beach,* by Alex Garland, and the popular film of the same name featuring Leonardo DeCaprio, tells the tale of the impossibility of modern Utopia, the very thing that so many Asian adventurers seek.

Carol Hollinger's *Mai Pen Rai Means Nevermind* is a personal history of time spent in the kingdom some 30 years ago, but the cultural insights are quite current. *Patpong Sisters* by Cleo Odzer and *Sex Slaves* by Louise Brown are both interesting exposés of the Thai sex industry. Though not about Thailand exclusively, Tiziano Terzani's book, *A Fortune-Teller Told Me,* is a well-crafted portrait of the interlocking cultures of Asia and of the Westerner's search for personal destiny.

Books on Thai Buddhism are many. Try Phra Peter Parrapadipo's *Phra Farang,* literally "The Foreign Monk," which tells the story of an Englishman turned Thai Buddhist monk. The writings of Jack Kornfield, particularly *A Path With Heart,* are a good introduction.

## VIETNAM

*The Quiet American,* by Graham Greene, which was made into a Hollywood film starring Michael Caine in 2002, is a classic tale of espionage in the old colony. In fact, much of what is written—or popular—about Vietnam chronicles the country's recent strife, particularly the American War years. The list is long. Here are but a few:

*In Retrospect: The Tragedy and Lessons of Vietnam,* by former American Secretary of Defense Robert S. McNamara and Brian DeMark, is quite popular in Vietnam (a copy stands in a glass case at the War Museum in Ho Chi Minh City), as it tells the tale of American deceit and misinformation from the perspective of one of its more remorseful arbiters. *A Bright Shining Lie,* by Neil Sheehan, is a similar explication. Pulitzer Prize–winning *Fire in the Lake,* by Francis Fitzgerald, is a sociological exploration of the war years and aftermath.

Personal accounts like *Dear America: Letters Home from Vietnam* by Bernhard Edelman or the Vietnamese classic *The Sorrow of War* by Bao Ninh tell of personal experiences of soldiers and civilians caught in the fray. *The Girl in the Picture: The Story of Kim Phuc and the Photograph That Changed the Course of the Vietnam War,* by Denise Chong, is self-explanatory.

Robert Olen Butler won a Pulitzer Prize for *A Good Scent from a Strange Mountain,* a collection of short stories recounting the legacy of war through disparate voices. *Catfish and Mandala,* by Andrew X. Pham, is a Vietnamese American's travel odyssey and coming to terms with the past.

The Vietnam War was fertile terrain for Hollywood in the 1980s, with award-winning classics like Francis Ford Coppola's *Apocalypse Now, The Deer Hunter* with Robert DeNiro, and Oliver Stone's *Platoon* and *Born on the Fourth of July,* a true story about returnee Ron Kovic. Films like Tran Anh Hung's *The Scent of Green Papaya* and *Cyclo* are more tranquil, studied views of Vietnamese culture. And *Indochine* starring Catherine Deneuve is a historic portrait of the tumultuous end of colonialism in Vietnam. *The Fog of War* is a uniquely candid hindsight look by Robert McNamara, the secretary of defense during the war.

---

### FAST FACTS: Southeast Asia

*ATM Networks* Note that Laos and Cambodia have no international ATMs; however, international ATMs abound in the major cities of most countries in Southeast Asia. See the "Money" section, earlier in this chapter, or in each specific country chapter.

*Car Rentals* See the "Getting Around" section in each country's chapter. In most places, it's best to hire a driver when renting a car because road conditions and traffic rules (or the seeming lack thereof) can make self-driving a bit harrowing; if this sounds like a luxury, hiring a driver for a day is affordable, for the most part, and drivers are often great sources of local information.

*Currency* See "Money," earlier in this chapter.

*Driving Rules* See "Getting Around Southeast Asia," earlier in this chapter.

*Drugstores* You'll find over-the-counter medications readily available in each country. It's best to bring enough of any medication that you require regularly, and know the generic name of the medicines you carry, in case you lose one or run out.

*Electricity* Most countries run on 220 volts, with two-pronged (flat or round) plugs. Use a converter for U.S. appliances (some hotels actually run on 110 volts), and use a surge protector for a laptop.

*Embassies & Consulates* See the "Fast Facts" sections in each country's chapter.

*Emergencies* Check the "Fast Facts" sections in each country's chapter.

*Etiquette & Customs* Customs vary, but in the mostly Buddhist and Muslim countries of Southeast Asia, modesty in dress and conduct is the general rule. Check the culture sections in specific country chapters.

**Appropriate Attire:** Though the cultures and religions of the many nations of Southeast Asia are more different than alike quite often, they all agree on respect for one another and staying covered in public. Ratty clothes are out of place here, as anywhere.

**Gestures:** See individual country chapters because there are some varied specifics here. Everywhere a scooping form of the wave that Westerners use to say "hello" in Southeast Asia means "come here." Be aware of issues in most countries over eating with only the right hand (the left is considered dirty) or of how to offer things to people (commonly with both hands). Check individual country chapters under "Etiquette."

**Business Etiquette:** Be on time, shake hands when greeting, and look people in the eye: The basics are all the same here, but it gets tricky when different cultural modes of thought and communication come into play (volumes are written on the subject). You might have to change your definition of "Yes" and "No," for example. Check individual country chapters.

**Photography:** Be aware that there are some superstitions about photography among hill tribes. In general, it's a good idea to ask before shooting portraits or taking photos in houses of worship. Be careful not to photograph police or military installations or activity.

*Film* Film is easy to get in all of these countries and is usually much cheaper than in the West (the exceptions being Singapore and Hong Kong, where it costs about the same). Digital camera supplies are readily accessible.

*Holidays* See "Holidays, Celebrations & Festivals," earlier in this chapter, or in the introductory material in each individual country chapter.

*Hot Lines* **Alcoholics Anonymous** has a strong presence in the region. There is an Intergroup office in Bangkok that can connect you with appropriate contacts elsewhere through the e-mail address on its website (www.aathailand.org) or its 24-hour hot line in Bangkok (© 02/ 231-8300). AA Cambodia also has a website (www.aacambodia.org), as does Bali (www.aa-bali.org).

*Information* See "Visitor Information," earlier in this chapter.

*Internet Access* The Internet is accessible just about anywhere and everywhere you'll travel. The farther you are from urban centers, the slower the dial-up connections (at slightly inflated prices), but the region's boom in young backpacker travelers means that you'll find a cybercafe in any location.

*Language* English is spoken everywhere in the countries of Southeast Asia, and wherever you go you'll be sure to find helpful folks eager to practice a few phrases on you (certainly touts and people who want your tourist dollars will know a few words). Don't let this distract you from picking up some of the local lingo; a little goes a long way.

*Laundry* Laundromats are few and far between, but affordable laundry service is available everywhere. Though often prohibitively expensive in large hotels, a short walk usually brings you to a local launderer where you'll pay by the kilo, extra for delicate items that require special care or ironing. Do not expect same-day service, as most rely on air drying.

*Liquor Laws* Drinking ages vary (in most countries it's either 18 or 20), but you won't find too many constraints placed on the purchase or consumption of alcohol in the region. Bars in the major cities are open late and, in some rural areas or at beachside, are mandated only by the whims of the owner. Beer, wine, and liquor, both familiar imports and local rice-based varieties, are sold anywhere and everywhere.

*Lost & Found* Be sure to tell all of your credit card companies the minute you discover that your wallet has been lost or stolen, and file a report at the nearest police precinct. Your credit card company or insurer might require a police report number or record of the loss. Most credit card companies have an emergency toll-free number to call if your card is lost or stolen; they might be able to wire you a cash advance immediately or deliver an emergency credit card in a day or two. Visa's U.S. emergency number is ℂ **800/847-2911** or 410/581-9994. American Express cardholders and traveler's check holders should call ℂ **800/221-7282**. MasterCard holders should call ℂ **800/307-7309** or 636/722-7111. For other credit cards, call the toll-free number directory at ℂ **800/555-1212**.

If you need emergency cash over the weekend when all banks and American Express offices are closed, you can have money wired to you via **Western Union** (ℂ **800/325-6000**; www.westernunion.com).

Identity theft and fraud are potential complications of losing your wallet, especially if you've lost your driver's license along with your cash and credit cards. Notify the major credit-reporting bureaus immediately; placing a fraud alert on your records could protect you against liability for criminal activity. The three major U.S. credit-reporting agencies are **Equifax** (ℂ **800/766-0008**; www.equifax.com), **Experian** (ℂ **888/397-3742**; www.experian.com), and **TransUnion** (ℂ **800/680-7289**; www.transunion.com). Finally, if you've lost all forms of photo ID, call your airline and explain the situation; they might allow you to board a plane if you have a copy of your passport or birth certificate and a copy of the police report you've filed.

*Mail* Postage rates are comparable to those in Western countries, although service is often less reliable and very slow, especially from the developing counties of Laos or Cambodia. Express services such as DHL or Fed Ex are growing in number and abundant in large cities (many souvenir or antiques dealers can arrange shipping on items large and small).

*Newspapers & Magazines* In the major urban centers, Hong Kong, Singapore, and Bangkok, foreign-press material is available anywhere. There are good local English-language papers, like the *Bangkok Post* or Singapore's *StraitsTimes* and the *Asian Wall Street Journal,* that will keep you connected. Don't pass up small-press editions or *Time Out* guides to local happenings and attractions; expat newspapers are also a good glimpse into daily life in each country.

*Passports* **For Residents of the United States:** Whether you're applying in person or by mail, you can download passport applications from the U.S. State Department website at **http://travel.state.gov**. For general information, call the **National Passport Agency (© 202/647-0518)**. To find your regional passport office, either check the U.S. State Department website or call the **National Passport Information Center** toll-free number (**© 877/487-2778**) for automated information.

**For Residents of Canada:** Passport applications are available at travel agencies throughout Canada or from the central **Passport Office,** Department of Foreign Affairs and International Trade, Ottawa, ON K1A 0G3 (**© 800/567-6868**; www.ppt.gc.ca).

**For Residents of the United Kingdom:** To pick up an application for a standard 10-year passport (5-yr. passport for children under 16), visit your nearest passport office, major post office, or travel agency or contact the **United Kingdom Passport Service** at © **0870/521-0410,** or search its website at www.ukpa.gov.uk.

**For Residents of Ireland:** You can apply for a 10-year passport at the **Passport Office,** Setanta Centre, Molesworth Street, Dublin 2 (© **01/671-1633**; www.irlgov.ie/iveagh). Those under age 18 and over 65 must apply for a €12 3-year passport. You can also apply at 1A South Mall, Cork (© **021/272-525**), or at most main post offices.

**For Residents of Australia:** You can pick up an application from your local post office or any branch of Passports Australia, but you must schedule an interview at the passport office to present your application materials. Call the **Australian Passport Information Service** at © **131-232,** or visit the government website at www.passports.gov.au.

**For Residents of New Zealand:** You can pick up a passport application at any New Zealand Passports Office or download it from its website. Contact the **Passports Office** at © **0800/225-050** in New Zealand or 04/474-8100, or log on to www.passports.govt.nz.

*Police* See the "Fast Facts" sections in individual country chapters.

*Restrooms* Public restrooms are often a bit of a shocker for first-time visitors. Especially in rural areas, it's common that toilets flush manually, with a few scoops of water from a larger cistern, and paper is to be deposited not in the loo, but in a separate wastebasket. Standards of cleanliness vary, but many public toilets would make a run-down roadside gas station in the U.S. seem like a temple. Squat toilets are common, but most major hotels have amenities familiar to the Western visitor.

*Safety*  See "Health & Safety," earlier in this chapter.

*Smoking*  The region is more or less a smoker's paradise, and there are few restraints on the habit in most destinations. In fact, in rural areas of the developing countries, smoking is even allowed on buses (a bit much, really). New laws in Bangkok ban smoking in restaurants, and similar rules are in place in the larger cities. If you're a smoker, be sure to read the rules before heading to Singapore.

*Taxes*  Each country has its version of a VAT tax added to restaurant and hotel bills. It can go as high as 20%, so be sure to inquire beforehand.

*Telephones*  See the "Fast Facts" sections in individual country chapters.

*Time Zone*  The countries of Southeast Asia are between 7 and 8 hours ahead of Greenwich Mean Time (that means 12 or 13 hr. ahead of New York, and 3 or 4 hr. behind Sydney).

*Tipping*  Though not as common as in the U.S., a small gratuity for taxi drivers, bellhops, and restaurant staff is appreciated.

*Useful Phone Numbers*  U.S. Dept. of State Travel Advisory ✆ 202/647-5225 (manned 24 hr.); U.S. Passport Agency ✆ 202/647-0518; U.S. Centers for Disease Control International Traveler's Hot Line ✆ 404/332-4559.

*Water*  Apart from in urban Singapore, **don't drink the water.** Buy inexpensive bottled drinking water, available everywhere. Some restaurants serve safe, treated ice and water.

# 4

# Thailand

*by Charles Agar*

Traffic and tranquillity, beaches and bargains, rural roads, ancient palaces and stunning temples: Thailand has much to offer anyone, from the casual visitor in search of affordable luxury to the rugged backpacker jumping off the grid. What brings visitors back time and again is the allure of the ephemeral: seemingly spontaneous festivals, chance meetings, and whimsical moments in an unpredictable land of ancient culture and elusive wisdom.

In bustling Bangkok, find canal and riverside communities, a sprawling Chinatown, an ultramodern cityscape, and giant outdoor markets that are a heady mix of sights, sounds, and smells.

Beyond urban Thailand are flat plains carpeted with rice paddies and dotted with tiny villages, mountains of luxuriant teak forests where elephants once roamed wild, long stretches of white-sand beach, acres of coconut palms and rubber plantations, and clear-blue waters against towering rock cliffs. Rural life is languid and hospitable and behind every warm Thai smile there is true kindness.

Outdoor adventure opportunities abound: sail, paddle, dive, and snorkel in the sea; trek to villages; ride the rivers; or go on 4WD adventures in the rugged upcountry. Rural Thailand is ripe for exploration by bus, train, car, motorbike, and boat, and visitors are only limited by their tolerance for adventure.

Gorgeous tropical island beaches play host to laid-back bungalow guesthouses and posh, Thai-style five-star resorts. The cuisine is captivating, a unique blend of sweet, sour, and salty tastes tempered with fiery spice. And whether shopping the sprawling bazaars or visiting Thailand's notorious nightlife, you're sure to have some *sanuk,* or "fun" Thai-style.

The world has caught on to Thailand's magic, though, and even through the hard years after economic crisis in 1997, the SARS scare of 2002 (no cases were reported in-country), the avian bird flu of 2004, recent unrest in the south, and the deadly tsunami of December 2004 the country enjoys a steady stream of tourists. And with the current flourishing domestic economy, Thailand welcomes visitors in style. A new subway in Bangkok, a deluxe international airport under construction, and an ever-higher standard of accommodations and amenities mean that while venturing into the unknown you will rarely feel uneasy.

## 1 Getting to Know Thailand

### THE LAY OF THE LAND

Thailand is in the center of Southeast Asia, roughly equidistant from China and India, and shares cultural affinities with both. It borders Burma (Myanmar) to the north and west, Laos to the northeast, Cambodia (Kampuchea) to the east, and Malaysia to the south. Thailand's southwestern coast stretches along the

Andaman Sea, and its southern and southeastern coastlines border the Gulf of Thailand (still often called the Gulf of Siam).

Thailand covers approximately 289,668 sq. km (112,970 sq. miles)—about the size of France. The country, which the Thais often compare in shape to the profile of an elephant's head, facing right, is divided into six major geographic zones, within which there are 73 provinces.

## THE REGIONS IN BRIEF

**NORTHERN THAILAND**   Northern Thailand (the forehead of the elephant) is a relatively cool mountainous region at the foothills of the Himalayas. Like most of Thailand, the cool hills in the north are well suited for farming, particularly for strawberries, asparagus, peaches, litchis, and other fruits. At higher elevations many hill-tribe farmers cultivate opium poppies, a crop that is rarely profitable (and ruinous to farmers who become addicted), though the agricultural program advanced by the king is introducing more productive crops. The cities in the north covered in this chapter are Chiang Mai and Chiang Rai.

**THE CENTRAL PLAIN**   The Central Plain is an extremely fertile region, providing the country and the world with much of its abundant rice crop. The main city of the area is Phitsanulok, northeast of which are the impressive remains of Sukhothai, Thailand's first capital. To the south is Lopburi, an ancient Mon-Khmer settlement.

**THE SOUTHEAST COAST**   The southeast coast is lined with seaside resorts, such as Pattaya and the islands Ko Samet and Ko Chang. Farther east, in the mountains, is Thailand's greatest concentration of sapphire and ruby mines.

**WESTERN THAILAND**   On the opposite side of the country, west of Bangkok, are mountains and valleys carved by the Kwai River, made infamous during World War II by the "Death Railway," built by Allied prisoners of war who worked and lived under horrifying conditions, and a bridge (made famous by the film *Bridge on the River Kwai*) over the river near Kanchanaburi. Just to the north of Bangkok (which is in every way the center of the country, along the Chao Phraya River banks) is Ayutthaya, Thailand's second capital after Sukhothai.

**THE SOUTHERN PENINSULA**   The long, narrow Southern Peninsula (the elephant's trunk) extends south to the Malaysian border. It was on the west coast of the peninsula, in the Andaman Sea, that the "Christmas Tsunami" struck on December 26, 2004. The result of a 9.0 earthquake in Aceh Indonesia, the waves claimed 5,000 victims in Thailand alone. Coastal Phuket was buffeted by the waves, but reconstruction was quick, while areas in Phang Nga Province, particularly Khao Lak, as well as the popular resort island of Ko Phi Phi near Krabi were flattened. International aid continues to flow in. The eastern coastline along the Gulf of Thailand, unaffected by the disaster, extends more than 1,802km (1,117 miles); the western shoreline runs 716km (444 miles) along the Andaman Sea. This region is the most tropical in the country, with heavy rainfall during monsoon seasons. The northeast monsoon, roughly from November to April, brings clear weather and calm seas to the west coast; the southwest monsoon, March to October, brings similar conditions to the east coast. There are glamorous beach resorts here (people visit them even during the rainy season; it doesn't rain all day), such as the western islands of Phuket and nearby Ko Phi Phi. The east coast islands of Koh Samui and Ko Phangan are comparable.

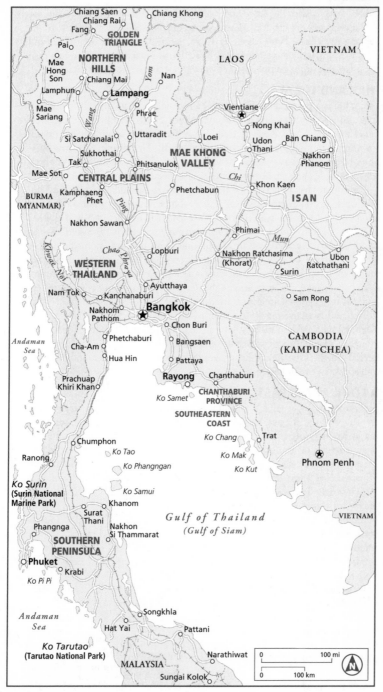

# Thailand

Chiang Saen
Chiang Rai
Fang
Chiang Khong

**GOLDEN
TRIANGLE**

Pai

**NORTHERN
HILLS**

LAOS

VIETNAM

Mae
Hong
Son

Chiang Mai

Nan

Lamphun

Lampang

Mae
Sariang

Phrae

Vientiane

Nong Khai

Si Satchanalai

Uttaradit

Loei

Udon
Thani

Ban Chiang

Sukhothai

Tak

Phitsanulok

**MAE KHONG
VALLEY**

Nakhon
Phanom

Mae Sot

**CENTRAL PLAINS**

Chi

Khon Kaen

**ISAN**

BURMA
(MYANMAR)

Kamphaeng
Phet

Phetchabun

Nakhon Sawan

Phimai

Mun

Chao Phraya

Lopburi

Nakhon Ratchasima
(Khorat)

Ubon
Ratchathani

**WESTERN
THAILAND**

Surin

Ayutthaya

Sam Rong

Nam Tok

Kanchanaburi

Nakhon
Pathom

**Bangkok**

*Andaman
Sea*

Chon Buri

**CAMBODIA
(KAMPUCHEA)**

Phetchaburi

Bangsaen

Cha-Am

Hua Hin

Pattaya

**Rayong**

Chanthaburi

*Ko Samet*

**CHANTHABURI
PROVINCE**

Prachuap
Khiri Khan

**SOUTHEASTERN
COAST**

*Ko Chang*

Trat

Chumphon

*Ko Tao*

*Ko Mak*

Ranong

*Ko Phangngan*

*Ko Kut*

Phnom Penh

*Ko Surin*
(Surin National
Marine Park)

*Ko Samui*

Khanom

*Gulf of Thailand
(Gulf of Siam)*

VIETNAM

Phangnga

Surat
Thani

Nakhon
Si Thammarat

**SOUTHERN
PENINSULA**

**Phuket**

Krabi

*Ko Pi Pi*

*Andaman
Sea*

Songkhla

Hat Yai

Pattani

*Ko Tarutao*
(Tarutao National Park)

Narathiwat

**MALAYSIA**

Sungai Kolok

| 0 | | 100 mi |
| 0 | | 100 km |

**ISAN**   Finally, Isan, the broad and relatively infertile northeast plateau (the ear of the elephant), is the least developed region in Thailand, bordered by the Mekong River (Mae Nam Khong in Thai). Isan is dusty in the cool winter and muddy during the summer monsoon. Fewer tourists make their way to Isan than any other part of the country, so we've opted not to cover it in this chapter.

## THAILAND TODAY

Today, under a pyramid of king, nation, and religion, Thais enjoy far more freedom and stability than any of their neighbors. The government is a constitutional monarchy, and King Bhumibol Adulyadej holds a position outside of government but is recognized as the defender of all Thai people. On a few occasions, he has put his foot down when government monkey business has not been beneficial to his people; his word is always heeded.

The country has seen a conservative shift with the ascendancy of Prime Minister Thaksin Shinawatra, a strong leader who is enacting aggressive fiscal and infrastructural reforms in an effort to make Thailand a leader in Asia. The PM's "War on Dark Influences" is more than your average PR campaign, but an across-the-board crackdown on corruption. His techniques, including the wholesale assault on drug traffickers and heavy-handed dealings with Muslim fundamentalism in the far south, has come under close international scrutiny. Palm greasing and kickbacks are still the norm in local government and business, but laws once ignored are now being strictly enforced.

Thailand is recovering famously from the economic crisis of the late '90s, when the value of the Thai baht plummeted. The baht has stabilized, and recent growth in manufacturing and trade means that Thailand is poised for real exponential growth. One look at Bangkok and its civic improvements and construction speaks of expansion.

## A LOOK AT THE PAST

Archaeologists believe that Thailand was a major thoroughfare for *Homo erectus* en route from Africa to China and other parts of Asia. Modern civilization did not arrive in Thailand until about a thousand years ago, when waves of people migrated from central and southern China, settling primarily in what is now Vietnam, Laos, Thailand, and Burma. These people, who are called *Tai,* became dispersed over a vast area of space, sharing a cultural and linguistic commonality. The **early Tais** lived in nuclear families with household collectives, called *muang,* or village, establishing loosely structured feudal states.

From the 6th century, Southeast Asia underwent a gradual period of **Indianization.** Merchants and missionaries from India introduced Brahmanism and Buddhism to the region, as well as Indian political and social values and art and architectural preferences. At the same time the **Mon,** migrants from Burma, were responsible for establishing Sri Lankan Buddhism in central Thailand.

By the early 9th century, the expansionist **Khmer** Empire had risen to power in Cambodia, engulfing the region. Magnificent Khmer temples, originally built for the worship of Hindu deities before conversion to Buddhism and distinguished by their corncob-shaped *prang,* or towers, were constructed in outposts increasingly farther afield until the Khmer's eventual collapse in the 13th century. You can still find many Khmer ruins in Thailand, especially in Isan.

In 1259, several powerful centers of Tai power in northern Thailand, southern China, and Laos were united by **King Mengrai,** who established the first capital of the **Lanna Kingdom** at Chiang Rai in 1263, and later at Chiang Mai in 1296. The Lanna Kingdom saw the rise of a scholarly Buddhism, with strict

adherence to orthodox ways. Citizens enjoyed the benefits of infrastructure projects for transportation and irrigation, developed medicine and law, and created
artistic expression through religious sculpture, sacred texts, and poetry. But the
Mongols, under the fierce expansionist leadership of **Kublai Khan,** forced their
way into the region. Mengrai, forming strategic alliances with neighboring king-
doms, succeeded in keeping the Mongols at bay.

In the vacuum left by the departing Khmers, a tiny kingdom based in
**Sukhothai** rose to fame after its crown prince, Rama, single-handedly defeated
an invasion from neighboring Mae Sot at the Burmese border. Upon his coronation in 1279, **Ramkhamhaeng,** or "Rama the Bold," set the scene for what is
recognized as the first truly Siamese civilization, mixing all the people of the central plains—Tai, Mon, Khmer, and indigenous populations, with threads of
India and China interwoven in their cultural tapestry. In response to the
Khmer's hierarchical rule, Ramkhamhaeng established himself as an accessible
king. He was a devout Buddhist, adopting the orthodox and scholarly Theravada Buddhism. A patron of the arts, the king commissioned many great Buddha images, initiated splendid architectural projects, and developed the modern
Thai written language. After his death in 1298, his successors failed to rule
wisely and Sukhothai's brilliant spark faded almost as quickly at it had ignited.

Next came the kingdom of **Ayutthaya,** which swallowed what was left of
Khmer outposts and the Sukhothai kingdom. Incorporating the strengths of its
population—Tai military manpower and labor, Khmer bureaucratic sensibili-
ties, and Chinese commercial talents, the empire grew wealthy and strong. Following Khmer models, the king rose above his subjects atop a huge
pyramid-shape administration. A huge fortified city was built, with temples that
glittered as any in Sukhothai. This was the Kingdom of Siam that the first Europeans, the Portuguese, encountered in 1511.

**Burmese invasion** forces took Chiang Mai's Lanna Kingdom in 1558 and
finally Ayutthaya in 1569. However, during the occupation, **Prince Naresuan,**
descended from Sukhothai kings, in a historic battle scene atop an elephant,
challenged the Burmese crown prince and defeated him with a single blow.
Ayutthaya continued through the following 2 centuries in grand style, and while
its Southeast Asian neighbors were falling under colonial rule, the court of Siam
retained its own sovereignty. Thailand has the distinction of being the only
Southeast Asian nation never to have been colonized, a point of great pride for
Thais today. Unfortunately, the final demise of Ayutthaya was two more
Burmese invasions in the 1760s.

The Siamese did not hesitate to build another kingdom. **Taksin,** a provincial
governor, rose to power on the merits of his military excellence, charisma, and a
firm belief that he was divinely appointed to rule. Rebuilding the capital at
Thonburi, on the western bank of the Chao Phraya River (opposite present-day
Bangkok), within 3 years he reunited the lands under the previous kingdom. But
Taksin suffered from paranoia—he had monks killed, along with eventually his
own wife and children. Regional powers were quick to get rid of him—he was
swiftly kidnapped, covered in a velvet sack, and beaten to death with a sandalwood club.

These same regional powers turned to **Chaophraya Chakri** in 1782 to lead
the land. Crowned **King Ramathibodi,** he was the first king of Thailand's present dynasty, the **Chakri Dynasty.** He moved the capital across the river to
Bangkok, where he built the **Grand Palace** and great temples. The city grew
around a network of canals, with the river as the central channel for trade and

commerce. Rama I reinstated Theravada Buddhist doctrine, reestablished the state ceremonies of Ayutthaya, and revised all laws. He also wrote the *Ramakien,* based upon the Indian *Ramayana,* a legend that has become the subject for many Thai classical arts.

**King Mongkut** (1851–68) with his son, **King Chulalongkorn** (1868–1910), lead Siam into the 20th century as an independent nation, establishing an effective civil service, formalizing global relations, and introducing industrialization-based economics.

It was King Mongkut who hired Anna Leonowens (of *The King and I*) as an English tutor for his children. Thai people want everyone to know that Mongkut was not the overbearing, pushover fop described in her account. Historians side with the Thais, for she is barely mentioned in court accounts—the story had its origins more in her imagination than in realty.

During the reign of **King Prajadhipok,** Rama VII (1925–35), the growing urban middle class became increasingly discontent. Economic failings and bureaucratic bickering weakened the position of the monarchy, which was delivered its final blow by the Great Depression. In 1932, a group of midlevel officials staged a coup d'etat, and Prajadhipok abdicated in 1935.

**Democracy** had a shaky hold on Siam. Over the following decades, government leadership changed hands fast and frequently, many times the result of hostile takeover with the military at the helm. In 1939, the nation adopted the name Thailand—"Land of the Free."

During **World War II,** democracy was stalled in the face of the Japanese invasion in 1941. Thailand chose to side with the Japanese, but at the war's end, no punitive measures were taken against Thailand; the Thai ambassador in Washington had failed to deliver his country's declaration of war against the Allies.

Thailand managed to stay out of direct involvement in the **Vietnam War;** however, it continues to suffer repercussions from the burden of refugees. The U.S. pumped billions into the Thai economy, bringing riches to some and relative affluence to many, but further impoverishing the poor. Communism became an increasingly attractive political philosophy, and a full-scale insurrection seemed imminent. In June 1973, thousands of Thai students demonstrated in the streets, demanding a new constitution and the return to democratic principals. Tensions grew until October, when armed forces attacked a demonstration at Thammasat University in Bangkok, killing 69 students and wounding 800, paralyzing the capital with terror and revulsion.

The constitution was restored, a new government was elected, and democracy once again wobbled on. Many students, however, were not yet satisfied and continued to complain that the financial elite were still in control and still resisting change. In 1976, student protests again broke out, and there was a replay of the grisly scene of 3 years before at Thammasat University. The army seized control to impose and maintain order, conveniently spiriting away some bodies and prisoners, and another brief experiment with democracy was at an end. Thanin Kraivichien was installed as prime minister of a new right-wing government, which suspended freedom of speech and the press, further polarizing Thai society.

In 1980, Prem Tinsulanonda was named prime minister, and during the following 8 years, he managed to bring remarkable political and economic stability to Thailand. The Thai economy continued to grow steadily through the 1980s, fueled by Japanese investment and Chinese capital in flight from Hong Kong. Leadership since then has seen quite a few changes, including a military coup in 1991 and another student crackdown in 1992. It was under

Gen. Chavalit Yongjaiyudh's administration that the economic crisis hit Thailand in July 1997. While his government sat on its hands in indecision over how to proceed, connections between public officials and bad financial institutions became more apparent and international investors lost confidence in Thailand. While in August 1997 Thailand accepted $17 billion in bailouts from the International Monetary Fund, political in-fighting stalled the government's action until November of the same year, when Chuan Leekpai, a previous prime minister, was elected into office again to try to straighten things out. It has been a long hard push to the present political and economic stability, but in 2004 Prime Minister Taksin Shinawatra paid back the $17 billion loan in full, and Thailand is prospering.

## THAILAND'S PEOPLE & CULTURE

Thailand is a true melting pot of people and cultures. Thais descended from people of southern China, who for centuries absorbed Mon, Khmer, Laotian, Persian, Indian, and Malay people and influences. The hill-tribe peoples of the north descended from Tibeto-Burman people who migrated from the Himalayas.

### RELIGION

Thai culture cannot be fully appreciated without some understanding of **Buddhism,** which is followed by 90% of the population. Although Buddhism first came to Thailand in the 3rd century B.C., when missionaries were sent from India, it was not until the 14th century that the *sangha* (monastic order) was established. Even Thai kings humbly don the monk's robes at age 13.

Other faiths in Thailand include Islam, Christianity, Hinduism, and Sikhism. Sunni Islam is followed by more than two million Thais, mostly in the south.

### ETIQUETTE

Disrespect for the royal family and religious figures, sites, and objects will cause great offense. While photography is generally permitted in temples, never stand above a Buddha image or point your feet in the direction of the Buddha. Women should never touch a monk and, when handing a monk an offering, he will provide a cloth for you to lay the item upon, and he will collect it.

To Thais, the feet are the lowest part of the body, so even pointing your feet at someone is offensive. Shoes should be removed when entering a temple or private home. And don't ever step over someone's body or legs. Alternately, the head, as the highest part of the body, should never be touched, not even in jest.

In public it is important to avoid confrontation or shows of anger or frustration. While banging your fist on the counter might get you better service back home, in Thailand you'll be promptly ignored. You catch more flies with honey.

A lovely Thai greeting is the *wai:* Place your palms together, raise the tips of your fingers to your chin, and make a subtle bow from the waist while bending your knees slightly. The person of lower social status initiates a wai. In general, you should not wai to children and to someone providing a service to you. Also, don't expect a monk to return a wai; they're exempt from the custom.

Address a Thai person by his or her first name preceded by "Khun." Don't be surprised if you are solely addressed by your first name—such as Mr. John or Ms. Mary. Close friends will use nicknames, which are much easier to remember.

Though a tropical climate, it is offensive to bare oneself in public, wear bathing suits around town, or go topless on the beach. It is particularly inappropriate for men or women to wear shorts, halter tops, or miniskirts in temples. Cover thyself in the presence of the Buddha.

## THAI CUISINE: FROM TIGER PRAWNS TO PAD THAI

Thai cuisine is the best of Chinese food ingredients and preparation combined with the sophistication of Indian spicing and topped off with red and green chilis. Basic ingredients include a cornucopia of shellfish, fresh fruits, and vegetables—asparagus, tamarind, bean sprouts, carrots, mushrooms of all kinds, various kinds of spinach, and bamboo shoots, combined with pungent spices such as basil, lemon grass, mint, chili, garlic, and coriander. Thai cooking employs coconut milk, curry paste, peanuts, and a variety of noodles and rice.

Among the dishes you'll find throughout the country are: *tom yum goong,* a Thai hot-and-sour shrimp soup; satay, charcoal-broiled chicken, beef, or pork strips skewered on a bamboo stick and dipped in a peanut-coconut curry sauce; spring rolls; *larb,* a spicy chicken or ground-beef concoction with mint and lime flavoring; salads, most with a dressing of onion, chili pepper, lime juice, and fish sauce; *pad thai* (Thai noodles), rice noodles usually served with large shrimp, eggs, peanuts, fresh bean sprouts, lime, and a delicious sauce; *khao soi,* a northern curried soup served at small food stalls; a wide range of curries, flavored with coriander, chili, garlic, and fish sauce or coconut milk; spicy *tod man pla,* one of many fish dishes; sticky rice, served in the north and made from glutinous rice, prepared with vegetables and wrapped in a banana leaf; and Thai fried rice, a simple rice dish made with whatever the kitchen has on hand. "American fried rice" usually means fried rice topped with one egg, over easy, and meat.

*A word of caution:* Thais enjoy incredibly spicy food, normally much more fiery than is tolerated in even the most piquant Western cuisines. Protect your own palate by saying *"Mai phet, farang,"* meaning "Not spicy, foreigner."

For dessert, the local fruit, from pineapple to papaya, is delicious. Also try local favorites like rambutan (like lycee), jackfruit, and pungent durian.

## LANGUAGE

Thai is derived from Mon, Khmer, Chinese, Pali, Sanskrit, and, increasingly, English. It is a tonal language, with distinctions based on inflection—low, mid, high, rising, or falling tone—rather than stress, and it can elude most speakers of Western languages. One interesting aspect of the language that can be confusing to first-time visitors is that the polite words roughly corresponding to our *sir* and *ma'am* are determined not by the gender of the person addressed, but by the gender of the speaker; females say *ka* and males say *krap.* Unfortunately, there is no universal transliteration system, so you will see the usual **Thai greeting** written in Roman letters as *sawatdee, sawaddi, sawasdee, sawusdi,* and so forth. **Central Thai** is the official language, but there are regional dialects.

### USEFUL THAI PHRASES

*Note:* All phrases end in "krup" for men and "ka" for women.

| | |
|---|---|
| Hello | **Sa-wa-dee-krup** (male); **sa-wa-dee-ka** (female) |
| How are you? | **Sa-bai-dee-mai-krup/ka?** |
| I am fine. | **Sa-bai-dee-krup/ka.** |
| Excuse me. | **Kor-tod-krup/ka.** |
| I understand. | **Kao-jai-krup/ka.** |
| I don't understand. | **Mai-kao-jai-krup/ka.** |
| Do you speak English? | **Khun-pood-pa-sa-ang-rid-dai-mai-krup/ka?** |
| Not spicy, please. | **Kor-mai-ped.** |
| Thank you | **Kop-koon-krup/ka** |
| Do you have . . . ? | **Mi . . . mai-krup/ka?** |

| | |
|---|---|
| Drinking water | **Nam-deum** |
| Coffee/tea w/milk/sugar | **Cafe/Nam cha-sai/num/wan** |
| How much? | **Tao-rai?** |
| That's expensive. | **Paeng** or **Paeng maak!** (very) |
| Can I get a discount? | **Lod-dai-mai-krup/ka?** |
| Where is the toilet? | **Hong-nam-yoo-tee-nai-krup/ka?** |
| Bus station | **Satani-rot-meh** |
| Train station | **Satani-rot-fai** |
| Stop here. | **Yood-tee-nee-krup/ka.** |

## 2 Planning Your Trip to Thailand

### VISITOR INFORMATION

The **Tourism Authority of Thailand (TAT)** publishes pamphlets and maps and current schedules for festivals and holidays. Visit its useful site: **www.tat.org**. Once in the country, you'll also find many free tourist maps and resources.

### ENTRY REQUIREMENTS

All visitors to Thailand must carry a valid **passport** with **proof of onward passage** (either a return or through ticket). Visa applications are not required if you are staying up to 30 days and are a national of 1 of 41 designated countries, including Australia, Canada, Ireland, New Zealand, the U.K., and the U.S. New Zealanders may stay up to 3 months. The **Immigration Division of the Royal Thai Police Department** is at 507 Soi Suan Phu (off Sathorn Tai Rd. south of Silom area and Sala Daeng BTS station; ℂ **02287-3101**). A visa extension costs a whopping 1,900B ($48). It is best to always have a proper visa and exit the country by the date stamped in your passport (or make the proverbial "visa run" over border points with Myanmar, Laos, Cambodia, or Malaysia). Visitors who overstay their visa will be fined 200B ($5) for each extra day, payable in cash upon exiting the country. For exhaustive visa particulars, try the unofficial but informative site www.thaivisa.com.

### CUSTOMS REGULATIONS

Tourists are allowed to enter the country with 1 liter of alcohol and 200 cigarettes (or 250g of cigars or smoking tobacco) per adult, duty-free. There are no restrictions on the import of foreign currencies or traveler's checks, but you cannot export foreign currency in excess of 10,000B ($250) unless declared to Customs upon arrival.

### MONEY

The Thai unit of currency, the **baht,** is written on price tags and elsewhere as the letter B crossed with a vertical slash (written "B" in this chapter, as in "100B"). One baht is divided into 100 **satang,** though you'll rarely see a satang coin. Yellow coins represent 25 and 50 satang; silver coins are 1B, 5B, and 10B. Bank notes come in denominations of 10B (brown), 20B (green), 50B (blue), 100B (red), 500B (purple), and 1,000B (khaki). While the rate is still experiencing some flux following the 1997 Asian economic crisis, it's still relatively stable, hovering around 40B per U.S. dollar.

For this edition we've used an exchange rate of **40 baht per U.S. dollar.** Obtain the latest money conversions before you plan your trip. For up-to-date conversions, visit the currency chart at www.xe.net/ict.

Most major banks in Bangkok now have **automated teller machines,** and ATMs are increasingly common in major tourist spots. The largest banks in

Thailand all perform account debit and cash advance services through the Cirrus/MasterCard or PLUS/Visa networks (try **Bangkok Bank, Thai Farmers Bank,** and **Bank of Ayudhya**). Things to keep in mind: The fee for a withdrawal is $1.25 per transaction, and time changes between here and home can affect your ability to withdraw cash on 2 consecutive business days.

Traveler's checks can be cashed in most banks or big hotels.

Nearly all international hotels and larger businesses accept **major credit cards.** Despite protests from credit card companies, many establishments add a 3% to 5% surcharge for payment. Use discretion in using your card—all major credit card companies list Thailand as a high-risk area for fraud. Don't let your card out of your sight, even for a moment, and be sure to keep all receipts. It's cash-only in rural parts.

**LOST/STOLEN CREDIT CARDS & TRAVELER'S CHECKS**    To report a lost or stolen credit card, you can call these service lines: American Express ✆ 02/273-0022; Diners Club ✆ 02/238-3660; MasterCard ✆ 02/232-2039; and Visa ✆ 02/256-7324.

**WIRING EMERGENCY FUNDS**    **Western Union** has branches in Bangkok and in many provincial capitals. The service allows you to either send or receive cash worldwide immediately at local branches connected with Western Union offices worldwide. *One word of warning:* Western Union's exchange rate is not favorable, so use this service only in emergency. Call the Western Union Customer Service Center in Bangkok at ✆ **02/254-7000.**

## WHEN TO GO

**CLIMATE**    Thailand has two distinct climate zones: tropical in the south and tropical savanna in the north. The northern and central areas of the country (including Bangkok) experience three distinct seasons. The hot season lasts from March to May, with temperatures averaging in the upper 90s Fahrenheit (mid-30s Celsius); April is the hottest month. This period sees very little rain, if any at all. The rainy season begins in June and lasts until October; the average temperature is 84°F (29°C), with 90% humidity. While the rainy season brings frequent showers, it's rare for them to last for a whole day or for days on end. Daily showers come in torrents, usually in the late afternoon or evening. The cool season, from November through February, has temperatures from the high 70s to low 80s Fahrenheit (mid- to upper 20s Celsius), with moderate and infrequent rain showers. In the north during the cool season (which is also the peak season for tourism), day temperatures can be as low as 60°F (16°C) in Chiang Mai and 41°F (5°C) in the hills.

The southern Malay Peninsula has intermittent showers year-round and daily ones during the rainy season (temperatures average in the low 80s Fahrenheit/high 20s Celsius). If you're traveling to Phuket or Koh Samui, it will be helpful to note that the two islands alternate peak seasons. Optimal weather on Phuket occurs between November and April, when the island welcomes the highest numbers of travelers. Alternately, Koh Samui's good weather lasts from about February to October. Refer to sections 16 and 11, respectively, for more information.

**PUBLIC HOLIDAYS**    Many holidays are based on the Thai lunar calendar, with many regional Buddhist fetes. The national holidays are: Makha Puja (Feb full moon), Chakri Day (Apr 6), Songkran (Thai New Year, Apr 12–14); Coronation Day (May 5), Visakha Puja (May full moon), Asalha Puja (July full moon), Her Majesty the Queen's Birthday (Aug 12), Chulalongkorn Day (Oct 23), His

## Sex for Sale

Everywhere in Thailand you will see Westerners enjoying the company of Thai women and men. Although prostitution is illegal, it is tolerated and is as much a tourist draw as the kingdom's hotels and beaches.

In poor, uneducated, rural families, where sons are counted on as farm labor, the sex trade has become an income-earning occupation for daughters who have few other job alternatives. While girls sent to the big cities as sex workers sometimes retire and return to their villages, for every happy ending, there are many more sad tales of abuse and addiction.

With a legacy of royal patronage and social acceptance, the oldest profession has been part of Thailand's economy for centuries. It is hard to get exact numbers for CSWs ("commercial sex workers") in Thailand (the number goes from 80,000 to 800,000, depending on the source), but it is interesting to note that foreigners engaging the services of prostitutes comprise only a fraction of the nationwide industry. Though efforts at cracking down on the trades are given much lip service, this just means that upfront, managed transactions at massage parlors and go-go bars decline while the many backroom deals, children bought and sold after being kidnapped and enslaved, carry on.

Thailand has made significant steps to counter the spread of **AIDS** and, through education and the introduction of condoms, have reputedly stemmed the tide of new cases from horrific numbers reported in the '90s. And while the 2004 AIDS convention, held in Bangkok, praised Thai efforts and groups like the Population & Community Development Association, a sober look at the data concludes that if there aren't greater changes regionwide, there may in fact be an epidemic of the disease to rival Africa.

Western embassies report numerous cases of tourists who are drugged in their hotel rooms by paid companions and wake 2 days later to find all their valuables gone. There are a shocking number of stories about young Western travelers found dead in their hotel rooms from unexplained causes. Exercise caution in your dealings with strangers.

Majesty the King's Birthday (Dec 5), and Constitution Day (Dec 10), as well as New Year's Eve (Dec 31) and New Year's Day (Jan 1).

## GETTING THERE
### BY PLANE

At the time of this writing a new international terminal was under construction, but until it opens Bangkok's busy Don Muang Airport still links Southeast Asia with all corners of the world. Even if you don't visit Thailand, many visitors to the region will pass through Bangkok en route.

The best way to ensure the most economical airfare on direct flights to Thailand is to call a registered travel agent for your reservations and booking.

**Thai Airways International** (in the U.S. ✆ **800/426-5204;** head office at 485 Silom Rd., Bangkok, ✆ **02/280-0060;** www.thaiair.com) covers virtually all Southeast Asian nations in its routing.

**FLIGHTS FROM NORTH AMERICA** Thai Airways International (© 800/426-5204) flies daily to Bangkok from Los Angeles. **United Airlines** (© 800/241-6522; www.ual.com) and **Northwest Airlines** (© 800/447-4747; www.nwa.com) can connect any airport in North America to Bangkok via daily flights. **Canadian Airlines International** (© 800/661-2227) flies to Bangkok from Vancouver via Hong Kong daily.

**FLIGHTS FROM AUSTRALIA** Thai Airways (© 300/651-960 toll-free within Australia, 7/3215-4700 in Brisbane, or 8/9322-7522 in Perth) services Bangkok from Sydney daily and from Brisbane, Melbourne, and Perth three times a week. **Qantas** (© 131211 toll-free within Australia; www.quantas.com) has, in addition to two dailies from Sydney and a daily flight from Melbourne, both direct, can also connect Adelaide, Brisbane, and Canberra daily. **British Airways** (© 2/8904-8800 in Sydney, 7/3223-3123 in Brisbane, 8/9425-7711 in Perth; www.british-airways.com) flies twice daily from Sydney.

**FLIGHTS FROM THE UNITED KINGDOM** Two or three flights daily, nonstop flights from London to Bangkok are offered by **British Airways** (© 0345/22-21-11 from anywhere within the United Kingdom; www.british-airways.com).

Note that while most international flights arrive in Bangkok, you can also fly direct to Phuket, Koh Samui, Hat Yai, and Chiang Mai from regional destinations like Hong Kong, Kuala Lumpur, Singapore, Vientiane and Luang Prabang in Laos, and Phnom Penh and Siem Reap in Cambodia.

Don't forget that if you leave Thailand by air, you're required to pay 500B ($13) **international departure tax.**

### BY TRAIN

Thailand is accessible via train from Singapore and peninsular Malaysia. **Malaysia's Keretapi Tanah Melayu Berhad (KTM)** begins in Singapore (© 65/222-5165), stopping in Kuala Lumpur (© 603/273-8000) and Butterworth (Penang) (© 604/323-7962) before heading for Thailand, where it joins service with the State Railway of Thailand. Bangkok's Hua Lamphong Railway Station is centrally located on Krung Kassem Road (© 02223-7010 or 1690).

The *Eastern & Oriental Express* (www.orient-express.com) operates a 2-night/3-day journey between Singapore and Bangkok that makes getting there almost better than being there. The romance of 1930s colonial travel is joined with modern luxury on this luxurious train. Departures are limited, and current fares start at $1,780 per person one-way during high season. There are also onward connections to Chiang Mai with return and a stop in Ayuthaya. Call © 800/524-2420 in the U.S., or 65/392-3500 in Singapore.

### BY BUS

From every major city in peninsular Malaysia (and even Singapore), you can pick up a bus to Thailand. VIP buses cost more but have reclining seats and more legroom; traveling overland along the length of the southern peninsula is best by train, however. Buses connect with Laos over the Lao-Thai Friendship Bridge to Vientiane and at other southern border crossings, and with Cambodia via Poipet.

## GETTING AROUND

Transportation within Thailand is accessible, efficient, and inexpensive. If your time is short, fly. But if you have the time to take in the countryside and you care to see a bit of provincial living, travel by bus, train, or private car.

## BY PLANE

Most convenient are domestic flights are on **Thai Airways,** part of Thai Airways International (6 Larn Luang Rd., Bangkok; (✆ **02535-2084**). Flights connect Bangkok and 27 domestic cities, including Chiang Mai, Chiang Rai, Mae Hong Son, Phitsanulok, Loei, Surat Thani, and Phuket. **Bangkok Airways** (Queen Sirikit Convention Center, New Ratchadaphisek Road, Bangkok; (✆ **02229-3456**) connects Bangkok with Koh Samui, Phuket, Ranong, U Tapao (near Pattaya), Sukhothai, and Chiang Mai, and with international flights from Singapore and Phnom Penh. **Air Andaman** (87 Nailert Bldg., 4th Floor, Unit 402a, Sukhumvit Rd.; (✆ **02251-4905**) handles short domestic hops. And the latest budget carrier, **Air Asia** (✆ **02515-9999** in Bangkok; www.airasia.com), flies between Bangkok and Chiang Mai, Phuket, Hat Yai, and Khon Kaen for supercheap (book ahead).

## BY TRAIN

Bangkok's **Hua Lampong Railway Station,** now easily reached by subway, is a convenient, user-friendly facility: Clear signs point the way to public toilets, coin phones, the food court, and baggage check area. A Post & Telegraph Office, Information Counter, police box, ATMs and money-changing facilities, convenience shops, baggage check, and restaurants surround a large open area.

From this hub, the State Railway of Thailand provides regular service to destinations north as far as Chiang Mai, northeast to Udon Thani, east to Pattaya, and south to Thailand's southern border with continuing service to Malaysia. Complete schedules and fare information can be obtained at any railway station or by calling **Hua Lampong Railway Station** directly at (✆ **02223-7010,** or call the information hot line at 1690.

There are various fare classes of trains based on speed and comfort. The fastest is the Special Express, which is the best choice for long-haul, overnight travel. These trains cut travel time by as much as 60% and have sleeper cars, which are a must for the really long trips. Rapid trains are the next best option. Prices vary for class, from air-conditioned sleeper cars in first class to air-conditioned and fan s..per or seats in second, on down to the straight-backed, hard seats in third class.

## BY BUS

Thailand has a very efficient and inexpensive bus system, highly recommended for budget travelers and short-haul trips. Options abound, but the major choices are public or private, air-conditioned or non-air-conditioned. Most travelers use the private, air-conditioned buses. Buses are best for short excursions; long-haul buses are an excellent value, but they can be slow and uncomfortable.

Bangkok has three major bus stations, each serving a different part of the country. All air-conditioned public buses to the west and the southern peninsula arrive and depart from the **Southern Bus Terminal** (✆ **02434-7192**) on Nakhon Chaisi and Phra Pinklao Road (near Bangkok Noi Station), west of the river over the Phra Pinklao Bridge from the Democracy Monument. Service to the east coast (including Pattaya) arrives and departs from the **Eastern Bus Terminal,** also known as **Ekkamai** (✆ **02391-2504**), on Sukhumvit Road opposite Soi 63 (Ekamai BTS skytrain station). Buses to the north arrive and leave from the **Northern Bus Terminal,** aka **Mo Chit** (✆ **02936-2841**), Kampaengphet 2 Rd., Mo Chit, near the **Chatuchak Weekend Market,** and a short taxi or bus ride from the Mo Chit skytrain station. VIP buses leave from locations in town.

## BY CAR

Renting a car is a snap in Thailand, although self-driving in Bangkok traffic is discouraged. Outside the city, it's a good option, though Thai drivers are quite reckless and American drivers must reorient themselves to driving on the left.

Among the many car-rental agencies, both **Avis** (© **02255-5300**) and **Budget** (© **02566-5067**) each have convenient offices around the country.

You can rent a car with or without a driver. All drivers are required to have an international driver's license. At press time, self-drive rates started at 1,500B ($38) per day for a small Suzuki four-wheel-drive.

Local tour operators in larger destinations like Chiang Mai, Phuket, or Koh Samui will rent cars for considerably cheaper than the larger, more well-known agencies. Sometimes the savings are up to 50%. These companies rarely require international driver's licenses. Always ask if you will still be covered by their insurance policy.

Thailand drives on the left side of the road at a maximum speed limit of 60kmph (37mph) inside a city and 80kmph (50mph) outside.

## TIPS ON ACCOMMODATIONS

Thailand accommodations run the gamut, but you can expect a high standard of comfort and service at affordable rates. In places like Phuket and Koh Samui, rainy season brings discounts of 30% and 50%. You can negotiate with hotel reservations agents—there are always special discounts, packages, or free service add-ons for extra value, and it never hurts to ask.

## TIPS ON DINING

Larger Thai cities and towns play host to many Western restaurants, but go for authentic Thai wherever possible. One-dish meals like noodle soup or fried-rice or noodles are popular for solo travelers, but Thai meals are best when shared family style. There are many regional variations, but the most notable are the barbecue, sticky rice, and spicy papaya salads in Isan (the northeast) and the fiery coconut curries of the south; always ask about regional specials. Most family meals consist of a meat or fish dish (often a whole fish), fried or steamed vegetables, a curry, stir-fried dishes of meat and vegetables, and a soup, such as fiery *tom yam*. Meals are lengthy and boisterous affairs, and food is picked at slowly (often accompanied by local beer, rice wine, or strong whiskey). Table manners are casual and practical.

Be cautious with street eats: Check out the stall to see that it's clean and the ingredients are fresh. Most places temper spices for foreigners, but always ask.

You're not expected to tip at a Thai restaurant, but rounding up the bill or leaving 20B (50¢) on top of most checks is acceptable.

## TIPS ON SHOPPING

Shopping is a full contact sport in Thailand. In markets and smaller shops, bargaining is the name of the game. If your suggested price is accepted, it is rude to walk away without finishing the sale. Keep in mind that in high-traffic tourist areas, prices are always inflated. In shopping malls and boutiques, prices are fixed. Some shops charge a 3% charge on credit card purchases.

### *FAST FACTS:* Thailand

*American Express* There is no specific agent that handles **American Express** services in Thailand anymore, but there is an **American Express**

office at 388 Pahonyothin Rd. in Bangkok. You can reach the office at
© 02273-5296 during business hours (Mon–Fri 8:30am–4:30pm) or call the
customer service hot line (© 02273-5544) with any problems or questions.

*ATM Networks*  Most major banks throughout the country have automated teller machines. MasterCard/Cirrus or Visa/PLUS network connection is available at most branches of Bangkok Bank, Thai Farmers Bank,
Siam Commercial Bank, or Bank of Ayudhya. See the "Money" section,
earlier in this chapter.

*Business Hours*  Government offices (including branch post offices) are
open Monday to Friday 8:30am to 4:30pm, with a lunch break between
noon and 1pm. Businesses are generally open 8am to 5pm. Shops often
stay open from 8am until 7pm or later, 7 days a week. Department stores
are generally open 10am to 7pm.

*Drugstores*  Pharmacies carry brand-name medication, and pharmacists
often speak some English and are very helpful.

*Electricity*  All outlets are 220 volts AC (50 cycles) with two flat- or round-
pronged holes. If you use a 110-volt hair dryer, electric shaver, or battery
charger, bring a transformer and adapter.

*Embassies & Consulates*  Most countries have consular representation in
Bangkok; the U.S., Australia, Canada, and the U.K. also have consulates in
Chiang Mai. Most embassies have 24-hour emergency services.

*Emergencies*  In any emergency call © 1699 or 1155 for the Tourist Police.
Don't expect many English speakers at normal police posts outside the
major tourist areas. It is a good idea to contact your embassy.

*Etiquette & Customs*  Practicing cultural sensitivity is very important in
Thailand and even longtime visitors are bound to come up against new
and different faux pas to trip them up. Pay close attention to what Thai
people do, especially in temples and at the table, and you'll be fine.

**Appropriate Attire:** You wouldn't know it by the current fashion trends in
urban Bangkok, where tiny miniskirts and bare midriffs are common, but
Thai people are quite modest. Conservative dress—longer shorts, trousers,
and shirts that cover the shoulder are the standard.

**Gestures:** The traditional Thai greeting is called the *wai,* a short bow with
hands in prayer, that is also used to say thank you and goodbye. You can
return the greeting, but are not obliged to do so when greeted by hotel
staff, for instance. In a business setting, a handshake is more appropriate.

Remember that in Thailand the head is the most sacred part of the
body, and the feet are the lowliest; therefore, do not touch another person's head or even tousle the hair of a child, and avoid pointing your feet
at people or Buddhist images. Pointing with the finger is also rude; Thais
use a palms-up hand gesture when signifying direction or indicating a person or thing. Beckoning looks like a wave goodbye.

Men and women should go easy on public displays of affection, though
this is changing. Women should never touch or sit next to a Buddhist monk.

**Avoiding Offense:** Funny, but the best way to avoid offending anyone in
Thailand is not to show your offense and express anger, a "face-losing"
proposition. Most Thais are Buddhist, and a person showing ill temper is

regarded with surprise and disapproval. A gentle approach will take you farther, and patient persistence is more effective in any situation.

"Thai Time" dictates that appointments are loosely kept and offense at someone's tardiness is met with confusion.

Be sensitive, particularly in places of worship, about photography.

*Hot Lines*  There are regular meetings of **Alcoholics Anonymous (AA)** in Thailand. See www.aathailand.org or call ✆ 02231-8300.

*Internet Access*  You'll find Internet cafes everywhere in Thailand. See the "Fast Facts" sections in specific destination chapters for details.

*Language*  Central (often called Bangkok) Thai is the official language. English is spoken in the major cities at most hotels, restaurants, and shops, and is the second language of the professional class.

*Liquor Laws*  The official drinking age in Thailand is 18, but laws are loosely followed—you can buy alcohol in most areas any time day or night, with exceptions for certain Buddhist holidays. All restaurants, bars, and nightclubs sell booze, and you can pick up take-away-size packages from just about anywhere. Nightlife spots now close between midnight and 2am.

*Lost & Found*  To report a lost or stolen credit card in Thailand, call: **American Express** (✆ 02273-5544); **Diners Club** (✆ 02238-3660); **MasterCard** (✆ 02260-8572); and **Visa** (✆ 02256-7326).

*Mail*  You can use *poste restante* as an address anywhere in the country. Address mail to Poste Restante, GPO, Name of City, and the mail is held for you at the post office or GPO until you pick it up. Airmail postcards to the United States cost 12B to 15B (30¢–40¢), depending on the size of the card; first-class letters cost 19B (50¢) per 5 grams (rates to Europe are about the same). Airmail delivery usually takes 7 days.

Air parcel post costs 606B ($15) per kilogram. Surface or sea parcel post costs 215B ($5.40) for 1 kilogram (3 or 4 months for delivery). International Express Mail (EMS) costs 440B ($11) from 1 to 250 grams, with delivery guaranteed within 4 days. See individual chapters for local post offices and their hours.

Shipping by air freight is expensive. Two major international delivery services have their main dispatching offices in Bangkok, though they deliver throughout the country; these are **DHL Thailand,** Grand Amarin Tower Building, Phetchaburi Road (✆ 02207-0600), and **Federal Express,** at Rama IV Road (✆ 02367-3222). **UPS Parcel Delivery Service,** with a main branch in Bangkok at 16/1 Soi 44/1 Sukhumvit Rd. (✆ 02712-3300), also has branches elsewhere in Thailand. Many businesses will also package and mail merchandise for a reasonable price.

*Maps*  The **TAT** gives out regional and city maps at its information offices, and there are a number of good privately produced maps, usually free, available at most hotels and many businesses.

*Newspapers & Magazines*  The major domestic English-language dailies are the *Bangkok Post* and *The Nation,* distributed in the morning in the capital and later in the day around the country. They cover the domestic political scene, as well as international news from AP, UPI, and Reuters wire services, and cost 20B (50¢).

*Police* In an emergency call the **Tourist Police** at © **1699** or 1155 to connect with English speakers 24 hours a day.

*Restrooms* The better restaurants and hotels will have Western toilets. Shops and budget hotels will have an Asian toilet, aka "squatty potty," a hole in the ground with foot pads on either side. Near the toilet is a water bucket or sink with a small ladle. The water is for flushing and cleaning the toilet. Don't count on these places having toilet paper. Some shopping malls have dispensers outside the restroom—2B (5¢) for some paper. Dispose of it in the wastebasket provided, not down the drain.

*Safety* Anonymous violent crime in Thailand is rare; however petty crime such as purse snatching or pickpocketing is common. Overland travelers should take care on overnight buses and trains for small-time thieves.

Beware of credit card scams; carry a minimum of cards, don't allow them out of your sight, and keep all receipts. Don't carry unnecessary valuables, and keep those you do carry in your hotel's safe.

*A special warning:* Be wary of strangers who offer to guide you (particularly in Bangkok), take you to any shop (especially jewelry shops), or buy you food or drink. This is most likely to occur near a tourist sight. Without exception, this is a scam of some kind. These folks want to sell you fake gems or waste your time and earn a commission. Just walk away.

Beware of bringing strangers to your hotel room. There are many incidents of drugging and robbery (especially by prostitutes).

*Taxes & Service Charges* Hotels charge a 7% government value-added tax (VAT) and typically add a 10% service charge; hotel restaurants add 8.25% government tax. Smaller hotels quote the price inclusive of these charges.

*Telephones* Major hotels in Thailand feature convenient international direct dial (IDD), long-distance service, and in-house fax transmission. Hotels charge a surcharge on local and long-distance calls, which can add up to 50% in some cases. Credit card or collect calls are a much better value, but most hotels also add a hefty service charge for them to your bill.

Major post offices have special offices or booths for overseas calls, as well as fax and telex service, usually open 7am to 11pm. Guesthouses and travel agents in tourist areas offer long-distance calling or call-back service on their private line or use very affordable net-to-phone connections of varying quality. Local calls can be made from any red or blue public pay telephone. Card phones are your best; buy a Telephone Organization of Thailand (TOT) card, for use in yellow phones, anywhere.

**To call Thailand:** If you're calling Thailand from the United States:

1. Dial the international access code: 011
2. Dial the country code: 66
3. And dial the number. So the whole number you'd dial for Bangkok would be 011-66-2-000-0000.

*Important note:* When making international calls to Thailand, be sure to omit the "0" that appears before all phone numbers in this guide (thus you will only dial 8 digits after the "66" country code).

**To make international calls:** To make international calls from Thailand, first dial 00 and then the country code (U.S. or Canada 1, U.K. 44, Ireland 353, Australia 61, or New Zealand 64). Next you dial the area code and number. For example, if you wanted to call the British Embassy in Washington, D.C., you would dial 00-1-202-588-7800.

For directory assistance: Dial ✆ **1133.**

*Time Zone* Thailand is 7 hours ahead of GMT (Greenwich Mean Time). During winter months, this means that Bangkok is exactly 7 hours ahead of London, 12 hours ahead of New York, and 15 hours ahead of Los Angeles.

*Tipping* If no service charge is added to your check in a fine dining establishment, a 10% to 15% tip is appropriate. In local shops, a small tip of 10B (25¢) or so is common. Airport or hotel porters expect tips, but just 20B to 50B (50¢–$1.25) is acceptable. Feel free to reward good service wherever you find it. Tipping taxi drivers is not expected but accepted. Carry small bills, as many cab drivers either don't have change or won't admit having any in the hope of getting a tip.

*Useful Phone Numbers* U.S. Department of State Travel Advisory ✆ 202/647-5225 (manned 24 hr.); U.S. Passport Agency ✆ 202/647-0518; U.S. Centers for Disease Control International Traveler's Hot Line: ✆ 404/332-4559.

*Water* Don't drink the tap water, even in the major hotels. Most hotels provide bottled water in or near the minibar or in the bathroom; use it for brushing your teeth as well as drinking. Most restaurants serve bottled or boiled water and ice made from boiled water, but always ask to be sure.

## 3 Bangkok

With an estimated population of over 10 million in a country of only 60 million, Thailand's capital is the urban and cultural heart of the land: where all trends originate, where all roads meet, an exaggeration of every aspect of life in the kingdom. Choked with traffic, polluted, and corrupt, the city is also the financial capital of one of the fastest-growing economies in the world. Central Bangkok is all columns of glass and steel, hulking shopping complexes, and hotels. Linked at the city center by an elevated monorail, the BTS skytrain, Bangkok now boasts a slick new subway too.

Bangkok was founded when King Rama I moved the city across the river from Thonburi in 1782. Today the capital's stunning temples share space with skyscrapers and Starbucks; luxury condominiums stand stridently just a stone's throw from labyrinthine slums along dirty canals; glittering shopping malls cast their shadows over dusty open-air street bazaars. The city is less "Asian" than what many visitors often expect, but there are still gems to find in and among the new construction and suburban sprawl, and exploring Bangkok is certainly a highlight.

Whatever your budget, lodging is affordable and Bangkok is a good place to splurge for far more comforts than the same prices afford you back home. And food? They've got it all in the Thai capital: fine dining on par with any large city as well as great local joints. A shopper's haven, the city has everything from luxury boutiques to sprawling markets. And nightlife? The proverbial "One Night in Bangkok," though tempered by restrictions, can still be found.

Wander in a day from luxury shopping districts to quiet temple compounds, cacophonous markets to tiny alleyways. Get lost and explore.

# ORIENTATION
## ARRIVING

Bangkok has a huge modern airport (and a newer version under construction), three bus terminals, and a centrally located train station. Affordable taxis and tuk-tuks (three-wheeled, motorized trishaws/pedicabs) cruise the broad avenues. The BTS skytrain, the city's elevated rail line, opened in late 1999 with service throughout downtown Bangkok, and the new Bangkok subway means direct connection between the domestic train station and northern bus terminal.

### By Plane

Bangkok is a major hub for air travel in Southeast Asia, with more than 70 airlines providing service. **Don Muang International Airport,** 22km (14 miles) north of the city center, is the hub. International and domestic flights arrive at different terminals, a 1km (half-mile) walk or a free shuttle ride apart. A new international airport, located to the south of the city, is also in the works.

Travelers arriving at the international terminal will find a wide range of services awaiting them, available 24 hours unless otherwise noted: luggage storage for 90B ($2.25) per day with a 3-month maximum; currency exchange banks with the same rates as in-town banks; ATMs; a post office with overseas telephone service; **Airport Information Booths** and **Tourism Authority of Thailand (TAT)** booths (Terminal 1 ✆ 02504-2701 and Terminal 2 ✆ 02535-2669), open 8am to midnight; a Thai Hotel Association desk that will assist you in finding available accommodations; restaurants serving both Thai and international food; a minimarket; and the **Amari Airport Hotel.**

The domestic terminal offers most of these services, though on a more limited schedule: luggage storage, for 90B ($2.25) a day with a 14-day limit, open 6am to 11pm; a post office in the departure wing with overseas telephone service; a foreign exchange bank; the Hotel Association desk open 24 hours; and a cafeteria-style coffee shop.

The airport provides **free shuttle service** between the international and domestic terminals, with buses every 15 minutes. If you have light luggage, you might find it more enjoyable (and sometimes faster) to walk.

Passengers on international flights must purchase a 500B ($13) departure tax ticket before you enter immigration. Children under 2 years are exempt.

**GETTING TO & FROM THE AIRPORT** From the town center it is about a half-hour ride with no traffic and up to 2 hours at rush hour. Most of the larger hotels offer pickup service for a fee. You can easily arrange for an air-conditioned minibus, taxi, or limousine to your hotel; these are found outside the arrival hall of both the international and domestic terminals (ground-floor level).

**Taxi stands** are just outside of both the domestic and international terminals. Charges will be according to the meter, plus a 50B ($1.25) service charge for airport service. The driver will ask if you would like to take the expressway, which costs an extra 40B ($1) but saves time.

**Private limousine services** have air-conditioned sedans for hire from booths in the arrival halls of both international and domestic airports. Trips to town start at 650B ($16). Advanced booking is not necessary.

**The Airport Bus** (✆ 02995-1252) is a convenient and inexpensive alternative with regular departures from both domestic and international terminals from 4:30am to 12:30am. Routes serve all parts of the city. Buy a ticket at curbside for just 100B ($2.50).

## By Train

The Thai rail network is extremely well organized, connecting Bangkok with major cities throughout the country. (You can also travel by train to Bangkok from Singapore, via Kuala Lumpur and Butterworth, Malaysia.)

All trains to and from the capital stop at **Hua Lampong Railroad Station** (© 02223-7010 or 1690), east of Chinatown at the intersection of Rama IV and Krung Kasem roads. The station has many services, including baggage check and a small food court. The Information Counter is helpful. Connect to your destination by subway, metered taxi, or tuk-tuk.

## By Bus

Bangkok has three major bus stations, each serving a different part of the country. Buses to the west and the southern peninsula arrive and depart from the **Southern Bus Terminal** (© 02434-7192) on Nakhon Chaisi, west of the river over the Phra Pinklao Bridge from the Democracy Monument. Service to the east coast arrives and departs from the **Eastern Bus Terminal,** also known as **Ekkamai** (© 02391-2504), on Sukhumvit Road opposite Soi 63 (Ekami BTS skytrain station). Buses to the north arrive and leave from the **Northern Bus Terminal,** aka **Mo Chit** (© 02936-2841), Kampaengphet 2 Rd., Mo Chit near the **Chatuchak Weekend Market** (easily reached by the BTS skytrain or the MRT subway). VIP buses leave from locations in town.

## VISITOR INFORMATION

The **Bangkok Tourist Bureau** has offices at major tour destinations throughout the city. Call with any questions at © 02225-7612 (www.bma.go.th).

The **Tourism Authority of Thailand (TAT)** offers general information about the provinces and operates a useful hot line: © 1672. It has a counter in Don Muang airport, open 8am to midnight. The branch office at Ratchadamnoen Nok Avenue (© 02282-9773) near the Grand Palace is helpful.

## CITY LAYOUT

Vintage 19th-century photographs of Bangkok show the Chao Phraya River bustling with humble longtail boats and elaborate royal barges. Built along the banks of the broad, S-shaped river, the city spread inland through a network of *klongs* (canals) that rivaled the intricacy—though never the elegance—of Venice.

The **Historic District** along the Chao Phraya River contains most of the city's historical sights, such as the Grand Palace, and most of the city's original *wats* (temples with resident monks). Following the river south, you'll run into the narrow lanes of Bangkok's **Chinatown** and, farther down, a row of the city's finest riverside hotels, including the Oriental and the Peninsula. Inland from the river, Bangkok's **central business district** is situated on Sathorn, Silom, and Surawongse roads, beginning at Charoen Krung (or "New") Road. Bangkok's **main shopping thoroughfare,** on Rama I Road, between Payathai and Ratchadamri roads, sports huge modern shopping complexes like the World Trade Center and Siam Square. East of Rama I, find Sukhumvit Road with its a acres of expatriate condos, restaurants, shopping, and nightlife.

Get to know the Thai word *soi,* meaning "lane." Larger thoroughfares in the city have names, and *sois* are the many numbered side streets along their length, odd and even numbers on alternate sides. For example, Sukhumvit Soi 5 is the home of the Amari Boulevard Hotel, while Sukhumvit Soi 8, a few minutes' walk east and across the street, is where you'll find Le Banyan restaurant. Note that closely numbered *sois* are not necessarily nearby.

# Bangkok Metro Lines

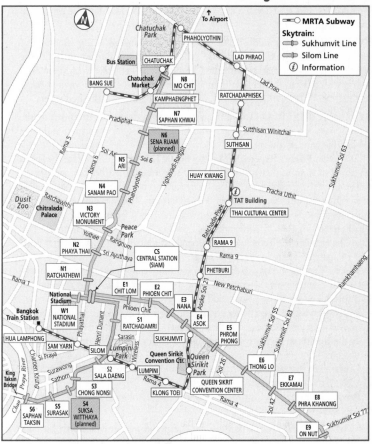

**STREET MAPS** Nancy Chandler's "Map of Bangkok" (160B/$4) is a detailed, colorful source for finding specific hotels, restaurants, and shopping. The free "Thaiways Map of Bangkok" and "Metropolitan Map" are both chock-full of adverts and good detailed city maps with specific insets (available in most hotels). Bus maps are many and helpful if you go that route.

## GETTING AROUND

It can take more than 2 hours by taxi to get from one side of town to the other during rush hour so it's best to avail yourself of the many new options below. Taxis are affordable, but at the wrong time of day can be a real nightmare.

**BY SKYTRAIN** The **Bangkok Mass Transit System (BTS skytrain)** is an elevated railways system high above the maddening traffic. Trains access Bangkok's central areas and now connect with the **MRTA subway.** Single-journey tickets cost from 10B to 40B (25¢–$1). Buy ticket cards at platform vending machines: Choose your numbered destination from a map, press the corresponding button on the map, and pay in a slot (get small change at the info counter as needed). Ticket cards let you through the turnstile and are required for exit so be sure to hang on to them during the ride. Also available are 1- and

3-day passes and stored-value cards. The skytrain operates daily between 6am and midnight.

**BY SUBWAY** Over budget and long overdue, Bangkok's new subway line opened in 2004 and makes a reverse "C" though town, conveniently linking Hua Lamphong Rail station with the Chatuchak market and bus terminal area, with connections to the BTS skytrain at Silom Road and on Sukhumvit at Asok. At the time of this writing, a flat fee of 10B (25¢) got you unlimited access.

**BY PUBLIC RIVERBOATS** Efficient and scenic, the public riverboats on the Chao Phraya are a great way to get around the sites in the city center and are a remarkable window on local life.

The **Chao Phraya Express Company** (② 02222-5330) boats trace the river's length, with stops at many piers (*tha* in Thai) on both the Thonburi side (west) and in central Bangkok (east). Good maps are posted at each stop. Most sight-seers will board near Saphan Taksin BTS station, the last stop on the Silom Line as it meets the river. The major stops going into town from Saphan Taksin are: Tha Ratchawong (in Chinatown off Ratchawong Rd.), Tha Thien (near Wat Po), Tha Chang (near the Temple of the Emerald Buddha), and Tha Maharaj (near Wat Mahathat). There is a range of boats.

**Tourist Express Boats** are the fastest and most convenient, with guides talking over a microphone about the sites you'll pass at riverside. Short trips start at 15B (40¢), and an all-day pass, good for all riverboats, is 75B ($1.90).

**Express boats** are long, white boats with pointed bow, bench seats, and open sides. Mention your destination when you board, and the attendant will tell you if it's the right boat (avoid the long-haul boats with colored flags on top). Trips start at just 6B up to 15B (15¢–40¢).

**Cross-river ferries** are another category and are useful for getting to places like Wat Arun or other sites in Thonburi.

**Private boats** are also for hire for tours. See "Exploring Bangkok," later in this section.

**BY PUBLIC BUS** Bangkok buses are cheap and frequent, if a little bit confusing (and ticket takers not always so helpful). Air-conditioned buses cost from 6B to 20B (15¢–50¢) and save you from inhaling lots of pollution. Buy a map, bring small change, and be careful of pickpockets.

**BY TAXI** Taxis are everywhere. It is 35B (90¢) for the flag-fall and the first 3km (2 miles); thereafter it's about 5B (15¢) per kilometer. It is a good idea to have your hotel concierge or a Thai friend write out any destination in Thai. Avoid drivers who want to barter a flat fare. Tipping is appreciated.

**BY CAR & DRIVER** You'd have to be a bit mad to drive yourself around Bangkok, what with the crazy traffic, left-side drive (if you're not used to it), and aggressive tactics of cabs and trucks. It is best to hire a car with a driver. Contact **Diethelm Travel** (② 02255-9150; www.diethelm-travel.com), a leader in the region. **Avis** (2/12 Wireless Rd.; ② 02255-5300) and **Budget** (Don Muang Railway St., near the airport; ② 02566-5067) also offer chauffeured cars at rates from 3,000B ($75) per day for a car with a driver.

**BY TUK-TUK** As much a national symbol as the elephant, the tuk-tuk, a small, three-wheeled, open-sided vehicle powered by a motorcycle engine, is noisy (named for the put-put sound it makes), smoky, and good fun. Drivers whip around city traffic like kamikazes. They are not good for long hauls or during rush hour, but for short trips or off-peak hours they're convenient and a real kick, especially for first-time visitors to Thailand.

All tuk-tuk fares are negotiated, usually beginning at 40B ($1) for short trips. Bargain hard, but remember you'll always end up paying more than locals.

*Warning:* Tuk-tuk drivers are notorious for talking travelers into shopping trips (and collecting commissions). Drivers will offer a very low fare (even just 10B/25¢) but will waste your time by stranding you at small, out-of-the-way gem and silk emporiums, all places that scam you and where the driver gets a cut. Insist on being taken where you want to go directly: Say, "No shopping!"

**BY MOTORCYCLE TAXI**   On every street corner, packs of drivers in colored vests play checkers, motorcycles standing by, waiting to shuttle passengers around the city. They are fast and can weave through traffic, but it is not so safe. Motorbike taxis are popular for short hops to the end of longer *sois,* or side streets, and cost from 10B (25¢) for short trips. Keep your knees tucked in.

**ON FOOT**   It is safe to walk around any part of town, but Bangkok is so spread out and the pollution so heavy that you'll want to stick to small areas.

## *FAST FACTS:* Bangkok

*American Express*   There is an office with limited services at 388 Pahonyothin Rd. (✆ 02273-5544).

*Banks*   Many international banks maintain offices in Bangkok, including **Bank of America,** next door to the Hilton at 2/2 Wireless Rd. (✆ 02251-6333); **Chase Manhattan Bank,** Bubhajit Building, Sathorn Nua Road (✆ 02234-5992); **Citibank,** 82 Sathorn Nua Rd. (✆ 02232-2000); **National Australia Bank,** 90 Sathorn Nua Rd. (✆ 02236-6016); and **Standard Chartered Bank,** Abdulrahim Place, 990 Rama IV Rd. (✆ 02636-1000). However, even if your bank has a branch in Thailand, your home account is considered foreign here—conducting personal banking will require special arrangements before leaving home.

*Bookstores*   **Asia Books** carries a wide selection of regional works at its main branch at 221 Sukhumvit Rd. between Soi 15 and 17 (✆ 02252-7277) and its many outlets in town and throughout the country.

**Bookazine** has a good selection at stores in Patpong on the first floor at CP Tower, 313 Silom Rd. (✆ 02231-0016); in Ploenchit on the third floor at Amarin Plaza, 494–502 Ploenchit Rd. (✆ 02256-9304); and at 286 Siam Square opposite Siam Center (✆ 02619-1015).

**Books Kinokuniya** has shops in Pathumwan at Isetan Department Store, Sixth Floor, World Trade Center, Ratchadamri Road (✆ 02255-9834), and on Sukhumvit at Emporium Shopping Complex, Third Floor, 622 Sukhumvit Rd. Soi 24 (✆ 02664-8554).

*Currency Exchange*   Most banks will exchange foreign currency Monday to Friday 8:30am to 3:30pm. Exchange booths affiliated with the major banks are found in all tourist areas, open daily from as early as 7am to as late as 9pm.

*Embassies & Consulates*   Your home embassy in Thailand can help you in emergencies medical and legal, and is the place to contact if you've lost your travel documents and need them replaced. The following is a list of major foreign representatives in Bangkok: **Embassy of the United States of America,** 120–22 Wireless Rd. (✆ 02205-4000); **Canada Embassy,** 15th floor, Abdulrahim Place, 990 Rama IV Rd. (© **02636-0540**); **Australian Embassy,** 37 S. Sathorn Rd. (© **02287-2680**); **New Zealand Embassy,** 93 Wireless Rd. (© **02254-2530**); and the **British Embassy,** 1031 Wireless Rd. (© **02253-0191**).

*Emergencies*   In any emergency, first call **Bangkok's Tourist Police,** which is a direct-dial four-digit number (© **1155**) or call 02678-6800. Someone at both numbers will speak English. **Ambulance service** is handled by private hospitals; see "Hospitals," below, or call your hotel's front desk. For operator-assisted **overseas calls,** dial © **100.**

*Hospitals*   The best facility going is luxurious **Bumrungrad Hospital,** 33 Soi 3, Sukhumvit Rd. (© **02667-1000**). **BNH Hospital** (the Bangkok Nursing Home) is at 9 Convent Rd., between Silom and Sathorn roads, south of Rama IV Road (© **02632-0052**). Bring your passport and be ready to put up a deposit as high as 20,000B ($500) before admittance. Bills must be settled before checking out.

*Hot Lines*   There are regular meetings of **Alcoholics Anonymous (AA)** in Bangkok and around Thailand. Check the regional website at www.aathailand.org or call the AA hot line at © **02231-8300.**

*Internet*   Most shopping malls and even the smallest hotel these days have at least a few terminals, and you can't take a step in places like Khao San Road, the backpacker area, or along busy Silom Road near Patpong without hearing the screech of a modem (still lots of dial-up). Prices range from 1B to 3B per minute (that's about $1.80–$4.80 per hr.). Big hotels charge exorbitant rates and are not worth it. Here are just two in the city central: **BKK Express** (1/18 Sukhumvit Soi 11) and **Time Internet Café** (Time Square Sukhumvit Soi 12 at Asok BTS).

*Lost Property*   If you have lost anything or had your valuables stolen, call the national police hot line at © **1155.** Believe it or not, there have been several reports of lost items being returned to the appropriate consulate by taxi drivers or bus attendants.

*Luggage Storage*   Both the domestic and international terminals of **Don Muang airport** offer luggage storage for 90B ($2.25) a day—7am to 10pm in the domestic terminal, 24 hours a day in the international terminal. Most hotels will allow you to store luggage while away on trips in the countryside.

*Mail*   See "Fast Facts: Thailand," earlier in this chapter, for rates. If shipping a parcel from Bangkok, take advantage of the packing service offered by the **GPO (Post and Telegraph Office),** Charoen Krung Road (© **02233-1050**), open 24 hours. Small cardboard packing cartons cost from just 10B (25¢) and packing service is available during normal office hours.

*Newspapers & Magazines* Bangkok Post and The Nation, English-language dailies, both cover local, national, and international news, plus happenings around town, TV listings, and other useful information (20B/50¢). Metro Magazine (100B/$2.50), found at most bookstores, is a good source of current information about what's happening in Bangkok, especially the entertainment and social scene. Falang spins tales of backpacker debauch and daring-do and, like Metro, has a listing section in the back with advice for travel in Thailand (100B/$2.50). Where, Look East, and *Thailand Magazine* are slick monthly English-language magazines distributed free and emphasizing events and features about Bangkok, with lesser coverage of other Thai cities and provinces.

*Pharmacies*  Bangkok has a great many pharmacies, though the drugs dispensed differ widely in quality and generic knockoffs are common. Bring any prescription medications you require and go to a hospital for refills.

*Police*  Call the **Tourist Police** at ℂ **1155** or 02678-6800 open 24 hours, for assistance. English is spoken.

*Post Office*  The **General Post Office (GPO) Post and Telegraph Office,** Charoen Krung Road (ℂ **02233-1050**), is open 24 hours. Telegraph and telephone service are available in the north end of the building. Ask at your hotel for branch offices located closer to you.

*Radio & TV*  In Bangkok, 88FM is hip "Radio No Problem," while 102.5 is pop music spun by Western DJs. Every day at 8am and 6pm, every radio station plays the national anthem and, in public places, Thais stand at attention (though the practice is dwindling).

Most hotels link to the **UBC (United Broadcasting Company)** satellite system, which hosts CNN, CNBC, Star Movies/Sports, HBO, and MTV.

*Safety*  Bangkok is a safe city, but be careful of pickpockets as you might anywhere. Don't seek out trouble—avoid public disagreements or hostility (especially with locals), and steer clear of gambling activities. It is safe, even alone at night in most parts of the city, but rely on your gut instincts—if you get a bad feeling about a place or situation, remove yourself from the scene to avoid getting caught in someone else's drama.

*Telephone, Telegrams & Telex*  Beware of hotel surcharges on international calls, usually 25% to 40% (check with the hotel operator).

Yellow, blue, or gray phones can be found in front of most convenience stores and in public places and accept prepaid cards or coins. For information within the Bangkok metropolitan area, dial ℂ **1133**. See "Fast Facts: Thailand," earlier in this chapter, for additional information.

## WHERE TO STAY

Bangkok supports a rich variety of rooms in all price categories, and luxury at a fraction of what you would pay elsewhere. Many hotels quote room rates in U.S. dollars. Rates listed are rack rate, so be sure and search for discounts. Prices do not include additional 7% service charge and the 7% value-added tax (VAT).

### ALONG THE RIVER
**Very Expensive**
**The Oriental** ✸✸  A high-ranking member in the pantheon of the world's finest hotels, The Oriental makes for perhaps the most memorable stay in Bangkok. Its history dates from the 1860s when the original hotel, no longer standing, was established by two Danish sea captains soon after King Mongkut (Rama IV) reopened Siam to world trade. The hotel has withstood occupation by Japanese and American troops and played host to a long roster of Thai and international dignitaries and celebrities, including adventurous authors Joseph Conrad, Somerset Maugham, Noël Coward, Graham Greene, John Le Carré, and James Michener. Rooms in the older wing, built in 1876, pack the most

# Where to Stay & Dine in Bangkok

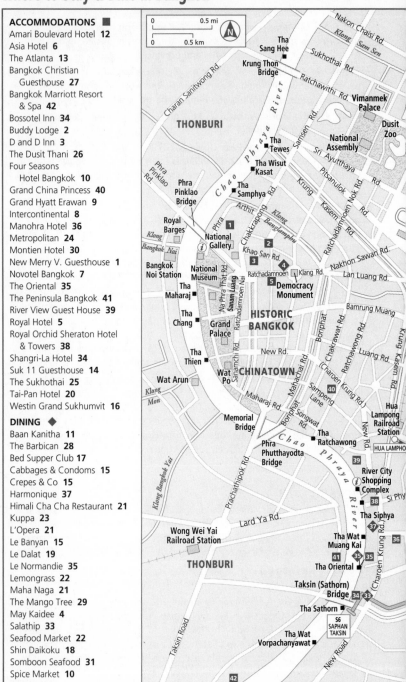

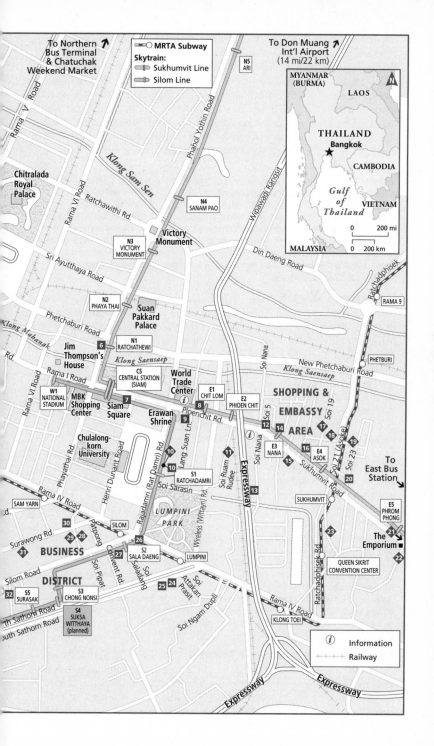

To Northern Bus Terminal & Chatuchak Weekend Market

**MRTA Subway**

**Skytrain:**
Sukhumvit Line
Silom Line

To Don Muang Int'l Airport (14 mi/22 km)

MYANMAR (BURMA)

LAOS

THAILAND
Bangkok ★

CAMBODIA

Gulf of Thailand

VIETNAM

MALAYSIA

| 0 | 200 mi |
| 0 | 200 km |

N5 ARI

N4 SANAM PAO

Chitralada Royal Palace

Rama V Road

Klong Sam Sen

Ratchawithi Rd.

Rama VI Road

Phahol Yothin Road

Wipawadi Rangsit

N3 VICTORY MONUMENT

Victory Monument

Sri Ayutthaya Road

Din Daeng Road

Ratchadphisek

RAMA 9

Klong Mahanak

Phetchaburi Road

N2 PHAYA THAI

Suan Pakkard Palace

Rd.

Jim Thompson's House

6 N1 RATCHATHEWI

Klong Saensaep

New Phetchaburi Road

Klong Saensaep

Soi Nana

PHETBURI

Rama I Road

CS CENTRAL STATION (SIAM)

World Trade Center

E1 CHIT LOM

SHOPPING & EMBASSY AREA

Soi 19

W1 NATIONAL STADIUM

Rama VI Road

MBK Shopping Center

7 Siam Square

Erawan Shrine

8

9

Ploenchit Rd.

E2 PHLOEN CHIT

Soi Nana

12

14

17

18

19

Soi 21 (Asoke)

Soi 23

Chulalongkorn University

Phayathai Rd.

Henri Dunant Road

10

Lang Suan Ln.

11

E3 NANA

16

E4 ASOK

15

Sukhumvit Road

20

To East Bus Station

10

Rajadamri (Rat Damri) Rd.

S1 RATCHADAMRI

Soi Sarasin

Soi Ruam Rudee

Expressway

E5 PHROM PHONG

SAM YARN

Rama IV Road

LUMPINI PARK

Patpong

Wireless (Wittayu) Rd.

13

SUKHUMVIT

23

The Emporium

21

30

SILOM

22

29 28

26

S2 SALA DAENG

LUMPINI

QUEEN SIKRIT CONVENTION CENTER

Ratchadphisek Rd.

31

Surawong Rd.

BUSINESS

27

Oriental Rd.

Soi Saladang

Silom Road

DISTRICT

32 S5 SURASAK

S3 CHONG NONSI

25 24

Soi Atakan Prasit

Rama IV Road

th Sathorn Road

S4 SUKSA WITTHAYA (planned)

Soi Ngam Dupli

KLONG TOEI

uth Sathorn Road

Expressway

Expressway

ℹ️ Information

+++++ Railway

colonial richness and charm but are smaller. Rooms in the newer buildings (ca. 1958 and 1976) are certainly more spacious, some with better views of the river, but they sacrifice some of that Oriental hotel romance. It's the level and range of service, however, that distinguishes the Oriental from the other riverfront hotels, and everyone from honeymooners and corporate execs to the well-heeled tourist is treated like a diplomat. Even if you don't stay, stop by for high tea in the oldest building, now called the Author's Wing and housing luxury suites. The area was recently renovated and is one of the best-preserved pieces of old Bangkok. A small buffet and tea service costs 942B ($24) and is as atmospheric as it gets in old Siam.

48 Oriental Ave., Bangkok 10500 (on the riverfront off Charoen Krung Rd./New Rd.). ℂ **800/526-6566** or 02236-0400. Fax 02236-1937. www.mandarin-oriental.com. 396 units. 12,300B–13,940B ($308–$349) double; from 18,000B ($450) suite. AE, DC, MC, V. 5-min. walk to Saphan Taksin BTS station. **Amenities:** 4 restaurants; lounge w/world-class live jazz performances; 2 outdoor pools; 2 lighted outdoor tennis courts; state-of-the-art fitness center; luxurious spa w/sauna, steam, massage, and traditional Thai beauty treatments; concierge; tour desk; car-rental desk; limo service; helicopter transfer service; tour boats for river excursions; business center; upmarket shopping arcade; salon; 24-hr. room service; babysitting; same-day laundry service/dry cleaning; nonsmoking rooms; executive-level rooms; cooking school. *In room:* A/C, satellite TV, minibar, fridge, hair dryer, safe.

**The Peninsula Bangkok** 🎡🎡🎡  Whether you land on the helicopter pad and promenade into the exclusive top-floor lounge, roll in from the airport in one of the hotel's Rolls-Royce limousines, or step lightly off the wood-decked, custom barges that ply the Chao Praya, you'll feel like you've "arrived" however you get to the Peninsula, one of Bangkok's most deluxe accommodations. Any possible amenity is available here, from elegant dining to great activities and top-of-the-line business services. Some of the largest in town, all rooms have river views and are done in a refined Thai and Western theme, a good marriage of Thai tradition and high-tech luxury with wooden paneling, silk wallpaper, and attractive carpets. The technical features of each room may make you may feel like you've walked into a James Bond film as each room is digitized in ways that only Agent Q could've conceived of; each bedside features a panel control that operates everything: the three phones, voice mail, climate control, TV, or even the mechanized room curtains. The large marble bathrooms have separate vanity counters and a large tub with a hands-free telephone and TV monitor built-in. "Ask and it will be done" seems the rule about service, and the multilingual staff is friendly and very accommodating.

333 Charoennakorn Rd., Klongsan, Bangkok 10600 (just across the Chao Praya River from Saphan Taksin station). ℂ **800/262-9467** in the U.S.; 02861-2888 in Bangkok. www.peninsula.com. 370 units. 12,300B–18,860B ($308–$472) deluxe; 40,180B–106,600B ($1,005–$2,665) suite. AE, DC, MC, V. **Amenities:** 3 restaurants; 2 bars; 60m (197-ft.) 3-tiered pool; tennis court; state-of-the-art fitness center; full spa service w/sauna, steam, massage, and aromatherapy; concierge; tour desk; car rental; fleet of Rolls-Royce limos; rooftop helicopter pad; tour boats and complimentary ferry service; business center; fine shopping; extensive salon; 24-hr. room service; babysitting; laundry service; dry cleaning; executive check-in. *In room:* A/C, satellite TV, minibar, hair dryer, safe, CD player.

### Expensive
**Royal Orchid Sheraton Hotel & Towers** 🎡  The Royal Orchid has the best view of the magnificent Chao Phraya of all the major riverfront inns, and it's an excellent base for shopping or sightseeing. The rooms are spacious, pastel hued, and trimmed with warm teakwood, lending a refined and distinctly Thai ambience. The Sheraton Towers, a hotel within a hotel on the 26th through 28th floors (with its own check-in desk and express elevator), offers more ornate decor and a higher level of service for a premium; Sheraton Tower suites, for

example, have personal fax machines in the sitting room, and all rooms are staffed by 24-hour butlers. Recent renovations added the luxurious Mandara spa and state-of-the-art fitness center. The large pool area makes it easy to forget the big, crowded city. Try the hotel's many fine dining options like "Etc. . . . " The hotel is a good home base for exploring the riverfront, and it has a walkway leading to the popular River City Shopping Complex next door.

2 Captain Bush Lane, Siphya Rd., Bangkok 10500 (next to River City Mall). ⓒ 800/325-3535 or 02266-0123. Fax 02236-8320. www.royalorchidsheraton.com. 740 units. 8,600B–11,300B ($215–$283) double; from 13,000B ($325) suite. AE, DC, MC, V. 15-min. walk to Saphan Taksin BTS station. **Amenities:** 4 restaurants; lounge; 2 outdoor pools open 24 hr.; outdoor lighted tennis court; brand-new 24-hr. fitness center w/sauna; new and luxurious spa w/private plunge pools, steam, massage, and beauty treatments; concierge; tour desk; car-rental desk; limo service; 24-hr. business center; small shopping arcade; 24-hr. room service; babysitting; same-day laundry service/dry cleaning; executive-level rooms. *In room:* A/C, satellite TV w/pay movies, minibar, fridge, hair dryer, safe, IDD phone.

**Shangri-La Hotel** ⭐⭐    The modern, opulent Shangri-La, on the banks of the Chao Phraya, boasts acres of polished marble, a jungle of tropical plants and flowers, and two towers with breathtaking views of the river. The higher-priced guest rooms have a view of the river, but all rooms are decorated with lush carpeting and teak furniture and have marble bathrooms. The views are terrific from the higher-floor deluxe rooms, and most have either a balcony or a small sitting room, making them closer to junior suites and a particularly good value for on-the-river upscale accommodations. For such an enormous place, the level of service and facilities is surprisingly good. The luxurious Krung Thep Wing adds another 17-story, riverview tower to the grounds, as well as a riverside swimming pool, restaurant, and breakfast lounge. Guests register in their spacious rooms, surrounded by colorful Thai paintings and glistening Thai silk.

89 Soi Wat Suan Plu, Charoen Krung Rd. (New Rd.), Bangkok 10500 (adjacent to Sathorn Bridge, w/access off Chaoren Krung Rd. at south end of Silom Rd.). ⓒ 800/942-5050 or 02236-7777. Fax 02236-8579. www.shangri-la.com. 850 units. 8,600B–12,300B ($215–$308) double; from 13,500B ($338) suite. AE, DC, MC, V. Next to Saphan Taksin BTS station. **Amenities:** 6 restaurants; lounge and bar; 2 outdoor pools w/outdoor Jacuzzi; 2 outdoor lighted tennis courts; 2 squash courts; fitness center w/Jacuzzi, sauna, steam, massage, and aerobics classes; concierge; tour desk; car-rental desk; limo service; helicopter transfer; city shuttle service; business center; small shopping arcade; salon; 24-hr. room service; same-day laundry service/dry cleaning; nonsmoking rooms; executive-level rooms; dinner cruise. *In room:* A/C, satellite TV, dataport, minibar, fridge, coffee/tea-making facilities, hair dryer, safe.

## Moderate

**Bangkok Marriott Resort & Spa** ⭐⭐ (Kids)    Formerly the Royal Garden Riverside Hotel, the name *resort* better describes this luxuriously sprawling complex. On the banks of the Chao Phraya across the river and a few miles downstream from the heart of Bangkok, the resort is best reached via longtail boat. It's a short trip down river, as you feel the crazy city release you from its grip. Once at the resort, the big city seems a distant memory. The three wings of the hotel surround a large landscaped pool area with lily ponds and fountains, and there is a wonderful spa for a very uniquely calming Bangkok experience. Boats go to and from the River City shopping mall every half-hour until evening. Choose the Bangkok Marriott if you want to explore Bangkok and at the same time escape.

257/1–3 Charoen Nakhorn Rd., at the Krungthep Bridge, Bangkok 10600 (on the Thonburi/east side of the Chao Phraya River, 15 min. by boat from River City). ⓒ 800/228-9290 or 02476-0022. Fax 02476-1120. www.marriotthotels.com. 413 units. 4,100B–6,000B ($103–$150) double; from 7,200B ($180) suite. AE, DC, MC, V. **Amenities:** 5 restaurants; bar and lounge; large, landscaped pool w/Jacuzzi; 2 outdoor lighted tennis courts; fitness center w/sauna; new spa w/massage and beauty treatments; children's recreation programs; concierge; tour desk; limo service; business center; adjoining shopping arcade; salon; 24-hr. room service;

babysitting; same-day laundry service/dry cleaning; nonsmoking rooms; dinner cruise. *In room:* A/C, satellite TV, dataport, minibar, fridge, safe, IDD phone.

## CHINATOWN

It's a trip to the past in the small streets and alleyways of busy Chinatown, really one of Bangkok's more out-of-the way destinations and a unique choice.

## Moderate

**Grand China Princess** Luxurious yet affordable, close to many attractions, and only a 5-minute walk from Ratchawong pier and the Chao Phraya ferry system, standing amid the bustling shophouses and businesses of colorful Chinatown, the Grand China Princess begins 10 stories above a shopping arcade and Chinese restaurant. Recent cosmetic improvements in guest rooms provide all of the contemporary necessities, amenities usually found in more expensive hotels, without sparing Oriental touches and character. Suites are especially large and done in muted tones of rose and gray. The 25th floor features Bangkok's first revolving lounge, with spectacular views over the city and Chao Phraya River.

215 Yaowarat Rd., Samphantawong, Bangkok 10100 (corner of Ratchawong Rd., just south of Charoen Krung/New Rd.). ✆ 02224-9977. Fax 02224-7999. www.grandchina.com. 155 units. 3,200B–3,500B ($80–$88) double; from 7,000B ($175) suite. AE, MC, V. **Amenities:** 3 restaurants; rooftop revolving lounge; small rooftop pool; active fitness center w/Jacuzzi, sauna, massage, and aerobics classes; concierge; tour desk; limo service; business center; 24-hr. room service; same-day laundry service/dry cleaning. *In room:* A/C, satellite TV, minibar, fridge, coffee/tea-making facilities, safe, IDD phone.

**Royal Princess** This first-class hotel near the Grand Palace in the Ratanakosin Island area is another of the many fine Dusit Thani Hotels and is great for travelers interested in the sights of old Bangkok. Public spaces are wall-to-wall marble and bustle with activity, yet the scale is intimate. Guest rooms are very tastefully furnished and bright. While higher-priced deluxe rooms have balconies overlooking the tropically landscaped pool, the superior rooms of the same style look out over the neighborhood. It's a 10-minute taxi ride to either the Grand Palace or Vimanmek Palace, and though the area lacks a diversity of dining, the authentic flavor of this old neighborhood more than compensates.

269 Larn Luang Rd., Pomprab, Bangkok 10100 (east of Wat Saket). ✆ 02281-3088. Fax 02280-1314. www.royalprincess.com. 170 units. 3,600B–3,900B ($90–$98) double; from 7,500B ($188) suite. AE, DC, MC, V. **Amenities:** 4 restaurants; lounge; small landscaped pool; fitness center w/massage; tour desk; shuttle bus service; business center; 24-hr. room service; babysitting; same-day laundry service/dry cleaning. *In room:* A/C, satellite TV, minibar, fridge, hair dryer, safe, IDD phone.

## Inexpensive

**River View Guest House** This special little place is deep in the heart of Chinatown, only 5 minutes from the railroad station, and a stone's throw from the river. It is not particularly comfortable, but the atmosphere of the busy neighborhood and nearby Chinese temples and shops (and, of course, the river views) attract visitors in search of an immersion experience. Part of the appeal is that to get here you'll have to wander through the neighboring *sois*, lanes, and labyrinthine alleys. Rooms are nothing special, just guesthouse basic, but some have great views and dining at the rooftop restaurant is an experience in itself. *Note:* Be sure to grab a business card at the front desk so you can find your way home once you've checked in (dropping breadcrumbs won't quite do it).

768 Soi Panurangsri, Songwat Rd., Sanjao Tosuekong, Taladnoi, Bangkok 10100 (500m/1,640 ft. southeast of railroad station, between the intersection of Songwat and Chaoren Krung roads and the river). ✆ 02234-5429. Fax 02237-5428. 45 units. 450B ($11) double w/fan; from 690B ($17) double w/A/C. MC, V. **Amenities:** Rooftop restaurant; laundry service. *In room:* Some w/A/C, TV, fridge.

## BANGLAMPHU & KHAO SAN ROAD

Most of the major tourist sights are located here, making sightseeing on foot more feasible, though it's quite a long ride from commercial Bangkok. For budget travelers, the widest range of low-price accommodations is found in this area around Khao San Road.

### Moderate & Inexpensive

**Buddy Lodge**    This is the newest in what is a likely trend of more upscale, air-conditioned accommodations in the Khao San area. Moderate-sized rooms are tidy but indistinct. Spillover from crazy Khao San just out front can get pretty raucous in the echoing hallways, but you're close to lots of convenient services.

265 Khao San Rd., Bangkok 10200 (on the eastern end of the Khao San strip). © **02629-4477**. Fax 02629-4744. www.buddylodge.com. 75 units. 1,500B–1,800B ($38–$45) double. MC, V. **Amenities:** Restaurant; bar; outdoor pool; tour desk; large adjoining shopping arcade (and busy Khao San out front); laundry service. *In room:* A/C, satellite TV, minibar, fridge, safe, IDD phone.

**D and D Inn**    A long-time "high-end" favorite for Khao San, D and D has nothing to do with dungeons or dragons, but lots to do with affordable, clean, basic rooms with air-conditioning. The place is often full, and service is characterized by a calm and calculated "Next!" because the rooms are in demand.

68–70 Khao San Rd., Phranakorn, Bangkok 10200 (right in the middle of Khao San). © **02629-5252**. Fax 02629-0529. 150 units. 600B ($15) double. No credit cards. **Amenities:** Restaurants and shopping in adjoining atrium and on the road out front; laundry service. *In room:* A/C, TV, fridge.

**Royal Hotel** ⭐    Near Thammasat University along the big, busy boulevard of Ratchadamnoen, the cozy Royal Hotel is just a 5-minute walk from the Royal Palace. It's good for the budget-minded sightseers who don't want to stay on crazy Khao San, but short of being near some of the major sites, the Royal isn't particularly convenient for getting around Bangkok. The glitzy lobby, with polished marble floors, chandeliers, and massive modern white Corinthian columns, was built in the 1950s and is a fun architectural pastiche from the Art Deco era. The hotel gained fame as the major field hospital during the May 1991 democracy demonstrations. Clean, kitschy rooms have lots of overly florid filigree and pink, ruffled dusters, but are spacious and have high ceilings. With a small pool and all the basic amenities, you're just a short walk from the useful tour services on Khao San, but it's quiet and a bit more grown-up.

Ratchadamnoen Ave., Bangkok 10200 (2 blocks east of National Museum). © **02222-9111**. Fax 02224-2083. 300 units. 1,300B ($33) double; from 4,000B ($100) suite. AE, MC, V. **Amenities:** 2 restaurants; lobby bar; outdoor pool; tour desk; car-rental desk; courtesy car or limo; salon; 24-hr. room service; same-day laundry service/dry cleaning. *In room:* A/C, satellite TV w/in-house video programs, minibar.

## THE BUSINESS DISTRICT

Don't be put off by the "Business District" name, which is merely to distinguish this area from the others. This part of town is connected by skytrain and subway and hosts Silom Road, the center of Bangkok nightlife.

### Very Expensive

**Metropolitan**    Just opening at the time of this writing and located on the site of the old YMCA, the Metropolitan is fashioned after the famed property in London and is Bangkok's newest house of style, a haven for pop stars and wannabes. The chic, modular lobby and crisply dressed staff could easily be mistaken for the velvet rope crowd at an upscale urban club. Rooms are elegantly angular but not minimalist (minimalism is "out," of course); there are lots of warm touches like earth-toned fabrics and overstuffed pillows to offset the crisp, contemporary lines. Bathrooms are large with big sunken tubs. This is a stylish little getaway with some cool new fine dining choices—one to watch.

27 S. Sathorn Rd., Tungmahamek, Sathorn, Bangkok 10120 (a short cab ride from Sala Daeng BTS station, soon just a short walk to the Lumpini subway stop). (*) 02625-3333. Fax 02625-3300. www.metropolitan. como.bz. 171 units. 9,850B–10,600B ($246–$265) double; from 12,300B ($308) suite. AE, MC, V. **Amenities:** 2 restaurants; bar; outdoor pool; great fitness center; spa w/massage, Jacuzzi, sauna, and steam; airport transfer; business center w/Internet; shopping arcade; 24-hr. room service; same-day laundry/dry cleaning. *In room:* A/C, satellite TV w/DVD and CD, minibar, fridge, safe, IDD phone.

**The Sukhothai** 🜲🜲🜲   Find a welcome, if studied, serenity in this hotel's maze of low pavilions, contemporary lines, and earthy textures and tones. Broad, colonnaded public spaces surround peaceful lotus pools. Symmetry and simplicity form the backdrop for brick *chedis* (stupas or mounds), terra-cotta friezes, and celadon ceramics evoking the ancient kingdom of Sukhothai. Large guest rooms are done in fine Thai silk, mellow teak, and celadon tile. Gigantic luxurious bathrooms feature oversize bathtubs, separate shower and toilet stalls, and two full-size wardrobes. The Sukhothai is second to none in service and privacy. Keep an eye out for the adjoining spa complex under construction.

13/3 S. Sathorn Rd., Bangkok 10120 (south of Lumphini Park, near intersection of Rama IV and Wireless roads, next to the YWCA). (*) 02287-0222. Fax 02287-4980. www.sukhothai.com. 220 units. 11,500B ($288) double; from 14,350B ($359) suite. AE, DC, MC, V. **Amenities:** 4 restaurants; bar and lobby lounge; 25m (82-ft.) outdoor pool; outdoor lighted tennis court; air-conditioned racquetball court; state-of-the-art fitness center w/Jacuzzi, sauna, steam, massage, and aerobics classes; concierge; limo service; 24-hr. business center w/cutting edge technology; salon; 24-hr. room service; babysitting; executive-level rooms. *In room:* A/C, satellite TV and in-house video, fax, dataport w/direct Internet access, hair dryer, safe, IDD phone.

## Expensive

**The Dusit Thani** 🜲 *Overrated*   "The Dusit" was once Bangkok's grandest address, but Bangkok has built up around the old girl though and now the Dusit lies in the shadow of the skytrain and a hulking highway flyover, but the location is still one of the best, just at the edge of the busiest part of Silom road and a short walk from both the skytrain, subway, and Lumpini Park. The lobby has splashing fountains and the large outdoor pool is surrounded by thick foliage and a great escape after a day of sightseeing. Rooms are a bit worn. Dining at Benjarong is a unique experience

Rama IV Rd., Bangkok 10500 (near Sala Daeng BTS station on the corner of Silom and Rama IV roads opposite Lumpini Park). (*) 02236-0450. Fax 02236-6400. www.dusit.com. 532 units. 7,800B ($195) double; from 10,660B ($267) suite. AE, DC, MC, V. **Amenities:** 8 restaurants; lounge; bar; library w/high tea service; small landscaped pool; driving range and chipping green; fitness center; spa w/massage, sauna, steam, and cafe; concierge; limo service; business center; shopping arcade; salon; 24-hr. room service; babysitting; same-day laundry service/dry cleaning; executive-level rooms. *In room:* A/C, satellite TV w/VCR, minibar, fridge, hair dryer, safe, IDD phone.

**Montien Hotel** 🜲   The Montien is a slick and comfortable business hotel in the very heart of Silom, right at the terminus of the two busy Patpong *sois*. Set up in two large wings, each with dark teak hallways and bright, pleasant rooms, the Montien has seen some good upgrades in recent years and offers lots of services and upmarket amenities at a cost that puts you in a dull cell in other parts of the world. Unique here, too, are the resident psychics at the mezzanine level's Astrologer's Terrace, open daily from 10:30am to 7pm. A glimpse at your future is just 500B ($13).

54 Surawong Rd., Bangkok 10500 (near Patpong). (*) 02233-7060. Fax 02236-5218. www.montien.com. 475 units. 5,500B–7,600B ($138–$190) double; from 9,000B ($225) suite. AE, DC, MC, V. 10-min. walk to Sala Daeng BTS station. **Amenities:** 3 restaurants; bar; lounge and karaoke; outdoor pool; fitness center w/sauna;

tour desk; limo service; business center; 24-hr. room service; babysitting; same-day laundry service/dry cleaning; executive-level rooms. *In room:* A/C, satellite TV, minibar, fridge, hair dryer, safe, IDD phone.

## Moderate

**Manohra Hotel**    This bright old standby, a 5-minute walk from the river and the famed Oriental, has a glitzy glass-and-stone lobby that faces a small indoor swimming pool. Guest rooms are compact and rather dimly lit but the hotel has a full range of amenities. It's often booked out by European tours.

412 Surawong Rd., Bangkok 10500 (between Charoen Krung/New and Mahesak roads). ℰ **02234-5070.** Fax 02237-7662. 250 units. 2,400B–2,600B ($60–$65) double. AE, DC, MC, V. **Amenities:** Restaurant; lounge; pool; small fitness center w/massage; tour desk; business center; salon; 24-hr. room service; same-day laundry service/dry cleaning. *In room:* A/C, satellite TV, minibar, fridge.

## Inexpensive

**Bangkok Christian Guesthouse**    A wholesome yin to the debaucherous yang of the nearby red-light district, the Bangkok Christian Guesthouse is on a small *soi* just one street back from Sala Daeng BTS station and is a convenient, quiet, and comfortable choice (just a short walk from sin to salvation, or vice versa). This tranquil two-story guesthouse, originally a Presbyterian missionary residence, was converted into a lodge in the late 1960s, and is now operated by the Church of Christ in Thailand. Large, recently refurbished rooms are simple. The best rooms are on the second floor overlooking the large lawn with its sitting area, goldfish pond, and teak pavilion. There's a large, cozy lounge and library, an affordable canteen restaurant, and a friendly and helpful staff.

123 Saladaeng, Soi 2, Convent Rd., Bangkok 10500 (1 block south of Silom Rd. off the corner of Convent Rd.). ℰ **02233-6303.** Fax 02237-1742. 30 units. 1,000B–1,400B ($25–$35) double; 1,800B ($45) triple; 2,200B ($55) quad. No credit cards. 10-min. walk to Sala Daeng BTS station. **Amenities:** Restaurant; laundry service. *In room:* A/C, no phone.

## SUKHUMVIT ROAD: THE SHOPPING/EMBASSY AREA

Accessed along its entire length by the convenient skytrain, Sukhumvit Road is the heart of upscale, commercial Bangkok. Here you'll find many of the town's finest large shopping complexes, good restaurants, and thronging street life.

## Very Expensive

**The Four Seasons Bangkok** 𝄞𝄞𝄞    The Four Seasons is a modern palace. The entry is grand with a sweeping staircase, giant Thai murals, and gold sunbursts on the vaulted ceiling. The impeccable service begins at the threshold, and an air of luxury pervades any stay in this modern city resort. Rooms are some of the largest in town and have Thai murals, and plush carpeted dressing areas next to each large bath. Unique cabana rooms face the large pool and terrace area, which is filled with palms, lotus pools, and all sorts of tropical greenery. If you can ignore the new condominium blocks overlooking the area, it is a real hideaway. The Four Seasons Spa is one of the best in Bangkok, and the in-house dining is excellent. The executive upgrade for just 1,400B ($35) is more than worth it

155 Ratchadamri Rd., Bangkok 10330 (adjacent to Ratchadamri BTS station, just south of Rama I Rd.). ℰ **02251-6127.** Fax 02253-9195. www.fourseasons.com. 358 units. 11,500B–12,300B ($288–$308) double; 17,200B–20,000B ($430–$500) cabana room/suite; from 15,500B ($388) suite. AE, DC, MC, V. **Amenities:** 7 restaurants; lobby lounge serving high tea and live jazz; landscaped outdoor pool; state-of-the-art fitness center; spa w/massage, sauna, and steam; concierge; limo service; 24-hr. business center; shopping arcade (w/Jim Thompson Silk); salon; 24-hr. room service; babysitting; same-day laundry service/dry cleaning; nonsmoking rooms; executive-level rooms; meeting rooms. *In room:* A/C, satellite TV, dataport, minibar, hair dryer, safe, IDD phone.

**Grand Hyatt Erawan** ★★★  Bangkok's old grand dame, the Grand Hyatt is tops in comfort, convenience, and style. Don't miss the hotel shrine, a monument to prosperity and good luck dating from the 1956 construction of the hotel. Public spaces are grand, with giant columns, balustrade staircases, and rich indoor landscaping. The works of dozens of contemporary Thai artists grace hallways and spacious rooms, where earth-toned silks, celadon accessories, antique-finish furnishings, parquet floors, Oriental rugs, large bathrooms, and city views abound. Rooms have just been given a technological upgrade and now feature individual reading lights, Internet access, and compact control panels. In addition to the facilities one expects from a five-star hotel, there is a delightful fifth-floor pool terrace, where a waterfall tumbles down a rocky wall into a full-size hot tub. The in-house dining is some of the best in the city.

494 Ratchadamri Rd., Bangkok 10330 (corner of Rama I Rd.). © **800/233-1234** or 02254-1234. Fax 02254-6308. www.hyatt.com. 387 units. 11,500B–12,500B ($288–$313) double; from 19,700B ($493) suite. AE, DC, MC, V. 5-min. walk to Chit Lom BTS station. **Amenities:** 8 restaurants; lounge; disco; wine bar; rooftop pool and garden; outdoor grass tennis court; 2 squash courts; fitness center w/Jacuzzi, sauna, steam, and massage; spa; concierge; tour desk; limo and helicopter service; 24-hr. business center; shopping arcade; salon; 24-hr. room service; babysitting; same-day laundry service/dry cleaning; nonsmoking rooms; executive-level rooms. *In room:* A/C, satellite TV, dataport, minibar, hair dryer, safe.

**Inter-Continental** ★★  Formerly the Le Meridien, the new Inter-Continental has a great location near Chit Lom BTS Station and downtown shopping. Rooms are immaculate, done in a bland but familiar high-end business hotel style and set in a glass-and-steel tower block with unobstructed views of the city. You pay a premium here, but you get perks like wireless Internet, excellent services, and fine dining; don't miss its branch of the popular Shin Daikoku Japanese restaurant (see "Dining," below). High-end business suites are without rival, and service is ultraprofessional and attentive.

973 Ploenchit Rd., Lumphini, Pathumwan, Bangkok 10330 (adjacent to Chit Lom BTS station, near intersection of Rama I and Ratchadamri roads). © **800/225-5843** or 02656-0444. Fax 02656-0555. www.lemeridien-bangkok.com. 381 units. 9,850B–11,000B ($246–$275) double; from 11,900B ($298) suite. AE, DC, MC, V. **Amenities:** 3 restaurants; tower lounge w/live music daily; karaoke; outdoor pools; fitness centers; spa w/Jacuzzi, sauna, steam, massage, and beauty treatments; concierge; tour desk; car-rental desk; limo service; business center; shopping arcade; salon; 24-hr. room service; babysitting; same-day laundry service/dry cleaning; nonsmoking rooms; executive-level rooms. *In room:* A/C, satellite TV, minibar, fridge, coffeemaker, hair dryer, safe, IDD phone.

## Expensive

**Amari Boulevard Hotel** ★  In the heart of the busy Nana shopping area of Sukhumvit Road (near the BTS Nana station), the Boulevard is a good value. The Krung Thep Wing has spacious rooms with terrific city views, while the original has less expensive rooms, some with balcony. Also see its popular business address, the **Amari Watergate** (© **02653-9000**), nearby.

2 Soi 5, Sukhumvit Rd., Bangkok 10110 (north of Sukhumvit Rd., on Soi 5). © **02255-2930.** Fax 02255-2950. www.amari.com. 315 units. 6,800B–8,400B ($170–$210) double; from 8,800B ($220) suite. AE, DC, MC, V. 5-min. walk to Nana BTS station. **Amenities:** Restaurant; rooftop pool; fitness center; concierge; tour desk; limo service; business center; 24-hr. room service; massage; babysitting; same-day laundry service/dry cleaning. *In room:* A/C, satellite TV, minibar, fridge, safe, IDD phone.

**Novotel Bangkok** ★★  This elegant and opulent high-rise hotel in the Siam Square shopping area is one of this French chain's best. The marble and glass entrance leads to an expansive gray stone interior, complemented by soft leather-upholstered sofas and chairs. Pastel tones carry over into guest quarters, where the rooms are spacious and fully equipped. Novotel is perfect for business or shopping trips and close to the skytrain. Don't miss the popular disco.

Travel Tip: He who finds the best hotel deal has more to spend on facials involving knobbly vegetables.

Hello, the Roaming Gnome here. I've been nabbed from the garden and taken round the world. The people who took me are so terribly clever. They find the best offerings on Travelocity. For very little cha-ching. And that means I get to be pampered and exfoliated till I'm pink as a bunny's doodah.

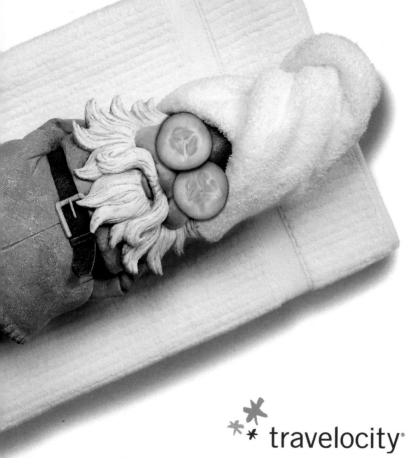

**travelocity**

1-888-TRAVELOCITY / travelocity.com / America Online Keyword: Travel

Siam Sq. Soi 6, Bangkok 10330 (in Siam Sq. off Rama I Rd.). ℂ **02255-6888**. Fax 02254-1328. 465 units. 5,100B–6,300B ($128–$158) double; from 7,200B ($180) suite. AE, DC, MC, V. Siam BTS station. **Amenities:** 4 restaurants; huge popular disco; outdoor pool; fitness center w/massage; concierge; tour desk; limo service; business center; shopping arcade; salon; 24-hr. room service; babysitting; same-day laundry service/dry cleaning; nonsmoking rooms; executive-level rooms. *In room:* A/C, satellite TV, minibar, fridge, safe, IDD phone.

## Moderate

**Asia Hotel**    With a second-floor connection directly to the skytrain (just one stop away from the central Siam station), Asia Hotel wins out over others in this category by virtue of location and affordability, but certainly not for style—the place could use a facelift, really. The Asia is near the main shopping boulevard and the skytrain access is tops. Rooms are like an American motel room, basic and clean. There are lots of in-house dining options, but the town is at your fingertips.

296 Phayathai Rd., Bangkok 10400 (between Petchaburi and Rama I roads). ℂ **02215-0808**. Fax 02215-4360. www.asiahotel.co.th. 650 units. 1,800B–3,600B ($45–$90) double; from 5,000B ($125) suite. AE, MC, V. Ratchathewi BTS station. **Amenities:** 5 restaurants; lobby lounge; 2 outdoor pools; small fitness center w/Jacuzzi, sauna, and massage; tour desk; car-rental desk; limo service; business center; 24-hr. room service; babysitting; same-day laundry service/dry cleaning. *In room:* A/C, satellite TV, minibar.

**Tai-Pan Hotel**  *Value*    This modern white tower rises above a quiet *soi* off Sukhumvit (which means the city is your oyster). The staff is attentive and helpful and the carpeted rooms have comfortable sitting areas and city views and all the facilities you'd expect from a more expensive hotel. The excellent coffee shop has bargain buffet breakfasts and lunches. This is a good value.

25 Sukhumvit Soi 23, Bangkok 10110 (1 block north of Sukhumvit Rd.). ℂ **02260-9888**. Fax 02259-7908. www.tai-pan.com. 150 units. 2,400B–2,800B ($60–$70) double; from 5,000B ($125) suite. AE, DC, MC, V. 10-min. walk to Asok BTS station. **Amenities:** Coffee shop; small pool; small fitness center; business center; 24-hr. room service; same-day laundry service/dry cleaning. *In room:* A/C, satellite TV, minibar, fridge, IDD phone.

## Inexpensive

**The Atlanta**  *Finds*    A great budget choice, the Atlanta is a real slice of history. The oldest "original" hotel in the city (without renovation), The Atlanta was built in 1952 by Dr. Max Henne, a Renaissance man and early expat (now managed by his son). For years the Atlanta was *the* foreigner visitor's address of note. If you don't believe it, have a look at the photo in the canteen of a young King Bhumibol playing saxophone along with a trumpeting Louis Armstrong and Benny Goodman on clarinet, while a grinning George H. W. Bush looks on from the background. Surreal. The lobby is original Art Deco and quite unique. Enjoy fine Thai food in the canteen (guests only) or grab a book from the small library or take in a film; a good youth hostel vibe pervades. There is a small pool out back and the hotel offers good travel service. Rooms are concrete basic and only a few suites have hot water. Service is quirky (a sign explains: NO COMPLAINTS AT THESE PRICES) but that's part of the charm. The works of journalists and photographers in residence line the walls. Management has a good "no drugs and no sex tourism" policy. The hotel is a 10-minute walk to Sukhumvit along Soi 2. It's often full so it's best to reserve by fax.

78 Soi 2, Sukhumvit Rd., Bangkok 10110 (at the very end of Soi 2, a 5-min. walk or a 10B/25¢ motorbike taxi ride). ℂ **02252-6069**. Fax 02656-8123. 49 units. 330B–450B ($8.25–$11) fan room; 500B–620B ($13–$16) A/C double. No credit cards. **Amenities:** Restaurant; small outdoor pool; small gym area; tour desk; laundry service; Internet corner; library (w/light table for photographers). *In room:* A/C, safe (bring your own lock).

**Suk 11 Guesthouse**  ⭐⭐    With convenient access to the skytrain at Nana and prices more befitting the budget spots on Khao San Road, this family-owned gem is often fully booked so call ahead (or book on the useful website). Rooms are basic: just plain linoleum floors and large beds in double rooms. Bathrooms are small, the shower-in-room variety, but clean. The rooms with shared bathrooms can be had for very little, but the single and double rooms with bathroom are the best bet. Common areas and hallways are done in a faux rustic style with wood-plank floors and are meant to look like old Thai streets. Suk 11 is a popular spot for folks studying Thai massage and a friendly camaraderie pervades.

1/13 Soi Sukhumvit 11 (behind 7-Eleven), Sukhumvit Rd., Bangkok 10110. ℂ 02253-5927. www.suk11. com. 75 units. 500B ($13) single; 600B ($15) double. No credit cards. **Amenities:** Restaurant; game room; laundry service; yoga room; Internet terminals; library. *In room:* A/C.

## THE AIRPORT AREA

Don Muang International Airport is anywhere from 30 minutes to 1 hour (or more) by car from the center of Bangkok depending on your destination and traffic. Traffic is lighter going into town in the evening, but if you have just a quick overnight or a long layover, there are a few good choices near the airport.

**Amari Airport Hotel** 🏵 This is the fanciest, the closest, and, if the budget is less of a concern, the best of all choices near the airport. An overpass connects the Amari with the international terminal (domestic is just a short shuttle ride away). The Airport Hotel has arrival and departure information monitors in the lobby and offers discount rates for "ministay" packages if you have a longer layover and want to shower and relax for a few hours. Spacious deluxe rooms have fine furnishings and are as cozy as any city business hotel.

333 Chert Wudthakas Rd., Don Muang, Bangkok 10210 (just west of international terminal, connected by an elevated footbridge). ℂ 02566-1020. Fax 02566-1941. www.amari.com. 434 units. 10,600B–11,500B ($265–$288) double; from 20,500B ($513) suite. AE, MC, V. **Amenities:** 3 restaurants; bar and lounge; outdoor pool; golf course nearby; fitness center w/sauna, massage, and spa; tour desk; limo service; business center; salon; 24-hr. room service; babysitting; same-day laundry service/dry cleaning; nonsmoking rooms. *In room:* A/C, satellite TV, minibar, fridge, safe, IDD phone.

## WHERE TO DINE

If you like your local Thai restaurant back home, you'll love the many choices in Bangkok, from simple noodle stands to sophisticated, upmarket joints. The city also offers a spectacular array of excellent European, Chinese, and other Asian cuisine that is expensive by local standards but a bargain in the West. Check local papers for any big "foodie" events, and get brave and try street food.

### ON THE RIVER
**Very Expensive**

**Le Normandie** 🏵🏵🏵 FRENCH The ultraelegant Normandie, atop the renowned Oriental hotel, with its panoramic views, is the apex in formal dining in Thailand. The room glistens in gold and silver, from place settings to chandeliers. Some of the highest-rated master chefs from France have made guest appearances at Normandie, adding their own unique touches to the menu. Choose from a limited selection of daily specials. The beef filet main course, in a red-wine sauce, is divine. The set also includes cheese, coffee, and a sinful dessert. Order any wine you can imagine from the extensive list.

The Oriental, 48 Oriental Ave. (off Charoen Krung/New Rd., overlooking the river). ℂ 02236-0400. Reservations required at least 1 day in advance. Jacket/tie required for men. Main courses 1,000B–1,600B ($25–$40); set menu w/wine selections 5,200B ($130). AE, DC, MC, V. Daily noon–2:30pm and 7–10pm; closed Sun lunch. 10-min. walk from Saphan Taksin BTS station.

**Expensive**

**Salathip** 🏵🏵 THAI Salathip, on the river terrace of the Shangri-La Hotel, is arguably Bangkok's most romantic Thai restaurant. Classical music and traditional cuisine are superbly presented under aging, carved teak pavilions perched over a lotus pond and overlooking the river (there are also air-conditioned dining rooms). Set menus introduce you to a range of courses. Here's an example: Thai spring rolls, pomelo salad with chicken, a spicy seafood soup, snapper with chili sauce, and your choice of Thai curries. There is live music nightly as well as Thai dancing and a culture show.

Shangri-La Hotel, 89 Soi Wat Suan Plu (overlooking Chao Phraya River, near Taksin Bridge). ℂ 02236-7777. Reservations recommended. Main courses 200B–450B ($5–$11). AE, DC, MC, V. Daily 6:30–10:30pm. Saphan Taksin BTS station.

## Moderate

**Harmonique** ⭐⭐ THAI    Hard to find, Harmonique is set in the courtyard of a century-old mansion and just oozes character—a great stop if touring the riverfront or visiting the antiques stores of nearby River City. Enter through the crook of a dangling banyan tree, and there is courtyard seating and an open-air dining area with Thai antiques. The cuisine is Thai tailored to Western tastes, but it's all still very good—the *tom yam* with fish is delicious, served only as spicy as you like and with enormous chunks of fish. The sizzling grilled seafood platter is nice and garlicky (chilis on the side). Harmonique also features good Western desserts like brownies, great with a cool tea on a hot day. It's an atmospheric spot to relax.

22 Chaoren Krung Rd. (New Rd.) Soi 34. ℂ 02630-6270. Main courses 70B–200B ($1.75–$5). AE, MC, V. Mon–Sat 11am–10pm. 15-min. walk from Saphan Taksin BTS station.

**Himali Cha Cha Restaurant** INDIAN    Mr. Cha Cha, the original owner and proprietor (now deceased), was on Lord Mountbatten's staff in India before he went on to cook for the diplomatic corps in Laos. This, the original restaurant, was built in 1980, and there are now three locations in greater Bangkok run by his children. House specialties include a mutton barbecue, chicken *tikka,* and chicken masala. The Indian *thali* plates (a large plate with a variety of items to sample—similar to an appetizer plate) are great, especially for lunch. The atmosphere is a bit bland, but the curries are good. Try the other locations: on Sukhumvit Soi 35 (near Phrom Pong BTS; ℂ **02258-8843**) or on Convent Road in Silom (near the Sala Daeng BTS station; ℂ **02238-1478**).

1229/11 Charoen Krung Rd. (on a side street off Charoen Krung/New Rd., corner of Surawong). ℂ 02235-1569. Main courses 58B–235B ($1.45–$5.90). AE, DC, MC, V. Daily 11am–3:30pm and 6–10:30pm. 15-min. walk from Saphan Taksin BTS station.

## BANGLAMPU—NEAR KHAO SAN ROAD

Khao San Road is Bangkok's busy backpacker ghetto and where you'll find every manner of food, from Israeli and halal cuisine to Italian as well as tasty Thai food served at street side. Have a seat somewhere along the busy road, order up a fruit shake, and watch the nightly parade of young travelers. Or try any of the following.

## Inexpensive

**May Kaidee** ⭐ *Finds* VEGETARIAN/THAI    Find this place. It's my favorite restaurant in Thailand. Don't come for atmosphere—it's more or less tables in a little alleyway—but bring your appetite for healthy and delicious Thai vegetarian dishes. Ms. May (pronounced *My*) has developed a real following, as much for her wry smile and kindness as for the great curries and soups she serves. The best *massaman* (potato and peanut) curry in Thailand and an array of dishes from sweet green curry to good stir-fries come with your choice of white or a

> **Tips** **Dining: Bangkok Street Eats**
>
> Ask any Bangkokian to take you to their favorite restaurant and you'll
> most likely be eating at street side or in a small, open-air eatery. In fact,
> the many night bazaars and hawker stalls are where you'll find the best
> eats throughout Thailand. Eating at street side will challenge your senses
> with the pungent aromas of garlic, chili, and barbecued meats, as well as
> the cacophony of music, lights, and voices. For the best open-air dining,
> try **Tong Lo,** a collection of busy stalls just adjacent to the Tong Lo BTS
> stop. **Suan Lum Night Bazaar** just next to Lumpini Park is another good
> choice.

unique short-grained brown rice. For dessert, don't pass up the black sticky rice
with mango. May has a good cookbook for sale and also offers cooking classes.

At the eastern terminus of Khao San Rd. in a small alley behind the first row of buildings (behind Burger King;
ask around—everyone knows this place). ✆ **02629-4839.** Main course 60B–120B ($1.50–$3). No credit
cards. Daily 7am–10pm.

## THE BUSINESS DISTRICT

Silom Road is where you'll find Patpong, the busy red-light district, a tourist
night market, and a host of good dining choices.

### Moderate

**The Barbican** ☆ INTERNATIONAL    A happenin' bar as much as anything,
The Barbican also serves good pasta entrees, goulash, and a tasty "Guinness pie."
Everything on the menu is good, and the atmosphere is a cool, steel-and-gran-
ite chic. The place is full at happy hour, and there are often live jazz acts.

9/4–5 Soi Thaniya, Silom Rd. (1 block east of Patpong between Silom and Surawong roads). ✆ **02234-3590.**
Reservations not necessary. Main courses from 120B ($3). AE, DC, MC, V. Daily 11:30am–2am. Sala Daeng
BTS station.

**The Mango Tree** ☆ THAI    In a lovely 80-year-old Siamese restaurant house
with its own tropical garden, Mango Tree offers a quiet retreat from the hectic
Patpong area. Live traditional music and classical Thai decorative touches fill the
house with charm, and the attentive staff serves well-prepared dishes from all
regions of the country. The mild green chicken curry and the crispy spring rolls
are both excellent—but the menu is extensive, so feel free to experiment. Only
trouble is, the food isn't exactly authentic, but it's still quite good.

37 Soi Tantawan, Bangrak (off west end of Surawong Rd., across from Tawana Ramada Hotel). ✆ **02236-
2820.** Reservations recommended. Main courses 90B–350B ($2.25–$8.75). AE, DC, MC, V. Daily
11:30am–midnight. 10-min. walk from Sala Daeng BTS station.

**Somboon Seafood** ☆☆ SEAFOOD    This one's for those who would sacrifice atmosphere for excellent food. Packed nightly, you'll still be able to find a
table (the place is huge). The staff is extremely friendly—between them and the
picture menu, you'll be able to order the best dishes and have the finest recommendations. Peruse the large aquariums outside to see all the live seafood
options like prawn, fishes, lobsters, and crabs (guaranteed freshness). The house
specialty, chili crab curry, is especially good, as is the *tom yang goong* soup (spiced
to individual taste).

169/7–11 Surawongse Rd. (just across from the Peugeot building). ✆ **02233-3104.** Reservations not necessary. Seafood at market prices (about 800B/$20 for 2). No credit cards. Daily 4–11pm.

## THE SHOPPING/EMBASSY AREA
### Expensive

**Baan Kanitha** ★★ THAI    Look no further than Baan Kanitha for authentic Thai in a comfortable, classy atmosphere. Down busy, traffic-choked Ruam Rudee, Baan Kanitha is an unexpected little oasis. You'll start off with a free tray of finger foods, the dried condiments for making your own little spicy spring rolls called mienkham, and then you'll graduate to shared dishes of curry, from spicy red to mellow yellow and green; light salads; and good seafood as you like it. The pomelo salad is a find. Follow up with good Thai desserts. Thais actually come here, a rarity for upscale Thai eateries, and the place is always packed: both good signs. Be sure to call ahead. There's another location at 36/1 Sukhumvit Soi 23 (✆ **02258-4128**).

49 Soi Ruam Rudee. ✆ **02253-4683**. Reservations highly recommended. Main courses 120B–350B ($3–$8.75). AE, MC, V. Daily 11am–2pm and 6–11pm. 5-min. walk from Ploen Chit BTS station.

**Bed Supper Club** ★★ INTERNATIONAL    This is the coolest place in Bangkok, hands down. Come for a drink in the bar, at least, and stick around for when the place busts open into a full-on club. It serves meals nightly for one sitting at 8:30pm and the best part is that, as the name suggests, you eat in long shared beds. The building is a giant cylinder and, walking up a concrete gang-plank, you enter via large airplane airlocks. One side is the bar, the other is the dining area where you'll be assigned your slot on one of the two big beds that line the walls. The two-story, glowing white-and-neon interior alone is unique. Four-course meals are ordered from a limited menu. I shared a tuna sashimi, tomato-and-basil soup, and a black cod filet artfully stacked on a bed of mashed potatoes and asparagus. Dessert is pure decadence of rich chocolate specials and cakes. Waitstaff wear tight spacesuits and angel wings, the music is funky trance stuff spun by a DJ, and the food is fantastic.

26 Sukhumvit Soi 11, Klongtoey-Nua, Bangkok 10110 (at the end of Soi 11, near the Nana BTS station). ✆ 02651-3537. www.bedsupperclub.com. Reservations required. Men should wear trousers, not shorts. Set menu: 790B ($20) weeknights; 990B ($25) weekends. AE, MC, V. Sun–Thurs 7:30pm–midnight; Fri–Sat 7:30pm–2am. Dinner is served promptly at 8:30pm (best to be early).

**Le Banyan** ★★ FRENCH    A spreading banyan tree on the edge of the gardenlike grounds inspires the name. The upscale dining area is warm in tone, furnished with sisal matting and white clapboard walls adorned with Thai carvings, old photos, and prints of early Bangkok. The house special is a dish for two: pressed duck with goose liver, shallots, wine, and Armagnac to make the sauce. Other fine choices include a rack of lamb a la Provençal and salmon with lemon grass. There are daily specials and a list of fine wines. If you come on foot, you'll run the gauntlet of all the girly bars at the entrance of the *soi,* but find this little upscale gem and enjoy an evening of fine dining and effusive service.

59 Sukhumvit Soi 8 (1 block south of Sukhumvit Rd.). ✆ 02253-5556. Reservations recommended. Main courses 350B–1,440B ($8.75–$36). AE, DC, MC, V. Mon–Sat 6–10pm. 10-min. walk from Nana BTS station.

**Maha Naga** ★★ THAI/WESTERN FUSION    Classy Maha Naga is an oasis of luxury Thai dining in the heart of the Sukhumvit area. The restaurant design features a fountain courtyard surrounded by high-peaked, lavishly decorated, and air-conditioned Thai pavilions and makes for a quiet, romantic evening or a fun night for private groups. The food is delicious, a bold marriage of Thai and Western traditions in unique dishes like pork chops with spicy Thai *som tam* (papaya salad) flavor, whole lobster done in a chili sauce, or imported New

Zealand grilled filet with Thai spice and mint. Elsewhere, fusion dishes come out rather bland, but the unique fare at Maha Naga breaks new ground.

2 Sukhumvit Soi 29, Klongteoy, Bangkok 10110 (*) **02662-3060**. Reservations recommended. Main courses 300B–800B ($7.50–$20). AE, DC, MC, V. Daily 11:30am–2:30pm and 6–11pm. A 10-min. walk south from Phrom Pong BTS station.

**Shin Daikoku** ★★ JAPANESE   With a track record of over 30 years as the home away from home for the many Japanese expatriates in Bangkok, Shin Daikoku serves delicious and authentic Japanese dishes, from hot apps and noodle dishes like *soba* and *udon,* to sushi, sashimi, and even *teppanyaki* steaks. Set in a quiet neighborhood off Sukhumvit (near the Asok skytrain stop) the restaurant is a sprawling compound of private *tatami* (mattress) rooms, and an open dining area surrounds a cavernous indoor garden and a pond full of koi (Japanese carp). Female staff wear summer kimonos and pad around politely, hovering over every detail of the meal. A la carte dishes are small and rather expensive (a la sushi the world over), but there are good set meals. Order some sake, take your shoes off, wrap your tie around your head, and say "Kampai!"

32/8 Soi Wattana, Sukhumvit 19, Klongtoey (a 5-min. walk down Soi 19 from Asok BTS station and on left after the first intersecting road, Wattana). (*) **02254-9981**. Reservations for big groups only. Main courses 100B–1,600B ($2.50–$40). AE, DC, MC, V. Daily 11:30am–2pm and 5:30–10:30pm. Asok BTS station.

## Moderate

**Kuppa** ★ INTERNATIONAL   This cafe restaurant is worth a visit if only to see the unique space, a former warehouse (reputedly a CIA hangout), now a chic, modern interior, housing the offices of owner and interior designer Robin Lourvanij, a woman who shares her time and heart between Bangkok and Australia. Come for the coffee and don't miss the hulking roaster machine, a centerpiece of the dining area where Kuppa roasts its own blend weekly. The food is delicious: a healthy sampling of unique Thai and Western fare and good stuff to fill the homesick tummies of expats and visitors. Grilled items are great, and there are lots of daily specials. Dessert is something sinful with good coffee. Kuppa is in a quiet neighborhood and has good couches for kicking back.

39 Sukhumvit Soi 16, Klongtoey, Bangkok (a long walk down Soi 16 from the Asok BTS skytrain station). (*) **02663-0495**. Main courses 165B–495B ($4.15–$12). AE, MC, V. Daily 10:30am–11:30pm.

**Lemongrass** ★★ THAI   Nouvelle Thai cuisine tailored to the Western tastes is the specialty of this pleasant restaurant. Just a short walk from the skytrain (near Phrom Pong) and just across from the hulking Emporium Shopping Center, Lemongrass is set in a small Thai mansion handsomely converted and furnished with antiques and a visit here makes it easy to forget busy Bangkok outside. Try house favorites pomelo salad or chicken satay. Also excellent is the *tom yang kung* (a spicy sweet-and-sour prawn soup with ginger shoots), and the lemon grass chicken is tender and juicy.

5/1 Sukhumvit Soi 24 (south of Sukhumvit Rd. on Soi 24). (*) **02258-8637**. Reservations highly recommended. Main courses 120B–550B ($3–$14). AE, DC, MC, V. Daily 11am–2pm and 6–11pm. Phrom Pong BTS station.

**L'Opera** ★ ITALIAN   With its sister restaurant in Vientiane, Laos, L'Opera Bangkok has been hosting visitors and expats since it first opened in the 1970s, when Soi 39 was but a dusty little alley with cows grazing out front. Now it's a sophisticated enclave and it's got the formula just right, dim lights in a glassed-in pavilion, cool jazz in the air, and good, affordable Italian. Come with friends and fill the table. We had biscotti appetizers followed by a decadent seafood

## Cricket, anyone?

Grasshoppers, beetles that look like cockroaches, scorpions, ants, and grubs are a favorite snack for folks from Isan, in the northeast, where bugs are in fact cultivated for the dining table and are an important source of protein. Don't miss the snack stands selling these on Sukhumvit or Khao San. How do they taste? Crickets are like popcorn, and the beetles are something like, hate to say it, crispy chicken. A great photo op.

salad. For a main course, go for the fresh fish done as you like or any of the grilled items or fine pastas. I had a delicious squid-ink linguini and clams. It's not to be missed.

53 Sukhumvit Soi 39, Klongtoe Bangkok. ℂ 02258-5606. Main courses 200B–880B ($5–$22). AE, MC, V. Daily 6–11pm. Near Phrom Pong BTS station.

**Seafood Market** ⭐ SEAFOOD   If you're a seafood fan, you're in the right place. Diners peruse large live tanks and choose the favorites, all priced by the kilo. Chefs cook your catch as you like and what comes out of the kitchen is always good. Cooking charges and corkage are paid separately at the end of the meal. The seafood is market price.

89 Sukhumvit Soi 24 (Soi Kasame), Bangkok. ℂ 02261-2071. Reservations suggested for weekend dinner. Market prices. AE, MC, V. Daily 11:30am to midnight.

### Inexpensive

**Cabbages & Condoms** ⭐⭐ THAI   Here's a theme restaurant with a purpose. Opened by local hero Mechai Viravaidya, founder of the Population & Community Development Association, the restaurant helps fund population control, AIDS awareness, and a host of rural development programs. Set in a large compound, the two-story restaurant has air-conditioned indoor dining—but if you sit on the garden terrace, you're in a fairyland of twinkling lights: quite romantic. Share a whole fish done as you like or try the *kai hor bai teoy* (fried boneless chicken wrapped in pandan leaves with a dark sweet soy sauce for dipping). There's also a large selection of vegetable and bean curd entrees.

Before you leave, be sure to check out the gift shop's whimsical condom-related merchandise. The restaurant hands out condoms instead of dinner mints.

10 Sukhumvit Soi 12. ℂ 02229-4610. Reservations recommended. 70B–200B ($1.75–$5). AE, DC, MC, V. Daily 11am–10pm. 15-min. walk from Asok BTS station.

**Crepes & Co** ⭐⭐ (Kids) EUROPEAN   Popular among Bangkok foreign residents (and their kids), this is the place to satisfy that sweet tooth. Crepes & Co. serves them up light and fluffy and filled with any of dozens of combinations, both savory and sweet—all of them delicious. It also serves good Mediterranean main courses. Everything is excellent. There's great coffee and a good selection of tea.

18/1 Sukhumvit Soi 12. ℂ 02653-3990. Reservations recommended. Main courses 100B–300B ($2.50–$7.50). AE, DC, MC, V. Mon–Sat 9am–midnight; Sun 8am–midnight. 15-min. walk from Asok BTS station.

## DINNER WITH THAI DANCE

For an evening of Thai culture and cuisine, try the **Sala Rim Nam** at the Oriental (ℂ 02437-2918) for an opulent evening from 1,680B ($42) per person. An affordable cultural evening can be found at the **Supatra River House** (ℂ 02411-0305) at riverside on Friday and Saturday nights. Call ahead.

## DINNER & LUNCH CRUISES ON THE CHAO PHRAYA

While there are a number of tour operators who offer dinner cruises along the Chao Phraya, if you want to eat the finest food, I only have one solid recommendation. The *Manohra* ★★, a reconverted antique rice barge, cruises the river nightly serving a six-course Thai dinner that's delicious (and not overly spicy). The quality of the food is excellent, especially considering most other dinner cruises serve lukewarm indescribable food. The set menu is 1,200B ($30) per person, and *Manohra* sets sail at 7:30pm (but you can pick it up at the Oriental pier, where it stops at about 7:40pm). Be sure to book in advance to make sure the boat isn't rented out for a private party. Call the **Bangkok Marriott Resort & Spa** (© 02476-0021).

The *Horizon II* makes daily trips to Ayuthaya and back as well as evening cruises in town for a romantic candlelit meal. Cruises start at just 1,400B ($35) and leave daily at 8am for all-day trips or 7:30pm for dinner cruises. Contact the **Shangri La Hotel** (© 02236-7777).

## EXPLORING BANGKOK

When Rama I established Bangkok as the new capital city in the 1780s, he built a new palace and royal temple on the banks of the Chao Phraya River. The city sprang up around the palace and spread outward from this point as population and wealth grew. Today this area contains most of Bangkok's major historical sites, including a great number of *wats,* or Buddhist temples, that were built during the last 200 years. If you're short on time, the most interesting and easily accessible *wats* to catch are Wat Phra Kaeo, the royal *wat* that houses the Emerald Buddha at the Grand Palace, and Wat Po, home of the reclining Buddha.

### BANGKOK'S WATERWAYS

The history of Bangkok was written on its waterways and Bangkok was once known as the "Venice of the East." Most of these *klongs* have been paved over, but the magnificent Chao Phraya River (River of Kings) cuts through the heart of the city. On the Thonburi side (opposite Bangkok), the labyrinthine *klongs* offer an intimate glimpse of traditional Thai life. You'll see people using the river to bathe and wash their clothes, and floating kitchens in sampans serve rice and noodles to customers in other boats. Hire a private boat to see the busy riverside area in style and to tour the narrow canals of neighboring Thonburi. Boat charter is available anywhere really, and the touts will find you, especially at the main sites. It is best to arrange hourly trips at the riverfront kiosk near the **River City Shopping**, at the **Grand Palace** (© 02225-6179), or at the skytrain exit at the **Saphan Taksin BTS** station. Trips cost 500B ($13) per hour, per boat. Be specific about destinations and times.

### BANGKOK'S HISTORICAL TREASURES

**The Grand Palace** ★★★    Rama I built the oldest buildings in the square-mile complex when he moved the capital from Thonburi to Bangkok in the 1780s. It was the official residence and housed the offices of the kings until 1946, when the royal family moved to Chitralada Palace. These days, the palace is used only for royal ceremonies. The focal point of the compound is the Chakri Maha Prasad, an intriguing mixture of Victorian architecture topped with a Thai temple-style roof that today houses the ashes of royal family members. The Amarinda Vinichai Hall is the venue for the highest royal ceremonies, including coronations. The Dusit Hall is a perfect example of Thai architecture in the highest order.

Near the river on Na Phra Lan Rd. near Sanam Luang. ℂ **02222-0094.** Admission 125B ($3.15). Price includes Wat Phra Kaeo and the Coin Pavilion inside the Grand Palace grounds, as well as admission to the Vimanmek Palace (near the National Assembly). Daily 8:30am–3:30pm; most individual buildings are closed to the public except on special days proclaimed by the king. Take the Chao Phraya Express Boat to the Tha Chang Pier, then walk east and south.

## Jim Thompson's House ★

Jim Thompson was a New York architect who served in the OSS (Office of Strategic Services, now the CIA) in Thailand during World War II and afterward settled in Bangkok. Almost single-handedly he revived Thailand's silk industry, employing Thai Muslims as skilled silk weavers and building up a thriving industry. After expanding his sales to international markets, Mr. Thompson mysteriously disappeared in 1967 while vacationing in the Cameron Highlands in Malaysia. Despite extensive investigation, his disappearance has never been resolved.

His Thai house is composed of six linked teakwood houses from central Thailand that were rebuilt according to Thai architectural principles, but with Western additions (such as a staircase and window screens). In some rooms, the floor is made of Italian marble, but the wall panels are pegged teak. Volunteers guide you through rooms filled with Thompson's splendid collection of Khmer sculpture, Chinese porcelain, Burmese carving (especially a 17th-century teak Buddha), and antique Thai scroll paintings.

Soi Kasemsan 2 (on a small *soi* off Rama I Rd., opposite the National Stadium). ℂ **02216-7368.** Admission 100B ($2.50). Daily 9am–4:30pm.

## The National Museum ★★

The National Museum, a short (15-min.) walk north of the Grand Palace and the Temple of the Emerald Buddha, is the country's central treasury of art and archaeology. It was originally the palace that the brother of Rama I built as part of the Grand Palace complex in 1782. Rama V converted the palace into a museum in 1884. Today it is the largest museum in Southeast Asia and takes quite a lot of time to see.

One important stop is the Red House, a traditional 18th-century Thai building that was originally the living quarters of Princess Sri Sudarak. Another essential stop is the Phuttaisawan (Buddhaisawan) Chapel, built in 1787 to house the Phra Phut Sihing, one of Thailand's most revered Buddha images, brought here from its original home in Chiang Mai. The main building of the royal palace contains gold jewelry, some from the royal collections, and Thai ceramics, including many pieces in the five-color *bencharong* style. The Old Transportation Room contains ivory carvings, elephant chairs, and royal palanquins. There are also rooms of royal emblems and insignia, stone carvings, wood carvings, costumes, textiles, musical instruments, and Buddhist religious artifacts. Fine art and sculpture are found in the newer galleries at the rear of the museum compound.

Na Phra That Rd. (about ½ mile north of the Grand Palace). ℂ **02224-1333.** Admission 40B ($1). Wed–Sun 9am–4pm. Free English-language tours: Buddhism culture, Wed 9:30am; art, culture, religion, Thurs 9:30am; call the museum or check a newspaper for more details and current schedule.

## Vimanmek Mansion Museum ★

Built in 1901 by King Chulalongkorn the Great (Rama V) as the Celestial Residence, this large, beautiful, golden teakwood mansion was restored in 1982 for Bangkok's bicentennial and was reopened by Queen Sirikit as a private museum with a collection of the royal family's memorabilia. An intriguing and informative hour-long tour takes you through a series of apartments and rooms (81 in all) in what is said to be the largest teak building in the world—the thought of all that gorgeous teakwood employed is staggering. The original **Abhisek Dusit Throne Hall** houses a display of Thai

# Exploring Bangkok

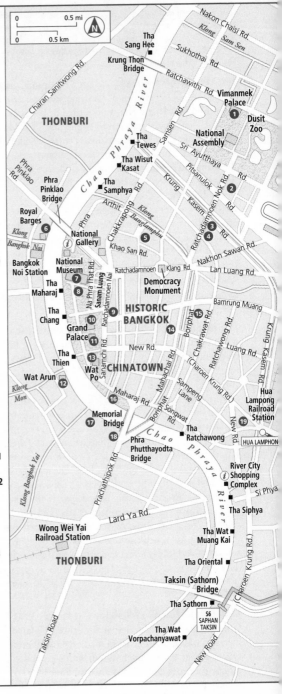

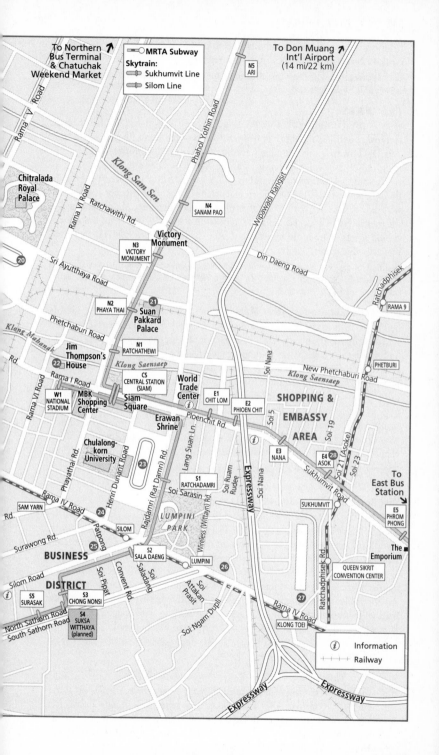

handicrafts, and nine other buildings north of the mansion display photographs, clocks, fabrics, royal carriages, and other regalia.

193/2 Ratchavitee Rd., Dusit Palace grounds (opposite the Dusit Zoo, north of the National Assembly Building). ℂ 02281-8166. Admission 50B ($1.25); included in Grand Palace fee. Daily 9:30am–4pm.

## THE WATS
### Wat Arun (Temple of Dawn) ★★★
The 86m-high (282-ft.) Khmer-inspired tower rises majestically from the banks of the Chao Phraya, across from Wat Po. This religious complex served as the royal chapel during King Taksin's reign (1809–24), when Thonburi was the capital of Thailand.

The original tower was only 16m (52 ft.) high, but it was expanded during the rule of Rama III (1824–51) to its current height. The exterior is decorated with flower and decorative motifs made of colorful ceramic shards donated to the monastery by local people at the request of Rama III. Wat Arun is a sight to behold shimmering in the sunrise, but truly the best time to visit is in late afternoon for the sunset.

West bank of the Chao Phraya, opposite Tha Thien Pier. ℂ 02465-5640. 20B (50¢) admission. Daily 8am–5:30pm. Take a water taxi from Tha Thien Pier (near Wat Po) or cross the Phra Pinklao Bridge and follow the river south on Arun Amarin Rd.

### Wat Benchamabophit (The Marble Wat)
Wat Benchamabophit, simplified for tourists as the Marble Wat because of the white Carrara marble of which it's constructed, is an early-20th-century temple designed by Prince Narai, the half brother of Rama V. It's the most modern and one of the most beautiful of Bangkok's royal *wats*. Unlike the older complexes, there's no truly monumental *wihaan* or *chedi* dominating the grounds. Many smaller buildings reflect a melding of European materials and designs with traditional Thai religious architecture. Even the courtyards are paved with polished white marble. Walk inside the compound, beyond the main *bot,* to view the many Buddha images that represent various regional styles. In the early mornings, monks chant in the main chapel, sometimes so intensely that it seems as if the temple is going to lift off.

Si Ayutthaya Rd. (south of the Assembly Building near Chitralada Palace). ℂ 02281-2501. 20B (50¢) admission. Daily 8am–5pm.

### Wat Mahathat (Temple of the Great Relic) ★
Built to house a relic of the Buddha, Wat Mahathat is one of Bangkok's oldest shrines and the headquarters for Thailand's largest monastic order. Also the home of the Mahachulalongkorn Buddhist University, the most important center for the study of Buddhism and meditation, Wat Mahathat offers some programs in English.

Adjacent to it, between Maharat Road and the river, is the city's biggest amulet market, where a fantastic array of religious amulets, charms, talismans, and traditional medicine is sold. Each Sunday, hundreds of worshippers squat on the ground studying tiny images of the Buddha with magnifying glasses, hoping to find one that will bring good fortune or ward off evil.

Na Phra That Rd. (near Sanam Luang Park, between the Grand Palace and the National Museum). ℂ 02222-6011. 20B (50¢) donation. Daily 9am–5pm.

### Wat Phra Kaeo ★★★
When Rama I built the Grand Palace, he included this temple, the royal temple most revered by the Thai people. The famed Emerald Buddha, a 0.6m-tall (2-ft.) northern Thai-style image made from green jasper, sits atop a towering gold altar. The statue dons a different costume for each of the three seasons in Thailand, changed by the king himself, who climbs up to the image because it can be lowered for no one.

Historians believe that artists created the statue in the 14th century. The Emerald Buddha hid inside a plaster Buddha image until 1434, when movers accidentally dropped it, setting it free. The king at Chiang Mai demanded that it be brought to his city, but three attempts failed. Each time the elephant transporting the image stopped at the same spot in Lampang, so the king gave in to the will of the spirits and built a *chedi* (a sacred monument) for it there. Thirty-two years later, King Tiloka of Chiang Mai brought the image to Chiang Mai. The Emerald Buddha stayed in the Wat Chedi Luang until 1552, when a later king from Luang Prabang carted it off to Laos. When the king moved the capital of Laos to Vientiane, the image followed him. Rama I finally recaptured the statue in a successful invasion of Laos and placed it in Wat Phra Kaeo, where it remains today.

The *wat* compound is a small city in itself, including a library with stunning Ayutthaya-style mother-of-pearl inlay doors; a reliquary like a golden bell-shape Sri Lankan–style *chedi;* a *wihaan* (hall) bejeweled with chipped porcelain mosaics; and a miniature model of Angkor Wat, the sprawling temple complex at the ancient Khmer capital, with its corn-shape chedis. Murals on the surrounding walls tell the story of the *Ramayana* (one of the two great epics of India).

In the Grand Palace complex. ℂ 02222-0094. Admission, 125B ($3.15); included in Grand Palace fee. Daily 8:30am–3:30pm. Take the Chao Phraya Express Boat to Tha Chang Pier, then walk east and south.

**Wat Po** ★★★ Wat Po (Wat Phra Chetuphon), the Temple of the Reclining Buddha, was built by Rama I in the 16th century and is the oldest and largest Buddhist temple in Bangkok. Considered Thailand's first public university, the temple's many monuments and artworks explain principles of religion, science, and literature.

Most people go straight to the enormous Reclining Buddha in the northern section. It's more than 46m (151 ft.) long and 16m (53 ft.) high, and was built during the mid-19th-century reign of Rama III. The statue is brick, covered with layers of plaster and always-flaking gold leaf; the feet are inlaid with mother-of-pearl illustrations of 108 auspicious *laksanas* (characteristics) of the Buddha. Behind the Buddha, a line of 108 bronze bowls, each also representing one of the *laksanas,* awaits visitors to drop coins (acquired nearby for a 20B/50¢ donation for luck).

Outside, the grounds contain 91 *chedis* (stupas or sacred mounds), four *wihaans,* and a *bot* (the central shrine in a Buddhist temple). The Traditional Medical Practitioners Association Center teaches traditional Thai massage and medicine. Stop in for a massage (250B/$6.25 per hr.), or ask about the 7- to 10-day massage courses.

Maharat Rd., near the river (about ½ mile south of the Grand Palace). ℂ 02222-0933. 20B (50¢) admission. Daily 8am–5pm; massages offered until 6pm.

**Wat Saket (The Golden Mount)** ★ Wat Saket is easily recognized by its golden *chedi* atop a fortresslike hill near the pier for Bangkok's east-west *klong* ferry. The *wat* was restored by King Rama I, and 30,000 bodies were brought here during a plague in the reign of Rama II. The hill, which is almost 80m (262 ft.) high, is an artificial construction begun during the reign of Rama III. Rama IV brought in 1,000 teak logs to shore it up because it was sinking into the swampy ground. Rama V built the golden *chedi* to house a relic of Buddha, said to be from India or Nepal, given to him by the British. The concrete walls were added during World War II to keep the structure from collapsing.

The Golden Mount, a short but breathtaking climb that's best made in the morning, is most interesting for its vista of old Rattanakosin Island and the rooftops of Bangkok. Every late October to mid-November (for 9 days around the full moon), Wat Sakhet hosts Bangkok's most important temple fair, when the Golden Mount is wrapped with red cloth and a carnival erupts around it, with food and trinket stalls, theatrical performances, freak shows, animal circuses, and other monkey business.

Ratchadamnoen Klang and Boripihat roads. Entrance to *wat* is free; admission to the *chedi* 5B (15¢) donation. Daily 9am–5pm.

**Wat Suthat and the Giant Swing**    The temple is among the oldest and largest in Bangkok, and Somerset Maugham declared its roofline the most beautiful. It was begun by Rama I and finished by Rama III; Rama II carved the panels for the *wihaan's* doors. It houses a beautiful 14th-century Phra Buddha Shakyamuni that was brought from Sukhothai, and the ashes of King Rama VIII, Ananda Mahidol, brother of the current king, are contained in its base. The wall paintings for which it is known were done during Rama III's reign.

The huge teak arch—also carved by Rama II—in front is all that remains of an original giant swing, which was used until 1932 to celebrate and thank Shiva for a bountiful rice harvest and to ask for the god's blessing on the next. The minister of rice, accompanied by hundreds of Brahman court astrologers, would lead a parade around the city walls to the temple precinct. Teams of men would ride the swing on arcs as high as 25m (82 ft.) in the air, trying to grab a bag of silver coins with their teeth. Due to injuries and deaths, the dangerous swing ceremony has been discontinued.

Sao Chingcha Sq. (near the intersection of Bamrung Muang and Ti Thong roads). © 02222-0280. 20B (50¢) donation. Daily 9am–9pm.

**Wat Traimit (The Golden Buddha)**    Thirteenth-century Wat Traimit is notable only for its central statue, a nearly 3m-high (10 ft.), 5-ton Buddha in gold. The statue was discovered by accident in 1957 when an old stucco image was being moved from a storeroom by a crane, which dropped it and shattered the plaster shell, revealing the shining gold beneath. The graceful seated statue was cast during the Sukhothai period and later covered with plaster to hide it from the Burmese.

Traimit Rd. (west of Hua Lampong Station, just west of the intersection of Krung Kasem and Rama IV roads). 20B (50¢) donation. Daily 9am–5pm. Walk southwest on Traimit Rd. and look for a school on the right with a playground; the *wat* is up a flight of stairs overlooking the school.

## CULTURAL PURSUITS

Thai culture is not something to observe, but to participate in, and festivals, classes and cultural activities abound. Check with the TAT (© **01155**) or the **Bangkok Tourism Bureau** (see the information offices around the city or call

---

### Organized Tours

There are numerous travel agencies offering local tours. **Diethelm Travel** (© 02255-9150; www.diethelm-travel.com), a leader in the region, can arrange tours of any length. **World Travel** (© 02233-5900) and **Sea Tours** (© 02216-5783) also have good services with branches in some hotels. Any hotel concierge can make the necessary arrangements.

© 02225-7612) and keep an eye on magazines like *Metro* or local newspapers, *The Nation* and *The Bangkok Post,* for major events during your stay.

## THAI COOKING

Fancy a chance to learn cooking techniques from the pros? Thai cooking is fun and easy, and there are a few good hands-on courses in Bangkok. Learn about Thai herbs, spices, and unique local veggies (you'll never look at a produce market the same again). Lectures on Thai regional cuisine, cooking techniques, and menu planning complement classroom exercises to prepare all your favorite dishes. The best part is after, when you get to eat them. **The Blue Elephant** (© 02673-9353; www.blueelephant.com) is the best in town, with classes starting at 2,800B ($70). **The Oriental Cooking School** (© 02437-6211) holds multiple-day courses at the famed riverside hotel and books special cooking packages.

## THAI MASSAGE

A traditional **Thai massage** is a must-do for visitors in Thailand and is quite unique. You don't just lie back and passively receive a Thai massage; instead, you are an active participant as masseurs manipulate your limbs to stretch each muscle, then apply acupressure techniques to loosen up tense muscles and get energy flowing. It's been described as having yoga "done" to you and your body will be twisted, pulled, and sometimes pounded in the process.

The home of Thai massage, **Wat Po,** is school to almost every masseuse in Bangkok, and has cheap massages in an open-air pavilion within the temple complex—a very interesting, but not necessarily relaxing, experience (see "The Wats," above; © 0222-0933; 200B/$5 per hr.).

Bangkok supports some fine **spas,** most in the larger hotels. **Le Banyan Tree Spa** (© 02679-1054; www.banyantree.com) and the **Oriental**'s spa (see "Where to Stay"; © 02439-7613) are two of the finest places going, but just two of the many fine spas in town (in hotels and out).

There are countless massage places around Bangkok, and many offer fine services at very reasonable rates (as low as 210B/$5.25 per hr.). Many places have NO SEX or other blatant signs indicating the place is hanky-panky free (and if you're looking for hanky-panky, those signs are just as blatant).

## THAI BOXING

**Muaythai,** or **Thai boxing**, is Thailand's national sport and a visit to the two venues in Bangkok, or the many fight-nights in towns all over Thailand (as much festival as sport), is a fun window into Thai culture. The pageant of the fighters' elegant prebout rituals, live musical performances, and the frenetic gambling activity are a real spectacle. In Bangkok, catch up to 15 bouts nightly at either of two stadiums. The **Ratchadamnoen Stadium** (Ratchadamnoen Nok Ave.; © 02281-4205) hosts fights on Monday, Wednesday, Thursday, and Sunday, while the **Lumphini Stadium** (Rama IV Rd.; © 02251-4303) has bouts on Tuesdays, Fridays, and Saturdays. Tickets are 1,500B ($38) for ringside seats, 800B ($20) for second class, and 500B ($13) for nose-bleed seats. Go for second-class seats. Not for the squeamish.

## MEDITATION

**Wat Mahathat,** or the Temple of the Great Relic (see "The Wats," earlier in this chapter), serves one of Thailand's largest Buddhist universities and has become a popular center for **meditation lessons and practice,** with English-speaking monks overseeing students of Vipassana, or Insight Meditation. Call ahead to get the schedule and to make an appointment (© 02222-6011).

## STAYING ACTIVE
### Fitness
Most hotels, certainly the finest five-star properties, support quality fitness centers complete with personal trainers and top equipment. **California,** just along Silom Road near Patpong at Liberty Square (℃ **02631-1122**), is a large convenient facility open to day visitors.

### Golf
Enthusiasts will be happy to know that you don't have to go far to enjoy some of Thailand's best courses; there are a number of courses, some of championship quality, in or near the city center.

- **Kantarat,** Thai Airports Authority Gate, 1km (half-mile) south of the airport domestic terminal (℃ **02534-3840**), is also known as Don Muang or the Old Royal Thai Air Force course, because this long 18-hole course sits between the two primary runways at Bangkok's Don Muang International Airport. Best to make reservations for weekend play (greens fees: weekdays 600B/$15; weekends 800B/$20).
- **Pinehurst Golf & Country Club,** 73 Phaholythin Rd., Klong Luang, Pathum Thani (℃ **05321-1911**), sports three 9-hole courses at par 27 each. This prestigious club served as the venue for the 1992 Johnnie Walker Classic (greens fees: 1,500B/$38 weekdays, 2,000B/$50 weekends).
- **Rose Garden Golf Club,** 53/1 Moo 4, Petchkasem Highway, Sam Phran, Nakhon Pathom (℃ **02253-0295**), an esteemed par-72 course, offers a pretty game, with scenery enhanced by wooded surrounds (greens fees: weekdays 450B/$11; weekends 1,110B/$28).
- **Royal Thai Army Golf Club,** 459 Ram Indra Rd., Bang Kaen, Bangkok, (℃ **02521-1530**), has both an old course and a new course to choose from. This well-maintained course was host to the Thai Open (greens fees: weekdays 600B/$15; weekends 800B/$20).
- **Unico Golf Club,** 47 Moo 7, Krungthep Kretha Road, Prawet, Bangkok (℃ **02377-9038;** fax 02379-3780), is a well-established city course with many challenging holes (greens fees: weekdays 535B/$13; weekends 1,070B/$27).

## SHOPPING
You're bound to shop in Bangkok. With the abundance of **Thai silk,** good tailors, artwork, hill-tribe crafts, silver, gems, and porcelain, shopping is inevitable, but prices are low and the whole process is good fun—bargain hard! At the city's many **street bazaars** you can find cheap batik clothing, knockoff watches, jeans, designer wear, and all sorts of souvenirs. Buy a bag to tote it all back home.

The best hotel shopping arcades are those at the Oriental, the Four Seasons, and the Peninsula hotels; prices are high. Pick up a copy of Nancy Chandler's *The Market Map* (160B/$4) with detailed insets of specific shopping areas. If you encounter problems with merchants, contact the **Tourist Police** (℃ **1155**).

For silk outlets, try **Jim Thompson Thai Silk Company,** the town's most famous (main store is at 9 Surawong Rd., near Silom; ℃ **02632-8100**) or **T. Shinawatra Silk** (94 Sukhumvit Soi 23; ℃ **02258-0295**).

## ON THE WATER
One of the finest collections of art and antiques dealers anywhere in the kingdom is at **River City,** a large convention hall at riverside near Bangkok's finest hotels. Sticker shock is the rule, but you get what you pay for and quality is what

you get at River City. Nearby **Charoen Krung Road** hosts lots of high-end shopping venues, from jewelry to antiques, carpet, and fine tailoring. All shops arrange shipping.

## SUKHUMVIT ROAD

This area is lined with shops from one end to the other as well as some of Bangkok's biggest shopping malls (see "Department Stores & Shopping Plazas," below). For antiques, try **L'Arcadia** (12/2 Sukhumvit Soi 23; ✆ **02259-1517**) where you'll find fine Burmese and Thai furniture and carvings. **Celadon House,** on 85 Ratchadapisek (near Sukhumvit; ✆ **02253-9237**) carries fine displays of attractive celadon ceramic. For gems, try **Uthai's Gems** down Ruam Rudee, a busy short-cut *soi* parallel to Wireless just south of Ploen Chit (28/7 Soi Ruam Rudee; ✆ **02253-2993**).

For fine tailoring, try the many shops along Sukhumvit Soi 11. Most ship your order off to have clothes made in a factory, but you can get good deals if you bargain. **Ambassador Fashion** (28–28 Sukhumvit Soi 19; ✆ **02253-2993**) has been in the business for years and provides good service (near Asok BTS station).

## SILOM ROAD

This area is packed with outdoor shopping (see the Patpong Night Market discussed below) and there are any number of fine jewelry shops, silk retailers, and tailors.

## MARKETS

Visiting Bangkok's many markets is as cultural as it is a consumer experience; the markets are where the Thai economy happens. The bargaining is fast and furious. The **Weekend Market (Chatuchak)** (near the Mo Chit BTS stop) is the city's most famous, covering a vast area and overcrowded on any given Saturday or Sunday. The riverside **Chinatown** area is a labyrinth of shopping. **Khao San Road,** the popular backpacker area, is a great place to pick up anything from travel trinkets to cool T-shirts and the city's two night markets, **Patpong Night Market** (Patpong Soi 1 off Silom) and **Suan Lum Night Market** (east of Lumpini Park on Rama IV Rd.), are great stops for souvenirs and more.

## DEPARTMENT STORES & SHOPPING PLAZAS

The size and opulence of Bangkok's many malls and shopping areas are a shock to first-time visitors in search of the exotic. Thai malls are where the rubber meets the road with old and new in Siam. Below are the highlights.

**The Emporium** (622 Sukhumvit Soi 24; ✆ **02664-8000**), Bangkok's finest shopping area, has all of the designer outlets you could imagine, a great food court, and a cinema. **Siam Discovery Center** (on Rama I Rd.; ✆ **02658-1000**), opposite the Siam stop on the BTS skytrain, adjoins **Siam Center** for some of the largest acreage of high-end shopping in Bangkok. Also near Siam, **Mah Boon Krong,** or **MBK,** and **Tokyu Department Store** (at the intersection of Rama I and Phayathai; National Stadium BTS station; ✆ **02217-9111**) is a real

---

### *Warning* Jewelry Scams

For every reputable gems dealer in Bangkok, there are at least 100 crooks waiting to catch you in the latest scam. To avoid being ripped off, follow this simple rule: Refuse offers from touts for free city shopping junkets.

trip to teenie-bopper Thailand and supports lots of more affordable local shops—a crowded exercise in how Bangkok shops.

## BANGKOK AFTER DARK

One night in Bangkok, right? Despite recent legislation restricting bar hours, the action is still fierce and furious in Thailand's hedonistic capital and a rollicking good time can be found. If the Bangkok debauch isn't your scene, know that the town is not all red-light by any means: There are all kinds of events, clubs, and bars. Check *Metro Magazine* (100B/$2.50), the *Bangkok Post* or *The Nation* for current happenings.

### THE PERFORMING ARTS

There are a number of Thai dance and dinner theaters for tourists (see "Dinner with Thai Dance," earlier in section 3, for specific recommendations.)

There are two major theaters for Thai and international performances: **The National Theater** (1 Na Phra That Rd.; ℭ **02224-1342**) and the **Thailand Cultural Center** (Thiem Ruammit Rd. off Ratchadaphisek Rd., Huai Khwang; ℭ **02247-0028**), both with a regular schedule of performances. Contact them directly or check local papers.

**The Joe Louis Theater** (in the Suan Lum Night Market adjacent to Lumpini Park; ℭ **02252-9683**) holds nightly **puppet theater** performances of stories from the *Ramakien* as well as comic vignettes of rural Thai life. Shows are nightly at 7:30 and 8:30pm. Tickets start at just 250B ($6.25).

For a bit of tongue-in-cheek theater, a couple of cabaret shows in Bangkok feature Katoeys (transsexuals aka "Lady-Boys") in 6-inch heels and feather boas performing to pop hits, rather hilarious extravaganzas really. **Calypso Cabaret** at the Asia Hotel (296 Phayathai Rd.; ℭ **02261-6355**) and **Mambo** (Washington Square, Sukhumvit Soi 22; ℭ **02259-5128**) have nightly shows. Contact for details.

### THE CLUB & BAR SCENE

There are nighttime adventures to be found down any *soi* in the town. If you'd just like to unwind with an evening cocktail, check out what's happening at your hotel's lobby bar; many set up jazzy live music to entertain folks. Don't miss the **Bamboo Bar at the Oriental** (Oriental Lane off Charoen Krung Rd.; ℭ **02236-0400**), with classy live jazz—some of the best in the city.

### Silom Road & Patpong

Most visitors won't leave Bangkok without a stroll around Patpong, the famous sex strip and night market with myriad vendors and blocks of bars and clubs. The Patpong scene centers around Soi Patpong 1 and Soi Patpong 2 between Surawong and Silom roads. It's the home of Bangkok's raunchier sex shows, but most visitors come to wander the market area (lots of pirated goods). Be prepared for crowds, pickpockets, and grinning touts with menu boards telling of "ping-pong ball shows" and other circuslike spectacles. These upstairs **"sex show"** places charge an entrance fee or have a one or two drink minimum. **Go-go bars** are open to the street and passersby get a peek at the groups of scantily clad young ladies crowding together on a central catwalk (and looking pretty bored, really). There is no entrance fee, but it's more or less a "drink or leave" policy.

Despite its rep as a go-go center, there are lots of good bars in Patpong. **O'Reilly's Irish Pub** (62 Silom Rd., on the corner of Soi Thaniya just east of Patpong; ℭ **02632-7515**), is a lively bar full of locals and travelers. **The Barbican** (9/4–5 Soi Thaniya off Silom Rd.; ℭ **02234-3590**) is a stylish hangout with great food and live music. **The Irish Exchange** across from Patpong on Convent Road (next to Silom Complex at 1/5–6 Sivadon Building; ✆ **02266-7160**) caters to expatriates with Irish-pub style and live music after office working hours. Head to Silom Soi 4 (between Patpong 2 and Soi Thaniya off Silom Rd.), where you'll find small home-grown clubs spinning great music as well as the city's prominent gay clubs: **Telephone Bar** (114/11–13 Silom Soi 4; ✆ **02234-3279**) and the **Balcony** (86–8 Silom Soi 4; ✆ **02235-5891**).

## Siam Square

Siam Square, on Rama I Road between Henri Dunant and Phayathai roads, is where you'll find **Bangkok's Hard Rock Cafe,** featuring good live bands, 424/3–6 Siam Square Soi 11 (✆ **02254-0830**).

A great disco, **Concept CM²,** goes nightly with live or DJ music—a very popular place in the basement of the **Novotel Siam** (Siam Sq. Soi 6; ✆ **02255-6888**). **Spasso,** in the Grand Hyatt Erewan Hotel (494 Ratchadamri Rd.; ✆ **02254-1234**), is a great Italian restaurant that turns upscale club featuring live music acts nightly.

A little bit north of this area (a short cab ride away), near the Victory Monument BTS station (a cab ride up Phayathai Rd.), check out live jazz and blues at **Saxophone Pub and Restaurant** (✆ **02246-5472**).

## Khao San Road

The backpackers on Khao San Road still party on despite more and more restrictions. Start at **Gulliver's** on the corner of Khao San and Chakrabongse roads, then explore the back lanes off Khao San for small dance clubs (some the size of broom closets) and hangouts. You'll find lots of travelers in their 20s, and the atmosphere is always laid-back and anything goes. In the middle of Khao San, don't miss **Lava** (249 Khao San Rd.; ✆ **02281-6565**) a popular basement dance club. For a more laid-back evening, head west of Khao San to riverside **Phra Athit Road,** where there are any number of small cafes with live music.

## Sukhumvit Road

One of the most happenin' areas of Bangkok, the small *sois* along busy Sukhumvit host Bangkok's top clubs and good bars. **Q Bar** ☆☆ (34 Sukhumvit Soi 11; ✆ **02252-3274**) is *the* place for the slick urban hip of Bangkok; its only rival is the similarly ab-fab **Bed Supper Club** ☆☆☆ (see "Where to Dine," earlier in this section; 26 Sukhumvit Soi 11; ✆ **02651-3537**). Both are ultramodern, have great expat DJs, and boom-boom-boom late into the night 7 days a week. The newly built **Conrad Hotel** (87 Wireless Rd., just across from the U.S. Embassy; ✆ **02690-9999**) hosts two of Bangkok's newest and best spots: **87** is an ultrachic, ultraexclusive club and its **Diplomat Bar** ☆ fills with, well, diplomats from the U.S. embassy as well as Bangkok's hip and happenin' hobnobbers.

For bars along Sukhumvit, try the **Bull's Head** (Sukhumvit Soi 33/1; ✆ **02259-4444**), a fun local pub that draws crowds with frequent theme parties and a clubhouse attitude. **Larry's Dive Bar** (8/3 Sukhumvit Soi 22; ✆ **02663-4563**) is a laid-back little place, like a little island getaway in the busy city and just as affordable. **Bruahaus Bangkok** (President Park, at the end of Sukhumvit Soi 24; ✆ **02661-1111**) is a popular brewpub, as is **Taurus Brew House** (Sukhumvit Soi 26; ✆ **02661-2207**), which packs them in—especially on weekends—for home brews and live pop music.

For live music head for **Riva's** (Sheraton Grande Sukhumvit Hotel, 250 Sukhumvit Rd.; ✆ **02653-0333**), with international bands and lots of dancing.

> **Tips** **When you go clubbing . . .**
>
> At all clubs and bars, be sure to ask upfront about cover charges, drink charges, and show charges—these places can really try to rip you off. If you are presented with an exorbitant bill, your only recourse is to pay up and then call the **Tourist Police (© 1155)**.

**Cheap Charlie's** 👁 is in a little alleyway off of Soi 11 (near Suk 11 guesthouse). It's like a small beach bar, but in the middle of Bangkok and drinks are, as advertised, "affordable."

Similar to the Patpong sex show scene, Sukhumvit's **Nana Plaza** just on Sukhumvit Soi 4 or **Soi Cowboy,** the oldest go-go scene dating from Vietnam War days (between Soi Asoke and Sukhumvit Soi 21), are popular go-go spots.

## THE BANGKOK SEX SCENE

Since the 1960s—and particularly since the Vietnam War—Bangkok has been the sin capital of Asia, with sex clubs, bars, massage parlors, and prostitutes concentrated in the Patpong, Nana Plaza, and Soi Cowboy districts. Sex is for sale in many quarters in Bangkok, and surprise at seeing the many older Western gentlemen strutting about town with lovely young Thai ladies is a common impression for first-time visitors.

Despite recent efforts and restrictions by the Taksin government, Bangkok's skin trades are thriving. Go-go bars and clubs are really little more than fronts for prostitution, and very thinly veiled fronts at that. The men and women in the clubs are all available to take out of the bar for a "bar fine." "Modern" or "physical" massage parlors are where patrons choose ladies by number from behind glass for an oil massage and more with negotiations. If this is your scene, take great care: Apart from the condom thing (use one), prostitutes are known to slip you drugs (which happens), rob your hotel room while you're sleeping (which happens), or get you mixed up with illegal activities (which also happens). Child prostitution, slavery, and violence against sex workers are still common. If you encounter any problem, report it to the **Tourist Police (© 1155)**.

A startling increase in HIV-positive cases in the last 20 years brought on mandated as well as grass-roots efforts to educate about use of condoms, but AIDS is still a major concern among sex workers.

## SIDE TRIPS FROM BANGKOK
### EASY 1-DAY EXCURSIONS

The **Floating Market at Damnoen Saduak** 👁, Ratchaburi, is about 40 minutes south of Nakhon Pathom. Some tours combine the Floating Market with a visit to the Rose Garden or with the River Kwai sights (see below for more on each). See "visitor information" for tour companies.

At a real floating market, food vendors sell their goods from small boats to local folk in other boats or in *klong*-side homes. Damnoen is as precise a duplicate as you could imagine and great for photographers.

## ROSE GARDEN COUNTRY RESORT

Besides its rose garden, this attractive if somewhat touristy resort is known for its all-in-one show of Thai culture that includes Thai classical and folk dancing, Thai boxing, sword fighting, and cock fighting—a convenient way for visitors with limited time to digest some canned Thai culture. It's located 32km (20 miles) west of Bangkok on the way to Nakhon Pathom on Highway 4 (© **02295-3261**). Admission is 10B (25¢) for the grounds; 220B ($5.50) for the show. It's open daily from 8am to 6pm; the cultural show is at 2:45pm. Call for details.

## KANCHANABURI
120km (74 miles) NW of Bangkok

Really more than a 1-day trip (best as an overnight), Kanchanaburi is home of the famed Bridge over the River Kwai and the notorious internment camps for Allied troops forced into servitude (and death) by the Japanese during World War II in an effort to link Burma and Thailand by rail. Made legendary by the film of the same name, the Bridge over the River Kwai lives on in name only; the existing bridge is just a little rattle-trap trestle that crosses not the River Kwai but a tributary (but that doesn't stop souvenir hawkers and the tourist infrastructure that has grown up around the bridge). There are, however, lots of good excursions in the area, many caves and waterfalls in the surrounding hills, and a few good hotels and riverside guesthouses; it's a popular escape from the heat, traffic, and pollution of Bangkok. You can connect by railway from Bangkok's **Hua Lampong Station** (© **1690**) on regular weekend junkets starting in the early morning, or go by daily ordinary trains from **Bangkok Noi Station** (© **02411-3102**) with slow, daily connections to Kanchanaburi Station (© **03456-1052**); rail trips here are quite scenic and a great experience (though a long, hot ride). There are also frequent regular buses from the **Southern Bus Terminal** (© **02434-5557**), but, if by road, it's perhaps best by rented car (see "Getting Around," earlier in this section, for info). The best place to stay is the **Felix River Kwai Resort** (9/1 Moo 3 Tambon, Kanchanaburi; © **03451-5061**). The Felix has rooms starting at 1,800B ($45) and is the best for comfort, but places like the **Jungle Raft Resort** (Lam Khao Ngu; © **02377-5556**) which is just as it says, a bunch of jungle rafts, are certainly far more atmospheric and adventurous. Budget guesthouses are chockablock at riverside near the bridge.

## AYUTTHAYA
76km (47 miles) N of Bangkok

From 1350 until its fall to the Burmese in 1767, Ayutthaya was Thailand's capital and home to 33 kings and numerous dynasties. At its zenith and until the mid–18th century, Ayutthaya was a majestic city with three palaces and 400 splendid temples on an island threaded by canals—a site that impressed European visitors.

The architecture of Ayutthaya is a fascinating mix of Khmer, or ancient Cambodian, style, and early Sukhothai style, with large cactus-shaped obelisks called *prangs* the hallmark.

Train and bus connections are frequent from Bangkok's **Hua Lampong Railway Station** (© **1690**) and Bangkok's **Northern Bus Terminal** (© **02936-2841**), respectively. **All-day river cruises** are a popular option to and from Ayuthaya. Contact **River Sun Cruises** at (© **02266-9316**) directly or book through any riverside hotel; departure points are the **Oriental** (© **02236-0400**), **Shangri-La Hotel** (© **02236-7777**), or River City pier daily at approximately 7:30am (and include a stop at Bang Pa-In). The *Manorha* ★★, a 60-year-old teak rice barge converted to a luxury liner, makes regular trips (40,000B/$1,012 for two; © **02476-0021**).

The town is encircled by water and the central island area of Ayuthaya is itself the site; modern buildings and busy canal-side streets are in and among the ruins of this once-great city. It is flat, so going by rented bicycle is a good choice.

Highlights are **Wat Mahathat,** a crumbling but stunning example of the Ayuthaya style (don't miss the Buddha head in the tree trunk), and **Wihaan Phra Mongkol Bopit,** which houses a massive Buddha. The **Ayutthaya Historical Study Center** and nearby **Chao Sam Phraya National Museum** offer useful background information. The TAT (at the museum) offers a detailed map.

If you're stuck overnight, the **Krungsri River Hotel** (7/2 Rojana Rd.; © 03524-4333) near the train station is the best choice in town. Convenient but basic is the **Ayothaya Hotel** (12 Moo Tessabarn Soi 2; © 03523-2855).

## 4 The Eastern Seaboard

Tracing the coastline directly east of Bangkok, there are a few resort spots that are attractive as much for their proximity to Bangkok as anything. Closest is Pattaya, one of Thailand's earliest holiday developments and famous (or infamous) for its wild nightlife. The town is always hoppin' late into the night and guys come from all over the world to live it up. Continuing east from Pattaya, **Ko Samet,** in Rayong Province, is a small island with loads of affordable, makeshift bungalow resorts. It is a low-luxe, laid-back little retreat reached by a short ferry ride from the mainland at the town of Ban Phe (via Rayong). And **Ko Chang,** the last stop before Cambodia to the east, has earned a hushed following among young budget travelers because its remote location has kept development to a minimum. The cement trucks are rolling though, and the island, Thailand's third largest, has sprouted a few high-end resorts. Ko Chang is reached via nondescript Trat.

## 5 Pattaya

147km (91 miles) E of Bangkok

The current incarnation of Pattaya claims its founders day as June 29, 1959, when a few truckloads of American troops stationed in nearby Isan arrived in overflowing trucks, rented houses along the beach, and had such a hoot that they told their friends. Word spread and, over time, the town became the R&R capital for war-weary American troops for the next many years. The legacy of those early visitors is today's adult playground: with hundreds of go-go clubs, beer bars, and massage parlors at beachside.

Tourism boomed in the 1980s, and unchecked resort development was not accompanied by infrastructure upgrades such that beaches became veritable toilets of raw sewage. Despite cleanup projects, the beach is not at all pleasant.

Pattaya supports a host of international resorts, retreats set in sprawling, manicured seaside gardens. Pattaya would like to be a family destination, and, along with fine accommodations, there are some family activities, but Pattaya's mammoth sex tourism industry kind of puts the kibosh on any wholesome family fun. Neighboring Jomtien is a popular alternative with less seedy activities and cleaner beaches but mostly just condominiums—good for day visits.

## ESSENTIALS
### GETTING THERE
**By Plane**   There's no airport in Pattaya, the nearest being in U Tapao, an hour east of the city (© 03824-5595).

**By Train**   Once-a-day train service leaves from Bangkok's **Hua Lampong station** at 6:55am and returns from Pattaya at 2:50pm. The 5-hour trip through the countryside is pleasant and costs only 31B (80¢). Call Hua Lampong in

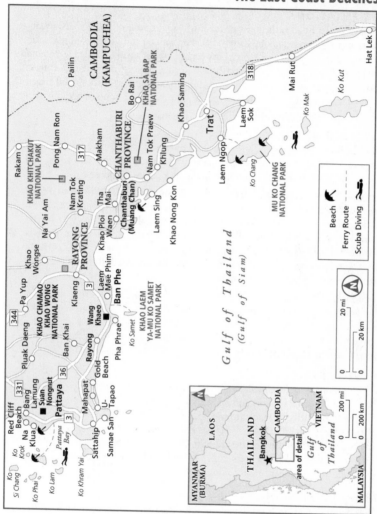

Bangkok (© **02223-7010** or 1690) or in Pattaya at © 03842-9285. A shared *songtao* (pickup truck) to town from the Pattaya train station is just 20B (50¢).

**By Public Bus**  Buses depart from Bangkok's **Eastern Bus Terminal** on Sukhumvit Road (opposite Soi 63 at the BTS Ekamai station; © **02391-2504**) every half-hour beginning from 5am until 10pm every day. For air-conditioned coach the fare is 90B ($2.25). There's also regular bus service from Bangkok's **Northern Bus Terminal (Mor Chit)** (© **02936-2841**).

The bus station in Pattaya for air-conditioned buses to and from Bangkok is on North Pattaya Road (© **03842-9877**). A *songtao* to town is 20B (50¢).

**By Taxi**  Taxis from the Don Muang airport taxi counter go for 1,250B ($31) and any hotel concierge can negotiate with a metered taxi driver to take you to or from Pattaya resort, door to door, for about 1,500B ($38).

## ORIENTATION

Pattaya Beach Road is the heart of the town, a long strip of hotels, bars, restaurants, and shops overlooking Pattaya Bay. Pattaya 2nd and Pattaya 3rd roads run parallel to Beach Road and form a busy central grid of small, crowded *sois* bound by North Pattaya Road and South Pattaya Road and bisected by Central Pattaya Road. At both the far northern (Dusit Resort) and southern (Royal Cliff Beach Resort) ends of the strip are two bluffs. Due south is condo-lined Jomtien Beach, a 15-minute ride from Pattaya.

## GETTING AROUND

**By Minibus or *Songtao***    *Songtao* (called baht buses here) follow regular routes up and down the main streets. Fares in Pattaya start at 10B (25¢) and about 30B (75¢) for Jomtien (bargain hard!). Some hotels operate minibuses.

**By Car**    Avis is at the **Dusit Resort** (© 03836-1628) with self-drive rates from about 1,500B ($38) per day for a Suzuki Caribian 4WD sport vehicle to 2,000B ($50) and up for a compact sedan. **Budget Car Rental** has an office at Liabchayhard Beach Road (© 03871-0717) and offers comparable rates. **VIA Rent-a-Car,** 215/15–18 Pattaya 2nd Rd. opposite Royal Garden Plaza (© 03872-3123), has a good reputation and, like the many along Pattaya Beach Road, offers better rates (from 900B/$23). Read contacts closely.

**By Motorcycle**    Let's be honest, Pattaya's busy roads are full of drunk and reckless foreign drivers on motorbikes, but the brave (or foolish) can rent 150cc motorcycles for 200B ($5) a day (no insurance). Big choppers and Japanese speed bikes (500cc) will go for from 500B to 900B ($13–$23) per day. Demand a helmet and, as always, "renter beware."

## FAST FACTS

There are many independent **money-changing booths,** bank exchanges (with better rates) open 24 hours, and ATMs at every turn in town. The post office is on **Soi Post Office** near the Royal Garden Plaza (© 03842-9341). **Bangkok Pattaya Hospital** (© 03842-7751) has full services and English-speaking staff. In Pattaya, the number for the **Tourist Police** is © 01699 or 03842-9371. Internet service in Pattaya costs 20B per minute ($30/hr.; expensive for Thai) and there are a number of cafes along the water (try Soi Yamato).

## WHAT TO SEE & DO

**Wat Khao Prayai** is a small temple complex high above town to the south, with a 10m (33-ft.) gold Buddha surveying town. For something completely unusual, the **Ripley's Believe It or Not** showcase (3rd Floor, Royal Garden Plaza, 218 Beach Rd.; © 03871-0294), is open 10am to midnight daily (admission 320B/$8), is hilarious, with unusual exhibits and oddities. Equally strange is **Mini Siam** (North Pattaya City; © 03842-1628), a novelty park of the kingdom in miniature. The **Pattaya Elephant Village** (see info at the Tropicana Hotel, Beach Rd.; © 03842-8158), stages elephant shows daily at 2:30pm and offers jungle treks, and **Ngong Nooch** (© 03842-2958) is a botanical garden with a culture show on the outskirts of town.

## WHERE TO STAY

Pattaya accommodations ranges from seedy to stylish, and the town supports a few more isolated, peaceful getaways. Reserve ahead in high season.

# Pattaya

**ACCOMMODATIONS** ■
Amari **2**
Cabbages & Condoms **10**
Dusit Resort **1**
Hard Rock Hotel Pattaya **4**
Pattaya Marriott Resort & Spa **7**
The Royal Cliff Beach Resort **9**
Siam Bayview Hotel **5**

**DINING** ◆
Benihana **8**
Henry J. Bean's **2**
PIC Kitchen **3**
Shere "E" Punjab **6**

Phothisan Rd.

To Bangkok

*Wong Amat Beach*

North Pattaya Rd.

Soi 1
Soi 2
Soi 3
Soi 4
Soi 5
Soi
Soi 6
Soi Sairong

Second Rd.
Yodsak
Pattaya Third Rd.

*Town Beach*

*Pattaya Bay*

Beach Rd.

Central Pattaya Rd.

Soi 7
Soi 8
Soi 9
Soi 10
Soi 13

Second Rd.

Pattaya Third Rd.

Sukhumvit Rd.

**Railway Station**

**Pier**

P

Post Office
Pattayaland

South Pattaya Rd.
Soi 14
Soi 15

Soi 17

Pha Lam Nak Rd.

Cliff Rd.

Thappaya Rd.

ⓘ

THAILAND

Bangkok
★
**Pattaya**

*Dong Tharn Beach*

*Gulf of Thailand (Gulf of Siam)*

**Pattaya Park**
Pedestrians Walkway

Thep Prasit Rd.

To Sattahip

Jomtien Beach Rd.

**Jomtien Beach**

ⓘ Information
╟──┤ Major Railway
⊠ Post Office
🐟 Scuba Diving
P Tourist Police

## EXPENSIVE

**Amari** ✪ On the northern end of busy Pattaya, just out of the fray but close enough to walk there, the Amari has tidy rooms, good amenities, and a helpful staff. The open-air lobby is inviting and guest rooms are large, trimmed in dark wood with parquet floors with pleasing, contemporary lines. There's a playground and lots of space in the grassy central area. Amari also has good in-house dining (see "Henry J. Bean's," under "Where to Dine," below).

Pattaya Beach, Pattaya 20150 (on the very northernmost end of the beachfront rd). ✆ 02255-3767. Fax 02255-3718. 236 units. 9,000B–9,800B ($225–$245) double; from 11,000B ($275) suite. **Amenities:** 3 restaurants; 3 bars; outdoor pool; 9-hole minigolf; 2 tennis courts; fitness center; Jacuzzi; playground and kids' club; tour desk; business center w/Internet; gift shop; salon; 24-hr. room service; babysitting; laundry service; dry cleaning; nonsmoking rooms. In room: A/C, satellite TV, minibar, fridge, safe, IDD phone.

**Dusit Resort** ✪ This sprawling, landscaped resort straddles the bluff on the north end of the main beach and is chock-full of fine amenities: watersports, two pools, access to two small beach coves, several dining outlets, and a small shopping arcade. Most of the balconied rooms overlook Pattaya Bay, but the garden view rooms are a great value. Tasteful, modern rooms are trimmed with stained wood with fine furnishings and all-marble bathrooms. It has a bland "chain hotel" vibe, but some rooms have cool outdoor showers and balconies.

240/2 Pattaya Beach Rd., Pattaya 20150, Chonburi (north end of Pattaya Beach). ✆ 03842-5611. Fax 03842-8239. www.dusit.com. 462 units. 6,000B–6,800B ($150–$170) double; from 9,300B ($233) suite. AE, DC, MC, V. **Amenities:** 3 restaurants; lobby bar w/live music; 2 large free-form pools; 2 outdoor tennis courts; small fitness center; spa w/massage, sauna, and steam; watersports equipment; games; concierge; tour desk; car-rental desk; limo service; small business center w/Internet; shopping arcade; 24-hr. room service; babysitting; same-day laundry service/dry cleaning; nonsmoking rooms. In room: A/C, satellite TV, minibar, fridge, coffeemaker, hair dryer, safe, IDD phone.

**Hard Rock Hotel Pattaya** ✪✪ (Kids) New and ultramodern Hard Rock Hotel is a rollicking, good-time oasis in the heart of sordid Pattaya. This is one place in town you might feel okay bringing the kids, and they're sure to have a ball in the fun sandy-edged pool, game area, and Internet cafe. Rooms are compact and purposely sparse in immaculate whites set against bright blue or orange. Each room features larger-than-life murals of your favorite rock-'n'-roll idols, from Elvis to John Lennon. Large family suites are a good option. The lobby and adjoining Hard Rock Cafe features the chain's typical minimuseum of musical memorabilia; the Lil' Rock Kid's Club is one of the best going; the poolside spa is tops; and the pool area is compact but has lots of shady areas and massage *salas*, a kind of low, Thai-style pavilion that is a better alternative than the beach.

Beach Road, P.O. Box 99, Pattaya 20260 (next to Montien Hotel). ✆ 03842-8755. Fax 03842-1673. www. hardrockhotels.net. 320 units. 4,180B–5,060B ($105–$127) double; from 5,330B ($133) suite. AE, MC, V. **Amenities:** 3 restaurants; Hard Rock Cafe w/live rock music; huge outdoor lagoon-style pool; fitness center; spa w/massage, Jacuzzi, sauna, and steam; watersports equipment and activities; Lil' Rock Kid's club; game room; tour desk; limo service; shopping arcade; salon; 24-hr. room service; babysitting; same-day laundry service/dry cleaning; nonsmoking rooms; executive-level rooms; "e-bar" Internet lounge. In room: A/C, satellite TV, minibar, fridge, coffeemaker, hair dryer, safe, CD player, IDD phone.

**Pattaya Marriott Resort & Spa** ✪✪ (Kids) Right in the center of Pattaya Beach and adjoining the Royal Garden Plaza shopping complex, the Marriot has a quiet courtyard garden and landscaped pool area so you can almost forget Pattaya City just beyond the walls. Spacious balconied rooms have views of the gardens or the sea and are done in a tidy, upscale-chain style with lots of nice little Thai touches. This resort makes for a great retreat full of all of the requisite creature comforts. The adjoining Royal Garden Plaza means access to fine dining, and entertainment and the hotel pool is the largest in Pattaya.

218 Beach Rd., Pattaya 20150, Chonburi. ✆ **03841-2120.** Fax 03842-9926. 300 units. 5,000B–7,000B ($125–$175) double; from 14,000B ($350) suite. AE, DC, MC, V. **Amenities:** 3 restaurants; lounge; pool w/swim-up bar; 2 lighted grass tennis courts; large fitness center; spa w/Jacuzzi, sauna, and steam; Thai herbal spa; watersports equipment; children's programs; game room; tour desk; limo service; shopping mall w/more than 50 shops; salon; 24-hr. room service; babysitting; same-day laundry service/dry cleaning; non-smoking rooms; executive-level rooms; Ripley's Believe It or Not Museum; Motion Master Theater. *In room:* A/C, satellite TV w/in-house movies, minibar, fridge, coffee/tea-making facilities, safe, IDD phone.

**The Royal Cliff Beach Resort** ★★★ Comprised of the Royal Cliff Grand, The Royal Wing and Spa, and the Royal Cliff Resort (and Terrace), this large, luxurious compound provides a range of accommodations and is tops in Pattaya. Each property has its own charm. High-end **Royal Cliff Grand** and **Royal Wing** are the best choices and cater to the well-heeled business traveler. Everything is luxurious: from the columned public spaces, chandeliers, and fountains to large and opulent guest rooms. The Grand's spacious rooms are set in a contemporary, scallop-shaped tower and have deluxe appointments like marble bathrooms with separate shower stalls and twin sinks. The Royal Club on the sixth floor boasts a private spa with massage, Jacuzzi, and sun deck. The **Royal Cliff Beach Hotel,** the most affordable choice, is Pattaya's top family resort. Rooms are spacious with bleached wood and pastel decor and large terraces, most with bay views. Two-bedroom suites are perfect for families. Even the more modest rooms in this cliff-top perch look out over the bay of Pattaya and the hotel amenities are without rival. It's far from town and very quiet.

353 Phra Tamnuk Rd., Pattaya, Chonburi 20150 (on cliff, south end of Pattaya Bay). ✆ **03825-0421.** Fax 03825-0514. www.royalcliff.com. 1,072 units. 5,200B–7,400B ($130–$185) deluxe double rooms; from 10,000B ($250) suite. AE, DC, MC, V. **Amenities:** Full facilities sharing w/all Royal Cliff Beach Resort properties, including 10 restaurants; 6 bars (many w/live music); 5 outdoor landscaped pools; golf course; 3-hole putting green; 6 outdoor lighted tennis courts; large, completely equipped fitness center w/spa, sauna, steam, and massage; Jacuzzi; watersports rentals; concierge; tour desk; limo service; business center; salon; 24-hr. room service; babysitting; same-day laundry/dry cleaning; nonsmoking rooms. *In room:* A/C, satellite TV, minibar, fridge, hair dryer, safe.

## MODERATE

**Cabbages & Condoms** This new, lush, comfortable resort was built by Khun Meechai and the same folks who support sustainable rural development and health education throughout Thailand (see their restaurants in both Bangkok and Chiang Rai). Rooms are cozy here and the resort, just recently up and running, is a luxurious oasis in the far south of Pattaya. An atmospheric, affordable escape.

366/11 Moo 12 Phra Tam Nak 4 Rd., Nongprue, Banglamung, Chonburi (south of town on the hilltop, not far from Royal Cliff). ✆ **03825-0556.** Fax 03825-0034. 53 units. 2,200B–5,800B ($55–$145) double; from 10,000B ($250) suite. AE, MC, V. **Amenities:** Restaurant; large outdoor pool; spa w/massage; tour desk; limited room service; laundry service. *In room:* A/C, satellite TV, minibar, fridge.

**Siam Bayview Hotel** Managed by the same people as the nearby Siam Bayview Resort (✆ **03842-8678**), a comparable property, the Siam Bayview is set in a spacious garden at the town center. The Bayview is more city hotel than resort and rooms are bland but comfortable. Some rooms have balconies. Go for the seaview rooms on upper floors.

Beach Rd., Pattaya, Chonburi 20260 (center of beach, between *sois* 9 and 10). ✆ **03842-3871.** Fax 03842-3879. www.siamhotels.com. 270 units. 3,000B–4,500B ($75–$113) double; from 8,000B ($200) suite. AE, MC, V. **Amenities:** 3 restaurants; lounge; 2 outdoor pools; 2 lighted tennis courts; fitness center; tour desk; business center; limited room service; babysitting; same-day laundry service/dry cleaning. *In room:* A/C, satellite TV, minibar, fridge, coffeemaker, hair dryer, IDD phone.

## WHERE TO DINE

Busy Pattaya is chockablock with small storefront bars and eateries. You'll find the big fast-food chains well represented (including two Starbucks along the beachfront road) and the Royal Garden Shopping Complex (south of town), as well as the large Big C Festival Center (on Pattaya 2nd Rd., north end of town) support a number of very familiar restaurants.

### MODERATE

**Benihana** JAPANESE/AMERICAN  Most American readers are thinking, "Benihana? In Thailand?" Well, if you've had your fill of *tom yam* and *pad thai*, this place is a welcome respite. It's got all the fun of any Benihana's—*teppanyaki* grill displays performed by chefs who have as much humor as skill, and the food is just great. Come for a good time and a lot of laughs.

2nd Level, Royal Garden Plaza. 𝒸 03842-5029. Set menus 150B–500B ($3.75–$13). AE, DC, MC, V. Daily 11am–10pm.

**Henry J. Bean's** TEX-MEX  Part of the Amari resort complex, Henry J. Bean's is a big, busy bar and restaurant at beachside (on the very north end of the beachside strip). There are live bands nightly and the food is a delicious mix of good Western fare, burgers, steaks and fries, and good Tex-Mex of anything from flaming fajitas to tasty quesadillas. You'll also find good margaritas and a range of fine cocktails.

Pattaya Beach Rd. (north end). 𝒸 03842-8161. Main courses 190B–350B ($4.75–$8.75). AE, MC, V. Daily 11am–1am.

**PIC Kitchen** ☆ THAI  Named for the Pattaya International Clinic (PIC) Hospital next door (don't worry, they're unrelated), PIC has a nice atmosphere of small Thai teak pavilions, both air-conditioned and open-air, and both Thai-style floor seating and romantic tables. Delicious and affordable Thai cuisine is served a la carte or in lunch and dinner sets. The spring rolls and deep-fried crab claws are mouthwatering. Other dishes come pan-fried, steamed, or charcoal grilled, with spice added to taste. At night, groove to a live jazz band from 7pm to 1am.

Soi 5 Pattaya 2nd Rd. 𝒸 03842-8374. 75B–320B ($1.90–$8). AE, DC, MC, V. Daily 8am–midnight.

**Shere "E" Punjab** NORTHERN INDIAN  An inviting little storefront right along the main beach road at town center, Shere "E" Punjab has candle-lit tables in air-conditioned comfort. It offers a range of northern Indian cuisine and tandoori grilled dishes. Everything is cooked to order with fresh ingredients and everything is authentic, a far better choice than the faux-Western eateries in town.

216 Soi 11 Beach Road. 𝒸 03842-0158. Main courses 120B–280B ($3–$7). AE, MC, V. Daily noon–1am.

## OUTDOOR ACTIVITIES IN PATTAYA
### WATERSPORTS

Efforts at cleanup are ongoing, but the bay in Pattaya is still quite polluted. Sad that development ruined the one thing that drew travelers here in the first place. Beach sand is coarse and swimming, if you dare, is best either at the very north of Pattaya Beach or a 15-minute drive south, over the mountain, to Jomtien Beach. The bay is full of boats ready to take you to **outlying islands** like Ko Khrok, Ko Lan, and Ko Sok for a day of private beach lounging or snorkeling starting at 500B ($13) per head on a full boat (more for a private charter). It'll cost you a bit more to far-flung Bamboo Island or Ko Man Wichai—some

2,000B ($50). **Paragliding** around the bay behind a motorboat is a popular beachfront activity and a 5-minute flight costs from 250B ($6.25).

Jomtien Beach hosts **windsurfing** and **sea-kayaking;** boards and boats are rented along the beach for from 200B ($5) per hour.

Contact **Adventure Divers,** 219/56 Soi Yamato (✆ **03871-0899**), for scuba.

## GOLF

The hills around Pattaya are known as the "Golf Paradise of the East" with many international-class courses in a short 40km (25-mile) radius of the city.

- **Bangphra International Golf Club,** 45 Moo 6, Tambon Bang Phra, Sri Racha (✆ **03834-1149**), is the finest course in Pattaya, although it's a long drive (greens fees: weekdays 840B/$21; weekends 1,500B/$38).
- **Laem Chabang International Country Club,** 106/8 Moo 4 Tambon Bung, Sri Ratcha (✆ **03837-2273**), is a 9-hole course designed by Jack Nicklaus with very dramatic scenery (greens fees: weekdays 1,500B/$38); weekends 2,500B/$63).
- **Siam Country Club,** 50 Tambol Poeng, Banglamung (✆ **03824-9381;** fax 03824-9387), is a short hop from Pattaya and believed to be one of the country's most challenging courses (greens fees: all week 1,100B/$28).

## PATTAYA AFTER DARK

Pattaya is all flashing neon and blaring music down even the smallest *soi,* an assault on the senses. Places like the South Pattaya pedestrian area, "Walking Street," are lined with open-air watering holes with bar girls luring passersby: The nightlife finds you in this town with an imploring, "You, mister, where you go?" Go-go bars are everywhere and red-light "Bar Beer" joints are springing up as fast as local officials can close them down. The city is a larger version of Bangkok's Patpong, complete with "Boyz Town," a row of gay go-go clubs in south Pattaya. The same debauch that brings so many to Pattaya is pretty sad in the light of day, though, when bleary-eyed revelers stumble around streets once glowing with neon, now bleak and strewn with garbage.

Sex for money in Pattaya is a simple and direct business. Pattaya's "physical" massage parlors, where clients choose ladies from behind glass by number for an oil massage, are on Pattaya 2nd Road in northern Pattaya. All-night companionship is a matter of a small payment to a club owner (a bar fine) and simple negotiations. Most hotels have small security desks where girls must register with security guards before coming up to guest rooms (often for a fee). There's also a very active *Katoey* (transsexual) scene. Stories of laced drinks and theft (or worse) abound and AIDS and other STDs are a concern, as in all of Thailand (see the "Sex for Sale" box at the beginning of this chapter).

There are a few spots without the sleaze. **Hopf Brewery** (219 Beach Rd.; ✆ **03871-0650**) makes it's own fine brand of suds and the in-house Hopf Band plays everything from old Herb Alpert tunes to newer jazzy sounds. **Shenani-gan's** is a fun Irish bar hangout at the Royal Garden Complex (near the Marriott), with the front entrance on Pattaya 2nd Road (✆ **03871-0641**) and **Henry J. Bean's** (on the beach near the Amari Hotel; ✆ **03842-8161;** see "Where to Dine," above) has a live band and a light, friendly atmosphere.

The town's campy cabaret shows are touristy good fun. Pattaya's most beautiful *Katoeys* (transsexuals) don sequined gowns and feather boas to strut their stuff for packed houses nightly. Both **Tiffany's** (464 Moo 9, 2nd Road ;✆ **03842-9642**) and **Alcazar** (78/14 Pattaya 2nd Rd., opposite Soi 5; ✆ **03841-0505**) have hilarious shows much like those in other tourist towns in Thailand. The biggest disco, **Palladium** (78/33–35 Pattaya 2nd Rd.; © **03836-1376**), is a cavernous dance hall with pulsing music, karaoke, and snooker.

## 6 Ban Phe & Ko Samet ✹

220km (136 miles) E of Bangkok on Highway 3 via Pattaya, or 185km (115 miles) on Highway 3 via the Pattaya bypass. Ban Phe is 35km (22 miles) east of Rayong city.

Tiny Ko Samet first became popular with Thais from the poetry of Sunthon Phu, a venerated 19th-century author and Rayong native who set his best-known epic on this "tropical island paradise." Just 1km (half-mile) wide, Samet is split by a rocky ridge. The east coast is lined with budget bungalows. Samet is a national park (you'll pay 200B/$5 to enter Diamond Beach) but it's unclear what's being protected here. It's best to arrive on a weekday for ease in finding a room, but stick around for the weekend to join in with big groups from Bangkok.

## ESSENTIALS
### GETTING THERE

**By Bus**   Buses leave Bangkok every hour between 5am and 7pm for the 3½-hour journey, departing from **Ekamai**, Bangkok's Eastern Bus Terminal on Sukhumvit Road opposite Soi 63 (© **02391-2504**). The one-way trip to Rayong costs 117B ($2.95) and from there it's a 20B (50¢) shared *songtao* to Ban Phe and the ferry landing (some buses go directly to Ban Phe). From Pattaya, you'll have to wait on the highway and flag down anything heading east.

**By Minibus**   Samet Island Tour (109/22 Moo 10 Pratumnak Rd., Pattaya; © **03871-0676**), runs regular routes from Pattaya (trip time: 1 hr.; 300B/$7.50 round-trip). Private cars can also be arranged.

**By Car**   Take Highway 3 east from Bangkok along the longer, more scenic coastal route (3½–4 hr.), or the quicker route via Highway 3 east to Pattaya, then Highway 36 to Rayong, then the coastal Highway 3 to Ban Phe (about 3 hr.).

### GETTING TO KO SAMET

**By Ferry**   Connect by bus from central Rayong to the ferry pier at Ban Phe. From there, ferries leave for the island's northern ferry terminal at Na Dan every half-hour (trip time: 40 min.; 40B/$1) or when full. The first boat departs at 9:30am and the last at 5pm. Several agents at the pier in Ban Phe sell passage directly to Vong Deuan beach for as little as 50B/$1.25.

After arriving at the ferry terminal on the northern tip of Samet Island you can catch a *songtao* to other beaches for between 10B and 50B (25¢–$1.25). There is one road on Samet connecting the main town, Samet Village, halfway down the eastern shore of the island to Vong Deuan. You can rent scooters with good suspension for about 400B ($10) per day.

### FAST FACTS

Ko Samet has no banks or ATMs, but any resort can change money. The post office is at the Naga Bar along the main road south of Diamond Beach.

### WHERE TO STAY

With few exceptions, accommodations are basic though rates are higher than at other "undeveloped" island resorts because food and water must be imported from the mainland. Hotel and transport touts pounce at the pier.

### AO PRAO

This is the only beach on the west coast and reached by pickup or motorbike from the ferry or directly by ferry (contact Ao Prao Resort, below).

**Ao Prao Resort**    This is as grand as it gets. A collection of midrange bungalows on a quiet hillside overlooking the sea, Ao Prao Resort has good basic
amenities, and the highest standard rooms are worth the outlay. It's the only
western-facing beach area on Samet and viewing a sunset from your bungalow
is memorable; however, the surly service isn't. It has direct connections from its
office just north of the main ferry pier. Contact the resort directly for arrangements. **Le Vinara Cottages** (✆ **03864-4104**) is Ao Prao's more upscale, boutique sister property just next door. There's a pool and more luxurious
bungalows start at 7,000B ($175).

60 Moo 4 Tumbong Phe, Rayong 21160 (on the northwest end of the island, best by direct boat, otherwise
rough island rd. far from Diamond Beach and the ferry landing). ✆ **03861-6881**. Fax 03861-6885. 56 units.
2,889B ($72) standard; 4,120B–5,297B ($103–$132) deluxe; from 8,560B ($214) suite. MC, V. **Amenities:**
Restaurant; bar; watersports rentals; tour desk; massage; laundry service. *In room:* A/C, satellite TV, minibar,
fridge.

### HAT SAI KAEO/DIAMOND BEACH

**Sai Kaew Beach Resort** (✆ **01874-8081**) dominates Hat Sai Kaew but there
are any number of simple budget numbers, basic bungalows, starting at 250B
($6.25), as well as the biggest concentration of restaurants and bars. Just a short
jaunt south of Diamond Beach, you'll reach Ao Phai; there, try **Ao Phai Hut**
(✆ **03874-4075**) for cozy, rustic bungalows set on a hillside (from 500B/$13).

### VONG DEAUN

This area is the most happenin' beach in Samet. Busy, with lots of bungalows
and open-air eateries, Vong Deaun has a good vibe in the evening and it's a fun
party spot on the weekend. The beach is about halfway down the island and can
be reached by ferry directly from Ban Phe for just 60B ($1.50) one-way.

   **Malibu Garden Resort** (✆ **03864-4020**) has clean, spartan rooms starting
at just 920B ($23) at its central motel-style campus. It has an in-house tour
operator and provides direct boat connection. **Vong Deaun Resort** (✆ **03864-
4171**) is a similar budget standard just next door.

## WHERE TO DINE

All of the bungalows offer some sort of eating experience, mostly bland local
food and beer, with some Western breakfast offerings. In the evenings on Vong
Deuan beach, tables are set up under twinkling lights alongside big seafood barbecues brimming with the day's catch. It's very pretty. Try **Sea Horse.**

## 7 Trat & Ko Chang

400km (248 miles) E of Bangkok

Trat's dramatic, wooded landscape crests at the Khao Bantat Range, which separates Thailand's easternmost province from neighboring Cambodia. Local
economy relies on rubber and chili plantations, fish farming and fishing. Memories of territorial conflicts with nearby Cambodia are fresh, but the situation is
calm. Trat Province is the gateway to the tranquil, unspoiled acres of Ko Chang
National Park, 52 heavily wooded islands, most accessible by ferry from the cape
at Laem Ngop. Ko Chang is scenically beautiful, and very, very quiet.

## ESSENTIALS

### GETTING THERE

**By Public Bus**    There are numerous daily departures from Bangkok's Eastern
or **Ekamai Bus Terminal** to Trat (✆ **02391-2504;** trip time: 5–6 hr.;
190B/$4.75). From Pattaya, you'll have to flag down westbound buses along

Sukhumvit Road and it is a 3½-hour trip (Pattaya tour companies can arrange direct minivans).

**By Car** Take Highway 3 east from Bangkok to Chonburi, then Highway 344 southeast to Klaeng (bypassing Pattaya and Rayong), then the coastal Highway 3 east through Chanthaburi and south to Trat (about 5–6 hr.).

## GETTING TO THE ISLAND FROM TRAT

From Trat you'll hop a shared *songtao* to the pier at Ao Thammachat for just 30B (75¢). Seven ferries depart Ao Thammachat daily from 7am to 7pm (trip time: 30 min.; 30B/75¢) and land at Ao Sapparos ferry terminal on Ko Chang. From there you can hop a *songtao* to your destination starting at 30B (75¢) for a 15-minute ride to White Sand Beach (touts from the many bungalows will offer free rides if you stay at their bungalow). Less frequent boats leave from Laem Ngop pier (50B/$1.25), a similar 30B (75¢) ride from Trat.

## VISITOR INFORMATION

The **TAT** has an office in Trat (Moo 1 Trat-Laem Ngop Rd.; ℂ 03959-7259) and provides information about the nearby islands.

## WHAT TO SEE & DO IN KO CHANG

Ko Chang, Thailand's second-largest island after Phuket, is the anchor of the 52-island Mu Ko Chang National Park. Thickly forested hills rise from its many rocky bays, forming a swaying hump reminiscent of a sleeping elephant (*chang* means elephant). Cambodia is visible from the eastern shore. **Hat Sai Khao (White Sand Beach),** on the island's west coast, is the most popular beach. Twenty minutes by boat farther south is **Hat Khlong Phrao,** with clusters of bungalows, an inland canal and fishing settlement. There is good snorkeling off Ko Chang's South coast (contact tour operators for details and passage by boat).

## WHERE TO STAY & DINE

If you're arriving in the late evening and get stranded in Trat, the **Muang Trad Hotel,** 4 Sukhumvit Rd. (ℂ 03951-1091), 1 block south of the bus terminal, has rooms from 650B ($16) with air-conditioning.

### EXPENSIVE

**Panviman** ⓐ The newly opened Panviman on Ko Chang is the island's most luxurious choice, far exceeding the many bungalow resorts. Rooms are set in high-peaked, Thai-style buildings with arching *naga* roofs; the spacious grounds are meticulously manicured and the pool is a beautiful little meander flanked on one side by a casual bar, on the other by the resort's fine dining, and all are oriented to great views of the sea (great sunsets). Check out the little garden gnomes all about. Rooms are done in tile and teak, each with canopy bed, large sitting area, balcony, and large stylish bathrooms. Bathrooms are huge. It's not a private beach, but the resort is far south of central White Sand Beach so even in high season you might have a vast stretch of sand to yourself.

8/15 Klong Prao Beach, Koh Chang Trat 23120 (a short ride south of White Sand Beach on the west coast of the island). ℂ 03955-1290, in Bangkok 02910-8660. Fax 03955-1283. 50 units. 5,000B–6,000B ($125–$150) double. MC, V. **Amenities:** Restaurant; bar; outdoor pool; fitness center; Jacuzzi; watersports rentals; tour desk; car rental; transfer services; limited room service; massage; laundry service; Internet. *In room:* A/C, satellite TV, minibar, fridge, coffeemaker, safe, IDD phone.

### MODERATE

**Banpu** (9/11 Moo 4, White Sand Beach; ℂ 03955-1234) is typical of the atmospheric bungalows along White Sand Beach. Rooms start at 2,000B ($50).

Further south, **Ko Chan Resort** (© **02277-5256**) is a similarly affordable and cozy.

## 8 Southern Peninsula: The East Coast & Islands

Thailand's slim Malay Peninsula extends 1,250km (775 miles) south from Bangkok to the Malaysia border. The towns of Cha Am and royal Hua Hin are just a short hop south of Bangkok, and the ancient temples of Phetchaburi, the last outpost of the Khmer Empire, are a good day trip from there. Passing through coastal towns like Prachuap Kiri Khan and Chumpon, heading further south you come to Surat Thani, a popular jumping-off point for islands in the east: Koh Samui, Koh Pha Ngan, and Koh Tao. If the beach resorts of Phuket dominate the tourist landscape on the west coast, so too, Koh Samui, a developed but laid-back resort island in the Gulf of Siam, dominates the east. Nearby Koh Pha Ngan, famed for it's wild full-moon parties, is gaining prominence as a rustic resort destination, as is Koh Tao for its access to some of Thailand's best dive sites.

With its fine islands and beaches, the Gulf of Siam is the Thai paradise of legend and there's an adventure or a little bit of heaven for everyone among palm-draped beaches, lacy coral reefs, Muslim fishing villages, and even Buddhist temples that welcome foreign spiritual seekers.

## 9 Hua Hin & Cha-Am

Hua Hin is 265km (164 miles) S of Bangkok; 223km (138 miles) N of Chumphon. Cha-Am is 240km (149 miles) S of Bangkok; 248km (154 miles) N of Chumphon.

Hua Hin and Cha-Am, neighboring towns on the Gulf of Thailand, are together the country's oldest resort area. Developed in the 1920s as a relaxing getaway for Bangkok's elite, the beautiful seaside of "Thailand's Riviera" was a mere 3 or 4 hours' journey from the capital by train, thanks to the southern railway's completion in 1916. The royal family was the first to embrace these two small fishing villages as the perfect location for both summer vacations and health retreats. In 1924, King Vajiravudh (Rama VI) built the royal Mareukatayawan Palace amid the tall evergreens that lined these stretches of golden sand. At the same time, the Royal Hua Hin Golf Course opened as the first course in Thailand. As Bangkok's upper classes began building summer bungalows along the shore, the State Railways opened the Hua Hin Railway Hotel for tourists, which stands today as the Hotel Sofitel Central, and to this day the King of Thailand spends much of his time at his regal residence just north of town (note the constant presence of coast guard cutters and battleships just off shore). Today, the area's clean sea and beaches support some unique resorts, and nearby Phetchaburi (see "Side Trips from Hua Hin & Cha-Am," later in this section) is a fascinating and easy day trip to experience a bit of Thai history and culture.

Plan your trip for the months between November and May for the most sunshine and least rain, but note that from about mid-December to mid-January, Hua Hin and Cha-Am reach peak levels and bookings should be made well in advance (at a higher rate). Low season means more rain, but not all day long.

## ESSENTIALS
### GETTING THERE
**By Plane**    There is an airport, but no domestic connections.

**By Train**    Both Hua Hin and Cha-Am are reached via the train station in Hua Hin. Ten trains make the daily trek from Bangkok's **Hua Lampong Railway Station** (© **02223-7010** or 1690). The trip is just over 4 hours.

The **Hua Hin Railway Station** (℄ 03251-1073) is at the tip of Dam-noenkasem Road, which slices through the center of town straight to the beach. Pickup truck taxis *(songtao)* or tuk-tuks to town start at 50B ($1.25).

**By Bus**   The bus is the most efficient choice for travel from Bangkok. Buses depart from Bangkok's **Southern Bus Terminal** (℄ 02434-7192) every 20 minutes from 5am to 10pm (128B/$3.20). There are also five daily buses to Cha-Am between 5am and 2pm (113B/$2.85).

Buses from Bangkok arrive in **Hua Hin** at the air-conditioned bus station (℄ 03251-1230) on Srasong Road, 1 block north of Damnoenkasem Road. From here it's easy to find a *songtao* or tuk-tuk to take you to your destination. The **Cha-Am bus station** is on the main beach road (℄ 03242-5307).

**Minibuses** can be arranged at any hotel or travel agent in either Bangkok or Hua Hin. Regular minivan departures leave from the traffic circle at Bangkok's busy **Victory Monument** (a stop on the BTS skytrain) and cost 140B ($3.50).

**By Car**   From Bangkok, take Route 35, the Thonburi-Paktho Highway, south-west and allow 2 to 4 hours, depending on traffic.

## SPECIAL EVENTS

The annual **King's Cup Elephant Polo Tournament** comes to Hua Hin each September. Teams from as far away as Europe and Sri Lanka play three-a-side polo, much like equine polo only with longer mallets on a smaller field. Sponsored by the **TAT** at **Anantara Resort & Spa** (℄ 03252-0250; see "Where to Stay," below), the event raises money for the National Elephant Institute.

## ORIENTATION

Despite all the tourist traffic, Hua Hin is easy to navigate. The main artery, Petchkasem Road, runs parallel to the waterfront about 4 blocks inland. The wide Damnoenkasem Road cuts through Petchkasem and runs straight to the beach. On the north side of Damnoenkasem toward the waterfront, you'll find a cluster of guesthouses, restaurants, shopping, and nightspots lining the narrow lanes.

Smaller Cha-Am is a 25-minute drive north of Hua Hin along Petchkasem Road. Ruamchit Road, also known as Beach Road, hugs the shore and is lined with shops, restaurants, hotels, and motels. Cha-Am's resorts line the 8km (5-mile) stretch of beach that runs south from the village toward Hua Hin.

## GETTING AROUND

**By *Songtao***   Pickup truck taxis follow regular routes in Hua Hin, passing the railway station and bus terminals at regular intervals. Flag one down that's going in your direction. Fares range from 10B to 20B (25¢–50¢) within town, while stops at outlying resorts will be up to 50B ($1.25). Trips between Hua Hin and Cha-Am cost between 100B and 200B ($2.50–$5).

**By Tuk-Tuk**   Tuk-tuks rides are negotiable, as always, but expect to pay as little as 20B (50¢) for a ride within town.

**By Motorcycle Taxi**   Within each town, motorcycle taxi fares begin at 20B (50¢). The taxi drivers, identifiable by colorful numbered vests, are a good way to get to your resort if you're in Cha-Am after hours (about 100B/$2.50).

**By *Samlor***   Trishaws, or *samlors,* can be hired for short distances in town (from 20B/50¢). You can also negotiate an hourly rate.

**By Car or Motorcycle**   **Avis** has a desk at both the Hotel Sofitel Central in Hua Hin (℄ 03251-2021) and the Dusit Resort and Polo Club in Cha-Am (℄ 03252-0008). **Budget** has an office at the Grand Hotel (℄ 03251-4220).

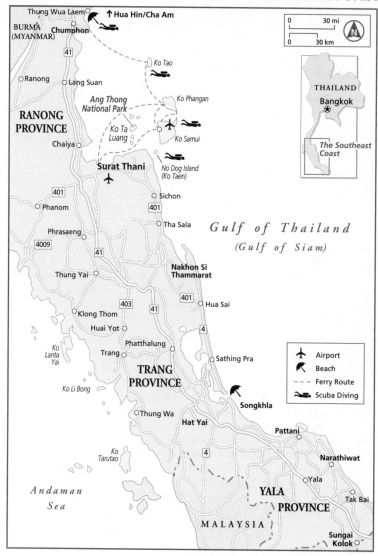

## The Southern Peninsula: East Coast

Thung Wua Laem
↑ Hua Hin/Cha Am

BURMA
(MYANMAR)

Chumphon

41

Ranong

Lang Suan

Ko Tao

Ang Thong
National Park

Ko Phangan

RANONG
PROVINCE

Ko Ta
Luang

Chaiya

Ko Samui

Surat Thani

No Dog Island
(Ko Taen)

401

Phanom

401

Sichon

Phrasaeng

Tha Sala

*Gulf of Thailand*
*(Gulf of Siam)*

4009

41

Thung Yai

Nakhon Si
Thammarat

401

403

41

Hua Sai

Klong Thom

4

Huai Yot

Ko
Lanta
Yai

Phatthalung

Trang

Sathing Pra

TRANG
PROVINCE

Ko Li Bong

Songkhla

Thung Wa

Hat Yai

Airport
Beach
Ferry Route
Scuba Diving

Ko
Tarutao

4

Pattani

Narathiwat

YALA
PROVINCE

Yala

Tak Bai

*Andaman*
*Sea*

MALAYSIA

Sungai
Kolok

0    30 mi
0    30 km

THAILAND

Bangkok

The Southeast
Coast

Self-drive rates start at 1,500B ($38). Cheaper alternatives can be rented from
stands near the beach on Damnoenkasem Road. A Suzuki Caribian goes for
around 1,000B ($25) per day, and 100cc motorbikes are available for 200B ($5)
per day.

## VISITOR INFORMATION
The **Hua Hin Tourist Information Center** (✆ 03251-1047 or 03253-2433) is
in the center of town tucked behind the city shrine at the corner of Damnoenkasem and Petchkasem roads. Opening hours are from 8:30am to 4:30pm
daily. In Cha-Am, the **TAT office** (✆ 03247-1005 or 03247-1006) is inconve-
niently located on the corner of Petchkasem Road and Narathip Road.

## FAST FACTS

**IN HUA HIN**   All major banks are along Petchkasem Road to the north of Damnoenkasem, and there are many money changers throughout the town. The **main post office** (℡ 03251-1350) is on Damnoenkasem Road near the Petchkasem intersection. Both Hua Hin and Cha-Am have Internet cafes along the more-traveled shopping streets. The **Hua Hin Hospital** (℡ 03252-0371) is located in the north of town along Petchkasem Road. Call the **Tourist Police** for either town at ℡ 03251-5995.

**IN CHA-AM**   Banks are centered along Petchkasem Road, and the post office is on Beach Road. The **Thonburi Cha-Am Hospital** (℡ 03243-3903) is off Narathip Road. Internet access is available along the beach road.

## WHAT TO SEE & DO

The stunning Khmer-style temples of **Phetchaburi** ★★ (see "Side Trips," at the end of this section) are the most significant cultural sites near Hua Hin and Cha-Am, but most folks are here to escape Bangkok and enjoy the beaches.

The 80-year-old **Sofitel Hotel,** originally built for Thai royals and their guests, is itself a site and visitors are welcome to tour the grounds or enjoy **high tea** in a quaint garden area (daily 3:30–5pm; 370B/US$9.25).

Hua Hin's **Night Market** (on Dechanuchit Rd. on the northern end at town center) is busy from dusk to late with small food stalls and vendors.

## WHERE TO STAY IN HUA HIN
### VERY EXPENSIVE

**Chiva-Som International Health Resort** ★★★   Chiva-Som is a new beginning for many. One of the finest high-end health resorts in the region, this peaceful campus is a sublime collection of handsome pavilions, bungalows, and central buildings dressed in fine teak and sea-colored tiles nestled in landscaped grounds just beyond a pristine beach. But what brings so many to Chiva-Som are its spa programs: From Chi Gong to chin-ups, muscle straining to massage, a stay at Chiva-Som is a chance to escape the workaday world and focus on development of body and mind. Leave the kids at home, turn off the cellphone, and change the suit for loose-fitting cotton because, whether just to relax or to start a new chapter in life, a visit to Chiva-Som is proactive. Upon check-in, you'll fill out an extensive survey, have a brief medical check, and meet with a counselor who can tailor a program to fit your needs, goals, and budget or package you have booked (there is a wide range). From there, guests might focus on early-morning yoga, stretching, and tough workouts, or go for gentle massages, aromatherapy, even isolation chambers and past-life regression workshops. The choices are many and personal trainers, staff, and facilities are unmatched in the region. The resorts spa cuisine is not all granola and oats, but simple, healthy fare, and there is a nice bond that develops between guests and staff in weekly barbecues and frequent mocktail parties. The spa treatments are fantastic: Don't pass up the signature Chiva-Som Massage. Day spa visitors welcome.

73/4 Petchkasem Rd., Hua Hin, 77110 Thailand (5-min. drive south of Hua Hin). ℡ 03253-6536. Fax 03251-1615. www.chivasom.net. 57 units. All rates are quoted per person: 14,150B ($354) oceanview double; 16,400B ($410) pavilion; from 24,400B ($610) suite. Nightly rate includes 3 spa cuisine meals per day, health and beauty consultations, daily massage, and participation in fitness and leisure activities. Contact the resort about other packages. AE, DC, MC, V. **Amenities:** 2 restaurants; ozonated indoor swimming pool and outdoor swimming pool; golf course nearby; amazing fitness center w/personal trainer and exercise classes; his-and-hers spas w/steam and hydrotherapy treatments, massage, beauty treatments, floatation, and medical advisement; watersports equipment; bike rental; concierge; tour desk; limo service; salon; 24-hr. room service; same-day laundry service/dry cleaning; nonsmoking rooms; library. *In room:* A/C, satellite TV, minibar, fridge, safe, IDD phone.

## EXPENSIVE

### Anantara Resort & Spa ★★

The Anantara is a collection of teak pavilions surrounded by lily ponds, and from the hotel's most luxurious rooms you can hear chirping frogs and watch buzzing dragonflies from wide balconies. More affordable rooms cluster around a manicured courtyard. Rooms are furnished Thai style with teak-and-rattan furniture. Superior rooms have a garden view and deluxe rooms overlook the sand and sea. Beach terrace rooms have large patios perfect for private barbecues. Junior suite rooms have enormous aggregate bathtubs that open to guest rooms by a sliding door. Fine dining options are many and the resort's spa is large and luxurious. The Anantara holds the annual Elephant Polo in Hua Hin, an event gaining worldwide attention.

43/1 Petchkasem Beach Rd., Hua Hin 77110. © 03252-0250. Fax 03252-0259. 197 units. 6,800B–7,600B ($170–$190) double; 8,400B ($210) terrace double; suite from 9,000B ($225). AE, DC, MC, V. **Amenities:** 4 restaurants; lounge; outdoor pool w/children's pool; outdoor lighted tennis courts; fitness center; spa w/sauna, steam, massage; Jacuzzi; watersports equipment and instruction; bike and motorcycle rental; children's playground; concierge; tour desk; car-rental desk; limo service; shopping arcade; salon; 24-hr. room service; babysitting; same-day laundry service/dry cleaning; nonsmoking rooms. *In room:* A/C, satellite TV, minibar, fridge, coffee/tea-making facilities, hair dryer, safe.

### Hilton Hua Hin Resort and Spa ★★

Right in the heart of downtown Hua Hin, this massive tower overlooks the main beach. It's a Hilton, which means a fine room standard and courteous staff. The marble lobby with quiet reflection pools is welcoming, the beachside pool is luxurious, and everything is well maintained and sparkling clean. The Hua Hin Resort is a top international standard and the best location for strolling the main beach area, in-town shopping, and nightlife.

33 Narsdamri Rd., Hua Hin 77110 (on the main beach and in the heart of downtown shopping). © 03251-2888. Fax 02250-0999. www.huahin.hilton.com. 296 units. 6,800B–8,400B ($170–$210) double; from 10,400B ($260) suite. AE, DC, MC, V. **Amenities:** 3 restaurants; 2 bars; outdoor pool; 2 tennis courts; health club; spa w/massage, Jacuzzi, sauna, and steam; concierge; tour desk; car-rental; shopping arcade; salon; 24-hr room service; laundry service; dry cleaning; babysitting. *In room:* A/C, satellite TV w/in-house movies, minibar, fridge, coffeemaker, hair dryer, safe, IDD phone.

### Hotel Sofitel Central ★★★

The original Hua Hin Railway Hotel opened in 1922 and is the classiest, most luxurious accommodations going. There's a cool, calm colonial effect to the whitewashed buildings, shaded verandas and walkways, fine wooden details, red-tile roofs, and immaculate gardens with topiaries. There is a small hotel museum of photography and memorabilia, and the original 14 bedrooms are preserved for posterity. Subsequent additions and renovations over the years have expanded the hotel into a large and modern full-facility hotel without sacrificing a bit of its former charm. The original rooms have their unique appeal, but the newer rooms are larger, brighter, and more comfortable. With furnishings that reflect the hotel's old beach resort feel, they are still modern and cozy. Sofitel's three magnificent outdoor pools are finely landscaped and have sun decks under shady trees. The new Spa Health Club, in its own beachside bungalow, provides full-service health and beauty treatments, and the fitness center is extensive.

1 Damnoenkasem Rd., Hua Hin 77110 (in the center of town by the beach). © 800/221-4542 in the U.S., or 03251-2021. Fax 03251-1014. www.sofitel.com. 214 units. 6,150B–7,050B ($154–$176) double; from 9,700B ($243) suite. DC, MC, V. **Amenities:** 5 restaurants; lounge and bar; 3 outdoor pools; putting green and miniature golf; golf course nearby; outdoor lighted tennis courts; new fitness center; spa w/massage; watersports

equipment; bike rental; kids' club; concierge; tour desk; car-rental desk; limo service; business center; shopping arcade; salon; 24-hr. room service; babysitting; same-day laundry service; dry cleaning; nonsmoking rooms; executive-level rooms; daily craft and language lessons; nature tours; billiards room. *In room:* A/C, satellite TV, minibar, fridge, hair dryer, safe, IDD phone.

**Hua Hin Marriott Resort & Spa** ✪    From the giant swinging couches in the main lobby to the large central pavilions, the hotel is done in a grand, if exaggerated, Thai style. The Marriott attracts large groups, but is a good choice for families. Ponds, pools, boats, golf, tennis, and other sport venues dot the junglelike grounds leading to the open beach area. There is a good kids' club. The hotel is relatively far from the busy town center and provides shuttle service. Deluxe rooms are the best choice—large, amenity-filled, and facing the sea. Terrace rooms at beachside are worth the bump up. The spa is luxurious, too.

107/1 Petchkasem Beach Rd., Hua Hin 77110. ✆ 800/228-9290 in the U.S., or 03251-1881. Fax 03251-2422. 216 units. 6,400B ($160) double; 7,300B–8,800B ($183–$220) beach terrace; from 14,300B ($358) suite. AE, DC, MC, V. **Amenities:** 3 restaurants; lounge; outdoor pool; golf course nearby; outdoor lighted tennis courts; fitness center; spa; watersports equipment; bike rental; children's playground and zoo; concierge; tour desk; car-rental desk; limo service; shopping arcade; salon; 24-hr. room service; massage; babysitting; same-day laundry service/dry cleaning; nonsmoking rooms. *In room:* A/C, satellite TV, minibar, coffee/tea-making facilities, hair dryer, safe.

**MODERATE**

For affordable, in-town accommodations, try **PP Villa** (11 Damnoenkasem Rd., ✆ 03253-3785) with tidy rooms from 1,000B ($25) or adjacent **Sirin Hotel** (✆ 03251-1150) with motel-style accommodations from 1,500B ($38).

## WHERE TO STAY IN CHA-AM
**EXPENSIVE**

**Dusit Resort and Polo Club** ✪    A "polo club" in theme only, the Dusit has all the amenities of a fine resort. The elegant marble lobby features bronze horses and hunting-and-riding oil paintings, and hall doors have polo mallet handles and other equine-themed artwork and decor. Guest rooms carry the same theme and are spacious, with big marble bathrooms. Room rates vary with the view, although every room's balcony faces the lushly landscaped pool. Ground-floor rooms are landscaped for privacy with private verandas leading to the pool and the beach. Suites are enormous with elegant living rooms, full pantry area, and dressing area. For all its air of formality, the resort is great for those who prefer swimsuits and T-shirts to riding jodhpurs and a relaxed holiday air pervades. All sorts of watersports are available on the quiet beach. It's a bit far from both Hua Hin and Cha-Am, but the resort is completely self-contained.

1349 Petchkasem Rd., Cha-Am 76120. ✆ 03252-0009. Fax 03252-0296. www.dusit.com. 300 units. 5,500B–6,000B ($138–$150) double; from 12,000B ($300) Landmark suite. AE, DC, MC, V. **Amenities:** 5 restaurants; lounge; huge outdoor pool; minigolf; golf course nearby; outdoor lighted tennis courts; squash courts; fitness center; Jacuzzi; sauna; watersports equipment; bike and motorcycle rental; billiards and game room; concierge; tour desk; car-rental desk; limo service; business center; shopping arcade; salon; 24-hr. room service; massage; babysitting; same-day laundry service/dry cleaning; nonsmoking rooms; executive-level rooms; equestrian center and horseback riding. *In room:* A/C, satellite TV, minibar, fridge, coffee/tea-making facilities, hair dryer, safe, IDD phone.

**MODERATE**

**The Regent Cha-Am** ✪    No relation to the Regent chain, the Regent Cha-Am is a sprawling property, the combination of three resorts for a total of some 708 rooms (at the Regent Resort and more luxury Regency Wing and Regent Chalet). There are lots of services, large pools, watersports, squash, and a small fitness area. The main resort is a massive courtyard, and the Chalet is a separate, quieter bungalow facility (the best choice). Standard rooms are comfortable and affordable, done up like the average chain hotel but very clean and cozy. The resort is on the road between Hua Hin and Cha-Am and a long ride to either. Come with your own wheels or you are stuck. The Regent is busy year-round, mostly on the weekends.

849/21 Petchkasem Rd., Cha-Am 76120. ☎ **03245-1240.** Fax 03245-1277. www.regent-chaam.com. 708 units. 3,800B–4,200B ($95–$105) double; from 5,600B ($140) suite. AE, MC, V. **Amenities:** 3 restaurants; lounge; 3 pools; outdoor lighted tennis courts; squash courts; fitness center; Jacuzzi; watersports equipment; bike and motorcycle rental; game room; tour desk; limo service; business center; salon; 24-hr. room service; massage; babysitting; same-day laundry service/dry cleaning. *In room:* A/C, satellite TV, minibar, fridge.

## WHERE TO DINE IN HUA HIN

The main piers in both Hua-Hin and Cha-Am are busy every morning when fishing boats return with their loads. Nearby open-air restaurants serve fresh seafood at a fraction of what you'd pay in Bangkok.

The Night Market, on Dechanuchit Road west of Petchkasem Road in the north end of town, is a great place for authentic local eats for very little. The resorts have more restaurants than there is room to list and no matter where you stay you'll have great dining options in-house. In town there are lots of small storefront eateries and tourist cafes as well.

There are lots of seafood places along the beach in the center of town. The best is **Meekaruna Seafood** (26/1 Naratdamri Rd. next to the pier; ☎ 03251-1932).

**Itsara** ⭐ THAI   In a two-story seaside home built in the 1920s, this restaurant has a real laid-back charm, from the noisy, open kitchen to the terrace seating and views of the beach—quite atmospheric and a good place to get together with friends, cover the table with dishes, and enjoy the good life. Specialties include a sizzling hot plate of glass noodles with prawn, squid, pork, and vegetables. A variety of fresh seafood and meats are prepared steamed or deep-fried, and can be served with either salt, chili, or red-curry paste.

7 Napkehard St., Hua Hin (sea side, a 50B/$1.25 *samlor* ride north from the town center). ☎ 03253-0574. Reservations recommended for Sat dinner. Main courses 60B–290B ($1.50–$7.25). MC, V. Mon–Fri 10am–midnight; Sat–Sun 2pm–midnight.

## ACTIVITIES
### Golf

Hua Hin is a golf getaway for Bangkokians. It's best to make reservations. The larger hotels run shuttles to all courses.

- **Palm Hills Golf Resort and Country Club,** 1444 Petchkasem Rd., Cha-Am; (☎ **03252-0800**), just north of Hua Hin, Palm Hills, is a picturesque course set among rolling hills and jagged escarpments (greens fees: 1,200B/$30).
- **Royal Hua Hin Golf Course,** Damnoenkasem Road near the Hua Hin Railway Station (☎ **03251-2475**), is Thailand's first championship golf course, opened in 1924. Don't miss the many topiary figures along its fairways (greens fees: 1,200B/$30; open daily 6am–6pm).
- **Springfield Royal Country Club,** 193 Huay-Sai Nua, Petchkasem Road, Cha-Am (☎ **03247-1303**), designed by Jack Nicklaus in 1993, is in a beautiful valley setting—the best by far (greens fees: 2,500B/$63).

### Watersports

Most resorts forbid noisy **jet skis,** but the beaches are lined with young entrepreneurs renting them out for 500B ($13) per hour. Windsurfers and Hobie Cats are for rent at most resorts or with small outfits along the beach (starting at 300B/$7.50 and 600B/$15 per hr., respectively).

Call **Western Tours** at © 03253-3303. Ask about **snorkeling trips** to outer islands for about 1,500B ($38) per person. The office is at 11 Damnoenkasem Rd. in the city center.

## SHOPPING

Damnoenkasem Road near the beach features local crafts, batik clothing, and handicrafts. At night the 2-block-long **Night Market** ☆ on Dechanuchit Road west of Petchkasem Road is a great stop for tasty treats and fun trinkets.

## NIGHTLIFE

For nightlife, your best bet is Hua Hin. A 15-minute stroll through the labyrinth of *sois* between Damnoenkasem, Poolsuk, and Dechanuchit roads near the beach reveals all sorts of small places to stop for a cool cocktail and some fun.

## SIDE TRIPS FROM HUA HIN & CHAN AM

### PHETCHABURI ☆☆

Phetchaburi dates from the same period as Ayutthaya and Kanchanaburi, and later served as an important military city. Phetchaburi's palace and historically significant temples highlight an excellent day trip. It's just 1 hour from Hua Hin. The main attraction is **Phra Nakhorn Khiri,** a 19th-century summer palace of King Mongkut (Rama IV) in the hills overlooking the city (reachable by cable car). Also find a collection of important royal temples and the summer palaces of other kings. **Western Tours,** 11 Damnoenkasem Rd. (© 03253-3303), has day excursions from 700B ($18).

### KHAO SAM ROI YOT NATIONAL PARK

Just 40 minutes drive south of Hua Hin, Khao Sam Roi Yot, or the "Mountain of Three Hundred Peaks," offers great short hikes to panoramic views of the sea. Of the park's two caves, Kaew Cave is the most interesting, housing a *sala* pavilion that was built in 1890 for King Chulalongkorn.

## 10 Surat Thani

644 km (399 miles) S of Bangkok

Surat Thani is believed to have been an important center of the Sumatra-based Srivijaya Empire in the 9th and 10th centuries. Today, it's known to foreigners as the gateway to beautiful Koh Samui and to Thais as a rich agricultural province.

Surat is the main jumping-off point for the eastern islands **Koh Samui, Koh Pha Ngan,** and **Koh Tao,** as well as the navigable jungles of **Khao Sok National Park** and nearby **Wat Suan Mohkk,** a forest monastery that holds monthly meditation retreats for Thais and foreigners (see " Day Trips from Surat Thani," below, for details).

Surat is known for its **oysters,** farmed in Ka Dae and the Tha Thanong Estuary (30km/19 miles south of town) where more than 6,475 hectares (15,993 acres) are devoted to aquaculture. Fallow rice paddies now support young *hoi takram,* or tilam oysters, which cling to bamboo poles submerged in brackish water. Surat Thani's other famed product is the Rong Rian rambutan (*ngor* in Thai), a fruit with a spiky rind hiding a sweet, pitted fruit not unlike lychee. During the August harvest time there is a rambutan fair and parade.

## ESSENTIALS

### GETTING THERE

**By Plane** **Thai Airways** (in Bangkok © 02535-2084) has two daily flights from Bangkok to Surat Thani (trip time: 70 min.). If you've rolled into town on the morning train you can just hop on one of the travel agent buses to the ferry—either Songserm or Phanthip has buses waiting. Otherwise you can grab a shared minivan to town for 80B ($2). Thai Airways office is at 3/27–28 Karoonrat Rd. (© 07727-2610), just south of town.

**By Train**    Ten trains leave daily from **Bangkok's Hua Lampong station** (© 02223-7010 or 1690) to Surat Thani (trip time: 13 hr.); second-class sleepers are 468B ($12), a second-class seat 288B ($7.20). The Surat Thani train station is very inconvenient, but minitrucks meet trains to transport you to town for 20B (50¢) shared ride.

**By Bus**    Two VIP 24-seater buses leave daily from **Bangkok's Southern Bus Terminal** (© 02434-7192; trip time: 10 hr.; 590B/$15). Air-conditioned buses leave daily from Phuket's Bus Terminal off Phang-nga Road opposite the Royal Phuket City Hotel (© 07621-1977; trip time: 5 hr.; 150B/$3.75). Also from Phuket, minivans travel to Surat Thani daily (trip time: 4 hr.; 160B/$4). Find them across from the Montri Hotel on Suthat Road. The Surat Thani Bus Terminal is on Kaset II Road a block east of the main road.

**By Minivan**    The best way to travel between southern cities is by privately operated air-conditioned minivans. They are affordable and run regular schedules from Surat Thani to/from Chumphon, Ranong, Nakhon Si Thammarat, Hat Yai, and beyond. The best way to arrange these trips is to consult your hotel's front desk. You can go door-to-door to the hotel of your choice, usually for little more than 100B ($2.50).

**By Car**    Take Highway 4 south from Bangkok to Chumphon, then Highway 41 south direct to Surat Thani.

## VISITOR INFORMATION
For information about Surat Thani, Koh Samui, and Koh Pha Ngan, contact the **TAT** office, 5 Talad Mai Rd., Surat Thani (© 07728-8818), near the Wang Tai Hotel.

## ORIENTATION
Surat Thani is built up along the south shore of the Tapi River. Talad Mai Road, 2 blocks south of the river, is the city's main street, with the TAT office at its west end, and the bus station and central market at its east end. Frequent *songtao* run along Talad Mai; prices are based on distance but rarely exceed 20B (50¢).

## FAST FACTS
Major **banks** along Talad Mai Road have ATMs and will perform currency exchanges. The **Post Office** and **Overseas Call Office** are together on Na Muang and Chonkasean roads near the center of town. The **Taksin Hospital** (© 07727-3239) is at the north end of Talad Mai Road. The **Tourist Police** (© 07728-1300) are with the TAT on Talad Mai Road.

## WHAT TO SEE & DO
Surat is a typical small Thai city and, for most foreign visitors, little more than a transportation hub to the islands (Samui and Pha Ngan). Most people will want to press on. If it is your only stop in Thailand (on the way to Samui, for example), give the town a wander and see what Thai life is all about (go small streets and find a *wat*). Outside of town, popular day trips include the **Monkey Training College** (24 Moo 4, Tambon Thungkong; © 07722-7351), where monkeys are trained to get coconuts, and, far from town, find **Wat Suan Mohk,** a Buddhist temple that accepts foreign students for monthly retreats (see "Day Trips from Surat Thani," below).

## WHERE TO STAY

For most, Surat Thani is just a stopping-off point for trips to the islands. If you have a layover, the best choice in town is the **Wang Tai Hotel** (1 Talad Mai Rd.; ℭ **07728-3020**) just south of the town center, with large, clean rooms from 950B ($24). More convenient to the market and town transport is the **BJ Hotel** (17/1 Donnok Rd.; ℭ **07721-7410**), with bare-bones rooms from 500B ($13). The **Siam Thara** (1/144 Donnock Rd.; ℭ **07727-3740**) is a similar standard but showing some age.

## WHERE TO DINE

You can sample Surat Thanis famous oysters at any streetside cafe, and there is a small cluster of open-air eateries along Talad Mai near the turn to BJ Hotel.

In the north end of town near the bus station, **Lucky's Restaurant** (452/84–85 Talad Mai Rd.; ℭ **07727-3267**) has an open-air dining room and an air-conditioned hall, both filled with locals enjoying the inexpensive Thai fare.

## DAY TRIPS FROM SURAT THANI
### CHAIYA TOWN & SUAN MOKKH

**Suan Mokkhabalarama,** or Suan Mokkh (Garden of Liberation), is a large forest monastery and retreat center, the legacy of Ajahn Buddhadasa, a widely published monk and scholar. From the first to the tenth day of each month, foreigner visitors are invited to practice meditation, learn about Thai Buddhism, and experiment with austere living. Arrive before the 31st and be prepared to stay the whole 10 days and get your Buddhist freak on.

### KHAO SOK NATIONAL PARK

Khao Sok is known for its stunning scenery and exotic wildlife, and is convenient to Surat Thani or Phuket. The park is some 646 sq. km (252 sq. miles) in area and is traced by jungle waterways and steep trails among craggy, limestone cliffs—imagine the jutting formations of Phangnga Bay or Krabi, only inland. Rising some 1,000m (3,280 ft.), and laced with shaggy patches of forest, the dense jungle habitat of the park is literally crawling with life. Among the dense underbrush and thick vines hanging from the high canopy, tigers, leopards, golden cats, and even elephants still wander freely, and visitors commonly spot Malaysian sun bear, gibbons, mangur, macaques, civets, flying lemur, and squirrels. Keep your eye peeled for the more than 200 species of birds, like hornbills, woodpeckers, and kingfishers. As for the flora, there is every variety and the Raffelesia, the largest flower in the world and a parasite, finds vines from which to draw its nourishment (the largest are up to 1m/3¼ ft. wide).

One of the best ways to get up close with the varied fauna of the park is by kayak along the nether reaches of the large reservoir. Jungle animals are skittish and your chances of seeing something rare by noisily tromping through the bush are slim at best. Contact the folks at **Paddle-Asia** in Phuket (53/80 Moo 5, Thambon Srisoonthon, Thalang, Phuket 83110; ℭ **07631-1222;** fax 07631-3689; www.paddleasia.com) for details.

## 11 Koh Samui

644km (399 miles) S of Bangkok to Surat Thani; 84km (52 miles) E from Surat Thani to Koh Samui

The island of Koh Samui lies 84km (52 miles) off the east coast in the Gulf of Thailand, near the mainland commercial town of Surat Thani. Since the 1850s, Chinese merchants sailed from as far as Hainan Island in the South China Sea to trade coconuts and cotton, the island's two most profitable products.

# Koh Samui

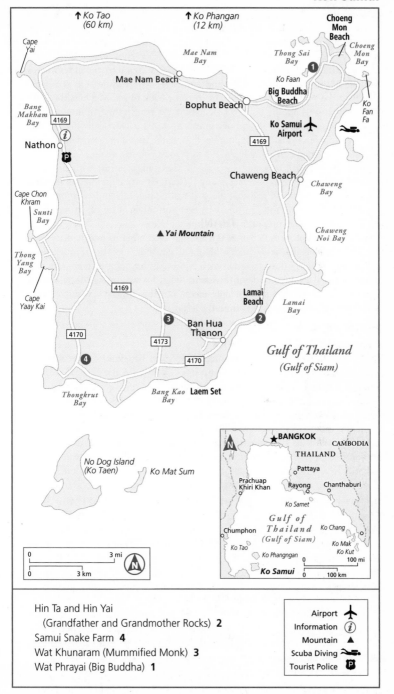

Hin Ta and Hin Yai
(Grandfather and Grandmother Rocks) **2**
Samui Snake Farm **4**
Wat Khunaram (Mummified Monk) **3**
Wat Phrayai (Big Buddha) **1**

Airport ✈
Information ⓘ
Mountain ▲
Scuba Diving
Tourist Police 🅿

Since the 1970s though, the islands early merchant visitors have been replaced by a strange, camera-toting breed whose patronage has swollen the ranks of hotels and guesthouses to a phenomenal number along the popular beaches. Once a popular hippie haven of pristine beaches, idyllic bungalows, and thatched eateries along dirt roads, Samui is now an international resort area with all of the attendant comforts and crowding. If you came here as a backpacker in the past, you may not want to come back to see McDonald's and a Wal-Mart–style shopping outlet where hammocks once hung. An international airport was opened in 1988 and now greets up to 20 packed daily flights. Fine hotels and large resorts are popping up all over the island and any comparison with Phuket, once a far more luxurious west coast cousin, are apt.

Koh Samui is still in some places an idyllic tropical retreat with fine sand beaches and simple living—in fact, many Western visitors are settling in for their retirement on the island and talk of good real estate deals and vacation time-shares is all the buzz. You can find whatever you might want on Samui, from rustic hideaways to luxury resorts to rockin' nightlife.

The high season on Koh Samui is from mid-December to mid-January. January to April has the best weather, before its gets hot. October through mid-December are the wettest months, with November bringing extreme rain and winds that make the east side of the island rough for swimming. August sees a brief increase in visitors, a mini–high season, but the island's west side is often buffeted by summer monsoons from the mainland.

## ESSENTIALS
### GETTING THERE
**By Plane**   **Bangkok Airways** (© **02265-5555** in Bangkok) connects Samui with Bangkok and Phuket. From Singapore, **Silk Air** (in Bangkok © **02236-5301-3**) flies daily, as does **Bangkok Airways.**

Koh Samui Airport (© **07742-5012**) is a little slice of heaven—open-air pavilions with thatch roofs surrounded by gardens and palms. If you're staying at a larger resort, airport minivan shuttles can be arranged when you book your room. There's also a convenient minivan service. Book your ticket at the transportation counter upon arrival and you'll get door-to-door service for 100B ($2.50). If you depart Koh Samui via the airport, there's an additional 150B ($3.75) airport tax that's usually added to your ticket charge.

**By Ferry**   If you're traveling overland, **Songserm** (© **07728-7124** in Surat Thani) runs a convenient ferry loop from Surat Thani with stops in Koh Samui, Koh Pha Ngan, and Koh Tao, finishing at Chumphon (and back again). The total trip is about 4 hours, while the Surat-Samui leg is 2 hours. Rates are as follows: Surat-Samui 150B ($3.75); Samui–Pha Ngan 100B ($2.50); Pha Ngan–Koh Tao 250B ($6.25); Koh Tao–Chumphon 400B ($10). The morning boat leaves at 8am. There are a number of smaller companies that make boat connection (also speedboats), but Songserm is the best.

If you book ahead at a resort, most will arrange transport from the Samui ferry pier at Nathon to your hotel; otherwise, *songtao* make the trip to most beaches on the east coast for as little as 30B (75¢) if they can get a packed truckload from the boat landing (and it can be very packed). If you have no accommodations booking, drivers will make stops along the way to help you find a place.

## ORIENTATION
With a total area of 233 sq. km (91 sq. miles), you can trace Samui's entire coastline by car in about 2½ hours. The island is hilly, densely forested, and rimmed

with coconut palm plantations. The Koh Samui airport is in the northeast corner of the island. The hydrofoils, car ferry, and express boats arrive on the west coast, in or near (depending on the boat) Nathon. The island's main road (Hwy. 4169, also called the "ring road") circles the island. The long east coast stretch between Chaweng and Lamai beaches is the most popular destination for visitors and, consequently, where you'll find the greatest concentration of hotels and bungalows. The south coast has a few little hideaways. **Nathon,** the ferry arrival point on the west coast, is just a tiny town; you'll find a few banks, the TAT office, and main post office, but few visitors spend much time here.

## VISITOR INFORMATION

The **TAT Information Center** is on Thawiratchaphakdi Road just north of the main fairy terminal in Nathon (© 07742-0504). You'll find a host of free small-press magazines and maps at all retailers in Samui.

## GETTING AROUND

**By *Songtao*** *Songtao* are the easiest and most efficient way to get around the island. They advertise their destinations—to such beaches as Lamai, Chaweng, and Mai Nam—with colorfully painted signs and all follow Route 4169, the ring road, around the island. For many trips, you have to change trucks between north and south routes. You can hail one anywhere along the highway and along beach roads. To visit a site off the beaten track (or one other than that painted on a truck's sign), ask the driver to make a detour. Most stop running regular routes after sundown, after which some will hang around outside the discos in Chaweng to take night owls home to other beaches. The cost is 30B to 40B (75¢–$1) one-way, with steep fares (up to 300B/$7.50) after hours.

**By Rental Car** Koh Samui's roads are narrow, winding, and poorly maintained, with few lights at night to guide you. Road accidents are many and renting a car is a far better idea than going on a motorcycle. Your defensive driving skills will be required to navigate around slow-moving trucks and motorcycles at the side of the road, not to mention the occasional wandering dog.

**Budget Car Rental** has an office at the Samui Airport. It rents a host of vehicles starting with **Suzuki Caribians** at just 1,500B ($38) a day. Contact Budget at © 07742-7188. **Avis** has an office at the Santiburi Dusit Resort (© 07742-5031) and offers similar services and does pickup and delivery.

Beachside rental companies and travel agents rent for as low as 700B ($18) per day, but don't expect solid insurance coverage.

**By Motorcycle** Road accidents injure or kill an inordinate number of tourists and locals each year on Samui, mostly motorcycle riders; but still, two wheels and a motor is still the most popular way to get around the island. The roads on Samui are busy, so stay left and close to the shoulder of the road to make way for passing cars and trucks and go easy. Hot-shotting around the island lands so many in the hospital, or worse. It's a 500B ($13) fine for not wearing a helmet (but enforced irregularly). Travel agencies and small operators rent motorcycles in popular beach areas. Honda scooters go for as little as 150B ($3.75) per day.

## FAST FACTS

All the major **banks** are in Nathon along waterfront Thawiratchaphakdi Road. In Chaweng you'll find numerous money changers and ATMs: Try Krung Thai Bank (opposite Starbucks). Hotels and guesthouses also accept traveler's checks. The main **post office** (© 07742-1013) is on Chonwithee Road in Nathon, but you'll probably not hike all the way back to the main pier for posting. Any hotel or guesthouse will handle it for you, and stamps can be purchased in small provision shops in beach areas. For **Internet service,** there are a number of options in Chaweng. Try the kind folks at **Multi Travel and Tour** (164/3 Moo 2 Chaweng; ℭ **07741-3969**) among the many. **Bandon International Hospital** (ℭ **07742-5382**) is a fine facility located north of Chaweng with English-speaking physicians who make house calls. For **tourist police** emergencies, dial ℭ **07742-1281.**

## WHERE TO STAY ON KOH SAMUI

Twenty years ago there were but a few makeshift beachside bungalow compounds along the nearly deserted coast of Samui. Today, luxury resorts stand shoulder-to-shoulder with homey guesthouses, chic modern facilities next to motel cellblocks, and all vying for supremacy for the choicest beachside real estate. Even if your budget is tight, you can still enjoy the same sand as those is the more exclusive joints.

## MAE NAM BAY

**Mae Nam Bay** is 12km (7½ miles) from the ferry pier, at the midpoint of Samui's north shore, facing nearby Koh Pha Ngan. The beach is narrow and long, with coarse sand and shaded by trees. The water is deep enough for swimming.

### VERY EXPENSIVE

**Santiburi Dusit Resort** ★★★    The Santiburi Dusit is the ultimate in relaxed luxury on the island. The resort design is influenced by late Thai royal architecture, with spacious and airy interiors—a simplicity accented with luxurious Jim Thompson Thai silks and tidy floral arrangements. The gardens and beachfront are picturesque and quiet and the staff is motivated to please, making this not only the finest resort on the island, but comparable to any of the fine properties in the kingdom. The resorts top villas front the beach, while the others are set among lush greenery around a central pool and spa. Each bungalow is a luxe suite, with living and sleeping areas divided by glass and flowers. The bathroom is masterfully fitted in wood and black tiles, the centerpiece a large, round sunken tub. Standard features such as a video player and stereo system make each villa as convenient as your own home. Guests can take advantage of windsurfing and sailing on the house. Santiburi Dusi also has its own gorgeous Chinese junk anchored in the bay for dinner cruises or for hiring out to tour surrounding islands.

12/12 Moo 1, Tambol Mae Nam, Koh Samui, Surat Thani 84330. ℭ **07742-5031.** Fax 07742-5040. www. dusit.com. 71 units. 15,600B–18,700B ($390–$468) deluxe suites; 18,850B–40,600B ($471–$1,015) villas; AE, DC, MC, V. **Amenities:** 2 restaurants; 2 bars; lounge; outdoor pool; outdoor lighted tennis courts; fitness center; spa; Jacuzzi; sauna; watersports equipment; concierge; car-rental desk; limo service; salon; 24-hr. room service; massage; babysitting; same-day laundry service/dry cleaning; Internet. *In room:* A/C, satellite TV and DVD w/disc library, minibar, fridge, hair dryer, safe, wireless Internet, stereo system, IDD phone.

### MODERATE/INEXPENSIVE

**Coco Palm Samui**    A good budget choice, Coco Palm's bungalows are basic and comfortable, all with air-conditioning, minibar, and TV. It attracts lots of families on a budget, but still it is quite peaceful. Deluxe bungalows are worth a bump-up; though still with just shower-in-room baths, they are airy with vaulted cathay ceilings and seaside bungalows are worth the next bump-up for location.

26/4 Moo 4, Maenam Beach, Koh Samui 84330. ℭ **07724-7288.** Fax 07742-5321. www.cocopalmsamui. com. 86 units. 800B–1,000B ($20–$25) double; 1,300B–1,600B ($33–$40) deluxe; 2,000B–2,500B ($50–$63) suite. MC, V. **Amenities:** Restaurant; small outdoor pool; jeep and motorcycle rental; tour desk; transfer service; laundry service. *In room:* A/C, minibar, no phone.

**Mae Nam Resort** ⭐ *(Value)*    These 36 bungalows form a little secluded village in jungle gardens with tall lush greenery. Each has teak paneling and floors, rattan furnishings, a small bathroom in tidy tiles, and a small deck in front. Beachfront bungalows will have you stepping off your balcony right into the silky, palm-shaded sand for very little considering the neighboring Santiburi Dusit Resort's beachfront villa run about 32,800B ($820). Okay, Mae Nam Resort can't compare to five-star luxury, but it's the same sand and view.

Mae Nam Beach, Koh Samui, 84330 Surat Thani (next to the Santiburi Dusit). ☎ 07724-7287. Fax 07742-5116. maenamrs@samart.co.th. 41 units. 1,000B–1,200B ($25–$30) double w/fan; 1,600B ($40) A/C bungalow. AE, MC, V. **Amenities:** Restaurant; jeep and motorcycle rental; transfer service; limited room service; laundry service. *In room:* No phone.

**Seafan Beach Resort**    With Thai ambience and low-key elegance, these semideluxe beach bungalows are connected by wooden walkways covering 3 hectares (7½ acres) of landscaped grounds fronting the bay. Each rustic rattan and coconut-wood house has two queen-size beds, an extra rattan daybed, built-in bamboo furnishings, and large, all-tiled bathroom with nice robes and slippers for padding about. Bungalows are well spaced and private (some directly on the water), but sadly a new multifloor hotel is going up next door and the higher floors will peek down onto the bungalows (Seafan is planting large trees to fix the problem). A small pool with kiddy pool and a snack bar overlook the beach. The restaurant features Thai, Continental, and good seafood. Rates include use of windsurfing boards, snorkeling gear, and other watersports activities. Service is attentive.

Mae Nam Beach, Koh Samui 84330, Surat Thani (west end of beach). ☎ 07742-5204. Fax 07742-5350. www.samui-hotels.com/seafan. 36 units. 4,500B ($113) double; slightly more for seafront; special rates available. AE, DC, MC, V. **Amenities:** Restaurant; lounge; outdoor pool and children's pool; watersports equipment; children's playroom; tour desk; limo service; massage; same-day laundry service/dry cleaning. *In room:* A/C, minibar, hair dryer, safe.

## BOPHUT BEACH

**Bophut Beach** is on the north coast just east of Mae Nam. The beach is thin and the sand is coarse but the little commercial strip is fun and convenient.

## MODERATE

**Peace Resort** ⭐⭐    Once just a few family-owned bungalows, that same relaxed spirit pervades at the Peace Resort, but these newest free-standing bungalows are small luxury suites, really. All have vaulted ceilings with design schemes that are either finely crafted wood or cooler, almost Mediterranean numbers in pastel tiles with designer flat-stone masonry and smooth stucco. Spring for the larger seaside rooms. The central pool is not particularly large but cozy and near the beach. There's a small, open-air restaurant where you can enjoy a cool drink, the company of good friends, and the calm of this tranquil bay with the big Buddha winking from the next beach. Peace indeed.

Bo Phut Beach, Koh Samui 94320 (central Bo Phut). ☎ 07742-5357. Fax 07742-5343. www.peaceresort.com. 102 units. 2,450B–3,100B ($61–$78) garden bungalow; 3,400B–4,500B ($85–$113) beachview bungalow. MC, V. **Amenities:** Restaurant; bar; outdoor pool; spa (across the road); kids' club and playground; tour desk; car and motorbike rental; limited room service (6am–11:30pm); babysitting; laundry service; Internet. *In room:* A/C, satellite TV, minibar, fridge, safe, no phone.

## BIG BUDDHA BEACH

**Nara Garden Beach Resort**    The Nara is one of the island's older inns, with attached rooms as similar to an American motel as you'll come in Koh Samui. A well-kept lawn leads to the beach and quite bay. The Nara has large connecting rooms for families. Spring for a superior.

81 Moo 4, Bophut, Koh Samui 84320, Surat Thani (Big Buddha Beach). © **07742-5364.** Fax 07742-5292. naragarden@sawadee.com. 43 units. 1,800B ($45) standard; 2,100B–2,700B ($53–$68) superior–deluxe; 3,000B ($75) suite. MC, V. **Amenities:** Restaurant; bar; outdoor pool; tour desk; transfer service; babysitting; laundry service. *In room:* A/C, satellite TV, minibar, fridge.

## TONGSAI BAY
### The Tongsai Bay ★★   This luxe resort dominates this stunning, rocky section of coast. Built amphitheatrically down a hillside, the white-stucco, red-tile-roofed bungalows and buildings remind one of the Mediterranean, though the palm trees are pure Thai. Between the half-moon cove's rocky bookends, the coarse sand beach invites you to idle away the days. This all-suite resort has some very unique touches that set it apart—each unit has plenty of outdoor terrace space with sea views or a nice private walled courtyard. Terrace suites have outdoor bathtubs, while the Grand Tongsai Villas have not only tubs but also gazebos. The villas are designed in a unique harmony with nature, some even have small stands of trees growing though the middle of them and you'll find plenty of spots to hide out with a hammock under a shade tree. Service is tiptop. The only drawback: the steep steps between buildings.

84 Moo 5, Ban Plailaem, Bophut, Koh Samui 84320, Surat Thani (northeast tip of island). © **07742-5015.** Fax 07742-5462. (Bangkok reservations office 02254-0056; fax 02254-0054.) www.tongsaibay.co.th. 83 units. 11,000B ($275) beachfront or cottage suite; 22,000B ($550) Tongsai Grand Villa. AE, DC, MC, V. **Amenities:** 3 restaurants; 2 bars; outdoor pool; outdoor lighted tennis court; fitness center; spa w/massage and beauty treatments; watersports equipment; tour desk; car-rental desk; limo service; limited room service; same-day laundry service/dry cleaning; snooker room; Internet center. *In room:* A/C, satellite TV, minibar, fridge, coffee/tea-making facilities, hair dryer, safe, DVD player (disks available at small library), IDD phone.

# CHOENG MON
**Choeng Mon** is a gracefully shaped crescent about 1km (½ mile) long. Palm trees shading sunbathers reach right to the water's edge; swimming is excellent, with few rocks near the central shore. Choeng Mon is isolated, but there are many good local services and transport.

## VERY EXPENSIVE
### Samui Peninsula Spa and Resort ★★   If you can, do stay at the Peninsula Resort; you'll be treated like royalty in a fine private suite or your own luxury pool villa with incredible views from this rocky promontory on the cusp of Choeng Mon and Bophut. It's a long walk to the beach proper, but you may not want to leave this ultracomfy compound. Rooms are sanctuaries done in dark wood and silk, and brimming with Thai features and classical style. The central pool has scenic views, and resort dining and services are tops. Honeymooners delight.

24/73 Moo 5, Bo Phut Beach, Koh Samui 84320 (on the rocky point between Mae Nam and Bo Phut). © **07742-8100.** Fax 07742-8122. 43 units. 10,250B–14,350B ($256–$359) suite; from 22,550B ($564) villa. AE, MC, V. **Amenities:** 2 restaurants; bar; outdoor pool; watersports equipment; tour desk; car rental; limo service; 24-hr. room service; massage; same-day laundry/dry cleaning; Internet. *In room:* A/C, satellite TV w/in-house movies; minibar, fridge, safe, IDD phone.

## EXPENSIVE
### The Imperial Boathouse ★   You've a pretty unique concept here—34 authentic teak rice barges have been dry-docked and converted into charming free-standing suites. The less-expensive rooms in the three-story buildings are fine but not nearly as atmospheric. Hotel facilities are extensive and if you can't get a boat suite you can swim in the boat-shaped swimming pool.

83 Moo 5, Tambon Bophut, Koh Samui 84320, Surat Thani (southern part of beach). ✆ **07742-5041.** Fax 07742-5460. www.imperialhotels.com. 210 units. 5,500B–6,500B ($138–$163) double; 9,225B ($231) boat suite. AE, DC, MC, V. **Amenities:** 2 restaurants; bar; 2 outdoor pools; fitness center; spa; Jacuzzi; sauna; water-sports equipment; concierge; tour desk; car-rental desk; limo service; business center; 24-hr. room service; massage; babysitting; same-day laundry service/dry cleaning. *In room:* A/C, satellite TV, minibar; fridge, hair dryer, safe, IDD phone.

**The White House** ★★    This resort in the graceful Ayutthaya style, built around a central garden with a lotus pond and swimming pool, is by far the top choice in Choeng Mon for comfort at cost. The lobby is impeccably decorated with original Thai artwork. Spacious and elegant rooms flank a central walkway that's lined with orchids. Houses accommodate four rooms each, which are large with separate sitting areas, huge beds, fine furnishings, and large bathrooms. By the beach there's a pool with a bar and an especially graceful teak *sala.* The resort's quality Swiss management team is very efficient and assures a pleasant stay. This is top comfort spilling onto a beautiful stretch of white-sand beach.

59/3 Moo 5, Choeng Mon Beach, Koh Samui 84320, Surat Thani. ✆ **07724-5315.** Fax 07724-5318. www.samuidreamholiday.com. 40 units. 5,000B–5,600B ($125–$140) double; 6,200B ($155) suite. AE, MC, V. **Amenities:** 2 restaurants; bar; outdoor pool; Jacuzzi; jeep and motorcycle rental; tour desk; transfer service; massage; laundry service. *In room:* A/C, satellite TV, minibar, fridge, coffee/tea-making facilities, safe.

## MODERATE/INEXPENSIVE
**P.S. Villa** (24/2 Moo 5; ✆ **07742-5160**) is exemplary of the cozy, family-run bungalow compounds in the area. Rustic rooms start at 700B ($18).

## CHAWENG & CHAWENG NOI BAYS
The beaches at Chaweng are the most popular and the most overdeveloped on Samui. If you came to get away from it all, go elsewhere, but most of the resorts are private, cozy, affordable, and convenient to the busy strip. North Chaweng beaches are rocky; the south is better for swimming.

### Expensive
**Amari Palm Reef Resort** ★★    This is the finest of Amari's many hotels in Thailand by virtue of the luxury suites at beachside and the comfortable design of the oceanside pool and dining. Older accommodations in the main block are not particularly luxurious, though very clean with parquet floors. New suite rooms face the sea and are designed in a seamless marriage of contemporary and traditional Thai with large decks giving way to huge glass sliders, lovely sunken seating areas, massive, plush beds situated in the center of the rooms and behind which you'll find designer bathrooms with separate shower, tub, and his-and-her sinks. The central pool area is lovely and the staff is kind and helpful. The rocks and coral along the beach mean you'll have to take a bit of a walk for swimming, but the scenery is lovely and you can expect the same high standard of service as at all Amari hotels. The resort is far enough from Chaweng strip to be quiet and comfortable (but close enough to party). Great for families.

Chaweng Beach, Samui 84320 (north end of the main strip). ✆ **07742-2015.** Fax 07742-2394. www.amari.com. 104 units. 6,150B ($154) superior; 7,400B ($185) deluxe; 10,250B ($256) suite. AE, MC, V. **Amenities:** 3 restaurants; 2 outdoor pools; squash court; spa w/massage, Jacuzzi, sauna, and steam; bike rental; kids' club; tour desk; car rental; small boutique shopping; babysitting; same-day laundry/dry cleaning service; non-smoking rooms. *In room:* A/C, satellite TV, minibar, fridge, coffeemaker, hair dryer, safe, IDD phone.

**Coral Bay Resort** ★    Far from the boom-boom bass of Chaweng but close enough to commute, the Coral Bay crests a picturesque hill on the northern end of Chaweng and is a collection of large, upscale thatch bungalows. Rooms are in rows along the hillside (a bit of trudging to get to some) and each has a large balcony, some shared with adjoining rooms. Room decor is lavish with bamboo and coconut-inlaid cabinets, intricate thatch, and fine hangings, and some rooms feature unique, graphic mosaics: nothing like it on Samui. Spring for a deluxe room with canopy bed. Baths are small garden landscapes with waterfall showers and designer flat-stone masonry. The central pool area is high above the rock and coral beach below (not good for swimming) and large thatch pavilions house the open lobby and fine dining. Coral Bay offers a good standard of comfort and service throughout and it provides good information about self-touring (or can make arrangements). Rooms do not have TVs but there is a library and video lounge.

9 Moo 2, Bophut, Chaweng Beach, Koh Samui 84320 (north end of Chaweng as the road crests the first big hill). ⓒ 07742-2223. Fax 07742-2392. www.coralbay.net. 53 units. 3,700B ($93) superior; 5,000B ($125) deluxe; from 10,000B ($250) deluxe family suite; all rooms add beachfront surcharge. AE, MC, V. **Amenities:** 2 restaurants; bar; pool; spa; Jacuzzi; sauna; kids' club; tour desk; car rental; small shop; massage; babysitting; laundry service; nonsmoking rooms; Internet; library and video lounge. *In room:* A/C, minibar, fridge, safe, IDD phone.

### Imperial Samui Hotel ⓐ

A member of the large, Thai-owned Imperial group, the hotel is set in a large hill-top grove of coconut palms a short drive south of busy Chaweng. You can't walk it, but it does have frequent shuttle service to town for 50B ($1.25) and the resort, unlike most on or near Chaweng, is quiet. The large saltwater pool has an organic design with large boulders, a central island, and a vanishing edge overlooking the bay below: charming. Spacious rooms have large balconies with sea views, lots of floral prints and rattan, large bathrooms with potted plants, and easy access (via steps) to the beach. The sprawling hillside location means a bit of hill hiking to some of the furthest rooms, but for seclusion and comfort, this is a good choice.

86 Moo 3, Ban Chaweng Noi, Koh Samui 84320, Surat Thani (middle of Chaweng Noi Beach). ⓒ 07742-2020. Fax 07742-2396. www.imperialhotels.com. 155 units. 5,750B ($144) double; 7,175B ($179) premiere sea-facing; from 7,800B ($195) suite. AE, DC, MC, V. **Amenities:** 2 restaurants; lounge; 2 outdoor pools (freshwater and seawater); outdoor lighted tennis courts; Jacuzzi; watersports equipment and dive center; bike rental; concierge; tour desk; car-rental desk; limo service; 24-hr. room service; massage; babysitting; same-day laundry service/dry cleaning; snooker and badminton. *In room:* A/C, satellite TV w/free in-house movies, minibar, fridge, coffeemaker, hair dryer, safe, IDD phone.

### Muang Kulaypan Hotel ⓐ

Like a museum "installation" as much as a hotel, the rooms of the Muang Kulaypan are gracefully simplistic in natural woods and rich local textiles in clean, contemporary minimalist lines. The name is derived from an ancient Thai-Javanesse tale and pieces of the story are spelled out in calligraphy on some room walls. The design can be almost harsh it is so spartan but you are meant to like it that way, and the overall effect of the interiors is not displeasing. Almost all rooms have sea views. That same clean, lined minimalism of the rooms only works when it is in fact "clean," though, and the sprawling public spaces and central courtyard are getting a bit run-down. The black tiled pool is lovely, though, and the Budsaba Restaurant serves fine Thai cuisine in private thatched *salas*. The staff is smartly dressed and snaps to. A good place for that postmodern honeymoon.

100 Moo 2, Chaweng Beach Rd., Koh Samui 84320, Surat Thani (northern end of Chaweng Beach). ⓒ 07723-0850. Fax 07723-0031. www.kulaypan.com. 40 units. 2,600B–4,800B ($65–$120) double; from 5,500B ($138) suite. AE, DC, MC, V. **Amenities:** Restaurant; lounge; outdoor pool; small fitness center; tour desk; car and motorcycle rental; limo service; limited room service; massage; babysitting; same-day laundry service/dry cleaning. *In room:* A/C, minibar, fridge, safe.

### Poppies Samui Resort ⓐⓐ

The famed Balinese resort features this popular annex in Samui. On the south end of busy Chaweng, Poppies is indeed an oasis. Luxury cottages, all the same, have thatch roofs and Thai-Balinese appointments.

Privacy and service is the hallmark here. Rooms are set close together but well situated for optimum privacy. This is a popular honeymoon choice and the service and standards throughout are tops. The central pool is small but cozy and the hotel dining is some of the best going (see "Where to Dine," below).

P.O. Box 1, Chaweng, Koh Samui 84320 (on the south end of the Chaweng strip). *C* **07742-2419.** Fax 07742-2420. www.kohsamui.net/poppies. 24 units. 8,200B ($205) double w/seasonal fluctuations. AE, MC, V. **Amenities:** Restaurant; pool; spa; tour desk; shopping; limited room service; massage; laundry service. *In room:* A/C, satellite TV, minibar, fridge, coffee and tea, safe, IDD phone.

**The Princess Village** ★★  If you've wondered what sleeping in Jim Thompson's House or in a Thai Palace might be like, try the regal Princess Village. Traditional teak houses from Ayutthaya have been restored and placed around lushly planted ponds and gardens dotted with comfortable Thai *salas*. Each room is on stilts (some above private lotus ponds) and use-worn stairs lead up to large verandas where complimentary afternoon tea and cakes are served. Inside each picturesque pavilion, you'll find a grand teak bed covered in embroidered silk, antique furniture, and fine artwork. Small, carved dressing tables and spacious bathrooms contain painted ceramics, silverware, a porcelain dish, a large khlong jar for water storage, and other Thai details side-by-side with modern conveniences. Traditional shuttered windows on all sides have no screens, but lacy mosquito netting and a ceiling fan, combined with sea breezes, create fine ventilation. There is air-conditioning for skeptics.

101/1 Moo 3, Chaweng Beach, Koh Samui 84320, Surat Thani (middle of Chaweng Beach). *C* **07742-2216.** Fax 07742-2382. www.samuidreamholiday.com. 14 units. 3,800B ($95) gardenview double; 4,200B–5,000B ($105–$125) seaview double; from 5,200B ($130) suite. AE, MC, V. **Amenities:** Restaurant; jeep and motorcycle rental; tour desk; massage; laundry service; daily Chinese tea service. *In room:* Minibar, coffee/tea-making facilities, safe.

## Moderate

**Chaweng Resort** ★  Like a small-time Florida development, the Chaweng Resort consists of two columns of free-standing bungalows leading to the sea. Cottages are basic but spacious with lots of overdone filigree. Bathrooms are plain but spotless. The larger suites are a good value for families. The grounds are nicely landscaped and there's cosmetic renovation going on that will mean a carved concrete lobby not unlike a Hindu temple (or a wedding cake), and there are lots of fun Thai touches and statues throughout. The central pool is small but cozy and the Thai/Continental restaurant overlooks the beach. The place is not luxurious, but a good family choice bustling with activity.

Chaweng Beach, Koh Samui, 84320 Surat Thani (middle of Chaweng Beach). *C* **07742-2230,** or 02651-0016 in Bangkok. Fax 07751-0018. www.chawengresort.com. 70 units. 2,200B–2,800B ($55–$70) double; 3,000B ($75) suite. AE, DC, MC, V. **Amenities:** Restaurant; pool; tour desk; massage; laundry service; Internet. *In room:* A/C, satellite TV, minibar, fridge.

**Tradewinds**  Tradewinds was one of the earliest hotels in Chaweng and still a good choice on the south end of the strip. From the higher-priced bungalows you can step right off your front porch into the sand, while standard bungalows are in a secluded garden not far from the beach. Rooms are not particularly luxurious but have large beds and rattan furnishings, good for travelers who want the intimate feeling of a bungalow village but don't want to sacrifice modern conveniences. Tradewinds has just opened a new motel-style block, but stick to the bungalows. Tradewinds is also home of Samui's catamaran sailing center.

17/14 Moo 3, Chaweng Beach, Koh Samui 84320, Surat Thani. *C* **07723-0602.** Fax 07723-1247. 20 units. 2,500B–3,000B ($63–$75) double. AE, DC, MC, V. **Amenities:** Restaurant; bar; catamaran sailing center; laundry service. *In room:* A/C, minibar, fridge.

## LAMAI BAY

The long sand beach on **Lamai Bay** is comparable to Chaweng's, but caters more to the young backpacker set. There are a few comfy new resorts in and among the budget bungalows though, and the wide range of services, cafes, and nightlife make Lamai the best budget choice and a popular spot.

### Very Expensive

**Buriraya Resort and Spa** ★★    Newly opened in the fall of 2003, Buriraya is the height of luxury and service in the hills high above busy Lamai Beach (once just a backpacker spot). Rooms in the larger tower block are very chic and comfortable with large puffy beds covered in sumptuous silk, rich wood floors, and fine Thai appointments. Larger, free-standing villas set in the resorts verdant gardens (all with private Jacuzzi and pool) are luxurious hideaways with fine traditional decor done on a grand scale. The pool is lovely, the spa is luxurious, and there are great fine dining options. The views of sand and sea from this exclusive perch are breathtaking and everything is new and orderly.

208/1 Moo 4, T. Maret, Lamai, Koh Samui 84310 (on the northeast end of Lamai on the hilltop). ℂ 07742-9300. Fax 07742-9333. www.buriraya.com. 77 units. 10,000B ($250) deluxe double; from 21,000B ($525) suite; from 18,000B ($450) villa. AE, DC, MC, V. **Amenities:** 3 restaurants; outdoor pool; health club; spa w/Jacuzzi, sauna, and steam; watersports rentals (sea kayaks free); bike rentals; children's center; tour desk; car rental; business center; shopping; limited room service; babysitting; same-day laundry service/dry cleaning. *In room:* A/C, satellite TV w/DVD and CD, minibar, fridge, coffeemaker, safe, IDD phone.

### Expensive

**Pavilion Samui Boutique Resort** ★    The newly renovated Pavilion is more the rococo of a small-time mafia Don's private sanctuary than "boutique," but it is a tidy hotel and service is good. Public spaces are surrounded by lots of greenery. Deluxe rooms run the gamut from fine private bungalows, some still a rustic thatch and others new, updated and with a clean Mediterranean flare in colored concrete. Honeymoon suites and spa rooms have huge luxury bathrooms, some even a courtyard area where guests can enjoy a Jacuzzi and shower under the stars. There's a fine new spa, the small pool and dining pavilion are right on the surf, and proximity to Lamai's nightlife is a plus for most guests.

124/24 Moo 3, Lamai Beach, Koh Samui 84310, Surat Thani (north end of Lamai Beach). ℂ 07742-4030. Fax 07742-4029. www.pavilionsamui.com. 62 units. 5,000B–6,500B ($125–$163) bungalow; from 8,000B ($200) suite. AE, DC, MC, V. **Amenities:** Restaurant; bar; outdoor pool; spa; Jacuzzi; steambath; tour desk; car-rental desk; transfer service; limited room service; laundry service. *In room:* A/C, TV, minibar, safe.

### Moderate

**Samui Yacht Club**    This tidy bungalow complex, a yacht club in name only, has an almost exclusive access to a small cove north of Lamai Beach. It is very quiet. The rocky beach is not for swimming but good snorkeling further out. Each bungalow has a porch, canopy beds with mosquito netting (for effect), clean tiled floors, and rattan furnishings. Best are the beachfront bungalows right on the sand. The restaurant is fine for breakfast, but go out for dinner. This place is best for people who want to be left alone and aren't looking for many services.

Ao Tongtakian, between Chaweng and Lamai beaches, Koh Samui 84320, Surat Thani (3km/1¾ miles north of Lamai). ℂ 07742-2225. Fax 07742-2400. www.samuiyachtclub.com. 43 units. 1,800B–2,800B ($45–$70) garden bungalow; 3,300B ($83) beachfront bungalow. AE, MC, V. **Amenities:** Restaurant; outdoor pool; motorcycle rental; laundry service. *In room:* A/C, satellite TV, minibar, fridge, safe.

**Spa Samui Resorts** ★ (Value    For long-term stays or just a daytime spa visit, the Spa Samui Resorts is a unique choice offering a "healthy good time." The popular cleansing-and-fasting series rejuvenates your system with prepared detox drinks and tablets plus twice daily colonic enema. Some balk at the thought of paying 10,660B ($267) per week, on top of room rental, to "not eat," but it is a good, professional program. The laid-back spa resort on the sea just north of Lamai has been around for years and is still in full swing, a rustic grouping of old bungalows and open-air dining and massage pavilions, but it's just built a new, more comfortable property in the south of Lamai, high in the hills above town. Rooms at the new resort range from simple, affordable bungalows to large private suites with large balconies. All rooms are fitted with a colonic board for daily enemas. The new spa has a cozy pool, herbal steam bath in a large stone grotto, massage, body wraps, and facial treatments. Classes and workshops on yoga, meditation, and massage techniques can fill your day or you can just put your feet up, colon all sparkling clean, and have a go at that novel you've been lugging around (or writing). All of the spa services are available for day visitors. The vegetarian Spa Restaurant serves excellent dishes with particular care to cleansing the body (see "Where to Dine," below).

Lamai Beach, Koh Samui 84320, Surat Thani (just south, in the hills over Lamai Beach). ✆ 07723-0855. Fax 07742-4126. www.spasamui.com. 44 units (plus 16 at the old resort). 800B–3,000B ($20–$75). MC, V. **Amenities:** Restaurant; juice bar; pool; spa; sauna; massage; laundry service. *In room:* A/C, minibar, fridge, safe.

## LAEM SET BAY
### Laem Set Inn ★★
Unique in a landscape of cookie-cutter, high-end resorts, the Laem Set Inn sets its own standard of style, traditional luxury, and fine service in this isolated corner of paradise. This cozy hideaway on the far southern end of the island is a collection of uniquely designed Thai suites ranging from rustic thatch bungalows to private pool villas. Some suites are built from the rural teak homes from outlying islands that were saved from the wrecking ball (or desertion) and moved here and carefully rebuilt: very unique. There are secluded places for anyone from the honeymoon couple to the rowdy family (and the property is designed to keep said groups far apart). Family suites have bunk beds, private baths for kids, and small family dining nooks. The most exclusive accommodations are the private two-bedroom suites decorated with hand-hewn furniture and a certain regional grace. Large porches bookend all villas and provide a perch for drinking in views beyond the pounding surf to nearby No Dog Island. Kayaks, mountain bikes, and snorkel gear are available to explore this location's stunning scenery. Wireless Internet comes standard in all areas free of charge. The elevated pool seamlessly blends with the gulf, reflecting sea and sky, and the pavilion restaurant serves gourmet fare and delicious Thai seafood. This boutique inn is true rustic luxury, far from the crowds—an ideal getaway.

110 Moo 2, Hua Thanon, Laem Set, Koh Samui 84310, Surat Thani. ✆ 07742-4393. Fax 07742-4394. www.laemset.com. 30 units. 3,100B ($78) seafront bungalow w/fan; 4,900B–7,600B ($123–$190) standard double; from 8,200B ($205) suite. MC, V. **Amenities:** 2 restaurants; bar; outdoor pool; fitness center; Jacuzzi; sauna; watersports equipment; bike and motorcycle rental; children's programs; concierge; tour desk; car-rental desk; limo service; business center; limited room service; massage; babysitting; same-day laundry service. *In room:* A/C, minibar, fridge, coffee/tea-making facilities, hair dryer, safe, wireless Internet, IDD phone.

## WEST COAST
### Le Royal Meridien Baan Taling Ngam ★★★
A true five-star, Le Royal Meridien is peaceful and isolated on the western side of the island some 40 minutes' drive from the Samui Airport. Built on the side of a hill, the resort's accommodations include deluxe rooms and suites, as well as one- to three-bedroom beach and cliff villas. The hilltop lobby and restaurant, as well as the guest rooms, have fantastic views of the sea and resort gardens, and the main pool appears to spill over its edges into the coconut palm grove below. Guest rooms

combine Thai furniture, fine textiles, and louvered wood paneling, including the sliding doors to the huge tanning terrace. Bathrooms feature oversize tubs and sophisticated black slate and wood paneling. The two-bedroom villas afford the most value and convenience for families. The resort's only drawback is that the beach is small, and while some may seek out the privacy this resort promises, the cost is isolation from the "action" on the other parts of the island—at least a 30-minute drive away. Le Royal Meridien has kayaks, catamarans, snorkeling gear, and windsurfers for rent, as well as tennis, mountain bikes, a fine spa, PADI dive school, and no fewer than seven outdoor swimming pools so no one gets bored. Dining at the hilltop Lom Talay is as gorgeous as the Thai and Asian cuisine served, while the Promenade serves locally caught fresh seafood by the beach.

295 Moo 3, Taling Ngam Beach, Koh Samui, Surat Thani 84140. © 800/225-5843 in the U.S., or 07742-3019. www.lemeridien.com. 72 units. 18,000B–20,500B ($450–$513) double; 31,150B ($779) suite; 31,150B–90,600B ($779–$2,265) villa. AE, DC, MC, V. **Amenities:** 3 restaurants; lounge; 7 pools; outdoor lighted tennis courts; fitness center; spa w/massage; Jacuzzi; sauna; watersports equipment and dive center; bike rental; concierge; tour desk; car-rental desk; limo service; salon; 24-hr. room service; babysitting; same-day laundry service/dry cleaning. In room: A/C, satellite TV, minibar, fridge, IDD phone.

## WHERE TO DINE IN KOH SAMUI
### CHAWENG BEACH

Chaweng is where you'll find the most variety, from McDonald's to fine dining.

**Betelnut** ✿ INTERNATIONAL   California cuisine, anyone? Down a quiet *soi* off the south end of Chaweng, you'll be greeted at the door by Jeffrey Lord, owner, proprietor, and rollicking raconteur who hands out fine wit and witticisms along with good victuals. The menu is divided into "Eats Big" and "Eats Small," not necessarily apps and main courses but could be, and runs the gamut from "Buddha Jumped Over the Wall" (an ostrich steak) to clam chowder with green curry. I had a delicious sesame-encrusted salmon Katsu, indicative of the international fare here. The blackened tuna with salsa and soft-shell crabs with green papaya and mango salad are also good choices. Come with friends, order a spread of tapas choices, and pick from among the fine wine selections for a great evening.

46/27 Chaweng Blvd., Chaweng (south of Tradewinds Hotel and the town center, down a small *soi*). © 07741-3370. Main courses 225B–625B ($5.65–$16). MC, V. Daily 6pm–last order.

**Poppies** THAI/INTERNATIONAL   Known for its Balinese flare, Poppies is equally famous for fresh seafood by the beach. The romantic atmosphere under the large thatch pavilion is enhanced by soft lighting and live international jazz music. Guest chefs from around the world mean the menu is ever-changing, but you can be sure the seafood selections are some of the best catches around. A good place, especially if you're romancing someone special.

South Chaweng Beach. © 07742-2419. Reservations recommended during peak season. Main courses 80B–240B ($2–$6). AE, MC, V. Daily 7am–10pm.

**Vechia Napoli** ✿ ITALIAN   Listen to the dulcet tones of quiet Italian folk music and watch lazy fans languidly churn cool air as you lean back in a rattan chair; you might think you've been transported to a small town in rural Napoli, and the simple authentic cuisine of this restaurant completes the picture. Tomato and mozzarella with a splash of pesto, a glass of red, and good conversation; you won't believe you're just a stone's throw from busy Chaweng (down a little alley with seedy massage places and bars, but somehow lends to the atmosphere). You'll find it all here: great pastas, grilled specials, pizza, and the house special—shellfish soup with king prawns, fresh crab, mussels, and clams done in a special Neapolitan broth. Follow it up with a real gelato or tiramisu and espresso. I make a kissing sound with fingertips to lips and lift them in the air joyfully and smile.

166/31 Moo 2, Chaweng Beach, Koh Samui 84320 (central Chaweng). (℃ 07723-1229. Main courses 120B–420B ($3–$11). MC, V. Daily 11am–11pm.

## LAMAI BEACH

**The Spa Restaurant** VEGETARIAN   Not just for veggies here at the Spa Restaurant (you'll find a few seafood and chicken dishes as well), but to anyone who'd like to enjoy a healthful, tasty dish. Go for the delicious curries, or try the excellent local dishes. But leave plenty of time for an herbal steam and massage at the Health Center. I think for a vacation activity, this is tops for relaxation— an afternoon of pure indulgence, and it's good for you!

Route 4169, between Chaweng and Lamai beaches. (℃ 07723-0855. Reservations recommended in peak season. Main courses 30B–250B (75¢–$6.25). MC, V. Daily 7am–10pm.

## BOPHUT BEACH

For good baked goods try **Angela's Harbourside Café** ((℃ 07742-7212).

**The Mangrove** ★★ INTERNATIONAL   For romantic, elegant dining, the Mangrove is the best on Samui. It's on a quiet stretch of rural road (near the airport) and though far from the bustling tourist areas like Chaweng, that is in fact the very appeal here and the restaurant is but a short ride from Chaweng (near Bophut Beach). The casual, cozy, open-air dining area overlooks a grove of mangroves of course and echoes with the sounds of forest and jungle. The menu changes monthly to cater to the oft-returning expatriate clientele. For a starter, try the crab salad and ask about any daily specials. I had a delicious lamb chop marinated in herbs de Provence. The place is run by a friendly young (but very experienced) French/Belgian couple who go to great lengths. Don't scrimp on dessert; try the rich chocolate mouse and follow it up with a Rum Ginger, the Mangrove's signature after-dinner drink.

32/6 Moo 4, Bophut, Koh Samui 84320 (on the airport rd. between Bophut and Big Buddha). (℃ 07742-7584. Main courses 430B–520B ($11–$13). Daily 5pm–last order (closed on the last 3 days of each month).

## WHAT TO SEE & DO

Busy Samui supports all kinds of activities, from scuba diving to bungee jumping, jungle trekking to cooking schools. Most folks come here for beach fun and frolic and you'll find all kinds of activities—sailing, jet skis, and parasailing— among them, at beachside.

**Na Muang Trekking** ((℃ 07741-8681) is one of many small tour and trekking agencies arranging day trips to the sites below; however, self-drive, best by car rather than motorbike, will get you there just as easily.

The gold-tiled **Wat Phrayai (Big Buddha),** more than 24m (79 ft.) tall, sits atop Koh Faan (Barking Deer Island), a small islet connected to the shore by a dirt causeway almost 305m (1,000 ft.) long. Though of little historic value, it's an imposing presence on the northeast coast and is one of Samui's primary landmarks. It's open all day; a 20B (50¢) contribution is recommended. It's easy to reach, just hop on any *songtao* going to Big Buddha Beach. You can't miss it.

Koh Samui's famed **Wonderful Rocks**—the most important of which are the unique **Hin Ta and Hin Yai,** or Grandfather and Grandmother Stones, shaped like the male and female anatomy—are located at the far southern end of Lamai Beach. To get there, flag down any minitruck to Lamai Beach.

The **Mummified Monk** at Wat Khunaram is certainly worth a visit if your bend is to roadside oddities. He died in the meditation mudra, legs folded lotus style, and he was embalmed that way; you can see him behind glass in a small pavilion at the right as you enter Wat Khunaram, itself a worthy example of a typical Thai town temple. At the entrance to the monks' pavilion, a few coins are the cost of the resident monks blessing with water. Take off your shoes, smile, and kneel, and he will put water on your head and say a few good words for whatever it's worth. The site is along the main road, Route 4169, as it shoots inland far south of Lamai.

The **Samui Monkey Theater** (© 07724-5140) is just south of Bophut village on 4169 Road. A vaudeville-style act demonstrates how monkeys collect coconuts—more fun for kids than for adults. Show times are 10:30am, 2pm, and 4pm daily; the cost is 150B ($3.75) for adults, 50B ($1.25) for children.

Samui's snake farm is at the far southwest corner of the island on 4170 Road (© 07742-3247), with daily shows at 11am and 2pm; tickets cost 250B ($6.25).

## SCUBA & SNORKELING

Local aquanauts agree that the best **scuba diving** is off Koh Tao, a small island north of Koh Pha Ngan and Koh Samui, and many of the operations on Samui coordinate with larger on-site dive centers there while also offering good day trips from Samui. Conditions vary with the seasons (best Oct–Mar). The cluster of tiny islands south of Samui, Mu Koh Angthong National Park, are often more reliable destinations. Follow the advice of a local dive shop on where to go because many have schools on Samui and offer trips ranging further afield.

Try **Samui International Diving School** (© 07742-2386; www.planet-scuba.net), **Easy Divers** (© 07741-3373), or **Big Blue** (© 07745-6179).

## KAYAKING

**Blue Stars Sea Kayaking,** at the Gallery Lafayette next to the Green Mango in Chaweng (© 07723-0497) and easy to contact through most booking agents, takes people kayaking and snorkeling to the Marine National Park. The rubber canoes are perfect for exploring the caverns underneath limestone cliffs. The 4-hour trip costs 2,000B ($50) per person.

## ROCK CLIMBING

Here's a fun one: **Samui Rocks** (© 07742-2232) is a little bar at the base of a road-cut cliff a few clicks south of Chaweng on the way to Lamai. Can't miss it. There are a number of top-rope routes set up for beginners (one climb is 200B/$5) and hold courses in lead climbing (1,800B/$45 per day).

## COOKING COURSE

For daily Thai cooking and fruit-carving lessons, **Samui Institute of Thai Culinary Arts** (SITCA; © 07741-3172; www.sitca.com) is a professional operation and a great way to have fun—especially if your beach plans get rained out. A lunchtime course goes for 995B ($25) and a dinner course is 1,400B ($35).

## KOH SAMUI SPAS

The spa scene on the island has really taken off. All of the big resorts offer "spa" services of varying quality and there are a number of good day spas on the island. Whether as an escape from the kids on a rainy day or as part of a larger health-focused mission in Thailand, Samui has all the services.

**Ban Sabai** (at Big Buddha Beach; © 07724-5175; www.ban-sabai.com) is a great choice for relaxing seaside massage and offers all treatments, from aromatherapy to body waxing, in their lush, Thai-style compound. Personal attention is Ban Sabai's hallmark and a well-informed staff can tailor a program to your every need. Treatments start at just 1,000B ($25) for a 1-hour massage. **The Spa Resort** (✆ 07723-0855; www.spasamui.com) in Lamai has been a leader on the island for years and continues to provide good, affordable day programs as well as the signature fasting retreat and all-inclusive packages. **Tamarind Retreat** (✆ 07723-0571; www.tamarindretreat.com) is a more exclusive (and expensive) choice set apart in a jungle area just off the beach at Lamai.

Traditional massage is available in any number of storefronts in Chaweng and everywhere along the beach. Expect to pay between 200B and 400B ($5–$10) per hour for services much the same as the average spa.

## KOH SAMUI AFTER DARK

Any given evening along the Chaweng strip is certain to be disrupted at least a few times by roaming pickup trucks with crackling PA systems blaring out advertisements in Thai and English for local **Thai boxing bouts.** Grab one of their flyers for times and locations, which vary.

Many of the hotels and resorts have culture shows featuring Thai dance that are worth seeing, and it wouldn't be a Thai beach without Koh Samui's drag queen review. **Christy's Cabaret** (✆ 01676-2181 cellular) on the north end of Chaweng puts on a hilarious show that's free of charge. Come well before the show starts at 11pm to get a better seat, and be prepared to make up for that free admission with cocktail prices.

For **bars and discos,** Chaweng is the place to be. A mainstream kind of fun seems to always be happening at the **Reggae Pub** (indicated on just about every island map—back from the main road around the central beach area). A huge thatch mansion, the stage thumps with some funky international acts, the dance floor jumps (even during low season it does a booming business) and the upstairs pool tables are good for sporting around. Just outside is a collection of open-air bars, also found along Chaweng's beach road.

The **Green Mango** has its own street just off the beachfront road in the northern end of Chaweng and boom-boom-booms late every night as the town's number-one dance location. Don't think of going before 10 or 11pm.

Irish-owned and -managed **Tropical Murphy's** (across from McDonald's in the south of Chaweng; ✆ 07741-3614) is indeed a slice of Ireland along the Chaweng strip. It's always full and open late and the best place to have a friendly pint and be assured not to have to scream over the thumping base of house music. Good Irish bands visit from time to time.

**Zico's,** a unique Brazilian restaurant, has a slick, big-city kind of bar that will be a comfort to any Hollywood-style "players" who miss the playground. Zico's modern facade looks over the busy main drag in the south of Chaweng near the Central Resort compound (✆ 07723-1560).

Over at Lamai Beach, there are some open-air bars geared to budget backpackers, but many are the sleazier bar-beer variety. **Bauhaus,** located in the center of town on the beach road, is at its best a stompin' club and at its worst hosts only a few tables of the lads there to watch English football. It's usually going strong in high season.

On Bophut Beach, be sure to stop by friendly and laid-back **Frog and Gecko Bar** (in Fisherman's Village; ✆ 07742-5248), especially for its popular pub quiz on Wednesday evenings.

Sunday afternoons, be sure to truck on over to the **Secret Garden Pub** ★★ on Big Buddha Beach (✆ 07724-5253) for live music and a barbecue on the beach. Many a famous performer (Gerry played here, man!) has jumped up on stage and there have been times where the pub has hosted thousands. It is not exactly "secret," but highly recommended.

## SIDE TRIPS FROM KOH SAMUI
### ANG THONG NATIONAL MARINE PARK ✦

Forty islands northwest of Koh Samui have been designated a national park. **Ang Thong National Marine Park** is known for its scenic beauty and rare coral reefs. Many of these islands are limestone rock towers (similar to Phangnga Bay off Phuket), once used by pirates marauding in the South China Sea.

You can book a private boat from Nathon Pier, or you can take a day trip in sea kayaks, paddling through the scenery for better views. A day trip runs about 2,000B ($50) with **Blue Stars** in Chaweng (✆ **07723-0497**).

## 12  Koh Pha Ngan

644km (399 miles) S of Bangkok to Surat Thani; 75km (47 miles) E from Surat Thani to Koh Pha Ngan

Like the kids in Alex Garland's novel *The Beach,* many come to Thailand to find that island paradise that has been unspoiled by the tacky trappings of mass tourism. The message of that novel is a perfect example of what eventually happens—paradise seekers inevitably bring their own standards of comfort and values, ironically turning their utopia into what they have strived to escape. Koh Pha Ngan still attracts an adventurous young crowd, but the bloom is off the rose.

Visible from Koh Samui and about two-thirds its size with similar terrain and flora, Koh Pha Ngan does have some beautiful beaches and the further reaches of the island, the rugged north and west coast areas accessible only by bumpy road or special boat, feature a few cozy resorts and a measure of rustic tranquillity.

The southeastern peninsula of **Haad Rin** is the locus of the monthly **Full Moon Party,** a multiday beachside rave with all the day-glow, strobe-lights, and debauch you can handle; attendance at the raves, especially in high season, numbers in many thousands of partiers moving to the mix of a European DJ, gobbling tabs of Ecstasy and magic mushrooms, and letting loose, very loose: something like Ibiza meets a Fish show at the beach. The aftermath of the party is a beautiful white-sand beach strewn with party garbage and buzzing with flies.

If you're interested in attending, boats from piers at either Big Buddha Beach or Bophut on Koh Samui leave at regular intervals all day and night (stopping at around 1am) and many revelers just make a night of it, crash on the beach, and come back to Samui in the morning. *A word of warning:* Beware of theft at Full Moon Parties—do yourself a favor and lock all your valuables in a hotel safe.

At other times, when not filled with wild-eyed revelers, the small area of Haad Rin is all New Age crystal, trinket, and T-shirt shops; vegetarian restaurants; bars playing DVD films; masseurs; cheap beers; magic-mushroom cake vendors; and $5 bungalows just a Frisbee throw away from a white-sand beach.

Don't be too put-off by Pha Ngan's party reputation. Haad Rin can be avoided altogether and, even during the full moon, you can find peace in any of a number of cozy hideaways on the island.

## GETTING THERE

**By Boat**    Frequent boats link Surat Thani, Koh Samui, Koh Pha Ngan, Koh Tao, and Chumphon and back again. From Samui's Nathon Pier, the trip to Koh Pha Ngan takes just over an hour and costs 95B ($2.40). Contact **Songserm** in Koh Samui (✆ **07742-0157**). *Note:* Unfortunately, the muster point in Pha Ngan is

## Just say "Mai!"

"Mai" means "no," and Nancy Reagan's ardent, much-parodied plea couldn't be more apt. Thai authorities hope to put the kibosh on Haad Rin's monthly Full Moon (and other "Half-moon" and "No-moon" excuses to rage). This means undercover drug busts by the very guy who just sold you that bag of oregano and bribing your way out of police custody.

not well organized, just a bare pier and one gruff attendant. Come armed with the patience of Buddha, especially any time near full moon.

Special boats from Samui's Big Buddha Beach or Bophut Beach also make regular trips for 100B ($2.50, more during Full Moon Parties at inflated rates).

## FAST FACTS

The tourist police operate a small information kiosk on the north end of the ferry offices at Thong Sala pier; contact them at ✆ **07742-1281** for info or ✆ 1155 in an emergency. There are branches of **Siam City Bank** with exchange and **ATM service** along both the main street of Thong Sala and in Haad Rin. Internet service is chockablock around the island; prices are 2B (5¢) per minute.

## GETTING AROUND

**Jeep and motorbike rental** on Koh Pha Ngan is available anywhere in Haad Rin or near the ferry pier at Thong Sala (Caribeener jeeps from 900B/$23; regular motorbikes from 150B/$3.75). The island roads are steep and treacherous, especially the popular southern reaches east of Thong Sala near Haad Rin. Many interior roads, including the trek to the secluded Thong Nai Pan area in the north, are hilly, muddy tracks. *Songtaos* (covered pickups) follow regular routes between Thong Sala ferry pier and Haad Rin as well as up the west coast and cost from 30B(75¢), more at night or during party time.

## WHAT TO DO & SEE

The rugged roads of Pha Ngan beg to be explored, and interior roads connect small towns worth seeing as a window into a way of laid-back island living that is slowly disappearing.

**Wat Kow Tahm** 🏃 is a well-known international meditation center and temple compound just north of the road near Thong Sala pier. Since 1988, Steve and Rosemary Weissmann (from the U.S. and Australia, respectively) have been offering courses in Insight Meditation, or Vipassana. The emphasis is on the development of compassionate understanding through the practice of formal walking and sitting meditation. There are frequent Dharma talks and 10- and 20-day retreats are for meditators of all experience levels (costs from 3,500B/$88 for 10 days). The temple is also open to day visitors and has an overlook with one of the best views on the island. Check its informative website at www.watkowtahm.org or write for information to: RETREATS, Wat Kow Tahm, P.O. Box 18, Koh Pah Ngan, Surat Thani 84280.

## WHERE TO STAY
### BAAN TAI BEACH

Just east of the ferry landing at Thong Sala, Ban Tai Beach is a quiet stretch of sand. The water is shallow and not great for swimming, but the beaches are lovely and there are a few convenient little resorts far from the hubbub of Haad Rin but close enough to visit. Try **First Villa** (145/1 Moo 1, Bantai Beach;

*C* 07737-7225) with basic bungalows from 1,200B ($30), or nearby **Mac Bay Resort** (Baan Tai Beach, Koh; *C* 07723-8443) with a similar plain standard and rates.

## HAAD RIN

Haad Rin is a narrow peninsula on the island's southeast tip, with a large number of bungalows on both the west and east sides and busy shopping streets and footpaths leading between them. There are lots of small bungalow resorts on Haad Rin but all are quite basic. On the busier west side try **Phangan Buri Resort & Health Spa** (120/1 Haad Rin Nai Beach, Haad Rin; *C* 07737-5481). Or check out hilltop **Sea Breeze Bungalow** (94/11 Moo 6, Haad Rin; *C* 07737-5162), a quiet, lofty perch high enough above town for a bit of quiet but close enough to walk down and join the festivities. Rooms start at 400B ($10) for fan only (double at Full Moon).

The **Sanctuary** bills itself as an alternative, boutique resort. It offers all kinds of healthy activities like yoga, massage, and fasting programs. Accommodations range from 60B ($1.50) dorms to cozy bungalows for 1,000B ($25). You'll need to arrange a taxi boat from Haad Rin to Haad Tien (50B/$1.25). Contact the resort at: P.O. Box 3, Koh Pha Ngan 84280; no phone, but e-mail through the website (www.sanctuaryresorts.com).

## WEST COAST

The west coast has good beaches and is far from the monthly "do" at Haad Rin, a relief for many. Resorts here are quiet and affordable and growing in number and quality of amenities. **Green Papaya** (Haad Salad, on the far northwest of the island; *C*/fax 07737-4230) is a mellow little courtyard hotel with rooms from 1,680B ($42), and **Salad Beach Resort** (*C* 07734-9274) next door is same-same.

Closer to the main ferry terminal is **Long Bay Resort** (11km/7miles north of Thong Sala; *C* 07737-7289), a low-luxe option with rooms from 600B ($15).

## NORTHEAST/THONG NAI PAN

Secluded on its own stretch of beach 17km (11 miles) from the ferry pier and north of busy Haad Rin, this area features great beaches with a few budget stops as well as the island's best resort. Thong Nai Pan is a scenic choice, easily reached by boat (contact Panviman below) or, less easily, by bumpy dirt road. **Panviman** ⚘ (22/1 Moo 5, Thong Nai Pan Noi Bay; *C*/fax 07723-8543; www.panviman.com) is the best standard on Pha Ngan and has picturesque rooms overlooking the bay, lots of services, and a unique tiered pool area.

## WHERE TO DINE

Cheap eats abound in busy Haad Rin, but your best bet for a good meal outside of your chosen resort is limited to mostly budget storefronts blaring DVD movies at high decibels. One bright spot is **Om Ganesh** (*C* 07737-5123) near the main ferry pier; it has great curries and set menus (all you can eat Indian *tali* meals) for little: authentic, delicious, and very popular.

## 13 Koh Tao

Tiny **Koh Tao** developed differently from its neighbors—it skipped the slow-growth years of thatch shacks and candlelit meals and went straight to corrugated tin roofs and video-playing bars. There are still lots of rustic choices on the island, but the current trend is small, all-inclusive resorts owned and operated by dive companies with head offices in Samui and elsewhere. Visitors spend their days out on the water on **scuba tours** to the fine coral sites around the island, then return to the comfort of private bungalows where they can debrief from the day's exploration and relax (many of these places even have air-conditioned classrooms for studying diving specifics). Avoid Koh Tao in the stormy November-to-December season, when the monsoon whips up and winds cloud the normally transparent seas. **Songserm** connects from nearby islands: from Chumphon the fare is a steep 400B ($10); from Koh Samui, 300B ($7.50); and from Koh Pha Ngan, 250B ($6.25). Contact Songserm in Samui (© **07742-0157**), Chumphon (© **07750-6205**), and Koh Tao (© **07745-6274**). Once you get to the main town, you'll find scuba operators and accommodations booking offices.

For advanced booking with a dive service, contact a dive office. Try:

- **Big Blue Diving Koh Tao** in Mae Haad, © **07745-6050** (www.bigblue diving.com).
- **Easy Divers** in Mae Haad Town (at catamaran jetty), © **07745-6010** (www.thaidive.com).

## 14 The Far South & on to Malaysia

From Surat Thani going south, Thailand slowly gives way to Malay culture and Buddhism, predominant elsewhere in the kingdom, is replaced by rich Islamic influence, a more gradual process than about any precise border. Nakhon Si Thammarat is an ancient Buddhist city of note with many temples worth visiting. Far southern Hat Yai is a major transport hub and a destination more popular with Malay and Singaporean tourists and mostly a stopover for onward travel to (or connecting from) Malaysia.

### NAKHON SI THAMMARAT

Nakhon Si Thammarat, one of the oldest cities in south Thailand, has long been a religious capital. **Wat Mahatat** houses a hair of the Buddha and is the town's central attraction and important pilgrimage point for Thai Buddhists. This region is the locus for traditional Thai puppet play, and **Ban Nang Thalung Suchart Subsin** (Mr. Subsin's House of Shadow Plays) at 110/18 Si Thammasok Soi 3 (© 07534-6394) makes for an interesting visit.

**Thai Airways** and **PB Air** each connect Nakhon with Bangkok. All north-south trains make a stop and affordable minivans can be arranged from any hotel (the best way to get around the south).

**Thai Hotel** (1375 Ratchadamnoen Rd; © 07534-1509) is a basic standard and convenient with rooms starting at 390B ($9.75).

### HAT YAI

It's a town full of tourists behaving badly really, mostly men from nearby Malaysia and Singapore attracted by this rowdy, slightly sleazy, inexpensive, consumer playground. For Westerners, Hat Yai is mostly a gateway to Malaysia by train or bus or a stepping-off point for rugged Tarutao National Park. Hat Yai's busy Night Market is certainly worth a wander and the beaches at nearby Songkhla are not a bad day trip.

**Hat Yai International Airport** welcomes flights from Malaysia and Singapore frequently throughout the week via Silk Air, Malaysia Airlines, and Thai Airways, and there are available connections to Bangkok and Phuket.

A major rail hub, five trains depart daily from Bangkok's **Hua Lampong Station** to Hat Yai (© 02223-7010 or 1690) and there are daily connections with

Malaysia. Minibuses connect from other parts of the region and long-distance buses connect with the Bangkok **Southern Bus Terminal** (© 02435-1199).

A number of fine hotels cater to Malay tourists. Try the **Regency Hotel** (23 Prachathipat Rd.; © 07423-4400), with rooms from 900B ($23), or the popular backpacker haunt, **Cathay Guest House** (93/1 Niphat Uthit 2 Rd; © 07424-3815), with dorms from 100B ($2.50) and reasonable singles from 160B ($4).

Hat Yai is also the gateway to **Tarutao National Park,** a chain of 51 islands originally settled by sea gypsies and later used as prison colonies. The jumping-off point for Tarutao is Ban Pak Bara, a port city reached by bus from Hat Yai.

## 15 Southern Peninsula: The West Coast & Islands

This stunning length of coast, dotted by some of the finest resorts in the region, is now well known for the tragic events of December 2004 when a massive tsunami struck the shores here, leaving a path of destruction. Many lives were lost and this long, heavily populated coast was left in ruins. However, most resorts were up and operating days after the disaster, and folks in this region are eager to reassure any tourists who have misplaced fears about another similar tragedy.

The island of **Phuket** was one of the earliest tourist developments in the kingdom and from humble origins has grown into a top international resort area: the best choice for comfort and services on the West Coast. Phuket may be the largest and best known, but is but one of many in the brilliant blue Andaman Sea; rocky islets, atolls, and leafy jungle coastline play host to a roster of island resorts and getaways. It is a great area to island hop by bus and ferry connections and there are opportunities for snorkeling, trekking, and laid-back luxury in every quarter.

Officially part of Krabi Province but often visited from Phuket, the island of **Koh Phi Phi** followed Phuket's development model though on a smaller scale. Phi Phi was hit hard by the tsunami, but the central beach area is quickly being rebuilt.

The province of **Krabi** encompasses all the land east of Phuket, including Koh Phi Phi and Koh Lanta, but "Krabi" typically refers to the small port town and nearby beaches of the **Krabi Resort Area** and **Ao Nang Beach.** In places like Railay beach, you'll find dynamic stone-tower landscapes (famous for rock climbing), great beaches, and a range of resorts. It's a popular alternative to busy Phuket.

**Koh Lanta** is a large island southeast of Krabi Town. Only marginally developed as yet, the cement trucks are rolling here and the islands western stretch promises a paved road soon (instead of the current grooved mud track). Here you'll find, apart from the island's one top-end resort, a rag-tag collection of budget resorts and bungalows (for some, just the ticket, though).

The high season on the west coast is from November to April—bookings must be made in advance, especially on Phuket, and discounted rates are hard to come by. Still, Western winter months are the time for water activities, when the Andaman is calm and the skies clear (when the snow falls thick in many parts of the world). In superpeak season, from the Christmas holiday through New Year's to about January 10, most places tack on steep surcharges.

## 16 Phuket

At its best, this island in the Andaman Sea is idyllic: It has long sandy beaches (some with dunes), warm water, excellent snorkeling and scuba diving off Koh Similan, ideal windsurfing conditions, mountains, fine resorts, and some of the best seafood in all of Thailand. At its worst, it is overdeveloped, overrun with

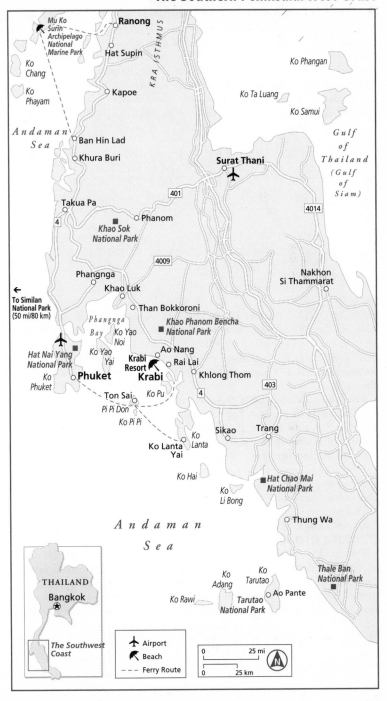

Mu Ko Surin Archipelago National Marine Park

**Ranong**

Ko Chang

Hat Supin

Ko Phayam

Kapoe

Ko Phangan

Ko Ta Luang

Ko Samui

*Andaman Sea*

Ban Hin Lad

Khura Buri

**Surat Thani**

*Gulf of Thailand (Gulf of Siam)*

401

4014

Takua Pa

Phanom

4

*Khao Sok National Park*

4009

Phangnga

Khao Luk

*Nakhon Si Thammarat*

To Similan National Park (50 mi/80 km)

Than Bokkoroni

*Khao Phanom Bencha National Park*

*Phangnga Bay*

Ko Yao Noi

Ao Nang

Ko Yao Yai

**Krabi Resort**

Rai Lai

*Hat Nai Yang National Park*

**Phuket**

**Krabi**

Khlong Thom

403

Ko Phuket

Ton Sai

Ko Pu

4

*Pi Pi Don*

*Ko Pi Pi*

Sikao

Trang

Ko Lanta Yai

Ko Lanta

Ko Hai

*Hat Chao Mai National Park*

Ko Li Bong

*Andaman Sea*

Thung Wa

THAILAND

Bangkok

Ko Adang

Ko Tarutao

*Thale Ban National Park*

Ko Rawi

Ao Pante

*Tarutao National Park*

*The Southwest Coast*

✈ Airport

⏷ Beach

--- Ferry Route

0          25 mi

0          25 km

N

tour groups and areas like busy Patong's pulsing commercial strip and raucous nightlife are a bit too much for those in search of beachside tranquillity.

Over the years, the Thai government has granted economic incentives to encourage developers to shape the island into an international first-class resort. Hotels—some of them enormous—line every beach. As groups pour in from Singapore, Hong Kong, and Europe, backpackers head off to nearby Koh Phi Phi, or islands on the eastern Gulf like Samui and Pha Ngan.

But many of the resorts are attractive and elegant and designed to give you the illusion of tropical solitude in busier areas. It's nearly impossible to find a totally secluded beach, but there are a number of very attractive and comfortable facilities with a high level of service—not a bad trade-off for those in search of all the luxuries. If on a family holiday, Phuket is a good choice.

The name "Phuket" is derived from the Malay "Bukit," meaning hill, and hills dominate much of the island's interior. There are still some rubber plantations and a few open-pit mining operations going on. Going by rented car or taking a fun but touristy "safari" is a good way to get into the jungle or up the hills from which you'll have great views of the beaches below and the many surrounding islands and islets. Most folks come for the beaches, though, and Phuket's are indeed some of the best in Thailand. Take your shoes off, find a hammock, and relax.

## ARRIVING

**BY PLANE**    **Thai Airways** (© 02525-2084 for domestic reservations in Bangkok) flies 13 times daily from Bangkok from 7am to 9:30pm (trip time: 1 hr., 20 min.) and has a daily flight from Hat Yai (trip time: 45 min.). In Hat Yai, its office is at 190/6 Niphat Uthit Rd. (© 07423-3433). Thai Airways' office in Phuket is at 78 Ranong Rd. (© 07621-1195 domestic or 07621-2499 international).

**Bangkok Airways** (© 02229-3434 in Bangkok or 07724-5601 on Koh Samui) connects Phuket with Koh Samui at least two times daily. The Bangkok Airways office in Phuket is at 158/2–3 Yaowarat Rd., Phuket Town (© 07622-5033, or 07632-7114 at Phuket Airport).

**Phuket Airlines** (© 02535-6382) also has daily flights (leaving in the morning, returning in evening). Thailand's newest budget airline, **Air Asia** (© 02515-9999; www.airasia.com), flies between Bangkok and Phuket for about the same price as the train.

**Thai Airways** (© 02525-2084) connects Phuket with international flights to and from Frankfurt, Hong Kong, Perth, Singapore, and Tokyo. **Silk Air** (© 02236-5301-3 in Bangkok) has daily connections with Singapore.

The attractive, modern **Phuket International Airport** (© 07732-7230) is located in the north of the island, about 40 minutes' drive from town or from Patong Beach. There are banks, money-changing facilities, car-rental agents (see "Getting Around," below), and a post office. The Phuket Tourist Business Association booth can help you make hotel arrangements if you haven't booked a room.

Many resorts will pick you up at the airport upon request for a fee, usually steep, though some include this with your booking. The airport limousine counter, operated by **Tour Royale** (© 07634-1214), offers many options for getting to your hotel from the airport. The cheapest way is the minibus, which operates every hour on the hour from 9am to 11pm daily. Stopping between Patong, Kata, Karon, and Phuket Town, prices run from 80B to 180B ($2–$4.50), depending on how far you're going (180B/$4.50 gets you as far south as Kata

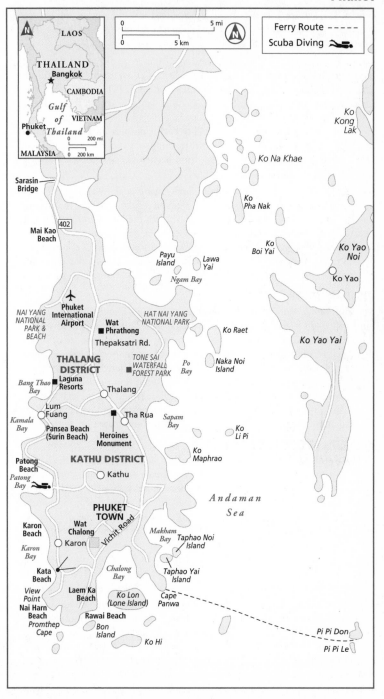

Beach). **Taxi service** from the airport, also arranged at the limousine counter, will cost from between 400B ($10) to Phuket Town and 590B ($15) to Kata beach. There are many VIP options as well.

**BY BUS** Three air-conditioned 24-seat VIP buses leave daily from Bangkok's **Southern Bus Terminal** (*©* 02434-7192), best as an overnight, and cost from 755B ($19). Regular air-conditioned buses cost 486B ($12). Standard buses make frequent connections to Surat Thani and nearby towns on the mainland (to Surat is 6 hr. and 105B/$2.65).

The intercity bus terminal is at the **City Park Complex** on Phangnga Road (*©* 07621-1480), east of Phuket Town just opposite the Royal Phuket City Hotel. For information on how to get from here to the beaches, see "Getting Around," below.

**BY MINIVAN** Minivans to and from Surat Thani, Krabi, Nakhon Si Thammarat, Ranong, and other southern cities leave on regular schedules throughout the day. In each city, minivan operators work with the hotels and arrange free pickup, so it's best to book through your hotel front desk or a travel agent (also the operators who man the phones at minivan companies rarely speak English). Tickets to destinations in the south, to places like Surat Thani or Hat Yai, go for between 100B and 250B ($2.50–$6.25).

## VISITOR INFORMATION

The **Tourism Authority of Thailand** has an office in Phuket Town at 73–75 Phuket Rd. (*©* 07621-2213), but there is far better information at any hotel concierge or tour desk. There are lots of free maps on offer (all are full of advertisements) and for driving around the island, pick up the very detailed *Periplus Editions Map of Phuket* at bookstores. Restaurants and hotel lobbies are good places to pick up any of a number of free local publications: *Phuket Food-Shopping-Entertainment* is packed with dining suggestions and ads for many of the island's activities; *What's on South* has some useful information on Phuket, Koh Phi Phi, and Krabi; and there a few fun ultraglossy local magazines for sale.

## ISLAND LAYOUT

Phuket Town, the island's commercial center, is in the southeast of the island. Phuket's picturesque stretches of sand dot the stretch of western coast from Nai Harn, on the southern tip, to Bang Tao, about 30km (19 miles) north. Beginning in the south, you'll find Kata Noi, Kata, Karon, Patong, Surin, and a number of smaller beaches all along this corridor. A busy coastal road links the popular tour towns in the south, but stops north of Patong require short detours from the main highway. Inland Phuket, with its winding mountain roads, buzzes with traffic and many visitors rent vehicles to tour the island's smaller byways or make the trip to jungle parks like Khao Phra Thaeo Wildlife Park in the northeast of the isle, famed for diverse flora and fauna.

**THE BEACHES** There's a beach for everyone in Phuket, from exclusive hideaways with luxury hotels to backpacker towns and even campgrounds. Each beach is distinct and selecting the appropriate area makes all the difference.

**Nai Harn,** in the far south of the busy west coast of Phuket, is an isolated beach area with a few fine resorts. Going north, find **Kata, Kata Noi,** and **Karon beaches.** Developed but not overwhelmingly so (far from over-the-top Patong), along these beaches you'll find resorts large and small. In general this is the least expensive area on Phuket with still a few hold-out budget places that haven't been bulldozed and made high-end yet. Sandy beaches are long and picturesque and the water is deep with some nice wave breaks. This beach area has more restaurants than the remote bays, and some shopping, nightlife, and travel agent options as well. But you won't find rowdy crowds here and, even with all the development, the area manages to maintain a laid-back character.

North of the Kata and Karon bays you'll pass through **Relax Bay,** a small cove with a few resorts, before rolling down the mountain to **Patong Beach,** the most famous (perhaps infamous) strip on the island. Patong's draw is its raucous nightlife, busy shops and restaurants, and brash neon-radiating pulse: Can you hear the bass? Accommodations run the gamut.

Still north of Patong, **Kamala Bay, Surin Beach,** and **Pan Sea Beach** have more secluded resorts on lovely beaches for those who still want the convenience of nearby Patong, but cherish the serenity of a quiet resort. Just north is **Bang Tao Beach,** home to the Laguna Resort Complex of luxury hideaways. Beautiful **Haad Nai Yang National Park** is a remote area with good diving, just north of Laguna, and, in the far north are **Mai Khao** and the JW Marriott Phuket.

## GETTING AROUND

Public transportation is a problem on Phuket that never seems to get solved. If you've spent any time in other parts of the country, you'll know that the covered pickup trucks that cruise the streets picking up and dropping off passengers are called *songtao,* while the noisy motorized three-wheel demon vehicles are known as tuk-tuks. Not so on Phuket! Here, the people call the minitrucks tuk-tuks, while *songtao* are the giant colorful buses that ply the main roads (a few people also call them "baht buses"). Tuk-tuk drivers, in an attempt to generate more business, have lobbied successfully for exclusive rights to transport people *between* beaches. This means the *songtao* buses are only permitted to travel from each beach to Phuket Town. You can't hop from beach to beach on them. For these trips you have to negotiate with the tuk-tuk drivers (see below for tips).

**BY *SONGTAO*** The local bus terminal is in front of the Central Market on Ranong Road in Phuket Town. Fares to the most popular beaches range from 20B to 30B (50¢–75¢). *Songtaos* leave when full, usually every 30 minutes, from 7am to 6pm between Phuket Town and the main beaches on the west coast. They do not operate routes between beaches.

**BY TUK-TUK & DAIHATSU MINI** Within Phuket Town, tuk-tuks cost about 20B to 40B (50¢–$1) for in-town trips: a good way to get to the bus station or to Phuket Town's restaurants; in the west-coast beaches, tuk-tuks and small Daihatsu minitrucks roll around town honking at any tourist on foot, especially in Patong, and charge more, about 120B ($3) from Patong Beach to Karon Beach for example, and more late at night

**BY MOTORCYCLE TAXI** Drivers, identifiable by colored vests, make short trips in Phuket Town or along Patong Beach for 20B–40B (50¢–$1).

**BY CAR** Self-drive is popular in Phuket but extreme caution applies. Roads between the main beaches in the west and connecting with Phuket Town across the center of the island are dangerously steep and winding with more than a few hairpin turns and lots of traffic and motorbikes zipping around unpredictably. As in other parts of the kingdom, drivers pass aggressively, even on blind curves, and self-driving visitors will want to be very defensive and alert at all times.

**Avis** has a counter at **Phuket Airport** (✆ 07653-1243). Plan on spending around 1,500B to 1,800B ($38–$45) per day for a Suzuki Caribian 4WD sport vehicle. **Budget** (✆ 07620-5396) is a bit cheaper and has an airport location as well as counters at a number of hotels (JW Marriott, Evason Resort, and Club

Andaman Beach Resort in Patong). Both companies offer sedans, and both also have sound insurance coverage available, which is highly recommended.

Inexpensive Suzuki Caribians can be rented from almost all travel agents and from hotels at the beach areas. Prices start at 1,200B ($30) per day. Independent agents hang around under umbrellas along Patong Beach and offer great bargains if you negotiate. Caribians go for as little as 900B ($23) a day (negotiable!), and 1,500B ($38) and over for open-top jeeps and souped-up four-wheel-drive off-road vehicles.

**BY MOTORCYCLE**    Also along the Patong strip, the same car-rental guys will provide you with a bike for cheap. A 100cc Honda scooter goes for 200B ($5) per day, while a 400cc Honda CBR or a 600cc Honda Shadow chopper will set you back at least 600B ($15) per day. Significant discounts can be negotiated if you plan to rent for a longer time. Wear your helmet (sometimes-enforced fines of 500B/$13 for going without), keep to the left, and let cars pass. You're sure to meet up with a few road-rashed travelers in any beach area and there is no quicker way to end a vacation than on slippery, treacherous roads, especially for inexperienced riders, so take caution.

---

### FAST FACTS: Phuket

*Banks*    Banks are located in Phuket Town, with many larger branches on Ranong and Rasada roads. There are bank offices at the airport, as well as branches of major Thai banks at Kata, Karon, and Patong beaches. See each section for more complete information. **Money changers** are in major shopping areas on each beach, and at most resorts. Banks offer the best rates.

*Hospitals*    The **Bangkok Phuket Hospital** at 2/1 Hongyok-Uthit Rd. (off Yaowarat Rd. in Phuket Town; ✆ 07625-4421) has English-speaking staff, high-quality facilities, and accepts international medical insurance.

*Internet*    Internet service is fairly easy to find on the island. There are cafes aplenty in Patong; the best are further away from the beach.

*Police*    The emergency number for the **Tourist Police** is fast-dial four digit ✆ 1155. For **Marine Police** call ✆ 07621-4368.

*Post Office*    The General Post Office in Phuket Town (✆ 07621-1020) is at the corner of Thalang and Montri roads.

---

## SPECIAL EVENTS

If you are on Phuket in October, don't miss the **Vegetarian Festival,** a colorful tradition passed down from early Thai-Chinese settlers. For 9 days not only do devotees refrain from meat consumption, many also submit to physical self-mutilation through extreme body-piercing with long skewers or swords and walk over coals, all acts of merit making and penance to the spirits who helped early inhabitants ward off malaria. Early morning processions follow through the streets of Phuket Town, with onlookers clad in white for the occasion.

## THINGS TO DO & SEE

If Phuket is your only destination in Thailand, you'll certainly want to get to some of the small rural temples and Phuket Town, but touring Phuket pales in

comparison to culturally rich areas like Bangkok or Chiang Mai. Beach and outdoor activities top the list of things to do and there's certainly something for
everyone (see "Exploring Phuket," at the end of this section). Opportunities
abound to tour the islands rustic bays and many beaches or take day trips to scenic **Phang Nga Bay** to the north or the island's jungle interior.

There are a few Buddhist temples on the island that are quite notable; the
most unique is **Wat Pra Tong,** located along Highway 402 in Thalang just south
of the airport. The most famous temple among Thai visitors is **Wat Chalong.**
Chalong was the first resort on Phuket, back when the Thais first started coming to the island for vacations. Nowadays, the discovery of better beaches on the
west side of the island has driven most tourists away from this area, but the temple still remains the center of Buddhist worship. While the temple compound
itself is pretty standard in terms of modern temples, the place comes to life during Buddhist holy days. The temple is on the Bypass Road, about 8km (5 miles)
south of Phuket Town.

**Sea Gypsies,** the indigenous people of the southern islands, are fast disappearing from Phuket. Commercial fishing interests and shoreline development
continue to threaten their livelihood of subsistence fishing. Gypsy villages are
simple, floating shacks, and longtail boats. Visits to some of the larger settlements in Pha Nga Bay are included in many island day trips.

## WHERE TO STAY

The island's hotels, resorts, and restaurants below are divided into beach areas to
simplify choice. Hotels in this section are listed by the high-season rack-rate, an
almost fictitious fee but a good point of departure for gauging price. Expect to
pay from 30% and as much as 50% below the listed rate, especially in low season (see "Tips on Accommodations," in chapter 3).

### PHUKET TOWN

Most just pass through the island's commercial hub, but there are some high-class
facilities if you're stuck and a few restaurants worth the trip, especially if Phuket
Island is your only destination (see "Where to Dine," later in this chapter).

If you're in a pinch and looking for a budget spot, **The Tavorn Hotel** (74
Rasada Rd., Amphur Muang, Phuket 83000; ⓒ **07621-1333**) is an old standby
at the town center with rooms starting at 550B/$14. The hotel has seen better
days, though; in fact, it has seen much better days and there is a little museum
in the beat old lobby that testifies to the fact. A careful renovation could bring
the old gal back to her former glory days, when she was the choice of kings, but
for now it's pretty rough. **Phuket Island Pavillion** (133 Satoon Rd.; ⓒ **07621-
0444**) has better rooms starting at just 1,500B/$38.

### Expensive

**The Metropole**    Just around the corner from the Royal Phuket City Hotel, the
Metropole is a similar fine business hotel. Public spaces are all spit-and-polish
(though not especially grand) and the rooms are large and fully appointed (if
bland) with good black-and-white tile bathrooms. Service is professional but curt.

1 Soi Surin, Montri Rd., Phuket Town 83000. ⓒ 07621-5050. Fax 07621-5990. www.metropolephuket.com.
248 units. 3,200B–3,800B ($80–$95) double; 6,000B ($150) suite. AE, MC, V. **Amenities:** 2 restaurants;
lounge and bar; pool; small fitness corner; tour desk; business center; shopping; salon; 24-hr. room service;
laundry service; dry cleaning. *In room:* A/C, satellite TV, minibar, fridge, safe, IDD phone.

### Royal Phuket City Hotel ⭐    For a small town like Phuket, this hotel is sur-
prisingly cosmopolitan. A true city hotel, Royal Phuket's facilities include one of

the finest fitness centers going, a full-service spa with massage, large outdoor swimming pool, and a very professional executive business center. Above the cavernous marble lobby, guest rooms are smart—in contemporary hues and style, but dull with views of the busy little town below that pale in comparison to the beachfront just a short ride away. Pickles Restaurant serves international cuisine and the Chinatown Restaurant is one of the most posh in town. Few indeed stay in Phuket Town, but if you're stuck here, go for style.

154 Phang-Nga Rd., Amphur Muang, Phuket 83000 (located to the east of Phuket Town, across from the inter-city bus terminal). © 07623-3333. Fax 07623-3335. www.royalphuketcity.com. 251 units. 3,500B–4,200B ($88–$105) double; from 6,000B ($150) suite. AE, DC, MC, V. **Amenities:** 2 restaurants; lobby lounge; out-door pool; golf course nearby; fitness center w/sauna, steam, massage, and spa; tour desk; limo service; busi-ness center; 24-hr. room service; babysitting; same-day laundry service/dry cleaning; nonsmoking rooms; executive-level rooms. *In room:* A/C, satellite TV, dataport, minibar, fridge, hair dryer, safe, IDD phone.

## NAI HARN BEACH
### Very Expensive

Just up the road from the Le Meridien you'll find rustic bungalows at **Jungle Beach Resort** (11/3 Viset Rd.; ©/fax **07638-1108**). There are no services to speak of, but it's not a bad little getaway. Rooms start at 800B ($20).

**Le Royal Meridien Phuket Yacht Club** ⋆⋆   Perched above the northern edge of Nai Harn beach, overlooking the public beach and yachts beyond, the Yacht Club is one of the earliest luxury accommodations in Phuket yet still rivals nearly anything on the island for setting and comfort. Staff members in pith hel-mets greet with heel-clicking salutes and, as you enter, the pagoda-style foyer gives way to the terraced gardens overflowing with pink and white bougainvil-lea. Common areas are terra-cotta tile and open air with views. All rooms have large balconies for viewing the beach, the Andaman Sea, and Promthep Cape from every angle. Interiors are spacious and decorated with cheerful fabrics and wicker furniture; bathrooms are huge, many with sunken tubs, and feature lux-ury amenities. The resort is more sedate and romantic than the many noisy fam-ily resorts on the island, exemplified by the Yacht Club's sister property, Le Meridien Phuket.

23/3 Viset Rd., Nai Harn Beach, Phuket 83130 (above Nai Harn Beach, 18km/11 miles south of Phuket). © **0800/225-5843** or 07638-1156. Fax 07638-1164. www.lemeridien.com. 110 units. 13,500B–14,350B ($338–$359) double; from 17,200B ($430) suite. AE, DC, MC, V. **Amenities:** 3 restaurants; patio lounge; out-door pool; 2 outdoor lighted tennis courts; small fitness center; spa w/Jacuzzi, steam, massage, and face and body treatments; extensive watersports equipment; tour desk; car-rental desk; limo service; business center; small boutique; salon; 24-hr. room service; babysitting; same-day laundry service/dry cleaning; nonsmoking rooms. *In room:* A/C, satellite TV w/pay movies, minibar, fridge, coffee/tea-making facilities, hair dryer, safe, IDD phone.

## KATA BEACH

Arguably one of the nicest beaches in Phuket, Kata is a wide strip of soft sand and rolling surf. Rent an umbrella for 100B ($2.50) per day, get a massage, or grab a kayak or surfboard and hit the waves (okay, the small waves, mostly). Unfortunately the most choice real estate near the beach is taken up by the sprawling **Phuket Club Mediterranee** (© **07633-0455;** www.clubmed.com), a branch of the famous luxury chain.

### Expensive

**Kata Beach Resort** ⋆   Under major cosmetic renovations at the time of this writing, the new-and-improved Kata Beach will still reign in central Kata. With its soaring granite-and-marble lobby and fine rooms, it is the most formal facility on the Kata coast and attracts not only individual tourists looking for comfort, but a burgeoning international conference market. Go for a deluxe beachview room in the central building—the slightly higher-priced choice, but the view really is lovely. All rooms have balconies and are attractively decorated.

5/2 Patak Rd., Kata Beach, Phuket 83100 (in the Kata Beach strip). ✆ 07633-0530, or 02939-4062 in Bangkok. Fax 07633-0128. 200 units. 4,600B ($115) superior double; 5,000B ($125) deluxe double (sea view); from 6,000B ($150) suite. AE, DC, MC, V. **Amenities:** 2 restaurants; outdoor pool; fitness center w/sauna and massage; watersports; children's center; concierge; tour desk; limo service; business center; shopping arcade; salon; limited room service; babysitting; same-day laundry service/dry cleaning. *In room:* A/C, satellite TV, minibar, fridge, hair dryer, safe.

**Kata Thani Hotel** ✸    The Kata Thani is the best option on the cul-de-sac of lovely Kata Noi Beach and is a haven of quiet luxury. Though just completing a major renovation at the time of this writing, the cosmetic upgrade of this long-popular gem promises an even higher standard for the same good value. Neighboring Kataburi Hotel is under the same management and offers similar comfortable rooms without sea views for a slight discount. Wide, well-groomed lawns surround sizable pools and lead to the graceful curve of the pristine cove. There is a nightly poolside buffet. The Kata Thani's best feature is that it's right on the beach and all rooms have good sea views. Kata Noi is a bit out of the fray, a few clicks south of the main Kata beach and far from the raucous strip at Patong, but the hotel is self-contained enough and can arrange transport for any excursion.

3/24 Patak Rd., Kata Noi Beach, Phuket 83100 (north end of Kata Noi Beach). ✆ 07633-0124. Fax 07633-0426. www.katathani.com. 530 units. 6,400B–7,200B ($160–$180) double; from 7,700B ($193) suite. AE, DC, MC, V. **Amenities:** 5 restaurants; lounge; 3 outdoor pools; golf course nearby; 2 outdoor lighted tennis courts; fitness center; aromatherapy spa; Jacuzzi; sauna; watersports equipment/scuba diving; game room; tour desk; car-rental desk; limo service; salon; 24-hr. room service; massage; babysitting; same-day laundry service/dry cleaning; library. *In room:* A/C, satellite TV, minibar, coffee/tea-making facilities, hair dryer, safe.

**Mom Tri's Boathouse (aka "The Boathouse")** ✸✸    At the quieter south end of Kata Beach, this small inn is a long-time favorite with many returning visitors. More inn than resort, there's a real home-style feeling here. Comfortable, attractive rooms all face the sea, each with a terrace overlooking courtyard pool and beach beyond but not particularly luxurious (though clean and adequate). Nothing about the hotel calls attention to itself really; instead, it's the friendly, attentive staff that makes it very special. The Boathouse grill, the first-floor restaurant, is a long-time favorite for the visiting connoisseur (see "Where to Dine," later in this chapter). For a very special stay, stop in at Mom Tri's latest venture, **Villa Royale,** a collection of superluxe suites. These large, luxury rooms are perched over a steep cliff with stunning views of the sea and are sumptuously decorated in a unique mix of local materials: dark teaks, mosaics of bamboo and coconut, black tile with stone inlay, and elegant weavings. Mom Tri's Kitchen, the hotel companion restaurant, offers some of the best dining on the island (see "Where to Dine," later in this chapter). It offers good cooking classes, too.

Kata Beach, Phuket 83100. ✆ 07633-0015. Fax 07633-0561. www.boathousephuket.com. 36 units at the Boathouse; 6 units at Villa Royale. 7,000B–13,000B ($175–$325) Boathouse double; from 12,000B ($292) Villa Royale suite. AE, DC, MC, V. **Amenities:** 3 restaurants; lounge; outdoor pool; golf course nearby; fitness center; Jacuzzi; limo service; limited room service (7am–10:30pm); massage; babysitting; same-day laundry service/dry cleaning; library. *In room:* A/C, satellite TV, minibar, fridge, coffee/tea-making facilities, hair dryer, safe, IDD phone.

## Moderate

**Marina Phuket** ✸    These simple cottages, tucked in the jungle above a scenic promontory between Kata and Karon beaches, are quite comfortable and the best choice of the many midrange places nearby. Rates vary according to the view, but all have a jungle bungalow charm, connected by hilly walkways and boardwalks past the lush hillside greenery (keep your eyes peeled for wildlife). Guest rooms are decorated in Thai style but are not particularly luxurious: standard rooms are just plain tile floors and basic built-in furniture; superior rooms are just a bit larger with more flourish like fine Thai fabrics, higher ceilings and good views. It is a hike down to the rocky shore and the swimming isn't great, but it has a good seaside restaurant (under major renovation at the time of this writing) and the in-house **Marina Divers** (② **07638-1625**) is a PADI International Diving School which conducts classes, rents equipment, and leads good multiday expeditions. The front desk staff is professional enough, friendly and playful.

47 Karon Rd., Karon Beach, Phuket 83100 (on bluff at south end of Karon Beach Rd.). ② 07633-0625. Fax 07633-0516. www.marinaphuket.com. 104 units. 4,400B–7,040B ($110–$176) double. MC, V. **Amenities:** Restaurant; pool; dive center; limited room service; same-day laundry service. *In room:* A/C, satellite TV, minibar, no phone.

## Inexpensive

**Katanoi Bay Inn**   Here's a no-muss-no-fuss pick for Phuket. This budget accommodation provides you with a comfortable, very clean room without paying out the nose for resort facilities you may not even use. Bright rooms have balconies and good firm beds and there is little else in the way of facilities, but there's quiet Kata Noi Beach just across the road (near the Katatani Hotel). This small place is a bit remote, which for some is a plus.

4/16 Moo 2 Patak Rd., Kata Noi Beach, Phuket 83100 (Kata Noi is south of Kata Beach). ②/fax 07633-3308. www.phuket.com/katanoibayinn. 28 units. 1,200B ($30) double. MC, V. **Amenities:** Restaurant; tour desk; car-rental desk; same-day laundry service/dry cleaning; Internet terminal. *In room:* Fridge, no phone.

## KARON BEACH

Karon Beach is a long, straight stretch of beach lined with upper and midrange hotels and resorts. You'll find heaps of tailors, gift shops, small restaurants, Internet service, and minimarts on the north end of the beach.

## Expensive

**Andaman Seaview Hotel** ★★   Here's one I recommend heartily if you can book it (the word is out and it is often full). Bright and airy public spaces done in Mediterranean hues of light blue and white, a Sino-Portuguese theme, are flanked by ponds and give way to a large central courtyard, garden, and meandering pool. Rooms overlook the pool area and are large and nicely appointed, better than most in this category. There is a charm throughout that is less about luxury than the warm welcome, tidy appearance of the place, and the friendly crowd this attracts. The restaurant is a hotel coffee shop de rigueur but you'll want to dine at poolside: In fact, do everything at poolside. There's a small spa and you're just across the street from Karon Beach.

Karon Rd., Phuket 83100 (along the main strip at Karon Beach). ② 07639-8111. Fax 07639-8177. www. andamanphuket.com. 161 units. 6,900B ($173) superior double; 8,800B ($220) deluxe double. AE, MC, V. **Amenities:** Restaurant; bar (poolside); 2 outdoor pools; small fitness center; spa; Jacuzzi; gift shop; 24-hr. room service; massage; same-day laundry service/dry cleaning; Internet corner; tailor. *In room:* A/C, satellite TV, minibar, fridge, coffee/tea-making service, safe, IDD phone.

**Hilton Phuket Arcadia Hotel** ★★   Just rebranded as a Hilton hotel, this modern, full-facility resort is a massive presence on Karon Beach, and quite pleasant if a bit expensive for a not-so-great beach area. Rooms are attractive but rather bland, with standard bathroom facilities, all overlooking the beach and ocean. If you're traveling with children, the studio double, with more space, will fit a couple of extra beds. The landscaping is a little stark, but the elevated pool and sun deck offer wonderful views of the bay.

78/2 Patak Rd., Karon Beach, Phuket 83100 (middle of Karon Beach Rd.). ☎ **07639-6433**. Fax 07639-6136. www.phuketarcadia.com. 475 units. 4,000B–8,400B ($100–$210) double; from 5,000B ($125) studio. AE, DC, MC, V. **Amenities:** 5 restaurants; lounge and karaoke; large outdoor pool; golf course nearby and putting green on-site; outdoor lighted tennis courts; fitness center w/Jacuzzi, sauna, steam, and massage; game room; tour desk; limo service; salon; 24-hr. room service; babysitting; same-day laundry service/dry cleaning. *In room:* A/C, satellite TV, minibar, coffee/tea-making facilities, safe.

**Thavorn Palm Beach Hotel** ✪    Near the beach and next to the Hilton (above), this large resort covers a lot of territory, providing plenty of facilities. Only recently renovated, most rooms have fine views of the Karon dunes and sea beyond. The decor is plain but pleasant, with tiled floors, rattan furnishings, and small balconies. Suites are decorated in Thai style featuring teak woodcarvings and local textiles. The large central pool is a highlight, and the traditional Thai restaurant, Old Siam, serves fine cuisine on low tables—big cushions are comfy—and there is live music nightly. Overall a good, familiar, convenient choice.

128/10 Moo 3, Karon Beach, Phuket 83110 (in mid–Karon Beach area). ☎ **07639-6091**. Fax 07639-6555. www.thavornpalmbeach.com. 209 units. 4,000B–9,850B ($100–$246) double; from 23,760B ($594) suite. AE, DC, MC, V. **Amenities:** 5 restaurants; lounge; 4 outdoor pools; golf course nearby; outdoor lighted tennis courts; fitness center; watersports equipment; game room; concierge; tour desk; car-rental desk; limo service; 24-hr. room service; massage; babysitting; same-day laundry service/dry cleaning. *In room:* A/C, satellite TV, minibar, fridge, hair dryer, IDD phone.

## Moderate

**Karon Beach Resort**    This is the only Karon Beach property with direct beach access (from all others you'll have to walk across the road). It is quite often full up, and the hotel maintenance has a real time of it to keep up with the constant traffic, but this is a good, cozy choice at beach side and a good, affordable choice for young couples. Rooms are midsize, with dark wooden entries, clean tile floors, and some Thai touches in decor, but are most noteworthy for their orientation to the sea: Balconies are stacked in receding, semicircular tiers and all look on the pool below (first floor with direct pool access) or to the beach and sea beyond. You'll find good nearby watersports rentals.

51 Karon Rd., Tambon Daron, Phuket 83100 (the south end of Karon Beach, just as the road bends up to cross to Kata). ☎ **07633-0006**. Fax 07633-0217. www.katagroup.com. 81 units. 4,600B ($115); from 6,000B ($150) suite. AE, MC, V. **Amenities:** 2 restaurants; 2 outdoor pools; tour desk; car rental; courtesy car and airport transfer; massage; laundry service; Internet corner. *In room:* A/C, satellite TV, minibar, fridge, safe (charge of 50B/ $1.25), IDD phone.

## Inexpensive

**Golden Sand Inn**    One of only a few acceptable budget accommodations on this part of the island (they're either getting converted into swanky digs or falling into disrepair as in Patong), the Golden Sand is clean, reasonably quiet, and well maintained. The location isn't bad, on the northernmost end of Karon and not far from all the town services and the beach. Rooms are large and like a beat-up roadside motel. It does have a nice coffee shop, though, and a small swimming pool. Off-season rates are cheap-cheap.

Karon Beach, Phuket 83100 (across hwy. from north end of beach above traffic circle). ☎ **07639-6493**. Fax 07639-6117. 125 units. 1,800B–2,500B ($45–$63) double. AE, DC, MC, V. **Amenities:** Restaurant; pool; laundry service. *In room:* A/C, TV, minibar, fridge, safe.

## RELAX BAY

**Le Meridien Phuket** ✪ *(Kids)*    Le Meridien Phuket is tucked away on secluded Relax Bay, with a lovely 549m (1,800-ft.) beach and 16 hectares (40 acres) of tropical greenery. This is one of the largest resorts on the island, and throughout the year it is packed with Asian and European vacationers. The advantages of a larger resort are its numerous facilities—two big swimming pools, watersports, four tennis courts, putting green and practice range, and a fine fitness center; the disadvantage is the crowds (during recent low occupancy due to SARS the hotel was almost giving away rooms and the place was packed). The staff is helpful but harried and can often be found "dug in" behind the front desk like soldiers in a trench for the onslaught of the many big groups here. The resort caters to families, though, and there are lots of activities and a good day-care center that kids just seem to love. The large building complex combines Western and traditional Thai architecture, and one of the advantages to its U-shape layout is that it ensures that 80% of the rooms face the ocean. The modern furnishings in cheerful rooms are of rattan and teak, each with a balcony and wooden sun deck chairs. No fewer than 10 restaurants give you all kinds of choice.

8/5 Tambol, Karon Noi, P.O. Box 277, Relax Bay, Phuket 83000. ✆ 0800/225-5843 or 07634-0480. Fax 07634-0479. www.lemeridien.com. 470 units. 11,500B–13,500B ($288–$338) double; from 18,000B ($450) suite. AE, DC, MC, V. **Amenities:** 10 restaurants; 4 pubs w/games and live shows; 2 large outdoor pools; golf driving range and on-site pro; minigolf; outdoor lighted tennis courts; squash courts; fitness center; watersports equipment and dive center; bike rental; excellent children's center; game room; concierge; tour desk; car-rental desk; limo service; business center; shopping arcade; salon; 24-hr. room service; massage; babysitting; same-day laundry service/dry cleaning; nonsmoking rooms. *In room:* A/C, satellite TV, minibar, fridge, coffee/tea-making facilities, hair dryer, safe.

## PATONG

Patong's got it all, but it's all stacked in a heap and glowing with neon. The area pulses with activity, shopping, dining, and nightlife, late into the evening. In the downtown it's all touts catcalling and the beeping horns of passing tuk-tuks wanting to take you for a ride (quite literally); but Patong has tons of services and some good accommodations (the best find creative ways to make you feel like you're not in Patong).

### Very Expensive

**Diamond Cliff Resort** ✾ The Diamond Cliff is a gleaming hilltop resort, with rooms done in soothing sea greens, blues, and light wood trim; all command great ocean views. The grounds are attractively landscaped and common areas are luxurious. It has irregular shuttle service to cover the distance down the hill and into town; after the one long walk you take on the special boardwalk to Patong that winds through the rocky coastline, you'll want to get some wheels. The hotel does have quite a selection of good facilities and the place is in tiptop shape. Comparable to Novotel next door.

284 Prabaramee Rd., Patong, Phuket 83150 (far south end, on road to Kamala Beach). ✆ 07634-0501. Fax 07634-0507. www.diamondcliff.com. 330 units. 10,500B–11,000B ($263–$275) double; from 12,500B ($313) suite. AE, DC, MC, V. **Amenities:** 8 restaurants; lounge; outdoor pool; minigolf; outdoor lighted tennis courts; fitness center; small spa; dive center; game room; concierge; tour desk; car-rental desk; limo service; salon; 24-hr. room service; massage; babysitting; same-day laundry service/dry cleaning. *In room:* A/C, satellite TV, minibar, safe.

### Expensive

**Amari Coral Beach Resort** ✾✾ The Coral Beach stands on the rocks high above Patong, at the southern tip well away from the din of Patong's congested strip, but close for access to the mayhem. The beachfront below is rocky, but the whole resort, from the very grand terraced lobby, guest rooms, and fine pool, is situated toward incredible views of the huge bay below. The rooms have seafoam tones, cozy balconies, and all the comforts of home. There is live music nightly and the hotel's Italian restaurant, La Gritta (see "Where to Dine," later in this section), is tops.

2 Meun-ngern Rd., Phuket 83150 (south and uphill of Patong Beach). ℭ **07634-0106.** Fax 07634-0115. www.amari.com. 200 units. 6,800B–7,950B ($170–$199) double; from 10,300B ($258) suite. AE, DC, MC, V. **Amenities:** 3 restaurants; lounge; 2 outdoor pools; outdoor lighted tennis court; fitness center; brand-new spa; dive center; game room; tour desk; car-rental desk; limo service; salon; 24-hr. room service; massage; babysitting; same-day laundry service/dry cleaning. *In room:* A/C, satellite TV, minibar, safe.

**Holiday Inn Resort Phuket** ✸✸ (*Kids*)    The older buildings at this Holiday Inn are modern, concrete blocks and not particularly luxurious, but the new Busakorn Wing features more stylish rooms in Thai decor with teak appointments, carving, and pottery. If on a honeymoon, go for the newer rooms; if with the kids, the old block will do the trick (and save some money). In fact, what distinguishes the Holiday Inn is its excellent offerings for traveling families. The central pool areas have elaborate fountains and a fun meander suited to kids of all ages, and the hotel has active kids' programs and a children's center, not to mention babysitting for when mom and dad need a night out. There are lots of family activities and excursions to choose from. There are even family suites, with separate "kids rooms" that have jungle or pirate theme decor, TV with video and PlayStation, stocked toy boxes, and some with bunk beds. The hotel also has self-service launderette so you don't have to pay hotel laundry prices for the biomass of play clothes your kids will rip through: quite unique. Also unique is the hotel's minibar scheme, whereby rooms have just a bare fridge and guests visit a small convenience store in the lobby and choose what they would like and have it delivered to their room at a cost of only a small bump-up from retail price.

52 Thaweewong Rd., Patong Beach, Phuket 83150 (Patong Beach strip). ℭ **0800/HOLIDAY** or 07634-0608. Fax 07634-0435. www.phuket.holiday-inn.com. 369 units. 5,200B ($130) standard double; 6,800B ($170) Busakorn studio or family suite. AE, DC, MC, V. **Amenities:** 3 restaurants; lounge; 4 outdoor pools; fitness center; spa w/massage, sauna, and steam; tiptop children's center and programs; tour desk; car-rental desk; limo service; business center; 24-hr. room service; massage; babysitting; same-day laundry service/dry cleaning; self-service launderette. *In room:* A/C, satellite TV, minibar, fridge, coffee/tea-making facilities, hair dryer, safe, IDD phone.

**Impiana Phuket Cabana Resort** ✸✸    This is the only accommodation in Patong with direct beachfront access and that alone sets it apart, but there's a nice feel to the place, too, a clean but rustic chic. Deluxe cabanas are quiet and have exposed wood beams, dark lacquered bamboo and rattan wall coverings, and stone floors. There's a small but very stylish pool and busy Patong Beach is accessed by a verdant garden—no need to cross the street as in all other resorts. Amenities are limited but the restaurant is one of the best in Patong and public areas are scenic and stylish. Rooms are a real value for the price. A good choice.

41 Thaweewongse Rd., Patong Beach, Phuket 83150 (middle of Beach Rd.). ℭ **07634-0138.** Fax 07634-0178. www.impiana.com. 80 units. 5,400B–6,600B ($135–$165) double; 7,000B ($175) family room; from 10,800B ($270) suite. AE, DC, MC, V. **Amenities:** 3 restaurants; pool; watersports equipment; concierge; tour desk; car-rental desk; limo service; limited room service; babysitting; same-day laundry service/dry cleaning; Internet center. *In room:* A/C, satellite TV, minibar, fridge, hair dryer, safe, IDD phone.

**Novotel Carolia Phuket** ✸    Just next to the Diamond Cliff Resort (above) and a similar standard on the north end of Patong, the Novotel is a lovely hilltop hideaway. It is typical of Accor hotels anywhere: good services and comfortable rooms done in a local style. What sets this apart is the three-tiered pool at the center of the property and its dynamic view of the beach and sea from this towering point. The lobby is under an enormous steep Thai roof, and from its luxury massage pavilions to the many fine dining choices, you are constantly reminded of Thai culture and wrapped in comfort.

Kalim Beach Rd., Patong Beach 83150 (on the hill north of town, just as the road heads uphill). ✆ 07634-2777. Fax 07634-2168. www.novotelphuket.com. 215 units. 6,500B–8,500B ($163–$213); from 11,000B ($275) suite. AE, MC, V. **Amenities:** 3 restaurants; 3 bars; pool w/multiple tiers; 2 tennis courts; fitness center; sauna; kids' club; tour desk; car-rental desk; business center w/Internet; shopping; 24-hr. room service; massage; babysitting; laundry service; dry cleaning. *In room:* A/C, satellite TV, minibar, fridge, safe, IDD phone.

## Moderate

Budget accommodations are best along Kata and Karon beaches in the southern end of the island. In Patong, budget hotels are generally run-down, even seedy, owing to the hostess bar and go-go scene, but among the better choices is **Blue Ocean Resort** (210/23 Soi Kepsap; ✆ 07634-5191), with rooms from 960B ($24).

## THE NORTHWEST COAST: PANSEA BEACH (SURIN BEACH)

Also known as Surin Beach, the Pansea area has coconut plantations, steep slopes leading down to the beach, and small, private coves dominated by two of the most secluded and divine hotels on the island.

### Very Expensive

**Amanpuri** 🏵🏵🏵  The discreet and sublime Amanpuri is the Phuket address for international celebrities. It is the most elegant and secluded resort in Thailand and quite possibly all of Southeast Asia. The lobby is an open-air pavilion with a standing Buddha near a lovely swimming pool and stairs leading to the beach. Free-standing pavilion suites dot the dense coconut palm grounds; each is masterfully designed in a traditional Thai style, with teak-and-tile floors, sliding teak doors, exquisite built-ins, and well-chosen accents, including antiques. Private *salas* (covered patios) are perfect for romantic dining or secluded sunbathing.

Pansea Beach, Phuket 83110 (north end of cove). ✆ 07632-4333. Fax 07632-4100. 53 units. 21,500B–26,250B ($538–$663) gardenview pavilion; 33,000B–55,440B ($825–$1,386) seaview pavilion. AE, DC, MC, V. **Amenities:** 2 restaurants; pool; golf course nearby; outdoor lighted tennis courts; squash courts; fitness center; spa; sauna; watersports equipment and instruction; private yacht fleet; concierge; limo service; limited room service; babysitting; same-day laundry service/dry cleaning; library. *In room:* A/C, minibar, fridge, stereo.

**The Chedi Phuket** 🏵🏵  Like its august neighbor Amanpuri (above), The Chedi commands an excellent view of the bay below and has its own private stretch of sand. From the exotic lobby (with columns and lily pond) to sleek and handsome private bungalows, it is one of the most handsome properties on the island. It's quality with a big price tag, but this romantic getaway has it down to the details. Each room is a thatched minisuite with a lovely private sun deck and top amenities. The black-tile swimming pool is large and luxurious. The snappy staff can arrange any watersports, sightseeing tour, or activity. The fine service here caters to the likes of honeymooners and celebrities, and everyone is a VIP. While it may not be as outwardly impressive as its extraordinary neighbor, The Chedi is quiet, comfortably informal, and very relaxing with fine dining options. There's a new, top-notch cooking school as well.

118 Moo 3, Choeng Talay, Pansea Beach, Phuket 83110 (next to the Amanpuri). ✆ 07632-4017. Fax 07632-4252. www.ghmhotels.com. 108 units. 15,580B–27,800B ($390–$695) 1-bedroom cottage; 20,000B–34,850B ($500–$871) 2-bedroom cottage. AE, DC, MC, V. **Amenities:** 3 restaurants; bar; outdoor pool; 2 outdoor lighted tennis courts; spa; watersports equipment; children's center; game room; concierge; tour desk; car-rental desk; limo service; 24-hr. room service; massage; babysitting; same-day laundry service/dry cleaning; volleyball and badminton. *In room:* A/C, satellite TV, minibar, coffee/tea-making facilities, safe.

## BANG THAO BAY (THE LAGUNA RESORT COMPLEX)

Twenty minutes south of the airport and just as far north of Patong beach on the western shore of Phuket, this isolated area is Phuket's "integrated resort" of five high-end properties that share the island's most top-rated facilities. Among them you'll find world-class health spas, countless restaurants, and the island's best golf course. The grounds are impressively landscaped, and the hotel properties are scattered among the winding lagoons, all navigable by boat. The best thing about staying here is that you can dine at any of the fine hotel restaurants, connecting by boat or free shuttle, and be charged on one simple bill at whatever resort you choose.

## Very Expensive

**Banyan Tree Phuket** ★★★    Banyan Tree is a famous hideaway for honeymooners and high society (paparazzi-free for your protection). There is nothing like it for people of means who need an escape. Private villas with walled courtyards (many with private pool or Jacuzzi) are spacious and grand, lushly styled in teakwood with outdoor bathtubs. Style throughout is low Thai pavilions and there are good Thai touches like platform beds and large Thai murals depicting the Ramakien, an ancient Thai saga. The resort can arrange private barbecues at your villa, and private massage in the room or in outdoor pavilions. The reception area is a large open *sala* with lovely lotus pools. A small village in itself, the spa provides a wide range of beauty and health treatments in luxurious rooms. The Tamarind Restaurant serves delicious, light, and authentic spa cuisine. The main pool is truly impressive—a free-form lagoon, landscaped with greenery and rock formations—with a flowing water canal. There's a top-notch golf course onsite and private tour office. The Banyan Tree garners many international awards.

33 Moo 4, Srisoonthorn Rd., Cherngtalay District, Amphur Talang, Phuket 83110 (north end of beach). ✆ 0800/525-4800 or 07632-4374. Fax 07632-4375. 121 units. 23,800B ($595) Jacuzzi villa; 36,000B ($900) pool villa; 49,000B ($1,225) spa pool villa; from 57,400B ($1,435) for 2-bedroom suites. AE, DC, MC, V. **Amenities:** 6 restaurants; lounge; outdoor lagoon-style pool; golf course; 3 outdoor lighted tennis courts; fitness center; award-winning spa w/spa pool, sauna, steam, and massage; watersports equipment; tour desk; car-rental desk; limo service; 24-hr. room service; babysitting; same-day laundry service/dry cleaning. *In room:* A/C, satellite TV w/pay movies, minibar, fridge, coffeemaker, safe, IDD phone.

**Dusit Laguna Resort** ★ (Kids    The Dusit hotel group has some fine properties in Thailand, and the Dusit Laguna is no exception. The rooms are midsize and done with pastel tiles, faux columns, and bathrooms that open to the living area by wide, wooden doors. Spring for a deluxe room with a balcony and ocean view for not much more than standard. Suites are large and luxurious. There are lots of Thai touches throughout, some tacky, others, like some of the large, traditional hangings, are quite pleasing. The hotel features some fine dining options; particularly of note is the quaint Italian restaurant, La Trattoria, serving authentic Italian in a chic but laid-back garden-side pavilion decorated in cool whites and blues. The well-landscaped gardens at seaside have an especially delightful waterfall and an excellent pool, and the grounds open onto a long, wide, white-sand beach flanked by two lagoons. Facilities for kids are great: a Kids Corner, babysitting, a playground, and computer games.

390 Srisoontorn Rd., Cherngtalay District, Phuket 83110 (south end of beach). ✆ 07632-4320. Fax 07632-4174. www.dusit.com. 226 units. 12,300B–13,900B ($308–$348) double; from 19,000B ($475) suite. AE, DC, MC, V. **Amenities:** 4 restaurants; lounge; free-form outdoor pool; golf course nearby and pitch and putt on premises; outdoor lighted tennis courts; fitness center; spa w/Jacuzzi, sauna, steam, and massage; watersports equipment; bike rental; tour desk; car-rental desk; limo service; business center; shopping arcade; salon; 24-hr. room service; babysitting; same-day laundry service/dry cleaning; nonsmoking rooms. *In room:* A/C, satellite TV, minibar, fridge, coffee/tea-making facilities, safe, IDD phone.

**Sheraton Grande Laguna Phuket** ★★    The granddaddy of the lagoon in terms of size, the Sheraton is a sprawling, luxury campus of two- and three-story hotel-style pavilions. Rooms are quite large and luxurious with tile floors, cozy sitting areas, large balconies, and some bathrooms with sunken tubs. On a large island, the hotel design carefully traces the natural lines, the coves and jetties, of the surrounding lagoon and the area is quiet and very private. The pool is a long, winding meander and there are good amenities for kids of all ages, from a kids' club (called VIK or Very Important Kids) to beach games and sailboat rental at the private, sandy put-in at the lagoon. With both fine dining and more casual eateries and cafes (including a good bakery) and a very professional staff, the Sheraton is a fine, reliable, familiar choice.

10 Moo 4, Bang Tao Bay, Phuket 83110. ℂ **07632-4101.** Fax 07632-4108. www.starwood.com. 335 units. 11,500B–21,300B ($288–$533) double; from 23,400B ($585) suite. AE, DC, MC, V. **Amenities:** 6 restaurants; bar and lounge; free-form outdoor pool; golf course nearby; 2 outdoor lighted tennis courts; fitness center; spa; watersports equipment; bike rental; kids' club; tour desk; car-rental desk; limo service; business center w/Internet; shopping; 24-hr. room service; babysitting; same-day laundry service/dry cleaning; nonsmoking rooms. *In room:* A/C, satellite TV, minibar, fridge, coffeemaker, hair dryer, safe, IDD phone.

## NAI YANG BEACH

Nai Yang National Park is a long stretch of shoreline peeking out from underneath a dense forest of palms, casuarina, and other indigenous flora. It's good if you want to leave the crowds behind, but be warned that it is isolated and, short of the one hotel here, it's quite rustic. It's become an area known for the yearly release of baby turtles into the wild. For accommodations, your only choice is **Pearl Village** (ℂ **07632-7006;** www.pearlvillage.co.th), one of the first on the island (and a little worse for wear) with rooms starting at 4,500B ($113).

## MAI KHAO BEACH

Mai Khao is a marvelous beach on the northeastern shore near the airport. It's where sea turtles lay their eggs during December and January and efforts are ongoing to protect the breeding grounds—turtle eggs are a local delicacy.

### Very Expensive
### JW Marriott Phuket Resort and Spa ⭑⭑⭑   The clean-lined luxury of the

JW Marriott could make a haiku poet out of anyone. Along the windswept stretch of sand and roaring surf along desolate Mai Khao Beach, this resort is a masterpiece of luxury and service. Arrivals at night will awe to the opulence of oversize torches lining the circular drive, and the wide, low pavilions of the lobby surround an enormous, black reflecting pool that sparkles with torchlight. There are no services outside of the hotel and it is a 30-minute drive to the nearest tourist area—there are regular shuttles—but the resort facilities are complete and guests needn't leave. Rooms are private getaways with open-plan bathrooms, a small meditation and reading corner with Thai cushions and lovely balconies that give way to sumptuous gardens: a hidden Eden. The service standard is high. Very professional. Come and leave it all behind, enjoy fine spa treatments, sports, activities, and fine dining. And you can write that haiku in your private meditation corner. The hotel can arrange transport anywhere on the island and there are a host of fine excursions to choose from at the helpful tour desk.

231 Moo 3, Mai Khao, Talang, Phuket 83110. ℂ **07633-8000.** Fax 07634-8360. www.marriott.com. 21,500B–24,000B ($538–$600) deluxe double; from 55,300B ($1,383) suite. AE, DC, MC, V. 265 units. **Amenities:** 5 restaurants; 3 bars; 2 outdoor pools; 2 tennis courts; top-notch fitness center w/lots of activities; extensive spa; Jacuzzi; sauna; watersports equipment (Hobie Cat and runabouts); bicycles (free to guests); children's center and kids' club; teen activity center w/computers; concierge; tour desk; car-rental desk; limo service; business center; shopping arcade; salon; 24-hr. room service; massage; babysitting; same-day laundry/dry cleaning; nonsmoking rooms; executive-level rooms w/private check-in. *In room:* A/C, satellite TV w/in-house movies, dataport (modem connection), minibar, fridge, coffeemaker, hair dryer, safe, IDD phone.

## WHERE TO DINE

From tip to tip, north to south, it's over an hour drive on Phuket, but hired tuk-tuks, hotel transport, or even self-drive vehicles mean that for dining and nightlife, you can choose from any on the island. The beach areas in the west are chockablock with small, storefront eateries and Patong features everything from the obligatory McDonald's and Starbucks to designer sushi chains.

### PHUKET TOWN

A long ride from the west-coast beach areas, a night out in Phuket Town is worth it for some fine meals and a taste of local culture.

**Ka Jok See** ★★ *Finds* THAI   This is one of those special finds in Thailand. A classy, exclusive restaurant peopled by hotel bigwigs and local businessmen hides behind an unassuming storefront hanging with ivy—there is no sign (look for the small Indian restaurant next door). Wood-beamed ceilings, antiques lit by candlelight and classic jazz set the stage. Ka Jok See is smart and chic, cozy, and intimate. The cooks prepare fabulous dishes like the house specialty, *goong-saroong*—vermicelli-wrapped shrimp fried quick and light and served with a velvety mustard dipping sauce. There are great daily specials and entrees like smoky grilled eggplant and shrimp salad or stir-fried beef curry. This place is well worth a venture from the beach for an evening.

26 Takuapa Rd., Phuket Town (a short walk from central Rasada Rd.). ✆ 07621-7903. Reservations recommended for weekends. Main courses 150B–380B ($3.75–$9.50). No credit cards. Tues–Sun 6pm–midnight (kitchen closes around 11pm).

**Salvatore** ★ ITALIAN   *"Va bene!"* It's the real thing here: pasta, grilled dishes, huge salads, and great pizza in a large air-conditioned dining room at the town center. The wine list is great and Salvatore himself comes to your table and will make you something special. There are lots of Italian restaurants in all of the resort areas of Thailand, but this one is the best with an unpretentious atmosphere and good food that brings many regular customers. Fine pasta, lasagna, steaks, cacciatore dishes, and a range of daily specials are all made with fresh ingredients and all the extras—like the important spices, garnish, even prosciutto and, of course, the wine—are imported. Don't miss the dessert of Limoncello Truffle, a liqueur meringue that will melt your palate and goes great with the strong coffee.

15 Rasada Rd., Tambol Taladyai, Phuket (central Phuket Town). ✆/fax 07622-5958. Main courses 140B–650B ($3.50–$16). AE, MC, V. Open daily 11:30am–3pm and 6–11pm.

### KATA & KARON

The busy road between Kata and Karon (as well as the many side streets) are chockablock with small cafes and restaurants serving affordable Thai and Western food. Stop by **Euro Deli** (58/60 Karon Rd.; ✆ 07628-6265) for a good sandwich (open 8am–1am).

#### Expensive

**The Boathouse and Mom Tri's Kitchen** ★★★ THAI/INTERNATIONAL   So legendary is the Thai and Western cuisine at the Boathouse, that the inn where it resides offers popular holiday packages for visitors who wish to come and take lessons from its chef. A large bar and separate dining area sport nautical touches and through huge picture windows diners can watch the sun set over the watery horizon. Cuisine combines the best of East and West and chefs use only the finest ingredients. If you're in the mood for the works, the Phuket lobster is one of the most expensive dishes on the menu, but is worth every baht.

The Boathouse also has an excellent selection of international wines—420 labels. And if that doesn't tickle your taste buds, **Mom Tri's Kitchen,** the latest upscale venture from the folks at the Boathouse, is just up the hill and serves similar fine cuisine from its luxury perch. Bon appétit.

The Boathouse Inn, 114 Patak Rd. © 07633-0557. Reservations recommended during peak season. Main courses 280B–850B ($7–$21); seafood sold at market price. AE, DC, MC, V. Daily 7am–10:30pm.

### Moderate
**On the Rock**    Part of the Marina Phuket (see "Where to Stay," earlier in this section), this little unassuming restaurant serves tiptop Thai meals from a scenic deck high above the south end of Karon Beach. Just finishing construction at the time of this writing, the new restaurant promises even finer, but still laid-back and rustic, atmosphere with some of the best views of Karon Beach below. Try the seafood basket, a medley of grilled and fried ocean critters. There are steaks and French entrees like chicken *cordon bleu,* but stick with the better Thai dishes for a great meal in a great atmosphere.

47 Karon Rd., Karon Beach, Phuket 83100 (on bluff at south end of Karon Beach Rd.). © 07633-0625. Fax 07633-0516. www.marinaphuket.com. Main courses 120B–580B ($3–$15). AE, MC, V. Daily 8am–11pm.

## PATONG
Some of the best seafood dining in busy Patong doesn't come from any upscale restaurant, but at the small **Seafood Night Market** in the north end of Patong along busy, central Rat-U-Thit Road. It's really just a collection of outdoor restaurants sharing a large open-air dining area. Visitors who approach or show any interest will be attacked with menus and implored to choose from among the restaurants. Can be a bit off-putting, but just pick a menu or a kind face (the others will disperse) and order from a wide selection of fresh seafood as you like it (all the seafood is displayed on iced countertops, so have a look). It's good food at a fraction of restaurant price.

**Baan Rim Pa** 🌟 THAI    In a beautiful Thai-style teak house, Baan Rim Pa has dining in a romantic indoor setting or with gorgeous views of the bay from outdoor terraces. Among high-end travelers, the restaurant is long one of the most popular stops on the island, so be sure to reserve your table early. Thai cuisine features seafood, with a variety of other meat and vegetable dishes, including a rich duck curry and a sweet honey chicken dish. The seafood basket is a fantastic assortment of prawns, mussels, squid, and crab. The owner of Baan Rim Pa has opened up a few other restaurants on the cliffside next to Baan Rim Pa; most notable is the Japanese restaurant Otowa (© **07634-4235**).

223 Kalim Beach Rd. (on the cliffs just north of Patong Beach). © 07634-0789. Reservations necessary. Main courses 250B–1,200B ($6.25–$30). AE, DC, MC, V. Daily noon–2:30pm and 6–10pm.

**La Gritta** 🌟 ITALIAN    Similar to the Amari chain's other fine Italian restaurants of the same name, this one is notable for it's views of Patong beach below, the best in town, really. It's classic northern Italian cuisine, antipastas, salads, soups, and grilled entrees and pastas accompanied by an extensive wine list. The cooks use all fresh ingredients and serve a colorful antipasto plate that makes a great shared appetizer while watching the fireworks of a Phuket sunset.

At the Amari Hotel; 2 Meun-ngern Rd., Phuket 83150 (south and uphill of Patong Beach). © 07634-0106. Main courses 170B–520B ($4.25–$13). AE, MC, V. Daily 11am–10pm.

**Patong Seafood Restaurant** SEAFOOD    Take an evening stroll along the lively Patong Beach strip and you'll find quite a few open-air seafood restaurants displaying their catch of the day on chipped ice buffet tables out front. The best choice of them all is the casual Patong Seafood, for the freshest and the best selection of seafood, including several types of local fish, lobster, squid (very tender), prawn, and crab. The menu has a fantastic assortment of preparation styles—with photos of popular Thai noodles and Chinese stir-fry dishes. Service is good and it's popular enough that it doesn't employ a carnival barker like most along the strip; it just attracts with the food rather than promote with ploys.

Patong Beach Rd., Patong Beach. ℂ 07634-0247. Reservations not accepted. Main courses 80B–250B ($2–$6.25); seafood at market price. AE, DC, MC, V. Daily 7am–11pm.

**Sala Bua** ✪ THAI   One of the only restaurants in Patong that enjoys a beach-side location, fine dining at Sala Bua is romantic and stylish with the roll and hush of surf for a soundtrack. The lunch menu features light Thai dishes, and Western sandwiches and burgers. More pricey evening fare includes southern-Thai-style seafood favorites—local Phuket lobster, huge juicy tiger prawns, and fresh fish steaks in a variety of local preparation styles—expensive but a good value. The imported New Zealand tenderloin is award winning. For dessert, try the unique sticky rice sushi rolls with sweet coconut milk and mango. Sala Bua is a far more intimate option from the crowded seafood joints across the street. Under the pavilion, candlelight and local decor make for a romantic atmosphere, but to see the beach you must sit on the patio.

In the Phuket Cabana Hotel, 94 Thaweewong Rd., Patong Beach (at the north end of the beach at Phuket Cabana Hotel). ℂ 07634-2100. Reservations recommended for weekends. Main courses 180B–1,360B ($4.50–$34). AE, DC, MC, V. Daily 6:30pm–midnight.

## BANG THAO BAY (THE LAGUNA RESORT COMPLEX)

The many hotel restaurants of the five-star properties in the Laguna Complex could fill a small guidebook of its own. You can't go too wrong in any of the hotels, really, and here, more than anywhere, it's a question of getting what you pay for; from superluxurious fine dining to laid-back hotel grills or snack corners, they cover it all. One restaurant just outside the complex is worth mentioning (it's where all the hotel managers eat when they get out of work).

**Tatanka** ✪✪ INTERNATIONAL   Billed as "Globe-trotter Cuisine," dining at Tatanka is indeed a foray into the realm of a culinary nomad. Harold Schwarz, the young owner and well-traveled chef, puts to use his many years in hotel restaurants around the world (his resume is written on the bathroom wall, each tile features another of Harold's many stops). "Fusion" is a battered and broken term in restaurant parlay, but dishes here are a creative melding of Mediterranean, Pan-American, and Oriental influence. The emphasis is on variety, and selections from the tapas menu include vegetable quesadillas, California crab cakes, stuffed calamari cups, wanton wafers, and rolls. The menu is updated frequently and depends on what is fresh that day, but features anything from Peking duck to pizza, gazpacho to Thai *tom yam* (hot and sour soup with shrimp). Ask what's good and enjoy.

382/19 Moo 1, Srisoontorn Rd., Cherngtalay, Phuket 83110 (at the entrance of the Laguna Resort in Bangtao Bay). ℂ/fax 07632-4349. Main courses 150B–420B ($3.75–$11). MC, V. Daily 6pm–last order.

## CHALONG BAY

One good bet for fresh seafood is in the far south of the island in Chalong Bay at **Kan Eang Seafood** (9/3 Chaofa Rd., Chalong Bay; ℂ 07638-1323). Whole fish and specials like Phuket lobster just jump out of the nets and onto your plate. If you've rented wheels, a ride down this way makes for a fun day.

# EXPLORING PHUKET

Lots to do in Phuket. Beachfront areas are full of tour operators, each vying for your business and offering similar trips (or copycat tours).

## BEACHFRONT WATERSPORTS

Most of the noisier watersports activities are concentrated along Patong Beach—so swimmers can enjoy other beaches without the buzz of a jet ski or power boat. **Jet skis** are technically illegal, but can still be rented for 30 minutes at 700B/$18. A 10-minute **parasailing ride** is 600B ($15) and you can rent outboard runabouts by the hour or the day. **Hobie Cats** go for 600B ($15) per hour; **windsurf boards** for 200B ($5) per hour. There are no specific offices to organize these activities, just small operators with hand-painted signs at the beaches.

## DAY-CRUISING

For a different view of the gorgeous Phang-Nga Bay, book a trip aboard the *June Bahtra,* a restored Chinese sailing junk, to cruise the islands. Full-day trips include lunch and hotel transfers. Adults are 2,200B ($55) per person (alcoholic beverages not included), children up to 12 are 1,500B ($38) each. Contact **East West Siam,** 119 Rat-U-Thit 2000 Year Rd., Patong (© **07634-0912**).

## GOLF

There are some fine courses on Phuket and golf junkets bring vacationing expats and international tourists alike.

- The best course is the **Banyan Tree Club & Laguna,** 34 Moo 4, Srisoonthorn Road, at the Laguna Resort Complex on Bang Tao Bay (© **07627-0991;** fax 07632-4351), a par-71 championship course with many water features (greens fees: 2,900B/$73; guests of Laguna resorts receive a discount).
- The **Blue Canyon Country Club,** 165 Moo 1, Thepkasattri Road, near the airport (© **07632-7440;** fax 07632-7449; www.bluecanyonclub.com), is a par-72 championship course with natural hazards, trees, and guarded greens (greens fees: from 2,900B/$73).
- An older course, the **Phuket Country Club,** 80/1 Vichitsongkram Rd., west of Phuket Town (© **07632-1038;** fax 07632-1721; www.phuketcountry club.com), has beautiful greens and fairways, plus a giant lake (greens fees: 2,400B/ $60).

## HORSEBACK RIDING

A romantic and charming way to see Phuket's jungles and beaches is on horseback. **Phuket Riding Club,** 95 Viset Rd., Chaweng Bay (© **07628-8213**), and **Phuket Laguna Riding Club,** 394 Moo 1, Bangthao Beach (© **07632-4199**), welcome riders of all ages and experience levels and can provide instruction for beginners and children. Prices start at 500B ($13) per hour.

## SCUBA DIVING

With access to the nearby **Similan Islands,** Phuket is a popular scuba destination, one of the most affordable (and safe) places to get certified. There are three decompression chambers on the island and a strong dive community. The problem is, there are something like 40 companies and all can arrange day trips to the nearby coral wall and wrecks as well as overnight or long-term excursions to the Similan Islands (also PADI courses, Dive Master courses, or 1-day introductory lessons and open-water certification). Open-water courses can cost as little as 10,000B ($250).

Many storefront operations are just consolidators for other companies, so ask if they have their own boats and that they are PADI certified. Also check about the ratio of divers to instructor or Divemaster; anything more than five to one is not acceptable, and more like two to one for beginner courses. Below are a few choices:

- The folks at **Scuba Cat** (94 Thaweewong Rd., Patong; © **07629-3120;** www.scubacat.com) have got the best thing going in Phuket. With some 10 years experience, a large expatriate staff, and its own fleet of boats, it's a very professional outfit offering the full range of trips for anyone from beginner and expert (and at competitive prices). You can't miss the small practice pool in front of its beachside Patong office (in fact, you have to cross a small bridge to get in the place), and the staff is very helpful and welcoming.
- **Fantasea Divers** is another reputable firm on Phuket. The main office is at Patong Beach at 219 Rat-U-Thit Rd. (© **07634-0088;** fax 07634-0309; www.fantasea.net). Dive packages include live-aboard trips to the Burmese coast and 4-day PADI certification courses, in addition to full-day dives around Phuket.
- **Sea Bees Diving** (1/3 Moo 9, Viset Rd., Chalong Bay; ©/fax **07638-1765;** www.sea-bees.com) is another good outfit offering day trips.
- **Dive Master's EcoDive 2000** has mostly live-aboard trips and with a focus on education and marine biology. Contact 75/20 Moo 10, Patak Road, Chalong (© **07628-0330**).
- **Dive Asia** (P.O. Box 70, Kata Beach, Phuket 83100; © **07633-0598**) offers similar services, dive training, day trips, and live-aboard trips.

## SEA KAYAKING

**Phang-Nga Bay National Park,** a 1½-hour drive north of Phuket (3 hr. by boat) hosts great day trips by sea kayak. The scenery is stunning, with limestone karst towers jutting precariously from the water's surface, creating more than 120 small islands. These craggy rock formations (the backdrop for the James Bond classic, *The Man with the Golden Gun*) look straight out of a Chinese scroll painting. Sea kayaks are perfect for inching your way into the many breathtaking caves and chambers that hide beneath the jagged cliffs. All tours include the hour-plus rides to and from Pha Nga, the cruise to the island area, paddle guide, kayak, and lunch. The company to pioneer the cave trips is **Sea Canoe** (main office in Phuket Town, P.O. Box 276, Muang Phuket 83000; © **07621-2252;** www.seacanoe.net). It's much imitated, but still the best choice for day trips through island caves to central lagoons (called *hongs*). The standard day trip runs 2,970B ($74) per person. It's touristy and you'll be sitting two to an inflated boat and be paddled by a guide going in and out of the caves (frustrating if you like to actually paddle), but the scenery is great and the caves are stunning (and there's free time for paddling on your own later). It also offers multiday and more adventurous "self-guided" tours.

The folks at **Paddle-Asia** (53/80 Moo 5, Thambon Srisoonthon, Thalang, Phuket, 83110; © **07631-1222;** fax 07631-3689; www.paddleasia.com) make Phuket their home and do trips throughout the region, with a focus more on custom adventure travel, not day junkets. It has great options for anyone from beginner to expert and on any trip you'll paddle real decked kayaks, not inflatables. A highlight is Paddle-Asia's trip to Khao Sok National Park (p. 160), a 3-day adventure in which you're sure to see some amazing jungle wildlife. In Phuket it can arrange offshore paddling to outlying islands or custom adventures.

## TREKKING

To experience the wild side of Phuket's interior, try a **rainforest trekking journey** through the Khao Phra Thaew National Park. **Phuket Nature Tour** takes small groups through 3.5km (2.25 miles) of jungle paths past waterfalls and swimming holes. A typical half-day excursion includes hotel transfers, English-speaking jungle guides, and drinks. Call 𝄞 **07625-5522.**

Then there's **elephant trekking,** a perennial favorite for children, and a great time for adults too. Elephants are not indigenous to Phuket so what you get here is more or less a pony ride, but arguments over captive elephant tour programs aside, the kids dig it (and the elephants do better here than when paraded around city streets for owners to collect coins). **Siam Safari Nature Tours** coordinates daily treks on elephants, Land Rovers, and river rafts. The three-in-one Half-Day Eco-Adventure includes 4 hours of elephant treks through jungles to rubber estates, jeep tours to see local wildlife, and a light river-rafting journey to Chalong Bay. A full-day tour is the three-in-one plus a trek on foot through Khao Pra Thaew National Park and a Thai lunch. Siam Safari's office is at 70/1 Chaofa Rd. in Chalong (𝄞 **07628-0116;** www.phuket.com/safari). **Siam Adventures** (60/4 Rat-U-Thit Rd. Patong Beach; 𝄞 **07634-1799**) arranges similar adventures and is a leader in Phuket.

## YACHTING

The crystal-blue waters of the Andaman Sea near Phuket are an old salt's dream. Every December Phuket hosts the increasingly popular **King's Cup Regatta,** in which almost 100 international racing yachts compete. For more information, check out www.kingscup.com.

There are more and more options for chartering yachts in Phuket. Contact **Thai Marine Leisure** for details (c/o Phuket Boat Lagoon, 20/2 Thepkasatri Rd., Tambon Koh Kaew, Phuket 83200; 𝄞 **07623-9111;** www.thaimarine.com) or **Sunsail Asia Pacific** (Phuket Boat Lagoon, 20/5 Moo 2, Thepkrasattri Rd., Phuket 83200; 𝄞 **07623-9057;** www.sunsail.com).

## OTHER ACTIVITIES

The **Jungle Bungy Jump** awaits. If you have the nerve to jump out 50m (164ft.) over the water, call the "bungee hot line" at 𝄞 **07632-1351.** It's in Kathu near Patong. The charge is 1,400B ($35) per jump.

## NATURAL TREASURES

**Haad Nai Yang National Park,** 90 sq. km (35 sq. miles) of protected land in the northwest corner of the island, offers a peaceful retreat from the rest of the island's tourism madness. There are two fantastic reasons to make the journey out to the park. The first is for Phuket's largest coral reef in shallow water, only 1,400m (460ft.) from the shore. The second is for the giant leatherback turtles that come to nest every year between November and February. Park headquarters is a very short hop from Phuket Airport off Highway 402.

**The Gibbon Rehabilitation Project** 🐾🐾, off Highway 4027 at the Bang Pae waterfall in the northeastern corner of the island (𝄞 **07626-0492**), cares for mistreated gibbons, placing them in more caring and natural surroundings (among other gibbons). Volunteer guides offer tours. Open daily from 10am to 4pm; admission is free, but donations are accepted and appreciated.

## PHUKET'S SPAS 🐾🐾🐾

If you've come to Phuket to escape and relax, there's no better way to accomplish your goal than to visit one of Phuket's spas. Even the smallest resort now offers full spa services (of varying quality) and you can find good, affordable massage along any beach and in storefronts in the main tourist areas.

For luxury treatments, the most famous and exclusive facility here is the **Spa at the Banyan Tree Phuket** (p. 195). In secluded garden pavilions you'll be treated regally and may choose from many types of massage, body and facial treatments, or health and beauty programs. To make reservations call ℭ 07632-4374 (www.lagunaphuket.com/spa). Expect to pay for the luxury—figure at least 2,000B ($50) per individual treatment.

Another high-end resort in the furthest southeast part of the island, **Evason,** makes for a great day-spa experience. It is a full-featured five-star with all the trimmings and the spa is renowned (similar to Banyan Tree's prices). It's at 100 Vised Rd., Rawai Beach, Phuket 83130 (ℭ **07638-1010;** fax 07638-1018; www.sixsenses.com).

**Let's Relax** is a more affordable little day spa in and among many similar services (some a bit dodgy really but this one is okay) just off of Patong (Rat-U-Thit Rd.; ℭ **07634-0913**). One-hour Thai massage begins at 350B ($8.75).

## SHOPPING

Patong Beach is the center of handicraft and souvenir shopping in Phuket and the main streets and small *sois* are chockablock with storefront tailors, leather shops, jewelers, and ready-to-wear clothing boutiques. Vendors line the sidewalks selling everything from batik clothing, T-shirts, pirated CDs, local arts and handicrafts, northern hill-tribe handicrafts, silver, and souvenir trinkets. Vendors everywhere in Patong have the rotten habit of hassling every passerby. Prices are a bit inflated, but a bit of haggling gets you the same cool goods you can only find in the far north or Bangkok.

## PHUKET AFTER DARK

From the huge billboards and glossy brochures, **Phuket FantaSea** , the island's premiere theme attraction, seems like it could be touristy and ridiculous. Surprise—it is! But it's fun in the same way Atlantic City can be fun. Phuket FantaSea is a big theme park with a festival village lined with glitzy shops, games, entertainment, and snacks. A wander here will keep you busy until the show starts. There's a huge buffet in the palatial Golden Kinaree Restaurant and then visitors proceed to the Palace of the Elephants for the show. Frankly, the shopping is expensive and the dinner is not too good (you can buy a ticket for the show only, no dinner), but the big spectacle is incredibly entertaining and very professional. There are rumors that the elephants are drugged so they can endure the fireworks, and that the show is just stage one of what will be a huge casino. The in-your-face advertising for the place alone is enough to put you off (trucks driving around town with loudspeakers and posters plastered on anything flat), but it's worth a trip. Many places include transport in the price of the ticket. The show is at Kamala Beach, north of Patong, on the coastal road. Call ℭ **07627-1222** for reservations. The stage is dark on Thursdays. The park opens at

### *Moments* The Best Sunset

From the cliffs atop Promthep Cape on the southern tip of the island, the view of the sky as it changes colors from deep reds to almost neon yellows can't compete with the best fireworks. The place isn't exactly a secret so get there early (around 6pm or so) on weekends.

5:30pm; the buffet begins at 6:30pm and the show at 9pm. Tickets for the show are 1,000B ($25) for adults and 750B ($19) for children, while dinner and transfer fees usually add 500B ($13) for adults and 300B ($7.50) for children. Ask about the rates at any hotel concierge, they often have deals.

Phuket also has a resident cabaret troupe at **Simon Cabaret,** 100/6–8 Moo 4, Patong Karon Road (© **07634-2011**). There are shows at 7:30 and 9pm nightly for 600B ($15); it's on the south end of Patong. It's a featured spot on every planned tour agenda that draws busloads. This glitzy transsexual show caters mostly to Asian tourists and lip-sync numbers of popular Asian pop songs keep the audience roaring. It can be a lot of fun. In between the comedy are dance numbers with pretty impressive sets and costumes.

Every night you can catch Thai boxing at **Vegas Thai Boxing** in Patong at the Patong Simon Shopping Arcade on Soi Bangla. Bouts start every night from 7pm and last until 3am. Fight-night info is all over town and admission is free.

**Patong nightlife** is wild. Lit up like a little Las Vegas, the beach town hops and it's Saturday every night of the week. Shops and restaurants stay open late, and there is an array of bars, nightclubs, karaoke lounges, snooker halls, massage parlors, go-go bars, and dance shows a la Bangkok's Patpong or the streets of Pattaya. Bangla Road, perpendicular to the beach road on the north end of Patong, is the little red-light district in town and the hostess girls line up and reel in passersby (it goes something like: "Hey, handsome man, where you go?"). It's pretty seedy and you might want to keep the little ones away to avoid any lengthy explanations later, but it's a funny scene. A few bars about halfway down the road are always packed for views of the informal tabletop dancing. The curvaceous, costumed dancers are mostly transsexuals (*Important:* no photos!).

**Scruffy Murphy's** (© **07629-2590**), along the main strip in Patong, is the obligatory beachside Irish pub with only a few scruffy ones wandering about, mostly young UK tourists revving up to make a night of it and a good place to get started of an evening. There are a few discos in town; just ask around to find out what's going on.

## 17 Krabi (Ao Nang, Raillay & Khlong Mouang Beaches)

814km (505 miles) S of Bangkok; 165km (102 miles) E of Phuket; 42km (26 miles) E of Koh Phi Phi; 276km (171 miles) N of Satun; 211km (131 miles) SW of Surat Thani

Krabi is a popular alternative to busy Phuket. Ferries and minivans connect the town of Krabi (few stay) to the nearby beach and tourist strip at Ao Nang and to the farther-flung beaches: Haad Raillay, the famed "climbers beach" with its stunning karst towers, is accessed by boat and Khlong Mouang Beach, only recently developed, is north of Ao Nang.

## ESSENTIALS
### GETTING THERE

There are boat and bus connections between Krabi and Phuket or connecting via Surat Thani with the east-coast islands of Samui and Pha Ngan.

**By Plane    Thai Airways** flies at least twice daily from Bangkok (© **02535-2084**). **Air Andaman** has a daily flight via Phuket (© **02251-4905** for Bangkok reservations). From the airport you can catch a minivan to town for 60B ($1.50), more for further beaches. Taxis start at 300B ($7.50).

**By Boat**  Thrice-daily trips leave from Koh Phi Phi to Krabi (trip time: 2 hr.; 200B/$5). There are two daily boats from Koh Lanta to Krabi in the high season (trip time: 2½ hr.; 150B/$3.75).

**By Bus**  Two air-conditioned VIP 24-seater buses leave daily from **Bangkok's Southern Bus Terminal** (© 02435-1199; trip time: 12 hr.; 710B/$18) to Krabi Town. Frequently scheduled air-conditioned minibuses leave daily from Surat Thani to Krabi (trip time: 2¾ hr.; 150B/$3.75). Three air-conditioned minibuses leave daily from Phuket town to Krabi (trip time: 3½ hr.; 200B/$5).

## VISITOR INFORMATION

There's a small branch of the TAT on the north end of the esplanade along the river in Krabi Town (© 07561-2740). Free maps and info available at hotels.

## ORIENTATION/FAST FACTS

Most services in Krabi town are on Utarakit Road, paralleling the waterfront (to the right as you board the ferry). Here you'll find the **TAT Office** (© 07562-2163) and a number of **banks** with ATM service. The **post office** and police station (© 07563-7208) are located south on Utarakit Road, to the left as you leave the pier. There are a few banks in Ao Nang, near the Phra Nang Inn.

## GETTING AROUND

**Krabi Town** is the commercial hub in the area, but few stay. There is frequent *songtao* (pickup truck) service between Krabi Town and Ao Nang beach; just flag down a white pickup (trip time: 30 min.; 20B/50¢). **Raillay Beach** is not an island but is cut off by its high cliffs from the mainland and reached only by boat from the pier in Krabi Town (45 min.) or from the beach at Ao Nang (at the small pavilion across from the Prah Nang Inn; just 20 min.). **Khlong Mouang beach** is some 25km (16 miles) from Krabi Town.

## WHAT TO SEE & DO

Most head straight for the beaches to relax and play. Popular activities are day boat trips, snorkeling, and rock climbing at Raillay.

Just north and east of Krabi Town, however, you'll find **Wat Tham Sua (The Tiger Temple),** a stunning hilltop pilgrimage point and meditation center. The beaches and stunning cliffs of **Raillay Beach** are certainly worth a day trip even if you don't stay there (see "Where to Stay," below). Longtail boats wait just offshore at Ao Nang and boat drivers consolidate passengers at a small pavilion just across from the Phra Nang Inn for the 50B ($1.25) ride (20 min). From the docks in Krabi Town it costs 80B ($2) (40 min). Daytime only.

The craggy karst cliffs of Raillay make it one of the best-known **rock climbing** spots in the region (if not the world). It is "sport climbing" done on mapped routes with safety bolts already drilled into the rock and there are a number of companies offering full- and half-day courses. There are many routes suitable for beginners. Start with a lesson at **King Climbers** (© 07563-7125; www.railay.com) or **Cliffs Man** (© 07562-1768; www.cliffsman.com). Half-day courses start at about 800B ($20) and full-day courses are from 1,500B ($38).

**Full-day boat trips and snorkeling** can be arranged from any beachfront tour agent or hotel near Krabi and take you to a few small coral sites as well as any number of secluded coves starting at 800B ($20) for a half-day.

Day **kayak tours** to outlying islands or the mangroves near **Ao Luk** are becoming popular for visitors to Ao Nang. Contact **Sea, Land and Trek Co.** (© 07563-7364) or **Sea Kayak Krabi** (© 07563-0270).

# WHERE TO STAY
## RAILLAY BEACH
### Very Expensive

**Rayavadee** ★★★    Rayavadee is one of the finest resorts in Thailand. Handsome two-story rounded pavilions are large and luxurious, offering every modern convenience and utmost privacy—first-floor sitting areas have a central hanging lounger with cushions, and second-story bedrooms are all silk and teak. Private bathrooms have big Jacuzzi tubs and luxury products. The resort grounds lie at the base of towering cliffs on the island's most choice piece of property, a triangle of land where each point accesses the island's beaches. Dining is great and the staff is very professional and friendly, but all with an over-the-top price tag. The sun sets the same for the bungalow dwellers next door, but everything at Rayavadee is tiptop, and from your airport pickup to private boat transfer to hotel service you are given the regal treatment.

214 Moo 2, Tambol Ao Nang, Amphur Muang, Krabi 81000 (30 min. northwest of Krabi Town by longtail boat or 70 min. from Phuket on the resort's own launch). ✆ 07562-0740. Fax 07562-0630. www.rayavadee.com. 77 units. 35,000B ($875) deluxe pavilion; 41,000B ($1,025) hydro-pool pavilion; 51,000B ($1,275) family pavilion; from 146,000B ($3,650) specialty villas. AE, DC, MC, V. **Amenities:** 2 restaurants; lounge and library; outdoor pool w/children's pool; outdoor lighted tennis courts; air-conditioned squash court; fitness center; spa w/massage; Jacuzzi; sauna; watersports equipment and scuba center; concierge; 24-hr. room service; massage; same-day laundry service. *In room:* A/C, satellite TV, minibar, fridge, safe, IDD phone.

### Moderate/Inexpensive

**Sand Sea Resort** (✆ 07562-2170; www.krabisandsea.com), just next to Rayavadee, is typical of the good midrange bungalows here, with clean air-conditioned rooms from 900B ($23). **Diamond Cave Resort** (north end of Raillay Beach; ✆ 07562-2589) has small private fan bungalows from 500B ($13).

## AO NANG BEACH
### Moderate

**Krabi Resort**    The Krabi Resort is the only property in Ao Nang with direct beach access. It is a compound of 2 hotel blocks and an array of free-standing beachside bungalows. Tidy grounds surround a fine swimming pool but other resort amenities are unused and aging. More private seaview bungalows are the best choice; they are large and clean with parquet floors, high ceilings, rattan furnishings, and lots of little Thai touches. It's just north of the main shopping and restaurant area at Ao Nang, but a lovely beach walk. Ask about overnight trips to rustic bungalows on nearby Poda Island.

53–57 Patthana Rd., Ao Nang Beach, Krabi 81000 (overlooking beach at Ao Nang). ✆ 07563-7051. 75 units. 4,600B–6,100B ($115–$153) bungalow; 4,000B–8,800B ($100–$220) suite. MC, V. **Amenities:** Restaurant; lounge; pool; outdoor lighted tennis courts; fitness center; watersports equipment; bike rental; tour desk; limited room service; massage; same-day laundry service. *In room:* A/C, satellite TV, minibar, fridge, safe, IDD phone.

**Phra-Nang Inn** ★    The eccentric Phra-Nang Inn is a rustic woodland lodge of pine and palms, with *papasans* (those round comfy sink-in chairs) arranged overlooking central gardens. Rooms are an upscale guesthouse standard but furnished in a unique mix of Chinese tiles, concrete furnishings built into the walls, seashell and stucco mosaics, and a twisted wood canopy bed hung with strands of shells. Bathrooms have unique concrete and slate built-in showers. The hotel's two wings are on either side of the busiest intersection in Ao Nang but rooms are oriented away from the road to private courtyards (thus quiet).

119 Ao Nang Beach (P.O. Box 25), Krabi 81000 (overlooking beach at Ao Nang-Raillay boat dock). ✆ 07563-7130. Fax 07563-7134. 88 units. 2,700B–4,000B ($68–$100) double; from 5,000B ($125) suite. DC, MC, V.

**Amenities:** 2 restaurants; 2 bars; small pool; spa w/massage; sauna; tour desk; 24-hr. room service; laundry service; Internet. *In room:* A/C, satellite TV w/in-house movies, minibar, fridge, safe, IDD phone.

## KHLONG MOUANG BEACH
### Very Expensive
**Sheraton Krabi Beach Resort** ⚲⚲    This expansive resort is set in a U-shaped configuration, the buildings connected by boardwalks suspended over tidal mangrove flats. Moderate-size rooms are immaculate and done in fine tile and dark-wood furnishings. The pool is large and luxurious at beachside and the fine health and fitness area has good programs (from kickboxing to meditation). The spa, too, is a real treat. The service is excellent.

155 Moo 2, Baan Khlong Mouang Beach, Nong Talay, Krabi 81000 (15km/9 miles north of Ao Nang, 26km/16miles from Krabi Town). ✆ 07562-8000. Fax 07562-8028. www.sheraton.com. 246 units. 10,600B–11,700B ($265–$293) double; 24,000B ($600) suite. AE, DC, MC, V. **Amenities:** 3 restaurants; 3 bars; outdoor pool; tennis court (shoe and racket rental available); fitness center; spa w/massage; Jacuzzi; sauna; sailboat and kayak rental; mountain bike rental; kids' club; library area w/games, video, and Internet; tour desk; car-rental desk; shopping arcade; babysitting; 24-hr. room service; laundry service; nonsmoking rooms; meeting facilities. *In room:* A/C, satellite TV, dataport, minibar, fridge, coffeemaker, hair dryer, safe, IDD phone.

## WHERE TO DINE
Outside of the resorts you'll find just small storefront eateries and tourist cafes. In Ao Nang, try **Ao Nang Cuisine** for good Thai fare or any of the small beachside eateries. On Raillay, there are lots of little beachside bars and restaurants.

## 18  Koh Phi Phi

814km (505 miles) S of Bangkok, then 42km (26 miles) W of Krabi; 160km (99 miles) SW of Phuket

The December 26, 2004, tsunami devastated Phi Phi; most of the central isthmus of this tiny island was wiped out and the loss of life was considerable, but recovery is underway and the resilient folks here are working hard in hopes of luring tourists back.

Phi Phi is two islands: Phi Phi Don is the main barbell-shaped island whose central isthmus (the barbell handle) is packed with amenities; all visitors arrive at the busy ferry port in Phi Phi Don's Loh Dalam Bay and the sandy beaches at Tonsai (just opposite) are good for swimming. Smaller Phi Phi Lei is south of the main island and famed for its coveted swallow nests and the courageous pole-climbing daredevils who go get them (the nests fetch a hefty price for the making of a gourmet soup). The smaller island is protected as a natural park but is visited as part of most day trips. Phi Phi is where the filmmakers of *The Beach* chose to stage their Hollywood version of tropical Utopia, and some tours will take you to Makan, the site of the filming. Small beachfront outfits rent snorkel gear and conduct longtail boat tours to quiet coves for as little as 500B ($13).

## HOW TO GET THERE
Ferries make regular connections from both Phuket and Krabi. Boats from the pier in central Krabi Town run three times daily (9 and 10:30am; 1pm; more in high season) for 200B ($5). From Phuket, ferry services leave from the pier near Phuket Town with rates as low as 250B ($6.25) for the 2-hour trip.

## WHERE TO STAY
Much of the accommodations on the central isthmus were badly damaged by the 2004 tsunami, but **PP Princess** (✆ 07562-2079; www.ppprincess.com), a compact resort compound at the very center of it all, is likely to rebuild quickly and has good rooms from 2,600B ($65). On the leeward side of the island and

little affected by the wave, **Pee Pee Island Village** (© 07621-5014; www.pp island.com) is a self-contained low-luxe resort reached only by boat.

## 19 Koh Lanta

About 70km (43 miles) SE of Krabi

Small Muslim fishing villages dot the east coast of Lanta Yai (Big Lanta), a less-developed region of the south. You'll have to cross Lanta Noi (Small Lanta) to get to the main beach areas of Lanta Yai and, apart from luxury Pimalai, an island unto itself on the southern coast, accommodations on the island are backpacker basic. Some stretches of beach are rocky and good swimming is only at a few choice sites in the south, but this is a good off-the-track choice.

### GETTING THERE

Minivans from Krabi town and Trang make connections to Lanta (cost is from 150B/$3.75 for bus/boat/bus door-to-door). After two short ferry crossings, most transport stops in **Saladan** near the ferry pier on the northern tip of Lanta Yai. There are chartered boat options from Krabi Town or even Phuket and Phi Phi in the high season (see individual chapters for private boat charter information) and Pimalai Resort (below) arranges luxury boat transport when booking.

### WHERE TO STAY
#### VERY EXPENSIVE

**Pimalai Resort and Spa** 🐦🐦   From Krabi Town or the airport you can ride in style: first by luxury van, then a picturesque private boat ride directly to the resort in high season (a short 4WD ride to another pier in low season). Getting there is an adventure in itself that pays dividends when you check in to your own luxury suite. A fine marriage of comfort and proximity to nature, large, free-standing villas are partly walled compounds with rooms done in hardwoods and luxurious bathrooms with outdoor showers. Each room has a large veranda, some overlooking the sea or at least in earshot of the crashing surf of the picturesque beach below (a good swimming beach). High-end suites are spectacular. The resort is remote, but thoroughly self-contained (with services like a library, a beautiful spa, and good day trips).

99 Moo 5, Ba Kan Tiang Beach, Lanta Yai Island, Krabi 81150 (on the far southeast coast of Lanta Yai). © 07560-7999. Fax 07560-7998. www.pimalai.com. 86 units. 10,500B–14,500B ($263–$363) double; 20,000B–30,000B ($500–$750) pavilion suite; 25,000B–60,000B ($625–$1,500) beach villa. AE, DC, MC, V. **Amenities:** 3 restaurants; bar; pool; spa w/massage; Jacuzzi; watersports rentals; mountain bike rentals; dive center; tour desk; car-rental desk; limo transfer; business center w/Internet; 24-hr. room service; same-day laundry service; library w/good book selection. *In room:* A/C, satellite TV (some w/CD and DVD players), mini-bar, fridge, safe, IDD phone.

#### MODERATE/INEXPENSIVE

Budget accommodations along the west coast of Lanta are basic bungalows starting as low as 300B ($7.50; keep an eye out for new hotels). **Moonlight Bay Resort,** (69 Moo 8, Klongtob; © 07568-4401), is typical of the few good bungalow resorts and offers cozy accommodations and basic services starting as low as 300B ($7.50).

## 20 Central Thailand

Going north from Bangkok, travelers tracing the route of the Chao Phraya River travel back in time as they push upstream and beyond. Starting with the ruins of Ayuthaya (see "Side Trips from Bangkok," earlier in the chapter), the towns as you go north are the successive historical capitals of old Siam, and the vast Central Plains and the nation's greatest architectural wonder, Sukhothai, are the very founding point of the Thai kingdom in 1238. Further north is the land of Lanna and the distinct ancient kingdom once centered around Chiang Mai (see section 22 below).

It's a good area to discover Thailand's historical past; central Thailand's smaller work-a-day towns provide a window into rural culture and lifestyles of another time. A vast area, known as the "Great Rice Bowl" for its agricultural abundance, the Central Plains are washed by rivers, tessellated with rice fields and dotted by architectural sites like the temples at Sukhothai.

**Phitsanulok** (377km/234 miles north of Bangkok) is the commercial hub of the region, but despite a visit to the town's noted **Wat Yai,** an important Thai pilgrimage temple, most just pass through on their way to Sukhothai. Phitsanulok has regular air and rail connection with Bangkok (for rail contact **Hua Lamphong Station** in Bangkok at ✆ **1690** or the **Phitsanulok Station** at ✆ **05525-8005**). If you're stuck for the night, try **Topland Hotel** (68/33 Akathodsarod St.; ✆ **05524-7800;** www.toplandhotel.com) with 1,400B ($35) rooms.

## 21 Sukhothai & Si Satchanalai Historical Parks

Sukhothai: 427km (265 miles) N of Bangkok; 58km (36 miles) E of Phitsanulok. Si Satchanalai: 56km (35 miles) N of Sukhothai

The emergence of Sukhothai (which means "Dawn of Happiness" in Pali) in 1238 as an independent political state signified the birth of the first unified kingdom known as Thailand. Today Sukhothai is a world-renowned historical site; it is to Thailand what Angkor Wat is to Cambodia.

The Sukhothai Historical Park, the main attraction, is situated 12km (7½ miles) west of the town of New Sukhothai. Si Satchanalai, far north of New Sukhothai, is another legacy of the Sukhothai Kingdom. The ancient city is crumbling and that's part of its charm, really, and certainly worth the 1-day detour. If you're traveling from Phitsanulok, the drive takes you across wide plains of rice paddies, cotton fields, and mango and lemon groves—a glimpse into another era.

## ESSENTIALS
### GETTING THERE
**By Plane**    **Bangkok Airways** has a private airport near Sukhothai with at least one daily flight connecting Bangkok, Sukhothai, and Chiang Mai. Call in Bangkok at ✆ **02229-3456,** Chiang Mai at ✆ **05328-1519,** or at the airport at ✆ **05564-7224.**

**By Train**    Phitsanulok is the nearest railroad station.

**By Bus**    Three daily standard air-conditioned buses leave from Bangkok (trip time: 7 hr.; 256B/$6.40), departing from the **Northern Bus Terminal** (✆ **02936-2841**). There's also air-conditioned bus service from Chiang Mai six times daily (trip time: 5½ hr.; 171B–220B /$4.30–$5.50) from the **Arcade Bus Station** (✆ **05324-2664**).

**By Local Bus from Phitsanulok**    Buses leave hourly for New Sukhothai (trip time: 1 hr.; 30B/75¢) from the intercity terminal on Highway 12.

**By Car**    Take Singhawat Road east from Phitsanulok, then Highway 12.

## ORIENTATION

**New Sukhothai,** built along the banks of the Yom River, is the access point for **Sukhothai Historical Park** (or Muang Kao, Old City) some 12km (7½ miles) east of New Sukhothai center. **Si Satchanalai Historic Park,** also along the Yom River, is 56km (35 miles) north of new Sukhothai.

## SPECIAL EVENTS

**Loi Krathong** is a visually delightful, 3-day festival held nationwide on the full moon of the 12th lunar month (usually Oct/Nov) in honor of the water spirits. Crowds gather at ponds, klongs, rivers, and temple fountains to float small banana-leaf boats bearing candles, incense, a flower, and a coin in offering to wash away the past year's sins. Since this festival dates from the Sukhothai era, celebrations are widespread throughout the province.

## WHERE TO STAY
### VERY INEXPENSIVE

**Ban Thai Guesthouse** (38 Pravet Nakhon Rd; on west side of Yom River; ℂ 05561-0163) is a collection of A-frame teak bungalows starting from 200B ($5). It's quite basic, but a good place to get useful local info.

### INEXPENSIVE

**Lotus Village** ⍟ Garden paths connect a basic guesthouse block with other teak floor, semiluxe numbers. Spring for the large, sturdy, air-conditioned rooms done in polished wood or one in the two-story pavilions toward the back. Owned by a Franco-Thai husband-and-wife team, Lotus Village offers certified guides and drivers for a day at the temples and cozy dining in a rustic, colonial-style common area.

170 Ratchathanee St., Sukhothai 64000 (short walk north along the river from the main market). ℂ 05562-1484. Fax 05562-1463. www.lotus-village.com. 28 units. 500B ($13) fan room; 900B–1,000B ($23–$25) A/C room. No credit cards. **Amenities:** Small restaurant; tour desk; car-rental desk; laundry service. *In room:* Minibar, fridge in top standard only, no phone.

**Pailyn Sukhothai Hotel** ⍟ Close to the temples, this roadside resort is the most luxurious Sukhothai has to offer. Comfortable, carpeted rooms lay in two four-story wings, one of which encircles a small pool and sun deck. Rates vary according to room size and amenities; higher rates bring minibars and TVs.

10/2 Moo 3, Jarodvithithong Rd., Sukhothai 64210 (4km/2½ miles east of historical park, 8km/5 miles from the town center). ℂ 05561-3310. Fax 05561-3317. 238 units. 800B ($20) double; from 1,200B ($30) suite. MC, V. **Amenities:** 2 restaurants; disco; pool; fitness center; sauna; tour desk; limited room service; massage; same-day laundry service. *In room:* A/C, satellite TV, minibar, fridge.

## WHERE TO DINE

Like most small cities and towns in Thailand, you can find good eats at the central market from early 'til late. **Dream Café** (86/1 Singhawat Rd.; ℂ 05561-2081) is a great choice, with fine, funky Thai atmosphere and great eats.

## EXPLORING SUKHOTHAI ⍟⍟⍟

Named a UNESCO World Heritage site in 1978, a 1988 preservation project kept the monuments upright and added the museum and park facilities.

**GETTING TO THE SITE** Reach the historic park of Sukhothai by public bus, a three-wheeled motorcycle taxi called a *samlor,* or private car. The *samlors* that cruise around New Sukhothai can be hired to trek you out to the monuments and for a 3-hour tour around the park for about for 300B ($7.50).

**TOURING THE SITE**    A basic map is available at the museum but the best maps are to be found at the bicycle rental shops near the entrance. It's best to either go by guided tour in a car, by *samlor,* or by rented bicycle (available at the entrance). The sites are too spread out to walk. There are also tram tours.

The historical park is open daily 6am to 6pm. Purchase a combination ticket with admission to the National Museum, Historic Park (all areas), and Si Satchanali National Park for 150B ($3.75)—good value.

## SEEING THE HIGHLIGHTS

A network of walls and moats defines the perfect rectangle that is the central city. **The Ramkamhaeng National Museum,** with its detailed models and artifacts from the site, is a good place to start. **Wat Mahatat,** composed of several small towers and *chedis,* is an imposing monument and the site's most important. Don't miss the fine relief work on the southeast corner. The remains of the **Royal Palace** and **Wat Sri Sawai** are also highlights. Don't miss the temples, pottery kilns, and small pilgrimage mounds outside of the city walls. A visit to **Sri Satchanalai,** some 56km (35 miles) north, makes for a good day trip.

## 22  An Introduction to Northern Thailand

If lazy beach days aren't your thing, the historic cities of **Chiang Mai, Chiang Rai,** and the small but interesting **Golden Triangle** (Chiang Saen), a former cowboy town for the opium trade, are a welcome change for visitors who want to experience Thailand's rugged rural beauty.

Northern Thailand is composed of 15 provinces that share borders with Burma (Myanmar) to the north and west, and Laos to the northeast. This verdant, mountainous terrain, which includes Thailand's largest mountain, Doi Inthanon, at 2,563m (8,407 ft.), supports nomadic farming and teak logging at high altitudes and systematic agriculture in the valleys. Traditionally, opium poppies were the main cash crop for the people here, but government efforts have largely replaced their cultivation with rice, tobacco, soybeans, corn, and sugarcane.

The majority of northern Thais trace their heritage to the Tai people who migrated from southern China in waves between the 1st and 8th centuries. King Mengrai, a brilliant leader who united the Tai tribes, established the first capital of the Lanna Kingdom at Chiang Rai in 1262. It was about this time that Kublai Khan invaded Burma. For added protection, King Mengrai forged ties with the Sukhothai Kingdom to the south, and in 1296 he moved his capital to Chiang Mai. For the next century, the Lanna Kingdom absorbed most of the northern provinces and, in alliance with the Sukhothai, held off invasion from the Mons and Khmers. After taking control of Sukhothai, Ayutthaya tried to conquer Chiang Mai and failed each time. The Lanna Kingdom enjoyed wealth and power until 1556, when the Burmese captured the capital. It remained in their hands until 1775, when King Taskin (of Ayutthaya) took it for Siam.

Northern Thailand is home to the majority of Thailand's more than half a million **ethnic hill tribes,** which are classified in six primary groups: the Karen, Akha, Lahu, Lisu, Hmong (Meo), and Mien (Yao), each with subgroups that are linked by history, lineage, language, costume, social organization, and religion. With close ethnic, cultural, and linguistic ties to the cultures of their Laotian, Chinese, Burmese, and Tibetan ancestors and neighbors, each group retains, to this day, traditional costume, religion, art, and daily practices.

## WEATHER

November to May is the best time for trekking, with February, March, and April (when southern Thailand gets extremely hot) usually being the least crowded months. *Trekkers beware:* During the rainy season, June to October, paths become mudslides due to frequent showers.

## 23  Chiang Mai

Chiang Mai (New City) was founded in 1296 by King Mengrai as the capital of the first independent Thai state, Lanna Thai (Kingdom of One Million Rice Fields). It became the cultural and religious center of the northern Tai, those people who had migrated from southern China to dwell in Thailand, and remained through the turbulent period of recurring Burmese attacks. The Burmese were occupiers; in fact, Burmese influence on culture is still strong, and ongoing Thai-Burmese conflicts led to alliances with Siam and, in 1939, the city became Thai.

These days, Chiang Mai is a booming town of some 167,000 people (in a province of some 1.5 million). Chiang Mai's heart is the Old City, an area surrounded by vestiges of walls and moats originally constructed for defense; yet Chiang Mai is a modern city with a growing infrastructure of modern shopping malls and condominiums. The contrast is part of the town's charm.

## ARRIVING

**BY PLANE**   **Lao Aviation** (℃ **05340-4033**) connects Chiang Mai to Vientiane and Luang Prabang three times each week, while both **Thai Airways** (℃ **05321-0431**) and **Air Mandalay** (℃ **05327-6884**) have limited flights to Yangon and Mandalay, in Myanmar (Burma). **Silk Air** (℃ **05327-6459**), the regional arm of Singapore Airlines, connects with Singapore.

Within Thailand, **Thai Airways** (240 Propokklao Rd.; ℃ **05321-0431**), **Bangkok Airways** (℃ **05328-1519** or 02229-3434 in BKK), and budget **Air Asia** (℃ **02515-9999** in Bangkok; www.airasia.com) fly Bangkok to Chiang Mai daily (trip time: 1 hr., 10 min.) and make regional connections.

The **Chiang Mai International Airport** has several banks for changing money, a post and overseas call office, and an information booth.

Taxis from the airport are a flat 100B ($2.50) to town. Buy a ticket from the taxi booth in the arrival hall, then proceed to the taxi queue.

**BY TRAIN**   Of the seven daily trains from Bangkok to Chiang Mai, the 8:30am Sprinter (11 hr.; 481B/$12 second-class A/C seat) is the quickest, but you sacrifice a whole day to travel and spend the entire trip in a seat. Other trains take between 13 and 15 hours. For overnight trips, second-class sleeper berths are a good choice (741B/$19 upper berth with A/C; 681B/$17 lower berth with A/C). In Bangkok contact **Hua Lampong Railway Station** (℃ **02223-7010** or 1690) up to 90 days in advance. For local train information in Chiang Mai call ℃ **05324-5363;** for advance booking call ℃ **05324-2094.** Reservations cannot be made over the phone, but you can check availability.

**BY BUS**   Buses from Bangkok to Chiang Mai are many and varied—from rattle-trap, open-air numbers to fully reclining VIP buses. The trip takes about 10 hours. From Bangkok's **Northern Bus Terminal** (℃ **02936-2841**) there are numerous departures (about 625B/$16). There's also frequent service between Chiang Mai and Mae Hong Son, Phitsanulok, and Chiang Rai.

Chiang Mai's **Arcade Bus Station** (℃ **05324-2664**) is on Kaeo Nawarat Road, 3km (2 miles) northeast of the Tha Pae Gate; some arrive at the Chang

# Northern Thailand

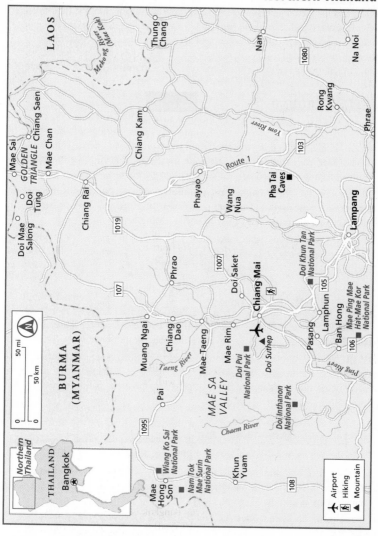

Puak station (℃ **05321-1586**) north of the Chang Puak Gate on Chotana Road.

## VISITOR INFORMATION

The **TAT** office is at 105/1 Chiang Mai-Lamphun Rd., 400m (1,312 ft.) south of the Nawarat Bridge on the east side of the Ping River (℃ **05324-8604**). Around town, find lots of free local magazines with maps and lists of events.

## ORIENTATION

The heart of Chiang Mai is the **Old City,** completely surrounded by a moat and a few remains of the massive wall, laid out in a square aligned on the cardinal directions. Several of the original gates have been restored and serve as handy reference points, particularly Ta Pae Gate to the east. All major streets radiate from the Old City. The main business and shopping area is the 1km (half-mile) stretch between the east side of the Old City and the Ping River. Here you will find the Night Bazaar, many shops, trekking agents, hotels, and restaurants. To the west of town and visible from anywhere in the city is the imposing wall of Doi Suthep mountain where, at its crest, you'll find the most regal of all Chiang Mai Buddhist compounds, Wat Phra That Doi Suthep.

## GETTING AROUND

**BY SONGTAO**   *Songtaos* (covered pickups) cover all routes. These red pickup trucks fitted with two long bench seats are also known locally as *seelor* (four wheels). Hail one going in your general direction and tell the driver your destination. (*Tip:* Have your hotel or guesthouse concierge write your destination in Thai before you head out.) Ask the price and bargain hard.

**BY TUK-TUK**   The ubiquitous tuk-tuk (motorized three-wheeler) is the next best option to the *songtao.* Fares are negotiable—and you will have to bargain hard to get a good rate—but expect to pay at least 40B ($1) for any ride.

**BY CAR   Avis** has an office conveniently located at the airport (© 05320-1574) and **Budget** (© 02203-0250) will deliver; prices start at 1,500B ($38). **North Wheels** (127/2 Moonmuang Rd.; © 05321-6189), is a good choice and typical of the more budget services in town.

**BY MOTORCYCLE**   Many guesthouses along the Ping River and shops around Chaiyapoom Road (north of Tha Pae Gate in the Old City) rent 100cc to 150cc motorcycles for about 200B ($5) per day (discounts for longer duration). 250cc Hondas (and larger) are also available. Wear a helmet.

**BY BICYCLE**   Cycling in the city is fun and practical, especially for getting around to the temples within the Old City. Bikes are available at any of the many guesthouses in or around the old city and go for about 30B (75¢) per day.

---

### FAST FACTS: Chiang Mai

*Airport*  See "Arriving," above.

*ATMs*  For ATMs and money changers, go to Chang Klan Road and Charoen Prathet Road, around the Night Bazaar, for the most convenient major bank branches.

*Bookstores*  **Backstreet Books** (© 05387-4143) and **Gecko Books** (© 05387-4066) are neighbors on Chang Moi Kao, a side street north of eastern Ta Pae Road just before it meets the city wall. Both have a good selection of new and used books and do exchanges at the usual rate (two for one, depending on the condition). **Bookazine** (ground floor, Chiang Inn Plaza, 100/1 Chang Klan Rd.; © 05328-1370)—is cramped but has a comprehensive selection. Also try **Suriwong Book Centre,** 54/1–5 Sri Dornchai (© 05328-1052), and **D. K. Books,** 234 Tha Pae Rd. (© 05325-1555).

*Car Rentals*  See "By Car," in "Getting Around," above.

*Consulates*  There are many representative offices in Chiang Mai. Contacts are as follows: **American Consulate General** (© 05325-2629), **Canadian Honorary Consul** (© 05385-0147), **Australian Honorary Consul** (© 05322-1083), and **British Consul** (© 05320-3405).

*Emergencies*  Dial © **1699** to reach the Tourist Police in case of emergency.

*Hospitals*  In Chiang Mai, hospitals offer excellent emergency and general care, with English-speaking nurses and physicians. The best private hospital is **McCormick** on Kaeo Nawarat Road (© **05324-1311**) out toward the Arcade Bus Terminal.

*Internet*  In the Old City, there are numerous small, inexpensive cafes with service sometimes costing only 15B (40¢) per hour. Try **NET Generation** at 404/4 Ta Pae Rd. (© **01568-7470**) or **Buddy Internet** near Gad Suan Kaew/Central Department Store (© **05340-4550**).

*Post Office*  The most convenient branch is at 186/1 on Chang Klan Road (© **05327-3657**). The General Post Office is on Charoen Muang (© **05324-1070**), near the train station.

# WHERE TO STAY
## NEAR THE PING RIVER
### Expensive

**The Imperial Mae Ping Hotel** ★   This imposing, crescent-shaped tower hotel is one of the city's most popular choices for its style and good location—just a short stroll from the Night Bazaar, yet far enough to get a good night's sleep. The unusual two-story lobby interprets Thai architectural elements in bold white-and-gold accents and the decor throughout is a nice mix of modern and traditional. Large, bright guest rooms are modern and feature traditional blond teak furnishings and contemporary Thai elements like sculpted lamp bases, reproductions of temple murals, and Thai weavings. Beds are big. Deluxe rooms have better-than-average amenities for just a small jump in price. Be sure to ask for a room with a mountain view.

153 Sri Dornchai Rd., Chiang Mai 50100 (corner of Kampaengdin Rd., 2 blocks southwest of Night Bazaar). © 05327-0160. Fax 05327-0181. 371 units. 3,500B–5,500B ($88–$138) double; from 8,000B ($200) suite. AE, DC, MC, V. **Amenities:** 3 restaurants; lounge and beer garden; outdoor pool; fitness center; tour desk; limo service; business center; salon; 24-hr. room service; massage; babysitting; same-day laundry service/dry cleaning; nonsmoking rooms, executive-level rooms. *In room:* A/C, satellite TV, minibar, fridge.

**Royal Princess Hotel** ★   This northern cousin of Bangkok's Dusit Thani is a first-rate city hotel. While the lobby has a faux-colonial feel, recent cosmetic renovations lend a chic air to upstairs common areas. Guest rooms are done in a mix of cool pastels set against panels, or whole walls, of saturated primary colors featuring poetry in elegant Thai calligraphy. Upper-floor deluxe rooms have an interesting Japanese theme. The downtown location means easy access to shopping and nightlife, and all guest rooms have a good vantage on the glittering lights of the city. You're right in the heart of it here, so be warned that stepping out of the hotel means that touts and tuk-tuk drivers pounce.

112 Chang Klan Rd., Chiang Mai 50100 (located just south of the Night Bazaar). © 05328-1033. Fax 05328-1044. www.royalprincess.com. 198 units. 3,200B–3,500B ($80–$88) double; from 10,500B ($263) suite. AE, DC, MC, V. **Amenities:** 3 restaurants; lobby lounge and pub; small outdoor pool; concierge; tour desk; limo service; 24-hr. room service; massage; babysitting; same-day laundry service/dry cleaning. *In room:* A/C, satellite TV, minibar, fridge, hair dryer, safe.

**The Sheraton Chiang Mai** ★★   Chiang Mai's best high-rise hotel is just a short ride south of town. This is "the" place if you're coming for business. From the enormous pillars, chandeliers, frescoes, and filigree of the grand lobby to its international standard of guest rooms and service, everything is tiptop. What the

Sheraton lacks in "local" touches it more than makes up for with comfortable familiarity. Complimentary shuttles to Night Bazaar and airport help offset the out-of-the-way locale.

318/1 Chiangmai-Lamphun Rd., Chiang Mai 50007 (south of city center, across Mengrai Bridge on east bank of river). © 05327-5300. Fax 05327-5299. www.sheraton-chiangmai.com. 526 units. 6,200B–7,200B ($155–$180) double; 8,500B ($213) executive deluxe; from 14,500B ($363) suite. AE, DC, MC, V. **Amenities:** 3 restaurants; lounge; outdoor pool; golf course nearby; fitness center; sauna; concierge; tour desk; car-rental desk; limo service; business center; 24-hr. room service; massage; babysitting; same-day laundry service/dry cleaning; nonsmoking rooms; executive-level rooms. In room: A/C, satellite TV, minibar, fridge, hair dryer.

## Moderate
### Chiang Inn Hotel ✴
The renovated Chiang Inn is just behind the Chiang Inn Plaza, an arcade of Western chain eateries and shops, but it's set back from the lively street and quiet. Location and convenience are its best features, adding special value for money to this modest hotel. The compact, teak-paneled lobby has a homey feel and is always crowded with Europeans. Spacious rooms are clean but are decorated in a bland fashion and a bit worse for wear. Bathrooms are big but could use a bit of grout solvent and elbow grease. While hotel facilities are limited, with so many dining and entertainment options nearby you won't be spending much time in your room. After touring the city and its sights, you'll appreciate relaxing around the pool and sun deck.

100 Chang Klan Rd., Chiang Mai 50100 (2 blocks south of Tha Pae Rd., 2 blocks west of river, just north of Night Bazaar). © 05327-0070. Fax 05327-4299. chianginn@chiangmai.a-net.net.th. 190 units. 1,600B ($40) double; from 6,000B ($150) suite. AE, DC, MC, V. **Amenities:** 2 restaurants; lobby lounge; small pool; tour desk; business center; limited room service; massage; babysitting; same-day laundry service/dry cleaning. In room: A/C, satellite TV, minibar, fridge.

### Chiang Mai Plaza Hotel
These two 12-story towers, completed in 1986, are a bland, modern Western hotel, but guest rooms are large, plush, and offer city and mountain views. The lobby is so spacious that the decorative furniture seems almost lost in acres of brilliantly polished granite. The Plaza is also well located—in town, but just far enough away, toward the Ping River, to be out of the congestion. It's very popular with group tours but the place is so big you won't know they're there. The swimming pool is surrounded by Lanna-style pavilions and the newly built spa area is a catacomb in deep umber tones, dim lights, and Thai decoration where you'll find the gamut of affordable but high-quality health and beauty treatments.

92 Sri Dornchai Rd., Chiang Mai 50100 (between Chang Klan and Charoen Prathet roads, midway between Old City and river). © 05327-0036. Fax 05327-2230. 445 units. 2,500B–3,000B ($63–$75) double; from 12,200B ($305) suite. AE, DC, MC, V. **Amenities:** Restaurant; lounge; outdoor pool; fitness center; spa w/massage and sauna; tour desk; car-rental desk; business center; limited room service; massage; babysitting; same-day laundry service/dry cleaning; nonsmoking rooms. In room: A/C, satellite TV, minibar, fridge, hair dryer.

### The Empress Hotel ✴
This 17-story tower, opened in 1990, is south of the main business and tourist area, which makes it especially quiet. The hotel has all the amenities and even when swarming with tourist groups doesn't seem over-run. The impressive public spaces are filled with glass, granite, and chrome and have integrated Thai touches and flairs. Large rooms with picture windows are done in a tasteful, modern interpretation of Asian decor of rose and peach tones. Bathrooms are small but decked out in marble and offer good complimentary amenities. Ask to be on the mountain side and there are nice views from upper floors.

199/42 Chang Klan Rd., Chiang Mai 50100 (15-min. walk south of Night Bazaar, 2 blocks from river). © 05327-0240. Fax 05327-2467. www.empresshotels.com. 375 units. 3,000B–4,000B ($75–$100) double; from 8,400B ($210) suite. AE, DC, MC, V. **Amenities:** 3 restaurants; lobby lounge and disco; pool; fitness

# Where to Stay & Dine in Chiang Mai

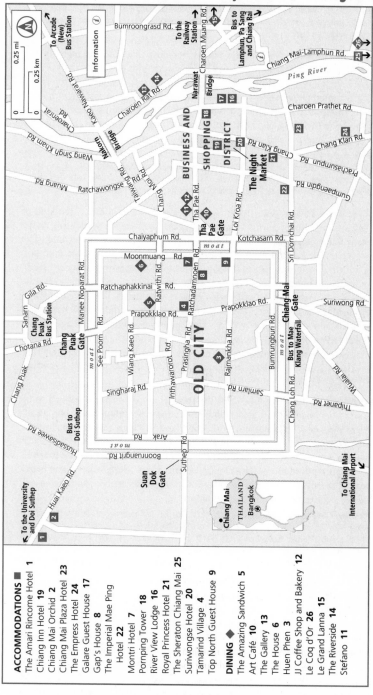

Bumroongrasd Rd.

To Arcade (New) Bus Station

Information (i)

To the Railway Station

Bus to Lamphun, Pa Sang and Chiang Rai

Charoen Muang Rd.

Narawat Bridge

Chiang Mai-Lamphun Rd.

Ping River

0.25 mi

0.25 km

Kaeo Nawarat Rd.

Charoenrat Rd.

Charoen Rat Rd.

Nawarat Bridge

Charoen Prathet Rd.

BUSINESS AND SHOPPING DISTRICT

Chang Klan Rd.

Chang Klan Rd.

The Night Market

Wang Singh Kham Rd.

Ratchawongse Rd.

Muang Rd.

Tawang Rd.

Chang Moi Rd.

Tha Pae Rd.

Chang

Tha Pae Gate

Loi Kroa Rd.

Prachasumpun Rd.

Gumpaengdin Rd.

Chaiyaphum Rd.

moat

Kotchasarn Rd.

Sri Donchai Rd.

Moonmuang Rd.

Ratwithi Rd.

Ratchadamnoen Rd.

Chiang Mai Gate

Suriwong Rd.

Gila Rd.

Sanam

Chang Puak Bus Station

Manee Noparat Rd.

Ratchaphakkinai Rd.

Prapokklao Rd.

Prapokklao Rd.

Bumrungburi Rd.

Chotana Rd.

Chang Puak Gate

moat

See Poom

Wiang Kaeo Rd.

Prasingha Rd.

Rajmankha Rd.

Bus to Mae Klang Waterfall

Chang Puak

Bus to Doi Suthep

Inthawarorot Rd.

OLD CITY

Samlarn Rd.

Chang Loh Rd.

Thipanet Rd.

Wulai Rd.

Hussadisawee Rd.

Huai Kaeo Rd.

Singharaj Rd.

Arak Rd.

moat

Suan Dok Gate

Suthep Rd.

Boonruangrit Rd.

To Chiang Mai International Airport

To the University and Doi Suthep

Chiang Mai

THAILAND

Bangkok

## ACCOMMODATIONS ■

The Amari Rincome Hotel  1
Chiang Inn Hotel  19
Chiang Mai Orchid  2
Chiang Mai Plaza Hotel  23
The Empress Hotel  24
Galare Guest House  17
Gap's House  8
The Imperial Mae Ping Hotel  22
Montri Hotel  7
Pornping Tower  18
River View Lodge  16
Royal Princess Hotel  21
The Sheraton Chiang Mai  25
Suriwongse Hotel  20
Tamarind Village  4
Top North Guest House  9

## DINING ◆

The Amazing Sandwich  5
Art Café  10
The Gallery  13
The House  6
Huen Phen  3
JJ Coffee Shop and Bakery  12
Le Coq d'Or  26
Le Grand Lanna  15
The Riverside  14
Stefano  11

217

center w/sauna; concierge; tour desk; business center; Internet; shopping arcade; salon; 24-hr. room service; massage; babysitting; same-day laundry service/dry cleaning; executive-level rooms. *In room:* A/C, satellite TV, minibar, fridge, hair dryer.

**Pornping Tower**   Right in the heart of the busy shopping and nightlife area near the Night Bazaar, this 20-story hotel bustles with evening activity. Public spaces are full of polished marble, glass, and mirrors; rooms use cool colors and have a contemporary style. There's an excellent pool with an inviting sun deck, good in-house dining, attentive service, and top location—ingredients that combine to make this one of the best buys in the city. Be sure to check out the happenin' Bubble Disco (when it's happenin', that is—weekend nights mostly).

46–48 Charoen Prathet Rd., Chiang Mai 50100 (corner of Loi Kroa Rd., 1 block from river). ⓒ 05327-0099. Fax 05327-0119. 318 units. 1,500B–2,200B ($38–$55) double; from 5,000B ($125) suite. AE, DC, MC, V. **Amenities:** 3 restaurants; popular disco, lounge, and karaoke; outdoor pool; tour desk; 24-hr. room service; babysitting; same-day laundry service/dry cleaning. *In room:* A/C, satellite TV, minibar, fridge.

**River View Lodge** 🏾🏾   River View has a great location and is the kind of place where people return to again and again (well-known guide-map maker Nancy Chandler, for instance, makes this her home when she is researching). The hotels riverside location makes for a peaceful retreat, and yet it's only a short hop to the city's main business and shopping district. What with the quaint, shady garden, small but cozy riverside pool, open-air cafe, and quiet sitting areas scattered about, there's a good laid-back vibe here. The staff is friendly enough and informed if a bit "eccentric," to give it a word. Large guest rooms have fresh terracotta tile floors with simple wood furnishings and no-fuss decor set against one wall of red-brick facing (some have balconies). Bathrooms have shower stalls only.

25 Charoen Prathet Rd., Soi 2, Chiang Mai 50100 (on river 2 blocks south of Tae Pae Rd.). ⓒ 05327-1109. Fax 05327-9019. www.riverviewlodgch.com. 36 units. 1,450B–1,800B ($36–$45) double. MC, V. **Amenities:** Restaurant; small pool; laundry service. *In room:* A/C.

**Suriwongse Hotel** 🏾 *(Value)*   For the shopper or party animal looking to be close to the Night Bazaar area, this hotel is tops. The unique hardwood paneling in the lobby lends warmth to the place and spacious, teak-trimmed rooms have clean carpet, large, firm beds, and are done in cool off-white and pastel (if you can ignore the red bordello drapes). This is one of Chiang Mai's better values. Higher-priced rooms have similar amenities but offer a balcony and better views. The town's McDonald's and Starbucks franchises are both within a stone's throw (if throwing stones is your thing).

110 Chang Klan Rd., Chiang Mai 50100 (corner of Loi Kroa Rd., just southwest of Night Bazaar, halfway between Old City and river). ⓒ 05327-0051. Fax 05327-0063. www.suriwongsehotels.com. 180 units. 2,200B–2,800B ($55–$70) double; from 4,700B ($118) suite (seasonal rates available). AE, DC, MC, V. **Amenities:** 2 restaurants; lounge; pool; tour desk; business center; shopping; limited room service; massage; babysitting; same-day laundry service/dry cleaning; nonsmoking rooms. *In room:* A/C, satellite TV, minibar, fridge, IDD phone.

### Inexpensive

**Galare Guest House**   If the River View Lodge (see listing above) is booked or you want to save the baht, try the smaller Galare, almost next door. It's a Thai-style, three-story, brick-and-wood motel, with broad covered verandas overlooking a pleasant garden and courtyard. Rooms are small but have air-conditioning and king-size beds. It's low-luxe linoleum floors and bamboo catay on the walls but comfortable. The restaurant serves breakfast, lunch, and dinner on a covered deck overlooking the river. An in-house trekking agency organizes trips to hill-tribe villages as well as local tours of Chiang Mai. Up to 20% discounts are available in the off season.

7 Charoen Prathet Rd., Soi 2, Chiang Mai 50100 (on river south of Tha Pae Rd.). © 05381-8887. Fax 05327-9088. 35 units. 880B ($22) double. MC, V. **Amenities:** Restaurant; tour desk; car rental; Internet access; laundry service. *In room:* TV, fridge.

## IN THE OLD CITY
### Moderate

**Tamarind Village** ★★    Passing down a long, shaded lane lined with new-growth bamboo, follow meandering walkways among the whitewashed buildings of this stylish little hideaway in the heart of the Old City. It's hard to believe that you're in Chiang Mai. Newly built and always busy, rooms at the Tamarind are marvels of concrete flatwork burnished to an almost shining glow and, complimented by straw mats and chic contemporary Thai furnishings, make for a pleasing minimalist feel (if you're a minimalist, that is). Bathrooms are spacious with large double doors connecting with vaulted ceiling guest rooms. There's an almost Mediterranean feel to the whole complex what with all of the arched, covered terra-cotta walks joining buildings in a village-style layout. Short of the fine pool and a dandy restaurant, amenities are sparse, but the staff is helpful and the atmosphere quite unique.

50/1 Rathcadamnoen Rd., Sriphom, Chiang Mai 50200 (a short walk toward the center of the Old City from Ta Pae Gate). © 05341-8896. Fax 05341-8900. 40 units. 3,600B–5,100B ($90–$128) double; 6,150B ($154) deluxe. **Amenities:** Restaurant; bar; outdoor pool; tour desk; same-day laundry service/dry cleaning. *In room:* A/C, satellite TV, minbar, fridge, hair dryer, IDD phone.

### Inexpensive

**Gap's House**    Gap's House is tucked down a quiet lane just inside the city wall at Ta Pae. An upmarket guesthouse, really, the hotel atmosphere is calm with a leafy central garden area surrounding a large, teak, Lanna Thai pavilion. Rooms are in free-standing teak houses and feature woven rattan beds and small tiled bathrooms. Time is taking a toll on the room facilities here so the rustic charm borders on just plain old. Avoid the budget singles in a separate cement building.

3 Soi 4, Ratchadamnoen Rd., Chiang Mai 50000 (1 block west of Tha Pae Gate on left). ©/fax 05327-8140. 19 units. 390B–650B ($9.75–$16) double. MC, V. **Amenities:** Restaurant; cooking courses; laundry service. *In room:* A/C, no phone.

**Montri Hotel** ★ *Value*    The earliest address of note for foreigners in Chiang Mai, the Montri is still a convenient, inexpensive gem located just inside the Old City and across from Ta Pae Gate. Newly renovated rooms with built-in cabinets, valances, and new furniture are attractive, comfortable, and a very good value, and the rest are pretty basic cells but comfy and clean. Dark parquet floors are standard throughout and bathrooms are shower-in-rooms style. Ask for a back-facing room; you'll get more peace and from higher floors can see Doi Suthep. If you're arriving by plane make sure you request a free airport transfer when you make your booking.

2–6 Ratchadamnoen Rd., Chiang Mai 50100 (just northwest across from Tha Pae Gate). © 05321-1069. Fax 05321-7416. 75 units. 575B–695B ($14–$17) double; 750B ($19) superior. MC, V. **Amenities:** Restaurant; tour desk; small business center; laundry service. *In room:* A/C, satellite TV, minbar, fridge.

**Top North Guest House**    South of Ta Pae and down one of the Old City's narrow lanes, laid-back Top North is comfortable and affordable. The small central pool is unique in this category and is a popular hangout for backpackers going upscale. There are many room standards. All have high ceilings and the top category rooms (500B/$13) are large and clean with tile floors and large bathrooms with bathtubs. Time is not kind to budget hotels, though, and indeed some of the room furnishings look like they've gone a few rounds with an angry, caged ape. Rooms on the lower echelon vary in price and amenities (with or without air-conditioning or TV) but all have hot-water showers. Top North has a good tour operation and an Internet cafe on premises, and shows DVDs in the bar in the evenings. Its sister property, **Top North Hotel** (© 05327-9623-5), is an old standby just south of the Ta Pae Gate within the Old City and offers a slightly higher class of rooms but seems to attract a rougher lot; it's good in a pinch, though.

15 Moon Muang Rd., Soi 2, Chiang Mai 50100. © 05329-8900. Fax 05327-8485. 90 units. 500B ($13) double w/A/C; 300B ($7.50) double w/fan. MC, V. **Amenities:** Restaurant; outdoor pool; bike and motorcycle rental; tour desk; laundry service; Internet cafe. *In room:* A/C, TV.

## WESTSIDE/UNIVERSITY AREA
### Expensive
**The Amari Rincome Hotel** ⋇   This tranquil hotel complex is a favorite because of its elegant, yet traditional, Thai atmosphere. The public spaces are decorated with local handicrafts, and the professional staff wears intricately embroidered costumes. The large, balconied guest rooms are elaborately adorned with Burmese tapestries and carved wood accents in local style, and the bathrooms are plush. There is a gorgeous garden and pool area, the dining at **La Gritta** is great, and the hotel is located near some of the better upscale shopping and galleries in town. The staff is as professional as they come, will know your name from the moment you cross the threshold, and can help with any eventuality (tours, transport, etc.). A very comfortable choice.

1 Nimmanhaeminda Rd., off Huay Kaeo Rd., Chiang Mai 50200 (near superhighway northwest of Old City). © 05322-1130. Fax 05322-1915. www.amari.com. 158 units. 4,300B–5,300B ($108–$133) double; from 10,500B ($263) suite. AE, DC, MC, V. **Amenities:** 3 restaurants; lounge; 2 outdoor pools; outdoor lighted tennis court; concierge; tour desk; limo service; business center; shopping arcade; salon; 24-hr. room service; massage; babysitting; same-day laundry service/dry cleaning; nonsmoking rooms; executive-level rooms. *In room:* A/C, satellite TV, minibar, fridge, hair dryer.

**Chiang Mai Orchid** ⋇   The Orchid has attractive facilities and friendly service and is located just next to the town's most popular hangout, Gad Suan Kaew Shopping Complex. Spacious, quiet rooms are large, familiar and pleasantly decorated with local woodcarvings. The lobby and other public spaces are furnished with clusters of chic, low-slung rattan couches and chairs and decorated with flowers. The Orchid covers all the bases in amenities, from dining to car rental and a knowledgeable tour desk.

100–102 Huai Kaeo Rd., Chiang Mai 50200 (northwest of Old City, next door to Gad San Kaew/Central Shopping Complex). © 05322-2099. Fax 05322-1625. 267 units. 2,800B–3,500B ($70–$88) double; from 9,000B ($225) suite. AE, DC, MC, V. **Amenities:** 3 restaurants; lounge and pub; outdoor pool; fitness center; sauna; children's playground; tour desk; car-rental desk; limited room service; massage; babysitting; same-day laundry service. *In room:* A/C, satellite TV, dataport, minibar, fridge.

## SANKAMPAENG ROAD
### Very Expensive
**Mandarin Oriental Dhara Dhevi Chiang Mai** ⋇⋇   The same folks who set the standard for riverside luxury in their historic property in Bangkok now bring a new ultraluxe resort to Chiang Mai. Just finishing the first phase of construction at the time of publication, the resort promises luxury to match the popular Four Seasons Resort (below). The resort is east of town along the busy stretch of Sankampaeng Road. Arranged like a Lanna village, villa suites surround a verdant, central compound of rice terraces and gardens. Rooms are appointed for royalty, in rich teak, silk, and all the finest fittings. Luxury suites are all free-standing villas styled in a unique combination of Lanna-style rice barns and traditional

Siamese rooflines. A high standard of style and service comes with a price tag to match. This is just the first phase of what will be a larger and more luxurious campus, certainly one to watch.

51/4 Chiang Mai–Sankampaeng Rd., Moo 1 T Tasala, Chiang Mai 50000 ℂ 05388-8929. Fax 05399-9928. www.mandarinoriental.com. 142 units. 18,000B–240,000B ($450–$6,000). AE, MC, V. **Amenities:** 3 restaurants; 2 bars; outdoor pool; tennis court; health club; extensive spa; children's center; concierge; tour desk; car rental; limo service; business center; shopping village; 24-hour room service; massage; babysitting; laundry service; dry cleaning; cooking school; library. *In room:* A/C, satellite TV, minibar, fridge, coffeemaker, hair dryer, safe, IDD phone.

## OUTSIDE CHIANG MAI
### Very Expensive

**The Four Seasons Resort & Spa** ★★★   Northern Thailand's finest resort is isolated from the bustle of the city on 8 hectares (20 acres) of landscaped grounds in the Mae Rim Valley. The beautiful central area features terraced rice paddies and even a resident family of water buffalos used to work the fields. Two-story Lanna-style pavilions overlook the tranquil scenery. Spacious suites are understatedly elegant with polished teak floors and vaulted ceilings, decorated with traditional Thai fabrics and art, each with an adjoining private *sala.* Bathrooms are particularly large and luxurious. The pool is a spectacle with a vanishing edge overlooking fields and mountains. At night, torches are lit in the fields, lending a mysterious air to the views from the resort's restaurants. The resort location though gives you full access to the picturesque Mae Rim valley and guests are invited to borrow mountain bikes for self-guided exploration of the area. If you're worried about being far from Chiang Mai, there are regular shuttles to and from the main business and shopping district. There's a fine cooking school. The *pièce de résistance* is the Regent's luxurious Lanna Spa, which offers a standard of luxury and service without rival in the region.

Mae Rim–Samoeng Old Rd., Mae Rim, Chiang Mai 50180 (20 min. north of city off Chiang Mai-Mae Rim Rd.). ℂ **800/545-4000** in the U.S., or 05329-8181. Fax 05329-8190. www.fourseasons.com. 80 suites. 15,400B–19,000B ($385–$475) pavilion suite; from 36,900B ($923) residence suite. AE, DC, MC, V. **Amenities:** 3 restaurants; bar; 2 pools; 2 outdoor lighted grass tennis courts; fitness center w/sauna and steam; spa w/steam, massage, and salon; complimentary bicycles; children's activities; concierge; car rental; shuttle to town; business center; 24-hr. room service; babysitting; same-day laundry service/dry cleaning; library. *In room:* A/C, satellite TV w/in-house movies, minibar, fridge, hair dryer, safe.

## WHERE TO DINE

Northern-style cuisine, called Lanna, is influenced by the Burmese and other ethnic minorities who live in the area. Among the most distinctive northern Thai dishes are *khao miao* (glutinous or sticky rice), often served in a knotted banana leaf; *sai-ua* (Chiang Mai sausage); *khao soi* (a spicy, curried broth with vegetables and glass noodles); as well as many other slightly sweet meat and fish curries. The formal northern meal is called *khan toke,* referring to the custom of sharing a variety of main courses (eaten with the hands) with guests seated around *khan toke* (low, lacquered teak tables).

## NEAR THE PING RIVER
### Expensive

**Le Coq d'Or** ★★ FRENCH   In a romantic English country house setting, Le Coq d'Or is second to none in Chiang Mai for excellent atmosphere, food, presentation, and service. Professional waiters serve from a list of imported beef, lamb, and fish prepared in French and Continental styles. Presentation is done in fine white linen and real china. Try the chateaubriand, rare, with a delicate gravy and béarnaise on the side. The poached Norwegian salmon is a fine, light choice.

For starters, try the foie gras or a unique salmon tartar wrapped in smoked filet and served with toast, a sour cream-and-horseradish sauce, and capers. A nice wine list complements your meal. Don't wait for a special occasion.

68/1 Koh Klang Rd. (5-min. drive south of the Westin, following the river). ℂ 05328-2024. Reservations recommended for weekend dinner. Main courses 320B–1,800B ($8–$45). AE, DC, MC, V. Daily noon–2pm and 6–10:30pm.

## Moderate

**The Gallery** ⭒ THAI   Built in 1892 and one of the oldest original wooden structures in Chiang Mai, The Gallery is the most tranquil and romantic of the choice riverside restaurants on the eastern bank of the Mae Ping river. This was the auspicious spot where, during her visit to Chiang Mai in 1996, Hillary Clinton chose to set sail her float at the Loi Kratong Festival. I enjoyed an appetizer plate of "build-your-own" dishes that all required more origami skill than I could muster, but it was fun trying to figure it out with the help of a giggling staff. As an entree, the *hor mok curry,* a popular Chiang Mai dish, was delicious. Candlelight, soft Thai music and a great view of the river and the city's twinkling lights beyond top off a lovely evening of dining. Bring someone special.

25–29 Charoenrat Rd. (east side of river, north of Narawatt Bridge). ℂ 05324-8601-1. Main courses 90B–340B ($2.25–$8.50). AE, MC, V. Daily noon–1am.

**The House** ⭒⭒ PACIFIC RIM FUSION   This cozy bistro is set in an old colonial-style edifice decorated in placid pale tones, windows are draped in light curtains, and the seating is in rattan chairs around linen-draped tables. The menu is a constantly evolving roster of regionally influenced classical dishes, grilled items, imported steaks, lamb, and seafood when available fresh. A good stop for a light lunch when touring or an evening of fine dining.

199 Moonmuang Rd. (just north of Ta Pae Gate on the inside edge of the city moat). ℂ 05341-9011. Main courses 210B–450B ($5.25–$11). Daily 11am–2:30pm and 6–10:30pm.

**Le Grand Lanna** ⭒⭒ THAI   Chiang Mai's most opulent Thai restaurant is indeed grand. In the shopping area of Sankampaeng Road, the restaurant is on a large parcel of lush terrain. Atmosphere is your choice of deluxe Lanna Thai pavilions, various open deck areas, pond-side courtyards among banyan trees, or in unique theme rooms. Evening meals are all candlelight, outdoor torches, and the dulcet tones of traditional music. The fine Thai cuisine is good and very affordable. Try the white fish with lemon-coleslaw marinade. Curries are delicious and varied. I had *gaeng hang lan mop,* a dry, fiery red curry that will knock your socks off (best mollified by a sweet mango chutney). Follow up with great homemade ice cream with local litchi or taro flavors.

51/4 Chiang Mai–Sankampaeng Rd., Moo 1 T. Tasala, Chiang Mai 50000 (4km/2½ miles east on Charoen Muang near the end of shopper's row, follow signs and turn right/south down a small lane). ℂ 05326-2569. Main courses 100B–250B ($2.50–$6.25). AE, MC, V. Daily 11am–10pm.

**The Riverside** ⭒⭒ THAI/INTERNATIONAL   Casual and cool is what Riverside is all about. It's a tavern with riverside terrace views—make sure you get there before the dinner rush so you get your pick of tables. There's live music, from blues to soft rock, great Thai and Western food (including burgers), and a full bar. Even if you just stop by for a beer, it's a convivial place that always has a jolly crowd of travelers, locals, and expatriates. Riverside also operates a dining cruise at 8pm (boards at 7:15pm) for just 70B ($1.75) per person (drinks and dining a la carte). Call ahead.

9–11 Charoenrat Rd. (east side of river, north of Narawatt Bridge). ℂ 05324-3239. Main courses 65B–330B ($1.65–$8.25). AE, MC, V. Daily 10am–2am.

**Stefano** ⋆⋆ ITALIAN    Stefano is in a busy alley off of Ta Pae Road, a lively and popular place with an extensive catalog of Northern Italian cuisine, from steaks to excellent pastas. I had a fusilli with cream sauce and big local mushrooms: a delicious departure from curry, rice, and noodles. Portions are big, the wine list is deep and there are good daily set menus and specials. Meet lots of young backpackers splashing out after long, rugged journeys in the north.

2/102 Chang Mai Kao Rd. (just to the east of Ta Pae Gate). ℂ 05387-4189. Main courses 90B–300B ($2.25–$7.50). AE, MC, V. Daily 11am–11pm.

## AROUND THE OLD CITY
### Inexpensive
**The Amazing Sandwich** WESTERN    The recipe is simple here: Create your own "amazing" sandwich for eat-in or take-away. The pallet for your masterwork is a list of ingredients and you simply tick the appropriate boxes to your heart's delight. Even if you are more interested in local food, this is a great place if you want to pack a lunch for any self-guided day trips.

252/3 Phra Pokklao Rd. (near the Thai Airways office). ℂ 05321-8846. Main courses 60B–85B ($1.50–$2.15). No credit cards. Mon–Sat 9am–8:30pm.

**Art Café** INTERNATIONAL    This cheery corner cafe has black-and-white tile floors and cozy booths with picture windows overlooking the busy terminus of Ta Pae Road: a good spot for people-watching. The menu is ambitious and offers good, familiar fare, from steaks and pizza to Mexican dishes and meatloaf. Art Café has good cakes and coffee and it is a good place to meet people.

291 Ta Pae Rd. (just opposite Ta Pae Gate). ℂ 05320-6365. Main courses 50B–260B ($1.25–$6.50). MC, V. Daily 8am–11pm.

**Huen Phen** THAI    Near Wat Phra Sing, Huen Phen is an authentic local choice. There's an English menu, but just peek in the open kitchen and see what looks good to you. Huen Phen serves good *kao soi,* Chiang Mai's famed noodle stew, but try the specialty: *Khanom Jeen Namngeua,* a beef stew in a hearty broth. It'll keep you warm when those storms come blowing in off of Doi Suthep.

112 Rachamangla Rd. ℂ 05381-4548. Main courses 15B–50B (40¢–$1.25). No credit cards. Daily 9am–12:30am.

**JJ Coffee Shop and Bakery** ⋆⋆ INTERNATIONAL    A Thai-styled diner, tidy JJ's has three neat locations in town. The extensive menu includes sandwiches, burgers, fries, and all things familiar. Breakfasts are tops, and reasonably priced. The Ta Pae Road branch has a sandwich and salad bar in the evenings. There's a second branch at the Chiang Inn Plaza off the Night Bazaar and a third across the river at 129 Lampoon Rd.

Ta Pae Gate, Chiang Mai. ℂ 05323-4007. Main courses 40B–220B ($1–$5.50). V. Daily 6:30am–10:30pm.

## SNACKS & CAFES
**Kalare Food & Shopping Center,** 89/2 Chang Klan Rd., on the corner of Soi 6, behind the bazaar (ℂ 05327-2067; call for hours), is where you'll find a small food court next to the nightly Thai culture show.

**Bake and Bite** is on a small side street to the south of Ta Pae Gate (6/1 Kotchasarn Rd. Soi 1; ℂ 05328-5185) and has tasty baked goods, fine bread, and good coffee. It's open Monday through Saturday 7am to 6pm and Sunday 7am to 3pm.

# EXPLORING CULTURAL CHIANG MAI
## THE WATS

Chiang Mai has more than 700 temples, the largest concentration outside of Bangkok, and unique little sites are around every corner. In one very full day you can hit the highlights in Old Chiang Mai if you go by tuk-tuk.

**Wat Chedi Luang** ★★★ Because this temple is near the Ta Pae Gate, most visitors begin their sightseeing here, where there are two *wats* of interest. This complex, which briefly housed the Emerald Buddha now at Bangkok's Wat Phra Kaeo, dates from 1411 when the original *chedi* (mound) was built by King Saen Muang Ma. The already-massive edifice was expanded to 84m (276 ft.) in height in the mid-1400s, only to be ruined by a severe earthquake in 1545, just 11 years before Chiang Mai fell to the Burmese. (It was never rebuilt.) A Buddha still graces its exterior, and it's not unusual to spot a saffron-robed monk bowing to it as he circles the *chedi.*

**Wat Phan Tao,** also on the grounds, has a wooden *wihaan* (spirit house) and *bot* (central shrine in a Buddhist temple), reclining Buddha, and fine carving on the eaves and door. After leaving the temple, walk around to the monks' quarters on the side, taking in the traditional teak northern architecture and delightful landscaping.

Prapokklao Rd. south of Ratchadamnoen Rd. Suggested donation 20B (50¢). Daily 6am–5pm.

**Wat Chet Yot** ★★ Also called Wat Maha Photharam, Wat Chet Yot is one of the central city's most elegant sites. The *chedi* was built during the reign of King Tilokkarat in the late 15th century (his remains are in one of the smaller *chedis*), and in 1477, the World Sangkayana convened here to revise the doctrines of the Buddha.

The unusual design of the main rectangular *chedi* with seven peaks was copied from the Maha Bodhi Temple in Bodh Gaya, India, where the Buddha first achieved enlightenment. The temple also has architectural elements of Burmese, Chinese Yuan, and Ming influence. The extraordinary proportions, the angelic, levitating *devata* figures carved into the base of the *chedi,* and the juxtaposition of the other buildings make Wat Chet Yot (Seven Spires) a masterpiece.

The Lanna-style Buddha hidden in the center was sculpted in the mid–15th century; a door inside the niche containing the Buddha leads to the roof on which rests the **Phra Kaen Chan (Sandalwood Buddha).** There is a nice vista from up top, but only men are allowed to ascend the stairs.

Superhighway near the Chiang Mai National Museum (north of the intersection of Nimanhemin and Huai Kaeo roads, about 1km/half-mile, on the left). Suggested donation 20B (50¢). Daily 6am–5pm.

**Wat Chiang Man** Thought to be Chiang Mai's oldest *wat,* it was built during the 14th century by King Mengrai, the founder of Chiang Mai, on the spot where he first camped. Like many of the *wats* in Chiang Mai, this complex reflects many architectural styles. Some of the structures are pure Lanna. Others show influences from as far away as Sri Lanka; notice the typical row of elephant supports. Wat Chiang Man is most famous for its two Buddhas: Phra Sritang Khamani (a miniature crystal image also known as the **White Emerald Buddha**) and the marble **Phra Sri-la Buddha.** Unfortunately, the *wihaan* that safeguards these religious sculptures is almost always closed.

North of the intersection of Nimanhemin and Huai Kaeo roads, about 1km (half-mile), on the left.

**Wat Phra Singh** ★★★ This compound was built during the zenith of Chiang Mai's power, and is one of the more venerated shrines in the city. It's still the

# Exploring Cultural Chiang Mai

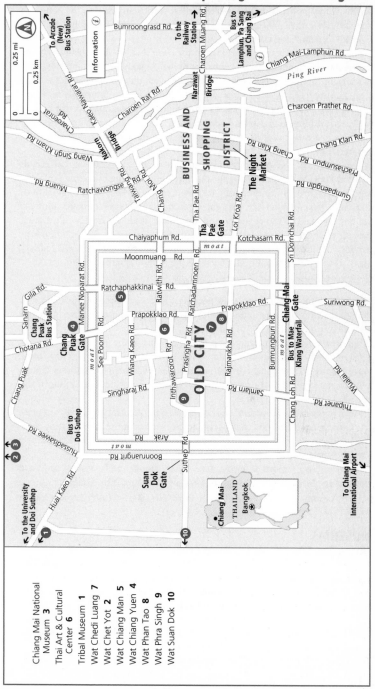

Chiang Mai National Museum **3**
Thai Art & Cultural Center **6**
Tribal Museum **1**
Wat Chedi Luang **7**
Wat Chet Yot **2**
Wat Chiang Man **5**
Wat Chiang Yuen **4**
Wat Phan Tao **8**
Wat Phra Singh **9**
Wat Suan Dok **10**

site of many important religious ceremonies, particularly during the Songkran Festival. More than 700 monks study here, and you will probably find them especially friendly and curious.

King Phayu, of Mengrai lineage, built the *chedi* in 1345, principally to house the cremated remains of King Kamfu, his father. As you enter the grounds, head to the right toward the 14th-century library. Notice the graceful carving and the characteristic roofline with four separate elevations. The sculptural *devata* (Buddhist spirits) figures, in both dancing and meditative poses, are thought to have been made during King Muang Kaeo's reign in the early 16th century. They decorate a stone base designed to keep the fragile *sa* (mulberry bark) manuscripts elevated from flooding and vermin.

On the other side of the temple complex is the 200-year-old **Lai Kham (Gilded Hall) Wihaan,** housing the venerated image of the Phra Singh or **Sighing Buddha,** brought to the site by King Muang Ma in 1400. The original Buddha's head was stolen in 1922, but the reproduction in its place doesn't diminish the homage paid to this figure during Songkran. Inside are frescoes illustrating the stories of Sang Thong (the Golden Prince of the Conch Shell) and Suwannahong. These images convey a great deal about the religious, civil, and military life of 19th-century Chiang Mai during King Mahotraprathet's reign.

Samlarn and Ratchadamnoen roads. Suggested donation 20B (50¢). Daily 6am–5pm.

**Wat Suan Dok**   This complex is special less for its architecture (the buildings, though monumental, are undistinguished) than for its contemplative spirit and pleasant surroundings.

The temple was built amid the pleasure gardens of the 14th-century Lanna Thai monarch, King Ku Na. Unlike most of Chiang Mai's other *wats* (more tourist sights than working temples and schools), Wat Suan Dok houses quite a few monks who seem to have isolated themselves from the distractions of the outside world.

Among the main attractions in the complex are the *bot,* with a very impressive **Chiang Saen Buddha** (one of the largest bronzes in the north) dating from 1504 and some garish murals; the *chedi,* built to hold a relic of the Buddha; and a royal cemetery with some splendid shrines.

There is also an informal "monk chat," where monks and lay visitors can share views, every Monday, Wednesday, and Friday from 5 to 7pm. Unique.

Suthep Rd. (from the Old City, take the Suan Dok Gate and continue 1.6km/1 mile west). Suggested donation 20B (50¢). Daily 6am–5pm.

## MUSEUMS
### Chiang Mai City Arts and Cultural Center
In the building adjacent to the Three Kings Monument in the heart of the Old City, this new museum houses a permanent exhibit that walks visitors through a tour of prehistory to the present. Another section houses short-term local exhibits of all types.

Propokklao Rd. © 05321-7793. Admission 90B ($2.25). Tues–Sun 9am–5pm.

### Chiang Mai National Museum
While its collection of historical treasures is not nearly as extensive as that of Bangkok's National Museum, this quick stop does provide something of a historical overview of the region, the city, and historical highlights. The Lanna Kingdom, Tai people, and hill tribes are highlighted in simple displays with English explanations.

Just off the superhighway northwest of the Old City near Wat Chet Yot. © 05322-1308. Admission 30B (75¢). Tues–Sun 8:30am–4pm.

## CULTURAL PURSUITS
### THAI COOKING SCHOOL

If you love Thai food and want to learn how to make it, look into a class at the **Chiang Mai Cookery School** 👍, the oldest establishment of its kind in Chiang Mai. It has five 1-day courses, each designed to teach Thai cooking basics but with a different menu (up to seven dishes) so you can attend as many days as you like and still gain quite a bit of skill. You'll have hands-on training, and a lot of fun. Classes start at 10am lasting until 4pm, and cost 900B ($23) for the day. Contact the main office at 1–3 Moonmuang Rd. opposite the Ta Pae Gate. Look for the RECOMMENDED BY FROMMER'S sign in the window (ⓒ **05320-6388;** fax 05320-6387; www.thaicookeryschool.com).

### MASSAGE SCHOOL

Northern-style Thai massage is something closer to yoga, where your muscles are stretched and elongated to enhance flexibility and relaxation. There are a number of schools in Chiang Mai. Try the **International Training Massage (ITM),** where a 5-day course is 2,400B ($60). Contact the school at 17/7 Morakot Rd., Hah Yaek Santitham (ⓒ **05321-8632;** fax 05322-4197).

### MEDITATION

The **Northern Insight Meditation Center** at Wat Rampoeng (Kan Klong-chonprathan Rd.) is a well-respected center for learning Vipassana meditation. "Are you ready?" is all they'll ask you upon arrival. Check its website (www.watrampoeng.cjb.net) or call ahead for info: ⓒ **05327-8620.**

## CHIANG MAI ACTIVITIES
### TOURS, TREKS & OUTDOOR ADVENTURE

**For jungle trekking,** there are a number of small outfits that arrange trips from Chiang Mai. **Contact Travel** (www.activethailand.com) is in a category all its own and can combine treks and village stays with multisport adventures by jeep, bicycle, and kayak. The office in Chiang Mai is 73/7 Charoen Prathet Rd. (ⓒ **05327-7178;** fax 05327-9505).

Small operators that cater to the backpacker market offer trips for as little as 500B ($13) per day. This can mean you'll be in a large group and care and feeding comes at a lower standard, but that's budget trekking. **Top North Tours** (41 Moonmuang Rd., Chiang Mai; ⓒ **05320-8788**) or **Queen Bee Travel Service** (5 Moonmuang Rd. Chiang Mai; ⓒ **05327-5525**) are both good.

### ELEPHANT RIDING

One of Thailand's greatest treasures, the domesticated Asian elephant has worked alongside men since the early history of Siam, and these gentle giants are an important symbol of the kingdom. There are a total of 14 elephant camps near Chiang Mai, some with animals in rather dire condition. Far above the rest is the **Young Elephant Training Center** in Lampang (see the Lampang section below) where visitors work with the animals. Of the others, try **Maetamann Elephant Camp** (535 Rimtai, Maerim, Chiang Mai 50180; ⓒ **05329-7060**). Day-tours include a few hours of hill trekking in a basket on elephant-back.

### GOLF

Golf is the activity du jour in Chiang Mai, especially among the many Western retirees and vacationing Thais. All courses below are open to the public and offer equipment rental. Call ahead to reserve a tee time.

- **Chiang Mai Green Valley Country Club,** located in Mae Rim, 20 minutes north of town on Route 107, 183/2 Chotana Rd. (© **05329-8249;** fax 05327-9386), is in excellent condition with flat greens and fairways that slope toward the Ping River (greens fees: weekdays 1,200B/$30; weekends 2,000B/$50).
- **Lanna Golf Club,** on Chotana Road 2km (1¼ miles) north of the Old City (© **05322-1911;** fax 05322-1743), is a challenging, wooded 27 holes and a local favorite with great views of Doi Suthep Mountain (greens fees: weekdays 600B/$15; weekends 800B/$20).
- **Chiang Mai–Lamphun Country Club,** Baan Thi Road, 10km (6¼ miles) east of Sankamphaeng (© **05324-8397;** fax 05324-8937), located in a valley to the east, is a fine 18-hole course (greens fees: weekdays 1,400B/$34; weekends 1,800B/$45).

## SPAS & MASSAGE

Most hotels offer massage and beauty treatments, and there are lots of street-side massage places of varying quality and reputation. **The Four Seasons Resort** (Mae Rim–Samoeng Old Rd.; © **05329-8181**) has some of the finest spa facilities in Thailand and, though it comes with a high price tag, the quality and service is over the top. **Baan Sabai** (17/7 Charoen Prathet Rd.; © **05328-5204**) is the bridge between the expensive services of a five-star spa and the affordable street-side places. **Let's Relax,** located in Chiang Mai Pavilion (on the 2nd floor above McDonald's, 145/27 Changklan Rd.; © **05381-8498**) has good rates and makes for a good break from shopping.

## SHOPPING

If you plan to shop in Thailand, save your money for Chiang Mai. Quality craft pieces and hand-made, traditional items still sell for very little and large outlets for fine antiques and high-end goods abound in and around the city. Many shoppers pick up an affordable new piece of luggage to tote their finds home and, if you find that huge standing Buddha or oversize Thai divan you've been searching for, all shops can arrange shipping.

## MARKETS

The **Night Bazaar,** on Chang Klan Road between the Old Town and the river, is the city's premier attraction. Shopping starts around 6pm each night and slows down at about 11pm. The actual Night Bazaar is a modern, antiseptic, three-story building, but the indoor and outdoor market extends south to Sri Dornchai Road and far beyond. Many shops and stalls remain open throughout the day and evening too, especially along Chang Klan Road. Some stalls have grandiose names, like Harrods (with the familiar logo), and most carry Bangkok-produced counterfeits of international name-brand clothing, watches, and luggage. There are thousands of pirated audiotapes and videodiscs, acres of burnished brown "bone" objects, masks, wood carvings, opium pipes, opium weights, you name it.

## SHOPPING IN THE CITY CENTER & OLD TOWN

Small shops and boutiques line the areas around the night bazaar and Old Town. Try **Ginger** (39/1 Loi Kroh; © **05320-6842**) with fine designer clothing and jewelry. Sleek designs steal the show at **Living Space** (276–278 Ta Pae Rd.; © **05387-4299**) with its collection of home furnishing, celadon, and laquerware. **Nova Collection** (201 Ta Pae Rd.; © **05327-3058**) carries a unique line of decorative jewelry in contemporary styles with Asian influences. **Princess Jewelry** (41 Changklan Rd. near Chiang Inn Plaza; © **05327-3648**) has customized and ready-made jewelry and good personalized service. For silk, try **City Silk** (336 Ta Pae Rd., 1 block east of the gate; © **05323-4388**).

## WEST SIDE OF THE OLD CITY

At 95 Nimanhemin Rd. across from Amari Rincome Hotel, **Nantawan Arcade** has many notable antiques, crafts, and curio shops that make for fun browsing. **Gong Dee Gallery** (© **05321-5768**) has a fine collection of gifts and original artwork, the best of the many here.

## SANKAMPHAENG ROAD

Shopaholics will be thrilled by the many outlets along the Chiang Mai–Sankamphaeng Road (Rte. 1006). Rent your own wheels or hop on the white *songtaos* that follow this busy road due east of town. After several kilometers you'll reach the many shops, showrooms, and factories extending along a 9km (5½ miles) strip. The many shops along Sankamphaeng feature anything from lacquerware to ready-made clothes, silver to celadon pottery. For pottery, try **Baan Celadon** (7 Moo 3, Chiang Mai–Sankamphaeng Rd.; © **05333-8288**); and **Siam Celadon** (38 Moo 13, Chiang Mai–Sankamphaeng Rd.; © **05333-1526**). There is also a **Shinawatra Thai Silk** outlet (145/1–2 Sankamphaeng Rd.; © **05333-8058**).

## CHIANG MAI AFTER DARK

The Night Bazaar area is the center of nighttime activity. There are lots of small bars, clubs, and go-go joints in the area. If you get tired and hungry along the way, you'll want to stop at **Kalare Food & Shopping Center** (89/2 Chang Klan Rd., on the corner of Soi 6, behind the bazaar; © **05327-2067**). There are free cultural dance shows nightly.

For a more studied **cultural performance,** the **Old Chiang Mai Cultural Center,** 185/3 Wulai Rd. (© **05327-4093**), stages a good show at 7pm every night for 270B ($6.75), which includes dinner and the show. Enjoy a *khan toke* meal and live music and dance. Yup, it's touristy, but a rollicking good time.

The following are just a few bars and clubs: **Good View** (13 Charoenrat Rd.; © **05324-1866**) and the **Riverside** (9/11 Charoenrat Rd.; © **05324-3239**) are both popular restaurants along the Mae Ping River and feature live music. Directly east of the Night Bazaar and in the large compound of the old Diamond Hotel, **River Bar** (33/11 Jarenprathat Rd.; © **05320-6169**) has live music nightly and is always full. The **Bubble Disco** in Pornping Tower (see "Where to Stay," earlier in this section; 46 Charoen Prathit Rd.; © **05327-0099**) and **Crystal Cave Disco at Empress Hotel** (Chang Klan Rd.; © **05327-0240**) are two popular haunts but seem to take turns getting shut down.

## SIDE TRIPS FROM CHIANG MAI

If you have time for only a 1 day trip, Wat Phra That Doi Suthep, Chiang Mai's famed mountain and temple, is the best choice.

### WAT PHRA THAT DOI SUTHEP ✿✿✿

The jewel of Chiang Mai, Wat Phra That glistens in the sun on the slopes of Doi Suthep mountain. At 1,000m (3,280 ft.), the temple occupies an extraordinary site with a cool refreshing climate, expansive views over the city, and the mountain's idyllic forests, waterfalls, and flowers.

In the 14th century, during the installation of a relic of the Buddha in Wat Suan Dok (in the Old City), the holy object split in two, with one part equaling the original size. A new *wat* was needed to honor the miracle. King Ku Na placed the new relic on a sacred white elephant and let it wander freely through the hills. The elephant climbed to the top of Doi Suthep, trumpeted three times, made three counterclockwise circles, and knelt down, choosing the site for Wat Phra That.

The site is highly revered and Thai visitors come to make an offering—usually flowers, candles, incense, and small squares of gold leaf that are applied to a favored Buddha or to the exterior of a *chedi*—and to be blessed. It's best to wear long trousers; visitors in shorts are offered a sarong for decency.

The site is open from 7am to 5pm. The suggested donation is 20B (50¢). To get there, take the 35B (90¢) minibus from Chiang Mai's Chang Puak Gate. Bring a sweater or jacket as it gets cold.

## LAMPANG ⊛

The sprawling town of Lampang (originally called Khelang Nakhon) was once famous for its exclusive reliance on the horse and carriage for transportation long after the car was introduced. In fact, old-style horse buggies can still be rented near the center of town next to the City Hall.

Sprawling Lampang has some of the finest Burmese temples in Thailand, and short tours by horse and carriage, the town's traditional mode of transport, are popular. Outside of town, don't miss the **Young Elephant Training Center** (54km/33 miles east of town; ℂ **05422-9042**). The center is not a tourist site per se and nothing like the pony-ride atmosphere of most elephant camps; instead, the focus at the Young Elephant Training Center is on the animals, their care, and their interaction with humans. It has unique programs where home stay visitors learn how to be elephant mahouts.

## DOI INTHANON NATIONAL PARK

Thailand's tallest mountain, **Doi Inthanon**—2,563m (8,406 ft.)—is 47km (29 miles) south of Chiang Mai. It crowns a 932-sq.-km (363-sq.-mile) national park filled with impressive waterfalls and wild orchids. There is a road to the summit, and along the way is the 30m-high (98-ft.) **Mae Klang Falls,** a popular picnic spot with food stands, and the best of the many falls. Admission is 200B ($5).

## THE MAE SA VALLEY

The picturesque Mae Sa Valley area is about 20km (12 miles) northwest of Chiang Mai. Current attractions include an elephant show, a snake show, bungee jumping, and a nature park, as well as orchid nurseries. Most of these attractions are packaged by Chiang Mai tour operators as a half-day trip.

### 24 Touring the Northern Hills

North of Chiang Mai and its satellite cities, travelers enter a mountainous region that promises lots of adventure. Rugged hills, proximity to Myanmar (Burma) and Laos, and the diverse ethnic hill-tribe groups living here distinguish northern Thailand from the rest of the country. The mighty Mekong River flows southeast from the Golden Triangle, the opium-producing region straddling Burma and Laos, and the river traces a path along dense jungles and teak forests. This is the land of the elephants, of the ancient Lanna culture, of backwater bordertowns and adventure around every turn.

## The Mae Hong Son Loop

Seasoned travelers, given the option, never backtrack, and the "Loop" through the rugged hills north and west of Chiang Mai is gaining popularity for that very reason. Connecting the towns of Pai and Mae Hong Son, the circuit continues to out-of-the way Mae Sariang before returning to Chiang Mai. For all but the adventurous, going by tour or a hired car with driver is recommended, but a self-drive means freedom to take side trips and explore at one's own pace. The road, especially on the northernmost points, is serpentine and precipitous and calls for good driving skills (watch for anything from smoke-belching buses to buffalos). Give yourself 4 days to do it, staying 1 night at least in each town.

The most useful resource for a self-guided tour by car or motorbike is a map entitled *Mae Hong Son, The Loop* (published *The Golden Triangle Rider* and priced at 175B/$4.40; www.gt-rider.com)

Your first stop is **Pai,** 135km (84miles) northwest of Chiang Mai. It's a quiet town, with mountains on all sides and a laid-back vibe (lots of travelers get "stuck" here). Overnight **rafting** trips on the Pai River with **Thai Adventure Rafting** (Rangsiyanon Rd.; ✆ **05369-9111**) are popular July to January.

**Belle Villa** (113 Moo 6, Tumol Viengtai; ✆ **05369-8226-7;** www. bellevillaresort.com) is the one high-end choice just outside of town, with cozy stilted villas starting from 2,943B ($74). Guesthouses abound in Pai. Try **Rim Pai Cottages** in the town center (✆ 05369-9133).

Between Pai and Mae Hong Son you'll find the **Lod,** or **Spirit Cave,** some 8km/5miles north of the highway. This large, awe-inspiring cave is filled with colorful stalagmites and stalactites and small caverns will keep you exploring for hours. Hire a guide with a lantern at the entrance (100B/$2.50) and pay for ferry crossings (200B/$5).

**Mae Hong Son,** the next stop on the loop, sits on the very edge of Burma and is the largest town amid the scenic woodlands, waterways, and unique hill-tribe villages of the area. The town is famed for cool weather, an eerie morning mist, and the bursts of fall foliage. It's a good base for trekking. Contact **Rose Garden Tours** (86/4 Khunlumprapas Rd.; ✆/fax **05361-1577**), which arranges treks and visits to nearby **Padung Villages** peopled by the famed **"long-neck Karen."**

The best place to stay in town is the luxury **Imperial Tara Mae Hong Son** (149 Moo 8, Tampon Pang Moo; ✆ **05361-1021**) with rooms from 4,000B ($100). A good in-town budget choice is **Bai Yoke Chalet** (90 Khunlumprapas, Chong Kham; ✆ **05361-1536;** from 1,400B/$35).

**Mae Sariang** is just a cozy river town and the best halfway stopover on the long southern link between Mae Hong Son and Chiang Mai. Driving in the area, along Route 108, takes you past pastoral villages, scenic rolling hills, and a few enticing side trips to small local temples and waterfalls. Mae Sariang offers only basic accommodations. Try **Riverhouse Hotel** (77 Langpanich Rd.; ✆ **05362-1201**).

## 25 Chiang Rai

780km (484 miles) NE of Bangkok; 180km (112 miles) NE of Chiang Mai

Chiang Rai is Thailand's northernmost province. The Mekong River makes its borders with Laos to the east and Burma to the west. The smaller yet scenic Mae Kok River, which supports many hill-tribe villages along its banks, flows right through the provincial capital of the same name.

Chiang Rai lies some 565m (1,853 ft.) above sea level in a wide fertile valley, and its cool, refreshing climate, tree-lined riverbanks, and popular Night Market lures travelers weary of traffic congestion and pollution in Chiang Mai. Although Chiang Rai has some passable hotels and restaurants and a few small attractions, most just use this as a base for trips to Chiang Saen and the Golden Triangle.

## ESSENTIALS
### GETTING THERE
**By Plane    Thai Airways** (☎ **05321-0431** in Chiang Mai) has four daily flights from Bangkok to Chiang Rai (85 min.) or Chiang Mai as well (30 min.).

The **Chiang Rai International Airport** (☎ **05379-3048**) is 10km (6¼ miles) north of town. Taxis to town are about 150B ($3.80).

**By Bus**    Three air-conditioned VIP 24-seat buses leave daily from Bangkok's **Northern Bus Terminal** (☎ **02936-2852**) to Chiang Rai (trip time: 11 hr.; 700B/$18). Buses leave from Chiang Mai's **Arcade Bus Terminal** (☎ **05324-2664**) hourly between 6am and 5:30pm (trip time: 3½ hr.; 66B/$1.65 non-A/C; 119B/$3 A/C). Chiang Rai's **Khon Song Bus Terminal** (☎ **05371-1369**) is near the Night Market just in the center of town. Tuk-tuks and *samlors* connect to hotels for 30B to 60B (75¢–$1.50).

**By Car**    The fast, not particularly scenic, route from Bangkok is Highway 1 north, direct to Chiang Rai. A slow, scenic approach on blacktop mountain roads is Route 107 north from Chiang Mai to Fang, then Route 109 east to Highway 1.

### VISITOR INFORMATION
The **TAT** (☎ **05374-4674**) is located at 448/16 Singhakai Rd., near Wat Phra Singh on the north side of town. Good free maps and info are available anywhere.

### ORIENTATION
Chiang Rai is a small city, with most services grouped around the main north-south street, Phaholythin Road. The Mae Kok River forms the north edge of town. The bus station is near the central Night Market just off Phaholythin Road.

### GETTING AROUND
Chiang Rai is small enough to explore on foot; however, there are *samlors* (pedicabs) and tuk-tuks, which charge 30B to 60B (75¢–$1.50) in town.

**By Motorcycle**    A good choice to get out of town. **Soon Motorcycle,** 197/2 Trirath Rd. (☎ **05371-4068**), charges 180B ($4.50) for a 100cc motorbike.

**By Car    Budget** has a branch at the Golden Triangle Inn (see "Where to Stay," below; 590 Phaholythin Rd.; ☎ **05371-1339**), offering a standard rate beginning at 1,500B ($38) for a Suzuki Caribian.

## FAST FACTS

Several **bank** exchanges are located on Phaholythin Road in the center of town and are open daily from 8:30am to 10pm. The **post office** is 2 blocks north of the Clock Tower on Uttarakit Road. There are a few **Internet cafes** along the main drag, Phaholythin Road, with average service for 20B (50¢) per hour. The **Overbrook Hospital** (© 05371-1366) is on the north side of town at Singhakai and Trairat roads, west of the TAT. The **Tourist Police** (© 05371-7796) are next to the TAT on Singhakai Road.

## THINGS TO SEE & DO

There are a number of fine *wats* in town: **Wat Phra Kaeo,** on Trairat Road on the northwest quadrant, is the best known of the northern *wats* because it once housed the Emerald Buddha now at Bangkok's royal Wat Phra Kaeo. **Wat Phra Singh,** a restored 15th-century temple, is 2 blocks east of Wat Phra Kaeo; and the Burmese-style **Wat Doi Tong** (Phra That Chomtong) sits atop a hill above the northwest side of town, up a steep staircase off Kaisornrasit Road, and offers an overview of the town and a panorama of the Mae Kok valley. It's said that King Mengrai himself chose the site for his new Lanna capital from this very hill.

The **Mae Kok River** is one of the most scenic attractions in Chiang Rai. You can hire a longtail boat for day trips to outlying villages.

## TREKKING & HILL-TRIBE TOURS

Most of the **hill-tribe villages** within close range of Chiang Rai have long ago been set up for routine visits by group tours (not recommended), but there are a few good outfitters. The best operation is **Golden Triangle Tours,** 590 Phaholythin Rd. (© 05371-1339; www.goldenchiangrai.com). It offers everything from 1-day hill-tribe treks to week-long adventures.

## WHERE TO STAY

With the exception of the two expensive resorts across the river, most hotels are within walking distance of the sights and shopping.

### EXPENSIVE

**Dusit Island Resort Hotel** ★★   Chiang Rai's best resort hotel occupies a large delta island in the Mae Kok River and is comfortable at the expense of atmosphere. The lobby is grand, with panoramic views of the river. Rooms are luxuriously appointed in pastel cottons and teak trim. The hotel has manicured grounds, pool, and numerous facilities that make the resort quite self-contained. Tenth-floor dining at the Peak offers sweeping views, and the Chinatown restaurant serves good Cantonese. Stop by the Music Room bar in the evening.

1129 Kraisorasit Rd., Amphur Muang 57000, Chiang Rai (over bridge at northwest corner of town). © 05371-5777. Fax 05371-5801. www.dusit.com. 271 units. 4,532B–5,179B ($113–$129) superior/deluxe double; from 7,769B ($194) suite. AE, DC, MC, V. **Amenities:** 3 restaurants; lounge and pub; outdoor pool; lighted tennis courts; fitness center w/Jacuzzi, sauna, steam, and massage; game room; concierge; tour desk; car-rental desk; limo service; 24-hr. room service; babysitting; same-day laundry service/dry cleaning; nonsmoking rooms; executive-level rooms. *In room:* A/C, satellite TV, minibar, fridge, safe.

### MODERATE

**Rimkok Resort Hotel** ★   It's a bit distant from town but thoroughly self-contained and done on a large scale. Guest rooms are airy with high ceilings and balconies and some Thai touches in an overall bland but comfortable setup. Public spaces are capped with high-peaked Thai roofs. Lushly planted lawns surround the large central pool. There are also regular shuttles to town.

6 Moo 4, Tathorn Rd., Amphur Muang, 57100 Chiang Rai (on north shore of Kok River, about 6km/3¾ miles north of town center). ✆ 05371-6445. Fax 05371-5859. www.rimkokresort.com. 256 units. 1,900B ($48) double; from 6,000B ($150) suite. AE, DC, MC, V. **Amenities:** 3 restaurants; bar and lounge; large outdoor pool; Jacuzzi; tour desk; limo service; business center; shopping; salon; limited room service; babysitting; same-day laundry service. *In room:* A/C, satellite TV, minibar, fridge.

**Wangcome Hotel** ✯   The Wangcome is located just a stone's throw from the Night Market and is the best downtown hotel. Rooms are small but comfortable, detailed with Lanna Thai touches like fine carved teak headboards. Central rooms face an outdoor swimming pool. There's a lively coffee shop and a moody cocktail lounge, a popular rendezvous spot after the Night Market closes.

896/90 Penawibhata Rd., Chiang Rai Trade Center, Amphur Muang 57000, Chiang Rai (west off Paholyothin Rd.). ✆ 05371-1800. Fax 05371-2973. 234 units. 1,600B ($40) double; from 2,000B ($50) suite. AE, DC, MC, V. **Amenities:** Restaurant; lounge; small pool; tour desk; limo service; business center; massage; laundry service. *In room:* A/C, satellite TV, minibar, fridge.

## INEXPENSIVE

**The Golden Triangle Inn** ✯✯   The Golden Triangle is set in its own quiet little garden patch. Large rooms have terra-cotta-tiled floors and traditional-style furniture and decoration. Staff is helpful and their in-house travel agency, **Golden Triangle Tours,** is the best choice in town for arranging travel in the area. The Thai restaurant is excellent.

590 Paholyothin Rd., Amphur Muang 57000, Chiang Rai (2 blocks north of bus station). ✆ **05371-1339.** Fax 05371-3963. 30 units. 900B ($23) double. MC, V. **Amenities:** Restaurant; tour desk; car-rental desk; laundry service. *In room:* A/C, no phone.

## WHERE TO DINE

After 7pm the **Night Market** is the best for budget eats, but beyond that there are a few good restaurants to choose from. Be sure to sample the town's delicacies like the huge *ching kong* catfish, caught in April to May; litchis, which ripen in June and July; and the sweet *nanglai* pineapple wine. Also find a branch of Bangkok's **Cabbages & Condoms** (620/25 Thanalai Rd.; ✆ **05371-9167**), a good Thai restaurant that promotes its unique humanitarian work. **The Golden Triangle Café** ✯ at the Golden Triangle Inn (see listing above) serves great regional treats from a menu that is a short course in Thai cuisine.

## 26 Chiang Saen ✯ & the Golden Triangle

935km (580 miles) NE of Bangkok; 239km (148 miles) NE of Chiang Mai

The small village of Chiang Saen has a sleepy, rural charm, as if the waters of the Mekong carry a palpable calm from nearby Burma and Laos. Chiang Saen was abandoned for the new Lanna Thai capitals of Chiang Rai, then Chiang Mai, in the 13th century, and today the decaying regal *wats,* crumbling fort walls, and overgrown moat contribute greatly to its appeal. After visiting the museum and local sites, most travelers head west along the Mekong to the Golden Triangle, the north's prime attraction.

The nearby **Golden Triangle** is less mysterious than its reputation and more like a row of souvenir stalls, but if you stand at the crook of the river, you can look to the right to see Laos and to the left to see Myanmar (Burma).

## ESSENTIALS
### GETTING THERE

**By Bus**   Buses from **Chiang Rai's Kohn Song Bus Terminal** leave every 15 minutes from 6am to 6pm (trip time: 1½ hr.; 20B/50¢). The bus drops you on

Chiang Saen's main street. The museum and temples are within walking distance. Public *songtao,* or pickups, make frequent trips between Chiang Saen and the Golden Triangle for about 20B/50¢.

**By Car**    Take the superhighway Route 110 north from Chiang Rai to Mae Chan, then Route 1016 northeast to Chiang Saen.

## VISITOR INFORMATION
The nearest **TAT** office is in Chiang Rai. Pick up a useful map at the Chiang Saen National Museum (see below).

## ORIENTATION
Route 1016 is the village's main street, also called Phaholythin Road, which terminates at the Mekong River. Along the river road there are a few guesthouses, eateries, and souvenir, clothing, and food stalls.

## GETTING AROUND
**By Bicycle & Motorcycle**    It's a great bike ride (45 min.) from Chiang Saen to the prime nearby attraction, the Golden Triangle. The roads are well paved and pretty flat. There are a few rental outlets along the river (30B/75¢ per day).

**By Samlor**    Motorized pedicabs hover by the bus stop in town to take you to the Golden Triangle for 60B ($1.50) one-way.

**By Songtao**    Songtao (truck taxis) can be found on the main street across from the market; rides cost only 20B (50¢) to the Golden Triangle.

**By Longtail Boat**    Longtail boat captains wait down by the river and offer Golden Triangle tours for as little as 400B ($10) per boat (seating eight) per half-hour. Many people enjoy the half-hour cruise, take a walk around the village of Sob Ruak after they've seen the Golden Triangle, and then continue on by bus.

## FAST FACTS
There's a **Siam Commercial Bank** in the center of Phaholythin Road, Route 1016, the main street, just close to the **bus stop, post, and telegram office.** There is a **currency exchange** booth at the Golden Triangle.

## WHAT TO SEE & DO
Allow a half-day to see all of Chiang Saen's historical sights before exploring the Golden Triangle. The **Chiang Saen National Museum** (702 Phaholythin Rd.; ✆ 05377-7102; 30B/75¢) is a good first stop, with an overview of artifacts from 15th- to 17th-century Lanna Thai. The temples of Chiang Saen are all within walking distance. **Wat Pa Sak** is the best preserved; the oldest is **Wat Phra Chedi Luang** and all are fine samples of Lanna temples.

## THE GOLDEN TRIANGLE
The infamous Golden Triangle (12km/7½ miles northwest of Chiang Saen) is the point where Thailand, Burma, and Laos meet at the confluence of the broad, slow, and silted Mekong and Mae Ruak rivers. Once a no man's land of the international drug trade, the area is a unique vantage point for life in the north.

The **Hall of Opium** ✺✺ (10km/6¼ miles northwest of Chiang Saen; ✆ 05365-2151; www.goldentrianglepark.org) is a sprawling museum overlooking the Mekong. It is a walk through the curious cultivation of poppies and the history of the opium trade. There is also information about the Thai war on drugs.

## Onward to Laos

Many make Chiang Rai or Chiang Saen their last port of call in the land of Thai and head overland to rugged but inviting Laos. It is possible to travel downriver 70km (43 miles) to Chiang Khong, a small border town from which you can catch a boat or bus into the Land of a Thousand Elephants, Laos. Buses and local *songtao* also make the connection from either Chiang Rai or Chiang Saen. For more info, see chapter 5, "Laos."

## WHERE TO STAY

**Anantara Resort and Spa Golden Triangle** ★★   The newly opened Anantara is a triumph of upscale, local design. Every detail reminds you that you're in the scenic hill-tribe region and the resort features fine local weavings, carved teak panels, and expansive views of the juncture of the Ruak and Mekong Rivers. The balconied rooms have splendid views and are so spacious and private you'll feel like you're in your own bungalow. Tiled foyers lead to large bathrooms and bedrooms are furnished in teak and traditional fabrics.

229 Moo 1, Chiang Saen 57150, Chiang Rai (above river, 12km/7½ miles northwest of Chiang Saen). ② 800/ 225-5843 in the U.S., or 05378-4084. Fax 05378-4090. www.anantara.com. 90 units. 4,100B–5,700B ($103–$143) double; 11,000B ($275) suite. AE, DC, MC, V. **Amenities:** 3 restaurants; lounge and bar; outdoor pool; outdoor lighted tennis courts; fitness center w/Jacuzzi, Mandara Spa w/sauna, and massage; bike rental; concierge; tour desk; car-rental desk; limo service; business center; shopping arcade; salon; limited room service; babysitting; same-day laundry service. *In room:* A/C, satellite TV w/in-house movies, minibar, fridge, coffee/tea-making facilities, hair dryer, safe.

The next step down from the luxurious Anantara is the **Imperial Golden Triangle Resort** (222 Golden Triangle, in Sob Ruak, 11km/7 miles northwest of Chiang Saen); ② **05378-4001**), a clean but uninspired hotel with rooms from 2,800B ($70). There are great views of the river from the top floor.

In tiny Chiang Saen, the **Chiang Saen River Hill Hotel** (714 Moo 3 Tambol Viang, Chaeng Saen; 5-min. *samlor* ride from bus stop; ② **05365-0826**) has clean, basic air-conditioned rooms from 800B ($20).

# 5

# Laos

*by Charles Agar*

**W**hen you leave, don't worry that you find it difficult to summarize your experiences in "The Jewel of Southeast Asia"; many travelers come away from Laos with only a vague sense that they'd like to return and do so quickly before that special "something" is gone. Fear not, though, for change comes slowly, and the genuine smiles of Laos's kind people endure.

Sixty percent of Lao people are practicing Buddhists, and that fact colors every facet of life. Temples and stupas dominate the architecture of even the smallest village, and you're sure to spot groups of monks in colorful robes—best on their early morning *pintabat,* or alms rounds, especially in Luang Prabang. Buddhist acceptance and compassion play an important part in Lao culture; arguments are the exception and the *sangha,* or monastic community, fosters a strict moral code. Even the shortest visit to Laos offers unique insight into Buddhist culture.

A developing country, one of the poorest in the world, rural Laos is heavily supported by international grants and nongovernmental organization (NGO) projects; the official white LandRovers of development workers can be seen everywhere in country. Opium production, once a major industry in the far north, has decreased to barely a trickle—an estimated 75% reduction—and legitimate trade with China and Thailand bodes well for the future.

Rugged Laos is popular for hearty backpackers willing to brave rough roads and basic accommodations for a bit of adventure. Opportunities for caving, kayaking, and trekking abound. There is something special about the traveler camaraderie and connection to locals on an all-day bumpy bus ride or lazy boat journey, and a trip to Laos is certainly about the journey, not the destination. There are some exciting eco-touring options for getting off-the-track in pristine jungle or among ethnic minorities, but only quiet villages and dusty, one-horse towns pass for tour destinations outside of the two major cities. Rural travel begs caution as only bare-bones accommodations and services are available.

Laos has a diverse geography and population. The north is a rich tapestry of ethnic minorities, and Lao people themselves support cultural and ethnic enclaves that differ from region to region, hill to plain. The mighty Mekong River and its tributaries form the spine of the land, and the country boasts vast tracts of deep jungle, open farmland, and even tropical river islands. Remnants of ancient civilizations are here as well, including the mysterious **Plain of Jars** in Phonsavan and **Wat Phu,** a Hindu site that predates Angkor Wat near the Cambodia border. **Luang Prabang,** the biggest burg up north, is a quiet city of colonial French architecture and was named a UNESCO World Heritage site.

With recent infrastructure development and rising tourism, many fear

## Warning  Travel Advisory

Travelers to Laos should refer to the U.S. State Department Travel Advisory regarding the present situation in the area (go to www.travel.state.gov and click "Travel Warnings"). Laos is not a dangerous destination, by any means, but it's important to remember that the current climate of calm and openness to visitors is quite short historically. Visitors should just keep in mind some late events and have an ear to the ground when in country.

In the winter and spring of 2003 there were a number of attacks on buses traveling on Route 13, the major north-south highway, just north of Vang Vieng. As a result, visitors are advised to avoid the journey between Vang Vieng and Luang Prabang (though the road is open to tourists) and stay abreast of the situation through the CDC or press. Attacks are attributed to Hmong rebels who have been fighting the Lao government for a number of years. Travelers in the countryside should also remember that bus and boat breakdowns are frequent, and road conditions and poor infrastructure make rural travel unpredictable. Hospital facilities, even in the capital, are rudimentary, at best, and any serious medical condition requires evacuation. UXO, unexploded ordnance left from years of conflict, is still a major concern, especially in Xieng Khouang near the Plain of Jars.

It should also be mentioned that Lao Airlines has yet to pass any international standards for safety.

for the natural and cultural resources of this peaceful land-locked nation. If Laos follows neighboring Thailand's model, as it does in many areas, its forests and waterways may be further exploited and, by packaging tourism for mass consumption, ethnic villages may become human zoos. Working with United Nations agencies, the Lao government is taking steps to see that rural development proceeds slowly in order to protect these vital resources.

Culturally, Laos is in fact moving West. Since the last edition of this book, for example, the mobile phone has arrived and little Vientiane is doing all it can to get cosmopolitan. To speak of a country's "innocence" is patronizing, but what is at stake with the DVD hip-hopification of Laos is the loss of a unique and gentle way of life. One woman explained it to me, saying, "When the girls trade the traditional skirt for the miniskirt, then it's all over."

Laos is a place to tread lightly, but foreign travelers are made quite welcome and encouraged to do their part to preserve and participate in cultural practices. The beauty of Laos exists not only along the Mekong at sunset, but in smiles at the market or impromptu Lao lessons on the street corner, things that are easily missed if you're in a hurry. It's an enchanting land that demands that you slow your pace to match its own, and even the shortest visit might add tranquility to your travels.

## 1 Getting to Know Laos

# THE LAY OF THE LAND

Comprising 147,201 sq. km (57,408 sq. miles), roughly the size of Great Britain or the state of Utah, Laos shares borders with China and Myanmar in the north and the northwest, Cambodia in the south, Thailand in the west, and Vietnam to the east. It is divided into 16 provinces. Seventy percent of its land is mountain ranges and plateaus, and with an estimated population of nearly 5.7 million, Laos is one of the most sparsely populated countries in Asia. Natural landmarks include the Annamite Mountains along the border with Vietnam, and the Mekong River, which flows from China and along Laos's border with Thailand. About 55% of the landscape is pristine tropical forest, sheltering such rare and wild animals as elephants, leopards, the Java mongoose, panthers, gibbons, and black bears.

# THE LAO PEOPLE & CULTURE

A group of Russian ethnologists on a recent survey estimated that there are more than 100 distinct ethnic groups in Laos, but it is commonly believed that Laotians fall into 68 different groups. Only 47 groups are fully researched and identified; sadly, many are disappearing by attrition or intermarriage. All Lao ethnicities fit into one of three categories. The lowlanders are **Lao Loum,** the majority group, who live along the lower Mekong and in Vientiane. The **Lao Theung,** low mountain dwellers, live on mountain slopes, and the **Lao Soung** are the hill tribes, or *montagnards.* Eighty percent of the population lives in villages or small hamlets, practicing subsistence farming.

The earliest **Lao religions** were animist, and most hill tribes still practice this belief, often in combination with Buddhism. In minority villages, you'll see elaborate spirit gates, small structures of bamboo and wood often depicting weapons to protect the village (tread lightly if you come across one of these markers because they are of great significance, and touching or even photographing them is a major faux pas). Buddhism predominates, though, and 60% to 80% of all Laotians are practicing Theravada Buddhists. In the morning, monks walk the streets collecting food or alms, eagerly given by the Laotians, who believe it will aid them in the next life. Laotians worship regularly and can often be seen making temple visits. Most young males spend at least 3 months in a *wat,* or monastery, usually around the time of puberty or before they marry. Impressive **religious art** and **architecture** is expressed in a singular Lao style, particularly the "standing" or "praying for rain" Buddha, upright with hands pointing straight down at the earth.

**Music and dance** are integral to the Lao character, and you'll get a taste of it during your stay. Folk or *khaen* music is played with a reed mouth organ, often accompanied by a boxed string instrument. The *lamvong* is the national folk dance, in which participants dance in concentric circles. Don't miss a **Baci ceremony,** where a circle of celebrants chant and sing to honor or bless an event.

Laotians are friendly and easygoing, but you might find it hard to make a close friend. Language will usually be a barrier. There is also a sense that the Lao people are just learning how to approach their foreign visitors. Solo travelers probably have the best chance of making entry into society, and any effort with the Lao language goes a long way. While Laos suffered brutally throughout its colonial history and most horrifically during the Vietnam War, the Lao people want to move on to peace and prosperity rather than dwell on the past. It's very unlikely that an American will be approached with recrimination, but memories are still fresh. Lao people still deal with war fallout literally and figuratively, a result of the unexploded bombs (or UXO) that litter 50% of the country.

## ETIQUETTE

The Lao are generally tolerant people, but there are a few things to keep in mind. First, upon entering a temple or *wat*, you must always remove your shoes. There will usually be a sign, but a good rule of thumb is to take them off before mounting the last flight of stairs. You should also take off your shoes before entering a private home, unless told otherwise.

**Dress modestly.** It's unusual to see bare Lao skin above the elbow or even above the midcalf. Longer shorts and even sleeveless tops are permissible for foreigners of both sexes, but short shorts or skirts and bare bosoms and navels will cause stares and possibly offense, especially in a *wat*.

Men and women should avoid public displays of affection.

Monks are not permitted to touch women or even to speak directly to them anywhere but inside a temple; therefore women should never try to shake hands with or even hand something directly to a monk. On buses, you'll find that Lao people will change seats so that monks sit only near men.

The **traditional greeting** (also a gesture of thanks and farewell) is called the *nop* or *wai*, a slight bow performed with hands in a prayer position. There are many subtleties to the gesture, but best to just return the greeting if you're given one.

The head is considered the most sacred part of the body, and the feet are the lowliest. Therefore, do not casually touch another person's head or even nonchalantly tussle the hair of a child. Don't sit with your legs crossed or otherwise point your feet at something or someone, especially Buddha images. As in most cultures, pointing with the finger is also considered rude; Laotians often use a palms-up hand gesture when signifying direction or indicating a person or thing. If you are seated on the floor, men may sit with the legs crossed, but women should tuck them to one side.

Lao people take a gentle approach to human relationships. A person showing violence or ill temper is regarded with surprise and disapproval. A calm approach will take you farther. Patient persistence and a smile always win out, especially when haggling. It is important to haggle, of course, but just one or two go-rounds are usually enough, and "no" means no.

## LANGUAGE

The **Lao language** resembles Thai, with familiar tones and sounds found in each. While some vocabulary words might cross over, the two tongues—spoken and written—are quite distinct. However, many Lao understand Thai (learned from school texts and TV), so if you've picked up some words and phrases in Thailand, they'll still be useful here and people will understand and correct you with the appropriate Lao phrase. Thankfully, many people in Vientiane and Luang Prabang speak **English,** and older citizens will usually be able to speak **French. Russian** is not uncommon, and **Chinese** is growing in accord with the rising Chinese population (mostly in the north).

Like Thai, Lao has no officially recognized method of Roman alphabet transliteration. As a result, even town and street names have copious spelling irregularities, so for the vocabulary below we have chosen to list only phonetic pronunciations. Most Lao will understand you, even without tones, and will very much appreciate your efforts to speak their language.

# Laos

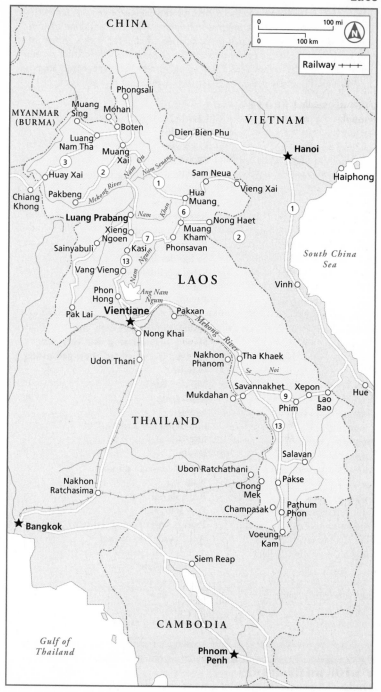

When trying to figure out the correct pronunciation of certain names, it's helpful to remember that the original transliteration of Lao was done by francophones, so consider the French pronunciation when faced with a new word. For example, in Vientiane (pronounced wee-en-*chan*), the wide central avenue spelled Lane Xang is pronounced *Lahn Sahng*. Also in Vientiane, Mixay sounds like *Mee*-sigh. Phonexay is *Pawn*-sigh. It takes awhile, but it's easy to catch.

## USEFUL LAO PHRASES

| English | Lao |
|---------|-----|
| Hello | **Sa bai dee** |
| Goodbye | **Laa kawn** |
| Yes | **Chow/ur** |
| No | **Baw/baw men** (Baw is also a tag to form questions.) |
| Thank you | **Khawp chai** |
| Thank you very much | **Khawp chai lai lai/khawp chai deu** |
| You're welcome/it's nothing | **Baw pen nyahng** |
| No problem | **Baw mi banhaa** |
| How are you? | **Sa bai dee baw?** |
| I'm fine!/ I'm not fine. | **Sabai dee!/ baw sabai.** |
| Where are you going? | **Pai sai?** |
| I'm going traveling/to the market/to eat. | **Pai tiao/Pai talaat/Pai kin kao.** |
| Excuse me | **Khaw thut** (rhymes with "put") |
| Where is the toilet? | **Hawng suam/Hawng nam yoo sai?** |
| May I wear shoes here? | **Sai Gup** (same as "put") **baw pen nyang baw?** |
| Do you have . . . ? | **Mii . . . Baw?** |
| drinking water | **nam-deum** |
| a room | **hawng** |
| a husband/wife | **mia** (common question) |
| Have/don't have | **Mii/baw mii** |
| I would like . . . | **Kaaw . . .** |
| coffee (black)/with cream | **Café daam/café sai noom** |
| tea | **Nam saa** |
| I want to go to . . . | **Koi yak pai . . .** |
| I don't understand. | **Baw kau jai.** |
| Do you speak English/French? | **Passah Angit/Falang dai baw?** |
| How do you say that in Lao? | **Ani Passah Lao nyang?** |
| How much kip/bot/dollar? | **Tao dai kip** (sounds like "keep") **/bot/dollah?** |
| Expensive/too expensive | **peng/peng pawt** |
| Can you make it cheaper? | **Lut dai baw?** |
| Help! | **Sue-wee dah!** |
| Call the police! | **Sue-wee un tam luat dah!** |

## 2 Planning Your Trip to Laos

### VISITOR INFORMATION

The Lao Tourism Authority serves as more of an administrative arm of the government than that of an information service for visitors. It provides some basic brochures if contacted at **National Tourism Authority of Lao P.D.R.,** 08/02

Lane Xang Ave., P.O. Box 2511, Vientiane, Lao P.D.R. (© **021/212-248** or 212-251; fax 021/212-769). The information office in Vientiane has a few good English speakers and is not a bad place to start.

The official Visit Laos website, **www.visit-laos.com**, is sponsored by both the Lao government and private organizations, and is now cross-referenced with other countries in Southeast Asia at **www.mekongcenter.com**. These sites are detailed and accurate, and are very useful supplements with links to other sources of information in the region. For current domestic and international news and government affairs, log on to **http://laoembassy.com**, sponsored and maintained by the Lao Embassy in Washington, D.C.

**Sayo Magazine** (www.sayolaos.com) is available at hotels and bookstores for $2.50 and features articles on local dining, fashion, and happenings.

## ORGANIZED TOURS & TRAVEL AGENTS
In chapter 3, "Planning Your Trip to Southeast Asia," we've outlined major tour operators that organize trips throughout the region. Getting around underdeveloped Laos can be difficult (see "Getting Around," below), so organized travel is, of course, the simplest option.

Independent travel is quite feasible, though, and the same companies that organize group tours can help with hotel and travel arrangements and even create independent tour itineraries.

The most established and widely represented tour operators provide basic, mainstream tours to most provinces for either short trips or extended visits. Destinations include in and around Vientiane, Luang Prabang, Xieng Khouang (Plain of Jars), and Champasak, plus trips to visit Laos's hill tribes or for adventure trips and eco-tourism. When arranging tours or travel with even the larger agents, be absolutely clear about the specifics (meals included, driver's expenses, taxes, etc.). Many tour companies offer the world and come up short.

- **Diethelm Travel,** Namphu Square, Setthathirat Road, P.O. Box 2657, Vientiane, Laos P.D.R. (© **021/213-833;** fax 021/217-151; www.diethelm-travel.com), is open Monday to Friday 8am to noon and 1:30 to 5pm, and Saturday 8am to noon. Operating almost like a de facto tourist information and help center, the folks at Diethelm are the most professional in the country and can arrange deluxe, personalized trips and cover all necessities. Offices are in all major towns (see the information sections in the coverage of each town).
- **Exotissimo Travel,** Pangkham Road (© **021/241-861;** fax 021/252-382; www.exotissimo.com), is a slick and helpful French-owned company. Exotissimo offers fine upscale group and individual, classic, and eco-tours.
- **Inter-Lao Tourism,** 07/073 Luang Prabang Rd., P.O. Box 2912, Vientiane, Laos P.D.R. (© **021/214-832;** fax 021/216-306; www.interlao.laopdr.com), is helpful and has convenient offices in Luang Prabang and Xieng Khouang.
- **Wildside Eco Group,** 54 Setthathirat Rd., Nam Phu Fountain Circle, Vientiane, Laos P.D.R. (© **021/223-022;** www.lao-wildside.com), offers some exciting rafting, kayaking, climbing, and trekking trips on anything from 1-day trips to 1-month expeditions. The helpful international staff caters to both budget travelers and well-heeled adventurers.

## AIR BOOKING
Making your own air arrangements from Vientiane and Luang Prabang is simple, and most travel offices can help for a small fee.

**Lao Airlines** has offices in Vientiane at 2 Pangkham Rd. (© **021/212-057;** reservations 021/214-427; www.laoairlines.com), the best place to book domestic flights. Smaller air booking offices, like **Lao Air Booking Co.** (44/3 Setthathirat Rd. just south of Namphu in Vientiane; © **021/216-761**) or **Blue Bird** (2 Pangkham Rd. across from the Laos Airlines office (bluebird@laotel. com), are good choices for regional connections on international carriers.

## ENTRY REQUIREMENTS

Visitors need a valid passport and visa to visit Laos. There are a number of entry sites where visas are granted upon arrival: by air to Vientiane or Luang Prabang, or when crossing from Thailand over the Friendship Bridge between Vientiane and Nong Khai, or between Chiang Khong and Houayxai in the far north, and Mukdaharn and Savannakhet or Chong Mek and Vung Tao (near Pakse) in the far south. When coming from Vietnam, be sure to have a prearranged visa. Thirty dollars gets you a 15-day visa. At an embassy outside of Laos, the going rate for a 30-day visa is $35, and you'll have to wait up to 5 days for processing, less in Bangkok. For a fee, travel agents in Thailand and other countries in the region can help you jump over the bureaucratic hurdles and get a visa in 1 day. Check the Lao Embassy site at http://laoembassy.com.

Once in Laos, you can extend your visa up to 30 days at $2 per day. It's best to do this through a travel agent. Many hotels, guesthouses, and tour operators offer the service as well (Diethelm has a counter devoted solely to visa affairs). **Lao Tourism** (08/02 Lane Xang Ave., adjacent to the National Tourism Authority; © **021/216-671**) is a government agency and a good choice.

Visa overstay costs $5 per day, levied when you exit the country.

## LAOS EMBASSY LOCATIONS OVERSEAS

**In the U.S.:** Embassy of the Lao People's Democratic Republic, 2222 S St. NW, Washington, DC 20008 (© **202/332-6416;** fax 202/332-4923; www.lao embassy.com); or the Lao P.D.R. Permanent Mission to the United Nations, 317 E. 51st St., New York, NY 10022 (© **212/832-2734;** fax 212/750-0039; www. laoembassy.com/laomission/index.html).

**In Australia:** 1 Dalmain Crescent, O'Malley, Canberra, ACT 2606 (© **02/ 6286-4595;** fax 02/6290-1910).

**In Thailand:** 520/502/1–3 Soi Sahakarnpramoon, Wangthonglang, Bangkok 10310, Pracha Uthit Road (end of Soi Ramkhamhaeng 39; © **539-6667-8** or 539-7341; fax 539-3827 or 539-6678; www.bkklaoembassy.com).

## CUSTOMS REGULATIONS

You may bring 500 cigarettes, 100 cigars, or 500g of tobacco; 1 liter of alcohol; two bottles of wine; and unlimited amounts of money, all for personal use, into Laos without taxation or penalty. Not that the Customs officials do much, if any, searching. However, if you purchase silver or copper items during your stay, you might be required to pay duty upon exiting Laos, according to their weight. Antiques, especially Buddha images or parts thereof, are not permitted to leave the country.

## MONEY

The **kip** (pronounced *keep*), the official Lao unit of currency, comes in denominations of 5, 10, 20, 100, 500, 1,000, 2,000, 5,000, and, only recently issued by the Lao government, 10,000 and 20,000 notes. The new notes are an improvement, but with the current exchange rate (10,000 kip to the dollar), that still means that the largest unit of currency is just $2. For your larger purchases, you'll want to use U.S. dollars, accepted widely, or Thai baht, commonly accepted but more popular near the border. Be prepared to handle bricks of Lao cash when you exchange foreign currency. You might enjoy the comical scene at local banks where businesses cash in and out by toting their large bundles of cash in brimming shopping bags.

**CURRENCY EXCHANGE & RATES**   At press time, the exchange rate was US$1 to 10,000 kip. I've used this rate as the standard for all currency conversions in this chapter.

Laos is very much a cash country, especially outside Vientiane. Virtually all hotel and guesthouse rates, up-market restaurant menus, transportation charges, and expensive purchases, are quoted in U.S. dollars. Payment is always accepted in either U.S. dollars, Thai baht, or Lao kip, so it doesn't always pay to convert all your currency into cumbersome wads of local scraps. For smaller purchases, local transportation, and pocket money, you can exchange currency at Wattay International Airport, in hotels, in banks, and on the black market, with the rate of exchange worst at hotels and best on the black market (though the difference is only negligible).

**Traveler's checks** in U.S. dollars and other major currencies are accepted in all banks in Vientiane and Luang Prabang, and some in Xieng Khouang and Pakse, but rarely by vendors. In other provinces, it's best to carry cash in U.S. dollars, Thai baht, or Lao kip. It's not a bad idea to change traveler's checks into U.S. dollars at a major bank before going for any extended time out of the larger towns (usually at a 2% charge). **Credit cards** are accepted only at major hotels or tour operators (Visa is the most widely accepted). Lao Airlines accepts American Express, MasterCard, and Visa. You can get cash advances from your Visa card at **La Banque pour le Commerce Extérieur Lao (BCEL)** and at **Lane Xang Bank** branches in larger towns throughout the country. Both banks have local ATM service but have yet to make the international link.

**LOST/STOLEN CREDIT CARDS & TRAVELER'S CHECKS**   To report a lost or stolen American Express card, contact **Diethelm Travel,** Setthathirat Road, Namphu Square, Vientiane (© **021/213-833** or 215-920). For other cards, call hot lines in Bangkok (p. 94).

## WHEN TO GO
**PEAK SEASON**   High season for tourism is November through March and the month of August, when weather conditions are favorable. Accommodations run at full capacity and transportation can be overbooked.

**CLIMATE**   Laos's tropical climate ushers in a wet monsoon season lasting from early May through October, followed by a dry season from November to April. In Vientiane, average temperatures range from 71°F (22°C) in January to 84°F (29°C) in April. The northern regions, which include Xieng Khouang, get chilly from November to February and can approach freezing temperatures at night in mountainous areas. Beginning in mid-February, temperatures gradually climb, and April can see temperatures over 100°F (38°C).

In order to avoid the rain and heat, the best time to visit the south is probably November through February. In the mountains of the north, May to July means still-comfortable temperatures.

**PUBLIC HOLIDAYS**   Businesses and government offices close for these holidays, but restaurants remain open. Ask about local festivals; on the full moon of each month, called a *boun,* there's always a festival somewhere—not to miss.

- **International New Year's Day:** January 1, nationwide. Your standard countdown and party sans Dick Clark.
- **Lunar New Year (Pimai Lao):** Full moon in mid-April, nationwide. The Luang Prabang festivities include a procession, a fair, a sand-castle competition on the Mekong, a Miss New Year pageant, folk performances, and cultural shows. Make sure you're booked and confirmed in hotels before you go.
- **Buddhist Lent:** At local temples, worshippers in brightly colored silks greet the dawn on **Buddhist Lent (Boun Khao Phansaa)** by offering gifts to the monks and pouring water into the ground as a gesture of offering to their ancestors. Lent begins in July and lasts 3 months. Monks are meant to stay at their temple throughout this time, for more rigorous practice. Lent ends in the joyous **Boun Ok Phansa** holiday in September, usually commemorated with boat races (below), carnivals, and the release of hundreds of candle-bearing paper and bamboo floats on the country's rivers.
- **Dragon Boat Races (Bun Song Heua):** Held at different times in late summer and early fall in every riverside town. These races celebrate the end of Buddhist Lent. Teams of 50 paddle longboats in a long sprint, and winners parade through town. The **Vientiane Boat Race Festival** (Vientiane and Savannakhet) is held the second weekend in October to mark the end of Buddhist Lent. The **Luang Prabang Boat Races** are held in early September along the Nam Kan, with a major market day preceding the races and festivities throughout the night on race day.
- **That Luang Festival:** Full moon in early November, Vientiane. This major Buddhist fete draws the faithful countrywide and from nearby Thailand. Before dawn, thousands join in a ceremonial offering and group prayer, followed by a procession. For days afterward, a combined trade fair and carnival offers handicrafts and flowers, games, concerts, and dance shows.
- **Hmong New Year:** End of November/beginning of December, in the north. Although this is not a national holiday, it's celebrated among this northern hill tribe.
- **National Day:** December 2, nationwide. The entire country celebrates a public holiday, while in Vientiane, you'll find parades and dancing at That Luang temple.

## HEALTH CONCERNS

In chapter 3, we discuss the major health issues that affect travelers to Southeast Asia and recommend precautions for avoiding the most common diseases.

No water in Laos is considered potable, so stick with bottled water. Also, Lao cuisine uses many fresh ingredients and garnishes, and condiments made from dried fish that might have been stored under unsanitary conditions. Exercise caution when eating from roadside and market stalls and smaller local restaurants.

In Laos, medical facilities are scarce and rudimentary. Emergency medical facilities exist in Vientiane, but outside the capital you'll require medical evacuation. Contact information is provided under "Fast Facts: Laos," below.

## GETTING THERE

Official land borders are with China, Vietnam, and Thailand *only,* and not all border points are open to Western nationals. For example, to China, the crossing point is at Boten, and though it looks encouraging on a map, you cannot cross north of Muang Sing. Similarly, the Laos/Vietnam borders in the north at Dien Bien Phu or Sam Neua are not open; only in the south at Lao Bao can you cross to and from Vietnam.

**BY PLANE**    Bangkok is Laos's main link with global air routes. In addition, regular flights from neighboring Vietnam and Cambodia make it easy to hop a direct flight from anywhere in Indochina. See each individual country chapter for carriers to the countries mentioned above.

**Lao Airlines** (formerly Lao Aviation) runs domestic and international routes. The main office in Vientiane is at 2 Pangkham Rd. (© **021/212-057;** reservations © 021/214-427; www.laoairlines.com). Lao Aviation connects Vientiane with Bangkok, Hanoi, Ho Chi Minh City, Phnom Penh, and Siem Reap. It's also possible to fly from Bangkok or Chiang Mai directly to Luang Prabang. Other convenient routes link Cambodia (Phnom Penh and Siem Reap) and Pakse.

Thai Airways International, Angel Air (from Thailand), Bangkok Air, Vietnam Airlines, and Myanmar Airways all provide service to Laos.

Check www.bangkokair.com for information about Bangkok Airways and new routes between the UNESCO World Heritage sites of Bangkok, Sukhothai, Luang Prabang, and Hue.

*Note:* There is an **international departure tax** of $10, payable in any currency (dollars/euros/bath/kip) at immigration.

**BY TRAIN**    The State Railway of Thailand's northeastern line originates at Bangkok's Hua Lampong Railway Station (© **02223-7010** or © 1690). Running north, it connects many major provincial capitals in Isan, Thailand's northeastern region, before terminating at Nong Khai, opposite Vientiane.

Once in Nong Khai, hire a tuk-tuk from the train station to the immigration checkpoint at the Thai-Lao Friendship Bridge (about 30B/70¢ for the trip; open daily 8:30am–5pm). Once across to Laos, take a taxi or tuk-tuk to Vientiane (from B150/$3.75 with hard bargaining). There is also infrequent bus service to the Morning Market in Vientiane for just 1,000 kip (10¢).

Connecting with Pakse in the south of Laos is also possible by train from Bangkok via the Thai terminus at Ubon Ratchathani. From Ubon to the Lao border and on to Pakse means two long bus rides (the best you'll get from the Lao border to Pakse is an overcrowded *songthaew,* or pickup truck).

**BY BUS**    Tourist buses—the VIP, reclining-seat, air-conditioned variety—connect Bangkok and Vientiane via the Friendship Bridge. The overnight trip can be booked from most tour services for about B700 ($16) and will leave you at the Thai side of the border. From Vietnam, a lot of people choose to take the bus overnight from Danang or Hué to Savannakhet. In Danang, the bus leaves at 7pm every Monday, Wednesday, Thursday, and Sunday. Talk to **Vietnamtourism** (83 Nguyen Thi Minh Khai; © **0511/823-660**); the cost is 37,000 VND ($2.45). From Hue, the bus leaves at 7pm on Tuesday and Saturday. Contact Huong Giang Tourist Company (17 Le Loi St.; © **054/832-220**) for more information.

**BY BOAT**    The Mekong border crossing between Thailand's Chiang Khong (near Chiang Mai) and Laos's Houayxay is popular. From the border, it's a lazy 2-day boat ride on the Mekong to Luang Prabang (see "Getting Around," below). At the time of this writing, a 15-day visa was available on arrival.

Additional ferry crossing points along the Mekong are between Mukhdahan (Thailand) and Thakhek (Laos), and between Mukhdahan (near Ubon in Thailand) and Chong Mek (Laos).

## GETTING AROUND

Laos's underdeveloped infrastructure begs caution. See the travel warnings at the head of the chapter and note poor road conditions, especially during the rainy season and in the north. Often-overcrowded public transport relegates road and river travel to the hearty.

That said, these very obstacles are what attract many to traveling in Laos; there's nothing like the feel of pulling into a northern town covered in dust or hopping from a boat to a muddy riverbank in a rural village to be greeted by a friendly delegation of kids. For many, though, the difficulties outweigh (or overshadow) any reward. Arm yourself with current information if you're traveling far out of Vientiane and Luang Prabang, and consider carefully the travel options below.

**BY AIR**   Contact **Lao Airlines** (© 021/212-057; www.laoairlines.com), about domestic routes. Ticket prices range from about 370,000 kip ($37) from Luang Prabang to Xieng Khouang, to 950,000 kip ($95) from Vientiane to Pakse. Lao Airlines accepts payment in U.S. dollars, traveler's checks, Lao kip, and most major credit cards.

**Lao Westcoast Helicopter Company** (© 021/512-023) will be more than happy to charter a whirlybird to take you where you need to go at your convenience. Similarly, **Lao Flying Service** (© 021/222-687; laofly@laotel.com) offers chartered fixed-wing options (strictly small planes) and sells blocks of time and package deals for charter, air taxi, and aerial survey throughout the country.

**BY BUS**   Korean-made **public buses and minibuses** connect most towns; however, many areas (especially in the north) are still serviced only by *songthaew,* four-valve pickup trucks fitted with open-sided covers and bench seats. Private companies handle long-haul routes from Vientiane north to Luang Prabang and south to Savannakhet. Buses are often overcrowded, which can mean sitting on a plastic chair in the center aisle with a bag of chickens or pigs wriggling at your feet. Buses stop frequently for new passengers and rest stops are rural roadsides. It's good grist for travel journals, but harrowing.

**BY CAR**   One alternative is to hire a **private vehicle,** a car with a driver (self-drive vehicles are virtually impossible to find). Find contacts for private vehicle hires in each corresponding section to follow.

**BY BOAT**   **Tour boats** operated by **LuangSay Cruises** (© 071/252-553 in Luang Prabang; © 021/215-958 in Vientiane; www.mekongcruises.com) are a luxury option along the Mekong both in the north between Thailand and Luang Prabang and in the south from Pakse. See each section for details.

**Riverboats** ply the length of the Mekong in Laos, and smaller boats of the longtail variety navigate smaller waterways throughout the country (particularly in the north). On some routes, departures are so infrequent that travelers need to charter boats for themselves, a true exercise in patience. The 2-day **slow boat** from the Thai border town of Houayxay (with an overnight in Pak Beng) is popular.

Another alternative is a **speedboat** hire, which gets you there much faster but via a bone-jarring ride that, though brief, is more uncomfortable than riding the barge (I recommend ear plugs, and many opt for the helmets offered).

Local boats from Pakse to Champasak and farther south are a possibility but are similarly uncomfortable and loosely scheduled.

Navigating on foot through Laos's small cities is easy. You can use **taxis** and **tuk-tuks** (covered carts behind motorbikes) in Vientiane, Luang Prabang, and Pakse, or you can rent **bicycles** and **motorbikes** in Vientiane, Luang Prabang, and Vang Vieng.

## TIPS ON ACCOMMODATIONS, DINING & SHOPPING

Book your hotel early during the peak season (Aug and Nov–Mar), using travel agents and tour operators as necessary. Standards and prices are good.

Lao cuisine is varied and interesting, with sticky rice (or glutinous rice) a staple that, over a longer visit, often loses its appeal through redundancy. Lao fare mixes Thai and Chinese traditions, with a bit of French thrown in for good measure (and a few unique regional favorites). Try it at real restaurants whenever possible because the street stands aren't up to those in neighboring countries. French colonial influence is clear in the many excellent Continental options in Vientiane and Luang Prabang.

You'll undoubtedly leave with a few pieces of hand-woven Lao textiles, hand-crafted silver, and other lovely objects. Many things are one of a kind, so if you see something you like, get it. Remember that the Lao do, of course, haggle. For foreigners the starting price might be high, but bargaining here is not as relentless as with Laos's neighbors.

### FAST FACTS: Laos

**American Express** The country's one Amex representative is **Diethelm Travel,** Namphu Square, Setthathirat Road, Vientiane (© 021/213-833 or 215-920).

**Business Hours** With a few exceptions, hours are 8:30am to noon and 1:30 to 5pm on weekdays and 8am to noon on Saturday. Restaurants are open from about 11am to 2pm and 6 to 10pm daily, and many are closed for lunch on Sunday.

**Doctors & Dentists** Medical care in Laos is primitive by Western standards. For major problems, most foreigners choose to hop the border to Thailand for the Nong Khai Wattana General Hospital (just over the Friendship Bridge). In an emergency, call © 66-42/465-201. Vientiane has one 24-hour International Medical Clinic, Mahosot Hospital, on Fa Ngum Road at the Mekong riverbank (© 021/214-022). For emergency evacuation, call **Lao Westcoast Helicopter Company** in Vientiane at © 021/512-023.

**Drug Laws** Opium is openly grown in northeast Laos and is easily available, as is marijuana. Neither are legal, and although you might see many travelers indulging, it is highly recommended that you don't. You could face high fines or jail if you're caught.

**Electricity** Laos runs on 220-volt electrical currents. Plugs are two-pronged, with either round or flat prongs. If you're coming from the U.S. and you must bring electrical appliances, bring your own converter and adapter. Outside of Vientiane and Luang Prabang, electricity is sketchy, sometimes available for only a few hours a day. A surge protector is a must for laptops.

**Embassies** **U.S.:** Thatdam Bathrolonie Road (© 021/212-582; fax 021/212-584). **Australia:** Nehru Road, Bane Phonsay (© 021/413-600). The Australian embassy also assists Canada, New Zealand, and U.K. nationals.

**Emergencies** In Vientiane, for police dial © 191; for fire, dial © 190; and for ambulance, dial © 195. For medical evacuation, call **Lao Westcoast Helicopter Company** at © 021/512-023.

*Internet/E-mail* You can find Internet access in the main tourist towns. Prices vary with proximity to Vientiane because most service is patched throughout the capital; it's often overpriced and too slow to be worth it. In Vientiane and Luang Prabang, the connections are generally not bad and prices are reasonable.

*Language* The national language of Laos is *Lao*. If you've picked up a bit of Thai, feel free to use it here because many understand (the languages are similar and Thai TV is popular). Many people in Vientiane and Luang Prabang speak **English**. A rare few also speak Russian and French, and Mandarin Chinese is growing concurrently with the Chinese population (mostly in the north). See "Language," p. 240.

*Liquor Laws* There are no real liquor laws in Laos, but most bars refuse to admit patrons under the age of 18. Bars usually close around midnight.

*Post Offices/Mail* A letter or postcard should take about 10 days to reach the U.S. Overseas postage runs about 21,000 kip ($2.10) for 100g, and up to 92,000 kip ($9.20) for 500g. Postcards are 4,000 kip (40¢). The mail service is unreliable, however, so if you're sending something important, use an express-mail service. **FedEx** (*ⓒ* **021/223-278**) and **DHL** have offices in the major cities.

*Safety* Buddhist Laos is an extremely safe country by any standard. Violent or even petty crime is not a big risk for tourists. There have been rare instances of robbery or rape in remote areas. Solo travelers should take care when getting remote, even on a day hike. Some of the country's highways, like Route 13 near Kasi and Route 7 in the northeast, have seen rebel and bandit attacks in the past. Ask around before going too far off the beaten track. Of course, petty crime does exist. Watch your belongings, and don't leave valuables in your hotel rooms.

When trekking in the north near the Plain of Jars or in the south around the Ho Chi Minh Trail, **beware of unexploded bombs.** Don't stray into remote areas, and don't touch anything on the ground.

*Telephone & Fax* The international country code for Laos is 856. Phone rates are as follows: 1 minute to the U.S., the U.K., or Canada: 23,000 kip ($2.30); to Australia: 11,500 kip ($1.15); and to New Zealand: 22,000 kip ($2.20). Buy a stored-value phone card at any post office or telecom center to use at international phone booths (there are just 300 phone booths in the whole country, and only a small percentage are international). Most newer hotels have international direct dialing at surcharges of about 10%. Collect calls are impossible anywhere, and the long-distance companies haven't made it to Laos yet. Internet cafes often have Internet phone service at 5,000 kip (50¢) per minute and charge 2,000 kip (20¢) for callback service. See the "Telephone Dialing Info at a Glance" box below for more information. Local calls are 100 kip (1¢) per minute. Like the international phone booths, local phone booths accept only prepaid phone cards. Laos has no coins.

Mobile phones have come to Laos. If you have a GSM phone with a replaceable SIM card, you can arrange prepaid service in any telecom outlet in the country. Coverage is surprisingly extensive. **Lao Telecom** (www.laotel.com) and **Tango** (*ⓒ* **021/253-001**) are the best.

*Time Zone*  Laos is 7 hours ahead of Greenwich Mean Time, in the same zone as Bangkok. That makes it 12 hours ahead of the U.S. and 3 hours behind Sydney.

*Tipping*  Tipping has arrived in Laos, particularly in Vientiane. Feel free to tip bellhops, chauffeurs, and tour guides, and to leave 5% to 10% or round up your bill in upscale restaurants. Foreign currency, especially U.S. dollars, is appreciated.

*Toilets*  You'll find Western toilets (sit-down style) in most hotels for foreigners. Out in the boonies it's mostly Asian-style (squatty-potty). Bring your own paper, and sanitary hand wipes are a good idea too. You'll notice a bowl and a pail of water nearby for flushing (put two or three buckets in). On rural roads, buses just pull to the side for bathroom breaks. In villages, find a convenient tree.

*Water*  Drink only boiled or bottled water, available everywhere for 1,000 kip (10¢). Be wary of ice in any but the finest restaurants. Some even use boiled or bottled water for tooth brushing.

## 3 Vientiane

Vientiane (wee-en-*chan*) has to be one of the world's unique capitals. Vientiane's population of 280,000 in a country of just under 6 million reflects the nation's rural makeup, and despite growth and the infusion of foreign aid, the infrastructure even here in the capital is basic. Just a short ride in any direction from Lane Xang, the main north-south avenue, will quickly carry you into the beginnings of rural Laos. Vientiane does play host to a few luxury hotels and some fine restaurants, however.

The city's small scale means you'll be constantly confronted by startling incongruities: pious monks in vermilion robes hard at work on their website or playing games online at the local Internet cafe; cell phones in the hands of every Vientiane urbanite, though you'll be hard-pressed to find a public phone even in the city center; gleaming sport utility vehicles and European sedans parked alongside rusty tuk-tuks and old Russian trucks.

The city was ransacked by the Vietnamese in 1828, so it lacks some of the ancient history you find in the former capital of Luang Prabang, but many of Vientiane's temples have been beautifully reconstructed. **That Luang** is the preeminent Buddhist temple in the country and the scene of a huge festival every November. **The Patuxay victory monument** is a peculiarly Lao version of the Arc de Triomphe. The **Morning Market** has a full city block of goods to explore. And the **Mekong,** lined with picturesque colonials and cozy thatched bars, rolls through the very heart of the city and glows pink at sunset—not to be missed. It is worth a stay of several days to take it all in and enjoy Vientiane's laid-back atmosphere while it lasts.

### VISITOR INFORMATION

There is a tourist information office on Lane Xang Avenue just north of the Morning Market. Also see the "Organized Tour & Travel Agents" section (p. 243) for tour providers in Laos, all of which have helpful offices in Vientiane. The *Vientiane Times* (www.vientianetimes.org.la) is the local English-language paper, a fun read with good listings of local events.

## Telephone Dialing Info at a Glance

- **To place a call from your home country to Laos,** dial the international access code (011 in the U.S., 0011 in Australia, 0170 in New Zealand, 00 in the U.K.), plus the country code (856), plus the city or area code (21 for Vientiane, 71 for Luang Prabang) and the 6-digit phone number (for example, 011 + 856 + 21/000-000).
- **To place a call within Laos,** dial the city or area code preceded by a 0, and then the 6-digit number (for example, 021/000-000). A local call costs 45 kip (1¢) a minute from a phone booth. You must use a phone card, which you can buy at the post office, the telephone office, and minimarts.
- **To place a direct international call from Laos,** dial the international access code (00) plus the country code, the area or city code, and the number (for example, 00 + 1 + 212/000-0000).
- **International country codes** are as follows: Australia: 61; Burma: 95; Cambodia: 855; Canada: 1; Hong Kong: 852; Indonesia: 62; Malaysia: 60; New Zealand: 64; the Philippines: 63; Singapore: 65; U.K.: 44; U.S.: 1; Vietnam: 84.

## GETTING THERE

**BY AIR**   Vientiane is Laos's major international hub for air travel. For information on arriving by plane or by train, see "Getting There," on p. 247. If you're arriving via Wattay International Airport in Vientiane, a taxi to town is 30,000 kip ($3). Drivers will say 50,000 kip ($5), but be persistent.

**BY BUS**   The bus station at the **Morning Market** (☎ 021/216-507) connects Vientiane with all destinations in Laos (also Nong Khai, Thailand).

## GETTING AROUND

The city lies on the east side of the Mekong River (the western bank is Thailand). The main streets, running parallel to each other, are Samsenthai and Setthathirat, with Lane Xang, the north-south artery, intersecting them. The heart of the city is Nam Phu Fountain, and many of the directions in this chapter are given in relation to it.

Central Vientiane is easily covered on foot. You can also hire a **tuk-tuk,** a covered cart behind a motorbike, or a **jumbo,** a bigger version of the same. Drivers charge about 5,000 kip to 10,000 kip (50¢–$1) around town. You should settle the price before you ride.

**Motorcycles** can be rented for 80,000 kip ($8) or so a day—look around the Nam Phu Fountain or along Samsenthai (or try **Douang Deuane Hotel;** see "Where to Stay," below; ☎ 021/222-301).

**Bicycles** are available at Orchid Guest House (as well as other storefronts) along Fa Ngum Road near the river or along Samsenthai. Bikes are a great way to get around town.

You can also rent a car with a driver for 600,000 kip ($60) a day. Call **Asia Vehicle Rental** at ☎ 021/217-493 (www.avr.laopdr.com) or inquire at any hotel front desk.

## FAST FACTS: Vientiane

*Banks/Currency Exchange*  **Banque Pour Le Commerce Extérieur Lao** is on Pangkham Street down by the river, just west of the Lane Xang Hotel (© 021/213-200), or just a short distance from the river at **Lao May Bank,** at 39 Pankham St. (© 021/330-001). At these and most other banks, you can exchange money in all major currencies, change traveler's checks to U.S. dollars, and withdraw cash on Visa cards. You can also exchange money at **Banque Setthathirat,** near Wat Mixay. All banks are open Monday to Friday 8:30am to 3:30pm. Other banks line Lane Xang Avenue, and exchange counters dot the city.

*Emergencies*  For police, dial © **991;** for fire, dial © **190;** and for ambulance, dial © **195.** For medical evacuation, call **Lao Westcoast Helicopter Company** at © **021/512-023.**

*Internet/E-mail*  There are a number of Internet cafes on riverside Fa Ngum or on parallel Setthathirat or Samsenthai (each 1 block further from the river). Connections are generally good. **Lanexang Internet Service** (© 020/555-5955) is fast. Find them on Setthathirat west of the fountain—look for the giant Pepsi can over the door. Services start from 100 kip per minute (under $1 per hr.) at most. Hotel business centers charge at least three times this rate for the same service.

*Post Office/Mail*  The General Post Office is on the corner of Khou Vieng Road and Lane Xang Avenue, opposite the Morning Market. Hours are Monday to Friday 8am to noon and 1 to 5pm, and Saturday and Sunday 8am to noon only. EMS and FedEx services are just next door.

*Telephone/Fax*  The central telephone office, where you can place local and international direct dialing (IDD) calls, is located on Setthathirat Road just east of Nam Phu Circle (Nam Phu Fountain), and is open from 8am to 10pm daily. You can also send faxes.

## WHERE TO STAY

Vientiane has some good options that range from luxury rooms to backpacker dives. Book ahead, especially in late November and early December, and ask for a discount if you come during the rainy season (some places post their low-season rates). Hotels accept U.S. dollars, Lao kip, or Thai baht. Be warned that the prices listed do not always include a government tax of 10%, or any additional service charges (sometimes applicable in high season).

### EXPENSIVE

**The Lao Plaza Hotel** ⟨★⟩  Popular with business travelers, the Lao Plaza is the most familiar international hotel in Laos. The hotel is in a convenient, central location, and accommodation is bland but comfortable. Sizable rooms are either beige or blue, with solid wood furniture, thick rugs, firm beds, and small marble-tiled bathrooms with hair dryers and terry-cloth robes. Nonsmoking rooms are available on two floors. The pool is big and inviting. Lao Plaza's staff is professional enough, but not especially friendly or helpful. The May Yuan restaurant has admirable Chinese food, and Dok Champa is a cheery cafe, with buffet meals and a deli/bakery. The Plaza is sufficiently self-contained and convenient

# Vientiane

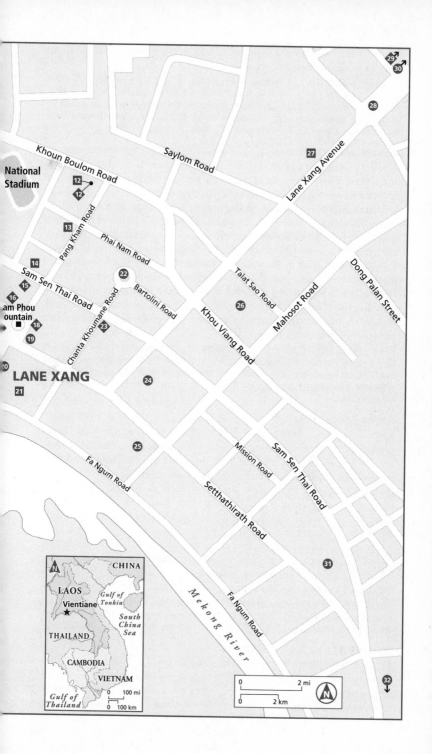

National Stadium

Khoun Boulom Road

Saylom Road

Lane Xang Avenue

27

28

29
30

12
12

Pang Kham Road

Phai Nam Road

13

14

Sam Sen Thai Road

15

16

am Phou
ountain

18

19

22

Bartolini Road

Chanta Khoumane Road

23

Talat Sao Road

Mahosot Road

26

Khou Viang Road

Dong Palan Street

0

LANE XANG

21

24

25

Fa Ngum Road

Mission Road

Setthathirath Road

Sam Sen Thai Road

31

Mekong River

Fa Ngum Road

32

CHINA

LAOS

Gulf of
Tonkin

Vientiane

South
China
Sea

THAILAND

CAMBODIA

VIETNAM

Gulf of
Thailand

0          100 mi
0          100 km

N

0          2 mi
0          2 km

N

to any destination in town, and one of only a few accommodations in Laos where you might forget that you're in Laos.

63 Samsenthai Rd., P.O. Box 6708, Vientiane. ℭ **021/218-800**. Fax 021/218-808. www.laoplazahotel.com. 142 units. $100–$120 superior single/twin; $130–$140 executive single/twin; $220–$420 suite. AE, MC, V. **Amenities:** 2 restaurants; bar; popular nightclub; beer garden; nice pool; gym (guests are charged $8); Jacuzzi; sauna; business center w/Internet; bookstore and gift shop; massage; laundry; conference rooms; banquet facilities. *In room:* A/C, satellite TV, minibar, IDD phone.

### Novotel Hotel Vientiane 🌟

Just a short ride west of the town center, the Novotel Vientiane is a pleasant oasis from the dusty streets and downtown tuk-tuk clamor. The lobby is decorated in a classic Art Deco theme, with stylish rounded woodwork and a domed ceiling painted in a muted pastel yellow—an attractive invitation to Novotel's fine rooms and services. Renovated deluxe rooms have attractive carpets, fine wood furniture, and marble bathrooms with big counters. Standard rooms are done in pastel with cane furnishings and plain tile bathrooms. Everything is ultratidy. All rooms feature hangings and artwork that keep your mind in Indochina. Adjoining the lobby is a well-appointed Continental restaurant with indoor and outdoor by-the-pool seating. The staff is friendly and helpful, and the hotel offers a wealth of facilities and services, including use of its smart business center and chic executive lounge. It's a bit far from town, but has very convenient amenities and good transportation. Their busy disco, Dtec, is always happenin'.

Unit 9, Samsenthai Rd., P.O. Box 585, Vientiane. ℭ **800/221-4542** or 021/213-570. Fax 021/213-572. www.novotel.com. 168 units. $70 standard; $90 superior; $180 deluxe; $320–$450 suite. AE, MC, V. **Amenities:** Restaurant; bar; nice outdoor pool; tennis; health club; sauna; steam bath; free and frequent transport to the town center; gift shop; 24-hr. room service; massage. *In room:* A/C, satellite TV, minibar, coffeemaker, hair dryer, IDD phone.

### Settha Palace Hotel 🌟🌟

By far the best choice in Vientiane is this masterfully restored, early-20th-century French colonial mansion. Once the distinguished address for visitors from the adjacent colonies of Indochina, the building traced a long history of decline before its multimillion-dollar face-lift and 1999 reopening. A small circular drive leads to the columned marble entry, where light coming through the large windows lends a softness to the lobby that is not unlike stepping into a sepia photograph of a distant time. Rooms are cozy, with antique detail and dark wood reproduction furnishings and stalwart four-poster beds. Bathrooms are small but elegant. If a stay at the Palace is a trip to the past, modern amenities like in-room Internet access and satellite TV will keep you connected in the present. The hotel's elegant restaurant, La Belle Epoque (see "Where to Dine," below), serves excellent Continental cuisine. With service unmatched in town, the Palace offers quality far exceeding its price tag.

6 Pangkham (P.O. Box 161), Vientiane. ℭ **021/217-581**. Fax 021/217-583. www.setthapalace.com. 29 units. $150 deluxe; $250 junior suite; $350 suite. AE, MC, V. **Amenities:** Restaurant; bar; outdoor pool (nonguests welcome for $4); Jacuzzi; laundry. *In room:* A/C, satellite TV, Internet connection, minibar, safe, IDD phone.

## MODERATE

### Royal Dokmaideng Hotel 🌟

The Royal is owned and managed by a Taiwanese group and often fills with big groups or conventioneers. The hotel has large rooms that are devoid of character and many are a bit musty or use too much aerosol to cover it up (ask to see the room first). The suites are large and good for families, and the Chinese restaurant is bright and inviting, as is the small courtyard pool. With a central location on Lane Xang Avenue, just north of the Morning Market, the Royal Dokmaideng is a favorite for businessmen.

Be sure to ask for a nonsmoking room. There's a popular karaoke area on the second floor.

Lane Xang Ave., P.O. Box 3925, Vientiane. ☎ **021/214-455**. Fax 021/214-454. 40 units. $60–$70 double; $100 suite. AE, MC, V. **Amenities:** Restaurant; bar; small courtyard swimming pool; basic gym; sauna; conference room; laundry. *In room:* A/C, TV, minibar, IDD phone.

### Tai-Pan Hotel ★★ *Value*    This very attractive midsize hotel is convenient to downtown, on a quiet street just off the Mekong, and offers the amenities and service of its larger, high-end competition. Standard rooms are compact, with double beds only, and the deluxe rooms are spacious. All are spotless and cheerful, with dark parquet floors and painted wood furniture set against bright floral bedspreads and decoration. Sizable bathrooms are done in white, with clean tile and bathtubs. Ask for a third-floor room with a balcony and river view. With a sister property in Bangkok, the Tai-Pan is popular for business travelers and the long-staying humanitarian workers. The lobby restaurant is tops, the location can't be beat, and the hotel just opened a new pool and tidy fitness center.

22/3 François Nginn Rd., Ban Mixay, Muong Chanthabury, Vientiane. ☎ **021/216-906**. Fax 021/216-223. www.travelao.com. 44 units. $58 double; $61 deluxe; $71 junior suite; $80–$136 suite. AE, MC, V. **Amenities:** Restaurant; bar; small swimming pool; health club; Jacuzzi; sauna; airport transfer; conference rooms; computer rental; Internet. *In room:* A/C, satellite TV, minibar, IDD phone.

## INEXPENSIVE

### Anou Hotel *Value*    Here's a bargain for you. The Anou has clean, bright, good-size rooms, some with tidy beige carpeting and others with hardwood floors. The beds are comfortable and the bathrooms are liveable, with tile floors and spiffy marble counters. Some are the shower-in-room variety, without bathtubs, so let the hotel know if that matters to you. The suites are simply huge and all have wood floors, but they're just oversize versions of the standard rooms (with a larger fridge). The downstairs restaurant is inviting, and the hotel has a good location in downtown Chinatown. Surrounded by shops and restaurants, the area is abuzz with activity into the evening and can get pretty noisy.

01–03 Heng Boun St., Vientiane. ☎ **021/213-630**. Fax 021/213-632. anouhotel@laonet.net. 48 units. $20 double; $30–$40 suite. AE, MC, V. **Amenities:** Restaurant; bar; laundry. *In room:* A/C, TV, minibar, IDD phone.

### Day Inn Hotel ★★ *Finds*    This charming little inn in the shadow of the Lao Plaza was once the Indian embassy, and it retains some of that urban, colonial dignity in its large, airy rooms, with their high ceilings and tall French doors. Though it's all a bit stark and simple, you're in an ideal downtown location. Rooms are furnished in basic but tidy wicker, with hard beds and clean but basic bathrooms (some with a tub). The Day Inn is like an upscale guesthouse, really, but it has the basic in-room amenities of a proper hotel (satellite TV and IDD phone). Ask for a spot in the front, where doors and windows open to small private balconies. With a young and friendly staff, a fine Lao restaurant, and a laid-back feel, the Day Inn is popular with tourists who need some amenities but are here to relax and learn about "Lao Time."

059/3 Pangkham Rd., P.O. Box 4083, Vientiane. ☎ **021/223-847**. Fax 021/222-984. dayinn@laotel.com. 25 units. $25 single; $30 double; $45 suite. No credit cards. **Amenities:** Restaurant; laundry; Internet service in lobby. *In room:* A/C, satellite TV, minibar, IDD phone.

### Douang Deuane Hotel *Value*    Popular with tour groups, this is a clean and basic budget option just off the Mekong and close to the center of town. Rooms have tacky fluorescent paintings and discolored wallpaper, but they are spacious, with wood floors and large, tiled bathrooms (the shower-in-room variety). Call

ahead; the word is out on the value of this little spot and the place is often booked. Bike and scooter rentals are available out front. A basic breakfast buffet is included.

Nokeo Koummane Rd., Ban Mixay, P.O. Box 6881, Vientiane. (C) **021/222-301.** Fax 021/222-300. www. bookings-asia.com/la/hotels/douangdeuane. 30 units. $18 single; $23 double. MC, V. **Amenities:** Restaurant; motorbike rental; laundry. *In room:* A/C, TV, minibar.

**Lane-Xang Hotel** ⭐   This 44-year-old hotel, once the prize of Vientiane, has seen better days, but there's a certain fallen-angel quality here, like an old Vegas casino or your favorite greasy spoon, that makes for an interesting stay. Be sure to ask for a higher floor facing the river where the views are great. For the many hotel facilities, you can't beat the price. Recent minor renovations, part of a larger effort to eventually bring the Lane-Xang back to its former glory, have at least improved cosmetic detail, but be sure to ask to see the room before you check in. The rooms are a nice size and comfortable, with clean beds and wood floors. Despite recent efforts, they're a bit rundown, with chipped furniture and old polyester bedspreads. The suites aren't much to write home about—just larger versions of the standard rooms. If the cigarette holes and stained carpet could talk, it might be a good story, but it makes for less than an ideal stay. Check out the snooker area and nightclub just outside for a bizarre late-night local scene.

Fa Ngum Rd., P.O. Box 280, Vientiane. (C) **021/214-102.** Fax 021/214-108. 72 units. $22 single; $25 double; $45–$55 suite. AE, V. **Amenities:** 2 restaurants; bar; outdoor pool; tennis; basic gym w/sauna and massage; car rental; business center; shopping; salon; room service; snooker/billiard parlor; meeting rooms. *In room:* A/C, TV, minibar, IDD phone.

## WHERE TO DINE

French is very big in the Lao capital, and good international restaurants of this ilk actually outnumber those serving Lao fare. You'll find some great, affordable fine dining. A few local specialties to watch out for are *khao poun,* rice vermicelli with vegetables, meat, or chiles, in coconut milk; *laap,* minced meat, chicken, or fish, tossed with fresh mint leaves; or a tasty Lao-style pâté. Try sticky rice, eaten with the hands, as an accompaniment to most Lao dishes (it's a thrice-a-day staple for Laotians).

### EXPENSIVE

**La Belle Epoque** ⭐⭐ FRENCH/CONTINENTAL   In the atmospheric Settha Palace Hotel (p. 256), you can't beat the atmosphere of La Belle Epoque—colonial elegance mixed with Vientiane's laid-back charm. The service is efficient, and the menu covers a wide range of French and Continental specialties, with meat, game, and seafood prepared to order. Imported Australian steaks and salmon top off a fine list of specialties, like grilled lamb with ratatouille or

---

### Tips   Budget Options

**Lakeo Guest House,** near the Patouxay Arc de Triomphe ((C) **021/214-930;** www.lakeo.laopdr.com) is popular with NGO workers. Twenty-three air-conditioned rooms range from $10 up to $35. They're a bit far from the tourist center, however.

The **Orchid Guesthouse** (33 Fa Ngum Rd.; (C) **021/252-825)** is friendly, laid-back, and right in the thick of things along the river. There are 22 rooms with air-conditioning, priced from $10. Bicycle rental is available.

Guesthouses from $2 are abundant on the streets near the river.

terrine of duck liver marinated in wine. Try one of the creative appetizers, like the goat-cheese pastry. Don't pass up the crème brûlée. You would pay an arm and a leg for such a meal anywhere but here.

Settha Palace Hotel, 6 Pangkham St., P.O. Box 1618. ℂ 021/217-581. Reservations recommended. Main courses $6–$13. AE, MC, V. Daily 6am–10:30pm.

**Le Na Dao** ★★ FRENCH    Once a hush-hush eatery of just a few tables, where ordering a souffle meant a long, languid wait, Le Nadao's Lao-born and French-trained chef and owner, Mr. Sayavouth, is reaching a wider market at his larger location adjacent to the Patuxay Monument, Vientiane's Arc de Triumph. Le Na Dao means "Stars in the Ricefield," and indeed this little star now plays host to Vientiane's best and brightest business folks and dignitaries. The dining room is a converted teak house, all very rustic and soothing, with a corrugated metal ceiling showing through rough slats, warm indirect lighting, and live local music. Mr. Sayavouth's menu is classic French; no fusion, no foolin'. I shared a meal starting with smoked salmon delicately presented on saucer tortillas and a dish of calamari pan-fried in cream Catalonian-style, followed by roast partridge in a rich gravy with potatoes and a lightly fried Mekong filet with lemon, capers, and local organic brown rice. Dessert is chocolate mousse so rich you melt, or a unique "tulip" of pastry with local fruit and ice cream. Bring someone special and make a long evening of it.

Patouxay, Vientiane (on the west side of the Victory Monument roundabout). ℂ 020/550-4884. Main courses $7–$40. No credit cards. Daily 11am–2pm and 6–10:30pm.

**L'Opera** ★★ ITALIAN    For over 10 years, L'Opera has been serving up "real Italian" cuisine and garnering nothing but praise. It features homemade egg-noodle pasta, fine grill and broiled specialties, and fantastic desserts and espresso. There is also a large selection of pizza Lao, which is a surprisingly good combination of tomatoes, cheese, chiles, Lao sausage, and pineapple. The ambience is good—a rather formal Italy-meets-Lao—with linen tablecloths, brick walls, and wood-beam ceilings in a large, open setting. Lao staff in fine restaurants often act as if their foreign patrons are armed and dangerous, but here the service is confident and professional. There are daily specials, and groups of four or more can try the Opera Menu of nine different special appetizers, pastas, and main courses for $25 per person.

On the Fountain Circle. ℂ 021/215-099. Main courses $5–$13. AE, V. Daily 11:30am–2pm and 6–10pm.

## MODERATE
**KhopChaiDeu** ★ LAO/INTERNATIONAL    The name means "Thank you very much." Even if your time in Vientiane is brief, you can't miss this place if you want to. Just south and west of the Nam Phu Fountain and set in a large colonial building, KhopChaiDeu is the crossroads for expats, backpackers, and tourists. Folks come to get connected with the local scene as much as anything. The menu is extensive, with some tasty barbecue and good Lao selections. Consider the Lao Discovery set, which walks you through various short courses of typical Lao dishes. The old standbys of fried rice, noodles, and spring rolls are featured on the menu's "backpackers page," while the "expatriate relief page" has pizza, spaghetti, and other microwavable favorites from home. Sit on one of the many balconies of this multitiered building, or pull up a chair in the courtyard or at the bar and get into some NGO shop-talk or meet with English teachers and backpackers sharing notes. KhopChaiDeu is abuzz late into the evening, and the 5,000 kip (50¢) draft beer flows freely.

54 Setthathirat Rd., southwest of Nam Phu Fountain. ✆ **021/212-106**. Main courses $2–$5; set menu $5.70. MC, V. Daily 7am–10:30pm. Bar open late.

**Kua Lao** ★★ LAO   Kua Lao serves excellent Lao fare in a traditional atmosphere that makes for a unique dining experience. Set in a restored colonial mansion, there is music and Lao dancing each evening. It's a bit of tourist kitsch, but the staff is very kind and their desire to infuse your dining experience with Lao culture is quite genuine. Nowhere else will you find such an extensive menu of Lao food with English descriptions (and pictures), and many will appreciate the numerous options for vegetarians, not to mention a whole page of tempting Lao desserts. Try the *laap* (or larp), a mince of fish, chicken, or beef mixed with spices and mint; it's excellent when accompanied by a basket of sticky rice and eaten by hand. The set menus are a bargain at $10, especially for smaller groups hoping to sample a larger selection. Staff answers questions or will find someone who can. If you're going upcountry or heading out to the back of beyond, this is a good place for a primer in Lao cuisine.

111 Samsenthai Rd., Box 1873 (at the intersection w/Chanta Khoumane). ✆ **021/214-813**. Fax 021/215-777. Main courses $2–$6; set menu $10. Daily 11am–2pm and 5–11:30pm.

**La Terrasse** *Value* FRENCH   La Terrasse is where you'll find French expats lingering over leisurely lunches or over glacés late in the evening. The Provincial French cuisine is good, heavy on fine grilled items, steak, and hearty salads and pasta. The atmosphere is "get-out-of-the-heat" air-conditioning with a tidy, fern-dotted tile interior. Come for coffee and dessert even if you have your main course elsewhere, as they offer fine cakes and daily specials.

Rue Nokeokoumane, Ban Mixay. ✆ **021/218-550**. Main courses $2–$5. MC, V. Mon–Sat 11am–2pm and 6–10pm.

**Le Provençal** FRENCH/CONTINENTAL   The pizza here is affordable, beginning at just $3, and hearty, with excellent cheeses and toppings. I ordered the supreme and was greeted with a proper pizza topped off with a fried egg smack in the middle—odd, but not a bad addition to an old favorite. Le Provençal also has good French fare, grilled items, and salad.

78/2 Pangkham Rd. (on the northern edge of Nam Phu Fountain). ✆ **021/219-685**. Main courses $3–$9.50. MC, V. Mon–Sat 11:30am–2pm and 6–10pm.

**Le Silapa** ★★ *Finds* FRENCH/CONTINENTAL   For cozy atmosphere and authentic French cuisine, this is a find in Vientiane (if you can find it). The effusive French proprietor will make you feel welcome. There's a great wine list, and tasty meals like whitefish subtly garnished with capers, lemon, and parsley. The food is a lot more sophisticated than you might expect from such an unassuming storefront.

17/1 Sihom Rd., Ban Haysok. ✆ **021/219-689**. Main courses $4.75–$13; set lunch $5.50. MC, V. Mon–Sat 11:30am–2pm and 6–10pm.

**Sticky Fingers** ★★ INTERNATIONAL   Started by Australians who came to Laos with the UN and are involved in NGO work, Sticky Fingers serves up soups, salads, sandwiches, and snacks in a relaxed atmosphere. It's got the corner on the casual business lunch and the after-work crowd. Try a burger, sandwich, or steak, and be sure to choose from the impressive list of homemade dips and sauces (available for carry-out). This is the place to get your hummus fix or grab a falafel and a respite from the afternoon heat.

10/3 François Nginn Rd., P.O. Box 7034, across from the Tai-Pan Hotel. ✆ **021/215-972**. Main courses $2.50–$7.50. Daily 10am–11pm.

(Finds **Vientiane's Street Fare**

The busy area of **Ban Haysok** on the western edge of the town center is Vientiane's small **Chinatown** and an excellent place for an evening stroll and some great snacks. One-dish meals of rice or noodles, Lao/Chinese desserts, and supersweet banana pancakes are sold by street vendors. It's an area that stays up late for sleepy Vientiane, and its charm is in the clamorous chaos. Don't miss it.

The many storefronts along riverside **Fa Ngum Road** are popular gathering spots for travelers, and across the street, on the riverside, are a row of **thatched-roof eateries** serving all the basics. This is a great spot for viewing the Mekong and neighboring Thailand at sunset.

## INEXPENSIVE

**Nazim Restaurant** (★) INDIAN    For great Indian cuisine at affordable prices, Nazim has cornered the market in Laos and now has branch locations in Vang Vieng and Luang Prabang. Serving up anything from biryani to tandoori to any kind of curry you can imagine, Nazim offers a survey of Indian cuisine (and the beer to wash it down) in a no-frills storefront along the Mekong. The food is tasty and the prices are reasonable, making this a popular backpacker spot and an expat standby. In the evenings in high season it's packed, and you might find yourself seated family style with other travelers, crackin' beers, swappin' tales, and making friends. Enjoy.

Fa Ngum Rd. (✆) 021/223-480. www.nazim.laopdr.com. Main courses $1–$2.30. No credit cards. Daily 11am–11pm.

## SNACKS & CAFES

Formerly the **Healthy and Fresh Bakery,** now **Joma Bakery Café** (across from the fountain on Setthathirat Rd.; (✆) 021/215-265) is renovated and spruced up, with the same fine breads and good coffee.

The **Scandinavian Bakery,** off Nam Phu Fountain Circle, has good fresh bread and is always packed with travelers. It's a good place to pick up a foreign newspaper and people-watch on the terrace. **Xayoh Café,** just across from the Lao National Culture Hall (✆ 020/612-051), serves pub grub of all sorts and is a good place to relax and have a beer or a coffee anytime.

**PVO,** an open-air storefront on Samsenthai near the Lao-Paris Hotel, serves great Vietnamese *bo bun* (cold noodles and spring roll) and is a longtime traveler's favorite.

For ice cream, crepes, and desserts, don't miss **La Terrasse** in Ban Mixay (see "Where to Dine," above).

## WHAT TO SEE & DO

Most sights are within the city limits, which means you'll be able to cover them by bicycle or even on foot, getting to know the city intimately—and getting to know the city intimately might be the real attraction in this little burg.

**Buddha Park** (★★) (Finds    It's said that if a fool persists in his folly, he will become wise. Buddha Park is a fanciful sculpture garden full of Hindu and Buddhist statues, and it is a concrete testament to the obsession of Luang Pu, a shamanist priest who conceived and started building the park in the 1950s. The statues are captivating, whether they are snarling, reposing, or saving maidens in distress (or carrying them to their doom—it's hard to tell). The huge reclining Buddha is outstanding; you can climb on its arm for a photo. There is also a big concrete dome to climb, itself filled with sculptures. The half-hour jumbo ride to get here, if you choose that route, is very dusty but fulfilling: You get a clear view of Thailand across the Mekong.

About 24km (15 miles) southeast of town. Admission 500 kip (5¢), plus an additional 500 kip (5¢) for jumbo parking and 500 kip (5¢) to use a camera. Daily 7:30am–5:30pm.

**Ho Phra Keo** ✦✦   Built by King Setthathirat in 1565, Phra Keo was constructed to house an emerald Buddha that the king took from Thailand (which the Thais took back in 1779). Today there are no monks in residence, and the *wat* is actually a museum of religious art, including a Khmer stone Buddha and a wooden copy of the famous Luang Prabang Buddha. In the garden, there's a transplanted jar from the Plain of Jars (p. 284).

On Setthathirat Rd., opposite Wat Sisaket. Admission 5,000 kip (50¢). Daily 8am–noon and 1–4pm.

**Lao National Museum**   Housed in an interesting old colonial structure that was once used for government offices, the Museum of the Revolution has photos, artifacts, and re-creations of the Lao struggle for independence against the French and Americans. The exhibits (firearms, chairs used by national heroes, and the like) are rather scanty, barely scratching the surface of such a complicated subject, but most are in English at least. Archaeological finds and maps presented on the first floor (probably because there is no other museum to house them at present) help make a visit here worthwhile. Actually, one of the most interesting exhibits is in the last room before you exit, sort of a Laos trade and commodities exhibit of produce, handiwork, and manufactured goods. Though dated, it will give you some idea of Laos's geography and commerce.

Samsenthai Rd., near the Lao Plaza Hotel. Admission 5,000 kip (50¢). Daily 8am–noon and 1–4pm.

**Morning Market (Talaat Sao)** ✦✦   Full of surprises around every corner, the Morning Market is the hub of local commerce and really where the action is. Here you can find anything, from the Thai version of that Britney Spears CD you've been chasing after to a Buddhist keepsake from one of the tourist shops or small-time trinket salesmen. Bargain hard. This is the Laos version of "mall culture," and sometimes the everyday tool department or stationery area gives a special glimpse into everyday life. Enjoy a good wander and hassle-free shopping. There are few touts, but, as always in crowded places, mind your valuables.

On Talat Sao Rd., off Lane Xang Ave. Daily 7am–5pm.

**Patuxay (Victory Monument)** ✦   This monument was completed in 1968 and dedicated to those who fought in the war of independence against the French. Ironically, the monument is an arch modeled on the Parisian Arc de Triomphe. Its detailing is typically Lao, however, with many *kinnari* figures—half woman, half bird. It's an imposing sight, and you can climb up for a good city view. This is the town's main teenage strutting ground and is busy and crowded on weekends. The park is currently under renovation, with funds from the Chinese government, a telling sign for the future, perhaps.

At the end of Lane Xang Ave. Admission 2,000 kip (20¢). Daily 8am–4pm.

**Phra That Luang** ✦   This is the preeminent stupa in Lao, a national symbol and imposing at 44m (144 ft.) in height. It is not the original; the first, built in 1566 by King Setthathirat over the ruins of a 12th-century Khmer temple, was destroyed when the Siamese sacked Vientiane in 1828. It was rebuilt by the French in 1900, but the Lao people criticized it as not being true to the original. It was torn down in 1930 and remodeled to become what you see today. As you approach, the statue in front depicts Setthathirat. After you enter the first courtyard, look to the left to see a sacred bodhi tree, the same variety Buddha sat under to achieve enlightenment. It has a tall, slim trunk, and the shape of its foliage is almost perfectly round. According to the Laotians, bodhi trees appear only in sacred places. You'll never see one, for example, in someone's backyard. The stupa is built in stages. On the second level, there are 30 small stupas, representing the 30 Buddhist perfections, or stages to enlightenment. That Luang is the site of one of Laos's most important temple festivals, which takes place in early November.

At the end of That Luang Rd. Admission 5,000 kip (50¢). Daily 8am–noon and 1–4pm.

**That Dam (the Black Stupa)** This ancient stupa was probably constructed in the 15th century or even earlier, though it has never been dated. It is rumored to be the resting place of a mighty *naga,* or seven-headed dragon, that protected the local residents during the Thai invasion in the early 1800s. (**Note:** The name is pronounced *tat dahm,* not with the mildly invective intonation.)

In the center of the traffic circle at the intersection of Chanta Khumman and Bartholomie Rd.

**Wat Ong Teu** Wat Ong Teu is in a particularly auspicious location, surrounded by four temples: Wat Inpeng to the north, Wat Mixay to the south, Wat Haysok to the east, and Wat Chan to the west. Its name comes from its most famous inhabitant, a huge *(ongteu)* bronze Buddha. The temple, famous for its beautifully carved wooden facade, was built in the early 16th century and rebuilt in the 19th and 20th centuries. Home to the Patriarch of Lao Buddhism, the temple also serves as a national center for Buddhist studies.

Intersection of Setthathirat and Chau Anou roads. Daily 8am–5pm.

**Wat Si Muang** Another 1566 Setthathirat creation, this *wat* houses the foundation pillar of the city. According to legend, a pregnant woman named Nang Si, inspired by the gods to sacrifice herself, jumped into the pit right before the stone was lowered. She has now become a sort of patron saint for the city. The temple is very popular as a result and is the site of a colorful procession 2 days before the That Luang festival every November.

East on Samsenthai, near where it joins Setthathirat. Daily 8am–5pm.

**Wat Si Saket** Completed in 1818, Wat Si Saket is the only temple in Vientiane to survive the pillaging of the city by the Siamese in 1828, perhaps because the temple is built in traditional Thai style. It is renowned for the more than 10,000 Buddha images in the outer courtyard, of all shapes and sizes, in every possible nook and cranny. Look for Buddha characteristics that are unique to Laos: the standing or "praying for rain" Buddha; or the pose with arms up and palms facing forward, the "stop fighting" or "calling for peace" Buddha. The pose in which Buddha points the right hand downward signifies a rejection of evil and a calling to mother earth for wisdom and assistance. Lao Buddhas also have exaggerated nipples and square noses, to emphasize that Buddha is no longer human. The sim features a Khmer-style Buddha seated on a coiled cobra for protection.

At the corner of Setthathirat Rd. and Lane Xang Ave. Admission 5,000 kip (50¢). Daily 8am–noon and 1–4pm.

## SHOPPING

Laos is famous for its hand-woven silk textiles. You can buy them as fabric or in ready-made wall hangings, accessories, and clothing. Finely crafted silver and ornamental objects are also popular souvenirs. The main shopping streets are **Samsenthai** and **Setthathirat,** around the Nam Phu Fountain area and the **Morning Market** (see "What to See & Do," above).

Perhaps best known (not just in town but worldwide) is **Carol Cassidy: Lao Textiles,** off Setthathirat on Nokeo Koummane Road (𝄢 021/212-123; www. laotextiles.com). Since 1990, Carol has employed local weavers. Using traditional Lao motifs as a base, she creates fine contemporary pieces. The cool colonial house alone is worth the visit, and be sure to stroll through the busy workshop area where up to 10 weavers work the looms and are happy to chat.

**Satri Lao Silk,** at 79/4 Setthathirat Rd., has fabrics, clothing, and housewares; and **Couleur d'Asie** (Namphu Sq.; 𝄢 021/223-008) has a fine ready-to-wear line. The unusual furniture and artworks displayed at **T'shop Lai Gallery** (Vat Inpeng Rd.; 𝄢 021/223-178) are also worth a visit. For anything from small carvings and authentic Buddhist doodads all the way up to priceless statues, furniture, and antiques, try **Oot-Ni,** just west of the Lao Cultural Hall on Samsenthai (𝄢 021/215-911). Check out the household linens, bedspreads, kitchen textiles, place settings, plus baby items in great colors and quality, at **Camacrafts** (Nokeo Koummane Rd.; 𝄢 021/416-597). And the **Mixay Boutic** sells a host of souvenirs from its two shops in the town center (Ban Mixay; 𝄢 021/216-592).

For a unique shopping experience in Vientiane, contact Sandra Yuck at her private studio, **Caruso,** housed in a charming colonial property west of the hospital on Fa Ngum Road (P.O. Box 7866, Vientiane; 𝄢 021/223-644; www. carusolao.com). Sandra carries a line of ebony wood boxes, trays, and accessories, as well as unique Lao bedspreads.

## BOOKS AND NECESSITIES

**Vientiane Book Center** (54/1 Pangkham Rd.; 𝄢 021/212-031), just across from the Lao Airlines office, is a good spot to pick up maps or exchange a novel.

For foreign goods, from Spam to fine French wine, check out **Phimphone Minimart** (110/1 Samsenthai Rd.; 𝄢 021/216-963) or the other **Phimpone Market** on Setthathirat (on the south end of the fountain; 𝄢 021/219-045).

## VIENTIANE AFTER DARK

At dusk, wander down to the riverside quay on Fa Ngum Road. The **Lane Xang Sunset Cruise** (𝄢 020/771-1003 or 020/551-7133) boards at 7pm and includes meals from $8 and affordable drinks. Passage is free on the weekends.

Back on land there are a few places to meet and greet. The **KhopChaiDeu** (see "Where to Dine," earlier), on the southwest corner of the Nam Phu Fountain, is the hot spot for expats and travelers, and a good place to find out what's going on in town. There is also a wine bar, **Le Cave de Châteaux,** on Fountain Circle. Also check out **Dtec Disco** at the **Novotel.** For live music, try **Chess Café** on Sakkaline Road, just off Fa Ngum Road east of town.

## HEALTH AND SPA

The **Lao Plaza Hotel** (𝄢 021/218-800) has a basic gym and good outdoor pool open to day visitors. There are a number of small massage storefronts along Fa Ngum Road, but for good spa treatments try new **Papaya Spa** (𝄢 021/216-550; www.papayaspa.com), a Vientiane trendsetter.

## 4 Vang Vieng

Vang Vieng is a picturesque little river town surrounded by beautiful limestone spires. Nothing Lao about it, the town itself is more or less a backpacker ghetto, with rows of budget guesthouses, small sit-on-the-floor eateries on raised bamboo platforms, and bars blaring techno or showing films (a rural version of Bangkok's Khao San Rd.). Anyone over 30 may feel ancient. Vang Vieng is, however, a great base for caving, trekking, and kayaking. It's a town for day-time adventures and twilight tall-tale telling. Stay a night or two and enjoy a single-day or multiday kayak tour in combination with trekking and cave exploration. If you're traveling by car, Ngam Ngum dam and lake, some 85 km (53 miles) north of Vientiane, is a good stop along the way.

### GETTING THERE

**By Bus**   Vang Vieng is a smooth 3-hour ride north on Highway 13 from Vientiane. There are numerous daily departures from the **Morning Market (②️ 021/216-507),** and tickets are just 35,000 kip ($3.50) on a regular bus (45,000 kip/$4.50 by minibus). Bus connection to Luang Prabang is a popular option, a rugged but scenic all-day ride for just 60,000 kip ($6). However, attacks just north of town mean that road travel must be undertaken with caution. Ask around about the current situation.

### INFORMATION AND TOURS

**Diethelm Travel** (see "Planning Your Trip to Laos," p. 242) includes Vang Vieng in many of its tours and can make any custom arrangements. The town itself is brimming with small operators. For good eco-tours, contact the local **Wildside Eco Group** (see "Outdoor Activities," below).

### WHERE TO STAY

**Ban Sabai Bungalow** ⭐⭐   This quiet collection of riverside bungalows provides a real lesson in the Lao language. *Ban* means "house"; *sabai* means "calm and relaxed"; and you'll pick up words like *ngiep* "quiet" and *baw mi banha* "no problem" if you stay long enough. Rooms are simple rustic bungalows, but clean and air-conditioned. One bungalow abuts the river, and the others form a quiet courtyard area. The riverside restaurant is tops.

Along the river just south and west of the town center. ②️ **023/511-088.** 10 units. $22 standard; $30 double. No credit cards. **Amenities:** Restaurant; bar; tour desk; laundry. *In room:* A/C.

**Bungalow Thavansouk and Sunset Restaurant** ⭐   Adjacent to the Hotel Nam Sang and also in a prime riverside spot, at the Thavansouk you'll find a range of neatly fitted, affordable bungalows. Accommodations start with a basic guesthouse standard and go all the way up to a unique riverside suite with, get this, a picture window next to the bathtub with views of the river. Rooms vary in age, quality, and mildew smell in this casual work in progress, so ask to have a peek before checking in. Lounge chairs on the lawn face the breathtaking wall of karst peaks across the river. The attached Sunset restaurant and bar serves good local fare and is a happening spot at dusk.

Along the Nam Song just south and west of the town center. ②️ **023/511-096.** Fax 023/511-096. www.geo cities.com/thavonsouk/index.html. 29 units. $16–$35 bungalow; $50 suite. **Amenities:** Restaurant; concierge can arrange tours and all rentals; laundry. *In room:* A/C. hot water.

**Hotel Nam Song**   Named for the river that rolls by out front, and just a stone's throw from the major takeout point for most kayaking or tubing trips on the Nam Song, this is a basic, tidy, and comfortable option in Vang Vieng. With clean tile floors, the air-conditioned rooms are small but cozy, and the spacious, shaded common area viewing the river is a fine spot to while away some lazy days. It's about a 10-minute walk from town.

Along the river just southwest of the town center, in Vang Vieng. ✆ **023/511-016.** 16 units. $30–$35 double (seasonal discount available). **Amenities:** Restaurant; concierge can arrange tours and all rentals; laundry. *In room:* A/C, hot water.

## WHERE TO DINE

There are lots of small eateries of the storefront variety all over town, and you can get good, basic traveler's fare (fried noodles and rice and "faux-Western") for next to nothing. **Nazim Restaurant,** on the main drag (✆ **023/511-214**), serves the same good, affordable Indian cuisine as in its other locations in Laos. **Xayoh Café,** at the main intersection in town (✆ **023/511-440**), serves good burgers and basics.

## OUTDOOR ACTIVITIES

Eco-tour operators offering kayak tours now line the main road, but the folks at **Wildside Eco Group,** at the main intersection in town (✆ **023/511-440;** www.lao-wildside.com), are your best bet for a fun day in inflatable two-man kayaks on the small rapids of the Nam Song. The trip will take you to some of the local caves, including one where you'll actually swim in wearing headlamps. Another option is a day on the **Nam Lik River,** a more exciting white-water journey (done by raft, depending on the season) just a few hours by pickup from town. Check in with these guys and ask about other trips, like their trekking and kayaking connection back to Vientiane and adventurous trips on the Nam Ngum. Day trips start at $8 (competing companies offer similar options and prices).

## 5 Luang Prabang

Luang Prabang is a town that wakes early each day when, beginning ever so faintly, the bells, gongs, and drums of local temples crescendo around 5am to send Luang Prabang's estimated 1,000 resident monks and novices on their morning alms rounds. Making a circuit around the small peninsula formed by the Nam Khan and Mekong, the crisp column of barefoot, orange-robed figures collect rice for their one daily meal. Visitors can even take part and do their good karmic deed for the day by giving rice or treats to the monks as they pass—a unique way to connect in a city that is alive with Buddhist culture and history. The colonial legacy and torch of French culture and custom is borne by Luang Prabang's colonial architecture and rich cuisine. Even the briefest visit to this magically tranquil town is memorable.

Designated a UNESCO World Heritage site in 1995, Luang Prabang is named after the golden statue that's kept here, the Prabang, or the "great holy image." Luang Prabang was the first capital of Laos and has mercifully remained relatively untouched by war, which means that many of the 33 temples are original, and the town's charm is ancient and authentic.

And there is certainly something magical about Luang Prabang. It's a place to wander, to watch street-side craftsmen, get lost in lazy back alleys amid stately colonials, and stop for a chat down by the river or in one of the many cozy street-side cafes. Allow yourself at least 3 days to sink into the city's languid rhythms, but beware: You might end up staying longer than you planned. Day trips by boat to **Pak Ou Caves,** outlying **weaving villages,** and **waterfalls** round out the experience.

# Luang Prabang

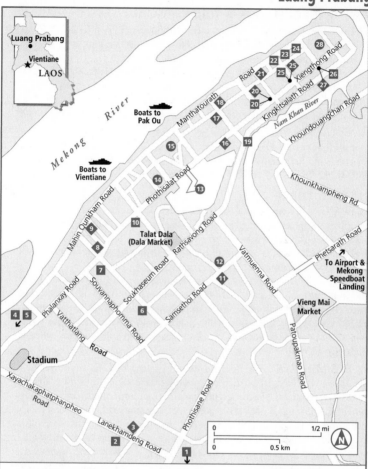

**ACCOMMODATIONS** ■
Aspara **14**
The Grand Luang Prabang
(Xieng Keo) **4**
La Residence Phou Vao **1**
Le Calao **24**
L'hotel Souvannaphoum **7**
Manoluk Hotel **2**
Mouang Luang Hotel **6**
Phousi Hotel **10**
Say Nam Khan Guest
House **19**
Sala Prabang **23**
Sayo Guesthouse **22**
Senesouk **26**
3 Nagas **25**
Villa Santi Hotel **20**
Villa Santi Resort **5**

**DINING** ◆
Café des Arts **16**
Café Regine **17**
Couleur Café
and Restaurant **18**
Indochina Spirit **8**
L'Elephant **21**
Malee Lao Food **3**
Nazim **11**
Somchan Restaurant **9**
3 Nagas **25**
Toum-Toum Cheng **27**
Villa Santi **20**

**ATTRACTIONS** ●
Mount Phousi **13**
Royal Palace Museum **15**
Wat Mai **14**
Wat Wisunalat/
Visounarath **12**
Wat Xieng Thong **28**

## VISITOR INFORMATION & TOURS

- **Diethelm Travel,** Sakarin Road, near the Villa Santi (© **071/212-277;** fax 071/212-032; www.diethelm-travel.com). Diethelm arranges city tours and excursions to out-of-town sights, and is the top agent.
- **Exotissimo,** offices in Ban Xieng Keo (© **071/253-851;** fax 071/253-027; www.exotissimo.com).
- **Inter-Lao Tourism,** in the Hotel Souvannaphoum on Phothisarat and on Kingkitsarath Road near the Talat Dala (Dala Market; © **071/212-200;** www.interlao.laopdr.com).

Small tour offices with good budget ticket service are chockablock in town, especially on "Restaurant Row." Try **All Lao Services** (5/7 Sisavangvong Rd.; © **071/252-785;** fax 071/253-522) for ticketing, rentals, and Internet use.

### GETTING THERE

**BY PLANE**    Lao Airlines (© **021/212-172;** reservations 021/214-427; www. laoairlines.com) has daily flights from Vientiane to Luang Prabang for $57 one-way. Some flights make a loop on to Xieng Khouang for $35 before heading back to Vientiane. There are no direct flights to the far north; for that you'll need to fly directly from Vientiane.

The Luang Prabang airport also handles international flights from Chiang Mai and Bangkok, Thailand, both with Lao Airlines and Bangkok Airways. The cost is $118 to Bangkok and $72 to Chiang Mai on Lao Air. Chiang Mai flights are $85 on Thai Air. On arrival, a visa is available at the airport. Airport transport is best arranged through any hotel. Otherwise, hop a shared, three-wheeled jumbo for $1 or so.

**BY BUS/MINIVAN**    The overland route to Luang Prabang from Vientiane takes about 10 hours by public bus, assuming there are no difficulties (breakdowns are common). There are international warnings about travel on this stretch (p. 238), and though it has been quiet in recent years, ask around before hitting the road. The trip is bumpy and winding and local buses are often packed. The jaw-dropping scenery, past the mountains and limestone formations at Vang Vieng and several Hmong hill villages, is well worth it, however. The bus costs 70,000 kip ($7) and has a few morning departures from Vientiane's Morning Market (© **021/216-507**). Go early to get a seat. Luang Prabang's NaLuang (Southern) bus station is a 5,000 kip (50¢) per person shared tuk-tuk from the town center. There are daily connections to Phonsavan (60,000/60¢) and the far north.

**BY CAR/JEEP**    The mountain route by rented vehicle takes 7 hours and costs about 2,300,000 kip ($230), plus 600,000 kip ($60) per day, *plus* extra for the driver's meals and accommodations. If it seems steep, blame all the nongovernmental organizations operating in Laos for driving up the prices—they all get reimbursed from expense accounts (in case you were wondering where your charity money ends up).

**BY BOAT**    Boat travel to and from Luang Prabang is quite popular. The local boat (called the **slow boat**) from Houayxay (near the Thai border) departs for Luang Prabang every morning. Arrive early at the riverside quay. The trip costs 120,000 kip ($12) and takes about 1½ days to complete. You'll stay overnight in Pak Beng, a village with basic accommodation, before arriving in Luang Prabang in the afternoon of the next day (assuming no engine trouble or other delay.) Be

> ⌒ *Tips*  **Where the Streets Have No Names**
>
> In Luang Prabang, though you'll see street signs, the same road can change names as it progresses through the city, making things confusing. For example, the main street (I refer to it as "Restaurant Row" at the town center) is Chao Fa Ngum, Sisavongvong, or Sakkarine Road, depending on where you are. Locals use village names, not streets, to navigate, and villages are commonly named for the local *wat*. When checking into your hotel, get a business card or ask the name of the local *wat* to tell taxi and tuk-tuk drivers. Also note that the Western spelling of many streets and *wat* names is very inconsistent. Just sound it out.

prepared for all kinds of discomfort, but you'll have many tales to tell sitting in the cafes or getting a massage in Luang Prabang. The chug upriver from Luang Prabang takes up to 3 days and is not recommended.

**Speedboats** also connect Luang Prabang with Houayxay if they get enough passengers to make the trip worthwhile (contact the main port at ✆ 021/215-924). Speedboat travel is uncomfortable, noisy, and dangerous. Haggle for any fare, but expect to pay about $20 for a full-day trip.

**LuangSay Cruises** also operates tour boats on the same route between Thailand and Luang Prabang (contact the agency at Ban Vat Sene, Sakkarine Rd., Luang Prabang, near Diethelm Travel; ✆ 071/252-553; www.mekongcruises). Starting at $351 for a single in high season ($300 per person for a shared double; contact them directly for exact prices), the 2-day trip takes you on the river in style, catered and comfortable, with a 1-night stop at the **LuangSay Lodge,** a charming, rustic eco-lodge that's the most luxurious choice in Pak Beng.

On all other river routes, like the Nam Tha between Luang Nam Tha and Pak Beng and the Nam Ou from Nong Kiao to Luang Prabang, you essentially have to charter your own boat with other tourists. Contact any travel agent or tour provider listed to make arrangements or get more details (availability varies with season).

## GETTING AROUND

Luang Prabang is easy to cover on foot or bicycle, and if you get tired, tuk-tuks and jumbos cost about 5,000kip (50¢) per trip (less with more people and some haggling).

*Note:* Citing the many accidents in recent years, local officials have put the kibosh on any motorbike rental outlets (which also ensures work for local transportation providers). Luang Prabang is a town for walking, really, but it is a shame you can no longer go put-putting out to the waterfalls. Instead it's now a cramped jumbo ride with no view.

**Vatthanaluck Vehicle Rental** (✆ 071/212-838), just around the corner from the Villa Santi, covers all the bases for rentals and is the best bet of the many competitors. Bicycles go for just $1 per day and a rented car with driver is $25.

For sights outside the city, jumbos and tuk-tuks usually gather along Xieng Thong Road across from the popular cafes and restaurants; prices are negotiable.

**Longtail boats** are for hire at Luang Prabang's main pier and can take you to adjacent villages and the **Pak Ou Caves.** See "Sites Outside the City", p. 279.

## FAST FACTS: Luang Prabang

*Banks/Currency Exchange* The **Lane Xang Bank** is at Phothisarat Road near the post office. Hours are Monday to Saturday 8:30am to 3:30pm; closed Sunday and holidays. You can exchange cash and traveler's checks in most major currencies to kip. You can also withdraw cash using a Visa card. There's another Lane Xang money-changing office on Xieng Thong Road next to the Luang Prabang Bakery. **Banque pour le Commerce Exterieur Lao** (① 071/252-983) also has an office on "Restaurant Row." U.S. dollars and Thai baht are accepted widely.

*Emergencies* For police, dial ① **071/212-453**; for a medical emergency, call ① **071/252-049**.

*Internet* Service was once patched through Vientiane, but now cable and satellite connections mean you can easily keep in touch from Luang Prabang. Internet cafes line the busy block of Phothisarat, "Restaurant Row," and are also scattered about town. Service is good. Expect to pay between 200 and 350 kip per minute ($1.20–$2.10 per hr.).

*Post Office/Mail* The post office is on the corner of Phothisarat and Kitsalat roads, across from Luang Prabang Travel and Tourism. Hours are Monday to Friday 8am to noon and 1 to 5pm, and Saturday 8am to noon.

*Telephone* The city code for Luang Prabang is 71. Dial a 0 first inside Laos. The telephone center in town consists of two booths around the corner from the post office on Kitsalat Road. You can buy local and international phone cards in an office across the street.

## WHERE TO STAY

Luang Prabang's UNESCO World Heritage status mercifully prevents large-scale construction in the historic center. As a result, developers have renovated existing hotels and completed boutique conversions on old guesthouses. A few resorts have also sprung up on the outskirts of town to keep up with demand. Promotional and low-season rates are available at most hotels, but be aware that a surcharge is often levied in the busy months. Book ahead from November through March.

### EXPENSIVE

**The Grand Luang Prabang (Xieng Keo)** 🐦🐦   Despite new road signs and advertising, you won't get far in a taxi if you ask to go to "The Grand." The site will forever be known to locals by its former name, Xieng Keo, in reverence to its previous owner, Lao nationalist and peace broker Prince Petsarath. Suffering years of exile, Petsarath followed his country, in and out of power, from colony to communism. The site of Petsarath's former palatial home is on a high, sloping hill at the apex of a wide bend in the Mekong. Words can't describe the views of river and mountains from the open campus. The hotel's aptly named Sunset Bar overlooks such an impressive vista that you might want to make a visit here just to see the afterglow during "magic hour." Without a swimming pool and only just developing amenities, any billing of the Grand as a "resort" comes up a bit short, but it's a popular spot for conventions and is attracting more individual travelers. The rooms are average in size but are quite lovely, with teak floors and high ceilings. Tile bathrooms are smallish but spotless, and the one wall left in rough brick is a unique touch. All rooms have a balcony and a view of either the colonnaded walkways and the courtyard or the majestic Mekong. Prince Petsarath's home stands at the middle of the compound and promises to be a museum honoring his legacy. The biggest drawback is the distance from town, though the hotel runs regular shuttles. From October 1 to March 31 the hotel runs private boat tours for groups up to 20.

Baan Xiengkeo, Khet Sangkalok, Luang Prabang (about 6km/3¾ miles south of the town center). ℂ 071/ 253-851-7. Fax 071/253-027-8. www.grandluangprabang.com. 78 units. $150 deluxe; $250–$300 suite. AE, MC, V **Amenities:** 2 restaurants; bar; Exotissimo Travel tour desk; airport and city shuttle; handicapped-access rooms. *In room:* A/C, satellite TV, minibar.

## La Résidence Phou Vao ★★    Luang Prabang's finest hotel offers deluxe accommodation, fine service, and a lofty perch away from the fray of the busy town center. Rooms are priced accordingly but worth it. The Phou Vao is named for the hill on which it stands. Shallow ponds trace the courtyards that connect the buildings, and bushes of bougainvillea, palm, and frangipani frame views of Phoussi hill in the distance. The views are especially lovely from the pool area and the balconies of the more choice rooms. The rooms are like small suites, decorated with a bamboo-and-wood inlaid headboard, fine rosewood furniture, and retro fixtures like fans and mosquito netting. The large marble bathrooms feature oversize tubs, dark-teak sink stands, and wooden slat blinds that open to reveal private balconies with low, Lao-style divans. The Phou Vao combines the amenities of a city hotel (safe, IDD phone, satellite TV) with a boutique, upscale rustic charm. There's a good indoor French/Lao restaurant with a bar overlooking the main courtyard. Frequent shuttle service to town is very efficient. The vanishing-edge pool is a showpiece.

Phou Vao St., P.O. Box 50, Luang Prabang. ℂ 071/212-194. Fax 071/212-534. www.pansea.com. 34 units. $200 deluxe double (low-season discount available); $290 residence suite. AE, MC, V. **Amenities:** Restaurant; bar; outdoor pool; shopping; limited room service; massage; babysitting; laundry; library and Internet area. *In room:* A/C; satellite TV; minibar; fridge; safe; IDD phone.

## 3 Nagas ★    This new hotel's original structure was built in 1898 as an unofficial reception area for the royal family before being converted into an ice-cream factory in the 1930s. The inspired recent renovation has just the right mix of style, convenience, and connection with local living and history. Style can be seen in the clean-lined rosewood interiors, contemporary Asian furniture, and local touches like ladders to upper floors and woven Lao floor mats in each room. Bathrooms are done in dark wood, shower and all. Convenience points are earned because the hotel is close to the town center, but far enough from the din for some peace. The connection to history and culture comes as the staff welcomes you as their own to a place that provides a glimpse into an aristocratic Indochine of a bygone era. At the time of publication, 3 Nagas was completing a major renovation to a building just across the street that would add another eight rooms and also a small swimming pool, the only one in the town center. Each room has a balcony overlooking the street, the hotel dining (see "Where to Dine," below) is tops, and the staff is very professional. All rooms have Internet connection.

P.O. Box 772, Luang Prabang (just further along the peninsula from "Restaurant Row"). ℂ 071/252-079. www.3nagas.com. 15 units. $72–$150 double. MC, V. **Amenities:** Restaurant; cafe/bar; outdoor pool; bike rentals; tour desk; laundry; Internet corner. *In-room:* A/C, fridge, minibar, hair dryer.

## Villa Santi Hotel ★    For charm and convenience, the Villa Santi is the top in-town residence. Formerly the home of Lao princess Manilay, this low-key

villa reopened in 1992. Whether in the original building, in the nearby annex, or at the latest venture some 6km (3¾ miles) from town (see Villa Santi Resort, below), you'll find peaceful elegance and a connection with culture and nature. Rooms have parquet floors and rosewood furniture. The decor is deluxe colonial with overstuffed pillows, fine linen, mosquito nets, and local weaving. The tile bathrooms are small but neat. There are nice touches like old-fashioned sun umbrellas available for borrowing, and fresh flowers in every room. The newer annex just across the street from the original has common balcony sitting areas and a charm all its own. Only four rooms have king beds, so be sure to specify when you book if that's what you want. The staff is friendly and professional. The downtown location is terrific, right in the thick of things.

P.O. Box 681, Sakkarine St., Luang Prabang. ℂ **071/212-267.** Fax 071/252-158. www.villasantihotel.com. 25 units. Low season $80 deluxe, $200 suite; high season $120 deluxe, $250 suite (Internet rates available). AE, MC, V. **Amenities:** Restaurant; bar; tour desk; limited room service; laundry service; dry cleaning. *In room:* A/C, minibar, fridge, safe, IDD phone.

**Villa Santi Resort** ✸   This resort is a roomier rural companion to the popular downtown Villa Santi and similarly sophisticated without being stuffy. Tucked among lush rice paddies and picturesque hills, this little Eden has a tranquil stream that tiptoes through the grounds, a placid pond, and an open garden area. The buildings seem at ease with the surroundings, and from the open-air, high-ceilinged lobby to the two-story villas scattered about, there's a certain harmony to the place. Rooms are larger versions of those at the downtown Villa Santi, with TVs augmenting similar tile floors, dark rosewood trim, and local decoration. The resort is just getting up and running, which means there are some kinks to work out. Still, the staff is kind and courteous, and will ensure efficient transport to and from town (as with the other resorts, distance is the biggest drawback).

Santi Resort Rd., Ban Nadeuay, P.O. Box 681, Luang Prabang (6km/3¾ miles from town, a 10-min. drive). ℂ **071/253-470.** $170 deluxe double; $300–$500 suite. **Amenities:** Restaurant; bar; limited room service; laundry. *In room:* A/C, satellite TV w/in-house movies, minibar, fridge, hair dryer, IDD phone.

## MODERATE
**Le Calao** ✸✸   This restored 1904 villa stands near the tip of Luang Prabang's peninsula on the banks of the Mekong. Unique and picturesque, it has a location, size, and style all its own. The second-floor rooms are a nice size, with high, sloping ceilings of exposed under-tile, wood furniture, neat tile floors, and beds that are firm and comfortable. Bathrooms have wood cabinetry but are otherwise rather spartan, with no bathtubs. The staff is, well . . . hey, where did the staff go? What sells these rooms and commands the seemingly high price tag is that each room has a large private balcony facing the majestic Mekong. The casual ambience at the Calao comes at a premium but is quite popular (be sure to book ahead). The newly renovated downstairs suite (formerly a kitchen and staff room) has two double beds and a private balcony, perfect for a family with kids.

Khaem Khong Rd. (on the Mekong River, close to Wat Xieng Thuong), Luang Prabang. ℂ **071/212-100.** Fax 071/212-085. www.calaoinn.laopdr.com. 6 units. $60–$70 double. V. **Amenities:** Cafe/bar; laundry. *In room:* A/C.

**Manoluk Hotel**   An interesting choice, the Manoluk; it's eccentric but comfy and affordable. You're a bit away from town, though, which is a drawback. Rooms are large and have polished wood floors, high ceilings, big clunky tables and chairs, and comfortable beds. The bathrooms are similarly large, clean and finished with tile. The huge restaurant and second-floor lounge, complete with wooden deer heads, give the place the feel of a lodge. If your taste runs to good quality kitsch, the Manoluk is the "Velvet Elvis" of Luang Prabang: You'll appreciate the many large carved elephants, fluorescent village-scene paintings, and shiny bedspreads with fringe. The one suite is fancy in a way that your eccentric uncle might like. The staff seems to be nonexistent, save for a person or two at the front desk watching the lobby television. Somehow, that seems to suit the laid-back, private feel of the place. There are motorcycles and bikes for rent.

121/3 Phou Vao St., Luang Prabang. ✆ 071/212-250 or 071/212-509. Fax 071/212-508. 30 units. $40–$45 double; $70–$80 suite. MC, V. **Amenities:** Restaurant; bar; motorcycle rental; laundry. *In room:* A/C, TV, IDD phone.

**Mouang Luang Hotel** ✦    A 10-minute walk from town on a quiet street north of the Souvanophoum, the Mouang Loung is adorned in traditional Lao temple-style roofs. Comparable to the Manoluk (above) in amenities and value, the rooms at the Mouang Luang are clean, with parquet floors and marble-tiled bathrooms (all with smallish tubs). Street-side rooms have balconies. There's an open-air Lao restaurant in the back, and just above it is an enormous balcony reserved for Baci ceremonies. Mouang Luang has the distinction of being one of the only hotels in town with a pool (there's a charge of $4 for nonguests). The staff is very friendly, and the place is popular with groups. If it's full, try **Le Parasol Blanc,** its sister property (✆ **071/252-124**).

Bounkhong Rd, P.O. Box 779, Luang Prabang. ✆ **071/212-791.** Fax 071/212-790. mgluang@laotel.com. 35 units. Low season $35 single, $40 double; high season $40 single, $45 double. AE, DC, MC, V. **Amenities:** Restaurant; outdoor swimming pool; laundry/dry cleaning; conference room. *In room:* A/C, TV, minibar, IDD phone.

**Phousi Hotel**    For overall comfort, price, and convenience, this is a good middle-of-the-road bet in Luang Prabang. The rooms are neat and clean, with teak furniture, floral fabrics, and little touches like Lao carvings and prints. Bathrooms are large and tidy, and the more expensive doubles have wood floors and are a bit larger; they're certainly worth the upgrade. The hotel is situated in a prime downtown spot, across from the market. At night the Phousi glitters with strings of lights and hums to the tune of live Lao musicians and the happy chatter of the many tour groups who call this home for a few days. Sadly, the word is out and the hotel is overworked, with nicks and scrapes on furniture, disinfectant smells, and halls and carpets that look like cattle have been herded through them.

Setthathirat Rd., Luang Prabang. ✆ **071/212-192.** Fax 071/212-719. phousi@laotel.com. 43 units. $42 standard; $48 superior; $67 family rooms (seasonal rates available). MC, V. **Amenities:** Restaurant; bar; tour desk; car-rental desk; laundry. *In room:* A/C, TV, IDD phone.

**Sala Prabang** ✦✦ *Finds*    Here's a trendsetter in developing Luang Prabang: an old riverside colonial that's been refurbished and refitted, the walls reinforced with stone, and good hot water showers and air-conditioning installed. The renovation was done with some panache, with beams and supports made of rough natural wood, sponge painting, and cool neutral tans throughout. The lobby area is a chic open-air space overlooking the Mekong, and the three top-end rooms on the second floor are large and have great balcony views. Sala Prabang is a boutique guesthouse at its best, and a model that will likely be copied.

Mekong Riverside Rd., 102/6 Thanon Ounkham, Xieng Mouane, P.O. Box 902, Luang Prabang. ✆ 071/252-460. Fax 071/252-472. www.salalao.com. 22 units. $40–$60 double. MC, V. **Amenities:** Cafe; airport transfer; laundry. *In room:* A/C, hair dryer; IDD phone in top-end rooms.

## INEXPENSIVE

**Say Nam Khan Guest House** ✦   Here is an unassuming little gem. In a renovated colonial on the banks of the Nam Khan River, Say Nam Khan is basic but centrally located, with its own quiet, riverside charm. Rooms are small, with comfortable beds and wood furniture. Nothing here is plush. Bathrooms are basic tile, with shower-in-room. The recent renovations mean clean parquet flooring can be found throughout. The hotel is close to "Restaurant Row" and has a laid-back balcony area for watching the sun go down.

Ban Wat Sene (off Kingkitsalath Rd., near the Nam Khan River), Luang Prabang. ℂ **071/212-976.** Fax 071/213-009. saynamkhane_lp@hotmail.com. 14 units. $30–$35 front rooms w/view; $25 back side. No credit cards. **Amenities:** Bar; laundry. *In room:* A/C.

**Sayo Guesthouse** ✦   This guesthouse isn't trying to be anything more than it is, and that is its charm. Service is nonexistent, and the lobby is just a little hallway, but the rooms on the second floor are enormous. Ceilings are practically barn height, and the rooms are done up with tasteful Lao decorations. Bathrooms are clean, large, and of the all-in-one variety (shower and toilet together). The rooms in the back are smaller, with exposed brick and unique loft spaces like little crow's nests. Sayo Guesthouse is basic, but it's an eccentric place with a lot of character. The location is convenient to the main street.

In front of Vat Xieng Mouane (between main rd. and the Mekong), P.O. Box 1060, Luang Prabang. ℂ 071/252-614. 10 units. $15–$40. No credit cards. **Amenities:** Laundry. *In room:* Fan, hot water.

Other good budget choices are atmospheric **Toum-Toum Cheng** (see "Where to Dine," below; ℂ **071/253-224**) with cozy rooms from $20, or **Senesouk** (Ban Vat Sene; ℂ **071/212-074**) with tidy, quiet rooms from $15.

## WHERE TO DINE

New, up-market bistros, many run by foreign restaurateurs, have added to the culinary diversity of little Luang Prabang. Affordable open-air Lao eateries still cater to hungry backpackers returning from the back of beyond, and Luang Prabang remains a wonderful place to explore authentic Lao cuisine or savor some excellent French and Western meals. It's local practice to linger after a long repast, and whether viewing the Mekong, meeting other travelers along "Restaurant Row," or enjoying a romantic corner of a quiet neighborhood, dining in this sleepy northern burg is a delight.

## EXPENSIVE

**L'Elephant** ✦✦ FRENCH   This stylish bistro is where it's at for fine dining in Luang Prabang. Run by French expats, it has a laid-back, retro-chic atmosphere inside a high-ceilinged colonial. There are daily and weekly specials, and just about everything is good, especially the imported steaks. Tasty cheeses and wines are also imported, though local stock is used whenever possible. Boar and venison specials are popular, for example. The wine list could hold its own in a much larger city, and it's unlikely that you'll stump the barman. Daily special set menus explore the best of what's available in the kitchen. A range of tasty dishes from coq au vin to grilled buffalo to a vegetarian savory baked eggplant cover all the bases. L'Elephant is very expensive for Laos but more than worth it. Be sure to make a reservation because it's quite often fully booked.

Ban Vat Nong, P.O. Box 812, Luang Prabang. ℂ 071/252-482. www.elephant-restau.com. Main courses $6–$13. MC, V. Daily 10:30am–2:30pm and 5:30–10pm.

**3 Nagas** ✦✦ LAO   You can get real Lao cuisine done right at this new openair spot on the quiet end of "Restaurant Row." Dining here is as sumptuous an affair as a stay at the connected 3 Nagas boutique hotel (see "Where to Stay," above). Meals are based on the culinary styles of the chef's own hometown, presented by a meticulous and capable waitstaff on fine china. You won't find the bones and gristle of traditional Lao restaurants. Start your meal with betel leaf soup before moving on to sautéed local mushrooms (when in season), *laap*, and grilled delicacies, from chicken satay to whole chunks of hearty river fish, lightly marinated in lemon grass and chiles. For dessert, go for the Lao-style crème brûlée, a custard of pumpkin and coconut with sugar on top that's divine. Great coffee, too.

P.O. Box 772, Luang Prabang (just further along the peninsula from "Restaurant Row"). ℂ 071/252-079. www.3nagas.com. Main courses $2–$12. AE, MC, V. Daily 9am–9pm.

## MODERATE

**Café Reginé** ★★ FRENCH/MEDITERRANEAN    Café Regine is run by French expatriates Xavier and Sylvie, and they have a simple formula, serving good salads, pastas, and pizzas made with fine ingredients and executed with panache. The atmosphere is laid-back—just a small storefront a short walk from the main drag, a great place to duck out of the heat. Their pizzas are the best going, thin-crusted and made with fresh ingredients left to do the talking. I love both the Flaine pizza, topped with cream, onions, bacon, and cheese, and the regular Neopolitan, with oregano and cheese. Sublime. Great breakfasts are also available here.

72/6 Sisavangvatthana Rd., Ban Xieng Mouane. ℂ 071/253-397. Main course $2.30–$6. No credit cards. Daily 7:30am–noon and 6pm–last customer.

**Couleur Café and Restaurant** ★ LAO/FRENCH    This unassuming but atmospheric down-alley bistro features affordable fine dining. The decor is elegantly sparse, with colonial-size high ceilings and walls adorned with the work of local artists. Though run by a young French expat, the bistro has Lao specialties like steamed fish with coconut in banana leaf, or fried prawns in oyster sauce. Both are served, of course, with sticky rice. Eggplant, mushrooms, and crispy green beans are combined in a tasty Casserole Luang Prabang. There is also a popular beef fillet. Order up some Mekong seaweed for an interesting appetizer, and ask about the fine Lao whiskey and imported wines. It's a quiet little getaway for next to nothing.

48/5 Ban Vat Nong, Luang Prabang. ℂ 020/562-1064. Main courses $1–$2. No credit cards. Daily 8am–10pm.

**Indochina Spirit** ★ LAO/THAI/WESTERN    Housed in a restored 70-year-old wooden home, Indochina Spirit, as its name denotes, dishes up as much atmosphere as it does good grub. This gorgeous traditional Lao home has been put to lovely use and now features traditional Lao music most evenings from 7:30 to 8pm (check the chalkboard in front to make sure). Indochina Spirit has done a great job with the simple local decor inside and charming garden dining outside. The menu is an ambitious list of Lao, Thai, and Western dishes. It's a good place to have a drink, enjoy an affordable appetizer plate, and hear some good music before strolling the city at night.

Ban Vat That 52, opposite the fountain across from L'Hotel Souvannaphoum. ℂ 071/252-372. Main courses 70¢–$3. No credit cards. Daily 8am–11pm.

**Toum-Toum Cheng** ★★ *(Finds)* LAO    In a new location on "Restaurant Row," this is an excellent spot for a relaxed or romantic meal. Owners Chandra, a Lao chef of note, and Elizabeth, a long-time expat from Hungary, will certainly make you feel welcome. The atmosphere in the first-floor open-air dining room is chic and comfortable, and decor is Laos original. The food is fantastic. Portions are hearty, but the fare is light, with fresh, local ingredients left to speak for themselves and not overly sauced or cooked away. The spring rolls are without rival, a perfect warm-up for the unique fried-rice salad, fine local curries, or one of many vegetarian specials. If you like what you eat, be sure to sign up for a **cooking course** and find out how to make it back home. Students meet at 9am at the restaurant, take a short ride to the market and shop for the necessary ingredients, and then spend a fun and informative day learning not only about Laos food, but also about Laos culture and history. Chef Chandra is a wealth of information. Classes are $20 for 1 day and $45 for 3 days; they come with the bonus of being able to eat your creations.

On Sisavangvong ("Restaurant Row") across from the Scandinavian Bakery. ℭ 071/253-224. Main courses $2–$4.50. No credit cards. Daily 8am–10pm.

**Villa Santi** ⭐⭐ LAO/CONTINENTAL   On the upper floor of the popular hotel's main building (see "Where to Stay," earlier), this atmospheric open-air perch has just the right angle on the busy street below. With linen and silver, a candlelight table on the balcony is hands down the town's most romantic spot. The food is local and traditional Lao, along with some creative Asian-influenced Continental (on the whole, though, it's a bit uninspired—stick to Lao and Thai specials, and sample one of the fine curries). The daily set menus are always a good choice and walk you through a few courses of local cuisine. The desserts are scrumptious: bananas flambéed in Cointreau, or fruit salad in rum. There are more casual offerings for lunch, including hamburgers. Most evenings there is traditional music and dancing in the courtyard below, and the restaurant is casual enough to allow you to stroll to the window for a look.

Sakkarine St., Luang Prabang (in the Villa Santi Hotel). ℭ 071/212-267. Main courses $2–$6. V. Daily 7am–10pm.

## INEXPENSIVE

For good, cheap eats and the company of many fellow travelers, don't miss what we've called **"Restaurant Row"** (it's hard to miss on any trip to Luang Prabang). It is the only place in town alive past 9pm, though it quickly dies at 11pm. This fun, affordable place is great for exploring—almost like a Khao San Road.

**Café des Arts** ⭐ FRENCH/CONTINENTAL   Pasta, hamburgers, crepes, *filet de boeuf,* and tartines round out the very appetizing menu here. Breakfast has omelets galore. Open-air like all the others on "Restaurant Row," Café des Arts has a better atmosphere than most, with real tables and chairs (not plastic), linen tablecloths, and a gallery of local artwork for sale.

Xieng Thong Rd. (on "Restaurant Row"). ℭ/fax 071/252-162. Main courses 50¢–$1.65. No credit cards. Daily 7am–11pm.

**Malee Lao Food** ⭐ LAO   Malee Lao dishes up inexpensive and delicious local cuisine in a large, casual, open-air setting. It's an old-time favorite for Laos's wayfarers, the kind of place to have a full-table banquet when returning from rough roads or longboat rides in the north. Curries predominate; try the chicken curry soup, which is actually big pieces of chicken and potato in sauce. Don't be daunted by menu items like "chicken cut up into small pieces eaten with green vegetables"—where they're short on linguistic pizzazz, they're long on taste. Try the *aulam,* a curry soup flavored with a unique bitter root.

Near the intersection of Phu Vao and Samsenthai. © 071/252-013. Main courses 35¢–$2. No credit cards. Daily 10am–10pm.

**Nazim** 🏵 INDIAN    Just like the other Nazim outlets in Vientiane and Vang Vieng, Nazim serves a fine compliment of good curries and halal food. The dining area is kind of grubby, but the food is great and Nazim is always packed. There's another location on "Restaurant Row," Sisavangvong Road, at the town center (© 071/253-493).

78/4 Ban Visoun, Visounnarath Rd. © 071/252-263. www.nazim.laopdr.com. Main courses 80¢–$2.50. No credit cards. Daily 8:30am–11pm.

**Somchan Restaurant** 🏵🏵 LAO    In a corner building at the edge of Ban Wat That, the old silversmith's neighborhood that is now a backpacker's ghetto, the Somchan serves up Lao specialties rivaled only by Malee Lao (above) for authenticity and price. There are lovely views of the river in the open-air dining room (more like a patio), but what sells this place is the grub, not the hubbub. Spicy coconut curries, flavored with the unique bitter-root *aulum,* fried dishes of all sorts, and various soups round out a menu that is refreshingly limited. The prices are a steal, and meals are followed up with complimentary fruit in season.

Soulingsvonsa Rd., near the Mekong in Ban Vatthat, Luang Prabang. © 071/252-021. Main courses 80¢–$1.80. No credit cards. Daily 10am–10pm.

## SNACKS & CAFES

For atmosphere, there is nowhere better than **L'étranger: Books and Tea** (booksinlaos@yahoo.com), in Ban Vat Aphay on the back side of Phousy Hill (the opposite side from the main street and royal palace) near the Nam Khan River. The friendly Canadian owners are full of good advice and lend books from their downstairs collection. Have a pot of tea or a cocktail (don't miss the *lao-lao* marguerita) in their atmospheric upstairs teahouse and gallery; it's also a good place in the steamy afternoons to choose from one of the old *National Geographic* magazines lining the walls and relax on the floor against a cozy Lao cushion. Young travelers descend for the films, played each day at 4 and 7pm.

A popular restaurant on "Restaurant Row," the **Luang Prabang Bakery** (11/7 Sisavangvong Rd.; © 071/212-617), serves some good pizza as well as a host of baked goods, and has an extensive collection of books. The **Scandinavian Bakery,** farther east at 52/6 Sisavangvong (© 071/252-223), and chic, air-conditioned **Joma** (© 071/252292), both serve similar fine coffee and baked goods and ensure that you won't go wanting for the delights of home. The same team of expats who run L'Elephant (see "Where to Dine") own **Café Vat Sene** (© 071/212-517), an atmospheric, open-air space with an upstairs gallery. Their desserts and coffee are excellent as are their light lunch specials (sandwiches and salads). Find them just across from the Villa Santi.

The best place in town for authentic French crepes, savory or sweet, **Dao Fa** on Sisavangvong Rd. (© 071/252-656), also has a good menu of fine pastas cooked to order and Mediteranean entrees—it's also a good spot for people-watching.

## WHAT TO SEE & DO

**Mount Phousi** 🏵🏵    Rising from the center of town, Phousi has temples scattered on all sides of its slopes and a panoramic view of the entire town from its top. **That Chomsi Stupa,** built in 1804, is its crowning glory. Taking the path to the northeast, you will pass **Wat Tham Phousi,** which has a large-bellied

Buddha, Kaccayana. **Wat Phra Bat Nua,** farther down, has a yard-long footprint of the Buddha. Be prepared for the 355 steps to get there. Try to make the hike, which will take about 2 hours with sightseeing, in the early morning or late afternoon, to escape the sun's burning rays. A great spot for sunset.

Admission 10,000 kip ($1). Daily dawn–dusk.

**Royal Palace Museum** 🜲🜲  The palace, built for King Sisavang Vong from 1904 to 1909, was the royal residence until the Pathet Lao seized control of the country in 1975. The last Lao king, Sisavang Vattana, and his family were exiled to a remote region in the northern part of the country and never heard from again. Rumor has it that they perished in a prison camp, though the government has never said so. The palace remains as a repository of treasures, rather scanty but still interesting. You can begin your tour by walking the length of the long porch; the gated open room to your right has one of the museum's top attractions, a replica of a golden standing Buddha that was a gift to King Fa Ngum from a Khmer king. Known as "The Prabang" (thus the town's name), which translates to "holy image," the original was cast in Sri Lanka in the 1st century A.D. Don't miss the busts of the last dynasty of kings. The central throne room is done in colorful glass mosaics dating from a renovation in the 1930s. Past the throne rooms is a compound of large, spartan bedrooms with what little finery was left after the departure of the last king. The temple at the compound entrance is a gilded wedding cake, and don't miss the large Soviet-made statue of Sisavang Vong, the first king under the Lao constitution, giving a stiff raised fist like a caricature of Lenin.

The palace hosts a growing troupe of dancers who perform at the Royal Theater. On Monday, Wednesday, and Friday, tourists can take part in a Baci ceremony and view the historical reenactment of the *Ramayana* (tickets are $5).

Phothisarat Rd. 🕾 071/212470. Admission 20,000 kip ($2). Mon–Sat 8–11am and 1:30–4pm. **(Warning:** At 11am they will kick you out, and you'll have to pay *again* to come back after lunch.)

**Wat Mai** 🜲🜲  Wat Mai is one of the jewels of Luang Prabang. Its golden bas-relief facade tells the story of Phravet, one of the last avatars, or reincarnations, of the Buddha. This *wat* held the Pra Bang Buddha from 1894 until 1947. Stop by at 5:30pm for the evening prayers, when the monks chant in harmony.

Phothisarat Rd., near the Lane Xang Bank. Daily dawn–dusk.

**Wat Wisunalat/Visounarath** 🜲  Wisunalat is known for its absolutely huge golden Buddha in the sim, the largest in town at easily 6m (20 ft.) tall. The wat was constructed in 1512 and held the famous Pra Bang Buddha from 1513 to 1894. On the grounds facing the sim is the famous **That Makmo,** or watermelon stupa, a survivor since 1504. Wat Aham is a few steps away from the Wisunalat sim.

At the end of Wisunalat Rd. Daily 8am–5pm.

**Wat Xieng Thong** 🜲🜲  Xieng Thong is the premier *wat* of Luang Prabang. Built in 1560 by King Say Setthathirat, it is situated at the tip of Luang Prabang's peninsula where it juts out into the Mekong. Xieng Thong survived numerous invading armies, making its facade one of the oldest originals in the city. To the left of the main temple, find the "red chapel" and its rare statue of a reclining Buddha that dates back to the temple's construction. The statue is one of the premier Buddha images in the country, with lines and an attitude sublime; the piece actually traveled to the World's Fair in Paris in 1931. The glass mosaics adorning

> **Moments** **Taking Refuge: Making Friends at the Temple**
>
> There is little that's spectacular on the sleepy peninsula of Luang Pra-bang. Time spent here is about soaking up the atmosphere and taking leisurely walks along dusty lanes lined with French colonial buildings. Another great local activity is to stop in at a temple—any temple, really—and meet up with monks or young novices. The monks are great sources of information and insight into Laos culture, Buddhism, or the vagaries of human existence. Language is a big part of their training, and they study Pali and Sanskrit as well as English and French (and even Chinese and Japanese). Novices are keen to practice their English on you or even get help with their homework. Women should be careful not to touch or sit too close to monks and novices, but all are welcome in the temple. Don't give in to any pleas for sponsorship (unless you want to); monks live through the generosity of the *sangha*, or monastic community, and don't need sponsors.

all external buildings date from only the 1950s but are fun depictions of popular folk tales and Buddhist history; note the "tree of life" on the side of the main temple. Facing the courtyard from the temple steps, the building on the right contains the funeral chariot of King Sisavang Vong with its seven-headed *naga* (snake) decor. The chariot was carved by venerated Lao sculptor Thid Tun. There are also some artifacts inside, including ancient marionettes.

At the end of Xieng Thong Rd. Admission 10,000 kip ($1). Daily 8am–6pm.

## SITES OUTSIDE THE CITY

**Kuangsi Waterfall** 🏛🏛 As famous now for its recent collapse as anything, Kuangsi was a tower of champagne-glass limestone formations until the whole structure fell in on itself in 2003. Locals say that tour operators became too greedy and neglected local spirits, called Pi. The falls are still beautiful, but less so. The ride there, however, is quite spectacular. You'll either have to trace the 30km (19 miles) by *songthaew,* at $5 per person if shared, or by boat and tuk-tuk for the same fee.

36km (20 miles) south of town. Admission 15,000kip ($1.50). Daily dawn–dusk.

**Pak Ou Caves** 🏛🏛 The 25km (16-mile) longtail boat ride on the Mekong is alone a worthy day trip. This stretch of river is lovely and from the base of the cave entrance you get a view of the high cliffs and swirling water of the Nam Ou river as it joins the Mekong. Inside the caves are enshrined a pantheon of Bud-dhist statuary. A day tour here costs $5 per person in a boat shared by many tourists—more for a private charter. Arrangements can be made at any hotel front desk at an inflated rate, or just go down along the Mekong and negotiate with boat drivers directly (these guys are sure to find you). The half-day trip often includes a visit to a weaving village or the **Lao Whiskey village,** where you'll have a chance to try some really potent local brew.

25km (16 miles) from town on the Mekong. Admission 10,000 kip ($1).

**Tad Se Waterfall** is 21km (13 miles) from town and good for swimming, even if it's less spectacular in height than Kuangsi. During the rainy season, the falls are stunning. Hire a driver for about $5 or pay a bit extra for a ferry boat.

Other sites outside of town include **Wat Phon Phao (Peacefulness Temple),** a golden stupa on a hilltop about 5km (3 miles) away, that's best viewed from afar—though the view back to town from its height is worth the trek. From there, visit nearby **Ban Phanom Weaving Village,** a now rather commercialized weaving collective where you can find deals on Lao Ikat patterns and hand-woven bags. Just past Ban Phanom and hidden in a jungle riverside area (signs point the way down the embankment), find the **Tomb of Henri Mouhot,** the 19th-century French explorer credited with the rediscovery of Cambodia's Angkor Wat. He died in Luang Prabang of malaria while hunting the source of the Mekong. Day trips **across the Mekong** to small temples and villages are also popular and can be arranged with boat drivers at quayside.

## OUTDOOR ACTIVITIES

Luang Prabang is a good base for exploring the jungly north. The folks at **Wild-side Eco Adventures** (✆ 071/212-093; www.lao-wildside.com) in the center of town are a top choice. You can also try **Tiger Trails** at Ban Wat That (✆ 071/252-655; www.tigertrails.com). Both offer tours and connections to the far north in Luang Nam Tha, in addition to multisport adventures along the Mekong and the picturesque Nam Ou out of Nong Kiaw (east of Luang Prabang).

## SHOPPING

Luang Prabang is a good place to find unique, hand-woven textiles. The **Night Market** opens at dusk each evening near Wat Mai along Phothisarat Road at the town center. Anything from good silk to jewelry to T-shirts sells for a song.

Check out the **Blue House** (✆ 071/252-383), near the Villa Santi, where there's a revolving display of local handicrafts. **OckPopTok,** in a two-story colonial between L'Elephant restaurant and the Mekong (✆ 020/570-148 or 071/253-219; www.ockpoptok.com), carries a fine line of contemporary Lao textiles (it also has a new outlet on "Restaurant Row" in the center of town.)

Natural papermaking has taken the town by storm, and **Baan Khily Gallery** on the eastern end of Sisavangvong Road (✆ 071/212-611) is where long-time German expat Oliver Bandmann produces and exhibits.

**Caruso,** Sandra Yuck's inspired collection of houseware, furnishings, and silk, has a new outlet in a renovated colonial along Sisavangvong as well as a display area above Ban Vat Sene (see "Snacks & Cafes," above).

**Lisa Regale** (✆ 071/253-224) has a unique collection of ready-to-wear silk, including some very unique antique pieces, at her gallery behind Wat Xieng Thong.

On "Restaurant Row," **Satri Lao Silk** has good, affordable cloth, and **Naga Creations** (✆ 071/212-775) presents an eclectic mix of jewelry.

## NIGHTLIFE

Luang Prabang is a morning town, really, but there are a few good spots for drinks and music. Backpackers fill the quiet lanes of Ban Wat That, the old silversmith quarter near the Mekong on the east end of town, and you'll sometimes find folks up late. Take a walk down any alley for budget guesthouses and adjoining bamboo bars.

**The Hive,** just next door to L'étranger (p. 277) and run by the same folks, plays drum and bass and hip-hop to a young crowd until late into the evening.

## MASSAGE

The **Red Cross of Luang Prabang,** near Wat Visoun to the southeast of the city, offers traditional massage and herbal sauna to raise money for its education programs. The Red Cross is the cheapest place in town, in addition to funding a good cause. The herbal sauna is open daily from 4:30 to 8:30pm; a 1-hour massage (9am–8:30pm) costs just $3.

## 6 Luang Namtha & the Far North

North of Luang Prabang, things get a little rough. It's where Laos travel separates the "travelers" from the "tourists." Roads are, in the main, just dirt tracks, and most towns are outposts, like the dusty main streets in the American Old West. This part of the country is best visited with a tour company (try **Diethelm** out of Luang Prabang; see "Visitor Information & Tours," in section 5) or with a private car and driver. The north has long been a favorite destination for intrepid individual travelers who brave the long, bumpy rides to meet with ethnic minority groups on treks or kayak expeditions in beautiful, rugged, mountainous jungle.

   **Luang Namtha** itself is not much to see, really—just a row of low concrete and wood storefronts on a dusty avenue and a few miles of bucolic road that takes you to the picturesque little **Old Town** (6km/3¾ miles down the main road); nonetheless, it's connected by air with Vientiane and is a great base to explore the surrounding countryside. Trekking, kayaking, and visiting remote villages in the phenomenal **Nam Ha Biodiversity Conservation Area** bring many up to this outpost. Come with the knowledge that travel here is off the track, you are far from all but the most basic medical assistance, and electricity flows only a few hours each day.

## VISITOR INFORMATION & TOURS

**Wildside Eco Group** puts together great kayak and raft trips in the pristine Nam Ha NBCA. You'll visit villages where they'll ask, through a translator, "Why are you here?" because foreign wayfarers are still an anomaly. The Nam Ha River is an exciting whitewater ride through cavernous jungle overgrowth or steep-walled gullies teeming with life. The folks at Wildside (© **086/211-484**) ensure that their clients set a good example and tread lightly in the villages. Find them at their small storefront on the main street. Highly recommended.

   **The NamHa Ecotourism,** working with the support of the government of New Zealand and UNESCO, offers multiday trekking to Khmu and Hmong villages in the area. Expect to pay from $13 per day to join a small group (no more than eight). This organization follows the truest tenets of eco-tourism, ensuring that Western visitors act properly in villages and that revenue generated from the program doesn't line the pockets of one village fat cat, but rather supports the building of schools and projects that benefit the whole village. Private tours can also be arranged. The guiding office is just 1 block off of the main street behind the post office (P.O. Box 7, Luang Nam Tha, 03000; © **086/312-150;** namhaguides@hotmail.com). Treks to a new region of the north, Vieng Phoukha, are also offered. Contact the Vieng Phoukha Guide Service (© **081/212-400;** www.theboatlanding.com)

## GETTING THERE

**BY AIR**   From Vientiane, there are a few flights each week, depending on the season, and they cost $80. The airport is 6km (3¾ miles) from town; a *songthaew* (covered pickup) will run about $3 with some friendly bargaining.

**BY BUS**   Luang Nam Tha is a major hub in the north, connecting by bus with **Jinhong, China** via Boten (you'll need to have a prearranged visa), **Muang Sing,** and **Houaysay** (Thai border). From Luang Prabang, you'll be bounced and jounced for 5 hours (25,000 kip/$2.50) until the dusty bus stop in **Oudomxay.** If your teeth are still in your head and buses are leaving (most buses have morning departures), you can connect with Luang Namtha for 20,000 kip ($2); sometimes there is no same-day connection, and travelers hole up for a $2 night in Oudomxay before the early-morning connection with Luang Namtha. Bus travel in the far north offers beautiful views and a chance to meet locals, but it is pretty grueling in the best of circumstances.

**BY CAR**   Contact **Diethelm** in Luang Prabang (✆ **071/212-277;** fax 071/212-032) for jeep/minivan rental. It's expensive, but a decent option for the north.

---

## FAST FACTS: Luang Namtha

**Bank and Post**   There are a few foreign exchange counters on the main road (Rte. 3), and **Lane Xang Bank** has a branch on the south end of town. You can change U.S. and Thai currency to kip in the central market.

**Internet**   There is one Internet cafe on the southern end of the main street with service at 600 kip/6¢ per minute.

**Telephone**   Most guesthouses can do callback service, and there are phone booths on the main road that are IDD-capable and require a local card (buy at any store or the post office).

---

## WHERE TO STAY & DINE

For lodging, **The Boat Landing** (✆ **086/312-398;** www.theboatlanding. laopdr.com) is a rustic little gem on the banks of the Nam Tha River some 6km (3¾ miles) from the town center (just past the old town in Luang Namtha). It has good local info and a good restaurant. In **Luang Namtha** proper, an array of budget accommodations start at $2. Try **Oudomsinh Hotel** (✆ **086/312-077**) or **Manichan Guesthouse** (✆ **086/312-398**) in Ban Phonsay.

## 7 Xieng Khouang Province: Phonsavan

Xieng Khouang Province is home to the Plain of Jars, a little-understood group of archaeological sites of enormous stone jars, or drums, buried in the earth. Phonsavan, the provincial capital and jumping-off point for exploring the area, still has an eerie "edge of the Earth" feeling; electricity is available only between 6 and 11pm, so bring a flashlight and some candles. Xieng Khouang is the land of "the secret war" waged by the CIA and American military against Communist forces in the border region of Vietnam. Bomb craters don't fill in too quickly and most will never grow grass again. Halved bombshells serve as pig troughs, metal tracks airlifted for makeshift runways are converted to convenient driveways, and there is even a village dedicated to and decorated by found shrapnel and bomb material. The jars themselves are a fun and interesting mystery. A visit to this region is certainly educational; you'll learn about the Hmong rebels, the mysterious recent history, and the many demining projects. Spring for a good guide to take you around to the many sites. *Note:* Higher altitude and weather patterns mean that it can get chilly here, especially in the rainy season, so bring a few layers.

---

*Warning*  **Beware of Unexploded Ordnance**

Xieng Khouang Province is one of the most heavily bombed areas on the Earth. UXO, or unexploded ordnance, is numerous, particularly in the form of small cluster bombs, blue or gray metal balls about the size of a fist. Don't stray into uninhabited unexplored areas without a good guide, and don't touch anything on the ground. The jar sites are safe.

---

## VISITOR INFORMATION & TOURS

At **Sousath Travel,** adjoining Maly Guesthouse, P.O. Box 649, Xieng Khouang (© **061/312-031;** fax 061/312-395) the effusive Mr. Sousath is the definitive source on local history and a true steward of the jar sites; he has been featured in a number of local history and archaeology books and was in a documentary, *Ravens,* about the covert CIA pilots who flew from the area during the Vietnam War. A tour with Mr. Sousath himself, if you are so fortunate, is one of the town's most interesting activities. A car and driver can be arranged.

**Diethelm** (© **061/211-118**), on the main road in Phonsavan, meets its usual high standard and can cater guided tours to any sites, local and remote.

Local guides will come and find you upon arrival or if you're wandering central Phonsavan. Gauge their English ability, be specific about the itinerary, and barter for price. Freelance guides usually charge about 311,250 kip $30 for tour and transport.

## GETTING THERE

**BY AIR**    Lao Airlines (© **021/214-427;** www.laoairlines.com) flies a loop starting from Vientiane to Luang Prabang and on to Phonsavan before back to the capital. You cannot fly back to Luang Prabang from Phonsavan. Flight schedules change with the seasons. Make sure you reconfirm your flight out *every day until you leave* to guarantee a seat back (flights overbook in the high season and get canceled in the low season).

**BY BUS**    Daily buses connect Phonsavan with Vientiane and Luang Prabang (6–8 hrs and 55,000 kip/ $5.50 from Vientiane; 6–8 hrs and 70,000 kip/ $7 from Luang Prabang). Route 7, a spur of the main north-south artery, Route 13, begins 150km (93 miles) north of Vientiane; the road, once a contender for the world's worst, is now in great condition. The ridge-top scenery is spectacular but buses are overcrowded and slow. The road is prone to landslides, so ask travel agents and fellow travelers about current conditions before setting out. Private vehicle hire is costly, but the best choice.

## FAST FACTS: PHONSAVAN

**Bank and Post**    There are a few foreign exchange counters on the main road (Rte. 7) near the central market, and Lane Xang Bank has a branch near the post office. *Note:* There is no Internet in Phonsavan.

## WHERE TO STAY & DINE

**Budget accommodations** line the main street (Rte. 7), and if you don't care to dine at your hotel, take a short stroll and you'll find a few good noodle and snack shops near the town center.

**Auberge de la Plaine des Jarres** ⚑    Throw another log on the fire and gaze across the deep green fields and rolling mountain scenery from the comfort of your own rustic bungalow. Nestled into a peaceful grove of pine on a mountain overlooking town, this is a great choice for atmosphere. Beds are spongy and some rooms musty, but fireplaces are a nice touch and the gas-powered showers are the best in town. The Auberge is light on amenities, so come with your own car and driver from town.

Atop Mount Phupadeng overlooking the town from the southeast. ℂ 061/312-044. plainjar@samart.co.th. $45–$60 double. No credit cards. **Amenities:** Restaurant; laundry. *In room:* Fireplace.

**Maly Hotel**   Owned and operated by local historian and raconteur Mr. Sousath, this is a good low-luxe but comfortable base for exploring the jars. Built pell mell in a series of additions, rooms vary and the decoration runs the gamut from comfortable wooden lodge to musty cell. Ask to see the room before checking in. A few luxe setups have floor-to-ceiling windows and fine views. Baths are guesthouse basic with fickle solar showers. Good Lao and Western food can be found in the popular lobby restaurant, the staff is friendly and helpful, and the convenient offices of **Sousath Travel** are the best place in town to arrange for a guide. There's some useful literature about the jars, and don't miss any chance to chat with Mr. Sousath. *Note:* This is the only credit card outlet in town.

P.O. Box 649, Xieng Khouang (short ride south from the town center). ℂ 061/312-031. sousathp@laotel. com. 24 units. $8–$55 double. MC, V. **Amenities:** Restaurant; tour service; car/jeep rental. *In room:* TV.

## WHAT TO SEE & DO

Thought to date back some 2,000 years, the archaeological finds at the **Plain of Jars** are stunning and mysterious. Hundreds of stone jars of varying sizes, the largest a bit over 2.7m (9 ft.) high, cover a plateau stretching across 24km (15 miles). Jars have been found in 15 different sites in the area so far. Visit these sites with a guide, if only to buoy up any fears over landmines (all areas within the sites are safe, though) and to get some perspective on local history. Be sure to get the obligatory "This is me in a jar!" shot before they make restrictions on touching or climbing on them. You can cover the main sites in one day, but you might want to take a few days and explore the surrounding Hmong villages. **Na Sala,** a busy Hmong village, is a good destination. Be sure to go with a guide who can translate and make introductions. **The Phonsavan Market** is standard for Laos, but very large, with unique trade items from nearby Vietnam.

**Site 1**  ⟨★★⟩   If you're short on time, this is the one to see. Set on a high hill is one of the largest of the jars, called the Doloman jar, amid a cockeyed collection of 300 jars. It's all quite surreal and a unique photo op; a visit here gives you a great perspective on the surrounding countryside. Burn scars still dot the area, and legend has it that a few enterprising members of the American military once tried to lift one of the jars with a helicopter and failed. This is the easiest site to access and the most picturesque.

11km (7 miles) from town, near Ban Hang Village. Admission 5,000 kip (50¢).

**Sites 2 and 3**  ⟨★⟩   These sites are both off the beaten track and require some fancy driving and a bit of picturesque rice paddy and pasture walking to reach, but they are certainly worth it. Site 2 is situated near a small waterfall and has some 60 jars in a grove atop a small hill. Site 3 will have you crossing a bamboo bridge and picking your way through fields to get to open pasture on a high hill with some 100 jars.

Site 2 is 22km (14 miles) from town, and Site 3 is just a short drive from there. Both have admission fees of 5,000 kip (50¢).

## 8 The Far South: Pakse & Champasak Provinces

South of Vientiane, Route 13 traces the Mekong River as it forms the border with Thailand. The river passes through Savannakhet, a French colonial outpost, then Pakse, a midsize town, before reaching the wide Mekong floodplain, where the river spreads into hundreds of rivulets before cascading over dynamic **Phapheng Falls** to Cambodia. What brings many to this little-visited region is **Wat Phou,** a pre-Angkorian ruin on a hilltop overlooking the river near the town of **Champassak.** The city of **Pakse** is the best base for exploring, and there are some great new luxury options, like a multiday cruise on LuangSay's **Wat Phou** riverboat. **Si Phan Don,** in the far south, literally means "the 4,000 islands." Here, the Mekong spreads out like the branches of a tree and you'll find stunning waterfalls and quaint island towns like **Don Khong.** The town of **Savannakhet** is a good stop for those connecting overland with Vientiane, and there are also some good rustic resorts like those at Tad Lo, Saravan, and the Bolavan Plateau. Arranging a tour with Diethelm (p. 243) or Exotissimo (p. 243), even just for transport, is a good choice.

### GETTING THERE

**BY PLANE   Lao Airlines** (℘ **021/214-427;** www.laoairlines.com) flies regularly from Vientiane to Pakse for $87. The airport in Pakse is on the opposite side of the river from the main town. Tuk-tuks connect to town for 8,000 kip (80¢) with bargaining.

**BY BUS**   Buses connect from Vientiane via Savannakhet. The road is good thanks to the many new Japanese-funded bridges, but it's 2 long days of travel. It is 8 hours from Vientiane to Savannakhet and then up to 10 hours from Savannakhet to Pakse. It's worth a flight, even if just one-way.

Pakse is just a short ride from the Thai border and a few hours by bus from Ubon Ratchatani.

### WHERE TO STAY

Accommodation choices are limited in the far south. **Champa Residence** (on Rte. 13, south of town in Ban Phonosath; ℘ **031/212-120**) has tidy rooms in a former colonial from $50. In the heart of town, **Hotel Pakse** (Street No. 5, Ban Watlouang; ℘ **031/212-131**), has basic concrete rooms with air-conditioning and cable from $18.

### WHAT TO SEE & DO

**Wat Phu** 👁👁   Predating the temples of Angkor (some time before the 9th century), this stunning hilltop site is a highlight in Laos. Wat Phu was built in homage to the Hindu god Shiva, on grounds once used for animist worship. Some archaeologists posit that the temple is also homage to the Mekong and a copy of a similar site along the Ganges in India. The compound is symmetrical, with a broad causeway as the central axis and expansive reflecting *barays,* or ponds, now gone dry, as flanks. The approach to the main temple site passes between two pavilions, crumbling but still grand, before ascending the steep central stair.

The upper level is the main sanctuary, which was converted to Buddhism in the 13th century and now houses nonhistoric Buddhist statues and an altar. The temple exterior is decorated in fine reliefs of Apsara, alluring mythical female dancers. The sanctuary was reportedly a site of human sacrifices from the pre-Wat

---

*Finds*  **Luxury on the Mekong: The Vat Phou Cruise**

The **Vat Phou Cruise** operated by the folks at LuangSay Cruises (© 021/ 215-958) in Vientiane; www.mekongcruises.com) offers 3-day, 2-night cruises between Pakse and the 4,000 Islands (Si Phan Don) in the far south. Trips cost a whopping $573 for a single ($441 per person in a shared double) in high season, but it's worth it. The boat is large and luxurious, with a top deck replete with quiet corners to relax and enjoy the passing scenery. Private state rooms are small but air-conditioned and comfortable. All trips begin in Pakse. Trips include stops at small villages, the unique pre-Angkorian ruins of Oum Muong, and, of course, the south's premeire attraction, **Wat Phou.** The food is ample, guides are informative and professional, and service is very friendly.

---

Phu temple era. Today, in a ceremony conducted on the 4th day of the waxing moon in the 6th lunar month, a bull is ritually slaughtered by members of a nearby Mon-Khmer (an ethnic group closely related to the Khmer) tribe in honor of the founding father of the temple. The view of the surrounding Mekong basin is spectacular. Don't miss the spring at the base of the cliff behind the main temple. The water is thought sacred and visitors anoint themselves to receive a blessing.

There is a small museum at the entrance featuring artifacts from the original site. Wat Phu is best visited with a tour. Diethelm (p. 243) and Exotissimo (p. 243) can make any arrangements. The *wat* is also a stop on the **Wat Phu Cruise** (see box above).

14km (8¾ miles) southwest of Champasak; 45km (28 miles) from Pakse. Admission 30,000 kip ($3). Daily 8am–4pm.

# 6

# Vietnam

*by Charles Agar*

"**V**ietnam is a country, not a war," goes the popular saying. Though memories lie just below the surface for all combatants and those who lived through the war in Vietnam and abroad, Vietnam is long a vibrant tourist destination and a visit of any length will dispel many preconceptions. From lush jungle terrain to beautiful coastline, cosmopolitan cities to friendly hamlets, or among Vietnam's many ethnic hill tribes, travelers can experience the gamut in only a short trip here.

Vietnam's more than 2,000 years of history is marred by occupation: the Chinese, French, and Americans left a brutal imprint on the Vietnamese story, but also left a rich cultural smorgasbord. Chinese and French food, language, and architecture have been assimilated smoothly into the already fascinating Vietnamese fabric of culture. An ancient Confucian university, a Zen monastery, a Buddhist temple built in the Hindu style, a Vietnamese puppet show, French country chalets, and gourmet restaurants—you'll find them all in Vietnam.

Vietnam hosts 54 minority groups, mostly in rural, mountainous areas. The distinct clothing, language, and customs of each indigenous group present another side of the country entirely. The Kingdom of Cham, an Indian- and Khmer-influenced nation, also made what is present-day Vietnam its home from the 2nd through 18th centuries, leaving a stunning legacy of art and architecture.

Vietnam is a land of rich natural beauty. From tall mountains and craggy limestone formations to dense jungles, river deltas, and pristine beaches, Vietnam's ecological treasures alone are worth a trip. Adventure and outdoor travel outfitters abound, and many travelers come to trek, bicycle, and paddle their way to scenic serenity.

If you want to see the country's past in terms of its wars, you can easily do so. Many sites, like the tunnel city of Vinh Moc, near Hue; crumbling pill-boxes of the DMZ (demilitarized zone); or old Viet Cong hideouts in the Mekong Delta or in the areas outside of Saigon are somber reminders of the past. American veterans and history buffs of all nationalities visit former bases and battle sites. The Vietnamese, though, would rather put their turbulent history behind them; the sentiment is almost a public policy, and you'll hear it like a mantra. You might have a chance to talk about the wars on a casual basis with people, and some might even share their stories, but expect no recrimination.

Instead, the Vietnamese are going forward to establish their country as a strong nation at peace. Since the inception of *doi moi,* the Communist Party's policy of loosening stringent economic restrictions and opening trade, Vietnam has enjoyed exponential growth. From the smallest northern village to frantic Saigon in the south, all are rushing for a slice of the pie. National infrastructure is growing, foreign investment flowing, and tourism booming. The Asian economic crisis is a distant memory and in larger cities, the central business districts rank with any in the world for quantity of glass and steel, and are peopled by an increasing number of Western businesspeople. Expat residents bring along their pocketbooks and appetites, and local hotels and restaurants rise to the challenge.

And it is easy to get around; English speakers are many and, though the touts are plenty, you'll have your pick of tour guides, ticket agents, and drivers. Vietnam's relatively good roadways and efficient air system make much of this small country within very easy reach of the casual traveler, and the country also hosts an ever-expanding collection of affordable, luxury resorts.

So, whether to close a chapter on the past, to experience a lively ancient culture, to see beautiful countryside, to get your adventure fix, or to just get a bit of beachside or cosmopolitan comfort, Vietnam has it all. Be sure to bring your camera: The whole country is a photo op in motion.

## 1 Getting to Know Vietnam

### THE LAY OF THE LAND

Vietnam is an S-shape peninsula that borders China to the north, Laos to the west, and Cambodia to the southwest. Covering about 331,520 sq. km (129,293 sq. miles), it is roughly the size of Italy. It has a varied and lush topography, with two deltas, tropical forests, craggy mountains and rock formations, and a coastline that stretches for 3,260km (2,021 miles), much of it white-sand beaches. Vietnam also claims thousands of islands off its coast.

### THE REGIONS IN BRIEF

**THE NORTH** The scenic northern highlands have craggy mountains hovering over sweeping green valleys. The inhabitants of the region are ethnic minorities and hill tribes, scratching out a living from subsistence farming and still somewhat isolated from civilization. Popular tourism destinations are **Sapa, Lao Cai, Son La,** and **Dien Bien Phu,** the former French military garrison. Vietnam's tallest mountain, Fansipan (3,143m/10,309 ft.), hovers over Sapa near the border with China in the northwest, part of the mountain range the French dubbed "The Tonkinese Alps." The **Red River** Delta lies to the east of the highlands. It is a triangular shape off the **Gulf of Tonkin,** an extension of the South China Sea. In the gulf is spectacular **Halong Bay,** 3,000 limestone formations jutting up from still blue waters. South of the highlands but still in the northern region is **Hanoi,** Vietnam's capital city.

**THE CENTRAL COAST** To the east is the central coastline, location of major cities **Hue, Hoi An,** and **Danang.** Hue is Vietnam's former capital and imperial city (1802–1945). Hoi An, a major trading port in the mid–16th century, still shows the architectural influences of the Chinese and Japanese traders who passed through and settled here, leaving buildings that are perfectly preserved. Danang, Vietnam's fourth-largest city, is a port town whose major attractions include the museum of Cham antiquities and nearby China Beach. Major flooding in the year 2000 caused immeasurable damage to the lowlands here, which will be apparent if you try to navigate Highway 1; at the printing of this book, the highway had yet to be repaired.

**THE SOUTH CENTRAL COAST & HIGHLANDS** The central highlands area is a temperate, hilly region occupied by many of Vietnam's ethnic minorities. Travelers are most likely to visit historic **Dalat,** a resort town nestled in the Lang Bien Plateau, established by the French at the turn of the century as a

# Vietnam

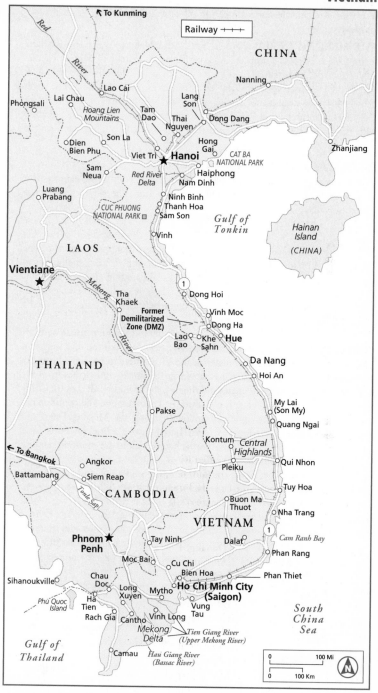

↖ To Kunming

Railway ┼┼┼┼

**CHINA**

Red River

Nanning

Lao Cai

Lai Chau

Phongsali

Lang Son

Tam Dao

Thai Nguyen

Dong Dang

Hoang Lien Mountains

Son La

Dien Bien Phu

Hong Gai

Viet Tri ★ **Hanoi**

Zhanjiang

CAT BA NATIONAL PARK

Sam Neua

Haiphong

Red River Delta

Nam Dinh

Luang Prabang

Ninh Binh

Thanh Hoa

Sam Son

CUC PHUONG NATIONAL PARK 🏛

Vinh

*Gulf of Tonkin*

*Hainan Island*

*(CHINA)*

**LAOS**

★ **Vientiane**

Tha Khaek

Mekong

① Dong Hoi

**Former Demilitarized Zone (DMZ)**

Vinh Moc

Dong Ha

Lao Bao

Khe Sanh

**Hue**

**THAILAND**

River

Da Nang

Hoi An

My Lai (Son My)

Quang Ngai

Pakse

Kontum

*Central Highlands*

← To Bangkok

Angkor

Siem Reap

Battambang

Pleiku

Qui Nhon

Tuy Hoa

**CAMBODIA**

Tonle Sap

Buon Ma Thuot

Nha Trang

**VIETNAM**

① *Cam Ranh Bay*

★ **Phnom Penh**

Tay Ninh

Dalat

Moc Bai

Cu Chi

Bien Hoa

Phan Rang

Sihanoukville

Chau Doc

Long Xuyen

Mytho

**Ho Chi Minh City (Saigon)**

Phan Thiet

*Phu Quoc Island*

Ha Tien

Rach Gia

Cantho

Vinh Long

Vung Tau

*South China Sea*

*Gulf of Thailand*

Camau

*Mekong Delta*

*Tien Giang River (Upper Mekong River)*

*Hau Giang River (Bassac River)*

0 ——— 100 Mi

0 ——— 100 Km

recreation and convalescence center. On the coast is **Nha Trang,** Vietnam's pre-eminent sea resort.

**THE MEKONG DELTA**    Farthest south, the Mekong Delta is a flat land formed by soil deposits from the Mekong River. Its climate is tropical, characterized by heat, high rainfall, and humidity. The delta's sinuous waterways drift past fertile land used for cultivating rice, fruit trees, and sugar cane. The lower delta is untamed swampland. The region shows the influences of ancient Funan and Khmer cultures, as well as the scars from war misery, particularly in battles with neighboring Cambodia. **Saigon (Ho Chi Minh City),** Vietnam's largest cosmopolitan area, lies just past its northern peripheries.

## A LOOK AT THE PAST

Vietnam began in the Red River Valley, around the time of the 3rd century B.C., with a small kingdom of Viet tribes called Au Lac. The tiny kingdom was quickly absorbed into the Chinese Qin Dynasty in 221 B.C., but as that dynasty crumpled, it became part of a new land called Nam Viet, ruled by a Chinese commander. In 111 B.C., it was back to China again, this time as part of the Han empire. It remained part of greater China for the next thousand years or so. The Chinese form of writing was adopted (to be replaced by a Roman alphabet in the 17th century), Confucianism was installed as the leading ideology, and Chinese statesmen became the local rulers. Few effectively challenged Chinese rule, with the exception of a nobleman's two daughters, the Trung sisters, who led a successful but short-lived revolt in A.D. 39.

In A.D. 939, the Chinese were finally thrown off and the Vietnamese were left to determine their own destiny under a succession of dynasties. The kingdom flourished and strengthened, enough for the Vietnamese to repel the intrusion of Mongol invaders under Kublai Khan from the north, and armies from the kingdom of Champa from Danang and the east, in the mid–13th century. Gathering strength, Vietnam gradually absorbed the Cham empire and continued to move south, encroaching upon Khmer land, taking the Mekong Delta and almost extinguishing the Khmer as well. There followed a brief period of Chinese dominance in the early 1400s, but the biggest risk to the country's stability was to come from the inside.

Torn between rival factions in court, the country split along north-south lines in 1545; the north followed the Le Dynasty, and the south followed the Nguyen. The country was reunited under Emperor Gia Long in 1802, but by the 1850s, the French, already settled and on the prowl in Indochina, launched an offensive that resulted in the Vietnamese accepting protectorate status 3 decades later.

Although the French contributed greatly to Vietnamese infrastructure, the proud people of Vietnam bridled under colonial rule. In 1930, revolutionary Ho Chi Minh found fertile ground to establish a nationalist movement. As in China, World War II and occupation by the Japanese in 1940 helped fuel the movement by creating chaos and nationalist fervor. Upon the retreat of the Japanese, Ho Chi Minh declared Vietnam an independent nation in August 1945.

The French did not agree, however, and the two sides fought bitterly until 1954. The French, having lost a decisive battle at Dien Bien Phu, agreed to a cease-fire at the Geneva Convention that year. The two sides determined that the country would be split along north and south at the 17th Parallel, with the Viet Minh (League for the Independence of Vietnam) having control of the north and the French supporters having control of the south. Elections were to be held in 2 years to determine who would lead a new, unified Vietnam.

Because of resistance to the American-supported regime in the south, led by Ngo Dinh Diem, the elections were never held. The communists continued to gain power, and Diem was assassinated, putting the southern regime in peril. Finally, in 1965, American president Lyndon Johnson dispatched the first American combat troops to Danang to prop up the south. The Soviet Union and China weighed in with assistance to the north. The rest is history. After a decade of heavy fighting that took 58,000 American and as many as 4 million Vietnamese lives, the communists took Saigon on April 30, 1975. In 1976, north and south were officially reunited. Rather than enjoying the newfound peace, Vietnam invaded Cambodia after border skirmishes in 1978. China, friend of Cambodia, then invaded Vietnam in 1979.

In the mid-1980s, Vietnam began moving toward *doi moi,* a free-market policy, to save itself from bankruptcy. To further ingratiate itself with the international community, it withdrew its army from Cambodia in 1989, and as the 1990s began, the country began opening to the world. It further reorganized its economy toward a market-oriented model, sought diplomatic relations, and in 1991 signed a peace agreement with Cambodia. In 1994, America capitulated and lifted its long-standing trade embargo against Vietnam, and the two countries established diplomatic relations in 1995. Vietnam also joined ASEAN (Association of Southeast Asian Nations).

## VIETNAM TODAY

The modern portrait of this once-troubled land is rosy. Today Vietnam is the world's third-largest rice exporter, and the country is tentatively finding its way in the global economy. Normalization of ties between the U.S. and Vietnam in 1995 was followed by a series of ongoing resolutions and agreements contingent upon Vietnamese complicity with international human rights and trade standards. President Clinton visited the reunified country in 2000, the first U.S. president since Richard Nixon in 1969, and Vietnam is now a member of the World Trade Organization (WTO).

American Secretary of Defense Donald Rumsfeld met with Vietnam's defense minister in Washington in 2003, and the USS *Vandergrift* pulled into port in Ho Chi Minh City at about the same time, the first U.S. navy ship to dock in a Vietnamese port since hasty withdrawal in 1975. Telling signs.

The road is not always smooth, however: pell-mell growth in certain industries, catfish and shrimp hatcheries for example, circumvents international standards, disrupting markets and raising U.S. ire; and continued reports of humanitarian violations are under close international scrutiny.

Per-capita income in Vietnam is estimated at a meager $500 per person, but increases steadily each year, especially in urban centers. Rural poverty and lack of good medical services is still a major problem. Vietnam hosted the Asian Games in 2003, putting its best foot forward in what was a coup for international opinion. Recent international airline agreements and new direct flights to the U.S. and Europe signify further international cooperation. As a stable, safe, rapidly developing nation, Vietnam appeals to travelers of all tastes and budgets.

## VIETNAMESE CULTURE

Vietnam has a cultural landscape as varied and colorful as its topography. The Viet ethnic group is well in the majority, comprising about 88% of the population, but there are 54 other minority ethnic groups, many of whom are hill tribes living in villages largely untouched by modern civilization.

Though Vietnam has rushed into modernization over the past several years, the economy has remained largely agrarian, with farmers, fishermen, and forestry workers accounting for 73% of the workforce and most of the population still residing in small villages. The Vietnamese have a strong sense of family and of community, and are accustomed to close human contact and far-reaching inter-relationships. This might be one of the reasons why, despite centuries of occupation by foreigners, Vietnamese cultural traditions have survived. Moreover, outsiders are still welcomed. Americans, in fact, will get a wide smile and a thumbs up, although the reception is better in the south than in the north.

## CUISINE

Each region has its specialties, but the hallmarks of Vietnamese food are light, fresh ingredients, heavy on the rice, pork, and fish, with fresh garnishes such as mint, coriander, fish sauce, and chile pepper. Two of the local dishes you're most likely to encounter are *pho,* a noodle soup in a clear broth, and *bun cha,* fresh rice noodles with barbecued pork in sauce. Chinese-influenced dishes can be found, including hot pot, a cook-your-own group activity in which fresh vegetables and chunks of meat and fowl are dipped into boiling broth and then consumed. The French have left their mark as well. Along with excellent restaurants, you'll find espresso and crusty French bread on every street corner.

## THE ARTS

Ancient, distinctive Vietnamese art forms remain today, like **water puppetry,** with wooden hand puppets actually dancing across water, and **cheo,** traditional **folk opera.** There is an emerging interest in fine arts, with countless galleries in almost every major Vietnamese city, and an emphasis on traditional techniques such as lacquer and silk painting and wood blocking. **Vietnamese music,** using string and woodwind instruments, bamboo xylophones, and metal gongs, is delicate, distinctive, and appealing. **Literature** has existed since the forming of the nation in folklore, proverbs, and idioms singular to each village and ethnic group, and passed down from century to century. Many of the old tales have been translated and printed in books that you can easily find in a foreign-language bookstore.

## RELIGION

About 70% of all Vietnamese are **Buddhists,** mainly Mahayana practitioners of Chinese influence (see "Buddha & Buddhism in Southeast Asia" box in chapter 2), 10% are **Catholics,** and the rest are **Confucianists, animists** (believing in gods of nature), or followers of the unique Vietnamese religion **Cao Dai** see the section on excursions from Ho Chi Minh on p. 403), an interesting combination of the major world faiths. **Islam** and **Protestantism** also have small pockets of believers. While we're on the topic of -isms, it's hard for the casual observer to see any observance of communism at all, other than the prevalence of state-owned entities and the bureaucratic hoops you might have to jump through.

## ETIQUETTE

Although the Vietnamese are generally tolerant of foreign ways, they dress very modestly. Foreigners displaying navels, chests, or shoulders, or wearing hot pants will attract stares. Swimsuit thongs and nude beach bathing are out of the question. Some temples flatly refuse to admit persons in shorts, and some smaller towns like Hoi An post signs asking tourists to dress "appropriately," which means you might have a run-in with the police if you don't.

Unfortunately, one byproduct of the relative newness of tourism in Vietnam is an eagerness to separate you from your money. The child hawkers, "tour guides," and cyclo drivers can be extraordinarily persistent, following you for blocks, grabbing your arm, and hounding you at temples and open-air restaurants. Saying "no" is just an invitation to turn up the sales pitch; even if you don't want to be rude, avoiding eye contact and saying nothing is the best way to extricate yourself. It can be wearying, but things have calmed down a bit in recent years. In tour centers like Hoan-kiem Lake in Hanoi or the major sites in Ho Chi Minh City, you'll still be besieged, though; remember that you're not going to hurt anyone's feelings by ignoring them (but it's hard to do).

## LANGUAGE

The ancient Vietnamese language, though not complex structurally, is tonal and therefore difficult for many Westerners to master. In its earliest written form, it was based on the Chinese pictographic writing forms, and you'll see remnants of that tradition on temple walls, but in the 17th century, a French scholar developed the Roman alphabet that is used today. Unlike other Asian countries, it looks like you can read this stuff, but the system of accent marks is quite involved (you'll still do double takes at some signs that look like you might be able to read them). Today most city dwellers seem to speak at least a little English, the older generation speaks some French, and, with increased influence from China (the Chinese comprise well more than 50% of all visitors here), younger people are increasingly studying Mandarin. Students especially will be eager to practice English with you. Solo travelers, being less intimidating, are at an advantage; you'll have many opportunities (and invitation) to have a squat on a street corner, drink a "Bia Hoi" (beer Hoi), and meet people.

### USEFUL VIETNAMESE PHRASES

| English | Vietnamese | Pronunciation |
|---|---|---|
| Hello | Xin chao | Seen chow |
| Good bye | Tam biet | Tam bee-et |
| Yes | Vang | Bahng |
| No | Khong | Kawng |
| Thank you | Cam on | Cahm un |
| You are welcome | Khong co gi | Kawng koe gee |
| Excuse me | Xin loi | Seen loy |
| Where is . . . | O dau . . . | Er dow . . . |
| Turn right | Re phai | Ray fie |
| Turn left | Re trai | Ray chrai |
| Toilet | Nha ve sinh | Nya vay shin |
| Hotel | Khach san | Kak san |
| Restaurant | Nha hang | Nya hahng |
| Potable water | Nuoc khoang | Nook kwang |
| I don't understand | Toi khong hieu | Toy kawng hew |
| How much? | Bao nhieu? | Baugh nyew? |
| When? | Luc nao? | Look now? |
| I need a doctor. | Toi can bac si. | Toy cahn back see |
| Hospital | Benh vien | Ben vee-in |
| Antibiotic | Thuoc khang sinh | Dook kahng shin |

## 2 Planning Your Trip to Vietnam

### VISITOR INFORMATION

Vietnam's national tourism administration has a fairly good website at www.vietnamtourism.com but it's more bureaucracy than information source. It operates mainly through state-run tourism agencies, **Saigontourist** (www.saigontourist.com) and **Hanoi Tourism** (hanoitourism.com.vn), which have offices all over Vietnam and provide comprehensive tours and booking services. The website of the Vietnam Embassy in the U.S. (www.vietnamembassy-usa.org) is also very helpful, or click on "Vietnam" at the Mekong subregion's cross-referenced site, www.visit-mekong.com. Also check out the Friends of Vietnam Heritage in Hanoi (© 04/942-0737; lefthanded2hanoi@yahoo.com), which supports cultural events and programs.

### ENTRY REQUIREMENTS

Residents of the U.S., Canada, Australia, New Zealand, and the United Kingdom need both passport and prearranged visa to enter Vietnam. A tourist visa lasts for 30 days and costs $65. You'll pay a bit more through an agent but will save yourself some paper shuffling (it can be done for a nominal fee at any travel agent in Bangkok). Getting a visa takes 5 to 7 days to process. Applicants must submit an application, a passport, and two passport photos. Tourist visas can be extended twice, each time for 30 days, best through a travel agent. Multiple-entry business visas are available that are valid for up to 3 months, but require a sponsor in Vietnam. Visas are good for any legal port of entry. *Note:* The visa begins on the date that you specify on your application.

### VIETNAMESE EMBASSY LOCATIONS
#### IN THE UNITED STATES
- **Vietnam Embassy:** 1233 20th St. NW, Suite 400, Washington, DC 20036 (© **202/861-0737;** fax 202/861-0917)
- **Consulate General of Vietnam:** 1700 California St., Suite 430, San Francisco, CA 94109 (© **415/922-1577;** fax 415/922-1848)
- **Permanent Mission of Vietnam to the United Nations:** 866 UN Plaza, Suite 435, New York, NY 10017 (© **212/644-0594;** fax 212/644-5732)

#### IN CANADA
- **Vietnam Embassy:** 470 Wilbrod St., Ottawa, Ontario, Canada K1N 6M8 (© **613/236-0772;** fax 613/236-2704)

#### IN THE UNITED KINGDOM
- **Vietnam Embassy:** 12–14 Victoria Rd., London W8-5RD, U.K. (© **0171/937-1912;** fax 0171/937-6108)

#### IN AUSTRALIA
- **Vietnam Embassy:** 6 Timbarra Crescent, Malley, Canberra, ACT 2606 (© **2/6286-6059;** fax 2/6286-4534)
- **Consulate General of Vietnam:** 489 New South Head Rd., Double Bay, Sydney, NSW 2028 (© **02/9327-2539;** fax 02/9328-1653)

#### IN THAILAND
- **Vietnam Embassy:** 82/1 Wireless Rd., Bangkok 10500 (© **251-7202,** 251-5835; fax 251-7201, 251-7203)

## Tours for Vietnam Veterans

U.S. veterans are returning to Vietnam, some to see how the story ended, others to stage memorial services, find closure by crossing the 17th Parallel, or just experience Vietnamese culture this time around.

**Tours of Peace (TOP),** a nonprofit organization started by Jess DeVaney, a retired U.S. Marine, runs tours where veterans not only come to terms with their past by visiting important sites in the Mekong Delta and the DMZ (among others), but also to participate in the future. The folks at TOP believe that through helping others, we heal ourselves, so humanitarian aid projects are part of every tour. Financial assistance is available. Check www.topvietnamveterans.org, or write to TOP Vietnam Veterans, 7400 N. Oracle Rd., Suite 100-W, Tucson, AZ 85704. Another popular veteran tour operator is **Nine Dragons Tours** (P.O. Box 24105, Indianapolis, IN 46224-0105; © **317/329-0350;** www.nine-dragons.com).

## CUSTOMS REGULATIONS

*Important:* **Do not lose your entry/exit slip,** the yellow piece of paper that will be clipped to your passport upon arrival; it is required for departure and loss means a fine. If you are entering the country as a tourist, you do not need to declare any items for personal use. You must declare cash in excess of $3,000 or the equivalent. You can also import 200 cigarettes, 2 liters of alcohol, and perfume and jewelry for personal use. Antiques are forbidden from export.

## MONEY

The official currency of Vietnam is the **dong (VND),** which comes in notes of 100,000, 50,000, 10,000, 5,000, 1,000, 500, and 200 VND.

**CURRENCY EXCHANGE & RATES**    At the time of publication, the exchange rate was 15,000 Vietnamese VND to 1 U.S. dollar. The U.S. dollar is used as an informal second currency, and most items that cost more than a few dollars are priced in the greenback. Prices in this guide are listed as they are quoted, in either U.S. dollars or Vietnam dong. Every hotel, no matter how small, will change money at a slightly lower rate or charge a small commission. Don't accept torn or very grubby bills. Tour areas have automated teller machines (ATMs) that dispense cash in Vietnam dong. Banks in any city can cash traveler's checks in U.S., Canadian, and Australian dollars or pounds sterling. A service charge of anywhere between $1 and $4 will be levied. Vendors and retailers usually don't accept traveler's checks, however.

Credit cards are accepted at major hotels, in upmarket restaurants, tour guide operators, in most big Hanoi and Ho Chi Minh outlets, and increasingly accepted outside these two major cities. Any Vietcombank branch, as well as big foreign banks, will handle credit card cash advance.

**LOST/STOLEN CREDIT CARDS & TRAVELER'S CHECKS**    To report lost or stolen cards or traveler's checks, call the nearest branch of Vietcombank. Otherwise, you can go to a post office to place a collect call to the card's international toll-free collect number for cash and a card replacement. The following international numbers are operational 24 hours: **Visa** Global Customer Assistance Service, © **410/581-3836,** and **MasterCard** Global Services, © **314/542-7111.** Note that foreigners aren't permitted to make collect calls, so you'll have to get a Vietnamese to assist you. Or, you can use AT&T, whose access number in Vietnam is ℂ **1/201-0288.** For American Express, visit or call the nearest representative office, listed below in "Fast Facts."

## WHEN TO GO

September through April are the peak months, but with a range of climatic variation in the different regions of the country, there are always areas of Vietnam where you can find favorable weather.

**CLIMATE**    Vietnam's climate varies greatly from north to south. The north has four distinct seasons, with a chilly but not freezing winter from November to April. Summers are warm and wet. The south (which means Nha Trang on down) has hot, humid weather throughout the year, with temperatures peaking March through May into the 90s (30s Celsius). The south has a monsoon season from April to mid-November, and Vietnam is affected by weather to the east, bearing the brunt of Pacific typhoons, especially from August through September.

If you follow a south-north or north-south sweep, you might want to avoid both the monsoons and heat in the south by going sometime between November and February. If you're planning a beach vacation, however, keep in mind that the surf on the south-central coast (China Beach, Nha Trang) is too rough for watersports from October through March (but is bringing out the windsurfers in droves). Dalat, a hill station in central Vietnam, stays cool all year, and Sapa in the far north is at some altitude and gets quite chilly. Otherwise, prepare for heat.

**PUBLIC HOLIDAYS**    Public holidays are New Year's Day (Jan 1), Tet/Lunar New Year (late Jan to mid-Feb; state holiday that lasts 4 days), Saigon Liberation Day (Apr 30), International Labour Day (May 1), and National Day of the Socialist Republic of Vietnam (Sept 2). Government offices and tourist attractions are closed at these times.

While **Tet** (the lunar new year, in late Jan/early Feb) is Vietnam's biggest holiday, it's very much a family-oriented time, something like American Thanksgiving. Folks travel far to get home for some of Mom's cooking. Beginning on the evening exactly 3 days from the Lunar New Year and lasting for 4 days, much of the country closes down, including stores, restaurants, and museums, and accommodations might be difficult to find.

## HEALTH CONCERNS

In chapter 3, we outline issues that affect the region. Health considerations are an important part of trip planning in Vietnam. You will need to get special vaccinations if rural areas are on your itinerary, and that means consulting a doctor at least a few weeks before your trip. Follow the guidelines here and those of your doctor and there's no reason you can't have a safe and healthy trip.

Your biggest safety precaution is to take care with food. **Drink only bottled or boiled water, without ice; wash your hands often** and follow the old adage: **Boil it, cook it, peel it, or forget it.**

### VACCINATIONS

It's always good to check the most recent information at the Centers for Disease Control: Search its website (www.cdc.gov) by region under the heading "Traveler's Health," or call **877/394-8747.**

The following vaccinations are important for Vietnam: Hepatitis A or immune globulin (IG) and typhoid vaccination. Injections for Japanese encephalitis are recommended if you plan to visit rural areas during the rainy season, and rabies if you're planning to go to rural areas where you might be exposed to wild animals. You should also consider booster doses for tetanus-diphtheria, measles, and polio.

According to the CDC, travelers in Vietnam should take an **oral prophylaxis** for **malaria** if traveling extensively in rural parts; malaria is not a problem anywhere in the Red River Delta, in coastal areas north of Nha Trang, nor in any of the major cities: Ho Chi Minh City, Hanoi, Haiphong, Nha Trang, or Danang. Consult a physician, but the common recommendations for malarial preventative are as follows: atovaquone/proguanil (Malarone), doxycycline, mefloquine (Larium), or primaquine in special circumstances. Side effects abound, so be sure to discuss with a medical professional and follow any treatment regimen to the letter. The best prevention is to cover exposed skin and to use an insect repellent that contains DEET (diethylmethyltoluamide).

## GETTING THERE
### BY PLANE

A new cooperative treaty between the U.S. and Vietnam means that there are now direct flights between the two ex-enemies. **United Airlines** now flies from the U.S. West Coast, and promotional rates are now available.

Most travelers connect to Vietnam via Bangkok, Hong Kong, Taipei, or Tokyo. See the section "Getting There," in chapter 3, for more international flight tips. Malaysia Airlines, Singapore Airlines, Thai Airways International, and Bangkok Airways fly regular routes from the big hubs. Vietnam Airlines connects Vietnam (Ho Chi Minh City) with Vientiane, Phnom Penh, Siem Reap, Bangkok, Kuala Lumpur, Singapore, and Manila.

Reconfirmation for flights 72 hours before departure from Vietnam is a must. Be prepared for a 200,000 VND ($13) departure tax for your international flight out (the 20,000 VND/$1.35 airport domestic departure tax is usually included in the ticket price).

### BY BUS

From Laos, it is possible to enter Vietnam overland via a bus ride from Savannakhet in the south. It's 520km (324 miles) to Danang ($27) or 405km (251 miles) to Hue ($22). Buses leave at midnight. In Laos, contact **Savanbanhao Tourist Co.** (© **041/212202**). It's a long, bumpy overnight, and the road often washes out in rainy season, so be sure to ask around.

### Have You Hugged Your Taxi Driver Today?

"Motorbike? Motorbike? Where you go?" You'll hear it on every street corner in most cities, the relentless ploys of the motorbike taxi drivers. These guys drive like maniacs, but, especially for the individual traveler, there is no better way to get around any town in Vietnam. Called Honda Om in Vietnamese, with Om meaning "hug"—thus, it's really a "hugging taxi." These huggers will, after bargaining, take you on a short ride for from 10,000 VND (65¢) or $2 per hour. Ask for a helmet, and don't be afraid to tap the guy's shoulder and give a "slow-down" hand signal.

## BY BOAT

Convenient boat service now connects Vietnam with neighboring Cambodia by way of one of the larger tributaries of the Mekong between Phnom Penh, Cambodia's capital, and the Mekong Delta border town Chau Doc. The trip takes all day and costs $15. Contact the **Capital Guesthouse** (© 023/724-104), Cambodia's budget travel cafe, or make more luxury arrangements on a private outboard speedboat with the **Victoria Chau Doc** (© 076/865-010). Be sure to have a prearranged Vietnam visa. The trip takes from morning until late afternoon, depending on water level and weather, and is an interesting adventure with great perspective on Indochine river life.

## GETTING AROUND

The large number of tour operators, from big, inefficient government operations to slick, high-end tour companies and on down to the many budget tourist cafes means that getting around Vietnam is quite easy. Stay with well-established agencies or recommendations in the "Visitor Information" of each section. Before booking any kind of transport, be sure to confirm details: meal inclusions, air-conditioning, transport, and so on.

**BY PLANE**   Vietnam Airlines is the country's only domestic air carrier, but prices are reasonable and the service is good. Seats are usually easy to come by. Purchasing tickets is also very easy; all travel agents book for a nominal fee, and many major hotels have V.A. agents in the lobby.

**BY TRAIN**   Vietnam's major rail network runs from Hanoi to Saigon and back, with stops along in Hue, Danang, and Nha Trang. To give you an idea of timing, from Hanoi all the way to Saigon is 34 hours on the express train; from Hanoi to Hue is about 14 hours on an overnight express. It's an interesting way to get around, although not much cheaper than flying. Soft-sleeper berths and special tourist cars are available on most routes and are worth the upgrade. Hard-sleeper berths are a good value, but you're stacked three high and cannot sit when the bunks are down. Air-conditioning will cost you an additional price per ticket but is definitely worth it.

It's not difficult to buy tickets at any station, but most hotels and tour agencies will gladly simplify the process and arrange tickets for you for only a nominal fee (check each section for contacts). Contact **Ratraco,** Vietnam's rail tour provider (just across from the station: 2nd floor, 95–97 Le Duan St., Hanoi; © 04/942-2889; ratraco@hn.vnn.vn), or book through any travel agent. From Hanoi to Lao Cai (Sapa) near the China border, be sure to check out the new luxury cars on either the **Victoria Express** (run by the **Victoria Sapa;** © 20/871-522; fax 20/871-539; www.victoriahotels-asia.com) or **Tulico Trains** (© 04/828-7806; www.tulico-sapa.com). See "Getting There" in specific destination sections.

---

### ⌐Tips  Smoker's Paradise

There is no such thing as "nonsmoking" in Vietnam. Only top-end restaurants serving Western cuisine are likely to have a **nonsmoking section,** and even then unlikely that there is any partition or distance to contain the fumes. Some hotels offer nonsmoking rooms or floors. Inquire when booking, especially at hotels popular with business travelers, because the rooms can get pretty musty.

---

**BY BUS/MINIVAN**    Public buses are recommended to only the most intrepid travelers. Local transport is slow, crowded, and prone to break down.

Begun as small storefronts making arrangements for early backpackers in the 1990s, Vietnamese **tourist cafes** are the best option for seat-in-coach tours. Now franchised, with offices dotting the country, these convenient outfits run **open-tour bus tickets** that connect all the major points: Saigon, Dalat, Phan Thiet, Nha Trang, Hoi An, Danang (optional), Hue, and Hanoi. You can travel either direction, north to south or vice versa, for under $30. The buses leave at set times (most in the morning, though a few overnights are possible), and you just decide the day before if you want to be on one. This gives you tremendous freedom to plan your own itinerary. In recent years, **Sinh Café,** which now has computerized reservation services, has really beat out the pack, but all of the cafes match prices and often consolidate services. **AtoZ Queen Café, Kim Café,** and **TM Brothers** (in the south) all have comparable service. Check "Visitor Information & Tours," later in this chapter and in each destination section.

**BY CAR**    For safety (and sanity) in Vietnam, it is best to rent a car only with a hired driver. Rates are reasonable and it is a good way to see things outside of urban centers or take a 1-day city tour of major sights. All major hotels and travel agents can arrange rental.

## TIPS ON ACCOMMODATIONS
Vietnam is gaining in popularity among travelers and tourists, so book early, especially during the high season of November/December; accommodations ranging from the glitziest five-stars to the grungiest guesthouses are often booked up or able to demand high rates. Always ask about seasonal reductions or promotional rates; low-season discounts can be as high as 50%.

There is a 20% value-added tax (VAT) on rooms, but some hotels charge as little as 10%. Inquire carefully.

## TIPS ON DINING
Many of the world's finest culinary traditions are represented in Vietnam, including French, Chinese, Japanese, and, of course, Vietnamese. Local French cuisine is affordable and authentic. There are some interesting new upscale Vietnamese food venues, but ask locals where to eat, and you'll get a blanket recommendation for the local market or street stalls. Whether with

### Piracy & the Proletariat

In October 2004, Vietnam committed to the Berne Convention for the Protection of Literary and Artistic Works, a consortium of over 150 nations working together to protect international copyright. Any stroll through a Vietnamese market will tell you that this pledge is a tall order. Vietnamese have long followed the socialist ideal that all intellectual property—literary, artistic, or scientific—benefits the collective and should be shared; in fact, copying, under the Communist regime, was encouraged. Today, this means rampant pirating of CDs and DVDs for resale. The tide is turning, and customs checks (when returning to Western countries) are increasingly sensitive to pirated material.

locals, or at high-end eateries, try local delicacies like *bun bo* (cold rice noodles with fried beef), *banh khoi* (crispy thin rice-based crepes filled with chopped meat and shrimp), and *chao* (rice porridge with garnishes of meat, egg, or chiles). Note that many upscale places levy a 10% government tax plus a 5% service charge.

## TIPS ON SHOPPING

Bring an empty suitcase—or buy one in-country for peanuts. Vietnam offers fabulous bargains on silk, as both fabric and made-to-order clothing, as well as lacquerware, silver, and fine art. Hanoi is probably best for most buys, particularly paintings; save the lacquerware and home furnishings for Saigon. Furthermore, all prices are negotiable except for those in the most upscale shops, and the more relentless bargainers can walk away with incredible deals on some unique finds.

---

### FAST FACTS: Vietnam

*American Express* Amex is represented by **Exotissimo Travel** (in Hanoi: 24–26 Tran Nhat Duat St.; ✆ 04/828-2150; in Ho Chi Minh City, Saigon Trade Center, 37 Ton Duc Thang St., HCMC; ✆ 08/825-1723). *Be warned:* It does not provide complete travel services, but can direct you if you lose your card. Hours are Monday to Friday 8am to 5pm.

*Business Hours* Vendors and restaurants tend to be all-day operations, opening at about 8am and closing at 9 or 10pm. Government offices, including banks, travel agencies, and museums, are usually open from 8 to 11:30am and 2 to 4pm.

*Crime* Violent crime isn't common in Vietnam, but petty thievery, especially against tourists, is a risk. Pickpocketing is rampant, and Ho Chi Minh City (HCMC), in particular, has a special brand of drive-by purse snatching via motorbike. Don't wear flashy jewelry or leave valuables in your hotel room, especially in smaller hotels. There are small-time rackets perpetrated against tourists by taxi and cyclo drivers, usually in the form of a dispute on the agreed-upon price after you arrive at your destination. Or, the driver doesn't seem to have change. Simply agree on a price by writing it down first, and always smile and demand change.

*Doctors & Dentists* Vietnamese health care is not yet up to Western standards. However, there are competent medical clinics in Hanoi and Saigon (see "Fast Facts," in individual sections) with international, English-speaking doctors. The same clinics have dentists. If your problem is serious, it is best to get to either one of these cities as quickly as possible. The clinics can arrange emergency evacuation. If the problem is minor, ask your hotel to help you contact a Vietnamese doctor. He or she will probably speak some English, and pharmacies throughout the country are surprisingly well stocked and require no prescriptions (check expiration).

*Drug Laws* Possessing drugs can mean a jail sentence, and selling them or possessing quantities in excess of 300g means a death sentence. Don't take chances.

*Electricity* Vietnam's electricity carries 220 volts, so if you're coming from the U.S., bring a converter and adapter for electronics. Plugs have either two round prongs or two flat prongs. If you're toting a laptop, bring a surge protector. Big hotels will have all these implements.

*Embassies* Embassies are located in Hanoi at the following addresses: **United States,** 7 Lang Ha St., Ba Dinh District (𝒸 **04/843-1500); Canada,** 31 Hung Vuong St., Ba Dinh District (𝒸 **04/823-5500); Australia,** 8 Dao Tan, Van Phuc Compound, Ba Dinh District (𝒸 **04/831-7755); New Zealand,** 32 Hang Bai St., Hoan Kiem District (𝒸 **04/824-1481); United Kingdom,** 31 Hai Ba Trung St., 4th Floor, Hoan Kiem District (𝒸 **04/825-2510).**

*Emergencies* Nationwide emergency numbers are as follows: For police, dial 𝒸 **113;** for fire, dial 𝒸 **114;** and for ambulance, dial 𝒸 **115.** Operators speak only Vietnamese.

*Hospitals* In Hanoi, **International SOS** medical services can be found at 31 Hai Ba Trung St.; call the 24-hour service center for emergencies at 𝒸 **04/ 934-0056.** They have both Vietnamese and foreign doctors. In Ho Chi Minh City, International SOS is at 65 Nguyen Du St., District 1 (24-hr. hot line 𝒸 **8/829-8424). The French Hospital,** at 1 Phuong Mai St. (𝒸 **574-0740),** provides fine medical attention at a fraction of the cost of SOS.

*Internet/E-mail* There are heaps of Internet cafes in cities throughout Vietnam, best in popular guesthouse and hotel areas. At cafes, rates are dirt cheap—usually around 4,000 VND per hour (a little less than 25¢). In rural areas, it can be as much as 500 VND per minute ($2 per hr.), and hotel business centers usually charge at least triple that. Take a short walk in most towns, and you can find affordable service.

*Language* Vietnamese is the official language of Vietnam. Older residents speak and understand French, and young folks are busily learning Chinese these days. While English is widely spoken among folks in the service industry in Hanoi and Saigon, it is harder to find in other tourist destinations. Off the beaten track, arm yourself with as many Vietnamese words you can muster (see "Useful Vietnamese Phrases," earlier in this chapter) and a dictionary.

*Liquor Laws* There are virtually no age restrictions laws limiting when or where you can buy or consume drink. It's not uncommon to find that your motorbike or taxi driver has had a few, so be cautious, especially at night.

*Police* You won't find a helpful cop on every street corner—just the opposite. Count on them only in cases of dire emergency. Police can even be part of the problem. Especially in the south, you and your car/motorbike driver might, for instance, be stopped for a minor traffic infraction and "fined." If the amount isn't too large, cooperate. Corruption is the rule, and palm greasing and graft pose as police process. Be aware.

*Post Offices/Mail* A regular airmail letter will take about 10 days to reach North America, 7 to reach Europe, and 4 to reach Australia or New Zealand. Mailing things from Vietnam is expensive. A letter up to 10g costs 13,000 VND (85¢) to North America, 11,000 VND (75¢) to Europe, and 9,000 VND (60¢) to Australia/New Zealand; postcards, respectively, cost 8,000 VND (55¢), 7,000 VND (45¢), and 6,000 VND (40¢). Express mail services such as FedEx and DHL are easily available and are usually located in or around every city's main post office.

*Safety*  Vietnam is a safe destination, but take heed of the following: First, the traffic is deadly, so be cautious when crossing the street anywhere; in big cities, pedestrians cross in groups and, if alone, wade out into it and maintain a steady pace. Second, women should play it safe and avoid going out alone late at night. Third, and most important, beware of unexploded mines when hiking or exploring, especially through old war zones such as the DMZ or My Son. Don't stray off an established path, and don't touch anything you might find lying on the ground.

*Taxes*  A 20% VAT was instituted for hotels and restaurants in January 1999, but expect variation in how it's followed. Upscale establishments might add the full 20%, and some might even tack on an additional 5% service charge. Others might absorb the tax in their prices, and still others will ignore it entirely. Inquire before booking or eating.

*Telephone & Fax*  Most hotels offer international direct dialing, but with exorbitant surcharges of 10% to 25%. It is far cheaper to place a call from a post office. There are plenty of phone booths that accept phone cards (local and international) that can be purchased at any post office or phone company branch. A local call costs 1,000 VND (5¢) per minute. See the "Telephone Dialing Information at a Glance" box, below, for more specific information.

*Time Zone*  Vietnam is 7 hours ahead of Greenwich Mean Time, in the same zone as Bangkok. It is 12 hours ahead of the U.S. and 3 hours behind Sydney.

*Tipping*  Tipping is common in Hanoi and in Saigon. In a top-end hotel, feel free to tip bellhops anywhere from 10,000 VND to 15,000 VND (about $1). Most upscale restaurants throughout the country now add a service surcharge of 5% to 10%. If they don't, or if the service is good, you might want to leave another 5%. Taxi drivers will be pleased if you round up the bill (again, mainly in the big cities). Use your discretion for tour guides and others who have been particularly helpful.

*Toilets*  Public toilets *(cau tieu)* are nonexistent in Vietnam outside of tourist attractions, but you'll be welcome in hotels and restaurants. Except for newer hotels and restaurants, squat-style toilets prevail. You'll often see a tub of water with a bowl next to the toilet. Throw two or three scoops of water in the bowl to flush. Finally, bring your own paper and antiseptic hand wipes—just in case.

*Water*  Water is not potable in Vietnam. Outside of top-end hotels and restaurants, drink only beverages without ice, unless the establishment promises that it manufactures its own ice from clean water. Bottled mineral water, particularly the reputable La Vie and "A&B" brands, is everywhere. Counterfeits are a problem, so make sure you're buying the real thing, with an unbroken seal. A sure sign is typos. "La Vile" water speaks for itself.

## 3 Hanoi

Vietnam's capital, Hanoi, ranks among the world's most attractive and interesting cities. Originally named Thang Long, it was first the capital of Vietnam in 1010, and even when the nation's capital moved to Hue under the Nguyen Dynasty in 1802 the city continued to flourish, especially after the French took control in 1888. In 1954, after the French departed, Hanoi was declared Vietnam's capital once again. The city boasts 1,000 years of history, and that of the past few hundred years is marvelously preserved.

Hanoi has a reputation, doubtless accrued from the American war years, as a dour northern political outpost. While the city is certainly smaller, slower, and far less developed than chaotic Saigon, and there are some vestiges of Soviet-influenced concrete monolith architecture, there are some beautiful, quiet streets and neighborhoods in Hanoi, and such placid air gives it a gracious, almost regal flavor. The city is dotted with dozens of lakes small and large, around which you can usually find a cafe, a pagoda or two, and absorbing vignettes of street life. Hanoi's 3.5 million residents all seem to be in constant motion, as part of the endless stream of motorbike and bicycle traffic, but there are plenty of quiet corners and tranquil neighborhoods to explore.

Among Hanoi's sightseeing highlights are the **Ho Chi Minh mausoleum and museum,** the **National Art Museum,** the grisly **Hoa Lo prison** (also known as the infamous Hanoi Hilton), and the **Old Quarter,** whose ancient winding streets are named after the individual trades practiced there. Hanoi is also Vietnam's cultural center. The galleries, puppetry, music, and dance performances are worth staying at least a few days to take in. You might also want to use the

## Telephone Dialing Information at a Glance

- **To place a call from your home country to Vietnam:** Dial the international code (011 in the U.S., 0011 in Australia, 0170 in New Zealand, or 00 in the U.K.), plus the country code (84), the city code (4 for Hanoi, 8 for Ho Chi Minh City, 54 for Hue, 511 for Danang, 510 for Hoi An, 63 for Dalat, 58 for Nha Trang), and the phone number (for example, 011 84 4 000-0000).
- **To place a call within Vietnam:** First dial 0 before the city code (as numbers are listed in this book). Note that not all phone numbers have seven digits after the city code.
- **To place a direct international call from Vietnam:** Most hotels offer international direct dialing, but with exorbitant surcharges of 10% to 25%. Faxes often have high minimum charges. To place a call, dial the international access code (00) plus the country code, the area or city code, and the number (for example, to call the U.S., you'd dial 00 01 000/000-0000).
- **International country codes are as follows:** Australia: 61; Cambodia: 855; Canada: 1; Indonesia: 62; Laos: 856; Malaysia: 60; New Zealand: 64; the Philippines: 63; Singapore: 65; Thailand: 66; U.K.: 44; U.S.: 1.
- Post offices in Vietnam also provide international calling services. If you must call home, this is your best cost-saving option.

# Hanoi

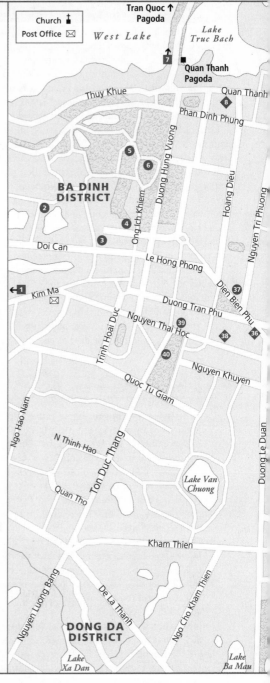

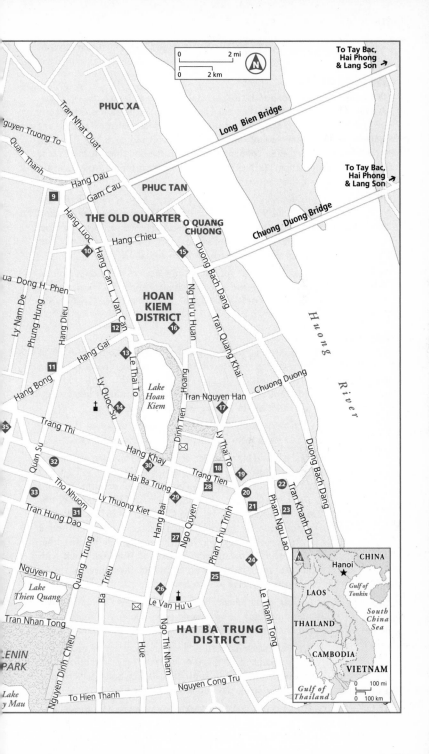

PHUC XA

Tran Nhat Duat

Nguyen Truong To

Quan Thanh

Hang Dau

Gam Cau

**9**

PHUC TAN

**THE OLD QUARTER**

O QUANG
CHUONG

Hang Luoc

Hang Chieu

**10**

Hang Can

L. Van Can

**15**

**HOAN
KIEM
DISTRICT**

ua Dong H. Phen

Ly Nam De

Phung Hung

Hang Dieu

**12**

**16**

Hang Gai

**13**

Le Thai To

**11**

Hang Bong

Ly Quoc Su

**14**

Lake
Hoan
Kiem

Ng Hu'u Huan

Duong Bach Dang

Tran Quang Khai

**35**

Trang Thi

Hoang Dieu

Dinh Tien

Tran Nguyen Han

Chuong Duong

**17**

Quan Su

**32**

Hang Khay

**30**

Ly Thai To

Tho Nhuom

**33**

Hai Ba Trung

Trang Tien

**18**

**19**

Tran Hung Dao

**31**

Ly Thuong Kiet

Hang Bai

**29**

**28**

**20**

**21**

**22**

Tran Khanh Du

**23**

Duong Bach Dang

Nguyen Du

Quang Trung

Ba Trieu

**27**

Ngo Quyen

Phan Chu Trinh

**24**

Pham Ngu Lao

Lake
Thien Quang

**26**

Le Van Hu'u

**25**

Le Thanh Tong

Tran Nhan Tong

Ngo Thi Nham

**HAI BA TRUNG
DISTRICT**

LENIN
PARK

Nguyen Dinh Chieu

Hue

Lake
y Mau

To Hien Thanh

Nguyen Cong Tru

H u o n g    R i v e r

Long Bien Bridge

To Tay Bac,
Hai Phong
& Lang Son

To Tay Bac,
Hai Phong
& Lang Son

Chuong Duong Bridge

0      2 mi
0      2 km

N

CHINA

Hanoi

Gulf of
Tonkin

LAOS

THAILAND

South
China
Sea

CAMBODIA

VIETNAM

Gulf of
Thailand

0      100 mi
0      100 km

city as a base for excursions to Halong Bay, to Cuc Phuong nature reserve, or north to Sapa.

## GETTING THERE

**BY PLANE**    Hanoi, along with Ho Chi Minh City, is a major international gateway. For details, see Vietnam's "Getting There" section, earlier in this chapter.

The airport is located about a 45-minute drive outside the city. If you haven't booked a hotel transfer through your hotel, an airport taxi costs $10. To save a few dollars, you can take the Vietnam Airlines minivan into town. It costs $2 for a drop-off at the Vietnam Airlines office, but sometimes for an extra buck you can get the driver to drop you at your hotel.

**BY TRAIN**    Hanoi Railway Station, on the western edge of Hoan Kiem district (120 Le Duan; © 04/942-3949), is a terminal stop on the Reunification Railroad. For $35, you'll get a comfortable, air-conditioned soft-berth to Hue, and the same is $87 to Ho Chi Minh. Buying tickets at the stations is easy (but takes time), and any travel agent can handle it for a small fee.

**BY BUS**    Traveler cafe open-tour options are numerous in the Old Quarter on Hang Bac or Hang Be. Service and price are similar: About $27 earns you an open-tour ticket from Hanoi to Saigon with all stops in between. See "Tourist Cafes," below.

## GETTING AROUND

Hanoi is divided into districts. Most sites and accommodations are in Hoan Kiem District (downtown), centered around picturesque Hoan Kiem Lake, and Ba Dinh (west of town) districts or Hai Ba Trung (south). Most addresses include a district name. You'll want to plan your travels accordingly because getting from district to district can be time-consuming and expensive.

**BY BUS**    Hanoi has only **buses** in the way of public transport. They are extremely crowded, and using them is difficult if you don't speak Vietnamese.

**BY TAXI**    Taxis can be hailed off the street, at hotels, and at major attractions. The meter should read 14,000 VND (90¢) to start, and 4,000 to 5,000 VND (about 30¢) for every kilometer thereafter. You can call ahead (or ask at any front desk or concierge) to contact a few companies, including **Vina Taxi (© 04/811-1111)**, **52 Taxi (© 04/852-5252)**, or **Taxi CP (04/826-2626)**. Make sure the cabbie turns on the meter. Be sure to get your change; drivers often seek a surreptitious tip by claiming that they don't have the change. Tell the driver that you'll wait until it's obtained, and it will materialize. **Warning:** Stick with accredited taxi companies; some independents rig meters. If you have any problems, take your case to the concierge of your hotel.

**BY CAR**    Renting a car is convenient. Book a car with driver from $33 a day (or $5 per hr., minimum 3 hr.). If an upscale hotel quotes you more, call a **tourist cafe** (combination eateries and travel agents) or any travel agent.

**BY MOTORBIKE**    Motorcycle taxis are a cheap and easy way to get around the city, but they go like madmen, so this is only for the brave. With haggling, pay about 10,000 VND (65¢) for short trips, or $1 by the hour. Self-rental at the tourist cafes starts at $6 for the day and is only for the brave.

**BY CYCLO**    Cyclos are two-seated carts powered by a man on a foot-pedal bike riding behind you. Flag them down anywhere (these guys find you). Being trundled along among whizzing motorcycles isn't always very comfortable, but it is a fun option for touring the Old Quarter. Pay as low as 10,000 VND (65¢) for a short ride, and 15,000 VND ($1) for a longer haul, or by the hour for about 30,000 VND ($2). If you're inclined, they'll let you try and ride just for fun.

**BY BICYCLE**    Rental costs about $1 from a hotel or tourist cafe. The traffic is daunting, but the brave learn quickly how to just join the flow.

## VISITOR INFORMATION & TOURS

Most tour companies are based in Saigon; however, many have branches in Hanoi. Operators can usually assist with local tours as well as countrywide services.

- **Ann Tours** (18 Duong Thanh St., Hoan Kiem District; ℭ **04/923-1366;** fax 08/832-3866; www.anntours.com). This company offers private deluxe tours to Halong Bay and elsewhere. Frommer's readers write to tell us of their good experiences with this operation.
- **Buffalo Tours** (13 Hang Muoi; ℭ **04/828-0702;** www.buffalotours.com). This reputable outfit offers a range of standard tours and some good eco-adventures, like cycling, trekking, and kayaking. Its boat, *The Jewel of the Bay,* is a great choice for trips in Ha Long. Friendly and professional staff.
- **Exotissimo** (26 Tran Nhat Duat St.; ℭ **04/828-2150;** fax 04/828-2146; www.exotissimo.com). Comprehensive services.
- **Handspan** (80 Ma May St.; ℭ **04/962-0446;** fax 04/926-0445; www.handspan.com). A good option for organized trips around Hanoi or adventures to the northern hills and Halong Bay.

## TOURIST CAFES

A good option for tours and transport or for 1- or 2-day excursions is to book with one of the tourist cafes, which are small eateries, Internet cafes, and travel agents all rolled into one. For good, affordable seat-in-tour coach, try:

- **Sinh Café** (25 Hang Be St., Hoan Kiem District; ℭ **04/926-1288;** fax 04/756-7862; www.sinhcafevn.com)
- **A–Z Queen Café** (65 Hang Bac, Hoan Kiem District; ℭ **04/826-0860;** fax 04/826-0300; www.azqueentravel.com)
- **Kim Tours** (82 Ma May St., Hoan Kiem District; ℭ **04/926-0804**)
- **An Phu Tours** (50 Yen Phu, Hanoi; ℭ **04/927-3585**)

### *FAST FACTS:* **Hanoi**

*Banks/Currency Exchange*  Major banks in Hanoi include: Australia New Zealand Bank (ANZ), 14 Le Thai To St. (ℭ **04/825-8190**); Citibank, 17 Ngo Quyen St. (ℭ **04/825-1950**); and Vietcombank, 198 Tran Quan Khai (ℭ **04/826-8045**). ATMs are located at ANZ Bank and Citibank and in various locations throughout the city. Money-changing offices abound in places like Hang Bac, in the heart of the backpacker area of the Old Quarter (Hanoi Sacombank, 87 Hang Bac, ℭ **04/261-392,** is typical of many). Black-market moneychangers will approach you outside of the major banks. Best to just avoid the temptation, as you'll often be left with a few counterfeit or out-of-circulation notes in the mix.

*Internet/E-mail*  The **Emotion CyberNet Café,** at 60 Tho Nhuom and 52 Ly Thuong Kiet (ℭ **04/934-1066**), across from the Hilton, sells snacks and Internet access. Small Internet storefronts are numerous in the Old Quarter on Hang Bac or Hang Be, and in all traveler cafes. **A–Z Queen Café,** at

65 Hang Bac (© **04/826-0860**), is a good bet with affordable service and a pay-as-you use honor system.

*Post Office/Mail* The General Post Office is located at 6 Dinh Le St., Hoan Kiem District (© **04/825-7036**). It's open daily 6:30am to 10pm. You can also send faxes or telexes and make international phone calls. FedEx (© **04/826-4925**) is located in the same building as the post office but has its own storefront.

*Telephone* The city code for Hanoi is 04. Most hotels provide international direct dialing, although none allows you to access an international operator or AT&T (whose Vietnam access code is 12010288). To do that, you will have to go to the General Post Office (above). There are public phone booths throughout the city for local calls that accept phone cards purchased from the post office.

## WHERE TO STAY

Hanoi has everything from historic charm to slick efficiency to a budget hole-in-the-wall. We list just three of the town's seven five-stars—others include the mammoth **Melia** (© **04/934-3343**), plush **Nikko** (© **04/822-3535**), and **Horizon** (© **04/733-0808**). Amenities and cleanliness levels are high across and prices low, making Hanoi a good place for an upgrade. Most hotels over $15 a night will have a phone, air-conditioning, in-room safes, and hair dryers. Children under 12 usually stay free. Ask for discounts. Prices shown here are rack rates, and discounts abound. Hotels charge a VAT of up to 20%.

### VERY EXPENSIVE

**Hanoi Daewoo Hotel** ★★ Just 7 years in business, the Daewoo is the most popular choice in recent years for heads of state and dignitaries (with a long list including President Clinton and Jiang Zemin) and, fittingly, everything is done large—the hotel lobby, the bars, the rooms with king beds, and the 80m-long (262-ft.) curving pool. All interior space is tessellated in marble, deep-toned wood, or in sumptuous fabrics. It's almost a bit too much. The plush rooms are decorated with local accents, and 1,000 interesting modern works of Vietnamese artists grace the walls. Bathrooms are surprisingly small in the lower-end rooms but quite well appointed, with hair dryers and thick, soft linens and towels. There's an attractive lobby lounge and a pool bar. Overlooking the large park surrounding Thu Le Lake, the Daewoo is like a city unto itself. Café Promenade features Asian and European buffets, and Silk Road offers fine Chinese (Cantonese and Szechuan) food. There are three nonsmoking floors and a very efficient business center. The Daewoo is far from the town center, but the many amenities make it sufficiently self-contained.

360 Kim Ma St., Ba Dinh District. © **04/831-5000.** Fax 04/831-5010. www.hanoi-daewoohotel.com. 411 units. $199 double; $319 executive-floor double; $329–$1,500 suite. AE, DC, MC, V. **Amenities:** 4 restaurants; 2 bars; outdoor tennis court; elegant health club; spa; Jacuzzi; sauna; family play program; concierge; tour desk; car rental; limo service; business center; shopping arcade; salon; barber shop; 24-hr. room service; massage; babysitting; laundry service; dry cleaning; Internet. *In room:* A/C, satellite TV, dataport, minibar, fridge, coffeemaker, hair dryer, safe, IDD phone.

**Hilton Hanoi Opera** ★★ The Hilton is a reproduction colonial that describes an elegant arc around the perimeter of the splendid Hanoi Opera building. The inside matches the fine facade, with a lobby done on a grand scale.

Rooms are carpeted in rich, contrasting colors with unique cushioned wallpaper, subdued lighting, and faux Chinese lacquer cabinets that fit well. Rooms on the fifth floor have balconies. Suites offer services similar to standard rooms but are much larger and nicely appointed. Satellite TV, daily newspaper delivery, voice mail, and in-room broadband Internet access keep business travelers up to speed. The hotel also has plenty of features for vacation travelers, like in-house tour services with Exotissimo and a helpful concierge. There is fine dining at Turtle's Poem (try the dim sum for lunch), and Café Opera has gourmet sandwiches and baked goods. Hotel breakfasts are tops and JJ's Sports Bar is a good place to catch up on scores or play a game of pool. On the executive floor, business travelers can enjoy the luxury of private check-in, as well as an executive lounge with a bar and snacks. The courtyard pool area is inviting.

1 Le Thanh Tong St., Hoan Kiem, Hanoi. © 800/774-1500 or 04/933-0500. Fax 04/933-0530. www.hilton. com. 269 units. $210–$230 double; $250 executive room. AE, MC, V. **Amenities:** 3 restaurants; bar; club lounge; pool; fitness center; business center; meeting/executive services; handicapped rooms; ballroom. *In room:* A/C, TV, dataport, hair dryer, safe.

### Sheraton Hanoi Hotel ★★

Just a 10-minute ride north of town, this smart, upscale hotel sits on a peninsula jutting out into Hanoi's picturesque West Lake in a neighborhood popular with the local expat community (which means good restaurants and services in the area). The hotel makes up for any inconvenience to town by being completely self-contained, with fine dining options, a top fitness center, and hotel services that cover all bases, from local touring to business support. Rooms are done in an ultratidy, contemporary style typical of Sheraton hotels, certainly nothing to write home about but cozy and familiar. All rooms have fine views of the lake. Bathrooms are large, with big bathtubs, separate glass shower and fine wood and granite detail. In-house dining is tops and transport to town is available 24 hours. The hotel is just reopening after a delay of some 7 years after the economic collapse in 1997. It's a popular meeting destination and has space for many. It's still under construction and promises more rooms as the upper floors are completed.

K5 Nghi Tam, 11 Xuan Dieu Rd., Ho Tay District, Hanoi. © 04/719-9000. Fax 04/719-9001. www.sheraton. com. 156 units. $200–$270 double; from $320 suit. AE, MC, V. **Amenities:** 2 restaurants; bar; outdoor pool; tennis court; health club; Jacuzzi; sauna; concierge; tour desk; car rental; business center; shopping; 24-hr. room service; massage; babysitting; laundry service; dry cleaning; nonsmoking rooms; club-level rooms. *In room:* A/C, satellite TV, minibar, fridge, hair dryer, safe, IDD phone.

### Sofitel Metropole Hanoi ★★★

Hanoi's top choice. Built in 1901, the Metropole is a historical treasure. It's where invading, liberating, or civil armies have found billet and raised their flags, where the first film was shown in Indochina, where Charlie Chaplin spent his honeymoon, where Jane Fonda and Joan Baez took cover in a bomb shelter, and where heads of state and embassy officials resided for many years. In fact, the history of the Metropole is the history of the last hundred years in Hanoi, and the folks here have even published a short volume telling the tale. The hotel has been through numerous renovations, and a new building was added in 1994. Rooms in the new wing are more spacious, but go for the old wing and walk into a bit of history (keep an eye out for ghosts) in these medium-size rooms with wood floors, cane furniture, classic fixtures, and high ceilings. Modern bathrooms are large and have little touches like wood-frame mirrors, fresh flowers, and a fine line of in-house products. The staff couldn't be nicer or more efficient. The pool is small, but the adjoining Bamboo lounge is an oasis of calm in the city center. The health club with sauna and massage is superb and has a good street view. Le Beaulieu is popular in

Hanoi for classic French fare, and the Spices Garden is a great place to sample local delights (the lunch buffet is a safe and tasty place to try Hanoi street fare like *pho* and *bun cha*). The Metropole also offers cooking classes. The Sofitel's Met Pub is a casual spot to have a beer and listen to live music. The downtown location can't be beat, and there's a nice mix of tourists and businesspeople here.

15 Ngo Quyen St., Hanoi. ☎ **800/221-4542** or 04/826-6919. Fax 04/826-6920. Sofmet@netnam.org.vn. 232 units. $190–$245 double; from $255 suite. AE, DC, MC, V. **Amenities:** 4 restaurants; 3 bars; nice courtyard pool; top-notch health club; spa; Jacuzzi; sauna; concierge; tour desk; car rental; limo; business center; shopping; salon; massage; laundry; Internet. *In room:* TV, dataport, minibar, fridge, hair dryer, safe, IDD phone.

## EXPENSIVE

**De Syloia** 👁 The De Syloia is cozy little treasure just south of the city center. Rooms are large and clean, not especially luxurious but comfortable with tidy carpet, dark wood appointments and furniture, and large bathrooms with tubs (deluxe rooms and suites have Jacuzzis). The lobby is compact and clean but not particularly atmospheric, and the whole setup is a Hanoi minihotel gone upscale, but a good standard throughout. The staff is friendly on a good day, and the amenities are limited, but this is a popular choice away from the downtown traffic. Check the website for a 42% discounted Internet rate.

17a Tran Hung Dao St., Hoan Kem District, Hanoi. ☎ **04/824-5346.** Fax 04/824-1083. www.desyloia.com. 33 units. $90–$105 double; $115 deluxe; $145 suite (discount available). AE, MC, V. **Amenities:** Restaurant; bar; minigym; tour desk; car rental; business center; laundry; dry cleaning; small meeting room; Internet. *In room:* A/C, satellite TV, minibar, fridge, hair dryer, safe, IDD phone.

**Guoman Hotel** 👁👁 For a high standard of service and comfort in Hanoi, the Guoman is a real find. This uppity downtown four-star caters to the business crowd and is popular for semipermanent residents; however, with such a good location and amenities, it's a great choice for all. From the large central chandelier and toothed filigree of the stylish lobby to the subdued Helmsman lounge's live music and low-slung couches, there is a laid-back boutique feel here that's much finer than the low price tag. Rooms are big, carpeted, and nicely furnished if a bit bland, and they still have that brand-new feeling. Other highlights include comfy, just-right firm beds; fat pillows; and big spic-and-span marble-and-tile bathrooms. There is a good fitness center, and the second-floor restaurant serves a great breakfast and good Western and Asian cuisine (lots of promotional specials). There are two nonsmoking floors, a rarity in Vietnam. Service is excellent, and the staff can help you with any business or travel need.

83A Ly Thuong Kiet St., Hanoi. ☎ **04/822-2800.** Fax 04/822-2822. 149 units. $70–$75 double; $120–$180 suite. AE, MC, V. **Amenities:** 2 restaurants; 2 bars (live music); health club; dry sauna; concierge; tour desk; car rental; limo; business center; small gift shop; massage; babysitting; nonsmoking floors; meeting rooms. *In room:* A/C, satellite TV, dataport, minibar, fridge, coffeemaker, safe.

## MODERATE

**Army Hotel** 👁👁 *Value* In a sprawling complex owned by the Vietnamese military—thus the name—there's no need to salute here and the friendly staff won't ask you to drop for 20 push-ups. For comfort and value close to downtown (and a nice pool), the Army Hotel is a find. Located on a quiet street just a short walk east of downtown (behind the opera house), Army is popular with long-term visitors, especially couples who come to adopt in Vietnam. Rooms vary, so ask to see one before you check in; most are large and clean, with tile floors and nice-size bathrooms with a shower/bathtub combo. Each room has a balcony, some with direct pool access. The staff is friendly, the lobby business center is convenient, and the pool is inviting and unique in this price range. Ask about the eclectic suites, some with Japanese-style rooms, and a larger private balcony.

33 C Pham Ngu Lao St., Hanoi (just behind the opera house). ☏ **04/825-2896**. Fax 04/825-9276. armyhotel@
fpt.vn. 70 units. $50–$60 standard double; $70 deluxe; $72–$198 suite. AE, MC, V. **Amenities:** Restaurant; out-
door pool in large central courtyard; basic fitness equipment; sauna; small business center (Internet $3/hr.);
room service 6am–10pm; babysitting. *In room:* A/C, TV, fridge, hot water for coffee, hair dryer, IDD phone.

**Dan Chu Hotel** ★★  Pronounced "Zahn Shoe," the hotel was originally a
French government building, and the 100-year history and columned facade
lends character to the place. Best is the location, just a short walk from Hoan
Kiem Lake, in the heart of the downtown district. Rooms all have high ceilings
and are spacious but not luxurious at all (and some a bit musty). Deluxe rooms
are the best value and large enough for a game of racquetball. Bathrooms are
large and clean, but basic tile spaces with no counters. The hotel has plenty of
service: a travel counter, car rental, an affordable restaurant, and popular massage and sauna area. A long, common balcony overlooks the courtyard and
active street scene below. Rooms could do without the polyester bedspreads, and
the downtown location and many big groups that stay here makes for a bit of
street noise, but for history, character, and convenience, this place is a great
value. The lunch buffet is a virtual giveaway and not a bad meal.

29 Trang Tien St., Hanoi. ☏ **04/825-4344**. Fax 04/826-6786. 42 units. $40 standard; $55 superior; $65
deluxe; $75–$90 suite. AE, DC, MC, V. **Amenities:** Restaurant; bar; tour desk; car rental; small business center; massage. *In room:* Satellite TV, minibar, fridge, coffeemaker, safe, IDD phone.

**Galaxy Hotel** ★★  Popular with tour groups, the Galaxy is on a busy corner
just north of the Old Quarter and is a comfortable spot to begin exploring this
colorful part of the city. Converted from a 1929 factory, the recently renovated
building is colorless but comfortable. Good-size rooms are spotless, with familiar amenities at affordable rates. Decor is nondescript but tidy with nice touches
like flourishes of filigree here and there. Rooms are big, and tile baths are small
but neat. Corner suites are a great option, with windows facing two directions
over the Old Quarter. There is a good Asian restaurant on the premises and a
nice little lobby bar. Staff members will remember your name and are friendly
and helpful with advice and suggestions.

1 Phan Dinh Phung St., Hanoi. ☏ **04/828-2888**. Fax 04/828-2466. galaxyhtl@netnam.org.vn. 60 units. $50
double; $60 suite. Breakfast included. AE, DC, MC, V. **Amenities:** Restaurant; bar; tour desk; car rental; 24-hr.
room service; babysitting; laundry; dry cleaning. *In room:* A/C, satellite TV, minibar, fridge, coffeemaker, hair
dryer, safe, IDD phone.

**Hoa Binh Hotel** ★  Built in 1926 and recently renovated, the Hoa Binh is a
good, atmospheric choice. Comfort and history meet at a good level, and
whether you're walking up the big, creaky grand stair or opening French doors
onto a balcony overlooking the busy street, you know that you're in Hanoi here.
Sizable rooms have original light fixtures, molded ceilings, and gloss-wood furniture. Everything is done a bit "low-luxe" but the shiny, polyester bedspreads,
velveteen drapes, and spongy mattresses detract from the overall effect. Bathrooms are plain and small but spotless. The hotel is in a prime downtown location, and the bar has a view of the city. Ask to see a room before checking in
because they vary in size, shape, and degree of smoke or must; in general,
though, this is a good bet. It's popular with tour groups.

27 Ly Thuong Kiet St., Hoan Kiem District, Hanoi. ☏ **04/825-3315** or 04/825-3692. Fax 04/826-9818. www.
hoabinhhotel.com. 103 units. $60 double; $80–$130 suite. Breakfast included. AE, MC, V. **Amenities:** 2
restaurants; 2 bars; sauna; concierge; tour desk; car rental; small business center; shopping; limited room service; massage; laundry; dry cleaning (next day); nonsmoking rooms available. *In room:* A/C, TV, minibar, fridge,
hair dryer, safe.

## INEXPENSIVE

**Hong Ngoc Hotel** ★★   With three locations all right in the heart of the Old Quarter, this is a good no-frills option close to Hoan Kiem Lake. Friendly to a fault, the staff has a can-do attitude and can help you with any detail, like renting a car, motorcycle, or bicycle. Rooms are compact, but all have quality amenities of a proper hotel: phone, cable, air-conditioning, and minibar. Larger suites are a good choice, and all rooms are done in dark wooden trim. Baths are small and clean. This is top-notch downtown affordability, a minihotel with attitude—like a terrier who thinks himself a Great Dane.

14 Luong Van Can St., Hoan Kiem District, Hanoi. ℂ **04/826-7566.** Fax 04/8245362. 34 Hang Manh St., Hoan Kiem. ℂ **04/828-5053.** Fax 04/828-5054. 14 Hang Van Can St., Hoan Kiem. ℂ **04/826-7566.** Fax 04/824-5362. hongngochotel@hn.vnn.vn. Total of 78 units. $20–$30. MC, V. **Amenities:** Restaurant; tour desk; limited room service; Internet. *In room:* A/C, satellite TV, minibar, fridge, safe.

**Phuc Loi** ★   This is the standard Old Quarter minihotel, but everything at the Phuc Loi is supertidy and ornate. Rooms are small but spotless, with faux-wood floors and high ceilings. This place is relatively new and everything is in good shape. The bathrooms are a nice size, with shower/tub combo, granite counters, and patterned wall tiles. Try for one of the three large split-level VIP rooms; they're very comfortable and a steal at $35. Rooms on higher floors have great views of the Old Quarter. The staff is friendly and helpful.

128 HangBong St., Old Quarter. ℂ **04/928-5235.** Fax 04/828-9897. phucloihotel@fpt.vn. 20 units. $22–$50. **Amenities:** Bar; small gym room on top floor; bike rental. *In room:* A/C, satellite TV, minibar, fridge, hair dryer, IDD phone.

## WHERE TO DINE

It's hard to have a bad meal in Hanoi. The French influence is everywhere with both classical French and Vietnamese fusion fare, all priced for any budget. Almost every ethnic food variation is well represented in the city as well.

Hanoi has savory specialties that must be sampled. For that, hit the streets and dine in small local eateries. *Pho,* by far the most popular local dish, is noodles with slices of beef *(bo)* or chicken *(ga),* fresh bean sprouts, and condiments. *Bun cha,* a snack of rice noodles and spring rolls with fresh condiments, has made Dac Kim restaurant (at No. 1 Hang Manh, in the Old Quarter) city-renowned. And don't miss Cha Ca, Hanoi's famed spicy fish fry-up (see below under "Inexpensive").

### EXPENSIVE

**Emperor** ★★★ VIETNAMESE   For atmosphere and decor alone, the Emperor is Hanoi's address of note. A beautiful restored colonial stands sentinel at the busy street-side entrance and is the fine-dining area, posh and elegant. But this hushed elegance, a bit stiff really, gives way to an interior courtyard and a laid-back, classy, open-air dining space. With the torches and candlelight, the hush mumble of conversation, and the gliding forms of staff in traditional *ao-dai* dresses, you might think you've gone into a time warp. The entry ticket is none too dear by Western standards; basic dishes fit any budget, but specialty items like the ubiquitous bird's nest or shark's fin soup will run up the bill. This is Vietnamese fine dining at its best, a tourist and expat favorite. I enjoyed the steamed *garuppa* in a subtle "slightly dark" sauce after an appetizer of crabmeat and asparagus soup. Everything was excellent. Try the soft-shell crab, spicy grilled squid, or any seafood specials of the day. Whether sampling light in the bar area or putting on a spread in the main dining room, this is affordable elegance and the benchmark for comparison.

18b Le Thanh Tong St., Hoan Kiem District. ℂ 04/826-8801. Fax 04/824-0027. Reservations highly recommended. Main courses $4.75–$29. MC, V. Daily 11:30am–2pm and 5:30–10:30pm (pub open until midnight).

**The Green Tangerine** ★★ FRENCH   Green Tangerine is set in a lovingly restored 1928 colonial right in the center of the old quarter. The menu features rich, delicious French fare. There's a small courtyard area, great for an afternoon drink just a few steps off of busy Hang Be, and the air-conditioned dining room is a real sanctuary of luxurious dining. It's very popular with expats, and that makes for a constantly evolving menu to keep up with repeat customers. I had a delicious *mille-feuille* of scallops cooked in white wine and garnished with Parmesan and eggplant. For a main, it was savory lasagna made of wide noodles stuffed with a pâté of crab and broccoli cooked in cognac and layered with spicy mashed carrot: very original. Everything is rich and delicious. The rack of lamb served in coffee is unique and the set menus are popular. A luxurious evening.

48 Hang Be, Hoan Kiem District. ℂ 04/825-1286. Main courses $7.70–$15. AE, MC, V. Daily 9am–11pm.

**The Press Club** ★★ CONTINENTAL   Subdued and elegant, this place states firmly, in hushed tones, "power lunch" and offers cuisine and prices to match. The indoor restaurant is sizable yet private, done in dark tones of maroon and forest green with solid wood furniture and detailing. There is outdoor seating on the terrace facing a stage which features regular live acts. The service is impeccable. The menu is full of sumptuous Continental standards: antipasto starters, goat-cheese salad, tuna steak, smoked trout and baked grouper, and various wood-grilled imported steaks and meat dishes. Unique is the "deconstructed" Vietnamese *pho* noodle soup with lobster, foie gras, and truffle. For dessert, try the white-chocolate sticky rice or rich rice pudding. The second and third floors house event facilities and meeting rooms, and on the ground floor there's a casual coffee corner and **The Deli,** a good, cozy place to grab a local or international paper (and also browse a good book corner) and a relaxed lunch of sandwiches and gourmet pizzas, not to mention the Aussie pie with chips or "Mom's Meatloaf." A good choice for a casual dose of home.

59A Ly Thai To St., Hoan Kiem District. ℂ 04/934-0888. www.hanoi-pressclub.com. Reservations recommended. Main courses $12–$40. AE, MC, V. Daily 11am–3pm and 5–10:30pm. Weekend brunch 11am–3pm.

**Wild Rice (Lá Luá)** ★ ASIAN FUSION   Nothing about Lá Luá portends to be authentic Vietnamese, and everything from the decor to the dining is in fact an amalgam of traditions and customs. The place looks like an upmarket LA bistro borrowing Japanese themes, with tall stands of bamboo encased in glass, slate floors, and bright white walls that shine with the mellow glow of indirect lighting. The food is good Vietnamese-influenced fare. I had a grilled chicken in chile with lemon grass and it was deliciously spicy and savory. Try the barbecued squid or beef with coconut. Presentation is Zen simple, white linen with black chopsticks, a plate and bowl and a candle on the table; and it's as if the staff is always playing a game of chess on your table, rearranging things as if they'd rather not disturb the utensil still life. It's all a bit studied really, but the food is very good.

6 Ngo Thi Nham St., Ba Trung. ℂ 04/943-8896. Fax 04/943-6299. Main course 45,000 VND–160,000 VND ($3–$11). AE, MC, V. Daily 11am–2pm and 5:30–10pm.

## MODERATE

**Al Fresco's** ★★ TEX-MEX   Run by Australian expats, Al Fresco's is two floors of friendly, casual dining. With checkered tablecloths, good oldies music, and a great view from the second floor to the street below, this is the place to bring the kids (or yourself) when they're in need of a slice of home. The place serves very good Tex-Mex, pizza, chicken wings, and the like. The ribs are the house specialty. There are excellent imported and local Aussie steaks, and the burgers are the real deal, with all the fixin's. Desserts are good old standbys like brownies a la mode. The wine list is heavy on Australian and inexpensive South American reds. If you've had enough of fried rice or noodle soup, come here for something to stick to your ribs and have a chat with the friendly owner.

23L Hai Ba Trung St., Hoan Kiem District. ℂ **04/826-7782.** Main courses $5–$12. MC, V. Daily 9:30am–10:30pm.

**Brother's Café** 🐦 VIETNAMESE   Buffet only, Brother's is an inexpensive starting point to explore gourmet Vietnamese cuisine. Lunch includes dishes such as salted chicken, sweet-and-sour bean sprouts, shrimp, noodles, and spring rolls; a full dessert table of sweet tofu, sweet baby rice, dragon fruit, and other exotic offerings; and fresh lemon or melon juice. Dinner features grilled items—shrimp, fish, lamb, and pork—and a glass of wine. There are faux street stalls encircling the garden with Vietnamese favorites like *pho* (noodle soup) and *bun cha* (cold rice noodles, spring rolls, and lettuce eaten by dipping into a slightly sweet sauce with meat). Don't expect anyone to explain anything, though; the staff here does little more than schlep drinks and smilingly point to the buffet, but it's about the food, really, and a meal here is not without nice details like pressed linen napkins and tiny fresh flowers. There is nice seating in both the courtyard (under canvas umbrellas) and the casual corners of this lushly restored colonial. The word is out, though so, especially at lunch, it's not uncommon to see tour buses pulled up in front. Get there early or get ready for an old-time smorgasbord push and shove.

26 Nguyen Thai Hoc St. ℂ **04/733-3866.** www.brothercafe.com. Buffets 90,000 VND ($6) lunch; 178,000 VND ($12) dinner. AE, DC, MC, V. Daily 11:30am–2pm and 6:30–10pm.

**Indochine** 🐦 VIETNAMESE   Set in a beautifully restored colonial, this place is a long-time tourist favorite. The food is, like that at many restaurants in Hanoi, Vietnamese cuisine toned down for foreign palates, but Indochine does it well. Indochine fills with tour groups at lunchtime, which is a bit much, and brings a rise in the noise level and a drop in service quality. The spring rolls are great, as are both the banana flower salad and the crispy fried prawn-cakes with ginger. Ask about daily specials. With indoor and patio seating and traditional Vietnamese performances in the evening (call ahead for times), Indochine is well worth a visit for the beautiful colonial setting alone. Take a cab; it's hard to find.

16 Nam Ngu St., Hoan Kiem District. ℂ **04/942-4097.** Main courses $2–$6.50. MC, V. Daily 11:30am–10pm.

**Khazanna** 🐦🐦 NORTHERN INDIAN   This restaurant changes names and owners every 2 years, but the current incarnation, not unlike the last, serves a fine menu of good North Indian dishes. It's tidy Indian-themed Western decor here with excellent service and presentation: The curries are served in small metal crocks with brass ladles. The affordable lunch menu brings in crowds of businesspeople. In the evening, choose from an extensive menu of curries, grilled dishes, and good nan breads. Everything's good.

41B Ly Thai To St., Hoan Kiem District. ℂ **04/824-1166.** Main courses 39,000 VND–79,000 VND ($2.60–$5.25). MC, V. Mon–Sat 11:30am–2pm and 6:30–10pm.

**Restaurant Bobby Chinn** 🐦🐦 CALIFORNIA/VIETNAMESE/FRENCH   With a decor and panache that would hold its own on a side street of Soho or a lofty perch in the Bay Area, a visit to Restaurant Bobby Chinn makes for an interesting evening. The restaurant is on the southwest corner of Hoan Kiem

Lake, where longtime expat and raconteur Mr. Chinn holds court and runs the show from behind the proscenium of his large, open bar at the entrance. It's where to see and be seen these days in Hanoi, and it's a popular late-night spot where local jazz artists like to drop by. There's a good revolving collection of local artists' works on the walls and always good music playing (a KENNY G–FREE ZONE, a sign tells you on the door). The dining area out front is simple tables and a few booths at bar side with picture-window views of the lake and the street. Seating in the back is choice overstuffed couches and low tables in a maze of discreet nooks with hanging cloths blown by ceiling fans that offer fickle privacy. It's all quite cinematic, really. However you feel about the atmosphere, Mr. Chinn serves up a delightfully eclectic menu of fine French and Vietnamese-inspired dishes all with a playful, cross-cultural flair. There is an excellent, affordable tapas menu billed as "Zen-like" for simple elegance; try the rib sampler or "symphony of flavors" (a selection of all). Main courses like pan-roasted salmon with wasabi mashed potatoes, and green tea–smoked duck have a certain Franco-Japanese appeal all their own. The menu is a work in progress, so try to get a recommendation.

1 Ba Trieu St., Hoan Keim District. ℂ 04/934-8577. Reservations recommended. AE, MC, V. Main courses $7–$12; tapas menu from $2. Daily noon–2pm and 5pm to last customer.

**Seasons of Hanoi** 🛪 VIETNAMESE   The atmosphere is picture-perfect at Seasons: intimate, candlelit, romantic, earth-colored surroundings in a casual yet beautifully restored colonial with authentic native furniture. Sit on the first to avoid group tours that take over the second floor. The spring rolls are heaven, as are the tempura soft-shell crabs. They serve great fish as you like it—fried, boiled, on kabobs, and in hot pots. Try the sautéed eel with chile and lemon grass or fried chicken in panda leaves. Presentation is elegant and the wine list long.

95B Quan Thanh. ℂ 04/843-5444. Reservations recommended, especially for groups. Main courses 40,000 VND–80,000 VND ($2.65–$5.35). MC, V. Daily 11:30am–2pm and 6–11pm.

## INEXPENSIVE

**Cha Ca La Vong** 🛪🛪 *Finds* HANOI/VIETNAMESE   On a street called Cha Ca there's a restaurant called Cha Ca, and it serves one dish: You guessed it, Cha Ca. So what's the story with Cha Ca? Very simple. It's monkfish, a fine white fish, fried at high heat in peanut oil with dill, tumeric, rice noodles, and peanuts—and it's delicious. The place is pretty grungy, and to call the service "indifferent" would be to sing its praises, but that's the beauty here: It's all about the food. You order by saying how many you are, and how many bottles of beer or soda you'd like. Then it's do-it-yourself, with some gruff guidance, as you stir in the ingredients on a frying pan over a charcoal hibachi right at the table. It's a rich dish and great with some hot sauce (go easy on it at first), and it makes for a fun and interesting evening. Just say "Cha Ca," and any cab driver can take you there. Avoid copycats; the original Cha Ca La Vong is the only game in town.

14 Cha Ca St. ℂ 04/825-3929. Main courses 70,000VND per person ($4.66). No credit cards. Daily 10am–2pm and 4–10pm.

**Le Café des Arts de Hanoi** 🛪 BISTRO/CONTINENTAL   After strolling around Hoan Kiem Lake, stop off its northwest end for a drink or a bite at this friendly bistro-style eatery, run by French expats and open all day. Spacious, with tiled floors and shuttered windows looking into the narrow Old Quarter street below, the cafe has casual rattan furniture and a long, inviting bar, and it doubles as an art gallery, which explains the interesting paintings hanging throughout. The Vietnamese art crowd also provides some attractive local color. Most inviting, however, is the excellent food. Ask for the special of the day, and stick to bistro standbys like the omelets or a *croque madame*—toasted bread and cheese sautéed in egg—and house specialty *salade bressare* (very fresh chicken and vegetables in a light mayonnaise sauce). There is also good house wine by the glass and excellent lunch set specials.

11b Ngo Bao Khanh, Hoan Kiem District (in the Old Quarter). ✆ 04/828-7207. Main courses $6–$12. No credit cards. Daily 9am–11pm (bar open until midnight).

**Mediterraneo** ✿ ITALIAN  You'll find a tasty but typical range of northern Italian fare at this mellow, street-side cafe on Nha Tho, Hanoi's stylish cafe area (called Church Street). Prosciutto with melon, tomato, and mozzarella is a good starter. Follow with good, homemade pasta, choice of grilled dishes, or pizza. It's affordable, cozy, and casual. There are daily specials and a good wine list.

23 Nha Tho St., Hoan Kiem (near the Old Church). ✆ 04/826-6288. Main courses $3.30–$8.30. MC, V. Daily 10am–11pm.

**Tamarind Café** ✿✿ VEGETARIAN  Tamarind is a laid-back, friendly spot, and, even if you're not a vegetarian, this welcoming cafe's inventive menu will tickle your fancy. Soups like vegetarian wonton and two-color soup (spinach and sweet potato) take the chill off Hanoi winter nights and go great with the selection of sandwiches. Other inventive options here include Ratatofu, ratatouille over tofu, and an all-day breakfast served with delicious homemade fruit condiments. Fruit shakes and excellent teas round out the meal, and, with a bottomless cup of coffee for just $1, it's a great place to take a break from the hectic traffic of the Old Quarter and relax. There are street-side tables out front and funky, raised-floor seating in the back. A good place to meet other travelers and pick up advice.

80 Ma May St. ✆ 04/926-0580. Main courses $2–$5. MC, V. Daily 5:30am–11pm.

## SNACKS & CAFES

For great coffee and desserts, try **Moca Café** (14–16 Nha Tho St.; ✆ 04/825-6334). This area has become the popular spot for a growing little Bohemian community in Hanoi, and businesses are sprouting up all along Nha Tho, the street that extends from St. Christopher's Church. **Paris Deli** (13 Nha Tho St.; ✆ 04/928-6697) is a popular new spot with great breads and deli sandwiches.

One of the main attractions around Hoan Kiem Lake (for me) is **Fanny's Ice Cream** on the west side of the lake at 48 Le Thai To. Fanny's serves exquisite gelato-style ice cream. Also find local ice-cream shops along Trang Tien between the lake and the Dan Chu Hotel. For 3,000 VND (20¢), enjoy a cone and be part of the local scene.

**Pepperonis** (29 Ly Quoc Su; ✆ 04/928-5246) serves up the pizza that backpackers have been longing for along the tough travel trails throughout Asia. It's cheap and best on the popular bar street (across from Café des Arts).

**Little Hanoi** (21 Hang Gai St.; ✆ 04/828-8333), just north of the lake, is a little local-styled fast-food joint, with basic but tidy bamboo and wood decor. With a limited menu of local favorites like banana flower salad and noodle soup (without the resultant bellyache), it's a good place for a light meal (and a good central meeting point). Little Hanoi delivers, too.

**Highland's Coffee** is the local version of Starbucks and a popular place to beat the heat and have a good, strong cup. Find it at lakeside (38–40 Le Thai To St.; ✆ 04/828/7043) or on a perch at Hoan Kiem Terrace overlooking the north end of the lake (6th floor; ✆ 04/928-7369).

## Finds Have You Tried the Snake?

Six kilometers (3¾ miles) to the east of Hanoi, across the Red River, lies the town of Le Mat, also known as the "snake village." In among shanty houses and winding alleyways, find Chinese-style roofs sheltering elegant dining areas of flashy little restaurants, all strangely tucked away. What's the big secret? The town is the hub of the very taboo snake industry. The Vietnamese taboo is not much different than that in the West (something like "Eat snake? Ooooh, Yuck!"). Snake is also considered a male aphrodisiac, a kind of fried Viagra, so at night it's not uncommon to see groups of businessmen drunk as skunks piling into these places for a bit of medicine.

So, here's the drill. Finding it is half the battle (or adventure). Any taxi driver will be happy to take you to his friend's place in anticipation of a commission. Feel free to ask to see another restaurant (some of them are pretty grotty), but expect to pay about $5 to get there. There are lots of restaurants in Le Mat, but try **O Sin** (© **04/827-2984**).

You'll be greeted by a friendly owner who'll usher you back to the cages and put on quite a show of stirring up the snakes before selecting one he thinks will feed your party. He'll then quote you a ridiculous price, but expect to pay somewhere between $5 and $10 per person after bargaining.

Then the show begins. Before your eyes, the owner kills the snake, drains the blood into a jar of rice whiskey, and systematically disembowels the animal, extracting the liver and showing you the still-beating heart before adding it to the whiskey/blood concoction. The guest of honor eats the heart and takes the first sip of whiskey. Thus begins a lengthy seven-course meal, starting with fried snake skin, grilled snake filet, snake spring rolls, snake soup with rice cake, minced snake dumpling, copious amounts of rice whiskey, and orange wedges for dessert. It's a decent meal, really, and certainly something to write home about.

Be warned that many of these places are part of the underground market in endangered species, but the snakes are common cobras found everywhere in Vietnam, and a trip here makes for an interesting night. Be clear with the driver about where you want to go (i.e., not to a brothel afterward), and don't pay until you arrive at the destination.

## WHAT TO SEE & DO

While sightseeing, remember that state-owned attractions will usually close for lunch from 11:30am to 1:30pm. Be sure not to accept any extraneous pamphlets or unwanted guides at sites; all come with a nominal, but frustrating fee.

### BA DINH DISTRICT

**Army Museum** This building, opened in 1959, presents the Vietnamese side of the country's struggle against colonial powers. There are three buildings of odds and ends from both the French and American wars here, including evocative photos. Most interesting, though, is the actual war equipment on display, including aircraft, tanks, bombs, and big guns, some with signs indicating just how many of which enemy the piece took out. There is a tank belonging to the troops that crashed through the Presidential Palace gates on April 30, 1975, Vietnamese Liberation Day. Outside there is also a spectacular, room-size bouquet of downed French and U.S. aircraft wreckage. Also on the grounds is Hanoi's ancient flag tower (Cot Co), constructed from 1805 to 1812. The exhibits have English translations, which makes this an easy and worthwhile visit.

28A Dien Bien Phu St. ℂ 04/823-4264. Admission 10,000 VND (65¢). Tues–Thurs and Sat–Sun 8–11:30am and 1:30–4:30pm.

### Ho Chi Minh's Mausoleum 𝕒𝕒

In an imposing, somber granite-and-concrete structure modeled on Lenin's tomb, Ho lies in state, embalmed and dressed in his favored khaki suit. He asked to be cremated, but his wish was not heeded. A respectful demeanor is required, and the dress code mandates no shorts or sleeveless shirts. Note that the mausoleum is usually closed through October and November, when Ho goes to Russia for body maintenance of an undisclosed nature. The museum might be closed during this period as well. Note that the mausoleum is only open in the mornings.

On Ba Dinh Sq., Ba Dinh District. Tues–Thurs and Sat 8–11am.

### Ho Chi Minh Museum 𝕒𝕒

English-language explanations help to piece together the fragments of Ho's life and cause at this museum tribute, and there are personal items, photos, and documents detailing the rise of the nation's communist revolution. The rhetoric is laid on a bit thick, but all in all it's an interesting and informative display. Completely unique to Vietnam are the conceptual displays symbolizing freedom, reunification, and social progress through flowers, fruit, and mirrors. Have a look.

3 Ngo Ha (left of 1 Pillar Pagoda, near Ba Dinh Sq.), Ba Dinh District. ℂ 04/845-5455. Admission 10,000 VND (65¢). Tues–Sun 8–11:30am and 1:30–4pm.

### Ho Chi Minh's Residence 𝕒𝕒

Ho's residence, the well-known house on stilts, is behind the Presidential Palace, a gorgeous French colonial building built in 1901 for the resident French governor. Shunning the glorious structure nearby, Ho instead chose to live here from 1958 to 1969. Facing an exquisite landscaped lake, the structure does have its charm, and the spartan room is an interesting glimpse into the life of this enigmatic national hero. The basement was a meeting place for the politburo; upstairs are the bedroom and a study, and little details like his phone and walking cane are kept behind glass. Behind the house is a garden of fruit trees, many of them exotics imported from other lands, including miniature rose bushes and areca trees from the Caribbean.

Behind the Presidential Palace at Ba Dinh Sq. Admission 10,000 VND (65¢). Tues–Sun 8–11am and 1:30–4:30pm.

### Hun Tiep Lake and the Downed B-52

This is not a site that will knock you off your feet for its size or beauty; in fact, what brings many here is that it's an ordinary neighborhood, a maze of quiet lanes broken only by a small pond and, in the brackish water, the wreckage of an American B-52 shot down during the Christmas air raids of 1972. Many folks, veterans among them, find that a visit here puts a perspective on the war and that the rusting wreckage brings our abstract historical impressions back to the concrete present; others see landing gear, struts, and metal sheathing in a grungy pond. There's a partly submerged memorial plaque, and the area is cordoned off; entrance fees are soon to follow, no doubt. Most taxi drivers know it, or some creative charades will get the point

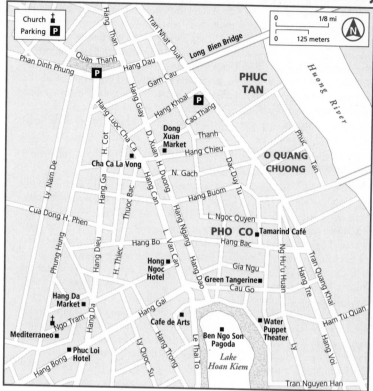

| Church ✝ | | 0 | | 1/8 mi |
| Parking P | | 0 | 125 meters | |

Phan Dinh Phung
Hang Than
Quan Thanh
Tran Nhat Duat
Long Bien Bridge
Hang Dau
Gam Cau
PHUC TAN
Huong River
Hang Giay
Hang Khoai
Cao Thang
Hang Luoc Cha Ca
H. Cot
Ly Nam De
D. Xuan
Dong Xuan Market
Thanh
Hang Chieu
Phuc Tan
O QUANG CHUONG
Cha Ca La Vong
Hang Ga
H. Duong
N. Gach
Dac Duy Tu
Cua Dong H. Phen
Thuoc Bac
Hang Can
Hang Buom
L. Ngoc Quyen
Hang Ngang
PHO CO ▪ Tamarind Café
Hang Bac
Phung Hung
Hang Dieu
H. Thiec
Hang Bo
L. Van Can
Hang Dao
Gia Ngu
Hong Ngoc Hotel
Green Tangerine ▪
Cau Go
Ng Hu'u Huan
Tran Quang Khai
Hang Tre
Hang Da Market ▪
Hang Da
Hang Gai
Cafe de Arts ▪
▪ Water Puppet Theater
Ngo Tram
Ham Tu Quan
Mediterraneo ▪
Ly Quoc Su
Hang Trong
Le Thai To
▪ Ben Ngo Son Pagoda
Hang Voi
Ly
▪ Phuc Loi Hotel
Hang Bong
Lake Hoan Kiem
Tran Nguyen Han

across. Drivers will drop you off at the head of the alley (Lane 55) leading to the site (a handwritten sign reads B-52 with an arrow).

Located just south of West Lake along Hoang Hoa Tham Rd., and a short walk down Lane 55 heading south.

**One-Pillar Pagoda** ✪  To the right of the Ho Chi Minh Museum is the unique One Pillar Pagoda, a wooden structure built in 1049 that sits on stilts over a lake. A king of the Ly Dynasty, Ly Thai Thong King, had it built after having a dream in which Bodhisattva Avalokitesvara, the goddess of mercy, presented him with a lotus flower. The existing pagoda is a miniature reproduction of the original, which was said to represent a lotus emerging from the water. It is certainly interesting, and a prayer here is said to bring fertility and good health. It's best to wear something full length (skirt or trousers), not shorts.

Right of Ho Chi Minh Museum, near Ba Dinh Sq. Ba Dinh District.

**Vietnam National Museum of Fine Arts** ✪✪  This very worthwhile arts museum features Vietnamese art of the 20th century, up to the 1970s or so. While the presentations are a bit crowded and rustic, there are explanations in English. Much of the art is outstanding, although you won't really see any works of an innovative or controversial nature. Entire rooms are devoted to the Vietnamese style of lacquer and silk painting, woodblock, and folk art. Techniques are explained—a nice touch. Interesting also are the modern works of wood statuary interspersed among the exhibits. Some are patriotic in nature, depicting daily life or events during the war or done in Soviet-influenced caricature with heavy-limbed peasants striking triumphant poses or depictions of the brotherhood of the army and the working class. The top floors are devoted to prehistoric artifacts and Buddhist sculptures, some of which are huge and impressive. Don't miss the famous 11th-century goddess of mercy (Kouan Yin), with her thousand arms and eyes in the far-left room on the second floor. Best of all, the museum itself is in an old colonial, and, unless there's a tour group milling around, you can stroll around in relative serenity and rest on one of the many benches provided (no napping). The gift shop has some modern works of well-known artists for sale.

66 Nguyen Thai Hoc St. ℂ 04/846-5801. Admission 15,000 VND ($1). Tues, Fri, Sun 8:30am–5pm; Wed and Sat 8:30am–9pm.

**West Lake** ★★   In Hanoi, West Lake is second only to Hoan Kiem as a nerve center for the city, steeped in legend and sporting several significant pagodas. Vietnam's oldest pagoda, **Tran Quoc,** was built in the 6th century and is located on Cayang Island in the middle of the lake, a beautiful setting. An actual fragment of the Bodhi tree under which Buddha achieved enlightenment was given as a gift from the Prime Minister of India in 1959 and now grows proudly in the main courtyard. Constructed by an early Zen sect and a famous center for Dharma study, and later as an imperial feasting grounds, the temple has a visitors' hall, two corridors, and a bell tower; it still houses a group of diligent monks. They recommend not wearing shorts here, but it is not enforced. Farther along the lake, **Quan Thanh Temple,** by the northern gate, was built during the reign of Le Thai To King (1010–28). It is dedicated to Huyen Thien Tran Vo, the god who reigned over Vietnam's northern regions. Renovated in the 19th century, the impressive temple has a triple gate and courtyard, and features a 3.6m (12-ft.) bronze statue of the god. West Lake is also a hub of local activity, particularly on weekends when families go paddle-boating on it.

Bordered by Thuy Khue and Thanh Nien sts.

## DONG DA DISTRICT
### Temple of Literature and National University (Van Mieu–Quoc Tu Giam) ★★
If Vietnam has a seat of learning, this is it. There are two entities here: Van Mieu, a temple built to worship Chinese philosopher Confucius in 1070; and Quoc tu Giam, literally "Temple of the King Who Distinguished Literature," an elite institute established in 1076 to teach the doctrines of Confucius and his disciples. It existed for more than 700 years as a center for Confucian learning. Moreover, it is a powerful symbol for the Vietnamese, having been established after the country emerged from a period of Chinese colonialism that lasted from 179 B.C. to A.D. 938. It is a testament to the strong cultural heritage of the Mandarins. As such, it stands for independence and a solidifying of national culture and values.

What exists today is a series of four courtyards that served as an entrance to the university. Architecturally, it is a fine example of classic Chinese with Vietnamese influences. Still present are 82 stone stelae—stone diplomas, really—erected between 1484 and 1780, bearing the names and birthplaces of 1,306 doctor laureates who managed to pass the university's rigorous examinations. Beyond the final building, known as the sanctuary, the real university began. Damaged in the French war, it is currently being restored.

Quoc Tu Giam St. ℂ 04/845-2917. Admission 5,000 VND (33¢); 3,000 VND (20¢) for English brochure. Daily 8am–5pm.

## HOAN KIEM DISTRICT

**Hanoi Opera House**    This gorgeous, historic Art Nouveau building was built near the turn of the century. Unfortunately, to get inside, you'll have to attend a performance, but that should be enjoyable as well (see "Hanoi After Dark," below).

1 Trang Tien St. ℰ 04/933-0113. Intersection of Le Thanh Tong and Trang Tien sts., District 1.

**Hoa Lo Prison (Hanoi Hilton)** ★★    For sheer gruesome atmosphere alone, this ranks near the top of the must-see list. It was constructed by the French in 1896 mainly to house political prisoners, and the Vietnamese took it over in 1954. It was subsequently used to house prisoners of war. From 1964 to 1973, it was a major POW detention facility. U.S. Sen. John McCain was a particularly famous inmate, as was Pete Peterson, the ambassador to Vietnam, and Lt. Everett Alvarez, officially the first American pilot to be shot down over Vietnam. Their stories are told from the Vietnamese perspective in photographs and writings grouped in one small room. To the west is the guillotine room, still with its original equipment, and the female and Vietnamese political prisoners' quarters. The courtyard linking the two has parts of original tunnels once used by a hundred intrepid Vietnamese revolutionaries to escape in 1945. Only part of the original complex is left; the rest of the original site was razed and is ironically occupied by a tall, gleaming office complex popular with foreign investors. There are basic English explanations, but this is a good spot to have a guide who is certain to be armed with a tale or two.

1 Hoa Lo St., off Quan Su St. ℰ 04/824-6358. Admission 10,000 VND (65¢). Tues–Sun 8am–4:30pm.

**National Museum of Vietnamese History**    This is an exhaustive repository of Vietnamese ancient and historical relics nicely displayed with some barebones explanations in English. Housed in a building that was the French consulate until 1910 and a museum in various incarnations since, this collection walks you from prehistoric artifacts and carvings to funerary jars and some very fine examples of Dong Son drums from the north, excavations of Han tombs, Buddhist statuary, and everyday items of early history. It's the kind of place where schoolchildren are forced to go (and be careful if you see buses out front), and for anyone but history buffs, you might feel just as bored as the kids. For those on any kind of historical mission in Vietnam, I recommend contacting a tour agency and booking a knowledgeable guide for an excellent overview and a good beginning to any trip.

1 Trang Tien St. (just east of the opera). ℰ 04/825-3518. Admission 15,000 VND ($1). Daily 8–11:30am and 1:30–4:30pm.

**Old Quarter & Hoan Kiem Lake** ★★★    The Old Quarter evolved from workshop villages clustered by trades, or guilds, in the early 13th century. It's now an area of narrow, ancient, winding streets, each named for the trade it formerly featured. Even today, streets tend to be for either silk, silver, or antiques. It's a fascinating slice of centuries-old life in Hanoi, including markets that are so pleasantly crowded that the street itself narrows to a few feet. Hoan Kiem is considered the center of the city. It is also known as the Lake of the Recovered Sword. In the mid–15th century, the gods gave emperor Le Thai To a magical sword to defeat Chinese invaders. While the emperor was boating on the lake one day, a giant tortoise reared up and snatched the sword, returning it to its rightful owners and ushering peace into the kingdom. Stroll around the lake in the early morning or evening to savor local life among the willow trees and see elders playing chess or doing tai chi. In the center of the lake is the Tortoise Pagoda; on the northern part is Ngoc Son pagoda, reachable only by the Bridge of the Rising Sun.

Bordered by Tran Nhat Duat and Phung Hung sts. Daily 8am–5pm.

**Quan Su Pagoda** ⭐   Quan Su is one of the most important temples in the country. Constructed in the 15th century along with a small house for visiting Buddhist ambassadors, in 1934 it became the headquarters of the Tonkin Buddhist Association and today it is headquarters for the Vietnam Central Buddhist Congregation. It's an active pagoda and usually thronged with worshippers; the interior is dim and smoky with incense. To the rear is a school of Buddhist doctrine. For good luck (or for fun), visitors of any stripe are welcome to buy sticks of incense and make offerings at the various altars and sand urns. It's easy to just follow suit, and folks will be glad to show you what to do.

73 Quan Su St., as it intersects Tran Hung Da, Hoan Kiem District. Daily 8–11am and 1–4pm.

## SIGHTS OUTSIDE THE CITY CENTER
**Vietnam Ethnology Museum** ⭐⭐   If you're interested in learning more about the 53 ethnic minorities populating Vietnam's hinterlands, make the jaunt out to this sprawling compound (go by cab). Vietnam's different ethnic groups, their history and customs, are explained in photos, videos, and displays of clothing and daily implements. Out back are a number of recreations of the village homes, from a low Cham house to the towering peak of a thatched Banhar communal home. You come away with a good historical perspective on the many groups you meet in the far north and in parts of neighboring Laos and Thailand.

Nguyen Van Huyen, 6km (3¾ miles) west of town. ☎ 04/756-2193. Admission 10,000 VND (65¢). Tues–Sun 8:30–11:30am and 1:30–4:30pm.

## ACTIVITIES
Bicycles are easily rented from almost every hotel for about $1 a day. Wake up early and join the hordes of people doing tai chi, stretching, walking, and running in the parks of Hanoi: This is a great place for people-watching and a little morning wake-up, best near the Botanical Gardens, Lenin Park, and Hoan Kiem Lake. Get your run in before about 6:30am, though, before traffic starts to snarl. The **Clark Hatch Fitness Center,** at the Metropole Hotel (☎ 04/826-6919), has top-end equipment, a sauna, and a Jacuzzi, with day rates for nonguests.

## SHOPPING
Hanoi is a fine place to shop for silk, silver, lacquer ware, embroidered goods, and ethnic minority crafts. Silk is good quality and an easy buy. Shops will tailor a suit in as little 24 hours, but allow yourself extra time for alterations. Many of the shops are clustered along Hang Gai Street, aka "Silk Street," on the northeast side of the Old Quarter. A silk suit will run from about $35 to $75, depending on the silk, and a blouse or shirt will cost $15 to $20. Virtually every shop takes credit cards (MC, V). Bargain hard for all but the silk; offer 50% of the asking price and end up paying 70% or so.

   **Khai Silk,** with branches in various hotel lobbies and at 96 Hang Gai St. (☎ 04/825-4237) and 121 Nguyen Thai Hoc St. (☎ 04/823-3508), is justly famous for its selection, silk quality, and relatively pleasant store layout. Also try **Thanh Ha Silk** (114 Hang Gai St.; ☎ 04/928-5348) and **Oriental House** (28 Nha Chung; ☎ 04/828-5542). **Tan My** (109 Hang Gai St.; ☎ 04/826-7081) has exquisite embroidery work, especially for children's clothing and bedding. **F Silk** (82 Hang Gai St.; ℂ 04/928-6786) has a fine line of silk ready-to-wear.

For decorative items and souvenirs, shopping is chockablock on the streets surrounding Hoan Kiem Lake. One good place to start is **Nha Tho Street,** also called "Church Street" as it terminates in the town's largest cathedral. Here you'll find the likes of silk and homeware designers in and among quiet cafes. Unique lacquerware and furnishings can be found at **DeltaDeco** or **La Casa** (12 Nha Tho St.; ℂ 04/828-9616; www.lacasavietnam.com). Nearby **Indochine House** (13 Nha Tho St.; ℂ 04/824-8071) has a good selection of handicrafts and souvenirs. These are just a few of the many here.

For silver, antique oddities, and traditional crafts, try **Hong Hoa** (18 Ngo Quyen St., near the Metropole Hotel; ℂ 04/826-8341). **Giai Dieu** (82 Hang Gai St.; ℂ 04/826-0222; also at 93 Ba Trieu St) has interesting lacquer paintings and decorative items.

For fine ceramics, look to **Quang's Ceramics** (22 Hang Luoc St.; ℂ 04/828-3440), in the Old Quarter. Wood, stone, and brass lacquer reproduction sculptures of religious icons are at **KAF Traditional Sculptures and Art Accessories** (31B Ba Trieu St.; ℂ 04/822-0022).

## ART GALLERIES

Vietnam has a flourishing art scene, and Hanoi has many galleries of oil, silk, water, and lacquer paintings. Don't forget to bargain here and know that any paintings you buy are not originals, but copies of well-known Vietnamese artists.

Galleries are chockablock in the Old Quarter and on the perimeters of Hoan Kiem. Try **Linh Gallery** (13 Hang Gai; ℂ 04/928-7013; www.vangallery.com) or **Van Gallery,** its sister shop on Trang Tien near the Dan Chu Hotel. **Nam Son** is next door at 41 Trang Tien (ℂ 04/826-2993).

Others include **Thanh Mai** (64 Hang Gai St.; ℂ 04/825-1618), **Apricot Gallery** (40B Hang Bong St.; ℂ 04/828-8965), and **Thang Long** (15 Hang Gai St.; ℂ 04/825-0740), in the Old Quarter.

## BOOKS

For foreign books in Hanoi, check out one of the many shops lining either Trang Tien or Ma May streets, where you'll find backpacker book repositories and some good deals on photocopied bootlegs. Also try the few similar shops on Bao Khan Street, a popular nightlife area.

## CONVENIENCE

To pick up good snacks for a long train or bus ride, check out **Intimex** (ℂ 04/825-6148), a spiffy grocery down a small alley at 22–23 Le Thai To St., on the west side of Hoan Kiem Lake. For Western wines and canned products from home, try the aptly named **Western Canned Foods** (66 Ba Trieu; ℂ 04/822-9217), just south of Hoan Keim.

# HANOI AFTER DARK

When it comes to nightlife, Hanoi is no Saigon, but there are a variety of pleasant watering holes about town and a few rowdy dance spots. Hanoi is also the best city in which to see **traditional Vietnamese arts** such as opera, theater, and water puppet shows. Invented during the **Ly Dynasty** (1009–1225), the art of water puppetry is unique to Vietnam. The puppets are made of wood and really do dance on water. The shows feature traditional Vietnamese music and depict folklore and myth. Book tickets for the popular puppets at least 5 hours ahead.

## THEATER & PERFORMANCE

The **Hanoi Opera House,** or Hanoi Municipal Theatre (1 Trang Tien St., Hoan Kiem District; C 04/933-0113), hosts performances by local and international artists. The **Hanoi Traditional Opera** (15 Nguyen Dinh Chieu, Ba Dinh District; C 04/826-7361), has shows on Monday, Wednesday, and Friday at 8pm.

**Central Circus** (in Lenin Park, Hai Ba Trung District; C 04/822-0277) has shows at 7:45pm every day except Monday. It's a real circus done on a small scale, so see it only if you're desperate to entertain the kids.

**Thang Long Water Puppet Theater** ★★★ *Finds* Shows are thrice daily at 5:15, 6:30, and 8pm. This might sound like one for the kids, but there is something enchanting about the lighthearted comedy and intricately skilled puppetry of this troupe. They perform numerous vignettes of daily life in the countryside and ancient tales, including the legend of Hoan Kiem Lake and the peaceful founding of the city of Hanoi. Puppeteers use bamboo poles to extend their puppets from behind the proscenium and up through the surface of a small pond that forms the stage. You will be amazed at their ingenuity, and it doesn't take much to suspend disbelief and get caught up in a magical hour of escape. The kids will like it, too. Buy tickets early in the high season. The theater is poorly raked, and that means that, though seats in the front cost a bit more, you'll have a better view—and not look at the back of someone's head—from the middle or the back (pick from a seating chart at the ticket office). You also get a better effect of verisimilitude from the back (looks more real).

57B Dinh Tien Hoang St., Hoan Kiem District. C 04/825-5450. Fax: 04/824-9494. Thanglong.wpt@fpt.vn. Admission 20,000 VND–40,000 VND ($1.35–$2.65).

## BARS, PUBS & DISCOS

**Bao Khanh Street,** just down a short lane in the northwest corner of Hoan Kiem Lake (near Café des Arts), is home to lots of popular bars and late-night spots. Some are a bit seedy, but there are a few comfortable laid-back places. Most popular is the **Funky Monkey** (15b Hang Hanh; C 04/928-6113), which has music, pool tables, pizzas, and a cool black-light menu. Also check out **Polite Pub** (5 Bao Khanh; C 04/825-0959), open 5pm–2 or 3am),or **Gecko Bar** (14b across from Café des Arts; C 04/928-6125). All of these spots are open late, and the street's always hoppin'.

**The Spotted Cow** (23C Hai Ba Trung, just next to Al Fresco; C 04/824-1028) is a good choice for a night out with the boys: There's just drinkin' and darts here.

For a more upscale experience, try a cocktail at the famous **Press Club** (59A Ly Thai To; C 04/934-0888), or just up the street at the **Diva Café** (57 Ly Thai To; C 04/934-4088), where bartenders put on a flamboyant and entertaining fire show when preparing their special Irish coffee.

**Cau Lac Bo Nhac Jazz Club,** in the heart of the Old Quarter (31 Luong Van Can St; C 04/828-7890), has no cover charge and offers some of the best local acts. Call ahead to see what's going on that evening.

**The New Century** (10 Trang Thi; C 04/928-5285), is a popular nightclub for locals—a bit seedy, really, but that's its very charm, according to many.

Also, the folks at **Restaurant Bobby Chinn's** (p. 314; 1 Ba Trieu St. on the south end of Hoan Kiem Lake; C 04/934-8577) can serve up just about any cocktail. It's kind of a hip, late-night hangout, depending on the crowd.

# EXCURSIONS FROM HANOI
## HALONG BAY ★★★

A Vietnamese fable tells that the towering limestone rock formations, called karst, at Halong were formed with the crash landing of a dragon sent by the gods of early Vietnamese animism to protect the country from an invading navy. The picturesque area did in fact play host to some important Vietnamese naval victories against Chinese forces, but the bay is most famous today by its UNESCO World Heritage status, its emerald-green water, and 3,000 islands of towering limestone in the Gulf of Tonkin. The bay itself is a 4-hour drive from Hanoi and a visit usually includes at least one overnight stay (though it can be done in 1 long day). Given the logistics, the trip is best done through an agent or with a group. When you book a tour with an overnight stay, you'll probably cruise on a junk for 4 to 6 hours along the bay, stopping to explore two grottos. You might pause for swimming or kayaking. Overnight trips can cost anywhere from $16 to upward of $150; it depends on whether you hire a bus or a private driver, where you stay, and what you eat. Sinh Café does a fine job on the low end, but don't expect much.

Our recommendation is to contact the helpful folks at **Buffalo Tours** (© 04/ 828-0702; www.buffalotours.com/jewel). Its luxury boat, *The Jewel of the Bay*, runs overnight trips that include kayaking, touring, and fine dining. Buffalo's boat now has a companion vessel, and it is just one of the best of a handful of operators: **Handspan** (www.handspan.com) runs similar tours from Hanoi, and **HuangHai** (www.halongtravels.com) manages a fleet of junks.

For a unique high-end experience, book passage aboard the *Emeraude,* a copy of a French steamer that once plied these waters in the early 20th century. Certainly the largest boat at 55m (180 ft.), the *Emeraude* offers real luxury in each of its 38 cabins, and it comes with a price to match. The 2-day, 1-night cruise is well worth it, though. Check its website at www.emeraude-cruises.com or call the offices at the Press Club in Hanoi at © 04/934-0888 (fax 04/934-0899).

**Eco-tourism** is taking off here, and the steep karst outcrops of the bay are not only beautiful, but ideal for **rock climbing.** You might also want to consider one of the 2- or 3-day **sea-kayaking** adventures that are becoming popular here. Contact Buffalo Tours or Handspan (see "Visitor Information & Tours," earlier in this chapter) for memorable, exciting packages starting from $180 for multiday trips.

## CUC PHUONG NATIONAL PARK

Cuc Phuong, established in 1962 as Vietnam's first national park, is a lush mountain rainforest with more than 250 bird and 60 mammal species, including tigers, leopards, and the unique red-bellied squirrel. The park's many visitors—and poachers—might keep you from the kind of wildlife experience you might hope for in the brush, however. It's still the perfect setting for a good hike, and it features goodies like a 1,000-year-old tree, a waterfall, and Con Moong Cave, where prehistoric human remains have been discovered. Cuc Phuong is a good day trip from Hanoi, and some tourist cafes offer programs for as little as $20 (if you have four people in your group). It is also possible to overnight there in the park headquarters.

## HOA LU

From A.D. 968 to 1010, Hoa Lu was the capital of Vietnam under the Dinh Dynasty and the first part of the Le Dynasty. It is located in a valley surrounded by awesome limestone formations, and is known as the inland Halong Bay. It is a similarly picturesque sight and much easier to reach. Most of what remains of the kingdom are ruins, but there are still temples in the valley, renovated in the 17th century. The first honors Dinh Tien Hoang and has statues of the king. The second is dedicated to Le Dai Hanh, one of Dinh's generals and the first king of the Le Dynasty, who grabbed power in 980 after Dinh was mysteriously assassinated. Hoa Lu can easily be seen on a day trip from Hanoi. Seat-in-coach tours from a tourist cafe run about $12 per person.

## 4 Sapa & the Far North

The north and northwest highland regions are popular destinations for hardy travelers. In addition to breathtaking landscapes of the **Tonkinese Alps** and off-the-map destinations like **Dien Bien Phu,** one of the main attractions are the **villages of the ethnic minority hill tribes.**

**Sapa** is a small market town that has been a gathering spot for many local hill tribes for nearly 200 years. Hmong and Yao people, among others, still come here to conduct trade, socialize, and attend an ephemeral **"love market"** where young men and women choose one another for marriage (it's not likely you'll see anything but a staged re-creation of it these days). Seeing this, French missionaries as early as 1860 said "Mon Dieu!" and set up camp to save souls; their stone church still stands sentinel and is well attended at the center of town. Sapa, with it's mercifully cool climate, became a holiday escape for French colonists, complete with rail connection, upscale hotels, and a tourist bureau as early as 1917. The outpost was retaken by the Vietnamese in 1950 and attacked and destroyed later by the French, followed by a brief occupation by Chinese troops. The town reopened for tourism in the 1990s.

Now connected by luxury train with Hanoi, Sapa boasts good accommodation and is a great jumping-off point for trekking and eco-tours. Even a 1- or 2-day trip, bracketed by overnight train journeys from Hanoi, will give you a unique glimpse of local hill-tribe culture. Trek out to nearby villages with or without a guide, or meet with the many hill-tribe people who come to town to sell their wares. Hill-tribe costumes are colorful embroidered tunics embellished with heavy silver ornaments that signify marital status or place in the group's hierarchy.

And the Tonkinese Alps are a feast for the eyes; hills striated by terraced rice-farms in vast, green valleys are like a stairway up to Mt. Fansipan, Southeast Asia's tallest mountain, which, at 3,143m (10,309 ft.), smiles down on all the proceedings. *Note:* Bring a few layers here because, especially in the winter months, it's can get chilly.

## GETTING THERE

**BY TRAIN**    Guests of the Victoria Hotel won't want to miss the **Victoria's Orient Express** train from Hanoi to Sapa. With wood-paneled luxury sleeping cars and a restaurant billed as the finest dining between Hanoi and Sapa, this is an exciting new option. Trains depart four times per week with a similar return schedule, making possible convenient 2- or 3-day trips with overnight transport. Prices range from $85 for a midweek round-trip in superior class to $220 in a deluxe compartment on the weekend. Children under 12 ride for 50% regular price. Contact the Victoria Sapa (© 20/871-522; www.victoriahotels-asia.com) for details and reservation.

A number of standard and tourist trains make the overnight run from Hanoi. You can make arrangements with any travel agent for a small fee, or do it yourself at the Hanoi Railway Station (where the western edge of Hoan Kiem district meets Dong Da district at 120 Le Duan; © **04/942-3949**). Prices range from $16 for a hard berth to $30 for a soft berth with air-conditioning. Trains passing through Lao Cai also continue north and make connections in China. (*Note:* This requires a Chinese visa.) **Tulico Trains** (© **04/828-7806;** www.tulico-sapa. com) is also a good bet, just one notch above the regular sleeper cars.

To get to Sapa from the train station in Lao Cai, you'll need to transfer by bus for the 2-hour ride from Lao Cai station. This can mean anything from a 25,000 VND ($1.65) fare in a rattle-trap Russian cast-off, or a price of $40 for a ride in a Japanese Pajero Mini (SUV). The road is cut into the hillside and is bumpy and windy, but the views of the terraced rice farms of the valley are beautiful as you ascend.

*Note:* All trains to Sapa leave from the **Hanoi Railway Station** at 120 Le Duan St., often confused with Hanoi's other station. Be sure to show any taxi the address.

**BY BUS**    Hanoi's tourist cafes all run frequent buses to Sapa for $12 one-way. Some include Sapa in larger tours of the north. You get what you pay for, and for my money, the train is the best option.

**BY CAR**    Any tourist cafe or travel agent in Hanoi can arrange trips by private jeep or a combo jeep-and-train tour. Apart from Sapa, the vast tracts of the north are untouristed and best visited with a company. Look under "Visitor Information & Tours" in the Hanoi section. **Ann Tours, Buffalo Tours,** and **Handspan** all offer comprehensive itineraries. Avoid the temptation to book budget tours with the tourist cafes, especially for areas off the beaten track.

## VISITOR INFORMATION

For tours and trekking in the region, the Danish outfit **Topas Travel** (20 Cau May, Sapa; © **020/871-331;** fax 020/871-596; www.topas.dk/vietnam), with offices worldwide and experienced guides, is a great option. Whether it's a day trek to nearby villages, an extended tour with home stays in villages, or the 5-day push to the top of Fansipan, these guys can cover it. There are a few storefront Internet cafes on Cau May Street. All hotels provide exchange service for traveler's checks and even credit card cash advances.

## WHERE TO STAY
### EXPENSIVE

**Victoria Sapa** ♔♔♔    This is Sapa's crème de la crème and one of the nicest rural resorts in Indochina. Set on a small hill with panoramic views of the town, the standard here, from the comfortable rooms and fine dining to the hilltop health club and pool, is without rival. Situated around a cozy courtyard, all rooms have balconies with wood-spindled railings and, inside, deep-toned wood floors offset by saturated wall colors, cane and fine wooden finish work, and local weavings and art. The decor in guest rooms and common areas work together in a nice unity to remind guests of the local hill-tribe culture. Beds are big and comfy, and the bathrooms are large, with fine granite counters, wood fixtures, and even a small heater to warm up the tiles. If you're here with the kids, family rooms are huge, with up to six beds and some with bunks (they can rearrange them), and are a great option. Suites are large with elegant canopy beds and sitting area. The heated pool and hilltop spa facilities are incredible, and with amenities like a billiard table, comfortable reading nooks, and scenic viewing points here and there, this hotel is so inviting and comfortable that many prolong their stay. Don't miss having at least one meal in the Tavanh restaurant (see "Where to Dine," below).

At the top of the hill overlooking town, Sapa District, Lao Cai Province. ℰ 020/871-522. Fax 020/871-539. www.victoriahotels-asia.com. 77 units. $135–$220 double; $250 suite (promotional rates available). AE, MC, V. **Amenities:** Restaurant; bar; indoor/outdoor pool (heated); tennis court; health club; sauna; kids' playroom; tour desk (can arrange treks w/Topas); car rental; salon; massage; laundry; nonsmoking rooms. *In room:* Satellite TV w/in-house movies, minibar, fridge, coffeemaker, hair dryer, safe, IDD phone.

## MODERATE

**Bamboo Sapa**   This good budget standby is a large concrete block suspended over the valley near the town center. Just over 2 years old, rooms are clean and quite large, done in shiny tile. Most have balconies and all are oriented to the valley view. Shower-in-room–style bathrooms are large and clean; mattresses are sturdy, hard foam; and the staff is quite friendly and has a good in-house tour operator (**Sapa Trekking Tour**) that can plan any trip. There is an open-air restaurant under the lobby that holds frequent, fun cultural dance shows.

Cau May St. ℰ 020/871-076. Fax 020/871-945. www.sapatravel.com. 30 units. $30–$40. No credit cards. **Amenities:** Restaurant; bar; motorbike rental; tour desk; car rental; laundry. *In room:* TV, IDD phone.

**Chau Long Sapa Hotel** ℛ   A tour-group favorite, the Chau Long has the look of an old hilltop castle in Europe, but that's just the facade. Rooms are none too special, but cleanly crafted in dark wood and with small, tidy bathrooms. Most rooms have balconies with good views. In a good location down a quaint off-the-main-drag street, the good views are blocked in part by a new minihotel (and a larger hotel under construction next door), so be sure to ask to see the room before checking in. The friendly staff will bend over backward to make your stay fun. And be sure to say hello to the Dalmatian or the unique, techno-colored lion-dog (even if you don't stay here, stop by and see this little guy). The roof-top restaurant is a unique stop to have a spot of grog and take in the valley below.

24 Dong Loi. ℰ 020/871-245. Fax 020/871-844. www.chaulonghotel.com. 35 units. $32–$48 double; $65 suite. MC, V. **Amenities:** Restaurant; bar; bike/motorbike rental; car rental; limited room service; laundry; Internet. *In room:* Satellite TV, hair dryer, IDD phone.

## INEXPENSIVE

**Cat Cat Guesthouse**   The view—that's what it's all about here. At this basic guesthouse, buildings are stacked like an unlikely pile of children's blocks against a steeply sloping hill. At the top of the hill there is a large guesthouse block and popular restaurant. Rooms are concrete and plain, a backpacker standard, but most have big windows and balconies. Stop for a coffee even if you don't stay.

Cat Cat Rd. (at the base of the town on the way down to the Cat Cat village). ℰ 020/871-946 or 020/871-387. Fax 020/871-133. catcatht@hn.vnn.vn. 20 units. $5–$25 double. No credit cards. **Amenities:** Restaurant; bar (w/best view in town). *In room:* Hot water.

**Royal Hotel** ℛ   It's backpacker central at this little five-story tower in the heart of town, the very terminus of central Cau May Street. The sparse tile-and-concrete decor, busy hallways, and hit-or-miss service are a bit of a turnoff. The hotel's Friendly Café is aptly named; waitstaff here seem to be chosen for their desire (read: not ability) to speak English, and the food is good, basic, affordable traveler fare (fried rice, fried noodles, and beer). Every room has a balcony, and some even come with a fireplace. Ask about Royal trains and travel services.

Cau May St. ℰ/fax 020/871-313. 30 units. $12–$15 double. AE, MC, V. **Amenities:** Restaurant; laundry. *In room:* TV, IDD phone.

## WHERE TO DINE

**The Gecko** ⭐⭐ FRENCH/VIETNAMESE   A good choice for a romantic evening with that someone special, The Gecko serves fine European and Viet cuisine in a cozy dining room. Candlelight gives a warm glow to the dark timbers and earth tone walls of this bar, salon, and dining room—taking the chill out of the brisk Sapa night. Try the fine grilled goose served with a rum-and-pepper-cream sauce, or chicken with Sapa mushrooms. Everything is good. The menu also includes pizza, burgers, boeuf bourguignon, good Vietnamese specials, and appetizers like carpaccio, tomato with real mozzarella, and Swiss Rosti or cheese fondue. It's one of those special places in the world where a gourmet meal costs about the same as buying a hot chocolate at the local ski hill. Set meals are a great value.

Just below the Victoria Sapa, Post Office Place, Ham Rong St. © 020/871-504. Fax 020/871-898. www.geckohotel.com. Main courses $4.50–$5.80. MC, V. Daily 7am–11pm.

**Tavanh** ⭐⭐ FRENCH/VIETNAMESE   This is the most elegant dining in the Tonkinese Alps. The menu is rich with imports; everything from lamb to filet and salmon steaks is shipped in. They serve all the right dishes to keep you warm on a chilly eve; be sure to try the cheese fondue. The dining room is candle-lit and romantic, done up with burgundy walls and rich wood floors and local hangings surrounding a central fireplace. There are good Vietnamese specials on an evolving menu, and the pastas are homemade and delicious.

At the Victoria Sapa Hotel. © 020/871-522. Main courses $6.50–$19. AE, MC, V. Daily 7am–10pm.

## WHAT TO SEE & DO

The town itself is the attraction here, and **Cau May Street,** the main drag, and the **central market area** (all very close together) are, on any given day, teeming with hill-tribe folks in their spangled finest, putting on and practicing the hard sell with some great weaving, fine silver work, and interesting trinkets like mouth harps and flutes. Especially on the weekend, it can be quite a scene. The small alleys and streets of the town are imminently wanderable, and a short walk in any direction offers great views.

**Cat-Cat Village** ⭐   At the base of the hill below the town of Sapa, this Hmong village is accessible by road most of the way, and cement path for the rest. The small waterfall is a good spot to kick back and rest. The whole trip can be made in just a few hours and offers a unique glimpse of rural life.

Admission fee (paid at the top of the hill) 20,000 VND ($1.35). You can walk all the way down or hire a motorbike/car taxi to pick up and drop off.

**Lao Cai to Tavanh** ⭐⭐   This is the premier day trip from Sapa and is convenient to the town center. It's a good chance to traipse around the rice terraces and experience a bit of rural village life. Hire a car or motorbike for the 9km (5½-mile) road down the valley from Sapa to the Hmong village of Lao Cai (some folks even walk it); it's a nice ride in itself, with great views of the lush terraces. From there, you'll just follow the valley for a few miles to the next town of Tavanh. Along the way, you'll walk through terraced rice fields and among some picturesque villages, and experience a bit of rural life (I had a chance to help with some rice threshing). The short trek walks you through a few different hill-tribe villages (Hmong, Zay, and Dao people), and it's good to have a guide to explain any customs or practices and perhaps translate. You're sure to see other tourists on the trail (and this puts many people off), but this is a good example of the many great treks in the area; ask at your hotel front desk, or contact Topas Travel (under "Visitor Information," above) for longer, less touristic treks. You'll still be greeted with "Bonjour, madam! Bonjour, monsieur!" wherever you go.

Admission is 5,000 VND (35¢). Drop-off at Lao Cai and later pickup at Tavan is about $4 by motorbike taxi and $25 by jeep (contact hotels for a guide).

**The Mission Church** ✿  An aging stone edifice, the church of the early French missionaries still stands on the high end of Cau May and is a popular meeting point for locals. There are masses held on Saturday night and throughout the day on Sunday.

## OTHER DESTINATIONS IN THE FAR NORTH

**Bac Ha Market** is a very popular hill-tribe market some 100km (62 miles) from Sapa, a more authentic version of Sapa's love market held on Sunday mornings early. **Mai Chau** is a gorgeous valley and home to ethnic Tai people about 4 hours from Hanoi. **Dien Bien Phu,** to the far northwest, is a former French commercial and military outpost, and the site of one of Vietnam's biggest military victories over the French. You can fly directly to Dien Bien Phu from Hanoi.

## 5 An Introduction to the Central Coast

Many of Vietnam's most significant historical sites and some of its best beaches are clustered along its central coast. Popular are Hue, the former Vietnamese capital, with its Imperial City and emperors' tombs, and Hoi An, a historic trading town with many original 17th-century buildings. Formerly the seat of the

### Who Are the Cham?

With little written history, what we do know of the Cham is from Chinese written texts, and the splendid religious art and artwork attributed to the Cham Empire (note the many Khmer-style Prang towers scattered along Vietnam's central coastline). Migrating from Indonesia, Cham people settled in central Vietnam in the 2nd century A.D. and fought Chinese incursions from their stronghold in and around Danang.

The Cham belong to the Malayo-Polynesian language family, and have their own Sanskrit-based script. Cham communities lived by rice farming, fishing, and trading pepper, cinnamon bark, ivory, and wood with neighboring nations via Hoi An. Hinduism was their dominant religion, with Buddhist influences and an infusion of Islam starting in the 14th century. In the middle of the 10th century, internal warfare, as well as battles against both the Khmer to the south and Dai Viet to the north, began to erode the Cham kingdom. By the mid-15th century, it had been almost entirely absorbed into Vietnam.

The Cham today are an ethnic minority; many are still Hindu, but many have converted to Islam. Cham enclaves subsist by fishing, farming, and sales of handicrafts. The premiere Cham site is at **My Son** (see "An Excursion to My Son," p. 356), but other Cham sites can be found near Nha Trang and as far south as Phan Thiet. The best Cham artifacts are on view at the Cham Museum (see "What to See & Do," in section 7).

Cham kingdom from the 2nd through 14th centuries, the central coast also has the greatest concentration of Cham relics and art. There are also a few good beach stops. Transport between each of these nearby towns is quite good.

## GETTING THERE

**BY PLANE**   You can fly into both Hue and Danang from Saigon or Hanoi.

**BY TRAIN**   Both Hue and Danang are stops on the north-south rail line.

**BY CAR/BUS/MINIVAN**   Tourist cafe buses connect all major towns in this region. Driving with a rented vehicle and driver is possible but will probably cost several hundred dollars and leave your teeth chattering from the bumpy roads.

## GETTING AROUND

**BY CAR/BUS/MINIVAN**   The three main coastal towns in the central part of the country are linked by roads that are prone to flooding. Potholes are an understatement, and the dust that gets kicked up dries out your throat pretty quickly. You can easily rent a car or get a seat on a bus or minivan in any of the towns or in a hotel or booking agency—if you take a bus, be prepared for the trip to take a bit longer than they advertise, due to the poor condition of the roads. From Hue to Danang is about 3½ hours; from Danang to Hoi An is about 90 minutes. See individual city listings for suggested prices.

## 6 Hue

Hue (pronounced "hway") was once Vietnam's imperial city, the capital of the country from 1802 to 1945 under the Nguyen Dynasty, and is culturally and historically significant. While much of Hue (tragically including most of Vietnam's walled citadel and imperial city) was decimated during the French and American wars, there is still much to see. Perhaps most captivating in Hue is simply observing daily life on the **Perfume River,** its many dragonboats, houseboats, and longtail vessels dredging for sand. You can visit many of the attractions, including the tombs of **Nguyen Dynasty emperors,** by boat. The enjoyable town has a seaside-resort sort of air, with a laid-back attitude; lowslung, colorful, colonial-style buildings; and strings of lights at outdoor cafes at night. There are many local cuisine specialties to sample as well.

You might want to plan for a full-day **American war memorial excursion** to the nearby demilitarized zone (DMZ), the beginning of the Ho Chi Minh trail, and underground tunnels at **Vinh Moc.**

## GETTING THERE

**BY PLANE**   Hue connects from both Hanoi and Saigon with Vietnam Airlines. A taxi from the airport costs 100,000 VND ($6.65). There's also an airport bus that picks you up at your hotel and covers the half-hour trip to the airport for 25,000 VND ($1.65). Book through your hotel's front desk or any tour operator.

**BY TRAIN**   Trains depart daily from both Hanoi and Saigon to Hue. A trip from Hanoi to Hue takes 14 hours on an express train; with two nightly departures, 7 and 11pm, these trains have soft-berth compartments with air-conditioning for about $35. From Saigon, in a soft-berth, it's about $50, which is a good way to go.

**BY CAR**   If you're coming from the south, Vietnamtourism Danang can arrange a car for the 3½-hour ride from Danang to Hue for $40. Contact travel agents in any section to rent a car with driver.

**BY BUS**    Many travelers choose to take a nerve-rattling overnight bus or mini-van from Hanoi to Hue. Tickets are $9 through one of Hanoi's tourist cafes (see "Visitor Information & Tours," below), and the trip takes an excruciating 17 hours. Hue is a major stop on any open-tour ticket, and open-tour cafe buses connect with Danang and Hoi An for just $2, or Nha Trang for $6 (these are long, bumpy trails but are cheap and convenient).

## GETTING AROUND

Taxis are much cheaper here than in Hanoi: 5,000 VND (35¢) starting out and 5,000 VND for each kilometer after. Flag 'em down or call **Gili** at ✆ **054/828-282** or **ThanhDo** at ✆ **054/835-835.** Because Hue is relatively small, renting a cyclo by the hour for 15,000 VND to 20,000 VND ($1–$1.35) works well. Even the tiniest hotel provides motorbike rentals at $3 to $5 per day and bicycles for $1.

## VISITOR INFORMATION & TOURS

There are a number of tour companies in Hue through which you can book boat trips and visits to the DMZ. Every hotel will also be able to assist you, although the tour companies will be cheaper, especially for car services.

**Huong Giang Tourist Company** (17 Le Loi St.; ✆ 054/832-220; www.huonggiangtourist.com) organizes good, personalized tours to the tombs and the DMZ at a premium, or you can join one of their group tours. This is Hue's most upscale and efficient group, and also the most expensive. A half-day tour by car and boat, with guide, to the Citadel and Thient Mu Pagoda is $25 for one, $30 for two. A private boat up the Perfume River will cost $29.

On the budget end, **Sinh Café** (7 Nguyen Tri Phuong or 12 Hung Vuong St.; ✆ 054/845-022; www.sinhcafevn.com) takes big groups upriver for $2 and has very reasonable junkets to the DMZ.

---

### FAST FACTS: Hue

**Banks/Currency Exchange**   Most hotels change currency in Hue. Vietcombank is at 46 Hung Vuong St. (✆ **054/846-058**). Vietinde, the foreign exchange bank, has an office at 41 Hung Vuong St. (on the roundabout at the terminus of the main tourist drag); it can do cash advances and is a Western Union representative.

**Internet/E-mail**   Sinh Café, at 07 Nguyen Tri Phuong, has good service for 10,000 VND (65¢) per hour, and there are many good spots on Hung Vuong (the main tourist street south of the river), Pham Ngu Lao Street (just across from the Century Riverside), and on Doi Cung Street.

**Post Office**   There are mini–post offices in both the Century and Huong Giang hotels. The main post office is at 8 Hoang Hoa Tham St., and is open from 7am to 9pm.

**Telephone**   The city code for Hue is 54. You can place IDD calls at the post office (above) and from most hotels.

---

## WHERE TO STAY

For the volume of tourists coming through this town, there isn't much in the way of quality accommodation, and even the best options are bland, with lots

# Hue

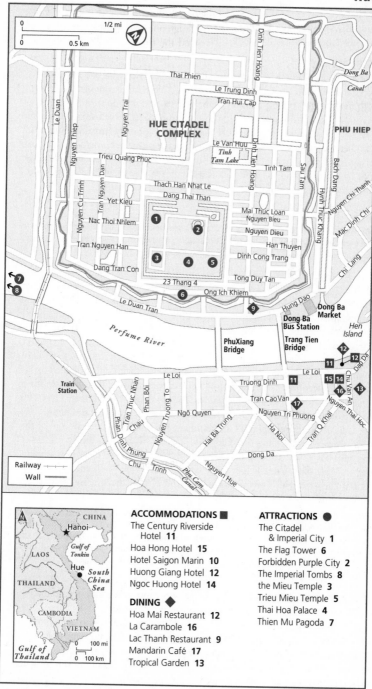

**HUE CITADEL COMPLEX**

Thai Phien

Le Trung Dinh

Tran Hui Cap

Dinh Tien Hoang

Le Duan

Nguyen Trai

Nguyen Thiep

Tri/Trieu Quang Phuc

Thach Han Nhat Le

Dang Thai Than

Yet Kieu

Nac Thoi Nhlem

Tran Nguyen Han

Dang Tran Con

23 Thang 4

Le Duan Tran

Nguyen Cu Trinh

Tran Nguyen Dan

Le Van Huu

*Tinh Tam Lake*

Tinh Tam

Sau Tam

Mai Thuc Loan

Nguyen Bieu

Nguyen Dieu

Han Thuyen

Dinh Cong Trang

Tong Duy Tan

Ong Ich Khiem

**PHU HIEP**

*Dong Ba Canal*

Bach Dang

Nguyen Chi Thanh

Mac Dinh Chi

Hynh Thuc Khang

Chi Lang

Hung Dao

**Dong Ba Market**

**Dong Ba Bus Station**

*Perfume River*

**PhuXiang Bridge**

**Trang Tien Bridge**

Hen Island

Dap Da

Train Station

Le Loi

Truong Dinh

Tran Cao Van

Nguyen Tri Phuong

Phan Boi Chau

Nguyen Truong To

Ngo Quyen

Hai Ba Trung

Ha Noi

Tran Thuc Nhan

Phan Dinh Phung

Chu

Trinh

*Phu Cam Canal*

Dong Da

Nguyen Hue

Nguyen Thai Hoc

Chu Van An

Tran Q. Khai

Railway ┼┼┼
Wall ▬▬▬

❶ ❷ ❸ ❹ ❺ ❻ ❼ ❽ ❾
⑪ ⑫ ⑬ ⑭ ⑮ ⑯ ⑰

CHINA
Hanoi ★
*Gulf of Tonkin*
LAOS
Hue ●
*South China Sea*
THAILAND
CAMBODIA
VIETNAM
*Gulf of Thailand*

0    100 mi
0    100 km

## ACCOMMODATIONS ■
The Century Riverside
  Hotel **11**
Hoa Hong Hotel **15**
Hotel Saigon Marin **10**
Huong Giang Hotel **12**
Ngoc Huong Hotel **14**

## DINING ◆
Hoa Mai Restaurant **12**
La Carambole **16**
Lac Thanh Restaurant **9**
Mandarin Café **17**
Tropical Garden **13**

## ATTRACTIONS ●
The Citadel
  & Imperial City **1**
The Flag Tower **6**
Forbidden Purple City **2**
The Imperial Tombs **8**
the Mieu Temple **3**
Trieu Mieu Temple **5**
Thai Hoa Palace **4**
Thien Mu Pagoda **7**

of "It's nice, but . . . ." Budget accommodation abounds, but there are some real duds. Always ask to see the rooms first. Hotel services are limited, but have basic tour services and include breakfast. Prices are flexible, so press for a discount.

## EXPENSIVE

### The Century Riverside Hotel ⓡ
Rooms at the Riverside are bland chain-hotel style and are showing their age, but it's clean, and comfortable enough with new tile-and-marble bathrooms (be sure to ask for a room with recent renovations). Standard rooms are rather small, with older carved-wood furniture. The riverview rooms are more than worth the extra outlay (usually about $10) and there are great views from upper floors of the busy river, longtail boats puttering by or fisherman paddling small dugouts. The pool is in a prime lounge spot by the river, and the Riverside Restaurant has nice views and serves good, familiar fare, if a bit bland. Renovation is imminent (we hope).

49 Le Loi St., Hue. Ⓒ **800/536-7361**, 054/823-390, or -391. Fax 054/823-394. www.centuryhotels.com. 138 units. $85–$125 double; $135–$300 suite. AE, MC, V. **Amenities:** 3 restaurants; 2 bars; outdoor pool overlooking river; 2 tennis courts; small gym; bicycles/motorbikes for rent; concierge; tour desk arranging popular boat trip to tombs; car rental; small business center; shopping in lobby; salon; 24-hr. room service; massage; laundry; postal service. *In room:* A/C, satellite TV, minibar, fridge, hair dryer, IDD phone.

### Hotel Saigon Morin ⓡⓡ
The Saigon Morin is a government-run, refurbished colonial block near the main bridge in town. A recent renovation of the third floor puts the Morin in a class of its own: junior deluxe rooms are the only international high standard in Hue, with built-in wooden cabinetry, fine linens, wood floors, and all working amenities like good cable TV and IDD phone. Large, stylish baths have a separate tub-and-glass standing shower and connect to the room via a fun "peek-a-boo" shuttered opening. The lower standard rooms are still the same Chinese business-hotel basic, with old laminated furniture and threadbare carpeting dotted with cigarette burns. The hotel forms a large courtyard around a central garden and pool area with dining. Over 100 years old, the Morin was originally the colonist's address of note and photos line the halls of this bygone era. It's interesting to note that the street in front of the Morin was where a young Ho Chi Minh carried his first placard in protest of foreign occupation. If he could only see the place now. The exterior maintains some of that old, colonial charm, but common areas are brash and busy, neon-lit and cluttered with souvenir stalls—all kind of fun, though, and service is a bit hit or miss, but usually friendly.

30 Le Loi St., Hue. Ⓒ **054/823-526.** Fax 054/825-155. www.morinhotel.com.vn. 127 units. $120–$140 double; $160 deluxe double; $250–$500 suite. AE, MC, V. **Amenities:** Outdoor buffet area, (breakfast included); lobby restaurant; 2 bars/cafe (1 on roof w/good views); small outdoor pool (in courtyard); small gym; Jacuzzi in executive suites; sauna; bicycle/motorbike rental; concierge; helpful in-house tour desk; car rental; shopping in lobby; salon; 24-hr. room service; massage; laundry; Internet; postal service. *In room:* A/C, satellite TV, minibar, fridge, coffeemaker, hair dryer, safe, IDD phone.

### Huong Giang Hotel ⓡⓡ
This hotel is a veritable Asian wonderland, so enamored is it of heavy carved wood and bamboo furnishings in its faux "imperial" theme. Tacky? Yes. But it's also kind of fun. Standard rooms are clean and comfortable, in basic bamboo, but the bathrooms are a disappointing dormitory style, with plastic shower curtains and no counter space. Try to get a good deal on one of the Royal Suites, with carved-wood walls, grandiose furniture with inlaid mother-of-pearl, and a massive wood room divider—sort of a minipagoda right in your room. The words *emperor* and *bordello* both leap to mind. The Royal Restaurant, worth a photo just for its gaudy gold-and-red-everything

design alone, is for prearranged group dinners, where the costumed staff serves a fancy traditional dinner at a hefty price (popular in town). The River Front Terrace Bar is the best place in Hue to have a drink and watch life on the river. Be sure to splurge for a riverview room and enjoy a fine meal at the Hoa Mai restaurant.

51 Le Loi St., Hue. © **054/822-122** or 054/823-958. Fax 054/823-102. 150 units. $55–$75 gardenview double; $65–$85 river view; $160–$230 suite. AE, MC, V. **Amenities:** 3 restaurants; 2 bars; pool; tennis court; basic health club; sauna; concierge; tour desk; car rental; small business center; cool, kitsch shopping area; salon; massage; laundry. *In room:* A/C, cable TV, minibar, fridge, hair dryer, IDD phone.

## MODERATE

**Hoa Hong Hotel** 🏨    Though showing it's age, the Hoa Hong has bargain rates and is still a popular group hotel and a good midrange choice. Rooms are nondescript—think navy and beige, with ugly polyester spreads—but all are comfortable, with good, firm beds. The bathrooms are a nice size and tidy, with bathtubs. Ask for a city view rather than a noisy streetview room. The suites are worth it and have authentic Asian furniture. There are two restaurants, one of which specializes in the popular "royal dinner" theme evenings, when both staff and guests dress like emperors and empresses. The lobby has a fun little bar and serves flowery umbrella drinks. Book early as they often fill up with tour groups.

1 Pham Ngu Lao St., Hue. © **054/824-377** or 054/826-943. Fax 054/826-949. hoahonghotel@dng.vnn.vn. 50 units. $30–$60 double; $80 suite. AE, MC, V. **Amenities:** Large restaurant (breakfast included); bar; tour desk; car rental; souvenir shop; 24-hr. room service; laundry; Internet in reception. *In room:* A/C, satellite TV, minibar, fridge, IDD phone.

**Ngoc Huong Hotel** 🏨    Comparable to Hoa Hong (above), Ngoc Huong is brand-spankin' new, clean, and already quite popular. Rooms have the unfortunate fluorescent polyester blankets and gawdy drapery of most minihotels, only here it is new and clean. Larger suite rooms overlook the river (peeking over the fronts of the Riverside and Huong Giang hotels—above), and the seventh-floor restaurant serves good Vietnamese fare and offers 180-degree views.

8–10 Chu Van An St., Hue. © **054/830-111.** Fax 054/829-316. www.ngochuonghotels.com. 45 units. $25–$70 double; $100 suite. AE, MC, V. **Amenities:** 2 restaurants; bar; tour desk; car rental; souvenir shop in lobby; laundry; Internet corner. *In room:* A/C, satellite TV, minibar, fridge, IDD phone.

## WHERE TO DINE

Hue cuisine is unique, featuring light ingredients in popular fresh spring rolls, or try *bun bo Hue,* a noodle soup with pork, beef, and shredded green onions; and *banh khoi,* a thin, crispy pancake filled with ground meat and crispy vegetables. Local dishes are best at street side, and there are a few good spots with English menus along the river and in the backpacker area, along Hung Vong.

## MODERATE

**Hoa Mai Restaurant** 🏨🏨 VIETNAMESE    Hoa Mai is decked out in kitschy bamboo furnishings and set in an open area on the top floor of the Huong Giang Hotel. Atmosphere aside, the Vietnamese fare is good and there are great views of the Perfume River. Try *banh rom hue,* triangular fried rolls stuffed with ground meat, shrimp, and vegetables. Daily special set menus are good; mine featured a unique fried cuttlefish with grapefruit, crab soup, and shrimp with fig and rice cake. The Muzak gets a bit much, and be sure to choose a table near the riverside window and away from any banquet-size setups that say RESERVED.

51 Le Loi St., 3rd floor, Huong Giang Hotel. © **054/822-122.** Main courses $2–$6; set menus $7–$15. AE, MC, V. Daily 6am–10pm.

**Tropical Garden** ✿✿ VIETNAMESE   Though a popular tour-bus stop, Tropical Garden has a good laid-back feel. The restaurant, with a sister location called **Club Garden** just down the road (08 Vo Thi Sau St.; ✆ **054/826-327**), serves fine Vietnamese fare from a good English menu, and there is a live music show nightly. Even when it's packed here, there are enough intimate corners that you'll feel comfortable. The place specializes in "embarrassing entrees," the kind of flaming dishes and multitiered platters that would impress that eccentric uncle of yours; I got spring rolls served on toothpick skewers around the rind of a hollowed pineapple with a candle in the middle, a la a Halloween jack-o'-lantern. It's all good fun, so just go with it. The food is good, but a bit overpriced for a la carte items. Set menus are quite reasonable and walk you through some house specialties, like the banana flower soup, the grilled chicken with lemon leaf, and the steamed crab with beer. As an appetizer, don't miss the grilled minced shrimp with sugar cane wrapped in rice paper and served with peanut sauce—unique and delicious. Service is a bit hit-or-miss, either fawning or forgetful.

27 Chu Van An St. ✆ **054/847-143**. Fax 054/828-074. adongcoltd@dng.vnn.vn. Main courses $2–$4; set menus $7–$25. Daily 8:30am–11pm. MC, V.

## INEXPENSIVE

**La Carambole** ✿✿ VIETNAMESE/CONTINENTAL   Good music is the first thing you might notice at La Carambole; I heard an unlikely mix from CCR to Beck in my relaxing evening. The decor is cheerful: cool indirect lighting, red tablecloths, and playful mobiles hang from the ceiling, all as welcoming as the kind waitstaff. The gregarious French proprietor, Christian, and his wife, Ha, will certainly make you feel at home, and the good "comfort items" on the menu, like spaghetti, burgers, pizzas, and various French-style meat-and-potatoes specials, will stick to your ribs. The set menus are a good deal (salad and pizza at $5, for example), and portions are ample. There's a game table, and you're sure to meet lots of other travelers.

19 Pham Ngu Lao St. ✆ **054/810-491**. Fax 054/826-234. Main courses $1.40–$5.50; set menu $4–$9. No credit cards. Daily 7am–midnight.

**Lac Thanh Restaurant** ✿ VIETNAMESE   Everybody knows Lac Thanh, so there's a good chance you'll run into some fellow wayfarers at this popular crossroad. The place is a bit grimy, but the food is great: try the good grilled pork wrapped in rice paper, sautéed bean sprouts, grilled crab, and the popular spareribs, among others. For dessert, try the local specialty, *ché nong*, a warm congee with coconut, bananas, and nuts. Sit on the second-floor balcony, and don't miss any opportunity to interface with Mr. Lac, the gregarious owner who speaks the international language of food and laughter despite his hearing impairment. Don't be fooled by the copycats next door (he has a RECOMMENDED BY FROMMER'S sign).

6A Dien Tien Hoang St. ✆ **054/824-674**. Main courses 7,000 VND–50,000 VND (45¢–$3.35). No credit cards. Daily 7am–midnight.

**Mandarin Café** ✿ VIETNAMESE/CONTINENTAL   In a busy storefront just a short walk from the riverside (near the Saigon Morin), Mandarin is always full of young backpackers, and for a reason: good, affordable Vietnamese fare, predominantly one-dish items like fried rice or noodles on top of a roster of comfort foods. Everything is good and this is a good casual choice for a meal and likely conversation with fellow travelers. Have a banana pancake and you are one with the universe. Owner Mr. Cu (pronounced *Coo*) is a practiced photographer and his works, classic images of rural Vietnam, line the walls and are for sale as postcards or prints. For the amateur shutterbug, the images are inspiring, and the best part is that Mr. Cu is more than happy to share secrets and talk shop.

3 Hung Vuong St., Hue City. ✆ 054/821-281. mandarin@dng.vnn.vn. Main courses 7,000 VND–25,000 VND (45¢–$1.65). No credit cards. Daily 6am–10pm.

## CAFES, BARS & NIGHTLIFE

Across from the major riverside hotels is the **DMZ Café,** which stays up late a la beer-swilling frat party, and along Hung Vuong you'll find a few backpacker bars open till midnight, but this is a pretty sleepy town. **Bar Why Not?** (21 Vo Thi Sau St.; ✆ **054/924-793**) is a cool open-air joint at the intersection of Pham Ngu Lao and Vo Thi Sau (near La Carambole, above) and has a good pool table and hot dogs cooked to order. **Newspace Bar** (22 Pham Ngu Lao; ✆ **054/810-310**) has a pool table fronting a chic, bistro/bar setup, with a gallery space next door. **Brown Eyes** (55 Nguyen Sinh Cung; ✆ **054/827-494**) is a late-night bar and cafe that's a short taxi ride from the town center.

## SHOPPING

All along Le Loi Street, you'll find souvenir stalls that vary from the cute to the kitschy. You can find good deals on commemorative spoons and Velvet Ho Chi Minh's here, but nothing too traditional or authentic; you will find a few good silversmiths, however. There are a few tailors in and among the souvenir shops, or stop by **Seductive** (40 Le Loi St.; ✆ **054/829-794**), a small ready-to-wear silk boutique. **Bambou Company** (21 Pham Ngu Lao St., next to La Carambole) produces unique T-shirts of local theme and design, all Western-size.

## WHAT TO SEE & DO

Except for the remains of its fabulous Imperial City, Hue in itself has sadly seen the worst of the French and American/Vietnam wars. Most of the star attractions other than The Citadel, therefore, involve half-day or day trips outside the city.

**The Citadel & Imperial City** 🌟🌟🌟    **The Citadel** is often used as a catchall term for Hue's Imperial City, built by Emperor Gia Long beginning in 1804 for the exclusive use of the emperor and his household, much like Beijing's Forbidden City. The city actually encompasses three walled enclosures: the Exterior Exclosure or Citadel; the Yellow Enclosure, or Imperial City, within that; and, in the very center, the Forbidden Purple City, where the emperor actually lived.

The Citadel is a square 2km (1¼-mile) wall, 7m (14 ft.) high and 20m (66 ft.) thick, with 10 gates. Ironically, it was constructed by a French military architect, though it failed to prevent the French from destroying the complex many years later. The main entrance to the Imperial City is the Ngo Mon, the southwest gate or "Noon" Gate, and is where you can get a ticket and enter.

Admission 55,000 VND ($3.65). Daily 7am–5:30pm.

### SITES WITHIN THE IMPERIAL CITY

**The Flag Tower** 🌟🌟    The focal point of the Imperial City, a large rampart to the south of the Noon Gate, this tower was built in 1807 during Gia Long's reign. The yellow flag of royalty was the first to fly here and was exchanged and replaced by many others in Vietnam's turbulent history. It's a national symbol.

**The Forbidden Purple City** 🌟    Once the actual home of the emperor and his concubines, this second sanctum within The Citadel is a large open area dotted with what's left of the king's court. Almost completely razed in a fire in 1947, a few buildings are left among the rubble. The new **Royal Theater** behind the square, a look-alike of the razed original, is under construction. The partially restored **Thai Binh Reading Pavilion,** to the left of it as you head north, is notable mostly for its beautifully landscaped surroundings, including a small lake with a Zen-like stone sculpture, and the ceramic and glass mosaic detailing on the roof and pillars, favored by flamboyant emperor Khai Dinh.

Catch a performance of the **Royal Traditional Theater** at the Hue Monuments Conservation Center. Eight performances daily, from 9am to 4pm, highlight the ancient art of *nha nhac,* courtly dance, at a cost of 20,000 VND ($1.35).

**The Imperial Tombs**    As befits its history as an Imperial City, Hue's environs are studded with tombs of past emperors. They are spread out over a distance, so the best way to see them is to hire a car for a half-day or take one of the many organized boat tours up the Perfume River. Altogether, there were 13 kings of the Nguyen Dynasty, although only seven reigned until their death. As befits an emperor, each had tombs of stature, some as large as a small town. Most tomb complexes usually consist of a courtyard, a stele (a large stone tablet with a biography of the emperor), a temple for worship, and a pond.

**Khai Dinh's Tomb** 🌟🌟    Completed in 1931, the tomb is one of the world's wonders. The emperor himself wasn't particularly revered, being overly extravagant and flamboyant (reportedly he wore a belt studded with lights that he flicked on at opportune public moments). His tomb, a gaudy mix of Gothic, baroque, Hindu, and Chinese Qing Dynasty architecture at the top of 127 steep steps, is a reflection of the man. Inside, the two main rooms are completely covered with fabulous, intricate glass and ceramic mosaics in designs reminiscent of Tiffany and Art Deco. The workmanship is astounding. The outer room's ceiling was done by a fellow who used both his feet and his hands to paint, in what some say was a sly mark of disrespect for the emperor. While in most tombs the location of the emperor's actual remains are a secret, Khai Dinh boldly placed his under his de facto tomb itself.

Admission 55,000 VND ($3.65). Summer daily 6:30am–5:30pm; winter daily 7am–5pm.

**The Mieu Temple** 🌟🌟    Constructed in 1921 to 1922 by Emperor Minh Mang, this temple has funeral altars paying tribute to 10 of the last Nguyen Dynasty emperors, omitting two who reigned for only days, with photos of each emperor and his empress(es) and various small offerings and knickknacks. The two empty glass containers to the side of each photo should contain bars of gold, probably an impractical idea today.

Across from The Mieu you'll see Hien Lam, or the Glorious Pavilion, to the far right, with the **Nine Dynastic Urns** in front. Cast from 1835 to 1837, each urn represents a Nguyen emperor and is richly embellished with all the flora, fauna, and material goods that Vietnam has to offer, mythical or otherwise.

**The Noon Gate (Cua Ngo Mon)** 🌟🌟    One of 10 entrances to the city, this southern entrance is the most dynamic. It was the royal entrance, in fact, and was built by Emperor Gia Long in 1823. It was used for important proclamations, such as announcements of the names of successful doctoral candidates (a list still hangs on the wall on the upper floor) and, most memorably, the announcement of the abdication of the last emperor, Bao Dai, on August 13, 1945, to Ho Chi Minh. The structure, like most here, was damaged by war but is now nicely restored, with classic Chinese roofs covering the ritual space, complete with large drums and an altar. Be sure to climb to the top and have a look at the view.

**Thai Hoa Palace**    Otherwise known as the Palace of Supreme Harmony, it was built in 1833 and is the first structure you'll approach at the entrance. It was used as the throne room, a ceremonial hall where the emperor celebrated festivals and received courtiers; the original throne still stands. The Mandarins sat outside. In front are two mythical *ky lin* animals, which walk without their claws ever touching ground and which have piercing eyesight for watching the emperor, tracking all good and evil he does. Note the statues of the heron and turtle inside the palace's ornate lacquered interior: The heron represents nobility and the turtle represents the working person. Folklore has it that the two took turns saving each other's lives during a fire, symbolizing that the power of the emperor rests with his people, and vice versa.

**Thien Mu Pagoda** ✿✿ Often called the symbol of Hue, Thien Mu is one of the oldest and loveliest religious structures in Vietnam. It was constructed beginning in 1601. The Phuoc Dien Tower in front was added in 1864 by Emperor Thieu Tri. Each of its seven tiers is dedicated to either one of the human forms taken by Buddha or the seven steps to enlightenment, depending upon whom you ask. There are also two buildings housing a bell reportedly weighing 2 tons, and a stele inscribed with a biography of Lord Nguyen Hoang, founder of the temple.

Once past the front gate, observe the 12 huge wooden sculptures of fearsome temple "guardians"—note the real facial hair. A complex of monastic buildings lies in the center, offering glimpses of the monks' daily routines: cooking, stacking wood, and whacking weeds. Stroll all the way to the rear of the complex to look at the large graveyard at the base of the Truong Son mountains, and wander through the well-kept garden of pine trees. Try not to go between the hours of 11:30am and 2pm, when the monks are at lunch, because the rear half of the complex will be closed.

On the bank of the Perfume River. Daily 8am–5pm.

**Tomb of Minh Mang** ✿ One of the most popular Nguyen emperors and the father of last emperor, Bao Dai built a restrained, serene, classical temple, much like Hue's Imperial City, located at the confluence of two Perfume River tributaries. Stone sculptures surround a long walkway, lined with flowers, leading up to the main buildings.

Admission 55,000 VND ($3.65). Summer daily 6:30am–5:30pm; winter daily 7am–5pm.

**Tomb of Tu Duc** ✿✿ With the longest reign of any Nguyen Dynasty emperor, from 1848 to 1883, Tun Duc was a philosopher and scholar of history and literature. His reign was unfortunate: His kingdom unsuccessfully struggled against French colonialism, he fought a coup d'état by members of his own family, and although he had 104 wives, he left no heir. The "tomb" was constructed from 1864 to 1867 and also served as recreation grounds for the king, having been completed 16 years before his death. He actually engraved his own stele, in fact. The largest in Vietnam, at 20 tons, it has its own pavilion in the tomb. The highlight of the grounds is the lotus-filled lake ringed by frangipani trees, with a large pavilion in the center. The main cluster of buildings includes Hoa Khiem (Harmony Modesty) Pavilion, where the king worked, which still contains items of furniture and ornaments. Minh Khiem Duong, constructed in 1866, is said to be the country's oldest surviving theater. It's great fun to poke around in the wings. There are also pieces of original furniture lying here and there, as well as a cabinet with household objects: the queen's slippers, ornate chests, and bronze and silver books. The raised box on the wall is for the actors who played emperors; the real emperor was at the platform to the left.

Admission 55,000 VND ($3.65). Summer daily 6:30am–5:30pm; winter daily 7am–5pm.

> **Tips  Taking a Boat to the Tombs**
>
> Expect to pay between $2 to $4 for a shared boat ride to the temples (depending on which agent you use), *plus* 55,000 VND ($3.65) for *each* tomb. Be prepared for when the boat pulls to shore at the first two tombs; you'll have to hire one of the motorcycle taxis at the bank to shuttle you to and from the site. You will not have enough time to walk there and back, so you're basically at their mercy. Haggle as best you can—about 10,000 VND (65¢) is a good starting point.

## DAY TRIPS FROM HUE

**Remnants of War: The DMZ and Vinh Moc Tunnels** ⭑⭑  If you're old enough to remember the Vietnam War, you'll know Hue from the large-scale battles waged there. A day trip to the nearby DMZ and Vinh Moc Tunnels is a sobering revisitation to that tumultuous time.

Under the Geneva Accords of 1954, an agreement struck to bring peace to Indochina after its struggle with French colonists, Vietnam was divided into North and South along the **17th Parallel.** What was meant to be a short-term political fix became a battle line and the 17th Parallel, aka the **DMZ** or demilitarized zone, became a tangle of barbed wire and land mines bombed and defoliated into a wasteland. The area is green with growth again and completely unremarkable except for its history. Nearby are strategic sites with names you may recognize: the Rockpile, Hamburger Hill, Camp Carroll, and Khe Sanh, a former U.S. marine base that was the site of some of the war's most vicious and deadly fighting. If you take a tour of the area, you will also visit Dakrong Bridge, an official entryway into the Ho Chi Minh trail. *Warning:* The route over Highway 9 to the sites is narrow and bumpy. Rethink this trip if it's a rainy day, or if you are faint of either heart or stomach.

Most tours to the DMZ area include a visit to the **Vinh Moc Tunnels,** a site that is a testament to human tenacity. Like the tunnels in the south at Cu Chi (see "Day Trips from Ho Chi Minh"), soldiers and civilians took to the underground, literally, digging over a mile of tunnels from 1965 to 1966 to support Viet Cong troops and confound U.S. battalions at this strategic position near the line of north-south demarcation. Up to 20m (about 66 ft.) below the surface, multilevel tunnels formed a real community haven, with "living rooms" for families, a conference and performance room, a field hospital, and exit points inland and along the coast. Visitors walk through about 300m (984 ft.) of the tunnels in a main artery that is 1.6m high by 1.2m wide (5¼×4 ft.), going down three stages. Wear your play clothes because it is dirty, clammy, and a bit claustrophobic. There is a museum at the entrance with photos and testimony of survivors. Admission is 25,000 VND ($1.65).

These sites are some 60km (37 miles) north of Hue. Contact Hue tourist cafes; the best is Sinh Café, or for good private tours try Huong Giang Tourist. See "Visitor Information & Tours," earlier.

**Lang Co Beach**  A good day stop along Route 1A between Hue and Danang/Hoi An, Lang Co Beach is a sweeping expanse of sand good for dipping your toes and taking a rest along the way. The absence of group tours and touts is the main draw, and for overnight and a spartan but cozy getaway, try the **Lang Co Beach Resort** (© 054/873-555; www.huonggiangtourist.com), whose stylish rooms at poolside start at $60.

## 7 Danang & China Beach

Danang, the fourth-largest city in Vietnam, is one of the most important seaports in the central region. It played a prominent historical role in the American war, being the landing site for the first American troops officially sent to Vietnam. Danang has nothing in the way of charm and there aren't any major attractions except for the **Cham Museum,** which has become just a quick stop on the tourist cafe buses between Hoi An and Hue. **Furama Resort,** a short ride from the city center, is one of the finest high-end resorts in Indochina, and there are some excellent-value hotels in town (some use this as a base to explore nearby Hoi An).

China Beach, or My Khe as it's known locally, is worth a stop. This former U.S. recreation base has a light-sand coast with excellent views of the nearby Marble Mountains, and is just beginning to draw international tourists.

## GETTING THERE

**BY PLANE** You can fly to Danang from both Hanoi and HCMC. A taxi from the airport costs about $3.

**BY BUS** If you're traveling on the open-tour ticket, Danang is not a specified stop, but they'll drop you off at the Cham Museum. You'll have to call the office in either Hue or Hoi An for pickup when you're ready to leave. Travelers to Laos should contact **Vietnamtourism** for buses to **Savanakhet** for $25.

**BY CAR** Danang is about 3½ hours by car from Hue, and the route covers the very scenic **Hai Van Pass.** You'll pay $40 for the trip. From Hoi An, it's about an hour and costs $25. This ride makes a good day trip along with the Marble Mountains (see "What to See & Do," below). Contact **Vietnamtourism** for good rentals.

## VISITOR INFORMATION & TOURS

**Vietnamtourism Danang** (83 Nguyen Thi Minh Khai; *©* **0511/823-660** or 822-142; fax 0511/821-560) can arrange trips to the Marble Mountains and My Son.

**Exotissimo Danang** (73 Ham Nghi, Thanh Khe District; *©* **0511/690-364;** fax 0511/891-553; www.exotissimo.com) can make any arrangements.

**An Phu Tourism** (147 Le Loi St, Danang; *©* **0511/818-366;** anphutourist@hotmail.com) is the local tourist cafe contact and can arrange any low-budget connections (there also are offices in Hoi An).

## FAST FACTS: DANANG

**Banks/Currency Exchange** Vietcombank is at 104 Le Loi St. (*©* **0511/821-955**).

**Telephone** The city code for Danang is 511.

## WHERE TO STAY
### EXPENSIVE

**Furama Resort Danang** *✸✸✸* The Furama is one of the finest destination resorts in the region. Just a short ride southwest of Danang and situated in elegant relation to a beautiful sandy beach, this popular upscale gem greets you in style with a grand lobby that is more or less the gilded frame to the beautiful scenery: sand, sun, and sky. Whether you're a sailor, a beach bum, or a comfort junky, you'll find what you want. There are two gorgeous swimming pools: one a multitiered minimalist still life overlooking the open beach, and the other a faux lagoon, complete with small waterfall and bridge, a romantic hideaway. It's a good place to just relax, but there is always something to do, too: The hotel offers local tours, yoga, tai chi, a spa, and a full aesthetic salon. Rooms are large and comfortable with wood floors, Vietnamese-style furniture and sliding doors to balconies that overlook the ocean or pool. Large marble bathrooms have all the amenities. Prices are determined by view, and oceanfront units are only steps from the beach and well worth it. Note that watersports are available only from February through September—the surf is far too rough the rest of the year. Resort amenities are extensive but they have to be because the site is quite isolated. There are shuttles to the city, but there isn't much to entice in bustling Danang.

68 Ho Xuan Huong St. (oceanside 11km/7 miles southwest of Danang). ℭ 0511/847-333. Fax 0511/847-220. www.furamavietnam.com. 200 units. $140–$160 garden view; $190–$200 ocean view; $400 suite. AE, MC, V. **Amenities:** 3 restaurants; 3 bars; 2 outdoor pools (in courtyard and multilevel w/ocean view); 4 lighted tennis courts; luxe health club; spa; sauna; diving; sailboat (Laser)/kayak rental; concierge; tour desk; business center w/Internet; lobby shopping (gallery); salon; 24-hr. room service; massage; laundry; conference/banquet rooms. *In room:* A/C, satellite TV, dataport, minibar, fridge, coffee/tea, hair dryer, safe, IDD phone.

## MODERATE

**Bamboo Green Hotel** 🖈🖈   The best choice in Danang proper, Bamboo Green is operated by Vietnamtourism and the best of its three properties in town (Bamboo Green II and III are comparable but less luxe). Rooms are large with clean beige carpets, and are well furnished in light wood (just try to overlook the hideous poly bedspreads). The nice-size marble bathrooms with hair dryers look brand new, and it is as cozy as any midrange U.S. chain. Ask for a room on the top floor for a good city view. There is a big restaurant with decent Asian/Vietnamese fare and good tour services. The staff is friendly and snaps to.

158 Phan Chau Trinh St. ℭ **0511/822-996** or 0511/822-997. Fax 0511/822-998. www.vietnamtourism-vitours.com. 46 units. $99–$119 superior; $119–$139 deluxe; $149–$169 suite. AE, MC, V. **Amenities:** 2 restaurants; bar; sauna; tour desk; motorbike/car rental; souvenir shopping; limited room service; massage; laundry; dry cleaning. *In room:* A/C, satellite TV, dataport, minibar, fridge, coffeemaker, hair dryer, IDD phone.

**Saigon Tourane Hotel** 🖈   Popular with European tour groups, it's comfort at low cost here in this nondescript, friendly hotel on the north end of town. Carpeted rooms are clean, with tidy, good-size bathrooms; some have good city views from upper floors. Nonetheless, it's all a bit low-luxe, with a general atmosphere marked by failing neon signs and worn carpets that speak of the volumes that pass through. The hotel is owned by Saigontourist, and guests of this three-star standard are well connected and can make any necessary arrangements with little hassle. The staff couldn't be any more kind. Be sure to ask for a room away from the karaoke—far away.

5 Dong Da St., Danang. ℭ **0511/821-021.** Fax 0511/895-285. 82 units. $50–$70 double; $80–$90 suite. **Amenities:** 2 restaurants; bar; basic gym; sauna; Saigontourist tour desk; car rental; business center; massage; laundry; dry cleaning; nonsmoking rooms; karaoke; basic souvenirs for sale. *In room:* A/C, satellite TV, minibar, fridge, hair dryer, IDD phone, complimentary water.

## WHERE TO DINE

If you're at Furama, that's where you'll find the best fine dining, but beachside seafood shacks adjacent to the resort also serve good barbecue for a fraction of resort prices. In Danang proper, choices are few, mostly small storefront restaurants. **Kim Do Restaurant** (180 Tran Phu St.; ℭ **0511/821-846**) is a popular Chinese restaurant of long standing, serving good stir-fries and steamed Cantonese specials. A notable find are the small storefronts adjacent to the Cham museum that serves good duck and rice dishes.

## WHAT TO SEE & DO

**The Cham Museum** ✪✪   The Cham Museum was established in 1936 (originally the École Française d'Extreme Orient) to house the relics of the powerful Hindu culture that once ruled vast tracts of Central Vietnam. The museum has the largest collection of Cham sculpture in the world, in works ranging from the 4th to 14th centuries, presented in a rough outdoor setting that suits the evocative, sensual sculptures well. The more than 300 pieces of sandstone artwork and temple decorations were largely influenced by Hindu and, later, Mahayana Buddhism. Among the cast of characters, you'll see symbols of Uroja, or "goddess mother," usually breasts or nipples; the linga, the phallic structure representing the god Shiva; the holy bird Garuda; the dancing girl Kinnari; the snake god Naga; and Ganesha, child of the god Shiva, with the head of an elephant. The sculptures are arranged by period, which are, in turn, named after the geographic regions where the sculptures were found. Note the masterpiece Tra Kieu altar of the late 7th century, with carved scenes telling the story of the Asian epic *Ramayana*. The story is of the wedding of Princess Sita. Side one tells of Prince Rama, who broke a holy vow to obtain Sita's hand. Side two tells of ambassadors sent to King Dasaratha, Prince Rama's father, to bring him the glad tidings. Side three is the actual ceremony, and side four depicts the celebrations after the ceremony. There is a permanent photo exhibition of the many Cham relics in situ at various locations throughout Vietnam.

At Tran Phu and Le Dinh Duong sts. Admission 20,000 VND ($1.35). Daily 7am–6pm.

**The Marble Mountains** ✪   The "mountains" are actually a series of five marble and limestone formations, which the locals liken to the shape of a dragon at rest. The hills are interlaced with caves, some of which are important Buddhist sanctuaries. The caves at the Marble Mountains, like so many in the country, served as sanctuaries for the Viet Cong during the American war. The highest mountain, Thuy Son, is climbable via a series of metal ladders beginning inside the cave and extending to the surface at the top. Ling Ong Pagoda, a shrine within a cave, is a highlight. The quarries in Non Nuoc village, at the bottom of the mountains, are as interesting as the caves are. Fantastic animals, and fanciful statues of folk tales and Buddhist figures are carved from the rock. Try to get a good look before you are set upon by flocks of hawkers. What's more, even if you're interested in the items they hawk—incredibly cheap mortise and pestle sets, some very nice chess sets, turtles, and small animals—any amount of marble adds considerable weight to luggage. You can easily see the mountains as part of your trip en route either to or from Hoi An; most cafe tour buses stop here.

11km (7 miles) south of Danang and 9.5km (6 miles) north of Hoi An along Hwy. 1. All tours stop here. Admission 30,000 VND ($2).

## 8 Hoi An

Hoi An was designated a UNESCO World Heritage site in 1999, and a visit to this old-world gem is a sure cultural highlight of any tour in Vietnam. From the 16th to the 18th centuries, the city was Vietnam's most important port and trading post, particularly of ceramics with nearby China. Today it is a quaint old town of some 844 structures protected as historical landmarks, and the unique influence of Chinese and Japanese traders who passed through (or settled) can still be felt. It's a picturesque town, small enough to cover easily on foot, and lots of good nooks and crannies, shops, and gastronomic delights to discover.

Wander among historic homes and temples, perhaps stop to lounge in an open-air cafe, gaze at the oddities and exotic foods in the market, or take a **sampan ride** down the lazy river. In the afternoons when school is out, the streets are thronged with skipping children in spotless white shirts and girls in their ao dai uniforms, and you can still see local craftsmen at work in some parts of the city.

On the full moon of every month, local shop owners turn off the electricity and hang lanterns bearing their shop's name, and a candlelight lantern procession, complete with a few small floats, makes its way through the Old Town and along the riverfront. It's well worth timing a visit to enjoy the spectacle and the postprocessional festivities.

## GETTING THERE

**BY PLANE OR TRAIN**    Major transport connections go through Danang. From there, you can take a car to Hoi An for between $8 and $25.

**BY BUS**    Hoi An is a major stop on all open-tour cafe buses. Connection with Danang is just $3.

## GETTING AROUND

Hoi An is so small that you'll memorize the map in an hour or two. Most hotels and guesthouses rent out bicycles for 5,000 VND to 7,000 VND (35¢–45¢) a day, a great way to explore the outer regions of the city or Cua Dai beach. **Motorbikes** are $3 to $5 per day and are not difficult to drive in this tiny, calm city. **Cyclos** are here and there; 10,000 VND (65¢) or so should get you anywhere within the city. Car rental is available anywhere. Try **Faifoo Travel** for a car by the hour or for the day (✆ **0510/914-580**).

## VISITOR INFORMATION & TOURS

- **The Hoi An Tourist Guiding Office** (01 Nguyen Truong To, ✆ **0510/ 861-327;** or 12 Phan Chu Trinh St., ✆ **0510/862-715;** www.hoianworld heritage.org), sells the entrance ticket to the Hoi An World Cultural Heritage. A one-ticket purchase offers limited admission to all of the town's museums, old houses, and Chinese assembly halls. For more information about the ticket, see "What to See & Do," later in this chapter.
- **Hoi An Tourist Service Company,** inside the Hoi An Hotel (6 Tran Hung Dao St.; ✆ 0510/861-373; fax 0510/861-636), books every type of tour of the city and surrounding areas, including China Beach and the Marble Mountains, and is a reliable operation.
- **The Sinh Café IV** (11 Le Loi St., Hoi An; ✆ **0510/863-948**), provides bus tours and tickets onward.
- **An Phu Tourist** (29 Phan Dinh Phung St.; ✆ **0510/862-643;** anphu tourist@hotmail.com) does everything that Sinh Café does.

---

### *FAST FACTS:* Hoi An

*Banks/Currency Exchange*    The Vietcombank branch at 4 Huong Dieu St. has an ATM, changes money of most major currencies, and does credit card cash withdrawal transactions. Hours are Monday to Saturday 7:30am to 7pm. Hoi An Incombank has offices, with exchange services, at 09 Le Loio St. and at 4 Hoang Diet St. Exchange Bureau #1, across from the Hoi An Hotel at 37 Tran Hung Dao, has exchange and ATM. There is also an ATM at the post office.

*Internet/E-mail* Along Le Loi, you'll find service at prices at about 100 VND per minute (40¢ per hour). Access is generally slow dial-up. **Min's Computer** (131 Nguyen Duy Hieu on the northern end of town; ☎ 0510/ 914-323) is as good as it gets.

*Post Office/Mail* The post office is at the corner of Trang Hong Dao and Huong Dieu streets and is open Monday to Saturday 6am to 9:30pm.

*Telephone* The city code for Hoi An is 510. You can place international phone calls from the post office listed above and from most hotels.

## WHERE TO STAY

Hoi An has seen a recent boom in upscale resorts and there are more on the way along Cua Dai Beach. Large-scale new construction in Hoi An proper is prohibited by UNESCO, but smaller hotels are going upmarket and there are a few new options closer to town.

### EXPENSIVE

**Hoi An Beach Resort** 🏵    Opened in 2000, this is the flagship of Hoi An Tourist, a government-owned company, and it's their answer to recent upscale development in town. The resort is across the road from Cua Dai beach and close to the small restaurant row and popular tourist sunbathing area. Everything from the casual open-air restaurant to the more expensive rooms and suites faces the De Vong River as it approaches the sea, offering a unique glimpse of everyday riverside life, and the hotel has just opened a bar and upscale access point to the beach where you can sit in private chairs without harassment from beachside sellers. All rooms here are nice, but the villas are certainly worth the extra few bucks: They're quite large, with high ceilings and large private balconies. Villas and suites have vaulted ceilings, and some have separate entrances with a shower area for cleanup after the beach. Service and general standards are comparable to the high-end competition in town. It's a popular choice for large European tours and can get a bit wild in the busy season, but it's all good fun. The two pools are large, dining is good, and there are frequent shuttles to town.

Cua Dai Beach. ☎ 0510/927-011 or 0510/927-015. Fax 0510/927-019. www.hoiantourist.com. 85 units. $100–$110 single/double garden deluxe; $120 oceanview and riverview villas; $200 suite. AE, MC, V. **Amenities:** Restaurant; 3 bars; 2 outdoor pools; tennis court; small health club; spa; Jacuzzi; sauna; steam bath; in-house tour desk; car rental; souvenir shops; salon; limited room service; foot massage; laundry; Internet. *In room:* A/C, satellite TV, minibar, fridge, coffeemaker, hair dryer, safe, IDD phone.

**Hoi An Riverside Resort** 🏵🏵    For upscale, tranquil, and intimate surroundings, you'll find no better than this lush little resort between road and river outside of Hoi An (just 3km/1¾ miles). The place has a cozy feel, as if guest rooms kind of grew around the winding path of the garden and tranquil courtyard pool. Rooms are neat and clean, not especially big, but with nice views of the meandering bend in the river here or the quiet garden. Vietnamese- or Japanese-theme rooms are a similar standard of amenities and comfort, with smallish but immaculate bathrooms and nice wood appointments throughout. The staff is invisible, meaning that this place carries on like an immaculately trimmed golf course that gets a once-over each night. The Song Do restaurant serves fine Vietnamese and Continental fare and a visit to their Faifo bar harkens back to another era. The central pool is a relaxing spot—great after wandering the town labyrinths. Staff is very professional and very informative. The resort offers Vietnamese cooking lessons or lazy canoe trips on the picturesque river.

Cua Dai Rd. 3km (1¾ miles) from Hoi An. ☏ 0510/864-800. Fax 0510/864-900. www.hoianriverresort.com. 60 units. $129 Vietnamese standard; $139 Japanese standard; $149 superior (river view); $189 deluxe (river view). Promotional rates available in off season. AE, DC, MC, V. **Amenities:** Restaurant; bar; outdoor pool; health club; business center w/Internet; nice souvenir shop; salon; 24-hr. room service; foot massage; babysitting; laundry; dry cleaning; small library; conference room; snooker/billiards room. *In room:* A/C, satellite TV, dataport, minibar, fridge, coffeemaker, safe, IDD phone.

## Life Resort Hoi An ⭐
New in 2004, the Life Resort is the only resort within walking distance of Hoi An—a good start. Chic, minimalist rooms have a certain spartan charm but are done in concrete and tile and already a bit musty. Views of the river are good, and deluxe rooms have quiet sitting areas out front perfect for meditation or a rest from the noonday sun. Rooms are split-level with the slightly raised sleeping area done in cooling slate tiles. Baths are large, open-plan affairs. The dining outlets, housed in a large faux-colonial block at riverside, are atmospheric; I like the quiet air-conditioned cafe with good coffee and desserts. The whole place has an overly studied feel—perhaps because it's just getting up and running—but, for location alone, it's a good choice.

1 Pham Hong Thai St., Hoi An Town. ☏ 510/914-555. Fax 510/914-515. www.life-resorts.com. 94 units. $110–$135 double. AE, MC, V. **Amenities:** 2 restaurants; 2 bars; outdoor pool; tour desk; limited room service; massage; laundry service. *Inroom:* A/C, satellite TV, minibar, fridge, safe, IDD phone.

## Victoria Hoi An Resort ⭐⭐
It's peace and palm trees just a short ride (4.8km/3 miles) from ancient Hoi An. The comfortable Victoria has all the amenities, lots of activities and begs at least a few days' stay. Guest rooms have it right in every detail, from fine rustic decor to in-room sandals and beach robes. Rooms are either the bungalow variety in low-slung buildings at beachside or set in parallel two-story rows to mimic Hoi An's ancient streets, not displeasing, but a bit like a theme park. Prices reflect beachside proximity, but even the least expensive rooms are laid-back and classy. Some bungalows are decorated in French country style, with canopy beds and wicker furniture; others are unique Japanese rooms, with open-timber construction, bamboo floors, and large bathtubs. All rooms are finished in dark wood, many with high, exposed tile ceilings and colorful, nonslip tile leading into large bathrooms. There is a certain flow to this property, from beach to garden, rooms to common spaces, that invites guests to wander; you'll find a small billiards room with gaming tables and reading nooks—all connected by catwalk. Amenities like the large oceanside pool, indoor gym, Jacuzzi, aesthetic salon, and massage are top-notch. The hotel's resident elephant, Darling, offers rides to kids of all ages (priced per hour) and gives demonstrations on elephant hygiene early each morning (he takes his bath). Convenient shuttles, one an old Renault bus, connect to town frequently; or rent a motorcycle with sidecar. There's a private boat for transfer to town, kayak rental, and kite-surfing equipment, and the resort offers cooking courses. Victoria Hoi An is the only hotel in the area with full body massage.

Cua Dai Beach, 5km (3 miles) from Hoi An. ☏ 0510/927-041. Fax 0510/927-041. www.victoriahotels-asia.com. 100 units. $150–$160 superior (river/sea view); $200–$240 deluxe (river/sea view); $300 suite. **Amenities:** 2 restaurants; 2 bars; outdoor pool (beachside); 2 tennis courts; nice health club; spa; Jacuzzi; kayak/windsurfer/Hobie Cat rental; children's play area; tour desk; car rental; shopping; extensive salon; 24-hr. room service; foot massage; babysitting; laundry; dry cleaning; small library; elephant rides; Internet; snooker/billiards room. *In room:* A/C, satellite TV, minibar, fridge, coffeemaker, safe, IDD phone.

# Hoi An

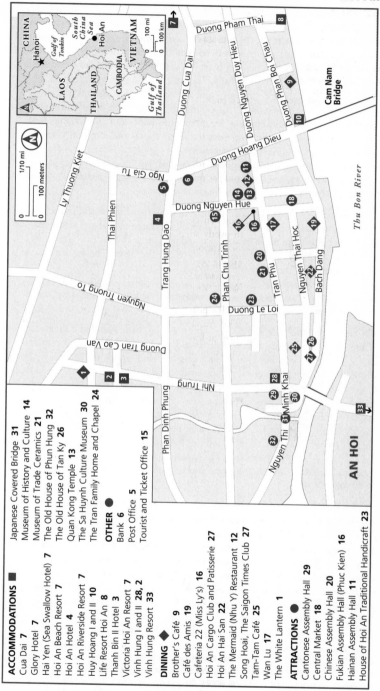

**ACCOMMODATIONS** ■
Cua Dai **7**
Glory Hotel **7**
Hai Yen (Sea Swallow Hotel) **7**
Hoi An Beach Resort **7**
Hoi An Hotel **4**
Hoi An Riverside Resort **7**
Huy Hoang I and II **10**
Life Resort Hoi An **8**
Thanh Bin II Hotel **3**
Victoria Hoi An Resort **7**
Vinh Hung I and II **28, 2**
Vinh Hung Resort **33**

**DINING** ◆
Brother's Café **9**
Café des Amis **19**
Cafeteria 22 (Miss Ly's) **16**
Hoi An Cargo Club and Patisserie **27**
Hoi An Hai San **22**
The Mermaid (Nhu Y) Restaurant **12**
Song Hoai; The Saigon Times Club **27**
Tam-Tam Café **25**
Wan Lu **17**
The White Lantern **1**

**ATTRACTIONS** ●
Cantonese Assembly Hall **29**
Central Market **18**
Chinese Assembly Hall **20**
Fukian Assembly Hall (Phuc Kien) **16**
Hainan Assembly Hall **11**
House of Hoi An Traditional Handicraft **23**

Japanese Covered Bridge **31**
Museum of History and Culture **14**
Museum of Trade Ceramics **21**
The Old House of Phun Hung **32**
The Old House of Tan Ky **26**
Quan Kong Temple **13**
The Sa Huynh Culture Museum **30**
The Tran Family Home and Chapel **24**

**OTHER** ●
Bank **6**
Post Office **5**
Tourist and Ticket Office **15**

## MODERATE

**Cua Dai** ⭐⭐    Another good budget gem on the beach road just out of town (like nearby Hai Yen above), the Cua Dai is a good marriage of affordability and comfort. It's easy to settle in here, with its open sitting areas of comfy wicker furniture on black-and-white tile and basic but comfy rooms. The very kind staff will make you feel right at home, too. The only drawback is the busy road out front, but all rooms have double glass and are relatively quiet. Rooms in the new wing in back have fine wooden appointments and creative, local decoration; older rooms in the main building are quite large, basic, and comfortable. Cua Dai is a good base to explore or meet the many expats and long-stay travelers here on cultural or humanitarian missions.

18A Cua Dai St. Ⓒ **0510/862-231** or 0510/864-604. Fax 0510/862-232. 27 units. $18–$25 double. MC, V. **Amenities:** Restaurant; bicycle/motorbike available; help w/any travel need; laundry. *In room:* A/C, TV, minibar, fridge, IDD phone.

**Glory Hotel**    On Cua Dau road just east of town (heading toward the beach), this new hotel has a fine standard of rooms, all very large and clean if rather spartan, set in a four-story block around a central pool area. The price is right, everything is new and clean, and the hotel covers all the bases. The pool is but a postage stamp, but the courtyard is tranquil.

06B Cua Dai St. Ⓒ **0510/914-445.** Fax 0510/914-445. www.gloryhotelhoian.com. 65 units. $60–$80 double; $95 suite. AE, MC, V. **Amenities:** Restaurant; bar; outdoor pool; tour desk; limited room service; laundry. *In-room:* A/C, satellite TV, minibar, fridge, IDD phone.

**Hai Yen (Sea Swallow Hotel)** ⭐    This is a good, basic standard on the edge of the old town (a short walk or ride toward the beach). Hai Yen is a popular choice for big, budget tour groups. Slick diagonal black-and-white (or blue-and-white) tile throughout gives everything a tidy edge, and rooms are big, but have funky Chinese relief carvings, overly fancy curtains, and shiny polyester spreads: an A for effort, but the general effect is kind of unsettling. The pool is a surprise luxury in this price range and is quite nice (if small). It's all a bit rough around the edges here, kind of a faded 1970s pallor over the whole place (and it's not so old). The staff is friendly, though, and can help with any detail.

22A Cua Dai St., Hoi An. Ⓒ **0501/862-445** or 0501/862-446. 41 units. $25–$30 double (seasonal). AE, MC, V. **Amenities:** Restaurant; bar; small outdoor pool; all rentals; tour desk; laundry. *In room:* A/C, satellite TV, minibar, fridge, IDD phone.

**Hoi An Hotel** ⭐⭐    Still the best and most convenient in-town address, the Hoi An Hotel was the first high-end hotel and works hard to keep that reputation. As a result, it's pretty busy here with lots of tour groups. The friendly staff does a great job, though, and handles large numbers with a modicum of grace. Don't expect anything fancy, but rooms are unusually large and impeccably clean, with tile floors and comfortable beds—older rooms are just as good, for my money. Basic tile bathrooms are in good condition. The newest building has upscale rooms with dark wood floors and a fun, contemporary Chinese theme. The central pool is large, though often overcrowded. The casual open-air dining facilities are good and the folks at the tour desk are very helpful. It's convenient to downtown sites.

6 Tran Hung Dao St. Ⓒ **0510/861-373.** Fax 0510/861-636. www.hoiantourist.com. 160 units. $50–$90 double; $100 suite. AE, MC, V. **Amenities:** Restaurant; garden bar; nice courtyard pool; tennis court; Jacuzzi; concierge; in-house tour desk; car rental; business center; lobby souvenir shops; 24-hr. room service; babysitting; laundry; dry cleaning. *In room:* A/C, satellite TV, minibar, fridge, hair dryer, IDD phone.

**Vinh Hung Resort** ⭐    Chinese-style entrepreneurs follow the model "Start small; go big," and that's what the folks at Vinh Hung have done (See Vinh

Hung I and II, below). Their small in-town properties are popular and they've turned that income back into this latest project: a self-contained, midlevel resort on Hoi An Island. The area, slated for further development in coming years, is just a 10- or 15-minute walk from the canal bridge at Hoi An center. Deluxe rooms are the best bet—large and tidy, with wood floors, Chinese tapestries and carpeted sitting areas. High-end rooms are enormous, some with Jacuzzis. Rooms encircle a central pool area and, though resort services are limited, and everything is a bit compact, Vinh Hung Resort is an affordable getaway and convenient. Some rooms overlook the wide river—a good choice. They have kayaks for rent, a unique commute to the town center, and cover all the basic amenities. The place is just getting up and running.

On Hoi Island (across the small bridge connecting to Hoi An near Bach Dang St. and a short ride to the opposite end of the island). © 0510/910-577. Fax 0510/864-094. www.vinhhunghotels.com. 82 units. $70–$90 double (priced by view); $100–$110 suite. AE, MC, V. **Amenities:** Restaurant; bar; outdoor pool; tennis court; small fitness center; Jacuzzi; sauna; kayak rental (can paddle to town); bike rentals; tour desk; car rental; salon; limited room service; babysitting; laundry. *In room:* A/C, minibar, fridge, safe, IDD phone.

## INEXPENSIVE

**Thanh Bin II Hotel** ⭐    The Thanh Bin II hotel is newer and nicer than its sister property, the Thanh Bin I over on Le Loi Street (a good location but just basic rooms; © **0510/861-740**). The three-story building has a Chinese-inspired lobby, with carved dark wood furnishings and cafe tables. Upstairs, the very clean and basic rooms are spacious. The decor is a color-coordinated mishmash. There's not a musty smell to be found, bathrooms are tidy, and the staff is really friendly. For fun, ask about one of the suites: It's a huge room that sports wood paneling, carved Chinese-style furnishings (and a mosquito net over the bed), a nice balcony with beaded curtains, and, in the center of the room, a large wooden carving of a fat, happy Buddha. Another location, **Thanh Bin III,** is on Nhi Trung St. (next to Thanh Bin II; © **0510/916-777**).

Nhi Trung St. © 0510/863-715. vothihong@dng.vnn.vn. 31 units. $12–$30 double. AE, MC, V. **Amenities:** Restaurant; rentals; laundry. *In room:* A/C, TV, minibar, fridge, IDD phone.

**Vinh Hung I and II** ⭐    Vinh Hung I, a downtown property set in an old wooden Chinese house, is a Hoi An institution; its two signature rooms are almost museum pieces and are alone worth a visit here, but they're not especially luxe or comfortable. Standard rooms in both Vinh Hung I and II are large, with wooden appointments and cool retro features like mosquito nets and Chinese latticework on wood balconies. Vinh Hung II is a tour-group favorite and often full, and for good reason (the central pool is unique in this category). Popularity means heavy use, though, and the place is getting a bit rough around the edges. The new Vinh Hung Resort (see above) is an improvement on an old theme.

Vinh Hung 1: 143 Tran Phu St.: © 0510/861-621. Fax 0510/861-893. **Vinh Hung II:** Nhi Trung St. © 0510/863-717. Fax 0510/864-094. www.vinhhunghotels.com. 64 units. $15–$30 double. AE, MC, V. **Amenities:** Restaurant; small outdoor pool; rentals; tour desk; laundry. *In room:* A/C, TV, IDD phone.

## WHERE TO DINE

Hoi An is a feast for the stomach as well as the eyes. Local specialties include *cao lau* (rice noodles with fresh greens, rice crackers, and croutons), white rose dumplings of shrimp in clear rice dough, and large, savory fried wontons. Good, fresh seafood is available everywhere (don't miss the morning market). There are some new high-end options in town alongside some popular standbys, and each of the resorts has its own fine dining (see "Where to Stay," above). The riverfront road, Bach Dang, has become the de facto "restaurant row," and below are listed a few good spots, but if you take a stroll down here any time in the day, you're sure to be besieged by some friendly but persistent touts who'll drag you bodily into their restaurants. All along Bach Dang are comparable in price and cuisine (fried rice and noodles), and it's sometimes fun to let the restaurant choose you.

*Note:* If you do eat on Bach Dang, choose a table a bit off the street and say a consistent and calm "No" to the many young Tiger Balm and chewing gum salesman if you'd like a quiet meal.

## EXPENSIVE

**Brother's Café** ✯✯✯ VIETNAMESE    Serving similar fine Vietnamese fare as its sister restaurant in Hanoi (but here it's a la carte, not buffet), Brother's Café is the town's top choice for cuisine and atmosphere. A bland street-side facade gives way to the lush, garden sanctuary formed by this grand U-shape colonial by the river. Indoor seating is upscale Indochina of a bygone era, and the courtyard is dotted with canvas umbrellas to while away a balmy afternoon or enjoy a candlelight evening riverside. The fare is gourmet Vietnamese at its finest, with changing daily set menus and great specials; be sure to ask for a recommendation. It's a good place to try local items like the white rose, a light Vietnamese ravioli, or *cao lao* noodles. Set menus are great here and change daily. With a group, it's a great spot to order up family style and sample it all. Brother's also features a cooking school (just ask the staff). Everything's good, the atmosphere is great, and the staff couldn't be friendlier. This is a strong recommendation.

27 Pham Boi Chau St. ✆ **0510/914-150.** Main courses $1.50–$12. AE, MC, V. Daily 10am–11pm.

**Hoi An Cargo Club and Patisserie** ✯ INTERNATIONAL    Ms. Vy expands her Hoi An empire (Nhy Y and White Lantern restaurants—the latter reviewed on p. 352—and Cua Dai Hotel) with a unique, open-air patisserie and French cafe. This stylish storefront serves light meals in a lounge bar on the first floor and, upstairs, is a refined restaurant specializing in contemporary Vietnamese cuisine. Good seafood dishes abound, like the crab in five spices or jumbo shrimp with tamarind sauce. Sandwiches, soups, and salads are good and served with fine fresh bread baked on sight. Upstairs seating is on a cool balcony overlooking the river or a chic indoor space, and the first floor is casual bar or lounge seating. Curries and good veggie dishes round out a good, affordable menu. Cargo Club is a good place to reconnoiter if traveling in a group or meet other travelers.

107/109 Nguyen Thai Hoc St. ✆ **0510/910-489.** www.hoianhospitality.com. Main courses 25,000 VND–65,000 VND ($1.65–$4.35). V, MC. Daily 7am–11pm.

**Song Hoai, The Saigon Times Club** ✯✯ VIETNAMESE    Set in the most picturesque period building in town, on a corner overlooking riverside Bach Dang, this Saigon-managed restaurant is as much about atmosphere as it is about dining. Rivaled only by Brother's, above, the two open floors here are true old Hoi An elegance. The second floor has great views of the river and is dramatic, with a high, exposed tile ceiling and languid ceiling fans. I had the Vietnamese-style ravioli, the local white rose specialty, and enjoyed fresh pan-fried shrimp. Song Hoai serves regional dishes like Hanoi *cha ca* and *mi quang* wide noodles. Presentation is arguably the classiest in town, with fine china, stemware, and lacquered dishes on linen, and the service is professional if a bit hovering. A good choice for a romantic evening of fine dining, Hoi An style.

119–121 Nguyen Thai Hoc St. ✆ **0510/910-369.** Fax 0510/910-436. Main courses $1–$11. AE, MC, V. Daily 10am–11pm.

**Tam-Tam Café** ✯✯ ITALIAN/CONTINENTAL    Tam-Tam is the place to be in Hoi An. The brainchild of three French expats, it is historic and laid-back, serving good, familiar food. The decor is authentic local style, with hanging bamboo lamps, a high wooden ceiling, and fantastic wooden figurines. The dinner menu, served in a separate restaurant room with checkered tablecloths, is simple—featuring generous portions of homemade pastas, steaks, and salads—but the food is delicious. The dessert menu includes flambéed crepes, sorbet, and hot chocolate. There are two bar rooms: The bigger one to the left of the entry has a pool table, a book swap shelf, comfortable lounge chairs, and sofas, and is the place to hang out in Hoi An. The extensive drink menu features all kinds of bang-for-the buck rum specials, and there's even a small counter on the balcony where you can sip a cocktail and watch life go by on the street below. Even for just a coffee, don't miss this place.

110 Nguyen Thai Hoc St. (on the 2nd floor). ✆ 0510/862-212. Main courses $2–$10. AE, MC, V. Daily 24 hrs.

## MODERATE
**Café des Amis** ✯✯ VIETNAMESE    What's on the menu? There isn't one. It's your choice of set menu, either seafood or vegetarian, and the details are, well, a surprise. And the surprise is always good; one of the best meals in Vietnam, if you ask me. But don't ask me. Read the straight dope from the many guests who come and sign their endorsements in Mr. Kim's lengthy guest book (you'll be asked to sign too, of course). I enjoyed a leisurely meal starting with a savory clear soup, fried wontons with shrimp, broiled fish, stuffed calamari, and scallops on the half shell. Sit back and surrender yourself to the surprises of the effusive Mr. Kim and his attentive staff. Mr. Kim is a practiced raconteur with rich material from his years as a taster for the army and a chef for heads of state. He is careful to explain the intricacies of each dish and even demonstrates how to eat some of the more unique entrees. The food is great, and a meal here makes for a memorable evening.

52 Bach Dang St. ✆ 0510/861-616. Set menu 65,000 VND ($4.35). No credit cards. Daily 6–10pm.

**Cafeteria 22 (Miss Ly's)** ✯    You're greeted by the kind proprietor herself, Miss Ly, always dressed to the nines and welcoming. The menu is limited, but that means everything is always available and fresh in this little hole-in-the wall cafe in the heart of the old town. Cafeteria 22 is the best place in Hoi An to try the town's famous fried wontons, a rice pastry stuffed with meat, shrimp, and onion and topped with Ly's special sauce, onion, and tomato—messy and delicious. And Ly has been at it for over 10 years now and has just the right formula. There's nothing fancy here, and that is the appeal for folks who tire easily of trumped-up atmosphere and overpriced, altered versions of local fare. Come meet Ly and try the real deal.

22 Nguyen Hue St., Hoi An. ✆ 0510/861-603. Main courses 8,000 VND–40,000 VND (55¢–$2.65). No credit cards. Daily 8am–11pm.

**Hoi An Hai San** ✯✯ VIETNAMESE/CONTINENTAL    Hai-san means "seafood" in Vietnamese and "hello" in Swedish: The owners, longtime Swedish expat Calle and Hoa, his Vietnamese wife, offer just that: "Hello, seafood!" This is one of the few spots on Hang Bac that won't drag you in because it's the food that brings folks here. I had delicious grilled, marinated tuna filet with ginger, garlic, and lemon grass and served in a light coconut milk. The sea scallops in cream sauce are a favorite. Everything's good here, and it's a good place to linger after a meal, enjoy the Swedish lingenberry (a kind of cranberry) ice cream, and watch the goings-on on busy Bach Dang.

64 Bach Dang St. © 0510/861-652. Main courses 20,000 VND–75,000 VND ($1.35–$5). Daily 9am–10pm.

**The Mermaid (Nhu Y) Restaurant** ⋐⋐ VIETNAMESE    This quiet spot in the heart of downtown is an ivy-draped, unassuming storefront that serves some of the best authentic Vietnamese food in town (for next to nothing). If you like what you eat, stick around and take a **cooking class** in the large adjoining kitchen that's open to the street: Here's a unique chance to bring some of Vietnam home to your kitchen. I had a scrumptious tuna filet cooked in a banana leaf with tumeric. The spring rolls are light and fresh, with a whole jumbo shrimp in each, and the Mermaid serves a most unique dish called white eggplant: It's eggplant covered in spring onion, garlic, and chile, and then pressed, sliced, and served in a light oil. Everything is good. The staff members also teach the class and are very friendly and can explain it all.

02 Tran Phu St. © 0510/861-527. www.hoianhospitality.com. Main courses 12,000 VND–40,000 VND (80¢–$2.65). No credit cards. Daily 7am–10pm.

**The White Lantern** ⋐⋐ VIETNAMESE    This is a very popular tour group stop, so try to get there early (or late); if you see buses parked out front, head for the hills. Everyone's here for good reason, though: delicious, affordable Vietnamese cuisine and mellow atmosphere. Strumming guitarists roam the tables playing old Beatles melodies and some nice local numbers, and the large open area on the first floor, with long tables for groups, and the second-floor balcony space are dimly lit and romantic. Owned by the same folks that run Nhu Y, above, this is a slightly upscale version. Set menus are a great bet; I had a fine meal of a delicate won-ton soup, spring rolls, and chicken in a light curry. It's a good find just north of the town center.

11 Nhi Trung St. © 0510/863-023. Main courses 30,000 VND–45,000 VND ($2–$3); set menu 75,000 VND–120,000 VND ($5–$8). MC, V. Daily 9am–10pm.

### INEXPENSIVE

**Wan Lu** ⋐    Pull up a chair and try the special, *cao lao,* a thick but tender white noodle in light soy with fresh vegetables, garnish, and croutons. This is where the locals eat it, and if it's not your cup of tea, then you're out only 6,000 VND (about 40¢). It's an open-air place, and the atmosphere is a little rough, but they serve a nice selection of local favorites, too, all for next to nothing. The portions are big and everything's authentic, right down to the kindness in this little Mom and Pop. There are no touts here; it's the food that brings 'em in.

27 Tran Phu St. © 0510/861-212. Main courses 5,000 VND–30,000 VND (35¢–$2). No credit cards. Daily 7am–11pm.

## WHAT TO SEE & DO

The whole town is an attraction, its narrow streets comprised of lovely historical buildings buzzing with open-air craft shops, woodworkers, and carvers. Tran Phu and Nguyen Thai Hoc streets are crowded with the shops of the original Chinese merchants and clan associations. Most Hoi An buildings have been lovingly restored and transformed into cafes, art galleries, and silk and souvenir shops, while still retaining their historical dignity. If you're an artist, bring your sketchpad and watercolors; photographers, bring plenty of film.

The Hoi An World Cultural Heritage Organization (www.hoianworldheritage. org.) has the dilemma of financing the restorations and maintaining the old portions of the town. They sell a 50,000 VND ($3.35) ticket that allows limited admission to the sights within the old town, each of which is listed below. "Limited" means a "one from column A, one from column B" formula. One ticket gets you one of the three museums, one of the three assembly halls, one of the four old houses, plus a choice of either the Japanese Bridge, the Quan Cong's Temple, or the local handicraft workshop; finally, a "wild card" lets you see one additional place in any category that you didn't see. So, to see everything, you'll have to purchase three tickets.

## THE MUSEUMS

### Museum of History and Culture 𝒜
This tottering building erected in 1653 houses works that cross 2,000 years of Hoi An history from Cham relics to ancient ceramics and photos of local architecture. There are English explanations, but they are scanty. If you're seeing only one museum, make it the Museum of Trade Ceramics (below). One interesting tidbit: The name Hoi An literally means "water convergence" and "peace."

7 Nguyen Hue St. Daily 8am–5pm.

### Museum of Trade Ceramics 𝒜𝒜𝒜
Located in a traditional house, this museum describes the origins of Hoi An as a trade port and displays its most prominent trade items. Objects are from the 13th through 17th centuries and include Chinese and Thai works as well. While many of the exhibits are in fragments, the real beauty of the place is that the very thorough descriptions are in English, giving you a real sense of the town's origins and history. Furthermore, the architecture and renovations of the old house are thoroughly explained, and you're free to wander through its two floors, courtyard, and anteroom. After all the scattered explanations at the other historic houses, you'll finally get a sense of what Hoi An architecture is all about.

80 Tran Phu St. Daily 8am–5pm.

### The Sa Huynh Culture Museum 𝒜
After local farmers around Hoi An dug up some strange-looking pottery, archaeologists identified 53 sites where a pre-Cham people, called the Sa Huynh, buried their dead in ceramic jars. The two-room display here includes some of the burial jars, beaded ornaments, pottery vessels, and iron tools and weapons that have been uncovered. English descriptions are sketchy. Upstairs, the little-visited Museum of the Revolution includes such intriguing items as the umbrella "which Mr. Truong Munh Luong used for acting a fortune-teller to act revolution from 1965 to 1967." Huh? This is for connoisseurs only.

149 Tran Phu St. Daily 8am–6pm.

## THE OLD HOUSES

### The Old House of Phun Hung 𝒜
This private house, constructed in 1780, is two floors of combined architectural influences. The first floor's central roof is four-sided, showing Japanese influence, and the upstairs balcony has a Chinese rounded "turtle shell" roof with carved beam supports. The house has weathered many floods. In 1964, during a particularly bad bout, its third floor served as a refuge for other town families. The upstairs is outfitted with a trap door for moving furniture rapidly to safety. You might be shown around by Ms. Anh, who claims to be an eighth-generation member of the family. Tour guides at every house make such claims; however, like Quan Thang's house, the family really does seem to live here.

4 Nguyen Thi Minh Khai St. Daily 8am–5pm.

**The Old House of Tan Ky** ✪   There have been either five or seven generations of Tans living here, depending on whom you speak with. Built over 200 years ago, the four small rooms are crammed with dark wood antiques. The room closest to the street is for greeting visiting merchants. Farther in is the living room, then the courtyard, and, to the back, the bedroom. The first three are open to the public. A guide who will greet you at the door will hasten to explain how the house is a perfect melding of three architectural styles: ornate Chinese detailing on some curved roof beams, a Japanese peaked roof, and a simple Vietnamese cross-hatch roof support. The mosaic decorations on the wall and furniture are aged, intricate, and amazing. Take your time to look around.

101 Nguyen Thai Hoc St. Daily 8am–5pm.

**The Tran Family Home and Chapel** ✪✪✪   In 1802, a civil service mandarin named Tran Tu Nhuc built a family home and chapel to worship his ancestors. A favorite of Viet Emperor Gia Long, he was sent to China as an ambassador, and his home reflects his high status. Elegantly designed with original Chinese antiques and royal gifts such as swords, two parts of the home are open to the public: a drawing room and an ancestral chapel. The house does a splendid job of conveying all that is exotic and interesting about these people and their period. It has even been featured as a stylish layout in a fashion magazine. The drawing room has three sections of sliding doors: the left for men, the right for women, and the center, open only at Tet and other festivals, for dead ancestors to return home. The ancestral altar in the inner room has small boxes behind it containing relics and a biography of the deceased; their pictures hang, a little spookily, to the right of the altar. A 250-year-old book with the family history resides on a table to the right of the altar. In back of the house are a row of plants, each buried with the placenta and umbilical cord of a family child, so that the child will never forget its home. As if it could.

21 Le Loi St. (on the corner of Phan Chu Trinh St.). Daily 8am–5pm.

## THE ASSEMBLY HALLS

**Cantonese Assembly Hall (Quang Trieu/Guangzhou Assembly Hall)**
Built in 1885, this hall is quite ornate and colorful. All of the building materials were completed in China, brought here, and then reassembled. The center garden sports a fountain with a dragon made of chipped pottery, the centerpiece. Inside, look for the statues depicting scenes from famous Cantonese operas and, in the rooms to each side, the ancestral tablets of generations past.

176 Tran Phu St. Daily 8am–6pm.

**Fukian Assembly Hall (Phuc Kien)**   This is the grandest of the assembly halls, built in 1697 by Chinese merchants from Fukian Province. It is a showpiece of classical Chinese architecture, at least after you pass the first gate, which was added in 1975. It's loaded with animal themes: The fish in the mosaic fountain symbolizes scholarly achievement, the unicorn flanking the ascending stairs symbolizes wisdom, the dragon symbolizes power, the turtle symbolizes longevity, and the phoenix symbolizes nobility. The main temple is dedicated to Thien Hau, goddess of the sea, on the main altar. To the left of her is Thuan Phong Nhi, a goddess who can hear ships in a range of thousands of miles, and on the right is Thien Ly Nhan, who can see them. Go around the altar for a view of a fantastic detailed miniature boat. There are two altars to the rear of the temple, the one on the left honoring a god of prosperity and the one on the right honoring a goddess of fertility. The goddess of fertility is often visited by local couples hoping for children. She is flanked by 12 fairies or midwives, each responsible for one of a baby's functions: smiling, sleeping, eating, and so forth. 46 Tran Phu St. Daily 7am–6pm.

## OTHER SITES

**Japanese Covered Bridge** 🐦🐦🐦 The name of this bridge in Vietnamese, Lai Vien Kieu, means "Pagoda in Japan." No one is exactly sure who first built it in the early 1600s (it has since been renovated several times), but it is usually attributed to Hoi An's Japanese community. The dog flanking one end and the monkey at the other are considered to be sacred animals to the ancient Japanese, and my guide claimed the reasoning is that most Japanese emperors were born in the year of either the monkey or the dog by the Asian zodiac. Later I read something else that claimed maybe it meant construction began in the year of the dog and was completed in the year of the monkey. I'm sure there are many other interesting dog and monkey stories going around. Pick your favorite. The small temple inside is dedicated to Tran Vo Bac De, god of the north, beloved (or cursed) by sailors because he controls the weather.

At the west end of Tran Phu St.

**Quan Kong Temple** 🐦 This temple was built in the early 1600s to honor a famous Chin Dynasty general. Highlights inside are two gargantuan 3m-high (10-ft.) wooden statues flanking the main altar, one of Quan Kong's protector and one of his adopted son. They are fearsome and impressive. Reportedly the temple was a stop for merchants who came in from the nearby river to pay their respects and pray for the general's attributes of loyalty, bravery, and virtue.

168 Tran Phu St. (on the corner of Nguyen Hue). Daily 8am–5pm.

## Attractions Not on the World Cultural Heritage Ticket

**Central Market** 🐦🐦 If you see one Vietnamese market, make it this one, by the river on the southeast side of the city. There are endless stalls of exotic foodstuffs and services, and a special big shed for silk tailoring at the east end (these tailors charge much less than the ones along Le Loi). Check out the ladies selling spices—curries, chile powders, cinnamon, peppercorns, and especially saffron—at prices that are a steal in the West. But don't buy from the first woman you see; the stuff gets cheaper and cheaper the deeper you go into the market. Walk out to the docks to see activity there (best early in the morning), but be careful of fish flying through the air, and stand back from the furious bargaining (best before 7am).

At Nguyen Hue and Tran Phu sts. along the Thu Bon River.

**Chinese Assembly Hall** 🐦 This hall was built in 1740 as a meeting place for all of the resident Chinese, regardless of their native province.

64 Tran Phu St. Daily 8am–5pm.

**Hainan Assembly Hall** The Chinese merchants from Hainan Island, in the South China Sea east of Danang, built this hall. Although it is newer than most and is mostly made of concrete, it is nice.

178 Nguyen Duy Hieu St. Daily 8am–5pm.

**House of Hoi An Traditional Handicraft** 🐦🐦 This is basically a silk shop with an interesting gimmick: On the first floor you can see both a 17th-century silk loom and a working, machine-powered cotton one. On the second, you can see where silk comes from: There are trays of silkworms feeding, then a rack of worms incubating, and then a tub of hot water where the pupae's downy covering is rinsed off and then pulled, strand by strand, onto a large skein. It's cool. They have the best selection of silks, both fine and raw, in many colors and weights good for clothing and for home interiors.

41 Le Loi St. Daily 8am–5pm.

## HITTING THE BEACHES

**Cua Dai beach** 🎐🎐 is a 25-minute bicycle ride from Hoi An on a busy road with vistas of lagoons, rice paddies, and stilt houses. Simply follow Tran Hung Dao Street to Cua Dai Street to the east of town and follow for 3km (2 miles). The beach is thin and crowded with hawkers, but there are cozy deck chairs (for a small fee) and the sand, surf, and setting, with views of the nearby Cham Islands, are worth the trip. Tour companies tout boat excursions in season (Mar–Sept) to the Cham Islands, a group of seven islands about 13km (8 miles) east of Hoi An; prices vary, but expect to pay about 30,000 VND ($2). Contact the traveler cafes in town. There are also boat trips on the Thu Bon River.

## AN EXCURSION TO MY SON 🎐🎐

My Son, some 40km (25 miles) from Hoi An (71km/44 miles from Danang), is an important temple ruin of the Cham people, a once-powerful Hindu empire. The temples were constructed as a religious center for citizens of the Cham capital, Danang, from the 7th through 12th centuries during the height of Cham supremacy. My Son (pronounced *mee sun*) might also have been used as a burial site for Cham kings after cremation. Originally, there were over 70 towers and monuments at the site, but bombing during the war with America (the Viet Cong used My Son as a munitions warehouse) has sadly reduced many to rubble. Additionally, many of the smaller structures have been removed to the Cham Museum in Danang. The complex is a very serene and spiritual setting, however, and what does remain is powerful and evocative. It's not hard to imagine what a wonder My Son must once have been.

Much of what remains today are structures built or renovated during the 10th century, when the cult of Shiva, founder and protector of the kingdom, was predominant in the Cham court. Each group had at least the following structures: a **kalan,** or main tower; a gate tower in front of that, with two entrances; a **mandapa,** or meditation hall; and a repository building for offerings. Some have towers sheltering stelae with kingly epitaphs. A brick wall encircles the compound.

Architecturally, the temple complex shows Indian influences. Each temple grouping is a microcosm of the world. The foundations are Earth, the square bases are the temple itself, and the pointed roofs symbolize the heavens. The entrance of the main tower faces east, and surrounding smaller towers represent each continent. A trench, representing the oceans, surrounds each group. Vietnamese architecture is represented in decorative patterns and boat-shape roofs.

Group A originally had 13 towers. A-1, the main tower, was a 21m-tall (69-ft.) masterpiece before it was destroyed in 1969. Group B bears the marks of Indian and Indonesian influence. Note that B-6 holds a water repository for statue-washing ceremonies. Its roof is carved with an image of the god Vishnu sitting beneath a 13-headed snake god, or **naga.** Group C generally followed an earlier architectural style called Hoa Lai, which predominated from the 8th century to the beginning of the 9th. Groups G and H were the last to be built, at around the end of the 13th century.

Arrange a half-day trip to My Son with any tourist agent in Hoi An (see "Visitor Information & Tours," in this section). Entrance to the site is 50,000 VND

($3.35), and a private half-day tour with a guide is $35 for a car and $43 for a van. The half-day seat-in-coach tour by Sinh Cafe costs $2 per person and is nothing more than a ride there, with no explanations. Less frequent tours also depart from Danang.

## SHOPPING

Southeast Asia is packed with would-be Buddhists, travelers on a real spiritual mission espousing lives of detachment from material desires. These folks usually walk away with just the "one suit, two shirts, trousers, and a tie package" when they leave Hoi An. Shopaholics wander the streets in a daze.

Hoi An is a silk mecca. The quality and selection are the best in the country, and you'll have more peace and quiet while fitting than in Hanoi. **Silk suits** are made to order within 24 hours for about $35; **cashmere wool** is $45. There are countless shops, and the tailoring is all about the same quality and fast. A good way to choose a shop is by what you see out front—if you see a style you like, it'll help with ordering. Make sure you take the time to specify your style, down to the stitch (it can come back looking pretty cheap without specifics). Try any of the shops along Le Loi; to recommend one in particular would be like recommending one snowflake over another. The tailoring is very fast, but not always great, so plan to have two or three fittings. Be choosy about your cloth, or go to the market and buy it yourself (**Hoi An Cloth Market** is at 01 Tran Phu St.), and haggle. It's not a bad idea to bring an actual suit or piece of clothing that you'd like a copy of. Get measurements from friends and relatives for good gifts.

**Yaly Couture** at 47 Nguyen Thai Hoc St. (© 0510/910-474) is a good answer to selecting your own tailor from the many budget places. Yes, the prices are higher, but quality comes with more of a guarantee and similar efficient service.

There are also skilled cobblers who make custom shoes at affordable rates. Find them near the market on Tran Phu Street.

Tran Phu Street is lined with **art galleries** and the good **pottery** and **carved-wood** vendors. Along the river, lots of places sell blue and white **ceramics.** However cumbersome your finds are, like those lovely **Chinese lanterns,** shopkeepers are masters at packing for travel and to fit in your luggage, and will do so before you've even agreed on a price or decided to buy. Haggle hard.

**Que Noi Gallery** (83 Nguyen Thai Hoc St.; © 0510/863-184) is exemplary of the fine high-end galleries springing up in town.

**Hand-painted Chinese scrolls** make a great souvenir, and Mr. Ly Si Binh (21 Nguyen Thai Hoc St.; © 0510/910-721), can script you anything from *Peace* or *Determination* to your best buddy's name (if it's wrong, he won't know the difference anyway). And it's fun to watch cheery Mr. Binh at work, too.

**Bambou Company** (96 Nguyen Thai Hoc St.) produces unique T-shirts of local theme and design, all Western-size cotton shirts.

## HOI AN AFTER DARK

For the most part, Hoi An is a town that sleeps early, but there are a few good night spots. **Tam-Tam Café** (p. 351) is long a popular spot for travelers, expats, and locals. **Hai's Scout Café** (98 Nguyen Thai Hoc St.; © 0510/863-210), is a popular late-night hangout for travelers and a good crossroads with your standard bar drinks as well as cappuccino and espresso and some great baked treats. **Treat's Same Same Café** (158 Tran Phu St., at the intersection with Le Loi; © 0501/861-125), is also usually hopping as late as it can and has a pool table and a guillotine (for show, of course). Also try **Same Same Not Different Café** on Phan Dinh Phung next to An Phu Tourist Co. (both locations are, in short, similar).

**The Yellow Star Café** (73 Nguyen Thai Hoc St.; ✆ **090/512-4422;** www.yellow starcafe.com), serves up drinks, while the next-door **ChamPa** (75 Nguyen Thai Hoc St.; ✆ **0510/862-974**), has comfy chairs, good wine, and a cozy, late-night atmosphere and frequent cultural dance performances.

**Lounge Bar** (102 Nguyen Thai Hoc St.; ✆ **0510/910-480**) is a laid-back, chic stop, and nearby **Mango Rooms** (111 Nguyen Thai Hoc St.; ✆ **0510/ 910-839**) is similarly new, hip, and mellow.

## 9 An Introduction to South Central Vietnam

South Central Vietnam is comprised of the highlands, a land of rugged mountainous terrain, as well as a stunning coastal area popular for Vietnamese vacationers. The area saw its share of fighting during the American war; names like Buon Me Thot and Pleiku will undoubtedly ring a bell. Dalat is a former French colonial outpost nestled among the hills, and it still retains a serene, formal air of another time—and cooler weather is welcome respite; it's a popular escape for expats and travelers and a popular honeymoon destination for Vietnamese. Nha Trang, not far from Dalat on the coast, is an easygoing seaside town that is growing into a top international resort destination.

### GETTING THERE
**BY PLANE**   Both Nha Trang and Dalat are easily accessible by plane from Hanoi and Saigon.

**BY TRAIN**   Nha Trang is a stop on the north-south railway line.

**BY BUS/MINIVAN**   Travel between the two major cities is a 6-hour ride by bus or minivan, easily organized through a local travel agency. Both towns are included on most tourist cafe open tours. For details, see "Getting There," in individual town listings.

## 10 Nha Trang

Welcome to Vietnam's Ocean City! The capital of Khanh Hoa Province, Nha Trang has a full-time population that stands at about 200,000 people, but it far exceeds that with the heavy local and international tourist influx, especially in the summer months. While it's not a particularly charming town, the surf isn't bad and the beach is breathtaking, with views of the more than 20 surrounding islands. There is a growing collection of fine, high-end hotels and resorts, as well as good budget options. Dining is all about good fresh seafood.

Nha Trang is also a very popular vacation spot for Vietnamese, and, especially in the summer months, the town is chockablock with tourists and young kids out "cruisin' the strip" on motorbikes—a bit much for folks looking to relax. It's a fine place to spend 2 or 3 days frolicking in the surf, snorkeling and diving, or taking a cruise to the nearby islands.

Culturally, there are a few things to keep you occupied: **The Pasteur Institute** offers a glimpse into the life and work of one of Vietnam's most famous expats; there also are the interesting **Long Son Pagoda** and the well-preserved **Po Nagar Cham Temple.**

Off season (Oct–Mar), the surf is far too rough for swimming and sports, and you might want to rethink stopping at Nha Trang at all.

### GETTING THERE
**BY PLANE**   Nha Trang is 1,350km (837 miles) from Hanoi and 450km (279 miles) from Saigon and there are daily connections on Vietnam Airlines with

# Nha Trang

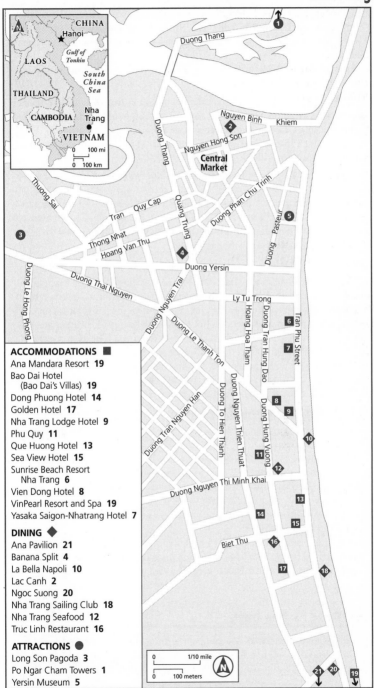

**ACCOMMODATIONS** ■
Ana Mandara Resort **19**
Bao Dai Hotel
 (Bao Dai's Villas) **19**
Dong Phuong Hotel **14**
Golden Hotel **17**
Nha Trang Lodge Hotel **9**
Phu Quy **11**
Que Huong Hotel **13**
Sea View Hotel **15**
Sunrise Beach Resort
 Nha Trang **6**
Vien Dong Hotel **8**
VinPearl Resort and Spa **19**
Yasaka Saigon-Nhatrang Hotel **7**

**DINING** ◆
Ana Pavilion **21**
Banana Split **4**
La Bella Napoli **10**
Lac Canh **2**
Ngoc Suong **20**
Nha Trang Sailing Club **18**
Nha Trang Seafood **12**
Truc Linh Restaurant **16**

**ATTRACTIONS** ●
Long Son Pagoda **3**
Po Ngar Cham Towers **1**
Yersin Museum **5**

Vietnam's urban centers and nearby Dalat (offices in Nha Trang: 91 Nguyen Thien Thuat St.; ℰ 058/826-768). The Nha Trang airport, once in the center of town, has traded places with a larger military facility and is now called **Cam Ranh Airport** some 35km (22 miles) north of town. The 30-minute ride costs 150,000 VND ($10) per taxi. The larger resorts offer more affordable group connections or limousine service.

**BY TRAIN**    Nha Trang is a stop on the Reunification Express and is 12 hours from Ho Chi Minh on a soft sleeper for $18, and 20 hours to Hanoi for $67. Buy your ticket at least 1 day in advance at the Nha Trang train station (17 Thai Nguyen St.; ℰ 058/822-113), or from any travel agent. There is a convenient overnight connection with Ho Chi Minh.

**BY CAR/BUS**    If you choose to drive from Hoi An to Nha Trang, it's a 10-hour trip and will cost you about $120 by car. An arduous 12-hour bus or minibus ride with a cafe tour bus will cost only $8. There are overnight schedules to Ho Chi Minh City and Hoi An; the trip is long and tiring, but it's a good option if you're short on time and don't want to waste your precious daylight hours looking out the window of a tour coach.

## GETTING AROUND

The main street in Nha Trang, **Tran Phu,** runs along a 4km (2½ miles) beach lined with the myriad minihotels and beach attractions that make the town center. **Biet Thu Street** runs perpendicular to Tran Phu and is where you'll find lots of smaller restaurants and budget tour operators (tourist cafes and so on). Taxis are scarce but a few tend to congregate around the major hotels. **Renting a bike** from your hotel for 15,000 VND to 30,000 VND ($1–$2) a day is a good option, as are cyclos, which you can rent for $3 per hour from your hotel. A **cyclo** across town will cost about 10,000 VND (65¢). In addition, **motorcycle taxis** can be had for 20,000 VND ($1.35) per hour and on short trips starting at 5,000 VND (35¢).

## VISITOR INFORMATION & TOURS

All hotels in Nha Trang can book city tours, day boat trips, or onward travel to your next destination.

One-day city tours visit Long Son Pagoda, Bao Dai's Villa, the Oceanographic Institute, and Cham Tower. Country tours take you to Ba Ho Waterfall and secluded Doc Let Beach, as well as Monkey Island. *Important:* No matter what anyone tells you, Monkey Island is not worth the trip, especially if you like animals and don't like wasting your time (you can just buy a "monkeys on bikes" postcard and be done with it).

For bus tickets and connection to Dalat, contact **TM Brothers Café** (22B Tran Hung Dao St.; ℰ **058/814-556**); **Sinh Café III** (10 Biet Thu St.; ℰ **058/ 811-981**); or **An Phu** (1/24 Tran Quang Khai St.; ℰ **058/524-471**).

### *FAST FACTS*: Nha Trang

*Currency Exchange/Banks*   Vietcombank's local branch is located at 17 Quang Trung St. (ℰ **058/821-483**). Hours are 7:30 to 11am and 1:30 to 4pm. It offers the usual currency and traveler's check exchange and credit card cash withdrawal services. Along Biet Thu, some of the tour operators will cash traveler's checks and change money—rates are the same as at the bank (except for a small service fee), and they're open longer hours.

*Internet/E-mail* Biet Thu has a cluster of Internet cafes for between 200 and 300 VND (a couple cents) per minute usage.

*Post Office/Mail* The main branch is at 4 Le Loi St. (℃ **058/823-866**). Hours are 6:30am to 10pm Monday to Saturday. DHL express mail services and Internet access are available. There is another branch at 50 Le Thanh Ton St.

*Telephone* The city code for Nha Trang is 58.

## WHERE TO STAY

There are 270 minihotels in Nha Trang, most quite basic and geared to the summer influx of Vietnamese vacationers and easy on the budget. Ana Mandara still stands in a class all its own, but recent construction means that there are a few mid- and high-range choices, and development on outlying islands (see Vin-Pearl and the new Evason Hideaway Ana Mandara) means there are lots of new options.

### VERY EXPENSIVE

**Ana Mandara Resort** ★★★   One of the finest resorts in the region, the Ana Mandara is a real seaside dreamscape. The name means "beautiful home" in the Cham language, and, though it comes with a price tag, the hospitality and kindness extended here is quite sincere. There are lots of return guests and staff is very kind, even make a point of learning your name. Such personalized service in a beautiful beachside setting, with a spa, pool, fine dining, and a host of activities, means that there's something for everyone—and you won't want to leave. A recent renovation includes a large, luxurious pool and the addition of a spacious new spa with designer outdoor massage areas at seaside. And it's the little things that make this resort special: native art and handiwork all about, the bowl with floating flowers in the bathroom, the basin of rainwater on your private veranda for rinsing sandy feet, the burning incense in the open-air lobby. Each room is double height and airy with wood beams, rattan ceiling, stylish furniture, and designer tile floors. When you check in, the bed sheets are set up in the most exquisite fan pattern, with flowers artfully scattered and a draping mosquito net over your private canopy. Bathrooms have a large window facing a private outdoor enclosure, like your own Zen garden. Thirty-six units face the beach, and others face a courtyard with lush, exotic plants. The restaurant, Ana Pavilion (see "Where to Dine," below), has the best food and atmosphere in town and the new beachside dining outlet is tops. The resort offers lots of great tours, like the informative "market tours" where guests can learn about Vietnam cuisine and find out where it all comes from.

Ask about its nearby sister resort, **Evason Hideaway Ana Mandara,** just a 20-minute boat ride away at Ninh Van Bay. Private, luxurious pool villas, some built right into unique rock formations, line this quiet stretch of beach and offer a new standard of comfort, style, and service.

Beachside, Tran Phu Blvd. ℃ **058/829-829.** Fax 058/829-629. www.sixsenses.com. 68 units. Low season $216–$278 double/villa, $407 suite villa; high season $245–$320 double/villa, $446 suite villa. AE, DC, MC, V. **Amenities:** 2 restaurants; 2 bars; 2 large outdoor pools w/hot tub; tennis court; health club; fine spa; Jacuzzi; sauna; watersports rentals; cyclo rental ($3/hr.); concierge; tour desk/in-house tour programs (can arrange diving); business center; boutique shopping; 24-hr. room service; massage; laundry; dry cleaning; non-smoking rooms; A/C library w/games and Internet. *In room:* A/C, satellite TV, dataport, minibar, fridge, coffeemaker, hair dryer, safe, nice touches like slippers and umbrella, IDD phone.

## EXPENSIVE

**Sunrise Beach Resort Nha Trang** 🌋   The massive Sunrise Beach Resort was just getting up and running at the time of publication. This grand edifice is all polished marble and white columns and is 10 floors of pomp, a bit like an over-size mafia don's palace, but everything about the place is shiny, new, and grand. Large rooms are clean-lined and tastefully decorated in a soothing off-white, all with great views of oceanside Tran Phu Street and the beach. The second-floor circular pool is surrounded by ostentatious columns, but is a luxurious getaway. Dining options are many, and the rooftop rotunda houses a classy lounge with great views of the big blue beyond.

12 Tran Phu St., Nha Trang. ⓒ **058/920-999.** Fax 058/822-866. www.sunrisenhatrang.com. 121 units. $138–$148 double; $168 deluxe; $178 studio; $198 club room; $298 junior suite; $398–$498 suite. AE, MC, V. **Amenities:** 3 restaurants (Japanese, Chinese, and Continental); 2 bars (1 rooftop); outdoor pool; tennis courts; small health club and spa; tour desk; car rental; business center; shopping arcade; 24-hr. room service; massage; babysitting; laundry; dry cleaning. *In room:* A/C, satellite TV, minibar, fridge, safe, IDD phone.

**VinPearl Resort and Spa** 🌋   "If you build it, they will come," or so the voices speak to some visionaries and entrepreneurs. The verdict is still out on the VinPearl (that is, whether or not they'll come), but this enormous new resort (500 rooms when complete) on Bamboo Island, a 10-minute boat ride from coastal Nha Trang, gets an A for effort. Everything on the island, from con-struction materials to the very water that comes out of the taps, is transported by large tankers—an incredible undertaking. Guests connect via a fleet of sturdy, high-speed crafts that keep a regular schedule (usually every 30 min.). Public spaces, like the double-height marble lobby rotunda, are grand in scale but rather uninteresting, but everything is new and tidy. Rooms are similarly large and comfortable, with all the amenities, but plain. The resort is designed in an arc around the vast acreage of the central pool, reputedly the largest in the region with lots of fun slides, meandering river areas, and bridges, all overlooking a secluded bay. The resort offers lots of daily activities, a top-notch watersport facility, scuba school, and lots of classes, from yoga and aerobics to "crazy cricket" (have to ask what it is when you go) and group trips. Dining is familiar but uninspired. It is just getting up and running—only half of the rooms are fin-ished—and good incentive packages are on offer. VinPearl is so far a favorite with wealthy Vietnamese weekenders and Korean group tours, but time will tell. They're talking about a casino in the future. The Shiseido Spa facility is luxe.

07 Tran Phu–Vinh Nguyen, Nha Trang (connect by boat from the pier on beachside Tran Phu just south of Ana Mandara). ⓒ **058/598-188.** Fax 058/598-199. www.vinpearlresort.com. 450 units. $150–$190 double (depending on view); $220 junior suite; $250–$1,750 presidential suite. AE, MC, V. **Amenities:** 2 restaurants; 3 bars; enormous outdoor pool; tennis courts; health club; Shiseido Spa; Jacuzzi; sauna; extensive watersport rental; children's center; concierge; tour desk; car rental (on mainland); business center; shopping; salon; 24-hr. room service; massage; babysitting; laundry. *In room:* A/C, satellite TV, minibar, fridge, coffeemaker, hair dryer, safe, IDD phone.

**Yasaka Saigon-Nha Trang Hotel** 🌋🌋   On the main strip overlooking Tran Phu and the ocean blue, this 5-year-old Japan/Vietnam joint venture bridges the gap between the ultraluxe resorts and low-end minihotels—a good compromise. All rooms have good, basic amenities, as cozy as your favorite highway hotel chain back home. Upper-level rooms have good views of the sea, some with bal-conies, and the view from corner suites is quite spectacular and worth the upgrade. The lowest standard, the superior, is quite comfortable and large, if bland; the deluxe room, an upgraded version of the superior and on higher floors, is the best bet for atmosphere, comfort, and price. Everything is done in cream or tan carpet, and rooms have flower-print spreads (no shiny polyester). Large, clean tile bathrooms are homey. Service is friendly, there are lots of good dining options on-site (the Red Onion is a local favorite), the rooftop pool is small but inviting, and it's just a short hop across busy Tran Phu Street to the beach. A good breakfast buffet is included.

18 Tran Phu St., Nha Trang. ℂ **058/820-090** or 058/825-227. Fax 058/820-000. www.yasanhatrang.com. 201 units. $98 superior; $118 deluxe; $158 senior deluxe; $178 executive; $198–$350 suite. AE, MC, V. **Amenities:** 4 restaurants; bar; night club; karaoke; liver-shape rooftop pool w/ocean view; roof-top tennis court; small health club; Jacuzzi by pool; sauna; all rentals available; Saigontourist tour desk; car rental; business center; 24-hr. room service; massage; laundry. *In room:* A/C, satellite TV w/in-house movies, minibar, fridge, upper standards w/coffeemakers, safe, IDD phone.

## MODERATE

### Bao Dai Hotel (Bao Dai's Villas) ★★
Built in 1923 as a seaside resort for then-Emperor Bao Dai, the hotel is a cluster of plain colonial-style buildings set high on an oceanside hill south of Nha Trang, so far south that you're in the next town, really. There's an interesting Gothic quality to the place, and one could certainly imagine a king wandering the promontory at night, watching the hotel's lighthouse scan the sea and sky, and worrying about the loss of his kingdom, which was the case. Bao Dai's very room is the master suite and makes for a memorable stay. The less-expensive rooms are musty monk's cells, but the villa-style rooms have high ceilings and large, shuttered windows overlooking the coast—a good bet. The more top-end rooms vary, but all are palatial in size even if they're wanting in amenities (the furniture can't keep up with the space). The bathrooms are nothing special but are sizable and clean, with bathtubs. Some of the buildings have creaky old winding wooden staircases and rooftop access. The restaurant, in its own building, serves buffet breakfast and delicious evening meals for little. The staff can arrange private boat trips.

Cau Da, Vinh Nguyen/Nha Trang. ℂ **058/590-147** or 058/590-148. Fax 058/590-146. www.vngold.com/nt/baodai. 45 units. $25–$50 standard; $70 superior; $80 suite. MC, V. **Amenities:** Restaurant; bicycle/motorbike rental; in-house tour desk for island/snorkeling trips; car rental; souvenir shop; limited room service; laundry; Internet terminal (500 VND/3¢ per min.). *In room:* A/C, satellite TV, minibar, fridge, hair dryer, IDD phone.

### Nha Trang Lodge Hotel ★
The 5-year-old lodge calls itself a "business hotel," and indeed it is a well-run and accommodating 12-story high rise. Average-size rooms are chain-hotel style, with clean carpet, floral bedspreads, and tidy, modern furnishings. The bathrooms are a nice size, with marble finishes. Spring for an oceanview room with balcony (on an upper floor away from street noise, if possible). The staff is professional, and this comfortable seaside address covers all the bases with amenities and services. It's a nice, uninspired, affordable standard here and a bit like the younger, less- accomplished brother of the Yasaka (above). Don't miss a meal in the popular outdoor seafood barbecue area.

42 Tran Phu St., Nha Trang. ℂ **058/810-500** or 058/810-900. Fax 058/828-800. www.nt-lodge.com. 121 units. $58 economy double; $87 deluxe; $110 superior; $169 suite. AE, MC, V. **Amenities:** 2 restaurants; bar; swimming pool; tennis court; small fitness center; sauna; tour desk; car rental; business center; souvenir shops in lobby; salon; 24-hr. room service; massage; laundry; dry cleaning; banquet/meeting rooms. *In room:* A/C, satellite TV, minibar, fridge, IDD phone.

### Que Huong Hotel
A Khanh Hoa Tourism property (a government company; see Vien Dong below), this 3-year-old hotel is a bright, bland, four-story block just across the street from the beach—quiet and convenient. Rooms surround a large central courtyard and pool. All are average size, with clean but worn carpets, warm pastel tones, nice padded wooden furniture, and balconies: It makes an overall good impression. There are signs of wear here and there, like crumbly

tile bathrooms, but suites are huge and are a nice option for families (some even have two bathrooms). This is the land of the tour group, though, and the staff is not versed in individual graces; in the high season, the front desk is run like a busy Manhattan Deli: "Next!" That said, it's affordable, clean, and close to the beach, and the pool is quite lovely. There are capable travel agents in the lobby and nice amenities, like the nice Asian/Continental restaurant, small pool hall, and fun little disco.

60 Tran Phu Blvd., Nha Trang. ⓒ **058/825-047** or 058/827-365. Fax 058/825-344. www.nhatrangtourist. com.vn. 56 units. $50–$60 single/double deluxe; $100 suite. MC, V. **Amenities:** Restaurant; bar/club/karaoke lounge; nice outdoor pool (courtyard); tennis; sauna; billiards; tour desk; car rental; small business center; salon; massage; laundry. *In room:* A/C, satellite TV, minibar, fridge, hair dryer, IDD phone, complimentary water.

**Vien Dong Hotel**    Connected with Hai Yen hotel, another large government tour agency hotel, the Vien Dong is showing her age after years of heavy tour-group use, but it's a relatively comfortable three-star with all the amenities. The large pool is a highlight. The Hai Yen, next door at 42 Tran Phu St. (ⓒ **058/ 810-500**), is a similar standard but *really* showing her age. Smallish rooms have tatty carpet, simple wood furnishing, and sturdy foam mattresses. Bathrooms are clean but bare. A college dorm room comes to mind. Suites are not worth it. There is an inviting outdoor restaurant featuring nightly music and a cultural dance show. You're sure to meet other travelers here, and the general atmosphere is friendly, which helps. It's just one row back from the beach. Staff, though taxed by the many large groups coming and going, is kind and helpful.

1 Tran Hung Dao St., Nha Trang. ⓒ **058/821-606** or 058/821-608. Fax 058/821-912. www.nhatrangtourist. com. 103 units. $30–$40 double; $70 suite. AE, MC, V. **Amenities:** Shared w/Hai Yen Hotel: large restaurant; bar (open-air at poolside and open late); big outdoor pool w/slide; tennis; sauna; all rentals available; tour desk; business center (Internet 500 VND/3¢ per min.); limited room service; massage; laundry; dry cleaning. *In room:* A/C, satellite TV, minibar, fridge, hair dryer, IDD phone.

## INEXPENSIVE

**Dong Phuong Hotel** ⓐ    It's function not form in this motel-style block that typifies the budget accommodation in town (this is one of three properties of the same name and standard in Nha Trang). Rooms are bright but spartan, with spotless tile and not much more than a bed and a good-size, shower-in-room style of bathroom. Some rooms have a good city view, and if you're lucky, you'll be blessed with a classy nude done in painted tile mosaic in the bathroom (the only decoration I could find throughout). Family rooms are large and a good value, and the penthouse room adjoins a huge rooftop area with 365-degree views of town. It's your standard minihotel service, though: just rooms.

103 Nguyen Thien Thuat St., Nha Trang. ⓒ **058/825-986** or 058/828-247. Fax 058/825-986. dongphuong nt@dng.vnn.vn. 30 units. $15–$20 double; $30–$40 deluxe (family). MC, V. **Amenities:** Restaurant; will arrange tours; laundry. *In room:* A/C, satellite TV, fridge, hair dryer, IDD phone.

**Golden Hotel**    It's little more than a surly welcome and room, but with no other expectations than these, you can't go too wrong. Private spaces in this over-size minihotel are in fact quite nice, done with dark wood trim, crown molding, and filigree, and more cozy than basic minihotels in the area. Amenities are bare bones: just good tour services and lobby safety box.

1K–2K Hung Vuong, Nha Trang. ⓒ **058/524-496.** Fax 058/524-498. 31 units. $12–$30. MC, V. **Amenities:** Tour desk; laundry. *In room:* A/C, satellite TV, fridge, IDD phone.

**Phu Quy** ⓐ    This is the granddaddy of Nha Trang's many minihotels. The Phu Quy is an interesting conglomeration of three properties, so rooms vary. (some of the passages between buildings require you to duck through the most unlikely doors too). Ask for something nice, and be sure to bargain a bit. All of the buildings sport small, bright, and very clean rooms with brand-new plastic furniture. The beds are comfortable and bathrooms are small, with shower-in-room facilities. There are no views to speak of, but go for the top floors to escape street noise. Of course, that means climbing lots of stairs. This place has no amenities whatsoever, but breakfasts are good and cheap, and, of course, the hotel will book tickets. This is backpacker central and an ant hill of activity, and that, along with the price, makes it worth a stay. The large, shaded penthouse area has hammocks and lawn chairs, and is a good place to relax (they'll deliver food to you there, too). It is family-run, and owner Mr. Quy is as nice as they come.

54 Hung Vuong St. ℂ 058/810-609 or 058/816-444. Fax 058/812-954. phuquyhotel@dng.vnn.vn. 47 units. $6–$16 double w/fan; $8–$25 w/A/C. V (w/4% commission). **Amenities:** Restaurant; bar; can arrange tours and any rentals; laundry. *In room:* Some A/C, some w/fan, some w/TV and phone.

**Sea View Hotel**    Here's another good, relatively new and clean, oversize minihotel comparable to those above. The Sea View is right in the heart of the busy backpacker area, and you'll have to be on higher floors to garner any actual sea view, but rooms are large, simple, and clean, with tile floors and shower-in-room style baths, some with balconies. Amenities are few, but the hotel is convenient to the busy downtown.

4 Biet Thu St. ℂ 058/524-333. Fax 058/524-335. seaviewhotel@dng.vnn.vn. 60 units. $12–$20 double. V, MC. **Amenities:** Tour desk; laundry. *In room:* A/C, satellite TV, fridge, IDD phone.

## WHERE TO DINE
### EXPENSIVE
**Ana Pavilion** ★★★ ASIAN/CONTINENTAL    Without question the finest dining on this beautiful stretch of coast, the Ana Pavilion is the jewel in the crown of the Ana Mandara resort and serves exquisite food in elegant, natural surroundings. Whether you're on the oceanfront veranda, under a canvas umbrella in the courtyard, or eating by candlelight over the open ocean on the seaside jetty, the location alone is breathtaking. The food is creatively prepared and beautifully presented, and portions are healthy. Chef David Thai serves from an ever-evolving roster of local and seasonal specials, fine East-West fusion, with anything from sandwiches made with bread baked on-site and imported cheese or imported Aussie steaks, to local favorites like banana flower salads and even sushi done to a T for the many Japanese guests. Don't miss the seafood hot pot served in a large, coal-fired crock and brimming with the catch of the day delicately stewed with vegetables. There is an excellent daily lunch buffet, and evening set menus are a great value. This is the best choice for romantic ambience and fine dining.

Tran Phu Blvd. (at the Ana Mandara Resort). ℂ **058/829-829**. Main courses $7–$19; prix-fixe menus $15–$22. AE, MC, V. Daily 6am–11pm.

### MODERATE
**La Bella Napoli** ★★ ITALIAN    It's all about the cheese here, and I'm talking homemade mozzarella served atop a fine thin-crust pizza done in a wood-fire oven with any topping you can imagine. Plus, you'll get great views of the beach. What else is there to say? Bring some friends, choose a nice wine, and enjoy. It's not just pizza, either, but a roster of specials from northern Italy. The effusive Italian proprietor always has some good daily specials and will keep you laughing with her good stories. Pizza by the South China Sea, anyone? Why not?

Tran Phu St. (beachside, across from the Nha Trang Lodge). ℂ **058/829-621**. Main courses $4.35–$8. No credit cards. Daily 8:30am–10pm.

**Ngoc Suong** ★★ SEAFOOD    Nha Trang has dozens of good seafood restaurants, but this one leads the pack. Whether in the very pleasant thatched outdoor pavilion or the vaguely nautical, softly lit interior, it's "seafood as you like it" served by a helpful, friendly staff. Whole fish and crustaceans can be chosen by pointing in the large tank and smiling greedily; the day's catch, including shrimp and crab, is ordered by the pound, grilled, fried, or boiled with basic spices like tamarind or pepper and lemon. The oysters, if they have them, are small but succulent. The name of the restaurant refers to a delicate marinated whitefish salad, one of the specialties and a great appetizer. This is a popular local and expat favorite.

96A Tran Phu (south of the town center at beachside) ✆ 058/827-030. Main courses 20,000 VND–240,000 VND ($1.35–$16). No credit cards. Daily 10am–midnight.

**Nha Trang Sailing Club** ★ VIETNAMESE/CONTINENTAL    Stop by this oceanside open-air bar/restaurant for a real Western breakfast, if nothing else. A good bet is the pancakes, not greasy (as usual) and served with real butter. There are other Western standbys, such as macaroni and cheese and hamburgers (tasty, if not authentic), as well as the usual Nha Trang seafood selections. The setting, in a large hut just off the beach, can't be beat, and there are now different "stations" for dining here, including good Japanese eats, an Italian menu, and even an Indian menu. You can lounge on the beach and buy or swap a book from the well-stocked rack, and book a boat tour or a day of scuba with Rainbow Divers. The bar swings at night.

72–74 Tran Phu St. ✆ 058/826-528. Main courses 30,000 VND–125,000 VND ($2–$8.35). No credit cards. Daily 7am–11pm. Bar open until 2am.

**Nha Trang Seafood** ★★ SEAFOOD/VIETNAMESE    Popular with Japanese groups (or local fat cats out to impress their mistresses), Nha Trang Seafood serves it up fresh and delicious as you like it: grilled, steamed, or fried. Viet-style preparation is sweet, sour and/or spicy; grilled items are good and the shrimp in coconut, clay-pot dishes, and hot pots are affordable and delicious. The atmosphere is plain, best by candlelight on the second floor when the place is crowded (dull by the light of day). The staff is fun-loving and friendly.

46 Nguyen Thi Minh Khai St. ✆ 058/822-664. Main course 25,000 VND–200,000 VND ($1.65–$13). No credit cards. Daily 9:30am–10pm.

## INEXPENSIVE

**Banana Split** ★ VIETNAMESE/WESTERN    Banana Split is traveler central, a good place to come for a snack and to meet fellow wanderers. This popular little storefront serves up good treats from home, like good burgers, soups, and sandwiches, for next to nothing. The owners and staff are very friendly, the list of fruit shakes is as long as a sunny beachside day, and the ice cream is aces. Go for the gargantuan banana split if you dare.

58 Quang Trung St. ✆ 058/829-115. Main courses 66¢–$4. No credit cards. Daily 7am–11pm.

**Lac Canh** ★★ CHINESE/VIETNAMESE    Two words: grilled shrimp. The Chinese-influenced Vietnamese cuisine here is all about ingredients, so go for the basics: fresh seafood in a light marinade that you grill yourself on a rustic, cast-iron brazier. The place is packed with locals and tourists. The new location is a little more airy, but try to sit outdoors because the atmosphere is smoky. This is definitely the local "greasy spoon," and it makes for a fun evening.

11 Hang Ca St. ✆ 058/821-391. Main courses $1.25–$7.95. No credit cards. Daily 7am–11pm.

**Truc Linh Restaurant** ⭐ VIETNAMESE    An eclectic menu here has anything from the backpacker standbys of fried rice and noodles to sirloin steak and T-bone: It kind of runs the gamut. There's a seafood smorgasboard out front from which you can choose your own jumbo shrimp, crab, squid, or fresh fish of the day and then have it weighed and cooked to your taste. It's got fondue and clay-pot specials, barbecued beef on clay tile, and rice-paper spring rolls with shrimp that are delicious.

21 Biet Thu St. ☎ **058/820-089** or 058/820-1259. Main courses 80¢–$10. Daily 6am–11pm.

## WHAT TO SEE & DO

**Alexandre Yersin Museum** ⭐⭐    Here you can get an inkling of the work of one of Vietnam's greatest heroes. Swiss doctor Yersin founded Dalat, isolated a plague-causing bacteria, and researched agricultural methods and meteorological forecasting, all to the great benefit of the Vietnamese. He founded the institute in 1895. On display are his desk, overflowing library, and scientific instruments.

In the Pasteur Institute, 10 Tran Phu St. ☎ **058/822-355.** Admission 26,000 VND ($1.75). Mon–Sat 8–11am and 2–4:30pm.

**Long Son Pagoda** ⭐    The main attraction at this 1930s pagoda is the huge white Buddha on the hillside behind, the symbol of Nha Trang. Around the base of the Buddha are portraits of monks who immolated themselves to protest against the corrupt Diem regime. After climbing the numerous flights of stairs, you'll also be rewarded with a bird's-eye view of Nha Trang.

Thai Nguyen St. Daily 8am–5pm.

**Po Ngar Cham Towers** ⭐    Starting in the 8th century, the Cham people, an early Hindu empire in Central Vietnam (see "Who Are the Cham," p. 330), built the Po Ngar Cham temple complex to honor Yang Ino Po Ngar, mother of the kingdom. Set on the site of an earlier wooden temple burned by the Javanese in A.D. 774, there were originally 10 structures here and just four remain. The main tower, or Po Ngar Kalan, is one of the tallest Cham structures ever built. Its square tower and three-story cone roof are exemplary of Cham style. It has more remaining structural integrity than many sites, giving you a good idea of how it might have looked in all its glory. In the vestibule can be seen two pillars of carved epitaphs of Cham kings, and in the sanctuary there are two original carved doors. The statue inside is of the goddess Bharagati, aka Po Ngar, on her lotus throne. It was carved in 1050. The Po Ngar temples are still in use by local Buddhists, and the altars and smoking incense add to the intrigue of the architecture. Detracting from the whole experience are kitsch stands and lots of hawkers.

2km (1¼ miles) out of the city center at 2 Thang 4, at the end of Xom Bong Bridge. Admission 10,000 VND (65¢). Daily 7:30am–5pm.

## SPORTS & OUTDOOR ACTIVITIES

**Diving** is big in Nha Trang, in season (Mar–Sept). There are a number of professionally run operations; whether you're a beginner or an expert, make your choice based on safety more than anything. **Rainbow Divers** has taken advertising to the level of pollution in Nha Trang, with seemingly every storefront claiming a connection, but whatever your belief is in truth in advertising, these guys are some of the best in town and you can book anywhere: Try the **Nha Trang Sailing Club** (see "Where to Dine," above; ☎ **058/826-528** or ☎ 058/829-946; www.divevietnam.com). For a guaranteed safe and fun time, try the folks at **Octopus Diving** (62 Tran Phu St.; ☎ **058/810-629;** octopusdiving club@yahoo.com), where the expert, mostly expat staff can devise dives for any and all (you can also contact them through the **Ana Mandara**). **Vietnam Explorer** (02 Tran Quang Khai; C **058/524-490**) is another good outfit.

Popular are the 1-day **boat cruises** to some of Nha Trang's 20 surrounding islands. For years, Nha Trang was famed for rowdy trips that were more like daytime raves. **Hahn's Green Hat Boat Tour** (2C Biet Thu St.; C **058/824-494**) is the old favorite, a remnant of the old "Mama Hahn" trips (Mama Hahn was famous for saying, "Smoke and drink! Don't be lazy!") but the trips have toned down significantly. **Mama Linh** (C **058/826-693**) offers similar tours, as do **Sinh Café** and **TM Brothers** (see "Visitor Information & Tours," at the beginning of this section). The going rate is $7 per day and includes 9am hotel pickup and afternoon drop-off. It's a mellow day of motoring through some lovely bays to three different islands, and you're guaranteed some snorkeling and a big feast for lunch; beer and drinks are available all day (at one point, you can swim out to a floating bar for complimentary wine) and there's a great spread of fruit in the afternoon. The tour terminates at a fish farm and a small harbor where you can rent a traditional bamboo-basket boat to paddle about. Just about everyone in town will want to book you on one of these tours, so ask at any hotel front desk and be sure to nail down all specifics (meals, transport included, etc.).

For **sailing,** contact the **Nha Trang Sailing Club** (C **058/826-528**) or the **Ana Mandara** (C **058/829-829**). Go for a Hobie Cat if it's available and hire a captain if you are not experienced; the strong ocean breezes and choppy waters make for a memorable sail. Runabouts and jet skis are also available.

There is also the popular **Thapba Mud Bath and Hotspring Resort** just outside town. Hire a car, or ask at any front desk to call them directly at C **058/ 834-939.**

## NHA TRANG AFTER DARK

Nha Trang has a few lively beachfront bars where tourists congregate to swap stories. The **Nha Trang Sailing Club,** at 72–74 Tran Phu St. across from the Hai Yen Hotel, has open-air bamboo huts and a dance scene on some nights until late (past midnight it gets pretty seedy). **Crazy Kim Bar,** at 19 Biet Thu St. in the backpacker area (C **058/816-072**), is open late and asks customers to "Be hot. Be cool. Be crazy. Just be." There are many versions of that walking around this place, and it's popular with the diving crowd and the few expats in town. **Guava** is next door to Kim's at 17 Biet Thu and is a similar scene.

## 11 Dalat

Known as "Le Petit Paris" by the early builders and residents of this hillside resort town, Dalat is still considered a kind of luxury retreat for city dwellers and tourists tired out from trudging along sultry coastal Vietnam. In Dalat you can play golf on one of the finest courses in Indochina, visit beautiful temples, and enjoy the town's honeymoon atmosphere and delightfully hokey tourist sites.

At 1,500m (4,920 ft.), Dalat is mercifully cool year-round—there's no need for air-conditioning here—and is a unique blend of pastoral hillside Vietnam and European alpine resort. Alexander Yersin, the Swiss geologist who first traipsed across this pass, established the town in 1897 as a resort for French commanders weary of the Vietnamese Tropics. In and around town are still scattered the relics of colonial mansions, as well as some serene pagodas in a lovely natural setting; you've escaped from big-city Vietnam for real. A few ethnic minorities, including the Lat and the Koho, live in and around the picturesque hills surrounding Dalat, and you can visit their small villages.

Dalat is a top resort destination for Vietnamese couples getting married or honeymooning. If the lunar astrological signs are particularly good, it's not unusual to see 10 or so wedding parties in a single day. Many of the local scenic spots, like the Valley of Love and Lake of Sighs, pander to the giddy couples. The waterfalls are swarming with vendors, costumed "bears," and "cowboys" complete with sad-looking horses and fake pistols. A carnival air prevails. It's tacky, but it's one of those "so bad that it's good" kind of tacky that's kind of fun.

## GETTING THERE

**BY PLANE**   The only direct flights to Dalat are from Ho Chi Minh City (flight time: 50 min). In Dalat, call to confirm your ticket, or direct inquiries to Vietnam Airlines at ℂ **063/822-895.** A taxi from the airport to the city is $3 and takes about 30 minutes.

**BY BUS/CAR**   Dalat is the first stop on the "open-tour" bus from Ho Chi Minh City. Buses from both north and south first stop at Phan Rang, an old Cham temple site, where the road turns inland for the hills of Dalat. The ride up is winding and spectacular, at one point following hairpin after hairpin underneath a large hydroelectric project. From Nha Trang (to the north) or Ho Chi Minh City (to the south), it is a 7-hour trip and costs $5 at any tourist cafe.

Hire a private car for the trip and save about an hour.

## VISITOR INFORMATION & TOURS

**Phat Tire Ventures** (73 Truong Cong Dinh; ℂ **063/823-104;** fax 063/829-422; www.phattireventures.com), offers a unique eco-tourist option in Dalat. Contact Brian and Kim (young U.S. expats), who can arrange anything from day treks to jungle expeditions, mountain biking (they have a stable of top-quality bikes and hold daily clinics), rock climbing, repelling, or canyoning. Daily rates for most activities start at $19 and include lunch, transport, and a knowledgeable guide. Safety and environmental stewardship are their trademark. They also book classic tours through their affiliate, **Dalat Tours.**

### BUDGET TOURS
- **Sinh Café** (4A Bui Thi Xuan St.; ℂ **063/822-663**), has an information and tour office adjacent to Trung Cang, the company's budget accommodation (see "Where to Stay," below).
- **TM Brothers** (02 Nguyen Chi Thanh St.; ℂ **063/828-282**), can book standard budget tours for you from its office on "cafe street."
- **An Phu Tourist Co.** (07 Hai Thuong St.; ℂ **063/823-631**) is here, too.

## GETTING AROUND

There are no cyclos in Dalat, but walking is very pleasant in the cool air. You can catch most of the city sites, like the market and the lake, **on foot.** On weekends, the busy streets of the central city are closed to motorbike and auto traffic.

For taxis in town, try **Dalat Taxi** at ℂ **063/830-830.** Dalat is a good place to rent a **motorbike,** cheapest with the street-side places on Nguyen Thi Minh Khai (between the market and the lake), for about $3 per day ($4–$5 from hotels and cafes). Be sure to check the brakes, and be sure the horn is working because you should beep-beep all the way, especially when passing or on curves. The hillside, windy roads will have you feeling like you're "born to be wild," if you can forget that you're riding the motorcycle equivalent of a hair dryer. This is a good, adventurous way to get to all the funky sites outside the city.

Another option is to get a **motorbike with a driver** for the day (about $1–$2 per hr., or fix a rate for the day and the destinations), or you can **rent a car** with a driver (about $25). Because most sites are outside city limits, it makes sense to take a **half- or full-day tour** through your hotel or a **tourist cafe.**

---

## FAST FACTS: Dalat

*Banks/Currency Exchange*  Industrial & Commercial Bank (46 Hoa Binh St.; ✆ 063/822-495) offers the best rate, but most hotels offer comparable exchange services for a small fee. There is no ATM service in Dalat.

*Internet/E-mail*  The most accessible Internet cafe in town is on the hill that overlooks the main market street—**Viet Hung Internet Café** (7 Nguyen Chi Thanh; ✆ 063/835-737). It charges VND 5,000 (35¢) per hour, but there are many scattered about.

*Post Office/Mail*  The main office is located at 14 Tran Phu St., across from the Novotel, and is open Monday to Saturday from 6:30am to 9:30pm.

*Telephone*  The area code for Dalat is 63.

---

## WHERE TO STAY

With its long history as a popular resort area for both foreigners and Viet-namese, Dalat offers some choice lodging. There are plenty of minihotels, but they're not of the quality you might find in Hanoi, for example. You'll note that no Dalat hotel has air-conditioning; with the year-round temperate weather, none is needed. Keep an eye on new developments in the hills outside the city center. Efforts are underway to restore and preserve the many '50s era French colonial homes, and many are converting to guesthouses. **Villa 28** (28 Tran Hung Dao; ✆ 063/822-764) is a very basic guesthouse but a harbinger of things to come.

### VERY EXPENSIVE

**Sofitel Dalat Palace** ✫✫✫    Built in 1922 as the address of choice for French colonists on holiday and once the home of Emperor Bau Dai, this recently ren-ovated beauty, with its understated old-world opulence, is one of the finest five-star choices in all of Indochina. From the huge fireplace and mosaic floor in the lobby to the hanging tapestries, 500 oil reproductions of classic European art, and thick swag curtains, it's a French country chateau with a Southeast Asian colonial flair. The large rooms, with glossy original wood floors, are finished with fine fabrics and throw rugs, and all beds are crowned with an ornate wooden housing for a mosquito net (purely for decoration). The bathrooms fea-ture hand-painted tiles and large, claw-foot bathtubs with antique-style fixtures. Genuine antique French clocks and working reproduction telephones complete the picture, yet nothing feels overdone. Every room has a foyer and a fireplace. Lakeview rooms open to a huge shared veranda with deck chairs. The high, high ceilings and huge corridors with hanging lamps contribute to the palatial feel-ing. Service is superb. All in all, this is an exquisite place that should not be missed. The in-house dining at Le Rabelais is unrivaled (see "Where to Dine," below). The whole place is the brainchild of the late Larry Hillblom, the enig-matic American entrepreneur and co-owner of DHL who invested heavily in the property out of love and generosity as much as anything. He is still remembered and revered by the many who knew him; Larry's Bar, a great little grotto establishment with a pool table, darts, and good pub grub, does his memory proud.

12 Tran Phu St., Dalat. ℂ 063/825-444. Fax 063/825-666. accorhotels.com/asia. 43 units. $169–$214 double; $319–$414 suite. Extra bed $40. Ask about discounts and specials. AE, DC, MC, V. **Amenities:** 2 restaurants; 3 bars; golf (can arrange); tennis; all rentals available; kids' playroom/outdoor playground; concierge; tour desk; business center; shopping boutique; limited room service; laundry; dry cleaning; horseback riding/carriage rental; hotel history corner. *In room:* Satellite TV, minibar, fridge, hair dryer, safe, IDD phone.

## EXPENSIVE

### Novotel Dalat Hotel ✷✷
This is the scaled-down companion hotel to the Sofitel Palace. It was renovated in 1997 from a 1932 building that was originally the Du Parc hotel, and a lovely job was done of it. The lobby has a unique wrought-iron lift. The smallish rooms have attractive historic touches: glossy wood floors, tastefully understated wood furniture, and molded high ceilings. A superior room (the lowest standard) is a bit cramped and not the greatest value ($119), but deluxe rooms are clean, compact, and classy and worth the upgrade ($139). Everything is tidy and convenient, with nice local artwork throughout and homey warmth in tone and atmosphere. The bathrooms are a nice size, efficient, and spotless, with sleek granite and dark wooden trim. The staff is businesslike and friendly, and the Novotel shares fine amenities with neighboring Dalat Palace (above).

7 Tran Phu St., Dalat. ℂ 800/221-4542 or 063/825-777. Fax 063/825-888. www.accorhotels-asia.com. 144 units $119–$139 double; $189 suite. Discounts and specials are common. AE, MC, V. **Amenities:** 2 restaurants; 3 bars; golf (can arrange); tennis; all rentals available; concierge; tour desk; business center; shopping. *In room:* Satellite TV, minibar, fridge, coffeemaker, safe, IDD phone.

## MODERATE

### Empress Hotel ✷✷
This Hong Kong/Vietnamese joint venture is a good, upscale but affordable oasis just a stone's throw from the lake and close to all the action. Tucked into the side of a hill, the hotel has rooms that form a courtyard, with the steep gable of a European lodge-style reception and restaurant on one side and two floors of rooms all facing the courtyard on the other. Comfortable rooms have dark wood walls, terra-cotta tile floors, rattan furniture, good indirect lighting, nice local artwork, and elegant cotton and silk bedspreads. Bathrooms are large, with granite counters and nice fixtures, some with bathtubs and others with an open arrangement with a combined shower/toilet area (like a guesthouse, but spotless). The suites are large and luxe, with a sunken tub and large sitting area, but for my money, I'll take a deluxe room ($80), which is a larger version of a standard and has views of the stone courtyard and lake below. There's a nice restaurant serving good local and Continental fare; if the staff is slightly cool, it's almost refreshingly real of them. They also have a great old Mercedes for rental or airport transfers. Go for a room on the second floor (1st-floor rooms are getting a bit musty).

5 Nguyen Thai Hoc St., Dalat. ℂ 063/833-888. Fax 063/829-399. empress@hcm.vnn.vn. $60–$80 double (superior/deluxe); $110–$198 suite. AE, MC, V. **Amenities:** Restaurant; tour desk; car rental (classic Mercedes to airport for $16); laundry; dry cleaning. *In room:* Satellite TV w/in-house movies, minibar, fridge, hair dryer, safe, IDD phone.

### Golf III Hotel ✷
The Golf is a three-star chain hotel and a good choice in Dalat (local Golf I and II are low-end versions). Large rooms are upholstered in purple with gawdy carved wood details. Some rooms are a bit frayed around the edges, but they're perfectly clean and comfortable. It's worth springing for a deluxe room ($50), a Vietnamese honeymooner favorite, with parquet floors rather than carpet and larger bathrooms with big sunken tubs. The constant

stream of Vietnamese wedding parties in and out lends a welcome festive air to the place, and this hotel is at its best when trying to be a little more than it is; blooming bonsais, overstuffed chairs, and a glitzy sheen over the lobby area stand testament. Golf III is right in the center of the busy market area, but set back far enough from the road that rooms are relatively quiet. Amenities are basic, like a rooftop steam, sauna, and massage area (a little seedy), and the lobby restaurant which serves a fine breakfast. As the name betrays, the Golf properties all have an arrangement with the local course at a good rate. The staff is happy you came.

4 Nguyen Thi Minh Khai St. (near the market). © **063/826-042** or 063/826-049. Fax 063/830-396. 78 units. $45–$60 double; $70–$100 suite. AE, MC, V. **Amenities:** Restaurant; bar; golf; sauna; steam; tour desk; small business center; limited room service; massage; laundry. *In room:* Satellite TV, minibar, fridge, safety box in higher standard rooms, IDD phone.

## INEXPENSIVE

**Hotel Dai Loi (Fortune Hotel)** ★★    If you want value for money, look no further. It's affordable, and even the lowest-priced rooms are terrific, with high ceilings, fresh paint, comfortable and firm mattresses, marble floors, new furnishings, and nicely tiled bathrooms. Most other places in this category have musty smells and dingy decor, but not the Fortune. The place is spotless, the location is far enough from the center of town for quiet yet close enough for access, and the price is right—most doubles are $14 to $15; the $25 rooms have two double beds and nice, large bathtubs, and most have balconies. The second-floor restaurant is open and inviting. The small lobby bar has white walls and white plastic chairs, and could be airlifted to a museum as a "minimalist installation," but there is nice black-and-white tile throughout to give it a nice, crisp look. The staff members speak little English but are quite helpful.

3A Bui Thi Xuan. © **063/837-333.** 39 units. $14–$25 double. AE, MC, V. **Amenities:** Restaurant; bar; all rentals available; laundry. *In room:* TV, minibar, fridge, IDD phone.

**Trung Cang Hotel** ★★    The Sinh Café expands its monopoly on budget traveler amenities here with this new, centrally located little gem. Rooms have clean tile floors and basic amenities; and any lack of decoration is compensated for by clean, airy rooms for next to nothing, though some even have nice filigreed ceilings and cool, subdued lighting. Time will tell with this place, but get there while it's new, ask to see a room, and do a bit of haggling. This is a good budget option and the folks at Sinh Café are always accommodating when arranging tours or getting you around town. All room rates include breakfast.

4A Bui Thi Xuan St. © **063/822-663.** 27 units. $10–$20. MC, V. **Amenities:** Restaurant; rentals available; tour desk; laundry service. *In room:* Satellite TV, minibar, fridge, IDD phone.

## WHERE TO DINE

Dalat dining is pretty basic. Meals are simply prepared and heavily influenced by Chinese cuisine. The huge variety of local ingredients, particularly fruit and vegetables, makes for freshly tasting food. Many small restaurants are located at Phan Dinh Phung Street, and some of the best dining, according to locals, is at the many stalls in the central market. Do try the artichoke tea and strawberry jam, two local specialties (and good souvenirs to take home from the market).

**Café de la Poste** ★★ CONTINENTAL    This cozy, colonial gem, part of the Dalat Palace Hotel, is located in an open, airy corner building across from the post office (go figure). It's more a restaurant than cafe, really, and has a great selection of light choices, sandwiches, and desserts on top of hearty entrees like spare ribs, T-bone steak, and fresh pasta. The salads are big and fresh, and they have a great French onion soup. Don't miss the cheesecake for dessert. It's pricey for Dalat, but it's worth it.

12 Tran Phu St. © 063/825-444. Main courses $4–$11. MC, V. Daily 6am–10pm.

**Dalat House** ✿ ASIAN/WESTERN   It's out of the town center, so you'll have to take a cab, but that somehow adds to the experience of this dolled-up new Western restaurant, a place where local businessman go to impress clients. Did someone hear the theme to *The Godfather?* It's a mix of Asian and Western cuisine served on fine white China at candlelit, linen-draped tables. The best local choices are the good stews that take the chill out of a cool Dalat evening: hot-pot dishes great for sharing, or baked clay-pot specials. Western meals are all country-club standbys: meat and potatoes, fish fillet, and pasta. For their steaks, a house specialty, guests have a choice of imported beef or locally grown at half the price; benefit from my experience and pay the extra for imported. Dessert is crème caramel, apple tart, or soufflé.

34 Nguyen Du (about 4 km/2½ miles east of town, past the railway station). © 063/811-577. Main courses 50,000 VND–350,000 VND ($3.35–$23). No credit cards. Daily 6am–10pm.

**Le Rabelais** ✿✿ FRENCH   Dining at Le Rabelais is an experience of genuine fine-dining French colonial style. Prices are high for this region, but so is the standard of preparation and service. The Sofitel people work closely with local organic farms, and all dishes are prepared with the finest fresh produce. In the tradition of the original 1922 Langbian Palace Hotel, Le Rabelais serves from a limited menu, which ensures that everything is done just right. Beginning with a tantalizing *amuse bouche,* a nouveau cuisine treat that changes nightly, dinner is a slow progression of delicious courses. I had rich lobster bisque and a beef sirloin, succulent and satisfying in a rich, savory pepper sauce. The wine list is long and, unique in the region, the staff knows the right suggestions for any given meal; in fact, the staff here is uniquely efficient and professional, attentive without either fawning or hovering and meticulous with every detail, making for a fluid, casual meal. For dessert, try the passion-and-raspberry trifles with sautern jelly. It's a great place to take that special someone for an evening of candlelit opulence. Follow up with coffee or after-dinner drinks and cigars down in the very atmospheric Larry's Bar.

12 Tran Phu St. (adjoining the lobby of the Sofitel Dalat Palace Hotel). © 063/825-444. Evening set menu $18–$35. MC, V. Daily 6am–10pm.

**Long Hoa** ✿✿ VIETNAMESE/CONTINENTAL   On a busy street just opposite the hilltop cinema, this small bistro has checkered tablecloths and a cozy atmosphere that attract passersby. The owner, a vivacious, self-taught linguist, is very welcoming and will walk you through any menu choices, travel recommendations, or local lore in the language of your choice. You'll feel like a regular, or will become one, even if you're here for only a few days. The menu is grouped by ingredients (chicken, beef, fish, etc.), and Long Hua has any kind of sauté or steamed dish you can imagine, as well as a variety of hot pots and soups for those cold Dalat nights. It's inexpensive, excellent local fare with a French flare here; I had a delicious meal of barbecued deer with french fries. Don't miss the homemade yogurt, a real treat.

6 Duong 3 Thang 2 (Duy Tan). © 063/822-934. Main courses $1–$4. No credit cards. Daily 10:30am–9:30pm.

**Lyla Hotel and Restaurant de Famille** ✿ VIETNAMESE/CONTINENTAL   It's real family dining, heavy on good French, in a closed, quiet dining room along Dalat's busy cafe street. This is a long-time expat favorite and everything is good. I had a "real" continental meal of French onion soup (absolutely delicious), french fries with mayonnaise and a nicoise salad (with French dressing, of course)—great steaks, pasta, and seafood too. A very friendly family.

18A Nguyen Chi Thanh. © 063/834-540. Main courses 19,000 VND–59,000 VND ($1.25–$3.95). V, MC. Daily 7am–10pm.

**Ngoc Hai Restaurant** ✿ VIETNAMESE/CHINESE   Just down the street from the market, this local spot is two floors of bright, clean, indoor/outdoor dining. It's nothing spectacular, but the staff at Ngoc Hai is friendly and the menu is ambitious; ask for anything, and you'll hear hearty replies of, "Have. Have." Selections from the Western end of the spectrum include roasted chicken with potatoes and a mock-up of British fish and chips, but go for the Chinese-influenced Vietnamese stir-fries, one-dish meals, and soups. Reasonable set menus vary daily and are a good bet. Good veggie selections, too.

6 Nguyen Thi Minh Khai St. © 063/825-252. Main courses $2–$5.35; set menus $3.35–$8. Daily 9am–10pm.

**V Café** ✿✿ *Finds* CONTINENTAL   It's good for the budget and good for the tummy here at homey V Café. Tell me where you can sit at a table with linen and candlelight and enjoy a great burger for a buck? Also, you'll find the only burritos in town here. The owner, V, and her husband, Michael, a long-time expat, serve up hospitality smothered in gravy and will welcome you as their own. With only a short time in business, the place is full of travelers and expats, but there's room for one more. Pull up a chair!

1/1 Bui Thi Xuan St. (across from Sinh Café). © 063/837-576. Main courses 10,000 VND–40,000 VND (65¢–$2.65). No credit cards. Daily 8:30am–10:00pm.

## CAFES
Nguyen Chi Thanh Street is lined with cafes, one indistinguishable from another in many ways. Each building hangs over the main market street and all serve ice cream, tea, and beer to oogling couples. Try **Coffee Artista** (© 063/821-749), at 9 Nguyen Chi Thanh St., for some good ice cream, classic rock, and friendly folks. Just next door the **Viethung Internet Café** (© 063/835-737) has laid-back porch seating.

For a peek into the local arts scene, see if you can find Mr. **MPK** (you have to ask him what it means). He makes his home at the back of a little villa guesthouse overlooking a beautiful valley (Khach San Van Khanh; 11/8 Khoi Nghia Bac Son, up in the hills near the Bao Dai Palace II). MPK is an inspired photographer, best when he is up close to his subject. He shoots with an old rusty camera and turns the lens backwards, shooting through a rough-hewn tube to get incredible macro close-ups. Have a coffee, peruse his photos, and buy something (if he's selling). A unique visit. Also see his works at V Café (see above).

## WHAT TO SEE & DO
Much of what there is to see in Dalat are natural sites: lakes, waterfalls, and dams dominate the tourist trail. Things are spread over quite some distance, so consider booking a tour or renting your own car or motorbike.

Remember to avoid visiting pagodas between 11:30am and 2pm, when nuns and monks will be having their lunch. You might disturb them and also miss a valuable opportunity for a chat. It is also correct to leave a thousand VND or two in the donation box near the altar.

**Bao Dai's Palace** ✿   Completed in 1938, this monument to bad taste provided Bao Dai, Vietnam's last emperor, with a place of rest and respite with his family. It has never been restored and, indeed, looks veritably untouched since the emperor's ousting and hasty exile; on a busy weekend in high season, you might get a rush by imagining you're there to liberate the place and are part of the looting masses—that's not hard to imagine, with the crowds ignoring any velvet ropes and posing for pictures in the aging velvet furniture. You'll be asked to go in stocking feet or wear loose shoe covers, which make it fun for sliding around the home's 26 rooms, including Bao Dai's office and the bedrooms of the royal family. You can still see the grease stains on Bao Dai's hammock pillow and the ancient steam bath in which he soaked. The explanations are in English, and most concern Bao Dai's family. There is pathos in reading them and piecing together the mundane fate of the former royals: This prince has a "technical" job, while that one is a manager for an insurance company. There are three other Bao Dai palaces in town, the Sofitel Dalat Palace Hotel among them, but this is the most choice.

South of Xuan Huong Lake and up the hill behind "Crazy House." Admission 5,000 VND (35¢). Daily 7am–8pm.

**Dalat Market (Cho Da Lat)** ★★★   Huge, crowded, and stuffed with produce of all varieties, this is the top stroll-through destination in Dalat. Here's where you can see all the local specialties—and even have a try! Some of the vendors will be happy to give you a sample of some local wine or a few candied strawberries. Dalat in general is low on the hassling tourist touts that plague the big towns and tourist sites in Vietnam, and entreaties from the merchants are friendly; you can walk around without too much hassle here because the locals are doing all the shopping.

Central Dalat.

**Dalat Railway Station (Cremaillaire Railway)**   Built in 1943, the Dalat station offers an atmospheric slice of Dalat's colonial history. You can see an authentic old wood-burning steamer train on the tracks to the rear, and stroll around inside looking at the iron-grilled ticket windows, empty now. Although the steamer train no longer makes tourist runs, a newer Japanese train makes a trip to Trai Mat Street and the Linh Phuoc pagoda (below). A ride costs $5 and leaves when full.

Near Xuan Huong Lake, off Nguyen Trai St. Daily 8am–5pm.

**The French Quarter** ★★   The whole town has the look and feel of a French replica, but on the ridge-running road, Tran Hung Dao, don't miss the derelict shells of the many French colonial summer homes once populated and popular; it's where the connected and successful came to escape the Saigon heat in summer. Most are owned by the folks at Sofitel, and who's to say what will become of them in years to come, but they are a beautiful and eerie reminder of the recent colonial past. The road itself, one you'll take to many of the sites outside of town, offers panoramic views.

Best visited by motorbike or in a car w/driver. Follow Tran Hung Dao Rd. a few kilometers southeast from town. Some of the houses are on private roads at the end of promontories.

**Hang Nga Guest House and Art Gallery** ★★   Otherwise known as the "Crazy House," this Gaudi-meets-Sesame Street theme park is one not to miss. It's a wild mass of wood and wire fashioned into the shape of a giant tree house and smoothed over in concrete. It sounds simple, but there's a vision to this chaos; just ask the eccentric owner/proprietor and chief architect, Ms. Dang Viet Nga. Daughter of aristocracy, Ms. Nga is well heeled after early schooling in China and has a degree in architecture from university in Moscow. In Dalat she has been inspired to undertake this shrine to the curved line, what she calls an essential mingling of nature and people. The locals deem her eccentric for some reason, but she's just misunderstood; don't pass up any opportunity to have a chat with the architect herself. On a visit here, you'll follow a helpful guide and are sure to have fun clambering around the concrete ladders, tunnels, and hollowed-out nooks, and in the unique "theme" rooms of this huge fantasy tree trunk. It's an actual guesthouse, too. There's a small family shrine in a large common area at the back. It all spoke to me about Vietnam's refreshingly lax zoning laws, but to many it's an interesting, evolving piece of pop art. This is a fun visit.

3 Huynh Thuc Khang St. © **063/822-070**. Admission 6,000 VND (40¢). Daily 7am–7pm.

**Lake of Sighs (Ho Than Tho)** ⭐ This lake has such romantic connotations for the Vietnamese that you would think it was created by a fairy godmother rather than French dam work. Legend has it that a 15-year-old girl named Thuy drowned herself after her boyfriend of the same age, Tam, fell in love with another. Her gravestone still exists on the side of the lake, marked with the incense and flowers left by other similarly heart-broken souls, even though the name on the headstone reads "Thao," not "Thuy." The place is crammed with honeymooners in paddleboats and motorboats.

Northeast of town, along Ho Xuan Huong Rd. Admission 5,000 VND (35¢). Daily 7am–5pm.

**Lam Ty Ni Pagoda: Home of Thay Vien Thuc, "The Crazy Monk"** A visit with the man is a highlight for some and is just plain creepy for others. The temple itself is nothing special, though the immaculate garden in the back is nice; the attraction here is the large studio of Mr. Thuc, a Vietnamese Zen practitioner who seems to be painting, drawing, and scribbling his way to nirvana. It's a unique glimpse into the inner sanctum of a true eccentric, and though locals say that he's not a real monk, just a painter and salesman, it's an interesting visit. A polyglot afflicted with graphophilia perhaps (a language genius who can't stop drawing), Mr. Thuc has a message of peace and connectedness characteristic of the Zen sect, and he conveys that message in Vietnamese, Chinese, French, English, Japanese, German, and Swedish as he continually cranks out poems with small stylized drawings when you talk with him. Your part in the plan is that for $1 (bargain if you will), he'll scribble an original before your eyes and pose for a photo; he has tentative plans to visit everyone who buys one of his paintings and bring us all together. Hmm. You're free to ask him questions, browse his stacks of finished works in the studio, and sign the guest book. This is a standard stop on city/country tours.

2 Thien My. © **063/822-775**. Admission free, but most feel obliged (or compelled) to buy one of his paintings.

**Linh Phuoc Pagoda** ⭐ Here is another example of one of Vietnam's fantasyland glass and ceramic mosaic structures. Refurbished in 1996, this modern temple features a huge golden Buddha in the main hall, and three floors of walls and ceilings painted with fanciful murals. Go to the top floor for the eye-boggling Bodhisattva room and views of the surrounding countryside. In the garden to the right, there is a 3m-high (10-ft.) dragon climbing in and out of a small lake. You'll find very cool little nooks and crannies to explore.

At the end of Trai Mat St. (20 min. by car/bike). Daily 8am–5pm.

**Prenn Falls** ⭐ The falls are actually quite impressive, especially after a good rain. You can ride a rattle-trap little cable car over them if you're brave or follow a stone path behind the falling water (prepare to get your feet wet). That is a little thrill, of course, but the true Prenn experience is all about staged photos for

Vietnamese tourists: couples preening, boys looking macho, and girls looking wan and forlorn. Professional photographers run the show and pose their willing actors on a small wooden bridge, on the back of a costumed horse, with an arm around a guy in a bear suit, on a small inflatable raft in front of the falls, or perched in one of the cool tree houses high above (be careful of the loose rungs when climbing up). Come here to have a laugh and observe until you find out that, as a foreign tourist, it's you that's being observed; in that case, say "Xin Chao" or return a few "hellos" and go from there (you'll be getting your photo snapped for sure). You might walk away with some new chums, not to mention some good tourist tchotchke, if that is your wont (plastic samurai sword, anyone?).

At the foot of Prenn Mountain pass, 10km (6¼ miles) from Dalat. Admission 6,000 VND (40¢). Daily 7am–5pm.

**Thien Vuong Pagoda** ★  Otherwise known as the "Chinese Pagoda," built as it was by the local Chinese population, this 1958 structure is unremarkable except for its serene setting among the hills of Dalat and the very friendly nuns who inhabit it. It does have three awe-inspiring sandalwood Buddhist statues that have been dated to the 16th century: Dai The Chi Bo Tat, god of power; Amithaba or Sakyamuni, Buddha; and Am Bo Tat, god of mercy. Each is 4m (13 ft.) high and weighs 1½ tons.

3km (2 miles) southeast of town at the end of Khe Sanh St. Daily 9am–5pm.

**Truc Lam (Bamboo Forest) Zen Monastery** ★★  What's refreshing is that you can walk around Truc Lam with no harassment, unlike many other temples and most pagodas in Vietnam. This is a working temple, and though it's packed with tourists at certain times of the day, you'll be wandering amid meditation halls and classrooms that are utilitarian, not museum pieces. You'll get to see monks at work and have an informative glimpse into the daily rhythms of temple life. The complex was completed in 1994 with the aim of giving new life to the Truc Lam Yen Tu Zen sect, a uniquely Vietnamese form of Zen founded during the Tran Dynasty (1225–1400). Adherents practice self-reliance and realization through meditation. The shrine, the main building, is notable mainly for its simple structure and peaceful air, and there is a large relief sculpture of Boddhidarma, Zen's wild-eyed Indian heir, at the rear of the main temple. The scenery around the monastery, with views of the nearby man-made lake, Tuyen Lam Lake, and surrounding mountains is breathtaking. Truc Lam can now be reached by a scenic **tram ride** from a hilltop overlooking Dalat; a motorbike or taxi to the tram station costs little, and the round-trip is 50,000 VND ($3.35).

Near Tuyen Lam Lake, 6km (3¾ miles) from Dalat. A popular spot on any countryside tour. Daily 7am–5pm.

**Valley of Love** ★★  The Valley is scenic headquarters in Dalat and a popular stopover for honeymooners. It's a good place to find some real bizarre kitsch, the kind whose precedent can only be roadside America; here I mean guys in bear suits and huge-headed cowboys with guns that spout "bang" flags. There are a few nice walking paths among the rolling hills and quaint little lakes, and everyone enjoys the antics of Vietnamese honeymooners zipping around on motorboats and posing for pictures with guys in fuzzy jumpsuits. Don't miss it.

Phu Dong Thien Vuong St., about 3.2km (2 miles) north of town center. Admission 5,000 VND (35¢). Daily 6am–5pm.

**Xuan Huong Lake** ★★  Once a trickle originating in the Lat village, Dalat's centerpiece, Xuan Huong, was created from a dam project that was finished in 1923, demolished by a storm in 1932, and reconstructed and rebuilt (with heavier stone) in 1935. You can rent windsurfing boards and swan-shape paddleboats,

although in two visits here I have yet to see anyone actually using them—
I cannot vouch for the cleanliness of the water.

Central Dalat.

## SPORTS & OUTDOOR ACTIVITIES

Dalat is the perfect setting for **hiking and mountain biking.** Check with the
folks at **Phat Tire Ventures** (73 Truong Cong Dinh; ℂ **063/823-104;** see "Visitor Information & Tours," earlier in this section), for some remote jungle treks
in among hill-tribe towns, good mountain biking, or any kind of day trip (these
folks are extremely amenable and can customize to your needs).

**Golfers** can try the **Dalat Palace Golf Club**'s impressive 18-hole course. One
round costs Sofitel Palace or Novotel guests $65; all others pay $85, plus a
mandatory caddie fee ($6 for 9 holes, and $12 for 18 holes). For reservations,
call ℂ **063/821-201.** Rental clubs and shoes are available; private lessons, by
appointment, begin at $30 for a half-hour. There is a nice driving range.

## 12  Phan Thiet Town & Mui Ne Beach

This is one of the best laid-back getaways in Vietnam. The town of Phan Thiet
itself is a bustling little fishing port, quite picturesque and good for a day's visit,
but you'll want to get out to the long stretch of beach to the east: the sprawling
sandy shore at Mui Ne. This is a popular weekend getaway from nearby Saigon,
and development in recent years has been rapid. Still, there are some very nice
upscale resorts and comfy little boutique bungalow properties.

Nick Faldo's golf course at the Novotel in Phan Thiet is a big draw, and the
consistent winds of Mui Ne bay bring wind- and kitesurfers from all over the
world. Farther east and north along the coast there are vast sand dunes, like a
beachside Sahara, and inland there is the famous and strangely verdant Silver
Lake amid the towering, shifting sands—a good day trip. These spots, as well as
other small fishing villages, make for great day trips. There are also some local
Cham ruins, and the town of Phan Thiet, famous for a brand of fish sauce *(nuoc
mam)* made here, is worth exploring (especially the market). Phan Thiet is a good
getaway from Saigon or to take a break as you make your way down the coast.

## GETTING THERE

**By Bus/Car:** Phan Thiet is just 3 hours from Saigon. The tourist cafe buses connect here from Nha Trang and Dalat as well as Saigon, and **Sinh Café** covers all
the bases from its new **Mui Ne Resort** (144 Nguyen Dinh Chieu St., Ham Tien,
Mui Ne; ℂ **062/847-542;** www.sinhcafevn.com) and **TM Brothers** has an
office at Km 10, Nguyen Dinh Chieu St. (ℂ **062/741-166**). Any hotel front
desk can make the necessary arrangements for car rental or return bus tickets.

## WHERE TO STAY

The Novotel is the only international standard in the town of Phan Thiet. Along
the beach at Mui Ne, about 9km (5½ miles) to the east, find a growing clutch of
luxury resorts that cover all the bases. Many folks find that they plan to stay only
a short time and end up in a hammock for a few extra days. *Note:* Addresses are
listed by their distance from Phan Thiet.

Find **Internet service** at most resorts at inflated prices, or check out **Coco Café**
(Km 13.5; ℂ **062/847-729**), the only reasonably priced and efficient place going.

### EXPENSIVE

**Novotel Coralia Ocean Dunes Phan Thiet** ⭐    "Fore!" Sandwiched between
Nick Faldo's golf course and an open lawn and sandy beach on the other, the

Novotel is a popular choice for golfers and Saigon expats on holiday. It's got all the amenities of a resort, and rooms and facilities are in a "traditional" hotel style, with clean carpet and floral prints. The original hotel is an old Soviet-era resort, and concrete block rooms are limited to the original build—they're small but comfy and not particularly luxe. Every room has a balcony, and prices are according to the view of either the beach or the golf course. The hotel is right in the town of Phan Thiet but is insulated by the surrounding golf course and far from any road so no honking. It's about 9km (5½ miles) to the popular beaches of Mui Ne. The beach is narrow and rocky, but the pool area and surrounding yard is expansive, great for kids (there's even a jungle gym). The hotel has lots of activities and children's programs and rents jet skis and sailboats.

1 Ton Duc Than St., Phan Thiet. © 062/822-393. Fax 062/828-045. www.accorhotels-asia.com. 123 units. $110–$125 golf/sea view; $156 suite. AE, MC, V. **Amenities:** Restaurant (indoor/outdoor seating); 2 bars (poolside and inside); golf; 2 tennis courts; health club; kids' room; concierge; tour desk; car rental; business center; lobby shopping; salon; massage; babysitting; laundry; nonsmoking rooms; Internet. *In room:* A/C, TV, minibar, fridge, coffeemaker, hair dryer, safe, IDD phone.

**Victoria Phan Thiet Resort** ★★   Just as the road descends from Phan Thiet to meet with the sandy beaches of Mui Ne, the Victoria stands on a quiet little knoll overlooking the sea. It's a grass-and-garden campus traced by small brick pathways that connect tidy, upscale bungalows. It's a unique layout, with cat-walks connecting the main buildings, most made of rough stone. The overall atmosphere is comfortable, laid-back, and private. The pool area is a great place to while away the day, and there's a good massage facility in a seaside grove. Guest rooms are large, private bungalows, some with two tiers and all done in terra cotta, bamboo catay, and dark wood; it's refined comfort with nice touches like stylish indirect lighting disguised as pottery, large ceiling fans, and local art-work. Family bungalows have multiple sleeping areas and a pullout couch. Shower and toilet are in separate rooms in most, and are compact and neat. Their newer rooms, further from the beach, are double height and quite spacious. The beach is rocky, but the resort overlooks its own quiet cove and there are beachside thatch awnings. Service is good, and the resort has all the amenities of a much larger property, only here done in intimate and friendly miniature. Come for the weekend, and you'll stay for the week.

Km 9, Phu Hai, Phan Thiet. © 062/813-000. Fax 062/813-007. www.victoriahotels-asia.com. 50 units. $140–$180 bungalow; $220 villa. AE, MC, V. **Amenities:** Restaurant (indoor/outdoor dining); large thatch-roofed poolside bar area; outdoor pool w/Jacuzzi; tennis court; small health club; all rentals available; private tours available; shopping arcade below reception; massage; laundry; Internet; billiards. *In room:* A/C, satellite TV, minibar, fridge, coffeemaker, safe, IDD phone.

## MODERATE

**Coco Beach** ★★   This is that little slice of heaven you've been looking for in your hard travels along the coast. On the main strip in Mui Ne, Coco Beach doesn't look like much from the road—just a wall to keep out the noise—but it is a real seaside, garden oasis. It was the first to build along the strip at Mui Ne, and it's still the best. Rooms are wooden bungalows on stilts, each with a comfy balcony area with a couch and table. It's a nice standard, intimate and tidy, and the real wood and thatch gives it an authentic rustic luxury, a comfy "Margari-taville" atmosphere (and maintenance here is tops: no musty smells, and so on). Spacious bungalows—the best are the Oceanside villas—have high vaulted ceil-ings, dark beams, exposed thatch roofs, bamboo catay lanterns, mosquito nets and subdued, indirect lighting. Bathrooms are small and basic but tidy, with glass stall showers. Rooms are priced by their proximity to the beautiful sandy beach, where you'll find comfy private lounge chairs and umbrellas. Service is attentive and genuine, the best along the main strip of Mui Ne. Coco Beach has two restaurants: seaside Paradise Beach Club and the more upscale Champa, are the best in town (see "Where to Dine," below). There are no TVs so there are no distractions (though there's a library and video area), and this is a good place to have a go at that novel you've been wanting to start (whether reading or writing) or just relax in the quiet garden after a day of swimming or boating. A great open-air massage facility at the center.

Km 12.5 Ham Tien, Phan Thiet. ✆ 062/847-111. Fax 062/847-115. 31 units. $70–$85 bungalow; $140–$170 2-room villa (long-stay rates available). **Amenities:** 2 restaurants; pool/beach bar and shop; central pool; Jacuzzi at poolside; motorboat/sailboat rental; family programs; in-house tour programs; car rental; business center; limited room service; massage; laundry. *In room:* A/C, minibar, fridge, IDD phone.

### Mui Ne Sailing Club ✸    This new seaside spot is owned by the same Aussie folks who run the popular Sailing Club in Nha Trang. Rooms run the gamut from budget rooms with a fan, comfortable but like an American motel, to top-notch bungalows at seaside. All rooms have terra-cotta tile with bamboo matting, cloth hangings, and bamboo floor lamps. There is an American Southwest feel in the artful beveled edges of the plaster walls and in the similarly rounded built-in night stands. Large bathrooms are nicely appointed in tile and dark wood trim and are separated from the bedroom by only a hanging cloth, a nice touch. The high-end bungalows are the best choice and certainly worth the upgrade. The pool is small, but in a picturesque seaside courtyard adjoining the open-air colonial-style restaurant. This is a popular stop for windsurfers and kitesurfers, and they rent equipment and give lessons. Be sure and ask to see a room before checking in. Some are a bit musty.

24 Nguyen Dinh Chieu St., Han Tien Ward, Phan Thiet. ✆ 062/847-440. Fax 062/847-441. www.sailing clubvietnam.com. 30 units. $30 fan double; $45 A/C double; $50–$90 bungalow. AE, MC, V. **Amenities:** Restaurant; bar; outdoor pool; all rentals; tour desk; business center; room service 7am–10pm; babysitting; laundry; Internet. *In room:* A/C, IDD phone.

### Pandanus Beach Resort    The best of a new clutch of resorts under construction at the foot of the famous Red Sand Dunes north of Phan Thiet, this large new resort is as self-contained as any in Mui Ne proper, but here just a bit more remote. The resort is large and spread out; the central pool area is cozy; the beach is expansive, but dirty and unused. It's just opened and is not attracting big numbers yet so good promotional prices are available. Rooms run the gamut, but all are comfortable with cooling terra-cotta tile offset by dark wood trim, good in-room amenities, and all surrounding ponds and manicured greens.

Quarter 5, Mui Ne, Phan Thiet. ✆ 062/849-849. Fax 062/849-850. www.pandanusresort.com. 134 units. $59–$74 double; $109–$119 suite. MC, V. **Amenities:** Restaurant; bar/lounge; outdoor pool; small fitness center; spa; tour desk; car-rental desk; shopping arcade; limited room service; massage; laundry. *In room:* A/C, satellite TV, minibar, fridge, IDD phone.

### Saigon Mui Ne Resort ✸    The Saigon Mui Ne is the most popular spot in town for larger group tours. Run by Saigontourist, the resort has all the amenities but not a lot of charm. Rooms are comparable to any in this category in town, but there's that hazy indifference of a government-run, tour-group hotel. The good news is the price tag and the many amenities. It's a sprawling campus of manicured lawns and tidy bungalows with terra-cotta tile floors, unique wrought-iron furniture, and bathrooms with granite counters and bamboo latticework. The hotel block rooms are spacious, but go for a bungalow with balcony, best facing the sea or the central pool area. There is talk of a casino soon, heaven help us.

Km 12.3 Ham Tien, Phan Thiet, Binh Thuan. © 062/847-302. Fax 062/847-307. www.saigonmuineresort.com. 69 units. $50–$95 double (bungalow or hotel block); $125 large family room. AE, MC, V. **Amenities:** Restaurant; beachside bar; nice courtyard pool w/Jacuzzi; tennis; sauna; all rentals; Saigon tour desk; salon; 24-hr. room service; massage; laundry; Internet. *In room:* A/C, TV, minibar, fridge, IDD phone.

**Budget accommodations** line the main drag in Mui Ne. The scene is constantly changing, but expect to pay between $8 and $15 for basic guesthouse accommodation. If you come by cafe bus, they will take you around to shop for the spot you'd like. It gets cheaper and more rustic the farther east you go on the main road.

**Sinh Café,** ever expanding its monopoly on the budget tourist market in Vietnam (they run all the buses), has just opened the **Mui Ne Resort** (144 Nguyen Dinh Chieu St., Ham Tien, Mui Ne; © **062/847-542;** www.sinhcafevn.com), a 48-room budget hotel on the furthest end of Mui Ne. If you come by one of its buses, it'll strand you there as long as it can in the hopes that you'll stay. Rooms start at $20 and aren't a bad bet. There's a pool and all the basics. A festive atmosphere pervades (lots of young partiers).

Another good choice in the budget department is **Full Moon Beach,** a popular spot for kitesurfers and windsurfers. Rooms vary from wood perches overlooking the beach to midrange comfort in the newest building. Contact Phuong or Pascal at © **062/847-008** (14km/8¾ miles from Phan Thiet, Thon 3–Xa Ham Tien, Muin Ne; fax 062/847-160; www.windsurf-vietnam.com).

## WHERE TO DINE

**Paradise Beach Club** ✹ SEAFOOD    Set in a soothing, seaside pavilion at the popular Coco Beach Resort (see "Where to Stay," above), the Paradise Beach Club Dine is the place for fine fresh seafood and barbecue. Choose from a raw bar and have it cooked to order as you like. The menu is a long roster covering anything from light snack and sandwiches to hearty Western meals. For dessert, they make the most unique sundaes I've ever seen. Check it out. The resort's more upscale restaurant, **Champa,** is also a great choice.

At the Coco Beach Resort (Km 12.5 Ham Tien, Phan Thiet). © **062/847-111.** Main courses 30,000 VND–200,000 VND ($2–$13). V, MC. Daily 6:30am–11pm.

Also try the **Mui Ne Sailing Club** (24 Nguyen Dinh Chieu St., Han Tien Ward, Phan Thiet; © **062/847-440**), which serves good, basic Western in a nice open-air building at poolside overlooking the ocean. Farther east, **Full Moon Beach** (14km/8¾ miles from Phan Thiet, Thon 3–Xa Ham Tien, Muin Ne; © **062/847-008**) is a good stop for coffee or breakfast on your way to Silver Lake or the big dunes north of town.

Thatched-roof eateries line the main beachside road in Mui Ne. **Luna d' Autuno** (Km12 Ham Tien; © **062/847-591**), a popular Saigon pizzeria, has a cool new restaurant under a high thatched roof, and there is also a **Good Morning Vietnam Restaurant** (Km 11.8 Ham Tien; © **091/802-2760**), Vietnam's pizza and pasta franchise that serves good, affordable, familiar meals for little.

**The Hot Rock** (Km 12.5, across from Bien Xanh Resort; © **062/847-608**) is a good late-night hangout. They also serve good, basic, Western fare.

## WHAT TO SEE & DO

**Cape Mui Ne** ✹✹, at some 20km (12½ miles) northeast of town are Mui Ne's sprawling sand dunes, and a trip out this way brings you though lots of quaint seaside villages that are well worth a look. Coming from Mui Ne Beach, you'll first reach a small fishing town and can explore its fine little rural market—great in the early morning. Heading inland away from the beach, you'll first come to the towering **Red Dunes** ✹✹. A walk to the top offers great views of the town and surrounding countryside, and you're sure to be followed by a gaggle of friendly kids trying to sell you on the idea of renting one of their plastic sleds for the ride down the steep dune slopes—kind of fun. From the Red Dunes, if you have time, the unique **Silver Lake** ☆☆ is reached only after a long bumpy ride, but the views of the coast are dynamic and this unique little verdant lake in the large, parched silver dune makes the trip worth it. It's a long day, though. Ask at any hotel or resort for tours. Expect to pay $10 per person for two or more to go to the tip of the cape and the Red Dunes, and more to go inland.

At the highest point on the road between Phan Thiet Town and Mui Ne beach, you won't miss **Cham Tower,** an impressive spire of crumbling brick. The tower dates from the end of the 13th century and is worth a stop if you weren't able to catch any of the Cham sites near Hoi An and Danang. Any taxi will be happy to make a brief stop on the way. There are also Cham sites some 2 hours' drive inland near Phan Rang, and all hotels and resorts can arrange tours.

**Phan Thiet Market** ☆ is a large but pretty standard central market in town. It's certainly worth a wander. This is where you can pick up a bottle of locally made *nuoc mam* (fish sauce). Go early for the bringing in of the day's catch, and don't forget your camera.

## OUTDOOR ACTIVITIES

The wind conditions in Mui Ne are steady and strong in the dry season (Oct–May), and the beach is becoming a real kitesurfing and windsurfing mecca (it's over 12 knot winds for two-thirds of the year). **Jibe's** (Km 14, Ham Tien, Muin Ne; ✆ **062/847-008;** www.windsurf-vietnam.com), a popular rental shop, windsurfer club, and bar, is a good place to check in or rent a board and a great opportunity for first-time kite-surfers. A day with an IKO-certified instructor starts at just $85; the focus is on safety, of course, and the savings is significant (similar lessons elsewhere cost a mint).

Sailors will want to contact the folks at the **Mui Ne Sailing Club** (24 Nguyen Dinh Chieu St., Han Tien Ward, Phan Thiet; ✆ **062/847-440**) or at any hotel or resort about renting Hobie Cat and Laser sailboats, windsurfers, jet skis, and runabouts.

The outstanding Nick Faldo–designed **Ocean Dunes Golf Course** (1 Ton Duc Than St., Phan Thiet; ✆ **062/821-511**) is a big draw here in town.

### 13 Ho Chi Minh City (Saigon)

Ho Chi Minh City, or, Saigon as it is once again commonly known, is a relatively young Asian city, founded in the 18th century. Settled mainly by civil-war refugees from north Vietnam and Chinese merchants, it quickly became a major commercial center. When the French took over the country they would call Cochin China, Saigon became the capital. After the French left in 1954, Saigon remained the capital of south Vietnam until national reunification in 1975.

Saigon is still Vietnam's commercial headquarters, brash and busy, with a keen sense of its own importance. Located on the Saigon River, it's Vietnam's major port and largest city, with a population of almost 7 million people. True to its reputation, the city is noisy, crowded, and dirty, but the central business district is rapidly developing in steel-and-glass precision to rival any city on the globe. The old Saigon still survives in wide downtown avenues flanked by pristine colonials. Hectic and eclectic, Ho Chi Minh City has an attitude all its own.

Some of Saigon's tourism highlights include the **Vietnam History Museum;** the grisly **War Remnants Museum;** and **Cholon, the Chinese district,** with its pagodas and exotic stores. Dong Khoi Street—formerly fashionable Rue Catinat during the French era and Tu Do, or Freedom Street, during the American war—is still a strip of grand colonial hotels, chic shops, and cafes. The food in Saigon is some of the best Vietnam has to offer, the nightlife sparkles, and the shopping is good. The city is also a logical jumping-off point for excursions to other southern destinations: the **Mekong Delta,** the **Cu Chi tunnels,** and **Phan Thiet beach.**

## GETTING THERE

**BY PLANE**    Most regional airlines connect with Ho Chi Minh, including Malaysian Airlines, Thai Airways, Bangkok Airways, Silk Air/Singapore Airlines, Lao Aviation, Garuda Indonesia, Philippine Airlines, United, and Cathay Pacific (from Hong Kong). Vietnam Airlines usually has the best fare, thanks to government controls. If you're flying to Vietnam directly from North America, check the new United Flights or check with Cathay Pacific for good fares and itineraries. Domestically, Saigon is linked by Vietnam Airline flights from Hanoi, Hue, Danang, Hoi An, Nha Trang, and Dalat.

At the airport in Saigon, you can change foreign currency for VND, but taxi drivers to town don't mind payment in U.S. dollars, either. Arranging a hotel limousine to greet you will certainly make life a bit easier, but taxis are aplenty outside the arrivals hall. The trip to town is $5.

In town, the Vietnam Airlines office is at 116 Nguyen Hue, District 1 (© **08/ 829-2118;** fax 08/823-8454). Call to book a flight or confirm your reservation.

To get to the airport, if you can't find a taxi, you can call Airport Taxi at © **08/844-6666.** There is an international departure tax of $12. The departure tax for domestic flights is 20,000 VND ($1.35).

**BY BUS/MINIVAN**    By bus, Saigon is about 5½ hours from Dalat, the nearest major city. All of the cafes connect here, of course; and line the streets around the Pham Ngu Lao area. See the tour information below.

**BY CAR**    For safety reasons alone, if you're taking wheels, it is better to book a minivan with a tour or group.

## GETTING AROUND

**BY BICYCLE & MOTORBIKE**    Saigon is blessed with the country's most chaotic traffic, so you might want to think twice before renting a motorbike or bicycle, which aren't as easily available as in other towns. You can, however, hop a motorcycle taxi—a quick trip is 5,000 VND (35¢), while hourly booking can be in the ballpark of 15,000 VND ($1) per hour with some haggling. It's a bit hair-raising sometimes but is a good way to get around.

**BY CYCLO**    Cyclos are available for an hourly rental of about 20,000 VND ($1.35), but they simply are not a good option in Saigon, especially outside District 1. First, drivers have an odd habit of not speaking English (or indeed, any other language) halfway through your trip and taking you to places you never asked to see, or simply driving around in circles pretending to be confused. Second, riding in a slow, open conveyance amid thousands of motorbikes and cars is unpleasant and dangerous, and cyclo passengers are low to the ground and in the front, something like a bumper. Third, drive-by thefts from riders are common even during daylight hours!

**BY TAXI**    Taxis are clustered around the bigger hotels and restaurants. They cost 12,000 VND (80¢) at flag fall and 6,000 VND or so (40¢) for every kilometer after. You can call Airport Taxi (© **08/844-6666**) or Saigon Taxi (© **08/ 822-6688**), among others.

# Ho Chi Minh City (Saigon)

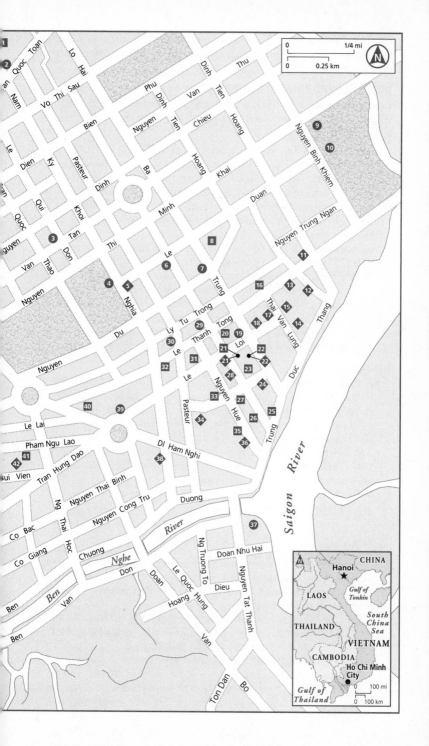

**BY CAR**   You can simplify your sightseeing efforts if you hire a car and driver for the day from Ann Tours or Saigontourist (see "Visitor Information & Tours," below).

## VISITOR INFORMATION & TOURS

Every major tourist agency has its headquarters or a branch in Saigon. They will be able to book tours and travel throughout the city and the southern region, and usually the countrywide as well.

- **Ann Tours** (58 Ton That Tung St., District 1; ℂ **08/833-2564** or 833-4356; fax 08/832-3866; www.anntours.com) has a great reputation that is well deserved. Ann's specializes in custom tours for individuals or small groups. They can be relatively expensive, but that's in comparison to the seat-in-coach cattle-drive tours. These guys will help you do virtually anything you want to in Vietnam. Ask for director Tony Nong, and tell him Frommer's sent you.

- **Exotissimo** (Saigon Trade Center, 37 Ton Duc Than, District 1; ℂ **08/825-1723;** fax 08/829-5800; vietnam@exotissimo.com) has a chic downtown office and can arrange just about any tour or international itinerary. It's popular for expats and has convenient offices throughout the region.

- **Saigontourist** (49 Le Thanh Ton St., District 1; ℂ **08/824-4554;** fax 08/822-4987; www.saigontourist.net.), is a large government-run group, but it'll get you where you want to go and is a far better choice than the budget cafes (below). It mans desks in the Majestic, Rex, and Sheraton hotels.

### BUDGET

- **Sinh Café** (246–248 De Tham St., District 1; ℂ **08/369-420** or 08/836-9322; sinhcafevietnam@hcm.vnn.vn), is a backpacker choice for inexpensive trips and tours. On paper, the tours seem exactly the same as others offered at private tour agents, but with a cheaper price tag—actually, they're pretty standard tours. This is a good option for shoestring travelers.

- **TM Brothers** (269 De Tham St. or 139 Bui Vien St., District 1; ℂ **08/836-1791**), is pure "same-same but different here" on the cafe tip. This is a good place to check in comparison with Sinh.

- **TNK** (230 De Tham St.; ℂ **08/837-8276;** www.tnktravelvietnam.com) is just another of the many.

---

*FAST FACTS:* **Ho Chi Minh City**

*Banks/Currency Exchange*   As with elsewhere in Vietnam, you can change money in banks, hotels, and jewelry stores. The exchange rate in Saigon is better than in many smaller cities.

Major banks in Saigon include these: ANZ Bank, 11 Me Linh Square, District 1 (ℂ **08/829-9319**); Citibank, 115 Nguyen Hue St. (ℂ **824-2118**); HSBC, 75 Pham Hong Thai St., District 1 (ℂ **08/829-2288**); and Vietcombank, 29 Ben Chuong Duong, District 1 (ℂ **08/829-7245**).

There is a good currency exchange at 4C Le Loi Street right in the town center. It's a good spot for the right rates on traveler's checks.

ATMs dispensing dollars and dong around the clock are at HSBC, ANZ Bank, and Citibank.

*Embassies & Consulates*   For embassies, see "Fast Facts: Vietnam," earlier in this chapter. Consulates are all in District 1, as follows: United States,

4 Le Duan St. (© **08/822-9433**); Canada, 235 Dong Khoi St. (© **08/ 824-5025**); Australia, 5B Ton Duc Thang St. (© **08/829-6035**); New Zealand, 41 Nguyen Thi Minh Khai St. (© **08/822-6908**); and United Kingdom, 25 Le Duan St. (© **08/829-8433**).

*Emergencies* For police, dial © **113**; for fire, dial © **114**; and for ambulance, dial © **115**. Have a translator on hand, if necessary; operators don't speak English.

*Internet/E-mail* Almost every upscale hotel provides Internet services in Saigon, and you can bet they charge a pretty penny. You won't find any service on Dong Khoi, but a short walk in any direction brings you to service for an average of 200 VND (1¢) per minute. My personal favorite: Thumbs up to **Café Cyber Business Center** for serving drinks as well as providing full business center services in a laid-back, plush atmosphere with very private terminals. It's at 48 Dong Du St., just off Dong Khoi in District 1 (© **08/823-3668**; info@cgcybercfe.com; 300 VND/2¢ per min.). Also try **Welcome Internet** (15B Le Thanh Ton St.; © **08/822-0981**). Service in the Pham Ngu Lao backpacker area is fast, and cheap; Internet cafes line De Tham and charge 5,000 VND per hour (3¢ per min.).

*Post Office/Mail* The main post office is located at 2 Coq Xu Paris, District 1 (© **08/823-2541** or 08/823-2542), just across from Notre Dame Cathedral. It's open daily from 6:30am to 10pm. All services are available here, including long-distance calling and callback, and the building itself is a historic landmark (see "What to See & Do," later in this chapter). Postal service is available in most hotels and at various locations throughout the city.

*Safety* The biggest threat to your health in Saigon is likely to be the street traffic. Cross the wildly busy streets at a slow, steady pace. If you're having a really hard time getting across, find a local who is crossing and stick to his heels!

Pickpocketing is a big problem in Saigon, especially motorbike drive-bys with someone slashing the shoulder strap, grabbing the bag, and driving off. Keep your bag close and away from traffic. Hang on to your wallet, and don't wear flashy jewelry. Be especially wary in crowded places like markets. Women should avoid wandering around in the evenings alone past 11pm or so. Contact your consulate or your hotel if you have a serious problem. If you insist on going to the local police, bring a translator. Also, the Saigon police tend to throw up their hands at "minor" infractions such as purse snatching or thievery.

*Telephone* The city code for Saigon is 8. When dialing within Vietnam, the city code should be preceded by 0.

*Toilets* There are no public toilets, per se. Seek out hotels, restaurants, and tourist attractions.

## SAIGON'S DISTRICTS

Saigon is divided into districts, as is Hanoi, and is very easy to navigate. Be sure to know the district along with any addresses, and try to group your travels accordingly (try not to criss-cross districts in a day). Most of the hotels, bars, shops, and restaurants are in District 1, easily covered on foot, while sightseeing attractions are spread among Districts 1, 3, and 5 (Cholon).

## WHERE TO STAY

Saigon presents the best variety of hotels in Vietnam, from deluxe business and family hotels to spotless smaller options. Most hotels are clustered around Nguyen Hue Street in District 1, as are the restaurants, shops, and bars.

If you're traveling on a tight budget, head for De Tham, a backpacker haven loaded with guesthouses and minihotels; a fan-cooled room with a cold-water shower goes for as little as $5 per night, or an air-conditioned room with hot water for around $15. Most of these places are very basic (and a bit noisy from street traffic) but are tidy, well run, and friendly.

Remember that prices listed here are the "rack rate" and should be considered only a guideline. Internet, group, and standard promotional rates are the rule, and especially in the off season (Mar–Sept), expect discounts up to 50%. Remember that many hotels levy a VAT of up to 20%.

### VERY EXPENSIVE

**Caravelle Hotel** ✿✿✿   Named for a type of light, fast ship, this sleek downtown address gives you that very impression. A French company built the original in 1956 and, after honeymoon years as the town's address of note, the hotel became a shabby hangout for wartime journalists and fell into obscurity as the Doc Lap (Independence) Hotel in postwar years. The Caravelle was renovated and expanded beyond recognition in 1998 and is now an extremely attractive, efficient, and well-appointed hotel. With five-star amenities and stylish rooms, luxury accommodations here attract business travelers and well-heeled tourists. The big, new rooms are large and plush, with neutral furnishings and firm beds; higher floors have great views. Bathrooms are sizable, in marble. The executive signature floors have fax machines, computer hookups, VCRs, and CD players in each room. The suites are luxe beyond belief. And the classic character of the old hotel lives on in the rooftop Saigon Saigon bar, an open-air colonial throwback with rattan shades, low-slung chairs, and twirling ceiling fans. If you let your imagination go, you might just see Graham Greene or a war-time correspondent sidling up to the bar. The popular restaurant, Port Orient, serves fine international and Vietnamese fare. There is new competition from the nearby Sheraton and the soon-to-open Hyatt around the corner, but that just ups the ante on service, and the Caravelle, with its long tradition of excellence, is sure to top any list. There is also an ATM machine, great bar area, and small casino.

19 Lam Son Sq., District 1, Saigon. ✆ 08/823-4999. Fax 08/824-3999. www.caravellehotel.com. 335 units. $190–$270 double; $310–$980 suite. AE, DC, MC, V. **Amenities:** 2 restaurants; 3 bars; lovely rooftop pool; top-notch health club; spa; Jacuzzi; sauna; all rentals available; tour desk; expensive but extensive business center; salon w/facials and manicures; 24-hr. room service; massage; laundry; dry cleaning; executive-level rooms; banquet facility for 250; rooms for travelers w/disabilities. *In room:* A/C, satellite TV, fax,; dataport, minibar, fridge, coffeemaker, hair dryer, safe, IDD phone.

**Hotel Majestic** ✿   This 1925 landmark on the picturesque, riverside corner of Dong Khoi St. (formerly Catinat) still has some historical charm despite many renovations and is a real picture-postcard colonial from the outside. Owned by Saigontourist and the jewel in the crown of its local empire, the Majestic is always full, and it is a good, affordable, atmospheric choice. Botched details abound on the interior, like tacky decor where something plain would stand, and vice versa, but rooms and facilities here are classy and comfortable for the cost. High ceilings, original wood floors, and retro fixtures are a nice touch in all rooms. Bathrooms are large, all with tubs and old-style taps. Majestic suites have large Jacuzzis. The small central courtyard pool area is lined with picturesque shuttered windows and walkways; in fact, the best choices are the fine deluxe rooms facing this quiet spot. Suites are just larger versions of deluxe rooms, and standards are small and quite basic. Buffet meals at the fine restaurant, Cyclo, are accompanied by either piano or traditional music and sometimes dance. The staff couldn't be nicer and has a genuine desire to make your stay memorable, whether that means explaining the eccentricities of Vietnamese cuisine or hailing you a taxi. Don't miss the great views from the rooftop Sky-Bar, a good spot to have a chat and popular for weddings and parties.

1 Dong Khoi St., District 1, Saigon. (C) **08/829-5514**. Fax 08/829-5510. 122 units. $130 single; $150 standard double; $165–$185 superior; $195–$215 deluxe; $295–$575 suite. AE, DC, MC, V. **Amenities:** 2 restaurants; 2 bars; small courtyard pool; basic health club; sauna; Saigontourist tour desk; car rental; business center; shopping; massage; babysitting; laundry; dry cleaning. *In room:* A/C, satellite TV w/HBO, minibar, fridge, hair dryer, safe, IDD phone.

## New World Hotel Saigon ★★
This first-rate hotel is where President Clinton called home during his brief stay in Saigon and is a fine choice indeed, whether you're a business traveler, a tourist, or a world leader. Everything's big, flashy, and deluxe. The location is in the very center of town and a short walk from Ben Thanh Market (see "What to See & Do," later in this chapter). It has a popular park out front, and there's a nice bustle and feeling of connectedness to the place uncommon to similar self-contained luxury hotels. The impeccable, plush rooms are done in a soothing array of neutrals, and the bathrooms are a sharp contrast in black-and-gray marble. The fat pillows are a little mushy and the beds are a bit too firm, but you can't have everything. The place is loaded with amenities. The four executive floors, with an executive lounge, have an impressive list of benefits: late check-out, all-day refreshments, free pressing, computer hookups, and free access to financial newswire information. If convenience is your game, it is well worth the $30 more you'll pay over a standard double room. The staff snaps to; service is ultraefficient. It's also one of the few places to ask straight away if you'd like a nonsmoking room.

76 Le Lai St., District 1, Saigon. (C) **08/822-8888**. Fax 08/823-0710. www.newworldvietnam.com. 570 units. $140 double; $170 executive floor; from $300 suite. AE, DC, MC, V. **Amenities:** 2 restaurants; bar; outdoor pool; lighted tennis court; health club; spa; sauna; rentals available; concierge; tour desk; business center; shopping arcade; 24-hr. room service; massage; babysitting; laundry; dry cleaning; executive/club rooms; banquet facilities. *In room:* A/C, satellite TV, minibar, fridge, coffeemaker, safe, IDD phone.

## Omni Saigon Hotel ★★
Once quarters for the U.S. CIA and later army, the edifice recalls a Soviet-era post office. Inside is another story. The lobby, with a colonial period flavor and Art Deco details, is gorgeous and welcoming. The rooms are quite comfortable, and the amenities, like the many fine-dining outlets, popular Irish pub Mulligan's, or extensive fitness center, rival any in town. Here's the drawback: Though it's just 10 minutes from the airport, you're in District 3 and some 15 minutes from town. Shuttles and taxis are consistent, but traffic can be hellish and you might feel distanced from the action. There are many perks, though: Rooms are luxurious and well equipped, done in a somewhat formal but immaculate decor. The executive floor has a small business center, in-room faxes and broadband hookup, and a particularly elegant lounge. The Omni is most popular for Asian travelers and businessmen.

251 Nguyen Van Troi St., Phu Nhuan District (District 3), Saigon. (C) **08/844-9222**. Fax 08/844-9198. www.omnisaigonhotel.com. 240 units. $110–$120 double; $150–$160 club floor; $200–$500 suite. (long-stay rates available). AE, DC, MC, V. **Amenities:** 5 restaurants; bar; outdoor patio pool; health club; nice spa; Jacuzzi; sauna; steam; tour desk; car rental; business center; shopping; salon; 24-hr. room service; massage; babysitting; laundry; book-borrowing corner. *In room:* A/C, TV, dataport (special in-room broadband for executive floor), minibar, fridge, hair dryer, safe, IDD phone.

**Renaissance Riverside Hotel Saigon** ⟨★⟩ Managed by Marriot, the Renaissance Riverside is a convenient, downtown address. The lobby is done in a colonial theme with a small central domed ceiling and a grand spiral stair connecting to the mezzanine. Rooms have black-and-white tile entries, tidy carpeting, and light furnishings all done in a cool eggshell and pastel. Electric control-panels near the headboard are like a 1970s bachelor pad. Bathrooms have black marble countertops and an antique black-and-white tile pattern throughout. You could be anywhere really, and everything's nice in the same way an upscale hotel might be nice in Bangkok, Paris, or Pittsburgh; nevertheless, the amenities, like the small rooftop pool and health club, are good. The Riverside is a popular business hotel, and that means smoking everywhere: all public spaces are a bit musty and rooms, even on designated nonsmoking floors, smell like a bar after closing time. Be sure to ask for nonsmoking and ask to see it before checking in. Don't miss the dim sum lunch at the fine Cantonese restaurant, Kabin.

8–15 Ton Duc Thang St., District 1, Saigon. **08/822-0033.** Fax 08/823-5666. www.renaissancehotels.com/sgnbr. 349 units. $95 single/double; $220–$550 suite. AE, MC, V. **Amenities:** 2 restaurants; bar; rooftop pool w/great city view; health club; nice massage/spa facility; can arrange all rentals; business center; shopping; 24-hr. room service; babysitting; nonsmoking floor; executive/club floor. *In room:* A/C, satellite TV, dataport, minibar, fridge, coffeemaker, iron, safe, IDD phone.

**Sheraton Saigon** ⟨★★⟩ The tallest, newest, most expensive hotel in Ho Chi Minh, the Sheraton is the talk of the town (keep an eye on the Hyatt set to open up in mid-2005). Everything is done on a grand scale, from colossal meeting rooms and top business facilities to enormous, plush guest rooms. It's high-end comfort from a brand that you can bank on. Rooms have it all: large, flat-screen TVs, broadband Internet, large desks with workstations, and great views of town. Bathrooms are huge, with separate shower and bath. The Sheraton covers every amenity, from a host of fine dining options, a health and spa area with squash courts and an outdoor pool, to their popular **Top of 23** nightspot, a double-height rotunda space that plays host to live bands on the very top of the city (23 floors is the highest point for now). All public areas are oversize and luxurious, and, from the moment your car pulls up out front, you'll know you've arrived, as every guest is given the red-carpet treatment. Executive services, like separate executive check-in area, lounge, and meticulous business services, make any transition smooth and easy. The hotel was just getting up and running from 2004, but they are always booked out, so be sure to contact them in advance.

88 Dong Khoi St., District 1, Ho Chi Minh City. ⓒ **08/827-2828.** Fax 08/827-2929. www.sheraton.com/saigon. 382 units. $285–$305 double; $335–$1,950 suite. AE, MC, V. **Amenities:** 3 restaurants; 2 bars; outdoor pool; tennis court; health club; spa; Jacuzzi; sauna; concierge; tour desk; car rental; business center; shopping arcade; 24-hr room service; massage; babysitting; laundry; dry cleaning; executive-level rooms (separate check-in). *In room:* A/C, satellite TV, minibar, fridge, coffeemaker, hair dryer, safe, IDD phone.

**Sofitel Plaza Saigon** ⟨★★⟩ The Sofitel hotel chain is famous in Southeast Asia for finding grand old colonial dames and converting them into the most charming hotel properties. This is not one of them. Opened in 1999, the Sofitel Plaza is one of the shiny new towers on the Saigon skyline; what it lacks in colonial charm, however, it more than compensates for in luxury, convenience, and comfort. Guest rooms are handsome, with fine Art Deco touches like the curving, clean-lined desks in most rooms. You'll never be wanting for any amenity here, and the staff is helpful and professional. In a convenient spot just across from the former U.S. and French embassies, this is a popular choice for the international business crowd and long-stay executives, who enjoy the sleek executive floor with a private lounge, daily buffet, drinks, and business services.

17 Le Duan Blvd., District 1, Saigon. © 800/221-4542 (in the U.S.) or 08/824-1555. Fax 08/824-1666. www.accorhotels.com/asia. 290 units. $150 superior; $200–$210 double; $360–$1,450 suite. AE, MC, V. **Amenities:** 2 restaurants; bar; luxury rooftop pool; health club; spa; sauna; steam; concierge; car rental; business center; 24-hr. room service; massage; babysitting; laundry; dry cleaning; nonsmoking floor; club rooms; meeting rooms for 500. *In room:* A/C, satellite TV, dataport, minibar, fridge, coffeemaker, safe, IDD phone.

## EXPENSIVE

**Duxton Hotel Saigon** ★★   Formerly the Prince before becoming part of the popular Australian chain—the Duxton Saigon is efficient, affordable and stylish (if a bit studied). Beige rooms are a nice size, tasteful, and comfortable, with plush beds, carpets, and coffeemakers. The bathrooms are smart black-and-white marble. The lobby, entered by swooping stairs from a circular drive and, inside, circled by a mezzanine, is classy but not overly grand: It's a good downtown meeting point. This place is popular with business travelers, especially those on an extended stay, who come here for all the comforts of home at cost. The staff is efficient and personable. The second-floor spa offers excellent Hong Kong massage service, along with steam and Jacuzzi (ask about special midweek spa rates). Also try the authentic Japanese restaurant on the mezzanine floor.

63 Nguyen Hue Blvd., District 1, Saigon. © 08/822-2999. Fax 08/824-1888. www.duxton.com. 203 units. $70$–150 deluxe; $220–$270 suites. Promotional and long-stay rates available. AE, DC, MC, V. **Amenities:** 2 restaurants; bar, nightclub; small health club; Jacuzzi; sauna; steam; concierge; tour desk; car rental; business center; shopping; 24-hr. room service; massage; laundry; dry cleaning; nonsmoking rooms; meeting rooms. *In room:* A/C, satellite TV, minibar, fridge, coffeemaker, safe, IDD phone.

**Grand Hotel** ★★   This 1930s colonial, another owned and renovated by Saigontourist, is done just right (okay, close, at least). The renovated Grand has a serene, tasteful atmosphere, and there are some choice features, like the lovingly restored iron elevator at center. The Grand is at its best when taking advantage of its long history, and rooms in the older block are much more charming than the more bland, chain-hotel units in the new wing. Deluxe rooms clustered in the old building near the elevator have classic high ceilings, rich wood floors, and a comfortable colonial charm for the price tag ($125). All rooms are big, with simple dark wood furniture and large wardrobes, and without the musty smell that plagues many Saigon hotels. The bathrooms are small but have big counters and hair dryers. The lobby is bright, the staff is friendly, and the location on Dong Khoi couldn't be better—right in the thick of it. The quiet atmosphere here suggests tourists rather than business, though, and it's got all the right amenities: Most notable are the quiet sitting areas and bar, and the central courtyard's small but peaceful pool area, a unique escape from busy Ho Chi Minh City.

8–24 Dong Khoi St., District 1, Saigon. © 08/823-0163. Fax 063/823-5781. www.grandsaigon.com. 107 units. $85–$125 double; $160 deluxe suite; $260–$490 grand/presidential suite. AE, MC, V. **Amenities:** Restaurant; 2 bars; outdoor pool (nice courtyard); small health club; Jacuzzi; sauna; steam; Saigontourist tour desk; car rental; business center; shopping; massage; laundry; dry cleaning. *In room:* A/C, satellite TV, minibar, fridge, safe, complimentary water, IDD phone.

**Hotel Continental** ★   This hotel is a big shame. It's not that it's so bad really, but it could be a world-class heritage hotel and instead it's a shambles thanks to the shortsightedness of the folks at Saigontourist. Built in 1890, it is the preeminent historic hotel in Saigon, of Graham Greene's *The Quiet American* fame. Its last renovation was in 1980. The very heart of Saigon's downtown, the colonial facade attracts shutter-clicking tourists and admirers, but that's where the love affair ends. The lobby is gawdy, with oversize chandeliers, Chinese vases, and that fake, semigloss shine of a low-end business hotel. Rooms are enormous, with high ceilings, but it's the red velveteen curtains, tatty red carpets, and general run-down feel that spoil the fantasy. It looks more like an aging cathouse, really, and the furniture can't seem to fill the big, empty space. Bathrooms are done plain, like a guesthouse, but are big and clean and have bathtubs. "First-class rooms," for $120, are big and comfy, with roll-top desks, ornate columns, and a wood archway separating a small sitting area—a good bet. The restaurant is a lovely period piece. Hotel staff is friendly but more or less dazed and confused. With a renovation, this historic gem could be a contender.

132–134 Dong Khoi St., District 1, Saigon. © 08/829-9201. Fax 08/824-1772. www.continentalvietnam.com. 83 units. $100–$130 double; $160–$170 suite. AE, MC, V. **Amenities:** 2 restaurants; 2 bars; small fitness center; tour desk; car rental; small business center in lobby; shopping; limited room service; massage; laundry; dry cleaning. *In room:* A/C, satellite TV w/video rental, minibar, fridge, safe (in higher standard only), IDD phone.

**Norfolk Hotel** ★★   This snappy little business hotel has one of the highest occupancy rates in town, and for good reason: It's affordable and convenient, and covers all the bases. Rooms are large and bright, furnished in slightly mismatched chain-hotel style, but everything is like new. The beds are soft and deluxe, and the TVs are large. Each room has a safe. Bathrooms are small but finished with marble. Staff is efficient and helpful. The restaurant is bright and upscale, featuring extensive breakfast and lunch buffets, as well as monthly themes and special menus. It's perfect for the business traveler or tourist seeking amenities, like a good business center, health club, a sauna, room service, and a travel desk to cater to any need—all at reasonable prices. Book early.

117 Le Thanh Ton St., District 1, Saigon. © 08/829-5368. Fax 08/829-3415. www.norfolkgroup.com. 104 units. $100–$140 double; from $220 suite. Promotional and Internet rates available. AE, MC, V. **Amenities:** Restaurant; bar/club; small health club; sauna; steam; concierge; tour desk; business center; 24-hr. room service; massage; laundry; nonsmoking rooms; meeting facilities. *In room:* A/C, satellite TV, minibar, fridge, coffeemaker, safe, IDD phone.

## MODERATE

**Huong Sen Hotel**   This is a good hotel for the price and downtown location, but Huong Sen is just another of the many government-owned places whose service is marked only by varying levels of indifference. The decor is kind of a downer, too. It's a popular choice for big tour groups, and great group rates (and Internet prices) are available. Rooms are big and newly renovated, with simple, colorfully painted wood furniture and floral drapes and headboards. Nice touches include molded ceilings and marble-topped counters in the spotless bathrooms. Some rooms have balconies. Beds are ultracomfortable. The hotel is comparable to any other in this category, but quite bland.

66–70 Dong Khoi St., District 1, Saigon. © 08/829-9400. Fax 08/829-0916. www.vietnamtourism. com/huongsen. 50 units. $52–$95 double. AE, DC, MC, V. **Amenities:** Restaurant; bar; sauna; car rental; business center; limited room service; massage; laundry; dry cleaning; Internet. *In room:* A/C, TV, minibar, fridge, IDD phone.

**Kim Do Royal City Hotel** ★★   This is a good bargain right downtown. The Kim Do is the kind of place with a wooden tree trunk clock in the lobby, pink plastic hangers, polyurethane slippers in the closet, and shiny polyester bedspreads. There's a rooftop massage area with a hot tub surrounded by plaster reliefs of sea nymphs and electric-light blinking stars on the ceiling. The original hotel was built nearly 100 years ago and underwent a renovation in 1994, and everything is still in good shape. All rooms are quite large and have interesting Asian carved furniture, tidy carpeting, and rock-hard beds (you can request a soft one). Bathrooms are clean but basic (no counter space). Basic but comfortable and it offers great discounts if you book directly through the website.

133 Nguyen Hue Ave., District 1, Saigon. © 08/822-5914 or 08/822-5915. Fax 08/822-5913. www. kimdohotel.com. 138 units. $99–$129 double; $169–$269 suite. AE, DC, MC, V. **Amenities:** Rooftop restaurant; bar; steam bath; all rentals; concierge; tour desk; car rental; business center; 24-hr. room service; massage; nonsmoking floor; Internet. *In room:* A/C, TV, minibar, fridge, coffeemaker, hair dryer, safe, IDD phone.

**Palace Hotel**   This downtown tower has been around for a while. In fact, it was popular for U.S. soldiers on R&R during the war years. There have been some recent updates, but the history shows. Standard rooms are nondescript, really, and a bit run down, with older carpet and lots of chipped paint. The high-end suites have large beds, desks, and sitting areas that are raised on parquet and with decent views—a good bet. It offers good group and Internet rates and so attracts lots of big groups, but the friendly staff isn't yet jaded. Unique is the small rooftop pool; small is the operative word, like a bathtub, really.

56–66 Nguyen Hue Blvd., Dist 1, Saigon. © 08/824-4231. Fax 08/824-4229. www.palacesaigon.com. $55–$80 double; $110–$165 suite. AE, MC, V. **Amenities:** 2 restaurants; 2 bars; rooftop pool; sauna; rentals available; business center; 24-hr. room service; massage; laundry. *In room:* A/C, TV, minibar, fridge, IDD phone.

**Rex Hotel** ★★   The Rex has an unorthodox history; it used to be a French garage, was expanded by the Vietnamese, and then was used by the United States Information Agency (and some say the CIA) from 1962 to 1970. The hotel was transformed in a massive renovation and opened in 1990 as the hugely atmospheric government-run place it is today. There are a variety of rooms, but all are large and clean, with fluffy carpets and bamboo detailing on the ceilings, the mirrors—everywhere, in fact. The lampshades are big royal crowns, which are a hoot. There is good indirect lighting throughout. Some of the suites have beaded curtains and Christmas lights over the bathroom mirrors. The beds and pillows are incredible, firm but fat, and there are good views from some balconies. Each suite has a fax machine. The Rex is in a fabulous location downtown, across from a square that has a lively carnival atmosphere at night. It is also known for its rooftop bar, with its panoramic Saigon view. The pool is small, just a toe-dipper, but is in a quiet courtyard. Amenities here cover all the bases, if you can find them in this labyrinth. Much-needed renovations planned.

141 Nguyen Hue Blvd., District 1, Saigon. © 08/829-2185 or 08/829-3115. Fax 08/829-6536. www.rexhotel vietnam.com. 207 units. $120–$140 double; $156–$520 suite. AE, MC, V. **Amenities:** 2 restaurants; 2 bars; outdoor pool; tennis; small health club; Jacuzzi; sauna; tour desk; car rental; business center; shopping; salon; 24-hr. room service; massage; babysitting; laundry; dry cleaning; nonsmoking rooms; Internet. *In room:* A/C, satellite TV w/in-house movies, safe, IDD phone.

## INEXPENSIVE

**Bong Sen Hotel Annex**   This small annex to the large Saigontourist-owned Bong Sen provides many of the same amenities at a lower price. Rooms are very basic, but tidy with light wood furniture, thin carpet, and blue tile bathrooms. Everything is kind of on the small side, though, and the economy rooms have only one small window (even a junior suite isn't much bigger). Make sure you're getting the Annex and not the main Bong Sen, which, though recently renovated, isn't much of a value. Service is indifferent, but this is a good place to just lay your head for cheap. You can arrange any travel necessities elsewhere.

61–63 Hai Ba Trung St., District 1, Saigon. © 08/823-5818. Fax 08/823-5816. www.hotelbongsen.com. 57 units. $50–$65 double; $80 junior suite. AE, MC, V. **Amenities:** Restaurant; rentals available; tour desk; laundry. *In room:* A/C, TV, minibar, fridge, hair dryer, IDD phone.

**Hong Hoa Hotel** ★★   You found it! This minihotel is the top dog of the lower-end category in the Pham Ngu Lao backpacker area. Rooms are small but tidy with real light wood furniture and tile floors. It's backpacker basics here, with low foam beds and little charm, but the satellite TV and IDD phones are a real luxury in this category. Downstairs is a popular Internet center, and the room rate includes free access. It's a funny spot: If it looks like two addresses, it is, with one entrance through a small grocery storefront on busy De Tham street and the other off Pham Ngu Lao. It's cozy, safe, and friendly, and if you stay here long enough, you'll be adopted (and certainly learn some Vietnamese). If the place is full, which is more often than not the case, with just seven rooms, ask for a recommendation and they'll point you to a good neighbor.

185/28 Pham Ngu Lao St., 250 De Tham St., District 1, Saigon. ℂ 08/836-1915. www.honghoavn.com. 7 units. $12–$18 double. Includes tax and service charge. MC, V. **Amenities:** Rentals available; tour information; laundry; good Internet service; small grocery connected. *In room:* A/C, satellite TV, IDD phone.

**Que Huong–Liberty 3**   As the name suggests, the Liberty 3 is part of a chain. No. 3 is right in the heart of the Pham Ngu Lao backpacker area and arguably the best choice down that way. Rooms have all the amenities of a proper hotel but are priced just above the average minihotel. It's thin office carpets and bland decor throughout, but everything is clean. Standard rooms are a bit too small; a superior is your best bet. Be sure to ask for a window and ask to see the room before checking in, as some are worse than others (and many are musty from smoking guests). The adjoining **Allez Boo** bar and restaurant is an old backpacker standby and now managed by the hotel. The chain's flagship hotel, the Metropole (148 Tran Hung Dao; ℂ **08/920-1937**), is a popular business address.

187 Pham Ngu Lao, District 1, Saigon. ℂ **08/836-9522.** Fax 08/836-4557. www.libertyhotels.com.vn. 60 units. $45–$65 double. AE, V, MC. **Amenities:** Restaurant; tour desk; laundry. *In-room:* A/C, satellite TV, fridge, minibar, hair dryer, safe in high-end units, IDD phone.

**Riverside Hotel** ⭐   Wedged into an old colonial storefront area between the hulking Renaissance Riverside and the wedding cake Majestic, the Riverside is a good little budget stop. It's popular with young Japanese tourists and most services cater to them (tours and shopping). Public spaces are a bit banged and battered (worn carpets all around), but private spaces are expansive for the price and everything is clean. It's an old building and some rooms conform to the angled footprint in unique ways. Bathrooms are huge, plain affairs with small tub and shower units, a simple sink, and no counter space, but, again, tidy if simple. Deluxe rooms are worth the upgrade; they're much larger and have new carpet and better amenities (large TVs, safety boxes). The leopard-skin pattern synthetic blankets are kind of fun. The staff is quite helpful.

18–20 Ton Duc Thang St., District 1, Saigon. ℂ 08/822-4038. Fax 08/825-1417. www.riversidehotelsg.com. 73 units. $50–$60 standard double; $70 deluxe; $90–$120 suite. MC, V. **Amenities:** 2 restaurants; tour desk; business center; laundry. *In room:* A/C, satellite TV, fridge, minibar, hair dryer, safe in high-end rooms, IDD phone.

**Spring Hotel (Mua Xuan)** ⭐⭐   If you don't care about fancy amenities and want to be downtown, look no further than the Spring, with nicer rooms than many hotels twice the price. Accommodations here are neat and clean, with comfy double and superking beds, big TVs, well-finished bathrooms done in decorated tiles, and nice, solid dark wood or light rattan furniture. The floral motif isn't bad, and the carpeted floors are impeccably clean. Go as high up as you can to escape street noise, which is the hotel's one failing (and the elevator's kind of slow, too). Lowest-priced "economy" rooms have no windows. Suites are large, with couches in large, separate sitting rooms. The Spring has an unsettling Greco-Roman motif, with statues and filigreed molding here and there; if the lobby's hanging ivy, colonnades, and grand staircase are a bit over the top, rooms are a bit more toned down, utilitarian, and pleasant. A short walk from Dong

Khoi and the central business district, this is a popular choice for long-term business travelers. The staff couldn't be nicer or more helpful.

44–46 Le Thanh Ton St., District 1, Saigon. ✆ 08/829-7362. Fax 08/822-1383. 45 units. $34–$51 double; $65 suite. Includes breakfast. AE, MC, V. **Amenities:** Restaurant; bar; can arrange rentals and tours; room service 7am–10pm; laundry; free Internet in lobby (but slow). *In room:* A/C, TV w/HBO, minibar, fridge, wooden safe, IDD phone.

## WHERE TO DINE

Saigon has the largest array of restaurants in Vietnam, and virtually every world cuisine is represented. The area around Dong Khoi has lots of fine dining choices. Ask locals where to eat, though, and they'll point you to the Ben Thanh Market or a local vendor on wheels. Ho Chi Minh's famous street stalls serve up local specials like *mien ga,* vermicelli, chicken, and mushrooms in a delicate soup; *lau hai san,* a tangy seafood soup with mustard greens; and, of course, *pho,* Vietnam's staple noodle soup.

### EXPENSIVE

**Amigo** 🍽🍽 ARGENTINE/STEAKHOUSE    One of the best steaks I've ever had was here, and I don't mean just in Saigon. This is one of those little expat gems you'll want to seek out. In a roomy two-floor downtown setting, it's a cozy and atmospheric Argentinean steakhouse theme (maybe the only in Asia), laid back but classy. You'll be greeted at the door by a kindly maitre d' who will make you feel at home, as will the friendly staff and chummy atmosphere around the imposing wooden bar. But it's the food that sells this place, and here I mean imported steak done just how you like it, chargrilled to perfection, not panfried, as is common in this part of the world. I had a filet mignon with red shallots that would hold its own in the heart of Chicago. There is a full raw bar and a roster of seafood specials and salads. Entrees come with big baked potatoes and corn; for a real slice of home, follow it up with apple strudel or ice-cream roulade. There's also a great wine list featuring good Argentine and Chilean reds, among others, and a full-service bar.

55 Nguyen Hue St., District 1, Saigon. ✆ 08/836-9890. Main courses 59,000 VND–350,000 VND ($4–$23). AE, MC, V. Daily 11am–2pm and 5–11pm.

**Bi Bi** FRENCH/MEDITERRANEAN    The food is the star at this small restaurant and art cafe, although the atmosphere has its charms as well. Bi Bi's cozy interior is fashioned with bright Mediterranean-style furnishings and Impressionist paintings; the collection changes periodically. Chairs are all embossed with names of notorious or beloved expat patrons past and present. A table near the front is devoted to drinking and card playing, and upstairs there are a few sofas for drinking and lounging. The menu is an interesting mix: cannelloni, ratatouille, pastas, and veal escalope, with fine hot and cold starters like salad with goat cheese and grill items. The beef tenderloin is *trés bien.* For dessert, there are perfectly done staples like crème brûlée, mousse, or homemade ice cream. The starters are almost as expensive as the main courses, and the short wine list comprises pricey selections, making this one of Saigon's more expensive choices. The food is well worth it, though, and service is seamless.

8A/8D Thai Van Lung, District 1, Saigon. ✆ 08/829-5783. Main courses 90,000 VND–190,000 VND ($6–$13). MC, V. Daily 11:30am–2pm and 5:30–10:30pm.

**Camargue** 🍽 FRENCH/CONTINENTAL    Camargue is two floors of enchanting renovated colonial. Choose from softly lit interior or spacious outdoor terrace seating surrounded by palm fronds. The menu changes regularly. A sampling from our visit included warm goat cheese salad, roast pork rondalet, and venison. Camargue also seems to have given tourists the nod by adding ubiquitous, lower-priced pasta dishes. The food, alas, isn't as perfect as the surroundings and the service is substandard, but it's a quaint, laid-back spot downtown. The first floor bar, **Vasco's,** is very popular and open late on Fridays.

16 Cao Ba Quat St., District 1, Saigon. © **08/824-3148.** Reservations recommended on weekend nights. Main courses $5–$12. AE, DC, MC, V. Daily 5:30–11pm.

**Hoi An** ⭐⭐ VIETNAMESE   Run by the same folks who bring you Mandarin just around the corner (see below), Hoi An serves a similar compliment of fine, authentic Vietnamese; here the focus is on central Vietnam's lighter fare and cuisine from Hoi An, Hue, and Saigon. On busy Le Thanh Ton Street just north of the town center, the building is a nice re-creation of a traditional Vietnamese home, and the upstairs dining room is an interesting faux-rustic blend of wood and bamboo. Presentation here is original; witness the hollowed coconut used to serve fine crab and asparagus. Try the drunken shrimp, large prawns soaked in rice whiskey and pan-fried at tableside. Order a cover-the-table meal for a group, and you're sure to go away smiling. Call ahead to ask about the authentic Vietnamese classical music (most nights).

11 Le Thanh Ton St., District 1, Saigon. © **08/823-7694.** Main courses $5.70–$34. AE, MC, V. Daily 5:30–11pm.

**Mandarin** ⭐⭐ VIETNAMESE/CHINESE   On a quiet side street between busy Le Than Thon and the river, cross the threshold at Mandarin and you enter a quaint, elegant oasis that will have you forgetting the seething city outside. Decor is an upscale Chinese motif with timber beams, fine Chinese screen paintings, and artwork on two open-plan floors. It's plush but not stuffy, and you'll feel comfortable in casual clothes or a suit. The staff is professional and attentive but doesn't hover, and it is helpful with suggestions and explanations. Ask about daily specials and set menus. I had an excellent spicy sautéed beef served in bamboo with rice. For a memorable meal, don't miss the famed duck done in a sweet "Mandarin style." The steamed garlic in lobster is as good as it sounds and the seafood steamboat for four is a real coupe. The restaurant features a live classical trio (call ahead for schedule).

11A Ngo Van Nam, District 1, Saigon. © **08/822-9783.** Fax 08/825-6185. Main courses $5.70–$18; set menu from $17 per person (minimum 2). AE, MC, V. Daily 11am–2pm and 5:30–10pm.

**Skewers** ⭐ MEDITERRANEAN   The best food at this chic bistro does in fact come on skewers; barbecue entrees, particularly the lamb kebabs, are delicious. Also try the moussaka, good baked fish and seafood, grilled Moroccan sea bass, good pastas, or barbecue entrees like vodka-flamed beef or ribs dipped in honey. All the flame-bursting barbecuing is done in an open-air kitchen at the front of the restaurant—fun to watch. The salads are large and delicious, and Skewers serves great light meals and apps, with great dips like hummus and baba ganoush. The atmosphere is candlelit and cozy, a great spot for a romantic evening.

9A Thai Van Lung St., District 1, Saigon. © **08/829-2216.** Main courses 50,000 VND–150,000 VND ($3.35–$10). V, MC. Mon–Fri 11:30am–2pm; daily 6–10:30pm.

**Sushi Bar** ⭐⭐ JAPANESE   The food speaks for itself (in Japanese, no less) at this friendly little corner sushi bar. At the end of Le Thanh Ton, an as-yet dubbed "Little Tokyo," this is one of many Japanese eateries popping up and is popular among longtime residents. It's a typical busy, big-city sushi bar, complete with a friendly, wise-cracking sushi master from Japan. Upstairs there are tatami mat rooms, and the place always seems full, which is a good sign. Everything's fresh, and the lunch specials are a good bargain, but it's good sushi and sashimi, worth the price.

2 Le Thanh Ton, District 1, Saigon. © 08/823-8042. A la carte dishes $1–$5.35; set menu $2.35–$12. MC, V. Daily 11:30am–2pm and 5:30–11:30pm. Delivery until 10pm.

## MODERATE

**Al Fresco's Café and Grill** *(Kids)* ⚘ WESTERN    Just like the popular Al Fresco's in Hanoi, this new location in the heart of HCMC (just a stone's throw from the Sheraton), serves good Western favorites. Meat dishes like burgers, steaks and their popular ribs, good pizzas, pastas, and hearty salads all stick to your ribs. Vietnam's answer to TGI Friday's. Good starters are chicken wings, satay, or fried calamari. Meal combos like the "Happy Homer" (as in Homer Simpson) include pizza, pasta, and salad. Al Fresco's is the best choice for Western comfort foods or for something familiar—kids love it. Expat management and ultrafriendly waitstaff make a visit here a welcome slice of home.

27 Dong Du, District 1, Saigon. © 08/822-7317. Main course 40,000 VND–210,000 VND ($2.65–$14). MC, V. Daily 10am–10:30pm.

**Augustin** ⚘ FRENCH    On the quaint, up-and-coming "restaurant row" Ngueyen Thiep (just off Don Khoi), this is a bright, lively little French restaurant, a favorite with French expats and tourists. The food is simple yet innovative French fare, including beef *pot-au-feu* and sea bass tartare with olives. Try the seafood stew, lightly seasoned with saffron and packed with fish, clams, and shrimp. The seating is quite cozy, especially because the restaurant is always full, and the Vietnamese wait staff is exceptionally friendly, speaking both French and English. The menu is bilingual, too. A large French wine list and classic dessert menu finish off a delightful meal.

10 Nguyen Thiep. District 1, Saigon. © 08/829-2941. Main courses 60,000 VND–150,000 VND ($4–$10). No credit cards. Daily noon–2pm and 6–11pm.

**Café Mogambo** AMERICAN    Run by American expat Mike and his Vietnamese wife, Lani, Mogambo is a long-time laid-back Yank hangout in Saigon. It's a small, dimly lit place with cane ceilings and walls, animal head trophies, and memorabilia. There is a long bar with television and a row of regulars bellied up to it. Before long, you'll be joining in the conversation and hanging out longer than you planned. Long, diner-style banquettes that stick to your ribs are one contribution to an American experience. The other is the beef; the hamburgers and steaks are the real thing, as are the sausages and meat pies. Entrees are all quite affordable; it's just the steaks that jack up the high end of the price range. Dessert is apple pie, of course, and a plain, hearty cup of coffee.

20 Bis Thi Sach St., District 1, Saigon. © 08/825-1311. Main courses $4–$13. MC, V. Daily 7am–11pm.

**Chao Thai** THAI    Chao Thai is two floors of an elegant, roomy Thai longhouse, with wide plank wood floors, black-and-white photos of Thai temples, and some small statuary. The restaurant is famous for its fiery papaya salad, fried catfish with basil leaves, and prawn cakes with plum sauce. The flavors are subtle and not overdone; you won't leave feeling drugged on spices or too much chile. It's a popular lunch spot, but the atmosphere is most warm and welcoming in the candlelit evening. The service is gracious and efficient.

16 Thai Van Lung, District 1, Saigon. © 08/824-1457. Reservations recommended only for groups of 5 or more. Main courses 35,000 VND–75,000 VND ($2.35–$5); set lunch menu from 90,000 VND ($6). AE, MC, V. Daily 11am–2pm and 6–10:30pm.

**Lemongrass** VIETNAMESE   The atmosphere is candlelit and intimate, very Vietnamese, with cane furniture and tile floors, yet it's not overly formal. On a small romantic side street that's becoming it's own "restaurant row" in the downtown area, this restaurant is three floors of subdued cool and fine dining; a great place to duck out of the midday sun. Set lunches are an affordable and light option: soup, spring rolls, and a light curry for $2. The long menu emphasizes seafood and seasonal specials. Particularly outstanding are the deep-fried prawns in coconut batter and the crab sautéed in salt and pepper sauce. The portions are very healthful, Asian family-style, so go with a group, if at all possible, and sample as many delicacies as possible.

4 Nguyen Thiep St., District 1, Saigon. ✆ 08/822-0496. Main courses 30,000 VND–190,000 VND ($2–$13); lunch set menus from 30,000 VND ($2). AE, MC, V. Daily 11am–2pm and 5–10pm.

**Temple Club** ✦✦ VIETNAMESE   For atmosphere alone, the Temple Club is a must-see in Ho Chi Minh. As the name suggests, this is a turn-of-the-20th-century Chinese temple with original wood and masonry. Though it has gone upscale with recent renovations, that special air about the place remains. The ceiling is high, and the walls are exposed brick. The floor is terra cotta draped in antique throw rugs, and there are some great Buddhist tapestries and statuary about. There's a classic old wooden bar and a formal but comfortable dining room, as well as a lounge area in the back for coffee and dessert. The cuisine is standard Vietnamese from all parts of the country. This place does a good Hanoi-style *cha ca,* fried monkfish, and the *tom me,* a dish of prawns in tamarind sauce, is a good choice. There's a "Western Corner" that serves sandwiches and salad. For dessert, the banana coconut cream pudding, served with sesame seeds, is decadent, and the coffee is the real thing, even cappuccino. This is one of the most atmospheric and romantic spots in town.

29 Ton That Thiep St., District 1, Saigon. ✆ 08/829-9244. Main courses $3–$8. Daily 10am–2pm and 5–11pm.

## INEXPENSIVE

**Ngon Restaurant** ✦✦✦ *(Finds)* VIETNAMESE   *Ngon* means "delicious," and, for authentic Vietnamese, this restaurant lives up to its name and gets my vote for the best in Vietnam. Ngon has become a real Ho Chi Minh institution and is always packed with both locals and tourists; they've even built a new location nearby to handle the overflow. The atmosphere is chaotic: a cacophony of laughing, chattering guests, shouting waiters, and clanging pots and pans. Fans blow mist to quell the smoky cooking fires of the open-air kitchen. Seating is a mix of regular table dining in the central colonial or in the balcony or courtyard out back. The main building is surrounded by cooking stations, each serving a regional specialty; it is like someone went around the country head-hunting all of the best street-side chefs. Waitstaff simply act as liaisons among the many cooks. The menu is a survey course in Vietnamese cooking, and the tuition is low. Go with a Vietnamese friend, if you can, or someone who can explain some of the regional specialties. If you're alone, just point and shoot. Everything is good. There's Hue-style *bun bo,* cold noodles with beef; a catalog of *pho,* noodle soup; and all kinds of seafood prepared the way you like. Meals here are best as leisurely, many-course affairs, but go just for a snack if you're visiting the Reunification Palace or any sites downtown. Don't miss it!

138 Nam Ky Khoi Nghia, District 1, Saigon. ✆ 08/829-9449. Main courses 7,000 VND–55,000 VND (45¢–$3.65). AE, MC, V. Daily 6:30am–11pm.

**Restaurant 13** ✦ VIETNAMESE   With all the upscale eateries popping up in the downtown area, you might miss out on an old-school standby like this little

## Zen & the Art of *Pho*

*Pho*, or Vietnamese noodle soup, has become a popular dish in the West, but in Vietnam it is a national obsession, a dish eaten any time of day. Its simplicity is the attraction: beef stock with rice noodles garnished as you like, with meat and herbs, all ingredients left to speak for themselves. You can eat *pho* on any street corner and in any market, but there are a few good places in Saigon with English menus and a high standard of cleanliness. Try these: **Pho 2000,** on Tran Hung Dao just catty-corner to the Benh Thanh Market is a Saigon institution and a beehive of activity day or night. Bill Clinton even made a visit here, and if Bubba liked it, it has to be good. **Pho 24** on Nguyen Thiep Street, a little restaurant row off of busy Don Khoi, serves a busy crowd all day in a cool, clean storefront. On Don Khoi, across from the Grand Hotel, look for the large **Pho** sign and Japanese characters at 37 Don Khoi St.; inside the place is covered in woodcarvings and serves great soups—popular with Japanese tourists.

storefront. Tucked between high rises and just off Dong Khoi, this is one of many restaurants whose name is its street number (if this one is busy, try no. 19). The atmosphere is plain, but it serves excellent traditional Vietnamese food without any bells, whistles, or sticker shock. The place is jolly and filled with locals, tourists, and expats. Ask what's good, and try the seafood, anything done in coconut broth, or the sautéed squid with citronella and red pepper. The food is carefully prepared and the waitstaff is very professional for this price range.

13 Ngo Duc Ke, District 1, Saigon. © 08/239-314. Main courses 18,000 VND–60,000 VND ($1.20–$4). No credit cards. Daily 7am–10:30pm.

### SNACKS & CAFES

While shopping on Dong Khoi, stop to savor a few moments at the **Paris Deli** (31 Dong Khoi St.; © 08/829-7533), a retro spot with fantastic pastries and sandwiches. There's another storefront at 65 Le Loi St. (© 08/821-6127), which serves the same good sandwiches and treats.

**Bach Dang** ☞, at 26 Le Loi Street in the heart of old Saigon, is three floors of fun, always crowded and the best place in town for good ice cream and to meet local people. It's a Saigon institution, really.

**Café Central,** in the Sun Wah Tower (115 Nguyen Hue, District 1; © 08/821-9303), is a great little international deli. Stop in for breakfast or a sandwich any time; the kind staff makes you feel like you've stepped into an old greasy spoon (with all the same standbys on the menu).

**Ciao Café** (02 Hang Bai St., downtown; © 08/822-9796) is a good spot for snacks and ice cream. **Fanny,** just below the Temple Club (48 Le That Thiep; © 08/821-1630), serves the real-deal French glacées.

**Brodard Café** (131 Dong Khoi St., District 1; © 08/822-3966) is a cozy international diner-style stop with lots of familiar choices, good coffee, and air-conditioning—a good spot to beat the heat when shopping along Dong Khoi.

**Café L'Opera** (11–13 Cong Truong Lam Son, District 1; © 08/827-5946) is a cozy, upmarket coffee corner right next to the Caravelle Hotel.

# WHAT TO SEE & DO
## ATTRACTIONS IN DISTRICT 1

**Ben Thanh Market** ⭐⭐⭐   The clock tower over the main entrance to what was formerly known as Les Halles Centrale is the symbol of Saigon, and the market might as well be, too. Opened first in 1914, it's crowded, a boon for pickpockets with its narrow, one-way aisles, and loaded with people clamoring to sell you cheap goods (T-shirts, aluminum wares, silk, bamboo, and lacquer) and postcards. There are so many people calling out to you that you'll feel like the belle of the ball or a wallet with legs. Watch for pickpockets. The wet market, with its selection of meat, fish, produce, and flowers, is interesting and hassle-free; no one will foist a fish on you. In open-air stalls surrounding the market are some nice little eateries. The adventurous can try all kinds of local specialties for next to nothing.
At the intersection of Le Loi, Ham Nghi, Tran Hung Dao, and Le Lai sts., District 1.

**City Hall**   Saigon's city hall was constructed between 1902 and 1908, a fantastic ornate example of colonial architecture. Unfortunately, it's not open to the public.
Facing Nguyen Hue Blvd.

**General Post Office (Buu Dien)** ⭐   In a grand old colonial building, you can check out the huge maps of Vietnam on either side of the main entrance and the huge portrait of Uncle Ho in the rear. The specialty stamps counter has some great collector sets for sale.
2 Coq Xu Paris, District 1. Daily 6:30am–10pm.

**Ho Chi Minh City Museum** ⭐   Formerly the Revolutionary Museum, this central behemoth attracts more newlyweds posing for photos on the front steps than anything. Originally built in 1890 by the French as a commercial museum, then a governor's palace and later committee building, the museum covers a broad range, from archaeology to ethnic survey and early photos of the city and documents from its founding in the 1600s. The second floor is heavy on Vietnam's ongoing revolution, with displays of weaponry and memorabilia from the period of struggle against Imperialism and many flags, placards, and dispatches from the rise of Communism, beginning with the August Revolution of 1945 all the way to the fall of Saigon. The bias is heavy, of course, and it is in fact an important rendering of Vietnam's protracted struggle and ideologies, but it is interesting to note how the displays, not unlike socialist ideals, are a bit frayed around the edges in a land that is going pell-mell toward a market economy. The grounds are picturesque, thus the young couples posing for wedding photos, and there is an interesting collection of captured U.S. fighter planes, tanks, and artillery in the main courtyard. Underneath the building is a series of tunnels (closed to the public) leading to the Reunification Palace, once used by former president Ngo Dinh Diem as a hideout before his execution in 1962.
65 Ly Tu Trong St. ☎ 08/829-8250. Admission 10,000 VND (65¢). Daily 8:30am–4:30pm.

**Notre Dame Cathedral** ⭐   The neo-Romanesque cathedral was constructed between 1877 and 1883 using bricks from Marseilles and stained-glass windows from Chartres. The cathedral is closed to visitors except during Sunday services, which are in Vietnamese and English. Whatever your faith is, don't miss it.
Near the intersection of Dong Khoi and Nguyen Du sts., District 1.

**Reunification Palace** ⭐   Designed as the home of former President Ngo Dinh Diem, the U.S.-backed leader of Vietnam in the '60s, this building is most notable for its symbolic role in the fall of Saigon in April 1975, when its gates were breached by North Vietnamese tanks and the victor's flag hung on the balcony; the very tanks that crashed through the gates are enshrined in the entryway and photos and accounts of their drivers are on display. Built on the site of the French governor general's home, called the Norodom Palace, the current modern building, designed when "modern" meant "sterile," was completed in 1966. Like the Bao Dai Palace in Dalat, the Reunification Palace is a series of rather empty rooms that are nevertheless interesting because they specialize in period kitsch and haven't been gussied up a single bit. Tour private quarters, dining rooms, entertainment lounges, and the president's office that feel like everybody just up and left. Most interesting is the war command room, with its huge maps and old communications equipment, as well as the basement labyrinth. There is an ongoing screening of a propagandistic video about the war years in the basement.

106 Nguyen Du St. Admission 15,000 VND ($1). Daily 7:30–11am and 1–4pm.

**Saigon Opera House (Ho Chi Minh Municipal Theater)** This magnificent building was built at the turn of the century and renovated in the 1940s. Three stories and 1,800 seats are inside. Today it does very little in terms of performances, but it is a stalwart atmospheric holdout amid steel-and-glass downtown.

At the intersection of Le Loi and Dong Khoi sts.

**Vietnam History Museum** 🗲🗲 Housed in a rambling new concrete, pagodalike structure, the museum presents a clear picture of Vietnamese history, with a focus on the south. There is an excellent selection of Cham sculpture and the best collection of ancient ceramics in Vietnam. Weaponry from the 14th century onward is on display; one yard is nothing but cannons. One wing is dedicated to ethnic minorities of the south, including photographs, costumes, and household implements. Nguyen Dynasty (1700–1945) clothing and housewares are also on display. There are archaeological artifacts from prehistoric Saigon. Its 19th- and early-20th-century histories are shown using photos and, curiously, a female corpse unearthed as construction teams broke ground for a recent housing project. There are even some general background explanations in English, something missing from most Vietnamese museums.

2 Nguyen Binh Khiem. © 08/829-8146. Admission 10,000 VND (65¢). Daily 8–11:30am and 1:30–4:30pm.

## OTHER DISTRICTS

**Cholon (District 5)** 🗲🗲 Cholon is a sizable district bordered by Hung Vuong to the north, Nguyen Van Cu to the east, the Ben Nghe Chanel to the south, and Nguyen Thi Nho to the west. Cholon is the Chinese district of Saigon and probably the largest Chinatown in the world. It exists in many ways as a city quite apart from Saigon. The Chinese began to settle the area in the early 1900s and never quite assimilated with the rest of Saigon, which causes a bit of resentment among the greater Vietnamese community. You'll sense the different environment immediately, and not only because of the Chinese-language signs.

A bustling commercial center, Cholon is a fascinating maze of temples, restaurants, jade ornaments, and medicine shops. Gone, however, are the brothels and opium dens of earlier days. You can lose yourself walking the narrow streets, but it makes sense to take a cyclo by the hour to see the sites.

Start at the **Binh Tay Market** 🗲🗲, on Phan Van Khoe Street, which is even more crowded than Ben Thanh and has much the same goods, but with a Chinese flavor. There's much more produce, along with medicines, spices, and cooking utensils, and you'll find plenty of hapless ducks and chickens tied in heaps.

From Binh Tay, head up to Nguyen Trai, the district's main artery, to see some of the major temples on or around it. Be sure to see Quan Am, on Lao Tu Street off Luong Nhu Hoc, for its ornate exterior. Back on Nguyen Trai, Thien Hau pagoda is dedicated to the goddess of the sea and was popular with seafarers making thanks for their safe trip from China to Vietnam. Finally, as you follow Nguyen Trai Street past Ly Thuong Kiet, you'll see the Cholon Mosque, the one indication of Cholon's small Muslim community.

**Emperor Jade Pagoda (Phuoc Hai)** ✿✿  One of the most interesting pagodas in Vietnam, the Emperor Jade is filled with smoky incense and fantastic carved figurines. It was built by the Cantonese community around the turn of the century and is still buzzing with worshippers, many lounging in the front gardens. Take a moment to look at the elaborate statuary on the pagoda's roof. The dominant figure in the main hall is the Jade Emperor himself; referred to as the "god of the heavens," the emperor decides who will enter and who will be refused. He looks an awful lot like Confucius, only meaner. In an anteroom to the left you'll find Kim Hua, a goddess of fertility, and the King of Hell in another corner with his minions, who undoubtedly gets those the Jade Emperor rejects. It's spooky.

73 Mai Thi Luu St., District 3. Daily 8am–5pm.

**Giac Lam Pagoda** ✿  Giac Lam Pagoda, built in 1744, is the oldest pagoda in Saigon. The garden in the front features the ornate tombs of venerated monks, as well as a rare bodhi tree. Next to the tree is a regular feature of Vietnamese Buddhist temples, a gleaming white statue of Quan The Am Bo Tat (Avalokitesvara, the goddess of mercy) standing on a lotus blossom, a symbol of purity. Inside the temple is a spooky funerary chamber, with photos of monks gone by, and a central chamber chock full of statues. Take a look at the outside courtyard as well.

118 Lac Long Quan St., District 5. Daily 8am–5pm.

**War Remnants Museum** ✿✿  The War Remnants Museum is a comprehensive collection of the machinery, weapons, photos, and documentation of Vietnam's wars with the both the French and American (the emphasis is heavily on the latter). The museum was once called the War Crimes Museum, which should give you an idea of whose side of the story is being told here. Short of being outright recrimination, this museum is a call for peace and a hope that history is not repeated—visitors are even asked to sign a petition against the kind of aerial carpet-bombing that so devastated the people of Vietnam. The exhibit begins to the right of the entrance with a room listing war facts: troop numbers, bomb tonnage, and statistics on international involvement in the conflict and numbers of casualties on both sides. Next is a room dedicated to the journalists who were lost in wartime. The exhibits are constantly evolving, and the museum was under renovation throughout 2004. One room is devoted to biological warfare, another to weaponry, and another to worldwide demonstrations for peace. The explanations, which include English translations, are very thorough. There is a large collection of bombs, planes, tanks, and war machinery in the main courtyard. Kids will love it, but you might want to think twice before taking them inside to see things like wall-size photos of the My Lai massacre and the bottled deformed fetus supposedly damaged by Agent Orange. There is also a model of the French colonial prisons, called the Tiger Cages, on the grounds.

28 Vo Van Tan St., District 3. ✆ 08/829-0325. Admission 10,000 VND (65¢). Daily 7:30–11:30am and 1:30–5:15pm.

## DAY TRIPS FROM HO CHI MINH

See "Visitor Information & Tours," earlier in this section, for tour providers to the following sites.

**Cao Dai Holy See Temple** ✦✦    The Cao Dai religion is less than 100 years old and is a broad, inclusive faith that sprang from Buddhist origins to embrace Jesus, Mohammed, and other nontraditional, latter-day saints such as Louis Pasteur, Martin Luther King, and Victor Hugo. Practitioners of Cao Daism are pacifists, pray four times daily, and follow a vegetarian diet for 10 days out of every month. Cao Daism is practiced by only a small percentage of Vietnamese people, mostly in the south, but you'll see temples scattered far and wide—easily recognizable by the all-seeing eye, which, oddly enough, looks something like the eye on the U.S. dollar. Often included with trips to the **Cu Chi Tunnels** (below), the temple at Tay Ninh is the spiritual center, the Cao Dai Vatican if you will, and the country's largest. Visitors are welcome at any of the four daily ceremonies, but all are asked to wear trousers covering the knee, remove their shoes before entering, and act politely, quietly observing the ceremony from the balcony area. The temple interior is a colorful wedding cake, with bright murals and carved pillars. Cao Dai supplicants wear either white suits of clothing or colorful robes, each color denoting what root of Cao Daism they practice: Buddhist, Muslim, Christian, or Daoist. On the ride there you'll pass through the town of Trang Bang, site of the famous photo of 9-year-old Kim Phuc, who was burned by napalm. The road also passes Nui Ba Den, the Black Virgin Mountain, which marked the end of the Ho Chi Minh trail from the north and was a Viet Cong stronghold during the war era.
Daily dawn–dusk.

**Cu Chi Tunnels** ✦✦    Vietnamese are proud of their resolve in the long history of struggle against invading armies, and the story of the people of Cu Chi is indicative of that spirit. Just 65km (40 miles) northwest of Saigon, the Cu Chi area lies at the end of the Ho Chi Minh trail and was the base from which Ho Chi Minh gorillas used to attack Saigon. As a result, the whole area became a "free fire zone" and was carpet-bombed in one of many American "scorched-earth" policies. But the residents of Cu Chi took their war underground, literally, developing a network of tunnels that, at its height, stretched as far as Cambodia and included meeting rooms, kitchens, and triage areas, an effective network for waging guerilla warfare on nearby U.S. troops. The U.S. Army's 25th Infantry Division was just next door, and there are detailed maps denoting land that was either U.S.-held, Vietminh-held, or in dispute.

Visitors first watch a war-era propaganda film that is so over the top it's fun. The site supports a small museum of photos and artifacts, as well as an extensive outdoor exhibit of guerilla snares and reconstructions of the original tunnels and bunkers. Wear your "play clothes" if you choose to get down in the tunnels; the experience is dirty and claustrophobic. There is also a shooting range where, for $1 per bullet, you can try your hand at firing anything from a shotgun to an AK-47. At the end of the tour visit the dining hall and try the steamed tapioca that was a Cu Chi staple. Souvenir hawkers abound. A half-day trip can be arranged with any tour company in Saigon, often including a visit to the Cao Dai Temple (above).
Daily dawn–dusk. Entry 65,000 VND ($4.35).

## SPORTS & OUTDOOR ACTIVITIES

There are two excellent 18-hole golf courses at the **Vietnam Golf and Country Club.** Fees are $50 to $80 during the week for nonmembers, depending on which course you want to play, and $100 on Saturday and Sunday. The clubhouse is at Long Thanh My Ward, District 9 (© 08/733-0126; fax 08/733-0102).

**Tennis** enthusiasts can find courts at **Lan Anh International Tennis Court** (291 Cach Mang Than Tam, District 10; © 04/862-7144).

The pool and well-equipped gym and spa at the **Caravelle Hotel** (see "Where to Stay," earlier in this section) are available for nonguests at a day rate of $12.

## SHOPPING

Saigon has a good selection of silk, fashion, lacquer, embroidery, and house-wares. Prices are higher than elsewhere in Vietnam, but the selection is more sophisticated. Stores are open daily from 8am until about 7pm. Credit cards are widely accepted, except for the markets.

Dong Khoi is Saigon's premier shopping street. Formerly Rue Catinat, it was a veritable Rue de la Paix in colonial times. Notable shops include **Heritage** (53 Dong Khoi St.; © 08/823-5438) for woodcarvings and other ethnic arts. **Les Epices** (25 Dong Khoi St.; © 08/823-6795) also has a nice collection of lacquerware and other gift items, and **Authentique Interiors** (38 Dong Khoi St.; © 08/822-133) specializes in fine pottery and table settings. **Viet Silk** (21 Dong Khoi St.; © 08/823-4860) has a quality selection of ready-made clothing and can, of course, whip something up for you in a day.

**Khai Silk** has a fine outlet right in the heart of the city (107 Dong Khoi St.; © 08/829-1146) and offers fine ready-to-wear and fitted silk clothing.

Nearby Le Thanh Ton Street is another shopping avenue. Look for **Kenly Silk** (132 Le Thanh Ton St.; © 08/829-3847), a brand-name supplier with the best ready-to-wear silk garments in the business. Unique, tasteful, hand-embroidered pillows, table linens, and hand-woven fabrics can be found at **MC Decoration** (92C5 Le Thanh Ton St., across from the Norfolk Hotel; © 08/822-6003).

### ART GALLERIES

The **Ho Chi Minh Fine Arts Museum** (97A Pho Duc Chinh St., District 1; © 08/829-4441; Tues–Sun 9am–4:45pm; admission 10,000 VND/65¢), is the place to start if you're truly keen; it is an evolving collection, featuring local artists' works in sculpture, oil, and lacquer: a good glimpse into the local scene. **Lac Hong Art Gallery,** located on the ground floor of the museum (© 08/821-3771), features the works of many famous Vietnamese artists.

There are galleries throughout the city, many clustered around Dong Khoi and near all the major hotels. Reproduction artists are everywhere. Here are a few popular galleries in town: **Ancient Gallery** (50 Mac Thi Buoi St., District 1, near Saigon Sakura Restaurant; © 08/822-7962); **Hien Minh** (32 Dong Khoi St., District 1; © 08/829-5520); **Particular Art Gallery** (123 Le Loi St., District 1; © 08/821-3019); and **101 Catinat** (101 Dong Khoi St.; © 08/822-7643). If these pique your curiosity, pick up a copy of *Vietnam Discovery* or *The Guide,* two local "happenings guides," for further listings.

### BOOKSTORES

HCMC's official foreign-language bookstore, Xuan Thu (85 Dong Khoi St., across from the Continental Hotel; © 08/822-4670) has a good selection of classics, as well as some foreign-language newspapers. There are also several small bookshops on De Tham Street in the backpacker area.

## SAIGON AFTER DARK

When Vietnam made a fresh entry onto the world scene in the mid-1990s, Ho Chi Minh City quickly became one of the hippest party towns in the East. The mood has sobered somewhat, but it's still a fun place. Everything is clustered in District 1; ask expats in places like **Saigon Saigon** or **Maya** (below) about any club happenings. As for cultural events, Saigon is sadly devoid of anything really terrific, except for a few cultural dinner and dance shows.

### BARS AND CLUBS

**Q Bar,** in the basement of the central opera house(7 Cong Truong Lam Son; ✆ **08/824-6325;** www.qsaigon.com), is the town's hippest club, a funky little catacomb with good music, cozy cocktail nooks, and an eclectic mix of homo sapiens. They've also just opened up a chic new restaurant space called **Qucina.**

**Saigon Saigon,** at the top of the Caravelle Hotel (19 Lam Son Sq.; ✆ **08/823-4999**) is a very popular spot featuring live music and a terrific view. Next door, at the Sheraton (88 Dong Khoi St.; ✆ **08/827-2828**), the **Top of 23** is a double-height rotunda overlooking town; it has good live bands. It's Indochina meets the Hard Rock Cafe on any given evening. **Maya's,** a posh martini bar also serving Latin cuisine, is always good for a chic evening of cocktails. **Vasco's Bar,** on the first floor of the Camarque restaurant (16 Cao Ba Quat St.; ✆ **08/824-3148**), is a chic, atmospheric choice. On Nguyen Thiep Street, a little alleyway off of Dong Khoi that is becoming a chic little restaurant row, also find new **Alibi** (6 Nguyen Thiep St.; ✆ **08/822-8855**), a cozy bar and club.

Don't miss the brick-walled Irish pub **O'Briens** (74A Hai Ba Trung St.; ✆ **08/829-3198**) for pints and pizza. **Sheridan's** (17/13 Le Thanh Ton St.; ✆ **08/823-0793**) is another good, friendly watering hole with character.

The Pham Ngu Lao area stays up late, and **Allez Boo** (187 Pham Ngu Lao; ✆ **08/837-2505**), is always up late, as are the many little street-side beer stalls selling Bia Hoi for pennies a glass.

### MUSIC & THEATER

A few hotels stage traditional music and dance shows a la dinner theaters. The **"Au Co" Traditional Troupe** has performed abroad but calls home the Skyview Restaurant at the **Mondial Hotel** (109 Dong Khoi St., District 1; ✆ **08/849-6291**). The **Rex Hotel** (141 Nguyen Hue Blvd.; ✆ **08/829-2185**), has regular performances as well. Call each place ahead of time to double-check the performance schedule.

## 14 The Mekong Delta

Don't leave without seeing the Mekong Delta, even for just a day. The delta is a region of waterways formed by the Mekong, covering an area of about 60,000 sq. km (37,200 sq. miles) and with a population of 17 million, most engaged in farming and fishing. Often called the bread basket of Vietnam, the Mekong Delta accounts for more than an estimated 50% of rice production. The land is tessellated with bright green rice paddies, fruit orchards, sugarcane fields, and vegetable gardens, and its waters are busy with boats and fish farms.

The regions urban centers, Can Tho and Chau Doc, are good bases for tours and exploration of the countryside by road and canal. As you cruise slowly along the meandering canals, you'll see locals living right beside the water on stilt houses or houseboats—a fascinating glimpse into a way of life that has survived intact for hundreds of years. In the many floating markets, trade is conducted from boat to boat in areas teeming with activity and sellers touting their wares.

Delta people are friendly and unaffected, and the cuisine is delicious—lots of good seafood, of course.

Coming south from Saigon, the town you'll probably reach first is **My Tho,** but you should try to make it down at least as far as **Can Tho,** the delta's largest city. It has a bustling riverfront and waterway. About 32km (20 miles) from Can Tho is **Phung Hiep,** the biggest water market in the region. **Chau Doc** is another picturesque town and a popular gateway to Cambodia. Find unique **floating markets,** weaving villages, and expansive fish farms, all visited on tours.

## VISITOR INFORMATION & TOURS

To cope with the necessary logistics, going with a tour agent is your best bet to the delta. Travel agents offer everything from day trips to "3-day, 4-night" tours. Our pick is **Ann Tours** (58 Ton That Tung St., District 1; © **08/833-2564** or 08/833-4356; fax 08/832-3866; www.anntours.com) for custom tours that take you off the beaten path (from $45 a day with a group).

**Saigontourist** (49 Le Thanh Ton St., District 1; © **08/829-8914;** fax 08/822-4987; www.saigon-tourist.com) is a large government tour operation that runs regular bus schedules and tours for groups large and small. Tour quality—and price—is higher than the budget tourist cafes.

The **tourist cafes** all run standard, affordable tours to the delta. Contact **Sinh Café** (246–8 De Tham St., District 1; © **08/369-420**) or **TM Brothers** (269 De Tham St. or 139 Bui Vien St., District 1; © **08/836-1791**), for 2- and 3-day tours starting at $10 per day (with optional connection to Cambodia).

## WHERE TO STAY

**Victoria Hotels** (www.victoriahotels-asia.com) has two unique properties on the Mekong Delta, in Can Tho (© **071/810-111**) and Chau Doc (© **076/865-010**). New but unique colonial-style rooms and services at riverside come priced from just $125. Nothing compares.

# 7

# Cambodia

*by Charles Agar*

It wasn't long ago that travel guides about Cambodia weren't much more than protracted warnings and lists of safety precautions, and for good reason: Following years of war, the chaos and genocide of Pol Pot's Khmer Rouge, and a long period of civil and political instability, Cambodia was until recently an armed camp closed to foreign visitors (or open only to travelers of the danger-seeking variety). But Cambodia is healing, and, though this is a process that will take years, the country is enjoying a period of relative stability under a coalition government. Cambodia offers travelers a host of experiences, from the legacy of ancient architecture to a growing urban capital and beautiful countryside. Even the shortest visit is a window into a vibrant ancient culture and a chance to meet with a very kind and resilient people.

What brings so many to this Buddhist land of smiles is **Angkor Wat,** the ancient capital and one of the man-made wonders of the world. The temple complex at Angkor is stunning, a pilgrimage point for temple aficionados and a place of spiritual significance to many. Most travelers limit their visit to a few days at the temples and the major sites in the growing capital, **Phnom Penh,** but travel in rural Cambodia, once unheard of, is now limited only by your tolerance for bumpy roads and rustic accommodation. Bouncing around the hinterlands of Cambodia still begs caution, though, and travelers should be aware of the mass amounts of UXO (unexploded mines), poor road conditions, and the absence of proper medical services. But dusty roads pay off when they connect hamlets rarely visited by outsiders or lead to unexplored rural ruins. Any of the larger tour operators are a good bet for arranging trips to the likes of mountainous **Rattanakiri,** in the northeast, the Thai border area, or rural riverside towns along the Mekong. The country's only port, **Sihanoukville,** is a little beach destination that's growing in popularity. Intrepid travelers commonly rent motorcycles or brave rattletrap buses.

Known for warm, beguiling smiles, smiles that have weathered great hardship, Khmer people are very friendly, approachable, and helpful; but be warned that the hard sell is on in Cambodia, and you're sure to be harried, especially by the persistent young sellers at Angkor Wat. Nevertheless, travelers here are sure to meet with great kindness.

For years, the lawlessness of Cambodia attracted some rather dubious foreign visitors who came in droves for budget drugs and prostitution. Phnom Penh's expatriate community was notorious during years of instability. Even the UN troops that arrived in 1992 were as much a part of the problem in their support of local vice as they were in maintaining order and ensuring fair elections. "Sexpats" and drug tourists are on the wane in Cambodia, but, sadly, there still is a contingent of folks who come to take advantage of Cambodia's seedier stock-in-trade. There are new extradition treaties in place whereby foreign sex offenders in Cambodia can be tried for their crimes in their home country, but the prosecution process is still full of gaping loopholes and offenders easily fall through the cracks.

Tourism is growing in leaps and bounds, though, and there are many **nongovernmental organizations (NGOs)** here to do their part to rebuild and support the growing nation. Their activities, centered in offices in Phnom Penh, are what keep social services and the infrastructure at subsistence levels. Volunteer opportunities abound. The number of foreign aid workers means increased quality of services, and the hotels and restaurants in Siem Reap and Phnom Penh are on par with any in the region, although outside of these two centers it's sparse.

A visit to **Angkor Wat,** the monumental Hindu temple compound of behemoth block temples, towering spires, giant carved faces, and ornate bas-reliefs, is a once-in-a-lifetime experience. And **Phnom Penh,** the capital, is tatty but charming, with crumbling French colonial architecture and a splendid palace. Cambodia is resplendent with natural gifts; the **Mekong River** is the country's lifeline and connects with **Tonle Sap,** or Great Lake, Southeast Asia's largest lake, surrounded by fertile lowlands. For the Angkor temples alone, the trip to Cambodia is well worth it, the chance to see a beguiling land shaking off the shackles of a devastating recent history to become an exciting tourist destination.

## 1 Getting to Know Cambodia

### THE LAY OF THE LAND

About the size of Missouri, some 181,035 sq. km (70,604 sq. miles), Cambodia's 20 provinces are bordered by Laos in the north, Vietnam in the east, Thailand to the west, and the Gulf of Thailand to the south. There is just one marine port in Cambodia: Sihanoukville, connected via a major American-built highway with the capital and largest city, Phnom Penh.

The mighty Mekong enters from Laos to the north and nearly bisects the country. The river divides into two main tributaries at Phnom Penh before it traces a route to the delta in Vietnam, and most areas of population density lie along the river valleys and fertile plains of this great river and its tributaries. Near Siem Reap, the Tonle Sap (Great Lake) is the largest lake in Southeast Asia. In the monsoon summer months, when the Mekong is swollen from the snows of Tibet, the river becomes choked with silt and backs up on the Mekong Delta. The result is an anomaly: The Tonle Sap river relieves the pressure by changing the direction of its flow and draining the Mekong Delta hundreds of miles in the opposite direction and into the Tonle Sap lake.

The northeast of the country, Ratanakiri Province, and areas bordering Vietnam are quite mountainous and rugged, as are the Thai border areas defined by the Dangrek Mountains in the northwest and the Cardamom Mountains in the southwest. These jungle forest regions are a rich source for timber in the region, and steps toward preservation come slow.

### A LOOK AT THE PAST

Some 2 millennia ago, a powerful people known as the Khmer ruled over much of present-day Southeast Asia, including parts of what is now eastern Thailand, southern Vietnam, and Laos. Theirs was a kingdom that seems to have been created in a dream, full of wondrous temples, magnificent cities rising from steamy jungles, and glorious gods.

# Cambodia

The story of Khmer civilization is one of a slow decline from the zenith of the powerful Angkor civilization of the 11th century. War and years of alternating occupation by neighboring Thailand to the west and Vietnam to the east, later by the French and Japanese, had Cambodia bouncing like a strategic ping-pong ball, and the Khmer kingdom's size was chiseled away considerably. Remaining is what we know today as Cambodia, a tiny land half the size of Germany.

The name Cambodia is an Anglicized version of the French *Cambodge,* a bastardized name of the northern Indian tribe from which the Khmer are said to descend. Both citizens and language are alternately referred to as Khmer or Cambodian. Whatever the origins, the name Cambodia hardly evokes thoughts of ancient glory. To those of us born in the late 20th century, especially in the West, Cambodia suggests instead a history of oppression, civil war, genocide, drug running, and coups d'état. Constant political turbulence, armed citizenry, bandits, and war fallout, such as unexploded mines and bombs, have given the country a reputation as one of the world's most dangerous places to travel rather than a repository of man-made and natural wonders. It's important to have perspective on the country's troubled history in order to understand the present. Only then can we appreciate the present civil order and the fact that citizens have been or are being disarmed, and that Cambodia is making the slow push into this new century.

## A TURBULENT POLITICAL PAST

Cambodia is populated by people of the **Mon-Khmer** ethnic group, who probably migrated from the north as far back as 1,000 B.C. The area they settled was part of the kingdom of Funan, a Southeast Asian empire that also extended into Laos and Vietnam, until the 6th century, when it was briefly absorbed into a rebel nation called Chenla. It then evolved into its glorious Angkor period in the 8th century, from which sprung many of Cambodia's treasures, most notably the lost city of Angkor.

By the late 12th century the Angkor kingdom began a decline, marked by internal rebellions. Angkor was lost to the Kingdom of Siam in 1431. Vietnam jousted with Siam and also had a hand in controlling the kingdom, to some degree, beginning in the early 17th century. The French took over completely in 1863, followed by the Japanese, and then the French again. Cambodia finally regained independence in 1953 under the leadership of **Prince Norodom Sihanouk.**

Vietnamese communist outposts in the country drew Cambodia into the Vietnam conflict. The country was heavily bombed by American forces in the late 1960s. A U.S.–backed military coup followed in 1970, but in 1975 the infamous **Khmer Rouge,** led by the tyrannical **Pol Pot,** took over Cambodia, renamed it Kampuchea, and established a totalitarian regime in the name of communism. Opposition—even imaginary opposition—was brutally crushed, resulting in the death of over 2 million Cambodians. The civil and Vietnam wars decimated Cambodian infrastructure. Cambodia became, and still is, one of the world's poorest nations, with a mainly agrarian economy and a literacy rate of about 35%.

In response to Khmer Rouge infractions into its country, Vietnam invaded Cambodia in 1978 and occupied it with a small number of troops until 1989, installing a puppet regime led by Hun Sen as prime minister. When Vietnam departed, the United Nations stepped in and engineered a fragile coalition government between the Sihanouk and Hun Sen factions. There was never full agreement, however, and Hun Sen took over in a violent 1997 coup. The Khmer Rouge subsequently waned in power, and its former leader, Pol Pot, died in 1998.

In November 1998, a new coalition government was formed between the two leading parties, leading to relative political peace. Cambodia is now leaning toward a war crimes tribunal for Khmer Rouge perpetrators, but it still has not decided how to confront its vicious and bloody past and move forward.

## THE PRESENT

July 2003 elections went off without incident, but it took nearly a year for the negotiation of a government coalition. Hun Sen still reigns as prime minister, but now alongside the FUNCINPEC Party and Prince Norodom Ranariddh. They have a dizzying backlog of legislation. In the fall of 2004, King Norodom Sihanouk, Cambodia's longtime standard-bearer through the many violent regime changes and trying times, abdicated, selecting his son Norodom Sihamoni, a retired ballet dancer, to take up the symbolic post of king.

Cambodia's economy is experiencing a 5% annual growth rate, mostly spurred by tourism, but the scene in rural Cambodia is bleak. Basic medical services are nonexistent and education and job training are out of reach for rural peasantry. International monitors and aid organizations look to the youthful population (some 60% under the age of 20), the survivors and the next generation after genocide, to foster peace and productivity. The forecast is not good. The proliferation of new AIDS cases in Cambodia, and the inability to treat patients, is a major concern. Rural travel entails following safety precautions to the letter (see below) and staying abreast of the current political situation—instability being the hallmark—

but know that the Cambodia of today is a much safer and saner land than only a few years ago. Our tourist dollars are a big reason why.

## THE KHMER PEOPLE

Ninety percent of Cambodia's 11 million people are ethnic Khmer, the remainder a mix of ethnic Vietnamese, Chinese, hill tribes, and a small pocket of Cham Muslims. Cambodia's history is a road map of incursions and invasion. Cambodia is a geographic and cultural crossroads of the two powers, India and China, that shaped Southeast Asia and, more than any country in the region, reflects the French term *Indochine*. Khmer culture, like nearby Laos, is defined by Theravada Buddhism, but in other matters, one gets the distinct impression that Cambodia is still searching for its identity.

## ETIQUETTE

Traditions and practices in Cambodia, like neighboring Thailand and Laos, are closely tied with Theravada Buddhism. Modest dress is expected of all visitors, and bare midriffs or short shorts are an offense to many and will cause a stir. Men and women should go easy on public displays of affection. As in all Buddhist countries, it is important to respect the space around Buddhist monks; women especially should avoid touching and even speaking to the men in orange robes anywhere outside the temple.

In personal interaction, keep it light and friendly, especially when bargaining or handling any business affairs. If Khmer people are confused, misunderstand, or are in disagreement, they do what many Westerners find inconceivable: smile, nod, and agree while whole in the knowledge that they will do something different. This is difficult to understand, but try to remember that if you're angry and lots of people around you are smiling, you're unlikely to have achieved your desired aim (in short, you're doomed). Direct discourse is certainly not standard procedure here, and many Western visitors can feel cheated by that misunderstanding. Be clear in what you expect from someone—whether a guide, a motorbike driver, or a business associate—and get firm affirmation of that fact. Listen closely to what comes after the *but* in "Yes, but . . .."

On the list of cultural no-nos, it's important to remember that the feet are considered dirty and that the head is sacred and pure. This means that even pointing the feet in the direction of another or stepping over someone, thus exposing the soles of the feet, is impolite. Touching someone's head, even tussling a child's hair, should be avoided.

Hospitality has its own elaborate rules, and, like in any culture, it is important to accept when possible, or comfortable, and say thank you, *Awk Koun.*

## LANGUAGE

The language of Cambodia is called either Cambodian or Khmer, a term that refers to the ethnic majority of the country but is also used to describe all things Cambodian: Khmer people (the Khmer), Khmer food, or Khmer culture. The Khmer language belongs to the Mon-Khmer family and is a derivative of Sanskrit and Pali, the language spoken by Buddha. Unlike in neighboring Thailand and Laos, the Khmer language is not tonal and is thus more merciful to the casual learner. Basic pronunciation is still frustrating and difficult, though. Khmer script is based on a south Indian model and is quite complex.

Khmer embraces many loan words from French, Chinese, and now English, especially technical terms. Older Khmers still speak French, and young people are quite keen to learn and practice English. In the major tour centers, speaking slowly and clearly in basic English phrases will do the trick, but a few choice phrases in Khmer will get you far.

## USEFUL KHMER PHRASES

| | | |
|---|---|---|
| Hello | **Soa s'day** | Sew sadday |
| Good bye | **Lia haoy** | Lee howie |
| Thank you | **Awk koun** | Awk coon |
| Thank you very much | **Awk koun chelan** | Awk coon chalan |
| How are you? | **Sohk sabai?** | Sook sabai? |
| I am fine. | **Sohk sabai.** | Sook sabai. |
| Yes (man) | **Baat** | Baht |
| Yes (woman) | **Jaa** | Jya |
| No | **Te** | Tay |
| I'm sorry | **Sohm To** | Sum too |
| Do you have _____? | **Men awt men? (lit. do you have or don't you?)** | Men ought men? |
| Water? | **Tuhk?** | Took? |
| Toilet? | **Bawngku uhn?** | Bangku oon? |
| How much? | **Th'lai pohnmaan?** | Tlai bawn mahn? |
| Can you make it cheaper? | **Som joh th'lai?** | Sum joe tlai? |

## 2 Planning Your Trip to Cambodia

### VISITOR INFORMATION

You'll find a wealth of information at www.gocambodia.com, or click on "Cambodia" at www.visit-mekong.com. The Cambodian Embassy to the U.S. sponsors www.embassy.org/cambodia.

- **In the U.S.:** 4500 16th St. NW, Washington, DC 20011 (© **202/726-7742;** fax 202/726-8381; www.embassy.org). **In NY:** 866 UN Plaza, Suite 420, New York, NY 10017 (© **212/421-7626;** fax 212/421-7743).
- **In Australia/New Zealand:** No. 5 Canterbury Crescent, Deakin, ACT 2600, Canberra (© **61-6/273-1259;** fax 61-6/273-1053; www.embassyofcambodia.org.nz).
- **In Thailand:** No. 185 Rajdammri Rd., Lumpini Patumwan, Bangkok 10330, Thailand (© **662/254-6630;** fax 662/253-9859; recanbot@loxinfo.co.tlt).

### WORKING WITH A TOUR OPERATOR

Many visitors choose to see Cambodia with the convenience of a guided tour, which is a good idea: It's not only safer and easier, but it also means that you won't miss the finer details of what you're seeing and can visit rural Cambodia in as much comfort as possible. Being part of a larger group tour is a good, affordable option. Even if you travel independently, you might want to sign up with a local tour operator (like Diethelm or Exotissimo, below) once you're there.

### RECOMMENDED TOUR OPERATORS:
### International

- **Abercrombie & Kent.** 1520 Kensington Rd., Suite 212, Oakbrook, IL 60523-2141 (© **800/323-7308;** fax 630/954-3324; www.aandktours.com).
- **Asia Transpacific Journeys.** 2995 Center Green Court, Boulder, CO 80301 (© **800/642-2742** or 303/443-6789; fax 303/443-7078; www.asiatranspacific.com).

## Regional

- **Diethelm Travel.** No. 65 St. 240, P.O. Box 99, Phnom Penh, Cambodia (© **023/219-151;** fax 023/219-150; www.diethelm-travel.com). **In Siem Reap:** House no. 4, Road no. 6, Krum no. 1, Sangkat no. 2, Phum Taphul, Siem Reap, Cambodia (© **063/963-524;** fax 063/963-694).
- **Exotissimo.** 46 Norodom Blvd., Phnom Penh, Cambodia (© **023/218-948;** fax 023/426-586; www.exotissimo.com).

## ENTRY REQUIREMENTS

All visitors are required to carry a passport and visa. A 1-month visa can be issued on arrival at the Phnom Penh or Siem Reap airports for about 80,000R ($21), and an overland visa-upon-arrival is available from both Thailand (overland from Poipet) and Vietnam (by boat from Chau Doc or by bus through Moc Bai) for $22. Bring two passport photos for your application. For other entry points, you must obtain your visa before arrival. There is an overland crossing between Laos and Cambodia via Stung Treng, but it is a trip reserved for the hearty.

Tourist visas can be extended three times for a total of 3 months. Any travel agent can perform the service for a small fee. Business visas, for just $25 upon entry, can be extended indefinitely.

## CUSTOMS REGULATIONS

For visitors 18 years or older, allowable amounts of goods when entering are as follows: 200 cigarettes or the equivalent quantity of tobacco; one opened bottle of liquor; and a reasonable amount of perfume for personal use. Currency in possession must be declared on arrival. Cambodian Customs on the whole is not stringent. With a long, sad history of theft from the Angkor temples, it is forbidden to carry antiques or Buddhist reliquary out of the country, but Buddhist statues and trinkets bought from souvenir stalls are fine.

## MONEY

Cambodia's official currency is the riel, but the Cambodian economy is tied to the fate of its de facto currency, the U.S. dollar. Greenbacks can be used anywhere. The exchange rate at the time of publication was **3,900 riel = US$1.** It's important to have riel for smaller purchases, but there is no point in exchanging large amounts of foreign currency into the local scrap. Prices for all but the smallest purchases are in U.S. dollars and are listed as thus in this chapter. The **Thai Bhat** is widely accepted in the western region of the country. You'll commonly receive small change in riel. The riel comes in denominations of 100, 200, 500, 1,000, 2,000, 5,000, 10,000, 50,000, and 100,000. You cannot change Cambodia's riel outside the country, so anything you carry home is a souvenir.

**ATMs**    There are no ATMs with international capabilities in Cambodia.

**CURRENCY EXCHANGE**    You can change traveler's checks in banks in all major towns. Because the U.S. dollar is the de facto currency, it's not a bad idea to change traveler's checks to dollars for a 1% or 2% fee and make all purchases in U.S. cash.

**TRAVELER'S CHECKS**    Traveler's checks are accepted in most major banks for exchange, but not commonly at individual vendors. American Express is a good bet and is represented by **Diethelm** (see tour operators above).

**CREDIT CARDS**    Cambodia has a cash economy, but credit cards are becoming more widely accepted. Most large hotels and high-end restaurants accept the majors, but you'll want to carry cash for most transactions and certainly in the countryside. To report a lost or stolen card, see the "Fast Facts" section (p. 417).

## WHEN TO GO

**CLIMATE**    Cambodia's climate falls into the pattern of the southern monsoons that also hit neighboring Thailand and Vietnam from May to November. There is little seasonal temperature variation, meaning that it's always hot (a yearly mean of about 82°F/28°C), and the best time to go is in the dry season from December to April.

**CLOTHING CONSIDERATIONS**    Keep it light and loose; it's always hot. "Less is more" applies here; bulky luggage is an albatross in Cambodia. Loose, long-sleeve shirts and long pants are recommended. Cotton is the best choice, and long trousers are better than shorts. First, long pants are the best way to fend off mosquitoes. Second, culturally, shorts are worn by children, not adults (although long shorts are more accepted, especially for young men), and for women only rarely (with sporting events being the exception). A wide-brimmed hat is essential protection from the sun, and some even carry an umbrella to be used either as a parasol or as cover from sporadic rains. Sandals are acceptable in most arenas.

**PUBLIC HOLIDAYS & EVENTS**    **Independence Day** is November 9 (1953) and is celebrated throughout the country like the American July Fourth. October 31 is **King Sihanouk's Birthday,** and **Khmer New Year** is in the middle of April. There are water festivals and boat races at the end of November, and the **Angkor Festival** is held at the end of July.

## SAFETY

It is recommended that you check with your home country's overseas travel bureau or with the **United States Department of State** (click "Travel Warnings" at www.state.gov) to keep abreast of travel advisories and current affairs that could affect your trip.

The days of the Khmer Rouge taking backpackers hostage are long gone, and the general lawlessness and banditry that marked Cambodia as inaccessible and dangerous only a short time ago has abated. Gun-toting thugs, once a common sight in any town, have been disarmed. Old habits die hard, however, and in general travelers should take caution. Poverty in rural areas breeds desperation and a volatile climate.

## DRUGS

Cambodia is one of the world's biggest producers of cannabis—not to mention heroin, amphetamines, and other substances—and peddlers abound. You might be tempted to buy or sample substances offered, but if caught, you could face a lengthy jail sentence, which is guaranteed to be uncomfortable. Enough said.

## HEALTH CONCERNS & VACCINATIONS

In chapter 3, we outlined information about health concerns and general issues that affect the region. Health considerations should comprise a good part of your trip planning for Cambodia, even if you're going for only a few weeks.

---

*Warning*    **Medical Safety & Evacuation Insurance**

The Cambodian medical system is rudimentary at best and nonexistent at worst. Make sure that you have medical coverage for overseas travel and that it includes emergency evacuation. For details on insurance, see chapter 3. There are a few clinics in Phnom Penh and Siem Reap, but for anything major, evacuation to Bangkok is the best option.

---

*Warning*   **Some Important Safety Tips**

- Remember that the police and military of Cambodia are not there to protect and serve. Any interaction with the constabulary usually results in frustration and/or your coming away short a few dollars. Contact your embassy for major problems, and call for police assistance only in cases of theft or extreme danger. Demand a ticket if threatened with a fine of any sort although often, especially for small traffic infractions, it's best to just cough up a buck or two.
- Rural travel is really opening up, and you'll find a hearty welcome in even the most remote hamlet, but roads are rough and travel of any distance is best done in an off-road conveyance with a sturdy suspension: Motorbike or four-wheel-drive trucks are best. Know too that you're really on your own out in the sticks, with no hospitals and limited support services.
- Especially at night, travelers should stay aware, not unlike in any big city at night; purse snatching is not uncommon in Phnom Penh, and pickpockets are as proficient here as anywhere in the region, so take care.
- Land mines and unexploded ordnance can be found in rural areas in Cambodia, but especially in Battambang, Banteay Meanchey, Pursat, Siem Reap, and Kampong Thom provinces. Don't walk in heavily forested spots or in dry rice paddies without a local guide. Areas around small bridges on secondary roads are particularly dangerous.

You'll need to cover all the bases to protect yourself from tropical weather and illnesses, and you will need to get special vaccinations if rural areas are on your itinerary. You should begin your vaccinations as necessary weeks before your trip to give them time to take effect. If you follow the guidelines here and those of your doctor, however, there's no reason you can't have a safe and healthy trip.

**Malaria** is not a concern in Phnom Penh and any of the larger towns, but upcountry and even in and around Siem Reap and Angkor Wat, it's quite common. Many travelers take preventative medication. Check with the Centers for Disease Control (CDC) at www.cdc.com for current information. An **antimalarial prophylaxis** is recommended everywhere but in Phnom Penh. Take atovaquone proguanil (brand name Malarone), doxycycline, or mefloquine (brand name Lariam). If you plan to travel extensively in the rural areas on the western border with Thailand, primaquine is the only effective preventative.

Other mosquito-borne ailments, such as **Japanese encephalitis** and **dengue fever,** are also prevalent. Your best protection is to wear light, loose-fitting clothes from wrist to neck and ankles, wear a bug repellent with DEET, and be particularly careful at sunset or when out and about early in the morning.

**Hepatitis** is a concern, as it is anywhere. Reliable statistics on **AIDS** are not out, but with rampant prostitution and drug abuse, Cambodia is certainly fertile ground for the disease. Recent efforts to educate needle users about the dangers of substance abuse and the importance of clean needles, as well as increased condom use, are positive signs, but recent statistics show that the tide of new AIDS cases is rising.

## Telephone Dialing Information at a Glance

- **To place a call from your home country to Cambodia:** Dial the international code (011 in the U.S., 0011 in Australia, 0170 in New Zealand, or 00 in the U.K.), plus the country code **855**, the city code (**23** for Phnom Pehn, **63** for Siem Reap), and the phone number (for example, 011 855 23 000-000). *Important note:* Omit the initial "0" in all Cambodian phone numbers when calling from abroad.
- **To place a call within Cambodia:** Dial 0 before the city code (as numbers are listed in this book). Note that all phone number are six digits after the city code.
- **To place a direct international call from Cambodia:** Most hotels offer international direct dialing, but with exorbitant surcharges of 10% to 25%. Faxes often have high minimum charges. To place a call, dial the international access code **(001)** plus the country code, the area or city code, and the number (for example, to call the U.S., you'd dial 001 1 000/000-0000).
- **International country codes are as follows:** Australia: 61; Myanmar: 95; Canada: 1; Hong Kong: 852; Indonesia: 62; Laos: 856; Malaysia: 60; New Zealand: 64; the Philippines: 63; Singapore: 65; Thailand: 66; U.K.: 44; U.S.: 1; Vietnam: 84.

## FOREIGN EMBASSIES IN CAMBODIA

If you encounter problems during your visit, go to your embassy. Addresses for embassies in Phnom Penh are as follows: **U.S.:** #16 St. 228 between streets 51 and 63 (✆ **023/216-436;** http://phnompenh.usembassy.gov); **Canada:** #11, Senei Vanna Vaut Oum, St. 254 (✆ **023/213-470**); **Australia:** (Also serves New Zealanders) #11, Senei Vanna Vaut Oum, St. 254 (✆ **023/213-466**); and **U.K.:** #27–29 Botum Soriyavong, St. 75 (✆ **023/427-124**).

## GETTING THERE

**BY AIR** International flights to Cambodia from neighboring countries are many and affordable. Cambodia's two main hubs, **Siem Reap Airport** and Phnom Penh's **Ponchentong Airport,** are served by the following: Bangkok Airways from Thailand; Malaysia Airlines from Kuala Lumpur; Lao Airways from Vientiane; Vietnam Airways from Ho Chi Minh and Hanoi; and Silk Air from Singapore. Shanghai Air, EVA, President, and China Southern provide connections between Phnom Penh and points in China. There is a $25 international departure tax.

**BY BUS** Pickup trucks and limited bus service connect with Poi Pet, near Thailand, a journey that is like crossing the craters of the moon—you'll come away dust-caked and exhausted and this trip is only recommended for the rough and ready. Arriving from Vietnam, private minibuses and taxis can be chartered from the border near Moc Bai to Phnom Penh. The ride is bumpy but manageable, though flying in or out of Phnom Penh or Siem Reap is recommended.

**BY BOAT** There are daily boats between Phnom Penh and Vietnam's border town, Chau Doc. From Vietnam, contact the **Victoria Chau Doc Hotel** (✆ **076/865-010**) for expensive, private services, or one of the traveler cafes, such as **Sinh Café** (✆ **08/369-420**) for a budget trip. From Phnom Penh, make arrangements through any hotel or travel agent.

## GETTING AROUND

**BY AIR**    Connection between Phnom Penh and Siem Reap is frequent and regular on President Air and Siem Reap Airways. There is a $6 domestic departure tax in both Phnom Penh and Siem Reap.

**BY BUS**    Most travelers find local buses rough going in the extreme. Contact the folks at an old traveler standby, **Capitol Tour** (#14 AEO, Rd. 182, Sangkat Beng Prolitt; ✆ **023/217-627**), for inexpensive seat-in-coach connections and tours throughout the country. **Ho Wah Genting Transport Company** (Rd. 67 just west of the Central Market, Phnom Penh; ✆ **023/210-859**) provides service between Siem Reap and Phnom Penh for just $3.50. **Mekong Express** (87 Sisowath Quay, Phnom Penh; ✆ **023/427-518**) connects Phnom Penh and Siem Reap with daily luxury (well, A/C) buses for just $6.

**BY CAR/MOTORBIKE**    Hiring a car with a driver, driving yourself, or going by rented motorbike is a great way to see Cambodia's rural highways and byways. Rough country roads mean that you'll need to hire the most durable of vehicles, with good suspension. Hiring a driver is recommended; traffic is unpredictable. Contact hotels and travel agents.

**BY BOAT**    Speed boats make the 5-hour trip between Phnom Penh and Siem Reap. The costs is $25 and any hotel can arrange a ticket. Boats leave from the pier near the Japanese Bridge in the north end of town or connect with Siem Reap's Tonle Sap docks by taxi. **Mekong Express Tour Boat** charges $35 for a ride on its larger, more comfortable boat. Visit its offices adjacent to the ferry terminal (87 Sisowath Quay, Phnom Penh; ✆ **023/427-518**).

## TIPS ON ACCOMMODATIONS

Be warned that accommodations often fill up in the winter high season, especially at the finer hotels near Angkor Wat. There is a 10% VAT charge at most hotels. Expect discounts in the low season. The only quality accommodations that you'll find are in Phnom Penh and Siem Reap, but their standard is high. Some budget properties are updating to rustic boutique properties.

## TIPS ON DINING

In this old French colony, the cuisine is heavily French, all affordable and often quite good. There's also good Thai, and tourist centers are chockablock with storefronts that serve up reasonable facsimiles of Western favorites.

## TIPS ON SHOPPING

There are lots of antique stores and boutiques in the major tour centers, but shopping for trinkets and memorabilia is best at the big markets: the Russian Market and Central Market in Phnom Pehn, and the Old Market in Siem Reap.

### FAST FACTS: Cambodia

*Business Hours* Vendors and restaurants tend to be all-day operations, opening at about 8am and closing at 9 or 10pm. Government offices, including banks, travel agencies, and museums, are usually open from 8am to 4 or 5pm with an hour break for lunch.

*Crime* Once a place where violence and banditry were an everyday occurrence, Cambodia has become much safer in recent years. The civilian population is more or less disarmed and civil authorities have firm control, but be on your toes. It's best not to be out on the roads too late at night and be careful to lock valuables in hotel safes. In the event of trouble, comply and report any incidents to local officials.

*Drug Laws* Availability can look like permission, but it's often not the case. It's said that you can bribe your way out of (or into) anything in corrupt Cambodia, but it is best not to test the theory. Police are crooked and may be the ones who sell (out of uniform) in order to collect the bribe. Like anywhere, dabbling in this arena makes you friends in all the wrong places, and Cambodia is not a good place to have the wrong friends.

*Electricity* Cambodia runs on 220-volt European standard electricity, with rounded, two-prong plugs. Bring an adapter if you're coming from the U.S., in addition to a surge protector for delicate instruments.

*Embassies* Australia and Canada: #11 St. 254 (✆ **023/426-000**); United Kingdom: #27–29 St. 75 (✆ **023/427-124**); United States: #27 St. 240 (✆ **023/426-436**).

*Emergencies* In Phnom Penh, dial ✆ **117** for police, or ✆ **119** for ambulance.

*Hospitals* You'll want to take care of any medical or dental issues before arriving in Cambodia. The **SOS Clinic** in Phnom Penh, #161 St. 51 (✆ **023/216-911**), is your best bet in a pinch.

*Internet/E-mail* Reliable service can be found in the major centers, with prepaid wireless connections a recent innovation.

*Language* The Cambodian language is Khmer, an amalgam of ancient Sanskrit and Pali. English and French are spoken widely, as is Mandarin.

*Police* Khmer Police exist to harass and collect, not to protect and serve. Contact them only in the event of a major emergency, ✆ **117**. The expat hot line is ✆ **023/724-793**.

*Post Offices/Mail* Hotels usually sell stamps and send postcards. See specific cities for post office locations.

*Telephone & Fax* Phones in the major centers are reliable and international direct dial is common—for a price. See telephone dialing, below.

*Time Zone* Cambodia is 7 hours ahead of Greenwich Mean Time, in the same zone as Bangkok. It is 12 hours ahead of U.S. Eastern Standard Time during the winter months, and 3 hours behind Sydney.

*Tipping* Tipping is not obligatory but appreciated. A blanket 10% to 20% is exorbitant. It's best to just round up any check, or leave a buck or so.

*Toilets* Public toilets are a little rough. Many are the Asian "squatty-potty" variety, rather grungy with an attendant at the door charging a small fee for entrance and a few squares of gritty paper. It's not a bad idea to bring your own bog roll (toilet paper) and maybe some germ-fighting hand lotion. Facilities in Western accommodations will be more familiar.

*Water* No tap water is potable. Buy bottled water, which is widely available.

## 3 Phnom Penh

Founded in the mid–14th century by the Khmers as a monastery, Phnom Penh replaced Angkor Thom a century later as the country's capital. The city has long been a vital trading hub at the confluence of three rivers: the Mekong, Tonle Sap, and Bassac. The city's most dramatic history was when it lay vacant; following an eviction order from Pol Pot, the city was deserted in a period of hours. Almost all of Phnom Penh's residents moved to the countryside in 1975, not to return until 1979 under the authority of Vietnamese troops.

It has been a long road to the peaceful and growing Phnom Penh of today. There were many years of frontier-style anarchy after the city was repopulated in 1979. Drugs and prostitution are still a big downtown commodity, but it's unlikely that you'll be caught in the crossfire, something you couldn't say 4 or 5 years ago. Today Phnom Penh enjoys its own kind of harmony of opposites. Visitors are offered peaceful moments like a sunset at riverside, as well as dusty, motorbike-choked labyrinthine alleys and cacophonous markets. The city is an incongruous cluster of crumbling French colonials, and the central riverside area has a pace all its own that's great for wandering.

There's also much of historic interest in Phnom Penh. Its **Royal Palace** is a stone showpiece of classical Khmer architecture, and the **Silver Pagoda,** on the palace grounds, is a jewel-encrusted wonder. Throughout the city, you'll see the faded glory of aged **French colonial architecture.** There are also many notable *wats,* Buddhist temples with resident monks.

Of more grisly interest is the **Tuol Sleng,** or Museum of Genocide, a schoolhouse-turned-prison where up to 20,000 victims of Pol Pot's excesses were tortured before being led to the **Choeung Ek,** otherwise known as The Killing Fields, about 16km (10 miles) from Phnom Penh. It's a town certainly worth exploring for a few days.

### VISITOR INFORMATION & TOURS
#### DELUXE
- **Diethelm Travel.** 65 St. 240, P.O. Box 99, Phnom Penh, Cambodia (© **023/219-151;** fax 023/219-150; www.diethelm-travel.com). In Siem Reap: House no. 4, Road no. 6, Krum no. 1, Sangkat no. 2, Phum Taphul, Siem Reap, Cambodia (© **063/963-524;** fax 063/963-694).
- **Exotissimo.** 46 Norodom Blvd., Phnom Penh, Cambodia (© **023/218-948;** fax 023/426-586; www.exotissimo.com).

#### BUDGET
- **Capitol Guesthouse Tours.** #14 AEO, Road 182, Sangkat Beng Prolitt (© **023/217-627**). This is the town's budget travel cafe and a good place to arrange inexpensive rural and local tours and onward connections by bus and boat. Remember that you get what you pay for, but the services are convenient.
- Small tour operators and ticket shops abound along Sisowath. For flights and other services, try **K.U. Travel and Tours** (© **023/723-456;** www.kucambodia.com) at #77 St. 240 (in the cafe and gallery area).

## GETTING THERE

**BY AIR**    All major airlines in the region connect here. Ponchentong Airport is just a 15-minute drive from the city center and a cab costs $7, a ride on the back of a motorbike just $2.

**BY BOAT**    Speedboats connect with Siem Reap and leave every morning from the main dock on the north end of town. Tickets are available just about anywhere in town. The price is $25 from most hotels or the Capitol Guesthouse (above). **Mekong Express Tour Boat** charges $35 for the 5-hour trip on a larger, more comfortable boat. Contact Mekong Express just across from the ferry terminal (87 Sisowath Quay; © 023/427-518; www.mekongexpresstourboat.com).

**BY BUS**    Buses connect with neighboring Vietnam and points throughout the country. From Vietnam, contact **Saigontourist** (© 08/829-8914) or **Sinh Café** (© 08/369-420). From Cambodia to Vietnam, ask at any travel agent, hotel, or the Capitol Guesthouse (see above). A tourist bus to Siem Reap takes 6 to 7 hours and costs $5. **Ho Wah Genting Transport Company** (© 023/210-859), with an office just west of the Central Market, sells tickets to all the major stops and minor hamlets in the country. **Mekong Express** (see "By Boat," above) has daily connections to Siem Reap on an air-conditioned bus for $6.

## GETTING AROUND

Phnom Penh's downtown is accessible on foot, and it's easy to find your way because the streets are arranged in a numbered grid. For sites farther afield, like The Killing Fields or any temples, you'll need wheels. Metered taxis are everywhere in town, and any hotel can arrange daily car rental (with driver). Or, contact the folks at **Lucky! Lucky!** (413 Monivong Blvd.; © 023/212-788), who rent high-quality motorbikes for rural touring (available for long-term rental) as well as jeeps and even luxury cars.

**Motorcycle taxis,** called **motodups,** can be hired anywhere and cost about 2,000 riel (about 50¢) for short trips in town. Bargain hard. These guys are everywhere, especially on the riverside, and the competition is in your favor. Then again, what the heck is 50¢? Tip and you'll have a friend for life.

---

### FAST FACTS: *Phnom Penh*

*American Express*  For basic American Express services (reporting lost checks, etc.) contact **Diethelm** at: #65 St. 240, P.O. Box 99, Phnom Penh, Cambodia (© 023/219-151; www.diethelm-travel.com).

*Banks/Currency Exchange*  **Canadia Bank**, at #265 St. 110 (© 023/215-284); **Mekong Bank**, at #1 St. 114 (© 023/217-112); and **Cambodian Commercial Bank** (CCB) at #26 Monivong Rd. (© 023/426-208) are just three of many in the downtown area that can cash traveler's checks and give cash advances. There is a **Western Union** office at Cambodia Asia Bank (© 023/210-900) in the Naga, a floating casino behind the Cambodiana Hotel.

*Emergency*  For police, dial © 117; for fire, dial © 118; and for the expat hot line, dial © 023/724-793.

*Clinics*  The **International SOS Medical and Dental Clinic,** at #161 St. 51 (© 023/216-911), is the best place for minor emergencies. **Naga Clinic,** at #11 St. 254 (© 011/811-175), is another. For any major emergency or injury, however, you'll want to arrange medical evacuation.

# Phnom Penh

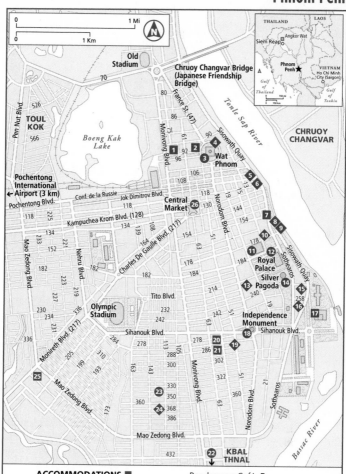

## ACCOMMODATIONS ■
Amanjaya, Pancam Hotel **7**
Golden Gate Hotel **20**
Goldiana **21**
Hotel Cambodiana **17**
Hotel Intercontinental
  Phnom Penh **25**
Raffles Hotel Le Royal **1**
Sunway Hotel **2**

## DINING ◆
Bali Café **9**
The Boddhi Tree **24**
Comme a la Maison **19**
Foreign Correspondents'
  Club (FCC) **8**
Le Deauville **4**
Mith Samlan (Good Friends)
  Restaurant **10**
Origami **15**

Rendezvous Café **5**
River House **6**
Tamarind Café **13**
Topaz **16**

## ATTRACTIONS ●
"The Killing Fields," Choeung
  Ek Memorial **22**
Central Market **26**
Independence Monument **18**
National Museum **11**
Royal Palace **12**
Silver Pagoda **14**
Tuol Sleng, Museum of Genocide **23**
Wat Phnom **3**

*Internet/E-mail* Internet outlets line the riverside Sisowath Street. Hourly access starts at $1. **Friendly Web,** near Capitol Guesthouse, has good access from its office at #199 EO, St. 107 (at the corner of Rd. 182; © **012/843-246**). **KIDS** is an NGO where American owner Bill Herod brings Internet technology to Khmer students. It has good, inexpensive access in its offices at #17A St. 178 (© **023/218-452**; kids@camnet.com.kh).

*Hot Lines* Alcoholics Anonymous holds meetings in Phnom Penh. Check its website at www.aacambodia.org.

*Post Office* The post office is located in the north end of town on Street 13, east of Wat Phnom. It's open daily 6:30am to 5pm, and has standard delivery service and an international phone. **DHL** has an office on #28 Monivong Rd. (© **023/427-726**), and **FedEx** is at #701D Monivong Rd. (© **023/216-712**).

*Telephone* The local code for Phnom Penh is 23. International direct dialing is available in most hotels and at the post office. Storefront Internet cafes along Sisowath offer inexpensive Internet calls or direct dialing. Cellphones are very popular in the city, and you'll find street-side stalls on wheels where you can make local and international calls for next to nothing, with a good cellular connection.

## WHERE TO STAY

There are some choice hotels in town, from old, upscale gems to budget mini-hotels and even a few small boutique properties. I recommend spending a little more for bargain luxury because the midrange properties of Phnom Penh are run-down, at best. Always ask about seasonal rates. Some hotels charge a 10% VAT.

### VERY EXPENSIVE

**Hotel Inter-Continental Phnom Penh** 🏵🏵🏵    This is a true five-star property. For the high-end business traveler, the Inter-Continental is definitely the place. This luxury behemoth has every amenity and every in-room convenience, including wireless Internet. You can also get fine fitness, health, and beauty services. You're just a short ride from the city center, but there's no reason to leave this self-contained, upscale gem. Rooms are done in tidy carpet, elegant dark wood furnishings, overstuffed couches, floral curtains that match the spreads on the large king beds, and fine marble detailing in the entry. All is large and luxe and beds are fluffy and comfortable. Well-appointed bathrooms are large and come with separate shower and bath. Art Deco oak desks and floor-to-ceiling windows give guests that "power broker" feel (even if you're just a small fish). The large outdoor pool has a fun elephant fountain and elegant water-level bar, and the Clark Hatch fitness center is the best in town. Dining is fine Chinese and Western. The lobby is pure marble elegance, and the staff is superefficient and professional. Executive check-in comes with an addition of just $18, and services in the fine executive lounge are certainly worth it. The regency suite is fit for kings, literally. Toto, I don't think we're in Cambodia anymore.

P.O. Box 2288, Regency Sq., 296 Blvd. Mao Tse Toung. © **023/424-888.** Fax 023/424-885. www.interconti.com. 354 units. $190 single; $220 double; $330–$1,500 suite. Seasonal and Internet rates available. AE, MC, V. **Amenities:** 2 restaurants; 2 snack bars; bar; outdoor pool; great fitness center; sauna; children's playroom; concierge; tour desk; car rental; business center; shopping; 24-hr. room service; massage; babysitting; laundry service; dry cleaning; banquet facilities; Internet. *In room:* A/C, satellite TV, dataport, minibar, fridge, safe, IDD phone.

**Raffles Hotel Le Royal** ⭐⭐   Built in 1929, this is Phnom Penh's most atmospheric hotel, an authentic Art Deco and colonial classic. Reopened and expanded with a new wing in 1997, everything from the vaulted ceilings in the lobby to the classic original central stairs breathes history and charm. Rooms are done with fine tiled entries, high ceilings, indirect lighting, a sitting area with inlaid furniture, and ornate touches like antique wall sconces and fine drapery. The scale is large but not imposing, and bathrooms are good-size and done in painted decorative tile with marble counters. Landmark rooms, just one step above the standard, are a good choice in the older building and are larger, with nice appointments like claw-foot tubs. It's luxury with a price tag, but it's worth it. There are some interesting theme suites named for famous visitors, including Stamford Raffles. Even Jacqueline Kennedy has a room dedicated to photos and memorabilia of her 1967 visit. The central pool area is a tranquil oasis divided by a unique pavilion, and the amenities throughout, such as the fine massage facility, are luxe. The staff is very professional.

92 Rukhak Vithei Daun Penh (off Monivong Blvd.), Sangkat Wat Phnom. ℂ 023/981-888. Fax 023/981-168. www.raffles.com. 208 units. $290–$320 double; $350–$2,000 suite. AE, MC, V. **Amenities:** 3 restaurants; 2 bars; 2 outdoor pools; health club; Jacuzzi; sauna; kids' club; concierge; tour desk; car rental; business center; shopping; 24-hr. room service; massage; babysitting; laundry service; dry cleaning; Internet. *In room:* A/C, satellite TV, minibar, fridge, coffeemaker, hair dryer, safe, IDD phone.

## EXPENSIVE

**Hotel Cambodiana** ⭐⭐   They've got it all at the Cambodiana. With a convenient location, atmosphere, and all the amenities, this is a good jumping-off point for the sites downtown. The building looks like a giant gilded wedding cake, and its vaulted Khmer-style roofs dominate the sky in the southern end of downtown. The lobby is abuzz with activity, whether it's visiting dignitaries or disembarking tour buses, but the helpful staff handles it all with grace. The large riverside pool is great, and there are some fine choices in international dining. Rooms are priced according to their view of the river, and executive floors are a fine high standard. Everything is tidy, but decoration is a chain-hotel style in plain wood and office carpet; it's a bit dull, and some floors reek of pungent deodorizers. Deluxe riverview rooms are the best bet. The high-end suites are richly decorated and the executive privileges on the top floors are luxe. Wireless Internet (with prepaid cards) is available in all public spaces. All rooms have picture windows and good views of town or the river.

313 Sisowath Quay. ℂ 023/426-288. Fax 023/982-380. www.hotelcambodiana.com. 267 units. $175–$180 double; $200 on Chactomuk floors; $225–$500 suite. AE, MC, V. **Amenities:** 4 restaurants; bar; outdoor pool; tennis court; small health club; Jacuzzi; sauna; concierge; car rental; business center; shopping; limited room service; massage; laundry service; dry cleaning; executive-level rooms; banquet facilities; Internet. *In room:* A/C, satellite TV, minibar, fridge, safe, IDD phone.

**Sunway Hotel** ⭐⭐   The Sunway is a very comfortable high-end choice. Just west of Wat Phnom in the north end of town, the facade and entry are grand, and the small wrought-iron chandelier suspended at mezzanine level in the cool marble of the lobby completes the fine effect. The staff snaps to and is courteous even when busy. The Sunway covers all the bases for amenities, with a good health club and large downstairs esthetic salon and massage area. The fine dining room and laid-back lobby lounge are stylish and inviting. Rooms are chain-hotel bland but are large, clean, and very comfortable. Done in a carpet of tight geometric design, white walls, and ceiling broken nicely by wooden valances, rooms have a good feel—though sadly they could do without the bad "hotel art." Still, it's a very comfortable standard. Bathrooms are large, with shower/tub combos and granite counters.

#1 St. 92, Sangkat Wat Phnom, P.O. Box 633. © 023/430-333. Fax 023/430-339. www.sunway.com.kh. 138 units. $140–$160 deluxe; $280–$850 suite. AE, MC, V. **Amenities:** Restaurant; cafe; bar/lounge (live entertainment nightly); health club; Jacuzzi; sauna; steam room; concierge; tour desk; car rental; business center; shopping arcade; 24-hr. room service; massage; babysitting; laundry service; dry cleaning; Internet; small book corner. *In room:* A/C, satellite TV, dataport, minibar, fridge, coffeemaker, safe, IDD phone.

## MODERATE

**Amanjaya, Pancam Hotel** ★★   Riverside at Sisowath Quay, this three-story corner building is a true house of style. The porous laterite walls of the lobby, the same stone used in Angkor, and Buddhist statues throughout contribute to a cool boutique vibe. Though sparse in services and amenities, rooms are spacious, done in rich red silk hangings and bedspreads that contrast boldly with the dark wood trim and floors. All rooms have king beds. The suites are enormous and worth the extra outlay. All bathrooms are immaculate affairs done in wood and tile, with neat shower/tub units in standard rooms and separate shower and tub in suites, delineated by unique large-stone gravel paths in concrete. Rooms vary in size and shape, with the corner suites the best, offering panoramic views of the river and busy street below. Noisy traffic is the only drawback.

#1 St. 154, Sisowath Quay. © 023/214-747. Fax 023/219-545. 21 units. $95–$125 single; $105–$145 double; $175–$215 suite. MC, V. **Amenities:** Restaurant; limited room service; laundry service; dry cleaning. *In room:* A/C, satellite TV, minibar, fridge, safe in suites only, IDD phone.

**Juliana Hotel** ★   The Juliana is a good distance from the center of town and popular with group tours. Rooms are situated around a luxuriant central pool shaded by palms and with a terrace and lounge chairs: a bright spot in an otherwise dull landscape. The hotel is Thai-owned and managed and popular with regional businessmen. Standard rooms aren't especially attractive and have aging red carpeting and the nicks and scrapes of heavy use. That said, superior and deluxe rooms are large and well appointed in tidy carpet and light wood trim. Regal headboards top large beds, and there are nice rattan furnishings throughout. Be sure to request a nonsmoking room and check it out before checking in. Billing as a "city resort" kind of comes up short, but the Continental restaurant is inviting and the pool is a standout, even if the rooms don't quite pass muster.

16 Juliana 152 Rd., Sangkhat Vealvong. © 023/366-070-72 or 023/880-530-31. Fax 023/366-070-72. www.julianacambodia.com 93 units. $70 standard; $120 superior; $160 deluxe; $240 suite. AE, MC, V. **Amenities:** 2 restaurants; small lobby bar; outdoor pool; small health club; sauna; car rental; business center; shopping; salon; room service 5am–11pm; large downstairs massage complex; babysitting; laundry; banquet facilities; Internet. *In room:* A/C, satellite TV, minibar, fridge, IDD phone.

## INEXPENSIVE

**Golden Gate Hotel** ★   Standard $15 rooms here are basic but clean and quite livable. The Golden Gate also has deluxe rooms that are larger but just as plain. This is a popular spot for long-staying expat business visitors and NGO folks, and the suites, with kitchenette and small living room, are like one-room apartments. Rooms are done in either tile or office carpet and have mismatched but tidy cloth and rattan furniture. Baths are the small shower-in-room type typical of guesthouses. The best choice is a deluxe room on a higher floor (with view). Be sure to ask to see the room first, as they really vary.

#9 Rd. 278, Sangkat (just south of the Independence Monument). © 023/7211-161. Fax 023/721-005. golden gatehtls@hotmail.com. $15 standard single; $20 standard double; $30 deluxe; $40 suite. MC, V. **Amenities:** Restaurant; car rental; business center; limited room service; laundry; Internet. *In room:* A/C, satellite TV, minibar, fridge, IDD phone.

**Goldiana** ★★   A labyrinthine complex, the result of many construction phases, the Goldiana is one of the best budget choices in the Cambodian capital. The hotel is just south of the Victory Monument and a short ride from the main sites. It's low luxe but squeaky clean. Rooms are very large and have either carpet or wood flooring. The hotel's maintenance standard, unlike similar hotels in town, is meticulous. Although that new-car smell is long gone, it's low on the mildew and musty odors of its in-town competition. Bathrooms are smallish but comfortable, with a shower/tub combo and granite tile. The third-floor pool is a real bonus in this category. The lobby is a designer muddle of heavy curtains, large pottery with fake flowers, mirrors, and bright-colored carved wood, but it acquires a certain appeal once it becomes familiar. The staff is kind and helpful and is used to the questions and concerns of long-staying patrons, tourists, and business clients. Even guests on short stays, however, will be made to feel at home.

#10–12 St. 282, Sangkat Boeng Keng Kang 1. ℭ 023/219-558. Fax 023/219-490. www.goldiana.com. 154 units. $35 single; $45 double; $55–$95 suite. MC, V. **Amenities:** Restaurant; outdoor pool (rooftop); basic gym; car rental; courtesy car; business center; room service 6am–10pm; laundry service; dry cleaning; Internet. *In room:* A/C, TV, minibar, fridge, IDD phone.

## BUDGET

Affordable accommodation abounds in the Cambodian capital but can be a bit rough—thin-walled cacophony, bad smells, surly proprietors, and poor security are the hallmarks. In and around Sisowath Quay, the busy riverside boulevard, you'll find minihotels and budget lodging of all kinds starting at about $10 per night. The eastern shore of the **Boeung Kak Lake** just north of town is also a popular backpacker ghetto. It's cheap sleeps and eats with no frills (or nothing even close to frills), but you're sure to meet some fellow travelers.

A good budget option is the **Last Home Guesthouse,** on the promenade south of Wat Phnom (#47 St. 108; ℭ **023/724-917**), with concrete-block basic rooms above a popular little storefront eatery. Rooms range from $2 to $8.

**Capitol Guesthouse** (#14 AEO, Rd. 182; ℭ **023/217-627**) is the town's backpacker information center and offers very basic concrete rooms from $2.

## WHERE TO DINE

Between remnants of French colonialism and the recent influx of humanitarian aid workers, international cuisine abounds in the Cambodian capital. Some restaurants themselves are actually NGO (nongovernmental organization) projects designed to raise money for local causes or provide training. Ask Khmer folks where to eat, and you'll certainly be pointed to any of the street-side stalls or storefront Chinese noodle shops south of the Central Market, but good eats can also be had from riverside Sisowath or in and among the lazy alleys of the town center.

---

### *Finds*  Prek Leap

For an interesting evening of local fun and frolic, cross the Cambodian-Japanese Friendship bridge on the Tonle Sap River in the north end of town and follow the main road a few short clicks to the town of **Prek Leap,** a grouping of large riverside eateries always crowded with locals on the weekend. Some of these places put on popular variety shows, combining the universal language of slapstick with a good chance to eat, talk, and laugh with locals. The restaurants serve similar good Khmer and Chinese fare. Go by taxi and pick the most crowded place; the more, the merrier.

---

## EXPENSIVE

**Foreign Correspondents Club (FCC)** ✯ CONTINENTAL   With a long
history as Phnom Penh's place to see and be seen, the FCC is as much a tour
stop as a restaurant. Once the gathering place of the dust-caked, camera-toting,
intrepid breed who came to chronicle the country's troubled times, the FCC is
now a multifloor affair of restaurant, bar, and shops done in dark wood and terra
cotta. There are low reclining chairs in the cafe area, a fine dining room, and a
dark bar that serves as the stalwart centerpiece. The whole second floor is oriented to the fine views of the river and busy Sisowath below. Ceiling fans dan-
gle from the high, exposed roof and spin oblong patterns, and geckos, as
everywhere in town, chase along the walls. Come for a drink or to pretend you're
here on assignment. The food is uninspired Western, but the execution is good.
The FCC makes fine pizza in its wood-fired oven and has good snacks like
nachos and enchiladas, as well as treats like "Death by Chocolate," a fudge cake
with mousse and ice cream. The upstairs bar is very popular in the evening, and
the place is abuzz with activity day and night, whether power lunches or late-
night laughs. There is also wireless Internet (buy a prepaid card). The FCC is a
good place to pick up information on travel, volunteering, or work in the area.
#363 Sisowath St. ✆ 023/724-014. Main courses $5–$19. MC, V. Daily 7am–midnight.

**Origami** ✯✯ JAPANESE   Sushi in Cambodia? Go figure. There are a number of Japanese restaurants in town, in fact, but Origami serves fine sushi and all
manner of good, authentic Japanese that'll have you saying *"Oishi!"* From
*tonkatsu,* deep-fried pork over rice, to real Japanese ramen (noodle soup), Ms.
Kimura, the genial proprietor, covers all the bases. Essential ingredients are
imported from Japan, and everything is priced accordingly. The sushi is the real
deal, and the presentation and decor of this little park-side gem could have been
lifted straight out of Tokyo. Popular with the many Japanese expats on humanitarian assignment, the restaurant is itself an NGO offering training in Japanese
language and culture to Khmer kids.
#88 Sothearos St. (near main downtown sites). ✆ 012/968-095. Main courses $3–$12; set menu $10–$20.
No credit cards. Mon–Sat 11am–2pm and 6–9:30pm.

**River House** ✯✯ FRENCH/CONTINENTAL   One of many along the riverside, this bar and restaurant, like the nearby FCC (above), stands out by virtue of
size and style. A classic corner colonial, its downstairs is an open-air bar area with
quaint patio seating under canvas umbrellas. There's also a new, elegant air-conditioned dining room. Upstairs is a bass-thumping, dimly lit club with a dance
floor that is a popular late-night haunt. Elegant rattan chairs, two stately bars in
wood and glass, and the fine linen and silver presentation are luxurious far
beyond the price tag. The food is excellent, characterized by fine French specials
like duck done as you like, coq au vin, and a popular chateaubriand with morel
mushrooms. Come for a romantic dinner and stay for dancing.
#6 St. 110 (corner of Sisowath). ✆ 023/212-302. Main courses $6.80–$32. AE, MC, V. Daily 10:30am–mid-
night.

**Topaz** ✯✯ FRENCH/CONTINENTAL   Good familiar food and atmosphere that's sophisticated but not stuffy are the hallmarks of Topaz, an 8-year-
old French bistro. In air-conditioned comfort, diners choose from informal
booth seating near the comfortable bar or at elegant tables with fine linen, silver, and real stemware in a formal dining room unrivaled in town. The menu
features great steaks, pasta, and salad. The Caesar salad is noteworthy. Daily

lunch sets are popular with the business crowd, and daily specials are contingent on the day's imports of fish or fine steaks. Wine racks line the dining room walls, with some great choices. *Bon appétit!*

#100 Sothearos Blvd. (near downtown sites). ℂ 023/211-054. Main courses $8.20–$35. MC, V. Daily 11am–2pm and 6–11pm.

## MODERATE

**Bali Café** ⊛ INDONESIAN/WESTERN   This smart little second-floor cafe has a vaulted ceiling and open plan that faces busy Sisowath and the picturesque riverside: a good spot to relax and beat the heat. The unique Indonesian cuisine is heavy on curry of the sweet, coconut milk variety. I had the *gado gado,* a popular Indonesian dish of steamed mixed vegetables in peanut sauce. Come with friends and order up a table-covering repast for very little. Views from the window seats are good, but go for a spot in the raised central area where comfy chairs have the best high angle on the busy street below. It's also a popular bar in the evening.

#379 Sisowath St. ℂ 023/982-211. Main courses $3–$5. No credit cards. Daily 7am–10pm.

**Comme á la Maison** ⊛ CONTINENTAL   Expats love this place. It's quiet, with the most commotion coming on weekend mornings when a steady stream of deliveries leaves the bakery. Light fare tops the bill, with good soups and salads perfect for sopping up with something freshly baked. Comme á la Maison also features heartier French entrees and meat and cheese platters, as well as good pizzas and pastas. Follow up with fresh yogurt, fruit, and tasty desserts. Breakfast is good, too. The quiet courtyard area is at the top of the list for escaping the chaos of busy Phnom Penh.

#13 St. 57 (around corner from Goldiana, southwest of town center). ℂ 023/360-801. www.commeala maison-delicatessen.com. Main courses $3–$8. No credit cards. Daily 6am–3pm and 6–10pm.

**Le Deauville** ⊛ FRENCH   This open-air French bar and brasserie is a good, mellow choice. On the north end of the Wat Phnom roundabout, the folks at Le Deauville serve fine, affordable French and Khmer dishes. The atmosphere is unpretentious and cozy, with a large open bar at the center and tables scattered in the street-side courtyard and shielded from the traffic by a wall of potted greenery. Daily lunch set menus give you a choice of salad and entree, and you can select from local specialties like filet of Mekong fish with lime or fine medallion de boeuf. The restaurant serves good pizzas and spaghetti, and has a wine list that fits just about any taste and budget. Le Deauville is also a popular spot for a casual drink in the evening.

Kj St. 94 (just north of Wat Phnom). ℂ 012/843-204. Main courses $2–$6. V. Daily 7am–11pm.

**Rendezvous Café** ⊛ CONTINENTAL   There are so many little eateries lining the riverfront of Sisowath Road, it's hard to pick. Here's one of the best, an open-air corner bar with big, comfy rattan chairs in a prime people-watching location on the north end of Sisowath Quay, the riverside road. The Rendezvous serves solid Western pub grub: burgers, steaks, and chicken dishes, as well as good pizzas and sandwiches. This is a great place to have a cold beer and a good meat-and-potatoes meal, or a groovy fruit shake and a simple salad or sandwich. The staff here couldn't be nicer; they're amenable to suggestions (such as burgers cooked to order), and they'll make you feel like a local from the get-go. The bar hops late into the night.

#127Eo, corner of Sisowath Quay and St. 108. ℂ 023/986-466. Main courses $3.80–$6.80. No credit cards. Daily 6am–11pm.

**Tamarind Café** ✻ FRENCH/MEDITERRANEAN  Good tapas, *mezze* (Middle Eastern appetizers), salads, and a host of French and Mediterranean entrees make Tamarind's cool perch overlooking busy Street 240 an excellent choice. This spot in the popular cafe and gallery area is perfect for Dad to grab a book or a local rag at the nearby London Book center and prop his feet up while Mom goes boutiquing. The pastas and pizzas are delicious, and fresh salads and light menu items are just right on a hot day. The bar is always busy, and stays open late.

#31 St. 240. ✆ **012/830-139**. Main courses $4.50–$11. MC, V. Daily 10am–last customer.

## INEXPENSIVE

There are lots of affordable open-air cafes along riverside Sisowath. Also try:

**The Boddhi Tree** ✻ ASIAN/KHMER  Include lunch here with a trip to nearby Tuol Sleng prison (p. 430), a site that doesn't inspire an appetite, really, but The Boddhi Tree is a peaceful oasis and not a bad spot to collect your thoughts after visiting vestiges of Cambodia's late troubles. Named for the tree under which the Buddha "saw the light," this verdant little garden courtyard and rough-hewn guesthouse has comfy balcony and courtyard seating, and seems to serve up as much calm as the coffee, tea, and light fare that make it so popular. There are daily specials and often visiting chefs. All the curries are good, as are the great baguette sandwiches. Established in 1997 as a way to drum up funds and support to help Khmer kids and families in challenging circumstances, the folks here welcome your suggestions and invite visitors to get involved in their important work.

#50 St. 113, Beong Keng Kong (across from Tuol Sleng Museum). ✆ **011/854-430**. www.boddhitree.com. Main courses $2–$3.75. No credit cards. Daily 7am–9pm.

**Mith Samlanh (Good Friends) Restaurant** ✻✻ KHMER/INTERNATIONAL  Not to be missed is this friendly little gem, an NGO project where Khmer street kids are given shelter and taught useful skills for their reintegration into society: It's a unique opportunity to meet friendly mentors and young folks who've found a new lease on life. The food is great, mind you, an ever-changing tapas menu of local and international favorites like spring rolls, fried rice, good salads, and a host of desserts. I had a delicious sweet sticky rice with a nice mix of local fruit. This is a great spot to cool off and have a light bite while touring the city center (right across from the "must-see" National Museum); the place is a cozy open-air colonial in a courtyard done up in primary-color murals of the kids' drawings. The name of the restaurant means "good friends"; in fact, you might find yourself giving English lessons, laughing, and smiling with these young survivors. The helpful mentoring staff members are happy to talk about their many efforts, including drug and AIDS programs and a 500-student vocational facility. They also run a boutique next door called **Friends and Stuff,** which sells reconditioned electronics and new crafts from their training center.

#215 St. 13 (across entrance to National Museum). ✆ **012/802-072**. www.streetfriends.org. Main courses $1–$3. No credit cards. Daily 11am–2pm and 5–9pm.

## SNACKS & CAFES

**Java Café and Gallery** (#56 E1 Preah Sihanouk Blvd.; ✆ **012/833-512**) is a good spot in town to relax and escape the midday heat. Just south of the main sites (near the Independence Monument), this popular second-story oasis has casual seating on a large balcony and an open gallery interior. It serves real coffee and cappuccino as well as good cakes and other baked goods. Evenings can feature live music. Open 7am to 10pm.

**The Shop** is a nice little stop on popular Street 240 (✆ **023/986-964**), now with a new location on the north end of Sisowath Quay. It serves fine baked goods and great teas and coffees in a friendly and comfortable storefront at each location. There are neat details, like butcher-block tables and fresh flowers, and The Shop can arrange picnic lunches for day trips from Phnom Penh.

**Sugar Palm Café** (#19 St. 240; ✆ **023/220-956**) serves good Khmer dishes at street side or from its upstairs balcony. The interior also functions as a gallery, with local crafts. This is a great place to relax and enjoy real Khmer atmosphere.

**Pizza** can be found at any number of storefronts on the crowded riverside; **Happy Pizza** (#223 Sisowath Quay; ✆ **012/559-114**) is among them. Beginning with the name, there are cute little codes in play here, so to be direct: Say "Please don't put marijuana on my pizza," unless you want it. Same drill at **Ecstatic Pizza** (193 Norodom Blvd.; ✆ **023/365-089**). Both are good and will deliver.

## WHAT TO SEE & DO

All sites in the city center can be reached on foot, but you'll want to hire a car with a driver or, for the brave, a motorcycle taxi to reach sites outside the city center. **Tuol Sleng** and **The Killing Fields** can be visited together, and arrangements can be made in any hotel lobby.

**Central Market**    This Art Deco behemoth, built in 1937, is a city landmark and, on any given day, a veritable ant hill of activity. The building has a towering rotunda with busy wings extending in four directions. The eastern entrance is the best spot to find T-shirts, hats, and all manner of trinkets and souvenirs, as well as photocopy bootlegs of popular novels and books on Cambodia. Goldsmiths, watch repair, and sales counters predominate in the main rotunda, and you can find some good deals. Spend some time wandering the nooks and crannies, though, and you're sure to come across something that strikes your fancy, whether that's a chaotic hardware shop, a cobbler hard at work with an awl, or just the cacophony and carnival-barker shouts of salesman and haggling shoppers. Be sure to bargain for any purchase.
Between sts. 126 and 136 in town center. Daily 5am–5pm.

**Independence Monument**    Built in the late 1950s to commemorate Cambodia's independence from the French on November 9, 1953, this towering obelisk is crowned with Khmer *nagas* and is reminiscent of Angkor architecture and Hindu influence. The area is at its most majestic when all lit up at night.
South of town center at intersection of Norodom and Sihanouk boulevards.

**"The Killing Fields," Choeung Ek Memorial**    Originally a Chinese cemetery before becoming the execution grounds for the Khmer Rouge during their maniacal reign under Pol Pot from 1975 to 1979, the site is a collection of mounds, mass graves, and a towering monument of catalogued human skulls. It's often visited in conjunction with a tour of Tuol Sleng (below).
15km (9¼ miles) south of Phnom Penh. Arrange a private car or motorcycle.

**National Museum** ★★★    What the British Museum is to the Elgin Marbles of Greece's Parthenon, the National Museum of Phnom Penh, opened in 1920 by King Sisowath, is to the statuary of Angkor Wat. This important storehouse holds artifacts and statuary from all over the country. The sad fact is that many pieces didn't make it here, but were plundered and smuggled out of the country. Nevertheless, this grand red sandstone edifice has a beautiful and informative collection of Khmer pieces. From the entrance, begin on your left with a room of small prehistorical artifacts. A clockwise loop around the central courtyard walks you through time, from static, stylized pieces of stiff-legged, standing Buddhas, to contra-posed and contorted forms in supplication. There are good accompanying descriptions in English, but this is not a bad place to have a knowledgeable guide (ask in the lobby). The central courtyard features a *Shiva lingum* (icon of the god Shiva) and large temple fragments. At the more signifi-cant works (the statue of Javaryman, for example) elderly ladies, looking like museum docents, hand out incense and flowers and instruct visitors to place them on makeshift altars. Don't feel obliged—it's kind of off-putting to some. If you do participate, drop a few riel and ignore entreaties for a larger donation.

Just north of Royal Palace at St. 178, and short walk from the river. Admission $3. Daily 8–11am and 2–5:30pm.

## Royal Palace and Silver Pagoda ★★★   Don't miss this glittery downtown campus, the ostentatious jewel in the crown of Cambodia's monarchy. Built in the late 1860s under the reign of Norodom, the site comprises many elaborate gilded halls, all with steep tile roofs, stupa-shaped cupolas, and golden temple *nagas* denoting prosperity. The grand **Throne Hall** at the center is the coronation site for Khmer kings and the largest gilded cathedral in the country. Don't miss the many royal busts and the gilded umbrella used to shade the king when in proces-sion. The French built a small exhibition hall on the temple grounds, a building that now houses the many gifts given to the monarchy, among them cross-stitch portraits of the royal family and all manner of bric-a-brac. Just inside the door, don't miss an original by Cézanne that has suffered terrible water damage and hangs in a ratty frame like an unwanted diploma: a shame. The balcony of the exhibition hall is the best bird's-eye view of the gilded temples. The facade of the neighboring **Royal Residence** is just as resplendent and is still the home of the now abdicated King Sihanouk and his son and successor.

The **Silver Pagoda** is just south of the palace and entrance is included in the same ticket. The floors of this grand temple are covered with 5,000 blocks of sil-ver weighing more than 6 tons. The temple houses a 17th-century Buddha made of Baccarat crystal, and another made almost entirely of gold and decorated with almost 10,000 diamonds. That's not exactly what the Buddha had in mind per-haps, but it's quite beautiful. The temple courtyard is encircled by a covered walkway with a contiguous mural of Cambodia's history and mythology. On the southern end of the complex is a small hill covered in vegetation and said to model the sacred Mt. Meru; there's a large Buddha footprint and a small temple that provokes very devout practice in Khmer visitors.

Between sts. 240 and 184 on Sothearos (entrance on east side facing the river). Admission $3 ($5 w/still camera; $8 w/video camera). Daily 7:30–11am and 2:30–5pm.

## Russian Market   This bustling market in the south end of town is compara-ble to the Central Market and equally worthy of a visit (it's a good stop on the return trip from The Killing Fields; otherwise go by cab). The real deal on sou-venirs can be had here, though it takes hard haggling to get the best prices on neat items like opium paraphernalia, carvings, and ceramics. It's all authentic-looking, even if it's made in China.

South of town center between sts. 440 and 450. Daily dawn to dusk.

## Tuol Sleng, Museum of Genocide ★★   The grounds of this high-school-turned-prison-and-torture-chamber are like they were in 1979 at the end of Cam-bodia's bloody genocide. A stop here is a visceral revisiting of some very horrible events, and guides are often just as brutal in their portrayal of it, too much for

some visitors. From 1975 until 1979, an estimated 17,000 political prisoners, most just ordinary citizens, were tortured at Tuol Sleng and died, or were executed in the nearby Killing Fields. If you don't come with a guide, you'll certainly want to hire one at the entrance, although you're free to roam the grounds on your own. Local guides often have personal experience with the prison and are vital sources of oral history. They are open to questions, but go easy on any debate. Recrimination against the perpetrators of these horrible events is an important issue here; Cambodians hope to move on into the future, but they fear revisiting the past in the current international tribunals. The prison population of Tuol Sleng, also known as S-21, was carefully catalogued; in fact, the metal neck brace employed for holding subjects' heads in place for the admitting photograph is on display. There are some written accounts in English, paintings done by a survivor, and gory photos of the common torture practices in the prison, but perhaps what is most haunting is the fear in the eyes of the newly arrived; one wing of the buildings is dedicated to these very arrival photos. This site is a bit overwhelming for some, so be prepared.

South of town at corner of sts. 350 and 113. Admission $3; guide fees vary (usually $2–$3 per person). Daily 8am–noon and 1–5pm.

**Wat Phnom** 🌟🌟    This is Cambodia's "Church on the Hill." Legend has it that in the 14th century, a woman named Penh found sacred Buddhist objects in the nearby river and placed them here on the small hill that later became a temple. Well, the rest is history. *Phnom,* in fact, means "hill," so the name of the city translates to "Penh's Hill."

The temple itself is a standard Southeast Asian *wat,* with *naga* (snakes) on the cornered peaks of the roof and didactic murals of the Buddha's life done in day-glow allegories along interior walls. Don't miss the central ceiling, which, unlike the bright walls, is yet to be restored and is gritty and authentic.

The hillside park around the temple was once a no-go zone peopled by armed dealers and pimps, and in the evening you should still be careful, though now it's a laid-back little park. You're sure to meet with some crafty young salesmen here who'll offer you the chance to show your Buddhist compassion by buying a caged bird for a dollar and letting it go; if you stick around long enough, you'll get to see the bird return to the comfort of the cage.

## SHOPPING & GALLERIES

The best shopping in town, for everything from souvenirs and trinkets to the obligatory kitchen sink, is at any of the large local markets (see the Central Market and Russian Market under "What to See," above).

Shops and galleries are growing in number in the developing capital. All along Street 178 interesting little outlets are springing up and include a few affordable silk dealers like **Lotus Pond** (#57Eo St. 178; ℂ 012/833-149) and **House Kravan** (#13Eo St. 178; ℂ 012/771-936). **Asasax Art Gallery** (#192 St. 178; ℂ 023/217-795; www.asasaxart.com.kh) features unique local works. **Photo Click Gallery** (#65 St. 178) features the tinted, black-and-white images of long-time expat and photographer Pier Poretti.

Take a stroll along Street 240, which is also developing its own cafe culture and has a few little hole-in-the-wall antique shops and boutiques like **Bliss** (#29 St. 240; ℂ 023/215-754), which sells some unique beaded and embroidered cushions and quilts, or **Le Lezard Bleu** (ℂ 012/767-417), which features traditional and contemporary designs and accessories.

**Bazar**, near the Independence Monument (28 Sihanouk Blvd.; ✆ **012/866-178**), has a small but refined collection of Asian antiques and furniture.

For CDs, DVDs, and cool T-shirts and hip-hop fashions, stop by **The Boom Boom Room,** on Street 93 in the backpacker area near Boeung Kok Lake or at its new location just across from the Golden Gate Hotel (#1C St. 278; ✆ **012/560-944**).

For essentials and Western groceries, stop by the **Lucky Market** (#160 Sihanouk Blvd.; ✆ **023/426-291**), and for fresh organic produce and fine canned goods, try **Veggy's** (#23 St. 240; ✆ **023/211-534**).

**Monument Books** (#111 Norodom Blvd.; ✆ **023/217-617**) has a great selection of new books; it's a good spot to find books on Khmer language and culture. At #51 St. 240, among new bistros and cafes, stop by **The London Book Centre** and exchange or buy new and used books; there's a good selection.

## AFTER DARK

Phnom Penh is notorious for some of the seedier nightlife in all of Southeast Asia. There are some good, friendly bars in town, though many are the "hostess bar" variety. Most good romps start or end at the town's counterculture hub, **The Heart of Darkness** (#38 St. 51, Pasteur), open 7pm to sunrise. Done in burgundy tones and cluttered with statuary and memorabilia, the Heart, as it's called, has had a face-lift in recent years and is not as seedy as its reputation of yore (though it's still bit of a relief to see the metal detectors). It's where to go to find out what's on in town.

The downtown area along the riverside is chockablock with small storefront bars and a few upscale spots. **The Rising Sun** (#20 St. 178; ✆ **023/986-270**) is one of the more comfy holes in the wall, a dark wooden stopover great for a few pints and a game of darts near the town center. **Tom's Irish Bar** (#170 St. 63, near the Golden Gate Hotel; ✆ **023/363-161**) is a comparable and friendly choice south of town, a longtime local and tourist favorite that has a classy wooden bar as well as comfy low-slung chairs in the roadside courtyard.

## SPORTS

The **Clark Hatch Fitness Center** (✆ **023/424-888**), at the Hotel Inter-Continental, has got it all in the way of equipment. Daily visitors are invited for a fee ($8), with pool and sauna included. It's open weekdays from 6am to 10pm and weekends from 8am to 8pm.

## DAY TRIPS FROM PHNOM PENH
### OUDONG

Following defeat at Angkor by the Thais, the Khmer capital moved to Oudong, and kings ruled from there for more than 100 years until the power center shifted to nearby Phnom Penh in 1866. The area was a monastic center, and the 13th-century temples, like most others, pale in comparison to those of the Angkor complex. Still, the hills of Oudong offer breathtaking views. It's 1 hour west of Phnom Penh and is best reached by rented vehicle.

### PHNOM CHISOR & TONLE BATI

If you've been or are going to Angkor Wat, these temples will pale in comparison, but the ride through the countryside and among rural villages makes for a good day. Tonle Bati (33km/20½ miles south of Phnom Penh) is a small collection of Angkor-style temples. Admission is $3. Nearby Phnom Chisor is a group of 10th-century ruins atop a picturesque hill. Phnom Penh travel agents can make all the arrangements.

## SIHANOUKVILLE

Your only bet for a dip in the ocean and beachside R & R in Cambodia is in Sihanoukville, some 230km (143 miles) south of Phnom Penh on the American-built highway. A popular summertime spot for Khmers, Sihanoukville is really a port town and though the beaches don't stack up to the likes of Thailand, they are not bad. Trips to outlying islands for scuba diving and snorkeling are attracting more and more Western tourists. To get there, contact **Capitol Tour** (© 023/217-627) or **Ho Wa Genting Bus Co.** (© 023/210-859), each with daily connections for the 3- to 4-hour ride. Contact any hotel front desk or travel agent about renting a car for the ride from Phnom Penh.

Where once it was only low-end accommodation or seedy casinos, there is now the **Sokha Beach Resort and Spa** (© 034/935-999; www.sokhahotels.com), with 180 upmarket rooms starting at $120. Amenities include a nice central pool and frontage on a stretch of private beach. There are a number of smaller hotels and guesthouses: try **Orchidee Guesthouse** (© 034/933-639; www.orchidee guesthouse.com) or **Golden Sand Hotel** (© 034/933-607; www.hotel goldensand.com), a business hotel with bland but clean rooms.

For dining, you'll find good seafood at low prices, and there are lots of little oceanside budget stops. Don't miss a visit to the unique **Snakehouse** (© 012/782-873), a restaurant and menagerie of local cold-blooded inhabitants (for viewing, not eating).

For tours to outlying islands, contact the folks at **EcoAdventures South East Asia LTD** (in the Samudera Market, Town Center, Sihanoukville; © 012/654-104; www.ecosea.com). It arranges great day tours with stops in remote coves where clients can snorkel or take a course in scuba.

## 4 Siem Reap & Angkor Wat

The ruins of the ancient city of **Angkor,** capital of the Khmer kingdom from 802 until 1295, are one of the world's marvels. The largest religious monument ever constructed, it's a vast and mysterious complex of hulking laterite and sandstone blocks. Unknown to the world until French naturalist Henri Mouhot literally stumbled onto it in 1861, the area of Angkor existed for centuries only as a myth—a wondrous city (or cities, to be exact), its exact location in the Cambodian jungle unknown.

The temple complex covers some 96.6 sq. km (38 sq. miles) and carries the remains of passageways, moats, temples, and palaces that represent centuries of building in the capital. The temples are served by the nearby town of Siem Reap, some 6km (3¾ miles) to the south.

A 3- or 4-day visit will suffice (though many do it in fewer). More than a few visitors come away with a newfound love for ancient cultures, Asian religions, and sunsets.

## GETTING THERE

**BY PLANE**    Siem Reap Airways, Royal Phnom Penh Airways, President Airlines, and Bangkok Air all fly the 1-hour connection to Siem Reap from Phnom Penh.

If you just want to see the great temples at Angkor, the process is simplified with international arrivals: Bangkok Airways flies directly from Bangkok, and you can check flights by Silk Air, Lao Aviation, Vietnam Airlines, and Royal Camboge Airline for other routes. *Note:* The international departure tax (from both Phnom Penh and Siem Reap) is $25; the domestic tax is $10 to $14, depending on where you're flying.

**BY BOAT**   A ride on the 5-hour boat connection between Phnom Penh and Siem Reap costs $25. Contact any hotel or travel agent, as they all sell the same tickets at the same price. The trip connects to Siem Reap via the great Tonle Sap Lake, with some good scenery en route. Also see the new **Mekong Express** (*©* **023/427-518;** www.mekongexpresstourboat.com) special, with a ride on its more luxurious boat for $35.

**BY BUS   Capitol Tour** (#14 AEO, Rd. 182, Sangkat Beng Prolitt; *©* **023/ 217-627**) runs daily minivans along the much-improved road between Phnom Penh and Siem Reap. Tickets for the all-day ride are just $5.

## GETTING AROUND

You'll need some kind of wheeled conveyance to make your way around Siem Reap and to and from the temples. Any hotel front desk or travel agent can make arrangements.

A rented **car with driver** is about $25 (double that with a guide). A **motorcycle taxi** is a good, cheap option for $8 per day, and there are also motorbikes that pull small, **covered trailers for two** (kind of fun, really), for about $11 per day.

Riding **your own motorbike** was once the most popular choice, but local officials have put a stop to it, citing many road accidents.

The temple roads are flat and well paved, and **bicycles** are a popular choice. They rent for $2 to $3 per day from guesthouses and hotels. Take care in the scorching midday heat and drink plenty of fluid.

## VISITOR INFO & TOURS

- **Diethelm.** No. 4, Airport Rd. No. 6, Siem Reap; *©* **063/963-524;** fax 063/963-694; dtc@dtc.com.kh. All local and regional services.
- **Exotissimo:** No. 300, Airport Rd. No. 6, Siem Reap; *©* **063/964-323;** fax 063/963-621; www.exotissimo.com; Cambodia@exotissimo.com. All local and regional services.

---

### *FAST FACTS:* Siem Reap

*Banks/Currency Exchange* **Canadia Bank** (on the western side of the Old Market; *©* **063/964-808**) is as good as any in town. You can change traveler's checks in some hotels and in any bank; **Cambodia Commercial Bank (CCB)** (130 Siwatha Blvd.; *©* **063/380-154**) and **Mekong Bank** (43 Siwatha Blvd.; *©* **063/964-420**) can do credit card cash advances. There are no ATMs in Siem Reap.

*Emergency* There is a tourist police station near the entrance to the temples. For local police, dial *©* **117.** In the event of medical emergency, contact **International SOS Clinic** in Phnom Penh (*©* **023/216-911**).

*Internet/E-mail* Small storefront offices aplenty surround the Central Market area. On the main street, try **E-Café** (#011 Siwatha Blvd.) an air-conditioned facility with speedy ADSL, for just over $2 per hour. If you have a wireless-capable laptop, you can connect using prepaid PIC cards at the **FCC** restaurant or the **Raffles Grand** and **Sofitel** hotels.

*Post Office* The post office is located on Pokambor Avenue at riverside near the town center (next to the FCC; see "Where to Dine," later). It's open daily 7am to 5pm and can handle foreign and domestic regular and parcel post.

# Siem Reap

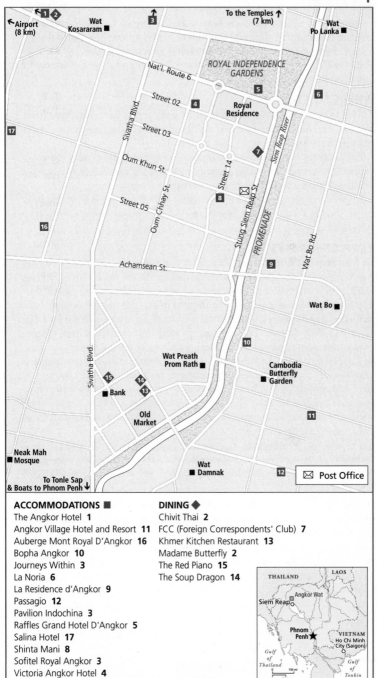

**ACCOMMODATIONS** ■

The Angkor Hotel **1**
Angkor Village Hotel and Resort **11**
Auberge Mont Royal D'Angkor **16**
Bopha Angkor **10**
Journeys Within **3**
La Noria **6**
La Residence d'Angkor **9**
Passagio **12**
Pavilion Indochina **3**
Raffles Grand Hotel D'Angkor **5**
Salina Hotel **17**
Shinta Mani **8**
Sofitel Royal Angkor **3**
Victoria Angkor Hotel **4**

**DINING** ◆

Chivit Thai **2**
FCC (Foreign Correspondents' Club) **7**
Khmer Kitchen Restaurant **13**
Madame Butterfly **2**
The Red Piano **15**
The Soup Dragon **14**

*Telephone* The code for Siem Reap is **63**. Most hotels have international direct dialing (IDD). Many of the Internet cafes around the Old Market have better rates and offer callback service or Internet phone.

## WHERE TO STAY

Tourist levels are high, and development is really revved up in tiny Siem Reap. Visitors can choose from some of the finest upscale accommodations in the region—more 5-star properties than we can list.

For midrange hotels (below $100), there are lots of bland choices, especially on the airport road, but smaller properties are sprucing themselves up to a more boutique standard and there are some atmospheric gems.

In the high season, high-end accommodation often fills up, so be sure to book ahead. During the low season be sure to ask for a discount. Most hotels levy a 10% VAT.

### VERY EXPENSIVE

**La Résidence d'Angkor** ★★ Formerly the Pansea, La Résidence d'Angkor is a stylish, self-contained sanctuary managed by the people at Orient-Express. You'll cross a small moat to enter the cool interior of the steeply gabled, dark wooden lobby with its grand Angkor-inspired reliefs. The tranquil central court-yard is lined with palms and dominated by a small but stylish pool fed by a font of stylized Shiva lingum. The resort area is small, but everything from the gardens to the room decor is tidy and designed for quiet privacy. Rooms are large, well appointed, open, and elegant, with cloth divans, retro fixtures, and nice local touches. Large bathrooms connect with bedrooms by a bamboo sliding door, and another glass slider opens to a small private balcony with views of the courtyard and cool lounges. The lobby restaurant offers good fine dining. There are some great open sitting areas for drinks, as well as a library with books, chess, and a conference table.

River Rd., Siem Reap. ✆ 063/963-390. Fax 063/963-391. www.pansea.com. 55 units. $290–$340 deluxe double; $440 suite. AE, MC, V. **Amenities:** Restaurant; bar; outdoor pool; all rentals available; shopping; 24 hr. room service; laundry service; dry cleaning; Internet; library area. *In room:* A/C, satellite TV, dataport, minibar, fridge, hair dryer, safe, IDD phone.

**Raffles Grand Hotel D'Angkor** ★★★ For luxury, atmosphere, and convenience, there is no better choice in Siem Reap. Rebuilt in 1994 from the shell of a classic 1929 structure, you'll find authentic old Indochina that's neither museum piece nor overly stuffy. Right in the center of town, the imposing colonial facade gives way to a marble lobby, connected by neat black-and-white tile halls to the many rooms and fine services. There's an open metal elevator, an original period piece that's still functional. Staterooms are large, with classic French doors and windows, tiled entries, fine furnishings, antique standing lamps, and an almost out-of-place high-tech entertainment module. Landmark rooms, the next higher standard, are similar but have four-poster beds, a balcony with rattan furniture, and nice touches like porcelain bathrooms and more antique detail. The courtyard pool is large and inviting—like a commercial set—and the nearby massage and health facilities are quite something. It's expensive, very expensive, but the price includes very fine service and a unique revisiting of old Indochina that you can't find elsewhere. Nightly, there's an *apsara* dance show (women's traditional temple dance to welcome goddesses).

1 Vithei Charles de Gaulle, Khum Svay Dang Kum, Siem Reap. ✆ 063/963-888. Fax 063/963-168. www.raffles.com. 131 units. $310–$390 double; $410–$1,900 suite. AE, MC, V. **Amenities:** 4 restaurants; 2 bars; outdoor pool; 2 tennis courts; health club; spa; Jacuzzi; sauna; steam room; kids' club; concierge; tour desk; car rental; shopping; massage; laundry service; dry cleaning; wireless Internet. *In room:* A/C, satellite TV, dataport, minibar, fridge, coffeemaker, hair dryer, safe, IDD phone.

### Sofitel Royal Angkor ★★
Sofitel is famed for bringing life back to the classic hotels of old Indochina, but in Siem Reap they started fresh in 2000 with a project limited only by the designer's imagination. The lobby is an old-world Indochine replica with an antique Khmer pagoda and a menagerie of overstuffed European furniture. Design and decor throughout nicely marry Khmer and French styles, with vaulted *naga* roofs high above the sculpted central garden and tranquil pond area. The courtyard pool is large, open, and fun, including a short river meander crossed by a small bridge that's great for kids. The massage facility is tops, and the private massage areas are resplendent with private baths. Rooms are spacious, with dark wood floors and rich touches like designer throw rugs and elegant built-in cabinetry. All bathrooms are large, with tubs and granite counters. Spring for a superior room with a balcony and a view of the central courtyard: It's worth it. Not surprisingly, there's an Angkor theme throughout, but the statuary is not overdone and is quite pleasing in both common areas and sleeping quarters (unique in a town of gaudy reproductions of the sites). Be sure to find a moment, preferably near the magic hour of sunset (though any time will do), to take it all in from the island pagoda in the central pond.

Vithei Charles de Gaulle (on the way to temples, just north of town center), Khum Svay Dang Kum, Siem Reap. ✆ 063/964-600. Fax 063/964-610. www.accor.com. 238 units. $338 superior double; $360 deluxe double; $320–$1,815 suite. AE, MC, V. **Amenities:** 4 restaurants; 3 bars; large outdoor pool; health club; Jacuzzi; sauna; steam room; concierge; tour desk; business center; shopping; 24-hr. room service; fine massage facility; laundry service; dry cleaning; nonsmoking floor; banquet facilities; wireless Internet; small library. *In room:* A/C, satellite TV w/in-house movies, fax, dataport, minibar, fridge, coffeemaker, hair dryer, safe, IDD phone.

### Victoria Angkor Hotel ★★
The Victoria expands its empire of fine Indochine hotels (mostly in Vietnam) with this latest offering. Brand spankin' new, Victoria Angkor is an oversize but tasteful replica of a French colonial era hotel, only with all of the amenities and functionality of a modern five-star. Public spaces are done in earth tones, with rattan and wood accents, designer diamond tiles, and fun local bric-a-brac. The effect is at times reminiscent of days of pith helmets and griping about local inefficiency. A large central atrium with a period-piece elevator and a towering courtyard staircase greets the visitor to this downtown campus, just a stone's throw from the Raffles (above). The central pool is large and inviting, and there are good spa services. Fine dining at the bistro is tops. Rooms are typical of Victoria hotels: large, luxurious, and decorated with location in mind (i.e., you know you're in Cambodia). Floors are wood with a border of fine tile that matches luxurious woven bedspreads. All rooms have balconies. Bathrooms are midsize, with separate bath and shower. Service is efficient and the list of amenities is extensive.

Central Park, P.O. Box 93145, Siem Reap. ✆ 063/760-428. Fax 063/760-350. www.victoriahotels-asia.com. 130 units. $285–$320 double; $395 junior suite; $440 colonial suite. AE, MC, V. **Amenities:** 2 restaurants; bar; large outdoor pool; spa; Jacuzzi; bike rentals; children's center; concierge; tour desk; car rental; business center; shopping arcade; 24-hr. room service; massage; babysitting; laundry. *In room:* A/C, satellite TV, minibar, fridge, coffeemaker, hair dryer, safe, IDD phone.

## EXPENSIVE
### The Angkor Hotel ★
Of the many newer hotels along the airport road, Route 6, the Angkor Hotel is the best (and only slightly more expensive than the

rest). Popular with group tours, the hotel is large and ostentatious, with high, Khmer-style roofs and large reproductions of temple statuary in the entry. Everything is clean and comfortable, if a bit sterile. Ask for a room in the new building in the back. Guest rooms are bland but large, with crown molding, clean carpet, and good, familiar amenities like a minibar and safe. The bathrooms are a little small. This is a good, comfortable step down from the glitzier hotels in town, and the best choice if they're full. The lobby is always busy with tour groups, but the staff remains friendly and expedient. The hotel is sufficiently self-contained, with good basic amenities, an outdoor pool in the courtyard, a good restaurant, and all necessary services. The two caged bears in the hotel's garden are enough to make you cry, though.

Rte. 6, Phum Sala Kanseng. (C) **063/964-301.** Fax 063/964-302. www.angkor-hotel-cambodia.com. 193 units. $125 standard double; $145 deluxe; $190 suite. V. **Amenities:** Restaurant; bar; outdoor pool; basic gym; tours; car rental; shopping; massage; laundry; Internet. *In room:* A/C, TV, minibar, fridge, hair dryer, safe, IDD phone.

**Angkor Village Hotel** ★★   For comfortable rustic atmosphere, Angkor Village is without rival. Located in a quiet neighborhood not far from the main market, this peaceful little hideaway is a unique maze of wood bungalows connected by covered boardwalks surrounding a picturesque ivy-draped pond. Rooms are rustic wooden affairs with high bamboo cathay ceilings, wood beams, built-in cabinetry, comfortable beds, and decorative touches like traditional Khmer shadow puppets and statuary. Top units have balconies overlooking the central pond. Bathrooms are all large, with a shower/tub combo and sinks set in oversize ceramic cauldrons. The central lobby is a series of platforms and private sitting areas, a good place to rest after a day at the temples. Staff is very welcoming. The pool is small but picturesque, in a verdant courtyard at the rear. The Auberge de Temples Restaurant is on a small island in the central pond and serves fine French and Khmer cuisine. The hotel's **Apsara Theater Restaurant,** just outside the gate, has Khmer-style banquet dining and performances of Khmer Apsara dancing nightly. The whole place is infused with Khmer culture and hospitality, and so popular is the original that it's expanded. **Angkor Village Resort,** a new venture on the edge of town, is due to open in 2005. This hotel is often full so be sure to book ahead.

Wat Bo Rd., Siem Reap. (C) **063/963-5613.** Fax 063/963-363. www.angkorvillage.com. 52 units. $89–$165 (off-season discounts). AE, MC, V. **Amenities:** Restaurant; bar; outdoor pool; business center; shopping; limited room service; laundry; Internet; small library. *In room:* A/C, minibar, fridge, coffeemaker, safe, IDD phone.

**Shinta Mani** ★   A member of the Sanctuary Resorts group, a Hong Kong–based hotel organization dedicated to sustainable tourism, environmental stewardship, and holistic practices, Shinta Mani is both a small boutique hotel and school of hospitality. One of its goals is to create opportunities in health, beauty, and hospitality professions for the next generation of underprivileged kids in Siem Reap. While the public spaces are done on a small scale—the pool is quite tiny—fine rooms and cool minimalist decor set this hotel apart. Each unit is large and stylish, with cool tile and buff-polished wood features. Bathrooms connect to the main room via large sliding doors. The overall effect is chic, clean, and luxurious.

Junction of Oum Khum and 14th St. (near FCC). (C) **063/761-998.** Fax 063/761-999. www.sanctuary resorts.com/shintamani. $144–$160 double. MC, V. **Amenities:** Restaurant; bar; small outdoor pool; limited room service; massage; laundry. *In room:* A/C, satellite TV, fridge, IDD phone.

## MODERATE
**Salina Hotel** ★   This recently renovated and expanded hotel is popular with tour groups and offers clean, utilitarian comfort. Affordable rates bring 'em in in

droves. The new pool at this unpretentious three-star is small but cozy. New rooms are clean, large, and well appointed, with fresh carpeting, new wood furnishing, and that new-car smell. Baths are small but tidy. The staff is friendly and can help arrange necessities, like guides and rentals. This is an overall good value, but there's little atmosphere to speak of. Tour groups also mean crowds at times.

#125 Rd. 6, Siem Reap. ℂ **063/380-221.** Fax 063/380-224. www.salinahotel.com. 133 units. $45 single; $55–$65 double; $100 suite. AE, MC, V. **Amenities:** Restaurant; 2 bars; outdoor pool; small gym; car rental; tour desk; business center; limited room service; laundry; Internet. *In room:* A/C, satellite TV, minibar, fridge, IDD phone.

## INEXPENSIVE

The downtown area of Siem Reap, on either side of the main road, is brimming with budget accommodation.

### Auberge Mont Royal D'Angkor ★★    Down a lazy lane just to the west of the town center, this quiet inn is a much better choice than the larger tourist hotels in this category. This cozy and comfortable hotel is Canadian-owned and managed. The staff is genial, the restaurant inviting, and standard rooms are quite chic for the low price tag. Terra-cotta tile covers all open areas and rooms, and there are atmospheric touches like canvas lamps, carved wood beds, cushions, and traditional hangings, curtains, and bedspreads. The traditional decor is pleasant and inviting. Bathrooms are done in clean tile but aren't particularly large or luxe. Deluxe rooms are worth the upgrade.

West of town center. ℂ **063/964-044.** www.auberge-mont-royal.com. 28 units. $30 standard; $50 deluxe double. AE, MC, V. **Amenities:** Restaurant; bar; tour desk; car rental; laundry. *In room:* A/C, satellite TV, minibar, fridge, no phone.

### Bopha Angkor ★    With its popular nightly dance show and Khmer restaurant, there is a certain "cultural theme park" vibe to this place, but Bopha Angkor is tidy, affordable, and quite genuine about providing a culturally infused visit to Siem Reap. Rooms are arranged in a U-shaped courtyard around a lush central garden. Private spaces are large but not luxe and feature fun local accents like mossy nets and souvenir-shop trinkets on the walls. Bathrooms are small. The staff is friendly and the hotel is close to the old market area.

0512 Acharsvar St. (across canal from market). ℂ **063/964-928.** Fax 063/964-446. www.bopha-angkor.com. 22 units. $42–$68 double. V, MC. **Amenities:** Restaurant w/nightly dance show; bar; tour desk; laundry. *In room:* A/C, satellite TV, minibar, fridge.

### La Noria ★★    With a similar sister property, Borann Auberge de Temples, La Noria is a mellow group of bungalows connected by a winding garden path. The guesthouse is near the town center but you wouldn't know it in the hush of this little laid-back spot. Rooms are basic but have nice local touches. Terra-cotta floors, wooden trim, and small balconies are all neat and tidy, and fine hangings and details like shadow puppets and authentic Khmer furniture round out a pleasing traditional decor. Bathrooms are small and basic but clean, with a guesthouse-style shower-in-room setup. The place is light on amenities but has a small pool and makes up for any deficiency with gobs of charm. The open-air restaurant is a highlight, serving good Khmer and French. The hotel is affiliated with Krousar Thmey "New Family," a humanitarian group doing good work, and there is a helpful information board about rural travel and humanitarian projects.

Down small lane off Rte. 6 to the northeast of town. ℂ **063/964-242.** Fax 063/964-243. 28 units. $29 w/fan; $39 w/AC. No credit cards. **Amenities:** Restaurant; outdoor pool; laundry. *In room:* A/C (optional).

**Passagio** ✪   This unpretentious little workhorse of a hotel is convenient to downtown and adjoins its own helpful travel agent, Lolei Travel. Rooms are large and tidy and not much more, but that's the beauty here: three floors that are something like a motel in the U.S., complete with tacky hotel art. The one suite has a bathtub; all others have just stand-up showers in bathrooms that are nondescript. The tile is plain, but it's neat and new. The friendly staff can arrange any detail and is eager to please.

Watdamanak Village (across river to east of town). ✆ **063/760-324.** Fax 063/760-163. 17 units. $33 double; $69 suite. AE, MC, V. **Amenities:** Restaurant (breakfast only); travel agent; car rental; business center; laundry; Internet. *In room:* A/C, satellite TV, minibar, fridge, no phone.

**Pavillon Indochina** ✪✪   This converted traditional Khmer house and garden is the closest you'll get to the temples and is quite peaceful, even isolated, in a quiet neighborhood. It's an upscale guesthouse really, charming and surprisingly self-contained, with a good restaurant and a friendly, knowledgeable French proprietor whose staff can help arrange any detail in the area. Just 2 years old, rooms are large, clean, and airy, with terra-cotta tile and wood trim, though they're not particularly luxe. The courtyard area has a picturesque garden dotted by quiet sitting areas with chairs or floor mats and comfy pillows. A good information corner provides the ins and outs on current happenings in town and at the temples.

On back rd. to temples, Siem Reap. ✆ **012/804-952.** www.pavillon-indochine.com. $25–$30. V. **Amenities:** Restaurant; tour desk; car rental; outdoor massage pavilion; laundry. *In room:* A/C, no phone.

## WHERE TO DINE

Dining in Siem Reap is not a pricey affair. The major hotels all have fine upscale eateries, in addition to the freestanding spots listed below. The area around the Old Market is a cluster of storefronts, most of little distinction from one another, but all are affordable and laid-back.

### MODERATE

**Chivit Thai** ✪✪ THAI   You found it! Authentic Thai in an atmospheric, traditional wood house. The food is great, the price is low, and there's casual floor seating and a rustic but comfortable dining room, romantic in candlelight. Name your favorite Thai dish and they do it here, and do it well. The *tom yum* (sweet, spicy Thai soup) is excellent, and Chivit Thai has good set menus comprising many courses that are much finer than its low price tag. Enjoy!

House 129, Rd. 6 next to Angkor Hotel. ✆ **012/830-761.** Main courses $2.50–$5. No credit cards. Daily 7am–10pm.

**FCC (Foreign Correspondent's Club)** ✪✪ CONTINENTAL   The glowing white modern cube of the FCC would be at home in a nouveau riche California suburb or a Jacques Tati film, but it is a bit jarring canal-side in the center of Siem Reap. The first floor is boutique shopping and the second floor is an elegant open space with high ceilings: a modern colonial. There is an Art Deco bar, low lounge chairs at the center, and standard dining space on the balcony. The main room is flanked on one end by an open kitchen. The FCC is the town's runway and holds numerous functions and hosts live music. The menu is the same as the original FCC in Phnom Penh, with good soups, salads, and Western standards like pasta, steaks, and wood-fired pizzas. The staff still can't believe they work here, and service is hot and cold but very friendly. Even if just for drinks, you won't want to miss this place. It has wireless Internet and is the de facto Starbucks in Siem Reap.

Pokambor Ave. (next to the Royal Residence). ✆ **012/900-123**. Main courses $4–$18. MC, V. Daily 6am–midnight.

**Madame Butterfly** ★★ KHMER/THAI   Serving the finest authentic Khmer- and Thai-influenced cuisine in town, the setting is very pleasant and alone worth a visit. In a converted traditional wooden home, seating is in low rattan chairs, and the decor is characterized by a tasteful collection of Buddhist and Khmer artifacts. Candlelight mingles with mellow indirect lighting, and the whole effect is casual and romantic. There are daily specials, and the menu reads like a short course in local cuisine. Entrees are heavy on good curries and hot-pot dishes; the helpful staff and French proprietor will gladly explain. I had a delicious poached fish in coconut sauce with sticky rice. The *masaman curry* is divine and the *mchou pous*, a chicken-and-shrimp bisque, is rich and tasty. For a leisurely evening, this is a great pick.

Short ride west on No. 6, airport rd. ✆ **016/909-607**. Main courses $3–$10. V. Daily 6am–10:30pm.

**The Red Piano** ★★ INTERNATIONAL   Ever since Angelina Jolie and cast and crew of the film *Tomb Raider II* made this their second home while filming at the temples, this atmospheric corner bar and restaurant has been "the place" to be in town. Imported steaks, spaghetti, sandwiches, salads, and international specialties like Indian samosas or chicken *cordon bleu* round out a great menu of familiar fare. This place is always hoppin' late into the evening. Due to popular demand (it's sometimes hard to get a seat and they take no reservations), they've expanded onto a second floor. Renovations throughout provide the place with a tidy, upscale charm. The best choice in town.

50m (164 ft.) northwest of the Old Market. ✆ **063/963-240**. Main courses $2.50–$9. No credit cards. Daily 7am–midnight.

## INEXPENSIVE

**Khmer Kitchen Restaurant** ★★ KHMER   This busy little storefront hides itself down an alley on the north end of the Old Market, but draws a busy crowd nightly for big portions of simple, delicious Khmer fare. Good curries and Khmer stir-fries share menu space with unique dishes like baked pumpkin. It's about the food here, not the service, but these folks are friendly enough considering how busy they usually are.

Down alley just north of the Old Market. ✆ **012/763-468**. Main courses $2–$3. No credit cards. Daily 10am–10pm.

**The Soup Dragon** ★ VIETNAMESE/KHMER   This long-time popular street-side cafe in the center of the Old Market area serves up good Khmer and Western dishes, though its fame comes from authentic Vietnamese fare like *pho*, fresh spring rolls, and all manner of wok-fried dishes. Two floors of open-air dining overlook the busy street at the center of town and are always packed, making this a good place to meet up with other travelers.

#369 Group 6, Mondol 1 Siem Reap (north of the Central Market). ✆ **063/964-933**. Main courses $2.50–$8. No credit cards. Daily 6am–10pm.

## DINING AT THE TEMPLES

Across the busy parking lot closest to Angkor Wat, you're sure to spot the snazzy **Angkor Café** (✆ **012/826-346**). This little gallery and souvenir shop serves, for a mint by Khmer standards, good coffee, tea, and sandwiches.

   For a very affordable and hearty meal while touring the temples, try **Sunrise Angkor** (✆ **012/946-595**), one of many open-air eateries and the first one you'll see behind and to the left of Angkor Café. It has good breakfasts for very little.

In and among all the major temples, you'll see lots of small, bamboo-roofed eateries, and all will implore you to enter. The competition means that you have more leverage when haggling: "Are you sure this Coke is $2? Someone over there said it was . . .." You get the picture.

## SNACKS & CAFES

For a good breakfast, real coffee, baked goods, and snacks, try **Blue Pumpkin** (365 Mondol 1; ✆ **063/963-574**), a posh little cafe north of the market.

**Butterfly Café** ✪ is one not to miss. This netted enclosure is a butterfly farm and menagerie of local flora and fauna, including a pond filled with Japanese carp. There are detailed descriptions of all the plants and some individual butterflies, but you're sure to meet the friendly U.K.-born owner, Ian, who's a great source of local information and will gladly explain or answer questions. The cafe serves drinks and a limited lunch menu daily from 8am to 5pm. Located just across the river and north of the market, admission is $2.

## WHAT TO SEE

Angkor Wat is the Disneyland of Buddhist temples in Asia. The temple complex covers 97 sq. km (38 sq. miles) and requires at least a few busy days to get around the major sites thoroughly. Everyone has their favorite, but I've highlighted a few must-sees below. Be sure to plan carefully and catch a sunrise or sunset from one of temple's more prime spots; it's a photographer's dream. *Note:* The temples are magnificent in and of themselves, and days spent clambering around are inherently interesting, but be careful not to come away from a visit to ancient Angkor with a memory of an oversize rock collection or jungle gym. There's much to learn about Buddhism, Hinduism, architecture, and Khmer history; it's useful to hire a well-informed guide or join a tour group. There are also subtleties to temple touring, and a good guide is your best chance to beat the crowd and catch the intricacies, or be in the right place for the magic moments of the day. Contact any hotel front desk or the tour agencies listed at the beginning of this section.

**THE TEMPLES**   Entrance fees for Angkor Wat are as follows: A 1-day ticket is $20, a 3-day ticket is $40, and a 1-week ticket is $60. Tickets are good for all sites within the main temple compound, as well as Banteay Srei, to the north, and the outlying temples of the Roluos Group.

**Angkor Thom** ✪✪✪   The temple name means "the great city" in Khmer and is famed for its fantastic 45m (148-ft.) central temple, **Bayon.** The vast area of Angkor Thom, over a mile on one side, is dotted with many temples and features; don't miss the elaborate reliefs of the **Terrace of the Leper King** and the **Terrace of Elephants.**

The **Bayon** is a Buddhist temple built under a later king, Jayavarman VII (1190), but the temple nevertheless adheres to Hindu cosmology and can be read as a metaphor for the natural world. It has four huge stone faces, with one facing out and keeping watch at each compass point. The curious smiling image, thought by many to be a depiction of Jayavarman himself, is considered by many to be the enigmatic Mona Lisa of Southeast Asia. Bayon is also surrounded by two long walls with bas-relief scenes of legendary and historical events, probably painted and gilded originally. There are 51 smaller towers surrounding Bayon, each with four faces of its own.

Just north of the Bayon is the stalwart form of the **Baphuon,** a temple built in 1066 that is in the process of being put back together in a protractive effort that gives visitors an idea of what original temple construction might've been like.

**Angkor Wat** ★★★    The symbol of Cambodia, the four spires of the main temple of Angkor are known the world over. In fact, this is the most resplendent of the Angkor sites, one certainly not to miss even in the most perfunctory of tours.

Built under the reign of Suryavarman II in the 12th century, this temple, along with Bayon and Baphuon, is the pinnacle of Khmer architecture. From base to tip of the highest tower, it's 213m (669 ft.) of awe-inspiring stone in the definitive, elaborate Khmer style.

The famous bas-reliefs encircling the temple on the first level depict the mythical "Churning of the Ocean of Milk," a legend in which Hindu deities stir vast oceans in order to extract the elixir of immortality. This churning produced the Apsaras, Hindu celestial dancers, that can be seen on many temples.

The most measured and studied of all the sites, Angkor Wat is the subject of much speculation: It's thought to represent Mt. Meru, home of Hindu gods and a land of creation and destruction. Researchers measuring the site in *hat,* ancient Khmer units of measure, deduce that the symmetry of the building corresponds with the timeline of the Hindu ages, as a map or calendar of the universe, if you will. The approach from the main road crosses the *baray* (or reservoir) and is an ascending progression of three levels to the inner sanctum. The T-shirt hawkers are relentless, and the tricky steps and temple height are a challenge to those with vertigo, but the short trip is inspiring and the views from the top are breathtaking. *Note:* There is a guide rope on the southern face (and often a long line up).

---

## ⌒ *Moments*  The Magic Hours at Angkor Wat

The skies over Angkor always put on a show. With just a bit of prior planning, you can see the dawn or the day's afterglow framed in temple spires, glowing off the main *wat,* or reflected in one of the temple reservoirs. Photographers swoon. Here are a few hints for catching the magic hours at the temples.

The sunrise and sunset views from the upper terraces of **Angkor Wat,** the main temple, are some of the best, though it's a tough climb for some. At dusk, temple staff start clearing the main temple area just as the sun dips. Smile; avoid them; and try to stay for the afterglow.

For the classic photographers' view of the main temple, Angkor Wat, at sunset—with the image of the temple reflected in a pool—enter the first wall of the temple compound, walk halfway down the front gangway and then take a right, down a set of stairs, and out into the field. The view from the water's edge, with warm light bouncing off the temple, is stunning.

Okay, so it's a bit crowded, but the views from **Phnom Bakeng (Bakeng Hill),** just a short drive past the entrance to Angkor Wat, are stunning at both sunrise and sunset. It's a good little climb up the hill; those so inclined can go by elephant.

The open area on the eastern side of **Banteay Kdey** (see map looks over one of Angkor's many reservoirs, this one full and a great reflective pool for the rising glow at sunrise.

For the best view of the temples, hands down, contact **Helicopters Cambodia Ltd.** ★ at ℂ 023/213-706. For a hefty fee, you can see the sites from any angle you choose. There are also balloon rides available.

**Ta Prohm** ⭐⭐⭐   The jungle foliage still has its hold on this dynamic temple. Ta Prohm was the only one left in such a ruinous state when early archaeologists freed the rest of the Angkor Wat temples from the jungle. Ta Prohm is a favorite for many; in fact, the ruinous roots appeal to most. As large around as some tree trunks, the roots of fig, banyan, and kapok trees cleave massive stones in two or give way and grow over the top of temple ramparts. It's quite dramatic, and there are a few popular photo spots where the collision of temple and vine are most impressive. Sadly, Ta Prohm was looted quite heavily in recent years, and many of its stone reliquaries are lost.

## ATTRACTIONS FARTHER AFIELD

**Banteay Srei** ⭐⭐   True temple buffs won't want to miss this distinct complex. Located some 32km (20 miles) north of the main temples, the 10th-century buildings of Banteay Srei are done in a style unique to the high spires of Angkor. The site is a collection of low walls surrounding low-rise peaked structures of deep red sandstone. Translated as "The Citadel of Women," it has well-preserved relief carvings on the squat central buildings and intricate tellings of ancient Hindu tales. Go with a guide who can explain the finer details of temple inscriptions.

**Kabal Spean** *Finds*   Known as the "River of a Thousand Linga" (a linga is a phallic symbol representing the Hindu god Shiva), Kabal Spean lay undiscovered by Westerners until a French researcher stumbled across it only recently. Dating from the early 11th century, the relief carvings that line the stream beds are said to purify the water before it fills the reservoirs (called *barays*) of Angkor. It's the journey here that's really interesting, some rough roads through rural villages north of Banteay Srei, and there's a fun little forest hike of about 30 minutes to the first waterfall. Khmer folks come to picnic, and it's a good spot to swim or follow the path that trips along at brook side; from there, you can view the many carvings in relief on the banks and creek bed.

5km (3 miles) north of Banteay Srei. Admission $3.

**Land Mines Museum**   You won't find signs leading you to this seemingly impromptu museum; Cambodian officials prefer their own rhetoric to that of the owner and curator, Mr. Akira. The museum itself is just a corrugated-roof area stacked high with disarmed ordnance and detailed data on the country's UXO (unexploded ordnance). Most interesting is the small grove out back, an exhibit of how mines are placed in a real jungle setting. The museum is a call to action for demining in the country. Resist any temptation to volunteer (unless properly trained), but you're sure to have a chance to chat with Mr. Akira, peruse his recent book on the subject, and sign a petition (he's hoping to achieve NGO status). It's an interesting visit.

On the main rd. to the temples, just before the checkpoint and a few clicks east. Go by motorbike or taxi. Daily 7am–5pm. Free admission (voluntary contributions).

**Roluos Group**   About 13km (8 miles) east of the town center, these three temples are best viewed in the context of Angkor architecture's progression, as the forefathers of the more dynamic of Angkor's main temples. A visit to these temples is included in the main temple ticket, but will cost you a bit extra for transport.

## SHOPPING

The **Old Market,** in the center of Siem Reap, is still the best place to find all kinds of Buddhist trinkets, souvenirs like T-shirts, and even good books on the temples. Just outside the market, you'll find a whole array of small storefront boutiques.

Large, mall-style souvenir venues line the road just north of town on the way to the temples and are a good stop for the obligatory collector's minispoon or plastic replica of the temples.

**The Lazy Mango Bookshop** (1 block west of the Old Market; lazy mangobooks@yahoo.com), is where you can exchange that novel you've been dragging around for a new one and talk with Don, the kind American owner.

## AFTER DARK

Siem Reap is a town where most visitors are up with the sun and out visiting the temple sites, but there are a few good evening options.

**Apsara dance** is an ancient art in Cambodia. Dancers in traditional gilded costume practice their slow art, characterized by the elegant contortions of a dancer's wrists. Combined with a fine buffet dinner in the traditional indoor banquet-house theater, this is a fun evening out. Contact the folks at the **Angkor Village** (© **063/963-5613**) to make reservations for the nightly show. Dinner begins at 7pm, and the show starts at 7:30pm (tickets cost $20).

The Raffles Grand Hotel D'Angkor has a similar show in an open pavilion on the lawn at the front of the hotel. Call © **063/963-888** (same time and price as above).

**Dr. Beat (Beatocello) Richner** plays the works of Bach and some of his own comic pieces between stories and vignettes about his work as director of the **Kanth Bopha Foundation** (www.beat-richner.ch), a humanitarian hospital just north of the town center. Admission is free, but donations are accepted in support of their valiant efforts to serve a steady stream of destitute patients, mostly children, who suffer from treatable diseases such as tuberculosis. Dr. Richner is as passionate about his music as he is about his cause. You're in for an enjoyable, informative evening. Performances are every Saturday at 7:15pm, just north of the town center on the road to the temples.

There are a few popular bars near the Old Market in Siem Reap. The **Angkor What?** (1 block west of the Old Market) seems to be where it's at, and next door the **Easy Speaking Café and Pub** handles the spillover. The whole street, in fact, hops late into the evening. Nearby, the black-lit, funky **Laundry,** on a side street to the north of the Old Market, has good special events. **Dead Fish Tower** (© **012/630-6377**), on the main road heading toward the temples, is set up like the rigging of a tall ship, with precarious perches, funky nooks, and unique drinks.

# 8

# Singapore

*by Jennifer Eveland*

Singapore thrives on a history that has absorbed a multitude of foreign elements over almost 2 centuries, melding them into a unique modern national identity. Beginning with the landing of Sir Stamford Raffles in 1819, add to the mix the original Malay inhabitants, immigrating waves of Chinese traders and workers, Indian businessmen and laborers, Arab merchants, British colonials, European adventure seekers, and an assortment of Southeast Asian settlers—this tiny island rose from the ingenuity of those who worked and lived together here. Today, all recognize each group's importance to the heritage of the land, each adding unique contributions to a culture and identity we know as Singaporean.

With all its shopping malls, fast-food outlets, imported fashion, and steel skyscrapers, Singapore could look like any other contemporary city you've ever visited—but to peel through the layers is to understand that life here is far more complex. While the outer layers are startlingly Western, just underneath lies a curious area where East blends with West in language, cuisine, attitude, and style. At the core, you'll find a sensibility rooted in the cultural heritage of values, religion, superstition, and memory. In Singapore, nothing is ever as it appears to be.

For me this is where the fascination begins. I detect so many things familiar in this city, only to discover how these imported ideas have been altered to fit the local identity. Like the Singaporean shophouse—a jumble of colonial architectural mandates, European tastes, Chinese superstitions, and Malay finery. Or "Singlish," the unofficial local tongue, which combines English language with Chinese grammar, common Malay phrases, and Hokkien slang to form a patois unique to this part of the world. This transformation of cultures has been going on for almost 2 centuries. So, in a sense, Singapore is no different today than it was 100 years ago. And in this I find my "authentic" travel experience.

## 1 Getting to Know Singapore

On a world map, Singapore is nothing more than a speck nestled in the heart of Southeast Asia, at the tip of the Malaysian peninsula. In the north, it's linked to Malaysia by a causeway over the Strait of Johor, which is its only physical connection to any other body of land. The country is made up of one main island, Singapore, and around 60 smaller ones, some of which—like Sentosa, Pulau Ubin, Kusu, and St. John's Island—are popular retreats. The main island is shaped like a flat, horizontal diamond, measuring in at just over 42km (26 miles) from east to west and almost 23km (14 miles) north to south. With a total land area of only 584.8 sq. km (228 sq. miles), Singapore is almost shockingly tiny.

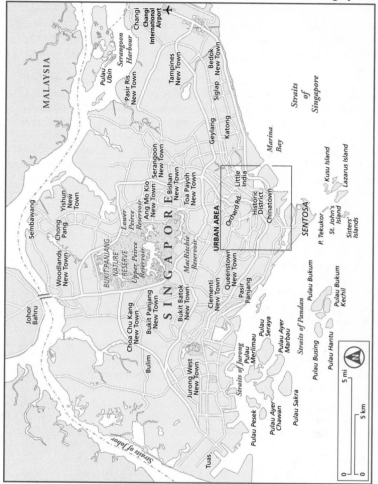

Singapore's geographical position, sitting approximately 137km (85 miles) north of the equator, means that its climate features uniform temperatures, plentiful rainfall, and high humidity.

Singapore is a city-state, which basically means the city *is* the country. The urban center starts at the Singapore River at the southern point of the island. Within the urban center are neighborhoods that are handy for visitors to become familiar with: The Historic District, Chinatown, Orchard Road, Kampong Gelam, and Little India.

Beyond the central urban area you'll find older suburban neighborhoods such as Katong, Geylang, or Holland Village, neighborhoods that feature prewar homes with charming architectural details. Travel farther and you'll find New Towns—for example, Ang Mo Kio or Toa Payoh—which are clusters of government-subsidized housing that have sprung up around the island, supported by their own shopping malls, schools, and clinics, and many of them connected by the subway system.

**THE CITY**   The urban center of Singapore spans quite far from edge to edge, so walking from one end to the other, say from Kampong Gelam to Chinatown, will be too much for a relaxed walk. But within each neighborhood, the best way to explore is by foot, wandering along picturesque streets, in and out of shops and museums.

The main focal point of the city is the **Singapore River,** which on a map is located at the southern point of the island, flowing west to east into a marina. It's along the banks of this river that Sir Stamford Raffles landed and built his settlement for the East India Trading Company. As trade prospered, the banks of the river were expanded to handle commerce, behind which neighborhoods and administrative offices took root. In 1822, he developed a town plan which allocated neighborhoods to each of the races who'd come in droves to find work and begin lives. The lines drawn then remain today, shaping the major ethnic enclaves held within the city limits.

On the south bank of the river, go-downs, or warehouses, lined the waterside. Behind, offices and residences sprang up for the Chinese community of merchants and "coolie" laborers who worked the river and sea trade. Raffles named this section **Chinatown,** a name that stands today.

Neighboring Chinatown to the southwest is **Tanjong Pagar,** a small district where wealthy Chinese and Eurasians built plantations and manors. With the development of the steamship, Keppel Harbour, a deep natural harbor just off the shore of Tanjong Pagar, was built up to receive the larger vessels. Tanjong Pagar quickly developed into a commercial and residential area filled with workers who flocked there to support the industry.

In the early days both Chinatown and Tanjong Pagar were amazing sights of city activity. Row houses lined the streets with shops on the bottom floors and homes on the second and third. Chinese coolie laborers commonly lived 16 to a room, and the area flourished with gambling casinos, clubs, and opium dens for them to spend their spare time and money. Indians also thronged to the area to work on the docks, a small reminder that although races had their own areas, they were never exclusive communities.

As recently as the 1970s, a walk down the streets in this area was an adventure: The shops housed Chinese craftsman and artists. On the streets, hawkers peddled food and other merchandise. Calligrapher scribes set up shop on sidewalks to write letters for a fee. Housewives would bustle, running their daily errands. Overhead, laundry hung from bamboo poles.

Today, both of these districts are sleepy in comparison. New Towns offering affordable housing have siphoned residents off to the suburbs, and though the government has renovated many of the old shophouses in an attempt to preserve history, they're now tenanted by law offices and architectural, public relations, and advertising firms. About the only time you'll see this place hustle any more is during weekday lunchtime, when all the professionals dash out for a bite.

The **north bank** was originally reserved for colonial administrative buildings and is today commonly referred to as the **Historic District.** The center point was The Padang, the field on which the Europeans would play sports and hold outdoor ceremonies. Around the field, the Parliament Building, Supreme Court, City Hall, and other municipal buildings sprang up in grand style. Government Hill, the present day **Fort Canning Hill,** was home of the governors. The Esplanade along the waterfront was a center for European social activities and music gatherings, when colonials would don their finest western styles and walk the park under parasols or cruise in horse-drawn carriages. These days the Historic District is still the center of most of the government's operations and home to numerous high-rise hotels and shopping malls. The area on the bank of the river is celebrated as Raffles' landing site.

To the northwest of the Historic District, in the area along **Orchard Road and Tanglin,** a residential area was created for European and Eurasians. Homes and plantations were eventually replaced by apartment buildings and shops, and in the early 1970s luxury hotels ushered tourism into the area in full force. In the 1980s, huge shopping malls were erected along the sides of Orchard Road, turning the Orchard-scape into the shopping hub it continues to be. The Tanglin area is home to most of the foreign embassies in Singapore.

The natural landscape of **Little India** made it a natural location for an Indian settlement. Indians were the original cattle hands and traders in Singapore, and this area's natural grasses and springs provided their cattle with food and water while bamboo groves supplied necessary lumber for their pens. Later, with the establishment of brick kilns, Indian construction laborers flocked to the area to find work. Today many elements of Indian culture persist, although Indians make up a small percentage of the current population. Shops, restaurants, and temples still serve the community, and on Sundays Little India is a true mob scene, when all the workers have their day off and come to the streets here to socialize and relax.

**Kampong Gelam,** neighboring Little India, was given to Sultan Hussein and his family as part of his agreement to turn Singapore over to Raffles. Here he built his Istana (palace) and the Sultan Mosque, and the area subsequently filled with Malay and Arab Muslims who imported a distinct Islamic flavor to the neighborhood. The area is still a focal point of Muslim society in Singapore thanks to Sultan Mosque, and the Istana has recently been opened as a new exhibit celebrating Malay culture. **Arab Street** is a regular draw for both tourists and locals who come to find deals on fabrics and local and regional crafts.

Two areas of the city center are relatively new, having been built atop huge parcels of reclaimed land. Where the eastern edges of Chinatown and Tanjong Pagar once touched the water's edge, land reclamation created the present-day downtown business district which is named after its central thoroughfare, **Shenton Way.** This Wall Street–like district is home to the magnificent skyscrapers that grace Singapore's skyline, and to the banks and businesses that have made the place an international financial capital. During weekday business hours, Shenton Way is packed with scurrying businesspeople; after hours and on weekends it's nothing more than a quiet forest of concrete, metal, and glass.

The other area is **Marina Bay,** on the opposite side of the Marina, just east of the historic district. **Suntec City,** Southeast Asia's largest convention and exhibition center, is located here and has become the lynchpin of a thriving hotel, shopping mall, and amusement zone.

## OUTSIDE THE URBAN AREA

The heart of the city centers around the Singapore River but outside the city proper are suburban neighborhoods and rural areas. In the immediate outskirts of the main urban area are the older suburban neighborhoods, such as **Katong, Geyland,** and **Holland Village.** Beyond these are the newer suburbs, called **HDB New Towns.** The HDB, or Housing Development Board, is responsible for creating large towns, such as **Ang Mo Kio** and **Toa Payoh;** each have their own network of supporting businesses: restaurants, schools, shops, health-care facilities, and sometimes department stores.

## 2 Planning Your Trip to Singapore

The long arm of the **Singapore Tourism Board (STB)** reaches many overseas audiences through its branch offices, which will gladly provide brochures and booklets to help you plan your trip, and through its website, at **www.visit singapore.com**.

### ENTRY REQUIREMENTS

To enter Singapore, you must have a passport valid for at least 6 months from your date of entry. Visitors from the United States, Canada, Australia, New Zealand, and the United Kingdom are not required to obtain a visa prior to arrival. A Social Visit Pass (with combined social and business status) good for up to 30 days (up to 90 days for U.S. visitors) will be awarded upon entry for travelers arriving by plane, or for 14 days if your trip is by ship or overland from Malaysia or Indonesia. Immigration officers are not required to grant you the maximum amount of days allotted, but rather have discretion to grant you as many days as they feel you need.

For information on obtaining a passport, please see "Passports" in the "Fast Facts" section in chapter 3.

### CUSTOMS
#### WHAT YOU CAN BRING INTO SINGAPORE

There's no restriction on the amount of currency you can bring into Singapore. For those over 18 years of age who have arrived from countries other than Malaysia and have spent more than 48 hours outside Singapore, allowable duty-free concessions are 1 liter of spirits; 1 liter of wine; and 1 liter of either port, sherry, or beer, all of which must be intended for personal consumption only. There are no duty-free concessions on cigarettes or other tobacco items. If you exceed the duty-free limitations, you can bring your excess items in upon payment of goods and services tax (GST) and Customs duty.

**PROHIBITED ITEMS**   It is important to note that Singapore has some very unique prohibitions on the import of certain items. While pretty much every country in the world, including Singapore, prohibits travelers from bringing items like plutonium, explosives, and firearms through Customs—same goes with agricultural products such as live plants and animals, controlled substances, and poisons—Singapore adds to the list any type of printed or recorded pornography; pirated movies, music, or software; and toy or decorative guns, knives, or swords. A detailed rundown of prohibited items can be found on the net at the Ministry of Home Affairs home page, www.mha.gov.sg.

**SINGAPORE'S DRUG POLICY**   With all of the publicity surrounding the issue, Singapore's strict drug policy shouldn't need recapitulation, but here it is: Importing, selling, or using illegal narcotics is absolutely forbidden. Punishments are severe, up to and including the death penalty (automatic for morphine quantities exceeding 30g, heroin exceeding 15g, cocaine 30g, marijuana 500g, hashish 200g, opium 1.2kg, and methamphetamines 250g). If you're carrying smaller sums (anything above morphine 3g, heroin 2g, cocaine 3g, marijuana 15g, hashish 10g, opium 100g, and methamphetamines 25g) you'll still be considered to have intent to traffic, and may face the death penalty if you can't prove otherwise. If you're crazy enough to try to bring these things into the country and you are caught, no measure of appeal to your home consulate will grant you any special attention.

# MONEY

The local currency unit is the **Singapore dollar.** It's commonly referred to as the "Sing dollar," and retail prices are often marked as S$ (a designation I've used throughout this book). Notes are issued in denominations of S$2, S$5, S$10, S$50, S$100, S$500, and S$1,000. S$1 bills exist but are rare. Notes vary in size and color from denomination to denomination. Coins are issued in denominations of S1¢, S5¢, S10¢, S20¢, S50¢, and the fat, gold-colored S$1. Singapore has an interchangeability agreement with Brunei Darussalam, so don't be alarmed if you receive Brunei currency with your change, as it's legal tender.

At the time of this writing, exchange rates on the Singapore dollar were as follows: US$1 = S$1.70, C$1 = S$1.38, £1 = S$3.07, A$1 = S$1.26, and NZ$1 = S$1.14. The exchange rate used throughout this book is US$1 = S$1.70, which I've calculated to be the average exchange rate during the year 2004. Before you begin budgeting your trip, I suggest you obtain the latest conversions so you don't suffer any last-minute surprises. A neat and easy customizable currency conversion program can be found on the Internet through **www.xe.com**.

**CURRENCY EXCHANGE**    It's not an absolute necessity to buy Singapore dollars before your trip, since you can find ATMs that accept cards from the Cirrus and PLUS networks at the Arrival Halls of **Changi Terminals 1 and 2** as you exit the baggage claim area. If you do need currency changed, there are a few banks that operate money-changing booths, plus an **American Express Foreign Exchange** office at Changi Terminal 2 (© 65/6543-0671), open from noon to midnight daily.

In town it's best to exchange currency or traveler's checks at a local authorized money changer, found in most shopping malls throughout the city. They'll give you the best rate. You'll lose money with the high rates at banks, hotels, and shops.

**ATMs**    ATMs are linked to an international network that most likely includes your bank at home. **Cirrus** (© 800/424-7787; www.mastercard.com) and **PLUS** (© 800/843-7587; www.visa.com) are the two most popular networks in the U.S. as well as in Singapore. ATMs operated by local or regional banks are ubiquitous in cosmopolitan Singapore. Look for them in shopping malls, MRT stations, and along streets with a lot of pedestrian traffic. You'll get the best exchange rate if you withdraw money from an ATM, but keep in mind that many banks impose a fee every time a card is used at an ATM in a different city or bank. Some local banks in Singapore will add their own charge of up to S$5 (US$2.95).

**TRAVELER'S CHECKS**    Traveler's checks are something of an anachronism from the days before the ATM (automated-teller machine) made cash accessible at any time. However, you're likely to be charged an ATM withdrawal fee if the bank is not your own, so if you're withdrawing money every day, you might be better off with traveler's checks—provided that you don't mind showing identification every time you want to cash one.

You can get traveler's checks at almost any bank. **American Express** offers denominations of $20, $50, $100, $500, and (for cardholders only) $1,000. You'll pay a service charge ranging from 1% to 4%. You can also get American Express traveler's checks over the phone by calling © **800/221-7282;** Amex gold and platinum cardholders who use this number are exempt from the 1% fee. AAA members can obtain checks without a fee at most AAA offices.

Visa, MasterCard, and Thomas Cook all offer traveler's checks, however they are not as widely recognized in Singapore, and may not be accepted at some establishments.

# Urban Singapore Neighborhoods

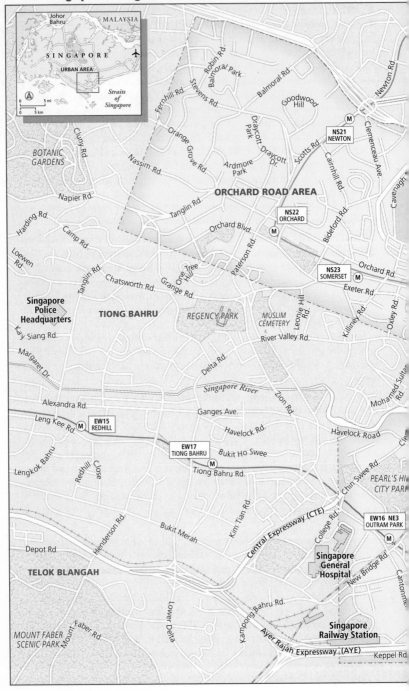

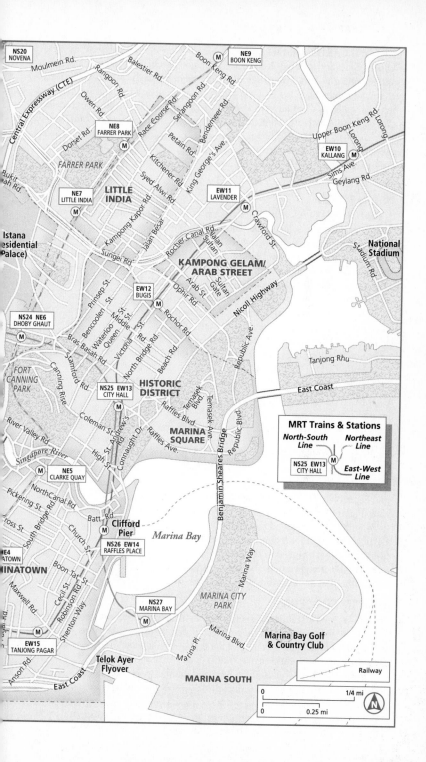

NS20
NOVENA

Moulmein Rd.

Rangoon Rd.

Balestier Rd.

Boon Keng Rd.

NE9
BOON KENG

Owen Rd.

Dorset Rd.

Race Course Rd.

Serangoon Rd.

Bendemeer Rd.

Upper Boon Keng Rd.

Lorong

Lorong

NE8
FARRER PARK

Petain Rd.

King George's Ave.

Kitchener Rd.

EW10
KALLANG

FARRER PARK

Sims Ave.

Geylang Rd.

NE7
LITTLE INDIA

LITTLE
INDIA

Syed Alwi Rd.

EW11
LAVENDER

Bukit
ah Rd.

Kampong Kapor Rd.

Jalan Besar

Crawford St.

Istana
esidential
Palace)

Sungei Rd.

Rochor Canal Rd.

Jalan
Sultan

KAMPONG GELAM/
ARAB STREET

National
Stadium

Stadium Rd.

Prinsep St.

EW12
BUGIS

Arab St.

Sultan
Gate

Ophir Rd.

Nicoll Highway

NS24 NE6
DHOBY GHAUT

Bencoolen St.

Middle St.

Queen St.

Victoria St.

St.

Rochor Rd.

Beach Rd.

Republic Ave.

Tanjong Rhu

FORT
CANNING
PARK

Bras Basah Rd.

Waterloo St.

North Bridge Rd.

HISTORIC
DISTRICT

East Coast

Stamford Rd.

Canning Rise

Coleman St.

St. Andrew's

NS25 EW13
CITY HALL

Raffles Blvd.

Temasek Blvd.

Temasek Ave.

River Valley Rd.

Singapore River

High St.

Connaught Dr.

Raffles Ave.

MARINA
SQUARE

Republic Blvd.

MRT Trains & Stations

NS25 EW13
CITY HALL

North-South
Line

Northeast
Line

East-West
Line

NE5
CLARKE QUAY

NorthCanal Rd.

Benjamin Sheares Bridge

Pickering St.

oss St.

South Bridge Rd.

Batt. Rd.

Clifford
Pier

Marina Bay

Church St.

NS26 EW14
RAFFLES PLACE

Boon Tat St.

E4
ATOWN

INATOWN

Cecil St.

Robinson Rd.

NS27
MARINA BAY

MARINA CITY
PARK

Marina Way

Maxwell Rd.

Shenton Way

Marina Pl.

Marina Blvd.

Marina Bay Golf
& Country Club

Anson Rd.

2

EW15
TANJONG PAGAR

Marina

Telok Ayer
Flyover

MARINA SOUTH

East Coast

Railway

0                    1/4 mi

0          0.25 mi

N

**CREDIT CARDS**   In Singapore, American Express, Visa, MasterCard, and Diners Club are accepted at virtually all major hotels, restaurants, nightclubs and shopping centers. Even taxis accept payment by credit card. Smaller food and retail merchants generally don't accept plastic, and be advised, if you are trying to negotiate a discount with a vendor, you will always get a better price with good old-fashioned cash. Some retailers will insist on adding a credit card "service charge" to your bill. While it is true that the credit card companies charge the retailers a small fee each time a customer uses a card, it is a cost the retailers are supposed to bear themselves. If anyone tries to foist this charge onto you, sadly your only recourse is to report him to your credit card company.

## WHEN TO GO

A steady supply of business travelers keep occupancy rates high year-round in Singapore, however, some hotels report that business travel gets sluggish during the months of July and August, when they target the leisure market more aggressively. This is probably your best time to negotiate a favorable rate. Peak season for travel falls between December and June, with "superpeak" beginning in mid-December and lasting through the Chinese Lunar New Year, which falls in January or February, depending on the moon's cycle. During this season, Asian travel routes are booked solid and hotels are maxed out. Favorable deals are rare, since most of Asia takes annual leave at this time.

There are 11 **official public holidays:** New Year's Day, Hari Raya Haji, Chinese New Year or Lunar New Year (2 days), Good Friday, Labour Day, Vesak Day, National Day, Hari Raya Puasa, Deepavali, and Christmas Day. On these days, expect government offices, banks, and some shops to be closed.

**CLIMATE**   Singapore lies between two monsoon winds, and rainfall varies greatly. The Northeast Monsoon arrives the beginning of November and stays until mid-March, when temperatures are slightly cooler, relatively speaking, than other times of the year. The heaviest rainfall occurs between November and January, with daily showers that sometimes last for long periods of time; at other times, it comes down in short heavy gusts and goes quickly away. Wind speeds are rarely anything more than light. The Southwest Monsoon falls between June and September. Temperatures are much higher and, interestingly, it's during this time of year that Singapore gets the *least* rain (with the very least reported in July).

By and large, year-round temperatures remain uniform, with a daily average of 81°F (27°C), afternoon temperatures reaching as high as 87°F (31°C), and an average sunrise temperature as low as 75°F (24°C). Relative humidity often exceeds 90% at night and in the early morning. Even on a "dry" afternoon, don't expect it to drop much below 60%. (The daily average is 84% relative humidity.)

## HEALTH CONCERNS

Singapore doesn't require that you have any vaccinations to enter the country, but recommends immunization against diphtheria, tetanus, hepatitis A and B, and typhoid for anyone traveling to Southeast Asia in general. If you're particularly worried, follow their advice; if not, don't worry about it.

Singapore's climate guarantees heat and humidity year-round, you should remember to take precautions. Give yourself plenty of time to relax and regroup on arrival to adjust your body to the new climate (and to the new time, if there is a time difference for you). Also, drink plenty of water. Avoid overexposure to the sun. The tropical sun will burn you like thin toast in no time at all. You may also feel more lethargic than usual. This is typical in the heat, so take things easy and you'll be fine. Be careful of the air-conditioning, though. It's nice and cooling, but if you're prone to catching a chill, or find yourself moving in and out of air-conditioned buildings a lot, you can wind up with a horrible summer cold.

If you do need medical attention, Singapore has a fantastic health-care system that is top-quality and affordable. A centrally located 24-hour emergency clinic can be found at **Mount Elizabeth Hospital,** 3 Mt. Elizabeth Rd., off Orchard Road near the York Hotel (© **65/6737-2666**). All hotels are prepared to contact medical assistance for you in the event of an emergency.

## GETTING THERE
### BY PLANE

If you're hunting for the best airfare, there are a few things you can do. First, plan your trip for the low-volume season, which runs from September 1 to November 30. Between January 1 and May 31, you'll pay the highest fares. Plan your travel on weekdays only, and, if you can, plan to stay for at least a full week. Book your reservations in advance—waiting until the last minute can mean you'll pay sky-high rates. Also, if you have access to the Internet, there are a number of great sites that'll search out decent fares for you.

In my experience, the best deals are offered through Asian carriers. Compare fares at Japan Airlines (www.jal.co.jp), Korean Air (www.koreanair.com), Cathay Pacific Airways (www.cathaypacific.com), Malaysia Airlines (www.malaysia airlines.com), and Thai Airways International (www.thaiair.com). Otherwise, I've listed information for a few major airlines below.

Singapore's national carrier, **Singapore Airlines** (www.singaporeair.com; (© **800/742-3333** in the U.S. and Canada; © **0870/608-8886** in the U.K.; © **131011** in Australia; © **0800/808-909** and 65/6223-8888 in Singapore), is arguably one of the finest airlines in the world, with reliable service that is second to none. It's the most luxurious way to fly to Singapore, but also the most expensive as well. It connects major cities in North America, Europe, Australia, and New Zealand to Singapore with daily flights.

From North America, **United Airlines** (© **800/241-6522** in the U.S., or 65/6873-3533 in Singapore; www.ual.com) and **Northwest Airlines** (© **800/447-4747** in the U.S. or 65/6336-3371 in Singapore; www.nwa.com) link all major U.S. cities with Singapore.

**British Airways** and **Qantas** collaborate to provide flights to Asia Pacific from major cities in the U.K. and Australia (British Airways: www.britishairways.com; © 0870/850-9850 in the U.K.; © 1300/767-177 in Australia; © 65/6589-7000 in Singapore. Qantas: www.qantas.com; © 0845/774-7767 in the U.K.; © 131313 in Australia; and © 65/6589-7000 in Singapore).

From New Zealand, **Air New Zealand** has daily flights from Auckland and Christchurch (www.airnewzealand.co.nz; © **0800/737-000** in New Zealand or © **65/6535-8266** in Singapore).

## GETTING INTO TOWN FROM THE AIRPORT

Most visitors to Singapore will land at **Changi International Airport,** which is located toward the far eastern corner of the island. Compared to other international airports, Changi is a dream come true, providing clean and very efficient space and facilities. Expect to find in-transit accommodations, restaurants, duty-free shops, money changers, ATMs, car-rental desks, accommodation assistance, and tourist information all marked with clear signs. When you arrive, keep your eyes peeled for the many Singapore Tourism Board brochures that are so handily displayed throughout the terminal.

The city is easily accessible by public transportation. A taxi trip to the city center will cost around S$22 to S$25 (US$13–US$15), which is the metered fare plus an airport surcharge, usually S$3 to S$5 (US$1.75–US$2.95) depending on the time of pickup. It takes around 20 minutes to reach the city; double it if you're traveling during weekday rush hours. You'll traverse the wide Airport Boulevard to the Pan-Island Expressway (PIE) or the East Coast Parkway (ECP), past public housing estates and other residential neighborhoods in the eastern part of the island, over causeways, and into the city center.

If you've got a lot of people and luggage, **CityCab** offers a six-seater maxicab to anywhere in the city for a flat rate of S$35 (US$21). You can inquire at the taxi queue or call © **65/6542-8297.**

There's an **airport shuttle,** a six-seater maxicab that traverses between the airport, all major hotels plus stops at Orchard Road, Chinatown, and Bugis Junction. A booking counter at both terminals is open daily from 6am to 2am. When you book your trip into town, you can also make an advanced reservation for your departure. Pay S$7 (US$4.10) for adults or S$5 (US$2.95) for children directly to the driver, but try not to pay with bills that are US$50 or larger. Call the counter at © **65/6542-8297.**

The **MRT,** Singapore's subway system, now operates to the airport, linking you with the city and areas beyond. STB will tell you the trip takes 30 minutes, but really, give yourself at least an hour, since you'll need time to wait for the train to arrive, then you'll have to transfer trains at Tanah Merah station, and if you're arriving in Terminal 1, you'll need to hop on yet another train—a shuttle between terminals. Once you get to your station in town, you'll still have to find your way, with your luggage, to your hotel. Personally, I think it's a pain in the neck, but hey, it only costs S$1.40 (US80¢) to get to City Hall station. Trains operate roughly from 6am to midnight daily.

A couple of **buses** run from the airport into the city as well. SBS bus no. 36 is the best, saving time by hopping on East Coast Parkway before making stops through the Historic District and along Orchard Road. Pick up the bus in the basement of either terminal. The trip will take over an hour, and you'll need to get exact change before you board. A trip to town will be roughly S$1.40 (US80¢).

For arrival and departure information, you can call **Changi International Airport** at © 65/6542-4422.

## GETTING AROUND SINGAPORE

The many inexpensive mass transit options make getting around Singapore pretty easy. Of course, taxis always simplify the ground transportation dilemma. They're also very affordable and, by and large, drivers are helpful and honest if not downright personable. The **Mass Rapid Transit (MRT) subway service** has lines that cover the main areas of the city and out to the farther parts of the island. Buses present more of a challenge because there are so many routes snaking all over the island, but they're a great way to see the country while getting where you want to go.

Of course, if you're just strolling around the urban limits, many of the sights within the various neighborhoods are within walking distance, but walking between the different neighborhoods can be a hike, especially in the heat. The STB Visitors Centres carry a variety of free city maps and walking tour maps of individual neighborhoods to help you find your way around.

**Stored-fare EZ-Link fare cards** can be used on both the subway and buses, and can be purchased at TransitLink offices in MRT stations. These save you the bother of trying to dig up exact change for bus meters. The card does carry a S$5 (US$2.95) deposit—for a S$15 (US$8.80) initial investment, you'll get S$10 (US$5.90) worth of travel credit.

When you pick up your EZ-Link card, I recommend purchasing the latest edition of the *TransitLink Guide* for about S$3.90 (US$2.30) at the TransitLink office where you buy your card. This tiny book details both MRT and bus routes, with maps of each MRT station surrounds and indicating connections between buses and MRT stations. It also tells you fares for each trip.

## BY TAXI

Taxis are by far the most convenient way to get around Singapore. Fares are cheap, cars are clean and drivers speak English. Taxi queues can be found at every hotel, shopping mall, and public building; otherwise you can flag one down from the side of the road. Most destinations in the main parts of the island can be reached fairly inexpensively, while trips to the outlying attractions can cost from S$10 to S$15 (US$5.90–US$8.80) one-way. That said, I caution against becoming too dependent on them. During the morning and evening rush you can wait a maddening long time in the queue, and sometimes if you're at a destination outside the main city area, they're few and far between. If it's raining, you might as well stay put, you'll never get a cab.

If you do find yourself stranded, there are a few things you can do. If you're at an attraction or a restaurant, you can ask the cashier or help desk to call a taxi company and book a cab for you. If you're near a phone, you can call yourself: **CityCab** (© 65/6552-2222), **Comfort** (© 65/6552-1111), and **TIBS** (© 65/6555-8888) to make your own booking. There's an extra charge for the booking: for CityCab it's S$3 (US$1.75), Comfort S$3.20 (US$1.90), and TIBS S$2.80 (US$1.65).

Taxis charge the metered fare, which is S$2.40 (US$1.40) for the first kilometer (½ mile) and S10¢ (US5¢) for each additional 225m to 240m or 30 seconds of waiting. Extra fares are levied on top of the metered fare depending on where you're going and when you go. At times, figuring your fare seems more like a riddle. Here's a summary:

Trips during peak hours: Between the hours of 7:30 and 9:30am Monday to Friday, 4:30 to 7pm Monday to Friday, and 11:30am to 2pm on Saturdays, trips will carry an additional S$1 (US60¢) peak-period surcharge. But if you're traveling outside the Central Business District (CBD), you won't need to pay this surcharge during the morning rush. (To accurately outline the boundaries of the CBD, I'd need to fill a couple of encyclopedic volumes, so for this purpose, let's just say it's basically Orchard Rd., the Historic District, Chinatown, and Shenton Way.)

Additional charges rack up each time you travel through an Electronic Road Pricing (ERP) scheme underpass. On the Central Expressway (CTE), Pan-Island Expressway (PIE), and selected thoroughfares in the CBD, charges from S30¢ to S$1.70 (US18¢–US$1) are calculated by an electronic box on the driver's dashboard. The driver will add this amount to your fare.

And for special torture, here are some more charges: From midnight to 6am, add 50% to your fare. From 6pm on the eve of a public holiday to midnight the following day, you pay an additional S$1 (US60¢). From Changi Airport add S$5 (US$2.95) if you're traveling Fridays, Saturdays, or Sundays between 5pm and midnight. Other times, it's S$3 (US$1.75). And for credit card payments (yes, they take plastic!), add 10%.

## BY MASS RAPID TRANSIT (MRT)

The MRT is Singapore's subway system. It's cool, clean, safe, and reliable, providing service around the central parts of the city, extending into the suburbs around the island. There are stops along Orchard Road into the Historic District, Chinatown, and Little India—chances are there will be a stop close to your hotel (see the MRT map in this chapter for specifics).

Fares range from S80¢ to S$1.80 (US47¢–US$1.05), depending on which stations you travel between. System charts are prominently displayed in all MRT stations to help you find your appropriate fare, which you pay with an EZ-Link fare card. Single-fare cards can be purchased at vending machines inside MRT stations. See above for information on stored-fare cards for multiple trips. (*One caution:* A fare card cannot be used by two people for the same trip; each must have his own.)

MRT operating hours vary between lines and stops, with the earliest train beginning service daily at 5:15am and the last train ending at 12:47am. For more information, call the **TransitLink Hotline** at ℂ **1800/767-4333** (daily 24 hr.).

## BY BUS

Singapore's bus system comprises an extensive web of routes that reach virtually everywhere on the island. It can be intimidating for newcomers, but once you get your feet wet, you'll feel right at home. Start off by purchasing an EZ-Link stored value card, so you can pay for your trips, and TransitLink Guide, so you can find your way around (see above for more details). All buses have a gray machine with a sensor pad close to the driver. Tap your EZ-Link card when you board and alight, and the fare will be automatically deducted. It'll be anywhere between S80¢ and S$1.80 (US47¢–US$1.05). If you're paying cash, be sure to have exact change; place the coins in the red box by the driver and announce your fare to him. He'll issue a ticket, which will pop out of a slot on one of the TransitLink machines behind him.

For more information, contact either of the two operating bus lines during standard business hours: **Singapore Bus Service (SBS)** (ℂ **1800/287-2727**) or **the Trans-Island Bus Service (TIBS)** (ℂ **1800/482-5433**).

## BY TROLLEY

You have a couple of trolley options; both services are offered for the convenience of travelers, making stops at most major tourist destinations. The **Singapore Explorer** shuttles down Orchard Road, through the Historic District and over the Singapore River, and down to Marina Square. For S$9 (US$5.30) adults and S$7 (US$4.10) children, you can enjoy unlimited rides for 1 day. Buy your tickets either from your hotel's front desk or directly from the driver. Call Singapore Explorer at ℂ **65/6339-6833.**

Singapore Airlines hosts the **SIA Hop-on bus.** Plying between Suntec City, the Historic District, the Singapore River, Chinatown, Orchard Road, and the Singapore Botanic Gardens, and Little India, the Hop-on comes every 30 minutes between the hours of 8am and 5pm. Unlimited rides for 1 day cost S$6 (US$3.50) adults and S$4 (US$2.35) children. If you flew Singapore Airlines to get here, you only have to pay S$3 (US$1.75) if you flash your boarding pass. Buy your tickets from your hotel's front desk, from a Singapore Airlines office, or from the bus drivers. For more information call **SH Tours** (ℂ **65/6374-9923**).

## RENTAL CAR

Visitors to Singapore rarely rent cars for sightseeing. Why? Because they cost a ton. At Avis, the lowest priced compact car rents for S$260 (US$158) per day. It's just

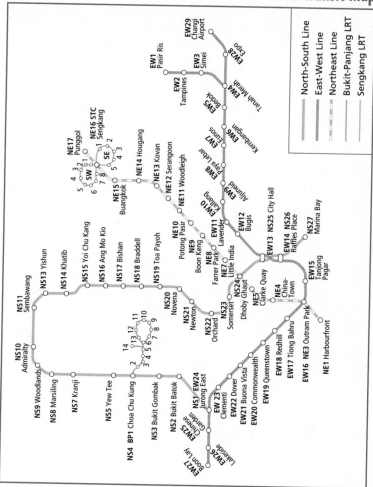

not worth it. Local transportation is excellent and affordable, you don't have to worry about adjusting to local driving rules and habits, and you don't have to worry about where to park the thing. Still, if you must, contact **Avis** at Changi Airport, Arrival Hall, Terminal 2 (© **65/6542-8855**), open daily 7am to 11pm.

## ETIQUETTE TIPS

While in Singapore, try to use only your right hand in social interaction. Why? Because in Indian and Muslim society, the left hand is used only for bathroom chores. Not only should you eat with your right hand and give and receive all gifts with your right hand, but you should make sure all gestures, especially pointing (and especially in temples and mosques), are made with your right hand. By the way, you should also try to point with your knuckle rather than your finger, to be more polite.

The other important etiquette tip is to remember to remove your shoes before entering places of worship (except for churches and synagogues) and all private residences.

In cosmopolitan Singapore, most people will shake hands in greeting, but it's good to remember that Muslim women are not allowed to touch men to whom they are not related by blood or marriage. Unless they initiate a handshake, a simple smile and nod is fine.

Also, it's common for Singaporeans to exchange business cards. Always receive cards with two hands, and always treat the card with respect—don't stash it in your pocket without paying attention to it.

If you're touring around during the day, shorts and a T-shirt is fine; however, if you plan to enter a temple or mosque, you will be required to cover your legs and upper arms. If you're dining in a restaurant, attending an event or business function, the dress code is "dress casual," meaning slacks and pressed shirt for men, and either slacks or skirt with a top for women, or a dress. For most business meetings a suit and tie is still necessary, but you needn't wear your jacket everywhere. For women, business suits are also expected.

If you would like to give a gift to a Singaporean, my advice is to consult your hotel concierge for appropriate gift recommendations. For example, avoid giving sweets or foods to Muslim friends, unless you are certain the gift is *halal* (permitted within Islamic dietary practice).

For the Chinese, it's more tricky. Gifts should never be knives, clocks, or handkerchiefs, and don't send anybody white flowers. (The sharp blades of knives symbolize the severing of a friendship; in Cantonese, the word for clock sounds the same as the word for funeral; handkerchiefs bring to mind tears and sadness; and white is the color of funeral mourning—you get the drift.)

The main rules regarding table manners revolve around the use of chopsticks. Don't stick them upright in any dish, don't gesture with them, and don't suck on them. Dropped chopsticks are also considered bad luck. Southern Indian food can be eaten with your hands, but make sure you wash them first, and always use your right hand.

## FAST FACTS: Singapore

*American Express* The American Express office is located at 300 Beach Rd., #18-01 The Concourse (© 65/6880-1333). It's open Monday to Friday 9am to 5pm and Saturday 9am to 1pm. There's a more convenient kiosk that handles traveler's checks and simple card transactions (including emergency check guarantee) on Orchard Road just outside the Marriott Hotel at Tangs (© 65/6735-2069). It's open daily from 9am to 9pm. An additional foreign exchange office is open at Changi Airport Terminal 2 (© 65/6543-0671). It's open from noon to midnight daily. See the "Money" section earlier in this chapter for more details on member privileges.

*Business Hours* Shopping centers are open Monday through Saturday from 10am to 9pm, and stay open until 10pm on some public holidays. Banks are open from 9:30am to 3pm Monday through Friday, and from 9 to 11am on Saturdays. Restaurants open at lunchtime from around 11am to 2:30pm, and for dinner they reopen at around 6pm and take the last order sometime around 10pm. Nightclubs stay open until 2am on weekdays and until 3am on Fridays and Saturdays. Government offices are open from 9am to 5pm Monday through Friday and from 9am to 3pm on Saturdays. Post offices conduct business from 8:30am to 5pm on weekdays and from 8:30am to 1pm on Saturdays.

*Car Rentals*  See "Getting Around Singapore," above..

*Climate*  See "When to Go," earlier in this chapter.

*Currency*  See "Money," earlier in this chapter.

*Documents*  See "Entry Requirements," earlier in this chapter.

*Drugstores*  **Guardian Pharmacies** fills prescriptions with name-brand drugs (from a licensed physician within Singapore), and carries a large selection of toiletry items. Convenient locations include #B1-05 Centre-point Shopping Centre (© **65/737-4835**), Changi International Airport Terminal 2 (© **65/545-4233**), #02-139 Marina Square (© **65/333-9565**), and #B1-04 Raffles Place MRT Station (© **65/535-2762**).

*Electricity*  Standard electrical current is 220 volts AC (50 cycles). Local electrical outlets are made for plugs with three square prongs. Consult your concierge to see if your hotel has converters and plug adapters in-house for you to use. If you are using sensitive equipment, do not trust cheap voltage transformers. Nowadays, a lot of electrical equipment—including portable radios and laptop computers—comes with built-in converters, so you can follow the manufacturer's directions for changing them over. *FYI:* Videocassettes taped on different voltage currents are recorded on machines with different record and playback cycles. Prerecorded videotapes are not interchangeable between currents unless you have special equipment that can play either kind.

*Embassies and Consulates*  Contacts for major embassies in Singapore are as follows: **U.S. Embassy,** 27 Napier Rd. (© **65/6476-9100**); **Canadian Embassy,** 80 Anson Rd. (© **65/6325-3240**); **U.K. Embassy,** Tanglin Road (© **65/6473-9333**); **Australian Embassy,** 391A Orchard Rd., Ngee Ann City Tower A, #15-06 (© **65/6836-4100**).

*Emergencies*  For **police** dial © **999.** For **medical** or **fire** emergencies call © **995.**

*Etiquette & Customs*  See "Etiquette Tips," earlier in this chapter.

*Holidays*  See the "When to Go," earlier in this chapter.

*Hospital*  A centrally located 24-hour emergency clinic can be found at **Mount Elizabeth Hospital,** 3 Mt. Elizabeth Rd, off Orchard Road near the York Hotel (© **65/6737-2666**).

*Internet Access*  Internet cafes are becoming common throughout the city, with usage costs about S$5 (US$2.95) per hour (keep in mind, if you use the Internet in your hotel's business center, you'll pay a much higher price). Almost every shopping mall has one, especially along Orchard Road, and there are cybercafes in both terminals at Changi Airport. In the Historic District, there are a few in Stamford House, just across from City Hall MRT Station. Check out **Chills Café,** #01-07 Stamford House, 39 Stamford Rd. (© **65/6883-1016;** open 9:30am–midnight daily).

*Language*  Singapore's four official languages are Malay, Chinese (Mandarin dialect), Tamil, and English. Malay is the national language while English is the language for government operations, law, and major financial transactions. Most Singaporeans are at least bilingual, with many speaking one or more dialects of Chinese, English, and some Malay.

*Liquor Laws* The legal age for alcohol purchase and consumption is **18** years—clubs rarely check foreigners. Bars and pubs will usually open in the afternoon and stay open until 1am on weeknights or until 2am on Fridays and Saturdays. Nightclubs and discos will open about 8pm and will stay open until 2am on weekdays or 3am on Fridays and Saturdays. Unless you come from New York, London, or Tokyo, alcohol can be very expensive here in comparison because of heavy "sin taxes."

*Mail* Most hotels have mail services at the front counter. Singapore Post has centrally located offices at #04-15 Ngee Ann City/Takashimaya Shopping Centre (✆ **65/6738-6899**); Chinatown Point, 133 New Bridge Rd. #02-42/43/44 (✆ **65/6538-7899**); Change Alley, 16 Collyer Quay #02-02 Hitachi Tower (✆ **65/6538-6899**); and at 231 Bain St. #01-03 Bras Basah Complex (✆ **65/6339-8899**). There are also five branches at Changi International Airport.

The going rate for international airmail letters to North America and Europe is S$1 (US60¢) for 20g plus S35¢ (US20¢) for each additional 10g. For international airmail service to Australia and New Zealand, the rate is S70¢ (US40¢) for 20g plus S30¢ (US20¢) for each additional 10g. Postcards and aerograms to all destinations are S50¢ (US30¢).

Your hotel will accept mail sent for you at its address.

*Maps* The STB Visitors Centres carry a variety of free city maps and walking tour maps of individual neighborhoods to help you find your way around.

*Newspapers and Magazines* Local English newspapers available are the *International Herald Tribune, The Business Times, The Straits Times, Today,* and *USA Today International.* Following an article criticizing the Singapore government, the *Asian Wall Street Journal* was banned from wide distribution in Singapore. Most of the major hotels carry it, though, so ask around and you can find one. *I-S Magazine* is a good resource for nightlife happenings. The STB Visitors Centres carry a few free publications for travelers, including *Where Singapore, This Week Singapore,* and *Singapore Business Visitor.* Major bookstores and magazine shops sell a wide variety of international magazines.

*Passports* For information on obtaining a passport, see "Passports" in the "Fast Facts" section in chapter 3.

*Pets* Singapore requires a mandatory 3 months quarantine for all pets entering from overseas.

*Police* Given the strict reputation of law enforcement in Singapore, you can bet the officers here don't have the greatest sense of humor. If you find yourself being questioned about anything, big or small, be dead serious and most respectful. For emergencies, call ✆ **999**. If you need to call the police headquarters, dial ✆ **1800/255-0000**.

If you are arrested, you have the right to legal council, but only when the police decide you can exercise that right. Bottom line: Don't get arrested.

*Smoking* It's against the law to smoke in public buses, elevators, theaters, cinemas, air-conditioned restaurants, shopping centers, government offices, and taxi lines.

*Taxes* Many hotels and restaurants will advertise rates followed by "+++." The first + is the goods and services tax (GST), which is levied at 5% of the purchase. The second + is 1% cess (a 1% tax levied by the STB on all tourism-related activities). The third is a 10% gratuity. The GST Tourist Refund Scheme lets you recover the GST for purchases of goods over S$300 (US$176) in value.

*Telephones* Public telephones can be found in booths on the street, or back near the toilets in shopping malls, public buildings, or hotel lobbies. Because most Singaporeans now carry mobile phones, public phones aren't always properly maintained. Local calls cost S10¢ (US5¢) for 3 minutes at coin- and card-operated phones. International calls can be made only from public phones designated specifically for this purpose. International public phones will accept either a stored-value phonecard or a credit card. Phonecards for local and international calls can be purchased at Singapore Post branches, 7-Eleven convenience stores, or money changers—make sure you specify local or international phonecard when you make your purchase.

**To call Singapore:** If you're calling Singapore from the United States: Dial the international access code 011, then dial the country code 65, then dial the 8-digit number. So the whole number you'd dial would be 011-65-0000-0000.

**To make international calls:** To make international calls from Singapore, first dial 001 and then the country code (U.S. or Canada 1, U.K. 44, Ireland 353, Australia 61, New Zealand 64). Next you dial the area code and number. For example, if you wanted to call the British Embassy in Washington, D.C., you would dial 001-1-202-588-7800.

**For directory assistance:** Dial 100 if you're looking for a number inside Singapore, and dial 104 for numbers to all other countries.

**For operator assistance:** If you need operator assistance in making a call, dial 104 if you're trying to make an international call and 100 if you want to call a number in Singapore.

**Toll-free numbers:** Numbers beginning with 1800 within Singapore are toll-free, but calling a 1-800 number in the States from Singapore is not toll-free. In fact, it costs the same as an overseas call.

*Time Zone* Singapore Standard Time is 8 hours ahead of Greenwich Mean Time (GMT). International time differences will change during daylight saving or summer time. Basic time differences are: New York –13 hours, Los Angeles –16, Montreal –13, Vancouver –16, London –8, Brisbane +3, Darwin +1, Melbourne +2, Sydney +3, and Auckland +4. For the current time within Singapore, call © 1711.

*Tipping* Tipping is discouraged at hotels, bars, and in taxis. Basically, the deal here is not to tip. A gratuity is automatically added into guest checks, and there's no need to slip anyone an extra buck for carrying bags or such. It's not expected.

*Toilets* Clean public toilets can be found in all shopping malls, hotels, and public buildings. Smaller restaurants may not be up on their cleanliness, and beware the "squatty potty" the Asian-style squat toilet, which you see in the more "local" places. Carry plenty of tissues with you, as they often run out.

*Useful Phone Numbers* U.S. Dept. of State Travel Advisory ℂ **202/647-5225** (manned 24 hr.); U.S. Passport Agency ℂ **202/647-0518**; U.S. Embassy in Singapore ℂ **65/6476-9100**; Canadian Embassy in Singapore ℂ **65/6325-3240**; U.K. Embassy in Singapore ℂ **65/6473-9333**; Australian Embassy in Singapore ℂ **65/6836-4100**; Singapore Tourism Board ℂ **1800/736-2000**; U.S. Centers for Disease Control International Traveler's Hot Line: ℂ **404/332-4559**

*Water* Tap water in Singapore passes World Health Organization standards and is potable.

## 3 Where to Stay

Budget accommodations are not a high priority on the island. Between the business community's demand for luxury on the one hand and the inflated Singaporean real estate market on the other, room prices tend to be high. Don't fret, though: I'm here to tell you that there's a range of accommodations out there—you just have to know where to find them.

In considering where you'll stay, think about what you'll be doing in Singapore—that way, you can choose a hotel that's close to the particular action that suits you. (On the other hand, since Singapore is a small place and public transportation is excellent, really nothing's ever too far away.)

**Orchard Road** has the largest cluster of hotels in the city, and is right in the heart of Singaporean shopping mania—the malls and wide sidewalks where locals and tourists stroll to see and be seen. The **Historic District** has hotels that are near museums and sights, while those in **Marina Bay** center more around the business professionals who come to Singapore for Suntec City, the giant convention and exhibition center located there. **Chinatown** and **Tanjong Pagar** have some lovely boutique hotels in quaint back streets, and **Shenton Way** has a couple of high-rise places for the convenience of people doing business in the downtown business district. Many hotels have free morning and evening shuttle buses to Orchard Road, Suntec City, and Shenton Way.

A newer trend is the boutique hotel. Conceived as part of the Urban Restoration Authority's renewal plans, rows of old shophouses and historic buildings in ethnic areas like Chinatown and Tanjong Pagar have been restored and transformed into small, lovely hotels. Places like Albert Court Hotel and The Inn at Temple Street are beautiful examples of local flavor turned into quaint accommodations. While these places can put you closer to the heart of Singapore, they do have their drawbacks—for one, both the hotels and their rooms are small and, due to building codes and a lack of space, they're unable to provide facilities like swimming pools, Jacuzzis, or fitness centers.

While budget hotels have very limited facilities and simpler interior stylings, you can always expect a clean room. What's more, service can sometimes be more personal in smaller hotels, where front desk staff has fewer faces to recognize and is accustomed to helping guests with the sorts of things a business center or concierge would handle in a larger hotel. Par for the course, many of the guests in these places are backpackers, and mostly Western backpackers at that. However, you will see some regional folks staying in these places. ***One note:*** The budget accommodations listed here are places decent enough for any standards.

While cheaper digs are available, the rooms can be dreary and depressing, musty and old, or downright sleazy.

Unless you choose one of the extreme budget hotels, there are some standard features you can expect to find everywhere. While no hotels offer a courtesy car or limousine, many have courtesy shuttles to popular parts of town. Security key cards are catching on, as are in-room safes. You'll also see in-house movies and, many times, CNN, ESPN, and HBO on your TV. Voice mail is gaining popularity, and fax services can always be provided upon request. You'll find most places have adequate fitness center facilities. Pools tend to be on the small side, and Jacuzzis are often placed in men's and women's locker rooms, making it impossible for couples to use them together. While tour desks are in some lobbies, car-rental desks are nonexistent.

Many of the finest restaurants in Singapore are located in hotels, whether they are operated by the hotel directly or just inhabiting rented space. Some hotels can have up to five or six restaurants, each serving a different cuisine. Generally, you can expect these restaurants to be more expensive than places located outside hotels. In each hotel review, the distinguished restaurants have been noted.

Rack rates for double rooms range from as low as S$75 (US$44) at the Strand on Bencoolen (a famous backpacker's strip) to as high as S$650 (US$382) a night at the exclusive Raffles Hotel. Average rooms are usually in the S$350 (US$206) range, but keep in mind that although all prices listed in this book are the going rates, they rarely represent what you'll actually pay. In fact, you should never have to pay the advertised rate in a Singapore hotel, as many offer promotional rates, often times up to 50% less than the official rack rate. When you call for your reservation, always ask what special deals they are running and how you can get the lowest price for your room. Hotels that have just completed renovations offer discounts, and most have special weekend or long-term stay programs. Also be sure to inquire about free add-ons. Complimentary breakfast and other services can have added value that makes a difference in the end.

For the purposes of this guide, I've divided hotels into the categories very expensive, S$450 (US$265) and up; expensive, S$350 to S$450 (US$206–US$265); moderate, S$200 to S$350 (US$118–US$206); and inexpensive, under S$200 (US$118).

**TAXES & SERVICE CHARGES**    All rates listed are in Singapore dollars, with U.S. dollar equivalents provided as well (remember to check the exchange rate when you're planning, though, since it may fluctuate). Most rates do not include the so-called "+++" taxes and charges: the 10% service charge, 5% goods and services tax (GST), and 1% cess (a tax levied by the STB on all tourism-related activities). Keep these in mind when figuring your budget. Some budget hotels will quote discount rates inclusive of all taxes.

**THE BUSY SEASON**    The busy season is from January to around June. In the late summer months, business travel dies down and hotels try to make up for

---

**Tips  Making Hotel Reservations Online**

The website www.asiarooms.com offers the best rates I've seen for Internet bookings, particularly for hotels in the Very Expensive and Expensive categories; however, they don't have deals for every hotel property. It's worth it to browse and compare.

# Where to Stay in Urban Singapore

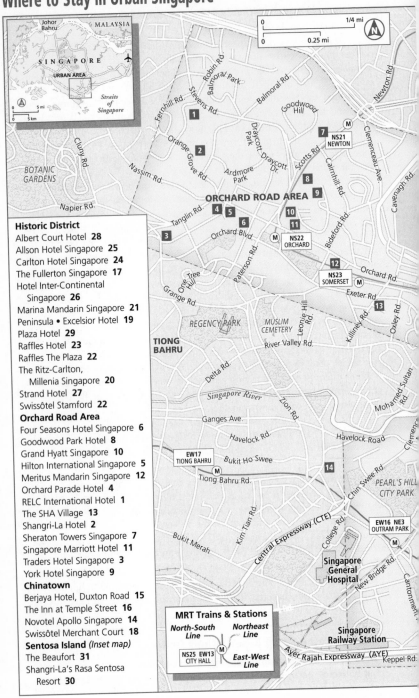

**Historic District**
Albert Court Hotel **28**
Allson Hotel Singapore **25**
Carlton Hotel Singapore **24**
The Fullerton Singapore **17**
Hotel Inter-Continental
  Singapore **26**
Marina Mandarin Singapore **21**
Peninsula • Excelsior Hotel **19**
Plaza Hotel **29**
Raffles Hotel **23**
Raffles The Plaza **22**
The Ritz-Carlton,
  Millenia Singapore **20**
Strand Hotel **27**
Swissôtel Stamford **22**

**Orchard Road Area**
Four Seasons Hotel Singapore **6**
Goodwood Park Hotel **8**
Grand Hyatt Singapore **10**
Hilton International Singapore **5**
Meritus Mandarin Singapore **12**
Orchard Parade Hotel **4**
RELC International Hotel **1**
The SHA Village **13**
Shangri-La Hotel **2**
Sheraton Towers Singapore **7**
Singapore Marriott Hotel **11**
Traders Hotel Singapore **3**
York Hotel Singapore **9**

**Chinatown**
Berjaya Hotel, Duxton Road **15**
The Inn at Temple Street **16**
Novotel Apollo Singapore **14**
Swissôtel Merchant Court **18**

**Sentosa Island** *(Inset map)*
The Beaufort **31**
Shangri-La's Rasa Sentosa
  Resort **30**

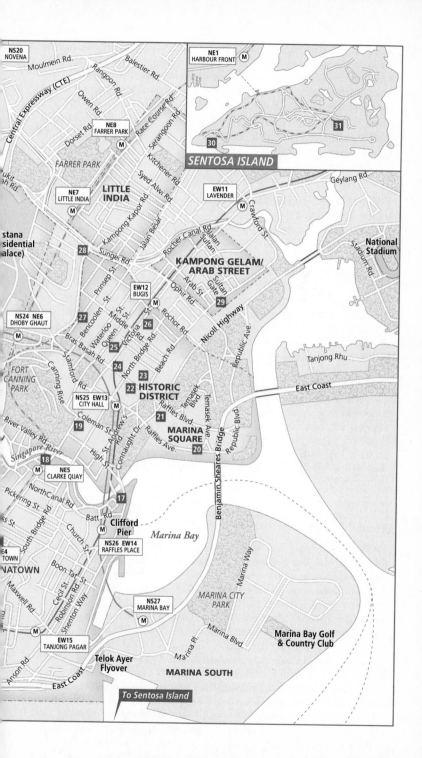

drooping occupancy rates by going after the leisure market. In fall, even tourism drops off somewhat, making the season ripe for budget-minded visitors. These may be the best times to get a deal. Probably the worst time to negotiate will be between Christmas and the Chinese New Year, when folks travel on vacation and to see their families.

**MAKING RESERVATIONS ON THE GROUND**   If you are not able to make a reservation before your trip, there is a reservation service available at Changi International Airport. The Singapore Hotel Association operates desks in both Terminals 1 and 2, with reservation services based upon room availability for many hotels. The desks are open daily from 7:30am to 11:30pm.

## THE HISTORIC DISTRICT
### VERY EXPENSIVE

**The Fullerton Singapore** 🏛🏛   The newest darling of Singapore's luxury hotel market, The Fullerton is giving competitors like Ritz-Carlton and Four Seasons a run for their money. Originally built in 1928, this squat administrative building at the mouth of the Singapore River once housed the General Post Office. Today it is flanked by the urban skyline, and its classical facade, with Doric columns and tall porticos, looks more mundane than opulent. But designers have done a superb job, restoring Italian marble floors, coffered ceilings, and cornices inside. The courtyard lobby is grand, with skylights above and courtyard guest-room windows lining the inner face of the building. Rooms have been cleverly arranged to fit the original structure, featuring vaulted ceilings and tall windows. While the architectural style is antique, the rooms are anything but. They feature large writing desks, deluxe stationery kits, flat-screen TVs, Sony PlayStations, and electronic safes big enough to hold your laptop. Big bathrooms have separate bath and shower stalls, mini-Stairmasters, and stylish Philippe Starck fixtures. The attentive service here is second to none.

1 Fullerton Sq., Singapore 049178. ℂ **800/44-UTELL** in the U.S. and Canada, 800/221-176 in Australia, 800/933-123 in New Zealand, or 65/6733-8388. Fax 65/6735-8388. www.fullertonhotel.com. 400 units. S$470–S$670 (US$276–US$394) double, from S$800 (US$471) suite. AE, DC, MC, V. 5-min. walk to Raffles Place MRT. **Amenities:** 3 restaurants; bar and lobby lounge; outdoor infinity pool w/view of the Singapore River; fitness center w/Jacuzzi, sauna, and steam; spa w/massage and beauty treatments; concierge; limo service; business center; shopping arcade; salon; 24-hr. room service; babysitting; same-day laundry service/dry cleaning; nonsmoking rooms; executive-level rooms. *In room:* A/C, satellite TV w/in-house movies, dataport w/direct Internet access, minibar, coffee/tea-making facilities, hair dryer, iron, safe.

**Raffles Hotel** 🏛🏛   Legendary since its establishment in 1887, and named after Singapore's first British colonial administrator, Sir Stamford Raffles, this posh hotel is one of the most recognizable names in Southeast Asian hospitality. Originally it was a bungalow, but by the 1920s and 1930s it had expanded to become a mecca for celebrities like Charlie Chaplin and Douglas Fairbanks, writers like Somerset Maugham and Noël Coward, and various kings, sultans, and politicians (the famous Long Bar, where the Singapore Sling was invented, is located here). Always at the center of Singapore's colonial high life, it's hosted balls, tea dances, and jazz functions, and during World War II was the last rallying point for the British in the face of Japanese occupation and the first place for refugee prisoners of war released from concentration camps. In 1987, the Raffles Hotel was declared a landmark and restored to its early-20th-century splendor, with grand arches, 4.2m (14-ft.) molded ceilings with spinning fans, tiled teak and marble floors, Oriental carpets, and period furnishings. Outside, the facade of the main building was similarly restored, complete with the elegant cast-iron portico and the verandas that encircle the upper stories.

Because it is a national landmark, thousands of people pass through the open lobby each day, so the hotel maintains a private inner lobby marked off for "residents" only. Each suite entrance is like a private apartment door: Enter past the small living and dining area dressed in Oriental carpets and reproduction furniture, then pass through louvered doors into the bedroom with its four-poster bed and period armoire, ceiling fan twirling high above. Raffles is the only hotel in Singapore where you can play out the colonial traveler fantasy, and it can be a lot of fun. Other unique features include a hotel museum, popular theater playhouse, and an excellent culinary academy.

1 Beach Rd., Singapore 189673. © 800/232-1886 in the U.S. and Canada, or 65/6337-1886. Fax 65/6339-7650. www.raffleshotel.com. 103 suites. S$650–S$6,000 (US$382–US$3,529) suite. AE, DC, MC, V. Next to City Hall MRT. **Amenities:** 8 restaurants; 2 bars; small outdoor pool; fitness center w/Jacuzzi, sauna, steam, and spa; concierge; limo service; business center; shopping arcade; salon; 24-hr. room service; babysitting; same-day laundry service/dry cleaning; billiard room; personal butler service. *In room:* A/C, satellite TV and VCR, fax, dataport w/direct Internet access, minibar, coffee/tea-making facilities, hair dryer, safe.

### The Ritz-Carlton, Millenia Singapore ✿✿✿    The ultimate in luxury hotels, The Ritz-Carlton blazes trails with sophisticated ultramodern design, sumptuous comfort, and stimulating art. Grand public spaces, lighted by futuristic window designs and splashed with artworks from the likes of Frank Stella, Dale Chihuly, David Hockney, and Andy Warhol, are a welcome change from international chain hotel design cliché. In comparison, guest rooms display a great deal of warmth and hominess. All rooms have spectacular views of either Kallang Bay or the more majestic Marina Bay. Even the bathrooms have views, as the huge tubs are placed under octagonal picture windows so you can gaze as you bathe. Guest rooms here are about 25% larger than most five-star rooms elsewhere, providing ample space for big two-poster beds, and full walk-in closets.

7 Raffles Ave., Singapore 039799. © 800/241-3333 in the U.S. and Canada, 800/241-3333 in Australia and New Zealand, 800/234-000 in the U.K., or 65/6337-8888. Fax 65/6338-0001. www.ritzcarlton.com. 610 units. S$515–S$595 (US$303–US$350) double; from S$698 (US$411) suite. AE, DC, MC, V. 10-min. walk to City Hall MRT. **Amenities:** 3 restaurants; lobby lounge; outdoor pool and Jacuzzi; outdoor lighted tennis court; fitness center w/sauna, steam, and massage; concierge; limo service; business center; shopping mall adjacent; 24-hr. room service; babysitting; same-day laundry service/dry cleaning; nonsmoking rooms; executive-level rooms. *In room:* A/C, satellite TV w/in-house movies, dataport w/direct Internet access, minibar, coffee/tea-making facilities, hair dryer, iron, safe.

## EXPENSIVE

### Carlton Hotel Singapore ✿✿✿    In April 2002 Carlton opened a new Premier Wing, a 19-story building just next door to its 26-story Main Wing. Leisure travelers will be most interested in the lower-priced superior and deluxe rooms in the Main Wing. While rooms in both categories are the same size and have all been smartly redone in contemporary neutral tones, deluxe rooms have broadband Internet access in-room, a flat-screen TV, plus marble bathroom decor (superiors are humble ceramic tile). The new building houses premier deluxe rooms, which, for a premium, feature larger bathrooms with separate bath and shower stall, an in-room safe to fit your laptop, and access to a coin-operated launderette. All public spaces have been upgraded as well. The location, in the center of the historic district, is terrific. Ask for a room with a view of the city.

76 Bras Basah Rd., Singapore 189558. © 65/6338-8333. Fax 65/6339-6866. www.carlton-hotel.net. 627 units. S$350–S$370 (US$206–US$218) double; from S$480 (US$282) suite. AE, DC, MC, V. 5-min. walk to City Hall MRT. **Amenities:** 2 restaurants; lobby lounge; outdoor pool; fitness center w/sauna, steam, and massage; concierge; tour desk; car-rental desk; limo service; shuttle service; business center; 24-hr. room service; babysitting; same-day laundry service/dry cleaning; nonsmoking rooms; executive-level rooms. *In room:* A/C, satellite TV w/in-house movies, minibar, coffee/tea-making facilities.

**Hotel Inter-Continental Singapore** ⭐ The government let Inter-Continental build a hotel in this spot with one ironclad stipulation: The hotel chain had to retain the original shophouses on the block and incorporate them into the hotel design. No preservation, no hotel. Reinforcing the foundation, Hotel Inter-Continental built up from there, giving touches of old architectural style to the lobby, lounge, and other public areas on the bottom floors while imbuing it with the feel of a modern hotel. Features like beamed ceilings and wooden staircases are warmly accentuated with Chinese and European antique reproductions, Oriental carpets, and local artworks. The second and third floors have "Shophouse Rooms" styled with such Peranakan trappings as carved hardwood furnishings and floral linens, and with homey touches like potted plants and carpets over wooden floors. These rooms are very unique, presenting a surprising element of local flair that you don't often find in large chain hotels. Guest rooms on higher levels are large, with formal European styling and large luxurious bathrooms.

80 Middle Rd., Singapore 188966 (near Bugis Junction). ℂ **800/327-0200** in the U.S. and Canada, 800/221-335 in Australia, 800/442-215 in New Zealand, 800/0289-387 in the U.K., or 65/6338-7600. Fax 65/6338-7366. www.intercontinental.com. 406 units. S$440–S$480 (US$259–US$282) double; from S$600 (US$353) suite. AE, DC, MC, V. Bugis MRT. **Amenities:** 3 restaurants; bar; lobby lounge; outdoor pool; fitness center w/Jacuzzi, sauna, and massage; concierge; limo service; business center; shopping mall adjacent; 24-hr. room service; babysitting; same-day laundry service/dry cleaning; executive-level rooms. *In room:* A/C, satellite TV w/in-house movies, minibar, coffee/tea-making facilities, hair dryer, safe.

**Marina Mandarin Singapore** ⭐⭐ There are a few hotels in the Marina Bay area built around the atrium concept, and of them, this one is the loveliest. The atrium lobby opens up to ceiling skylights 21 stories above, guest corridor balconies fringed with vines line the sides, and in the center hangs a glistening metal mobile sculpture in red and gold. One of the most surprising details is the melodic chirping of caged songbirds, which fills the open space every morning. In the evening, live classical music from the lobby bar drifts upward.

The guest rooms are equally impressive: large and cool, with two desk spaces and balconies standard for each room. Try to get the Marina view for that famous Shenton Way skyline towering above the bay. All bathrooms have double sinks, a separate shower and tub, and a bidet. Unique Venus Rooms, for women travelers, include potpourri, bath oils, custom pillows, and hair curler. One plus: The Marina Square Shopping Center, which is completing renovations by the end of 2005, adjacent to the lobby adds dozens of shops and services.

6 Raffles Blvd., Marina Square, Singapore 039594. ℂ **65/6845-1000.** Fax 65/6845-1001. www.marina-mandarin.com.sg. 575 units. S$380–S$430 (US$224–US$253) double; from S$600 (US$353) suite. AE, DC, MC, V. 10-min. walk to City Hall MRT. **Amenities:** 3 restaurants; English pub; lobby lounge; outdoor pool; outdoor lighted tennis courts; squash courts; fitness center w/Jacuzzi, sauna, steam, and massage; concierge; limo service; business center; shopping mall adjacent; salon; 24-hr. room service; babysitting; same-day laundry service/dry cleaning; nonsmoking rooms; executive-level rooms. *In room:* A/C, satellite TV w/in-house movies, minibar, coffee/tea-making facilities, hair dryer, safe.

**Raffles The Plaza** ⭐⭐⭐ This has to be the best location in the city. Above an MRT hub and next to one of the largest shopping centers in Singapore, you won't find any inconveniences here. The lobby is studied serenity with soft lighting and music, a lovely escape from the crazy mall and hot streets. Perhaps the best reason to stay is the Amrita spa and fitness center, the largest of its type. You get a huge state-of-the-art gym, a pool, hot and cold plunge pools, steam and sauna, and endless treatment rooms with Asian and European treatments for beauty and rejuvenation. Standard rooms are large and comfortable, having been recently updated with new soft goods. Premier deluxe rooms, however, are stunningly contemporary, with cushy bedding, big desk spaces, Bose Wave systems, and incredible bathrooms—crisp white tiles, glistening glass countertops, polished chrome fixtures, and a shower that simulates rainfall.

2 Stamford Rd., Singapore 178882. © **65/6339-7777**. Fax 65/6337-1554. www.rafflestheplazahotel.com. 769 units. S$380–S$420 (US$224–US$247) double; suites from S$1,100 (US$647). AE, DC, MC, V. City Hall MRT. **Amenities:** 10 restaurants; martini bar; lobby lounge; live jazz venue; outdoor pool; spa w/gym, Jacuzzi, sauna, steam, and massage; concierge; limo service; business center; shopping arcade adjacent; 24-hr. room service; babysitting; same-day laundry service/dry cleaning; nonsmoking rooms; executive-level rooms. *In room:* A/C, satellite TV w/in-house movies, coffee/tea-making facilities, hair dryer, safe.

**Swissôtel The Stamford** ⚐⚐ ⓥalue    You'd think a room in the tallest hotel in the world would cost a bundle, but this gem is reasonably priced. Besides, with an amazing location, right on top of a subway hub and a huge shopping complex, walking distance from many sights and attractions, this hotel is great value for money. On a clear day you can see Indonesia, so make sure you request a room with a view. Done in fresh white linens, cool neutral fabrics, and new furnishings in golden wood tones, these large rooms also feature private balconies and full toiletries in marble bathrooms. Executive rooms in The Stamford also have Bose hi-fi systems, ergonomically designed writing tables and chairs, multifunction printer, fax and copier, plus bathrooms with a view. It's managed by Raffles International, so you can be sure of friendly and professional service.

2 Stamford Rd., Singapore 178882. © **800/637-9477** in the U.S. and Canada, 800/121-043 in Australia, or 65/6338-8585. Fax 65/6338-2862. www.swissotel-thestamford.com. 1,200 units. S$360 (US$212) double; S$1,100 (US$647) suite. AE, DC, MC, V. City Hall MRT. **Amenities:** 10 restaurants; martini bar; lobby lounge; live jazz venue; outdoor pool; spa w/gym, Jacuzzi, sauna, steam, and massage; concierge; limo service; business center; shopping arcade adjacent; 24-hr. room service; babysitting; same-day laundry service/dry cleaning; nonsmoking rooms; executive-level rooms. *In room:* A/C, satellite TV w/in-house movies, minibar, coffee/tea-making facilities, hair dryer, safe.

## MODERATE

**Allson Hotel Singapore** ⚐ ⓥalue    In 2002 and 2003, Allson saw major renovations—just in time to save it from getting overly tatty. The facade got a complete facelift, adding a soundproofing layer to keep out traffic noise from busy Victoria Street below. Guest rooms have new carpeting, fresh paint, and drapes, bed coverings, and upholstery, for a fresher feeling. I'm happy that they kept the carved rosewood furniture in each room—doors, headboards, sidetables, and armchairs in quaint Ming-style carvings are an elegant touch for such a moderately priced accommodation. Bathrooms have been completely retiled with spotless grout. The small pool area and even smaller gym even saw some maintenance touch ups as well. With a good location and modest prices, Allson is a great choice for value-conscious leisure travelers.

101 Victoria St., Singapore 188018. © **65/6336-0811**. Fax 65/6339-7019. www.allsonhotels.com. 450 units. S$250 (US$147) double; from S$650 (US$382) suite. AE, DC, MC, V. 5-min. walk from Bugis Junction MRT. **Amenities:** 3 restaurants; lounge; small outdoor pool; fitness center w/Jacuzzi, sauna, steam, and massage; tour desk; business center; salon; 24-hr. room service; babysitting; same-day laundry service/dry cleaning; nonsmoking rooms; executive-level rooms. *In room:* A/C, satellite TV w/in-house movies, minibar, coffee/tea-making facilities, safe.

**Peninsula • Excelsior Hotel** ⚐⚐ ⓥalue    Recently, two of Singapore's busiest tourist-class hotels merged, combining their lobby and facilities into one giant value-for-money property. The location is excellent, in the Historic District within walking distance to Chinatown and Boat Quay. It's a popular pick for groups, but don't let the busloads of tourists steer you away. There are some great deals to be had here, especially if you request the guest rooms in the Peninsula tower. These are large and colorful, with big picture windows, some of which have stunning views of the city, the Singapore River, and the marina. Surprisingly, these rooms are priced about S$10 (US$5.90) lower than rooms in the Excelsior tower, which are smaller and, frankly, look like they haven't seen a decor update since the far-out 1970s.

5 Coleman St., Singapore 179805. ℂ **65/6337-2200.** Fax 65/6336-3847. www.ytchotels.com.sg. 600 units. S$240–S$260 (US$141–US$153) double; S$360–S$440 (US$212–US$259) suite. AE, DC, MC, V. 5-min. walk to City Hall MRT. **Amenities:** Restaurant; bar; lobby lounge; 2 outdoor pools; fitness center w/Jacuzzi; concierge; tour desk; business center; shopping mall adjacent; 24-hr. room service; babysitting; same-day laundry service/dry cleaning. *In room:* A/C, TV, minibar, coffee/tea-making facilities, hair dryer, safe.

**Plaza Hotel**    Situated just across from the Arab Street and Kampong Gelam areas, you're a little off the beaten track at the Plaza Hotel—you'll need to take buses or taxis just about everywhere—but the trade-off is that if you stick around you can take advantage of the attractive recreation and relaxation facilities, which include a half-size Olympic pool with a diving board, a Balinese-style tropical sundeck, and a Bali-themed poolside cafe, cooled by ceiling fans. Two gyms have plenty of space and new equipment, but the most exquisite facility of all is the exotic Bali-inspired spa. Guest rooms are midsize and quite nondescript, but good value, especially if you can negotiate a good rate.

7500A Beach Rd., Singapore 199591. ℂ **65/6298-0011.** Fax 65/6296-3600. www.plazapacifichotels.com. 350 units. S$270–S$370 (US$159–US$218) double; from S$435 (US$256) suite. AE, DC, MC, V. 20-min. walk to Bugis MRT. **Amenities:** 2 restaurants; lounge; outdoor pool; fitness center; spa w/Jacuzzi, sauna, steam, and massage; concierge; tour desk; limo service; business center; 24-hr. room service; babysitting; same-day laundry service/dry cleaning; executive-level rooms. *In room:* A/C, satellite TV w/in-house movies, dataport w/direct Internet access, minibar, coffee/tea-making facilities, hair dryer, safe.

## INEXPENSIVE

**Albert Court Hotel** ★★ *Value*    This hotel was first conceived as part of the Urban Renewal Authority's master plan to revitalize this block, which involved the restoration of two rows of prewar shophouses. The eight-story boutique hotel that emerged has all the Western comforts but has retained the charm of its shophouse roots. Decorators placed local Peranakan touches everywhere, from the carved teak furnishings in traditional floral design to the antique china cups used for tea service in the rooms. (Guaranteed: The sight of these cups brings misty-eyed nostalgia to the hearts of Singaporeans.) Guest-room details like the teak molding, bathroom tiles in bright Peranakan colors, and old-time brass electrical switches give this place true local charm and distinction and make this hotel stand out from all the rest. This hotel is especially attractive if you wish to spend a lot of time shopping and eating in Little India, which is just across the street.

180 Albert St., Singapore 189971. ℂ **65/6339-3939.** Fax 65/6339-3252. www.albertcourt.com.sg. 136 units. S$180–S$300 (US$106–US$176) double. AE, DC, MC, V. 5-min. walk to either Bugis or Little India MRT. **Amenities:** 3 restaurants; small lobby lounge; tour desk; limited room service; babysitting; same-day laundry service/dry cleaning. *In room:* A/C, satellite TV, minibar, coffee/tea-making facilities, hair dryer, safe.

**Strand Hotel** ★ *Value*    The Strand is by far one of the best of the backpacker places in Singapore. The lobby doesn't look or feel like a budget hotel, with marble floors, a smart bellhop, and a long reception desk. There's also an inviting cafe to one side, plus a small gift shop. Guest rooms are the largest I've seen in a budget hotel in Singapore, in fact larger than a lot of more expensive rooms as well. They're pretty funky, too, with brightly painted walls to offset very simple wooden furnishings. Whatever you do, don't go for the "special room," with the bathtub/shower separated from the main room by only a thin glass wall. Anybody for a free show?

25 Bencoolen St., Singapore 189619. ℭ **65/6338-1866**. Fax 65/6338-1330. 130 units. S$75–S$85 (US$44–US$50) double; S$120 (US$70) 4-person sharing. AE, DC, MC, V. 10-min. walk to City Hall or Dhoby Ghaut MRT. **Amenities:** Restaurant; 24-hr. room service; same-day laundry service. *In room:* A/C, TV.

# CHINATOWN
## MODERATE

### Berjaya Duxton Hotel Singapore ⭐ Formerly The Duxton, this was one
of the first accommodations in Singapore to experiment with the boutique hotel concept, transforming its shophouse structure into a small hotel and doing it with an elegance that earned it great international acclaim. From the outside, the place has old-world charm equal to any lamplit European cobblestone street, but step inside and there are very few details to remind you that you are in a quaint old shophouse—or in the historic Chinese district, for that matter. It's done entirely in turn-of-the-20th-century styling that includes reproduction Chippendale furniture, hand-painted wallpapers, and pen-and-ink Audubon-style drawings. Unfortunately, in recent years the hotel has dropped in service quality and the place has grown frayed around the edges. The recent takeover by Malaysian four-star hotel chain Berjaya is the first clue that this former luxury accommodation has gone downhill. Berjaya has no plans for refurbishment, which this place really needs. Each room is different (to fit the structure of the building), and some can be quite small with limited views. Garden suites feature a lovely little courtyard. There is no pool or fitness center.

83 Duxton Rd., Singapore 089540. ℭ **65/6227-7678**. Fax 65/6227-1232. www.berjayaresorts.com. 50 units. S$210–S$250 (US$124–US$147) double; S$290 (US$171) suite. AE, DC, MC, V. 5-min. walk to Tanjong Pagar MRT. **Amenities:** Restaurant; lobby bar; shuttle service; limited room service; babysitting; same-day laundry service/dry cleaning. *In room:* A/C, satellite TV w/in-house movies, minibar, coffee/tea-making facilities, hair dryer, safe.

### Novotel Apollo Singapore Novotel has just recently taken over the management of this property, an older hotel that in 2000 completed construction of a new wing. Called the Tropical Wing, it caters primarily to corporate travelers, featuring a fully modern facility with large rooms and new furnishings. The construction project also included enlargement of the lobby with a comfortable lounge, a new outdoor pool and Jacuzzi, outdoor tennis courts, and a huge ballroom. The old wing, called the Tower Block, has slightly less expensive rooms, but was also refurbished with new plush carpeting, bedspreads, drapery, and upholstery. If you're staying here, you may find yourself dependent on taxi transportation, as the MRT is a bit far, but the location is still within short taxi hops around the city.

405 Havelock Rd., Singapore 169633. ℭ **65/6733-2081**. Fax 65/6733-1588. www.novotelapollo.com. 480 units. S$240–S$260 (US$141–US$153) double; S$480 (US$282) suite. AE, DC, MC, V. Far from MRT. **Amenities:** 2 restaurants; lounge; outdoor pool; outdoor lighted tennis court; concierge; tour desk; business center; salon; 24-hr. room service; same-day laundry service/dry cleaning; nonsmoking rooms; executive-level rooms. *In room:* A/C, satellite TV, dataport w/direct Internet access, minibar, coffee/tea-making facilities, safe.

### Swissôtel Merchant Court ⭐ Merchant Court's convenient location and
facilities make it very popular with leisure travelers. Situated on the Singapore River, the hotel has easy access not only to Chinatown and the Historic District, but also to Clarke Quay and Boat Quay, with their multitude of dining and nightlife options. In 2003 it became even more convenient when the new MRT stop opened just outside its doors. While this hotel's guest rooms aren't the biggest or most plush in the city, I never felt claustrophobic due to the large

windows, uncluttered decor, and cooling atmosphere. Try to get a room with a view of the river or landscaped pool area. Convenience is provided by a self-service launderette, drink and snack vending machines on each floor, and unstocked minibar fridge, so you can buy your own provisions. The hotel touts itself as a city hotel with a resort feel, with a small but nicely landscaped pool area (with a view of the river).

20 Merchant Rd., Singapore 058281. (C) **800/637-9477** in the U.S. and Canada, 800/121-043 in Australia, 800/637-94771 in the U.K., or 65/6337-2288. Fax 65/6334-0606. www.swissotel-merchantcourt.com. 476 units. S$315–S$345 (US$185–US$203) double; from S$510 (US$300) suite. AE, DC, MC, V. Clarke Quay MRT. **Amenities:** Restaurant; bar; outdoor pool; fitness center and spa w/Jacuzzi, sauna, steam, massage, and beauty treatments; 24-hr. room service; babysitting; same-day laundry service/dry cleaning; nonsmoking rooms; executive-level rooms. *In room:* A/C, satellite TV w/in-house movies, dataport w/Internet access, minibar, coffee/tea-making facilities, hair dryer, safe.

## INEXPENSIVE
**The Inn at Temple Street** 🔍  They've done a lovely job with this boutique hotel. In the heart of Chinatown's tourism hustle and bustle, step into the small lobby to be greeted by pretty antiques and tasteful Chinese trappings. To the side of the lobby, a charming cafe serves Western and local meals three times a day. The front desk handles everything from business center services to arranging laundry, tours, and postal services, but never seems frazzled. Rooms are quite modern for this type of hotel, with keycard locks, in-room safe, minibar, and room service. Decor is atmospheric as well, with local touches of carved woods and rich fabrics. I like the black-and-white tiled bathrooms. This place is a welcome addition to Singapore's smattering of budget accommodations.

36 Temple St., Singapore 058581. (C) **65/6221-5333.** Fax 65/6225-5391. www.theinn.com.sg. 42 units. S$148–S$188 (US$87–US$111) double, S$228 (US$134) family. AE, DC, MC, V. 5-min. walk to Chinatown MRT. **Amenities:** Restaurant; lounge; room service; same-day laundry service/dry cleaning. *In room:* A/C, TV, minibar, coffee/tea-making facilities, in-room safe.

## ORCHARD ROAD AREA
### VERY EXPENSIVE
**Four Seasons Hotel Singapore** 🔍🔍🔍  Many upmarket hotels strive to convince you that staying with them is like visiting a wealthy friend. Four Seasons delivers this promise. The guest rooms are very spacious and inviting, and even the standard rooms have creature comforts you'd expect from a suite, such as complimentary fruit, terry bathrobes and slippers, CD and video disk players, and an extensive complimentary video disk and CD library that the concierge is just waiting to deliver selections from to your room. Each room has two-line speakerphones with voice mail and an additional dataport. The Italian marble bathrooms have double vanities, deep tubs, bidets, Neutrogena amenities, and surround speakers for the TV and stereo. Did I mention remote-control drapes? Everything here is comfort and elegance done to perfection (in fact, the beds here are so comfortable that they've sold almost 100 in the gift shop.) In the waiting area off the lobby you can sink into soft sofas and appreciate the antiques and artwork selected from the owner's private collection. The fitness center has a state-of-the-art gymnasium with TV monitors, videos, tape players and CD and video-disk players, a virtual-reality bike, aerobics, sauna, steam rooms, massage, facials, body wraps and aromatherapy treatments, and a staff of fitness professionals. Two indoor, air-conditioned tennis courts and two outdoor courts are staffed with a resident professional tennis coach to provide instruction or play a game. There are two pools: a 20m (66-ft.) lap pool and a rooftop sun

deck pool, both with adjacent Jacuzzis. Consider a standard room here before a suite in a less expensive hotel. You won't regret it.

190 Orchard Blvd., Singapore 248646. ℂ 800/332-3442 in the U.S., 800/268-6282 in Canada, or 65/6734-1110. Fax 65/6733-0682. www.fourseasons.com. 254 units. S$500–S$530 (US$294–US$312) double; from S$620 (US$365) suite. AE, DC, MC, V. 10-min. walk to Orchard MRT. **Amenities:** 2 restaurants; bar; 2 outdoor pools w/adjacent Jacuzzis; 2 outdoor lighted tennis courts and 2 indoor A/C tennis courts; Singapore's best-equipped fitness center; spa w/sauna, steam, massage, and full menu of beauty and relaxation treatments; concierge; limo service; business center; 24-hr. room service; babysitting; same-day laundry service/dry cleaning; nonsmoking rooms; executive-level rooms; billiards room. *In room:* A/C, satellite TV and in-room laserdisc player w/complimentary disks available, minibar, coffee/tea-making facilities, hair dryer, safe.

### Shangri-La Hotel 🏵🏵🏵
The Shangri-La is a lovely place, with strolling gardens and an outdoor pool paradise that are great diversions from the hustle and bustle all around. Maybe that's why visiting VIPs like George H. W. Bush, Benazir Bhutto, and Nelson Mandela have all stayed here.

The hotel has three wings: The Tower Wing is the oldest, housing the lobby and most of the guest rooms, which were completely redone. Instead of the usual square block hotel rooms of typical city hotels, Shang's added unusual angles and curves, sophisticated contemporary furnishings, and a refreshing wall of glass blocks that welcomes natural light into the giant bathroom and dressing area. Balconies were melded into the rooms to become reading nooks. The Garden Wing surrounds an open-air atrium with cascading waterfall and exotic plants. Rooms here are more resortlike, with natural textured wall coverings, tweedy carpeting, and woven bedspreads. These larger-size rooms also have bougainvillea-laden balconies overlooking the tropical landscaped pool area. The exclusive Valley Wing has a private entrance and very spacious rooms (I'd say the largest rooms in Singapore), linked to the main tower by a sky bridge that looks out over the hotel's 6 hectares (15 acres) of landscaped lawns, fruit trees, and flowers. These rooms, with large bathrooms and dressing areas, reopened in 2004 after a massive-scale renovation. The new decor reflects the exclusivity of the facility, an Oriental sanctuary. These rooms come with complimentary airport limousine, a champagne bar in the lobby, personalized butler service, and personalized stationery.

Orange Grove Rd., Singapore 258350. ℂ 800/942-5050 in the U.S. and Canada, 800/222-448 in Australia, 800/442-179 in New Zealand, or 65/6737-3644. Fax 65/6737-3257. www.shangri-la.com. 760 units. S$450 (US$265) Tower double; S$560 (US$329) Garden double; S$685 (US$403) Valley double; from S$1,000 (US$588) suite. AE, DC, MC, V. 10-min. walk to Orchard MRT. **Amenities:** 4 restaurants; lobby lounge; resort-style outdoor landscaped pool; 3-hole pitch-and-putt course; 4 outdoor lighted tennis courts; fitness center w/glass walls looking out into gardens, Jacuzzi, sauna, steam, and massage; concierge; limo service; business center; shopping arcade; salon; 24-hr. room service; babysitting; same-day laundry service/dry cleaning; nonsmoking rooms; executive-level rooms. *In room:* A/C, satellite TV w/in-house movies, minibar, coffee/tea-making facilities, hair dryer, iron, safe.

## EXPENSIVE

### Goodwood Park Hotel 🏵
This national landmark, built in 1900, resembles a castle along the Rhine—having served originally as the Teutonia Club, a social club for the early German community. During World War II, high-ranking Japanese military used it as a residence, and later it served as a British war crimes court before being converted into a hotel. Since then the hotel has expanded from 60 rooms to 235, and has hosted a long list of international celebrities and dignitaries.

For the money, there are more luxurious facilities, but while most hotels have bigger and better business and fitness centers (Goodwood has the smallest fitness center), only Raffles Hotel can rival Goodwood Park's historic significance. The poolside suites off the Mayfair Pool are fabulous in slate tiles and polished wood, offering direct access to the small Mayfair Pool with its lush Balinese-style landscaping. There are also suites off the main pool, which is much larger but offers little privacy from the lobby and surrounding restaurants. The original building has large and airy guest rooms in a classic European decor, but beware of the showers, which have hand-held shower heads that clip to the wall, making it difficult to aim and impossible to keep the water from splashing out all over the bathroom floor. Newer rooms in the main wing are renovated in stark contemporary style. The extremely attentive staff always serves with a smile.

22 Scotts Rd., Singapore 228221. ✆ **800/772-3890** in the U.S., 800/665-5919 in Canada, 800/89-95-20 in the U.K., or 65/6737-7411. Fax 65/6732-8558. www.goodwoodparkhotel.com.sg. 235 units. S$385 (US$226) double; from S$525 (US$309) suite. AE, DC, MC, V. 5-min. walk to Orchard MRT. **Amenities:** 6 restaurants; bar; lobby lounge; 2 outdoor pools; tiny fitness center; spa; concierge; limo service; business center; 24-hr. room service; babysitting; same-day laundry service/dry cleaning. *In room:* A/C, satellite TV w/in-house movies, minibar, coffee/tea-making facilities, hair dryer, safe.

### Meritus Mandarin Singapore ★

Smack in the center of Orchard Road is the Mandarin Hotel, a two-tower complex with Singapore's most famous revolving restaurant topping it off like a little hat. The 39-story Main Tower opened in 1973, and with the opening of the South Wing 10 years later the number of rooms expanded to 1,200. True to its name, the hotel reflects a Chinese aesthetic, beginning in the lobby with the huge marble mural of the "87 Taoist Immortals" and the carved wood chairs lining the walls. The South Wing is predominantly for leisure travelers, who have access to the tower via a side entrance. These guest rooms are the same size as those in the Main Tower but feel slightly smaller, most likely because of the dark wood modular units that fill up major wall space with imposing TV and minibar cabinets and a built-in seating area. Mandarin refurbished the carpets, drapes, and linens in this wing in 2003, which really freshened up these rooms from previous dull colors. While rooms in this wing are priced for greater value, be warned that this is where they put all the tour groups. Be prepared for large groups milling around the public spaces during peak tourist seasons.

333 Orchard Rd., Singapore 238867. ✆ **65/6737-4411.** Fax 65/6732-2361. www.mandarin-singapore.com. 1,200 units. S$350–S$450 (US$206–US$265) double; from S$580 (US$341) suite. AE, DC, MC, V. Near Orchard MRT. **Amenities:** 4 restaurants; revolving observation lounge; lobby lounge; outdoor pool; fitness center w/Jacuzzi, sauna, steam, and massage; concierge; tour desk; limo service; business center; shopping arcade; salon; 24-hr. room service; babysitting; same-day laundry service/dry cleaning; nonsmoking rooms; executive-level rooms. *In room:* A/C, satellite TV w/in-house movies, minibar, coffee/tea-making facilities, safe.

### Sheraton Towers Singapore ★★

One of the first things you see when you walk into the lobby of the Sheraton Towers is the service awards the place has won; check in, and you'll begin to see why they won them. With the deluxe (standard) room you receive a suit pressing on arrival, daily newspaper delivery, shoeshine service, and complimentary movies. These refurbished rooms are handsome with textured walls, plush carpeting, and a bed luxuriously fitted with down pillows and dreamy 100% Egyptian cotton bedding. Upgrade to a Tower room and you get a personal butler, complimentary nightly cocktails and morning breakfast, free laundry, free local calls, your own pants press, and free use of the personal trainer in the fitness center. The cabana rooms, off the pool area, have all the services of the Tower Wing in a very private resort room. The 23 one-of-a-kind suite rooms each feature a different theme: Chinese regency, French, Italian, jungle, you name it—very unique, with hand-picked furnishings. While Sheraton is a luxe choice, you can find better deals, price-wise.

39 Scotts Rd., Singapore 228230. ℂ **800/325-3535** in the U.S. and Canada, 800/073535 in Australia, 800/325-35353 in New Zealand, 800/353535 in the U.K., or 65/6737-6888. Fax 65/6737-1072. www.sheraton.com. 413 units. S$430–S$500 (US$253–US$294) double; from S$1,000 (US$588) suite. AE, DC, MC, V. 5-min. walk to Newton MRT. **Amenities:** 3 restaurants; lobby lounge; outdoor landscaped pool; fitness center w/sauna and massage; concierge; limo service; 24-hr. business center; 24-hr. room service; babysitting; same-day laundry service/dry cleaning; nonsmoking rooms; executive-level rooms. *In room:* A/C, satellite TV w/in-house movies, dataport w/direct Internet access, minibar, coffee/tea-making facilities, hair dryer, safe.

**Singapore Marriott Hotel** ✪✪   You can't get a better location than at the corner of Orchard and Scotts roads. Marriott's green-roofed pagoda tower is a well-recognized landmark on Orchard Road, but guest rooms inside tend to be smaller than average to fit in the octagonal structure. Luckily the recent refurbishing scheme added lively colors to brighten the spaces with natural greens and floral fabrics. The palatial lobby has been overtaken by the Marriott Cafe, with weekend buffets that are so popular with the locals that there's a long queue. Outside, the Crossroads Café, spilling out onto the sidewalk, is a favorite place for international and Singaporean celebrities who like to be seen. Service in this hotel is very personable and professional.

Marriott, which took over management of this property in 1995, caters to the business traveler, so the rooms on the club floors get most of the hotel's attention. The club lounge, for instance, has a great view and there's not a tacky detail in the comfortable seating and dining areas.

320 Orchard Rd., Singapore 238865. ℂ **800/228-9290** in the U.S. and Canada, 800/251-259 in Australia, 800/22-12-22 in the U.K., or 65/6735-5800. Fax 65/6735-9800. www.singaporemarriott.com. 373 units. S$380 (US$224) double; from S$650 (US$382) suite. AE, DC, MC, V. Orchard MRT. **Amenities:** 4 restaurants; lobby lounge; bar w/live jazz; dance club w/live pop bands; outdoor pool w/Jacuzzi; fitness center w/Jacuzzi, sauna, steam, and massage; concierge; limo service; 24-hr. business center; shopping arcade; 24-hr. room service; babysitting; same-day laundry service/dry cleaning; nonsmoking rooms; executive-level rooms; outdoor basketball court. *In room:* A/C, satellite TV w/in-house movies, dataport w/direct Internet access, minibar, coffee/tea-making facilities, hair dryer, iron, safe.

## MODERATE

**Grand Hyatt Singapore** ✪✪   Despite its fantastic location, this hotel was doing pretty poorly until they had a feng shui master come in and evaluate it for redecorating. According to the Chinese monk, because the lobby entrance was a wall of flat glass doors that ran parallel to the long reception desk in front, all the hotel's wealth was flowing from the desk right out the doors and into the street. To correct the problem, the doors are now set at right angles to each other, a fountain was built in the rear, and the reception was moved around a corner to the right of the lobby. Since then, the hotel has enjoyed some of the highest occupancy rates in town. Feng shui or not, the new decor is modern, sleek, and sophisticated, an elegant combination of polished black marble and deep wood. Terrace Wing guest rooms invite with plush duvet and golden colors, plus unique glass-enclosed alcoves looking over the hotel gardens. Bathrooms are large, with lots of marble counter space. If you've booked through a travel agent, these are the rooms you'll get. If you make your booking on your own, they'll more likely put you in a Grand Wing room. These are really suites with separate living areas, small walk-in closets, and separate work area. They're very deluxe since 2003 refurbishment to freshen up the decor. The pool and fitness center are amazing. Located in the center of this city hotel, a four-story waterfall provides the perfect soundscape to match a lush jungle garden hugging the free-form pool and state-of-the-art gym.

***Important note:*** Grand Hyatt no longer publishes a rack rate; rather, it selects the "best rate" for the dates of your stay. The result is that the rates can fluctuate from moderate to very expensive. Below, the rates reflect the average best rates for November 2004.

10 Scotts Rd., Singapore 228211. ℭ **800/223-1234** in the U.S. and Canada, or 65/6738-1234. Fax 65/6732-1696. www.singapore.grand.hyatt.com. 685 units. S$280–S$320 (US$165–US$188) double. AE, DC, MC, V. Near Orchard MRT. **Amenities:** 3 restaurants; lobby lounge; live music bar; landscaped outdoor pool; 2 outdoor lighted tennis courts; squash court; badminton court; excellent fitness center w/Jacuzzi, sauna, steam, massage, and spa treatments; concierge; limo service; business center; 24-hr. room service; babysitting; same-day laundry service/dry cleaning; executive-level rooms. *In room:* A/C, satellite TV w/in-house movies, dataport w/direct Internet access, minibar, coffee/tea-making facilities, hair dryer, iron, safe.

### Hilton International Singapore

If you count the luxury cars that drive up to the valet at the Hilton, you'd think this is a good address to have while staying in Singapore. Well, to be honest, this Hilton doesn't measure up with some of its other properties worldwide and definitely can't compete with other hotels in this price category in Singapore. The most famous feature of the Hilton is its glamorous shopping arcade, where you can find your Donna Karan, Louis Vuitton, Gucci—all the greats. Ask the concierge for a pager, and they'll page you for important calls while you window-shop or try some of the 45 fragrant vodkas at the lobby bar. With all this, the guest rooms should be pretty sumptuous, no? Well, no. The rooms are simpler than you'd expect, with nothing flashy or overdone. There are floor-to-ceiling windows in each, and while views in the front of the hotel are of Orchard Road and the Thai Embassy property, views in the back are not so hot. In this day and age when business-class hotels are wrestling to outdo each other, Hilton has a lot of catching up to do.

*Important note:* Hilton no longer publishes a rack rate; rather, it selects the "best rate" for the dates of your stay. The result is that the rates can fluctuate from moderate to very expensive. Below, the rates reflect the average best rates for November 2004.

581 Orchard Rd., Singapore 238883. ℭ **800/445-8667** in the U.S., or 65/6737-2233. Fax 65/6732-2917. www.singapore.hilton.com. 423 units. S$210–S$290 (US$124–US$171) double. AE, DC, MC, V. Near Orchard MRT. **Amenities:** 2 restaurants; lobby lounge; outdoor pool; fitness center w/sauna and steam; concierge; limo service; business center; shopping arcade; salon; 24-hr. room service; babysitting; same-day laundry service/dry cleaning; nonsmoking rooms; executive-level rooms. *In room:* A/C, satellite TV w/in-house movies, minibar, coffee/tea-making facilities, hair dryer, safe.

### Orchard Parade Hotel  ★★ (Value (Kids)

This fine hotel, after a US$24-million, 2-year renovation, sports a new swimming pool, guest rooms, lobby, driveway, front entrance, and food and beverage outlets, decorated in a Mediterranean theme integrating marble mosaics, plaster walls, beamed ceilings, and wrought-iron railings. The midsize pool on the sixth-floor roof features colorful tiles and draping arbors, a motif carried over through the new fitness center. Rooms also feature Mediterranean style in terra-cotta wall sconces, wrought-iron table legs, and shades of teal and aqua. If it's important to you, you need to specify a room with a view here. For good value, the Family Studio fits a king-size bed and two twins with separate family room and dining area and plenty of space for just S$100 (US$59) extra. Just outside, a long terrace along Orchard Road hosts many restaurant choices, the most popular of which, Modestos, serves good pasta and pizzas at an affordable price.

1 Tanglin Rd., Singapore 247905. ℭ **65/6737-1133.** Fax 65/6733-0242. www.orchardparade.com.sg. 387 units. S$280–S$300 (US$165–US$176) double; S$400 (US$235) family studio; from S$400 (US$235) suite. AE, DC, MC, V. Orchard MRT. **Amenities:** 5 restaurants; lobby lounge; outdoor pool; fitness center; concierge; tour desk; business center; salon; 24-hr. room service; babysitting; same-day laundry service/dry cleaning; executive-level rooms. *In room:* A/C, satellite TV, minibar, coffee/tea-making facilities, hair dryer.

**Traders Hotel Singapore** ★★    A fantastic bargain for leisure travelers in Singapore, Traders advertises itself as a "value-for-money" hotel. A spinoff of Shangri-La (see above), this hotel anticipates the special needs of travelers and tries on all levels to accommodate them. Rooms have an empty fridge that can be stocked from the supermarket next door (show your room card key at nearby Tanglin Mall for discounts from many of the shops); there are spanking-clean self-service launderette facilities with ironing boards on six floors; and there are vending machines and ice machines (a rarity in Asian hotels). There's even a hospitality lounge for guests to use after checkout, with seating areas, work spaces with dataports, card phones, safe-deposit boxes, vending machines, and a shower.

Guest rooms are smaller than average, but feature child-size sofa beds and large drawers for storage. The large, landscaped pool area has a great poolside alfresco cafe, Ah Hoi's Kitchen, serving up tasty local dishes at reasonable prices. Be sure to ask about promotion rates when you book your room. If you're planning to stay longer than 2 weeks, Traders has a long-stay program that offers discount meals, laundry and business center services, and half-price launderette tokens.

*One caveat:* The distance from MRT service and Orchard Road makes you dependent on taxi service. However, I like Trader's option to cross-sign with Shangri-La sister properties, giving you access to their awesome pools, spas, and fitness centers, plus Shangri-La's Rasa Sentosa Resort's beachfront access.

1A Cuscaden Rd., Singapore 249716. © **800/942-5050** in the U.S. and Canada, 800/222-448 in Australia, 0800/442179 in New Zealand, or 65/6738-2222. Fax 65/6831-4314. www.shangri-la.com. 547 units. S$255–S$280 (US$150–US$165) double; from S$425 (US$250) suite. AE, DC, MC, V. 15-min. walk to Orchard MRT. **Amenities:** 2 restaurants; bar; lobby lounge; outdoor pool; fitness center w/Jacuzzi, sauna, steam, and massage; spa; concierge; limo service; shuttle service; business center; salon; 24-hr. room service; babysitting; same-day laundry service/dry cleaning; self-service launderette; executive-level rooms. *In room:* A/C, satellite TV, dataport w/direct Internet access, minibar, coffee/tea-making facilities, hair dryer, iron, safe.

**York Hotel Singapore** ★★    This small tourist-class hotel can boast some of the most consistently professional and courteous staff I've encountered. A short walk from Orchard, York is convenient, though far enough removed to provide a relaxing atmosphere. A recent renovation has redressed previously flavorless rooms in a sharp contemporary style in light woods, natural tones, and simple lines. Combined with an already spacious room, the result is an airy, cooling effect. Bathrooms throughout are downright huge. Cabana rooms look out to a pool and sun deck decorated with giant palms. Despite surrounding buildings, it doesn't feel claustrophobic, as do some of the more centrally situated hotels. There's a Jacuzzi, but the business center is tiny as is the fitness center. The rates here have gone up a bit, so make sure you ask for promotional discounts.

21 Mount Elizabeth, Singapore 228516. © **800/223-5652** in the U.S. and Canada, 800/553-549 in Australia, 800/447-555 in New Zealand, 800/89-88-52 in the U.K., or 65/6737-0511. Fax 65/6732-1217. www.york hotel.com.sg. 406 units. S$290–S$310 (US$190–US$182) double; from S$460 (US$271) suite. AE, DC, MC, V. 10-min. walk to Orchard MRT. **Amenities:** Restaurant; lobby lounge; outdoor pool; fitness center; Jacuzzi; tour desk; business center; 24-hr. room service; babysitting; same-day laundry service/dry cleaning. *In room:* A/C, satellite TV, minibar, coffee/tea-making facilities.

## INEXPENSIVE

**RELC International Hotel** ★★ *Value*    RELC offers real value-for-money in terms of location (a 10-minute walk to Orchard Road) and an excellent facility. I found the service and convenience here superior to some hotels in the higher priced categories. RELC has four types of rooms—superior twin, executive twin, Hollywood queen, and alcove suite—but no matter what the size, none of the rooms ever feel cluttered, close, or cramped. All rooms have balconies, TVs with two movie channels, and a fridge with free juice boxes and snacks. Bathrooms are large, with full-length tubs. If you're interested in the higher-priced rooms, I'd choose the Hollywood queen over the alcove suite—its decor is better and it can sleep a family very comfortably. The "superior" rooms don't have coffee/tea-making facilities. A self-service launderette is available.

30 Orange Grove Rd., Singapore 258352. © **65/6885-7888.** Fax 65/6733-9976. www.relc.org.sg. 128 units. S$152–S$162 (US$89–US$95) double; from S$175 (US$103) suite. AE, DC, MC, V. 15-min. walk to Orchard MRT. **Amenities:** Restaurant; tour desk; same-day laundry service; self-service launderette; nonsmoking rooms. *In room:* A/C, TV w/in-house movies, dataport w/direct Internet access, fridge w/minibar, hair dryer.

**The SHA Villa** 🏿🏿 *Finds*   SHA Villa is an interesting pick. Formerly the Regalis Court, this charming colonial-style mansion has been restored beautifully and outfitted with Peranakan-inspired touches. Everything here will make you feel as if you're staying in a quaint guesthouse rather than a hotel, from the open-air lobby (under the porte-cochere) and corridors to the guest rooms, which have comforting touches like teakwood furnishings, textile wall hangings, Oriental throws over wooden floors, and bamboo blinds to keep out the sun. What makes this place truly unique is its management. SHA stands for Singapore Hotel Association—this property serves as a training ground for hospitality service staff, from bellhops to chefs. Everyone is eager to please because, well, they're being graded. Centrally located with just a 10-minute walk from Orchard Road, and with an excellent Western restaurant, you really can't go wrong at this place.

64 Lloyd Rd., Singapore 239113. © **65/6734-7117.** Fax 65/6736-1651. www.sha.org.sg. 40 units. S$145–S$165 (US$85–US$97) double. AE, DC, MC, V. 10-min. walk from Somerset MRT. **Amenities:** Restaurant; car-rental desk; babysitting; same-day laundry service; nonsmoking rooms. *In room:* A/C, TV, dataport w/direct Internet access, coffee/tea-making facilities, safe.

## 4 Where to Dine

So what do Singaporeans do for boredom relief? They eat. Dining out in Singapore is the central focus of family quality time, the best excuse for getting together with friends, and the proper way to close that business deal. That's why you find such a huge selection of local, regional, and international cuisine here, served in settings that range from bustling hawker centers to grand and glamorous palaces of gastronomy. But to simply say, "If you like food, you'll love Singapore!" doesn't do justice to the modern concept of eating in this place. The various ethnic restaurants, with their traditional decor and serving styles, hold their own special sense of theater for foreigners; but Singaporeans don't stop there, dreaming up new concepts in cuisine and ambience to add fresh dimensions to the fine art of dining. For a twist, new variations on traditions pop up, like the East-meets-West fusion cuisine dished up at Doc Cheng's. Theme restaurants turn regular meals into attractions; take, for example, Imperial Herbal's intriguing predinner medical examination or True Blue Cuisine's Peranakan home feeling.

It is estimated that Singapore has over 2,000 eating establishments, so you'll never be at a loss for a place to go. I'll begin by providing an overview of the main types of traditional cuisine to help you decide, and also list those signature dishes that each style has contributed to the "local cuisine," dishes that have crossed cultures to become time-honored favorites—the Singaporean equivalent to bangers and mash or burgers and fries. These suggestions are especially helpful when navigating the endless choices at hawker centers.

**CHINESE CUISINE**   The large Chinese population in Singapore makes this obviously the most common type of food you'll find, and by right, any good description of Singaporean food should begin with the most prevalent Chinese regional styles. Many Chinese restaurants in the West are lumped into one category—Chinese—with only mild acknowledgment of Szechuan and dim sum. But China's a big place, and its size is reflected in its many different tastes, ingredients, and preparation styles.

A lot of hawker center fare is inspired by regional Chinese home cooking. Local favorites like carrot cake (white radishes that are steamed and pounded until soft, then fried in egg, garlic, and chile), *Hokkien bak ku teh* (boiled pork ribs in a seasoned soup), *Teochew kway teow* (stir-fried rice noodles with egg, prawns, and fish), and the number-one favorite for foreigners, *Hainanese chicken rice* (boiled sliced chicken breast served over rice cooked in chicken stock). At the end of this section, I've provided an overview of the hawker food scene so you'll know where to find local food the way the locals eat it.

**MALAY CUISINE**    Malay cuisine combines Indonesian and Thai flavors, blending ginger, turmeric, chiles, lemon grass, and dried shrimp paste to make unique curries. Heavy on coconut milk and peanuts, Malay food can at times be on the sweet side. The most popular Malay curries are **rendang,** a dry, dark, and heavy coconut-based curry served over meat; **sambal,** a red and spicy chile sauce; and **sambal belacan,** a condiment of fresh chiles, dried shrimp paste, and lime juice.

The ultimate Malay dish in Singapore is **satay,** sweet barbecued meat kabobs dipped in chile peanut sauce. *Nasi lemak*—coconut rice surrounded by an assortment of fried anchovies, peanuts, egg, and sambal—is primarily a breakfast dish, but can be eaten anytime.

**PERANAKAN CUISINE**    This type of food came out of the Straits-born Chinese community and combines such mainland Chinese ingredients as noodles and oyster sauces with local Malay flavors of coconut milk and peanuts. *Laksa lemak* is a great example of the combination, mixing Chinese rice flour noodles into a soup of Malay-style spicy coconut cream with chunks of seafood. Another favorite, **popiah,** is the Peranakan version of a spring roll, combining sweet turnip, chopped egg, chile sauce, and prawns in a delicate wrap. **Otak-otak** is very unique. It's toasted mashed fish with coconut milk and chile, wrapped in a banana leaf and grilled over flames.

**INDIAN CUISINE**    **Southern Indian** food is a superhot blend of spices in a coconut milk base. Rice is the staple, along with thin breads such as *prata* and *dosai,* which are good for curling into shovels to scoop up drippy curries. Vegetarian dishes are abundant, a result of Hindu-mandated vegetarianism, and use lots of chickpeas and lentils in curry and chile gravies. **Vindaloo,** meat or poultry in a tangy and spicy sauce, is also well known.

**Banana leaf restaurants,** surely the most interesting way to experience southern Indian food in Singapore, serve up meals on banana leaves cut like place mats. It's very informal. Spoons and forks are provided, but if you want to act local and use your hands, remember to use your right hand only (see "Etiquette Tips," earlier in this chapter), and don't forget to wash up before and after at the tap.

One tip for eating very spicy foods is to mix a larger proportion of rice to gravy. Don't drink in between bites, but eat through the burn. Your brow may sweat but your mouth will build a tolerance as you eat, and the flavors will come through more fully.

**Northern Indian** food combines yogurts and creams with a milder, more delicate blend of herbs and chiles than is found in its southern neighbor. It's served most often with breads like fluffy nans and flat chapatis. Marinated meats like

# Where to Dine in Urban Singapore

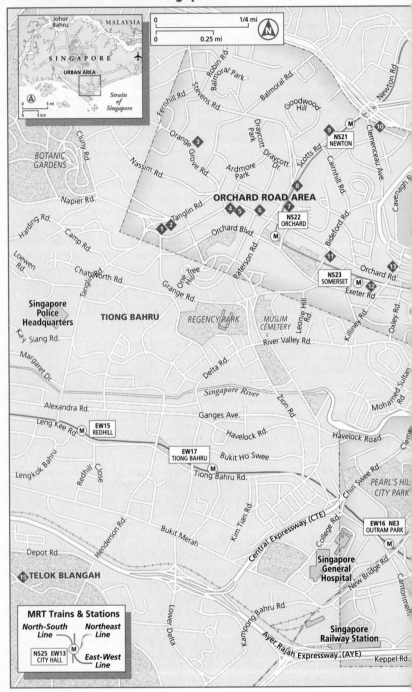

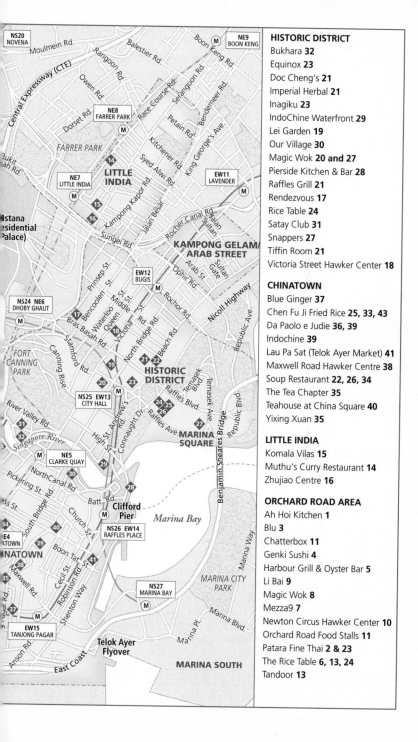

## HISTORIC DISTRICT
Bukhara **32**
Equinox **23**
Doc Cheng's **21**
Imperial Herbal **21**
Inagiku **23**
IndoChine Waterfront **29**
Lei Garden **19**
Our Village **30**
Magic Wok **20 and 27**
Pierside Kitchen & Bar **28**
Raffles Grill **21**
Rendezvous **17**
Rice Table **24**
Satay Club **31**
Snappers **27**
Tiffin Room **21**
Victoria Street Hawker Center **18**

## CHINATOWN
Blue Ginger **37**
Chen Fu Ji Fried Rice **25, 33, 43**
Da Paolo e Judie **36, 39**
Indochine **39**
Lau Pa Sat (Telok Ayer Market) **41**
Maxwell Road Hawker Centre **38**
Soup Restaurant **22, 26, 34**
The Tea Chapter **35**
Teahouse at China Square **40**
Yixing Xuan **35**

## LITTLE INDIA
Komala Vilas **15**
Muthu's Curry Restaurant **14**
Zhujiao Centre **16**

## ORCHARD ROAD AREA
Ah Hoi Kitchen **1**
Blu **3**
Chatterbox **11**
Genki Sushi **4**
Harbour Grill & Oyster Bar **5**
Li Bai **9**
Magic Wok **8**
Mezza9 **7**
Newton Circus Hawker Center **10**
Orchard Road Food Stalls **11**
Patara Fine Thai **2 & 23**
The Rice Table **6, 13, 24**
Tandoor **13**

chicken or fish, cooked in the tandoor clay oven, are always the highlight of a northern Indian meal.

Northern Indian restaurants are more upmarket and expensive than the southern ones, but while they offer more of the comforts associated with dining out, the southern banana leaf experience is more of an adventure.

Some Singaporean variations on Indian cuisine are *mee goreng*, fried noodles with chile and curry gravy, and **fish head curry**, a giant fish head simmered in a broth of coconut curry, chiles, and fragrant seasonings.

Muslim influences on Indian food have produced *roti prata,* a humble late-night snack of fried bread served with lentil gravy, and *murtabak,* a fried prata filled with minced meat, onion, and egg. Between the Muslims' dietary laws *(halal)* forbidding pork and the Hindus' regard for the sacred cow, Indian food is the one cuisine that can be eaten by every kind of Singaporean.

**SEAFOOD**   One cannot describe Singaporean food without mentioning the abundance of fresh seafood. But most important is the uniquely Singaporean **chile crab,** chopped and smothered in a thick tangy chile sauce. **Pepper crabs** and **black pepper crayfish** are also a thrill. Instead of chile sauce, these shellfish are served in a thick black-pepper-and-soy sauce.

**FRUITS**   A walk through a wet market at any time of year will show you just what wonders the Tropics can produce. Varieties of banana, fresh coconut, papaya, mango, and pineapple are just a few of the fresh and juicy fruits available year-round; in addition, Southeast Asia has an amazing selection of exotic and almost unimaginable fruits. From the light and juicy star fruit to the red and hairy rambutan, they are all worthy of a try, either whole or juiced.

Dare it if you will, the fruit to sample—the veritable king of fruits—is the *durian,* a large, green, spiky fruit that, when cut open, smells worse than old tennis shoes. The "best" ones are in season every June, when Singaporeans go wild over them. In case you're curious, the fruit has a creamy texture and tastes lightly sweet and deeply musky.

## TIPS ON DINING

Of course, in any foreign land, the exotic cuisine isn't the only thing that keeps you guessing. Lucky for you, the following tips will make dining no problem.

- Most restaurants are open for lunch as early as 11am, but close around 2:30 or 3pm to give them a chance to set up for dinner, which begins around 6pm. Where closing times are listed, that is the time when the last order is taken. If you need to eat at odd hours, food centers serve all day and some hawker centers are open all night—see the section "Hawker Centers," later in this section.
- Don't tip. Restaurants always add a gratuity to the bill. Sometimes I just leave the small change, but the government discourages this practice.
- Some restaurants, especially the more fashionable or upscale ones, may require that reservations be made up to a couple of days in advance. Reservations are always recommended for Saturday and Sunday lunch and dinner, as eating is a favorite national pastime and a lot of families take meals out for weekend quality time.
- Because Singapore is so hot, "dress casual" (meaning a shirt and slacks for men and a dress or skirt/slacks and top for women) is always a safe bet in moderate to expensive restaurants. For the very expensive restaurants, formal is required, which in Singapore means jacket and tie for men, and a dressier outfit for women. For the cheap places, come as you are, as long as you're decent.

**ORDERING WINE WITH DINNER**  Singaporeans have become more wine savvy in recent years, and have begun importing estate-bottled wines from California, Australia, New Zealand, Peru, South Africa, France, and Germany. However, these bottles are heavily taxed. A bottle of wine with dinner starts at around S$50 (US$29) and a single glass runs between S$10 and S$25 (US$5.90–US$15), depending on the wine and the restaurant. Chinese restaurants usually don't charge corkage fees for bringing your own.

**LUNCH COSTS**  Lunch at a hawker center can be as cheap as S$3.50 (US$2.05), truly a bargain. Many places have set-price buffet lunches, but these can be as high as S$45 (US$26). Indian restaurants are great deals for inexpensive buffet lunches, which can be found as reasonably as S$10 (US$5.90) per person for all you can eat.

**DINNER COSTS**  Prices for Western restaurants list the range for standard entrees and prices for Asian restaurants list the range for small dishes intended for two people to share. As a guideline, here are the relative costs for dinner in each category of restaurant, without wine, beer, cocktails, or coffee, and ordered either a la carte or from a set-price menu:

- **Very Expensive:** At a very expensive restaurant, you can expect to pay as much as S$145 (US$85) per person. The more expensive cuisines are Continental and Japanese, but a full-course Cantonese dinner, especially if you throw in shark's fin, can be well over S$150 (US$88) per person.
- **Expensive:** At an expensive restaurant, expect dinner to run between S$50 and S$80 (US$29–US$47) per person.
- **Moderate:** At a moderate restaurant, dinner for one can be as low as S$25 and as high as S$50 (US$15–US$29).
- **Inexpensive:** Some inexpensive dinners can be under S$5 (US$2.95) at hawker stalls, and up to around S$15 (US$8.80) for one if you eat at local restaurants.

Fortunately, Singapore is not only a haven for cultural gastric diversity, but it's also possible to eat exotic foods here to your heart's content, all while maintaining a shoestring budget.

## THE HISTORIC DISTRICT
### VERY EXPENSIVE
**Inagiku** 🐱🐱 JAPANESE  At Inagiku, you'll have excellent Japanese food that gets top marks for ingredients, preparation, and presentation. In delicately lighted and subtle decor, you can enjoy house favorites like sashimi, tempura, and *teppanyaki*—with separate dining areas for tempura and a sushi bar. The *tokusen sashimi morikimi* is masterful in its presentation: An assortment of raw fish—including salmon, prawns, and clams—is laid out in an ice-filled shell inside of which nestles the skeleton of a whole fish. It's odd and delightful at the same time. I recommend the tempura *moriawase,* a combination of seafood and vegetables that's very lightly deep fried. Also highly recommended are the *teppanyaki* prawns. In addition to sake, there is also a good selection of wines.

Raffles The Plaza Level 3, 80 Bras Basah Rd. 🕐 **65/6431-6156.** Reservations recommended. Set lunch S$42–S$60 (US$25–US$35); set dinner S$130–S$180 (US$76–US$106). AE, MC, V. Daily noon–2:30pm and 6:30–10:30pm.

### EXPENSIVE
**Doc Cheng's** 🐱🐱 FUSION  If you're growing tired of your travel partner, I recommend Doc Cheng's. The witty menu tells the story of Doc Cheng, a

mythological colonial figure who was a sought-after physician, local celebrity, and notorious drunk. His concept of "restorative foods" is therefore rather decadent, on the menu you'll find fabulous "fusion" dishes that are more flavorful than medicinal. Guest chefs make the menu ever-changing—the latest and greatest, a trio of beef cuts prepared in three different styles—Western, Indian, and Chinese—on the same plate, or the unique and mouthwatering Szechuan rack of lamb. The house wine is a Riesling (sweet wines are more popular with Singaporeans) from Raffles's own vineyard. Two dining areas allow you to dine alfresco under the veranda or in cool air-conditioning inside.

Raffles Hotel Arcade #02-20, Level 2. ✆ **65/6331-1612**. Reservations recommended. Main courses S$30–S$40 (US$18–US$24). AE, DC, MC, V. Daily noon–2pm and 7–10pm.

**Equinox** ✮ CONTINENTAL/ASIAN   What a view! From the top of the tallest hotel in Southeast Asia, you can see out past the marina to Malaysia and Indonesia—and the restaurant's three-tier design and floor-to-ceiling windows means every table has a view. It's decorated in contemporary style with nice Chinese accents. Lunch is an extensive display of seafood served in a host of international recipes, with chefs searing scallops to order. Dinner is a la carte, with a menu that's divided between Eastern and Western cuisine, plus some dishes that combine Eastern and Western ingredients and cooking styles, such as *yuzu* marinated cod with braised *enoki* and *tasoi* and grilled beef tenderloin with foie gras. For dessert, order the Equinox Temptation—a sample plate of desserts.

Raffles City, 2 Stamford Rd., Level 70. ✆ **65/6431-6156**. Reservations required. Daily buffet lunch S$48 (US$28), dinner main courses S$40–S$55 (US$24–US$32). AE, DC, MC, V. Daily noon–2:30pm and 7–10:30pm.

**IndoChine Waterfront** ✮✮✮ VIETNAMESE/LAO/CAMBODIAN/ FRENCH   IndoChine Waterfront shares the stately Empress Place Building with the Asian Civilisations Museum, enhancing the sophistication of its chic Oriental decor. The views over the water make for true romance. The menu combines the best dishes from the Indochinese region, many with hints of the French cuisine that was added into regional palates during colonial days. The two most popular dishes here are the house specialty, beef stew ragout, and the pepper beef with sweet-and-sour sauce. More traditional Vietnamese favorites, like spring rolls and prawns grilled on sugarcane, are fresh starters. After dinner, don't miss the Vietnamese coffee; it's mind-blowingly delicious. IndoChine has two sister restaurants, one in a quaint Chinatown shophouse (49B Club St.; ✆ **65/6323-0503**) and another in Wisma Atria (Orchard Rd. #01-18/23; ✆ **65/6238-3470**).

1 Empress Place, Asian Civilisations Museum. ✆ **65/6339-1720**. Reservations required. Small dishes S$22–S$38 (US$13–US$22). AE, DC, MC, V. Daily 11:30am–2:30pm and 6:30–10:30pm.

**Lei Garden** ✮✮ CHINESE/CANTONESE   Lei Garden lives up to a great reputation for the highest-quality Cantonese cuisine in one of the most elegant settings, nestled within the unique ambience of CHIJMES just outside its towering picture windows. One highly recommended dish is Buddha Jumps Over the Wall, a very popular Chinese soup made from abalone, fish maw (stomach), shark's fin, and Chinese ham. It's generally served only on special occasions. To make the beggar's chicken, the chefs take a whole stuffed chicken and wrap and bake it in a lotus leaf covered in yam, which makes the chicken moist with a delicate flavor you'll never forget. For either of these dishes, you must place your order at least 24 hours in advance when you make your dinner reservation. Also try the barbecued Beijing duck, which is exquisite. Dim sum here is excellent. A small selection of French and Chinese wines is available.

30 Victoria St., CHIJMES #01-24. ✆ **65/6339-3822.** Reservations required. Small dishes S$18–S$58 (US$11–US$34). AE, DC, MC, V. Daily 11:30am–2:30pm and 6–10:30pm.

**Raffles Grill** ★★★ FRENCH  Dining in the grande dame of Singapore achieves a level of sophistication unmatched by any other five-star restaurant. The architectural charm and historic significance of the old hotel will transform dinner into a cultural event, but don't just come here for the ambience; the food is outstanding as well. An ever-changing menu means that the dishes I recommend here might not be around by the time you make it, but I assure you, what you order will still be divine. The degustation menu, seven courses at S$180 (US$106), is the best way to explore their finest dishes if you have trouble choosing from an a la carte menu that features pigeon, lamb, suckling pig, veal, and a carving trolley of amazing cuts of beef prepared to perfection. The 400-label wine list (going back to 1890 vintages) could be a history lesson, and if you'd like you can request the cellar master to select a wine to match each course. The fabulously attentive service from the waitstaff will make you feel like you own the place. Formal dress is required.

Raffles Hotel, 1 Beach Rd. ✆ **65/6331-1612.** Reservations required. Main courses S$50–S$65 (US$29–US$38). AE, DC, MC, V. Mon–Fri noon–2pm and 7–10pm; Sat 7–10pm.

**Snappers** ★★ SEAFOOD  With a view of The Ritz-Carlton's lovely pool and gardens, this restaurant is hardly your typical poolside snack bar. Snappers invents mouthwatering recipes for new ways to enjoy fresh seafood—the menu is ever-changing. The crispy sea bass with eggplant and walnut coriander dressing melts in your mouth. The seafood platter is awesome. But if the a la carte menu doesn't have what you're looking for, you can have your choice of live seafood prepared to your specs. This is one of the city's top choices for delicious dining with a terrific wine list and impeccable service. You will never be disappointed.

The Ritz-Carlton, Millenia Singapore, Level 1, 7 Raffles Ave. ✆ **65/6434-5288.** Reservations recommended. Live seafood is priced by weight; average dish S$65 (US$38). Main courses S$32–S$38 (US$19–US$22). AE, DC, MC, V. Daily noon–2:30pm and 6:30–10:30pm.

**Tiffin Room** ★ NORTHERN INDIAN  Tiffin curry came from India and is named after the three-tiered containers that Indian workers would use to carry their lunch. The tiffin box idea was stolen by the British colonists, who changed around the recipes a bit so they weren't as spicy. The cuisine that evolved is pretty much what you'll find served at Raffles's Tiffin Room, where a buffet spread lets you select from a variety of curries, chutneys, rice, and Indian breads. The restaurant is just inside the lobby entrance of Raffles Hotel and carries the trademark Raffles elegance throughout its decor. Very British Raj.

Raffles Hotel, 1 Beach Rd. ✆ **65/6331-1612.** Reservations recommended. All meals served buffet style. Breakfast S$41 (US$24); lunch S$43 (US$26); high tea S$37 (US$22); dinner S$46 (US$27). AE, DC, MC, V. Daily 7–10:30am, noon–2pm, 3:30–5:30pm (high tea), and 7–10:30pm.

## MODERATE

**Bukhara** NORTHERN INDIAN  I like to recommend Bukhara for the buffet, which is a great way to savor many treats without going over the top with the expense. Tandoori lamb kabobs, fish, prawns, chicken, and more will make meat lovers' eyes pop—the food just keeps coming. *Plu*, tandoori veggies like cauliflower, and stuffed potatoes and peppers are quite good. The decor is a little bit India-kitsch, with carved stonelike accents and weathered wooden chairs.

The buffet includes breads and dhal. You can also order from an a la carte menu of standard northern Indian fare. If you're in Clarke Quay, this is the best choice in this price range—lunch is the better value.

3C River Valley Rd., #01-44 Clarke Quay. ② **65/6338-1411.** Reservations recommended. Buffet lunch Mon–Thurs S$15 (US$9.10), Fri–Sun S$18 (US$11); buffet dinner Mon–Thurs S$29 (US$17), Fri–Sun S$33 (US$19). AE, DC, MC, V. Daily noon–2:30pm and 6:30–10:30pm.

**Imperial Herbal** 🏵🏵 CHINESE HERBAL    People come again and again for the healing powers of the food served here, enriched with herbs and other secret ingredients prescribed by a resident Chinese herbalist. Upon entering, you'll be ushered to the herb counter. The herbalist, who is also trained in Western medicine, will ask for the symptoms of what ails you and take your pulse. While you sit and order (from an extensive menu of meats, seafood, and vegetable dishes that are delicious in their own right), he'll prepare a packet of ingredients and ship it off to the kitchen, where it'll be added to the food in preparation. Surprisingly, dishes turn out tasty, without the anticipated medicinal aftertaste. If all this isn't wild enough for you, order the scorpion.

The herbalist is in-house every day but Sunday. It's always good to call ahead, though, as he's the main attraction. When you leave, present him with a small *ang pau*—a gift of cash in a red envelope—maybe S$5 or S$7. Red envelopes are available in any card or gift shop.

Metropole Hotel, 3rd Floor, 41 Seah St. (near Raffles Hotel). ② **65/6337-0491.** Reservations recommended for lunch, necessary for dinner. Small dishes S$12–S$25 (US$7.10–US$15). AE, DC, MC, V. Daily 11:30am–2:30pm and 6:30–10:30pm.

**Pierside Kitchen & Bar** 🏵 SEAFOOD    A light and healthy menu centers on seafood prepared with fresh flavors in a wide variety of international recipes, like the house specialty cumin-spiced crab cakes with marinated cucumber and chile or grilled hazelnut-crusted king prawns in lobster-and–lemon grass sauce. Raw oysters are served with a tangy lime-and-chile sauce which is out of this world. The place itself is airy, sparsely decorated with light wood and white walls. Nothing can compete with the view, really—the panoramic view of the Esplanade Theatres and the marina is lovely. After sundown, the alfresco dining area cools off with breezes from the water and the stars make for some romantic dining. Relax, enjoy the scenery, and order dessert from the gorgeous selection of chocoholic sugar-coma treats.

Unit 01-01, One Fullerton, 1 Fullerton Rd. ② **65/6438-0400.** Reservations recommended. Main courses S$22–S$35 (US$13–US$21). AE, DC, MC, V. Mon–Fri 11:30am–2:30pm; Mon–Thurs 7–10:30pm; Fri–Sat 7–11pm.

## INEXPENSIVE

**Magic Wok** ✓Value THAI    Here's an excellent value-for-money restaurant in town. The decor doesn't do much, it's usually crowded, and staff don't pamper, but food is reliably good and cheap. Thai favorites include a spicy *tom yam* seafood soup that doesn't skimp on the seafood, a mild green curry with chicken, and sweet pineapple rice. If you come too late, the yummy fried chicken chunks wrapped in pandan leaf will be sold out. If you're adventurous, the fried baby squid look like cute, tiny octopi and are crunchy and sweet. During busy times, you'll have to wait in line, but it moves fast. Other outlets are located at **#04-22/24 Far East Plaza** on Scotts Road (② **65/6738-3708**) and **#02-05 Marina Liesureplex** (② **65/6837-0826**).

#01-20 Capitol Building, Stamford Rd. ② **65/6338-1882.** Reservations not accepted. Small dishes S$4–S$18 (US$2.35–US$11). MC, V. Daily 11am–10pm.

**Our Village** ✿ NORTHERN INDIAN   With its antique white walls stuccoed in delicate and exotic patterns and glistening with tiny silver mirrors, you'll feel like you're in an Indian fairyland here. Even the ceiling twinkles with silver stars, and hanging lanterns provide a subtle glow for the heavenly atmosphere—it's a perfect setting for a delicate dinner. Every dish here is made fresh from hand-selected imported ingredients, some of them coming from secret sources. In fact, the staff is so protective of its recipes, you'd almost think their secret ingredient was opium—and you'll be floating so high after tasting the food that it might as well be. There are vegetarian selections as well as meats (no beef or pork) prepared in luscious gravies or in the tandoor oven. The dishes are light and healthy, with all natural ingredients and not too much salt.

46 Boat Quay (take elevator to 5th floor). ✆ 65/6538-3058. Reservations recommended on weekends. Small dishes S$9–S$20 (US$5.30–US$12). AE, MC, V. Mon–Fri 11:30am–1:30pm and 6–10:30pm; Sat–Sun 6–10:30pm.

**Rendezvous** MALAY/INDONESIAN   I was sad when, after a few months away from Singapore, I couldn't find Rendezvous at its previous location in Raffles City Shopping Center, only to learn it had shifted to a nicer space at the new (coincidentally named?) Rendezvous Hotel. Line up to select from a large number of Malay dishes, cafeteria style, like sambal squid in a spicy sauce of chile and shrimp paste, and beef *rendang,* in a dark, spicy curry gravy. The waitstaff will bring your order to your table. The coffee shop setting is as far from glamorous as the last Rendezvous, but on the wall black-and-white photos trace the restaurant's history back to its opening in the early '50s. It's a great place to experiment with a new cuisine.

#02-02 Hotel Rendezvous, 9 Bras Basah Rd. ✆ 65/6339-7508. Reservations not necessary. Meat dishes sold per piece S$3–S$5 (US$1.75–US$2.95). AE, DC, MC, V. Daily 11am–9pm. Closed on public holidays.

## CHINATOWN
### MODERATE
**Da Paolo e Judie** ✿✿✿ ITALIAN   Beautiful ambience is created in this shophouse restaurant remodeled in contemporary elegance, with alfresco dining and a wine bar. The Italian fare features seafood in classic and modern recipes using fresh seafood. For starters, raw oysters are zesty; also try the delicate and tangy seabass tartare with rocket salad. For your main course, the lobster pasta in a tomato, olive oil, white wine, and garlic sauce is perfect—the lobster is soft and juicy and the pasta a perfect al dente. The wine list features labels from Italy. For the quality of food and service, the prices can't be beat. The owners have other branches that are equally satisfying: **Da Paolo il Ristorante** (80 Club St.; also in Chinatown; ✆ 65/6224-7081), **Da Paolo il Giardoni** (501 Bukit Timah Rd., #01-04 Cluny Court, beside the Singapore Botanic Gardens; ✆ 65/6463-9628), and **Da Paolo la Terrazza** (44 Jalan Merah Saga, #01-56, at Chip Bee Gardens in Holland Village; ✆ 65/6476-1332).

81 Neil Rd. ✆ 65/6225-8306. Reservations highly recommended for dinner. Main courses S$24–S$34 (US$14–US$20). AE, DC, MC, V. Mon–Sat 11:30am–3pm and 6:30–11:30pm.

### INEXPENSIVE
**Blue Ginger** ✿ PERANAKAN   The standard belief is that Peranakan cooking is reserved for home-cooked meals, and therefore restaurants are not as plentiful—and where they do exist, are very informal. Not so at Blue Ginger, where traditional and modern mix beautifully in a style so fitting for Singapore. Snuggled in a shophouse, the decor combines clean and neat lines of contemporary styling with paintings by local artists and touches of Peranakan flair like carved

wooden screens. The cuisine is Peranakan from traditional recipes, making for some very authentic food—definitely something you can't get back home. A good appetizer is the *kueh pie tee*: bite-size "top hats" filled with turnip, egg, and prawn with sweet chile sauce. A wonderful entree is the *ayam panggang* Blue Ginger, really tender grilled boneless thigh and drumstick with a mild coconut-milk sauce. One of the most popular dishes is the *ayam buah keluak* (my favorite), a traditional chicken dish made with a hard black Indonesian nut with sweet meat inside. The favorite dessert here is *durian chendol,* red beans and pandan jelly in coconut milk with durian purée. Served with shaved ice on top, it smells strong.

97 Tanjong Pagar Rd. ☎ 65/6222-3928. Reservations recommended. Small dishes S$6.50–S$23 (US$3.80–US$14). AE, DC, MC, V. Daily 11:30am–2:30pm and 6–10pm.

**Chen Fu Ji Fried Rice** SINGAPOREAN   With bright fluorescent lighting, the fast-food ambience is nothing to write home about, but once you try the fried rice here, you'll never be able to eat it anywhere else again, ever. These people take loving care of each fluffy grain, frying the egg evenly throughout. The other ingredients are added abundantly, and there's no hint of oil. On the top is a crown of shredded crabmeat. If you've never been an aficionado, you'll be one now. Other dishes are served here to accompany the fried rice, and their soups are also very good. Additional branches are **Chen Fu Ji Sing's Sensation** (Riverside Point, 30 Merchant Rd. #02-21; ☎ 65/6533-0166) and **Chen Fu Ji Noodle House** (Suntec City Mall, 3 Temasek Blvd. #03-020 Sky Garden; ☎ 65/6334-2966).

23 Smith St. ☎ 65/6323-0260. Reservations not accepted. Small dishes S$10–S$20 (US$5.90–US$12). No credit cards. Daily noon–2:30pm and 6–9:45pm.

**Soup Restaurant** ☆ CHINESE   Tasty, traditional, exotic, and affordable. This simple eatery specializes in Samsui Ginger Chicken, moist, fragrant steamed chicken dipped in ginger sauce and wrapped in lettuce. It is unique and delicious. The menu is limited, but simple dishes like stews of meats simmered in herbs served in "beggars' bowls" or baked in clay pots are as authentic as they come. The quaint coffee-shop decor is also a treat. Highly recommended for those who seek something they've never tried before. Other branches are located at 39 Seah St., across from Raffles Hotel (☎ 65/6333-9388); #B1-44 Paragon, 290 Orchard Rd. (☎ 65/6333-6228); and #B1-59 Suntec City Mall (☎ 65/6333-9886).

25 Smith St. ☎ 65/6222-9923. Reservations accepted. Small dishes S$6–S$24 (US$3.50–US$14). AE, DC, MC, V. Daily noon–2:30pm; Mon–Fri 6–10pm; Sat–Sun 5:30–10pm.

**Teahouse at China Square** CANTONESE/CHINESE   For those who dare, the Teahouse is a terrific place for dim sum served in traditional style. The coffee-shop atmosphere is as loud and chaotic as you'd imagine a Chinese eatery should be, but the dim sum is served in the authentic style, by waitstaff who push carts around to each table. They will tell you what is inside each dumpling and bun and what each meat treat is, if you ask. Baskets of goodies are slammed on the table as soon as you can wink, so make sure you get only what you order. But the dishes are mouthwatering. *My tip:* Arrive at the very beginning of meal time so you can get waitress' attention and spend less time shouting over the munching hoardes.

China Square Food Centre Level 3, 51 Telok Ayer St. ☎ 65/6533-0660. Reservations recommended. Small dishes S$2.20–S$6 (US$1.30–US$3.50). AE, DC, MC, V. Daily 11am–3pm and 6–10:30pm.

## LITTLE INDIA
### INEXPENSIVE

**Komala Vilas** ☆ SOUTHERN INDIAN   Komala Vilas is famous with Singaporeans of every race. Don't expect the height of ambience—it's pure fast food, local style—but to sit here during a packed and noisy lunch hour is to see all walks of life come through the doors. Komala's serves vegetarian dishes in southern Indian style, so there's nothing fancy about the food; it's just plain good. Order the *dosai,* a huge, thin pancake used to scoop up luscious and hearty gravies and curries. Even for carnivores, it's very satisfying. What's more, it's cheap: two samosas, *dosai,* and an assortment of stew-style gravies *(dal)* for two are only S$8 (US$4.70) with tea. For a quick fast-food meal, this place is second to none.

76/78 Serangoon Rd. (✆ **65/6293-6980.** Reservations not accepted. *Dosai* S$2 (US$1.20); lunch for 2 S$8 (US$4.70). No credit cards. Daily 11:30am–3pm and 6:30–10:30pm.

**Muthu's Curry Restaurant** SOUTHERN INDIAN    Muthu's is a local institution that is synonymous with one local delicacy, fish head curry, a giant fish head floating in a huge portion of delicious curry soup, its eye staring and teeth grinning. The cheek meat is the best part of the fish, but to be truly polite, let your friend eat the eye. The list of accompanying dishes is long and includes crab masala, chicken *biryani* (rice casserole), and mutton curry, with fish cutlet and fried chicken sold by the piece. We're not talking the height of dining elegance here, but Muthu's really has come a long way since its simple coffee-shop opening, with its recent shift to newer, larger digs, with matching tables and chairs! I miss the old grotty ambience, but still it's a good place to try this dish. Go either at the start or toward the end of mealtime, so you don't get lost in the rush and can find staff with more time to help you.

138 Race Course Rd. (✆ **65/6293-2389.** Reservations not accepted. Small dishes S$3.50–S$6.50 (US$2.05–US$3.80); fish head curry from S$18 (US$11). AE, DC, MC, V. Daily 10am–10pm.

# ORCHARD ROAD AREA
## EXPENSIVE

**BLU** ✮✮✮ CALIFORNIA    The top floor of the Shangri-La commands a lovely view of Orchard Road and the gardens of the most fashionable residential district in the city. BLU is Singapore's cutting edge in stylish dining, decorated with modern glass sculpture by Danny Lane, table lamps by Philippe Starck, and Wedgewood table settings. The menu changes frequently, as chefs constantly create new dishes. However, the Maine lobster paella with saffron, black mussel, and lobster chorizo jus was mind-blowing. Even your humble chicken is sumptuously flavored with apricots, foie gras, and Swiss chard. The wine list here is excellent. After hours BLU turns into an atmospheric lounge with live jazz Monday to Thursday till 12:45am, Friday and Saturday till 1:45am. BLU is my pick for the sexiest date venue.

24th floor, Shangri-La Hotel, 22 Orange Grove Rd. (✆ **65/6213-4598.** Reservations recommended. Main courses S$40–S$60 (US$24–US$35). AE, DC, MC, V. Mon–Sat 7–10:30pm.

**Harbour Grill & Oyster Bar** ✮✮✮ CONTINENTAL    Grilled seafood and U.S. prime rib are perfectly prepared and served with attentive style in this award-winning restaurant. The Continental cuisine is lighter than most, with recipes that focus on the natural freshness of their ingredients rather than on creams and fat. Caesar salad is made at your table so you can request your preferred blend of ingredients, and the oyster bar serves juicy fresh oysters from around the world. For the main course, the prime rib is the best and most requested entree, but the rack of lamb is another option worth considering—it melts in your mouth. Guest chefs from international culinary capitals are flown in for monthly specials. The place is small and cozy, with nautical inspired murals and a finishing kitchen in the dining room.

Hilton Singapore, Level 3, 581 Orchard Rd. ℂ **65/6730-3393.** Reservations recommended. Main courses S\$35–S\$60 (US\$21–US\$35). AE, DC, MC, V. Mon–Fri noon–2:30pm; Mon–Sat 7–10:30pm.

## MODERATE
**Chatterbox** SINGAPOREAN  If you'd like to try the local favorites but don't want to deal with hawker food, then Chatterbox is the place for you. The Hainanese chicken rice is highly acclaimed, and other dishes—like *nasi lemak, laksa,* and carrot cake—are as close to the street as you can get. For a quick and tasty snack, order *tahu goreng,* deep-fried tofu in peanut chile sauce. This is also a good place to experiment with some of those really weird local drinks. *Chin chow* is the dark brown grass jelly drink; *chendol* is green jelly, red beans, palm sugar, and coconut milk; and *bandung* is pink rose syrup milk with jelly. For dessert, order the ever-favorite sago pudding, made from the hearts of the sago palm. This informal and lively coffee shop dishes out room service for the Mandarin Hotel and is open 24 hours a day.

Mandarin Hotel, 333 Orchard Rd. ℂ **65/6737-4411.** Reservations recommended for lunch and dinner. Main courses S\$15–S\$39 (US\$8.80–US\$23). AE, DC, MC, V. Daily 24 hr.

**Li Bai** ✯✯✯ CHINESE CANTONESE  Chinese restaurants are typically unimaginative in the decor department—slapping up a landscape brush painting or two here and there is sometimes about as far as they go. Not at Li Bai, which is very sleekly decorated in contemporary black and red lacquer, with comfortable black leather seating. Creative chefs and guest chefs turn out a constantly evolving menu, refining specialties, and jade and silver chopsticks and white bone china add opulent touches to their flawless meals. Shark's fin soup and abalone creations are a requirement for any self-respecting Cantonese restaurant, and while Li Bai's preparation of these delicacies is tops, I recommend you bypass them—too much hype and expense. Go for the chef's special creations, which are always imaginative. Or, try the duck smoked with jasmine tea leaves, a succulent dish, as is the barbecued meats assortment. The crab fried rice is fabulous, with generous chunks of fresh meat, and the beef in mushroom-and-garlic brown sauce is some of the tenderest meat you'll ever feast upon. The wine list is international, with many vintages to choose from.

Sheraton Towers, Lower Lobby Level, 39 Scotts Rd. ℂ **65/6839-5623.** Reservations required. Small dishes S\$16–S\$48 and up (US\$9.40–US\$28). AE, DC, MC, V. Daily 11:30am–2:30pm and 6:30–10:30pm.

**Mezza9** ✯✯ FUSION  This is your best bet if your party can't agree on what to eat because Mezza9 offers an extensive menu that includes Chinese steamed treats, Japanese, Thai, deli selections, Italian, fresh seafood, and Continental grilled specialties. Start with big and juicy raw oysters in the half shell. If you want to consider more raw seafood, the combination sashimi platter is also very fresh. Grilled meats include various cuts of beef, rack of lamb, and chicken dishes with a host of delicious sides to choose from. The enormous 450-seat restaurant has a warm atmosphere, with glowing wood and contemporary Zen accents. Before you head in for dinner, grab a martini in their *très chic* martini bar.

Grand Hyatt, 10 Scotts Rd. ℂ **65/6416-7189.** Reservations required. Main courses S\$25–S\$45 (US\$15–US\$27). AE, DC, MC, V. Daily noon–3pm and 6–11:30pm.

**Patara Fine Thai** THAI  Patara may say fine dining in its name, but the food here is home cooking: not too haute, not too traditional. Seafood and vegetables are big here. Deep-fried *garoupa* (grouper) is served in a sweet sauce with chile that can be added sparingly upon request. Curries are popular, too. The roast duck curry in red curry paste with tomatoes, rambutans, and pineapple is juicy and hot. For something really different, Patara's own invention, the Thai taco, isn't exactly traditional, but is good, filled with chicken, shrimp, and sprouts. The green curry, one of my favorites, is perhaps the best in town. The Thai-style iced tea (which isn't on the menu, so you'll have to ask for it) is fragrant and flowery. A small selection of wines is also available. Patara has another outlet at Swissôtel The Stamford Level 3, Stamford Road (© **65/6339-1488**).

#03-14 Tanglin Mall, 163 Tanglin Rd. © **65/6737-0818.** Reservations recommended for lunch, required for dinner. Small dishes S$13–S$32 (US$7.65–US$19). AE, DC, MC, V. Daily noon–2:30pm and 6–10:30pm.

**Tandoor** 🏵🏵 NORTHERN INDIAN Live music takes center stage in this small restaurant, adorned with carpets, artwork, and wood floors and furnishings. Entrees prepared in their tandoor oven come out flavorful and not as salty as most tandoori dishes. The tandoori lobster is rich, but the chef's specialty is crab *lababdar:* crabmeat, onions, and tomato sautéed in a coconut gravy. Fresh cottage cheese is made in-house for fresh and light *saag panir* (spinach and cheese dish), a favorite here. Chefs keep a close eye on the spices to ensure the spice enhances the flavor rather than drowning it out—more times than not, customers ask them to add more spices. A final course of creamy masala tea perks you up and aids digestion.

Holiday Inn Parkview, 11 Cavenagh Rd. © **65/6730-0153.** Reservations recommended. Small dishes S$20–S$40 (US$12–US$24). AE, DC, MC, V. Daily noon–2:30pm and 7–10:30pm.

## INEXPENSIVE

**Ah Hoi's Kitchen** SINGAPOREAN I like Ah Hoi's for its casual charm and its selection of authentic local cuisine. The menu is extensive, specializing in local favorites like fried black pepper *kuay teow* (noodles), *sambal kang kong* (vegetable), and fabulous grilled seafood. The alfresco poolside pavilion location gives it a real "vacation in the Tropics" sort of relaxed feel—think of a hawker center without the dingy florescent bulbs, greasy tables, and sludgy floor. Also good here is the chile crab—if you can't make it out to the seafood places on the east coast of the island, it's the best alternative for tasting this local treat. Make sure you order the fresh lime juice. It's very cooling.

Traders Hotel, 1A Cuscaden Rd., 4th level. © **65/6831-4373.** Reservations recommended. Small dishes S$12–S$24 (US$7.10–US$14). AE, DC, MC, V. Daily 11:30am–2:30pm and 6:30–10:30pm.

**Genki Sushi** 🄥alue JAPANESE I ducked into Genki Sushi for lunch. I sat at the counter, where a tiny conveyor belt snaked along in front of me carrying colored plates full of glistening sushi, rolls, sashimi, and other treats. Just pick and eat—and pay per plate. So the goofy Japanese guy next to me got chatty. We discussed the conveyor-belt sushi bar concept and how much we both loved it, then he poked some buttons on his electronic translator and showed me the screen. "This name in Japan," he said. The translator spelled *revolution.* Makes sense, the "revolution" sushi bar, but now I'll never shake the image of Che Guevara sitting there plucking sushi off the belt.

#01-16 Forum The Shopping Mall, Orchard Rd. © **65/6734-2513.** Reservations not accepted. Revolving plates S$1.90–S$6.50 (US$1.10–US$3.80). AE, DC, MC, V. Sun–Thurs 11:30am–9pm; Fri–Sat 11:30am–10pm.

**The Rice Table** 🏵 INDONESIAN/DUTCH Indonesian Dutch *rijsttafel,* meaning "rice table," is a service of many small dishes (up to almost 20) with rice. Traditionally, each dish would be brought to diners by beautiful ladies in pompous style. Here, busy waitstaff brings all the dishes out and places them in front of you—feast on favorite Indo-Malay wonders like beef *rendang,* chicken satay, *otak-otak,* and *sotong assam* (squid) for a very reasonable price. It's an enormous amount of food and everything is terrific. Pay extra for your drinks and desserts. There's an additional outlet at Cuppage Terrace at 43-45 Cuppage Rd. (© **65/6735-9117**) and a new one at Suntec City Mall, #03-028 Sky Garden © **65/6333-0248**.

International Bldg., 360 Orchard Rd., #02-09/10. © **65/6835-3783**. Reservations not necessary. Lunch set S$13 (US$7.55), dinner set S$19 (US$11). AE, DC, MC, V. Tues–Sun noon–2:45pm and 6–9:45pm.

## RESTAURANTS A LITTLE FARTHER OUT

Many travelers will choose to eat in town for convenience, and while there's plenty of great dining in the more central areas, there are some other really fantastic dining finds if you're willing to hop in a cab for 10 or 15 minutes. These places are worth the trip—for a chance to dine along the water at UDMC Food Centre or go for superior seafood at Long Beach Seafood Restaurant. And don't worry about finding your way back: Most places always have cabs milling about. If not, restaurant staff will always help you call a taxi.

### MODERATE

**Halia** ☆ CONTINENTAL/FUSION    Most notable for its location within the Singapore Botanic Gardens, you really need to come to Halia for a daytime meal, either a weekend breakfast buffet, relaxing lunch, or weekday high tea, if you want to enjoy the lush greenery of the surrounds. Cuisine is contemporary fare, with ginger permeating quite a few of the recipes—*halia* being "ginger" in Malay. The specialty of the house is the chunks of seafood stewed in Asian flavors of chile and lemon grass served over a bed of papardelle pasta. To get there, ask the taxi driver to take you along Tyersall Avenue and look for the Halia signboard at the Tyersall Gate near the Ginger Garden.

1 Cluny Rd., in the Singapore Botanic Gardens, Tyersall Gate. © **65/6476-6711**. Reservations recommended. Main courses S$26–S$43 (US$15–US$25), breakfast buffet S$18 (US$11). AE, MC, V. Daily noon–3pm and 6:30–11pm; breakfast Sat–Sun 8–10:45am; high tea Mon–Sat 3–5:30pm.

**Original Sin** ☆ MEDITERRANEAN/VEGETARIAN    This cozy place is a perennial favorite with Singapore's expatriate population. Located in Holland Village, Singapore's expatriate enclave, the restaurant is close to shopping, pubs and numerous other dining choices that cater to this international group. This particular restaurant is a favorite, with generous portions of favorites like baba ganoush, *tzatziki* (cucumber and yogurt dip), and hummus served with olives, feta, and pita bread. And while the menu features standard Mediterranean fare like moussaka and risotto dishes, people always seem to go for the pizzas, which are loaded with interesting Middle Eastern toppings. The owners also run two other properties of equal quality and popularity in Chip Bee Gardens, Italian restaurants **Michelangelo's** (Block 44, Jalan Merah Saga #01-60; © **65/6475-9069**) and **Sistina** (Block 44, Jalan Merah Saga #01-58; © **65/6476-7782**). All of these restaurants have a casual, congenial bistro-style atmosphere inside, and sidewalk dining outside.

Block 43, Jalan Merah Saga, #01-62, Chip Bee Gardens, Holland Village. © **65/6475-5605**. Reservations recommended. Main courses S$22–S$26 (US$13–US$15). AE, DC, V, MC. Daily 11:30am–2:30pm and 6–10:30pm.

### INEXPENSIVE

**Long Beach Seafood Restaurant** SEAFOOD    They really pack 'em in at this place. Tables are crammed together in what resembles a big indoor pavilion, complete with festive lights and the sounds of mighty feasting. This is one of the best places for fresh seafood of all kinds: fish like *garoupa* (grouper), sea bass, marble goby, and kingfish, and other creatures of the sea from prawns to crayfish. The chile crab here is good, but the house specialty is really the pepper crab, chopped and deliciously smothered in a thick concoction of black pepper and soy. Huge chunks of crayfish are also tasty in the black-pepper sauce, and can be served in variations like barbecue, sambal, steamed with garlic, or in a bean sauce. Don't forget to order buns so you can sop up the sauce. You can also get vegetable, chicken, beef, or venison dishes to complement, or choose from their menu selection of local favorites.

1018 East Coast Pkwy. ✆ **65/6445-8833**. Reservations recommended. Seafood is sold by weight according to seasonal prices. Most dishes S$9–S$16 (US$5.30–US$9.40). AE, DC, MC, V. Daily 11am–3pm; Sun–Fri 5pm–midnight; Sat 5pm–1:15am.

## Samy's Curry Restaurant ✶ SOUTHERN INDIAN

There are many places in Singapore to get good southern Indian banana leaf, but none quite so unique as Samy's out at Dempsey Road. Because it's part of the Singapore Civil Service Clubhouse, at lunchtime nonmembers must pay S50¢ (US30¢) to get in the door. Not that there's much of a door, because Samy's is situated in a huge, high-ceilinged, open-air hall, with shutters thrown back and fans whirring above. Wash your hands at the back and have a seat, and soon someone will slap a banana leaf place mat in front of you. A blob of white rice will be placed in the center, and then buckets of vegetables, chicken, mutton, fish, prawn, and you name it will be brought out, swimming in the richest and spiciest curries to ever pass your lips. Take a peek in each bucket, nod your head yes when you see one you like, and a scoop will be dumped on your banana leaf. Eat with your right hand or with a fork and spoon. When you're done, wipe the sweat from your brow, fold the banana leaf away from you, and place your tableware on top. Samy's serves no alcohol, but the fresh lime juice is nice and cooling.

Block 25, Dempsey Rd., Civil Service Club. ✆ **65/6472-2080**. Reservations not accepted. Sold by the scoop or piece, S80¢–S$3 (US45¢–US$1.75). V. Daily 11am–3pm and 6–10pm. No alcohol served.

## True Blue Cuisine ✶✶ PERANAKAN

Katong, the central neighborhood of the Peranakan, or Straits Chinese, community, is also famous for excellent local cuisine. True Blue, housed in a restored prewar shophouse in this historic neighborhood, shares a block with other Peranakan heritage sites, like Rumah Bebe, a shop for Peranakan fashions. Inside, the restaurant is decorated with cultural trappings that will make Singaporeans nostalgic and foreigners feel as if they've been welcomed into a private home. Home cooked from family recipes (the owner's mother runs the kitchen), luscious favorites such as *ayam buah keluak,* which is a dish of chicken and mincemeat-stuffed nuts in a sourish curry, is some if the best I've ever tasted. The friendly staff will help you navigate other classics on the menu, like *otak-otak,* pounded fish and chile grilled in banana leaves, and beef *rendang,* beef stewed in a thick, mildly spicy coconut gravy. Tell your taxi driver to take you to East Coast Road at the junction with Joo Chiat Road. You can follow the shop numbers a short walk until you find the place. Taxis back to town are plentiful.

117 East Coast Rd., 2nd floor. ✆ **65/6440-0449**. Reservations required. Small dishes S$12–S$24 (US$7.10–US$14). AE, DC, MC, V. Daily 11am–2:30pm and 6–10pm.

## UDMC Seafood Centre ✶✶ SEAFOOD

Eight seafood restaurants are lined up side by side in 2 blocks, their fronts open to the view of the sea outside. UDMC is a fantastic way to eat seafood Singapore style, in the open air, in restaurants that are more like grand stalls than anything else. Eat the famous local chile crab and pepper crab here, along with all sorts of squid, fish, and scallop dishes. Noodle dishes are also available, as are vegetable dishes and other meats. But the seafood is the thing to come for. Of the eight restaurants, there's no saying which is the best, as everyone seems to have his own opinions about this one or that one (I like Jumbo at the far eastern end of the row; call ☎ 65/ 6442-3435 for reservations, which are recommended for weekends). Have a nice stroll along the walkway and gaze out to the water while you decide which one to go for.

Block 1202, East Coast Pkwy. No phone. Seafood dishes are charged by weight, w/dishes starting from around S$12 (US$7.10). AE, DC, MC, V. Daily 5pm–midnight.

## HAWKER CENTERS

**Hawker centers**—large groupings of informal open-air food stalls—were Singapore's answer to fast and cheap food in the days before McDonald's, and are still the best way to sample every kind of Singaporean cuisine. The traditional hawker center is an outdoor venue, usually under cover with fans whirring above, and individual stalls each specializing in different dishes. In between rows of cooking stalls, tables and stools offer open seating for diners.

Each center has an array of food offerings, with most dishes costing between S$3.50 and S$6.50 (US$2.10–US$3.80). You'll find traditional dishes like *char kway teow,* flat rice noodles fried with seafood; **fishball noodle,** soup with balls made from pounded fish and rice flour; **claypot chicken rice,** chicken and mushrooms baked with rice and fragrant soy sauce; *bak kut teh,* pork ribs stewed with Chinese herbs; **Hainanese chicken rice,** soft chicken over rice prepared in rich chicken stock; *laksa,* seafood and rice noodles in a spicy coconut chile soup; *popiah,* turnip, egg, pork, prawn, and sweet chile sauce wrapped in a thin skin; *rojak,* fried dough, tofu, cucumber, pineapple, and whatever the chef has handy, mixed with a sauce made from peanuts and fermented shrimp paste; plus many, many more Chinese, Malay, and Indian specialties. You'll also find hot and cold drink stalls and usually a stall selling fresh fruits and fruit juices.

If you want to become a real Singapore foodie, buy a copy of *Makansutra* by K. F. Seetoh (Makansutra Publishing) at any bookstore. Seetoh's the local guru of hawker foods, and has sniffed out the tastiest, most authentic local delicacies you can imagine.

Within the city limits, most traditional style hawker centers have been closed down, but you can still find a few. Singapore's two most famous, or notorious, hawker centers are **Newton** and the **Satay Club.** Newton, a 24-hour center near the Newton MRT stop, is a tour-bus darling; beware of gouging, especially when ordering seafood dishes, which are sold by the kilo. The Satay Club, at Clarke Quay, is a touristy version of a Singaporean institution. The original Satay Club was a simple gathering of stalls by the water where Esplanade—Theatres on the Bay is now located. This reincarnation of the Satay Club is certainly not as authentic, in atmosphere and in food quality, but generally hawkers here tend to be an honest lot.

For local-style hawker centers, in Chinatown you can find stalls at the **Maxwell Road Food Centre** at the corner of Maxwell and South Bridge roads, or you can try **Lau Pa Sat** at the corner of Raffles Way and Boon Tat Street. A new food attraction, a row of stalls along Smith Street called **Food Alley,** was conceived by the STB. Rumor has it, these guys are having a hard time making a living selling local food to the very touristy crowd that passes down this street in the evenings. In the Historic District, try the **small center next to Allson Hotel** on Victoria Street, or the one the locals call **S-11** located on Stamford Road behind the bus stop near the junction with Armenian Street.

Along Orchard Road, almost all have been obliterated. During most of 2004, they had a small hawker center pop up **across from Centrepoint,** open in the evenings. It was only supposed to be a 1-month deal, but they keep extending it because it's so popular. It might still be around into the future. In Little India, **Zhujiao Centre** features more Indian and Muslim hawker fare, as opposed to the mainstay Chinese cuisine at most places.

When you eat at a hawker center, the first thing to do is claim a seat at a table (local trick: If you put a tissue packet down on the table in front of your seat, people will understand it's reserved). Remember the number on your table so that when you order from each stall, you can let them know where you're seated. They will deliver your food to the table, and you must pay upon delivery. Change will be provided. When you are finished, there's no need to clear your dishes; it will be taken care of for you.

The modern version of the hawker center is the **food court.** Similar to hawker centers, food courts are air-conditioned spaces inside shopping malls and public buildings. They also have individual stalls offering a variety of foods and tables with free seating. Generally, food courts offer a more fast-food, less authentic version of local cuisine, but you also get greater variety—many food courts have a stall that sells Western burgers and fish and chips, and stalls with Japanese *udon* or Korean barbecue. Food courts also differ in that they're self-serve. When you approach the stall, you take a tray, pay when you order, then carry the food yourself to your own table, similar to cafeteria style. When you finish, you are not expected to clear your tray.

Food courts are everywhere within the city, most of them operated by popular chains like **Food Junction, Kopitiam,** and **Banquet.** You'll find them in shopping malls and public buildings, most likely on the top floor or in the basement. Your hotel's concierge will be able to point you to the nearest food court, no problem.

## 5  What to See & Do

The city's many old buildings and well-presented museum displays bring history to life. Chinese and Hindu temples and Muslim mosques welcome curious observers to discover their culture as they play out their daily activities, and the country's natural parks make the great outdoors easily accessible from even the most urban neighborhood. Singapore also has a multitude of planned attractions for visitors and locals alike. Theme parks devoted to cultural heritage, sporting fun, and even kitsch amusement pop up all over the island.

The places of worship listed in this section are open to the public and free of entrance charges. Expect temples to be open from sunup to sundown. Visiting hours are not specific to the hour, but, unless it's a holiday (when hours may be extended), you can expect these places to be open during daylight hours.

## THE HISTORIC DISTRICT

**Armenian Church** ✪   The first permanent Christian church in Singapore, it was funded primarily by the Armenian community, which was at one time quite powerful. Today few Singaporeans can trace their heritage back to this influential group of immigrants. The church was consecrated in 1836, and the last appointed priest serving the parish retired in 1936. Although regular Armenian services are no longer held, other religious organizations make use of the church from time to time. The cemetery in the back of the church is the burial site of many prominent Armenians, including Ashgen Agnes Joachim, discoverer of the Vanda Miss Joachim, Singapore's national flower.

60 Hill St., across from the Grand Plaza Hotel. © 65/6334-0141.

# What to See & Do in Urban Singapore

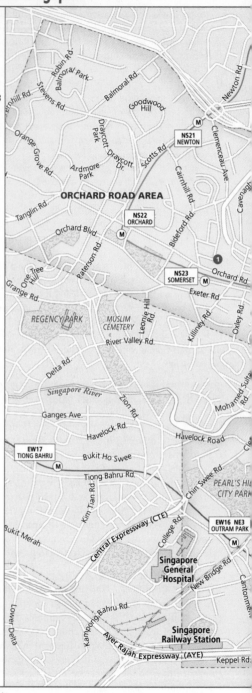

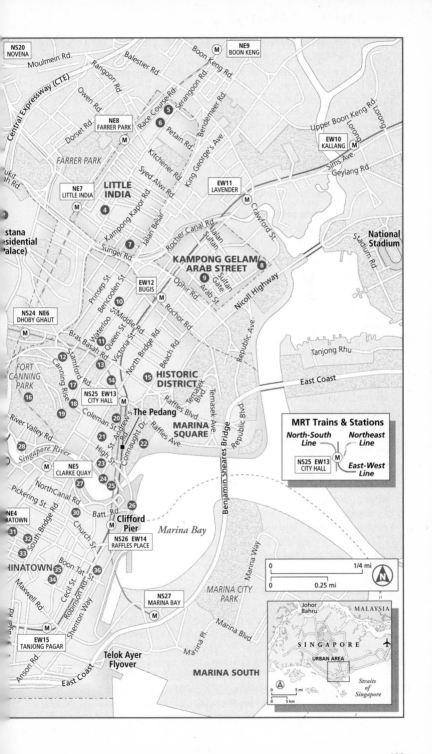

MRT Trains & Stations

North-South Line — Northeast Line

East-West Line

NS25 EW13 CITY HALL

0 — 1/4 mi
0 — 0.25 mi

0 — 5 mi
0 — 5 km

Johor Bahru    MALAYSIA

SINGAPORE

URBAN AREA

Straits of Singapore

**Asian Civilisations Museum, Armenian Street** ★★    The quaint Tao Nan School, which dates from 1910, was completely renovated and opened in 1997 to house this smaller branch of the Asian Civilisations Museum, which highlights Peranakan, or "Straits-born Chinese," heritage. This culture was born of intermarriage between early Chinese settlers and the local Malay women, resulting in a curious mix of aesthetic, religious, and culinary flavors. At this museum, beautiful collections of historical, cultural, and household objects, with detailed descriptions, illustrate the unique heritage of the Peranakans.

39 Armenian St. ✆ 65/6332-3015. www.nhb.gov.sg. Adults S$3 (US$1.75), children and seniors S$1.50 (US90¢), free Fri 7–9pm. Combined ticket for both ACM museums: adults S$5 (US$2.95), children and seniors S$2.50 (US$1.50). Mon noon–6pm; Tues–Sun 9am–6pm (Fri until 9pm). Free guided tours in English Tues–Fri 11am and 2pm, w/extra tour on weekends at 3:30pm. 15-min walk from City Hall MRT.

**Asian Civilisations Museum, Empress Place** ★★★    If you only have time for one museum, this is the one I recommend. The main branch of the Asian Civilisations Museum opened in March 2003. This fantastic and well-executed exhibit of Southeast Asian culture highlights the history of the region, and explores the Chinese, South Indian, and Islamic heritage that helped to shape regional cultures here. Well-planned galleries showcase fine arts, furniture, porcelain, jade, and other relics with excellent descriptions.

The Empress Place Building that houses the museum stood as a symbol of British colonial authority as sea travelers entered the Singapore River. The stately building was the headquarters for almost the entire government bureaucracy around the year 1905, and was a government office until the 1980s, housing the Registry of Births and Deaths and the Citizenship Registry.

Don't forget to stop at the Museum Shop (✆ **65/6336-9050**) to browse exquisite ethnic crafts of the region. Also, check out the museum's website to find out more about its free lecture series.

1 Empress Place. ✆ **65/6332-7798.** www.nhb.gov.sg. Adults S$3 (US$1.75), children and seniors S$1.50 (US90¢), free Fri 7–9pm. Combined ticket for both ACM museums: adults S$5 (US$2.95), children and seniors S$2.50 (US$1.50). Mon noon–6pm; Tues–Sun 9am–6pm (Fri until 9pm). Free guided tours in English Tues–Fri 11am and 2pm, w/extra tour on weekends at 3:30pm. 15-min. walk from City Hall MRT.

**Cathedral of the Good Shepherd**    This cathedral was Singapore's first permanent Catholic church. Built in the 1840s, it brought together many elements of a fractured parish—Portuguese, French, and Spanish—to worship under one roof. Designed in a Latin cross pattern, much of its architecture is reminiscent of St. Martin-in-the-Fields and St. Paul's in Covent Garden.

4 Queen St., at the corner of Queen St. and Bras Basah Rd. ✆ 65/6337-2036. Open to the public during the day.

**CHIJMES (Convent of the Holy Infant Jesus)**    CHIJMES (pronounced "Chimes") is a bustling enclave of retail shops, restaurants, and nightspots. It's difficult to imagine that this was once a convent that, at its founding in 1854, consisted of a lone, simply constructed bungalow. After decades of buildings and add-ons, this collection of unique yet perfectly blended structures was enclosed within walls, forming peaceful courtyards and open spaces encompassing an entire city block. In late 1983, the convent relocated to the suburbs, and some of the block was leveled to make way for the MRT headquarters. Thankfully, most of the block survived and the Singapore government, in planning the renovation of this desirable piece of real estate, wisely kept the integrity of the architecture. For an evening out, the atmosphere at CHIJMES is exquisitely romantic. At the same time, you can enjoy a special decadence when you party in one of the popular bars here.

30 Victoria St. Free admission. ☎ 65/6337-7810.

**City Hall (Municipal Building)**    During the Japanese occupation, City Hall was a major headquarters, and it was here in 1945 that Adm. Lord Louis Mountbatten accepted the Japanese surrender. In 1951, the Royal Proclamation from King George VI was read here declaring that Singapore would henceforth be known as a city. Fourteen years later, Prime Minister Lee Kuan Yew announced to its citizens that Singapore would henceforth be called an independent republic.

City Hall, along with the Supreme Court, was judiciously sited to take full advantage of the prime location. Magnificent Corinthian columns march across the front of the symmetrically designed building, while inside, two courtyards lend an ambience of informality to otherwise officious surroundings. For all its magnificence and historical fame, however, its architect, F. D. Meadows, relied too heavily on European influence. The many windows afford no protection from the sun, and the entrance leaves pedestrians unsheltered from the elements. In defining the very nobility of the Singapore government, it appears the Singaporean climate wasn't taken into consideration.

St. Andrew's Rd., across from The Padang. Entrance to the visitor's gallery is permitted, but all other areas are off-limits.

**Fort Canning Park**    When Stamford Raffles first navigated the Singapore River, he was already envisioning a port settlement and had designs to build his own home atop the hill that is today this park. His home, a simple wooden structure (at the site of the present-day lookout point), later became a residence for Singapore's Residents and Governors. In 1860, the house was torn down to make way for **Fort Canning,** which was built to quell British fears of invasion but instead quickly became the laughingstock of the island. In 1907, the fort was demolished to make way for a reservoir. Today the only reminders of the old fort are some of the walls and the Fort Gate, a deep stone structure. Behind its huge wooden door, you'll find a narrow staircase that leads to the roof of the structure.

Fort Canning was also the site of a **European cemetery.** To make improvements in the park, the graves were exhumed and the stones were placed within the walls surrounding the outdoor performance field that slopes from the Music and Drama Society building. A large Gothic monument was erected in memory of James Napier Brooke, infant son of William Napier, Singapore's first law agent, and his wife, Maria Frances, the widow of prolific architect George Coleman. Although no records exist, Coleman probably designed the cupolas as well as two small monuments over unknown graves. The Music and Drama Society building itself was built in 1938. Close by, in the wall, are the tombstones of Coleman and of Jose D'Almeida, a wealthy Portuguese merchant.

Inside the park, **The Battle Box** is an old WWII bunker displaying in wax dioramas and a multimedia show the surrender of Singapore. It's open Tuesday to Sunday from 10am to 6pm; adults S$8 (US$4.70), children S$5 (US$2.95); ☎ 65/6333-0510.

51 Canning Rise. ☎ 65/3663-3307. www.nparks.gov.sg Major entrances are from behind the Hill Street Building, Percival Rd. (Drama Centre), National Library Carpark, and Canning Walk (behind Park Mall). Free admission. Dhoby Ghaut or City Hall MRT.

**Kuan Yin Thong Hood Cho Temple**    It's said that whatever you wish for within the walls of Kuan Yin Temple comes true, so get in line and have your wishes ready. It must work because there's a steady stream of people on auspicious days of the Chinese calendar. The procedure is simple: Wear shoes easily slipped off before entering the temple. Light several joss sticks. Pray to the local god, pray to the sky god, and then turn to the side and pray some more. Now pick up the container filled with inscriptions and shake it until one stick falls out. After that, head for the interpretation box office to get a piece of paper with verses in Mandarin and English to look up what your particular inscription means. (For a small fee, there are interpreters outside.) Now for the payback: If your wish comes true, be prepared to return to the temple and offer fruits and flowers to say thanks (oranges, pears, and apples are a thoughtful choice and jasmine petals are especially nice). Be careful what you wish for. Once you're back home and that job promotion comes through, your new manager might nix another vacation so soon. To be on the safe side, bring the goods with you when you make your wish.

Waterloo St., about 1½ blocks from Bras Basah Rd. Open to the public during the day.

**Old Parliament House** The Old Parliament House is probably Singapore's oldest surviving structure, even though it has been renovated so many times it no longer looks the way it was originally constructed. It was designed as a home for John Argyle Maxwell, a Scottish merchant, but he never moved in. In 1822, Raffles returned to Singapore and was furious to find a residence being built on ground he'd allocated for government use. Maxwell never moved in, instead the government took over his house for its court and other offices. In 1939, when the new Supreme Court was completed, the judiciary moved into Maxwell's House; then, in 1953, following a major renovation, the small structure was renamed Parliament House and was turned over to the legislature.

Today, the building has been transformed once again—reopened in March 2004 as The Arts House at the Old Parliament, with lovingly restored spaces for visual and performance arts plus special cultural events. A couple highbrow eateries offer a variety of Thai and Western cuisine. Singapore's parliament now operates out of the new Parliament Building just next door.

1 Old Parliament Lane, at the south end of The Padang, next to the Supreme Court. ✆ 65/6332-6900. www.theartshouse.com.sg. Free admission; extra for tickets to events. 15-min. walk from City Hall MRT.

**The Padang** This large field—officially called Padang Besar but known as The Padang—has witnessed its share of historical events. It is bordered on one end by the Singapore Recreation Club and on the other end by the Singapore Cricket Club, and flanked by City Hall. The Padang is mainly used for public and sporting events—pleasant activities—but in the 1940s it felt more forlorn footsteps when the invading Japanese forced the entire European community onto the field. There they waited while the occupation officers dickered over a suitable location for the "conquered." Presently, they ordered all British, Australian, and Allied troops as well as European prisoners on the 22km (13½-mile) march to Changi.

An interesting side note: Frank Ward, designer of the Supreme Court, had big plans for The Padang and surrounding buildings. He would have demolished the Cricket Club, Parliament House, and the Victoria Theatre and Concert Hall to erect an enormous government block if World War II hadn't arrived, ruining his chances.

St. Andrew's Rd. and Connaught Dr.

**Raffles Hotel** ★★ Built in 1887 to accommodate the increasing upper-class trade, Raffles Hotel was originally only a couple of bungalows with 10 rooms, but, oh, the view of the sea was perfection. The owners, Armenian brothers named Sarkies, already had a couple of prosperous hotels in Southeast Asia (the Eastern & Oriental in Penang and The Strand in Rangoon) and were well versed in the business. It wasn't long before they added a pair of wings and completed the main building—and reading rooms, verandas, dining rooms, a grand lobby, the Bar and Billiards Room, a ballroom, and a string of shops. By 1899, electricity was turning the cooling fans and providing the pleasing glow of comfort.

As it made its madcap dash through the '20s, the hotel was the place to see and be seen. Vacancies were unheard of. Hungry Singaporeans and guests from other hotels, eager for a glimpse of the fabulous dining room, were turned away for lack of reservations. The crowded ballroom was jumping every night of the week. During this time Raffles's guest book included famous authors like Somerset Maugham, Rudyard Kipling, Joseph Conrad, and Noël Coward. These were indeed the glory years, but the lovely glimmer from the chandeliers soon faded with the stark arrival of the Great Depression. Raffles managed to limp through that dark time—and, darker still, through the Japanese occupation—and later pull back from the brink of bankruptcy to undergo modernization in the '50s. But fresher, brighter, more opulent hotels were taking root on Orchard Road, pushing the "grand old lady" to the back seat.

In the 1980s Raffles was brought back to its former glory. History-minded renovators selected 1915 as a benchmark and, with a few changes here and there, faithfully restored the hotel to that era's magnificence and splendor. Today, the hotel's restaurants and nightlife draw thousands of visitors daily to its open lobby, its theater playhouse, the Raffles Hotel Museum, and 65 exclusive boutiques. Its 15 restaurants and bars—especially the Tiffin Room, Raffles Grill, and Doc Cheng's, all reviewed earlier—are a wonder, as is its famous Bar and Billiards Room and Long Bar.

1 Beach Rd. ℭ 65/6337-1886. City Hall MRT.

## Raffles Landing Site
The polymarble statue at this site was unveiled in 1972. It was made from plaster casts of the original 1887 figure located in front of the Victoria Theatre and Concert Hall (see below), and it stands on what is believed to be the site where Sir Stamford Raffles landed on January 29, 1819.

North Boat Quay. 15-min. walk from City Hall MRT.

## St. Andrew's Cathedral
Designed by George Coleman and erected on a site selected by Sir Stamford Raffles himself, St. Andrew's was the colonial's Anglican Church. Completed toward the end of the 1830s, its tower and spire were added several years later to accord the edifice more stature. By 1852, because of massive damage sustained from lightning strikes, the cathedral was deemed unsafe and was torn down. The cathedral that now stands on the site was completed in 1860. Of English Gothic Revival design, the cathedral is one of the few standing churches of this style in the region.

Coleman St., between N. Bridge Rd. and St. Andrew's Rd., across from The Padang. ℭ 65/6337-6104. Open during daylight hours. City Hall MRT.

## Singapore Art Museum ⭐
The Singapore Art Museum (SAM) officially opened in 1996 to house an impressive collection of more than 3,000 pieces of art and sculpture, most of it by Singaporean and Malay artists. A large collection of Southeast Asian pieces rotates regularly, along with visiting international exhibits. Once a Catholic boys' school established in 1852, SAM has retained some visible reminders of its former occupants: Above the front door of the

main building, you can still see inscribed ST. JOSEPH'S INSTITUTION, and a bronze-toned cast-iron statue of St. John Baptist de la Salle with two children stands in its original place.

71 Bras Basah Rd. ☎ **65/6332-3222.** www.nhb.gov.sg. Adults S$3 (US$1.75), children and seniors S$1.50 (US90¢). Sat–Thurs 10am–7pm; Fri 10am–9pm. Free guided tours in English Mon–Fri 11am and 2pm, w/additional Sat–Sun tour at 3:30pm. 5-min. walk from City Hall MRT.

**Singapore History Museum** ★★   The original Singapore History Museum, located on Stamford Road, is closed from 2003 through 2006 for a massive renovation project that will double its exhibition space. In the interim, the national Heritage board has opened a small display at Riverside Point called "Rivertales." This special exhibit tells the history of the Singapore River through stories of the people who worked and lived along the river.

Riverside Point, 30 Merchant Rd., #03-09/17, across the river from Clarke Quay. ☎ **65/6332-3659.** www.nhb.gov.sg. Adults S$2 (US$1.20), children and seniors S$1 (US60¢). Fri free 7–9pm. Mon noon–6pm; Tues–Sun 9am–6pm (Fri until 9pm). 5-min. walk from Clarke Quay MRT.

**Singapore Philatelic Museum**   This building, constructed in 1895 to house the Methodist Book Room, recently underwent a nearly US$4-million restoration and reopened as the Philatelic Museum in 1995. Exhibits include a fine collection of old stamps issued to commemorate historically important events, first-day covers, antique printing plates, postal service memorabilia, and private collections. Visitors can trace the development of a stamp from idea to the finished sheet, and can even design their own. Free guided tours are available upon request.

23B Coleman St. ☎ **65/6337-3888.** www.spm.org.sg. Adults S$2 (US$1.20), children and seniors S$1 (US60¢). Mon noon–6pm; Tues–Sun 9am–6pm. 10-min walk from Clarke Quay MRT.

**Statue of Raffles**   This sculpture of Sir Stamford Raffles was erected on The Padang in 1887 and moved to its present position after getting in the way of one too many cricket matches. During the Japanese occupation, the statue was placed in the Singapore History Museum (then the Raffles Museum) and was replaced here in 1945. The local joke is that Raffles's arm is outstretched to the Bank of China building, and his pockets are empty. (**Translation:** In terms of wealth in Singapore, it's Chinese one, Brits nil.)

Victoria Theatre and Concert Hall. 15-min. walk from City Hall MRT.

**Supreme Court**   The Supreme Court stands on the site of the old Hotel de L'Europe, a rival of Raffles Hotel until it went bankrupt in the 1930s. The court's structure, a classical style favored for official buildings the world over, was completed in 1939. With its spare adornment and architectural simplicity, the edifice has a no-nonsense, utilitarian attitude, and the sculptures across the front, executed by the Italian sculptor Cavaliere Rodolpho Nolli, echo what transpires within. Justice is the most breathtaking, standing 2.7m (9 ft.) high and weighing almost 4 tons. Kneeling on either side of her are representations of Supplication and Thankfulness. To the far left are Deceit and Violence. To the far right, a bull represents Prosperity and two children hold wheat, to depict Abundance.

St. Andrew's Rd., across from The Padang. Closed to visitors, but worth seeing from the outside. 10-min. walk from City Hall MRT.

**Victoria Theatre and Concert Hall**   Designed by colonial engineer John Bennett in a Victorian Revival style that was fashionable in Britain at the time, the theater portion was built in 1862 as the Town Hall. Victoria Memorial Hall was built in 1905 as a memorial to Queen Victoria, retaining the same style of the old building. The clock tower was added a year later. In 1909, with its name changed to Victoria Theatre, the hall opened with an amateur production of the *Pirates of Penzance*. Another notable performance occurred when Noël Coward passed through Singapore and stepped in at the last moment to help out a traveling English theatrical company that had lost a leading man. The building looks much the same as it did then, though, of course, the interiors have been modernized. It was completely renovated in 1979, conserving all the original details, and was renamed Victoria Concert Hall. It housed the Singapore Symphony Orchestra until the opening of Esplanade—Theatres on the Bay, when it shifted to the larger digs.

9 Empress Place, at the southern end of The Padang. ✆ 65/6339-6120. 15-min walk from City Hall MRT.

## ALONG THE RIVER

The Singapore River had always been the heart of life in Singapore even before Raffles landed, but for many years during the 20th century life here was dead—quite literally. Rapid urban development that began in the 1950s turned the river into a giant sewer, killing all plant and animal life in it. In the mid-1980s, though, the government began a large and very successful cleanup project, and shortly thereafter, the buildings at Boat Quay and Clarke Quay were restored. Now the areas on both banks of the river offer entertainment, food, and pubs day and night.

**Boat Quay** ⭐   Known as "the belly of the carp" by the local Chinese because of its shape, this area was once notorious for its opium dens and coolie shops. Nowadays, thriving restaurants boast every cuisine imaginable, and the rocking nightlife offers up a variety of sounds—jazz, rock, blues, Indian, and Caribe—that are lively enough to get any couch potato tapping his feet. Remember to pronounce *quay* as "key" if you don't want people to look at you funny.

Located on the south bank of the Singapore River between Cavenagh Bridge and Elgin Bridge. 5-min. walk from Clarke Quay MRT.

**Chettiar's Hindu Temple (aka the Tank Road Temple)**   One of the richest and grandest of its kind in Southeast Asia, the Tank Road Temple is most famous for a ***thoonganai maadam,*** a statue of an elephant's backside in a seated position. It's said that there are only four others of the kind, located in four temples in India. The original temple was completed in 1860, restored in 1962, and practically rebuilt in 1984. Used daily for worship, the temple is also the culmination point of Thaipusam, a celebration of thanks, and the Festival of Navarathiri.

15 Tank Rd., close to the intersection of Clemenceau Ave. and River Valley Rd. ✆ 65/6737-9393. 20-min. walk from Clarke Quay MRT.

**Clarke Quay**   The largest of the waterfront developments, Clarke Quay was named for the second governor of Singapore, Sir Andrew Clarke. In the 1880s, a pineapple cannery, iron foundry, and numerous warehouses made this area bustle. Today, with 60 restored warehouses hosting restaurants and a shopping section known as Clarke Quay Factory Stores, the Quay still hops. **River House,** formerly the home of a *towkay* (company president), occupies the oldest building. In the evenings you can find **The Satay Club** here, a spot where satay sellers gather to sell the juicy little Malay meat kebabs dipped in yummy peanut chile sauce. Get up early on Sunday, forgo the comics section and take in the **flea market,** which opens at 9am and lasts all day. You'll find lots of bargains on unusual finds.

   Also here, G-Max Ultimate Bungy (3E River Valley Rd.; ✆ **65/6338-1146; www.gmax.com.sg**) will strap you and two buddies into a cage and fling you around at the end of giant bungee cords for only S\$30 (US\$18) each. You'll go up to 60m (197 ft.) high at 200kmph (124 mph). Woo! Stop by during weekdays from 3pm to midnight, and on weekends from noon 'til late.

River Valley Rd. west of Coleman Bridge. © 65/6337-3292. www.clarkequay.com.sg. Clarke Quay MRT.

**Esplanade Park**   Esplanade Park and Queen Elizabeth Walk, two of the most famous parks in Singapore, were established in 1943 on land reclaimed from the sea. Several memorials are located here. The first is a fountain built in 1857 to honor **Tan Kim Seng,** who gave a great sum of money toward the building of a waterworks. Another monument, **the Cenotaph,** commemorates the 124 Singaporeans who died in World War I; it was dedicated by the Prince of Wales. On the reverse side, the names of those who died in World War II have been inscribed. The third prominent memorial is dedicated to **Major General Lim Bo Seng,** a member of the Singaporean underground resistance in World War II who was captured and killed by the Japanese. His memorial was unveiled in 1954 on the 10th anniversary of his death. At the far end of the park, the Esplanade—Theatres on the Bay opened in October 2002. Fashioned after the Sydney Opera House, the unique double-domed structure is known locally as The Durians, because their spiky domes resemble halves of durian shells (the building itself is actually smooth—the "spikes" are sun shields).

Connaught Dr., on the marina, running from the mouth of the Singapore River along The Padang to Esplanade—Theatres on the Bay. Daily until midnight. 10-min. walk from City Hall MRT.

**Merlion Park**   The Merlion is Singapore's half-lion, half-fish national symbol, the lion representing Singapore's roots as the "Lion City" and the fish representing the nation's close ties to the sea. Bet you think a magical and awe-inspiring beast like this has been around in tales for hundreds of years, right? No such luck. Rather, he was the creation of some scheming marketers at the Singapore Tourism Board in the early 1970s. Talk about the collision of ancient culture and the modern world. Despite the Merlion's commercial beginnings, he's been adopted as the national symbol and spouts continuously every day at the mouth of the Singapore River.

South bank, at the mouth of the Singapore River, adjacent to One Fullerton. Free admission. Daily 7am–10pm. 15-min walk from either City Hall or Raffles Place MRT.

## CHINATOWN & TANJONG PAGAR

### Al-Abrar Mosque
This mosque was originally erected as a thatched building in 1827 and was also called Masjid Chulia and Kuchu Palli, which in Tamil means "hut mosque." The building that stands today was built in the 1850s, and even though it faces Mecca, the complex conforms with the grid of the neighborhood's city streets. In the late 1980s, the mosque underwent major renovations that enlarged the mihrab and stripped away some of the ornamental qualities of the columns in the building. The one-story prayer hall was extended upward into a two-story gallery. Little touches like the timber window panels and fanlight windows have been carried over into the new renovations.

192 Telok Ayer St., near the corner of Telok Ayer and Amoy sts., near Thian Hock Keng Temple. 15-min. walk from either Raffles Place or Tanjong Pagar MRT.

### Chinatown Heritage Centre 🏛🏛
This block of old shophouses in the center of the Chinatown heritage district has been converted into a display that tells the story of the Chinese immigrants who came to Singapore to find work in the early days of the colony. Walk through rooms filled with period antiques replicating coolie living quarters, shops, clan associations, and other places that were

prominent in daily life. It reminded me of the museum on Ellis Island in New York City that walks visitors through the immigrant experience of the early 1900s. Like Ellis Island, this display also has detailed descriptions to explain each element of the immigrant experience.

48 Pagoda St. *C* 65/6325-2878. www.chinatownheritage.com.sg. Adults S$8 (US$5), children S$4.80 (US$3). Daily 10am–7pm. English language tour every hour. 5-min. walk from Chinatown MRT.

## Jamae Mosque

Jamae Mosque was built by the Chulias, Tamil Muslims who were some of the earlier immigrants to Singapore, and who had a very influential hold over Indian Muslim life centered in the Chinatown area. It was the Chulias who built not only this mosque, but Masjid Al-Abrar and the Nagore Durgha Shrine as well. Jamae Mosque dates from 1827 but wasn't completed until the early 1830s. The mosque stands today almost exactly as it did then.

18 S. Bridge Rd., at the corner of S. Bridge Rd. and Mosque St. Chinatown MRT. 10-min. walk from Chinatown MRT.

## Lau Pa Sat Festival Pavilion

Though it used to be well beloved, the locals think this place has become an atrocity. Once the happy little hawker center known as Telok Ayer Market, it began life as a wet market, selling fruits, vegetables, and other foodstuffs. Now it's part hawker center, part Western fast-food outlets, and all tourist. Lau Pa Sat is one of the few hawker centers that's open 24 hours, in case you need a coffee or snack before retiring.

18 Raffles Quay, located in the entire block flanked by Robinson Rd., Cross St., Shenton Way, and Boon Tat St. 10-min. walk from Raffles Place MRT.

## Nagore Durgha Shrine

Although this is a Muslim place of worship, it is not a mosque, but a shrine, built to commemorate a visit to the island by a Muslim holy man of the Chulia people (Muslim merchants and money lenders from India's Coromandel Coast), who was traveling around Southeast Asia spreading the word of Indian Islam. The most interesting visual feature is its facade: Two arched windows flank an arched doorway, with columns in between. Above these is a "miniature palace"—a massive replica of the facade of a palace, with tiny cutout windows and a small arched doorway in the middle. The cutouts in white plaster make it look like lace. From the corners of the facade, two 14-level minarets rise, with three little domed cutouts on each level and onion domes on top. Inside, the prayer halls and two shrines are painted and decorated in shockingly tacky colors.

140 Telok Ayer St., at the corner of Telok Ayer St. and Boon Tat St. *C* 65/6324-0021. 15-min. walk from either Raffles Place or Tanjong Pagar MRT.

## Sri Mariamman Hindu Temple

As the oldest Hindu temple in Singapore, Sri Mariamman has been the central point of Hindu tradition and culture. In its early years, the temple housed new immigrants while they established themselves and also served as social center for the community. Today the main celebration here is the Thimithi Festival in October or November. The shrine is dedicated to the goddess Sri Mariamman, who is known for curing disease, but as is the case at all other Hindu temples, the entire pantheon of Hindu gods is present to be worshipped as well.

244 S. Bridge Rd., at the corner of S. Bridge Rd. and Pagoda St. *C* 65/6223-4064. 10-min. walk from Chinatown MRT.

## Thian Hock Keng Temple ★★★

Thian Hock Keng, the "Temple of Heavenly Bliss," is one of the oldest Chinese temples in Singapore. Before land reclamation, when the shoreline came right up to Telok Ayer Road, the first Chinese sailors landed here and immediately built a shrine, a small wood-and-thatch structure, to pray to the goddess Ma Po Cho for allowing their voyage to be safely completed. For each subsequent boatload of Chinese sailors, the shrine was always the first stop upon landing. Ma Po Cho, the Mother of the Heavenly Sages, was the patron goddess of sailors, and every Chinese junk of the day had an altar dedicated to her. The temple that stands today was built in 1841 over the shrine with funds from the Hokkien community. All of the building materials were imported from China, except for the gates, which came from Glasgow, Scotland, and the tiles on the facade, which are from Holland.

158 Telok Ayer St., ½ block beyond Nagore Durgha Shrine. © 65/6423-4616.

**Wak Hai Cheng Bio Temple** ✸✸  Like most of Singapore's Chinese temples, Wak Hai Cheng Bio had its start as a simple wood-and-thatch shrine where sailors, when they got off their ships, would go to express their gratitude for sailing safely to their destination. Before the major land-reclamation projects shifted the shoreline outward, the temple was close to the water's edge, so it was named "Temple of the Calm Sea Built by the Guangzhou People." It's a Teochew temple, located in a part of Chinatown populated mostly by the Teochews. The temple itself is quite a visual treat, with ceramic figurines and pagodas adorning the roof, and every nook and cranny of the structure adorned with tiny three-dimensional reliefs that depict scenes from Chinese operas. The spiral joss hanging in the courtyard adds an additional picturesque effect.

30-B Phillip St., at the corner of Phillip St. and Church St. 5-min. walk from Raffles Place MRT.

## LITTLE INDIA

Little India did not develop as a community planned by the colonial authorities like Kampong Gelam or Chinatown, but came into being because immigrants to India were drawn to business developments here. In the late 1920s, the government established a brick kiln and lime pits here that attracted Indian workers, and the abundance of grass and water made the area attractive to Indian cattle traders.

**Desire Paths** (65 Kerbau Rd.; © 65/6392-1772) will lease you a headset with an audio tour of Little India, guiding you through the streets and giving you all kinds of insight into this part of town. Headsets are available Tuesday through Saturday from 10am to 4pm for S$15 (US$8.80) each.

*A word of advice:* If you visit Little India on a Sunday, be prepared for a mob scene the likes of Calcutta! Sunday is the only day off for Singapore's many immigrant Indian and Bangladeshi laborers, so Serangoon Road gets a little difficult to navigate.

**Abdul Gafoor Mosque**  This charming little mosque is resplendent, thanks to a loving restoration completed in 2003. Nestled behind a row of shophouses, you really can't see it until you arrive at the gate. Inside the compound, the bright yellow-and-green facade and minarets reflect an Indian Muslim architectural preference, most likely imported with the mosque's builder Sheik Abdul Gafoor. The original mosque on this site, called Al-Abrar Mosque, was constructed of wood in 1859, and is commemorated on a granite plaque within the compound above what could have been either an entrance gate or part of the mosque itself. The newer mosque on the site was built in 1907 and includes some unusual features, including ornate European-style columns, and the sunburst above the main entrance. This "sundial" has 25 rays in Arabic calligraphy relief said to represent the 25 prophets in the Koran.

Inside the courtyard, an information office provides robes for those in shorts and sleeveless tops. As in every mosque, the main prayer hall is off-limits to non-Muslims.

41 Dunlop St., between Perak Rd. and Jalan Besar. ℂ 65/6295-4209. 15-min. walk from Little India MRT.

### Sakya Muni Buddha Gaya (Temple of a Thousand Lights)   Thai elements influence this temple, from the *chedi* (stupa) roofline to the huge Thai-style Buddha image inside. Often this temple is brushed off as strange and tacky, but there are all sorts of surprises inside, making the place a veritable Buddha theme park. On the right side of the altar, statues of baby bodhisattvas receive toys and sweets from worshippers. Around the base of the altar, murals depict scenes from the life of Prince Siddhartha (Buddha) as he searches for enlightenment. Follow them around to the back of the hall, and you'll find a small doorway to a chamber under the altar. Another Buddha image reclines inside, this one shown at the end of his life, beneath the Yellow Seraka tree. On the left side of the main part of the hall is a replica of a footprint left by the Buddha in Ceylon. Next to that is a wheel of fortune. For 50¢, you get one spin.

336 On Race Course Rd., 1 block past Perumal Rd. ℂ 65/6294-0714. 5-min. walk from Farrer Park MRT.

### Sri Perumal Temple   Sri Perumal Temple is devoted to the worship of Vishnu. As part of the Hindu trinity, Vishnu is the sustainer, balancing out Brahma the creator and Shiva the destroyer. When the world is out of whack, he rushes to its aid, reincarnating himself to show mankind that there are always new directions for development.

The temple was built in 1855 and was most recently renovated in 1992. During Thaipusam, the main festival celebrated here, male devotees who have made vows over the year carry *kavadi*—huge steel racks decorated with flowers and fruits and held onto their bodies by skewers and hooks—to show their thanks and devotion, while women carry milk pots in a parade from Sri Perumal Temple to Chettiar's Temple on Tank Road.

397 Serangoon Rd., ½ block past Perumal Rd. Best times to visit are daily 7–11am or 5–7:30pm. 5-min. walk from Farrer Park MRT.

### Sri Veerama Kaliamman Temple ☆☆   This Hindu temple is used primarily for the worship of Shiva's wife Kali, who destroys ignorance, maintains world order, and blesses those who strive for knowledge of God. The box on the walkway to the front entrance is for smashing coconuts, a symbolic smashing of the ego, asking God to show "the humble way." The coconuts have two small "eyes" at one end so they can "see" the personal obstacles to humility they are being asked to smash. Inside the temple in the main hall are three altars, the center one for Kali (depicted with 16 arms and wearing a necklace of human skulls) and two altars on either side for her two sons—Ganesh, the elephant god, and Murugan, the four-headed child god. To the right is an altar with nine statues representing the nine planets. Circle the altar and pray to your planet for help with a specific trouble.

On Serangoon Rd. at Veerasamy Rd. Daily 8am–noon and 5:30–8:30pm. 10-min. walk from Little India MRT.

## ARAB STREET & KAMPONG GELAM
### Hajjah Fatimah Mosque ☆☆   Hajjah Fatimah was a wealthy businesswoman from Malacca and something of a local socialite. She had originally built a home on this site, but after it was robbed a couple of times and later set fire to, she decided to build a mosque here and moved to another home. Inside the high walls of the compound are the prayer hall, an ablution area, gardens and mausoleums,

and a few other buildings. You can walk around the main prayer halls to the garden cemeteries, where flat square headstones mark the graves of women and round ones mark the graves of men. Hajjah Fatimah is buried in a private room to the side of the main prayer hall, along with her daughter and son-in-law.

4001 Beach Rd., past Jalan Sultan. ℂ 65/6297-2774. 20-min. walk from Bugis MRT.

**Malay Heritage Centre (Istana Kampong Gelam)**  When the Malay Heritage Centre opened its doors in November 2004, it became the first museum dedicated to the history, culture, and arts of this oftentimes marginalized ethnic group. The Centre has lovingly displayed exhibits that offer a glimpse into Singapore's early Malay settlements, the sultan's royal family, Malay arts, and 20th-century Malay life.

There's a bit of irony here. The museum is housed in the Istana Kampong Gelam, the former royal palace that housed the descendents of the original sultan that oversaw Singapore. In 1819, Sultan Hussein signed away his rights over the island in exchange for the land at Kampong Gelam plus an annual stipend for his family. After the Sultan's death, the family fortunes began to dwindle and disputes broke out among his descendants. In the late 1890s, they went to court, where it was decided that since no one in the family had the rights as the successor to the sultanate, the land should be reverted to the state. The family was allowed to remain in the house, but since they didn't own the property they lost the authority to improve the buildings. Over the years the compound fell into a very sad state of dilapidation. Eventually, Sultan Hussein's family was given the boot by the government to make way for this museum heralding the value of the Malay, and the Sultan's, cultural contribution to Singapore. Hmm.

Every day at 10am, 11:30am and 3:30pm there's a cultural show with live music, costumes, and dancing. Tickets cost S$15 (US$8.80) for adults and S$8 (US$4.70) children.

The house to the left before the main gate of the Istana compound is called **Gedong Kuning,** or Yellow Mansion. It was the home of Tenkgu Mahmoud, the heir to Kampong Gelam. When he died, it was purchased by local Javanese businessman Haji Yusof, the belt merchant. Today it houses a Malay restaurant, Tepak Sireh (ℂ 65/6393-4373; open daily 11:30am–2:30pm and 6:30–9:30pm.

85 Sultan Gate. ℂ 65/6391-0450. Adults S$3 (US$1.75), children S$2 (US$1.20). Daily 9am–7pm. 15-min. walk from Bugis MRT.

**Sultan Mosque** ⚘  Though there are more than 80 mosques on the island of Singapore, Sultan Mosque is the real center of the Muslim community. The mosque that stands today is the second Sultan Mosque to be built on this site. The first was built in 1826, partially funded by the East India Company as part of its agreement to leave Kampong Gelam to Sultan Hussein and his family in return for sovereign rights to Singapore. The present mosque was built in 1928 and was funded by donations from the Muslim community. The Saracenic flavor of the onion domes, topped with crescent moons and stars, are complemented by Mogul cupolas. Funny thing, though: The mosque was designed by an Irish guy named Denis Santry, who was working for the architectural firm Swan and McLaren.

Sultan Mosque, like all the others, does not permit shorts, miniskirts, low necklines, or other revealing clothing to be worn inside. However, they do realize that non-Muslim travelers like to be comfortable as they tour around, and they provide cloaks free of charge. They hang just to the right as you walk up the stairs.

3 Muscat St. Daily 9am–1pm and 2–4pm. © **65/6293-4405**. No visiting is allowed during mass congregation Fri 11:30am–2:30pm. 15-min. walk from Bugis MRT.

# ORCHARD ROAD AREA
## The Istana and Sri Temasek
This building serves as the official residence of
the President of the Republic of Singapore. Used mainly for state and ceremonial occasions, the grounds are open to every citizen on selected public holidays,
though they're not generally open for visits. The house's domain includes several
other houses of senior colonial civil servants.

Orchard Rd., between Claymore Rd. and Scotts Rd. 5-min. walk from Dhoby Ghaut MRT.

## Peranakan Place ✶
The houses along Emerald Hill have all been renovated,
and the street has been closed to vehicular traffic. As you pass Emerald Hill,
though, don't just blow it off as a tourist trap. Walk through the cafe area and out
the back. All of the terrace houses have been redone magnificently. The facades
have been freshly painted and the tiles have been polished, and the dark wood
details add a contrast that is truly elegant. When these places were renovated, they
could be purchased for a song, but as Singaporeans began grasping at their heritage in recent years, their value shot up, and now these homes fetch huge sums.

Located at the intersection of Emerald Hill and Orchard Rd. 5-min. walk from Somerset MRT.

# WESTERN SINGAPORE ATTRACTIONS
The attractions grouped in this section are on the west side of Singapore, beginning from the Singapore Botanic Gardens at the edge of the urban area all the
way out to the Singapore Discovery Centre past Jurong. Remember if you're traveling around this area that transportation can be problematic; the MRT system
rarely goes direct to any of these places, taxis can be hard to find, and bus routes
get more complex. Keep the telephone number for taxi booking handy. Sometimes ticket salespeople at each attraction can help and make the call for you.

## Bukit Timah Nature Reserve ✶✶
Bukit Timah Nature Reserve is pure pri-
mary rainforest. Believed to be as old as 1 million years, it's the only place on the
island with vegetation that exists exactly as it was before the British settled here.
The park is more than 81 hectares (200 acres) of soaring canopy teeming with
mammals and birds and a lush undergrowth with more bugs, butterflies, and
reptiles than you can shake a vine at. Here you can see more than 700 plant
species, many of which are exotic ferns, plus mammals like longtailed macaques,
squirrels, and lemurs. There's a visitor center and four well-marked paths, one of
which leads to Singapore's highest point. At 163m (535 ft.) above sea level, don't
expect a nosebleed, but some of the scenic views of the island are really nice.
Along another walkway is Singapore's oldest tree, estimated to be 400 years old.
Also at Bukit Timah is Hindhede Quarry, which filled up with water at some
point, so you can take a dip and cool off during your hike.

177 Hindhede Dr. © **1800/468-5736**. www.nparks.gov.sg Free admission. Daily 24 hrs. Newton MRT, then
bus no. 171 to park entrance.

## Chinese and Japanese Gardens
Situated on two islands in Jurong lake, the
gardens are reached by an overpass and joined by the Bridge of Double Beauty.
The **Chinese Garden** dedicates most of its area to "northern-style" landscape
architecture. The style of Imperial gardens, the northern style integrates brightly
colored buildings with the surroundings to compensate for northern China's
absence of rich plant growth and natural scenery. The Stoneboat is a replica of
the stone boat at the Summer Palace in Beijing. Inside the Pure Air of the Universe building are courtyards and a pond, and there is a seven-story pagoda, with

the odd number of floors symbolizing continuity. Around the gardens, special attention has been paid to the placement of rock formations to resemble true nature, and also to the qualities of the rocks themselves, which can represent the forces of yin and yang, male and female, passivity or activity, and so on.

I like the Garden of Beauty, in Suzhou style, representing the southern style of landscape architecture. Southern gardens were built predominantly by scholars, poets, and men of wealth. Sometimes called Black-and-White gardens, these smaller gardens had more fine detail, featuring subdued colors as the plants and elements of the rich natural landscape gave them plenty to work with. Inside the Suzhou garden are 2,000 pots of *penjiang* (bonsai) and displays of small rocks.

While the Chinese garden is more visually stimulating, the **Japanese garden** is intended to evoke feeling. Marble-chip paths lead the way so that as you walk you can hear your own footsteps and meditate on the sound. They also serve to slow the journey for better gazing upon the scenery. The Keisein, or "Dry Garden," uses white pebbles to create images of streams. Ten stone lanterns, a small traditional house, and a rest house are nestled between two ponds with smaller islands joined by bridges.

Toilets are situated at stops along the way, as are benches, to have a rest or to just take in the sights. Paddle boats can be rented for S$5 (US$2.85) per hour just outside the main entrance.

1 Chinese Garden Rd. ℂ 65/6261-3632. Free general admission; admission to bonsai garden adults S$5 (US$2.95), children S$3 (US$1.75). Daily 9am–7pm. Chinese Garden MRT.

### Haw Par Villa (Tiger Balm Gardens) 🐸

In 1935, brothers Haw Boon Haw and Haw Boon Par—creators of Tiger Balm, the camphor and menthol rub that comes in those cool little pots—took their fortune and opened Tiger Balm Gardens as a venue for teaching traditional Chinese values. They made more than 1,000 statues and life-size dioramas depicting Chinese legends and historic tales and illustrating morality and Confucian beliefs. Many of these were gruesome and bloody and some of them were really entertaining.

But Tiger Balm Gardens suffered a horrible fate. In 1985, it was converted into an amusement park and reopened as Haw Par Villa. Most of the statues and scenes were taken away and replaced with rides. Well, business did not exactly boom. In fact, the park lost money fast. But recently, in an attempt to regain some of the original Tiger Balm Garden edge, they replaced many of the old statues, some of which are a great backdrop for really kitschy vacation photos, and ditched the rides. They also decided to open the gates free of charge.

262 Pasir Panjang Rd. ℂ 65/6774-0300. Free admission. Daily 9am–5pm. Buona Vista MRT and transfer to bus no. 200.

### Jurong BirdPark 🐸 *Kids*

Jurong BirdPark, with a collection of 8,000 birds from more than 600 species, showcases Southeast Asian breeds plus other colorful tropical beauties, some of which are endangered. The more than 20 hectares (49 acres) can be easily walked or, for a couple dollars extra, you can ride the panorail for a bird's-eye view (so to speak) of the grounds. I enjoy the Waterfall Aviary, the world's largest walk-in aviary. It's an up-close-and-personal experience with African and South American birds, plus a pretty stroll through landscaped tropical forest. This is where you'll also see the world's tallest manmade waterfall, but the true feat of engineering here is the panorail station, built inside the aviary. Another smaller walk-in aviary is for Southeast Asian endangered bird species; at noon every day this aviary experiences a man-made thunderstorm. The daily guided tours and regularly scheduled feeding times are enlightening. Other bird exhibits are the flamingo pools, the World of Darkness (featuring nocturnal birds), and the penguin parade, a favorite for Singaporeans, who adore all things Arctic.

The **World of Hawks** show, at 10am and 4pm, features birds of prey either acting out their natural instincts or performing falconry tricks. The **All-Star Birdshow** takes place at 11am and 3pm, with trained parrots that race bikes and birds that perform all sorts of silliness, including staged birdie misbehaviors. Try to come between 9:30 and 10:30am for breakfast among hanging cages of chirping birds at the **Songbird Terrace.**

2 Jurong Hill. ☎ 65/6265-0022. www.birdpark.com.sg. Adults S$14 (US$8.25), children under 12 S$7 (US$4.10). Daily 8:30am–6pm. Boon Lay MRT and transfer to bus no. 194 or 251.

**Jurong Reptile Park**    The newly renovated Jurong Reptile Park (fixed up just in time because the older facility was smelling up the entire neighborhood) houses more than 50 species of reptiles from the region and around the world. Feedings are fun, as are the reptile shows (at 11:45am and 2pm daily). Snakes are happy to wrap themselves around your neck for a souvenir photo (10:30am and 5pm daily). In itself, it's no reason to trek out to Jurong, but it makes a convenient add-on to a visit to the Jurong BirdPark.

241 Jalan Ahmad Ibrahim. ☎ 65/6261-8866. Adults S$8 (US$4.70), children under 12 and seniors S$3.50 (US$2.10). Daily 9am–6pm. MRT to Boon Lay Station, transfer to SBS no. 194 or 251.

**Ming Village**    Tour a pottery factory that employs traditional pottery-making techniques from the Ming and Qing dynasties, and watch the process from mold making, hand throwing, and hand painting to glazing each piece. After the tour, shop from the large selection of beautiful antique reproduction dishes, vases, urns, and more. Certificates of authenticity are provided, which describe the history of each piece. They are happy to arrange overseas shipping for your treasures, or if you want to carry your purchase home, they'll wrap it very securely.

32 Pandan Rd. ☎ 65/6265-7711. Admission and guided tour free. Daily 9am–5:30pm. Clementi MRT then SBS no. 78.

**Singapore Botanic Gardens** ✸✸    In 1822, Singapore's first botanic garden was started at Fort Canning by Sir Stamford Raffles. After it lost funding, the present Botanic Garden came into being in 1859, thanks to the efforts of a horticulture society; it was later turned over to the government for upkeep. More than just a garden, this space occupied an important place in the region's economic development when "Mad" Henry Ridley, one of the garden's directors, imported Brazilian rubber tree seedlings from Great Britain. He devised improved latex-trapping methods and led the campaign to convince reluctant coffee growers to switch plantation crops. The garden also pioneered orchid hybridization, breeding a number of internationally acclaimed varieties.

Carved out within the tropical setting lies a rose garden, a sundial garden with pruned hedges, a banana plantation, a spice garden, and sculptures by international artists dotted around the area. As you wander, look for the cannonball tree (named for its cannonball-shape fruit), para rubber trees, teak trees, bamboos, and a huge array of palms, including the sealing wax palm—distinguished by its bright scarlet stalks—and the rumbia palm, which bears the pearl sago. The fruit of the silk-cotton tree is a pod filled with silky stuffing that was once used for stuffing pillows. Flowers like bougainvilleas and heliconias add beautiful color.

The **National Orchid Garden** is 3 hectares (7½ acres) of gorgeous orchids growing along landscaped walks. The English Garden features hybrids developed here and named after famous visitors to the garden—there's the Margaret

Thatcher, the Benazir Bhutto, the Vaclav Havel, and more. The gift shops sell live hydroponic orchids in test tubes for unique souvenirs.

The gardens have three lakes. Symphony Lake surrounds an island band shell for "Concert in the Park" performances by the local symphony and international entertainers like Chris de Burg. Call visitor services at the number below for performance schedules.

Main entrance at corner of Cluny Rd. and Holland Rd. ✆ 65/6471-7361. www.nparks.gov.sg. Free admission. Daily 5am–midnight. National Orchid Garden adults S\$2 (US\$1.20), children under 12 and seniors S\$1 (US60¢). Daily 8:30am–7pm. Orchard MRT then bus no. 7, 105, 106, or 174 from Orchard Blvd.

**Singapore Discovery Centre** *(Kids)*  This cool display of the latest military technology with hands-on exhibits that cannot be resisted—one of 19 interactive information kiosks, for instance, lets you design tanks and ships. Airborne Rangers, a virtual-reality experience, lets you parachute from a plane and manipulate your landing to safety. In the motion simulator, feel your seat move in tandem with the fighter pilot on the screen. The Shooting Gallery is a computer-simulated combat firing range using real but decommissioned M16 rifles. IMAX features roll at the five-story iWERKS Theatre regularly. When you get hungry, there's a fast-food court.

You can also have a 30-minute bus tour of the neighboring Singapore Air Force Training Institute free with SDC admission. Inquire about tour times at the front counter.

510 Upper Jurong Rd. ✆ 65/6792-6188. www.sdc.com.sg. Adults S\$9 (US\$5.30), children under 12 S\$5 (US\$2.95). Tues–Sun 9am–7pm. MRT to Boon Lay; transfer to SBS no. 192 or 193.

## CENTRAL & NORTHERN SINGAPORE ATTRACTIONS

The northern part of Singapore contains most of the island's nature reserves and parks. Here's where you'll find the Singapore Zoological Gardens, in addition to some sights with historical and religious significance. Despite the presence of the **MRT** in the area, there is not any simple way to get from attraction to attraction with ease. Bus transfers to and from MRT stops is the way to go—or you could stick to taxi cabs.

**Kong Meng San Phor Kark See Temple**  The largest and most modern religious complex on the island, this place, called Phor Kark See for short, comprises prayer and meditation halls, a hospice, gardens, and a vegetarian restaurant. The largest building is the Chinese-style Hall of Great Compassion. There is also the octagonal Hall of Great Virtue and a towering pagoda. For S50¢ (US30¢) you can buy flower petals to place in a dish at the Buddha's feet. Compared to other temples on the island, Phor Kark See seems shiny—having only been built in 1981. As a result, the religious images inside carry a strange, almost artificial, cartoon air about them.

88 Bright Hill Dr. Located in the center of the island to the east of Bukit Panjang Nature Preserve. Bright Hill Dr. is off Ang Mo Kio Ave. ✆ 65/6453-4046. Take MRT to Bishan, then take bus no. 410.

**Kranji War Memorial**  Kranji Cemetery commemorates the men and women who fought and died in World War II. Prisoners of war in a camp nearby began a burial ground here, and after the war it was enlarged to provide space for all the casualties. The Kranji War Cemetery is the site of 4,000 graves of servicemen, while the Singapore State Cemetery memorializes the names of more than 20,000 who died and have no known graves. Stones are laid geometrically on a slope with a view of the Strait of Johor. The memorial itself is designed to represent the three arms of the services.

Woodlands Rd., located in the very northern part of the island. ✆ 65/6269-6158. Daily 24 hrs. Kranji MRT.

**MacRitchie Nature Trail**    Of all the nature reserves in Singapore, the Central Catchment Nature Reserve is the largest, at 2,000 hectares (4,940 acres). Located in the center of the island, it's home to four of Singapore's reservoirs: MacRitchie, Seletar, Pierce, and Upper Pierce. The rainforest here is the secondary forest, but the animals don't care; they're just as happy with the place. There's one path for walking and jogging (no bicycles allowed) that stretches 3km (1.75 miles) from its start in the southeast corner of the reserve, turning to the edge of MacRitchie Reservoir and then letting you out at the Singapore Island Country Club.

Central Catchment Nature Reserve. No phone. www.nparks.gov.sg Free admission. From Orchard Rd. take bus no. 132 from the Orchard Parade Hotel; from Raffles City take bus no. 130. Get off at the bus stop near Little Sisters of the Poor. Follow the paved walkway, which turns into the trail.

**Mandai Orchid Gardens**    Owned and operated by Singapore Orchids Pte Ltd. to breed and cultivate hybrids for international export, the gardens double as an STB tourist attraction. Arranged in English-garden style, orchid varieties are separated in beds that are surrounded by grassy lawn. Tree-growing varieties prefer the shade of the covered canopy. On display is Singapore's national flower, the Vanda Miss Joaquim, a natural hybrid in shades of light purple. Behind the gift shop is the Water Garden, where a stroll will reveal many houseplants common to the West, as you would find them in the wild.

Mandai Lake Rd., on the route to the Singapore Zoological Gardens. © 65/6269-1036. Adults S$2 (US$1.20), children under 12 S50¢ (US30¢). Daily 8:30am–5:30pm. Ang Mo Kio MRT to bus no. 138.

**Night Safari** ★★★ (Kids    Singapore takes advantage of its unchanging tropical climate and static ratio of daylight to night to bring you the world's first open-concept zoo for nocturnal animals. Here, as in the zoological gardens, animals live in landscaped areas, their barriers virtually unseen by visitors. These areas are dimly lit to create a moonlit effect, and a guided tram leads you through "regions" designed to resemble the Himalayan foothills, the jungles of Africa, and, naturally, Southeast Asia. Some of the free-range prairie animals come very close to the tram. The 45-minute ride covers almost 3.5km (2 miles) and has regular stops to get off and have a rest or stroll along trails for closer views of smaller creatures.

Staff, placed at regular intervals along the trails, help you find your way, though it's almost impossible to get lost along the trails; however, it is nighttime, you are in the forest, and it can be spooky. The guides are there more or less to add peace of mind (and all speak English). Flash photography is strictly prohibited, and be sure to bring plenty of insect repellent. *A weirder tip:* Check out the bathrooms. They're all open-air, Bali style.

Singapore Zoological Gardens, 80 Mandai Lake Rd., at the western edge of the Bukit Panjang Nature Reserve, on the Seletar Reservoir. © 65/6269-3411. www.nightsafari.com.sg. Adults S$18 (US$11), children under 12 S$9 (US$5.30). Combination Zoological Gardens (see below) & Night Safari ticket: adults S$25 (US$15), children S$13 (US$7.35). Daily 7:30pm–midnight. Ticket sales close at 11pm. Entrance Plaza, restaurant, and fast-food outlet open from 6:30pm. Ang Mo Kio MRT to bus no. 138.

**Sasanaransi Buddhist Temple**    Known simply as the Burmese Buddhist Temple, it was founded by a Burmese expatriate to serve the overseas Burmese Buddhist community. His partner, an herbal doctor also from Burma, traveled home to buy a 10-ton block of marble from which was carved the 3.3m (11 ft.) Buddha image that sits in the main hall, surrounded by an aura of brightly colored lights. The original temple was off Serangoon Road in Little India and was moved here in 1991 at the request of the Housing Development Board. On the third story is a standing Buddha image in gold, and murals of events in the Buddha's life.

14 Tai Gin Rd., located next to the Sun Yat-sen Villa near Toa Payoh New Town. Daily 6:30am–9pm. Chanting Sun 9:30am, Wed 8pm, and Sat 7:30pm. Take MRT to Toa Payoh, then take a taxi.

### Singapore Zoological Gardens 🐾🐾 (Kids)

This is called the Open Zoo because, rather than coop the animals in jailed enclosures, they're allowed to roam freely in landscaped areas. Beasts of the world are kept where they are supposed to be using psychological restraints and physical barriers that are disguised behind waterfalls, vegetation, and moats. Some animals are grouped with other species to show them coexisting as they would in nature. For instance, the white rhinoceros is neighborly with the wildebeest and ostrich—not that wildebeests and ostriches make the best company, but certainly contempt is better than boredom. Guinea and pea fowl, Emperor tamarinds, and other creatures are free roaming and not shy; however, if you spot a water monitor or longtailed macaque, know that they're not zoo residents—just locals looking for a free meal.

Major zoo features are the Primate Kingdom, Wild Africa, the Reptile Garden, the children's petting zoo, and underwater views of polar bears, sea lions, and penguins. Daily performances include primate and reptile shows at 10:30am and 2:30pm, and elephant and sea lion shows at 11:30am and 3:30pm. You can take your photograph with an orangutan, chimpanzee, or snake, and there are elephant and camel rides, too.

The literature provided includes half-day and full-day agendas to help you see the most while you're there. The best time to arrive, however, is at 9am, to have breakfast with an orangutan, which feasts on fruits, putting on a hilarious and very memorable show. If you miss that, you can also have tea with it at 4pm. Another good time to go is just after a rain, when the animals cool off and get frisky.

Also see listing for "Night Safari," above.

80 Mandai Lake Rd., at the western edge of the Bukit Panjang Nature Reserve, on the Seletar Reservoir. ✆ 65/6269-3411. www.zoo.com.sg. Adults S$14 (US$8.25), children under 12 S$7 (US$4.10). Combination Zoo & Night Safari ticket: Adults S$25 (US$15), children S$13 (US$7.35). Daily 8:30am–6pm. Ang Mo Kio MRT to bus no. 138.

### Sungei Buloh Wetland Reserve 🐾

Located to the very north of the island and devoted to the wetland habitat and mangrove forests that are so common to the region, 87-hectare (215-acre) Sungei Buloh is out of the way, and not the easiest place to get to; but it's a beautiful park, with constructed paths and boardwalks taking you through tangles of mangroves, soupy marshes, grassy spots, and coconut groves. Of the flora and fauna, the most spectacular sights here are the birds, of which there are somewhere between 140 and 170 species in residence or just passing through for the winter. Of the migratory birds, some have traveled from as far as Siberia to escape the cold months from September to March. Bird observatories are set up at different spots along the paths. Also, even though you're in the middle of nowhere, Sungei Buloh has a visitor center, a cafeteria, and souvenirs. Go early to beat the heat.

301 Neo Tiew Crescent. ✆ 65/6794-1401. Adults S$1 (US60¢), children and seniors S50¢ (US30¢). Mon–Fri 7:30am–7pm; Sat–Sun and public holidays 7am–7pm. Audiovisual show Mon–Sat 9am, 11am, 1pm, 3pm, and 5pm; hourly Sun and public holidays. Kranji MRT to bus no. 925. Stop at Kranji Reservoir Dam and cross causeway to park entrance.

### Sun Yat-sen Nanyang Memorial Hall 🐾

Dr. Sun Yat-sen visited Singapore eight times to raise funds for his revolution in China, and made Singapore his headquarters for gaining the support of overseas Chinese in Southeast Asia. A wealthy Chinese merchant built the villa around 1880 for his mistress, and a later owner permitted Dr. Sun Yat-sen to use it. The house reflects the classic bungalow style, which is becoming endangered in modern Singapore. Its typical bungalow features include a projecting carport with a sitting room overhead, verandas with striped blinds, second-story cast-iron railings, and first-story masonry balustrades. A covered walkway leads to the kitchen and servants' quarters in the back.

Inside, the life of Dr. Yat-Sen is traced in photos and watercolors, from his birth in southern China through his creation of a revolutionary organization.

12 Tai Gin Rd., near Toa Payoh New Town. ✆ 65/6256-7377. Admission S$2 (US$1.20). Tues–Fri and Sun 9am–5pm; Sat 1–10pm. Toa Payoh MRT to bus no. 45.

## EASTERN SINGAPORE ATTRACTIONS

The east coast leads from the edge of Singapore's urban area to the tip of the eastern part, at Changi Point. Eastern Singapore is home to the Changi International Airport, nearby Changi Prison, and the long stretch of East Coast Park along the shoreline. The **MRT** heads east in this region but swerves northward at the end of the line. Not all attractions are served by MRT, and bus travel is time consuming. You're better off taking a taxi to these sights.

**Changi Museum** ✦   Upon successful occupation of Singapore, the Japanese marched all British, Australian, and allied European prisoners to Changi by foot, where they lived in a prison camp for 3 years, suffering overcrowding, disease, and malnutrition. Prisoners were cut off from the outside world except to leave the camp for labor duties. The hospital conditions were terrible; some prisoners suffered public beatings, and many died. In an effort to keep hope alive, they built a small chapel from wood and attap. Years later, at the request of former POWs and their families and friends, the government built this replica.

The museum displays sketches by W. R. M. Haxworth and secret photos taken by George Aspinall—both men POWs who were imprisoned here. Displayed with descriptions, the pictures, along with writings and other objects from the camp, bring this period to life, depicting the day-to-day horror with a touch of high morale.

1000 Upper Changi Rd., in the same general area as the airport. ✆ 65/6214-2451. www.changimuseum. com. Free admission. Guided tour adult S$6 (US$3.50), children S$3 (US$1.75). Daily 9:30am–4:30pm. Tanah Merah MRT to bus no. 2.

**East Coast Park**   East Coast Park is a narrow strip of reclaimed land, only 8.5km (5¼ miles) long, tucked in between the shoreline and East Coast Parkway. It serves as a hangout for Singaporean families on the weekends. Moms and dads barbecue under the trees while the kids swim at the beach, which is nothing more than a narrow lump of grainy sand sloping into yellow-green water that has more seaweed than a sushi bar. Paths for bicycling, in-line skating, walking, or jogging run the length of the park and are crowded on weekends and public and school holidays. On Sunday, you'll find kite flyers in the open grassy parts. The lagoon is the best place to go for bicycle and in-line skate rentals, canoeing, and windsurfing.

Because East Coast Park is so long, getting to the place you'd like to hang out can be a bit confusing. Many of the locators I've included sound funny (for example, McDonald's Carpark C) but are recognizable landmarks for taxi drivers. Sailing, windsurfing, and other sea sports happen at the far end of the park, at the lagoon, which is closer to Changi Airport than it is to the city. Taxi drivers are all familiar with the lagoon as a landmark. Unfortunately, public transportation to the park is tough—you should bring a good map and expect to do a little walking from any major thoroughfare.

East Coast Park is also home to **UDMC Seafood Centre** (p. 495), located not far from the lagoon.

East Coast Pkwy. No phone. Free admission. Bus no. 36 to Marine Parade and use the underpass to cross the highway.

### Escape Theme Park (Kids)

If you think your kids will pass out at the sight of another museum, Singapore's newest and best amusement park will keep them occupied. There are rides for small kiddies and families, plus exciting ones for big kiddies as well. The go-kart circuit is happening. There are also carnival games with prizes, plus snacks and beverages. If it gets too hot, visit Wild Wild Wet (see below). There is also a beach and good seafood hawker fare nearby.

Downtown East 1, Pasir Ris Close. *C* 65/6581-9112. www.escapethemepark.com.sg. Adult S$17 (US$9.70), children and seniors S$8.30 (US$4.90). Combo pass for Escape Theme Park and Wild Wild Wet adult S$23 (US$14), children and seniors S$14 (US$7.95). Open Sat, Sun, and public and school holidays 10am–10pm. Pasir Ris MRT.

### Malay Village

In 1985, Malay Village opened in Geylang as a theme village to showcase Malay culture. The Cultural Museum is a collection of artifacts from Malay culture, including household items, musical instruments, and a replica of a wedding dais and traditional beaded ceremonial bed. Kampung Days lets you walk through a *kampung* house (or Malay village house) as it would have looked in the 1950s and 1960s. The 25-minute **Lagenda Fantasy show** is more for kids, using multi-image projection, Surround Sound, and lights to tell tales from the Arabian Nights and the legend of Sang Nila Utama, the founder of Temasek (Singapore). The village is filled with shops that carry merchandise for the local Malay residents of Geylang.

Two in-house groups perform **traditional Malaysian and Indonesian dances** in the late afternoons and evenings. Call during the day on Saturday to find out if they'll be performing the **Kuda Kepang** in the evening. If you're lucky enough to catch it, it's a long performance but worth the wait because at the end the dancers are put in a trance and walk on glass, eat glass, and rip coconuts to shreds with their teeth. Arrive early because the place gets packed with locals.

39 Geylang Serai, in the suburb of Geylang, an easy walk from the MRT station. *C* 65/6748-4700 or 65/6740-8860. Free admission to village. Daily 10am–10pm. Paya Lebar MRT.

### Wild Wild Wet

Beat the heat at this waterpark, with flumes, raft slides, wave pool, plus lots of water activities for children. A locker room and food and beverage facilities are all convenient, plus water safety is provided by trained lifeguards. Wild Wild Wet and neighboring Escape Theme Park both opened in 2003, so the facilities haven't gotten that worn and tatty look that older theme parks take on after awhile.

Downtown East 1, Pasir Ris Close. *C* 65/6581-9135. www.wildwildwet.com. Adult S$13 (US$7.35), children and seniors S$8.30 (US$4.90). Combo pass for Escape Theme Park and Wild Wild Wet adult S$23 (US$14), children and seniors S$14 (US$7.95). Open Sat, Sun, and public and school holidays 10am–10pm. Pasir Ris MRT.

## SENTOSA ISLAND

In the 1880s, Sentosa, then known as Pulau Blakang Mati, was a hub of British military activity, with hilltop forts built to protect the harbor from sea invasion from all sides. Today, it has become a weekend getaway spot and Singapore's answer to Disneyland.

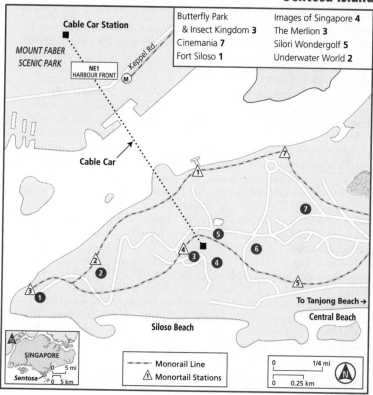

Cable Car Station

MOUNT FABER
SCENIC PARK

NE1
HARBOUR FRONT

Ⓜ

Keppel Rd.

| Butterfly Park & Insect Kingdom **3** | Images of Singapore **4** |
| Cinemania **7** | The Merlion **3** |
| Fort Siloso **1** | Silori Wondergolf **5** |
| | Underwater World **2** |

Cable Car

To Tanjong Beach →

Central Beach

Siloso Beach

SINGAPORE

0    5 mi

Sentosa    0    5 km

⋯⋯⋯ Monorail Line
⚠ Monortail Stations

0        1/4 mi

0      0.25 km

N

If you're spending the day, there are numerous restaurants and a couple of food courts. For overnights, the Shangri-La's Rasa Sentosa Resort and Spa, and the Sentosa Resort & Spa are popular hotel options. For general **Sentosa inquiries,** call ☏ **1800/736-8672,** or see www.sentosa.com.sg.

## GETTING THERE

Island admission is S$2 (US$1.20) for adults and children payable at the Visitors Centre upon entry, with tickets to additional attractions and activities purchased separately once inside.

The most entertaining way to get to the island is to take the cable car. From the Cable Car Towers (☏ **65/6270-8855**), cars leave daily between 8:30am and 9pm at a cost of S$8.90 (US$5.25) adults and S$3.90 (US$2.30) children round-trip. The view is nice (but too far from the city to see the skyline) and the ride is especially fun for kids. The cable cars also extend up Mt. Faber on the Singapore side, but if you choose to alight at this stop, note there are very few taxis to get you back to civilization.

There's also a bus that operates from the HarbourFront Bus Terminal (near Harbourfront MRT) operating daily from 7am to 11pm (until 12:30am Fri, Sat, and eve of public holidays), that costs S$1 (US60¢) per person, paid upon arrival at Sentosa. Or any city taxi can take you there; just pay the entrance fee once you cross the causeway, and the driver can drop you anywhere you'd like to go within the island.

## GETTING AROUND

Once on Sentosa, a free monorail operates from 9am to 10pm daily at 10-minute intervals to shuttle you around to the various areas. Four free shuttle bus lines snake around the island as well.

## SEEING THE SIGHTS

The most notable attractions that you get free with your Sentosa admission are the **Fountain Gardens and Musical Fountain,** staging fountain, lights and laser shows nightly (aimed at junior audiences); the **Dragon Trail Nature Walk,** a 1.5km (1-mile) stroll through secondary rainforest to see dragon sculptures and local flora and fauna; and the **beaches.**

Sentosa has three beaches. At **Siloso Beach,** deck chairs, beach umbrellas, and a variety of **watersports equipment** like pedal boats, aqua bikes, fun bugs, canoes, surfboards, and banana boats are available for hire at nominal charges. Bicycles are also available for hire. Shower and changing facilities, food kiosks, and snack bars are at rest stations. **Palawan Beach** has a greater assortment of beachside bars and restaurants, while **Tanjong Beach** is the more quiet and laid-back of the three.

The attractions on Sentosa that charge separate entrance fees include the **Butterfly Park and Insect Kingdom** (© 65/6275-0013; adults S$10/US$5.90, children S$6/US$3.50; daily 9am–6:30pm); **Sijori WonderGolf** (© 65/6275-2011;** adults S$8–S$10/US$4.70–US$5.90, children S$4–S$7/US$2.35–US$4.10; daily 9am–7pm); **Cinemania** motion ride (© 65/6275-0804; adults S$13/US$7.35, children S$8/US$4.70; daily 11am–8pm); and the **Carlsberg Sky Tower** (© 1800/736-8672; adults S$10/US$5.90, children S$6/US$3.50; daily 9am–9pm.) The best attractions, in my opinion, are as follows:

**Fort Siloso**    Fort Siloso guarded Keppel Harbour from invasion in the 1880s. It's one of three forts built on Sentosa, and it later became a military camp in World War II. The buildings have been outfitted to resemble a barracks, kitchen, laundry, and military offices as they looked back in the day. In places, you can explore the underground tunnels and ammunition holds, but they're not as extensive as you would hope they'd be.

© 65/6275-0131. Adults S$5 (US$2.95), children S$3 (US$1.75). Daily 9am–7pm.

**Images of Singapore** 🎫🎫    Images of Singapore is without a doubt one of the main reasons to come to Sentosa. There are three parts to this museum/exhibit: the Pioneers of Singapore and the Surrender Chambers—which date back as far as I can remember—and Festivals of Singapore, a recent addition.

Pioneers of Singapore is an exhibit of beautifully constructed life-size dioramas that place figures like Sultan Hussein, Sir Stamford Raffles, Tan Tock Seng, and Naraina Pillai, to name just a few pioneers, in the context of Singapore's timeline and note their contributions to its development. Also interesting are the dioramas depicting scenes from the daily routines of the different cultures as they lived during colonial times. It's a great stroll that brings history to life.

The powers that be have tried to change the name of the **Surrender Chambers** to the Sentosa Wax Museum, but it still hasn't caught on because the Surrender Chambers are oh so much more than just a wax museum. The gallery leads you through authentic footage, photos, maps, and recordings of survivors to chronologically tell the story of the Pacific theater activity of World War II and how the Japanese conquered Singapore. The grand finale is a wax museum depicting, first, a scene of the British surrender and, last, another of the Japanese surrender.

Recently, Images of Singapore added the **Festivals of Singapore,** another life-size diorama exhibit depicting a few of the major festivals and traditions of the Chinese, Malay, Indian, and Peranakan cultures in Singapore.

🕐 **65/6275-0426.** Adults S$8 (US$4.70), children S$5 (US$2.95). Daily 9am–9pm.

**Underwater World** ★ *Kids*   Underwater World is without a doubt one of the most visited attractions on Sentosa. Everybody comes for the tunnel: 83m (272 ft.) of transparent acrylic tube through which you glide on a conveyor belt, gaping at sharks, stingrays, eels, and other creatures of the sea drifting by, above and on both sides. At 11:30am, 2:30pm, and 4:30pm daily, a scuba diver hops in and feeds the fish by hand. In smaller tanks you can view other unusual sea life like the puffer fish and the mysteriously weedy and leafy sea dragons. Then there's the latest display of bamboo shark embryos, developing within egg cases—what's keeping you?

🕐 **65/6275-0030.** www.underwaterworld.com.sg. Adults S$17 (US$10), children S$11 (US$6.60). Daily 9am–9pm.

## ORGANIZED TOURS

While touring Singapore is simple enough for DIY travelers, visitors with little time, or who want to delve deeper into local sights, can take advantage of convenient organized activities.

### COACH TOURS

**Tour East** (🕐 **65/6738-2622**) organizes your typical half-day coach tour of the city (adults S$28/US$17, children S$14/US$8.25), full-day coach tour (adults S$69/US$41, children S$35/US$21) and half-day coach excursions to some of the main attractions around the island (S$29–S$59/US$17–US$35 adults, S$17–S$35/US$10–US$21 children), some with meals included. The more interesting tours include the Feng Shui Tour, to particularly auspicious sites with explanations about Chinese geomancy (adults S$38/US$22, children S$18/US$11) and the Peranakan Trail, taking visitors out to Katong, a suburban neighborhood that is the focal point of Peranakan heritage (adults S$39/US$23, children S$19/US$11).

For something different, go for the **DUCKTour** (🕐 **65/6338-6877;** www.ducktours.com.sg) a combined coach-and-boat tour in an amphibious vehicle, a decommissioned military craft, that circles you around the Historic District for a tour of the harbor. The hour-long tour starts every hour, departing from the Suntec City Mall Galleria, with additional transfers from the DUCKTours office on Orchard Road (at the corner of Cairnhill Rd.) Reservations are highly recommended; tickets are S$33 (US$19) for adults, S$17 (US$10) for children 4–12, and S$2 (US$1.20) for toddlers under 3. DUCKTours also operates the **HiPPO Tour** aboard an open-top double-decker bus, cruising Orchard Road, Little India, Kampong Gelam, Chinatown, and the Historic District. It's a hop-on kinda thing; pick it up at the DUCKTours office on Orchard Road or at Suntec City, then get on and off at sights that interest you along the way. The day ticket costs S$23 (US$14) adult, S$13 (US$7.65) children 4–12, and S$2 (US$1.20) for toddlers under 3. The evening ticket costs S$33 (US$19) adults, S$17 (US$10) children 4–12, and S$2 (US$1.20) for toddlers under 3.

### WALKING TOURS

The **Singapore History Museum** (🕐 **65/6332-4075;** www.nhb.gov.sg) also offers a selection of tours that I highly recommend. The Overview of Singapore History & Culture (S$22/US$13 adults and children) is a half-day historical look at the city's ethnic enclaves with guide Geraldine Lowe, Singapore's local authority on history and heritage. The Cemetery Tour (S$25/US$15 adults and children) takes you outside the city to see a side of local culture that is rarely explored.

**Singapore Walks** (© 65/6325-1631; www.singaporewalks.com) is another reputable outfit that organizes guided walking tours of the Historical District, Chinatown, Little India, Kampong Gelam, and other neighborhoods every day. Call them to find out the meeting time and place for the tour you want, pay S$15 (US$8.80) adults and S$12 (US$7.10) children, and enjoy.

### RIVER TOURS & CRUISES

**Singapore Explorer** (© 65/6339-6833; www.singaporeexplorer.com.sg) operates boats up and down the Singapore River and into the harbor from 9am to 11pm daily. A bumboat ride with recorded info about the riverside sights costs S$12 (US$7.10) for adults and children. If you want to ride in an air-conditioned glass-top boat, you'll pay S$15 (US$8.80) for adults, S$6 (US$3.50) for children. Singapore Explorer also offers a wine-and-dine cruise, but I say spend your time and money savoring the best food in one of the restaurants. The boats can be picked up from Esplanade, Merlion Park, Clarke Quay, and Riverwalk, plus a few other jetties along the river.

The *Imperial Cheng Ho* (Watertours: © 65/6533-9811; www.watertours. com.sg) is a huge boat modeled after the sort of Chinese junk that Admiral Cheng Ho might have sailed when he explored this region in the 15th century. The 2½-hour cruise takes you past the Singapore skyline, the mouth of the Singapore River, then out past Sentosa with a stop on Kusu island. I recommend the Morning Glory Cruise (10:30am, adults S$23/US$14, children S$11/US$6.50). There's also a High Tea Cruise (3pm, adults S$29/US$17, children S$14/US$8.25) and a dinner cruise (6:30pm, adults S$49/US$29, children S$25/US$15). Watertours can arrange hotel transfer with your booking.

### TRISHAW TOUR

These cycle rickshaws were once a staple form of public transportation. Now they're only permitted on busy streets with special permits, and only for guided tours. **Singapore Explorer** (© 65/6339-6833; www.singaporeexplorer.com.sg) coordinates regular outings through Chinatown. You can either call ahead to book a ride, or you can just show up at the corner of Sago and Terrenganu streets; you'll see the collection of trishaws under cover. The half-hour trip takes you through Chinatown's quaint streets for a charge of S$36 (US$21) per person. You can also combine the trishaw tour with a half-hour bumboat trip for only S$2 (US$1.20) extra. Singapore Explorer can arrange pickup from anywhere if you book in advance.

## 6 Sports & Recreation

### BEACHES

Besides the beach at East Coast Park and those on Sentosa Island (see above) you can try the smaller beach at Changi Village, called Changi Point. From the shore, you have a panoramic view of Malaysia, Indonesia, and several smaller islands that belong to Singapore. The beach is calm, and frequented mostly by locals who set up camps and barbecues to hang out all day. There are kayak rentals along the beach, and in Changi Village you'll find, in addition to a huge hawker center, quite a few international restaurants and pubs to hang out in and have a fresh seafood lunch when you get hungry. To get there take SBS bus no. 2 from either the Tanah Merah or Bedok MRT stations.

## BICYCLE RENTAL

Bicycles are not for rent within the city limits, and traffic does not really allow for cycling on city streets, so sightseeing by bicycle is not recommended for city touring. If you plan a trip out to **Sentosa,** cycling provides a great alternative to that island's tram system, and gets you closer to the parks and nature there. For a little light cycling, most people head out to **East Coast Park,** where rentals are inexpensive, the scenery is nice on cooler days, and there are plenty of great stops for eating along the way.

**AT EAST COAST PARK**    Bicycles can be rented at East Coast Park from **SDK Recreation** (② 65/6445-2969), near McDonald's at Carpark C; open 7 days from about 11am to 8 or 9pm. Rentals are S$3 to S$8 (US$1.75–US$4.70) per hour, depending on the type and quality bike you're looking for. Identification may be requested, or leave a S$50 (US$29) deposit.

**ON SENTOSA ISLAND**    Try **SDK Recreation** (② 65/6272-8738), located at Siloso Beach off Siloso Road, a short walk from Underwater World (see "Sentosa Island," above) and open 7 days from around 10am to 6:30 or 7pm. Rental for a standard bicycle is S$4 (US$2.35) per hour. A mountain bike goes for S$8 (US$4.70) per hour. Identification is required.

## GOLF

Golf is big in Singapore, and while there are quite a few clubs, many are exclusively for members only. However, many places are open for limited play by nonmembers. All will require you bring an international par certificate.

Most hotel concierges will be glad to make arrangements for you, and this may be the best way to go. Also, it's really popular for Singaporeans go on day trips to Malaysia for the best courses.

**Changi Golf Club**    Nonmembers can play at this private club only on weekdays. The 9-hole walking course is par 34, with greens fees of S$40 (US$24) and compulsory caddy fees of S$15 (US$8.80). While on weekdays they will accept walk-ins, the club recommends advanced booking. It may even be able to set you up with other players. The course opens at 7:30am. Last tee is 4:30pm.
20 Netheravon Rd. ② 65/6545-5133.

**Seletar Base Golf Course**    A public course, Seletar's 9-hole, par 36 course is open for everyone 7 days a week. Expect to pay greens fees of S$32 (US$19) on weekdays and S$42 (US$25) on weekends, with very low-cost golf cart and equipment rentals (all available with deposit). First tee is at 7am except for Monday, when first tee is at noon. Last tee is 5:30pm.
244 Oxford St., 3 Park Lane. ② 65/6481-4745.

**Sentosa Golf Club**    The best idea if you're traveling with your family and want to get in a game, Sentosa's many activities will keep the kids happy while you practice your swing guilt-free. This club's two 18-hole courses are each 72 par. This private course charges nonmembers S$231 (US$136) on weekdays and only allows weekend play on Sunday afternoons for S$315 (US$185). It's far more expensive than other courses around, but the chance to get off Singapore island for the day can be quite relaxing. Advance phone bookings are required.
27 Bukit Manis Rd., Sentosa Island. ② 65/6275-0022.

## SCUBA DIVING

The locals are crazy about scuba diving, but are more likely to travel to Malaysia and other Southeast Asian destinations for good underwater adventures. The most common complaint is that the water surrounding Singapore is really silty—sometimes to the point where you can barely see your hand before your face. See chapter 9 for scuba activities in Malaysia.

## SEA CANOEING

Rubber sea canoes and one-person or two-person kayaks are available for rent at Siloso Beach on Sentosa, the beach at East Coast Park (near MacDonald's Carpark C), and the beach at Changi Point. Prices range from S$6 to S$12 (US$3.50–US$7) per hour, depending on the type of craft you rent. Life jackets are provided. Just go to the beach and scout out the rental places on the sand; these places don't have telephones, so it's really impossible to call ahead.

## TENNIS

Quite a few hotels in the city provide tennis courts for guests, many floodlit for night play (which allows you to avoid the midday heat), and even a few that can arrange lessons, so be sure to check out listings for hotel facilities earlier in the chapter. If your hotel doesn't have tennis facilities, ask your concierge for help to arrange a game at a facility outside the hotel. Many hotels have signing agreements with sister hotel properties or special rates with independent fitness centers within the city.

## WATER-SKIING & WAKEBOARDING

The Kallang River, located to the east of the city, has hosted quite a few international water-skiing tournaments. If this is your sport, contact the Cowabunga Ski Centre, the authority in Singapore. Located at **Kallang Riverside Park** (10 Stadium Lane; ✆ **65/6344-8813;** www.extreme.com.sg), Cowabunga will arrange lessons for adults and children and water-skiing and wakeboarding trips. Beginner courses will set you back S$130 (US$76), while more experienced skiers and boarders can hire a boat plus equipment for 4 hours for S$300 (US$176) on weekdays and S$360 (US$212) on weekends. It's open Tuesday to Friday noon to 6:45pm, and Saturday, Sunday, and public holidays 9am to 6:45pm. Call in advance for a reservation.

## WINDSURFING & SAILING

You'll find both windsurf boards and sailboats for rent at the lagoon in East Coast Park, which is where these activities primarily take place. The largest and most reputable firm to approach has to be the **Pasta Fresca Seasport Centre** (1212 East Coast Pkwy.; ✆ **65/6449-5118**). For S$20 to S$25 (US$12–US$15) an hour you can rent a Laser or windsurf board. Expect to leave around S$30 (US$18) deposit.

## 7 Shopping

In Singapore, shopping is a sport—from the practiced glide through haute couture boutiques to skillful back-alley bargaining to win the best prices on Asian treasures. The shopping here is always exciting, with something to satiate every pro shopper's appetite.

**HOURS** Shopping malls are generally open from 10am to 8pm Monday through Saturday, with some stores keeping shorter Sunday hours. The malls sometimes remain open until 10pm on holidays. Smaller shops are open from around 10am to 5pm Monday through Saturday, but are almost always closed on Sunday. Hours vary from shop to shop. Arab Street is closed on Sunday.

**PRICES**    Almost all of the stores in shopping malls have fixed prices. Sometimes these stores have seasonal sales, especially in July, when they have the month-long **Great Singapore Sale,** during which prices are marked down, sometimes up to 50% or 75%. In the smaller shops and at street vendors, prices are never marked, and vendors will quote you higher prices than the going rate, in anticipation of the bargaining ritual. These are the places to find good prices, if you negotiate well.

**DUTY-FREE ITEMS**    Changi International Airport has a large duty-free shop that carries cigarettes, liquor, wine, perfumes, cosmetics, watches, jewelry, and other designer accessories. There's also a chain of duty-free stores in Singapore called **DFS.** The main branch is at #01-58 Millenia Walk, 9 Raffles Blvd., next to the Pan Pacific Hotel (© 65/6332-2188). The store is huge and impressive, but unfortunately, the only truly duty-free items are liquor, which you can arrange to pick up at the airport before you depart—everything else carries the standard 5% GST. Feel free to apply for the Tourist Refund Scheme here, though.

## THE SHOPPING SCENE, PART 1: WESTERN-STYLE MALLS

**ORCHARD ROAD AREA**    The malls on Orchard Road are a tourist attraction in their own right, with smaller boutiques and specialty shops intermingled with huge department stores. **Takashimaya** and **Isetan** have been imported from Japan. **John Little Pte. Ltd.** is one of the oldest department stores in Singapore, followed by **Robinson's. Tang's** is historic, having grown from a cart full of merchandise nurtured by the business savvy of local entrepreneur C. K. Tang. Boutiques range from the younger styles of **Stussy** and **Guess?** to the sophisticated fashions of **Chanel** and **Salvatore Ferragamo.** You'll also find antiques, oriental carpets, art galleries and curio shops, Tower Records and HMV music stores, Kinokuniya and Borders bookstores, video arcades, and scores of restaurants, local food courts, fast-food joints, and coffeehouses—even a few discos, which open in the evenings. It's hard to say when Orchard Road is not crowded, but it's definitely a mob scene on weekends, when folks have the free time to come and hang around, looking for fun.

Some of the larger and more exciting malls to check out are **Centrepoint,** 176 Orchard Rd.; **Ngee Ann City/Takashimaya Shopping Centre,** 391 Orchard Rd.; **Specialists' Shopping Center,** 277 Orchard Rd; and **Wisma Atria,** 435 Orchard Rd. The **Hilton Shopping Gallery,** 581 Orchard Rd., deals only in exclusive top-designer boutiques.

At **Far East Plaza** (14 Scotts Rd.) and **Lucky Plaza** (304 Orchard Rd.), there are some bargains to be had on electronics, camera equipment, and luggage, among other things, but be wary of rip-off deals. **Eyeglasses** are a surprising bargain in Singapore. A reputable outlet is Capitol Optical (#03–132, Far East Plaza; © 65/736-0365). **Royal Selangor,** the famous Malaysian pewter manufacturer since 1885, has eight outlets in Singapore. The Orchard branch is at #02–40 Paragon by Sogo, 290 Orchard Rd. The **Tanglin Shopping Centre** (Tanglin Rd., at the northern end of Orchard) is a treasure trove of antiques dealers and carpet shops. For the best selection of carpets, visit **Hassan's Carpets** (#03–01/06 Tanglin Shopping Center; © 65/737-5626).

**THE HISTORIC DISTRICT**    Although the Historic District doesn't have as many malls as the Orchard Road area, it still has some good shopping. **Raffles City** can be overwhelming in its size, but convenient because it sits right atop the City Hall MRT stop. One of my favorite places to go, however, is the very upmarket **Raffles Hotel Shopping Arcade,** where I like to window-shop and dream about actually being able to afford some of the stuff on display.

**Parco Bugis Junction** Here you'll find restaurants—both fast food and fine dining—mixed in with clothing retailers, most of which sell fun fashions for younger tastes. Victoria St. ✆ **65/6334-8831.**

**Raffles City Shopping Centre** Raffles City sits right on top of the City Hall MRT station, which makes it a very well-visited mall. Men's and women's fashions, books, cosmetics, and accessories are sold in shops here, along with gifts. 252 N. Bridge Rd. ✆ **65/6338-7766.**

**Raffles Hotel Shopping Arcade** These shops are mostly haute couture; however, there is the Raffles Hotel gift shop for interesting souvenirs. For golfers, there's a Jack Nicklaus signature store. 328 N. Bridge Rd. ✆ **65/6337-1886.**

## THE SHOPPING SCENE, PART 2: MULTICULTURAL SHOPPING

**CHINATOWN** For Chinese goods, nothing beats **Yue Hwa** ★★ (70 Eu Tong Sen St.; ✆ **65/6538-4222**). This five-story Chinese Emporium is an attraction in its own right. The superb inventory includes all manner of silk wear (robes, underwear, blouses), embroidery and house linens, bolt silks, tailoring services (for perfect mandarin dresses!), cloisonné (enamel work) jewelry and gifts, lacquerware, pottery, musical instruments, traditional Chinese clothing for men and women (from scholars' robes to coolie duds!), jade and gold, cashmere, traditional items, art supplies, herbs, home furnishings—I could go on and on. Prices are terrific. Plan to spend some time here.

For one-stop souvenir shopping, you can tick off half your shopping list at **Chinatown Point,** aka the **Singapore Handicraft Center** (133 New Bridge Rd.). The best gifts there include hand-carved chops, or Chinese seals. **Chinatown Seal Carving Souvenir** (#03-72; ✆ **65/6534-0761**) has an absolutely enormous selection of carved stone, wood, bone, glass, and ivory chops ready to be carved to your specifications. Simple designs are really quite affordable, while some of the more elaborate chops and carvings fetch a handsome sum. At **Inherited Arts & Crafts** (#03-69; ✆ **65/6534-1197**) you can commission a personalized Chinese scroll painting or calligraphy piece. The handiwork is quite beautiful. Amid the many jade and gold shops at Chinatown Point, **La Belle Collection** (#04-53; ✆ **65/6534-0231**) stands out for its jewelry crafted from orchids. The coating lets the flowers' natural colors show, while delicate gold touches add a little extra sparkle.

My all-time favorite gift idea? Spend an afternoon learning the traditional Chinese tea ceremony at **The Tea Chapter** (9–11 Neil Rd.; ✆ **65/6226-1175**). Pick up a tea set—it has a lovely selection of teapots, cups, and accessories, as well as quality teas for sale. When you return home, you'll be ready to give a fabulous gift—not just a tea set, but your own cultural performance as well, as you teach your friends a new art. Another neat place to visit is **Kwong Chen Beverage Trading** (16 Smith St.; ✆ **65/6223-6927**) for some Chinese teas in handsome tins. While the teas are really inexpensive, they're packed in lovely tins—great to buy lots to bring back as smaller gifts. For serious tea aficionados or those curious about Traditional Chinese Medicine (TCM), stop by **Eu Yan Sang** (269 S. Bridge Rd.; ✆ **65/6223-6333;** www.euyansang.com.sg), which has stocks of very fine (and expensive) teas, plus herb and herbal remedies for health.

For something a little more unusual, check out **Siong Moh Paper Products** (39 Mosque St.; ✆ **65/6224-3125**), which carries a full line of ceremonial items. Pick up some joss sticks (temple incense) or joss paper (books of thin sheets of paper, stamped in reds and yellows with bits of gold and silver leaf). Definitely a conversation piece, as is the Hell Money, stacks of "money" that believers burn at the temple for their ancestors to use in the afterlife. Perfect for that friend who has everything? Also, if you duck over to **Sago Lane** while you're in the neighborhood, there are a few souvenir shops that sell Chinese kites and Cantonese Opera masks—cool for kids.

**ARAB STREET**   Over on Arab Street, shop for handicrafts from Malaysia and Indonesia. I head straight for **Hadjee Textiles** (75 Arab St.; ✆ 65/6298-1943), for their stacks of folded sarongs in beautiful colors and traditional patterns. They're perfect for traveling, as they're lightweight, but can serve you well as a dressy skirt, a bedsheet, beach blanket, window shade, bath towel, or whatever you need—when I'm on the road I can't live without mine. Buy a few here and the prices really drop. If you're in the market for a more masculine sarong, **Goodwill Trading** (56 Arab St.; ✆ 65/6298-3205), specializes in *pulicat,* or the plaid sarongs worn by Malay men. For modern styles of batik, check out **Basharahil Brothers** (101 Arab St.; ✆ 65/6296-0432), for their very interesting designs, but don't forget to see the collection of fine silk batiks in the back. For batik household linens, you can't beat **Maruti Textiles** (93 Arab St.; ✆ 65/6392-0253), where you'll find high-quality place mats and napkins, tablecloths, pillow covers, and quilts from India. The buyer for this shop has a good eye for style.

I've also found a few shops on Arab Street that carry **handicrafts** from Southeast Asia. For antiques and curios, try **Gim Joo Trading** (16 Baghdad St.; ✆ 65/6293-5638), a jumble of the unusual, some of it old. A departure from the more packed and dusty places here, **Suraya Betawj** (67 Arab St.; ✆ 65/6398-1607), carries gorgeous Indonesian- and Malaysian-crafted housewares in contemporary design—the type you normally find for huge prices in shopping catalogues back home.

Other unique treasures include the large assortment of fragrance oils at **Alju-nied Brothers** (91 Arab St.; ✆ 65/6293-2751). Muslims are forbidden from consuming alcohol in any form (a proscription that includes the wearing of alcohol-based perfumes as well), so these oil-based perfumes re-create designer scents plus other floral and wood creations. Check out the delicate cut-glass bottles and atomizers as well. Finally, for the crafter in your life, **Kin Lee & Co.** (109 Arab St.; ✆ 65/6291-1411), carries a complete line of patterns and accessories to make local Peranakan beaded slippers. In vivid colors and floral designs, these traditional slippers were always made by hand, to be attached later to a wooden sole. The finished versions are exquisite, plus they're fun to make.

**LITTLE INDIA**   I have a ball shopping the crowded streets of Little India. The best shopping is on Serangoon Road, where Singapore's Indian community shops for Indian imports and cultural items. The absolute best place to start is **Mustapha's** ✮✮ (320 Serangoon Rd./145 Syed Alwi Rd., at the corner of Serangoon and Syed Alwi roads; ✆ 65/6299-2603), but be warned, you can spend the whole day there—and night, too, since Mustapha's is open 24 hours every day. This maze of a department store fills 2 city blocks full of imported items from India. Granted, much of it is everyday stuff, but the real finds are rows and rows of saris and silk fabrics; two floors of jaw-dropping gold jewelry in Indian designs; an entire supermarket packed with spices, packets of instant curries, and snacks; ready-made Indian-style tie-dye and embroidered casual wear; incense and perfume oils; cotton tapestries and textiles for the home . . . the list goes on. And prices can't be beat, seriously.

Little India offers all sorts of small finds, especially throughout **Little India Arcade** (48 Serangoon Rd.) and just across the street on Campbell Lane at **Kuna's** (#3 Campbell Lane; © 65/6294-2700). Here you can buy inexpensive Indian costume jewelry like bangles, earrings, and necklaces in exotic designs, and a wide assortment of decorative dots (called *pottu* in Tamil) to grace your forehead. Indian handicrafts include brass work, wood carvings, dyed tapestries, woven cotton household linens, small curio items, very inexpensive incense, colorful pictures of Hindu gods, and other ceremonial items. Look here also for Indian cooking pots and household items.

Across the street from Little India Arcade, the second floor of **Zhujiao Centre** is packed with stall after stall of inexpensive *salwar kameez,* or Punjabi suits, the three-piece outfits—long tunic over pants, with matching shawl—worn by northern Indian ladies. Don't be afraid to bargain for the best price.

**Punjab Bazaar** (#01-07 Little India Arcade, 48 Serangoon Rd.; © 65/6296-0067), carries a more upmarket choice of *salwar kameez,* in many styles and fabrics. If nothing strikes your fancy at Punjab Bazaar, try **Roopalee Fashions,** a little farther down at 84 Serangoon Rd. (© 65/6298-0558). Both shops carry sandals, bags, and other accessories to complement your new outfit.

## 8 Singapore After Dark

Major cultural festivals are highly publicized by the **Singapore Tourism Board (STB),** which will give you complete details at its Visitors Centres or on its website. A great source is the Life! Section of *Straits Times,* which lists events for each day, plus theater and cinema listings. *I-S Magazine,* a free publication, promotes Singapore's clubbing lifestyle.

**TICKETS** Two ticket agents, **TicketCharge** and **Sistic,** handle bookings for almost all theater performances, concert dates, and special events. You can find out about schedules before your visit through their websites: www.ticketcharge.com.sg and www.sistic.com.sg. When in Singapore, stop by one of their centrally located outlets to pick up a schedule, or call them for more information. Call TicketCharge at © 65/6296-2929 or head for Centrepoint, Forum—The Shopping Mall, Funan—The IT Mall, Marina Square Shopping Centre, or Tanglin Mall. For **Sistic** bookings call © 65/6348-5555, or see them at the Victoria Concert Hall Box Office, Parco Bugis Junction, Raffles Shopping Centre, Scotts, Specialists' Shopping Center, Suntec Mall, or Wisma Atria.

**HOURS** Theater and dance performances can begin anywhere between 7:30 and 9pm. Be sure to call for the exact time, and don't be late—at Esplanade latecomers are not allowed in. Many bars open in the late afternoon, a few as early as lunchtime. Disco and entertainment clubs usually open around 6pm, but generally don't get lively until 10 or 11pm. Closing time for bars and clubs is at 1 or 2am on weekdays, 3am on weekends. A rare few have extended hours until 6am.

**DRINK PRICES** Because of the government's added tariff, alcoholic beverage prices are high everywhere, whether in a hotel bar or a neighborhood pub. "House-pour" drinks (generics) are between S$8 and S$14 (US$4.70–US$8.25). A glass of house wine will cost between S$10 and S$15 (US$5.90–US$8.80), depending if it's a red or a white. Local draft beer (Tiger), brewed in Singapore, is around S$10 (US$5.90). Hotel establishments are, on average, the most expensive venues, while stand-alone pubs and cafes are better value. Almost every bar and club has a happy hour in the early evenings and discounts can be up to 50% off for house pours and drafts. Most of the disco and entertainment clubs charge covers, but they will usually include one drink. Hooray for ladies' nights—at least 1 night during the week—when those of the feminine persuasion get in for free.

**DRESS CODE** Many clubs will require smart casual attire. Feel free to be trendy, but stay away from shorts, T-shirts, sneakers, and torn jeans. Be forewarned that you may be turned away if not properly dressed. Many locals dress up for a night on the town, usually in elegant garb or fashionista threads.

**SAFETY** You'll be fairly safe out during the wee hours in most parts of the city, and even a single woman alone has little to worry about. Occasionally, groups of young men may catcall, but by and large those groups are not hanging out in the more cosmopolitan areas. You can always get home safely in a taxi, which fortunately isn't too hard to find even late at night, with one exception: When Boat Quay clubs close, there's usually a mob of revelers scrambling for cabs. (Note that after midnight, a 50% surcharge is added to the fare, so make sure you don't drink away your ride home!)

## THE BAR & CLUB SCENE

Singaporeans love to go out at night, whether it's to lounge around in a cozy wine bar or to jump around on a dance floor until 3am. And this city has become pretty eclectic in its entertainment choices, so you'll find everything from live jazz to acid jazz, from polished cover bands to internationally acclaimed guest DJs. The nightlife is happening. Local celebrities and the young, wealthy, and beautiful are the heroes of the scene, and their quest for the "coolest" spot keeps the club scene on its toes.

### BARS

**Anywhere Music Pub**    This perennial favorite has weathered fashion trends and the economic crisis to become one of the oldest and most established bars in the city. Resident band Tania plays pop and rock covers to packed crowds Monday through Saturday. It's a casual joint, come as you are, and a mixed crowd of mostly 30s and up, locals and foreign expatriates. Hours are Sunday to Thursday 6pm to 2am, Friday and Saturday 6pm to 3am. Happy hours are held on weekdays 6 to 9pm. 19 Tanglin Rd. #04-08/08, Tanglin Shopping Centre. ✆ 65/6734-8233.

**Brix**    In the basement of the Grand Hyatt Regency, Brix has inherited the spot once reserved for Brannigan's, a rowdy upmarket watering hole and pickup joint. Grand Hyatt decided to clean up its act, and had Brix move in instead. Decidedly more sophisticated than its predecessor, Brix has a new air of class, but somehow lacks a certain seedy spontaneity. Still, it's a nice new place on the scene for those who prefer a more discriminating kind of fun. The Music Bar features live jazz and R&B, while the Wine & Whiskey Bar serves up a fine selection of wines, Scotch, and cognacs. Hours are Sunday to Thursday 7pm to 2am, Friday and Saturday 7pm to 3am, and there is a nightly happy hour from 7 to 9pm. Basement, Grand Hyatt Singapore, 10–12 Scotts Rd. ✆ 65/6416-7108. Cover charge Thurs, Fri, and Sat S$20 (US$12).

**Carnegie's**    Carnegie's rocks. Here's the place where you'll hear rowdy old favorites to make the room shake from dancing and roar with singing, everything from the latest hot pop songs to cheesy old *Grease* medleys, disco, and drinking favorites. Time was, the rowdier girls would jump up on the bar to dance (including yours truly), but a recent controversial law banning bartop dancing in the city has put a damper on that (at least for now). It's a great time, but it's also a notorious *ang moh* place (*ang moh* being Hokkien for Westerners), so don't count on rubbing elbows with too many locals here. On busy nights sometimes the doorman will charge 10 bucks to let you jump the line. Hours are Sunday to Thursday 11am to midnight, Friday and Saturday 11am to 3am. There is a happy hour daily 11am to 9pm and a crazy hour 6 to 7pm except Saturday and Sunday. 44–45 Pekin St., #01-01 Far East Sq. (C) **65/6534-0850.**

**The Crazy Elephant**   Crazy Elephant is the city's address for blues rock. Hang out in cooling breezes blowing off the river while listening to classic rock and blues by resident bands. This place has hosted, in addition to some excellent local and regional guitarists, international greats such as Rick Derringer, Eric Burdon, and Walter Trout. It's an unpretentious place to chill out and have a cold one. Beer is reasonably priced as well. Hours are Sunday to Thursday 5pm to 1am, Friday and Saturday 5pm to 2am, with daily happy hour 5 to 9pm. 3E River Valley Rd., #01-06/07 Traders Market, Clarke Quay. (C) **65/6337-1990.**

**The Fat Frog Café**   More a cafe than a bar, Fat Frog draws folks who prefer conversation without intrusive music. The patio at the back of this place stays quiet in the afternoons, and at night fills up, but rarely becomes overcrowded. The main attraction is its location—behind the Substation, a hub for Singapore's visual and performing-arts scene, making this place a good stop after a show. Sometimes you can even run into performers and other majors from the local scene. Inside you'll find a bulletin board promoting current shows, performances, and openings. Around the patio courtyard walls local painters contribute mural work to the decor. There is a limited menu available. Hours are Sunday to Thursday 11:30am to midnight, Friday and Saturday 11:30am to 1am. 45 Armenian St. (behind the Substation). (C) **65/6338-6201.**

**Hard Rock Cafe**   The Hard Rock Cafe in Singapore is like the Hard Rock Cafe in your hometown. You probably don't go to that one, so don't bother spending your vacation time in this one either. Not that it's all bad—the Filipino bands are usually pretty good and, of course, so are the burgers. Other than that it's not much more than a tourist pickup joint. Bring mace. Hours are Sunday to Thursday 11am to 2am, Friday and Saturday 11am to 3am. Happy hour is daily 4 to 6pm and again Sunday from 10:30pm to 2am. #02-01 HPL House, 50 Cusacaden Rd. (C) **65/6235-5232.** Cover S$23 (US$14) Fri–Sat only (includes 1st drink). Sun–Mon 1 drink minimum charge.

**IndoChine**   Richly atmospheric, with graceful Southeast Asian decor, this fashionable lounge drips with exotic charm. Seating areas feel almost like cushiony opium dens, with low benches piled with pillows surrounding small candlelit tables. Music is moody and not too loud to talk over. This is a good place to start exploring all the watering holes along Club Street, and there are a few, all of them pretty hip. Open Monday through Thursday noon to 2:30pm and 6:30 to 10:30pm; Friday to Saturday noon to 2:30pm and 6:30 to 11:30pm. Closed Sundays. 49 Club St. (C) **65/6323-0503.**

**JJ Mahoney**   If you're looking for a real bar-type bar, JJ Mahoney comes pretty close. You have the tile floor, the dark wood bar and paneling, stools lining the sides, and everyday people sidling up for another round. The first floor is a nice place to hang out and meet people (until about 10:30pm, when the band kicks in with contemporary but rather loud music), and will broadcast soccer games from time to time. The second floor, up a wide hardwood staircase, has small tables where you can order drinks and play games like Scrabble, Yahtzee, chess, and checkers. The third floor is reserved for KTV, a karaoke lounge where you can sing without worrying about con-women hitting you up for overpriced and watered-down drinks. Hours are Sunday to Thursday 5pm to 1am, Friday and Saturday and the eve of public holidays 5pm to 2am. Happy hour is held nightly 5 to 8pm. 58 Duxton Rd. © 65/6225-6225.

**The Long Bar**   Here's a nice little gem of a bar, even if it is touristy and expensive. With tiled mosaic floors, large shuttered windows, electric fans, and punkah fans moving in waves above, Raffles Hotel has tried to retain much of the charm of yesteryear, so you can enjoy a Singapore Sling in its birthplace and take yourself back to when history was made. And truly, the thrill at the Long Bar is tossing back one of these sweet juicy drinks while pondering the Singapore adventures of all the famous actors, writers, and artists who came through here in the first decades of the 20th century. If you're not inspired by the poetry of the moment, stick around and get juiced for the pop/reggae band at 9pm, which is quite good. Hours are Sunday to Thursday 11am to 1am, Friday and Saturday 11am to 2am. Happy hour is nightly 6 to 9pm, with special deals on pitchers of beer and some mixed drinks. A Singapore Sling is S$18 (US$11), and a Sling with souvenir glass costs S$28 (US$17). Raffles Hotel Arcade, Raffles Hotel, 1 Beach Rd. © 65/6337-1886.

**Muddy Murphys**   This is one of a few Irish bars in Singapore. It's a favorite sports hangout, with big-screen viewing of international soccer and rugby matches and live bands on weekends (otherwise Irish music plays in the background). The ambience is created by the mostly Irish imported trappings around the place. Occasionally there will even be an Irish band. There is a limited menu for lunch, dinner, and snacks. Hours are Sunday to Thursday 11am to 1am, Friday and Saturday 11am to 3am. Happy hour is daily 11am to 7:30pm (happy hour begins earlier than at other places, but the discount is not as great). #B1-01/01-06 Orchard Hotel Shopping Arcade, 442 Orchard Rd. © 65/6735-0400.

**The Next Page**   Few bars stand out for ambience like The Next Page, which is a freaky Chinese dream in an old Singaporean shophouse. Creep through the front door into the main room, its old walls of crumbling stucco washed in sexy Chinese red, and lanterns glowing crimson in the air shaft rising above the island bar. The crowd is mainly young professionals who by late night have been known to dance on the bar (and not only on weekends). The back has a bit more space for seating, darts, and a pool table. There is a small snack menu available. Open daily 3pm to 3am; happy hour is daily 3 to 9pm. 17 Mohamed Sultan Rd. © 65/6235-6967.

**No. 5**   Down Peranakan Place there are a few bars, one of which is No. 5, a cool, dark place just dripping with Southeast Asian ambience, from its old shophouse exterior to its partially crumbling interior walls hung with rich wood carvings. The hardwood floors and beamed ceilings are complemented by seating areas cozied with Oriental carpets and kilim throw pillows. Upstairs is more conventional table-and-chair seating. The glow of the skylighted air shaft and the whirring fans above make this an ideal place to stop for a cool drink on a hot afternoon. In the evenings, be prepared for a lively mix of people. Open Monday to Thursday noon to 2am, Friday and Saturday noon to 3am, Sunday 5pm to 2am. Happy hour is daily noon to 9pm. 5 Emerald Hill. © 65/6732-0818.

## MICROBREWERIES

**Brewerkz**   Brewerkz, with outside seating along the river and an airy contemporary style inside—like a giant IKEA warehouse built around brewing kettles and copper pipes—brews the best house beer in Singapore. The bar menu features five tasty brew selections from recipes created by their English brew master: Nut Brown Ale, Red Ale, Wiesen, Bitter, and Indian Pale Ale (which, by the way, has the highest alcohol content). The American cuisine lunch, dinner, and snack menu is also very good—I recommend planning a meal here as well. Open Sunday to Thursday 5pm to 1am, Friday and Saturday 5pm to 3am. Happy hour is held daily 3 to 9pm with two-for-one beers. #01-05 Riverside Point, 30 Merchant Rd. © 65/6438-7438.

## JAZZ BARS

**Harry's**   The official after-work drink stop for finance professionals from nearby Shenton Way, Harry's biggest claim to fame is that it was bank-buster Nick Leeson's favorite bar. But don't let the power ties put you off. Harry's is a cool place, from airy riverside seating, to cozy tables next to the stage. Harry's is known for its live jazz and R&B music, which is always good. Of all the choices along Boat Quay, Harry's remains the most classy; and even though it's also the most popular, you can usually get a seat. Upstairs, the wine bar is very laid-back, with plush sofas and dimly lit seating areas. It's the hottest hub for musicians and other artiste-types. Open Sunday to Thursday 11am to 1am, Friday and Saturday 11am to 2am. Happy hour is daily 11am to 9pm. 28 Boat Quay. © 65/6538-3029.

**Raffles Bar & Billiards**   Talk about a place rich with the kind of elegance only history can provide. Raffles Bar & Billiards began as a bar in 1896 and over the decades has been transformed to perform various functions as the hotel's needs dictated. In its early days, legend has it that a patron shot the last tiger in Singapore under a pool table here. Whether or not the tiger part is true, one of its two billiards tables is an original piece, still in use after 100 years. In fact, many of the fixtures and furniture here are original Raffles antiques, including the lights above the billiards tables and the scoreboards, and are marked with small brass placards. In the evenings, a jazzy little trio shakes the ghosts out of the rafters, while from 6pm to 1am nightly people lounge around enjoying single malts, cognacs, coffee, port, champagne, chocolates, and imported cigars. Expect to drop a small fortune. Open daily 11:30am to 12:30am. Raffles Hotel, 1 Beach Rd. © 65/6331-1746.

**Round Midnight**   Here's a great little hole in the wall. This place opens late but stays open through the wee hours. Hosting a live band nightly, the real fun starts after hours, when Singapore's professional musicians finish their gigs at other bars and come here to hang out and jam for the rest of the night. It gets packed on weekends with a who's who of the local live music scene. It has absolutely no atmosphere to speak of, which is a refreshing change from Singapore's typically overly style-conscious clubs. It gets crowded and smoky, but people are friendly, especially if you want to talk about music. Open daily 10pm to 6am. 43A Cuppage Terrace © 65/9715-8721.

## CLUBS

**Bar None**   In Singapore's trendy club scene, nightclubs have been known to come and go. Bar None is one place that has enjoyed steady success, probably because it does a great job keeping up with its patrons' needs, with regularly scheduled theme parties and comedy nights. Resident band Energy is the best club band in town, playing a high-voltage mix of R&B, Top 40, and rock. Be prepared to line up to get in on weekends. Hours are Tuesday to Sunday 7pm to 3am, Monday 7pm to 2am. Happy hour is 7 to 9pm. Basement, Marriott Hotel, 320 Orchard Rd. © 65/6831-4656. Cover Fri–Sat S$26 (US$15), includes 1 drink.

**China Jump Bar & Grill** China Jump combines a disco, bar, and restaurant—sounds tame, but this place has been known to hop. It's especially famous for its Wednesday "Babe Central Night" that draws hordes of women after office hours. On any night, however, you can count on a fun crowd, dancing to pop and dance music. Restaurant cuisine is a passable American and Mexican grill offering, with huge portions. Open daily 5pm to 3am. No happy hour. 30 Victoria St., #B1-07/08 CHIJMES Fountain Court. ✆ 65/6338-9388. Cover Wed Ladies' Night, men pay S$18 (US$11). Cover Fri–Sat S$18 (US$11) for everybody.

**Thumper** Every time I update this book, there's a New Hot Spot which is full of spark, but by the time I make my next update it has either fallen asleep or is gone. Introducing Thumper, the latest "it" club. It does have one timeless feature, a really nice outdoor terrace for happy hour cocktails as the sun sets over Scotts Road. In the early evenings, you'll hear live soul singers, and later in the evening a live funk band gets the dance floor moving. Special events and parties happen a lot at the latest "it" places, and celebrities are known to pop in from time to time. At least until the next "it" club . . . until then, enjoy the scene. Open daily 11am to 3am. There is a happy hour daily 11am to 9pm. 76 Robertson Quay, Evason Hotel. ✆ 65/6333-8117. Cover S$28 (US$17).

**Top Ten** It's the most notoriously sleazy joint in Singapore, and throws a wild party every night of the week. The huge space is like an auditorium, with multilevel loungy seating areas looking down onto one of Singapore's best soundstages and dance floors. A cover band plays three sets of pop and rock 7 days a week, but people don't come here for the decor or the music: Top Ten is a pickup joint for Thai working girls. Other clubs in the building, called Orchard Towers, host ladies from other parts of the region, which is how the building got its unofficial name . . . Four Floors of Whores. No joke. Open daily 5pm to 3am with a happy hour daily 9 to 11pm. #04-35/36 Orchard Towers, 400 Orchard Rd. ✆ 65/6732-3077. Cover Fri–Sat S$18 (US$11), includes 1 drink.

**Zouk/Phuture/Velvet Underground** Singapore's first innovative danceteria, Zouk introduced the city to house music, which throbs nightly in its cavernous disco, comprised of three warehouses joined together. Zouk plays the best in modern music, so even if you're not much of a groover you can still have fun watching the party from the many levels that tower above the dance floor. If you need a bit more intimacy in your nightlife, Velvet Underground, within the Zouk complex, drips in red velvet and soft lighting—a good complement to the more soulful sounds spinning here. The newer addition to Zouk, Phuture, draws a younger, more hip-hop-loving crowd than VU. Including the wine bar outside, Zouk is basically your one-stop shopping for a party; in Singapore, this place is legendary. All clubs are open daily 6pm to 3am. Jiak Kim St. ✆ 65/7638-2988. Call for cover charges. Payment of highest cover charge among the 3 clubs in the complex allows admission to the other clubs; otherwise, additional charges will be incurred when moving between clubs.

## CABARET

**Boom Boom Room** Singapore's fun night out with female impersonators and somewhat bawdy vaudeville-style acts. Local TV stars Kumar and Leena perform regularly, in elaborate costumes, to Japanese and Bollywood hits in between bawdy jokes and audience participation. Drinks are moderately priced. Open only on Fridays and Saturdays 8:30pm to 3am. The show starts around 11pm. 130–132 Amoy St., Far East Sq., ✆ 65/6435-0030. Cover S$25 (US$16).

## GAY NIGHTSPOTS

Singapore's gay clubbing scene is alive and well, but still very underground. Bars come and go, so to get the absolute latest happenings you'll have to go beyond mainstream media. The Web has listings at www.utopia-asia.com, where you'll find the best updated information about the most recent parties and hangouts. For the latest info, I'd recommend one of the chat rooms suggested at the address above, and talk to the experts. Velvet Underground, part of the Zouk complex (see above), welcomes a mixed clientele of gays, lesbians, and straight folks.

## WINE BARS

**Beaujolais**   This little gem of a place, in a shophouse built on a hill, is smaller than small, but its charm makes it a favorite for loyal regulars. Two tables outside (on the Five-Foot-Way, which serves more as a patio than a sidewalk) and two tables inside doesn't seem like much room, but there's more seating upstairs. The owners believe that wine should be affordable, and so their many labels tend to be more moderately priced per glass and bottle. Hours are Monday through Friday 11am to midnight and Saturday 6pm to midnight. Happy hour is held from opening until 9pm. 1 Ann Siang Hill. © 65/6224-2227.

**Que Pasa**   One of the more mellow stops along Peranakan Place, this little wine bar serves up a collection of some 70 to 100 labels with plenty of atmosphere and a nice central location. It's another bar in a shophouse, but this one has as its centerpiece a very unusual winding stairway up the air shaft to the level above. Wine bottles and artwork line the walls. In the front you can order Spanish-style finger food—tapas, anyone?—and cigars. The VIP club on the upper floor has the look and feel of a formal living room, complete with wing chairs and board games. Hours are Sunday to Thursday 6pm to 2am, Friday and Saturday 6pm to 3am. 7 Emerald Hill. © 65/6235-6626.

## THE PERFORMING ARTS

The **Singapore Symphony Orchestra** (www.sso.org.sg) performs regularly in its new home at Esplanade—Theatres on the Bay (www.esplanade.com), with regular special guest appearances by international celebrities. The **Singapore Lyric Opera** (Stamford Arts Centre, 155 Waterloo St. #03-06; © 65/6336-1929), also appears regularly. The **Singapore Chinese Orchestra,** the only professional Chinese orchestra in Singapore, has won several awards for its classic Chinese interpretations. It performs every 2 weeks at a variety of venues (including outdoor concerts at the Botanic Gardens). Information is available through People's Association, Block B, Room 5, No. 9 Stadium Link (© 65/6440-3839). Ticket sales are handled by Sistic (© 65/6348-5555; www.sistic.com.sg).

## THEATER

Most international companies will perform at the new **Esplanade—Theatres on the Bay** (1 Esplanade Dr., 10-min. walk from City Hall MRT; © 65/6828-8222; www.esplanade.com). For local theater, the best are **ACTION Theatre** (42 Waterloo St.; © 65/6837-0842), **The Necessary Stage** (126 Cairnhill Arts Centre, Cairnhill Rd.; © 65/6738-6355), and the **Singapore Repertory Theatre** (DBS Arts Centre, 20 Merbau Rd., Robertson Quay; © 65/6733-0005).

   **Chinese Theatre Circle** (#5 Smith St.; © 65/6323-4862), stages 2-hour Cantonese opera shows on Fridays and Saturdays with excerpts from the most famous tales and explanations of the craft. Come at 7pm for the 2-hour show with dinner, or at 8pm to catch the last half with tea only. If you come for the dinner, don't expect anything special—it's basically chicken nuggets. Tickets are S$35 (US$21) for the former and S$20 (US$12) for the latter.

At **Malay Village** (39 Geylang Serai; 🕿 **65/6748-4700**), every Saturday and Sunday at 5pm (except during the fasting month of Ramadan), Indo-Malay dancers perform in traditional costume accompanied by a live gamelan orchestra. The times I've been, I've seen more locals than tourists.

# 9

# Malaysia

*by Jennifer Eveland*

Compared with spicy Thailand to the north and cosmopolitan Singapore to the south, Malaysia is a relative secret to many from the West, and most travelers to Southeast Asia skip over it, opting for more heavily traversed routes.

Boy, are they missing out. Those who venture here wander through streets awash with international influences from colonial times and trek through mysterious rainforests and caves, sometimes without another tourist in sight. They relax peacefully under palms on lazy white beaches that fade into blue, blue waters. They spy the bright colors of batik sarongs hanging to dry in the breeze. They hear the melodic drone of the Muslim call to prayer seeping from exotic mosques. They taste culinary masterpieces served in modest local shops—from Malay with its deep mellow spices to succulent seafood punctuated by brilliant chile sauces. In Malaysia, I'm always thrilled to witness life without the distracting glare of the tourism industry, and I leave impressed by how accessible Malaysia is to outsiders while remaining true to its heritage.

Malaysia just doesn't get the tourism press it deserves, but it's not because foreign travelers aren't welcome. True, the Malaysian Tourism Board has almost no international advertising campaign—and you'll be hard-pressed to get any useful information out of them—but everyone from government officials in Kuala Lumpur to boat hands in Penang seems delighted to see the smiling face of a traveler who has discovered just how beautiful their country is.

I'm going to cover the major destinations of peninsular Malaysia. We begin with the country's capital, **Kuala Lumpur,** then tour the peninsula's west coast—the cities of **Malacca (Melaka),** plus islands like the popular **Penang** and luxurious **Langkawi.** My coverage also includes **Taman Negara National Park,** peninsular Malaysia's largest national forest. Finally, we cross the South China Sea to the island of **Borneo,** where the Malaysian states of **Sarawak** and **Sabah** feature Malaysia's most impressive forests as well as unique and diverse cultures.

Malaysia is accessible to the rest of the world through its international airport in Kuala Lumpur. Or if you want to hop from another country in the region, daily flights to Malaysia's many smaller airports give you access to all parts of the country, and you can also travel by car, bus, or train from Singapore or Thailand.

## 1 Getting to Know Malaysia

Malaysia's territory covers peninsular Malaysia—bordering Thailand in the north just across from Singapore in the south—and two states on the island of Borneo, Sabah and Sarawak, approximately 240km (150 miles) east across the South China Sea. All 13 of its states total 329,749 sq. km. (127,316 sq. miles)

# Peninsular Malaysia

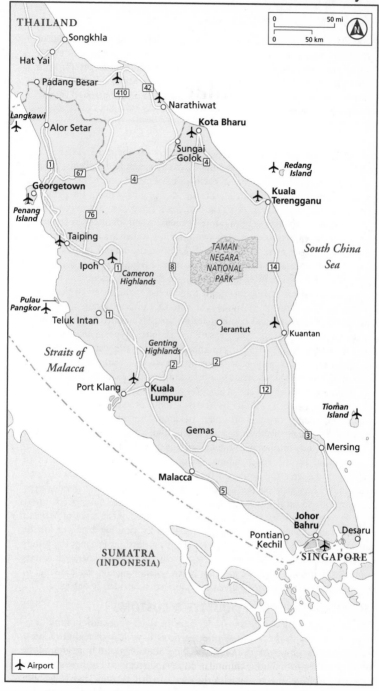

THAILAND

Songkhla

Hat Yai

Padang Besar

410   42

Narathiwat

Langkawi

Alor Setar

Kota Bharu

Sungai Golok

4

1   67   4

Redang Island

Georgetown

Penang Island

76

Kuala Terengganu

Taiping

Ipoh

1   Cameron Highlands

8

TAMAN NEGARA NATIONAL PARK

14

*South China Sea*

Pulau Pangkor

Teluk Intan

1

Genting Highlands

Jerantut

Kuantan

*Straits of Malacca*

2   2

Port Klang

Kuala Lumpur

12

Tioman Island

Gemas

3

Mersing

Malacca

5

Johor Bahru

Desaru

SUMATRA (INDONESIA)

Pontian Kechil

SINGAPORE

0        50 mi
0        50 km

✈ Airport

> **Tips  Abbreviating Malaysia**
>
> The first tip here is that people are always abbreviating Kuala Lumpur to KL. Okay, that's pretty obvious. But these people will abbreviate everything else they can get away with. So, Johor Bahru becomes JB, Kota Bharu KB, Kota Kinabalu KK—you get the picture. Malaysia itself is often shortened to M'sia. To make it easier for you, the only shortened version I've used in this book is KL.

of land. Of this area Peninsular Malaysia makes up about 132,149 sq. km. (51,023 sq. miles) and contains 11 of Malaysia's 13 states: Kedah, Perlis, Penang, and Perak are in the northwest; Kelantan and Terengganu are in the northeast; Selangor, Negeri Sembilan, and Melaka are about midway down the peninsula on the western side; Pahang, along the east coast, sprawls inward to cover most of the central area (which is mostly forest preserve); and Johor covers the entire southern tip from east to west, with two vehicular causeways linking it to Singapore, just over the Strait of Johor. Kuala Lumpur, the nation's capital, appears on a map to be located in the center of the state of Selangor, but it is actually a federal district similar to Washington, D.C., in the United States.

Tropical evergreen forests, estimated to be some of the oldest in the world, cover more than 70% of Malaysia. The country's diverse terrain allows for a range of forest types, such as montane forests, sparsely wooded tangles at higher elevations; lowland forests, the dense tropical jungle type; mangrove forests along the waters' edge; and peat swamp forest along the waterways. On the peninsula, three national forests—Taman Negara (or "National Forest") and Kenong Rimba Park, both inland, and Endau Rompin National Park, located toward the southern end of the peninsula—welcome visitors regularly, for quiet nature walks to observe wildlife or hearty adventures like white-water rafting, mountain climbing, caving, and jungle trekking. Similarly, the many national forests of Sabah and Sarawak provide a multitude of memorable experiences, which can include brushes with the indigenous peoples of the forests.

Surrounded by the South China Sea on the east coast and the Strait of Malacca on the west, the waters off the peninsula vary in terms of sea life (and beach life). The waters off the east coast house a living coral reef, good waters, and gorgeous tropical beaches, while more southerly parts host beach resort areas. By way of contrast, the surf in southern portions of the Strait of Malacca is choppy and cloudy from shipping traffic—hardly ideal for diving or for the perfect Bali Hai vacation. But once you get as far north as Penang, the waters become beautiful again. Meanwhile, the sea coast of Sabah and Sarawak counts numerous resort areas that are ideal for beach vacationing and scuba diving. In fact, one of the world's top 10 dive sites is located at Sipadan in Sabah.

## MALAYSIA'S PEOPLE, ETIQUETTE & CUSTOMS

The mix of cultural influences in Malaysia is the result of centuries of immigration and trade with the outside world, particularly with Arab nations, China, and India. Early groups of incoming foreigners brought wealth from around the world, plus their own unique cultural heritages and religions. Furthermore, once imported, each culture remained largely intact; that is, none has truly been homogenized. Traditional temples and churches exist side by side with mosques.

Likewise, **traditional art forms** of various cultures are still practiced in Malaysia, most notably in the areas of dance and performance art. Chinese opera, Indian dance, and Malay martial arts are all very popular cultural activities. Silat, originating from a martial arts form (and still practiced as such by many), is a dance performed by men and women. Religious and cultural festivals are open for everyone to appreciate and enjoy. Unique arts and traditions of indigenous people distinguish Sabah and Sarawak from the rest of the country.

Traditional **Malaysian music** is very similar to Indonesian music. Heavy on rhythms, its constant drum beats underneath the light repetitive melodies of the stringed gamelan (no relation at all to the Indonesian metallophone gamelan, with its gongs and xylophones), will entrance you with its simple beauty.

Questions of etiquette in Malaysia are very similar to those in Singapore, so please see chapter 8 for more information.

## 2 Planning Your Trip to Malaysia

The **Malaysia Tourism Board (MTB)** (www.tourismmalaysia.gov.my) can provide some information by way of pamphlets and advice before your trip, but keep in mind it is not as sophisticated as the Singapore Tourism Board. Much of the information it provides is vague, broad-stroke descriptions with few concrete details that are useful for the traveler—a lot of it quite outdated.

Within Malaysia, each state or tourist destination has its own tourism board that operates a website and local offices for tourist information. These are your best bets, as they have on-the-ground knowledge that's more current. For each destination, I have provided websites, telephone contacts, and locations of information offices.

## ENTRY REQUIREMENTS

To enter the country you must have a valid passport. Citizens of the United States do not need visas for tourism and business visits, and upon entry are granted a Social/Business Visit Pass good for up to 3 months. Citizens of Canada, Australia, New Zealand, and the United Kingdom can also enter the country without a visa, and will be granted up to 30 days pass upon entry. For other countries, please consult the nearest Malaysian consulate before your trip for visa regulations. Also, note that travelers holding Israeli passports are not permitted to travel within Malaysia (likewise, Malaysians are forbidden from traveling to Israel).

For information on obtaining a passport, please see "Passports" in the "Fast Facts" section in chapter 3.

If you are arriving from an area in which yellow fever has been reported, you will be required to show proof of yellow fever vaccination. Contact your nearest MTB office to research the specific areas that fall into this category.

## CUSTOMS REGULATIONS

With regard to currency, you can bring into the country as many foreign currency notes or traveler's checks as you please, but you are not allowed to leave the country with more foreign currency or traveler's checks than you had when you arrived.

Social visitors can enter Malaysia with 1 liter of hard alcohol and one carton of cigarettes without paying duty—anything over that amount is subject to local taxes. Prohibited items include firearms and ammunition, daggers and knives, and pornographic materials. Be advised that, similar to Singapore, Malaysia enforces a very strict drug abuse policy that includes the death sentence for convicted drug traffickers.

## MONEY

Malaysia's currency is the **Malaysian ringgit.** Prices are marked as RM (a designation I've used throughout this book). Notes are issued in denominations of RM1, RM2, RM5, RM10, RM20, RM50, RM100, RM500, and RM1,000. One ringgit is equal to 100 sen. Coins come in denominations of 1, 5, 10, 20, and 50 sen, and there's also a 1-ringgit coin.

Following the dramatic decline of the ringgit's value at the start of the East Asian economic crisis, the Malaysian government pegged its currency at an artificial exchange rate to ward off currency speculation. Since then, exchange rates have been a constant RM3.80 to US$1.

**CURRENCY EXCHANGE** Currency can be changed at banks and hotels, but you'll get a more favorable rate if you go to one of the money changers that seem to be everywhere; in shopping centers, in little lanes, and in small stores—just look for signs. They are often men in tiny booths with a lit display on the wall behind them showing the exchange rate. All major currencies are generally accepted, and there is never a problem with the U.S. dollar.

**ATMs** Kuala Lumpur, Penang, and Johor Bahru have quite a few automated teller machines (ATMs) scattered around, but they are few and far between in the smaller towns and nonexistent on smaller islands and remote beach areas. In addition, some ATMs do not accept credit cards or debit cards from your home bank. I have found that debit cards on the MasterCard/Cirrus or Visa/PLUS networks are almost always accepted at **Maybank,** with at least one location in every major town. Cash is dispensed in ringgit deducted from your account at the day's rate.

**TRAVELER'S CHECKS**     Generally, travelers to Malaysia will never go wrong with American Express and Thomas Cook traveler's checks, which can be cashed at banks, hotels, and licensed money changers. Unfortunately, they are often not accepted at smaller shops. Even in some big restaurants and department stores, many cashiers don't know how to process these checks, which might lead to a long and frustrating wait.

**CREDIT CARDS**     Credit cards are widely accepted at hotels and restaurants, and at many shops as well. Most popular are American Express, MasterCard, and Visa. Some banks may also be willing to advance cash against your credit card, but you have to ask around because this service is not available everywhere.

In Malaysia, to report a lost or stolen card, call **American Express** at its head office in Kuala Lumpur (✆ **03/2050-8888**); for **MasterCard** call ✆ **800/804-594;** and for **Visa** call ✆ **800/800-159.** Both numbers are toll-free from anywhere in the country.

## WHEN TO GO

There are **two peak seasons** in Malaysia, one in winter and another in summer. The peak winter tourist season falls roughly from the beginning of December to the end of January, covering the major winter holidays—Christmas, New Year's Day, Chinese New Year. Hari Raya Puasa, celebrating the end of Ramadan, shifts dates from year to year. If you plan to travel to Malaysia between November and January, I highly recommend calling MTB to find out exactly when this holiday will fall.

Singapore's school holidays occur from mid-May through to the end of June, and again during November and December, when families are likely to flock to Malaysia's seaside resorts, particularly the budget and midpriced properties. I hate to say it, but I've heard numerous complaints about resort holidays that have become nightmares when guests have to wrestle to get to the breakfast buffet and must suffer screaming children around the pool. Malaysia's school holidays fall about 1 or 2 weeks each during March, June, and August, then again from November through December.

The peak summer season falls in the months of June, July, and August, and can last into mid-September. During this period hotels are booked solid with families from the Middle East as this is school holiday season for many of the region's countries. After September it's quiet again until December. Both seasons experience approximately equal tourist traffic, but in summer months that traffic may ebb and flow.

**CLIMATE**     Climate considerations will play a role in your plans. If you want to visit any of the east coast resort areas, the low season is between November and March, when the monsoon tides make the water too choppy for watersports and beach activities. During this time many island resorts will close. On the west coast, the rainy season is from April through May, and again from October through November.

The temperature is basically static year-round. Daily averages are between 67°F and 90°F (19°C and 32°C). Temperatures in the hill resorts get a little cooler, averaging 67°F (19°C) during the day and 50°F (10°C) at night.

**HOLIDAYS**   During Malaysia's official public holidays, expect government offices to be closed, as well as some shops and restaurants, depending on the ethnicity of the shop owner or restaurant owner. During **Hari Raya Puasa** and **Chinese New Year** you can expect many shop and restaurant closings. However, look out for special sales and celebrations. Also count on public parks, shopping malls, and beaches to be more crowded during public holidays, as locals will be taking advantage of their time off.

Official public holidays fall as follows: New Year's Day (Jan 1), Hari Raya Haji (Jan 10 and Dec 31, 2006; and Dec 20, 2007), Chinese New Year (Jan 29, 2006; and Feb 18, 2007), Wesak Day (May 22, 2005; May 12, 2006; and May 1, 2007), Prophet Muhammad's Birthday (Jun 26), National Day (Aug 31), Hari Raya Aidi Fitri (also called Hari Raya Puasa, Nov 3, 2005; Oct 24, 2006; and Oct 13, 2007), Deepavali (Nov 1, 2005; Oct 21, 2006; and Nov 9, 2007), and Christmas (Dec 25). In addition, each state has a public holiday to celebrate the birthday of the state sultan.

## HEALTH

The **tap water** in Kuala Lumpur is supposedly potable, but I don't recommend drinking it—in fact, I don't recommend drinking tap water anywhere in Malaysia. Bottled water is inexpensive enough and readily available at convenience stores and food stalls. Food prepared in hawker centers is generally safe—I have yet to experience trouble and I'll eat almost anywhere. If you buy fresh fruit, wash it well with bottled water and carefully peel the skin off before eating it.

**Malaria** has not been a major threat in most parts of Malaysia, even Malaysian Borneo. **Dengue fever,** on the other hand, which is also carried by mosquitoes, remains a constant threat in most areas, especially rural parts. Dengue, if left untreated, can cause fatal internal hemorrhaging, so if you come down with a sudden fever or skin rash, consult a physician immediately. There are no prophylactic treatments for dengue; the best protection is to wear plenty of insect repellent. Choose a product that contains DEET or is specifically formulated to be effective in the tropics.

In 2003, SARS seemed to skip right over Malaysia, but avian influenza, or bird flu, did find its way here, particularly in the northern state of Kelantan. The U.S. Centers for Disease Control (CDC) advises travelers to Malaysia to avoid contact with live or raw poultry.

## SAFETY/CRIME

Malaysia has been having a terrible problem with thievery. "Snatch thieves" are becoming bolder and bolder, riding on motorcycles through heavily populated areas in KL, Johor Bahru, and other cities, snatching handbags from women's shoulders. Some victims have been dragged and seriously injured. When you're out, don't wear your handbag on your side that's facing the street, or better yet, don't carry a handbag at all.

The first thing I do when I check into a hotel is put my passport, international tickets, extra cash and travelers checks, plus any credit or ATM card I do not have immediate plans to use, straight into the safe, either in my room or behind the hotel's front desk.

Be careful when traveling on overnight trains and buses where there are great opportunities for theft (many times by fellow tourists, believe it or not). Keep your valuables close to you as you sleep.

For further health and safety information, see chapter 3.

# GETTING THERE
## BY PLANE

Malaysia has six international airports—at Kuala Lumpur, Penang, Langkawi, Kota Kinabalu, Kuching, and Johor Bahru—and 14 domestic airports at locations that include Kota Bharu, Kuantan, and Kuala Terengganu. Specific airport information is listed with coverage of each city.

A passenger service charge, or **airport departure tax,** is levied on all flights. A tax of RM6 ($1.60) for domestic flights and RM45 ($12) for international flights is usually included when you pay for your ticket.

Few Western carriers fly directly to Malaysia. If Malaysian Airlines does not have suitable routes from your home country, you'll have to contact another airline to work out a route that connects. I have found Malaysia Airlines service to be of a very good standard, not to mention they have possibly the lowest rates to Southeast Asia from North American destinations.

**FROM THE UNITED STATES** **Malaysia Airlines** (© 800/552-9264; www.malaysiaairlines.com) flies from Los Angeles and New York.

**FROM CANADA** North American carriers will have to connect with a Malaysian Airlines flight, either in East Asia or in Europe.

**FROM THE UNITED KINGDOM** **Malaysia Airlines** (© 0870/607-9090; www.malaysiaairlines.com) flies from London Heathrow airport to KL, Penang, and Langkawi, with domestic connections from Glasgow, Edinburgh, Teesside, Leeds Bradford, and Manchester. **From Australia, Malaysia Airlines** (© 1300/655-324; www.malaysiaairlines.com) flies directly to Kuala Lumpur from Perth, Adelaide, Brisbane, Sydney, and Melbourne, with an additional direct flight between Perth and Sarawak.

**FROM NEW ZEALAND** **Malaysia Airlines** (© 0800/777-747; www.malaysiaairlines.com) flies a direct route to KL from Auckland.

## BY TRAIN

**FROM SINGAPORE** The **Keretapi Tanah Melayu Berhad (KTM),** Malaysia's rail system, runs express and local trains that connect the cities along the west coast of Malaysia with Singapore to the south and Thailand to the north. Trains depart daily from the **Singapore Railway Station** (© 65/6222-5165), on Keppel Road in Tanjong Pagar, not far from the city center. Trains to Kuala Lumpur depart daily for fares from S$34 to S$68 (US$20–US$40). The trip takes around 6 hours. Kuala Lumpur's KL Sentral railway station (© 03/2267-1200) is a 10-minute taxi ride from the center of town, and is connected to the Putra LRT, KL Monorail city public transportation trains, and the Express Rail Link (ERL) to Kuala Lumpur International Airport (KLIA).

**FROM THAILAND** KTM's international service departs from the **Hua Lamphong Railway Station** (© 662/223-7010 or 662/223-7020) in Bangkok, with operations to Hua Hin, Surat Thani, Nakhon Si Thammarat, and Hat Yai in Thailand's southern peninsula. The final stop in Malaysia is at Butterworth (Penang), so passage to KL will require you to catch a connecting train onward. The daily service departs at 3:15pm and takes approximately 22 hours from Bangkok to Butterworth. There is no first- or third-class service on this train, only air-conditioned second class; upper birth goes for about $20, and lower is $23.

For a fascinating journey from Thailand, you can catch the **Eastern & Orient Express (E&O),** (www.orient-express.com) which operates a route between

Bangkok, Kuala Lumpur, and Singapore. Traveling in the luxurious style for which the Orient Express is renowned, you'll finish the entire journey in about 42 hours. Compartments are classed as Pullman (approximately $1,730 per person double occupancy), State ($2,570 per person double occupancy), and Presidential ($3,620 per person double occupancy). All fares include meals on the train. Overseas reservations for the E&O Express can be made through a travel agent, or from the United States and Canada call © 631/847-3716 (East Coast) or © 480/595-7602 (West Coast), from Australia © 1800/000-395, and from the United Kingdom © 2078/055-060. From Singapore, Malaysia, and Thailand contact the E&O office in Singapore at © 65/6392-3500.

### BY BUS

From Singapore, there are many bus routes to Malaysia. If you want to travel on land, I personally prefer the bus over the train from Singapore to Kuala Lumpur. Executive coaches operated by **Transnasional** have huge seats that recline, serve a box lunch on board, and show movies. Call Transnasional in Singapore at © **65/6284-7034.** Buses depart from the Lavender Street bus terminal for the 5-hour trip (S$30/US$18 one-way).

Buses to Johor Bahru and Malacca can be picked up at the Ban Sen terminal at the corner of Queen and Arab streets. Call © 65/6292-8149 for buses to Johor Bahru (S$2.40/US$1.40) and © 65/6293-5915 for buses to Malacca (S$11/US$6.30).

**From Thailand,** you can grab a bus in either Bangkok or Hat Yai (in the southern part of the country) heading for Malaysia. I don't recommend the bus trip from Bangkok. It's just far too long a journey to be confined to a bus. You're better off taking the train. From Hat Yai, many buses leave regularly to northern Malaysian destinations, particularly Butterworth (Penang).

### BY TAXI (FROM SINGAPORE)

From the Johor-Singapore bus terminal at Queen and Arab streets, the **Singapore Johor Taxi Operators Association** (© **65/6296-7054**) can drive you to Johor Bahru for S$40 (US$24).

### BY CAR

Major international car rental agencies operating in Singapore will rent cars that you can take over the causeway to Malaysia, but be prepared to pay a small fortune. They're much cheaper if you rent within the country. At Kuala Lumpur International Airport, find **Avis** at Counter B-16 at the arrival hall in the main terminal (© **03/8776-4540**). There's another branch at the international airport in Penang (© **04/643-9633**), or make a booking via www.avis.com.

## GETTING AROUND
### BY PLANE

The modernization of Malaysia has made travel here—whether it's by plane, train, bus, taxi, or self-driven car—easier and more convenient than ever. Malaysia Airlines has service to every major destination within the peninsula and East Malaysia, and now budget carrier AirAsia connects all major towns for cheap. Buses have a massive web of routes between every city and town. Train service up the western coast and out to the east provides even more options. And a unique travel offering—the outstation taxi—is available to and from every city on the peninsula. All the options make it convenient enough for you to plan to hop from city to city and not waste too much precious vacation time.

By and large, all the modes of transportation between cities are reasonably comfortable. Air travel can be the most costly of the alternatives, followed by outstation taxis, then buses and trains.

**Malaysia Airlines** (www.malaysiaairlines.com) links from its hub in Kuala Lumpur to the cities of Johor Bahru, Kota Bharu, Kota Kinabalu, Kuala Terengganu, Kuantan, Kuching, Langkawi, Penang, and other smaller cities not covered in this chapter. Malaysian Airline's national hot line (© **1300/88-3000**) can be dialed from anywhere in the country. Individual airport information is provided in sections for each city that follows. One-way domestic fares can average RM100 to RM372 ($26–$98).

A new budget airline competes with incredibly affordable rates. AirAsia links all the country's major cities with fares that average from RM35 to RM180 ($9.20–$47). Call its KL office at 1300/889-933, or visit the website at www.airasia.com.

Berjaya Air (© 03/2145-8689; www.berjaya-air.com) operates a small fleet of aircraft that services the peninsula's island resorts, with flights that link KL to Pankor, Langkawi, Tioman, and Redang islands with another flight between Singapore and Tioman.

## BY TRAIN

The **Keretapi Tanah Melayu Berhad (KTM)** provides train service throughout peninsular Malaysia. Trains run from north to south between the Thai border and Singapore, with stops between including Butterworth (Penang), Kuala Lumpur, and Johor Bahru. There is a second line that branches off at Gemas, midway between Johor Bahru and KL, and heads northeast to Tempas near Kota Bharu. Fares range from RM64 ($17) for first class between Johor Bahru and KL, to RM158 ($42) for first-class passage between Johor Bahru and Butterworth. Train station information is provided for each city in individual city headings below.

## BY BUS

Malaysia's intercity coach system is extensive and inexpensive, but I don't really recommend it. With the exception of executive coach services between KL and Singapore, which are excellent, standard coaches get dirtier and dirtier each year, maintenance issues are a question mark, and road safety is a roll of the dice. Still, if you must, for each city covered, I've listed bus terminal locations, but scheduling information must be obtained from the bus company itself.

## BY TAXI

You can take special hired cars, called **outstation taxis,** between every city and state on the peninsula. Rates depend on the distance you plan to travel. They are fixed and stated at the beginning of the trip, but many times can be bargained down. In Kuala Lumpur, go to the second level of the Puduraya Bus Terminal to find cabs that will take you outside the city or call the **Kuala Lumpur Outstation Taxi Service Station** (© **03/2078-0213**). A taxi from KL to Malacca will cost you approximately RM140 ($37), KL to Cameron Highlands RM220 ($58), and KL to Butterworth or Johor Bahru RM300 ($79). Outstation taxi stand locations are included under each individual city heading.

Also, within each of the smaller cities, feel free to negotiate with unmetered taxis for hourly, half-day, or daily rates. It's an excellent way to get around for sightseeing and shopping without transportation hassles. Hourly rates are anywhere from RM15 to RM25 ($3.95–$6.60).

## BY CAR

The cities along the west coast of the peninsula are linked by the North-South Highway. There are rest areas with toilets, food outlets, and emergency telephones at intervals along the way. There is also a toll that varies depending on the distance you're traveling.

Driving along the east coast of Malaysia is actually much more pleasant than driving along the west coast. The highway is narrower and older, but it takes you through oil palm and rubber plantations, and the essence of *kampung* Malaysia permeates throughout. As you near villages you'll often have to slow down and swerve past cows and goats, which are really quite oblivious to oncoming traffic. You have to get very close to honk at them before they move.

The speed limit on highways is 110kmph (68 mph). On the minor highways the limit ranges from 70 to 90kmph (43–56 mph). Do not speed, as there are traffic police strategically situated around certain bends.

**Distances between major towns are:** from KL to Johor Bahru, 368km (228 miles); from KL to Malacca, 144km (89 miles); from KL to Kuantan, 259km (161 miles); from KL to Butterworth, 369km (229 miles); from Johor Bahru to Malacca, 224km (139 miles); from Johor Bahru to Kuantan, 325km (202 miles); from Johor Bahru to Mersing, 134km (83 miles); and from Johor Bahru to Butterworth, 737km (457 miles).

**To rent a car in Malaysia,** you must produce a driver's license from your home country that shows you have been driving at least 2 years. There are desks for major car-rental services at the international airports in Kuala Lumpur and Penang, and additional outlets throughout the country (see individual city sections for this information).

## TIPS ON ACCOMMODATIONS

Peak months of the year for hotels in western peninsular Malaysia are December through February and July through September. For the east coast, the busy times are July through September. You will need to make reservations well in advance to secure your room during these months.

**TAXES & SERVICE CHARGES**   All the nonbudget hotels charge a 10% service charge and 5% government tax. As such, there is no need to tip. But bellhops still tend to be tipped at least RM2 (50¢) per bag, and car jockeys or valets should be tipped at least RM4 ($1) or more.

## TIPS ON DINING

Malaysian food seems to get its origins from India's rich curries, influenced by Thailand's herbs and spices. You'll find delicious blends of coconut milk and curry, shrimp paste, and chiles, accented by exotic flavors of galangal (similar to turmeric), lime, and lemon grass. Sometimes pungent, a few of the dishes have a deep flavor from fermented shrimp paste that is an acquired taste for Western palates. By and large, Malaysian food is delicious, but in multicultural Malaysia, so is the Chinese food, the Peranakan food, the Indian food—the list goes on. The Chinese brought their own flavors from their points of origin in the regions of southern China. Teochew, Cantonese, and Szechuan are all styles of Chinese cuisine that you'll find throughout the country. Peranakan food is unique to Malacca, Penang, and Singapore. The Peranakans, or "Straits Chinese," combined local ingredients with some traditional Chinese dishes to create an entirely new culinary form. And Indian food, both northern and southern, can be found in almost every city, particularly in the western part of the peninsula. And, of course, you'll find gorgeous, fresh seafood almost everywhere.

I strongly recommend eating in a hawker stall when you can, especially in Penang, which is famous for its local cuisine.

Also, many Malaysians eat with their hands off banana leaves when they are having *nasi padang* or *nasi kandar* (rice with mixed dishes). This is absolutely acceptable. If you choose to follow suit, wash your hands first and try to use your right hand because the left is considered unclean (traditionally, it's the hand used to wash after a visit to the toilet). While almost all of the food you encounter in a hawker center will be safe for eating, it is advisable to go for freshly cooked hot or soupy dishes. Don't risk the precooked items.

Also, avoid having ice in your drink in the smaller towns because it might come from a dubious water supply. If you ask for water, either make sure it's boiled or buy mineral water.

**TAXES & SERVICE CHARGES**    A 10% service charge and 5% government tax are levied in proper restaurants, but hawkers charge a flat price.

## TIPS ON SHOPPING

Shopping is a huge attraction for tourists in Malaysia. In addition to modern fashions and electronics, there are great local handicrafts. In each city section, I've listed some great places to go for local shopping.

For **handicrafts,** prices can vary. There are many handicraft centers, such as Karyaneka, with outlets in cities all over the country, where goods can be priced a bit higher but where you are assured of good quality. Alternatively, you could hunt out bargains in markets and at roadside stores in little towns, which can be much more fun.

**Batik** is one of the most popular arts in Malaysia, and the fabric can be purchased just about anywhere in the country. Batik can be fashioned into outfits and scarves or purchased as sarongs. Another beautiful Malaysian textile craft is *songket* weaving. These beautiful cloths are woven with metallic threads. Sometimes *songket* cloth is patterned into modern clothing, but usually it is sold as sarongs.

**Traditional woodcarvings** have become popular collectors' items. Carvings by *orang asli* groups in peninsular Malaysia and by the indigenous tribes of Sabah and Sarawak have traditional uses in households or are employed for ceremonial purposes to cast off evil spirits and cure illness. They have become much sought after by tourists.

Malaysia's **pewter products** are famous. Selangor Pewter is the brand that seems to have the most outlets and representation. You can get anything from a picture frame to dinner sets.

Silver designs are very refined, and jewelry and fine home items are still made by local artisans, especially in the northern parts of the peninsula. In addition, craft items such as *wayang kulit* (shadow puppets) and *wau* (colorful Malay kites) make great gifts and souvenirs.

## FAST FACTS: Malaysia

*American Express*   The main office for **American Express** is located in KL at The Weld, 18th floor, Jalan Raja Chulan (✆ **03/2050-0888**).

*Business Hours*   Banks are open from 10am to 3pm Monday through Friday and 9:30 to 11:30am on Saturday. Government offices are open from 8am to 12:45pm and 2 to 4:15pm Monday through Friday and from 8am to 12:45pm on Saturday. Smaller shops like provision stores may open as early as 6 or 6:30am and close as late as 9pm, especially those near the wet markets. Many such stores are closed on Saturday evenings and Sunday afternoons and are busiest before lunch. Other shops are open 9:30am to 7pm. Department stores and shops in malls tend to open later, about 10:30 or 11am till 8:30 or 9pm throughout the week. Note that in Kuala Terengganu and Kota Bharu the weekday runs from Saturday to Wednesday.

*Dentists & Doctors* All hotels and resorts have qualified physicians on call who speak English. These doctors will come directly to your room for treatment. If your condition is serious, he or she can help you to check in to a local hospital. Call © **999** for emergencies.

*Drug Laws* As in Singapore, the death sentence is mandatory for drug trafficking (defined as being in possession of more than 15g of heroin or morphine, 200g of marijuana or hashish, or 40g of cocaine). For lesser quantities you'll be thrown in jail for a very long time and flogged with a cane.

*Electricity* The voltage used in Malaysia is 220–240 volts AC (50 cycles). Three-point square plugs are used, so buy an adapter if you plan to bring any appliances. Also, many larger hotels can provide adapters upon request.

*Embassies* While in Malaysia, should you need to contact an official representative from your home country, the following contact information in Kuala Lumpur can help you out: **United States Embassy,** © 03/2168-5000; **Canadian High Commission,** © 03/2718-3333; **Australian High Commission,** © 03/2146-5555; **New Zealand High Commission,** © 03/2078-2533; and **the British High Commission,** © 03/2148-2122.

*Internet* Service is available to all of the nation, and I have found Internet cafes in the most surprisingly remote places. While the major international hotels will have access for their guests in the business center, charges can be very steep. I used to recommend Internet cafes in each city, but found that these small places came and went overnight, making it impossible for me to provide accurate information for this book. Wherever you are, your best bet is to ask your concierge or the local tourism information office for the best places close by. Usage only costs about RM5 to RM10 ($1.30–$2.65).

*Language* The national language is Malay, or Bahasa Malaysia, although English is widely spoken. Chinese dialects and Tamil are also spoken.

*Liquor Laws* Liquor is sold in pubs and supermarkets in all big cities, or in provision stores. If you're going to an island, your resort will have limited alcohol selections, otherwise bring your own. In Terengganu and Kelantan, liquor is strictly limited to a handful of Chinese restaurants. A recent ruling requires pubs and other nightspots to officially close by 1am nationwide, but there are places in KL that stay open until later.

*Newspapers & Magazines* English-language papers the *New Straits Times, The Star, The Sun,* and *The Edge* can be bought in hotel lobbies and magazine stands. Of the local KL magazines, *Day & Night* has great listings and local "what's happening" information for travelers.

*Passports* For information on obtaining a passport, please see "Passports" in the "Fast Facts" section in chapter 3.

*Postal Services*  Post office locations in each city covered are provided in each section. Overseas airmail postage rates are as follows: RM.50 (15¢) for postcards and RM1.50 (40¢) for a 100g letter.

*Taxes*  Hotels add a 5% government tax to all hotel rates, plus an additional 10% service charge. Larger restaurants also figure the same 5% tax into your bill, plus a 10% service charge, whereas small coffee shops and hawker stalls don't charge anything above the cost of the meal. While most tourist goods (such as crafts, camera equipment, sports equipment, cosmetics, and select small electronic items) are tax-free, a small, scaled tax is issued on various other goods such as clothing, shoes, and accessories that you'd buy in the larger shopping malls and department stores.

*Telephone*  **To place a call from your home country to Malaysia:** Dial the international access code (011 in the U.S. and Canada, 0011 in Australia, or 00 in the U.K., Ireland, and New Zealand), plus the country code (60), plus the Malaysia area code (Cameron Highlands 5, Desaru 7, Genting Highlands 9, Johor Bahru 7, Kuala Lumpur 3, Kuala Terengganu 9, Kota Bharu 9, Kota Kinabalu 88, Kuantan 9, Kuching 82, Langkawi 4, Malacca 6, Mersing 7, Penang 4, Tioman 9), followed by the six-, seven-, or eight-digit phone number (for example, from the U.S. to Kuala Lumpur, you'd dial 011-60-3/0000-0000).

**To place a direct international call from Malaysia:** Dial the international access code (00), plus the country code of the place you are dialing (U.S. and Canada 1, Australia 61, Republic of Ireland 353, New Zealand 64, U.K. 44), plus the area/city code and the residential number.

**To reach the international operator:** Dial Ⓒ 108.

**To place a call within Malaysia:** You must use area codes if calling between states. Note that for calls within the country, area codes are preceded by a zero (Cameron Highlands 05, Desaru 07, Genting Highlands 09, Johor Bahru 07, Kuala Lumpur 03, Kuala Terengganu 09, Kota Bharu 09, Kota Kinabalu 088, Kuantan 09, Kuching 082, Langkawi 04, Malacca 06, Mersing 07, Penang 04, Tioman 09).

*Television*  Guests in larger hotels will sometimes get satellite channels such as HBO, Star TV, or CNN. Another in-house movie alternative, Vision Four, preprograms videos throughout the day. Local TV stations TV2, TV5, and TV7 show English-language comedies, movies, and documentaries.

*Time*  Malaysia is 8 hours ahead of Greenwich Mean Time, 16 hours ahead of U.S. Pacific Standard Time, 13 ahead of Eastern Standard Time, and 2 hours behind Sydney. It is in the same zone as Singapore. There is no daylight saving time.

*Tipping*  People here don't really tip, except you might want to give your bellhop something. In a nicer hotel, at least RM5 ($1.30) per bag should be fine. In a budget hotel, they'll probably be shocked to be tipped.

*Toilets*  To find a public toilet, ask for the *tandas*. In Malay, *lelaki* is male and *perempuan* is female. Be prepared for pay toilets. Coin collectors sit outside almost every public facility, taking RM20¢ per person, RM30¢ if you want paper. Once inside, you'll find it obvious that the money doesn't go for cleaning crews. Public toilets are pure filth. They smell horrible and the floors are always an inch deep with stagnant water. While most toilets are of the "squatty-potty" variety (a porcelain bowl set into the floor), even if you find a seat-style toilet bowl, the locals always place their feet on the seat to squat! The best toilets are in hotels, upmarket shopping malls, and restaurants.

*Water*   Water in Kuala Lumpur is supposed to be potable, but most locals boil the water before drinking it—and if that's not a tip-off, I don't know what is. I advise against drinking the tap water anywhere in Malaysia. Hotels will supply bottled water in your room. If they charge you for it, expect inflated prices. A 1.5-liter bottle goes for RM7 ($1.85) in a hotel minibar, but RM2 (55¢) at 7-Eleven.

## 3 Kuala Lumpur

Kuala Lumpur (or KL, as it is commonly known) is more often than not a traveler's point of entry to Malaysia. As the capital it is the most modern and developed city in the country, with contemporary high rises and world-class hotels, glitzy shopping malls, and international cuisine.

Today the original city center at **Merdeka Square** is the core of KL's history. Buildings like the Sultan Abdul Samad Building, the Royal Selangor Club, and the Old Kuala Lumpur Railway Station are gorgeous examples of British style peppered with Moorish flavor. South of this area is KL's **Chinatown.** Along Jalan Petaling and surrounding areas are markets, shops, food stalls, and the bustling life of the Chinese community. There's also a **Little India** in KL, around the area occupied by Masjid Jame, where you'll find flower stalls, Indian Muslim and Malay costumes, and traditional items. Across the river you'll find **Lake Gardens,** a large sanctuary that houses Kuala Lumpur's bird park, butterfly park, and other attractions and gardens. Modern Kuala Lumpur is rooted in the city's **Golden Triangle,** bounded by Jalan Ampang, Jalan Tun Razak, and Jalan Imbi. This section is home to most of KL's hotels, office complexes, shopping malls, and sights like the KL Tower and the Petronas Twin Towers, the tallest buildings in the world (until some other country breaks the record).

### VISITOR INFORMATION

In Kuala Lumpur, the Malaysia Tourism Board·has several offices. The largest is at the **MTC,** the **Malaysia Tourist Centre** (see "What to See & Do," later in this chapter; 109 Jalan Ampang; © **03/2164-3929**) and open daily from 7am to midnight. In addition to a tourist information desk, MTC also has a money changer; ATM; tourist police post; travel agent booking for Taman Negara trips, city tours and limited hotel bookings; souvenir shops; an amphitheater; and Transnasional bus ticket bookings.

*Vision KL Magazine* is offered for free in many hotel rooms and has listings for events in KL and around the country, plus ads for restaurants and shops. At newsstands it costs RM6.80 ($1.80).

### GETTING THERE

**BY PLANE**   The **Kuala Lumpur International Airport (KLIA)** (© **03/8776-2000**) is located in Sepang, 53km (33 miles) outside the city. KLIA is a huge complex with business centers, dining facilities, a fitness center, medical services, shopping, post offices, and an airport hotel operated by **Pan Pacific** (© **03/8787-3333**). While there are money changers, they are few and far between, so

# Kuala Lumpur

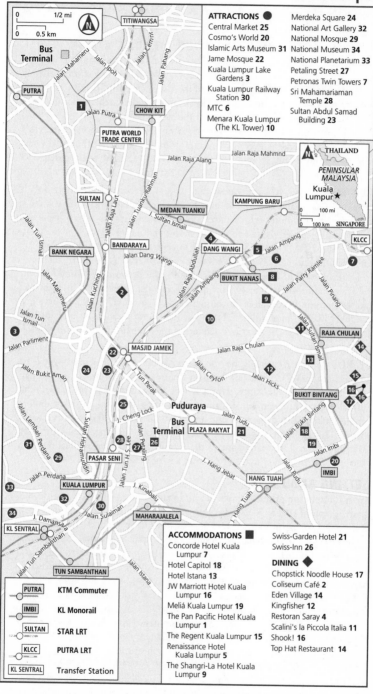

0 1/2 mi
0 0.5 km

Bus Terminal

TITIWANGSA

PUTRA

CHOW KIT

PUTRA WORLD TRADE CENTER

Jalan Putra

Jalan Ipoh

Jalan Mahameru

Jalan Pahang

Jalan Cemnt

Jalan Raja Alang

Jalan Raja Mahmnd

SULTAN

MEDAN TUANKU

KAMPUNG BARU

BANDARAYA

DANG WANGI

Jalan Ampang

KLCC

BANK NEGARA

Jalan Dang Wangi

BUKIT NANAS

Jalan Parry Ramlee

Jalan Pinang

Jalan Tun Ismail

Jalan Kuching

Jalan Tuanku Rahman

Jalan Raja Laut

Jalan Raja Abdullah

Jalan Ampang

Jalan Mahameru

Jalan Tun Ismail

Jalan Parliment

MASJID JAMEK

RAJA CHULAN

Jalan Sultan Ismail

Jalan Raja Chulan

Jalan Bukit Aman

Jalan Ceylon

Jalan Hicks

BUKIT BINTANG

J. Tun Perak

Puduraya Bus Terminal

PLAZA RAKYAT

Jalan Pudu

J. Cheng Lock

Jalan Bukit Bintang

Jalan Imbi

J. Sultan Hishamuddin

Jalan Peeling

PASAR SENI

IMBI

Jalan Lembah Perdana

J. Hang Jebat

Jalan Pudu

Jalan Perdana

KUALA LUMPUR

J. Kinabalu

HANG TUAH

J. Tun Sambanthan

KL SENTRAL

J. Damansa a

Jalan Sulaiman

MAHARAJALELA

J. Hang Tuah

Jalan Istana

TUN SAMBANTHAN

## ATTRACTIONS ●

Central Market 25
Cosmo's World 20
Islamic Arts Museum 31
Jame Mosque 22
Kuala Lumpur Lake Gardens 3
Kuala Lumpur Railway Station 30
MTC 6
Menara Kuala Lumpur (The KL Tower) 10

Merdeka Square 24
National Art Gallery 32
National Mosque 29
National Museum 34
National Planetarium 33
Petaling Street 27
Petronas Twin Towers 7
Sri Mahamariaman Temple 28
Sultan Abdul Samad Building 23

THAILAND

PENINSULAR MALAYSIA

Kuala Lumpur ★

0 100 mi
0 100 km    SINGAPORE

## ACCOMMODATIONS ■

Concorde Hotel Kuala Lumpur 7
Hotel Capitol 18
Hotel Istana 13
JW Marriott Hotel Kuala Lumpur 16
Meliá Kuala Lumpur 19
The Pan Pacific Hotel Kuala Lumpur 1
The Regent Kuala Lumpur 15
Renaissance Hotel Kuala Lumpur 5
The Shangri-La Hotel Kuala Lumpur 9

Swiss-Garden Hotel 21
Swiss-Inn 26

## DINING ◆

Chopstick Noodle House 17
Coliseum Café 2
Eden Village 14
Kingfisher 12
Restoran Saray 4
Scalini's la Piccola Italia 11
Shook! 16
Top Hat Restaurant 14

PUTRA — KTM Commuter
IMBI — KL Monorail
SULTAN — STAR LRT
KLCC — PUTRA LRT
KL SENTRAL — Transfer Station

551

hop on the first line you see, and don't assume there's another one just around the corner.

## GETTING INTO TOWN FROM THE AIRPORT

**BY TAXI**    City taxis are not permitted to pick up fares from the airport, (although you will find illegal gypsy cabs—avoid them!) but **special airport taxis** (© 03/8787-3030) operate round the clock, charging RM88 ($23) for a premier car (Mercedes) and RM63 ($17) for a standard vehicle (locally built Proton). Coupons must be purchased at the arrival concourse.

An **express coach** (© 03/8776-6595) connects KLIA to most of the city's major hotels. Operating every 30 minutes from 5:30am to 10:15pm daily, the trip takes 1 hour and 15 minutes and costs RM20 ($5.25) adult and RM13 ($3.40) child.

**BY TRAIN**    I love KL's shiny new train station, **KL Sentral.** Not only does it serve as a clean, safe, and orderly base from which to take the train, it's also a hub for local commuter train services around the city, it's got tons of facilities, money changers, ATMs, fast food, and shops; and it's got an easy taxi coupon system (about RM7–RM8/$1.85–$2.10 to central parts of the city). Cabs are really easy to find here. For KL Sentral information, call © 03/2267-1200.

The **Express Rail Link** (© 03/2267-8000) runs between KLIA and KL Sentral train station from 5am to 1am daily. Trains depart every 15 minutes and take 28 minutes to complete the journey. Tickets cost RM35 ($9.20) for adults and RM15 ($3.95) for children. From KL Sentral, taxis are always on hand and use a coupon system, or you can catch one of the city's commuter trains to a station near your hotel.

**BY BUS**    If you're arriving on the executive bus from Singapore, you'll be dropped at the MTC (Malaysia Tourism Centre) on Jalan Ampang in the center of town. Three other bus terminals—Puduraya Terminal, on Jalan Pudu; Putra Terminal, on Jalan Tun Ismail; and Pekililing Terminal, on Jalan Ipoh—handle intercity bus departures and arrivals to all parts of the country. If you arrive at Puduraya, the biggest of the three, good luck! It's congested—both with toxic fumes and traffic jams (one of the reasons I avoid standard bus travel in Malaysia). Taxis are not hard to find from any of these terminals.

## GETTING AROUND

Kuala Lumpur is a prime example of a city that was not planned, per se, from a master graph of streets. Rather, because of its beginnings as an outpost, it grew as it needed to, expanding outward and swallowing up suburbs. The result is a tangled web of streets too narrow to support the traffic of a capital city. Cars and buses weave through one-way lanes, with countless motorbikes sneaking in and out, sometimes in the opposite direction of traffic or up on the sidewalks. Expect traffic jams in the morning rush between 6 and 9am, and again between 4 and 7pm. At other times, taxis are a convenient way of getting around, but the commuter train systems, if they're going where you need to, is perhaps the best value and easiest route. City buses are hot and crowded with some very confusing routes. Walking can also be frustrating. Many sidewalks are in poor condition, with buckled tiles and gaping gutters. The heat can be prohibitive as well. However, areas within the colonial heart of the city, Chinatown, Little India, and some areas in the Golden Triangle are within walking distance of each other.

**BY TAXI**    If you ask me, KL cabbies should have their tires slashed. If you can get one to stop, the driver will almost always refuse to use the meter (which is against the law), quoting what seems to be the standard—RM10 ($2.65), usually for a trip that normally costs RM4 ($1.05). If it's raining, expect that quote to double. I usually don't dicker over the price since it's only a buck and a half. It's just frustrating when cab after cab passes you by. In some places within the city, taxi stands try to solve this problem. Be prepared for taxis to pull over, roll down the window and hear the pleas from those waiting in line before deciding upon which passenger to take, regardless of the order of the queue. Somewhere there are numbers to call for taxi booking—what a joke! Maybe they'll show, and maybe they won't. Don't even waste your time. Technically, the metered fare is RM2 (55¢) for the first 2km (1¼ mile) and an additional 10 sen for each 200m after that. Between midnight and 6am you'll be charged an extra 50% of the total fare.

**BY BUS**    I don't recommend travel on city buses. They're cheap but not dependable, with city routes that will get newcomers lost for sure. It's not the most relaxing way to get around.

**BY RAIL**    KL has a network of mass transit trains that snake through the city and out to the suburbs, and it'll be worth your time to become familiar with them, since taxis are sometimes unreliable and traffic jams can be unbearable. Trouble is, there are five train routes and each one is operated by a different company. How confusing! The lines don't seem to connect in any logical way.

The four lines that are most useful to visitors are the **Putra LRT,** the **Star LRT,** the **KL Monorail,** and the **Express Rail Link** to the airport. The latter route is explained under "Getting into Town from the Airport," above.

**Putra LRT** has stops at Bangsar (featured in "Nightlife," later in this section), KL Sentral (train station), Pasar Seni (Chinatown), Masjid Jamek, Dang Wangi, and KLCC shopping center. An average fare would be about RM1.40 (35¢).

The **Star LRT** is only convenient if you need to get to the Putra World Trade Centre. It also stops at Masjid Jamek and Plaza Rayat. An average trip will cost well under RM2 (55¢).

The newly opened **KL Monorail** provides good access through the main hotel and shopping areas of the city, including stops at KL Sentral, Imbi, Bukit Bintang (the main shopping strip), and Raja Chulan (along Jalan Sultan Ismail, where many hotels are). Fares run between RM1.20 and RM2.50 (30¢–65¢).

As a rough guide, all lines operate between 5 or 6am till around midnight, with trains coming every 10 minutes or so. Tickets can be purchased at any station either from the stationmaster or from single-fare electronic ticket booths.

**ON FOOT**    The heat and humidity can make walking between attractions pretty uncomfortable. However, sometimes the traffic is so unbearable that you'll get where you're going much faster by strapping on your tennis shoes and hiking it.

## FAST FACTS: KUALA LUMPUR

The **area code** for Kuala Lumpur is 03, and the city's phone numbers have an 8-digit format. Numbers in the rest of the country only have 7 digits.

The main office for **American Express** is located in KL at The Weld, 18th floor, Jalan Raja Chulan (© **03/2050-0888**). You'll also find headquarters for all Malaysian and many international banks, most of which have outlets along Jalan Sultan Ismail plus ATMs at countless locations throughout the city. Look for money changers in just about every shopping mall; they're a better bargain than banks or hotel cashiers.

KL's **General Post Office** (© 03/2274-1122), on Jalan Sultan Hishamuddin in the enormous Pos Malaysia Komplex Dayabumi, can be pretty overwhelming. If you can, try to use your hotel's mail service for a much easier time. Internet service in KL will run about RM3–RM6 (80¢–$1.60) per hour for usage. Internet cafes come and go, popping up in backpacker areas like Chinatown and the streets around BB Plaza. A combination Internet cafe and business center, Yoshi Connection, is near the MTC at Lot 2.34, 2nd floor, Bangunan Angkasa Raya, Jalan Ampang (© 03/2143-2500).

If you have a medical **emergency,** the number to dial is © **999.** This is the same number for **police and fire emergencies** as well.

## WHERE TO STAY

The hotels I've selected here represent only those properties I think are best for leisure travelers. Even the very expensive hotels I've chosen have qualities that extend beyond the business center. If you plan to travel to KL in July and August and want to stay in an upmarket hotel, you'll need to book your room well in advance. KL's superpeak season falls during these months, when travelers from the Middle East take a break from scorching temperatures back home.

### VERY EXPENSIVE

**The Regent Kuala Lumpur** ⭐⭐⭐    Of the best five-star properties in Kuala Lumpur, nobody delivers first-class accommodations with the finesse of The Regent. A landmark along KL's fashionable Jalan Bukit Bintang shopping strip, The Regent has an ever-bustling lobby to match the excitement along the sidewalks outside—the lobby lounge is filled night and day. Surprisingly, the staff always seems polite and professional despite the barrage. The Regent's guest rooms are spacious, quiet, and cool, with huge plush beds covered in soft cozy cotton sheets and down comforters. Bathrooms are large, marble affairs with plenty of counter space. The outdoor pool is a palm-lined free-form escape, and the fitness center is state of the art, with sauna, steam, spa, and Jacuzzi. During my last stay I noticed the plot next to the hotel may be starting construction of a new, mammoth shopping and apartment complex. Ask about it when you make your booking: Nobody wants to hear driving piles when they're trying to nap.

160 Jalan Bukit Bintang, 55100 Kuala Lumpur. © **800/545-4000** in the U.S. and Canada, 800/022-800 in Australia, 800/440-800 in New Zealand, 800/917-8795 in the U.K., or 03/2141-8000. Fax 03/2142-1441. 468 units. RM600 ($158) double; from RM980 ($258) suite. AE, DC, MC, V. 5 min. walk to Bukit Bintang Monorail station. **Amenities:** 3 restaurants; bar; lobby lounge; outdoor pool; 2 squash courts; 24-hr. fitness center w/Jacuzzi, sauna, steam, and massage; concierge; limo service; business center; 24-hr. room service; babysitting; same-day laundry service/dry cleaning; nonsmoking rooms; executive-level rooms. *In room:* A/C, satellite TV w/in-house movies, minibar, coffee/tea-making facilities, hair dryer, safe.

**Renaissance Kuala Lumpur Hotel** ⭐⭐ (Value)    The Renaissance is terrific value for the money. It's basically two hotels in one: the posh Renaissance and the New World Hotel, its budget neighbor with access to all Renaissance's facilities. Each hotel has its own entrance, connected in the middle where the ballroom and banquet rooms are housed. Guest rooms in the Renaissance Wing have an "official" feel to them—very bold and impressive, and completely European in style. In fact, you'll never know you're in Malaysia. The New World Wing is contemporary, with simpler decor, but is no less comfortable. The enormous outdoor pool, which sits between the two hotel towers, is second only to Shangri-La's.

Corner of Jalan Sultan Ismail and Jalan Ampang, 50450 Kuala Lumpur. © **800/HOTELS-1** in the U.S. and Canada, 800/251-259 in Australia, 800/441-035 in New Zealand, or 03/2162-2233. Fax 03/2163-1122. 910

units. Renaissance Wing RM565–RM595 ($149–$157), from RM955 ($251) suite; New World Wing RM490–RM520 ($129–$137) double, from RM680 ($179) suite. AE, DC, MC, V. 5-min. walk to Bukit Nanas Monorail and Dang Wangi LRT stations. **Amenities:** 3 restaurants; lounge; large landscaped outdoor pool; outdoor lighted tennis court; fitness center w/sauna and massage; concierge; limo service; business center; shopping arcade; salon; 24-hr. room service; babysitting; same-day laundry service/dry cleaning; nonsmoking rooms; executive-level rooms. *In room:* A/C, satellite TV w/in-house movies, minibar, coffee/tea-making facilities, hair dryer, safe.

## EXPENSIVE

**Hotel Istana** ⌾   Fashioned after a Malay palace, Hotel Istana is rich with Moorish architectural elements, and *songket* weaving patterns are featured in decor elements throughout. The guest rooms have Malaysian touches like hand-woven carpets and upholstery in local fabric designs, capturing the exotic flavor of the culture without sacrificing modern comfort and convenience. Located on Jalan Raja Chulan, Istana is in a favorable Golden Triangle location, within walking distance to shopping and some of the sights in that area.

73 Jalan Raja Chulan, 50200 Kuala Lumpur. ℂ 03/2141-9988. Fax 03/2144-0111. 516 units. RM550–RM650 ($145–$171) double; RM1,000 ($263) suite. AE, DC, MC, V. 5-min. walk to Raja Chulan Monorail station. **Amenities:** 4 restaurants; lobby lounge; outdoor pool; 2 outdoor lighted tennis courts; 2 squash courts; fitness center w/Jacuzzi, sauna, steam, and massage; concierge; limo service; business center; 24-hr. room service; babysitting; same-day laundry service/dry cleaning; executive-level rooms. *In room:* A/C, satellite TV w/in-house movies, minibar, coffee/tea-making facilities, hair dryer, safe.

**JW Marriott Hotel Kuala Lumpur** ⌾   Opened in July 1997, the Marriott is finding itself overshadowed by some of the newer properties opening up in the city. But the small lobby area still allows for a very dramatic entrance, complete with wrought-iron filigree and marble. The modern guest rooms have a European flavor, decorated in deep greens and reds with plush carpeting, large desks, and a leather executive chair that are all beginning to show some wear. If you've stayed at Marriott in other locations, this one might disappoint you. It's not their hottest property, yet the staff is very motivated and enthusiastic. Another great plus: The hotel is next door to some of the most upmarket and trendy shopping complexes in the city. Similar to The Regent, this hotel is adjacent to what appeared to be a new construction site, so ask about noise pollution when booking.

183 Jalan Bukit Bintang, 55100 Kuala Lumpur. ℂ **800/228-9290** in the U.S. and Canada, 800/251-259 in Australia, 800/221-222 in the U.K., or 03/2715-9000. Fax 03/2715-7000. 518 units. RM500 ($132) double, from RM800 ($211) suite. AE, DC, MC, V. 10-min. walk to Bukit Bintang Monorail station. **Amenities:** 4 restaurants; lounge; cigar bar; outdoor pool; outdoor lighted tennis court; fitness center w/Jacuzzi, sauna, and steam; new spa w/massage and beauty treatments; concierge; limo service; business center; shopping mall w/designer boutiques adjacent; salon; 24-hr. room service; babysitting; same-day laundry service/dry cleaning; executive-level rooms. *In room:* A/C, satellite TV, dataport, minibar, coffee/tea-making facilities, hair dryer, safe.

**The Pan Pacific Hotel Kuala Lumpur** ⌾   One thing you'll love about staying at the Pan Pacific is the view from the glass elevator as you drift up to your floor. The atrium lobby inside the main entrance is bright and airy and filled with the scent of jasmine. The hotel staff handles the demands of its international clientele with courtesy and professionalism, but when Pan Pac's running a full house, help can be a little weary and hard to find. The rooms are spacious and stately, in pale pastels. Sunken windows with latticework frame each view. The large shopping mall across the street makes this hotel more convenient, as does the LRT station close by. Otherwise it's a bit out of the city center—the inconvenience is felt during rush hour when it can take 30 minutes to make an otherwise 10-minute taxi hop.

Jalan Putra, P.O. Box 11468, 50746 Kuala Lumpur. ℂ **800/327-8585** in the U.S. and Canada, 800/252-900 in Australia, 800/969-496 in the U.K., or 03/4042-5555. Fax 03/4041-7236. 565 units. RM520–RM570

($137–$150) double; from RM1,000 ($263) suite. AE, DC, MC, V. 10-min. walk to Putra World Trade Centre LRT station. **Amenities:** 3 restaurants; lobby lounge; outdoor pool; outdoor lighted tennis court; squash court; fitness center w/Jacuzzi, sauna, and massage; concierge; limo service; business center; 24-hr. room service; babysitting; same-day laundry service/dry cleaning; nonsmoking rooms; executive-level rooms. *In room:* A/C, satellite TV w/in-house movies, minibar, coffee/tea-making facilities, iron, safe.

### The Shangri-La Hotel Kuala Lumpur ★★★    In 2003 Shangri-La emerged from a massive facelift which enhanced its "tropical oasis in the city" ambience. I'm a big fan of Shangri-La, an Asian hotel chain that seeks to create luxury accommodations within lush gardens—something different from the typically faceless city tower of most urban hotels. Complete renovations to the guest rooms included new carpets, soft upholstered furniture, drapes, and bed linens in bright, natural colors and textures. Flat-screen TVs and broadband access come standard (although Internet usage is not included in the cost of the room). Of all the upmarket hotels in the city, Shang has the most attractive facilities for leisure travelers, with a pretty landscaped outdoor pool and fitness center stocked with the latest equipment.

11 Jalan Sultan Ismail, 50250 Kuala Lumpur. ☎ **800/942-5050** in the U.S. and Canada, 800/222-448 in Australia, 0800/442-179 in New Zealand, or 03/232-2388. Fax 03/202-1245. 681 units. RM500–RM635 ($132–$167) double; from RM1,600 ($421) suite. AE, DC, MC, V. 10-min. walk to Bukit Nanas Monorail station. **Amenities:** 5 restaurants; outdoor pool; outdoor lighted tennis courts; fitness center w/Jacuzzi, steam, sauna, and massage; concierge; limo service; salon; babysitting; 24-hr. room service; same-day dry cleaning/laundry service; nonsmoking rooms; executive-level rooms. *In room:* AC, satellite TV w/in-house movies, Internet access, minibar, coffee/tea-making facilities, hair dryer, in-room safe.

## MODERATE
### Concorde Hotel Kuala Lumpur ★★ *Value*    Concorde is one of my favorites in this price category for its central location and quality accommodations at an incredible price. Although rooms are not as large as those in more expensive hotels, they're well outfitted with desks, side chairs, comfortable beds, and tidy bathrooms in an up-to-date style that can compete with the best of them. Concorde has a small outdoor pool with a charming cafe and small fitness center. The lobby lounge is noisy at night because it's popular. Hard Rock Cafe, also located on the premises, is one of the more fun clubs in town.

2 Jalan Sultan Ismail, 50250 Kuala Lumpur. ☎ **03/2144-2200.** Fax 03/2144-1628. 570 units. RM250–RM300 ($66–$79) double; from RM1,000 ($263) suite. AE, DC, MC, V. 5-min. walk to Bukit Nanas Monorail station and 10-min. walk to Dang Wangi LRT station. **Amenities:** 3 restaurants; lobby lounge; small outdoor pool; fitness center w/sauna, steam, and massage; concierge; limo service; business center; shopping arcade; salon; 24-hr. room service; babysitting; same-day laundry service/dry cleaning; executive-level rooms. *In room:* A/C, satellite TV w/in-house movies, minibar, coffee/tea-making facilities, safe.

### Meliá Kuala Lumpur ★ *Value*    This tourist-class hotel had nothing special to boast until recently. The opening of a KL Monorail station just outside, combined with the mind-bogglingly enormous Times Square shopping and entertainment complex across the street, has certainly added great value. The small lobby is functional, with space for tour groups and a very active and efficient tour desk. Newly renovated guest rooms have light wood furnishings, contemporary decorator fixtures, wall desks with a swivel arm for extra space, and large-screen TVs. Bathrooms, while small, are well maintained with good counter space. Mealtimes in the hotel's coffee shop can be a little crowded.

16 Jalan Imbi, 55100 Kuala Lumpur. ☎ **03/2142-8333.** Fax 03/2142-6623. www.solmelia.com. 301 units. RM350–RM400 ($92–$105) double; from RM750 ($197) suite. AE, DC, MC, V. Imbi Monorail station. **Amenities:** 2 restaurants; bar; karaoke lounge; small outdoor pool; health center w/massage; tour desk; small business center; shopping arcade; salon; 24-hr. room service; babysitting; same-day laundry service/dry cleaning; nonsmoking rooms. *In room:* A/C, satellite TV w/in-house movies, minibar, coffee/tea-making facilities, iron.

**Swiss-Garden Hotel** For midrange prices, Swiss-Garden offers reliable comfort, okay location, and affordability that attracts many leisure travelers to its doors. It also knows how to make you feel right at home, with a friendly staff (the concierge is on the ball) and a hotel lobby bar that actually gets patronized (by travelers having cool cocktails at the end of a busy day of sightseeing). The guest rooms are simply furnished, but are neat and comfortable. Swiss-Garden is just walking distance from KL's lively Chinatown district, and close to the Puduraya bus station (which unfortunately makes traffic ugly at rush hour).

117 Jalan Pudu, 55100 Kuala Lumpur. © 03/2141-3333. Fax 03/2141-5555. www.swissgarden.com. 310 units. RM350–RM425 ($92–$112) double; from RM580 ($153) suite. AE, DC, MC, V. **Amenities:** 2 restaurants; lobby lounge; small outdoor pool; small fitness center; spa w/massage; concierge; limo service; business center; 24-hr. room service; babysitting; same-day laundry service/dry cleaning; nonsmoking rooms. *In room:* A/C, satellite TV w/in-house movies, minibar, coffee/tea-making facilities, hair dryer, safe.

## INEXPENSIVE

**Hotel Capitol** ★ *Value* A top pick for a budget hotel, Capitol is located in an up-and-coming part of the city's popular Golden Triangle district, close to the junction of Jalan Sultan Ismail and Jalan Bukit Bintang. In the surrounding lanes you'll find small eateries and shops for necessities, and a short hop away is the giant megamall Times Square. The place has been refurbished and presents a face fitting for the new millennium, with a minimalist lobby that's function over frills. Inside the refurbished guest rooms, the wooden furniture seems like it's been around awhile, but the upholstery, bedding, carpeting, and drapes are all fresh. The big tiled bathroom also has a long bathtub. There are no leisure facilities to speak of, but if you've come to KL to sightsee, you won't miss them.

Jalan Bulan, off Jalan Bukit Bintang, 55100 Kuala Lumpur. © 800/448-8355 in the U.S. and Canada and 1800/221-176 in Australia, or 03/2143-7000. Fax 03/2143-0000. 225 units. RM160–RM250 ($42–$66) double. AE, DC, MC, V. 10-min. walk to Imbi Monorail station. **Amenities:** Restaurant; limited room service; same-day laundry service; nonsmoking rooms. *In room:* A/C, satellite TV w/in-house movies, minibar, coffee/tea-making facilities, hair dryer, in-room safe.

**Swiss-Inn** This minisize hotel is one of KL's most popular budget places. Tucked away in the heart of Chinatown, Swiss-Inn's best asset is its location, amid the jumble of vibrant night market hawkers. The place is small, and offers almost no facilities. Higher-priced rooms have a small window, a bit more space (but are still compact), and are somewhat better maintained. Budget rooms, on lower floors, are very small, the cheapest having no windows at all. The beige carpeting can use a deep cleaning, the walls can use a fresh coat of paint, and the bathrooms some new grout work. On my last visit, housekeeping wasn't up to snuff, which added to the problem. Still, these rooms can be had for as little as RM80 per night, which comes to about $20. Make sure you reserve your room early, because this place runs at high occupancy year-round. The cafe, hidden behind market stalls, is an interesting place to have a beer and people-watch.

62 Jalan Sultan, 50000 Kuala Lumpur. © 03/2072-3333. Fax 03/2031-6699. www.swissgarden.com. 110 units. RM150–RM184 ($39–$48) double. AE, DC, MC, V. **Amenities:** Restaurant; bar; tour desk; limited room service; babysitting; same-day laundry service/dry cleaning; nonsmoking rooms; Internet terminals for guest use (extra charge). *In room:* A/C, TV w/in-house movies, coffee/tea-making facilities.

## WHERE TO DINE

Kuala Lumpur is very cosmopolitan. Here you'll not only find delicious and exotic cuisine, but you'll find it served in some pretty trendy settings.

**Chopstick Noodle House** *Value* CANTONESE I was in the mood for something cheap and good in the center of town, and was thrilled to find this place.

The menu is vast, with no fewer than 20 kinds of noodles, served either in soup or dry (with soup on the side). The fresh prawn won ton noodle is light and flavorful and you can also get it fried. The Chopstick Noodle House has barbecue dishes—duck, pork, honey spare ribs—and seafood dishes are reasonably priced. Also good are the clay-pot dishes, with rice and meats baked in a clay pot with dark soy, mushrooms, and crunchy onions. A good alternative to formal dining.

Lot F 003, 1st Floor, KL Plaza, 179 Jalan Bukit Bintang. ✆ 03/2148-2221. Main courses RM9–RM22 ($2.35–$5.80). AE, DC, MC, V. Daily 11:30am–10:30pm.

**Coliseum Cafe** *(Finds* WESTERN/LOCAL   What can I say about Coliseum? Okay, the place is 84 years old, and so is the staff (seriously, some have worked here their whole lives). Located in the grottiest hotel I've ever witnessed, with stained white walls, worn tile floors, and threadbare linens, this is KL's authentic "greasy spoon." It sounds dreadful, but the place is legendary, and someday it will be gone and there will never be anything else like it. It used to be The Place for the starched-shirt colonial types to get real Western food back in the day. Now it's a favorite with the locals, who come for enormous sizzling steaks (which fill the place with greasy smoke), baked crabmeat served in the shell, and the house favorite, caramel custard pudding. Actually, the food is quite nice, and the prices are terrific for the steaks, which I highly recommend ordering. You either get this place or you don't.

98–100 Jalan Tuanku Abdul Rahman. ✆ 03/2692-6270. Reservations not accepted. Main courses RM8.90–RM34 ($2.35–$8.90). MC. Daily 8am–10pm.

**Eden Village** SEAFOOD   Uniquely designed inside and out to resemble a Malay house, Eden Village has great local atmosphere. It was once KL's most famous "fancy place" for a night out. Now it's visited by as many tourists as locals, but still retains some authenticity. Waitresses are clad in traditional sarong *kebaya,* and serve up popular dishes like braised shark's fin in a clay pot with crabmeat and roe, and the Kingdom of the Sea (a half lobster baked with prawns, crab, and cuttlefish). The terrace seating is the best in the house.

260 Jalan Raja Chulan. ✆ 03/2141-4027. Reservations recommended. Main courses RM18–RM100 and up ($4.75–$26). AE, MC, V. Mon–Sat noon–3pm and 7pm–midnight; Sun 7pm–midnight.

**Kingfisher** *☆☆* SEAFOOD   This street, lined with simple low-rise houses and commercial buildings in the center of KL's fashionable shopping and hotel district, has in recent years become a hot address for trendy restaurants and bars, the best of which is Kingfisher. The very freshest fishes are crafted into lovely haute cuisine dishes with delicate Asian accents for flavor. With the help of the friendly waitstaff, you select your fish of choice, then decide the best preparation style in a "one from column A, one from column B" approach. Everything is fresh and delicious—a good pick.

20 Changkat Bukit Bintang. ✆ 03/2141-9266. Reservations recommended. Main courses RM58–RM128 ($15–$33). MC, V. Mon–Sat noon–2:30pm and 6:30–10:30pm.

**Restoran Saray** *☆* TURKISH   Recently an intriguing little alley called "Asian Heritage Row" has popped up beside the Sheraton, and down this row you'll find about a dozen trendy bars and eateries. Saray is the most interesting of them all, serving a combination of Persian and Arab cuisines in a charming Turkish cafe setting. Some of the menu descriptions just beg you to try them: "curvaceous meat patties," "tender beef stew on a bed of yummy," and my all-time favorite, "green goody." Truly everything that passed my lips, from the hummus and shepherd's salad starters to the baklova and mint tea dessert, was food for angels. Portions seem small, but are surprisingly filling.

No. 60 Jalan Doraisamy, Asian Heritage Row. ℂ **03/2694-9724.** Reservations accepted. Main courses RM17–RM24 ($4.35–$6.20). MC, V. Mon–Fri noon–3pm and 6–11pm; Sat–Sun 6:30–11pm.

**Scalini's la Piccola Italia** ✸✸ ITALIAN   Four chefs from Italy create the dishes that make Scalini's a favorite among KL locals and expatriates. From a very extensive menu you can select pasta, fish, and meat, as well as a large selection of pizzas. The specials are superb and change all the time. Some of the best dishes are salmon with creamed asparagus sauce and ravioli with goat cheese and zucchini. Scalini's has a large wine selection (that is actually part of the romantic decor) with labels from California, Australia, New Zealand, France, and, of course, Italy.

19 Jalan Sultan Ismail. ℂ **03/2145-3211.** Reservations recommended. Main courses RM26–RM58 ($6.85–$15). AE, DC, MC, V. Sun–Thurs noon–2:30pm and 6–10:30pm; Fri noon–2:30pm and 6–11pm; Sat 6–11pm.

**Shook!** JAPANESE/CHINESE/ITALIAN/WESTERN GRILL   This place is unique for a number of reasons. First, Shook! is located on the ground floor of a shopping center, in a cavernous space decorated in a sort of Zen minimalism with splashes of color. Above, escalators glide shoppers to floors over the glass stage where the pop and jazz band plays nightly. Second, the menu features four different types of cuisine that are prepared in four separate show kitchens. It will take a few minutes to read the menu, which offers a mind-boggling selection of Japanese, Chinese, Italian, and Western grill specialties. Very inventive. A good spot if your party can't agree on where to eat—something for everyone. *One caveat:* The waitstaff sometimes seem lost in Shook's enormity.

Starhill Centre, Lower Ground Floor, 181 Jalan Bukit Bintang. ℂ **03/2716-8535.** Main courses RM20–RM200 ($5–$53). AE, DC, MC, V. Daily noon–2:30pm and 6:30–10:30pm.

**Top Hat Restaurant** ✸✸✸ *Finds* ASIAN MIX   Let me tell you about my favorite restaurant in Kuala Lumpur. First, Top Hat has a unique atmosphere. In a 1930s bungalow that was once a school, the place winds through room after room, its walls painted in bright hues and furnished with an assortment of mix-and-matched teak tables, chairs, and antiques. Second, the menu is fabulous. While a la carte is available, Top Hat puts together set meals featuring *nonya,* Malacca Portuguese, traditional Malay, Thai, Western, even vegetarian recipes. They're all brilliant. Desserts are huge and full of sin.

No. 7 Jalan Kia Peng. ℂ **03/2141-8611.** Reservations recommended. Main courses RM30–RM88 ($7.90–$23); set meals RM37–RM123 ($9.75–$32). AE, DC, MC, V. Mon–Fri noon–2:30pm; daily 6–10:30pm.

## WHAT TO SEE & DO

Most of Kuala Lumpur's historic sights are located in the area around Merdeka Square/Jalan Hishamuddin area, while many of the gardens, parks, and muse-ums are out at Lake Gardens. Taxi fare between the two areas should run you about RM5 ($1.30). If you plan to sightsee on a Monday, check below to make sure the attractions you plan to visit aren't closed.

City tours can be booked through **Tour Fifty-one,** located at the MTC (Malaysia Tourism Centre) on Jalan Ampang (ℂ **03/2161-8830**). It coordinates a half-day coach tour for RM25 ($6.60) adults and RM15 ($3.95) children. It swings by most of the places listed here, but is rushed.

**Central Market** ✸   The original Central Market, built in 1936, used to be a wet market, but the place is now a cultural center (air-conditioned!) for local artists and craftspeople selling antiques, crafts, and curios. It is a fantastic place for buying Malaysian and Asian crafts and souvenirs, with two floors of shops to chose from. The Central Market also stages evening performances (7:45pm on weekends) of Malay martial arts, Indian classical dance, or Chinese orchestra. Call the number below for performance information.

Jalan Benteng. © **03/2274-6542**. Daily 10am–10pm. Shops open until 8:30 or 9pm.

**Cosmo's World Theme Park** ★★★ *Kids*   I don't care if you have kids or not, Cosmo's rocks. The world's largest indoor amusement park is literally built into the walls of this 900-outlet shopping mall. You don't even need to ride the loop-ing roller coaster to feel that thrill in the pit of your stomach. Just stand and watch it overhead as it flashes by. It really takes your breath away. There are other rides for those more sane, plus a host of kiddie rides. Highly recommended for families with bored kids.

Berjaya Times Sq. Shopping Mall, No. 1 Jalan Imbi. © **03/2117-3118**. Adult RM25 ($6.60), child RM15 ($3.95). Daily 10am–10pm.

**Islamic Arts Museum** ★★   The seat of Islamic learning in Kuala Lumpur, the center has displays of Islamic texts, artifacts, porcelain, and weaponry in local and visiting exhibits.

Jalan Lembah Perdana. © **03/2274-2020**. Adult RM8 ($2.10), child RM4 ($1.05). Tues–Sun 10am–6pm.

**Jame Mosque (Masjid Jame)**   The first settlers landed in Kuala Lumpur at the spot where the Gombak and Klang rivers meet, and in 1909 a mosque was built here. Styled after an Indian Muslim design, it is one of the oldest mosques in the city. It is supposed to be opened to the public, but many foreigners, even those properly attired, have been shooed away at the gate.

Jalan Tun Terak. No phone.

**Kuala Lumpur Lake Gardens (Taman Tasik Perdana)**   Built around an artificial lake, the 92-hectare (227-acre) park has plenty of space for jogging and rowing, and has a playground for the kids. It's the most popular park in Kuala Lumpur. Inside the Lake Gardens find the **Kuala Lumpur Bird Park** ★ (Jalan Perdana; © **03/2273-5423;** adults RM28/$7.40, children RM20/$5.25; daily 9am–7pm) nestled in beautifully landscaped gardens, with over 3,000 birds within a huge newly built walk-in aviary. Quite impressive. **Kuala Lumpur Orchid Garden** (Jalan Perdana; © **03/2693-5399;** weekend and public holiday admission adults RM1/25¢, children RM.50/15¢; weekdays free; daily 9am–6pm) has a collection of over 800 orchid species from Malaysia, and it also contains thousands of international varieties. The **Kuala Lumpur Butterfly Park** (Jalan Cenderasari; © **03/2693-4799;** adults RM12/$3.15, children RM5/$1.30; daily 9am–6pm) has over 6,000 butterflies belonging to 120 species; this park has been landscaped with more than 15,000 plants to simulate the butterflies' natural rainforest environment. There are also other small ani-mals and an insect museum.

Enter via Jalan Parliament. No phone. Free admission. Daily 9am–6pm.

**Kuala Lumpur Railway Station**   Built in 1910, the KL Railway Station is a beautiful example of Moorish architecture.

Jalan Sultan Hishamuddin. No phone. Daily 7:30am–10:30pm.

**MTC (Malaysia Tourist Centre)**   At MTC you'll find an exhibit hall, tourist information services for Kuala Lumpur and Malaysia, and other travel-planning services. On Tuesdays, Thursdays, Saturdays, and Sundays there are cultural shows at 3pm, featuring Malaysian dance and music. Shows are RM5 ($1.30) for adults, free for children.

109 Jalan Ampang. ✆ **03/2164-3929**. Daily 9am–6pm.

**Menara Kuala Lumpur**   Standing 421m (1,381 ft.) tall, this concrete structure is the third-tallest tower in the world, and the views from the top reach to the far corners of the city and beyond. At the top, the glass windows are fashioned after the Shah Mosque in Isfahan, Iran.

Bukit Nanas. ✆ **03/2020-5448**. Adults RM15 ($3.95), children RM9 ($2.40). Daily 9am–10pm.

**Merdeka Square**   Surrounded by colonial architecture with an exotic local flair, the square is a large field that was once the site of British social and sporting events. These days, Malaysia holds its spectacular Independence Day celebrations on the field, which is home to the world's tallest flagpole, standing at 100m (328 ft.).

Jalan Raja. No phone.

**National Art Gallery**   The building that now houses the National Art Gallery was built as the Majestic Hotel in 1932 and has been restored to display contemporary works by Malaysian artists. There are international exhibits as well.

Jalan Temerloh, off Jalan Tun Razak. ✆ **03/4025-4990**. Free admission. Daily 10am–6pm.

**National Mosque (Masjid Negara)**   Built in a modern design, the most distinguishing features of the mosque are its 73m (239-ft.) minaret and the umbrella-shaped roof, which is said to symbolize a newly independent Malaysia's aspirations for the future. Could be true, as the place was built in 1965, the year Singapore split from Malaysia.

Jalan Sultan Hishamuddin (near the KL Railway Station). No phone. Daily 9am–6pm.

**National Museum (Muzim Negara)** 👁👁   Located at Lake Gardens, the museum has more than 1,000 items of historic, cultural, and traditional significance, including art, weapons, musical instruments, and costumes.

Jalan Damansara. ✆ **03/2282-6255**. Admission RM2 (55¢), children under 12 free. Daily 9am–6pm.

**National Planetarium** *(Kids)*   The National Planetarium has a Space Hall with touch-screen interactive computers and hands-on experiments, a viewing gallery with binoculars for a panoramic view of the city, and the Ancient Observatory Park with models of Chinese and Indian astronomy systems. The Space Theatre has shows at 11am, 2pm, and 4pm for an extra charge of RM3 (80¢) for adults and RM2 (55¢) for children.

Lake Gardens. ✆ **03/2273-5484**. Admission to exhibition hall RM1 (25¢), children free. Tues–Sun 10am–4pm.

**Petaling Street** 👁   This is the center of KL's Chinatown district. By day, stroll past hawker stalls, dim sum shops, wet markets, and all sorts of shops, from pawn shops to coffin makers. At night, a crazy bazaar (which is terribly crowded) pops up—look for designer knockoffs, fake watches, and pirate VCDs (Video CDs) here.

**Petronas Twin Towers** 👁   Standing at an awesome 452m (1,482 ft.) above street level, with 88 stories, the towers are the tallest buildings in the world. From the outside, the structures are designed with the kind of geometric patterns common to Islamic architecture, and on levels 41 and 42 the two towers are linked by a bridge.

Kuala Lumpur City Centre. ✆ **03/2051-7770**. Sky bridge Tues–Sun 10am–8pm (closed public holidays).

**Sri Mahamariaman Temple**    With a recent face-lift (Hindu temples must renovate every 12 years), this bright temple livens the gray street scene around. It's a beautiful temple tucked away in a narrow street in KL's Chinatown area, which was built by Thambusamy Pillai, a pillar of old KL's Indian community.

Jalan Bandar. No phone.

**Sultan Abdul Samad Building**    In 1897 this exotic building was designed by Regent Alfred John Bidwell, a colonial architect responsible for many of the buildings in Singapore. He chose a style called "Muhammadan" or "neo-Saracenic," which combines Indian Muslim architecture with Gothic and other Western elements. Built to house government administrative offices, today it is the home of Malaysia's Supreme Court and High Court.

Jalan Raja. No phone.

## GOLF

People from all over Asia flock to Malaysia for its golf courses, many of which are excellent standard courses designed by pros. The **Kuala Lumpur Golf & Country Club** (10 Jalan 1/70D, off Jalan Bukit Kiara; ✆ 03/2093-1111) has two 18-hole courses (par 71 and 72), designed by R. Nelson & R. Wright, with greens fees of RM180 ($47) weekdays, RM250 ($66) weekends and holidays. **Suajana Golf & Country Club** (Km 3, Jalan Lapangan Terbang Sultan Abdul Aziz Shah, 46783 Subang Selangor; ✆ 03/7846-1466; fax 03/7846-7818), has two 18-hole courses (each par 72), designed by Ronald Fream, with greens fees of RM199 ($52) weekdays, RM319 ($84) weekends and holidays.

## SHOPPING

Kuala Lumpur is a truly great place to shop. In recent years, mall after mall has risen from city lots, filled with hundreds of retail outlets selling everything from haute couture to cheap chic clothing, electronic goods, jewelry, and arts and crafts. The **major shopping malls** are located in the area around Jalan Bukit Bintang and Jalan Sultan Ismail. There are also a few malls along Jalan Ampang. Suria KLCC, located just beneath the Petronas Twin Towers, has to be KL's most upmarket mall, while Berjaya Times Square wins the prize for excess with 900 shops and food and entertainment outlets, plus the world's largest indoor amusement park.

Still the best place for Malaysian handicrafts, the huge **Central Market** on Jalan Benteng (✆ 03/2274-6542) keeps any shopper saturated for hours. There you'll find a jumble of local artists and craftspeople selling their wares in the heart of town. It's also a good place to find Malaysian handicrafts from other regions of the country. One specific shop I like to recommend for Malaysian handicrafts is **KL Craft Complex** (Section 3, Jalan Conlay; ✆ 03/2162-7533), with a warehouse selection of assorted goods from around the country, all of it fine quality. Don't forget to walk through the gardens to see the artists' village. In the bungalows towards the side of the building you'll find some of Malaysia's finest contemporary artists displaying their works for sale. And wear comfy shoes, you may need to walk back to the main road to get a cab.

Another favorite shopping haunt in KL is **Chinatown,** along Petaling Street. Day and night, it's a great place to wander and bargain for knockoff designer clothing and accessories, sunglasses, T-shirts, souvenirs, fake watches, and pirated videos.

**Pasar malam (night markets)** are very popular evening activities in KL. Whole blocks are taken up with these brightly lit and bustling markets packed with stalls selling everything you can dream of. They are likely to pop up anywhere in the city. Two good bets for catching one: Go to Jalan Haji Taib after dark until 10pm. On Saturday nights, head for Jalan Tuanku Abdul Rahman.

## KUALA LUMPUR AFTER DARK

There's nightlife to spare in KL, from fashionable lounges to sprawling discos to pubs perfect for lounging. Basically, you can expect to pay about RM11 to RM20 ($2.90–$5.25) for a pint of beer, depending on what and where you order. While quite a few pubs are open for lunch, most clubs won't open until about 6 or 7pm. These places must all close by 1 or 2am, so don't plan on staying out too late. Nearly all have a happy hour, usually between 5 and 7pm, when drink discounts apply on draft beers and "house-pour" (lower-shelf) mixed drinks. Generally, you're expected to wear dress casual clothing for these places, but avoid old jeans, tennis shoes, and very revealing outfits.

The center of nightlife, if you want to browse, begins at the corner of Jalan Sultan Ismail and Jalan P. Ramlee. Walk along P. Ramlee and you'll find bars of all kinds, plus cafes and coffee shops.

For a little live music with your drinks, the **Hard Rock Cafe,** Jalan Sultan Ismail connected to Concorde Hotel (© **03/2715-5555**), hosts the best of the regional bands, which play nightly for a crowd of locals, tourists, and expatriates who take their parties very seriously.

The biggest dance club in town is the newly opened **Zouk,** fashioned after the ultrasuccessful Zouk in Singapore. It's at 113 Jalan Ampang, down the street from MTC (© **03/2171-1997**). There's a cover charge of anywhere between RM25 and RM40 ($6.60–$11), depending on the event that's taking place inside.

**Bangsar,** just outside the city limits, is 2 or 3 blocks of bars, cafes, and restaurants that cater to a variety of tastes (in fact, so many expatriates hang out there, they call it Kweiloh Lumpur, "Foreigner Lumpur" in Mandarin). Every taxi driver knows where it is. Get in and ask to go to Jalan Telawi Tiga in Bangsar (fare should be no more than RM5 or RM6/$1.30 or $1.60), and once there it's very easy to catch a cab back to town. During the week, it's kinda quiet.

## SIDE TRIPS FROM KUALA LUMPUR
### TAMAN NEGARA NATIONAL PARK ★★★

Malaysia's most famous national park, **Taman Negara,** covers 434,300 hectares (1,072,721 acres) of primary rainforest estimated to be as old as 130 million years, and encompasses within its borders **Gunung Tahan,** peninsular Malaysia's highest peak at 2,187m (7,173 ft.) above sea level.

Prepare to see lush vegetation and rare orchids, some 250 bird species, and maybe, if you're lucky, some barking deer, tapir, elephants, tigers, leopards, and rhinos. As for primates, there are longtailed macaques, leaf monkeys, gibbons, and more. Malaysia has taken the preservation of this forest seriously since the early part of the century, so Taman Negara showcases efforts to keep this land in as pristine a state as possible while still allowing humans to appreciate the splendor.

There are outdoor activities for any level of adventurer. Short **jungle walks** to observe nature are lovely, but then so are the hardcore 9-day treks or climbs up Gunung Tahan. There are also overnight trips where you can observe animals up close. The jungle canopy walk is the longest in the world, and at 25m (82 ft.) above ground, the view is spectacular. There are also rivers for rafting and swimming, fishing spots, and a couple of caves.

If you plan your trip through one of the main resort operators, they can arrange, in addition to accommodations, all meals, treks, and a coach transfer to and from

Kuala Lumpur. Prices vary wildly, depending on the time of season you plan your visit, your level of comfort desired, and the extent to which you wish to explore the forests. The best time to visit the park is between the months of April to September; other times it will be a tad wet, and that's why it's called a rainforest.

**Mutiara Taman Negara Resort** ⚑, well established in the business of hosting visitors to the park, is the best accommodation in terms of comfort. It organizes trips for 3 days and 2 nights or for 4 days and 3 nights, as well as an a la carte deal where you pay for lodging and activities separately. Accommodations come in many styles: a bungalow suite for families; chalet and chalet suite, both good for couples; standard guesthouse rooms in a motel-style longhouse; and dormitory hostels for budget travelers. To get an idea of pricing, a 3-day/2-night package runs about RM399 ($105) per person, double occupancy in a chalet, with air-conditioning with attached bathroom, plus breakfasts and 1 dinner, plus one night-jungle walk and a day trek. What it doesn't include is bus transfer from KL (RM80/$21 per person round-trip) and the boat upriver from the park entrance (RM50/$13 per person round-trip), and other a la carte activities that run anywhere between RM40 to RM60 ($3.85–$11) per person, all of which the resort can arrange for you when you book. A la carte activities include a 3-hour jungle trek, a 1½-hour night-jungle walk, the half-day Lata Berkoh river trip with swimming, a 2-hour cave exploration, and a trip down the rapids in a rubber raft (Kuala Tahan, Jerantut, 27000 Pahang; ✆ **09/266-3500;** Kuala Lumpur sales office 03/2145-5585).

## GENTING HIGHLANDS

Malaysia's answer to Las Vegas, Genting comes complete with bright lights (that can be seen from Kuala Lumpur) and gambling. And while most people come here for the casino, there's a wide range of other activities, although most of them seem to serve the purpose of entertaining the kids while you bet their college funds at the roulette wheel.

The 24-hour casino charges a refundable deposit of RM200 ($53) entry for people over 21 years of age. Outside of the casino, there's also a pond, a bowling alley, and an indoor heated pool. The **Awana Golf and Country Club** (✆ **03/6101-3025**) is the premier golf course in these hills. For children, the **Genting Theme Park** covers 100,000 square feet of mostly rides, plus many Western fast-food eating outlets, games, and other attractions.

**Genting Highlands Transport** (✆ **03/6251-8398**) operates buses from KL every half-hour from 6:30am to 9pm daily from the Pekeliling Bus Terminal on Jalan Ipoh for RM2.60 (70¢). The hour-long trip lets you off at the foot of the hill, where you take the cable car to the top for RM3 (80¢). You can also get there by hiring an outstation **taxi.** The cost is RM40 ($11).

Genting has four hotels of varying prices within the resort. The **Genting Highlands Resort** is owned and operated by Resorts World Berhad, which will be glad to provide you with hotel reservations if you call ✆ **03/2718-1118.**

## CAMERON HIGHLANDS

Located in the hills, this colonial-era resort town has a cool climate, which makes it the perfect place for agriculture, as well as weekend getaways by Malaysians and Singaporeans who are sick of the heat. Temperatures in the highlands average 70°F (21°C) during the day and 50°F (10°C) at night.

There are **no visitor information services** here, but you'll find banks with ATMs and money-changing services along the main road in Tanah Rata, the main town.

Most of the sights can be seen in a day. I recommend trying **C. S. Travel & Tours** (47 Main Rd., Tanah Rata; ✆ **05/491-1200**), a highly reputable agency that will plan half-day tours for RM15 ($3.95) or full days starting from RM80 ($21). On your average tour you'll see the Boh tea plantation and factory, flower nurseries, rose gardens, strawberry farms, butterfly farms, and the Sam Poh Buddhist Temple. You're required to pay admission to each attraction yourself. C.S. Travel also provides trekking and overnight camping tours in the surrounding hills with local trail guides.

If you want to hit around some balls, **Padang Golf** (Main Rd. between Tanah Rata and Brinchang; ✆ **05/491-1126**) has 18 holes at par 71, with greens fees around RM42 ($11) on weekdays and RM63 ($17) on weekends. It provides club rentals, caddies, shoes, and carts.

The best choice for accommodations here is **The Smokehouse Hotel,** a picturesque Tudor mansion with pretty gardens outside and a charming old-world ambience inside (Tanah Rata, Cameron Highlands, Pahang Darul Makmur; ✆ **05/491-1215;** fax 05/491-1214; RM400–RM600/$105–$158 suite).

To get to Cameron Highlands, **Kurnia Bistari Express Bus** (✆ **05/491-2978**) operates between Kuala Lumpur and Tanah Rata daily for around RM10 ($2.65) one-way. Outstation taxis from KL will cost RM220 ($58) for the trip. Call ✆ **03/2078-0213** for booking.

## 4 Malacca

Malacca became the birthplace of Islam in Malaysia when Arab traders imported the faith in the early 1400s. Around that time, the port city rose to international attention as a major center for Southeast Asian trade with China and the Middle East. European powers conquered, first the Portuguese, then the Dutch and finally the British; however, over the centuries Malacca lost its status to neighboring Singapore. Today, the sleepy backwater town reveals remnants of past conquerors, settlers, and traders in its architecture.

### VISITOR INFORMATION
The **Malacca Tourism Centre** is on Jalan Kota at the Town Square next to the bridge (✆ **06/281-4803**).

### GETTING THERE
**BY TRAIN**  Malacca doesn't have a proper train station, but the **KTM** stops at Tampin (✆ **06/441-1034**), 38km (24 miles) north of the city. It's not the most convenient way in and out of Malacca, but if you decide to stop en route between Kuala Lumpur and Johor Bahru, you can easily catch a waiting taxi to your hotel in town for RM40 ($11).

**BY BUS**  From Singapore, contact **Malacca-Singapore Express** at ✆ **65/6293-5915.** Buses depart daily for the 4½-hour trip (S$11/US$6.45). **KL's Puduraya Bus Terminal** on Jalan Pudu, Transnasional (✆ **03/230-5044**) has hourly buses between 8am and 10pm for about RM6.80 ($1.80). The trip takes about 2 ½ hours.

The bus station in Malacca is at Jalan Kilang, within the city. Taxis are easy to find from here.

**BY TAXI**  **Outstation taxis** can bring you here from Kuala Lumpur for RM140 ($37). The outstation taxi stand in Malacca is at the bus terminal on Jalan Kilang.

## GETTING AROUND

Most of the historic sights around the town square are well within walking distance. For other trips **taxis** are the most convenient way around, but are at times difficult to find. They're also not as clearly marked as in KL or Johor Bahru. They are also not metered, so be prepared to bargain. Basically, no matter what you do, you'll always be charged a higher rate than a local. Tourists are almost always quoted at RM10 ($2.65) for local trips. Malaysians pay RM5 ($1.30). If you're feeling sporty, you can bargain for a price somewhere in between.

**Trishaws** (bicycle rickshaw) are all over the historic areas of town, and in Malacca they're renowned for being very, very garishly decorated (which adds to the fun!). Negotiate for hourly rates of about RM20 ($5.25) for two people.

## FAST FACTS: MALACCA

Malacca's **area code** is 06. Major **banks** are located in the historic center of town, with a couple along Jalan Putra. Internet places come and go. Your best bet is to ask your hotel's concierge or the Tourism Centre for the nearest cafes.

## WHERE TO STAY

Malacca is not very large, and most of the places to stay are well within walking distance of attractions, shopping, and restaurants.

**Century Mahkota Hotel Melaka**    Located along the waterfront, the hotel is in walking distance from sightseeing, historical areas, shopping, and commercial centers. Rooms are more like holiday apartments, with minikitchens and up to three bedrooms for family living—a big hit with Malaysian and Singaporean families. Each apartment has a tiled main room with clean cooking space at one end and simple rattan furnishings at the other—only bedrooms are air-conditioned. The views are of either the pools, the shopping mall across the street, or the muddy reclaimed seafront. The sprawling complex includes two outdoor pools, facilities for children, and is across from the largest shopping mall in Malacca. This place gets especially crowded during the school holidays in June and December.

Jalan Merdeka, 75000 Malacca. © 06/281-2828. Fax 06/281-2323. 617 units. RM208–RM408 ($55–$107) 1- to 3-bedroom apt. AE, DC, MC, V. **Amenities:** 3 restaurants; lounge; piano bar; 2 outdoor pools; outdoor lighted tennis courts; squash courts; fitness center w/sauna and massage; children's playground; game room; tour desk; car-rental desk; shuttle; business center; 24-hr. room service; babysitting; same-day laundry service/dry cleaning. *In room:* Satellite TV, coffee/tea-making facilities, hair dryer.

**Heeren House**    This is the place to stay in Malacca for a taste of the local culture. Started by a local family, the small guesthouse is a renovated 100-year-old building furnished in traditional Peranakan and colonial style and located right in the heart of historical European Malacca. All the bedrooms have views of the Malacca River, and outside the front door of the hotel is a winding stretch of old buildings housing antiques shops. Just walk out and wander. Small rooms have very basic amenities. The rooms on the second floor are somewhat larger. Laundry service is available, and there's a cafe and gift shop on the premises. Everybody is nice as pie. Reserve well in advance.

1 Jalan Tun Tan Cheng Lock, 75200 Malacca. © 06/281-4241. Fax 06/281-4239. 7 units. RM139 ($37) double; RM239 ($63) family suite. No credit cards. **Amenities:** Restaurant; souvenir shop; same-day laundry service. *In room:* A/C, TV.

**Hotel Puri** *(Value)*    In olden days, Jalan Tun Tan Cheng Lock was known as "Millionaire Row" for all the wealthy families that lived here. This old "mansion" has been converted into a guesthouse, its tiled parlor has become a lobby,

# Malacca

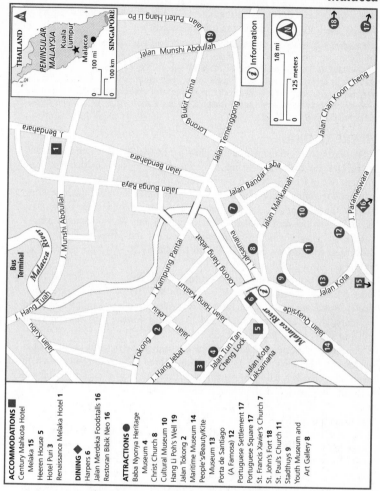

and the courtyard is where breakfast is served each morning. While Hotel Puri isn't big on space, it is big on value (discount rates can be pretty low). Rooms are very clean, and while not overly stylish, are comfortable enough for any weary traveler. Friendly and responsive staff add to the appeal.

118 Jalan Tun Tan Cheng Lock, 75200 Malacca. ☎ **06/282-5588.** Fax 06/281-5588. 50 units. RM150–RM200 ($40–$53) double; RM230 ($61) triple; suites from RM305 ($80). AE, MC, V. **Amenities:** Restaurant; tour desk; limited room service; babysitting; same-day laundry service. *In room:* A/C, satellite TV, fridge, coffee/tea-making facilities, hair dryer.

**Renaissance Melaka Hotel** ✪    Renaissance is one of the more posh hotels in Malacca, and, according to business travelers, is the most reliable place for quality accommodations—but aside from the pieces of Peranakan porcelain and art in the public areas, you could almost believe you weren't in Malacca at all. The hotel is, however, situated in a good location, though you'll still need a taxi to most of the sights. Renovations were completed 2 years ago to upgrade the guest rooms, which are fairly large and filled with Western comforts. Don't expect much from the views, as the hotel is in a more business-minded part of the city. No historical landmarks to gaze upon here.

Jalan Bendahara, 75100 Malacca. ℰ **800/228-9898** in the U.S. and Canada, 800/251-259 in Australia, 800/ 441-035 in New Zealand, 800/181-737 in the U.K., or 06/284-8888. Fax 06/284-9269. 294 units. RM420–RM480 ($111–$126) double; from RM540 ($142) suite. AE, MC, V. **Amenities:** 3 restaurants; bar; lobby lounge; outdoor pool; golf nearby; squash courts; fitness center w/sauna, steam, and massage; concierge; tour desk; limo service; business center; salon; 24-hr. room service; babysitting; same-day laundry service/dry cleaning; executive-level rooms. *In room:* A/C, satellite TV w/in-house movies, minibar, coffee/tea-making facilities, safe.

## WHERE TO DINE

In Malacca you'll find the typical mix of authentic Malay and Chinese food, and as the city was the major settling place for the Peranakans in Malaysia, their unique style of food is featured in many of the local restaurants.

A good recommendation for a quick bite at lunch or dinner if you're strolling in the historical area is the long string of open-air food stalls along Jalan Merdeka, just between Mahkota Plaza Shopping and Warrior Square. **Mama Fatso's** is especially good for Chinese-style seafood and Malay sambal curry. A good meal will run you about RM35 to RM40 ($9.20–$11) per person. And believe me, it's a good meal.

Try local Peranakan cuisine at **Restoran Bibik Neo** (No. 6, ground floor, Jalan Merdeka, Taman Melaka Raya; ℰ **06/281-7054**), a small coffee shop that's about as authentic as you can get. *Ikan assam* with eggplant is a tasty mild fish curry that's very rich and tart, and I always go for the *otak-otak* (pounded fish and spices baked in a banana leaf).

For a taste of Portuguese Malacca, the **Portuguese Settlement** (Jalan d'Albuquerque off Jalan Ujon Pasir) has some open-air food stalls by the water, where in the evenings hawkers sell an assortment of dishes inspired by these former colonial rulers, including many fresh seafood offerings (RM15–RM20/$3.95–$5.25). Saturday nights are best when, at 8pm, there's a cultural show with music and dancing. Other times it may be slow business.

My favorite place in town is **Harper's Restaurant** (Harper's Building, Jalan Hang Jebat; ℰ **06/282-8800**), which serves Nyonya, Chinese, and Western food in a terrific riverside ambience. This combination watering hole and bistro has a relaxed Asian feel, with open air verandahs and cane furnishings. Simple but atmospheric. The menu serves local dishes that can be adjusted for Western tastes upon request (if you need less chile, for example), and a selection of steaks prepared in Western style. Prices range from RM20 ($5.25) for simple Asian small dishes to up to RM45 ($12) for the surf and turf. It's open daily from 10am to 1:30am; however, the Asian kitchen is only open from noon to 2:30pm and 6 to 10:30pm. Western food is served anytime between noon and 11:30pm.

## WHAT TO SEE & DO

To get the most out of Malacca, it's best to have a bit of knowledge about the history of the place, which I've explained briefly in the intro to this section. Most of the preserved historical sites are on both sides of the Malacca River. Start at **Stadthuys** (the old town hall, pronounced "stat-highs") and you'll see most of Malacca pretty quickly.

### MUSEUMS

**Baba Nyonya Heritage Museum** ⭑ Called "Millionaire's Row," Jalan Tun Tan Cheng Lock is lined with row houses that were built by the Dutch and later bought by wealthy Peranakans; the architectural style reflects their East-meets-West lifestyle. The Baba Nyonya Heritage Museum sits at nos. 48 and 50 as a museum of Peranakan heritage. The entrance fee includes a guided tour.

48/50 Jalan Tun Tan Cheng Lock. ✆ 06/283-1273. Admission RM8 ($2.10) adults, RM4 ($1.05) children. Daily 10am–12:30pm and 2–4:30pm.

### The Cultural Museum (Muzium Budaya) 🀫   A replica of the former palace of Sultan Mansur Syah (1456–77), this museum was rebuilt according to historical descriptions to house a fine collection of cultural artifacts such as clothing, weaponry, and royal items. The gardens are quite nice.

Kota Rd., next to Porta de Santiago. ✆ 06/282-6526. Admission RM2 (55¢) adults, RM.50 (15¢) children. Daily 9am–5:30pm.

### The Maritime Museum and the Royal Malaysian Navy Museum   These two museums are located across the street from one another but share admission fees. The Maritime Museum is in a restored 16th-century Portuguese ship, with exhibits dedicated to Malacca's history with the sea. The navy museum is a modern display of Malaysia's less-pleasant relationship with the sea.

Quayside Rd. ✆ 06/282-6526. Admission RM2 (55¢) adults, RM.50 (15¢) children. Daily 9am–5:30pm.

### The People's Museum, the Museum of Beauty, the Kite Museum, and the Governor of Melaka's Gallery   This strange collection of displays is housed under one roof. The People's Museum is the story of development in Malacca. The Museum of Beauty is a look at cultural differences of beauty throughout time and around the world. The Kite Museum features the traditions of making and flying *wau* (kites) in Malaysia, and the governor's personal collection is on exhibit at the Governor's Gallery.

Kota Rd. ✆ 06/282-6526. Admission RM2 (55¢) adults, RM.50 (15¢) children. Tues–Sun 9am–5:30pm.

### Stadthuys—The Museums of History & Ethnography and the Museum of Literature 🀫   The Stadthuys Town Hall was built by the Dutch in 1650, and it's now home to the Malacca Ethnographical and Historical Museum, which displays customs and traditions of all the peoples of Malacca, and takes you through the rich history of this city. Behind Stadthuys, the Museum of Literature includes old historical accounts and local legends. Admission price is for both exhibits.

At circle intersection of Jalan Quayside, Jalan Laksamana, and Jalan Chan Koon Cheng. ✆ 06/282-6526. Admission RM2 (55¢) adults, RM.50 (15¢) children. Daily 9am–5:30pm.

### The Youth Museums and Art Gallery   In the old General Post office are these displays dedicated to Malaysia's youth organizations and to the nation's finest artists. An unusual combination.

Laksamana Rd. ✆ 06/282-6526. Admission RM1 (25¢) adults, RM.50 (15¢) children. Tues–Sun 9am–5:30pm.

## HISTORICAL SITES

**Christ Church**   The Dutch built this place in 1753 as a Dutch Reform Church, and its architectural details include such wonders as ceiling beams cut from a single tree and a Last Supper glazed-tile motif above the altar. It was later consecrated as an Anglican church, and mass is still performed today in English, Chinese, and Tamil.

Located on Jalan Laksamana. No phone.

**Hang Li Poh's Well**   Also called "Sultan's Well," Hang Li Poh's Well was built in 1495 to commemorate the marriage of Chinese Princess Hang Li Poh to

Sultan Mansor Shah. It is now a wishing well, and folks say that if you toss in a
coin, you'll someday return to Malacca.

Located off Jalan Laksamana Cheng Ho (Jalan Panjang). No phone.

**Jalan Tokong** 🐸  Not far from Jalan Tun Tan Cheng Lock is Jalan Tokong,
called the "Street of Harmony" by the locals because it has three coexisting
places of worship: the Kampong Kling Mosque, the Cheng Hoon Teng Temple,
and the Sri Poyyatha Vinayar Moorthi Temple.

**Porta de Santiago (A Famosa)** 🐸  Once the site of a Portuguese fortress
called A Famosa, all that remains today of the fortress is the entrance gate, which
was saved from demolition by Sir Stamford Raffles. When the British East India
Company demolished the place, Raffles realized the arch's historical value and
saved it. The fort was built in 1512, but the inscription above the arch, "Anno
1607," marks the date when the Dutch overthrew the Portuguese.

Located on Jalan Kota, at the intersection of Jalan Parameswara. No phone.

**Portuguese Settlement and Portuguese Square**  The Portuguese Settlement is an enclave once designated for Portuguese settlers after they conquered
Malacca in 1511. Some elements of their presence remain in the Lisbon-style
architecture. Later, in 1920, the area was a Eurasian neighborhood. In the center of the settlement, Portuguese Square is a modern attraction with Portuguese
restaurants, handicrafts, souvenirs, and cultural shows. It was built in 1985 in an
architectural style to reflect the surrounding flavor of Portugal.

Located down Jalan d'Albuquerque off of Jalan Ujon Pasir in the southern part of the city.

**St. Francis Xavier's Church**  This church was built in 1849 and dedicated to
St. Francis Xavier, a Jesuit who brought Catholicism to Malacca and other parts
of Southeast Asia.

Located on Jalan Laksamana. No phone.

**St. John's Fort**  The fort, built by the Dutch in the late 18th century, sits on
top of St. John's Hill. Funny how the cannons point inland, huh? At the time,
threats to the city came from land. It was named after a Portuguese church to
St. John the Baptist, which originally occupied the site.

Located off Lorong Bukit Senjuang. No phone.

**St. Paul's Church**  The church was built by the Portuguese in 1521, but when
the Dutch came in, they made it part of A Famosa, converting the altar into a
cannon mount. The open tomb inside was once the resting place of St. Francis
Xavier, a missionary who spread Catholicism throughout Southeast Asia, and
whose remains were later moved to Goa.

Located behind Porta de Santiago. No phone.

## SHOPPING
**Antique hunting** has been a major draw to Malacca for decades. Distinct Peranakan and teak furniture, porcelain, and household items fetch quite a price
these days, due to a steady increase in demand for these rare treasures. The area
down and around Jalan Hang Jebat and Jalan Tun Tan Cheng Lok called **Jonker
Walk** sports many little antiques shops that are filled with as many gorgeous
items as any local museum. You'll also find handmade crafts, ready-made batik
clothing and other souvenirs. Whether you're buying or just looking, it's a fun
way to spend an afternoon.

For crafts and souvenirs, you'll also find a row of shops along the lane beside Stadthuys. Most of the prices seemed fair, but you may need to do a little bargaining.

## 5 Penang

Penang is unique in Malaysia because, for all intents and purposes, Penang has it all. Malacca has historical sights and museums, but it doesn't have a good beach for miles. Similarly, while KL has shopping, nightlife, and attractions, it also has no beach resorts. Penang has all of it: beaches, history, diverse culture, shopping, food—you name it, it has it. If you have only a short time to visit Malaysia but want to take in as wide of an experience as you can, Penang is your place.

Since Malaysia's independence in 1957, Penang has had relatively good financial success. Today the state of Penang is made up of the island and a small strip of land on the Malaysian mainland. Georgetown is the seat of government for the state. Penang Island is 285 sq. km (111 sq. miles) and has a population of a little more than 1 million. Surprisingly, the population is mostly Chinese (59%), followed by Malays (32%) and Indians (7%).

### VISITOR INFORMATION

The main **Malaysia Tourism Board (MTB)** office is located at No. 10 Jalan Tun Syed Sheh Barakbah (© 04/261-9067), just across from the clock tower by Fort Cornwallis. There's another information center at **Penang International Airport** (© 04/643-0501) and a branch on the third level at **KOMTAR (Kompleks Tun Abdul Razak)** on Jalan Penang (© 04/261-4461).

### GETTING THERE

**BY PLANE**   **Penang International Airport** (© 04/643-4411) has flights that connect from all over the world. **Malaysia Airlines** (© 1300/883-000; www.malaysiaairlines.com) has about 20 flights each day from KL, plus connecting flights from all over the country and region. Other airlines that service Penang are: **Singapore Airlines** (© 800/742-3333; www.singaporeair.com), **Thai Airways** (www.thaiair.com), **Cathay Pacific** (© 800/233-2742; www.cathaypacific.com) and the popular budget carrier, **AirAsia** (© 1300/889-933; www.airasia.com).

There are also car rentals at the airport. Talk to **Avis** (© 04/643-9633).

**BY TRAIN**   By rail, the overnight trip from KL to Butterworth takes 10 hours and costs RM67 ($18) first-class passage, or RM37 ($9.75) for second class. The prices vary quite greatly depending on if you choose upper or lower berth, and what class passage you take. Call **KL Sentral** (© 03/2267-1200) for schedule information.

The train will let you off at the **Butterworth Railway Station** (© 04/323-7962), on Jalan Bagan Dalam (near the ferry terminal) in Butterworth, on the Malaysian mainland. From there, you can take a taxi to the island or head for the ferry close by.

**BY BUS**   Many buses will bring you to Butterworth or Georgetown, but I really only recommend it if you're a glutton for punishment. Transnasional stopped its executive coach service, and if you take a standard coach the trip will be horrible.

**BY FERRY**   The ferry to Penang is nestled between the Butterworth Railway Station and the Butterworth bus terminal. It operates 24 hours a day and takes 20 minutes from pier to pier. From 6am to midnight ferries leave every 10 minutes.

From midnight to 1:20am boats run every half-hour, and from 1:20 to 6am they run hourly. Purchase your passage by dropping 60 sen (15¢) exact change in the turnstile (there's a change booth if you don't have it). Fare is paid only on the trip to Penang. The return is free. The ferry lets you off at Weld Quay (© **04/261-0290**).

**BY TAXI** The outstation taxi stand is in Butterworth next to the bus terminal (© **04/323-2045**). Fares to Butterworth from KL will be about RM300 ($79).

## GETTING AROUND

**BY TAXI** Taxis are abundant, but be warned they do not use meters, so you must agree on the price before you ride. Most trips within the city are between RM3 and RM6 (80¢–$1.60). If you're staying out at the Batu Feringgi beach resort area, expect taxis to town to run RM20 ($5.25), RM30 ($7.90) at night. The ride is about 15 or 20 minutes, but can take 30 minutes during rush hour.

**BY BUS** Buses also run all over the island and are well used by tourists, who don't want to spring RM20 ($5.25) every time they want to go to the beach. The dark blue no. 93 and the white with blue no. 202 both operate between KOMTAR in Georgetown and the beach resorts at Batu Feringgi. Fare is anywhere under RM3 (80¢). Get exact change from your hotel's cashier before you set off, and ask the bus driver about the exact fare to your destination.

**CAR RENTAL** **Hertz** has an office in Georgetown at 38 Farquhar St. (© **04/243-0208**), but it does not rent self-drive vehicles. A car with chauffer goes for RM80 ($21) per hour, for a minimum of 3 hours. If you want to self-drive, call **Avis** at the Penang International Airport at © **04/643-9633.**

**BY BICYCLE** Along Batu Feringgi there are bicycles and motorcycles (little 100cc scooters, really) available for rent. I don't recommend hiring the scooters. You can never be certain of their maintenance record and Penang's drivers are careless about watching your back. A sad number of visitors are injured or worse because of scooter accidents.

**BY TRISHAW** In Georgetown it's possible to find some trishaw action for about RM20 ($3.95) an hour. It's kitchy and touristy and I completely recommend it for traveling between in-town sights, at least for an hour or two. Bargain hard; these guys are skilled negotiators.

**ON FOOT** I think everyone should walk at least part of the time to see the sights of Georgetown, because in between each landmark and exhibit there's so much more to see. A taxi, even a trishaw, will whisk you right by back alleys where elderly haircutters set up alfresco shops, bicycle repairmen sit fixing tubes in front of their stores, and Chinese grannies fan themselves in the shade. Georgetown is stimulating, with the sights of old trades still being plied on these living streets, the noise of everyday life, and the exotic smells of an old Southeast Asian port. Give yourself at least a day here. Start wandering early in the morning, by the waterfront, down the back alleys, before the heat of the sun takes hold—the lighting is perfect for photography and you will find fantastic subjects here.

## FAST FACTS: PENANG

Penang's **area code** is 04. The **banking center** of Georgetown is in the downtown area (close to Fort Cornwallis) on Leboh Pantai, Leboh Union, and Leboh Downing, but you'll find ATMs in KOMTAR and other smaller shopping plazas as well. **Internet** cafes come and go, so it's best to ask your hotel's

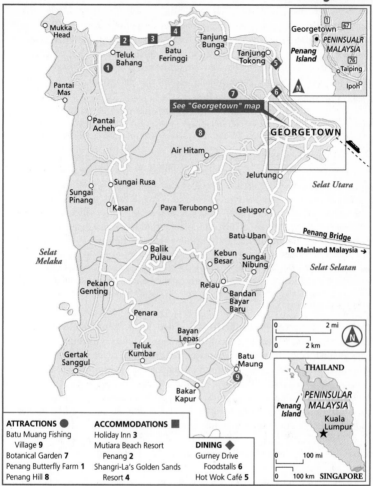

# Penang Island

**ATTRACTIONS** ●
Batu Muang Fishing
  Village **9**
Botanical Garden **7**
Penang Butterfly Farm **1**
Penang Hill **8**

**ACCOMMODATIONS** ■
Holiday Inn **3**
Mutiara Beach Resort
  Penang **2**
Shangri-La's Golden Sands
  Resort **4**

**DINING** ◆
Gurney Drive
  Foodstalls **6**
Hot Wok Café **5**

concierge for the closest place to your hotel. If you're in town, Chulia Street, the
main drag for backpacker tourists, has Internet access in a few places.

## WHERE TO STAY

While Georgetown has many hotels right in the city for convenient sightseeing,
most visitors choose to stay at one of the beach resorts 30 minutes away at Batu
Feringgi. Trips back and forth can be a bother (regardless of the resorts' free shuttle services), but if you're not staying in a resort, most of the finer beaches are
off-limits.

**Cheong Fatt Tze Mansion** ★★ *Finds*     Hands down the most unique and
memorable hotel experience in all of Malaysia—to sleep inside the walls of one
of Asia's most carefully restored heritage homes, the huge and opulent mansion
of 19th-century millionaire Cheong Fatt Tze. The lobby is a simple desk in the
courtyard, inside the only facilities to speak of are a courtyard breakfast area, a
library, and a TV room (guest rooms do not have TVs). Guest rooms are each

distinctive in shape and decor, all with plank floors, charming architectural detail, and furnished in antiques and replicas of the period. Double rooms have either twin beds or one king. Suites are also available. All are air-conditioned and have private bathrooms, though they are pretty small and bare. The experience is described by the management as an "owner-hosted home stay," which is quite accurate. Don't expect the professional polish of the Shangri-La, but then, with so much beauty around you, who cares?

13 Leith St., 10200 Penang. ⓒ **04/262-0006.** www.cheongfatttzemansion.com. 16 units. RM250 ($66) double; suites from RM420 ($111). AE, DC, MC, V. **Amenities:** Breakfast area w/tea and beverage service; laundry service; nonsmoking rooms; library; TV room; valet service. *In room:* A/C, coffee/tea-making facilities.

**The City Bayview Hotel, Penang**    This city hotel is perfect for those who visit Penang for its cultural treasures rather than its beaches. A good budget choice, it has a number of fair dining venues, including a rooftop revolving restaurant with excellent views of the island. Choose from guest rooms in the new wing, completed in 1999, or those in the old wing, which have been recently refurbished. Either choice offers cool rooms in neutral tones, not as elegant as many, but comfortable and definitely value for money.

25-A Farquhar St., Georgetown, 10200 Penang. ⓒ **04/263-3161.** Fax 04/263-4124. 320 units. RM350–RM400 ($92–$105) double. AE, DC, MC, V. **Amenities:** 3 restaurants; club w/live entertainment; lobby lounge; outdoor pool; concierge; limo service; business center; 24-hr. room service; babysitting; same-day laundry service/dry cleaning; nonsmoking rooms. *In room:* A/C, TV w/in-house movies, minibar, coffee/tea-making facilities, hair dryer, safe.

**Eastern & Oriental Hotel (E&O)** 👫👫    E&O first opened in 1884, established by the same Sarkies brothers who were behind Raffles Hotel in Singapore. Closed for many, many years (it was desperately in need of an overhaul), it reopened in April 2001. It is without a doubt the most atmospheric hotel in Penang, with manicured lawns and tropical gardens flanking a white colonial-style mansion, with a lacelike facade and Moorish minarets. Accommodations are all suites, with cozy sitting nooks and sleeping quarters separated by pocket sliding doors. You can expect molding details around every door and paned window, Oriental carpets over polished plank floorboards, and Egyptian cotton linens dressing each poster bed. Dining along the hotel's many verandas is gorgeous. One caveat—no beach, but the pool in the seafront garden is very pretty.

10 Farquhar St., 10200 Penang. ⓒ **04/222-2000.** Fax 04/261-6333. www.e-o-hotel.com. 101 units. RM530–RM650 ($140–$171). AE, DC, MC, V. **Amenities:** 2 restaurants; English-style pub; outdoor pool; small fitness center w/sauna; concierge; limo service; 24-hr. room service; same-day laundry service/dry cleaning. *In room:* A/C, satellite TV, minibar, coffee/tea-making facilities.

**Holiday Inn Resort Penang** 👶    This is a recommended choice for families, but be warned this resort has little appeal for vacationing couples or singles sans children. For families it has everything. Special KidSuites have a separate room for the wee ones with TV, video, and PlayStation, some with bunk beds—choose from jungle, treasure island, or outer-space themes. Holiday Inn also has a Kids Club, fully supervised day care with activities and games and a lifeguard. Older kids can join in beach volleyball, water polo, bike tours, and an assortment of watersports arranged by the staff. Guest rooms are in two blocks: a low-rise structure near the beach and a high-rise tower along the hillside, connected by a second-story walkway. Naturally, the beachside rooms command the greater rate. Beachside rooms also have better ambience and slightly larger space with wood floors and details, while tower rooms have less charm. The lack of dining options gets tiring.

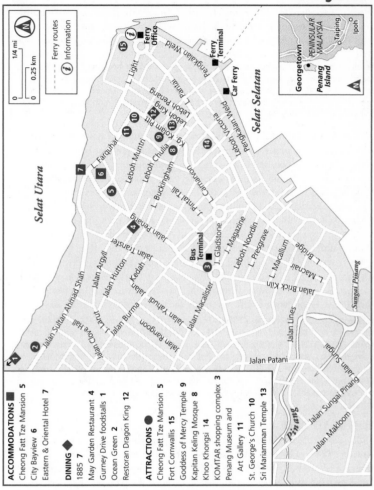

**Georgetown** map legend:

72 Batu Ferringhi, 11100 Penang. © **04/881-1601.** Fax 04/881-1389. www.penang.holiday-inn.com. 362 units. RM400–RM500 ($105–$132) hillview double; RM480–RM600 ($126–$158) seaview double; RM750 ($197) KidSuite; from RM750 ($197) suite. AE, DC, MC, V. **Amenities:** Restaurant; lobby lounge; 2 pools (outdoor and children's); outdoor lighted tennis courts; fitness center; watersports rentals; children's club; game room; concierge; tour desk; limo service; 24-hr. room service; massage; babysitting; same-day laundry service/dry cleaning. *In room:* A/C, satellite TV w/in-house movies, minibar, coffee/tea-making facilities, hair dryer, iron, safe.

**Mutiara Beach Resort Penang** 🏵🏵 With a superb secluded beach location combined with luxurious accommodations and beautiful grounds, Mutiara has remained a popular choice in Penang since it opened in 1988. The poolside is lush and scenic, and the private beach has all assortment of watersports available. I love the guest rooms here. Boring drapes are replaced by wooden louvered doors that open out to a small balcony with a cafe table and chairs—even gardenview rooms feel like an escape. Inside, rooms feel uncluttered, with rattan armchairs and Persian-style carpets covering parquet floors. Huge bathrooms have separate bathtubs and shower stalls, double vanity sinks and lots of closet space. The restaurants and lounge facilities, particularly the Italian La Farfalla, are excellent with attentive waitstaff. There's a children's club as well.

1 Jalan Teluk Bahang, 11050 Penang. ℂ **04/886-8888.** Fax 04/885-2829. 438 units. RM650–RM830 ($171–$218) double; from RM960 ($253) suite. AE, DC, MC, V. **Amenities:** 4 restaurants; lobby lounge; beachfront bar; 2 outdoor pools (1 for children); putting green; 4 outdoor lighted tennis courts; 4 squash courts; fitness center w/Jacuzzi, sauna, steam, and massage; watersports equipment; children's center; game room; concierge; tour desk; car-rental desk; limo service; shuttle service to Georgetown; business center; salon; 24-hr. room service; babysitting; same-day laundry service/dry cleaning. *In room:* A/C, satellite TV w/in-house movies, minibar, coffee/tea-making facilities, hair dryer, safe.

**Shangri-La's Golden Sands Resort** 🟡 🄺🄸🄳🅂 Shangri-La has been operating resorts on Penang longer than anyone else, and since it got here first you can bet it laid claim to the best beach. Shangri-La has two neighboring properties on this site, Golden Sands and its more exclusive sister, Rasa Sayang. A newer resort, Golden Sands is priced lower than the Rasa Sayang, so it attracts more families. The beach, pool area, and public spaces fill up fast in the morning, and folks are occupied all day with beach sports like parasailing and jet-skiing, and pool games. For the younger set, a kids' club keeps small ones busy while Mom and Dad do "boring stuff." Rooms are large with full amenities, and the higher-priced categories have views of the pool and sea. Bad news: Rasa Sayang, my favorite resort on Penang, closed in December 2004 for a massive 2-year renovation. Management at Golden Sands swear there will be no effect on the quality of service at their resort. Good news: I can't wait to see the new Rasa Sayang in 2006!

Batu Feringgi Beach, 11100 Penang. ℂ **800/942-5050** in the U.S. and Canada, 800/222-448 in Australia, 800/442179 in New Zealand, or 04/881-1911. Fax 04/881-1880. www.shangri-la.com. 395 units. RM490–RM680 ($129–$179) double; RM1,399 ($368) suite. AE, DC, MC, V. **Amenities:** 3 restaurants; lobby lounge; 2 outdoor lagoon-style pools; outdoor lighted tennis courts; watersports equipment; children's center; game room; concierge; tour desk; car-rental desk; limo service; shuttle service to Shangri-La Hotel in Georgetown; business center; salon; 24-hr. room service; babysitting; same-day laundry service/dry cleaning; self-service launderette. *In room:* A/C, satellite TV w/in-house movies, fridge, coffee/tea-making facilities, hair dryer, safe.

## WHERE TO DINE

**1885** 🟡🟡 CONTINENTAL If you're celebrating a special occasion while in Penang, 1885 will make the experience beyond memorable. The nostalgic romance of the E&O Hotel, its colonial architecture, interiors, and manicured lawns evoking times when tigers probably roamed the grounds after dark, provides the most incredible backdrop for a perfect meal. From an ever-changing menu, poultry, special cuts of meats, and fresh seafood are prepared in delicate contemporary Western style. Candlelight, starched linens, silver service, and extremely attentive staff create a magical experience. The wine list is extensive. By Malaysian standards, this is a very expensive meal, but if you compare the quality of the service and cuisine, plus the stellar surrounds, really, you will never find such elegance for this price in Europe or the States. Also, men are asked to kindly wear a shirt with a collar.

Eastern & Oriental Hotel (E&O), 10 Lebuh Farquhar. ℂ **04/222-0000.** Reservations recommended. Main courses RM50–RM100 ($13–$26). AE, DC, MC, V. Daily 7–10:30pm.

**Hot Wok Café** 🟡 PERANAKAN This place is the number-one-recommended Peranakan restaurant in the city, and small wonder: The food is great and the atmosphere is fabulous. Filled with local treasures such as wooden latticework, wooden lanterns, carved Peranakan cabinets, tapestries, and carved wood panels, the decor will make you want to just sit back, relax, and take in sights you'd only ever see in a Peranakan home. Their curry capitan, a famous local dish, is curry chicken stuffed with potatoes, with a thick delicious coconut-based gravy. The house specialty is a mean *perut ikan* (fish intestine with roe and vegetable).

125-D Desa Tanjung, Jalan Tanjung. ✆ **04/899-0858.** Reservations recommended for weekends. Main courses RM9–RM15 ($2.35–$3.95). AE, DC, MC, V. Daily 11am–3pm and 6–11pm.

**May Garden Restaurant** CANTONESE   This is a top Cantonese restaurant in Georgetown, and while it's noisy and not too big on ambience, it has excellent food. But how many Chinese do you know who go to places for ambience? It's the food that counts! Outstanding dishes include the tofu and broccoli topped with sea snail slices or the fresh steamed live prawns. May Garden also has suckling pig and Peking duck. Don't agree to all the daily specials or you'll be paying a fortune.

70 Jalan Penang. ✆ **04/261-6806.** Reservations recommended. Main courses start at RM8 ($2.10). Seafood is priced by weight. AE, DC, MC, V. Daily noon–3pm and 6–10:30pm.

**Ocean Green** ★★ SEAFOOD   I can't rave enough about Ocean Green. If the beautiful sea view and ocean breezes don't make you weep with joy, the food certainly will. A long list of fresh seafood is prepared steamed or fried, with your choice of chile, black-bean, sweet-and-sour, or curry sauces. On the advice of a local food expert, I tried the lobster thermidor, expensive but divine, and the chicken wings stuffed with minced chicken, prawns, and gravy.

48F Jalan Sultan Ahmad Shah. ✆ **04/226-2681.** Reservations recommended. Main courses from RM12 ($3.15); seafood priced according to market value. AE, MC, V. Daily 9am–11pm.

**Restoran Dragon King** PERANAKAN   Penang is famous around the world for delicious local Peranakan dishes, and Dragon King is a good place to sample the local cuisine at its finest. It was opened 20 years ago by a group of local teachers who wanted to revive the traditional dishes cooked by their mothers. In terms of decor, the place is nothing to shout about—just a coffee shop with tile floors and folding chairs—but all the curries are hand blended to perfection. Their curry capitan will make you weep with joy, it's so rich. But come early for the *otak-otak*, or it might sell out. While Dragon King is hopping at lunchtime, dinner is quiet.

99 Leboh Bishop. ✆ **04/261-8035.** Main courses RM8–RM20 ($2.10–$5.25). No credit cards. Daily 11am–3pm and 6–10pm.

## FOOD STALL DINING

No section on Penang dining would be complete without coverage of the local food stall scene, which is famous. Penang hawkers can make any dish you've had in Malaysia, Singapore, or even southern Thailand better. Penang may be attractive for many things—history, culture, nature—but it is loved for its food.

**Gurney Drive Foodstalls,** toward the water just down from the intersection with Jalan Kelawai, is the biggest and most popular hawker center. It has all kinds of food, including local dishes with every influence: Chinese, Malay, Indian. Find *char kway teow* (fried flat noodles with seafood), *char bee hoon* (a fried thin rice noodle), *laksa* (noodles and seafood in a tangy and spicy broth), *murtabak* (mutton, egg, and onion fried inside Indian bread and dipped in dhal), *oh chien* (oyster omelet with chile dip), and *rojak* (a spicy fruit and seafood salad). After you've eaten your way through Gurney Drive, you can try the stalls on Jalan Burmah near the Lai Lai Supermarket.

## WHAT TO SEE & DO
### IN GEORGETOWN

**Cheong Fatt Tze Mansion** ★★★  Cheong Fatt Tze (1840–1917), once dubbed as "China's Rockefeller" by the *New York Times,* built a vast commercial empire in Southeast Asia, first in Indonesia, then in Singapore. He came to Penang in 1890 and continued his success, giving some of his spoils to build schools throughout the region. His mansion, where he lived with his eight wives, was built between 1896 and 1904.

The mansion is a sight to behold. Mr. Cheong spent lavishly for Chinese detail that reflects the spirit of his heritage and the fashion of the day as well as the rules of traditional feng shui. Every corner is dripping with ambience, outfitted throughout with stained glass, carved moldings, gilded wood-carved doors, ceramic ornaments, lovely courtyard and gardens, plus seven staircases.

In 2000 the mansion won UNESCO's Asia-Pacific Heritage Award for Conservation, so lovingly has this historic treasure been preserved. Guided tours explain the history, personalities, and culture behind the home, plus the details of the conservation efforts. If you're really hooked, the owners host a home-stay program.

Lebuhraya Leith. ☎ 04/262-0006. Admission RM10 ($2.65). Daily guided tours at 11am and 3pm.

**Fort Cornwallis**  Fort Cornwallis is built on the site where Capt. Francis Light, founder of Penang, first landed in 1786. The fort was first built in 1793, but this site was an unlikely spot to defend the city from invasion. In 1810 it was rebuilt in an attempt to make up for initial strategic planning errors. In the shape of a star, the only actual buildings still standing are the outer walls, a gunpowder magazine, and a small Christian chapel. The magazine houses an exhibit of old photos and historical accounts of the old fort.

Lebuhraya Leith. No phone. Admission RM4 ($1.05) adults, RM2 (55¢) children. Daily 8am–7pm.

**Goddess of Mercy Temple**  Dedicated jointly to Kuan Yin, the goddess of mercy, and Ma Po Cho, the patron saint of sea travelers, this is the oldest Chinese temple in Penang. On the 19th of the second, sixth, and ninth months of the lunar calendar (the months that fall between February/March, June/July, and September/October, respectively), Kuan Yin is celebrated with Chinese operas and puppet shows.

Leboh Pitt. No phone.

**Kapitan Keling Mosque**  Captain Light donated a large parcel of land on this spot for the settlement's sizable Indian Muslim community to build a mosque and graveyard. The leader of the community, known as Kapitan Keling (or Kling, which ironically was once a racial slur against Indians in the region), built a brick mosque here. Later, in 1801, he imported builders and materials from India for a new, brilliant mosque. Expansions in the 1900s topped the mosque with stunning domes and turrets, adding extensions and new roofs.

Jalan Masjid Kapitan Keling (Leboh Pitt). No phone.

**Khoo Khongsi** ★  The Chinese who migrated to Southeast Asia created clan associations in their new homes. Based on common heritage, these social groups formed the core of Chinese life in the new homelands. The Khoo clan, which immigrated from Hokkien province in China, acquired this spot in 1851 and set to work building row houses, administrative buildings, and a clan temple around a large square. The temple here now was actually built in 1906 after a fire destroyed its predecessor. It was believed the original was too ornate, provoking the wrath of the gods. One look at the current temple, a Chinese baroque masterpiece, and you'll wonder how that could possibly be. Come here in August for Chinese operas.

Leburaya Cannon. ✆ 04/261-4609. Free admission. Daily 9am–5pm.

**Penang Museum and Art Gallery** 𝒜𝒜 The historical society has put together this marvelous collection of ethnological and historical findings from Penang, tracing the port's history and diverse cultures through time. It's filled with paintings, photos, costumes, and antiques among much more, all presented with fascinating facts and trivia. Upstairs is an art gallery. Originally the Penang Free School, the building was built in two phases, the first half in 1896 and the second in 1906. Only half of the building remains; the other was bombed to the ground in World War II. It's a favorite stop on a sightseeing itinerary because it's air-conditioned!

Leburaya Farquhar. ✆ 04/261-3144. Free admission. Sat–Thurs 9am–5pm.

**St. George's Church** Built by Rev. R. S. Hutchins (who was also responsible for the Free School next door, home of the Penang Museum) and Capt. Robert N. Smith, whose paintings hang in the museum, this church was completed in 1818. While the outside is almost as it was then, the contents were completely looted during World War II. All that remains are the font and the bishop's chair.

Farquhar St. No phone.

**Sri Mariamman Temple** This Hindu temple was built in 1833 by a Chettiar, a group of southern Indian Muslims, and received a major face-lift in 1978 with the help of Madras sculptors. The Hindu Navarithri festival is held here, whereby devotees parade Sri Mariamman, a Hindu goddess worshipped for her powers to cure disease, through the streets in a night procession. It is also the starting point of the Thaipusam Festival, which leads to a temple on Jalan Waterfall.

Leburaya Queen. No phone.

## OUTSIDE GEORGETOWN

**Batu Muang Fishing Village** If you'd like to see a local fishing village, here's a good one. This village is special for its shrine to Admiral Cheng Ho, the early Chinese sea adventurer.

Southeast tip of Penang. No central phone.

**Botanical Gardens** Covering 30 hectares (74 acres) of landscaped grounds, this botanical garden was established by the British in 1884, with grounds that are perfect for a shady walk and a ton of fun if you love monkeys. They're crawling all over the place and will think nothing of stepping forward for a peanut (which you can buy beneath the DO NOT FEED THE MONKEYS sign). Also in the gardens are a jogging track and kiddie park.

About a 5- or 10-min. drive west of Georgetown. ✆ 04/228-6248. Free admission. Daily 7am–7pm.

**Penang Butterfly Farm** The Penang Butterfly Farm, located toward the northwest corner of the island, is the largest in the world. On its 0.8-hectare (2-acre) landscaped grounds there are more than 4,000 flying butterflies from 120 species. At 10am and 3pm there are informative butterfly shows. Don't forget the insect exhibit—there are about 2,000 or so bugs.

Jalan Teluk Bahang. ✆ 04/881-1253. Admission RM5 ($1.30) adults, RM2 (55¢) children 5 and over; free for children 4 and under. Mon–Fri 9am–5pm; Sat–Sun 9am–6pm.

**Penang Hill**   Covered with jungle growth and 20 nature trails, the hill is great for trekking. Or, you can go to Ayer Hitam, a town in the central part of Penang, and take the Keretapi Bukit Bendera funicular railway to the top. It sends trains up and down the hill every half-hour from 6am to 9:15pm, and costs RM4 ($1.05) for adults and RM2 (55¢) for children, round-trip. If you prefer to make the trek on foot, go to the Moon Gate at the entrance to the Botanical Garden for a 5.5km (3.4-mile) 3-hour hike to the summit.

A 20- to 30-min. drive southwest from Georgetown. The funicular station is on Jalan Stesen Keretapi Bukit.

## SHOPPING

The first place anyone here will recommend you to go for shopping is **KOM-TAR.** Short for Kompleks Tun Abdul Razak, it is the largest shopping complex in Penang, a full 65 stories of clothing shops, restaurants, and a couple of large department stores. There's a **duty-free shop** on the 57th floor. On the third floor is a **tourist information center.**

Good shopping finds in Penang are batik, pewter products, locally produced curios, paintings, antiques, pottery, and jewelry. If you care to walk around in search of finds, there are a few streets in Georgetown that are the hub of shopping activity. In the city center, the area around Jalan Penang, Leburhaya Campbell, Leburhaya Kapitan Keling, Leburhaya Chulia, and Leburhaya Pantai is near the Sri Mariamman Temple, the Penang Museum, the Kapitan Keling Mosque, and other sites of historic interest. Here you'll find everything from local crafts to souvenirs and fashion, and maybe even a bargain or two. Most of these shops are open from 10am to 10pm daily.

Out at Batu Feringgi, the main road turns into a fun **night bazaar** every evening just at dark. During the day, there are also some good shops for batik and souvenirs.

## PENANG AFTER DARK

If you're looking for a bar that's a little out of the ordinary, visit **20 Leith Street** (11-A Lebuh Leith; ℰ **04/261-8873**). Located in an old 1930s house, the place has seating areas fitted with traditional antique furniture in each room of the house. Possibly the most notorious bar in Penang is the **Hong Kong Bar** (371 Lebuh Chulia; ℰ **04/261-9796**), which opened in 1920 and was a regular hangout for military personnel based in Butterworth. It has an extraordinary archive of photos of the servicemen who have patronized the place throughout the years, plus a collection of medals, plaques, and buoys from ships.

## 6 Langkawi

Where the beautiful Andaman Sea meets the Strait of Malacca, Langkawi Island positions itself as one of the best emerging island paradise destinations in the region. Since 1990, the Malaysian Tourism Board has dedicated itself to promoting the island and developing it as an ideal travel spot. Now, after a decade and a half of work, the island has proven itself as one of this country's holiday gems.

*Note:* Malaysia has declared Langkawi a duty-free zone, so take a peek at some of the shopping in town, and enjoy RM4 ($1.05) beers!

## GETTING THERE

**BY PLANE**   Malaysia Airlines (ℰ **1300/883-000;** www.malaysiaairlines. com) and **AirAsia** (ℰ **1300/889-933;** www.airasia.com) make Langkawi very convenient from either mainland Malaysia or Singapore. In addition, **Singapore Airlines** also flies to Langkawi.

# Langkawi

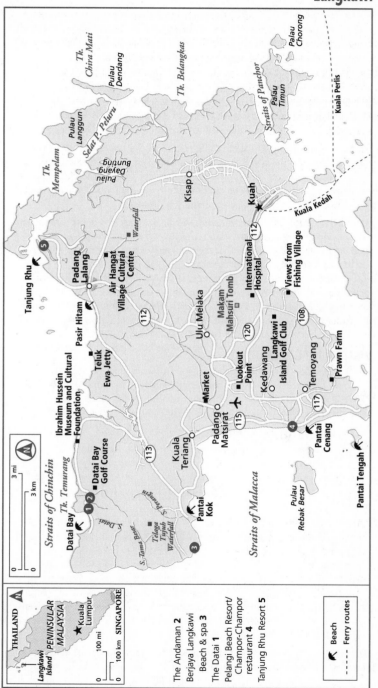

**THAILAND**

**PENINSULAR MALAYSIA**

Langkawi Island

★ Kuala Lumpur

**SINGAPORE**

0                100 mi
0        100 km

Straits of Chinchin

*Tk. Temurang*

Datai Bay

Datai Bay Golf Course

Ibrahim Hussein Museum and Cultural Foundation

Teluk Ewa Jetty

Pasir Hitam

Padang Lalang

Tanjung Rhu

*Tk. Mempelam*

*Pulau Langgun*

*Selat P. Peluru*

*Pulau Dayang Bunting*

*Tk. Chira Mati*

*Pulau Dendang*

*Tk. Belangkas*

*Straits of Panchor*

*Pulau Timun*

*Palau Chorong*

Kuala Perlis

Kisap

Kuah

Kuala Kedah

Air Hangat Village Cultural Centre

Waterfall

(112)

Ulu Melaka

Makam Mahsuri Tomb

International Hospital

Views from Fishing Village

(112)

(120)

(108)

Kedawang

Langkawi Island Golf Club

Temoyang

Prawn Farm

Lookout Point

Market

Padang Matsirat

(115)

(117)

Pantai Cenang

Kuala Teriang

(113)

*S. Datai*

*S. Panggai*

Telaga Tujuh Waterfall

*S. Tama Besar*

Pantai Kok

Pantai Tengah

*Pulau Rebak Besar*

*Straits of Malacca*

N

0   3 mi
0   3 km

The Andaman **2**

Berjaya Langkawi Beach & spa **3**

The Datai **1**

Pelangi Beach Resort/ Champor-Champor restaurant **4**

Tanjung Rhu Resort **5**

↙ Beach

- - - - Ferry routes

581

The best thing to do is prearrange a shuttle pickup from your resort; otherwise you can grab a taxi out in front of the airport. To Pantai Cenang or Pantai Tengah, the fare should be about RM25 ($6.60), while to the farther resorts at Tanjung Rhu and Datai Bay it will be as high as RM40 ($11).

**BY TRAIN**    Taking the train can be a bit of a hassle, because the nearest stop (in Alor Setar) is quite far from the jetty to the island, requiring a cab transfer. Still, if you prefer rail, hop on the overnight train from KL (the only train), which will put you in to Alor Setar at around 7am. Just outside the train station you can find the taxi stand, with cabs to take you to the Kuala Kedah jetty.

**BY BUS**    To be honest, I don't really recommend using this route. If you're coming from KL, the bus ride is long and uncomfortable, catching the taxi transfer to the jetty can be problematic, and by the time you reach the island you'll need a vacation from your vacation. Fly or use the train. If you're coming from Penang, the direct ferry is wonderfully convenient.

**BY FERRY**    From the jetty at Kuala Kedah, there are about five companies that provide ferry service to the island (trip time: about 1 hr. and 45 min.; cost: RM15/$3.95). Ferries let you off at the main ferry terminal in Kuah, where you can hop a taxi to your resort for RM30 to RM40 ($7.90–$11).

If you're coming from Penang, the ferry is the way to go. **Bahagia Express** has a morning and afternoon speedboat from Weld Quay in Georgetown for RM35 ($9.20). Call Bahagia in Penang at ✆ **04/263-1943** or visit its office across from the clock tower, just next to the main tourism board office. If you're heading from Langkawi to Penang, you can call Bahagia in Langkawi at ✆ **04/966-5784.**

## VISITOR INFORMATION
The MTB office is unfortunately situated in Kuah town on Jalan Persiaran Putra, far from the beach areas. For specific queries, you can call ✆ **04/966-7789.** If you're arriving by plane, there's another MTB office at the airport (✆ **04/955-7155**).

### GETTING AROUND
**BY TAXI**    Taxis generally hang around at the airport, the main jetty, the taxi stand in Kuah, and at some major hotels. From anywhere in between, your best bet is to ask your hotel's concierge to call a taxi for you. Keep in mind, if you're going as far as one side of the island to the other, your fare can go as high as RM40 ($11).

**CAR & MOTORCYCLE RENTAL**    At the airport and from agents in the complex behind the main jetty, car rentals can be arranged starting at RM60 ($16) per day. This is for the standard, no-frills model—actually, mine was more reminiscent of some of the junkers I drove throughout college, but it still got me around. Insurance policies are lax, as are rental regulations. My rental guys seemed more concerned with my passport documents than with my driver's license. If you're out on the beach at Cenang or Tengah, a few places rent jeeps and motorcycles from RM80 ($21) per day and RM30 ($7.90) per day, respectively. Pick a good helmet.

**BY FOOT**    The main beaches at Cenang and Tengah can be walked quite nicely; however, don't expect to be able to walk around to other parts of the island.

### FAST FACTS: LANGKAWI
The only major **bank** branches are located far from the beach areas, in Kuah town, mostly around the blocks across the street from the Night Hawker Center

(off Jalan Persiaran Putra). Money changers keep long hours out at Pantai Cenang and Pantai Tengah, but for other resorts you'll have to change your money at the resort itself. Along the Pantai Cenang and Pantai Tengah main road, you'll find at least a half dozen small **Internet** places.

## WHERE TO STAY

**The Andaman** ★★ *Kids*   You will be surprised how large this resort is, its buildings blend so perfectly with the jungle surrounding them. Andaman has far better landscaped garden areas than neighboring Datai (see below), with a sprawl of lush grounds hugging a beautiful white beach, as opposed to Datai, which is quite constricted architecturally by its hillside situation. On the other hand, I prefer Datai's mesmerizing tropical Asian simplicity. Sometimes The Andaman uses decorator ideas straight from the West, European-style furnishings and fabrics, which to me detract from the whole spirit of escapism. But one other advantage: The Andaman welcomes families, and has special facilities, including a kid's club, and a better beach. The entrance and main lobby are overpowering in size, but visually quite stunning in open-air local-style architecture with vaulted roofs built from polished hardwoods. Guest rooms, in two wings that span out to either side of the main building are big, with wall-to-wall carpeting and Western-style decor, save a few local textiles for effect. Ground-floor lanai rooms have a private sun deck with umbrella stand. The pool is huge with lots of shady spots, and the spa features traditional Malay herbal beauty and health treatments. Gulai House serves delicious Malay and Indian cuisine in a charming open-air Malay-style house by the beach.

Jalan Teluk Datai, P.O. Box 94, 07000 Langkawi, Kedah. ✆ 04/959-1088. Fax 04/959-1168. www.the andaman.com. RM900–RM1,950 ($237–$513) double; RM1,450 ($382) lanai double; from RM1,950 ($513) suite. Prices jump in Dec–Jan. AE, DC, MC, V. **Amenities:** 4 restaurants; 3 lounges; outdoor pools surrounded by gardens; golf course; 2 outdoor lighted tennis courts; fitness center; spa w/Jacuzzi, sauna, steam, and massage; watersports equipment; mountain-bike rental; concierge; limo service; 24-hr. room service; babysitting; same-day laundry service/dry cleaning; jungle trekking. *In room:* A/C, satellite TV w/in-house movies, minibar, coffee/tea-making facilities, hair dryer, safe.

**The Datai** ★★★   Aesthetically speaking, this is one of my favorite resorts in Southeast Asia, coming damn close to heaven. Datai is the epitome of sublime, its tropical resort design incorporating nature at every turn. Beyond the graceful open-air lobby, pass the lily pond courtyard to the Datai's brilliant lounge—a hillside veranda surrounded by lush jungle and suspended above a breathtaking bay. Rooms and villas, also built into the hillside, are expert in their studied Southeast Asian elegance. Minimalist in design, the color schemes stick close to nature, with rosewood tones, deep local tapestries, and regal celadon-colored upholstery. Even lower-priced deluxe rooms have a quaint seating area with a view, plus an oversize bathroom with designer body-care products, separate stall shower, and long bathtub. Guest facilities, which include two pools, a spa, and golf course, show the same meticulous attention to luxury. A top pick.

Jalan Teluk Datai, 07000 Langkawi, Kedah. ✆ 800/223-6800 in the U.S. and Canada, 800/181-123 in the U.K., or 04/959-2500. Fax 04/959-2600. www.ghmhotels.com/thedatai. RM1,325 ($349) double; RM1,520–RM1,985 ($400–$522) villa; from RM2,125 ($559) suite. Prices jump in Dec–Jan. AE, DC, MC, V. **Amenities:** 3 restaurants; lounge; 2 outdoor pools surrounded by jungle; golf course; 2 outdoor lighted tennis court; fitness center w/Jacuzzi, sauna, steam, and massage; spa; watersports equipment; mountain-bike rental; concierge; limo service; limited room service; babysitting; same-day laundry service/dry cleaning; library; jungle trekking. *In room:* A/C, satellite TV w/in-house movies, minibar, coffee/tea-making facilities, hair dryer, safe.

**Mutiara Burau Bay Beach Resort**   Burau offers beachside resort accommodations for less money than its upscale neighbors. Not nearly as ritzy, this place feels more like summer camp than a resort. All guest rooms are contained in cabanas, with simple decor that's a bit on the older side. For the price, though, they offer value for money. Burau also organizes golf, massage, jeep treks, jungle treks, mountain biking, tennis, canoeing, catamaran sailing, jet-skiing, scuba diving, snorkeling, fishing, water-skiing, windsurfing, and yachting.

Teluk Burau, 07000 Langkawi, Kedah. 🄯 **04/959-1061.** Fax 04/959-1172. 150 units. RM380 ($100) gardenview chalet; RM420 ($111) seaview chalet; RM550 ($145) family chalet; RM1,000 ($263) suite. AE, DC, MC, V. **Amenities:** 3 restaurants; beach bar; outdoor pool; outdoor lighted tennis courts; children's center; game room; concierge; activities desk; car-rental desk; shuttle service; business center; 24-hr. room service; massage; babysitting; same-day laundry service; nonsmoking rooms. *In room:* A/C, satellite TV w/in-house movies, minibar, coffee/tea-making facilities.

**Pelangi Beach Resort** 🄯    For those who prefer a more active vacation or are looking for a resort that's more family-oriented, I recommend Pelangi. A top-quality resort, this place stands out from neighboring five-star resorts for its sheer fun. A long list of organized sports and leisure pastimes make it especially attractive for families, but surprisingly I never found children to be a distraction here. Pelangi's 51 ethnic wooden chalets are huge inside, and are divided into either one, two, or four guest rooms. You'll be welcomed by vaulted ceilings, modern bathrooms, and large living spaces. But it's the little things you'll love—I didn't want to get out of bed and leave my squishy down pillows and snuggly bedding! In addition, Pelangi's location, near the central beach strip for island life, means you're not cloistered away from the rest of civilization.

Pantai Cenang, 07000 Langkawi, Kedah. 🄯 **04/952-8888.** Fax 04/952-8899. www.pelangibeachresort.com. 350 units. RM740–RM870 ($195–$229) double; from RM1,100 ($289) suite. AE, DC, MC, V. **Amenities:** 3 restaurants; 3 bars; 2 large outdoor pools w/swim-up bar; golf nearby; minigolf course; outdoor lighted tennis courts; squash courts; fitness center w/sauna, steam, and massage; Jacuzzi; concierge; tour desk and watersports center w/equipment rental, boating excursions, and jungle trekking; car-rental desk; limo service; shuttle service; business center; 24-hr. room service; babysitting; same-day laundry service/dry cleaning. *In room:* A/C, satellite TV w/in-house movies, minibar, coffee/tea-making facilities, hair dryer, safe.

**Tanjung Rhu Resort** 🄯🄯    Everyone on the island will agree that the beach at Tanjung Rhu wins first prize, no contest. It's a wide crescent of dazzlingly pure sand wrapped around a perfect crystal azure bay. Tree-lined karst islets jut up from the sea, dotting the horizon. Just gorgeous. This resort claims 440 hectares (1,086 acres) of jungle in this part of the island, monopolizing the scene for extra privacy, but it has its pros and cons. The pros? Guest rooms are enormous and decorated with a sensitivity to the environment, from natural materials to organic recycled-paper wrapped toiletries. The cons? Make sure you don't book your vacation during the months of June or December when Malaysia and Singapore celebrate school holidays, since the place draws families like flies. Still, during between-holiday downtime, I love this resort's friendly and casual atmosphere—and, of course, the beach.

Tanjung Rhu, Mukim Ayer Hangat, 07000 Langkawi, Kedah. 🄯 **04/959-1033.** Fax 04/959-1899. www.tanjungrhu.com.my. 138 units. RM1,100–RM1,500 ($290–$395) double; RM2,050 ($540) suite. AE, DC, MC, V. **Amenities:** 3 restaurants; bar; 2 outdoor pools (1 saltwater and 1 freshwater); golf nearby; outdoor lighted tennis courts; fitness center w/Jacuzzi, sauna, steam, and massage; concierge; activity desk w/watersports (nonmotorized), trekking, and boat tours; limo service; shuttle service; 24-hr. room service; babysitting; same-day laundry service/dry cleaning; library. *In room:* A/C, satellite TV and in-room video w/movie library, CD player, minibar, coffee/tea-making facilities, hair dryer, safe.

## WHERE TO DINE

If you're out at one of the more secluded resorts, chances are you'll stay there for most of your meals. However, if you're at Pantai Cenang or Pantai Tengah, I strongly recommend taking a stroll down to **Champor-Champor** ⚑, just across the road in the Pelangi Resort (© **04/955-1449**), which serves magnificently creative dishes at lunch and dinner—a local *roti canai* served like a pizza, and local fish catches doused in sweet sauces. Everything is incredibly fresh, wildly delicious, and amazingly inexpensive. As for decor, the imaginative catchall beach shack atmosphere really relaxes. After dinner, hang around the bar for the best fun on the island. Since Langkawi is an official duty-free port, one beer costs a wee RM4 ($1.05)!

If you're in Kuah town looking for something good to eat, the best local dining experience can be found at the evening **hawker stalls** just along the waterfront near the taxi stand. A long row of hawkers cook up every kind of local favorite, including seafood dishes. You can't get any cheaper or more laid-back. After dinner, from here it's easy to flag down a taxi back to your resort.

## WHAT TO SEE & DO

Fifteen years ago, Langkawi was just a backwater island supporting small fishing communities. When the government came in with big money to develop the place for tourism, it thought it needed a catch, so it dug up some old moldy "legends" about the island and have tried to market them as bona fide cultural attractions. Basically, any of these sorts of attractions are more hype than anything else. If you want to experience culture, take a ferry to Penang for an overnight in historical Georgetown. Now *that's* something to see.

In terms of beaches and watersports, most resorts are self-contained units, offering their own equipment rentals and planning their own outings.

Outside of your resort, there's some fairly decent diving to be had. **Asian Overland** (© **04/955-2002;** www.asianoverland.com.my) can arrange day trips with two dives to Payar Marine Park within Langkawi's extensive island network. It charges RM240 ($63). It'll take you out even if you're not PADI certified for an introductory dive, and then let you snorkel around for the afternoon. That trip is RM290 ($76) per person. There's an interesting snorkel attraction off Langkawi—a platform in the middle of the sea that floats above a coral reef. Day trips to the platform include rides in a glass-bottomed boat, snorkeling, and lunch on the platform. It's an all-day affair for RM220 ($58) per person, starting at 8am and getting you back to your resort just before dinnertime.

Asian Overland also plans round-island boat trips to "island-hop" at beaches and into mangrove swamps (interesting), with a stop at the Pregnant Maiden Lake (one of the before-mentioned overhyped places). See if you can get them to skip the lake and take you to the Batik Art Village instead. They'll cater your tour so you can see anything you want.

Perhaps one of the loveliest additions to Langkawi's attractions is the **Ibrahim Hussein Museum and Cultural Foundation** (Pasir Tengkorak, Jalan Datai; © **04/959-4669**). The artistic devotion of the foundation's namesake fueled the creation of this enchanting modern space designed to showcase Malaysia's contribution to the international fine-arts scene. If you can pull yourself from the beach for any one activity in Langkawi, this is the one I recommend. Mr. Hussein has created a museum worthy of international attention. Truly a gem. It's open daily from 10am to 5pm; admission is adults RM12 ($3.15), children RM3 (80¢).

## SHOPPING

Langkawi's designated duty-free-port status makes shopping here quite fun and very popular. In Kuah town, the **Sime Darby Duty Free Shop** (Langkawi Duty

Free, 64 Persiaran Putra, Pekan Kuah; (*C* **04/966-6052**) carries the largest selection.

## 7 East Malaysia: Borneo

Borneo for the past 2 centuries has been the epitome of adventure travel. While bustling ports like Penang, Malacca, and Singapore attracted early travelers with dollars in their eyes, Borneo attracted those with adventure in their hearts. Today, the island still draws visitors who seek new and unusual experiences, and few leave disappointed. Rivers meander through dense tropical rainforests, beaches stretch for miles, and caves snake out longer than any in the world. All sorts of creatures you'd never imagine live in the rainforest: deer the size of house cats, owls only 6 inches tall, the odd proboscis monkey, and the endangered orangutan, whose only other natural home is Sumatra. It's also home to the largest flower in the world, the rafflesia, spanning up to a meter wide. Small wonder this place has special interest for scientists and researchers the world around.

The people of Borneo can be credited for most of the alluring tales of early travels. The exotically adorned tribes of warring headhunters and pirates of yesteryear, some of whom still live lifestyles little changed (though both headhunting and piracy are now illegal), today share their mysterious cultures and colorful traditions openly with outsiders.

Add to all of this the fabulous tale of the White Raja of Sarawak, Sir James Brooke, whose family ruled the state for just over 100 years, and you have a land filled with allure, mystery, and romance unlike any other.

Malaysia, Brunei Darussalam, and Indonesia have divided the island of Borneo. Indonesia claims Kalimantan to the south and east, and the Malaysian states of **Sarawak** and **Sabah** lie to the north and northwest. The small sultanate of Brunei is nestled between the two Malaysian states on the western coastline.

### SARAWAK

Tropical rainforest accounts for more than 70% of Sarawak's total land mass, providing homes for not only exotic species of plants and animals, but for the myriad ethnic groups who are indigenous to the area. With more than 10 national parks and four wildlife preserves, Malaysia shows its commitment to conserving the delicate balance of life here, while allowing small gateways for travelers to appreciate natural wonders. The national parks located around the state's capital, **Kuching,** provide quick access to forest life, while longer, more detailed trips to northern Sarawak leads you deeper into the jungle to explore remote forests and extensive ancient cave networks. A web of rivers connects the inland areas to the main towns, and a boat trip from Kuching to visit tribal communities and trek into the surrounding forests is the most memorable attraction going.

The perfect introduction to Sarawak begins in its capital. Kuching's museums, cultural exhibits, and historical attractions will help you form an overview of the history, people, and natural wonders of the state. In Kuching your introduction to Sarawak will be comfortable and fun—culture by day and good food and fun by night. Kuching, meaning "cat" in Malay, also has a wonderful sense of humor, featuring monuments and exhibits to its feline mascot on almost every corner.

**VISITOR INFORMATION** The **Sarawak Tourism Board's Visitor Information Centre** has literature and staff that can answer any question about activities in the state and city. This is actually the best place to start planning any trips to Sarawak's wonderful national parks, as the main office for the National Parks

# East Malaysia's National Parks

& Wildlife Centre operates a Visitor Information Centre here as well. Both offices are incredibly informed and are so welcoming, feel free to take advantage. You'll find them at the Sarawak Tourism Complex in the Old Courthouse opposite the Kuching Waterfront (Sarawak Tourism Board: © 082/410-944; National Parks Centre: © **082/248-088; www.sarawaktourism.com**).

**GETTING THERE**   Almost all travelers to Sarawak enter via Kuching International Airport, just outside the city. **Malaysia Airlines** (© **1300/883-000;** www.malaysiaairlines.com) has international fights from Singapore and Perth, with domestic service from KL, Johor Bahru, and Kota Kinabalu. **AirAsia** (© **1300/889-933;** www.airasia.com) flies between Kuching and KL.

   Massive upgrading works to the airport have created some inconveniences, and nobody seems to know when they will be completed. Some estimates say 2008! Taxis from the airport use coupons that you purchase outside the arrival hall. Priced according to zones, most trips to the central parts of town will be about RM18 ($4.60).

**GETTING AROUND**   Centered around a *padang,* or large ceremonial field, Kuching resembles many other Malaysian cities. Buildings of beautiful colonial style rise on the edges of the field; many of these today house Sarawak's museums. The main sights, as well as the Chinatown area and the riverfront, are easily accessible on foot. Taxis are also available, and do not use meters; most rides around town are quoted at RM6 ($1.60). Taxis can be waved down from the side of the road, or if you're in the Chinatown area, the main taxi stand is near Gambier Road near the end of the India Street Pedestrian Mall.

**FAST FACTS**   Sarawak's area code is 082. Major **banks** have branches on Tunku Abdul Rahman Road near Holiday Inn Kuching, or in the downtown area around Khoo Hun Yeang Road. There are a few Internet cafes around town; it's best to ask your hotel's concierge for the nearest one before you start wandering around—they're constantly going out of business, then popping up elsewhere.

## WHERE TO STAY

**Holiday Inn Kuching**   Holiday Inn offers Western-style accommodations at a moderate price, and you'll appreciate its location in an excellent part of town. It sits along the bank of the Kuching River, so to get to the main riverside area you need only stroll 10 minutes past some of the city's unique historical and cultural sights, shopping, and good places to dine. Catering to a diverse group of leisure travelers and businesspeople, the hotel has spacious, modern, and comfortable rooms; and while there are few bells and whistles, you won't want for convenience. The outdoor swimming pool and excellent fitness center facility will help you unwind, and the small shopping arcade has one of the best collections of books on Sarawak that can be found in the city.

P.O. Box 2362, Jalan Tunku Abdul Rahman, 93100 Kuching, Sarawak, Malaysia. ⓒ 082/423-111. Fax 082/426-169. 305 units. RM225–RM265 ($59–$70) double. AE, DC, MC, V. **Amenities:** 3 restaurants; bar; outdoor pool; fitness center w/sauna; concierge; tour desk; limo service; business center; 24-hr. room service; babysitting; same-day laundry service/dry cleaning; nonsmoking rooms; executive-level rooms. *In room:* A/C, satellite TV w/in-house movies, minibar, coffee/tea-making facilities, hair dryer.

**Merdeka Palace Hotel** ⚑   Towering over the Padang Merdeka in the center of town is the Merdeka Palace, practically a landmark in its own right (as soon as you see the easily distinguishable tower, you'll always know where you are). This is one of the most fashionable addresses in the city, for guests as well as banquets and functions. From the large marble lobby to the mezzanine shopping arcade stuffed with designer tenants, its reputation for elegance is justified. Large rooms come dressed in European-inspired furnishings and fabrics. Try to get a view of the *padang,* as the less expensive rooms face the parking lot. The rooftop outdoor swimming pool is small, but the fully equipped fitness center has sauna and steam rooms, plus massage. The pub here is perhaps the most happening one in town.

Jalan Tun Abang Haji Openg, 93000 Kuching, Sarawak, Malaysia. ⓒ 082/258-000. Fax 082/425-400. www.merdekapalace.com. 214 units. RM390–RM495 ($103–$130) double. AE, DC, MC, V. **Amenities:** 2 restaurants; bar; outdoor pool; fitness center w/Jacuzzi, sauna, steam, and massage; concierge; limo service; business center; shopping arcade; salon; 24-hr. room service; babysitting; same-day laundry service/dry cleaning; nonsmoking rooms; executive-level rooms. *In room:* A/C, satellite TV, minibar, coffee/tea-making facilities, safe.

**Telang Usan Hotel** ⚑⚑ *Value*   While in Kuching I like to stay at the Telang Usan Hotel. It's not as flashy as the higher-priced places, but it's a fantastic bargain for a good room. Most guests here are leisure travelers, and in fact, many are repeat visitors. The small public areas sport murals in local Iban style, revealing the origin of the hotel's owner and operator. While rooms are small and decor is not completely up-to-date, they're spotless. Some rooms have only standing showers, so be sure to specify when making your reservation if a bathtub is important to you. The coffee shop is a fine place to try local food, but it has Western selections as well. The higher-priced rooms have minibars. There is an excellent tour agency under the same ownership at the hotel.

# Kuching

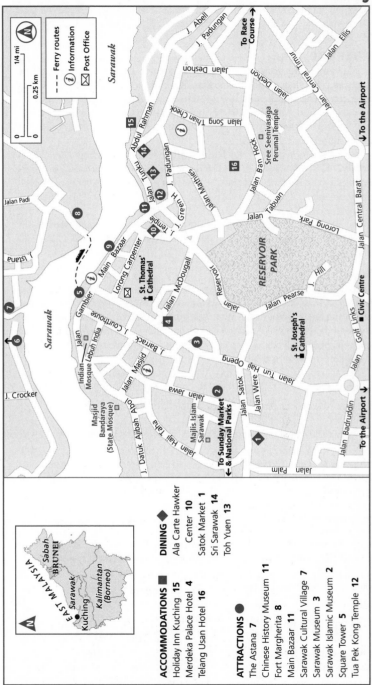

**ACCOMMODATIONS** ■
Holiday Inn Kuching **15**
Merdeka Palace Hotel **4**
Telang Usan Hotel **16**

**ATTRACTIONS** ●
The Astana **7**
Chinese History Museum **11**
Fort Margherita **8**
Main Bazaar **11**
Sarawak Cultural Village **7**
Sarawak Museum **3**
Sarawak Islamic Museum **2**
Square Tower **5**
Tua Pek Kong Temple **12**

**DINING** ◆
Ala Carte Hawker
    Center **10**
Satok Market **1**
Sri Sarawak **14**
Toh Yuen **13**

Ban Hock Rd., P.O. Box 1579, 93732 Kuching, Sarawak, Malaysia. ☎ 082/415-588. Fax 082/245-316. www.telangusan.com. 66 units. RM140–RM200 ($37–$53) double. AE, DC, MC, V. **Amenities:** Restaurant; limited room service; same-day laundry service; Internet service. *In room:* A/C, TV.

## WHERE TO DINE

If you want to try local cuisine, two places come highly recommended. **Sri Sarawak** (18th floor of the Crowne Plaza Riverside hotel; ☎ 082/247-777), has great city views and friendly and helpful waiters who are more than happy to help you navigate the menu, which includes Sarawak specialties such as *umai,* raw fish that's marinated in lime juice with onion, ginger, and chile. I'm addicted and want everyone to try it!

A more informal pick, the **Dulit Coffee House** at Telang Usan Hotel (☎ 082/415-588) has regular local food promotions. Try their *laksa,* vermicelli noodles and seafood in a rich and spicy coconut gravy, or the Sarawak black pepper steak, which is a house specialty. At both Dulit and Sri Sarawak, entrees are reasonably priced between RM8 and RM24 ($2.10–$6.30).

For culinary adventurers, head for the local food stalls at **Satok Market** out at Jalan Satok for excellent Malay, Chinese, and Sarawakian cuisine. Cheap and authentic.

## WHAT TO SEE & DO

**The Astana and Fort Margherita**   At the waterfront by the Square Tower you'll find water taxis to take you across the river to see these two reminders of the White Rajas of Sarawak. The Astana, built in 1870 by Raja Charles Brooke, the second raja of Sarawak, is now the official residence of the governor. It is not open to the public, but visitors may still walk in the gardens. The best view of the Astana, however is from the water.

Raja Charles Brooke's wife, Ranee Margaret, gave her name to Fort Margherita, which was erected in 1870 to protect the city of Kuching. Inside the great castle-like building is a police museum, the most interesting sights of which are the depictions of criminal punishment.

Across the Sarawak River from town. Museum: no phone. Fort: ☎ 082/244-232. Free admission. Tues–Sun 9am–5pm.

**Chinese History Museum**   Built in 1912, this old Chinese Chamber of Commerce Building is the perfect venue for a museum that traces the history of Chinese communities in Sarawak. Though small, it's centrally located and a convenient stop while you're in the area.

Corner of Main Bazaar and Jalan Tunku Abdul Rahman. No phone. Free admission. Daily 9am–5pm.

**Main Bazaar**   Main Bazaar, the major thoroughfare along the river, is home to Kuching's antiques and handicraft shops. If you're walking along the river, a little time in these shops is like a walk through a traditional handicrafts art gallery. You'll also find souvenir shops and some nice T-shirt silk screeners.

Along the river.

**Sarawak Cultural Village** ✦   What appears to be a contrived theme park turns out to be a really fun place to learn about Sarawak's indigenous people. Built around a lagoon, the park re-creates the various styles of longhouse dwellings of each of the major tribes. Inside each house are representative members of each tribe displaying cultural artifacts and performing music, teaching dart blowing, and showing off carving talents. Give yourself plenty of time to stick around and talk with the people, who are recruited from villages inland and love to tell stories about their homes and traditions. Performers dance and display costumes at 11:30am and 4:30pm daily. A shuttle bus leaves at regular intervals from the Holiday Inn Kuching on Jalan Abell.

Kampung Budaya Sarawak, Pantai Damai, Santubong. ✆ 082/846-411. Adults RM45 ($12), children RM23 ($5.90). Daily 9am–5pm.

**Sarawak Islamic Museum**    A splendid array of Muslim artifacts at this quiet and serene museum depicts the history of Islam and its spread to Southeast Asia. Local customs and history are also highlighted. While women are not required to cover their heads, respectable attire that covers the legs and arms is requested.

Jalan P. Ramlee. ✆ 082/244-232. Free admission. Sat–Thurs 9am–5pm; Fri 9am–12:45pm and 3–5pm.

**Sarawak Museum** ⚲    Two branches, one old and one new, display exhibits of the natural history, indigenous peoples, and culture of Sarawak, plus the state's colonial and modern history. The two branches are connected by an overhead walkway above Jalan Tun Haji Openg. The wildlife exhibit is a bit musty, but the arts and artifacts in the other sections are well tended. A tiny aquarium sits neglected behind the old branch, but the gardens here are lovely.

Jalan Tun Haji Openg. ✆ 082/244-232. Free admission. Sat–Thurs 9am–5pm; Fri 9am–12:45pm and 3–5pm.

**Square Tower**    The tower, built in 1879, served as a prison camp, but today the waterfront real estate is better served by a tourist information center. The Square Tower is also a prime starting place for a stroll along the riverside, and is where you'll also find out about cultural performances and exhibitions held at the waterfront. Call for performance schedules.

Jalan Gambier near the riverfront. ✆ 082/426-093.

**Tua Pek Kong Temple**    At a main crossroads near the river stands the oldest Chinese temple in Sarawak. While officially it is dated at 1876, most locals acknowledge the true date of its beginnings as 1843. It's still lively in form and spirit, with colorful dragons tumbling along the walls and incense filling the air.

Junction of Jalan Tunku Abdul Rahman and Jalan Padungan. No phone.

## TOURING LOCAL CULTURE ★★★

One of the highlights of a trip to Sarawak is a visit to a longhouse community. Trips can last from simple overnight stays to 2-week intensive discovery tours. It goes without saying that shorter trips only venture as far as those longhouse villages closest to Kuching. The benefit is that these communities are at ease with foreigners, and so are better able to demonstrate their culture. The drawback is that these villages are the ones most trampled by coach-loads of tourists looking to gawk at "primitive tribes." Basically, the more time you have, the deeper you will venture into the interior, the more time you will have to spend with different ethnic groups allowing greater insight into these fascinating cultures.

A typical longhouse trip starts with a van ride from Kuching followed by a longtail boat ride upriver, through gorgeous scenery. If you are only stopping in for the night, you'll be welcomed, fed, and entertained—the food is generally edible and always prepared under sanitary conditions. Fruits are delicious. Your guide, through translations, will help you chat with villagers and ask questions about their lifestyle and customs. At night you will sleep in a longhouse provided especially for guests. It's basic but cool, with mosquito nets (very necessary) provided. The following day includes a very brief jungle trek, plus hunting and fishing demonstrations before your departure back from whence you came.

If your trip is for longer, you will probably avoid the closer villages and head straight for more remote communities, depending on how much time (and money) you have.

Your average overnight longhouse tour will set you back up to $125 per person. Good tour operators to speak to about arranging a trip are **Borneo Adventure** (55 Main Bazaar; ✆ 082/245-175; fax 082/422-626) and **Telang Usan Travel & Tours** (Ban Hock Rd.; ✆ 082/236-945; fax 082/236-589). These agencies can also arrange trips into Sarawak's national parks.

## TOURING SARAWAK'S NATIONAL PARKS

The Sarawak National Parks & Wildlife Centre has opened access to all of Sarawak's national parks to DIY (do it yourself) travelers. From its booking center in Kuching, you can apply for parks permits and book reservations in state-run lodging within each park. Staff can also advise how to travel to and from each park: those closer to Kuching will only involve local road and river transportation, while more remote parks will require commercial flights to either Sibu or Miri, plus transfers to ground and river transportation and even chartered flights. If you have the time to plan your travel this way, you will be rewarded with the thrill of "getting there," experiencing local life a little closer to the ground.

Most people do not have the luxury of time, which is why I recommend booking trips that interest you through a tour operator who will arrange all transportation, parks permits, lodging, meals, and guides for you, freeing your time to experience the attractions themselves.

### NATIONAL PARKS NOT FAR FROM KUCHING

**Borneo Adventure** (55 Main Bazaar; ✆ 082/245-175; www.borneoadventure. com) costs a few dollars more than many of the other local operations, but you'll get experienced guides and reliable services, and you do not need to join a huge touristy coach group. Most of these trips are for small groups. The half-day trips from Kuching take the mystery out of local transportation—they can even be combined for longer itineraries so you can maximize your time. Borneo Adventure can also prepare customized itineraries and special theme tours based upon your special interests—for example, crafts, flora, or tribal cultures.

**Bako National Park** ✸✸✸, established in 1957, is Sarawak's oldest national park. An area of 2,728 hectares (6,738 acres) combines mangrove forest, lowland jungle, and high plains covered in scrub. Throughout the park you'll see the pitcher plant and other strange carnivorous plants, plus longtailed macaques, monitor lizards, bearded pigs, and the unique proboscis monkey. Because the park is only 37km (23 miles) from Kuching, half-day trips here are extremely convenient. A half-day trip for two costs RM188 ($49) per person.

**Gunung Gading National Park,** about a 2-hour drive west of Kuching, sprawls 4,106 hectares (10,142 acres) over rugged mountains to beautiful beach spots along the coast. Day-trippers and overnighters come to get a glimpse of the rafflesia, the largest flower in the world. The flowers are short-lived and temperamental, but the national parks office will let you know if there are any in bloom. A half-day tour for two people costs RM180 ($47) per person.

**Semenggoh Orang Utan Sanctuary** is a rehabilitation center for orangutans and other endangered wildlife species, who are either orphaned or recovering from illness and are being trained for eventual release into the forest. A half-day tour for two people costs RM160 ($42) per person.

## NATIONAL PARKS A LITTLE FARTHER OUT

**Borneo Adventure** (55 Main Bazaar; ✆ 082/245-175; www.borneoadventure. com) also books trips to national parks in other parts of the state. You'll have to fly to Miri or Sibu, as these two towns are the hop-off points for these excursions. Malaysia Airlines and AirAsia both service these two towns from KL and Kuching.

**Gunung Mulu National Park** provides an amazing adventure with its astounding underground network of caves. The park claims the world's largest cave passage (Deer Cave), the world's largest natural chamber (Sarawak Chamber), and Southeast Asia's longest cave (Clearwater Cave). No fewer than 18 caves offer explorers trips of varying degrees of difficulty, from simple treks with minimal gear to technically difficult caves that require specialized equipment and skills. Above ground is 544 sq. km (212 sq. miles) of primary rainforest, peat swamps, and mountainous forests teeming with mammals, birds, and unusual insects. Located in the north of Sarawak, Mulu is very close to the Brunei border. Borneo Adventure has a 2-day/1-night package for RM276 ($73) per person (minimum two people). The trip includes accommodation, ground transportation, and longboat rides, plus nature guides to see Deer Cave, Sarawak Chamber, and Clearwater Cave, plus some rainforest trekking (wear a hat in the caves to protect yourself from bat droppings). It can book your flights from Kuching, but you'll have to pay extra.

**Niah National Park,** while interesting to nature buffs, is more fascinating for those interested in archaeology. From 1954 to 1967 explorers excavated a prehistoric site inside Niah's extensive cave network. The site dates as far back as 40,000 years, and is believed to have been continuously occupied until some 2,000 years ago. The **Niah Great Cave,** which contains the site, revealed sharp stone implements, pottery vessels, and animal and botanical remains. Near the mouth of the cave is a burial ground dating from Paleolithic times. The Painted Cave, also within Niah's cave network, is a magnificent gallery of mystical cave paintings and coffins that were buried here between A.D. 1 and A.D. 780. Borneo Adventure has a day trip that includes lunch and airport transfer for RM300 ($79) per person, or a 2-day/1-night trip which includes accommodations, meals, and guides for RM606 ($160) per person (both trips are for minimum two people). Further information on the excavation sites can be obtained from the **Sarawak Museum** (✆ 082/244-232; fax 082/246-680).

## 8 Sabah ★★★

Sabah presents a wonderland of awe-inspiring natural scenery, lush primary rain forest, vibrant coral reefs, and mysterious indigenous cultures. It is, in my opinion, Southeast Asia's hidden treasure. A playground for adventure seekers, extreme sportsters, and bums in search of the ultimate beach, Sabah rewards those who venture here with a holiday in an unspoiled paradise.

Covering 73,711 sq. km (28,747 sq. miles) of the northern part of Borneo, the world's third-largest island, Sabah stretches from the South China Sea in the west to the Sulu Sea in the east, both seas containing an abundance of uninhabited islands, postcard perfect beaches, and pristine coral reefs bubbling with marine life. In between, more than half of the state is covered in ancient primary rainforest that's protected in national parks and forest reserves. In these forests, some rare species of mammals like the Sumatran rhino and Asian elephant (herds of them) take effort to witness, but other animals, such as the orangutan, proboscis monkey, gibbon, lemur, civet, Malaysian sun bear, and a host of others can be

---

### ⓘ *Warning* Exercise Caution

In April 2000, 22 people, including 11 foreign tourists, were kidnapped from a dive resort on Sipadan Island off the east coast of Sabah. This would be the first of four incidents of kidnapping, mostly of Malaysian workers, in this area by the Abu Sayyaf, a terrorist group in the southern Philippines with known links to Al-Qaeda. While Malaysia responded by placing security forces on 23 islands and 6 additional strategic locations, the U.S. Department of State still advises Americans to exercise caution when traveling in this area. Despite the warning, foreign visitor arrivals to Sipadan have doubled since the advisory was first issued.

---

seen on jungle treks if you search them out. Of the hundreds of bird species here, the hornbills and herons steal the show.

Sabah's tallest peak also happens to be the highest mountain between the Himalayas and Irian Jaya. At 4,095m (13,432 ft.), **Mt. Kinabalu** is the tallest in Southeast Asia, and a challenge to trek or climb. The state's interior has endless opportunities for jungle trekking, river rafting, mountain biking, and 4×4 exploration for every level of excitement, from soft adventure to extreme sports.

Not only does this state hold mysterious wildlife and geography, but people as well. Sabahans count among their many ethnic groups some 32 different tribes whose cultures and traditions are vastly different from the Malay majority that makes up the rest of the country. In fact, ethnic Malays are a minority in Sabah.

## KOTA KINABALU

The best place to begin exploring Sabah's marine wonders, wildlife and forests, adventure opportunities, and indigenous peoples is from its capital, Kota Kinabalu. A speck of a city on the west coast, it's where you'll find the headquarters for all of Sabah's adventure tour operators and package excursion planners. I recommend you spend at least a day here to explore all your options, then set out to the wilds for the adventure of a lifetime.

**VISITOR INFORMATION**   The **Sabah Tourism Board** (51 Jalan Gaya; ⓒ **088/212-121;** www.sabahtourism.com) provides the most comprehensive information about the state. It's open Monday through Saturday 8am to 5pm. While the national MTB has a small office on Jalan Gaya a block down from the Sabah Tourism office, almost all of its information promotes travel in other parts of the country. Still, if you're interested, stop by at the Ground Floor Uni. Asia Building, No 1 Jalan Sagunting (ⓒ **088/248-698**).

**GETTING THERE**   Because of Sabah's remote location, just about everybody will arrive by air via the **Kota Kinabalu International Airport** in the capital city (ⓒ **088/238-555**), about a 20-minute drive south of the central part of the city. A surprising number of direct international flights connect Sabah to the region. Malaysia Airlines flies from Hong Kong, Manila, Osaka, Seoul, Shanghai, Singapore, Tokyo, and other cities (ⓒ **1300/883-000;** www.malaysia airlines.com), and AirAsia from Bangkok (ⓒ **1300/889-933;** www.airasia.com). Australian Airlines, operated by Qantas (ⓒ **131313;** www.australianairlines. com.au), flies from Sydney.

Malaysia Airlines also has direct domestic flights to Kota Kinabalu from KL, Johor Bahru, Kuching, Sibu and Miri, with in-state service to Sandakan and other towns. AirAsia has direct domestic flights from KL and Johor Bahru.

# Kota Kinabalu

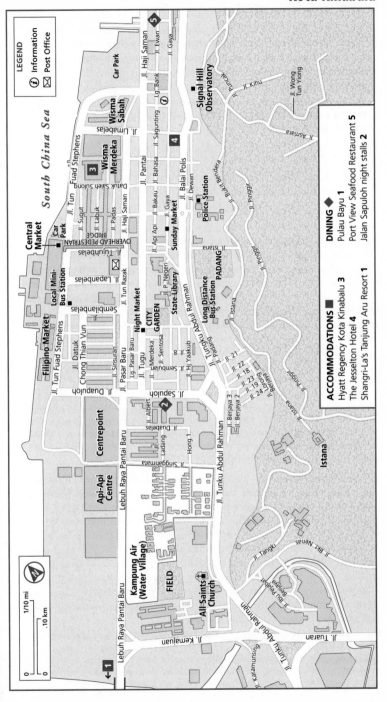

**LEGEND**
- ⓘ Information
- ⊠ Post Office

**South China Sea**

Central Market

Car Park

Wisma Sabah

Wisma Merdeka

Filipino Market

Local Mini-Bus Station

Centrepoint

Api-Api Centre

Kampung Air (Water Village)

FIELD

All Saints Church

Night Market

CITY GARDEN

State Library

Sunday Market

Police Station

PADANG

Long Distance Bus Station

Signal Hill Observatory

Car Park

Istana

**ACCOMMODATIONS** ■
Hyatt Regency Kota Kinabalu **3**
The Jesselton Hotel **4**
Shangri-La's Tanjung Aru Resort **1**

**DINING** ◆
Pulau Bayu **1**
Port View Seafood Restaurant **5**
Jalan Sapuloh night stalls **2**

Jl. Tun Fuad Stephens
Datuk Salleh Sulong
Jl. Sugut
Jl. Labuk
Jl. Padas
Jl. Haji Saman
Jl. Limbelas
Jl. Tuinbelas
Jl. Lapanbelas
Sembilanbelas
Jl. Tun Razak
Jl. Pasar Baru
Lg. Pasar Baru
Jl. Tugu
Jl. Sembulan
Jl. Merdeka
Lg. Sentosa
Jl. Datuk Chong Thian Vun
Jl. Tun Fuad Stephens
Jl. Duapuloh
Jl. Sinsuran
Jl. Sapuloh
Jl. Duabelas
Jl. Albert
Ladang
Hong 1
Jl. Singgahmata
Lebuh Raya Pantai Baru
Jl. Tunku Abdul Rahman
Lebuh Raya Pantai Baru
Jl. Kemajuan
Jl. Tuaran
Jl. Ibu Pejabat
Jl. Bkt. Nenas
Jl. Tangki
Jl. Karamunsing
Jl. Pinggir
Jl. Istana
Jl. Bkt. Bendera
Jl. Saguntung
Jl. Bahasa
Jl. Bakau
Jl. Api Api
Jl. Pantai
Jl. Balai Polis
Jl. Gaya
P. Negeri
Jl. Hj. Yaakub
Jl. Pasang
Jl. 21
Jl. 22
Jl. 18
Jl. 23
Jl. 19
Jl. 20
Jl. 24
Jl. Berjaya
Jl. Berjaya 3
Jl. Berjaya 2
Jl. Dewan
Jl. Pinggir
Jl. Asmara
Jl. Kihu
Jl. Wong Tun Yiong
Jl. Ewan
Jl. Gaya
Jl. Haji Saman
Lg. Bank
Jl. Pandan

OVERHEAD PEDESTRIAN BRIDGE

1/10 mi
.10 km

The most efficient way to get into town from the airport is via taxi. The cars line up outside the arrival hall and are supposed to use a coupon system—look for the coupon sales and taxi-booking counter close by. You'll pay about RM12 ($3.15) for a trip to town. Ignore the drivers who will try to lure you away from the coupon counter; they will always overcharge you.

**GETTING AROUND**   In the downtown area, you can get around quite easily on foot between hotels, restaurants, tour operators, markets, and the tourism office. For longer trips, a taxi will be necessary; in town trips cost about RM10 ($2.65). Taxis are flagged down on the street, or by your hotel's bellhop.

**FAST FACTS**   The **area code** for Sabah is **088.** Sabah time is 1 hour ahead of peninsular Malaysia. You'll find **banks** with ATMs conveniently located in the downtown area around Jalan Limabelas and along Jalan Gaya and Jalan Pantai. While there are no large Internet cafes, per se, you'll find access in small shop fronts around the main parts of town, especially near the shopping malls.

## WHERE TO STAY

**Hyatt Regency Kinabalu** 🌟   The only international business-class hotel in town, in some ways the Hyatt seems a little out of place in cozy Kota Kinabalu. Still, it's located close to the waterfront, near all major shopping and travel operators, and has a fantastic assortment of restaurants to choose from. Even if you're staying elsewhere in town, you may appreciate one of its dining options. As modern as you would expect the Hyatt chain to be, rooms here are large, and are presented in up-to-date furnishing styles that are not so Western that they take all the charm away from the room. Local tour and car-rental booking in the lobby make the place convenient for leisure travelers. One of the high points is Shenanigan's, the best bar in Kota Kinabalu, with live entertainment. It gets packed, mostly with locals and expatriates out for a sip.

Jalan Datuk Salleh Sulong, 88994 Kota Kinabalu, Sabah. 📞 **800/233-1234** in the U.S. and Canada, 800/441-234 in in Australia and New Zealand, or 088/221-234. Fax 088/225-972. http://kinabalu.hyatt.com. 288 units. ($60–$70) double; from ($135) suite. AE, DC, MC, V. **Amenities:** 3 restaurants; bar; outdoor pool; fitness center; concierge; tour desk; car-rental desk; limo service; business center; 24-hr. room service; babysitting; same-day laundry service/dry cleaning; nonsmoking rooms; executive-level rooms. *In room:* A/C, satellite TV w/in-house movies, minibar, coffee/tea-making facilities, hair dryer, safe.

**The Jesselton Hotel** 🌟🌟   Listen to me rave about The Jesselton. It's such a nice surprise to find this quaint boutique hotel in the center of Kota Kinabalu, just about the last real reminder in this city of a colonial presence. Even more lovely is the level of personalized service you receive, and the comfort of the rooms, which, though completely modern, retain their charm with lovely Audubon-style inks and attractive wallpapers and fabrics—sort of a cross between a cozy guesthouse and a top-class hotel. Due to lack of space in the building, there's no pool, fitness center, or business center, but the staff at the front desk can help you with tour information and transportation. The coffee house serves local and Western food, which is quite good. The Gardenia Restaurant looks more upmarket than it really is.

69 Jalan Gaya, 88000 Kota Kinabalu, Sabah. 📞 **088/223-333.** Fax 088/240-401. www.jesseltonhotel.com. 32 units. RM265–RM299 ($70–$79) double; RM650 ($171) suite. AE, DC, MC, V. **Amenities:** Restaurant; coffee shop; bar; lounge; tour desk; limo service; 24-hr. room service; babysitting; same-day laundry service; complimentary clothes pressing and shoe polishing; foreign currency exchange; nonsmoking rooms. *In room:* A/C, TV (movies available), minibar, coffee/tea-making facilities, hair dryer, safe.

**Shangri-La's Tanjung Aru Resort** 🌟🌟🌟 *Kids*   A short ride southwest of Kota Kinabalu and you're at Tanjung Aru, an amazingly gorgeous beach resort area—Sabah's Riviera. The Shangri-La here is located in a most impressive setting, surrounded on three sides by water. It serves the finest local Sabahan cuisine and freshest seafood you can get in the region. Book a room in the Tanjung Wing, which is nestled amid Shangri-La's signature lush garden setting, as the Kinabalu Wing, while newer, is more like a hotel block. Every room has a stunning view of either the sea or Mount Kinabalu, with a balcony for full appreciation. Tropical touches include rattan furnishings in cool colors and local fabrics with wood details. The tour desk can arrange everything from scuba to trekking and rafting, and the free shuttle gives you convenient access to town. Special activities for kids make this place a good choice for families.

Locked Bag 174, 88744 Kota Kinabalu, Sabah. *C* 088/225-800. Fax 088/217-155. www.shangri-la.com. 499 units. RM590–RM690 ($155–$182) double; RM850 ($224) suite. **Amenities:** 3 restaurants; beach bar; lounge; 2 outdoor lagoon-style pools; 4 outdoor lighted tennis courts; fitness center w/Jacuzzi, sauna, steam, and massage; concierge; tour desk; shuttle service; salon; 24-hr. room service; babysitting; same-day laundry service/dry cleaning; nonsmoking rooms. *In room:* A/C, satellite TV w/in-house movies, dataport w/direct Internet access, minibar, coffee/tea-making facilities, hair dryer, safe.

## WHERE TO DINE

On Wednesdays and Saturdays, **Pulau Bayu** at Shangri-La's Tanjung Aru Resort (*C* **088/225-800**) serves all varieties of the freshest fish, lobsters, prawns, squid, crabs, scallops, and clams in an extensive buffet with accompanying cultural show (RM58/$15 per person). Try the *hinava,* a mouthwatering local delicacy of raw fish marinated in lime juice, ginger, shallots, herbs, and chiles. The restaurant is on a small island connected to the resort by walkway, quite romantic. If you're not staying at the resort, the taxi ride from town is only about RM10 ($2.65).

If you're in town, you can also get fresh seafood (selected from tanks on the back wall) at **Port View Seafood Restaurant** (Jalan Haji Saman, across from the old Customs Wharf; *C* **088/252-813**). Prepared primarily in Chinese and Malay styles, dishes are moderately priced (sold by weight) and always succulent.

For a more local experience, food stalls provide the most authentic local cuisine at the best prices. Check out the night stalls on Jalan Sapuloh. Walk through and peek at all the offerings before ordering, and check for the most popular stalls and dishes. (When approaching a new hawker center, I always stroll around checking out what everybody else is eating. Locals always seem to know what's best.)

## WHAT TO SEE & DO

Sabah attracts **scuba** enthusiasts from around the world, who come to dive at Sipadan, an island resort off the east coast of the state. **Sipadan,** ranked as one of the top 10 dive sites in the world, is actually a tall limestone "tower" rising from the bed of the Celebes Sea, supporting vast numbers of marine species, some of which may still be unidentified. As of December 2004, the Malaysian government revoked the licenses of the five dive operators that managed resorts on the tiny island in an effort to prevent environmental degradation—Malaysia is also applying for UNESCO World Heritage site recognition for the area. The dive operators will move their base camps to surrounding islands, offering day trips to the area or running live-aboard trips.

**Borneo Divers** (9th floor, Menara Jubili, 53 Jalan Gaya; *C* **088/222-226;** www.borneodivers.com) was the first full-service dive operator in Borneo, and the pioneering operator to Sipadan. Starting in 2005, it will be housing divers at a new resort, taking half-day trips to Sipadan—the government will regulate the number of divers allowed, but Borneo Divers will take care of your permits. Most people go for a 5-day/4-night trip for about $690 per person, which includes accommodations, meals, airport transfers, and two dives a day. You'll have to pay extra for a round-trip flight into Tawau, which costs about RM190 ($50). Booking can be made through Borneo Divers. Equipment rentals come to $25 per day. Sipadan has good diving year round, but March through October has the best weather.

A newer spot, Layang Layang, located off the coast of northwest Borneo in the South China Sea, is also making a splash as an underwater bounty of marine life. **Layang Layang Island Resort** (head office in KL at Block A, ground floor, A-0-3, Megan Ave. II, 12 Jalan Yap Kwan Seng; ✆ **03/2162-2877**; www.layang layang.com) pioneered this area for divers. The standard package of 6 days/5 nights runs at about $900 per person, which includes accommodation, meals, and three dives a day. Equipment is extra, as is the chartered helicopter flight to the island, which is expensive at $200 round-trip (booked through the dive operator). Layang Layang closes during the monsoon season, from early September through February.

If you want to stay close to Kota Kinabalu, Borneo Divers (see above) makes day trips to **Tunku Abdul Rahman Marine Park.** This group of five islands about 8km (5 miles) off the coast of Kota Kinabalu have been protected since the mid-'70s. Throughout the park, waters are clear and visibility is good. While not as lauded as Sipadan and Layang Layang, if you're looking for some quick diving excitement but you have time and money constraints, it's highly recommended. A day trip that includes two boat dives and a shore dive costs $68, not including equipment rentals. Borneo Divers has a base camp on the smallest island, from which it also conducts complete PADI courses.

Sabah has many other dive sites, including sites such as Pulau Tiga, of *Survivor* TV fame. A couple of sites also offer wreck diving, so if you're interested, inquire when you make your booking.

For other types of watersports, your best bet is to either book these activities through your resort or plan a DIY trip to Tunku Abdul Rahman Marine Park. Catch a ferry at the Sabah Parks Jetty at the Customs House on Jalan Haji Saman opposite Port View Seafood Restaurant (RM15/$3.95 round-trip) to take you to the park. It's only 8km (5 miles) from Kota Kinabalu, so you can spend a day trip at one or more of the park's five islands sunning on the beach. **Snorkel** rentals go for RM10 ($2.65), parasailing charges run RM90 ($24). The latest thrill is **seawalking**—donning an enormous helmet connected to the surface with a tube, which allows you to breathe underwater without tanks. This costs RM200 ($54) a pop. *Tip for snorkelers:* Bring cotton socks to wear under your rental fins to prevent blisters. There are cafes and toilets near the jetties, plus rustic accommodations on two of the islands.

Sabah's rugged terrain makes for terrific hiking, camping, biking, and rafting for any level, be it soft adventure or extreme sports. **TYK Adventure** (Lot 48-2F, 2nd floor, Beverly Hill Plaza; ✆ **088/727-825**) was founded by a local Chinese award-winning tour guide Tham Yau Kong, who also happens to hold records for the longest cultural walk (1998) and for leading the first group to circumcycle Mt. Kinabalu (1999). Mountain-biking day trips around Papar or Penampang are RM220 ($58) per person, including hotel transfer, mountain bike, and helmet.

Many come to Sabah to climb **Mt. Kinabalu.** It's a terrific trip if you are prepared and if you hit it just right, in terms of weather and timing. It can only be done on an overnight trip, which includes a 4- or 5-hour hike from the park headquarters uphill to a ranger station, where you stay the night. Groups awake at 3am to begin the 3-hour hike to the summit. This is not light trekking, as some parts are steep, altitude sickness can cause headaches and nausea, and remember—you're tooling along in the pitch darkness, the whole point being to arrive at the summit in time for the spectacular sunrise. Come prepared with cold-weather snugglies, or at the very least a wool sweater or fleece, long pants, windbreaker, rain poncho, and hiking boots. Bring a good, strong flashlight, and pack plenty of trail mix and sports drinks for rejuvenation. And finally, there's no guarantee that the weather will cooperate with your itinerary. You might hit rain or find the summit covered in clouds. There's pretty much nothing any tour operator can do to guarantee you'll get a clear view. A good general tour operator, **Discovery Tours** (Wisma Sabah, Lot G22, Jalan Haji Saman; ✆ **088/221-244**), with offices at both Shangri-La resorts, takes groups on either 2-day/1-night or 3-day/2-night trips to climb Mt. Kinabalu (RM410/$108 and RM569/$150 per person, respectively, not including an extra RM100/$26) national parks entrance fee). Make sure you book early, because they need to make sure there's space availability at park accommodations. The price includes transfer, lodging, and your guide to the summit.

Discovery Tours also plans regular trips out to Sandakan, on the eastern coast of Sabah, for 2-day/1-night trips to see the **Sepilok Orang Utan Rehabilitation Center,** the largest orangutan sanctuary in the world, with facilities to house and train hundreds of orphaned orangutans for eventual release back into the wilds, and a boat trip to see the **Marine Turtle Conservation Park and Hatchery** (RM654/$172) per person, not including air transfer (about RM190/$50 round-trip.)

**Monsopiad Cultural Village,** a Kadazandusun heritage center with its creepy House of Skulls, is located in Penampang, not far from Kota Kinabalu. During the 3-hour visit to the village you'll tour the place and be treated to a cultural performance. It's about the height of "touristy" Sabah, but can be a fun half-day trip if you want to peep at a bit of local culture. Call ✆ **088/242-336** to make a booking. RM65 ($17) includes transportation to and from your hotel, the tour and show, plus a welcome drink. Tours leave daily between 9 and 9:30am and again between 2 and 2:30pm.

If you're not satisfied with the coach-tour approach to cultural experience, consider a **home-stay program.** Malaysia's Ministry of Culture, Arts and Tourism has worked with a handful of rural villages belonging to many different ethnic groups to host foreign visitors. Within these villages local families open their homes to guests who are interested in learning about their unique lifestyle and customs. Trips also include nature trekking and visits to nearby wildlife attractions, depending on what sights surround your home-stay village. Some home stays involve accommodations in lodges designed with basic foreign comforts. Check out www.sabah-homestay.com, a site developed by the Ministry of Tourism, for more information about the various villages and what makes each unique. **Nature Heritage Tours** (Wisma Sabah, Lot G06, Jalan Tun Razak; ✆ **088/318-747;** www.nature-heritage.com) will book your trip for you, and will also keep you well informed of the etiquette issues involved with submersing yourself in local culture. The most popular trips are to a village near Kudat. Most visitors go for a day trip (RM350/$92 per person), overnight trip (RM450/$118 per person), or 3 days/2 nights (RM550/$145 per person).

In 2000, the **North Borneo Railway** revived the old tradition of steam-train travel with the launch of a 1954, fully renovated British Vulcan steam locomotive pulling six restored carriages. Traversing a 58km (36-mile) route from Tanjung Aru, just outside Kota Kinabalu, to the rural town of Papar, the train passes lovely water and mangrove views, fishermen, and local sea crafts, through a deep mountain tunnel and out the other side into a vast scenery of paddy fields. Carriages are open air but comfortable, with soft seats and charming wood-and-brass accents. A swanky bar car and observation deck round out facilities that also include toilets. The train departs every Wednesday and Saturday at 10am, returning at 2pm. Contact the North Borneo Railway at Tanjung Aru Railway at © **088/263-933.**

For another unique view of the countryside, **Sabah Air** (Sabah Air Building, Old Airport Rd.; © **088/256-733;** www.sabahair.com.my) offers thrilling **tours via helicopter,** flying over Kota Kinabalu, tropical wilds, and the jewel-colored sea for 20 minutes. You can also book a 1-hour aerial tour of Mt. Kinabalu. You need a minimum of four people for each trip. The Kota Kinabalu trip is RM205 ($54) per person; the Mt. Kinabalu trip, RM605 ($159) per person.

# 10

# Bali (Indonesia)

*by Charles Agar*

A scenic land of active volcanoes, dense jungle, stunning beaches, and a rich, ancient culture, Bali is an island of tranquility in the often-tumultuous Indonesian archipelago. Bali's peaceful way of life—one marked by colorful ritual and genuine hospitality—has drawn tourists, artists, and escapists for generations. Sadly, recent events like the tragedy of October 2002, when more than 200 people lost their lives in a terrorist bombing in Kuta, the island's tourist hub, as well as terrorist incidents in nearby Jakarta, have shattered that image. Warnings from the U.S. government, among others, are still in place, and, though the Indonesian government has taken important steps to update security on its tourist cash cow, many balk at returning to Bali.

There has been a marked shift among Balinese, a realignment of priorities in the wake of tragedy and changing world opinion. Where in the past tourists were taken for granted, bilked for that extra rupiah at every turn and hurried along, many Balinese have reassessed what life is all about. Among tourists and expats, the impression is that the Balinese mastery of "living in the moment" and coexisting with nature has intensified. Visitors are sure to find Balinese eager to sit for a chat and share a laugh (though the transport lads are still pretty relentless). The Balinese always welcomed visitors warmly, a sense of hospitality that has even increased of late. A visit to Bali is, as always, replete with kingly comforts, beautiful resorts, fine dining, and immersion in an ancient culture amid an island dreamscape.

And people are coming back. The summer high season in 2004 saw record numbers of visitors, topping pre-2002 records. Hotels that suffered through a year of drought, many of which closed or changed hands, are operating near full capacity. The market has shifted slightly, however, reflecting a greater number of visitors from other parts of Indonesia and neighboring countries. Australians are coming back in big numbers, but Europeans and Americans are still slow to return.

Though in some places tourism has spawned over-development a la Thailand's Phuket, a brief ride out of Kuta or away from any resort area brings you to the pristine Bali of volcanic peaks, bubbling springs, tropical jungle, and stunning beaches.

Balinese people practice a unique amalgam of Indian Hindu traditions, Buddhism, ancient Javanese practices, and indigenous animistic beliefs. The beauty of this faith colors every aspect of life, from fresh flowers strewn everywhere in obeisance, to the calm of morning prayer at temple. During your visit you're sure to catch the soothing music of the gamelan, the music of the island, and Balinese dance is enchanting. Despite recent events, Bali is still the beautiful island paradise that has attracted so many for so long.

## 1 Getting to Know Bali

### THE LAY OF THE LAND

Tiny Bali has great topographical variety. Located in the center of Indonesia's vast archipelago, the island has an area of 5,620 sq. km (roughly 2,192 sq. miles), only the size of a large metropolis. The land is divided in half east to west by a volcanic mountain chain and is scored lengthwise by deep river gorges. White-sand beaches line the coast to the east, as well as near **Kuta** in the most populated area of wider lowlands to the south. Active volcanoes dot the island, including **Gunung Agung,** a dynamic peak and a power point of Balinese culture and belief. Central **Ubud** is one of the more beautiful spots, with mountainous scenery, lush vegetation, and Bali's famed terraced rice farms. The far west is the least developed area of the island, with mountainous terrain mostly given over to national park land.

### A LOOK AT THE PAST

As distinct as Balinese life is, its people and culture originated elsewhere. Evidence of settlement goes back to the Neolithic period of around 3000 B.C., but the culture flourished under Chinese and Indian influences, including the introduction of Buddhism and Hinduism beginning in 800 B.C. Bali was ruled periodically by the Javanese. With the rise of Islam on the mainland, the last Javanese Majapahit king fled Jakarta for Bali in 1515, cementing the island's Javanese influence and affecting a renaissance in art and culture that would survive years of Muslim incursion.

The first real Western presence was established in 1601 when a Dutch contingent came to set up formal relations and establish trade. Attempts to expand relations were largely rebuffed—even as the **Dutch East India Company** expanded throughout the area—but Balinese slaves were shipped to Dutch and French merchants. In the era of Napoleon, Holland's East Indian holdings passed first to the French and then to the British, who returned them to the Dutch in the peace agreement following Napoleon's Waterloo defeat in 1815. After protracted struggle, the Dutch fully secured control in 1909.

A steady stream of European settlers and visitors followed—doctors and teachers at first, followed by the first tourists, artists, and cultural explorers. By the 1930s, Bali's reputation as a magical paradise was spreading rapidly, and such figures as anthropologist Margaret Mead and artist Walter Spies frequented the island.

**World War II** saw an exodus of foreigners with the arrival of Japanese troops. For Indonesians, it was a time of both strain under the brief Japanese occupation and revelation in light of the withdrawal of Dutch control. Shortly after the end of the war in 1945, Nationalist Party founder **Sukarno,** a thorn in the side of the Dutch since the 1920s, announced a declaration of Indonesian independence and was named president. The Dutch withdrew under international pressure in 1949, allowing the creation of the Republic of Indonesia, a tentative federation.

Hindu Bali was suspect under the rule of Muslim Jakarta, and the island was hit very hard by economic collapse. In 1965, **Suharto** seized control in response to a staged communist coup, and bloody conflicts continued for several years. As many as 100,000 Balinese were killed as suspected communists or as ethnic Chinese.

Under Suharto, the military gained a far-reaching influence over national affairs. For the next 3 decades, until the major economic crisis of 1997, Indonesia enjoyed a period of prosperity in spite of Suharto's embezzling autocracy. During this time, and with government attention, Bali rose to prominence as a top tour destination in the region.

## BALI & THE INDONESIAN CRISIS

In just the last half century, Bali has undergone remarkable change and weathered turmoil on the Indonesian mainland. The riots and protests that erupted in Indonesia in 1998 were the result of 3 decades of military rule and struggles to bring the world's fourth most populous country into the modern global economy. Chafing under the yoke of President Suharto, the Indonesians finally revolted, with demonstrations turned into riots that made headlines around the world. In June 1999, Indonesians witnessed their first free parliamentary election since 1955, ousting Suharto. But riots, bombings, and separatist protests continued to plague the country, specifically in Aceh and Irian Jaya. On May 20, 2002, East Timor was internationally recognized as an independent state after a protracted struggle. Indonesia achieved a tentative peace under a provisional government headed by **President Megawati,** the daughter of Sukarno (predecessor to Suharto). Megawati inherited political instability and an economic crisis, but addressed corruption and the military's human rights record.

The elections in July 2004 brought ascendancy to **Susilo Bambang Yudhoyono,** and a certain peace prevails in the wake of a surge toward democracy. Despite the recent bombings in Jakarta and alleged terror cells throughout the archipelago, many countries have lifted travel restrictions as visitors rediscover Indonesia.

## BALI TODAY

The bombings in October 2002 brought the world's problems to paradise, and Balinese are doing what they can to repair the damage literally and spiritually. Security has been stepped up at individual hotels, ocean ports, and the airport. Bargain packages are luring new visitors to experience that special Balinese hospitality. For Indonesia, shining up the now-tarnished reputation of its tourist gem is an important step in putting forward a good image to the world.

As with any undiscovered paradise that isn't so undiscovered anymore, Bali buffs mourn the loss of the island's innocence and you're sure to meet one or two scruffy old expats who'll be more than happy to tell you about "how it once was" on the island. Where there were no hotels or even electricity only a few decades ago, the island is now spotted with cybercafes, upscale lodging, and pesky touts. Don't be dissuaded. The "real Bali" is wherever you look for it.

## CEREMONY & CELEBRATION: BALI'S PEOPLE & CULTURE
### RELIGION

Over 90% of the population is **Hindu,** with the minority made up of Muslims, Buddhists, and Christians. Religious ritual plays into every facet of life.

Balinese Hindus believe in the ascending (and confusing) pantheon of Hindu gods, as well as dharma and adharma, order and disorder, and the need for balance between the two and rituals to that end. The importance of karma, or the consequence of individual actions, plays into the peaceful daily rhythms, and forms of "making merit" are as many as the people who practice them. Whether placing daily offerings of flowers on someone's car or undertaking rigorous mountain pilgrimages, Balinese believe that, to achieve harmony, the forces of good must be saluted with offerings, while the forces of evil must be appeased.

# Bali

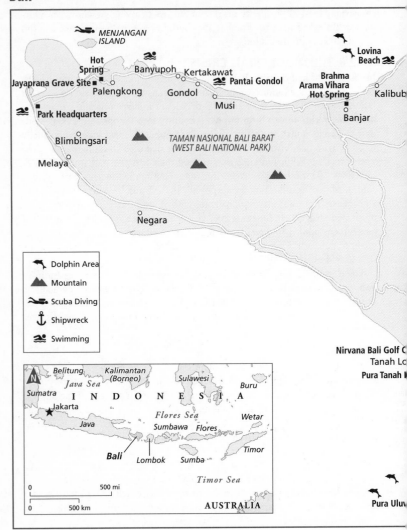

With an estimated 20,000 temples and shrines, Bali is known as the "Island of the Gods," and every village has at least one temple with buildings dedicated to Vishnu, Brahma, and Shiva (the Creator, the Preserver, and the Destroyer).

## CELEBRATIONS

**Tooth filing** is a rite of maturation, wherein the sharp front teeth, especially the canines, are filed down smooth (the idea being to differentiate humans from the animals). This can happen at any age, even after death, but is most often done to adolescents, who by that age have already been through the nearly dozen rituals that marked their first few days on the planet.

**Weddings** in Bali are unique, colorful affairs not to be missed, and surprisingly festive are **cremations.** Burning the body is the only way a soul can be

freed of its earthly self and travel to its next incarnation (or to enlightenment), and death is a joyous occasion in Bali, full of floats and fanfare. Complicated towers (the higher the caste, the higher the tower) hold the body, carried aloft by cheering men who turn the tower in circles to send the spirit to heaven as they carry it to the burning ground. It's an extraordinary and wonderful event; there are even tours that will take you, or ask at any *losmen* (hostel) or at your hotel's front desk. Cremations in Ubud are particularly noteworthy.

Compared to Western churchgoing, celebrations in Bali are very casual: Women gossip, children play, and dogs wander temple grounds freely, snacking on offerings. A priest chants, people pray and then get up, and others take their places. Ask before taking photos, and stay on your best behavior. Balinese are generally most welcoming and might even invite you for food or drinks.

## MUSIC & DANCE

The sounds of the **gamelan**—the bright-sounding metal percussion ensembles that accompany just about every celebration and ceremony here—will first turn your head. Music is everywhere in Bali, from the raucous *dangdut*, or Indonesian pop pouring from restaurants and shops to folk and the refined classical music that accompanies the many staged dance performances and temple worship.

If you have a chance, don't miss a performance of traditional dance. **Legong** and **Barong dances** are intricate ballets depicting scenes from the epic *Ramayana*. **Kecak dance** is a circle of up to 100 men chanting rhythmically and telling the saga of a monkey king and his warriors. It's a colorful, fun experience not to be missed. Many hotels hold shows and the **Palace** in Ubud is a good choice. If you're lucky, you'll find a real, nontourist performance in an outlying village.

*Wayang Kulit*, or **shadow puppet plays,** feature intricately cut leather figures that puppeteers use to project images against a screen. *Wayang Kulit* shows also depict tales from the Hindu epics and are accompanied by a gamelan ensemble and the voices of puppeteers (often injecting news, gossip, and bawdy jokes).

## ARTS & CRAFTS

Decoration and craft are as seamlessly woven into the fabric of life in Bali as are dance, music, and ritual. Fine carving and craftwork can be found adorning the most humble dwelling. Craftsmen are highly revered, and skilled wood and stone carvers turn out authentic works in street-side studios all over the island (concentrated in Ubud). Visitors are sure to walk away with some beautiful, original finds in wood and stone.

**Masks** used in traditional performance, many of the bug-eyed demoness Rangda, make fine souvenirs (*but beware:* Tradition has it that even tourist copies can be inhabited). There's a lot of mass-produced clutter, and lots of these works have been "aged" by an artful banging around on the sidewalk; authentic antiques are rare, so be cynical of claims of authenticity—though the copies are quite good.

Ancient stylized **paintings** of deities and the delicately carved "lontar" palm frond books are both still produced on the island. Expatriates have had as much influence on modern Balinese art as the ancients. As guiding patrons, men such as **Rudolf Bonnet,** a Dutchman, and **Walter Spies,** whose home on the site of the Tjampuhan Hotel in Ubud became central to the arts in Ubud, influenced local painters, opened societies, and brought the glory of Bali to the world at large. With a little searching, you can find some real masterpieces.

## LANGUAGE

The Balinese speak both Indonesian and Balinese—the former when out in public, the latter at home. Aside from the tendency toward seemingly jaw-breaking polysyllabic phrases, Indonesian is not that hard to learn—pronunciation is pretty straightforward, and spelling is phonetic. Balinese is much more complicated, not least because there are three levels—high, middle, and low—depending on the class and authority of the person to whom you are speaking.

English is spoken widely, and if you've learned a few words of Malay, you can give them a try here as the languages are quite similar.

## 2 Planning Your Trip to Bali

### VISITOR INFORMATION

The Department of Tourism operates **Information Centers** at a number of locations: at **Ngurah Rai International Airport** (*©* **361/751011**); in **Ubud** at the crossroad of Monkey Forest Road and Jalan Raya Ubud; in **Kuta** at Jalan Benasari 36B, Legian (© 361/754090); in **Denpasar** at Jalan Parman Niti Mandala (© 362/222387); and in **Singaraja** at Jalan Veteran 23 (© 361/ 225141). Better still is the efficient **Badung Government Tourist Office** in Kuta, Jalan Raya Kuta no. 2 (© 361/756176).

Some good online sources include **Bali Paradise Online** (www.bali-paradise. com), **Bali Online** (www.indo.com), and **Bali Guide** (www.baliguide.com). **Bali Echo** (www.baliecho.com) is an informative art and culture magazine.

There are lots of free flyers and pamphlets with listings, information, and maps: *Bali Plus* has general info; *The Beat* (www.beatmag.com), *What's Up Bali?*, and *Groove* are free guides to nightlife, dining, and activities. *The Yak* is a local glossy focused on nightlife in Seminyak. For information about surfing, check www.indosurf.com.au or pick up a copy of *Indo Surf Guide,* published by the same folks.

## ENTRY REQUIREMENTS

Visitors from the U.S., Australia, and most of Europe, New Zealand, and Canada do not need visas. Sixty-day stamps are available on entry through Ngurah Rai Airport or the seaports of Padang Bai and Benoa. For stays of longer than 60 days, a tourist or business visa must be arranged *before* coming to Indonesia. Tourist visas are valid only for 4 weeks and cannot be extended; business visas can be extended for 6 months at Indonesian immigration offices.

## CUSTOMS REGULATIONS

Customs allows you to bring in, duty-free, 200 cigarettes or 50 cigars and 2 pounds of tobacco; cameras and film; 2 liters of alcohol; and perfume clearly intended for personal use. Forbidden are guns, weapons, narcotics, pornography (leave it at home if you're unsure how it's defined), and printed matter with Chinese characters. Plants and fresh fruit might also be confiscated.

## MONEY

The currency of Indonesia is the **rupiah,** from the Sanskrit word for wrought silver, *rupya.* Coins are available in denominations of Rp25, 50, 100, and even occasionally 5 and 10. Notes are Rp100, 500, 1,000, 5,000, 10,000, 20,000, 50,000, and 100,000, thus the largest denomination is only about US$10.

**The following bills are no longer in circulation:** the 1992 pink Rp10,000, the 1992 greenish Rp20,000 bill, and the blue Rp50,000 featuring Suharto's picture.

**CURRENCY EXCHANGE & RATES**   The rate of exchange is relatively stable. At publication time it was **9,094 Indonesian rupiahs per U.S. dollar.**

Most major hotels have **exchange services** but offer less than favorable rates. Storefront exchange services line most streets and offer the best exchange, but it's important to be careful of scams such as counterfeit bills and damaged currency that won't be accepted anywhere. Ask first about commission, and be sure to count your bills before walking away. State-sponsored **Wartel Telecommunications Service** offices are the best bet.

**ATMs**   In Bali, ATMs are common in all major tourist areas and trade at good rates.

**LOST/STOLEN CREDIT CARDS & TRAVELER'S CHECKS**   To report a lost or stolen credit card, you can call these service lines: **American Express** (counter at the Grand Bali Beach Hotel), © 361/283970; **MasterCard** and **Visa,** © 361/759010.

## WHEN TO GO

**PEAK SEASON** The high tourist season is July and August and the weeks surrounding Christmas and New Year's, when prices are higher and tourist traffic is considerably increased. Try to avoid these times as well as February and March (given the increased heat and humidity).

**CLIMATE** Bali is just below the equator (so days are a consistent 12 hr.), and the temperatures always hover in the 80s Fahrenheit (upper 20s to low 30s Celsius). The rainy season lasts from October to April; rain usually comes in short, violent bursts that last an hour or so, and the humidity is at its crushing worst during this period. The hottest months are February, March, and April; remember that it gets a bit nippy at night up in the mountains, but a light sweater will certainly be enough.

**PUBLIC HOLIDAYS** Public holidays are New Year's Day (Jan 1), Idul Fitri (celebration of the end of Ramadan, in late Feb), Nyepi (a major purification ritual and a time when Balinese are supposed to sit at home, silent, in late Mar), Good Friday and Easter Sunday (late Mar/early Apr), Muslim New Year (mid-May), Indonesia Independence Day (Aug 17), Ascension Day of Mohammed (early Dec), and Christmas (Dec 25).

## HEALTH CONCERNS

In chapter 3, we outline general information about vaccinations and general issues that affect the region. **No inoculations are required** for Bali, but it's always a good idea to get shots for hepatitis A, tetanus, polio, and typhoid (likely you've already had some of these). Consult the CDC website (www.state.gov) or your doctor for details.

The CDC has declared Bali **malaria-free** though it is not uncommon on other islands in the Indonesian archipelago. Of concern, though, are the many stray dogs on Bali and rabies, so beware of strays.

**You can't drink the water on Bali,** but bottled water is cheap and readily available. Just about every hotel will supply you with a couple bottles or a jug of boiled water—to be extra cautious, use it to brush your teeth as well. Restaurants in tourist areas supply safe water and ice, but to be cautious ask for *air minum* (bottled drinking water) and no ice. Avoid "Bali belly" (the Indonesian version of Montezuma's Revenge) by sticking to foods that have been peeled or cooked.

## GETTING THERE

### BY PLANE

**Airport information** and connection to airline reservation counters is available by calling ☎ **361/651011,** ext. 1454.

**FROM THE U.S. & CANADA** Most visitors make a connection with Singapore, Bangkok, Taipei, or Japan via **China Air, Eva Air, Thai Airways,** and **Garuda Indonesia** or **Singapore Air.** Check with travel agents for deals and package rates, some with affordable overnight connections through Bangkok.

**FROM THE U.K.** Bali is served from Europe by **Cathay Pacific** via Hong Kong; tickets can be purchased from **British Air, Singapore Air,** or **Air France.**

---

**Tips  Remember the Departure Tax**

When you leave Bali, there will be an **airport departure tax** of Rp50,000 ($5.50).

> ## *Tips*  A Note on Addresses
> Street addresses can be as vague as "on the main street." In some areas, that's all that passes for an address. Don't worry, most are easy to find.

**FROM AUSTRALIA & NEW ZEALAND**    Flights from Australia and New Zealand can be booked through **Qantas.**

## GETTING TO YOUR DESTINATION FROM THE AIRPORT
**Ngurah Rai,** Bali's airport, is 13km (8 miles) southwest of Denpasar. Few travelers stop in the city, but connect directly with their resort area of choice.

It is a good idea to prearrange pickup through your hotel (the rate is comparable to the official rates at the airport); otherwise buy a ticket at the **official taxi counter** just outside of Customs and arrange a fixed rate ride to your destination. Avoid the temptation to go with unofficial cabs; you might get caught in a taxi scam that will leave you frustrated, overcharged, or in the wrong place.

## GETTING AROUND
**BY CAR**    Given how cheap and easy it is to hire someone to drive, many folks just avoid the headache of driving themselves. Note that, if you do drive, you will need an international driver's license or a locally issued tourist driving license; 1-month licenses are issued on the spot for Rp150,000 ($16) at the **Foreign License Service** (Jalan Agung Tresna No. 14, Renon, Denpassar; © **361/ 243939**). Traffic is on the left side, and "third-world rules" apply: the more aggressively honking, larger vehicle goes first. Traffic police are just bribe collectors.

**BY MOTORBIKE**    Riding a motorbike on Bali is a dangerous proposition and in even the shortest visit to the island you will see your share of crashes; renting a scooter or motorbike, however, is cheap (from $3 per day) and a fun way to see the island. Riding is safer and more beautiful in remote areas. The same driving license requirements for cars apply to motorbikes and scooters.

**BY PRIVATE TRANSPORTATION**    **Private taxis** are the most common choice of transport and can get you to any destination for a reasonable price. Ask around to find out the going rate and be sure to haggle. Guys offering "transport" and pantomime steering a car will be at your heels wherever you go and, depending on your luck, can be pretty helpful. Be sure to be specific about destination and price before setting out.

One other option is to ask at your hotel or a travel agent about the **tourist shuttles** that connect the main destinations on the island.

**BY PUBLIC TRANSPORTATION**    Blue and brown vans called *bemos* operate as buses in Bali. They have regular routes, but these aren't really written down. Just ask someone which bus and where to catch it. Prices are also similarly secretive, so ask around about how much the ride really should cost. *Bemos* are better for short hops (around town, for example) than long distances. Metered taxis, if you can find them, are your best bet. Be sure that the driver turns on his meter (you might have to insist more than once).

**BY BOAT**    Several companies offer **day diving, snorkeling trips,** and **sunset-** or **dinner-cruises,** as well as connection to the nearby islands of Nusa Penida and Nusa Lembongan. Both **Bounty Cruises** (© **361/726666;** http://balibounty cruises.com) and **Bali Hai Cruises** (© **361/720331;** www.balihaicruises.com)

run regular high-end tours from Bali's Benoa Harbor. **Sail Sensations** (© **361/ 725864;** www.bali-sailsensations.com) offers day sailing and overnights. The *Wakalouka* (© **361/484085**), a luxury catamaran, transports you in style to its exclusive property on Nusa Lembongan.

## TIPS ON ACCOMMODATIONS

Bali hotels range from bungalows at Rp40,000 ($4.40) to luxury villas serviced by a retinue of servants and at prices over $1,000. In between are an ever-increasing number of hotels and bungalows. Atmosphere is the rule here, and those who forgo Western chain-hotel comfort to stay in a *losmen* (traditional home stay, a bastardization of the Dutch word *logement*) or find their own **rustic bungalow** (all more or less "roughin' it") often come away from Bali with fond memories of the tranquility of this island and the beauty of Balinese hospitality. That said, Bali's resorts and fine Western hotels cost a fraction of what luxury accommodation would elsewhere, and many come to enjoy the upgrade.

**A NOTE ON PRICES**   Promotional and Internet rates are available at all hotels in Bali. Paying the rack rate, or published rate (which we list in this guide), even in high season, is almost unheard of. Especially in the off season, it pays to shop around, and you can show up at the front desk of even the largest hotels and ask for the best rate.

*Important:* Almost all the hotels charge a 21% government tax and service charge on top of the quoted rates. Some hotels tack on a charge in high season (the 2 or 3 weeks around Christmas and New Year's, and in July and Aug).

## TIPS ON DINING

The choices in Bali are many, but it's rare to find authentic Balinese or Indonesian on a menu for foreigners; for that, you'll have to go to a *warung,* a local cafe, and many visitors are dissuaded by the typical *warung*'s appearance (some are pretty grungy). If you're not put off by a bit of grime, a la an old greasy spoon in the U.S., the food at *warungs* is authentic, delicious, and cheap. Most visitors surrender to the call of high-quality international dining options, which are affordable and varied, with great options for vegetarians.

Indonesian dishes that you are most likely to encounter include *nasi goreng* (fried rice, usually topped with an egg), *mie goreng* (fried noodles), *nasi campur* (a plate of boiled rice with sides of meat and veggies and a house specialty), *ayam goreng* (fried chicken), *gado gado* (salad with peanut sauce, served hot or cold), and satay (small chunks of meat on skewers served with peanut sauce). Padang food (sold in little cafes called *rumah makan*) is spicy tidbits of fried fish, chicken, or veggies on a buffet; you pick what you want.

## TIPS ON SHOPPING

The quantity of Balinese arts and crafts available on the island is overwhelming. There's something for all budgets, from tourist trinkets to fine art and antiques. It's a shopper's paradise of fabrics, clothing, wood and stone carvings, paintings, and doodads of varying quality. You get what you pay for generally—but with a bit of haggling, can get a lot more for what you pay. Shop around; the same item gets cheaper the more you look at it, and it's really the same stuff everywhere. Ask the price, offer half, smile, and go from there. Even at inflated prices, you'll still come out ahead of the game.

Woodcarvers, jewelers, and craftspeople of all types line the streets around all tourist areas, particularly in and around Ubud and on the streets of Kuta.

## Telephone Dialing Info at a Glance

- **To place a call from your home country to Bali,** dial the international access code (011 in the U.S. and Canada, 0011 in Australia, 0170 in New Zealand, and 00 in the U.K.), plus Indonesia's country code (62), plus the area code (361 for Kuta, Jimbaran, Nusa Dua, Sanur, and Ubud; 362 for Lovina; 363 for Candi Dasa; and 370 for Lombok), followed by the six-digit phone number (for example, from the U.S. to Lovina, you'd dial 011 + 62 + 362 + 000000).
- **To place a call within Indonesia,** you must use area codes if calling between states. Note that, for calls within the country, area codes are all preceded by a 0 (Lovina is 0362, Candi Dasa is 0363, Lombok is 0370, and so on).
- **To place a direct international call from Indonesia,** dial the international access code (001), plus the country code of the place you are dialing, plus the area code, plus the residential number of the other party.
- **To reach the international operator,** dial 102.
- **International country codes** are as follows: Australia 61, Burma 95, Cambodia 855, Canada 1, Hong Kong 852, Laos 856, Malaysia 60, New Zealand 64, the Philippines 63, Singapore 65, Thailand 66, U.K. 44, U.S. 1, Vietnam 84.

## *FAST FACTS:* Bali

*American Express* There is a branch in the Grand Bali Beach Hotel in Sanur (© 361/283970).

*Business Hours* Most places keep "daylight hours," which on the equator pretty much means 6am to 6pm (or a little later).

*Doctors & Dentists* Ask your hotel for a referral—many have a doctor on call. In Kuta, try the **Bali International Medical Centre** (Jalan Bypass Ngurah Rai no. 100X; © 361/761263). It's open daily from 8am to midnight and sometimes will send someone to your hotel. There is a general hospital in Denpasar, but for any serious problems, go home as soon as possible for treatment. For dentists, ask your hotel for a referral.

*Drug Laws* Though you might be offered hash and marijuana at every turn, Indonesia officially takes drug offenses very seriously. Busts are regular and jail terms stiff.

*Electricity* Currents can be either 110 volts (50 AC); or 220 to 240 volts (50 AC).

*Embassies/Consulates* **United States:** Jalan Hayam Wuruk no. 188, Denpasar (© 361/233605). **Australia (Canada, New Zealand,** and **Great Britain** also have their representatives here): Jalan Prof. Moch, Yamin 51, Denpasar (© 361/235092). Or, in Jakarta: **Canada:** Wisma Metropolitan I, 5th floor, Jalan Jen. Sudirman, Kav. 29, Jakarta (© 021/510709). **Great Britain:** Jalan Thamrin 75, Jakarta (© 021/330904).

*Emergencies* The number for the police is 📞 **110**, ambulance is 📞 **118**, and fire is 📞 **113**. Search and rescue is 📞 **111/115/151**.

*Hospitals* There is a city hospital in Denpasar, but for any serious ailment, evacuate to Hong Kong, Singapore, Kuala Lumpur, or Bangkok. In Bali, try the **International SOS Bali** (JL Bypass Ngurah Rai, Kuta; 24-hour hot line, 📞 **361/710505**) or **Bali International Medical Centre** (JL Bypass Ngurah Rai, Kuta; 24-hour hot line, 📞 **361/761263**).

*Hot Lines* Alcoholics Anonymous holds meetings in tourist centers all across the island. Check its website at www.aa-bali.org or call the infoline at 📞 **081/8551811**.

*Internet/E-mail* Internet cafes are springing up all over Bali, but the connections can still be painfully slow. Expect to pay about $1.50 per hr.

*Language* The Balinese speak both Indonesian and Balinese—the former when out in public, the latter at home. English is widely spoken throughout Bali, particularly in the major tourist areas. While not everyone is fluent, most of the people you will be dealing with will speak enough English that you can communicate with them (see "Language," earlier in this chapter).

*Liquor Laws* You won't find liquor in *halal* restaurants catering to Muslims, but there are no restrictions elsewhere.

*Police* The phone number for the police is 📞 **110**.

*Post Office/Mail* Your hotel can send mail for you, or you can go to the post office in Denpasar, at Jalan Raya Puputan Renon (📞 **361/223566**). Other branches are in Kuta (Jalan Raya Kuta; 📞 **361/754012**), Ubud, and Sanur. For big items, there are packing and shipping services in all major tourist areas, but the price of shipping from Bali is exorbitant.

*Safety/Crime* Bali is by and large a safe place to be, even after dark. Violent crime is rare. However, pickpockets are not, so you should exercise considerable caution by using a money belt, particularly in crowded tourist areas, and be careful not to flash large wads of cash. If you find yourself in need of assistance, contact the **Guardian Angels Tourist Police** (there are 265 of these angels dressed in blue) at 📞 **361/763753** 24 hours a day.

Many hotels offer safety deposit boxes, and it is best to keep extra cash and other valuables in them. If nothing else, make sure your suitcase has a good lock on it. Even the best hotel can't always guarantee security for valuables left lying in plain sight.

*Telephones* Because many hotels charge a great deal even for using your calling card, you are better off using **Wartel's** privately owned public phones. There's one in every tourist center, though some work better than others. Some also have Internet services.

*Time* Bali is on Greenwich Mean Time plus 8 hours, except during daylight saving time, which it does not observe. That's 13 hours ahead of Eastern Standard Time in the U.S. and 16 hours ahead of Pacific Standard Time.

*Tipping* Tipping is not required and not even encouraged. Most restaurants include a service charge. Leave a small tip if you feel the need; more often than not, the recipient will be surprised.

*Toilets* Western-style toilets with seats are becoming more common than the Asian squat variety, though cheap *losmen*/home stays and some less touristic public places still have the latter. Always carry some toilet paper with you, or you might have to use your hand (the left one only, please) and the dip bucket.

*Water* Avoid tap water in Bali unless properly boiled. Bottled water is available everywhere, and restaurants in tourist areas seem to use it as a matter of course, but you should always ask to be sure.

## 3 Kuta

A quick 10 minutes from the airport, you'll be in Kuta, Bali's most developed area, a popular spot for budget travelers and a longtime favorite for weekend vacationers from nearby Australia. It's also where Abu Sayef chose to attack the island on the night of October 12, 2002, and, though it is again brimming with tourists, memories of that day are still fresh. At the time of this writing, a temple and small monument to commemorate the day were under construction.

Kuta is made up of narrow streets and alleys, and pedestrians share space with honking, mufflerless cars and motorbikes. You'll be harried by some of the most aggressive touts on the island, and the beaches are crowded with imploring sellers and masseurs; the tourist rush, however, means some of the best nightlife and dining on the island. Unfortunately, the current makes swimming difficult and dangerous.

The best compromise of all, short of staying elsewhere on the island, is to hit the quiet beaches just north of Kuta at Legian and Semniyak.

### GETTING THERE
Kuta is near the airport, and most hotels offer free airport pickup. Taxis for hire at the airport are best at the **official taxi counter,** where you'll pay a set fare.

### GETTING AROUND
Kuta is a big rectangle. The two main north-south streets are oceanside Jalan Pantai Kuta and Jalan Legian, and are connected east-west by Jalan Benesari, Poppies Gang I, and many quaint alleys. You can easily **walk** all of this or take the reasonably priced blue-and-yellow **metered taxis.**

## FAST FACTS: Kuta

*Banks/Currency Exchange* There are a number of ATMs in Kuta. **Wartel** outlets are found all around the main streets.

*Internet/E-mail* Internet cafes almost outnumber transport guides in Kuta and charge between Rp10,000 and Rp37,000 ($1.10–$4.05) per hour for reliable connection. Try **Internet Explorer** (explonet@hotmail.com) in the busy nightlife area of Dhyanapura in Seminyak.

*Post Office/Mail* There is a main post office on Jalan Raya Tuban, but it's far from the town center. There are also some postal agents, and your hotel can send mail for you.

*Telephones* The area code in Kuta is **361.**

## WHERE TO STAY

**Kuta Beach,** while still a booming resort, is quite noisy and busy. We've listed the better choices in town and at nearby Legian and Seminyak to the north.

### KUTA & LEGIAN BEACH
#### Expensive

**Hard Rock Hotel** 🎸🎸   You'll be disarmed by this hotel's fun, fanciful design. The lobby is typical Hard Rock Cafe, lined with once-used guitars and gold records, and the decor throughout is bright, with corridors done in varying rock themes. Rooms are light and airy, with photos of artists, and bathrooms are done in playful geometric patterns. The pool is the largest in Bali with slides and its own beach. There's an outdoor living room, an in-house radio station, and a recording studio where you can live out your own musician fantasies. Sure, rock blares around the clock in the lobby, which has a popular bar, and in other public areas, but the fabulous kids' playroom—"Little Rock"—and that pool make it a great option for boomer families. It's not really Bali, but it is good fun.

Jalan Pantai, Banjar Pande Mas, Kuta, Bali. ☎ **361/761869.** Fax 361/761868. www.hardrockhotels.net. 418 units. $190–$220 double; $370–$760 suite. AE, DC, MC, V. **Amenities:** 3 restaurants; 3 bars; outdoor pool (w/swim-up bar); health club; spa; kids' club; concierge; business center; shopping; salon; 24-hr. room service; massage; laundry service; dry cleaning; meeting rooms; Internet service; rock-'n'-roll library. *In room:* A/C, satellite TV (on-demand movies), dataport, minibar, fridge, safe, IDD phone, video games and in-room Internet available upon request.

**Padma Hotel** 🎸   You've got all that you need at the Padma, a self-contained, comfortable compound just the right distance from the fray at Kuta for quiet, but close enough to go play and shop. There's something for the whole family here, including a good kid's club, daily activities, a roster of day trips, the fine Mandara Spa, and cultural classes such as egg painting and musical demonstrations. Garden rooms have parquet floors and fine Balinese furnishings. Standard rooms, in a four-story high rise, all have balconies and great views. Family rooms open onto a patio and central garden. There is a nice grassy spot between the large pool and the beach for the kids to frolic (it's quiet and, happily, tout-free). The beach is not good for swimming, however.

Jalan Padma no. 1, Legian, Bali. ☎ **361/752111.** Fax 361/752140. www.hotelpadma.com. 403 units. $160 double; $180 chalet; $220–$1,500 suite. AE, DC, MC, V. **Amenities:** 3 restaurants; 3 bars; outdoor pool; game area w/Internet and PlayStation; tour desk; car rental; 24-hr. room service; babysitting; laundry service; club-level rooms and check-in; meeting rooms. *In room:* A/C, satellite TV, minibar, fridge, safe, IDD phone.

#### Moderate

**Bounty Hotel** 🎸🎸   The Bounty is popular with Australian revelers, especially at school-break times. The rooms are decidedly Western, but they have traditional wood floors and are decorated with Balinese fabric. The standard rooms are slightly smaller than the deluxe, with the wash basin in the room. The complex, arranged around an attractive pool, features stone carvings and red tile ornamentation. The hotel is within easy walking distance of the beach, the best shopping on Legian, and Kuta's many night spots (the same people own the **Bounty Bar & Restaurant,** a happening late-night spot). This is a good choice if you want to be right in the middle of the fray.

Poppies Gang II, Jalan Segara Batu Bolong no. 18, Kuta, Bali. ☎ **361/753030.** Fax 361/752121. 166 units. $93–$190 double. AE, DC, MV, V. **Amenities:** 2 restaurants; bar; 2 outdoor swimming pools; car rental; 24-hour room service; laundry service; dry cleaning. *In room:* A/C, cable TV, minibar, fridge, IDD phone.

**Hotel Restu Bali** 🎸   This little stop is on Kuta's main shopping drag of Jalan Raya, which means it's about a 10-minute walk to the beach while still right in the middle of nighttime action. The hotel is a long, narrow rabbit's warren of different tropical nooks and crannies, and, for all the hustle and bustle outside, it's unbelievably serene. Standard rooms have wicker furniture and stark but nice baths. The Puri Deluxe are bungalow style, with thatched roofs and woven mats covering the walls and private patios. Bathrooms are the same, but the sink is in the room. Two very nice swimming pools spill into gurgling fountain pools that trickle at all hours and can be heard from some rooms (which can be considered either peaceful or infuriating). Though not particularly luxe, good discounts are available.

Jalan Raya Legian no. 113, Kuta, Bali. ✆ 361/751251. Fax 361/751252. restubali@denpasar.wasantara. net.id. 38 units. $35–$55 double (w/breakfast). AE, MC, V. **Amenities:** Restaurant; bar; 2 outdoor pools; Jacuzzi; tour services; 24-hr. room service; laundry service; Internet service. *In room:* A/C, satellite TV, minibar (deluxe only), fridge, IDD phone.

**Inna Kuta Beach** ⭐    This is the only hotel in Kuta that is right on the beach, and the Inna Kuta Beach is right next to Kuta Square, convenient for downtown shopping or partying. The hotel has seen better days, though, and rooms are a bit drab and uninspired. The good news is that with the large pool area and many activities to keep you busy, it is unlikely that you'll spend much time in the room. Skip the more costly bungalows in back, which provide little more than a bit of privacy (the bathrooms are the same size as in the standard room). With lots of connecting rooms, proximity to the wackier side of Bali, and good rates, this is not a bad choice for families.

Jalan Pantai Kuta no. 1, P.O. Box 3393, Kuta, Bali. ✆ 361/751361. Fax 361/751362. www.innakutabeach. com. 137 units. $100–$110 double; $210–$410 suites (seasonal rates available). AE, DC, MC, V. **Amenities:** Restaurant; 2 bars; outdoor pool; tour desk; shopping; salon; 24-hr. room service; laundry service; dry cleaning; meeting rooms. *In room:* A/C, TV, IDD phone.

**Poppies Cottages I & II** ⭐⭐    This is by far the best midrange hotel in Kuta, with atmospheric thatched cottages set among gorgeous gardens abloom with a riot of bougainvillea. Both locations, separated by only 1 block at the town center, are comparable. Each has a small central pool that is designed to look like a natural pond and is surrounded by many lush garden nooks perfect for lounging. The rooms are a bit compact for the price, but the open-air bathrooms are done in marble, complete with sunken tubs, and it is all very clean and cozy.

Poppies Lane I, Kuta, Bali. ✆ 361/751059. Fax 361/752364. www.poppiesbali.com. 20 units (4 additional units at the older Poppies II). $85 double (seasonal rates available). AE, DC, MC, V. **Amenities:** Restaurant; bar; outdoor pool; business center; shopping; room service; laundry service; Internet service. *In room:* A/C, TV, IDD phone.

### Inexpensive
There are lots of budget options in busy Kuta. Small guesthouses crowd the back streets near the beach. Also try **Adi Dharma Hotel and Cottages** (Jalan Raya, at the town center) or **Fat Yogi's** (fatyogi@telkom.net), a collection of basic, clean bungalows.

## SEMINYAK
### Very Expensive
**Legian** ⭐⭐    This resort is a true Indonesian boutique. All rooms are suites, enormous and luxe, with terraces facing the sea and outdoor day beds that are almost too pretty to muss up. The architectural style of the entry is somewhat austere, and private spaces feel a bit like an upscale city hotel, but the sumptuous Western contemporary and Balinese design flairs round out the effect. Service is very professional and the location, right on the beach at Seminyak, is

rivaled only by the Oberoi (below). Its latest venture, **The Club,** features fine contemporary villas just across the street.

Jalan Laksmana, Seminyak, Kuta, Bali 80361. ✆ **361/730622.** Fax 361/730623. 70 units. $300–$1,000 suite. AE, DC, MC, V. **Amenities:** Restaurant; 2 bars; 2-tiered pool; spa; tour desk; shopping; massage; laundry service; dry cleaning; meeting rooms. In room: A/C, satellite TV w/in-house movies, minibar, fridge, hair dryer, safe, tea and coffee.

**Oberoi** ✮✮   The first hotel in Seminyak and one of the leading hotels of the world, the Oberoi has long attracted celebrities, from Henry Kissinger to Julia Roberts. The property is composed of individual *lanais*—native bungalows of coral stone with wood beams and thatch roofs. Rooms are cozy and strike a great balance between high-end comforts and local materials and style. Room amenities are first class all the way: raised futon beds, marble baths with sunken tubs facing private gardens, and goodies like slippers, robes, and flip-flops for the beach. Private pool villas are luxurious beyond belief. The beach here is great, with few touts and sellers to harry you and a nice expanse of sand. A mini–outdoor amphitheater hosts traditional dance performances. Service is genuinely warm and helpful without fawning, and you can feel at ease here without forgetting that you're in Bali. The fine spa is managed by Banyon Tree.

Jalan Laksmana, Seminyak, Kuta, Bali 80361. ✆ **361/730361.** Fax 361/730791. www.oberoihotels.com. 75 units, all w/bathroom. $255–$790 garden-view cottage or villa; $300–$850 ocean view. AE, DC, MC, V. **Amenities:** Restaurant; bar; outdoor pool; tennis court; fitness center; spa; sauna; tour desk; car rental; 24-hr. room service; massage; laundry service; dry cleaning. In room: A/C, satellite TV w/in-house movies, minibar, fridge, hair dryer, IDD phone.

## Expensive

**Royal Seminyak** ✮   Location, location, location. You're right on the beach here and the staff is friendly and helpful, though the place is not particularly luxe. The pool area is done up in gaudy-but-fun statuary depicting local dancers and provocative nudes. It's a real step down from the likes of the Oberoi and Legian (above), but there's a good vibe. Rooms are large, done in a mix of Chinese business hotel and boutique wannabe styling; what Balinese touches there are might have been bought at local souvenir shops. Still, the rooms are spacious and very clean. Opt for one of the affordable deluxe rooms. A popular choice for conferences and meetings, great deals can be found here.

JL Abimanyu (Dhyana Pura), Seminyak, Bali. ✆ **361/730730.** Fax 361/730545. 136 units. $220–$420 double; $500–$700 villas. AE, MC, V. **Amenities:** 2 restaurants; spa; Jacuzzi; tour desk; limo service; shopping; limited room service. In room: A/C, cable TV, minibar, fridge, IDD phone.

## Moderate

**Puri Cendana** ✮✮   Right near the ocean at the end of busy Dhyana Pura Street (Bali's newest nightlife spot), the Puri Cendana has a good balance of affordability, comfort, and location. Rooms in two-story motel blocks are oversize and try to fill the space with big canopy beds and sparse furnishings. It's very clean and the bathrooms are stylish, with aggregate tubs and windows looking onto private garden spaces. The pool is small and right near the road, as is the restaurant, but you're just a short walk from the beach at Seminyak in one direction and all of the services and nightlife of Dhyana Pura in the other. Puri Cendana is a hotel disguised as a guesthouse.

Jalan Abimanyu (Dhyana Pura), Seminyak, Bali. ✆ **361/730869.** Fax 361/730868. http://geocities.com/puri cendana. 24 units. $80–$100 double (big discounts available). AE, MC, V. **Amenities:** Restaurant; bar; outdoor pool; tour desk; airport transfer; 24-hour room service; laundry service; Internet. In room: A/C, TV, fridge, phone.

# WHERE TO DINE

The international variety in Kuta is a result of homesick tourists; unfortunately, this translates into mediocre copies of Western fare. There are a couple of standouts, listed below.

## KUTA BEACH

**Aroma's Café** INTERNATIONAL    Here's where to come to get a taste of the familiar in the middle of busy Kuta. This cafe serves up snacks like fries and samosas, great salads, and gourmet sandwiches. You can also get more substantial dishes like a tofu or tempeh burger, falafel, or pizza. Follow it up with strong local coffee or a cappuccino. Great breakfasts are also available, and this is a good spot to use as a meeting-up point for shopping in Kuta. "Ladies, we'll see you here at 5."

Jalan Legian, Kuta. © 361/761113. Main courses Rp10,000–Rp38,000 ($1.10–$4.15). MC, V. Daily 7am–11pm.

**Kori Restaurant and Bar** 🔾🔾 EUROPEAN/STEAKHOUSE    Valet parking in the narrow and chaotic Poppies Gang II? Finery uncharacteristic of Bali abounds at this chic dining venue. Choose to sit in the dining room, replete with linen and silver finery, or on one of the more romantic cushioned bamboo platforms that bridge the narrow garden oasis. The lunch menu is light, featuring dishes like *malai köfte,* spicy vegetarian fritters in a curry sauce, or the mouthburning Bali chile burger (if you dare). The dinner menu has all the bells and whistles of a Western steakhouse. Try the mixed grill of U.S. beef loin, spare ribs, pork cutlet, and Nuerberger sausages, or order up the Singapore chile crab, savory and spicy fresh black Bali crabs served with a big ol' bib. Topping the high end of the menu is the giant seafood grill, cooked and served on a hot lava stone. To finish off, there's a respectable stock of brandy and cognac.

Poppies Gang II, Kuta. © 361/758605. Main courses Rp30,000–Rp140,000 ($3.30–$15). AE, DC, MC, V. Daily 11:30am–11pm.

**Poppies Restaurant** 🔾🔾 INDONESIAN/EUROPEAN    Poppies has a 25-year tradition of serving Indonesian and international specials on the busy beach. It's the place for your "Western" fix on the island and certainly is the prettiest restaurant in the Kuta area: a garden setting with crawling vines overhead that keep the hot sun at bay, and babbling pools and waterfalls. Indonesian dishes include an outstanding *ikan pepes*—mashed fish cooked in a banana leaf with fine spices and very spicy local "pickles" (beware). The *mie goreng,* loaded with shrimp and vegetables, is also good. Service is slow, but this is a good place to dawdle.

Poppies Cottages, Poppies Lane I, Kuta. © 361/751059. www.poppiesbali.com. Reservations recommended. Men must wear shirts. Main courses Rp20,000–Rp50,000 ($2.20–$5.50). AE, MC, V. Daily 8am–11pm.

**TJ's Restaurant** 🔾🔾 MEXICAN    Set up more like a typical Asian bistro, TJ's is a real Bali original. Stop in if only for one of the famous frozen margaritas and to listen to some good tunes in this laid-back, open-air spot. Meals start with homemade corn chips, delicious dips, and an extensive menu of specials. They advertise the "best burgers in town," and though the jury is still out on that one, most everything from the quesadillas to the fish Veracruz is delicious. Order up, kick back, and enjoy the vibe in this popular spot.

Poppies Lane, Kuta. © 361/751093. Main courses Rp35,000–Rp55,000 ($3.85–$6.05). MC, V. Daily 11am–11pm.

## SEMINYAK

This northern stretch of the Kuta Beach area is *the place* for fine dining and hip nightlife. The restaurants listed below are only a few of the many little bistros popping up. Check out what's now called "Eat Street," the road that connects the main north-south thoroughfare with the Oberoi and Legian hotels north of town.

**Kafe Warisan** ⋆ FRENCH   It's fine international dining in a Balinese setting here in this open courtyard of frangipani trees overlooking rich, green rice paddies. The standards, service, and menu are equally sophisticated, and with so many choices, you might have to come back for a few meals. Be sure to try the raw oysters if you're game. Kafe Warisan serves the finest cuts of meat imported from Australia, and even local venison. On the lighter side, try the grilled Tasmanian salmon, seafood fricassee, or grilled rosemary chicken breast. You'll be treated to an extensive wine list and a range of California wines by the glass. Stop by the boutique to peruse the collection of beaded dresses, silk sarongs, jewelry, antique batik, and other collectibles.

Jalan Kerobokan, Seminyak. ⓒ 361/731175. Reservations required. Main courses Rp65,000–Rp145,000 ($7.15–$16). AE, MC, V. Mon–Sat 11am–4pm and 7–11pm.

**Ku De Ta** ⋆⋆ BISTRO   This is Kuta's "Europe meets Asia" international bistro, aimed at an upscale clientele. It's also one of the town's hippest catwalks. With a daytime ambience dominated by the nearby beach, at night it's all about romantic lighting in the restaurant's open-air, minimalist rotunda. Add an elegant bar and lounge area, and a cigar lounge—complete with putting green—and you've got an all-purpose evening out. Happily, what comes out of the kitchen makes you want to stay: Try the signature dish of slow-roasted, yellow curry duck, or the chile-and-sea-salted squid with a mango/papaya marmalade. The cigar lounge is open from 6pm until late. The place roars with the carefree laughter of the ridiculously rich.

Jalan Oberoi 9, Seminyak. ⓒ 361/736969. www.kudeta.net. Reservations recommended. Main courses Rp140,000–Rp330,000 ($15–$33). AE, MC, V. Daily 7am–midnight (food service).

**La Lucciola** ⋆ ITALIAN   If there's a see-and-be-seen spot among the Kuta crowd, it's La Lucciola. Even breakfast draws the beautiful people, and why not, with its prime beachfront location on this deserted stretch of Legian? Morning eye-poppers include tasty ricotta hot cakes and smoked salmon scrambled eggs on toasted focaccia. The dinner menu is equally enticing, with choice offerings such as lemon grass bok choy risotto with sesame ginger, and oven-baked snapper with braised shallots and oregano. The seafood specials, calamari and a unique prawn and snapper pie, are tops, in addition to a complement of good pasta and traditional Italian fare. End with a bracing espresso and tiramisu.

Oberoi Rd., Kayu Aya Beach, Legian. ⓒ 361/730838. Main courses Rp40,000–Rp150,000 ($4.40–$16). AE, MC, V. Daily 8am–midnight.

**Made's Warung** ⋆⋆ *Finds* INDONESIAN   This is a longtime Bali favorite, and for good reason. The atmosphere is lively and the Western and Indonesian dishes are great. The original location is an open-air place at street side in Kuta, but the new space in Seminyak is a big improvement—it's protected from the road and bustling with people, not beeping motorbikes. If it's busy, and it often is, don't be surprised if you end up sharing a table. *Gado gado*, satay, and curries are all recommended, and the price is right. Fun surprises on the menu include a bagel with smoked marlin, tofu burgers, and Caesar salad. Don't pass up the daily specials, particularly fresh fish dishes. Beverage choices range from iced coffee and juices to some very potent booze concoctions (be warned).

In Kuta: Br. Pando Mas, Kuta. ℂ 316/755297. In Seminyak: Jalan Raya Seminyak ℂ 316/732130. Main courses Rp12,000–Rp30,000 ($1.30–$3.30). AE, MC, V. Daily 8am–midnight.

**Ryoshi** ⋐ JAPANESE   If you're like me, you've got your favorite sushi place back home where you take that special someone to celebrate when some good news comes down the pike. At Ryoshi every day is special, the prices are reasonable for sushi, and they have all kinds of other Japanese fare that's done just right (just ask the many Japanese guests). Be sure to try the Butterfish, a deep-water whitefish with a rich texture and savory flavor. Not to miss. They have locations all over the island (see below), but the Seminyak outlet is by far the best (with their busy shop in Kuta a close second).

Seminyak: Jl Raya Seminyak No. 17 ℂ 361/731144. Kuta: Jalan Melasti 42A ℂ 361/761852 (also locations in Sanur, Ubud. 14 Roses and even on tiny Gili Trawangan island near Lombok). Main courses from Rp35,000 ($3.85) and a la carte sushi dishes from Rp10,000 ($1.10). MC, V. Daily 11am–10pm.

## OUTDOOR ACTIVITIES

**Surfing** is "gnarly" in Kuta (that means good), and enthusiasts from all over are drawn to its stupendous breakers, which are at their best between March and July. Surf shops line the main drags and can help with rentals or tide information. Any hotel can arrange a private or group lesson, or contact **Cheyne Horan School of Surf** (ℂ 361/735858; www.schoolofsurf.com). Beginners start off at Kuta or Legian (with soft-sand beaches), but the legendary surf is at the low reef breaks and "barrels" of **Kuta Reef** at the southern end.

Unfortunately, the same surf makes recreational **swimming** virtually impossible. Even past the breakers, the current can be too strong. Pay close attention to swimming warnings and restrictions, and be very careful if you do swim. Tanning and splashing to cool off are about all that are left to do.

You can book adventure tours to destinations across the island using Kuta as a hub. For day trips to Ubud, the volcanoes and/or the temples of central Bali, contact **Sobek Tours** (ℂ 361/287059) or **Bali Adventure Tours** (ℂ 361/721480). One smaller operator, **Matangi Tours** (ℂ 361/739820; www.traditionalbali tours.com), has unique cultural and adventure tours all across the island starting at $76 per day.

If money is no obstacle, take a ride on a helicopter to remote stretches of the island and pass over volcanoes and jungle scenery. Contact **Air Bali** (ℂ 361/767466; www.airbali.com).

And if the kids aren't getting enough of a kick out of the busy beach at Kuta, take 'em to the **Waterbom Park** in the south end of Kuta on Jalan Kartika Plaza (ℂ 361/755676).

## SHOPPING

Shopping in Kuta is inevitable. Even if you aren't interested in buying anything, the touts are quick to steer you none-too-subtly to their merchandise (usually by waving it in your face). The streets (particularly Poppies Gang II) are lined with stalls offering tie-dyed sarongs, shorts, swimsuits, knock-off brand-name cologne, hats, and wristwatches. Given the hard sell, this might be the best place to hone your bargaining skills. **Kuta Square** is the place to go for Western-style shopping—it might be called "Brand Name Row," with Nike, Polo, and Armani stores, and fast-food places such as McDonald's and KFC. **Matahari** is the large budget department store at the center.

Try **Jungle Surf** for all of your discount (and not so discount) beachwear and surfing gear, on Legian Street, at beachside near the Hard Rock Cafe, and in the Kuta Arcade (www.junglesurfworld.com).

For books, stop by **Periplus** with locations in Kuta Square (© 361/763988), in Seminyak near Made's Warung (© 361/734843), and even in the airport.

## SPAS

There are some fine spas in the area and most large hotels and resorts have at least basic spa services. Both the **Royal Seminyak** (p. 616) and **Padma** hotels (p. 614) offer extensive, high-end services. Also try the **Henna Spa** (© 361/701695; www.balquisse.com).

## KUTA & SEMINYAK AFTER DARK

Kuta is party central, going full-on from 11pm until dawn—every night. Clubs and bars abound, each with its own flavor, though they're mostly "same-same but different" with lots of pint-tilting scenes. Thankfully, it is all pretty family-friendly and not a go-go bar scene as in Thailand and other Southeast Asian destinations.

There are too many bars to mention, and many are pretty adolescent, but the **Hard Rock Hotel** (© 361/755661) is classy in its own way and sometimes has good live acts. **Kori Restaurant and Bar** (Poppies Gang II; © 361/758605) is relaxed, cozy, and pricey, with a chic cigar salon, a pool table, and even valet parking.

For clubbing in Kuta, try **Bounty Ship II** (like the first only bigger) on Jalan Legian (© 361/752529), which is built to look like a galleon and has a lively dance floor and bar. It's cheesy but fun. **Kama Sutra** (© 361/761999) is a busy stage-band club on the north end of Kuta; it has nightly shows and features local bands.

A new upscale scene has blossomed to the far north of Kuta. **Ku De Ta** ✪ (p. 618) is a chic beachside restaurant and club, open late. What's new in Seminyak is **Jalan Dhyana Pura**, a street lined with stylish clubs and bars that attracts quite the little paparazzi-ducking clientele. Check around for *The Yak,* a free local glossy magazine that lists nightly events. Try **Spy Bar, Oxygen** (© 361/730885) or **Liquid** (© 361/730894) any time after 10pm to "get thy freak on." The ultraconnected make the trip further north to **Hu'u Bali** (it's pronounced "Who"; © 361/736443), with dining, funky cocktails, and special DJ nights when it's all lounge and pose (and pout, darling, pout like you haven't eaten in a week). On the road just south of Dhyanapura and right on the beach is the busy **Double Six** (© 361/655661).

## DAY TRIPS FROM KUTA

**Uluwatu** is a spectacular pinnacle of land at the far south of Bali. At the right times of year, it has some of the best surfing in the world. Arrange trips to Uluwatu, Tanah Lot (below), or sites listed later in this chapter under "Day Trips from Ubud" by contacting any hotel concierge or tour desk. Daily car rental (with driver) comes as low as $20.

**Tanah Lot** Founded by a Brahmin priest in the 16th century, the temple at Tanah Lot is notable less for its construction than its spectacular setting, high on craggy bluffs overlooking the Java Sea. This is a truly magnificent example of how well temples in Bali are wedded to their locations, be they lakeside, mountainside, or seaside. Legend has it that a Brahmin priest had a rivalry with the local, established priest which nearly led to his expulsion from the order; instead, he meditated so hard he pushed Tanah Lot "out to sea," where it rests on an inlet that actually becomes an island at high tide. The walk from the car park is not as long or as steep as at many other sites, and there are no stairs. Non-Hindus cannot enter the temple, but may access the other parts of the complex strung out across the rocks. Many of these afford stunning views. Try to come at sunset, when Tanah Lot is truly glorious. Skip the touristy snake cave.

15km (9¼ miles) west of Denpasar. Admission Rp3,000 (30¢). Open during daylight hours.

## 4 Jimbaran Bay

Jimbaran has some of the best sandy beaches in South Bali, and the clear, calm water is great for swimming. Developers were quick to realize this and Jimbaran now hosts some of the finest high-end resorts on the island. Despite development, the town still looks like a fishing village and small mom-and-pop seafood shacks at beachside serve up some of the best fish dishes on the island. It's a worthy day trip from Kuta for good eats alone, and the many resorts make it comfy to stay.

## GETTING THERE
Jimbaran is on the road to Nusa Dua, south of Kuta. Cabs are many.

## WHERE TO STAY
**Four Seasons at Jimbaran Bay** 🐠🐠    The very picture of luxury, the exquisitely landscaped grounds of the Four Seasons are on a stunning hillside overlooking the bay. The layout is meant to suggest a series of Balinese villages, each thatched villa consisting of a large bedroom, generous dressing area, and marbled bathroom with oversize tub. The little things stand out: nice thick towels and fancy bath amenities, his and her sinks, cool garden showers, a library with books for borrowing and Internet connections, and snap-to service everywhere on the grounds. There are also top spa services, and a cooking school. The resort's horizon pool blends seamlessly with the ocean blue and there are other small dipping and soaking pools, plus lots of private corners to relax and escape from it all. Walk or be driven in a golf cart down to the beach, passing *bales* (open-air pavilions) and viewing spots along the way. The luxe beach club has all the same amenities as the pool.

Jimbaran 80361, Bali. ℂ 361/701010. Fax 361/701020. www.fourseasons.com. 147 units. From $450 1-bedroom villa; from $750 2-bedroom and Royal Villa. AE, DC, MC, V. **Amenities:** 3 restaurants; 2 bars; 2 outdoor pools; tennis courts; health club; spa; Jacuzzi; sauna; watersports rentals; concierge; tour desk; car rental; shopping; 24-hour room service; massage; babysitting; laundry service. *In room:* A/C, satellite TV, minibar, fridge, safe, IDD phone.

**Jimbaran Puri Bali** 🐠🐠    The pioneer resort on Jimbaran beach, the Puri Bali, originally the Pansea, has stylish, self-contained garden cottages set among lily ponds, coconut trees, and Balinese statuary, set back from the beach. All cottages have terraces, shaded by umbrellas, with privacy-providing bamboo catay screens and outdoor deck showers. Rooms are done in carved teak under thatched roofing, with mosquito netting and natural linen touches. Bathrooms have sunken tubs and all the goodies. The resort is a haven of privacy and calm, a good choice for getting away from it all.

Jalan Uluwatu, Jimbaran, Bali. ℂ **361/701605.** Fax 361/701320. www.pansea.com. 41 cottages. $190–$290 cottage. AE, MC, V. **Amenities:** 2 restaurants; bar; outdoor pool; tour desk; business center w/Internet; shopping; 24-hr room service; massage; babysitting; laundry service. *In room:* A/C, satellite TV, minibar, fridge, hair dryer, safe, IDD phone.

## WHERE TO DINE

Dining at Jimbaran's fine resorts is a good, safe option (try **PJ's** at the Four Seasons), but folks come from far and wide for the good, fresh seafood barbecue, priced by the pound, served at beachside. Lobster and snapper are served with dipping sauces, rice, cucumber salad, and spinach cooked in sweet chile. Follow it up with some fresh fruit. It's romantic at sunset and afterwards by candlelight. Cheap too!

## 5 Nusa Dua

In the 1970s, a French firm, commissioned by the Indonesian government, came up with the idea for a self-contained resort complex to "minimize the impact of tourism on the Balinese culture." It chose this 300-hectare (741-acre) tract of undeveloped land, devoid of any infrastructure, and basically transformed it into a theme park. Nusa Dua is now a roster of five-star, all-inclusive properties, all secluded and finely manicured. The beaches are clean and blissfully tout-free, but it can all seem a bit sterile. Still, it's suitable for families and business conventions.

### GETTING THERE

Things couldn't be easier. Most hotels in Nusa Dua offer airport pickup, but you can find shuttles and cheap taxis at the airport and in Kuta. (Be sure to take only the official blue-and-yellow metered taxis in Kuta.) Bemos from Denpasar go to Nusa Dua by way of Kuta and Jimbaran.

### GETTING AROUND

These big spreads make it so comfortable you won't want to or even have to leave the grounds—but even the most starry-eyed honeymooners might want a break from expensive hotel meals. Cabs are unreliable, and hotel transport, unless free, is at inflated prices. It's best to take a **local shuttle** with stops at all resorts.

### WHERE TO STAY

Nusa Dua is like a Disneyland of high-end hotels and resorts. You'll find a new **Conrad** resort (© **361/778788;** www.conradhotels.com), a **Grand Hyatt** (© **361/771234;** www.bali.grand.hyatt.com), and a **Melia Hotel** (© **361/ 771510;** www.meliabali.com), among others. Self-contained, these behemoth estates can handle any eventuality, including transport, tours, and money changing.

### VERY EXPENSIVE

**Amanusa** ★★★   It doesn't get any better than this. Typical of the refined Aman resorts in Ubud and Candi (among others), the Amanusa stands in a magnificent setting, on a high hilltop overlooking a golf course and the beaches of Nusa Dua beyond. It comes with quite a price tag, but a visit to Amanusa is an invitation to service that is gracious and intuitive, and rooms that are over-the-top luxurious while remaining in harmony with the surroundings. The name means "Peaceful Isle" and it is certainly that. Rooms are crafted in rich redwood with four poster beds, sunken indoor baths, and outdoor and indoor showers. Each suite has a small *bale,* or covered sitting area, with a stylish lounging daybed. The central 24m (79-ft.) pool is stunning. Cozy nooks abound, including the library, which offers Internet access. In-house dining at The Terrace is an experience in itself, with great views and delicious local cuisine. The beach club is just a short drive down the hill and is a collection of private *bales* that front the Bali Golf and Country Club property. They can arrange just about anything here, from local cycling tours, to island cruises, to cooking classes, shopping, or adventure tours.

Nusa Dua, Bali. © 361/772333. Fax 361/772335. www.amanresorts.com. 35 units. $650–$800 suite; $1,000–$1,300 pool suite. AE, MC, V. **Amenities:** 2 restaurants; bar; outdoor pool; beach club; golf course; 2 outdoor tennis courts; watersports rentals; bike rentals and tours; concierge; tour desk; courtesy car; business center; boutique shopping; 24-hour room service; in-room massage; babysitting; laundry service; dry cleaning; nonsmoking rooms; library. *In room:* A/C, TV w/DVD and stereo, minibar, fridge, hair dryer, safe, IDD phone.

## EXPENSIVE

**Nusa Dua Beach Hotel and Spa** 🐟🐟    One of the first resorts in Nusa Dua and owned by the Sultan of Brunei, this fine resort has a lot more local style than most, with a friendly, laid-back demeanor appropriate to the beachside. When things slowed during the period after the bombing in Kuta, folks here hunkered down and renovated and the place looks great. Regular rooms are rather ordinary, but the Deluxe and Palace rooms are large, with Balinese fabric on the beds and, for the Palace rooms, DVD players and Jacuzzi tubs. Both swimming pools are picturesque and luxurious. The exquisite spa has open-air, thatched massage pavilions and Bali-style beds set among fountains. The gym, too, is well equipped, and the amenities throughout, including many choices for fine dining (see **Raja's,** p. 624), are all top of the line. All rooms connect with the outdoors via elegant double sliding doors, and the wooden appointments throughout are elegant. The staff is as professional and as welcoming as they come. The hotel offers elaborate culture shows each evening, and there are lots of activities, from cycling tours to batik lessons, throughout the day. From families to honeymooners, this place is a great choice.

P.O. Box 1028, Denpasar, Bali. © 361/771219 or 361/771210. Fax 361/772617. www.nusaduahotel.com. 380 units. $150–$230 double; $300–$2,800 suite. AE, DC, MC, V. **Amenities:** 5 restaurants; 4 bars; 2 outdoor pools; golf (nearby); spa; Jacuzzi; sauna; kids' club; tour desk; business center; shopping; 24-hr. room service; massage; babysitting; laundry service; dry cleaning; meeting facilities; Internet. *In room:* A/C, satellite TV, minibar, fridge, safe, IDD phone.

**Sheraton Laguna Nusa Dua** 🐟    It's a Sheraton and you get all the benefits—and blasé basics—of the chain. The central pool is sprawling and always busy. The rooms are lavish but a bit flower-fussy, with a brash and brassy vaguely tropical decor. Bathrooms are large and done in marble. Additional luxury touches include optional in-room check-in and 24-hour butler service. The grounds are vast and manicured, but this can make getting to the beach an endeavor. If it's not luxe enough here, try the more upscale Westin next door; it's a bit short on character and cold for beachside, but popular for meetings and business arrangements.

P.O. Box 77, Nusa Dua Beach 80363, Bali. © 361/771327. Fax 361/771326. www.starwood.com/bali. 270 units. $258–$420 double; $515–$1,260 suite. AE, DC, MC, V. **Amenities:** 3 restaurants; 4 bars; 3 outdoor pools (and kid's pool); golf (nearby); tennis court; fitness center; spa; Jacuzzi; watersports rentals; tour desk; car/motorbike rentals; shopping; salon; 24-hr. room service; massage; laundry service; meeting room. *In room:* A/C, satellite TV w/in-house movies, minibar, fridge; hair dryer, IDD phone.

## TALUNG BENOA

Just north of Nusa Dua along the coast is the fishing village of Benoa. The labyrinth of streets in this town makes for a good stroll, certainly more interesting than sterilized Nusa Dua. The coast here is lined with upscale hotels and resorts, from the newest **Conrad** (© 361/778788; www.conradhotels.com) to a **Melia Hotel** (© 361/771510). This is a popular spot for jet ski and motorboat rental, as well as parasailing, so the beach is always busy.

## Expensive

**Novotel Coralia Benoa Bali** ✵✵    The Novotel here in Benoa is slightly more upscale than usual Novotels. Public spaces are grand and the design throughout reflects Bali. The resort straddles the main street: The ocean side is more expensive and has better beach access, while the "garden" side is quiet and secluded. Better still, for the price, are the "beach cabanas," even bigger suites in semiprivate bungalows (two per pavilion), complete with outdoor stone tubs— most of them honeymoon-worthy. Rooms throughout are big, bright, and airy, decorated in a minimalist Asian style with coconut wood. The three swimming pools all have their own flair, though none is very big. Lots of activities, including aerobics, soccer, a kid's club, and dance and cooking lessons, will keep you on the run, if you like. The free shuttle to Nusa Dua is convenient for touring, but given that this is the best of both worlds—a terrific resort and authentic Bali—it's hard to see that you would need it. The ocean up this way is much deeper and better for swimming, too.

Jalan Pratama Tanjung Benoa, P.O. Box 39, Nusa Dua 80361, Bali. ℰ **361/772239.** Fax 361/772237. www. novotelbali.com. 192 units. $150–$170 double; $270 beach cabana. AE, DC, MC, V. **Amenities:** 3 restaurants; 2 bars; 3 outdoor pools; tennis court; fitness center; spa; kid's club; tour desk; shuttle service; shopping; 24-hr. room service; massage; babysitting; laundry service; dry cleaning; meeting room; library. *In room:* A/C, satellite TV, minibar, fridge, safe, IDD phone.

## WHERE TO DINE

Nusa Dua has some fine dining, mostly at the hotels, all with high prices for this part of the world. There are few other options short of the small *warungs* in town. A good choice is **Raja's** (ℰ **361/771219**), which serves tasty traditional Balinese at the Nusa Dua Beach Hotel. Seafood places line Jalan Pantai Mengiat just outside the main shopping complex; try **Ulam** (ℰ **361/771590**).

## OUTDOOR ACTIVITIES & WATERSPORTS

Unlike Kuta, the surf here is a considerable distance offshore, making swimming in the clear blue-green water most pleasant at high tide (at low tide, it's only ankle-high). It's a popular surf, wind-surf, and jet-skiing spot. Dive excursions, all arranged by the hotels, will probably take you to areas closer to Sanur or to Amed and Tambulen in the northeast (p. 639).

The **Bali Golf and Country Club** (ℰ **361/771791**) sits at the southern tip of the island and has sweeping views of the beaches and clear waters off Nusa Dua. It has a fine course, worth the whopping $156 outlay to the serious enthusiast.

## 6 Ubud

For a thorough exploration of Balinese culture and tradition—and a good dose of comfort and quiet—Ubud is the place. Though unabashedly touristic, the town is the cultural pulse of the island, the richest region in Bali for art production, and the very reason why so many expat artists and collectors have made Bali their home. The town has a royal legacy and hosts the **Royal Palace,** a center for cultural performances and dance. In and among the smaller streets of town you'll find refined boutiques, chic galleries, and cool trinket shops, alongside open-air cafes that swallow passersby on lazy days. Outside the busy town labyrinth, the phosphorescent rice paddies, virgin jungle, gorges, and river valleys of this hilly Shangri-La are ripe for exploration. Ubud's central location makes the whole island accessible as a day trip. About the only thing it doesn't have is a beach, but they're all a short drive away.

## VISITOR INFORMATION

The information kiosk (© **361/973285**) on **Jalan Raya,** on the south side of the main street, near the intersection with Monkey Forest Road, is a good place to start. There are also tourist agencies all over town, each offering competitive prices for day trips and shuttles to other tourist areas.

## GETTING THERE

Many hotels in the area offer hotel pickup, and taxis connect from the airport, about an hour away. *Bemos* drop you in the center of town, while the tourist shuttles have their own stops, usually on one of the two main drags.

## GETTING AROUND

Transport touts in Ubud are quite aggressive and **minivans** are for hire on every corner for day trips or the short jaunt across town. Central Ubud is small enough to see **on foot,** and hotels away from the main action generally provide regular **shuttles** into town. The main street is Jalan Raya, which runs east-west; Monkey Forest Road runs perpendicular. Ubud is a good a place to **rent a motorbike** (about Rp50,000/$5.50 per day) if you're an experienced rider. **Bicycles** are available for hire at two or three street-side locations along Monkey Forest Road for about Rp10,000 (about $1.10).

### FAST FACTS: Ubud

*Banks/Currency Exchange* There are a number of small ATM outlets on Main Street and along Monkey Forest Road. Storefront money changers are at every turn.

*Internet/E-mail* There are Internet cafes every few steps in Ubud, but for the best service, find **Ubud Music** (© **361/971837**) next to Ary's Warung on Jalan Raya at the center of town, one of only a few with broadband.

*Post Office/Mail* The post office is on the main road, but very far to the east. Major hotels offer postal service.

*Telephone* The area code in Ubud is **361**.

## WHERE TO STAY

No matter what your budget is, Ubud has it all, from sublime honeymoon compounds to the humblest *alang alang* (thatch-roof) cottage. Here we've listed an assortment, both in central Ubud and outside of town. Staying at the more rural properties might mean a long walk or ride, but the scenery is breathtaking. Many come and spend a few nights before shopping around for something new.

### VERY EXPENSIVE

**Alila** Just one step down from the ultraluxe Amandari, the Alila has a beautiful campus with fine rooms, suites, and villas overlooking the stunning northern stretch of the Ayung gorge, one of the most scenic stretches of the popular rafting trips that go through here. This infinity-edge swimming pool was voted one of "The 50 Most Spectacular Pools in the World"; it's like a cube of water in otherworldly (or at least unlikely) suspension over the spectacular gorge. Rooms are large and luxe, with top amenities (though no bathtubs), and the Mandara Spa complex is as luxurious as they come. The resort is far from town, but there is regular shuttle service and the resort is perfectly self-contained.

Desa Melinggih Kelod, Payangan Gianyar. © 361/975963. Fax 361/975968. www.alilahotels.com. 64 units. $240–$260 double; $450 villa. AE, MC, V. **Amenities:** Restaurant; bar; outdoor pool; Mandara Spa; Jacuzzi; sauna; bike rentals; concierge; tour desk; airport transfer; boutique; 24-hour room service; massage; babysitting; laundry service; dry cleaning; library and TV room. *In room:* A/C, TV, minibar, fridge, coffeemaker, hair dryer, safe, IDD phone.

**Amandari** 🏵🏵🏵  If you have serious disposable income, a stay at the Amandari ensures the kind of luxurious seclusion afforded celebrities (it's where Mick Jagger and Jerry Hall got married). Laid out like a fanciful Balinese village, the plush rooms are housed within huge stone cottages roofed in thatch. Each suite is enclosed in its own walled compound and appointed with every kingly comfort, including some with private pool. Amandari is over-the-top luxurious without sacrificing local charm: there are outdoor baths, Balinese decoration, and a unique connection to the surrounding villages. Architects, anticipating local ceremonial processions, have designed pathways and openings in the covered walks for the passage of tall, ritual palanquins. Bathrooms are large and luxe with big indoor showers and outdoor tub basins. Village suites have a spacious, first-floor common room and a cozy upstairs loft bedroom done in wood, like a rustic treehouse with a quiet writing nook. And the service is unrivaled. The resort looks out over a beautiful jungle gorge and the Amandari's emerald green infinity-edge pool mimics the color, to blend seamlessly with the green beyond. There is a free shuttle to Ubud, but it's hard to imagine wanting to leave very often. The one terrific restaurant has a bar and serves local and European favorites.

Kedewatan, Ubud. © 361/975333. Fax 361/975335. www.amandari.com. 29 units. $600–$2,400 double; $3,100 villa. AE, MC, V. **Amenities:** Restaurant; bar; outdoor pool; golf course; tennis courts; health club; full spa; Jacuzzi; complimentary bicycles; concierge; tour desk; shopping; 24-hr. room service; massage; babysitting; laundry service; dry cleaning. *In room:* A/C, minibar, fridge, hair dryer, safe, IDD phone.

**Four Seasons Resort at Sayan** 🏵🏵  The Four Seasons here is a masterpiece of planning that takes full advantage of its extraordinary setting right on the River Ayung. It's incredibly posh, though not intimidatingly so. You enter across a long bridge leading to a pond that, almost unbelievably, rests atop the central lobby, all in an immense crater of rice terraces. The design throughout is ultra-modern, but with good references to Balinese tradition. Rooms are either in two-story suites (bedroom below the sitting area), deluxe suites, or high-end villas with private plunge pools. Interiors are done in gleaming woods and natural fabrics, and are full of precious local art and artifacts. Expect luxurious bathrooms (two to every suite/villa) with huge tubs, showers, and dressing areas, and more thick towels than a linen shop. Every room has views of the deep green gorge and/or the river, with in-room sound systems. The two-level horizon pool follows the serpentine shape of the river below. Pampering, of course, is at a maximum and includes "seamless" transfer between here and the resort at Jimbaran Bay; they take care of everything, including, if you wish, your packing. There is also a regular shuttle to Ubud.

Sayan, Ubud, Gianyar. . © 361/977577. Fax 361/977588. www.fourseasons.com. 46 units. $450 suite; $575–$3,000 villa. AE, DC, MC, V. **Amenities:** 2 restaurants; bar; outdoor pool; health club; spa; all rentals available; tour desk; shopping; 24-hr. room service; laundry service; dry cleaning; library w/games. *In room:* A/C, TV, minibar, fridge, safe, IDD phone.

**Ibah** 🏵🏵  Just a stone's throw from the real Ubud action, Ibah is the most romantic hotel you'll find close to town, a boutique resort that bills itself as a "hand-crafted meditation on the art of relaxation." It is indeed a special marriage of Balinese style and Western comfort. The large rooms have clean lines and are done in wood and natural fabrics. Four-poster canopy beds hung with mosquito netting are a nice touch. Good-size bathrooms have either outdoor or wood-floor showers, and oddly-placed toilets right in the middle of an open space. All rooms have spacious verandas. The grounds make good use of the hilly terrain, and there are lots of secret nooks and crannies, including romantic alcoves in the hotel's stylish pool area. Spa and massage services are in muslin-draped out-rooms. There is also a particularly luxe indoor Jacuzzi.

Campuhan, Ubud, P.O. Box 193., ℂ **361/974466.** Fax 361/974467. www.ibahbali.com. 15 units. $210–$315 double; $430 pool villa; $500 2-bedroom suite. AE, MC, V. **Amenities:** Restaurant; bar; outdoor pool; health club; spa; Jacuzzi; concierge; tour desk; salon; room service (6am–midnight); massage; babysitting; laundry service; dry cleaning. *In room:* A/C, TV, minibar, fridge, hair dryer, safe, IDD phone.

**Maya Ubud** 🐾🐾    Just 3 years old, this fine resort is a short hop outside of Ubud proper (just to the east) and is set in a quiet, mountainous area surrounded by rice fields. The hotel's design makes elegant use of local materials, blended in an immaculate, contemporary style. Rooms reflect refined simplicity, with cool white and yellow pastel colors set against the dark wood of fine, Art Deco furnishings. Floors are made of river stone and ceilings of thatch. The double-height lobby rotunda echoes the shape of a Dongsan Drum, a relic of an ancient culture and an important regional motif. The campus stretches in a line of low-profile, tranquil buildings all the way down to the river. An elevator transports you down the steep valley to the riverside, where the fine spa rooms literally hang over the rushing water; there's also a riverside pool with a vanishing edge and a small restaurant. Fine dining, spa facilities, and plenty of activities make the Maya quite self-sufficient, but regular shuttle service to town keeps you connected.

Jalan Gunung Sari Peliatan, Ubud. ℂ **361/977888.** Fax 361/977555. www.mayaubud.com. 108 units. $210–$230 double; $320–$1,200 villa. AE, DC, MC, V. **Amenities:** 2 restaurants; bar; 2 outdoor pools; tennis courts; comprehensive spa; Jacuzzi; bike rentals; tour desk; airport transfer; shopping; laundry service; dry cleaning; library w/Internet. *In room:* A/C, satellite TV, minibar, fridge, coffeemaker, hair dryer, safe, IDD phone.

## EXPENSIVE

**Bali Spirit Hotel and Spa** 🐾    Located a fair jaunt from central Ubud in the village of Nyuh Kuning, this is a reasonable alternative to the really high-end luxury hotels in the north of Ubud. At Bali Spirit you get a great setting and comfortable rooms at a good price, without all the bells, whistles, and fees. The stunning hillside setting overlooks a river gorge. Rooms are large and well-appointed, with small kitchen nooks. Local fabrics and materials are employed throughout and each room has a cozy deck area. The pool is just right, a cozy perch with lounges overlooking the gorge, and there are traditional Balinese bathing pools in the holy river below. A fine spa offers a full range of services. There are regular shuttles to town, in addition to a car available to take you wherever you want to go "at a moment's notice." The lack of TV in the rooms keeps your eyes on the beautiful hills.

P.O. Box 189, Nyuh Kuning Village, Ubud . ℂ **361/974013.** Fax 361/974012. www.balispirithotel.com. 19 units. $95–$135 double; $145 villa. Rates include breakfast. AE, MC, V. **Amenities:** Restaurant; bar; outdoor pool; full spa; mountain-bike rental; tour desk; car rental; airport transfer; 24-hr. room service; massage; laundry service; dry cleaning; Internet; cooking school. *In room:* A/C, TV, minibar, fridge, IDD phone.

**Komaneka Resort** 🐾    On Monkey Forest Road right in the center of town, the Komaneka is clean, modern, and chic. Tracing a long, narrow corridor ending in a small pool with an elegant vanishing edge, guest buildings are well away from street noise and have views of gardens and rice paddies. Deluxe rooms have unique bathrooms: some have outdoor-type showers and baths and others feature marble sunken tubs. Rooms are done in a cool, contemporary style with shiny marble tiles and Spartan wooden furnishings. The decor employs lots of natural woods and fabrics, and the beds are hung with cheeseclothlike netting suspended from the thatched ceiling, just enough to remind you that you're in Bali. Suites are larger versions of deluxe rooms. The owners have also just opened a new high-end resort north of town called **Komaneka Tanggayuda,** a more deluxe compound of suites and pool villas from $220.

Monkey Forest Rd., Ubud, Gianyar. ℂ **361/976090.** Fax 361/977140. www.komaneka.com. 20 units. $135–$190 double; $210–$344 garden and pool villa. AE, DC, MC, V. **Amenities:** Restaurant; outdoor pool; full spa; tour desk; car rental; shopping; 24-hr. room service; massage; laundry service; library. *In room:* A/C, minibar, fridge, IDD phone.

## MODERATE

**Agung Raka Bungalows** ⍟  Just south of central Ubud, these fine, two-story thatched bungalows are arranged around a series of working rice paddies and surrounded by a thriving village art community. Lower-end bungalows are basic two-story wood-and-bamboo constructions with rudimentary outdoor bathrooms and a staircase up to a cozy bedroom. Superior bungalows are single occupancy A-frames with teak and catay accents. The bathrooms here are large, modern courtyard facilities that include both a tile bathtub and a stone-floor shower. The suites are tip-top: a dizzying spectacle of stone and marble, big enough for four and great for two.

Pengosekan Village (2km/1¼ miles south of Ubud center), Ubud. ℂ **361/975757.** Fax 361/975546. www. agungraka.com. 21 bungalows. $70–$100 double; $135–$200 suite. MC, V. **Amenities:** Restaurant; bar; outdoor pool; motorbike rental; tour desk; car rental; shuttle service; laundry service. *In room:* A/C, TV, minibar, IDD phone.

**Alam Sari** ⍟⍟  This model hotel has an excellent combination of comfort, social responsibility, setting, and low price. Everything the Alam Sari does is with a thought toward the local economy, ecology, and culture. Room decor, such as brightly dyed fabric and wood furniture, is made locally. The hotel employs, almost exclusively, villagers from neighboring Keliki, to bolster the local economy. Environmentally friendly touches are everywhere, from solar water heaters to the use of recycled paper. Rooms are lovely, with views of the gorge and looming volcano. The hotel is sufficiently self-contained, making the 20-minute ride to town an only occasional necessity. Traditional music is featured at night.

Keliki, Tromoi Pos 03, Kantor Pos Tegallalang, Ubud, Gianyar.. (9km/5½ miles north of Ubud). ℂ/fax 361/ 240308. www.alamsari.com. 10 units. $106 double; $119 suite; $198 family unit. AE, MC, V. **Amenities:** Restaurant; bar; bicycle rentals; tour desk; car rental; laundry service; library. *In room:* A/C, minibar, fridge, safe, IDD phone.

**Ananda Cottages** ⍟  Just north of Ubud proper, Ananda Cottages is atmospheric enough for the Balinese experience you're hoping for, and situated far enough from the town center to discourage the tourist hoards. The rice fields and thatched cottages of this bungalow campus are almost more "Balinese" than real villages you might visit (where you'll find TVs instead of shrines, and roaring machines instead of hand tools). Cozy rooms are connected by paths along terraced retaining walls, which are lit at night with miniature coal-fed, torchlike flames. The cottages are bi-level brick huts with bamboo pavilion roofs. Downstairs rooms are the better choice and have outdoor baths and patio living rooms. Upstairs rooms have modern baths and small verandas. The pool is small, but on an interesting raised rice terrace. The new deluxe bungalows (just three of them) are very cozy and well worth the outlay (just $70).

Campuhan, Ubud. ℭ **361/975376**. Fax 361/975375. anandaubud@denpasar.wasantara.net.id. 54 units, all w/bathroom. $40–$50 double without A/C; $60–$70 double w/A/C; $175 suite villa. AE, MC, V. **Amenities:** Restaurant; bar; outdoor pool; shopping; 24-hr. room service; laundry service. *In room:* A/C (some rooms), minibar, fridge, IDD phone.

## Hotel Tjampuhan 🏵🏵

This hotel is a tropical sanctuary with terraces that lead to a beautiful gorge, the Tjampuhan River, and the 900-year-old Gunung Lebah Temple. The hotel was built in 1928 for guests of the prince of Ubud and was chosen by Western artists Walter Spies and Rudolf Bonnet as headquarters for their art association, Pita Maha. All units have Balinese thatched roofs. Air-conditioned rooms are larger and have better views than fan rooms. Splurge for a Raja Room (or even Spies's own villa), with verandas overlooking the gorge. The grounds are done in beautiful stonework, and immaculate gardens line the path down to the river. There are two very pretty pondlike pools and another with cold spring water, perfect for hot days.

Jalan Raya Campuhan, Ubud. ℭ **361/975368**. Fax 316/975137. 64 units. $70 double w/fan; $115 double w/A/C; $175 Walter Spies villa. Includes breakfast. AE, MC, V. **Amenities:** 2 restaurants; 4 bars; outdoor pool; full spa; tour desk; car rental; shopping; massage; babysitting; laundry service; dry cleaning; library. *In room:* A/C (some), minibar, fridge, IDD phone.

## Matahari Cottages 🏵

Matahari Cottages is just six quaint, private bunga-lows, and little else. Rooms are done in different themes, from Indian to Eliza-bethan, and the place is fun. There are little Jacuzzi nooks and even a library, though it's not particularly luxurious. Rooms are fan only.

Jalan Jembawan, Ubud. ℭ **361/975459**. Fax 361/975459. www.matahariubud.com. 6 units. $25–$50. MC, V. **Amenities:** Restaurant/bar; small pool; laundry service. *In room:* Fan (no A/C); no phone.

## Ubud Bungalow 🏵

These bungalows are a popular budget option in the mid-dle of town (call ahead as they're often full). Basic rooms, all with balconies out front, are stacked two high in a long column down the length of this quiet cam-pus. There's a small pool and restaurant. Otherwise, you just fend for yourself which, given the central location right in the middle of busy Monkey Forest Road, won't require the use of survival skills. This is a very good budget choice.

Monkey Forest Rd., Ubud. ℭ **361/975537**. Fax 361/971298. 18 units. $22 double w/fan; $33 double w/A/C. MC, V. **Amenities:** Restaurant, pool, laundry service. *In room:* A/C (some rooms); no phone.

## Ubud Sari Health Resort 🏵🏵

This place gets my top recommendation in this category. Nowhere else in Ubud will you find such lovely little cottages, small but immaculate, with real rustic charm. Rooms have air-conditioning, but are situated above a river and many guests just open the windows, hang the mossy net, and let the jungle sounds and rushing water sing them to sleep. Breakfast is served on your private balcony and the staff is attentive without fawning. There's nothing like it at these prices. Rooms connect with the spa area via a meandering garden path. Open to day visitors, this rustic spa offers a cold plunge-pool, herbal steam, a sauna, and a roster of fine massage treatments at discount prices. Once you've checked in, you may not want to leave.

#35 Jalan Kajeng, Ubud. ℭ **361/974393**. Fax 361/976305. www.ubudsari.com. 10 units. $35–$45 double. MC, V. **Amenities:** Restaurant; outdoor pool; extensive spa; whirlpool; Jacuzzi; steam; sauna; tour desk; lim-ited room service; massage; babysitting; laundry service. *In room:* A/C, no TV, no phone.

## INEXPENSIVE

**Puri Garden Bungalows** (Monkey Forest Rd.; ℭ/fax **361/974923**) is exem-plary of the good budget choices in town. Large, cozy guesthouse rooms with air-conditioning start from $19. Other budget choices line Monkey Forest Road and the Jalan Hanoman; better still, turn down any little alley or side street that cuts across them. One very good budget spot right in the center of town is **Sania House Bungalows,** a cool collection of filigreed low-rise bungalows around a central courtyard, with units starting at $12.

## WHERE TO DINE

Choices are many in Ubud, mostly international restaurants in the busy town center, though you'll also find small *warungs* or stands selling *babi guling* (suckling pig). Much of Ubud's fine dining comes with a Western price tag.

**Ary's Warung** ☆ MODERN INDONESIAN    Ary's gourmet European and Indonesian specialties have fans from around the world. Stop in at least for one of their honey-ginger-lime drinks (with or without the booze) and kick back in a couch at street side for a bit of people-watching. The metallic, angular construction of this two-floor, open-air bistro would look great in a big city gallery district, but is a bit at odds with ancient Hindu temples and the adjacent Royal Palace. It is the place to see and be seen, however, and Ary's is quite pleasant at night when tranquil trance music plays and candles light every corner. Second-floor dining gives you a good view of the busy street below or the bats swooping to catch bugs at dusk. The food is good; overpriced, but good. Try the gazpacho, a generous bowl full of icy fresh flavor—perfect for a hot day—or the grilled goat cheese salad. The grilled tuna and lamb cutlets are done to perfection, and the ponzu-grilled snapper is delicious. They offer a tasting menu for Rp220,000 ($24) which includes two glasses of house wine. Ary's also makes for a good meeting place, or for reconnoitering when the kids are trekking and mom is off shopping.

Main St., Ubud. ✆ 361/975053. www.dekco.com. Main courses Rp25,500–Rp75,000 ($2.80–$8.25) (duck, lamb, and salmon much higher—up to Rp150,000/ $16). MC, V. Daily 7:30am–1am.

**Batan's Waru** ☆☆ INDONESIAN/EUROPEAN    Tucked away on a pleasant side street, Batan's Waru is particularly atmospheric at night, when the street entrance is lit with candles. The very ambitious menu has traditional dishes beyond the usual suspects and plenty of vegetarian options. For an appetizer, try *urap pakis,* wild fern tips with roasted coconut and spices; or the *lemper ayam,* chicken dumplings simmered in a banana leaf. Uncle Karaman's Humus is spicy and comes with grilled-pepper flat bread and tomato-mint relish. Everything is served with a dish of spicy hot condiments. Finish off with a perfect cup of decaf Illy-brand espresso. The restaurant also does smoked duck and a *babi guleng* feast, with a day's advance order, and there is a full menu of pasta, sandwiches, and light fare.

Jalan Dewi Sita, Ubud. ✆ 361/977528. www.baligoodfood.com. Main courses Rp15,500–Rp43,000 ($1.70–$4.75). MC, V. Daily 8am–midnight.

**Bebek Bengil (Dirty Duck)** ☆☆ INDONESIAN/EUROPEAN    The Dirty Duck is the best place to try Ubud's famous dish. First stewed in local spices, then deep fried, the duck here is finger-lickin' good, but not quite as oily as in other restaurants. Another good choice is the stuffed chicken with shiitake, sprouts, and spinach. The menu also features salads, overstuffed crunchy sandwiches, and good veggie options. There are two locations, on either end of town.

Padang Tegel (at end of street as it hooks into Monkey Forest Rd.), Ubud. ✆ 361/975489. Main courses Rp12,500–Rp35,000 ($1.35–$3.85). MC, V. Daily 10:30am–11pm.

**Cafe Lotus** ☆ MODERN INDONESIAN/INTERNATIONAL    The food here isn't half bad, but the real reason to come to Cafe Lotus is for the chance to dine in the shadow of the Pura Saraswati temple (p. 633). It's cozy in the shaded dining area or on bamboo platforms overlooking the temple. The menu features some good Western dishes, pastas and such, some modified into fiery dishes with hot chiles, black olives, and hearts of palm. Try the Balinese Satay Lilit, a mixed fish kabob with a hint of coconut, served on skewers and presented on a plate the size of a boat. Their fresh health drinks are a delight, and it's a good place to just kick back when touring the town. No beef is served due to the restaurant's proximity to the temple.

Ubud Main Rd. ℂ 361/975660. Main courses Rp25,000–Rp54,000 ($2.75–$5.95). No credit cards. Daily 9am–10pm.

**Indus** ⭐ ECLECTIC   Indus provides two floors of open-air dining overlooking the stunning Tjampuhan Ridge. It's a bit like a mafia don's house, with marble tile and columns. The entrance is a small gallery and the dining area is under a high thatch roof with cozy, low-slung couches and chairs to one side. This is a great spot for coffee and escape from the heat, or for a long, languid lunch. The setting alone makes it worth the trip, and the food is tops. Sample the likes of beetroot and feta empanadas, grilled calamari tostada, or fine wraps and sandwiches. Be sure to try the Balinese *tenggiri* curry, a Spanish whitefish done in ginger and coconut (or, for a lighter choice, try the *tenggiri* salad). Indus has an extensive tapas menu and good fruit smoothies. Save room for the homemade ginger ice cream or coconut crème caramel.

Jalan Raya Sargingan, Campuhan, Ubud. ℂ 361/977684. www.casalunabali.com. Dress "neat casual." Main courses Rp27,000–Rp50,000 ($3–$5.50). MC, V. Daily 8:30am–11pm.

**Mozaic** ⭐⭐⭐ INTERNATIONAL   The word is out and hip Mozaic is the only place in town where you really need a reservation; make one. Chris Salons, the French-trained American chef and owner, brings his own distinctive French-American cooking techniques and presentation. He uses fresh local ingredients, all rich and delicious but healthy, with unique local dairy substitutes. The restaurant was just listed in Le Grande Tables du Monde, a prestigious French culinary fraternity. The level of innovation and service is unrivaled. A meal at Mozaic is a languid affair, best enjoyed in multiple courses, sopped up with good bread, chased with fine wine, and shared with friends. Give yourself at least 2 hours to really enjoy it. Daytime dining features good French light fare served in a quiet patio area. The evening meal is an extravaganza of French and continental specialties done with local flair and served in a lush garden dining area. Try the king prawns in chilled gazpacho, followed by a pan-seared Long-Nose Emperor filet done in a Laksa Indonesian yellow emulsion with rice noodles and baby turnips. Other specials include roasted lamb with toasted almond and bean fricassee, Australian beef tenderloin, and local favorites like *babi guling* and Ubud crispy duck. Finish with a fine sorbet combining melon, cherry, and pomello. The chocolate tart soufflé is sinfully rich. Service is ultraprofessional, attentive without being fawning or intimidating, and the atmosphere is the right mix of elegant and casual—the perfect romantic evening.

Jalan Raya Sanggingan, Ubud. ℂ 361/975768. www.mozaic-bali.com. Main courses Rp99,000–Rp175,000 ($11–$19); tasting menu Rp245,000–Rp265,000 ($27–$29). AE, MC, V. Daily noon–4pm and 6–10pm. Reservations required.

**Naughty Nuri's Warung and Grill** ⭐ BARBECUE/BALINESE   This old expat hangout has the best barbecue in town, with ribs so tender the meat falls right off the bone. On Thursday a regular shipment of fresh tuna arrives and the place fills right up. The burgers, dogs, and local curries and satay are also good.

Free-flowing drink (try their honkin' martinis) add to the laid-back atmosphere at street side. Bring your appetite, a high booze tolerance, and a good sense of humor.

Tromol Pos No. 219, Ubud (just across from the Neka Museum on the road leading north of town). © 361/ 977547. Main courses Rp15,000–Rp60,000 ($1.65–$6.60). Cash only. Daily 9am–10pm.

**Satri's Warung** ★★ INDONESIAN/BALINESE The house specialty of this funky, hidden courtyard is worth the hunt (and the wait). You need to order a day in advance for a feast of a whole chicken or duck marinated and glazed in a succulent sauce. The meat just falls off the bone, and the shared dish is artfully arranged and served with heaping plates of salad, cooked vegetables, and a large bowl of rice. Top it off with fresh-squeezed lemonade. Don't miss this restaurant, even if you don't have time for the chicken or duck; it's one of the finest *warungs* in all of Bali. The very friendly Mrs. Satri serves her exceptional Indonesian food in generous portions, and she also holds cooking classes by appointment. The restaurant is at the end of a dim little alley off of Monkey Forest Road. On approach, it looks a bit shady, but soldier on, have a seat, say hello, and ask for a recommendation. A good evening is guaranteed.

Monkey Forest Rd. (east side, 1-min. walk from Main Rd.; look for 2nd yellow beer sign). © 361/973279. Main courses Rp8,000–Rp17,000 (90¢–$1.85); banana chicken for 2 Rp125,000 ($14); duck for 2 Rp150,000 ($16). No credit cards. Daily 10am–10pm.

**TeraZo** ★★ MEDITERRANEAN The spacious interior of this hip bistro is simple yet welcoming, with terraces behind a nice garden with decorative fountains. The menu is extensive. Cool gazpacho made of ripe tomatoes is a welcome starter in the tropical heat, and the spring rolls are light and delicious. The eight-layer pie is a delicious pastry crust filled with smoked blue marlin, spinach, ricotta, and mushrooms. There's also a host of grilled items, fine pasta, and gourmet Asian-influenced dishes, like the *nasi kuning,* yellow coconut rice with raisins, cashews, and strips of egg; or the *kue tiaun,* stir-fried rice noodles, chicken, and local greens. You can also find a tempting breakfast menu with surprises like ricotta blintzes topped with honey and fresh yogurt.

Jalan Suweta, Ubud. © 361/978941. www.baligoodfood.com. Main courses Rp60,000–Rp134,000 ($6.60–$15). AE, MC, V. Daily 8am–11pm.

## SNACKS & CAFES

**Casa Luna** on Main Street (© 361/973282) is a longtime favorite with expats and offers a roster of local and international cuisine, coffee, and desserts. (It also has cooking classes.) **Tutmak Warung Kopi** (Jalan Dewi Sita near Batan's Waru; © 361/975754) is the town's best little coffee shop with great desserts and a whole range of good, healthy treats, from salads to light lunches. There's also a good menu for little kids.

**Zula Vegetarian Paradise** (Jalan Raya Ubud No. 25; © 361/972294), just across from the palace and east of the town center, is, as the name suggests, a great spot for a fresh fruit and vegetable juice or some excellent light fare like baba ganoush or a specialty sandwich made with light, healthy ingredients. For desserts and good ice cream, **Mumbul's Café** (© 361/975364) on the Main Street is a tasty choice in a serene garden terrace.

**Bali Buddha Cafe** (Jalan Jembawan #1, in front of the post office to the east of town; © 361/976324) is a happening little expat spot with a small grocery where you can pick up good fresh bread (most with no white flour), organic vegetables, healthy snacks, and supplements. The upstairs is a popular juice bar and a good place to meet long-staying folks or get info off of their bulletin board. It's New Age central here, more or less.

## WHAT TO SEE

**Pura Saraswati** ★★   The royal family commissioned this temple and water garden, dedicated to the Hindu goddess of art and learning, at the end of the 19th century. The main shrine is covered in fine carvings, and the *bale* houses (small pavilions) and giant *barong* masks are interesting. The restaurant **Cafe Lotus** is situated at the front, on the main street, so that diners can look out over the lovely grounds.

Jalan Raya Ubud. Ubud. Free admission. Daily during daylight hours.

**Puri Saren Agung, the Royal Palace** ★   From the late 19th century to the mid-1940s, this was the seat for the local ruler. It's a series of elegant and well-preserved pavilions, many of them decorated incongruously with colonial-era European furniture. Visitors are welcome to stroll around, though there are no signs indicating what you are looking at, so it palls quickly. Evening dance performances are held in the courtyard, and it is by far the best and most dramatic setting for these in Ubud.

Jalan Raya, Ubud. Free admission. Daily during daylight hours.

## MUSEUMS

Ubud has enjoyed a long relationship with foreign artists. As a result, there are a few good museums in town and many galleries. All give you a good crash course in authentic Balinese art, not to mention welcome respite from souvenir stalls.

There are a number of small museums in town. Those listed below are the best choices, but don't pass up the many small, free galleries around town, especially on Jalan Raya Sanggingan going north toward the more high-end resorts. Including those below, also see the **Seniwati Gallery of Art by Women** (Jln. Sriwedari 2B, Banjar Taman, Ubud; *℃* **361/975485;** free admission). **Agung Rai Museum and Gallery** (*℃* **361/974228;** www.nusantara.com/arma) is another popular local collection.

**Antonio Blanco's Gallery**   The gallery is an homage to Bali's famous Catalan expat. Born in the Philippines, Blanco arrived in Bali penniless and befriended the king, married, had children, and lived the life of Riley all his days. He was a favorite at court and the confidant of many powerful people on the island and in Indonesia. This grand gallery houses a collection of his work that is as much a romp through Blanco's sexual dalliances as anything, a collection of homespun, baroque pornography. Some paintings feature Blanco's raunchy prose poetry. Don't miss touring his studio space. The consummate egomaniacal artist, Blanco envisioned this monument to himself and participated fully in its creation before shuffling off this mortal coil in 1999. The museum grounds are a trip, with Blanco's menagerie of dachshunds, monkeys, and exotic birds still ruling the roost.

Jalan Campuhan, just past the bridge heading north of Ubud. *℃* **361/975502.** www.marioblanco.com or www.blancobali.com. Admission Rp20,000 ($2.20). Daily 9am–5pm.

**Neka Museum** ★★   Founded in 1982 by Suteja Neka, a former schoolteacher and patron of the arts, this museum is a good introduction to the Balinese school. Housed in several pavilions, works are labeled in English and provide informed access to rural traditions and modern movements on the island or locally in Ubud. The collection features the work of the Dutch-born Indonesian artist Arie Smit, as well as contemporary works both local and from abroad. Don't miss the view of the Campuhan Gorge from the Smit Pavilion, and see what inspires local artists (or get inspired yourself).

Jalan Raya Campuhan (about 10 min. north of central Ubud, near Ananda Cottages). ⓒ **361/975074** or 361/975034. www.museumneka.com. Admission Rp20,000 ($2.20). Daily 9am–5pm.

**Puri Lukisan** 🏵 A major renovation has turned this formerly dilapidated display into something nearly on par with the Neka Museum. The gorgeous gardens of lily ponds and rice paddies are worth a visit on their own. Founded in 1956 by a prince of Ubud and a Dutch artist, the collection of painting and sculpture here traces the evolution of Balinese art. One space is dedicated to a revolving exhibit of up-and-coming local artists.

Jalan Raya, Ubud. ⓒ **361/975136**. www.mpl-ubud.com. Admission Rp20,000 ($2.20). Daily 9am–5pm.

## OUTDOOR ACTIVITIES

**Elephant Safari Park** 🏵🏵 The **Elephant Safari Park,** run by **Bali Adventure Tours,** is less safari and more elephant ride, and it's a real hoot. These native Sumatra elephants are well cared for and live in large, lush enclosures. The owners have worked carefully with locals from Taro Village, previously one of Bali's most remote and untouched villages, to make sure they leave little more than elephant tracks. A safari starts with Pachyderm 101, as knowledgeable guides tell about the animals' care and feeding, local ecology, threats to the native population, and preservation efforts. Then, along with a mahout (a guide), you'll have a galumphing trip through the jungle. Don't miss the antics of their youngest pachyderm; he's just taken up the game of soccer and can usually be found pouncing on an oversize ball in the central pond. They have a fun elephant show twice daily at 12:30 and 3:30pm. The price is a bit dear, but they take good care of you here, with a tasty lunch buffet and attentive service.

Jalan Bypass Ngurah Rai, Pesanggaran. ⓒ **361/721480**. Fax 361/721481. www.baliadventuretours.com. Park entrance (including transport, buffet lunch, and show) is **$48, $68** w/elephant ride, kids **$33** and **$47**; family rates and Internet rates are available. Reservations are recommended.

**Monkey Forest** 🏵 Yes, there is a monkey forest at the southern end of Monkey Forest Road, and this is a popular day trip. The towering tree clusters here are home to a troop of bad-tempered but photogenic primates who swing from branches, cannonball into pools of water, and do everything short of putting on suits and paying taxes, all to the general delight of photo-snapping visitors. Signs warn you not to feed the monkeys, but locals stand under those very signs selling you bananas and nuts for precisely that purpose. Do so if you must, but do not tease the critters, who are grumpy enough as it is—just hand them the food. Make sure you have no other food on you: They will smell it. They're also known to snatch at dangling or glittering objects or gnaw on sandals. There's a small temple in the forest, and the track also leads to Nyuhkuning, a woodcarving village.

Monkey Forest Rd. Admission Rp3,000 (35¢). Daily during daylight hours.

## RAFTING & TREKKING

Just west of Ubud, the Ayung River has some good white-water rafting and kayaking. The rapids aren't too impressive for experienced rafters, but the scenery along the way is, with rice paddies, deep gorges, and photo-op waterfalls. Two-hour trips include all equipment, hotel pickup, and lunch; most hotels can make the reservations. You can also contact **Bali Adventure Tours** (ⓒ **361/721480;** www.baliadventuretours.com) or **Sobek** (ⓒ **361/287059**).

## SPAS

Repeat visitors to Ubud are escapists, spiritual seekers, and relaxation junkies. The best choice for the latter, and a very affordable option, is the **Ubud Sari Resort** (ⓒ **361/974393;** www.ubudsari.com) which has a range of packages including massage, sauna, and steam. The setting is a peaceful garden—low-luxe digs and high-luxe service. **The Ubud Body Works Center** (25 Hanuman Rd.; ⓒ **361/975720;** www.ubudbodyworkscentre.com) focuses on Balinese healing techniques. All of the high-end resorts have good spa services; **Ibah** (ⓒ **361/ 974466;** www.ibahbali.com) and the **Four Seasons Sayan** (ⓒ **361/977577;** www.fourseasons.com) are best among them.

## WALKING

Ubud is surrounded by fascinating villages, scenic rice paddies, gorges, and rivers, and roads and paths lead to all of them. You can just wander, but I strongly urge you to buy a copy of the *Ubud Surroundings* **map,** available in all shops. Then head for the picturesque village of **Penestanan** or go on the rigorous **Campuhan Ridge walk.** Hiring a local guide is also a good option.

Ever seen a Scarlet-headed Flowerpecker? For an interesting day, meet up with famed author and naturalist **Victor Mason** for his popular **Birdwatching Tour** 🍂 of Ubud. Tours cost $33 and leave every morning from the bridge at Tjampuhan in the northeastern end of town. To make arrangements, call ⓒ **361/975009** in the day or ⓒ **812/3913801** in the evening. You're bound to see a good many of Bali's 100 species of birds. The scenic walk includes lunch, water, and binocular use.

## SHOPPING

Ubud is the shopper's paradise of Bali, with everything from tacky plastic doohickeys to priceless works that will have you thinking of selling the SUV.

Start at **Ubud Market** at the southeast corner of Monkey Forest Road and Jalan Raya Ubud (open during daylight hours.). It's a real market—great noisy fun, with dozens of stalls selling produce and livestock along with tourist kitsch.

All along **Monkey Forest Road, Jalan Raya Ubud,** and **Jalan Hanoman,** shop after shop is filled with gorgeous sarongs, woodcarvings, mobiles, jewelry, incense, pottery, and gaily colored shirts. It's all geared to tourists, but the quality isn't bad. Elsewhere in town you can find jewelry, housewares, and textiles.

**Threads of Life,** Jalan Kajeng 24 (ⓒ **361/972187;** www.threadsoflife.com), a foundation that supports groups of weavers on the eastern islands of Indonesia, sells unique local patterns.

**Treasures, Toko,** and **Toko East** are fine boutiques owned by the folks at Ary's Warung; find them on Main Street in the center of Ubud or on the Internet at www.dekco.com. Other boutiques and galleries line the road running north of central Ubud toward the high-end resort area. The lace shop **Toko Uluwatu** (www.uluwatu.com) has outlets all over Bali. You can find its popular storefront on Monkey Forest Road in the center of Ubud. **Okrakartini,** east of the palace on the Main Road (ⓒ **361/975624**), is an upmarket boutique with fine cloth, jewelry, and antiques.

For books, stop by **Periplus** on Monkey Forest Road (ⓒ **361/975178**) or **Ganesh Bookshop,** Jalan Raya (ⓒ **361/973359;** www.ganeshabooksbali.com), adjacent to the popular Buddha Cafe.

## UBUD AFTER DARK

Ubud's nightlife scene is growing but still rather sedate. **Jazz Café** (Jalan Sukma 2, east of Monkey Forest Rd.; ⓒ **361/976594**), has good live jazz. There are lots of little laid-back places along Monkey Forest Road that are more than happy to stay open late. Upscale **Lamak** (ⓒ **361/974663**) also stays up, but nightlife is mostly calm. For a night of drinking and fun, hit **Naughty Nuri's** (p. 631; (p. 631;

## Scaling the Heights: Bali's Volcanoes

**Gunung Agung,** the tallest peak on the island at 3,014m (9,886 ft.), is quite a spectacle, visible from as far away as the island of Lombok or high buildings in busy Kuta. It is a grueling 5-hour climb to the top. Easier is nearby **Gunung Batur,** Agung's little brother, just a few hours' hike. Start before first light to catch the dawn. The views from the top are stunning: You can see the geothermally active surrounding crater, the volcanoes of nearby Lombok, and the looming peak of Agung.

Both Batur and Agung are still active volcanoes, with eruptions as recent as 1997. This is a stunning part of the island and certainly worth the trip. Lots of small storefront outfitters arrange group bus tours and private transport. The area makes for a good overnight, too. Rooms in the very basic lodging at the base of Mt. Batur start at Rp30,000 ($3.30). The town of Penelokan, a name that means "moved people" (a result of volcanic activity), stands at the rim of the crater. **Lakeview Hotel and Restaurant** (✆ 366/51394; www.indo.com/hotels/lakeview) is a good bet, with deluxe rooms from $30. All rooms face the lake (thus the moniker) and helpful staff can arrange transport and trekking at a cost just slightly higher than if you go down and make your own arrangements at the trail head.

You do need a guide. It's not just the rules, it's a good idea. The sad part is that the local mafia masks itself as a government agency and controls the mountain guides. It's best to arrange any hiking plans at your guesthouse or hotel. Be sure to be fastidious and specific about details: Is it a private tour? Is breakfast included? What route will you follow?

There are a few different routes up both peaks. Most follow the trail to the main viewing point near the top of Batur (there's a little lean-to where folks have breakfast and wait for the sunrise). From there you can follow a short loop to the various craters. You can arrange a basic tour and then offer the guide a little extra for an upgrade.

It's a fun morning and you can follow it up with a visit to the small hot springs near the lake.

---

✆ 361/977547) where most dinners turn into a romp. **Exiles Café** (Jln. Pengosekan; ✆ 361/974812), is where the disenfranchised come to fraternize and get anesthetized, particularly on Saturday nights; it's located just to the southeast of central Ubud.

## PERFORMANCES

There are usually several dance, music, and shadow puppet performances to choose from every night in Ubud, both at the **Palace** and on other nearby stages. A *barong* performance at the Ubud Palace is the best and most stimulating choice (the kids will even like it). Touts selling tickets are ubiquitous; ask at any front desk for a recommendation.

## DAY TRIPS FROM UBUD

Day hiking in and around Bali is the real attraction, with rice fields set among low hills and small towns as far as the eye can see. Ask at any tour desk about day trips to the **Sayan Rice Terraces** ⚐ just north of Ubud. This deep green valley striated in stunning tiers and hanging with palms is a photographer's dream.

**Basakih Temple** ⚐   Called the "Mother Temple," Basakih is Bali's premier Hindu site. Even if you come with your own guide, you'll have to hire a local to take you around the temple site; meet one out in front of the temple (he'll find you). The compound is a collection of 22 multitiered temples that look like Chinese pagodas. They're more interesting for their significance to Balinese culture than for their architectural qualities. This is a working temple complex, with each compound attended by families. There are no signs for tourists and ceremonies are often in progress—the compulsory guides help prevent tourists from treading where they're not welcome. Be respectful and certainly ask before taking pictures, though usually foreign visitors are made welcome. The temples were destroyed in eruptions in 1917, and damaged in another incident in 1963. This is a possible day trip from Ubud or Kuta, and most visitors include a trip to the nearby volcanoes (see "Scaling the Heights: Bali's Volcanoes," below).

40km (25miles) north of Klungklung. Admission Rp8,000 (90¢) and expect to pay about $2 for a guide.

## 7 Candi Dasa

The best reason to camp out in Candi Dasa is to take advantage of the peace, relaxation, and historical riches of the eastern corner of the island. The beaches are eroded and it's overdeveloped, but you can find some of the island's finest accommodations here. Many choose to stay in nearby **Padangbai,** an atmospheric little fishing village with some basic accommodations.

## GETTING THERE

There are shuttles from all major tourist areas to Candi Dasa, and most of the hotels offer airport pickup for a fee.

## GETTING AROUND

There isn't much to the town of Candi Dasa itself—just one road, parallel to the beach—so your feet will do you just fine. Hotels just outside the center generally offer regular **shuttles** into town. **Motorbike** rental and **bemos** are available, too.

---

### FAST FACTS: Candi Dasa

*Banks/Currency Exchange*  Money changers are up and down the main street, offering competitive prices.

*Car/Motorbike Rental*  **Safari,** on the main street (ℂ 363/41707), is a reliable and friendly tourist point, with a selection of cars, jeeps, and motorbikes.

*Internet*  Internet storefronts line the main street. Service is unreliable but only costs Rp2,400 per hour (30¢).

*Post Office/Mail*  **Asri Shop,** on the main street, offers postal services.

*Telephone*  Candi Dasa's area code is **363.**

# WHERE TO STAY
## VERY EXPENSIVE

**Amankila** 👁👁   The name of this ultraluxe resort means "beautiful hill," and it is just that. Private villas, luxurious beyond compare, open to the most stunning views of surrounding hills and ocean below. There is nothing typical about an Aman Resort, and this breathtaking perch is no exception. Private villas have it right in every detail. A solid-wood four-poster canopy bed dominates design in spacious units, and each has an enormous dressing area, ultraluxe bath with sunken tub, and cushioned window seats. The high-end suites have better views and private pools. The Amankila has the only beach in Candi Dasa with sand. Its most striking feature is the giant tiered pool at the center, with water that matches the color of the ocean it seems to spill into. One restaurant serves breakfast and lunch; another serves dinner. There's a very cozy library with real leather-bound volumes and Internet service. Amankila has every service, of course, and rooms and restaurants beyond compare, but what really sets this place apart is its anticipating, meticulous service. Everyone is a rock star here.

Manggis. ✆ 363/41333. Fax 361/771266. 34 units. $650–$1,000 suite. $1,300–$2,600 pool suite. AE, MC, V. **Amenities:** 2 restaurants; bar; outdoor pool; tennis court; spa; watersports equipment rental; motorbike rental; tour desk; car rental; 24-hr. room service; massage; laundry service; library. *In room:* A/C, satellite TV, minibar, fridge, coffeemaker, safe, IDD phone.

## EXPENSIVE

**Alila Manggis** 👁👁   From the outside, this comfortable, contemporary place looks more like a boxy, concrete apartment complex, but inside it's all stark luxury. Chic rooms have clean lines, and everything is new and tidy. The staff is very friendly, and there are nice little touches like afternoon tea and treats on your patio. The large, lush central lawn and pool area is surrounded by teak lounges and leads to a large pebble beach. Getting to town is a bit of a haul, but regular shuttles make it convenient. The hotel features its own line of special soaps which have spawned a local cottage industry. When you check in, you'll be asked your preference: coconut, loofah sponge, or seaweed (you'll also have your choice of aromatherapeutic oils). Be sure to carry some of their Sensatia products away with you. The hotel's new restaurant, Sea Salt, takes its name from nearby salt-producing villages. Days at their popular cooking school include a visit to these areas.

Buitan, Manggis, Karangasem. ✆ 363/41011. Fax 363/41015. www.alilahotels.com. 58 units. $180–$210 double; $350 suite. AE, MC, V. **Amenities:** Restaurant; bar; rentals; tour services; shuttle bus; room service; babysitting; laundry service; Internet. *In room:* A/C, satellite TV, minibar, fridge, IDD phone.

**Puri Bagus** 👁👁   The Puri Bagus is a short ride from the town center and a good compromise between Candi Dasa's ultraluxe options and the more run-down budget stops. Pretty and romantic, this hotel is the best of its class. It's set on land jutting out into the ocean, and steps lead right down to the beach. Good-size bungalows are airy and light, thanks to many large windows, and each has a small sitting area. Cool outdoor bathrooms have hand-held showers. The U-shaped swimming pool has a deep section for scuba practice and a large, shallow area for kids. Dance programs and movies are offered at night, plus there's a full range of free daily activities and good dining at seaside. You'll also find a beautiful new spa area.

P.O. Box 129, Candi Dasa, Karangasem. ✆ 363/41131. Fax 363/41290. www.bagus-discovery.com. 26 units. $115–$160 double; $235 2-bedroom villa. AE, DC, MC, V. **Amenities:** 2 restaurants; 2 bars; outdoor pool; tennis court (nearby); watersports equipment rentals; bike and scooter rentals; concierge; tour desk; car rental;

shopping; room service (7am–midnight); massage; laundry service. *In room:* A/C, minibar, fridge, IDD phone (better amenities, including fruit basket and sarong, in higher standards).

## MODERATE

**Kubu Bali** 🎇   A great value for the price, the Kubu Bali is comfortable and atmospheric. Just off the main street, this quiet little hillside sanctuary is sited in a ravine of rice terraces, cobblestone gardens, statues, benches, aviaries, and pavilions. Handsomely decorated individual bungalows are simple, bright, and airy, with comfortable amenities. The bathrooms have porcelain tile and stone showers open to the sky. Each cottage has a porch with lazy lounges in the shade. At the highest point on the grounds is a cozy pool area with views of the ocean.

Main St., Candi Dasa. ✆ 363/41532 or 363/41256. Fax 363/41531. 20 units. $55 double; $65 suite. MC, V. **Amenities:** Restaurant; outdoor pool; tour desk; car rental; shopping; room service (7am–10pm); massage; babysitting; laundry service. *In room:* A/C, minibar, fridge, hair dryer, safe, IDD phone.

**Watergarden** 🎇🎇   The simple thatched, individual bungalows of the Watergarden may not be spectacular but they're plenty comfortable. Each has a wide veranda overlooking the many lily ponds that give the hotel its name. The best, and most private, rooms are at the back. In-house dining at the Watergarden Café (see "Where to Dine," below) is some of the best in town. There is a small central pool and the place has a good laid-back feel that draws you in (and draws lots of return guests). The hotel is under new management, but they plan to carry on the tradition of quiet atmosphere and friendly service at a reasonable price.

Main St., Candi Dasa. ✆ 363/41540. Fax 363/41164. www.watergardenhotel.com. 14 units. $70–$85 double; $160 2-bedroom suite. AE, MC, V. **Amenities:** Restaurant; bar (popular TJ's); outdoor pool; tour desk; airport transfer; shopping; laundry service; games; library. *In room:* A/C (some), TV, minibar, IDD phone.

## INEXPENSIVE

**Dewa Bharata** on the north end of Main St. in Candi Dasa (✆ **363/41090**) is typical of the good, basic beachside accommodation available here. Rooms start at $35.

## WHERE TO DINE

Hotels offer some of the best dining choices among the myriad possibilities on the Candi Dasa strip. The **Watergarden Café** (✆ **363/41540**) and **Kubu Bali** (✆ **363/41532**) lead the pack with great local and Western fare (see "Where to Stay"). Also recommended is **Kedai** (✆ **363/42020;** www.dekco.com), a chic little bistro from the owners of Ubud's Ary's Warung.

## OUTDOOR ACTIVITIES & WATERSPORTS

Big, healthy reefs teaming with marine life are just a short trip from the shores of Candi Dasa. There are lots of storefront outfits in town able to arrange snorkeling and diving trips. Some spots are fit only for advanced divers; the wreck of the World War II USS *Liberty* is offshore at Tulamben. Hotels can arrange trips with operators along the main road, or try **Geko Divers** out of Padangbai to the south (✆ **363/41516;** gekodive@indosat.net.id).

## DAY TRIPS FROM CANDI DASA

Tracing the coast north from Candi Dasa, travelers have the chance to see volcanoes to the left and stunning coast to the right. The fishing village of **Amed,** about 2 hours north of Candi Dasa, is popular for snorkeling and diving. You can come on a day trip from Candi Dasa or even Ubud (it's easy to arrange land transport), though you might want to spend the night. Lodging options are limited to either *losmen* or the very posh **Hotel Indra Udhyana** (✆ **361/241107;**

www.indo.com/hotels/indra-udhyana). **Amed Café** (© **363/21991;** www.amed cafe.com) is a good budget choice at beachside, with rooms as low as $10.

Some 4 hours of driving north and west along the coast brings you to **Lovina.** Famous for the schools of dolphins swimming just off shore, Lovina is a collection of bungalows and hotels on a quiet stretch of beach far from the maddening crowd. **Damai Lovina Hotel,** Jalan Damai, Kayuputih (© **362/ 41008;** www.damai.com) has over-the-top luxury overlooking town (rooms from $250). **Puri Bagus Lovina** (© **362/21430**) offers less pricey luxury, with beachside rooms starting at $100. Budget accommodation is wall-to-wall along the beaches in Lovina. All accept cash only and cost between Rp80,000 and Rp150,000 ($8.80–$16). Check out **Angsoka,** Jalan Bina Ria, Lovina Beach (© **362/41841**), a clean, comfortable choice; some rooms have air-conditioning and there's a pool.

**Lombok,** a smaller island off the east coast of Bali, is a flight into the rugged landscape of unspoiled Indonesia. With a dry climate and dominated by central volcanic peeks, Lombok is a predominantly Muslim island and attracts travelers hoping to get off the track. Tourism infrastructure is limited, but beaches are unspoiled and it is a popular base for diving and trips to the outlying Gili Islands. With the recent drop in tourism, high-speed boats no longer connect, but there is a daily ferry from Padang Bai, just south of Candi Dasa (trip time is 5 hr.). **Merpati** (© **361/235358** in Bali; **370/636745** on Lombok) flies several times daily to Lombok's **Selaparang Airport** (20 min.; approximately $30) from Bali. From there connect to your destination by cab. The top choice for accommodations is the self-contained, luxurious **Oberoi Lombok,** cousin of the popular Kuta resort (Medana Beach, Tanjung, West Lombok; © **370/638444;** www.oberoihotels.com) on the far north of the island. Lombok's **Sengigi Beach** is dotted with budget accommodations.

# Index

# A Guide for Every Type of Traveler

### FROMMER'S® COMPLETE GUIDES

For independent leisure or business travelers who value complete coverage, candid advice, and lots of choices in all price ranges.

These are the most complete, up-to-date guides you can buy. Count on Frommer's for exact prices, savvy trip planning, sightseeing advice, dozens of detailed maps, and candid reviews of hotels and restaurants in every price range. All Complete Guides offer special icons to point you to great finds, excellent values, and more. Every hotel, restaurant, and attraction is rated from zero to three stars to help you make the best choices.

### UNOFFICIAL GUIDES

For honeymooners, families, business travelers, and anyone else who values no-nonsense, *Consumer Reports*-style advice.

Unofficial Guides are ideal for those who want to know the pros and cons of the places they are visiting and make informed decisions. The guides rank and rate every hotel, restaurant, and attraction, with evaluations based on reader surveys and critiques compiled by a team of unbiased inspectors.

### FROMMER'S® IRREVERENT GUIDES

For experienced, sophisticated travelers looking for a fresh, candid perspective on a destination.

This unique series is perfect for anyone who wants a cutting-edge perspective on the hottest destinations. Covering all major cities around the globe, these guides are unabashedly honest and down-right hilarious. Decked out with a retro-savvy feel, each book features new photos, maps, and neighborhood references.

### FROMMER'S® WITH KIDS GUIDES

For families traveling with children ages 2 to 14.

Here are the ultimate guides for a successful family vacation. Written by parents, they're packed with information on museums, outdoor activities, attractions, great drives and strolls, incredible parks, the liveliest places to stay and eat, and more.

**Visit Frommers.com**

# A Guide for Every Type of Traveler

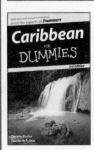

### FOR DUMMIES® TRAVEL GUIDES

For curious, independent travelers.

The ultimate user-friendly trip planners, combining the broad appeal and time-tested features of the For Dummies guides with Frommer's accurate, up-to-date information and travel expertise. Written in a personal, conversational voice, For Dummies Travel Guides put the fun back into travel planning. They offer savvy, focused content on destinations and popular types of travel, with current and extensive coverage of hotels, restaurants, and attractions.

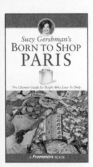

### SUZY GERSHMAN'S BORN TO SHOP GUIDES

For avid shoppers seeking the best places to shop worldwide.

These savvy, opinionated guides, all personally researched and written by shopping guru Suzy Gershman, provide detailed descriptions of shopping neighborhoods, listings of conveniently located hotels and restaurants, easy-to-follow shopping tours, accurate maps, size conversion charts, and practical information about shipping, customs, VAT laws, and bargaining. The handy pocket size makes it easy to carry them in your purse while you shop 'til you drop.

### FROMMER'S® $-A-DAY GUIDES

For independent travelers who want the very best for their money without sacrificing comfort or style.

The renowned series of guides that gave Frommer's its start is the only budget travel series for grown-ups—travelers with limited funds who still want to travel in comfort and style. The $-a-Day Guides are for travelers who want the very best values, but who also want to eat well and stay in comfortable hotels with modern amenities. Each guide is tailored to a specific daily budget and is filled with money-saving advice and detailed maps, plus comprehensive information on sightseeing, shopping, nightlife, and outdoor activities.

### FROMMER'S® PORTABLE GUIDES

For short-term travelers who insist on value and a lightweight guide, including weekenders and convention-goers.

Frommer's inexpensive, pocket-sized Portable Guides offer travelers the very best of each destination so that they can make the best use of their limited time. The guides include all the detailed information and insider advice for which Frommer's is famous, but in a more concise, easy-to-carry format.

**Visit Frommers.com**

WILEY

Now you know

## FROMMER'S® NATIONAL PARK GUIDES

Algonquin Provincial Park
Banff & Jasper
Family Vacations in the National
  Parks

Grand Canyon
National Parks of the American
  West
Rocky Mountain

Yellowstone & Grand Teton
Yosemite & Sequoia/Kings
  Canyon
Zion & Bryce Canyon

## FROMMER'S® MEMORABLE WALKS

Chicago
London

New York
Paris

San Francisco

## FROMMER'S® WITH KIDS GUIDES

Chicago
Las Vegas
New York City

Ottawa
San Francisco
Toronto

Vancouver
Walt Disney World® & Orlando
Washington, D.C.

## SUZY GERSHMAN'S BORN TO SHOP GUIDES

Born to Shop: France
Born to Shop: Hong Kong,
  Shanghai & Beijing

Born to Shop: Italy
Born to Shop: London

Born to Shop: New York
Born to Shop: Paris

## FROMMER'S® IRREVERENT GUIDES

Amsterdam
Boston
Chicago
Las Vegas
London

Los Angeles
Manhattan
New Orleans
Paris
Rome

San Francisco
Seattle & Portland
Vancouver
Walt Disney World®
Washington, D.C.

## FROMMER'S® BEST-LOVED DRIVING TOURS

Austria
Britain
California
France

Germany
Ireland
Italy
New England

Northern Italy
Scotland
Spain
Tuscany & Umbria

## THE UNOFFICIAL GUIDES®

Beyond Disney
California with Kids
Central Italy
Chicago
Cruises
Disneyland®
England
Florida
Florida with Kids
Inside Disney

Hawaii
Las Vegas
London
Maui
Mexico's Best Beach Resorts
Mini Las Vegas
Mini Mickey
New Orleans
New York City
Paris

San Francisco
Skiing & Snowboarding in the
  West
South Florida including Miami &
  the Keys
Walt Disney World®
Walt Disney World® for
  Grown-ups
Walt Disney World® with Kids
Washington, D.C.

## SPECIAL-INTEREST TITLES

Athens Past & Present
Cities Ranked & Rated
Frommer's Best Day Trips from London
Frommer's Best RV & Tent Campgrounds
  in the U.S.A.
Frommer's Caribbean Hideaways
Frommer's China: The 50 Most Memorable Trips
Frommer's Exploring America by RV
Frommer's Gay & Lesbian Europe
Frommer's NYC Free & Dirt Cheap

Frommer's Road Atlas Europe
Frommer's Road Atlas France
Frommer's Road Atlas Ireland
Frommer's Wonderful Weekends from
  New York City
The New York Times' Guide to Unforgettable
  Weekends
Retirement Places Rated
Rome Past & Present

**Travel Tip:** He who finds the best hotel deal has more to spend on facials involving knobbly vegetables.

Hello, the Roaming Gnome here. I've been nabbed from the garden and taken round the world. The people who took me are so terribly clever. They find the best offerings on Travelocity. For very little cha-ching. And that means I get to be pampered and exfoliated till I'm pink as a bunny's doodah.

**\*\*\* travelocity®**

-888-TRAVELOCITY / travelocity.com / America Online Keyword: Travel

Travel Tip: Make sure there's customer service for any change of plans — involving friendly natives, for example.

One can plan and plan, but if you don't book with the right people you can't seize le moment and canoodle with the poodle named Pansy. I, for one, am all for fraternizing with the locals. Better yet, if I need to extend my stay and my gnome nappers are willing, it can all be arranged through the 8oo number at, oh look, how convenient, the lovely company coat of arms.

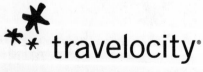

**travelocity**®